A W Bradley and K D Ewing

Constitutional and administrative law

Twelfth Edition

By A W Bradley MA, LLM
Emeritus Professor of Constitutional Law
in the University of Edinburgh; of the Inner Temple, Barrister

and

K D Ewing LLB, PhD
Professor of Public Law
in the University of London, at King's College

Longman
London and New York

Addison Wesley Longman
Edinburgh Gate
Harlow
Essex CM20 2JE
England
and Associated Companies throughout the world

Published in the United States of America
by Addison Wesley Longman, New York

© Addison Wesley Longman Limited 1997

First Edition 1931 (E C S Wade and G G Phillips)
Second Edition 1935 (E C S Wade and G G Phillips)
Third Edition 1946 (E C S Wade and G G Phillips)
Fourth Edition 1950 (E C S Wade and G G Phillips)
Fifth Edition 1955 (E C S Wade)
Sixth Edition 1960 (E C S Wade)
Seventh Edition 1965 (E C S Wade and A W Bradley)
Eighth Edition 1970 (E C S Wade and A W Bradley)
Ninth Edition 1977 (A W Bradley)
Tenth Edition 1985 (A W Bradley)
Eleventh Edition 1993 (A W Bradley and K D Ewing)
Twelfth Edition 1997 (A W Bradley and K D Ewing)

ISBN 0 582 30817 8 PPR

British Library Cataloguing-in-Publication Data
A catalogue record for this book is
available from the British Library

Set in Linotype Baskerville by 3
Printed and bound in Great Britain
by Biddles Ltd, Guildford and Kings Lynn

Contents

Preface

Since 1993, when the 11th edition of this book appeared, there have been few weeks in Britain when aspects of the law dealt with here have not featured prominently in the media. To name but two events of significance from a democratic standpoint: in 1996 the report of the Scott inquiry into the 'arms for Iraq' affair was published, which (inter alia) examined the use of public interest immunity certificates and the accountability of ministers to Parliament; and in 1997 at Westminster the long-running reverberations of 'cash for questions' are still felt, with the publication in July of the report of the Parliamentary Commissioner for Standards, Sir Gordon Downey.

Though Mr Major disclaimed interest in constitutional reform, his government actively promoted changes in managing the civil service and took steps towards a more open system of government. The 1992–97 Parliament was a prolific legislator, and the select committees at Westminster produced a rich but bewildering crop of reports into aspects of public policy. And it is now commonplace for judicial decisions to be made, whether in London, Luxembourg or Strasbourg, striking down or upholding the legality of ministers' action.

Two months before the 1997 general election, the Labour and Liberal Democrat parties realised that they shared much common ground on constitutional reform, and issued a lengthy statement of that consensus. The scale of Labour's victory on 1 May 1997 means that the government does not depend on Liberal Democrat support. However, its ability to fulfil election commitments on constitutional reform is subject to the constraints of the legislative process and to the competing pressures of social and economic issues.

At the time of writing, the Labour government has given priority to legislation preparing the way for a Scottish Parliament and a Welsh Assembly (see chapter 3). Under the Referendums (Scotland and Wales) Bill 1997, electors in each country will be asked to state whether they support devolution, in advance of Parliament approving detailed proposals for it; in Scotland the electors will also be asked whether a Scottish Parliament should have the power to vary taxation. The government intends to incorporate the European Convention on Human Rights in national law and to outline its proposals later in 1997. Two published Bills deal with more detailed points: the Special Immigration Appeals Commission Bill seeks to create an independent body for hearing appeals against deportation decisions 'not conducive to the public good' where it is for the deportee to remain (see chapter 20 B); and the Local Government (Contracts) Bill will protect those contracting with local authorities against the ultra vires rule (chapter 29 A). Such issues as freedom of information, reform of the House of Lords and the electoral system have been given a lower priority in the legislative pro- gramme.

Against this background, the structure of the book remains unchanged, but to a greater or lesser extent every chapter has had to be revised. Chapter 8 is newly written, and there is new material particularly in chapters 7, 11, 13, 14, 17, 21 and 31. Chapters 4 and 5 have changed places. Although the length of the book has increased more than we had intended, we must stress that, as with previous editions, the aim is not to say the last word on the subjects discussed, but to provide an outline of leading topics of public law as a basis for further study and research. We hope that it will be read alongside the valuable source books on public law that exist.

In 1930, when *Constitutional Law* by E C S Wade and G Godfrey Phillips was first published, it presented in short compass 'an outline of the law and practice of the constitution, including English local government, the constitu- tional relations of the British Empire and the Church of England'. The late Professor E C S Wade in fact bore the major responsibility for the book until 1970. Since then his name has continued to be associated with the book, despite the changes through which it has passed. For this edition, the publishers have made a further change in the book's designation to indicate the extent to which the book reflects the work of the present editors.

In the task of revision, we have been assisted in various ways by numerous people. In thanking them, we wish in particular to mention Barry Winetrobe and Oonagh Gay (of the Research Section of the House of Commons Library), Chris Himsworth (of Edinburgh University) and Sionaidh Douglas-Scott (of King's College London).

The text seeks to cover events occurring up to May 1997, but a few later developments are briefly mentioned. While we jointly accept responsibility for the entire book, the main task of preparation was divided between us as follows: chapters 1–7, 9–11, 15, 20 and 26–31 – A W B; other chapters – K D E.

In principle, case-references are to the main Law Reports; cases reported there are usually also found in the Weekly Law Reports and the All England Reports. Where cases are not included in the main Law Reports, citations are generally to All ER rather than to WLR. In the interests of space, abbreviated references are given to periodical articles and official publications; further details may be found in the periodicals concerned and in the lists of official publications issued by the Stationery Office.

Finally, we thank our respective families for their patience during the arduous months in which this new edition was being prepared.

Anthony Bradley and Keith Ewing
7 July 1997

Table of Legislation

United Kingdom Statutes

United Kingdom Orders and Statutory Instruments

Legislation from other jurisdictions

Australia

Canada

European Community

Germany

India

Ireland

New Zealand

Scotland

United States

International Conventions

Table of Cases

Abbreviations

In addition to the standard abbreviations used for the citation of reported cases, the following abbreviations are used for the principal journals and other sources cited.

AJCL *Americal Journal of Comparative Law*
AJIL *American Journal of International Law*
ALJ *Australian Law Journal*
APS *Acts of Parliament of Scotland*
BHRC *Butterworths Human Rights Cases*
BNIL *Bulletin of Northern Ireland Law*
BYIL *British Yearbook of International Law*
CL *Current Law*
CLJ *Cambridge Law Journal*
CLP *Current Legal Problems*
CMLR *Common Market Law Reports*
CML Rev *Common Market Law Review*
Crim LR *Criminal Law Review*
Edin LR *Edinburgh Law Review*
EHRR *European Human Rights Reports*
ELR *Education Law Reports*
EL Rev *European Law Review*
HC House of Commons Paper
HC Deb House of Commons Debates (Hansard)
HEL Sir William Holdsworth, *A History of English Law*
HL House of Lords Paper
HL Deb House of Lords Debates (Hansard)
HLE *Halsbury's Laws of England* (4th edn, 1973 onwards)
ICLQ *International and Comparative Law Quarterly*
ILJ *Industrial Law Journal*
JR *Juridical Review*
Kilbrandon Report Report of Royal Commission on the Constitution, vol. 1, Cmnd 5460, 1973
LQR *Law Quartely Review*
LS *Legal Studies*
MLR *Modern Law Review*
MPR Report of Committee of Ministers' Powers, Cmd 4060, 1932
NILQ *Northern Ireland Legal Quarterly*
NLJ *New Law Journal*
OJLS *Oxford Journal of Legal Studies*
PL *Public Law*
SI Statutory Instrument
SO Standing Order
SR & O Statutory Rule and Order
SLT *Scots Law Times*
TEU *Treaty on European Union (Maastricht, 1992)*
WA Written Answer
YBEL *Yearbook of European Law*

PART I

General principles of constitutional law

CHAPTER 1

Definition and scope of constitutional law

The starting-point for studying constitutional law should ideally be the same starting-point as for studying political philosophy, or the role of law and government in society. How is individual freedom to be reconciled with the claims of social justice? Is society founded upon a reciprocal network of rights and duties, or is the individual merely a pawn in the hands of state power?

These fundamental questions are often not pursued explicitly in the study of constitutional law. In fact constitutional law concerns the relationship between the individual and the state, seen from a particular viewpoint, namely the notion of law. As a historian stated, 'It is inherent in the especial character of law, as a body of rules and procedures, that it shall apply logical criteria with reference to standards of universality and equity'.[1] Law is not merely a matter of the rules which govern relations between private individuals (for example between employer and employee, or between landlord and tenant). Law also concerns the structure and powers of the state. The constitutional lawyer is always likely to insist that the relations between the individual and the state should be founded upon and governed by law.

But law does not exist in a social and political vacuum. Within a given society, the legal rules that concern relations between employer and employee will reflect that society's attitude to paid employment. So too the rules of constitutional law, that govern political relations, will within a given society reflect a particular distribution of political power. In a stable society, constitutional law expresses what may be a very high degree of consensus about the organs and procedures by which political decisions are taken. But when a community insists on taking political decisions by recourse to armed force or gang warfare, or by the might of industrial muscle, the rules of constitutional law are either non-existent, or at best are no more than a transparent cover for a power-struggle that is not conducted in accordance with anything deserving the name of law.

Within a stable democracy, constitutional law reflects the value that people attach to orderly human relations, to individual freedom under the law, and to institutions such as parliament, political parties, free elections, and a free press. Now the reality is often different from the rhetoric. Laws are the product of human decisions, not the gift of an all-perfect deity. As Lord Acton

---

[1] Thompson, *Whigs and Hunters*, p 262.

said, 'Power tends to corrupt and absolute power tends to corrupt absolutely'. But the weaknesses and imperfections of human nature are a reason for law, not a reason for discarding law as a means of regulating political conduct. The rules of football are often broken. But if we shoot the referee and tear up the rules, football as an organised activity ceases to exist.

Total disbelief in the value of the individual or in the possibility of public good is therefore a bad starting-point for studying constitutional law. But there is no need to go to the other extreme and hold the belief, fiercely savaged by Jeremy Bentham, that in Great Britain we have a 'matchless constitution'.[2] We ought not to be dominated by the lessons which our ancestors learned about constitutional government; nor should we reject those lessons out of hand, or from sheer ignorance. A modest claim founded upon the past may be made – that constitutional law is one branch of human learning and experience that helps to make life in today's world more tolerable and less brutish than it might otherwise be.

What is a constitution?

Applied to the system of law and government by which the affairs of a modern state are administered, the word constitution has two meanings. In the narrower meaning of the word, a constitution means a document having a special legal sanctity which sets out the framework and the principal functions of the organs of government within the state, and declares the principles by which those organs must operate. In those countries in which the constitution has overriding legal force, there is often a constitutional court which applies and interprets the text of the constitution in disputed cases. Such a court is the Supreme Court in the USA or the Federal Constitutional Court in the Federal Republic of Germany. In these countries, legislative or administrative acts may be held by the constitutional court to be without legal force where they conflict with the constitution.

In this sense of the word, the United Kingdom of Great Britain and Northern Ireland has no constitution. There is no single document from which is derived the authority of the main organs of government, such as the Crown, the Cabinet, Parliament and the courts of law. No single document lays down the relationship of the primary organs of government one with another, or with the people.[3] But the word constitution has a wider meaning. As Bolingbroke stated in 1733:

By Constitution, we mean, whenever we speak with propriety and exactness, that assemblage of laws, institutions and customs, derived from certain fixed principles of reason ... that compose the general system, according to which the community hath agreed to be governed.[4]

Or, in more modern words, constitution in its wider sense refers to 'the whole system of government of a country, the collection of rules which establish and regulate or govern the government'.[5] In this sense, the United Kingdom has a

---

[2] Bentham, *Handbook of Political Fallacies* (ed Larrabee), pp 154–63.
[3] For what such a document might contain, see *The Constitution of the UK* (Institute for Public Policy Research, 1991).
[4] From *A Dissertation Upon Parties* (1733), quoted in Wheare, *Modern Constitutions*, p 2.
[5] Wheare, op cit, p 1.

constitution since it has a complex and comprehensive system of government, which has been called 'one of the most successful political structures ever devised'.[6] This system is founded partly on Acts of Parliament and judicial decisions, partly upon political practice, and partly upon detailed procedures established by the various organs of government for carrying out their own tasks, for example the law and custom of Parliament, or the rules issued by the Prime Minister to regulate the conduct of ministers.[7]

The wider sense of the word constitution necessarily includes a constitution in the narrower sense. In Canada, the USA, India and many other states, the written constitution occupies the primary place amongst the 'assemblage of laws, institutions and customs' which make up the constitution in the wider sense. But no written document alone can ensure the smooth working of a system of government. A written document has no greater force than that which persons in authority are willing to attribute to it. Around a written constitution will evolve a wide variety of customary rules and practices which adjust the operation of the constitution to changing conditions.[8] These customary rules and practices may often be more easily changed than the constitution itself and their constant evolution will reduce the need for formal amendment of the written constitution.

Nor can a written constitution contain all the detailed rules upon which government depends. Thus the rules for electing the legislature are usually found not in the written constitution but in ordinary statutes enacted by the legislature within limits laid down by the constitution. Such statutes can when necessary be amended by ordinary legislation, whereas amendments to the constitution may require a more elaborate process, such as a special majority in the legislature or approval by a referendum.

The making of written constitutions

It was in the late 18th century that the word constitution first came to be identified with a single document, mainly as a result of the American and French Revolutions. The political significance of the new concept of constitutions was stressed by the radical Tom Paine:

A constitution is a thing *antecedent* to a government, and a government is only the creature of a constitution.... A constitution is not the act of a government, but of a people constituting a government, and government without a constitution, is power without a right.[9]

In the modern world, the making of a constitution normally follows some fundamental political event – the conferment of independence on a colony; a successful revolution; the creation of a new state by the union of states which were formerly independent of each other; a major reconstruction of a country's institutions following a world war. A documentary constitution

---

[6] Hailsham, *On the Constitution*, p 1.

[7] See *Questions of Procedure for Ministers*, first made publicly available in 1992; and ch 13 B.

[8] For the argument that all constitutions leave important things unsaid, see Foley, *The Silence of Constitutions*.

[9] *Rights of Man* (ed Collins), pp 93 and 207.

normally reflects the beliefs and political aspirations of those who have framed it. Within the United Kingdom, except between 1653 and 1660 when the country was governed under Cromwell's 'Instrument of Government', political circumstances have never required the enactment of a code of rules covering the whole of government. There have indeed been periods of acute political upheaval culminating in the reform of certain institutions, for example the revolution of 1688, which was the final act of the constitutional conflicts of the 17th century. Later there was the first major reform of the House of Commons in 1832 and the crisis over the Lords which led to the Parliament Act 1911. There have also been the union of England and Scotland in 1707, the union of Great Britain and Ireland in 1800, and the subsequent questions relating to the government of Ireland. There was the abdication crisis affecting the monarchy in 1936. And in 1973 the United Kingdom became a member of what was then the European Communities. But on none of these occasions was it necessary to reconstruct the whole system of government. Instead legislation was passed to give effect in law to the particular consequences of each political event. A pragmatic approach has predominated at the expense of declaring British political philosophy in terms of law. Evidence of the same approach was provided by the report of the Royal Commission on the Constitution in 1973: the reason for setting up the commission had been to examine the need for devolution of power within the United Kingdom and the majority took the view that a root and branch examination of the whole constitution had not been intended and would not have been practicable.[10]

Nevertheless, the Westminster system of government is not inherently incompatible with a written constitution. In the past, numerous written constitutions were framed for British territories overseas, whether as colonies or when they attained independence. Such constitutions contained no definition of responsible government and did not guarantee the rights of the citizen. Some of these older constitutions have stood the test of time virtually unchanged, for example the constitution of the Commonwealth of Australia, enacted in 1900. The need for constitutional reform has been much discussed by Australians and in 1986 surviving legal links with the United Kingdom Parliament were severed by the Australia Act; but in 1988 a group of constitutional amendments failed to receive popular support.[11] The Canadian constitution, contained in the British North America Act 1867 (now re-named the Constitution Act 1867), was amended when necessary by the Westminster Parliament to meet requests from Canada. In 1982 the Canada Act passed at Westminster gave full powers of constitutional amendment to Canada and also enacted the Canadian Charter of Rights and Freedoms as part of the Canadian constitution.[12] After 1945, a different approach to constitution-making prevailed as most British colonies acquired independence. It became common form for guarantees of rights and declarations of broad political purpose to be included in the constitutions of the newly independent countries, as in 1979 when the colony of Rhodesia achieved independence as

---

[10]   Kilbrandon Report, para 14. And see ch 3 B.
[11]   See H P Lee [1988] PL 535.
[12]   See Hogg, *Constitutional Law of Canada*; and app 1 of the 10th edn of this book.

the republic of Zimbabwe.[13] Within the United Kingdom, as we shall see, the arguments for having a written constitution have received more support as lessons are learnt from developments within Europe and the Commonwealth.

Legal consequences of the unwritten constitution

Where there is a written constitution, the legal structure of government may assume a wide variety of forms. Within a federal constitution, the tasks of government are divided into two classes, those entrusted to the federal (or central) organs of government, and those entrusted to the various states, regions or provinces which make up the federation. Thus in countries such as Canada, Australia or the USA, constitutional limits bind both the federal and state organs of government, which limits are enforceable as a matter of law. It may be desired to place certain rights of the citizen beyond reach of the organs of government created by the constitution; these fundamental rights may be entrenched by requiring a special legislative procedure if they are to be amended, or even by rendering them in essence unalterable, as in the Federal Republic of Germany.[14] Again, many constitutions seek to avoid a concentration of power in the hands of any one organ of government by adopting the principle of separation of powers, vesting legislative power exclusively in the legislature, executive power in the executive and judicial power in the courts.[15]

Within the United Kingdom, there is no written constitution which can secure these objects or serve as the foundation of the legal system. The resulting vacuum is occupied by the doctrines of the legislative supremacy of Parliament and the rule of law, their interrelation being one of the central questions of public law in Britain.[16] These doctrines will be examined later,[17] but one result is that formal restraints upon the exercise of power which exist elsewhere do not exist in the United Kingdom. For example, no truly federal system can exist so long as Parliament's legislative supremacy is maintained. Just as it was Parliament which passed the Government of Ireland Act 1920, devolving powers of self-government upon Northern Ireland, so in 1972 Parliament could suspend operation of the Act of 1920 by re-imposing direct rule upon Northern Ireland.[18] For a federal system to be established a written constitution would be necessary, limiting the powers of the Westminster Parliament and thus preventing it from taking back the devolved powers into its own hands. Without such a guarantee, if subordinate legislatures were to be established for Scotland and Wales, it might be politically difficult to abolish them: but their existence would be safeguarded by political factors rather than by law.

So too, in the absence of a written constitution, it is difficult to imagine how the courts could be entrusted with the function of protecting the rights

---

13   Zimbabwe Constitution Order 1979, SI 1979 No 1600, part III; and see de Smith, *The New Commonwealth and its Constitutions*, ch 5.
14   Basic Law of the Federal Republic of Germany, arts 19(2) and 79(3).
15   Ch 5.
16   See Allan, *Law, Liberty and Justice.*
17   Chs 4, 6.
18   Ch 3 A.

of minorities and individual citizens against legislative infringement by Parliament. Moreover, the absence of a written constitution means that there is no special procedure prescribed for legislation of constitutional importance. Before the Republic of Ireland could join the EC, a constitutional amendment had to be approved by referendum of the people. In the United Kingdom, while the European Communities Act 1972 was debated at length in Parliament, the Act was passed by essentially the same procedure as would apply to a Road Traffic Act or other ordinary legislation. British membership of the EC was in 1975 confirmed by a consultative referendum; but this was a product of divisions in the Labour party, not a constitutional requirement. By contrast with written constitutions, which may be described as *rigid* because of the special procedure required if they are to be altered, the United Kingdom has what at least in form is an extremely *flexible* constitution. It would seem that there is no aspect of our constitutional arrangements which could not be altered by the passing of an Act of Parliament.

The absence of a written constitution affects the sources of constitutional law. Instead of the constitution being the formal source of all constitutional law, greater importance attaches to Acts of Parliament and to judicial decisions, which settle the law on matters such as civil liberties and the principles of judicial review that have never been the subject of comprehensive legislation. Some major institutions, like the Cabinet, do not derive their authority from the law; many important constitutional rules are not rules of law at all.[19] To summarise, the absence of a written constitution means that the British constitution depends less on legal rules and safeguards than upon political and democratic principles.

Constitutionalism[20]

According to the principle of constitutionalism as it has developed in the democratic tradition, one primary function assigned to a written constitution is that of controlling the organs of government. 'Constitutions spring from a belief in limited government.'[21] As Professor Vile remarked:

Western institutional theorists have concerned themselves with the problems of ensuring that the exercise of governmental power, which is essential to the realisation of the values of their societies, should be controlled in order that it should not itself be destructive of the values it was intended to promote.[22]

It would be unfortunate if the absence of a written constitution were to suggest that no restraints or limits upon government were required. In the United Kingdom, the problem is no less acute than in countries with written constitutions. The absence of a written constitution makes the more necessary the existence of a free political system in which official decisions are subject to open discussion and scrutiny by Parliament. In 1973, the Royal Commission on the Constitution rejected a written constitution, but increasing dissatisfac-

---

[19]   Ch 2 B.
[20]   See Vile, *Constitutionalism and the Separation of Powers*, and McIlwain, *Constitutionalism, Ancient and Modern*.
[21]   Wheare, *Modern Constitutions*, p 7.
[22]   Vile, op cit, p 1.

tion with the British political system led later to strong advocacy for the idea;[23] in particular, many demands have been made for a new Bill of Rights that could give greater legal protection to individual liberties than the present unwritten constitution.[24] In 1988, a cross-party manifesto, Charter 88, called for a new constitutional settlement, and in 1991 the text of a complete constitution for the United Kingdom was published by a research institute.[25] At the general elections in 1992 and 1997, all parties except the Conservatives included constitutional reform in their manifestos; in 1997 agreement on specific reforms had been reached between the Labour and Liberal Democrat parties. The 1997 election made likely some structural reform, but not a systematic programme of comprehensive reform. Serious issues relating to the European Union remained to be resolved.

What is constitutional law?

There is no hard and fast definition of constitutional law. According to one very wide definition, constitutional law is that part of national law which governs the system of public administration, and the relationships between the individual and the state.[26] Constitutional law presupposes the existence of the state[27] and includes those laws which regulate the structure and functions of the principal organs of government and their relationship to each other and to the citizen. Where there is a written constitution, emphasis is placed on the rules which it contains and on the way in which they have been interpreted by the highest court with constitutional jurisdiction. One problem of definition in the United Kingdom is that many of the rules and practices under which our system of government operates do not have the force of law.[28] Without knowledge of these rules and practices, knowledge of the legal rules alone is incomplete and sometimes misleading. In the past this has been thought to be a problem peculiar to constitutional law. Today, it is recognised that in most branches of law the purpose and operation of legal rules can be understood only with a knowledge of the social background against which the rules operate: legal procedures for the resolution of disputes arising within a family, a trade union or a limited company are an incomplete guide to the role of these institutions in society.

A further problem of definition is that, unlike legal systems in which law is divided up into a series of codes, there is no hard and fast demarcation in Britain between constitutional law and other branches of law. A legal historian advised students of constitutional law that they should take a wide view of the subject: 'there is hardly any department of law which does not, at

---

23 Notably from Scarman, *English Law – the New Dimension*, and Hailsham, *The Dilemma of Democracy*. Contrast the provocative and witty defence of the unwritten constitution as an expression of political culture in Thompson, *Writing by Candlelight*, pp 191–256. And see Brazier, *Constitutional Reform*; Johnson, *In Search of the Constitution*; Mount, *The British Constitution Now*; and Norton, *The Constitution in Flux*.
24 Ch 19 C.
25 See note 3 above.
26 HLE, vol 8(2), para 1; and see Marshall, *Constitutional Theory*, ch 1.
27 For the impact on constitutional law of the changing concept of the state, see N MacCormick (1993) 56 MLR 1 and C M G Himsworth [1996] PL 639.
28 Ch 2 B.

one time or another, become of constitutional importance'.[29] For example, in the field of family law, important protection for family life is given by the European Convention on Human Rights,[30] and family status is an important basis for many rules of immigration control.[31] In employment law, the freedom of association and the law of picketing[32] are of constitutional importance. Numerous civil liberty issues arise out of criminal law and procedure. In property law, public control of private rights is a fertile field for the emergence of disputes involving a clash between public and private interests. These examples are not meant to suggest that constitutional law comprehends the whole of the legal system, but that the manner in which the legal system allocates rights and duties and arbitrates on disputes is of direct concern to constitutional law.

Constitutional law and administrative law

In the past, constitutional law gave more emphasis to the role of the state in maintaining public order and national security than it did to the individual's right to employment and housing, education and health services, and the conservation of the environment. Many people still look to the courts for protection in the sphere of public order and the criminal law. But in the administration of the social services, and in the exercise of economic regulation, individuals come into contact more often with officials than with judges. When a dispute arises out of these activities, a citizen may wish to go to the courts to assert his or her rights and often the procedure of judicial review enables this to be done.[33] Again, many prefer to seek redress of the grievance from a member of Parliament. Moreover, administrative tribunals and the Parliamentary Ombudsman provide important means of remedy for the citizen against official action or inaction.[34]

There is no precise demarcation between constitutional and administrative law in Britain. Administrative law may be defined as the law which determines the organisation, powers and duties of administrative authorities.[35] Like constitutional law, administrative law deals with the exercise and control of governmental power. A rough distinction is that constitutional law is mainly concerned with the structure of the primary organs of government, whereas administrative law is concerned with the work of official agencies in providing services and in regulating the activities of citizens. Within the vast field of government, questions often arise as to the sources of administrative power, the adjudication of disputes arising out of the public services and, above all, the means of securing a system of legal control over the activities of government which takes account of both public needs and the private interests of the individual.

---

[29]   Maitland, *Constitutional History*, p 538.
[30]   Arts 8 and 12. Ch 19 B.
[31]   Ch 20 B.
[32]   Ch 23.
[33]   Chs 29 and 30.
[34]   Ch 28.
[35]   Ch 26. Also Maitland, *Constitutional History*, pp 528–35, and Craig, *Public Law and Democracy in the UK and the USA*, pp 1–3.

Constitutional law and public international law

Public international law is that system of law whose primary function it is to regulate the relations of states with one another. The system

presupposes the state, a territorial unit of great power, possessing within its own sphere the quality of independence of any superior, a quality which we are accustomed to call sovereignty and possessing within that sphere the power and right to make law not only for its own citizens, but also for those of others.[36]

International law thus deals with the *external* relations of a state with other states; constitutional law deals with the legal structure of the state and its *internal* relations with its citizens and others on its territory. Both are concerned with regulating by legal process and values the great power which states wield. In the dualist tradition, national and international law operate at two distinct levels, but both are concerned with state power. Thus one important branch of constitutional law is the national law relating to a government's power to enter into treaties with other states and thus to create new international obligations.[37] So too, the procedure of extradition, by which a criminal who escapes from one state to another may be sent back to the state in which his crime was committed, operates in both international and national law: the government of a state which is party to an extradition treaty must acquire the powers necessary in national law if the state is to be able to fulfil its treaty obligations.[38] International organisations have today established new forms of cooperation between states and have set standards of conduct for the international community. Increasingly international law has become concerned with the treatment of minority groups and individuals by states. These developments make it necessary to reconsider the nature of internal sovereignty which the national system of constitutional law ascribes to the state. Thus the European Convention on Human Rights, to which the United Kingdom is a party, imposes international obligations which directly affect our constitutional law.[39]

Constitutional law and the law of the European Union

The European Union was created by the Maastricht Treaty out of the European Communities, themselves created by means of treaties between the member states, but the Union is very different from other international organisations to which the United Kingdom belongs. It is equipped with legislative, administrative and judicial organs, which exercise their powers with direct effect throughout the member states. The substantive rules of Community law in the economic and social fields lie outside the scope of this book. But there can be no doubt that the Community exercises powers of government over the member states, including the United Kingdom, in which the British electorate participate through elections to the Westminster and the European Parliaments: the public law of the United Kingdom has had to adapt to this reality. Accordingly, the main structure of the EU will be

---

[36]　C Parry, in *Manual of Public International Law* (ed Sorensen), p 3. And cf note 27 above.
[37]　Ch 15 B.
[38]　Ch 20 C.
[39]　Ch 19 B.

outlined and the implications of membership for constitutional law examined, including the relationship between Community law and national law.[40] In 1997, a keenly disputed issue was the extent to which the United Kingdom should take part in further European integration, requiring member states to relinquish aspects of national sovereignty in favour of European measures such as a common currency. It continued to be necessary for public law to be studied in a European perspective.

---

[40]   Ch 8.

CHAPTER 2

Sources and nature of the constitution

A. The sources of constitutional law

If the United Kingdom possessed a written constitution, the main rules of constitutional law would be contained within it. Alterations to these rules would be made by the procedure laid down for amendment of the constitution. In all probability, Parliament would be authorised to make detailed provision for such matters as the machinery of elections and the structure of the courts. If a court exercised the function of interpreting and applying the constitution in disputed cases, its decisions would be an authoritative indication of the meaning of the constitution. The sources of constitutional law would comprise: (a) the constitution itself, and amendments made to it; (b) Acts of Parliament dealing with matters of constitutional importance; (c) judicial decisions interpreting the constitution. By the word 'source' is meant the formal origin of a rule which confers legal force upon that rule. The word source may also be used in other senses: thus the historical sources of a written constitution include both the immediate circumstances in which it was framed and adopted, and also the long-term factors which influenced its making. So too there are broad political principles which influence the content of particular legal rules. Thus the general belief in democracy explains why the people of the United Kingdom have the right to vote in elections. Such principles are given practical effect in legislation by Parliament and may influence decisions that the courts take on disputed questions of law. But in this section we are concerned solely with the formal sources of the legal rules of the United Kingdom constitution. Those constitutional rules which do not have the force of law are discussed in section B.

Sources of legal rules

In the absence of a written constitution, the two main sources of constitutional law are the same as of legal rules in general, namely:

(a) Legislation (or enacted law) including Acts of Parliament; legislation enacted by ministers and other authorities upon whom Parliament has conferred power to legislate;[1] exceptionally, legislative instruments issued by

---

[1]   Ch 27.

the Crown under its prerogative powers;[2] and, since 1973, legislation enacted by organs of the European Community.[3]

(b) Judicial precedent (or case law) ie the decisions of the courts expounding the common law or interpreting legislation. Since 1973, this includes decisions of the European Court of Justice in relation to Community law.[4]

Another source of legal rules is custom, ie rules of conduct based upon social or commercial custom which are recognised by judicial decision as having binding force. Custom of this kind is not an important source of constitutional law. However, if a customary practice of government is challenged in judicial proceedings, evidence of the practice may lead the court to decide that it is lawful.[5] Moreover, many rules of the constitution which do not have the force of law are based on the customary usages of various organs of government, and these rules will be considered in section B. In the case of Parliament, each House of Parliament has authority to regulate its internal affairs: the 'law and custom of Parliament' (*lex et consuetudo Parliamenti*) is therefore an important source of constitutional rules and practice to which the distinction drawn in this chapter between the legal and non-legal rules of the constitution is not directly applicable.[6] Another secondary source of constitutional law is to be found in the opinions and conclusions of writers of books of authority.[7]

(a) Legislation

In the absence of a written constitution, many Acts of Parliament have been enacted which relate to the system of government. There are few topics of constitutional law which have not been affected by legislation. Unlike some branches of private law, for example the general law of contract, which may involve relatively little study of enacted law, a study of constitutional law involves frequent recourse to the statute book. Those statutes which deal with matters of constitutional law do not form sections of a complete constitutional code. If a collection were made of all the legislation (from medieval charters to the present day) which deals with the form and functions of government, the result would present a most imperfect description of the constitution.[8] Moreover, these enactments can each be repealed by another Act of Parliament. A few statutes, though in law in no different position from other Acts, have special constitutional significance.

1 Magna Carta.[9] Magna Carta, first enacted in 1215 and confirmed on numerous occasions thereafter, was passed by the English Parliament long before the formation of the present United Kingdom. The importance of Magna Carta lies in the fact that it contained a statement of grievances, the

---

[2] Ch 12 D.
[3] Ch 8.
[4] Ibid.
[5] See eg *Carltona Ltd v Commissioners of Works* [1943] 2 All ER 560; p 127 below.
[6] Section C.
[7] Ibid.
[8] See the statutes collected under the title 'Constitutional Law' in *Halsbury's Statutes*, 4th edn, vol 10 (1995 reissue).
[9] For a full historical account, see Holt, *Magna Carta*.

settlement of which was brought about by a union against the king of important classes in the community. The Charter set out the rights of various classes of the medieval community according to their different needs. The Church was to be free; London and other cities were to enjoy their liberties and customs; merchants were not to be subject to unjust taxation. The famous clauses which laid it down that no man should be punished except by the judgment of his peers or the law of the land, and that to none should justice be denied, have been described as the origin of trial by jury and the writ of habeas corpus. Trial by jury is in fact traced to another source, and the writ of habeas corpus had not yet been devised. But these clauses embodied a protest against arbitrary punishment and asserted the right to a fair trial and a just legal system. Today few provisions of Magna Carta remain on the statute book. Its historical and symbolic value is greater than its current legal force.

2 Petition of Right.   Another document enacted by the English Parliament at a later period of constitutional conflict is the Petition of Right 1628, enrolled on the statute book as 3 Car 1 c 1.[10] This contained protests against taxation without consent of Parliament, arbitrary imprisonment, the use of commissions of martial law in time of peace and the billeting of soldiers upon private persons. To these protests the king yielded, though the effect of the concessions was weakened by the view Charles I held that his prerogative powers were not thereby diminished.

3 Bill of Rights and Claim of Right.   The 'glorious revolution' of 1688 brought about the downfall of James II of England and James VII of Scotland from his two thrones and the restoration of monarchy in the two kingdoms on terms laid down by the English and Scottish Parliaments respectively. These terms were accepted by the incoming joint monarchs, William and Mary. In England it was the House of Lords and the remnants of Charles II's last Parliament who in 1689 approved the Bill of Rights which was later confirmed by the post-revolution Parliament.[11] This laid the foundations of the modern constitution by disposing of the more extravagant claims of the Stuarts to rule by prerogative right.

Its principal provisions (known as 'articles'), many of which are still in force as part of English law, declared:

(1) That the pretended power of suspending of laws or the execution of laws by regal authority without consent of Parliament is illegal.
(2) That the pretended power of dispensing with laws or the execution of laws by regal authority as it hath been assumed and exercised of late is illegal.
(3) That the commission for erecting the late court of commissioners for ecclesiastical causes and all other commissions and courts of like nature are illegal and pernicious.
(4) That the levying money for or to the use of the crown by pretence of prerogative without grant of Parliament for longer time or in other manner than the same is or shall be granted is illegal.
(5) That it is the right of the subjects to petition the king and all commitments and prosecutions for such petitioning are illegal.

---

[10] *Halsbury's Statutes*, vol 10, p 26.
[11] Ibid, p 38.

(6) That the raising or keeping of a standing army within the kingdom in time of peace unless it be with consent of Parliament is against the law.

(7) That the subjects which are protestants may have arms for their defence suitable to their conditions and as allowed by law.

(8) That election of members of Parliament ought to be free.

(9) That the freedom of speech and debates or proceedings in Parliament ought not to be impeached or questioned in any court or place out of Parliament.

(10) That excessive bail ought not be required nor excessive fines imposed nor cruel and unusual punishments inflicted.

(11) That jurors ought to be duly impannelled and returned. ...

(12) That all grants and promises of fines and forfeitures of particular persons before conviction are illegal and void.

(13) And that for redress of all grievances and for the amending, strengthening and preserving of the laws Parliaments ought to be held frequently.[12]

The Scottish Parliament enacted the Claim of Right in 1689. Its contents followed those of the Bill of Rights with certain modifications; for example, the distinction between the suspending and dispensing powers was not made, but all proclamations asserting an absolute power to 'cass [quash], annul or disable laws' were declared illegal.[13] Many provisions of the Claim of Right are still in force within Scotland.

4 The Act of Settlement.   The Act of Settlement 1700, passed by the English Parliament, not only provided for the succession to the throne, but added important provisions complementary to the Bill of Rights, especially:

That whosoever shall hereafter come to the possession of this crown shall join in communion with the Church of England as by law established.

That in case the crown and imperial dignity of this realm shall hereafter come to any person, not being a native of this kingdom of England, this nation be not obliged to engage in any war for the defence of any dominions or territories which do not belong to the crown of England, without consent of Parliament.

That no person who has an office or place of profit under the King or receives a pension from the crown shall be capable of serving as a member of the House of Commons.

That ... judges' commissions be made *quamdiu se bene gesserint* [so long as they are of good behaviour], and their salaries ascertained and established, but upon the address of both Houses of Parliament it may be lawful to remove them.

That no pardon under the great seal of England be pleadable to an impeachment by the Commons in Parliament.[14]

The Bill of Rights and the Act of Settlement marked the victory of Parliament over the claim of kings to govern by the prerogative. There was, however, nothing in these statutes to secure the responsibility of the King's ministers to Parliament. That important principle of parliamentary govern-

---

[12]   *Halsbury's Statutes*, vol 10, p 34. For judicial citation, see *Congreve v Home Office* [1976] QB 629 (art 4); *Williams v Home Office* [1981] 1 All ER 1151 (art 10); and *R v Home Secretary, ex p Herbage (No 2)* [1987] QB 1077 (art 10). Art 7, sometimes cited by the gun lobby, had no effect on the Firearms (Amendment) Act 1997. Art 9 was amended by the Defamation Act 1996, see ch 22 F.

[13]   APS IX, 38.

[14]   *Halsbury's Statutes*, vol 10, p 40.

ment developed in the 18th century and later, a product of constitutional practice rather than legislation.[15]

5 *Other statutes of constitutional importance.* It is not intended to catalogue other principal statutes that form part of constitutional law. It is sufficient to mention the Act of Union with Scotland 1707, the Parliament Acts 1911 and 1949, the Crown Proceedings Act 1947, the European Communities Act 1972, the Race Relations Act 1976, the Representation of the People Act 1983, and the Public Order Act 1986, all of which will be discussed in this book.

It is often said that in Britain it is not possible to distinguish statutes of constitutional significance from other statutes, since without a written constitution no statute can be labelled as constitutional. But in two respects a distinction is sometimes drawn between constitutional and other legislation. First, the House of Commons may refer Bills of constitutional significance for detailed consideration to a committee of the whole House rather than to a standing committee of the House,[16] but not all Bills of constitutional significance are treated in this way. Secondly, by the doctrine of implied repeal,[17] a later Act prevails over the provisions of an earlier Act which are inconsistent with the later Act; however, in the case of some statutes of special significance, the courts are sometimes reluctant to hold that they have been overridden by a later Act. Under this category might come such Acts as the Bill of Rights 1689, the Acts of Union with Scotland and Ireland and, for special reasons, the European Communities Act 1972.[18] As a senior judge said extra-judicially:

> In strict law there may be no difference in status ... as between one Act of Parliament and another, but I confess to some reluctance in holding that an Act of such constitutional significance as the Union with Ireland Act is subject to the doctrine of implied repeal or of obsolescence.[19]

(b) Case law

The other main source of rules of law is found in the decisions of the superior courts, stated in authoritative form in the law reports. Under the doctrine of precedent, or 'stare decisis' (ie the duty of courts to observe decided cases), these decisions are binding on inferior courts and may, according to the relative status of the courts in question, bind other superior courts.[20] Judge-made law takes two principal forms:

1 The common law proper. This consists of the laws and customs of the realm which have from early times been declared to be law by the judges in their decisions in particular cases coming before them. In the reports of these cases are to be found authoritative expositions of the law relating to the prerog-

---

[15] Ch 7.
[16] Ch 10 A.
[17] Ch 4 C.
[18] Ch 8 C.
[19] Report by the Committee of Privileges on the Petition of the Irish Peers (1966) HL 53 (Lord Wilberforce), p 73.
[20] See Cross and Harris, *Precedent in English Law*.

atives of the Crown,[21] the ordinary remedies of the subject against illegal acts by public authorities and officials[22] and the writ of habeas corpus,[23] which in English law protects against unlawful invasion of personal liberty.

Examples of judicial decisions are *Entick v Carrington,* (which held that a Secretary of State had no power to issue general warrants for the arrest and search of those publishing seditious papers[24] and, in modern times, *Burmah Oil Co v Lord Advocate,* (which held that the Crown was under a duty to compensate the subject for property taken in the exercise of prerogative powers,[25] *Conway v Rimmer,* (which held that the courts had power to order the production of documents in evidence for which Crown privilege had been claimed by the Home Secretary)[26] and *M v Home Office,* (holding that the Home Secretary had committed contempt of court in not obeying a judge's order to bring a deported Zairean teacher back to the United Kingdom.[27] These decisions, made by the most senior judges in the United Kingdom, declare important rules of public law which often would not have been enacted by Parliament. In the absence of a written constitution, such decisions provide what have been called the legal foundations of British constitutionalism.[28] Even so, they are not binding for all time since they may be set aside or amended by Parliament, even retrospectively.[29] If the case concerns rights under Community law, a House of Lords decision is subject to the European Court of Justice at Luxembourg;[30] in cases affecting human rights, the European Court of Human Rights may hold that the national decision conflicts with the European Convention on Human Rights.[31] One fundamental constitutional rule which owes its legal source to judicial decision is the doctrine of the legislative supremacy of Parliament.[32]

2 Interpretation of statute law. The courts have no authority to rule on the validity of an Act of Parliament (although they have such authority in the case of subordinate legislation)[33] but they have the task of interpreting enacted law in cases where the correct meaning of an Act is disputed. Important issues of public law may arise out of the interpretation of statutes. Two decisions of the Court of Appeal in 1996 illustrate this. In one, the court held, interpreting the Race Relations Act 1976, that police officers dealing with an attack by white youths on a Somali citizen must not discriminate on racial grounds, but that the chief constable is not vicariously responsible for such discrimination.[34] In the other, it was held that, although the British Nationality Act 1981

---

[21]   Ch 12 D.
[22]   Ch 30.
[23]   Ch 21 F and ch 30.
[24]   (1765) 19 St Tr 1030.
[25]   [1965] AC 75.
[26]   [1968] AC 910; ch 31 C.
[27]   *Re M* [1994] 1 AC 377; chs 18 B, 31 C.
[28]   See Allan, *Law, Liberty and Justice,* chs 1, 4. Also S Sedley, in Richardson and Genn (eds), *Administrative Law and Government Action,* ch 2 and (1994) 110 LQR 270.
[29]   The War Damage Act 1965 reversed the *Burmah Oil* decision above; ch 12 D.
[30]   For the *Factortame* litigation, ch 8 D.
[31]   Ch 19 B.
[32]   Ch 4.
[33]   Ch 27.
[34]   *Farah v Metropolitan Police Commissioner* [1997] 1 All ER 289; ch 31 A.

exempted the Home Secretary from giving reasons for refusing an application for citizenship, the minister must nonetheless act fairly.[35]

Since most powers of government are derived from statute, the judge-made law which results from the interpretation of statutes is of great importance in administrative law. Just as it is difficult to draft clear, accurate and intelligible legislation, so also is it to interpret the result. The experience of the courts has led to the growth of principles of statutory interpretation. Unfortunately, these principles are seldom conclusive and indeed may often contradict one another.[36] Two general approaches are intermittently followed by the courts. The literal approach to interpretation is based on the principle that it is the duty of the court to discover the true meaning of the words used by Parliament; this concentrates on the actual text of the legislation, and excludes consideration of legislative policy. Another approach is based on the principle that a court should endeavour to give effect to the policy of a statute and to the intentions of those who made it, a principle expressed in the mischief rule laid down in *Heydon's* case.[38] There was formerly a rule that the courts may not look at Hansard (the record of debates in Parliament) to discover the meaning of legislation, although limited use might be made of documents such as the reports of royal commissions and parliamentary committees as an aid to identifying the mischief which legislation was intended to remedy.[39] However, Hansard was used to discover the intention of Parliament in approving regulations which gave effect to a decision of the European Court of Justice.[40] In 1992, the House of Lords modified the former rule: a court may use Hansard as an aid to statutory construction where the legislation is ambiguous or obscure and the material relied on consists of clear statements made by a minister or other promoter of the Bill.[41]

Certain presumptions of interpretation are of constitutional importance. Thus many Acts do not in law bind central government departments, since the Crown is presumed not to be bound by legislation, unless this is expressly stated or necessarily implied.[42] In the past there has been a presumption that Parliament does not intend to take away common law rights by mere implication, as distinct from express words. Thus the courts have presumed that Parliament does not intend to take away the property of a subject without compensation[43] or to deprive a subject of access to the courts,[44] and have interpreted penal statutes strictly in favour of the citizen: thus a statute creating a criminal offence will not in the absence of express words be held to be retrospective.[45] These common law presumptions may not be very helpful

---

35   *R v Home Secretary, ex p Fayed* [1997] 1 All ER 228.
36   Report of the Law Commission, *The Interpretation of Statutes*, HC 256, 1968–69; Marshall, *Constitutional Theory*, ch 4; Cross, *Statutory Interpretation*; Bennion, *Statutory Interpretation*.
37   Cross, *Statutory Interpretation*, p 14.
38   (1584) 3 Co Rep 71.
39   *Black-Clawson International Ltd v Papierwerke AG* [1975] AC 591; *Davis v Johnson* [1979] AC 264.
40   *Pickstone v Freemans plc* [1989] AC 66.
41   *Pepper v Hart* [1993] AC 593.
42   *Lord Advocate v Dumbarton DC* [1990] 2 AC 580; ch 31 C.
43   *Central Control Board v Cannon Brewery Co* [1919] AC 744, 752.
44   *Chester v Bateson* [1920] 1 KB 829.
45   *Waddington v Miah* [1974] 2 All ER 377.

when applied to town and country planning law, where one object of the legislation is to restrict the common law rights of the landowner,[46] or to social security legislation, which creates a whole scheme of rights and duties unknown to the common law.

British membership of the European Union directly affects our traditional approaches to interpretation, since in most European legal systems the methods of legislative drafting and the rules of statutory interpretation are very different from those in Britain. Where it is necessary for a provision of a European treaty or regulation to be interpreted in a British court, art 177 of the EC Treaty enables the question of interpretation to be settled by the European Court of Justice.[47] British courts must follow that court's practice by giving a purposive construction to regulations intended to comply with EC directives.[48]

Whatever the rules of interpretation may be within a given legal system, it is now recognised that many legal rules have what has been called an open texture. As H L A Hart said:

Even when verbally formulated general rules are used, uncertainties as to the form of behaviour required by them may break out in particular concrete cases ... In all fields of experience, not only that of rules, there is a limit, inherent in the nature of language, to the guidance which general language can provide.[49]

However difficult the task of statutory interpretation, it is an essential principle of the concept of law that enacted laws should be interpreted by judicial bodies independent of the legislature which made the law: statutory provisions authorising the government to define the meaning of terms used in an Act of Parliament are contrary to basic legal principles.[50] In interpreting a statute, the judges seek to determine what Parliament intended, and are not free merely to decide what they believe to be in the public interest.[51]

B.   Non-legal rules of the constitution

Many important rules of constitutional behaviour, which are observed by the Sovereign, the Prime Minister and other ministers, members of Parliament, judges and civil servants, are contained neither in Acts nor in judicial decisions. It will be shown below that disputes which arise out of these rules rarely lead to action in the courts and that judicial sanctions are not applicable if the rules are broken. Constitutional writers have applied a wide variety of names to these rules: the positive morality of the constitution,[52] the unwritten maxims of the constitution,[53] and 'a whole system of political

---

46   *Westminster Bank Ltd v Beverley Borough Council* [1971] AC 508.
47   Ch 8 A.
48   *Litster v Forth Dry Dock and Engineering Co Ltd* [1990] 1 AC 546.
49   Hart, *The Concept of Law*, p 123.
50   Counter-Inflation Act 1973, Sched 3, para 1(1); and cf the *Black-Clawson* case, note 39 above.
51   *Duport Steels Ltd v Sirs* [1980] 1 All ER 529.
52   Austin, *The Province of Jurisprudence Determined*, p 259.
53   Mill, *Representative Government*, ch 5.

morality, a whole code of precepts for the guidance of public men'.[54] Dicey referred to them as:

conventions, understandings, habits or practices which, though they may regulate the conduct of the several members of the sovereign power ... are not in reality laws at all since they are not enforced by the courts.[55]

Under Dicey's influence, the most common name given to this phenomenon is constitutional convention.

This use of the word convention is quite different from its use in international law, where a convention is a synonym for a treaty, or binding agreement between states. But the notion of conventional conduct does include a strong element of what is customarily expected, in the sense of ordinary or regular behaviour. In common speech a person may be described as conventional or unconventional, depending on his or her capacity for conforming to or departing from accepted patterns of social behaviour and opinion. Most discussion of constitutional conventions has gone beyond description of conduct which is merely a customary practice and has suggested that conventions give rise to binding rules of conduct.[56] John Mackintosh described a convention as 'a generally accepted political practice, usually with a record of successful applications or precedents'[57] but other authors describe conventions as:

rules of constitutional behaviour which are considered to be binding by and upon those who operate the Constitution but which are not enforced by the law courts ... nor by the presiding officers in the House of Parliament.[58]

Mackintosh here regarded conventions as merely *descriptive* statements of constitutional practice, based on observation of what actually happens; the latter approach regards conventions as *prescriptive* statements of what should happen, based in part upon observation but also upon constitutional principle. We return later to the choice between these two approaches;[59] but at present we will assume that conventions are concerned with matters of obligation, and will explore the nature of that obligation.

In this section it is not possible to summarise all existing conventional rules; the aim is rather to discuss their general characteristics. Other chapters will examine the non-legal rules which apply to particular institutions. Some of the most important conventional rules will be discussed in the chapters dealing with responsible government, the Crown and the Cabinet. First, some examples will be given of non-legal rules and in each case relevant legal rules will be mentioned.

---

[54] Freeman, *Growth of the English Constitution*, p 109, quoted in Dicey, p 418. And see O Hood Phillips (1966) 29 MLR 137.

[55] Dicey, *The Law of the Constitution*, p 24.

[56] See eg Mitchell, *Constitutional Law*, p 39; Wheare, *The Statute of Westminster and Dominion Status*, p 10; and Marshall, *Constitutional Conventions*, chs 1 and 13.

[57] Mackintosh, *The British Cabinet*, p 13. Brazier, in *Constitutional Practice*, p 3, leaves it open whether the practices that he describes have the status of 'rules'; at (1992) 43 NILQ 262 he distinguishes conventions (which impose duties) from matters of practice.

[58] Marshall and Moodie, *Some Problems of the Constitution*, pp 22–3. Marshall, *Constitutional Conventions*, p 3, refers to conventions as 'non-legal rules of constitutional behaviour'.

[59] Page 29–30 below.

Non-legal rules of the constitution: some examples

1 It is a rule of common law that the royal assent must be given before a Bill which has been approved by both Houses of Parliament can become an Act of Parliament.[60] The manner in which the royal assent may be given is now regulated by statute and in certain circumstances the royal assent may be signified by others on behalf of the Sovereign.[61] These legal rules deal with a vital matter of legal form. But a more important conventional rule is that the royal assent is granted by the Sovereign on the advice of her ministers. Where a Bill has been passed by both Houses of Parliament, the royal assent will be given as a matter of course. The Sovereign's legal power to refuse assent was last exercised by Queen Anne in 1708, when (apparently with the approval of her ministers and without objection by Parliament) the royal assent was refused to the Scottish Militia Bill.[62] In the Irish crisis of 1912–14, the Unionists suggested to George V that he should withhold assent from the Bill to give home rule to Ireland. The Liberal Prime Minister, Asquith, advised the King against this and the royal assent was granted.[63] While the Sovereign may not of her own initiative refuse the royal assent the position may be different if ministers themselves advise this course, although this advice would have to be defended in Parliament and would provoke discussion.

2 At common law the Sovereign has unlimited power to appoint whom she pleases to be her ministers. Statutes provide for the payment of salaries to ministers, and limit the number of appointments which may be made from the House of Commons.[64] There is no rule of law which prevents the Sovereign appointing to ministerial office a person who is outside Parliament. But all appointments are made by the Sovereign on the advice of the Prime Minister and the principle of ministerial responsibility[65] requires that a minister should belong to one or other House of Parliament. If a non-member is appointed to ministerial office, either he must receive a peerage, or he must fight an early by-election to win a seat in the Commons (as did two Labour ministers after the general election in 1964, one (Cousins) succeeding at the by-election and the other (Gordon Walker) again being defeated). In 1983, when a Conservative minister (Mr Hamish Gray) was defeated at the general election, he became a life peer and continued to hold office; this also happened to Lady Chalker in 1992.

The only exception to the general rule is that the two Scottish Law Officers (the Lord Advocate and the Solicitor-General for Scotland) may not always have seats in Parliament, although the practice (dating from 1969) is for the Lord Advocate to receive a life peerage when he is not a member of the Commons. While therefore there is a definite rule that ministers of the Crown should hold seats in Parliament, limited exceptions to the rule are accepted.

---

60   Ch 4 C.
61   Royal Assent Act 1967, Regency Acts 1937–53; ch 10 A.
62   Hearn, *The Government of England*, p 61.
63   Jennings, *Cabinet Government*, pp 395–400. See also ch 12 B. Cf Brazier, *Constitutional Practice*, pp 189–92.
64   Ch 9 B.
65   Ch 7.

3 Although the conduct of a general election is governed by detailed statutory rules,[66] there is no legal rule which regulates the conduct of the Prime Minister when the result of the election is known. But there is a conventional rule that the government must have the confidence of a majority in the Commons. Therefore when it is clear from the election results that the Prime Minister on whose advice the election had been called has lost the election and another party has been successful, he must resign immediately without, as formerly, waiting for the new Parliament to meet.[67] Where the result of the election gives no party an overall majority in the Commons, the Prime Minister may continue in office for such period as is necessary to discover whether he is able to form a coalition or to govern with the support of other parties. In February 1974, when this situation arose, a period of three days elapsed before Mr Heath decided to resign, having learned that the Liberal MPs would not support him. In 1979, an Opposition motion of no confidence in the Labour government was carried by one vote (on 28 March 1979) and forced Mr Callaghan to call an election in May 1979. He resigned as Prime Minister as soon as it was clear that the Conservative party had won the election.

4 Superior judges in England and Wales hold their offices by statute during good behaviour, subject to a power of removal by the Sovereign on an address presented to her by both Houses; by statute they are disqualified from membership of the Commons.[68] Before appointment as a judge, a lawyer may have been active in party politics but a conventional rule requires him or her on appointment to sever links with the party which he or she had formerly supported. Although the legal tenure of judges in Scotland is different, the same conventional rule applies. In 1968, a Scottish judge, Lord Avonside, agreed to serve on a committee to consider the future constitution of Scotland which Mr Heath, then leader of the Opposition, had established. Within a few days, he resigned from the committee when his membership of the Conservative party's committee became a matter of public controversy.[69]

5 The office of Speaker of the House of Commons is recognised by statute.[70] His or her election is the first business of a newly elected House. Before being elected to the post, the Speaker will probably have been a member of one of the two main parties in the House. Once elected, he or she must sever links with that party and must act with complete impartiality. At the next general election, he or she stands as the Speaker, not as a member of a party.

6 The legal opinions which the Law Officers of the Crown give to the government are in law confidential and are protected by legal privilege from being produced as evidence in court proceedings. They may however be published by the government or quoted from in Parliament if (as rarely happens) a minister considers it expedient that the Commons should be told of their contents.[71] During the Westland affair, early in 1986, the Secretary of

---

[66] Ch 9 B.
[67] Ch 12 B.
[68] Ch 18 A.
[69] Ibid.
[70] Eg Parliament Act 1911, s 3. And see Griffith and Ryle, *Parliament*, pp 141–9.
[71] Edwards, *The Law Officers of the Crown*, pp 256–61.

State for Trade and Industry (Mr Brittan) authorised civil servants to leak to the press extracts from a confidential letter to him from the Solicitor-General, without first seeking the latter's consent. 'Cover' but not approval for the leak was sought from the Prime Minister's office. Under a storm of criticism for these events, Mr Brittan had to resign, thus reinforcing the authority of the rule which the Law Officers sought to defend.[72]

Many more examples of conventional rules could be given. They serve a wide variety of constitutional purposes and vary widely in importance. Such rules develop under every system of government, whether a written constitution exists or not. Their special importance in Britain is that it is through such rules and practices that the system of Cabinet government has developed. In earlier times, conventional rules were important in the process by which self-governing colonies in the British Empire attained dominion status,[73] and they determine the Queen's role today in Commonwealth countries where she is head of state.[74] When amendments to the Canadian constitution could be made only by Act of the Westminster Parliament, an elaborate system of conventions and practices evolved as to how the process of amendment should be set in motion.[75] With such a diversity of subject matter, what general characteristics, if any, do these rules possess?

General characteristics[76]

Although some long-established conventional rules (like the rule that the Queen's speech read at the opening of each session of Parliament is prepared by her ministers) have great authority and are universally known, many have developed out of a desire to avoid the formality, explicitness and publicity associated with changes in the law. The development of a regular practice may enable legislation on a point of principle to be avoided. The role of the Sovereign in the conduct of government has almost disappeared since the 18th century without a series of statutes removing one royal power after another. In the same way, many powers have been acquired by the Prime Minister by the operation of convention rather than as the result of legislation. Conventional rules may be used for discreetly managing the internal relationships of government while the outward legal form is left intact.

The informality of such rules is often accompanied by the fact that the rules themselves are not formulated in writing, for example, the rule that judges should not undertake party political activities. But this is not always the case. The government may give to the Commons an undertaking about the future use of its powers – for example, about the laying of treaties before the House to enable them to be debated[77] – or may convey to the House undertakings regarding future practice in the making of certain appoint-

---

72   See eg Linklater and Leigh, *Not Without Honour*, ch 11; and G Marshall [1986] PL 184.
73   Ch 15 C.
74   V Bogdanor and G Marshall [1996] PL 205.
75   Marshall, *Constitutional Conventions*, ch 11.
76   A full discussion by the Supreme Court of Canada is in *Reference re Amendment of the Constitution of Canada* (1982) 125 DLR (3d) 1. See also C R Munro (1975) 91 LQR 218, W Maley (1985) 48 MLR 121 and R Brazier (1992) 43 NILQ 262.
77   The so-called Ponsonby Rule: HC Deb, 1 April 1924, col 2001; ch 15 B.

ments by the Sovereign or Prime Minister. Such undertakings are publicly recorded.[78] One result of the current debate on ministerial responsibility is the publication of documents containing guidance for ministers and civil servants on their duties to Parliament.[79]

The development of unwritten rules is often an evolutionary process. In retrospect, it is possible to identify the time when the royal assent to a Bill was last refused (1708), when the Lord Chief Justice of England last held a seat in the Cabinet (1806) and when a member of the House of Lords last held office as Prime Minister (1902). The fact that each of these events is highly improbable today, and would be regarded as contrary to good constitutional practice, does not mean that this has been so ever since the last occurrence. At a given moment of time, it may be impossible to tell whether practice on a certain matter has hardened into a rule, particularly where the practice is negative in character.

It is for these reasons, as well as the fact that they operate in a political context, that disputes may arise about the existence and content of conventional rules. Moreover, different rules are enforceable in different ways. While the Prime Minister interprets and enforces the rules regarding the duties and collective responsibility of ministers,[80] the rules which forbid a judge to undertake political activities are primarily interpreted and applied by the judge, and depend on the force of public and political opinion. Disputes about the existence and content of legal rules are typically settled by judicial decision. If, as we have seen, many legal rules have an 'open texture', how much more 'open' will be the texture of non-legal rules where there is no definite procedure for resolving disputes about existence and content.

In the past, accounts of constitutional conventions often concentrated on the rules by which powers legally vested in the Sovereign came to be exercised by ministers of the Crown. Dicey considered that conventions were 'rules intended to regulate the exercise of the whole of the remaining discretionary powers of the Crown'.[81] In fact, many non-legal rules fall outside this category. It is more accurate to say that conventional rules regulate the conduct of those holding public office. Our constitutional system allots different roles to the Sovereign, ministers, judges, civil servants and so on. Anyone who would play one of these roles must observe the restraints which the system imposes on those who accept that office. Edward VIII was not willing to accept these constraints and was required to abdicate.[82] So too a minister who does not observe or does not accept the constraints of his office must resign. Mr Nicholas Fairbairn, Solicitor-General for Scotland, resigned after making comments to the press on the Glasgow rape case, one day before an important statement on the subject was to be made to Parliament by the Lord Advocate.[83] In January 1986, Mr Michael Heseltine, Secretary of State for Defence, walked out of a Cabinet meeting and resigned his post because he

---

[78] See HC Deb, 11 December 1962, cols 209–10 (appointment of Serjeant at Arms); and Cmnd 8323, 1981, para 23 (Comptroller and Auditor General).

[79] Ch 7.

[80] *Questions of Procedure for Ministers* (1992); and ch 13 B.

[81] Dicey, p 426.

[82] Ch 12 A.

[83] HC Deb, 21 January 1982, col 423.

was not prepared to accept Cabinet Office clearance for all further ministerial statements on the Westland affair.[84] Similar constraints operate at the institutional level. If the House of Lords does not accept its subordinate role when confronted with the determined will of the Commons, the House knows that it may lose its remaining legislative powers or be abolished.

Why are conventional rules observed?

Dicey, writing as a lawyer in a period dominated by Austinian jurisprudence according to which laws were observed because they could be enforced against the citizen by the coercive power of the state, said:

the sanction which constrains the boldest political adventurer to obey the funda-mental principles of the constitution and the conventions in which these principles are expressed, is the fact that the breach of these principles and of these conventions will almost immediately bring the offender into conflict with the courts and the law of the land.[85]

To support this view, Dicey argued that Parliament meets at least once a year because the government would be compelled to act unlawfully if this did not happen. This argument has been shown to be much weaker than Dicey had supposed.[86] In any event, the rule which the supposed legal sanction supports is antiquated. Today Parliament is expected not merely to meet once a year but to be in session at Westminster for about 34 weeks in the year, interspersed with holidays and the long summer recess. During these weeks there is a customary pattern of parliamentary work to be done. The Provisional Collection of Taxes Act 1968[87] imposes certain constraints upon the timetable of Parliament, but this in itself does not explain why Parliament requires to meet regularly throughout the year. That Parliament should do so is expected by politicians and citizens alike.

It is nearer the mark to say, as did Sir Ivor Jennings, that conventions are observed because of the political difficulties which arise if they are not.[88] As these rules regulate the conduct of those holding public office, possibly the most acute political difficulty which can arise for such a person is to be forced out of office. But an explanation merely in terms of political difficulties is inadequate since not every event which gives rise to political difficulties (for example an unpopular Bill) is a breach of a conventional rule. The Supreme Court of Canada stated that the main purpose of conventions is to ensure that the legal framework of the constitution is operated in accordance with the prevailing constitutional values of the period.[89] On this basis, conventions are observed for the positive reason that they express prevailing constitutional values and for the negative reason of avoiding the difficulties that may follow from 'unconstitutional' conduct.

---

[84]   See D Oliver and R Austin (1987) 40 Parliamentary Affairs 20; and note 72 above.
[85]   Dicey, pp 445–6.
[86]   Eg by Jennings, *The Law and the Constitution*, pp 128–9.
[87]   Ch 10 C.
[88]   *The Law and the Constitution*, p 134.
[89]   *Reference re Amendment of the Constitution of Canada* (1982) 125 DLR (3d) 1, 84.

The meaning of 'unconstitutional'

Where a written constitution ranks as fundamental law, legislative or executive acts which conflict with the constitution may be held unconstitutional and thus illegal. In the United Kingdom, the term 'unconstitutional' has no defined legal content. The 19th-century jurist, Austin, suggested that the Sovereign was acting unconstitutionally when he infringed the maxims of government which with popular approval he generally observed – but by definition the Austinian Sovereign could not act illegally.[90] For Freeman, unconstitutional conduct was conduct contrary to 'the undoubted principles of the unwritten but universally accepted constitution'.[91] It has been commented that 'for the Americans, anything unconstitutional is illegal, however right or necessary it may seem; for the British, anything unconstitutional is wrong, however legal it may be'.[92] The two senses of 'unconstitutional' were illustrated in the Canadian constitutional controversy of 1981–82, when the Supreme Court dealt separately with the issues of whether it would be (a) illegal and (b) in breach of convention for the Federal Parliament to adopt resolutions requesting amendments to the constitution which were opposed by eight of the ten provinces.[93] On the first question, the court held (by seven to two) that such action would not be illegal, but on the second question (by six to three) that it would be in breach of convention.

While conduct may be unconstitutional without being illegal, illegal acts may also be unconstitutional. British politicians who instigated or covered up criminal offences for political ends would be in breach of the code of behaviour recognised by public opinion, as well as being in breach of the criminal law. Ministers are restrained from exceeding their powers not only by the likelihood of legal sanctions but also by the obligation on government to conduct its affairs according to law. When used concerning executive decisions, 'unconstitutional' implies that a decision is not merely incorrect in law but also contrary to fundamental principle, for example where a policy of the Inland Revenue involved 'taxation by self asserted administrative discretion and not by law'.[94] It is in this sense that exemplary damages may in exceptional cases be awarded in the law of tort when public authorities or officials commit wrongful acts that are 'oppressive, arbitrary or unconstitutional'.[95]

However, it is often not easy to determine whether the boundary between constitutional and unconstitutional conduct has been crossed, especially where there is no universally accepted rule of conduct. Different politicians may take opposing views of the constitutional propriety of the acts of a government. Unpopular proposals for new legislation are not for that reason unconstitutional, but a Bill which sought to destroy essential features of the electoral system or to give the Cabinet power to overrule decisions of the courts could rightly be described as unconstitutional.

---

90   Austin, *The Province of Jurisprudence Determined*, pp 257–60.
91   Freeman, *The Growth of the English Constitution*, p 112.
92   Mallory, *The Structure of Canadian Government*, p 2.
93   Note 76 above.
94   *Vestey v Inland Revenue Commissioners* [1980] AC 1148, 1173.
95   *Rookes v Barnard* [1964] AC 1129.

Another difficulty in determining what is constitutional in a given situation is that there may be no relevant precedent. When in 1932 the Cabinet of the National government agreed to differ on a major issue of economic policy, an attack on the government for unconstitutional conduct was met by the rejoinder:

Who can say what is constitutional in the conduct of a National Government? It is a precedent, an experiment, a new practice, to meet a new emergency, a new condition of things . . .[96]

In 1975, the open disagreement of the Labour Cabinet over Britain's continued membership of the EEC was defended in similar terms.

Consequences of a breach of conventional rule

Various consequences may follow the breach of conventional rules. Loss of office or departure from public life would be the severest consequence as in 1990, when a member of Mrs Thatcher's Cabinet, Mr Ridley, made a strongly anti-European speech which departed from stated government policy towards the European Communities, and he resigned his ministerial post. The force of public opinion may simply force the offender to think again: thus the Scottish judge who in 1968 joined a committee established by the Conservative party resigned rather than prejudice the work of the committee.[97] In these instances, the outcome reinforces the established rule. A less serious consequence would be a reprimand or a reminder not to act similarly in the future, given by someone in a position to enforce the rule. If no adverse consequences follow, the matter becomes more open. It may be expedient that, for instance, the Prime Minister should turn a blind eye to acts of colleagues that breach a rule for ministers: but if such acts are repeatedly condoned, it must be asked whether the rule has been abandoned or modified.

As constitutional rules often give rise to reciprocal obligations, one consequence of a breach may be to release another office-holder from the normal constraints that would otherwise be binding. When Ian Smith's Cabinet in 1965 unilaterally declared Rhodesia's independence, the immediate response of the UK government, conveyed through the Governor-General of Rhodesia, was to dismiss the entire Cabinet. In the event this dismissal proved purely nominal. More significantly, the Southern Rhodesia Act 1965 was passed at Westminster to give the government full power to legislate for the domestic affairs of Rhodesia, thus overriding the previous convention that the Westminster Parliament would not exercise its sovereignty in such matters except with the agreement of the Rhodesian government.[98]

Another consequence may be the passing of legislation to avoid a similar breach in the future. When in 1909 the Lords rejected the Liberal government's Finance Bill, the crisis was resolved only by the Parliament Act 1911, which removed the power of the Lords to veto or delay money Bills. The 1911 Act contained other provisions intended to place the Lords–Commons

---

[96] Mr Baldwin, HC Deb, 8 February 1932, col 535.
[97] Ch 18 B.
[98] Cf *Madzimbamuto v Lardner-Burke* [1969] AC 645, 723.

relationship on a new footing.[99] These provisions led in turn to new conventional doctrine regarding the use by the House of Lords of its residual powers.

Should all constitutional rules be enacted as law?

In theory, all the non-legal rules of the constitution could be enacted in legal form by one or more Acts of Parliament. Written constitutions in the Commonwealth have adopted various means of incorporating conventions: express enactment of the main rules, wholesale adoption by reference to practice in the United Kingdom and so on.[100]

If a written constitution were to be drafted for the United Kingdom, many hard decisions on these matters would have to be made. It would, for example, be very difficult to anticipate every possible eventuality in which the Sovereign might be required to invite a new Prime Minister to form a government. There would be no real difficulty in framing the main principles of responsible government, but this would make little difference if the principles continued to govern an essentially political relationship between government and Parliament: to make the doctrine of responsible government enforceable by the courts would be to change its character entirely.[101]

While enactment may be useful in the case of particular rules that need to be clarified, there is little to be said for 'codifying' the non-legal rules of the constitution. They cover so diverse an area that they could not sensibly be included within a single code. Even if the attempt was made, it would be impossible to stop the process by which formal rules are gradually modified by informal rules, principles and practices from starting over again.

There is indeed an indistinct borderline between conduct which is a matter of habitual practice, and conduct which occurs as a result of what is felt to be constitutional obligation. Textbooks on constitutional law often exaggerate the extent to which rules govern political life.

In 1963, by a procedure without precedent, the 14th Earl of Home was chosen to follow Harold Macmillan as Prime Minister and renounced his title so that he could enter the House of Commons as Sir Alec Douglas-Home. Commenting upon these events, Professor Griffith coined two aphorisms as an antidote against a convention-dominated view of the constitution: 'the constitution is what happens' and 'if it works, it's constitutional'. His comment concluded: 'So let us delete those pages in constitutional textbooks headed Conventions, and talk about what happens and why what happened yesterday may not happen tomorrow.'[102] In other words, it is better to discuss why it would be politically impossible today for a Prime Minister to govern

---

[99]   Ch 10 B.
[100] de Smith, *The New Commonwealth and its Constitutions*, pp 78–87. For an Australian exercise in re-stating the conventions, see C Sampford and D Wood [1987] PL 231.
[101] In 1996, Sir Richard Scott (p 113 below) said that if ministers did not accept the obligations of accountability, a statutory duty requiring them to keep Parliament informed should be enacted and enforced by the courts: [1996] PL 410, 426.
[102] [1963] PL 401–2. For criticism of the distinction between law and convention, see Jennings, *The Law and the Constitution*, p 132, and Mitchell, *Constitutional Law*, pp 34–8; and in reply, Marshall, *Constitutional Theory*, pp 7–12. See also note 76 above.

from the House of Lords, than to try and read back into past events a rule to this effect.

One reply to this approach involves considering the relation between the reasons which give rise to a rule, and the rule itself. Legal rules, whether made by the judges or by Parliament, may continue long after the original reasons for them have been forgotten. In the constitutional field, the informality of many non-legal rules enables them to disappear or to change as the underlying reasons for the rule change. This does not mean that so long as the original circumstances continue, there is no rule. Within a stable political system, what is learned by experience can be expressed in the form of rules for future conduct. The abdication of Edward VIII and the reasons for it must have influenced Elizabeth II and her advisers. The early failure of the 'agreement to differ' in 1932 has not encouraged later Cabinets to repeat the experiment. One lesson from previous events is that short-term political expediency may be a temptation that an experienced government ought to resist, and that constitutional principle may provide more reliable norms of conduct. As Freeman wrote in 1872:

Political men may debate whether such and such a course is or is not constitutional, just as lawyers may debate whether such a course is not legal. But the very form of the debate implies that there is a Constitution to be observed, just as in the other case it implies that there is a law to be observed.[103]

The motives for human conduct are usually mixed. If we seek to understand the behaviour of the Sovereign, a politician or a judge, we may discover both a degree of enlightened self-interest and also a strong perception of constitutional obligation. If that perception is shared by others in a similar position, as well as by informed commentators, it is difficult to explain such behaviour without reference to the perceived obligation. Without understanding the rules that differentiate the actors in their various roles at the opening of a new session of Parliament, it is difficult to explain why, for example, the Sovereign's speech is so different in character from the Prime Minister's speech in the ensuing debate in the House of Commons. The fact that conventional rules may change without formal amendment does not mean that they are irrelevant to political behaviour.

The attitude of the courts

In this section it has been assumed that the rules under discussion are not capable of being enforced through the courts. If, when a rule has been broken, a remedy is available in the courts for securing relief or imposing a sanction upon the wrongdoer, this would indicate that the rule has the quality of law. Where a non-legal rule has been broken, no remedy will be available in the courts. Often the citizen's only recourse will be political action – a complaint to an MP, a letter to the press, a public demonstration or protest. In view of the political nature of most conventional rules, the stress on political or parliamentary remedies is appropriate. Moreover, many conventional rules, for example those relating to the Cabinet system, do not affect a citizen's rights closely enough for a judicial remedy to be justified.

---

[103]   *The Growth of the English Constitution*, p 112; cf Loughlin, *Public Law and Political Theory*, p 53.

It may however be necessary for a court to take into account the existence of a conventional rule in making its decision on a point of law. This is likely to happen in administrative law cases where the court's decision on the extent of judicial control may be affected by the doctrine of ministerial responsibility. The courts have taken judicial notice of the fact that civil servants take decisions in the name of ministers and of the fact that ministers may be called to account by Parliament for the decisions.[104] The Australian High Court took account of the conventional rules which in practice restricted legislation by the UK Parliament for Australia before the rules were enacted in the Statute of Westminster 1931.[105] But on an appeal from Rhodesia following the unilateral declaration of independence, the Judicial Committee, referring to the former convention by which Westminster would not legislate for Rhodesia except at the request of the Rhodesian government, stated that the convention had no legal effect and that the Judicial Committee were concerned only with the legal powers of Parliament.[106]

The Crossman diaries case is an outstanding illustration of the inter-relation of legal and non-legal rules. As a last resort, an attempt was made by the Attorney-General in the public interest to prevent the breach of a conventional rule and to establish the existence of a legal obligation. The court held that former Cabinet ministers could be restrained by injunction from publishing confidential information which came to them as ministers, since there was a legal obligation to respect that confidentiality.[107] But it would be wrong to state simply that the court was enforcing the convention of collective responsibility; that convention was no more than one factor taken into account by the judge in establishing the limits of the legal doctrine of confidence. In the different context of the Canadian constitution, by a reference procedure which permits Canadian courts to give wide-ranging advisory opinions, the Supreme Court of Canada in 1981 gave an opinion on the existence of the conventions governing the process of constitutional amendment.[108] It is difficult to imagine circumstances in which the British courts would have jurisdiction to give a similar opinion.

C. Other sources of the constitution

The law and custom of Parliament

While a distinction may be drawn between rules of the constitution which have the force of law and those which do not, it is difficult to classify the law and custom of Parliament under either heading. In earlier days, reference was often made to the 'High Court of Parliament'.[109] Each House has power over its own procedure and has certain privileges and immunities. The inherent authority of each House to control its own internal affairs is respected by the

---

104   *Carltona Ltd v Commissioners of Works* [1943] 2 All ER 560; p 127 below. And see *R v Environment Secretary, ex p Notts CC* [1986] AC 240.
105   *Copyright Owners Reproduction Society Ltd v EMI (Australia) Pty Ltd* (1958) 100 CLR 597.
106   *Madzimbamuto v Lardner-Burke* [1969] AC 645.
107   *A-G v Jonathan Cape Ltd* [1976] QB 752; ch 13 B.
108   Note 76 above. Cf *Adegbenro v Akintola* [1963] AC 614.
109   McIlwain, *The High Court of Parliament*, especially ch 2.

ordinary courts of law, who seek to avoid interfering in these matters.[110] Many rules of constitutional importance are contained in the standing orders of the House of Commons, as well as in resolutions of the House and in other sources of the practice of the House, such as rulings by the Speaker.[111]

As well as the formal powers of each House, many informal practices and understandings are observed between the two main parties in the Commons, between the two front benches and the back-bench members, and between the main parties and the smaller parties. These practices are not contained in standing orders, nor are they often mentioned in that authoritative guide to the procedure of Parliament, Erskine May, but they directly affect the conduct of parliamentary business. These practices have resemblances to the conventional rules of the constitution which apply outside Parliament. Departure from these practices could lead to changed conduct within Parliament, for example the withdrawal of cooperation between government and opposition (such as agreed pairing between absent MPs), and possibly to changes in the formal rules of parliamentary business.

Within Parliament, therefore, there are formal rules, informal rules, principles and practices; and the distinction between these various categories is often no more certain in Parliament than outside. In general the ordinary courts have no jurisdiction to apply and enforce the law of Parliament.

Legal and constitutional literature

In English law, as a general rule no legal textbook has intrinsic authority as a source of law: the authority of the most eminent textbook is confined to the extent to which a court considers that it accurately reproduces the law as enacted by the legislature or decided by earlier courts. Where a statute has not yet been judicially interpreted, or where no court has pronounced authoritatively on a matter of common law, then the opinions of textbook writers and academic authors may be of great value when a case arises for decision.[112] Dicey's *Law of the Constitution* has profoundly influenced academic and judicial reasoning; and the recent development of administrative law owes much to the writing of the late Professor de Smith and of Sir William Wade.

In Scots law, the position is very different as regards the past. A series of eminent legal authors between the mid-17th and early 19th centuries, including Viscount Stair, Professor John Erskine and Baron David Hume, are known as the institutional writers. Their work expounded the private law and criminal law of Scotland in a systematic manner which derived much from the institutional writers of Roman law: in the absence of other authority, a statement in their works is likely to be taken as settling the law.[113] The approach of the Scottish legal system to the question of legal authority was seen in *Burmah Oil Co v Lord Advocate*,[114] relating to the Crown's prerogative:

---

[110]   Ch 11 A.
[111]   Erskine May, *Parliamentary Practice*, pp 1–6, 181.
[112]   For clear recognition of this by the House of Lords, see *Woolwich BS v IRC (No 2)* [1993] AC 70, 163 (Lord Goff).
[113]   Walker, *The Scottish Legal System*, p 401.
[114]   [1965] AC 75; ch 12 D.

the case having reached the House of Lords on appeal from Scotland, counsel and judges referred extensively to the civilian writers of earlier centuries, in a manner untypical of the English common law.

Legal writers on the constitution are handicapped by the unreality of many of the legal terms which they must sometimes employ.[115] Statements about the prerogative powers of the Crown often seem archaic, or to be conferring despotic powers upon the Sovereign, until it is realised that they concern powers of government exercised by ministers, civil servants and other Crown servants.

In certain areas of the constitution, books such as Jennings's *Cabinet Government*, Mackintosh's *The British Cabinet*, Griffith and Ryle's *Parliament* and Brazier's *Constitutional Practice* are a valuable record of practice. Since they are founded in part upon historical sources and in part upon contemporary political accounts, it is not surprising that works on British government are seldom unanimous in their description of controversial events (for example, the differing interpretations of the political crisis in 1931 which led to the formation of the National government).[116] Rules of official secrecy may make it difficult to write about current practice. While most Cabinet papers are available in the Public Record Office after 30 years, the structure of Cabinet committees and the rules of conduct for ministers were until 1992 regarded as secret.[117] Another problem is that historical precedents are often of doubtful relevance to present issues. Jennings, whose book was first published in 1936, used constitutional precedents dating from 1841.[118] But the system of government has changed so much since 1900 that precedents from before, say, the Labour government of 1945 are of little more than historical interest.

In the field of parliamentary procedure, which is not affected by considerations of secrecy, a work which has especial authority is Erskine May's *Parliamentary Practice*. First published in 1844, this is revised regularly under the editorship of the Clerk to the House of Commons, and it summarises the collective experience of the Clerks of the House.[119] It is essentially a means of reference to the original sources, which are found in standing orders, in resolutions of the House, and in rulings given by the Speaker and recorded in Hansard.

Finally, there is a more diverse source of information, namely the unending flow from government and Parliament of reports of such bodies as royal commissions, departmental committees, committees of Parliament and tribunals of inquiry. Many of these reports have concerned important constitutional topics, the most notable in recent years being the first report of the Nolan committee on standards in public life and Sir Richard Scott's massive report on the 'arms for Iraq' inquiry.[120] There is also the prolific class of reports by select committees of the House of Commons into the activities of the government departments with which they are concerned.[121] The reports

---

115   Cf Bagehot, *The English Constitution*, pp 99–100.
116   See Bassett, *1931: Political Crisis*.
117   Ch 13 B.
118   Jennings, *Cabinet Government*, p 9.
119   See the 21st edn by C J Boulton, 1989.
120   Respectively Cm 2850–I (1995) and HC 115 (1995–96).
121   Ch 10 D.

of the Parliamentary Ombudsman give a more detailed insight into the methods of central departments than can be obtained from the law reports or Hansard alone. These publications do not reach heights of literary excellence, but they provide information about the working of government which is not given by formal legal sources nor by political authors. British membership of the European Union has given rise to a flow of official publications from the headquarters of the European Community.

D.   Constitutional government in Britain

Evolutionary development

The British constitution is flexible, not in the sense that it is unstable but in that many of its principles and rules can be changed by an Act of Parliament or the establishment of a new conventional rule. Perhaps because of this flexibility, the constitution has, at least since 1688, escaped those revolutionary convulsions which may occur in countries with more rigid constitutions but less stable political systems. Since the settlement of 1688, there have been innumerable changes in the system of government, some freely conceded but many fought for by political action. The result has been a complete change from personal rule by the monarch to the collective ascendancy of the Prime Minister and Cabinet. Many of the older forms and organs have survived from earlier times, and these are tolerated or respected because they represent historic continuity. Writing in 1867, Walter Bagehot in *The English Constitution* distinguished between the *dignified* parts of the constitution 'which excite and preserve the reverence of the population' and the *efficient* parts, 'by which it, in fact, works and rules'.[122] Bagehot called it the characteristic merit of the constitution 'that its dignified parts are very complicated and somewhat imposing, very old and rather venerable; while its efficient part, at least when in great and critical action, is decidedly simple and rather modern.'[123] Certainly the apparent continuity can be misleading. In 1973, the Royal Commission on the Constitution, who should have known better, were moved to say: 'The United Kingdom already possesses a constitution which in its essentials has served well for some hundreds of years.'[124] In complacent reflections of this kind, the term 'constitution' might well be replaced by a phrase such as 'system of government and politics'.

The evolutionary nature of the British system of government is illustrated by the changing position of the Sovereign; despite the vast changes that have occurred since 1688, it could not in 1997 be assumed that development in the monarchy had reached finality. As regards such matters as the accountability of government to Parliament, the electoral system, the internal structure of the United Kingdom and the protection of human rights, there were strong arguments in 1997 for further reform. The process of political evolution may

---

[122]   *The English Constitution*, p 61.
[123]   Ibid, p 65.
[124]   Kilbrandon Report, para 395.

have avoided lapsing into revolution, but there has been no simple, linear improvement in democracy.

The party system

Parliamentary government cannot be explained solely in terms of legal and conventional rules. It depends essentially upon the political base which underlies it, in particular on the party system around which political life is organised. Given the present political parties and the electoral system, it is accepted that, following a general election, the party with a majority of seats in the House of Commons will form the government. As the British system of politics is strongly centralised, power to direct national affairs passes to the leadership of the party which, in popular terms, has won the general election. Except for February 1974, every general election held between 1931 and 1997 produced an absolute majority in the Commons for one or other of the major parties. Even if that majority is counted in single figures (as it was in 1950–51, 1964–66 and after October 1974) it serves as a basis for the government's authority. In terms of the ability to govern for the time being, it is irrelevant that the majority of seats in the Commons represents only a minority of votes cast by the electorate – as it did in every election between 1906 and 1992 except in 1931 and 1935. The general election in 1997 led to a House of Commons in which there were 417 Labour MPs, 163 Conservative MPs, and 79 other MPs from the smaller parties. There was, as in all recent elections, a wide discrepancy between the seats won by the parties and their total votes.

The British system therefore appears to provide strong government, the continuance of the government in office being dependent mainly upon the ability of the governing party to retain its majority in the Commons. The concentration of power in the hands of the executive makes it necessary to emphasise that the British system is only tolerable because of the range of restraints upon government which exist. One restraint is the certainty of a general election, guaranteed by law to occur at least every five years and often likely to occur more frequently.

Another restraint is that government policies run the gauntlet of criticism from Opposition parties and others in Parliament. Another is that a government cannot ignore the force of public reaction to its measures (as was seen when Mrs Thatcher was ousted from power in 1990): legislation which has passed through Parliament may not be enforceable unless it is accepted by the majority of those to whom it is intended to apply. Moreover, it is salutary to a government to know that its majority of members in the Commons (417 out of 659, after the election in 1997) was elected by only a minority of the electors (some 44% of the votes cast in 1997).

While there have been periods since the partition of Ireland when it has been possible to think of the United Kingdom as forming a single political system, dominated by two national parties, this has not been possible since 1974. Difficult as this period has been for the third party (now the Liberal Democrats), electoral gains have been made at the expense of the two bigger parties. Moreover, from Scotland, Wales and Northern Ireland, other parties are represented at Westminster; in a closely balanced House of Commons, they have affected the outcome of important votes. Those parties come from smaller political 'systems' in which the general trends of party politics in England were not necessarily reproduced. In 1953, an elder statesman of the Conservative party wrote:

the two-party system has been the normal type to which, after occasional interludes, we have regularly reverted, for the very reason that it has always centred round the business of maintaining a majority in Parliament for a Government or securing its displacement by another Government.[125]

Certainly the Conservative and Labour parties have a common interest in seeking to maintain a rigorous two-party system. But the constitutional structure of Britain does not rest upon that system, even if for many politicians the ideal state of affairs is one in which they hold office with their party commanding an absolute majority in the Commons, as the Conservatives did after the elections in 1979, 1983, 1987 and 1992. Periods of minority government, as occurred between February and October 1974, and again between 1976 and 1979, may well lead to developments in government like the agreement between the Labour government and the Liberal party in 1977–78.[126] But there are no reasons based on constitutional principle for regretting such developments. Indeed, there would be real advantage from a democratic viewpoint if a government's proposals and performance could come under more effective scrutiny in the Commons than is possible when that House is dominated by the government. Nor can coalitions, electoral pacts and unwritten understandings between the parties be regarded as unconstitutional.[127] Nor should the occasional decision of an MP to switch allegiance to another party be seen as a threat to the democratic process.[128]

It is not possible in a book on constitutional law to give an account of the political system of the United Kingdom. The internal procedures of the parties are however often of constitutional importance – for example, the election of a leader, the relationship between the parliamentary party and other bodies, and the relationship between the party and interests such as the trade unions. We will be examining electoral law, including such rules as there are on the financing of the parties.[129] As between the parties, this book seeks to apply the theory behind electoral law, namely that in a society which recognises the freedom of association for political purposes, the law should maintain conditions of neutrality between all contesting parties.

Politicians, and the role of the parties in political life, are often criticised. It has been argued that the party system serves not so much to enable public opinion to be represented in Parliament, as to restrict the scope for popular participation in the process of government. One advocate of this view submits that participation of the people will be enhanced if the electoral system is changed to one of proportional representation, and if the referendum becomes more widely used as a means of taking national decisions.[130] These

---

[125]   Amery, *Thoughts on the Constitution*, p 43; and cf Jennings, *Parliament*, pp 23–4.
[126]   See Steel, *A House Divided: the Lib-Lab Pact and the Future of British Politics.*
[127]   See Butler (ed), *Coalitions in British Politics*; Butler, *Governing without a Majority: Dilemmas for Hung Parliaments in Britain*; Bogdanor, *Multi-party Politics and the Constitution.*
[128]   On MPs who cross the floor of the Commons between elections, see P Cowley [1996] PL 214.
[129]   Ch 9 B, III.
[130]   Bogdanor, *The People and the Party System.*

developments may yet occur, but if it continues to be accepted that the pendulum of government should merely swing at intervals between Labour and Conservative, those parties are unlikely to seek to modify the traditional process.

CHAPTER 3

The structure of the United Kingdom

A. The historic structure

While the external identity of a state is a matter for international law, it is constitutional law which regulates the internal relationships of the various territories which make up the state. In the past, writers often used the word 'English' in referring to the constitution, a usage liable to give the false impression that English law prevailed throughout the United Kingdom. Dicey and Bagehot, for example, wrote about the English constitution when they were dealing with the British constitution or, to be completely accurate, with what was then the constitution of the United Kingdom of Great Britain and Ireland. The active political consciousness of Ireland since the 19th century, and that of Scotland and Wales more recently, means that constitutional lawyers must now choose their geographical adjectives with care. When in 1969 a royal commission on the constitution was appointed, among its duties was 'to examine the present functions of the central legislature and government in relation to *the several countries, nations and regions* of the United Kingdom' and also to consider the constitutional and economic relationships between the United Kingdom and the Channel Islands and the Isle of Man.[1] Some of the deliberate vagueness of the words in italics was dispelled when the commission's report referred to England, Scotland, Wales and Northern Ireland as the four countries which make up the United Kingdom.

Legal definitions

In law, the expression 'United Kingdom' refers to the United Kingdom of Great Britain and Northern Ireland; it does not include the Channel Islands or the Isle of Man.[2] For purposes of international relations, however, the Channel Islands and the Isle of Man are represented by the UK government. So are the colonies and other dependent territories of the United Kingdom overseas.[3]

The expression 'British Islands' is defined in the Interpretation Act 1978 as

---

[1]   See section B below.
[2]   Interpretation Act 1978, Sched 1. By the British Nationality Act 1981, s 50 (1), the United Kingdom includes the Channel Islands and the Isle of Man for purposes of nationality law.
[3]   Ch 15 C.

meaning the United Kingdom, the Channel Islands and the Isle of Man. The British Islands do not in law include the Republic of Ireland, which is outside the United Kingdom.[4]

The expression 'Great Britain' refers to England, Scotland and Wales: these first became a single kingdom by virtue of art 1 of the Treaty of Union between England and Scotland in 1707.

The Wales and Berwick Act 1746 provided that where the expression 'England' was used in an Act of Parliament, this should be taken to include the dominion of Wales and the town of Berwick on Tweed. But the Welsh Language Act 1967, s 4, provided that references to England in future Acts should not include the dominion of Wales. Concerning the boundary between Wales and England, a long-standing controversy was brought to an end by the Local Government Act 1972, which declared that Monmouthshire was to be within Wales.[5]

The adjective 'British' is used in common speech to refer to matters associated with Great Britain or the United Kingdom. It has no definite legal connotation and one authority has described the expression 'British law' as hopelessly ambiguous.[6] In legislation 'British' is sometimes used as an adjective referring to the United Kingdom, particularly in the context of nationality.[7]

Historical development of the United Kingdom

1 Wales.[8]   While it is not possible to summarise the lengthy history by which the kingdom of England became a single entity, it is worthwhile briefly to examine the historical formation of the United Kingdom. The military conquest of Wales by the English reached its culmination in 1282, when Prince Llywelyn was killed and his principality passed by conquest to King Edward I of England. Thereafter the principality (which formed only part of what is now Wales) was administered in the name of the Prince, but the rest of Wales was subjected to rule by a variety of local princes and lords; at this period English law was not extended to Wales, where the local customs, laws and language prevailed. From 1471, a Council of Wales and the Marches brought Wales under closer rule from England and the accession of the Tudors did much to complete the process of assimilation. In 1536, an Act of the English Parliament united Wales with England, establishing an administrative system on English lines, requiring the English language to be used, and granting Wales representation in the English Parliament.[9] In 1543, a system of Welsh courts (the Courts of the Great Sessions) was established to apply the common law of England. The Council of Wales and the Marches was granted a statutory jurisdiction which it exercised until its abolition in 1689. In 1830, the Courts of the Great Sessions were abolished and in their

---

4   As to which, see Roberts-Wray, *Commonwealth and Colonial Law*, pp 32–5.
5   Ss 1(12), 20(7) and 269; Interpretation Act 1978, Sched 1.
6   Roberts-Wray, op cit, p 69.
7   British Nationality Act 1981. See ch 20 A.
8   Kilbrandon Report, ch 5, and Andrews (ed), *Welsh Studies in Public Law*, specially chs 2 (D Jenkins), 3 (H Carter) and 4 (I L Gowan).
9   27 Hen VIII, c 26. The Statute Law Revision Act 1948 called this Act the Laws in Wales Act 1535, but recent Welsh writers have called it the Act of Union of 1536: *Welsh Studies*, p 28.

place were set up two new circuits to operate as part of the English court system. After the union with England, Acts of Parliament applying exclusively to Wales were rare.[10]

The mid-19th century saw the beginning of a political and educational revival, and occasional Acts of Parliament applying only to Wales began again to be passed.[11] In 1906 the Welsh Department of the Board of Education was established, the first central department created specifically to administer Welsh affairs.[12] In 1914 was passed the Welsh Church Act, which disestablished and disendowed the Church of England in Wales. Thereafter, from time to time, the identity of Wales was recognised as new administrative arrangements were made. In 1949 a Council for Wales and Monmouthshire was established with the task of keeping the government informed of the impact of governmental activities on the life of the Welsh people: this Council gave way to the Welsh Economic Planning Council in 1966 and to the Welsh Council in 1968.[13] In 1964 following various ministerial experiments, the post of Secretary of State for Wales was established and the Welsh Office emerged as a department of the UK government.[14] Wales and England share a common legal system, but some statutes make special provision for Wales. By the Welsh Language Act 1967, the Welsh language may be spoken in any legal proceedings within Wales, by any person who desires to use it; and ministers are authorised to prescribe the use of Welsh versions of any official document or form. The Welsh Language Act 1993 created the Welsh Language Board, to further the principle in Wales that public services and the courts should treat the English and Welsh languages on a basis of equality.

2 Scotland.[15]   Unlike Wales, Scotland was able to maintain its national independence against English military and political pressures during the Middle Ages. Scotland retained its own monarchy and only in the 16th century did the two royal lines come closer together with the marriage to James IV of Scotland of Henry VII's daughter, Margaret. On the death of Elizabeth in 1603, James VI of Scotland, great-great-grandson of Henry VII, became James I of England. This personal union of the two monarchies had the legal consequence that persons born in England and Scotland after the union both owed allegiance to the same King.[16] During the conflicts of the 17th century, events took a broadly similar course in both countries and for a brief period under Cromwell, the Commonwealth of England, Scotland and Ireland was subject to a single legislature and executive. But apart from this, and despite the personal union of the monarchies, the constitutions of the two countries were not united and both the English and the Scottish

---

[10] See eg Welsh Bible and Prayer Book Act 1563: *Welsh Studies*, pp 38–9.
[11] See eg Sunday Closing (Wales) Act 1881: *Welsh Studies*, p 48.
[12] *Welsh Studies*, p 49.
[13] Ibid, pp 62–3.
[14] Section B below.
[15] Kilbrandon Report, ch 4; also Donaldson, *Scotland: James V–James VII*; Ferguson, *Scotland, 1689 to the Present*; HLE, vol 8(2), pp 54–72.
[16] *Calvin's* case (1608) 7 Co Rep 1a.

Parliaments maintained separate existences.[17] Following the ousting of James II/VII in 1688, the Scottish Parliament for the first time asserted independence of the royal will. There followed for some 20 years a contest of wills between the English and Scottish Parliaments, marked by religious disputation and by keen rivalry to profit from expanding ventures in world trade, against a deeply insecure European background. In 1704, the Scottish Parliament by the Act of Security went so far as to provide that if Anne died without heirs the Parliament would choose her successor, 'provided always that the same be not successor to the Crown of England', unless in the meantime acceptable conditions of government had been established between the two countries.[18] Following a strong initiative from the English government, the English and Scottish Parliaments authorised negotiations between two groups of commissioners representing each Parliament but appointed by the Queen. The Treaty of Union was drawn up by them and was approved by Act of each Parliament together with an Act to maintain Presbyterian church government within Scotland.[19]

The Treaty of Union came into effect on 1 May 1707: it united the two kingdoms of England and Scotland into one by the name of Great Britain; the Crown was to descend to the Hanoverian line after Anne's death; there was to be a Parliament of Great Britain including 16 Scottish peers and 45 elected members in the Commons. Extensive financial and economic terms were included in the Treaty. Guarantees were given for the continuance of Scottish private law (art 18) and the Scottish courts (art 19), as well as for the maintenance of the feudal jurisdictions in Scotland and the privileges of the royal burghs in Scotland. The Act to maintain the Presbyterian Church in Scotland was incorporated in the Treaty and also provided for the maintenance of the Scottish universities. While the Treaty was described as an incorporating union (ie it did not establish a federal system and did not maintain the previous Scottish and English legislatures for any purpose), it gave extensive guarantees to Scottish institutions. Guarantees of a similar kind for English institutions were not required as it was obvious that the English would be politically predominant in the new Parliament of Great Britain.[20]

In the years after 1707, the new unity of Great Britain was challenged by the Jacobite uprisings in 1715 and 1745 but without success. Various expedients were resorted to for governing Scotland from London, and from time to time new laws were made for Scotland by the Parliament of Great Britain. Some of these, for example the abolition of the Scottish feudal jurisdictions in 1747, were considered in Scotland to be a breach of the Treaty of Union. The Scottish Privy Council having been abolished in 1708, for much of the 18th and 19th centuries the Lord Advocate, the Crown's chief law officer in Scotland, occupied the primary role in politics and government, managing affairs in Scotland on behalf of the Crown. In 1885, a new post of Secretary for Scotland was created and in 1928 the post was raised to Cabinet status with the

---

[17] See Donaldson, op cit, ch 15, and Terry, *The Scottish Parliament 1603–1707.*
[18] APS XI, 136.
[19] Scottish Act: APS XI, 406, English Act: 6 Anne c 11; *Halsbury's Statutes*, vol 10, p 44. For the making of the union, see Riley, *The Union of England and Scotland.*
[20] On the legal effect of these guarantees, see ch 4 D.

title of Secretary of State for Scotland. Demands for home rule for Scotland were expressed from the late 19th century onwards: the response of the government was to develop the Scottish Office as the department responsible for Scottish affairs.[21] Political demands for a Scottish legislative assembly were firmly resisted, although greater use was made of committees of Scottish MPs in the Commons. Since 1707, Parliament has often legislated separately for the English and Scottish legal systems. In particular, the structure of private law, courts, education and local government in Scotland has always differed from the English pattern.

3 Northern Ireland.[22]   The constitutional history of Northern Ireland is inextricably linked with the history of Ireland itself. As an entity Northern Ireland dates only from the partition of Ireland in the early 1920s. Ireland itself first came under English influence in the 12th century when Henry II of England became Lord of Ireland. As settlers came from England, courts modelled on those in England were established. While an Irish Parliament began to develop, some English legislation was extended to Ireland by ordinance of the King of England. In 1494, the Irish Parliament passed the statute known as Poyning's Law, which required that all Irish Bills should be submitted to the King and his Council in England; only such Bills as the English Council approved were to be returned for the Irish Parliament to pass. In 1541, the title of Lord of Ireland was changed to King of Ireland. During the 17th century, Ireland had its share of religious bitterness and conflict. William of Orange defeated the former King James II at the Battle of the Boyne in 1690. There followed a dispute over the power of the Irish House of Lords to hear appeals from Irish courts, and in 1720 the British Parliament by statute declared that it retained full power to legislate for Ireland and deprived the Irish House of Lords of all its judicial powers. Pressure from Ireland for greater autonomy led in 1782 to the repeal of the Declaratory Act of 1720, and to the recognition by the British Parliament of the Irish Parliament's legislative independence of Britain, although there was no change in the position of the monarchy.[23] But legislative independence was shortlived and after the rising of the United Irishmen in 1798, the British government proceeded to a legislative union with Ireland.

The Union agreement between the two Parliaments was broadly similar to the Union with Scotland, although fewer constitutional guarantees were given to Ireland than had been given to Scotland. Article 1 created the United Kingdom of Great Britain and Ireland, and arts 3 and 4 provided for Irish representation in the new Parliament of the United Kingdom. Article 5 provided for the (Protestant) United Church of England and Ireland, whose continuance was stated to be an essential and fundamental part of the Union.

---

21   Section B below.
22   For the earlier history, see Donaldson, *Some Comparative Aspects of Irish Law,* for the 1920 Constitution, see Calvert, *Constitutional Law in Northern Ireland,* and Kilbrandon Report, ch 6. Also Hadfield, *The Constitution of Northern Ireland;* Hadfield (ed), *Northern Ireland: Politics and the Constitution;* C McCrudden, in Jowell and Oliver (eds), *The Changing Constitution,* ch 12; McEldowney, *Public Law,* ch 19; Morison and Livingstone, *Reshaping Public Power,* HLE, vol 8(2), pp 72–93.
23   Cf *Re Keenan* [1972] 1 QB 533.

Within the enlarged United Kingdom, all trade was to be free; the laws in force in Ireland were to continue, subject to alteration by the UK Parliament from time to time. As with the Scottish union, the terms of the Union were separately adopted by Act of each of the two Parliaments concerned.[24]

The Irish Union with Britain was less stable than the Anglo-Scottish Union of 1707. For much of the 19th century and until the present day, the Irish question proved to be one of the most difficult political and constitutional issues within the United Kingdom. Catholic emancipation occurred in 1829, opening the way for political demands for further constitutional reform, often associated with militant action and acts of violence. The Irish Church was disestablished in 1869 despite the guarantee for its existence contained in the Act of Union.[25] Gladstone's two Home Rule Bills in 1886 and 1893 were both defeated in Parliament, the first time in the Commons, the second in the Lords. After the Parliament Act 1911 had taken away the power of the House of Lords to veto legislation[26] the Government of Ireland Act 1914 became law, but it never came into effect because of the outbreak of world war; its parliamentary history had been marked by the extreme determination of Ulster Protestants not to be separated from Britain.

The Easter rising in Dublin in 1916 was further evidence of the nationalist feeling in Catholic Ireland. In 1919 the Sinn Fein movement established a representative assembly for what was proclaimed to be the Irish Republic. In 1920 the Government of Ireland Act was passed by the UK Parliament, providing for two Parliaments in Ireland, one for six northern counties and one for the remainder of Ireland, with cooperation between the two to be maintained by means of a Council of Ireland. The 1920 Act was ignored by Sinn Fein and, after a period of bitter civil war, an Anglo-Irish Treaty was formally concluded in 1922. This recognised the emergence of the Irish Free State, on which Westminster conferred what was then described as the status of a self-governing dominion within the British Empire.[27] The six northern counties were excluded from the Irish Free State, acquiring their own government and Parliament under the 1920 Act.

The dominion status of the Irish Free State proved no more than a transitional stage, and steps were taken by the state in the 1930s to assert a more complete independence of the United Kingdom. The Irish Constitution of 1937 declared that Eire was a sovereign independent state. During the Second World War, Eire was neutral. In 1949, the state became the Republic of Ireland and the UK Parliament at last recognised that Eire had ceased to be part of Her Majesty's dominions although it was, perhaps anomalously, also declared that Ireland was not to be regarded as a foreign country.[28]

The system of government established under the Act of 1920 in Northern Ireland survived in all essentials for 50 years. Dissatisfaction with that system led to civil unrest from 1968 onwards. The UK government was required to intervene increasingly in the affairs of Northern Ireland until, in 1972, direct

---

24 For the Union with Ireland Act 1800, see *Halsbury's Statutes*, vol 31 (1994 reissue), p 290.
25 *Ex p Canon Selwyn* (1872) 36 JP 54, and see Calvert, op cit, pp 20–1.
26 Ch 10 B.
27 Ch 15 C.
28 Ireland Act 1949, ss 1(1) and 2.

rule of Northern Ireland was resumed and the constitution of Northern Ireland was suspended.[29] In 1973, after a poll of the electorate had shown a clear majority in favour of Northern Ireland remaining part of the United Kingdom, the system of government under the 1920 Act was finally ended. In its place, a bold experiment was made to establish a new Assembly and a new form of executive based on the concept of power-sharing.[30] Elections for the Assembly were held in June 1973 by proportional representation, the Sunningdale agreement (to which the Dublin government was a party) was reached in December, and the executive came into office in January 1974. But the experiment failed after a few months. The Northern Ireland Act 1974 restored direct rule, making temporary provision for governing the province through the Secretary of State for Northern Ireland, and authorised the holding of an elected constitutional convention under the chairmanship of the Chief Justice of Northern Ireland. The convention met during 1975 but it failed to produce an agreed scheme[31] and direct rule from Westminster continued under temporary legislation which is renewed annually.

Later developments included the Anglo-Irish Inter-governmental Council, established in 1981 by the governments of the United Kingdom and the Irish Republic for the discussion of matters of common concern; the increase in Northern Ireland's representation at Westminster from 12 to 17 seats;[32] and the re-activation in 1982 of the Assembly first created in 1973.[33] Under the Northern Ireland Act 1982, elections for the Assembly were held in October 1982. The Assembly was authorised to make proposals to the Secretary of State for a total or partial resumption of the devolution of powers authorised by the Act of 1973. It was empowered to exercise a scrutinising function so long as direct rule continues, and for this purpose to establish a committee of Assembly members for each Northern Ireland department. The aim behind the 1982 Act was to bring together the parties of Northern Ireland, leaving to them the task of making further constitutional proposals, an aim which was not fulfilled.

A notable development in November 1985 was the signing of the Anglo-Irish Agreement by the British and Irish Prime Ministers at Hillsborough.[34] The Agreement gave the assurance that no change in the status of Northern Ireland would come about without the consent of the majority of its people, to increase cooperation between the two governments in relation to security and in economic and social matters, and to provide a framework (based on a standing Inter-governmental Conference) for discussion between the two governments of issues affecting Northern Ireland (such as human rights, security, criminal justice, and cultural cooperation). The Agreement endorsed the UK government's policy of seeking to devolve powers of government from the Secretary of State to democratic bodies within the

---

[29]   Northern Ireland (Temporary Provisions) Act 1972.
[30]   Cmnd 5259, 1973; Northern Ireland Assembly Act 1973; Northern Ireland Constitution Act 1973.
[31]   HC 1 (1975–76); Cmnd 6387, 1976.
[32]   House of Commons (Redistribution of Seats) Act 1979.
[33]   See Cmnd 8541, 1982; and C Gearty [1982] PL 518.
[34]   Cmnd 9690. And see Hadden and Boyle, *The Anglo-Irish Agreement*. Also for the background, Boyle and Hadden, *Ireland: A Positive Proposal*.

province; once devolved, such powers would go out of the remit of the Inter-governmental Conference.

This Agreement attracted much support, apart from Unionist parties in Northern Ireland, who protested vehemently at the increased recognition that it gave to the interest of the Dublin government in Northern Ireland affairs.[35] No effective progress was made in the devolution of powers to Belfast, but measures of cooperation resulted from the Agreement and further steps against discrimination were taken.[36]

Both direct rule and terrorist activity continued in the 1990s, as efforts were made to find a political solution. In December 1993, the 'Downing Street Declaration' of the two Prime Ministers sought to bring about by peaceful negotiation a final settlement for Northern Ireland. It confirmed that the status of the province could not be changed without majority consent, and that the British government would not oppose a united Ireland for which there was popular consent.[37] In August 1994, the IRA announced a cessation of military activities, and this was followed by a loyalist ceasefire. Despite this, little progress towards all-party talks was made, mainly because of disagreement over the conditions on which Sinn Fein might take part in talks. In 1995, the Prime Ministers outlined framework proposals for a Northern Ireland Assembly, a cross-border body with executive and consultative functions, and a Belfast/Dublin parliamentary forum.[38] The IRA resumed activities in February 1996, with the South Quay bombing in London. The British government caused elections to be held in May 1996[39] before the opening of multi-party talks in June, but only in October was some agreement reached on the agenda for discussion.

The Union with Ireland Act of 1800 (as amended) was in 1997 in force as regards Northern Ireland, but its existence pinpointed the division between the Protestant and Catholic communities. In one study, the province's difficulties were linked with deep-seated problems in the British approach to constitutionalism.[40] The general election in May 1997 may have made possible a new political initiative on Northern Ireland.

Three legal systems

For many purposes the United Kingdom may be described as a unitary state, since there is no structure of federalism. But this brief historical outline has sought to emphasise that constitutional and legal differences exist within the United Kingdom, and that diversity, as well as political and economic unity, is found. While the legislative competence of Parliament extends to all the United Kingdom, three distinct legal systems exist, each with its own courts and legal profession, namely, (a) England and Wales (b) Scotland (c) Northern Ireland. A unifying influence is that the House of Lords is the final

---

[35]   For an unsuccessful legal challenge, see *Ex p Molyneaux* [1986] 1 WLR 331. And cf
       McGimpsey v Ireland [1990] ILRM 441.
[36]   Eg Fair Employment (Northern Ireland) Act 1989; E Ellis [1990] PL 161.
[37]   Cm 2442, 1994.
[38]   Cm 2964, 1995.
[39]   Cm 3232, 1996; and Northern Ireland (Entry to Negotiations, etc) Act 1996.
[40]   Morison and Livingstone, op cit, note 22 above; cf McCrudden, op cit, note 22 above, pp
       324–6.

court of appeal from all three jurisdictions, except for criminal cases in Scotland. When Parliament legislates, it may legislate for the whole United Kingdom (for example, income tax or immigration law), for Great Britain (for example, social security or trade union law) or separately for one or more of the countries within the United Kingdom. But such legal differences are not always of political significance.

The Channel Islands[41]

Neither the Channel Isles, nor the Isle of Man, form part of the United Kingdom, except for the purposes of the British Nationality Act 1981. The islands are possessions of the Crown, and the British government is responsible for their defence and international relations. The laws of the Channel Islands are based on the ancient customs of the Duchy of Normandy, of which they formed part until 1204. The sovereignty of Her Majesty is admitted only in her right as successor to the Dukes of Normandy. These islands have never been colonies and enjoy wide autonomy for most domestic purposes, including taxation. They are subject to the legislative supremacy of the Westminster Parliament, in which they are not represented, but by a long-standing convention it is rare for Westminster to legislate directly for the Islands. Where this is intended it is usual for the Act of Parliament to authorise an Order in Council to be made applying the Act, as modified in the Order, to the Islands.

In Jersey the Sovereign is represented by the Lieutenant-Governor, who acts as the channel of communication between the UK government and the island authorities. He is entitled to sit but not to vote in the legislative body, the Assembly of the States, and also to sit in the Royal Court. The chief judicial and executive officer is the Bailiff who, like the Lieutenant-Governor, is appointed by the Crown. He presides over both the States and the Royal Court. The Assembly of the States consists of 12 senators, 12 constables and 28 deputies, chosen by various forms of election. The Assembly has power to make permanent laws, subject to their being approved by Orders of the Privy Council registered in the Royal Court, and also to make subordinate regulations without such approval. Civil and criminal jurisdiction is exercised by the Royal Court, constituted by the Bailiff and 12 elected jurats.[42]

The Bailiwick of Guernsey is separate from, but in a similar position to that of Jersey. The Bailiff is the head of the administration as well as President of the States of Deliberation (the legislature) and the Royal Court. The legislature consists of 12 conseillers, 33 deputies, 10 douzaine representatives and two representatives of Alderney. The States of Guernsey legislate also for the adjoining islands of Alderney and Sark, subject in the former case to the consent of the local States, and in Sark to that of the Chief Pleas. As with Jersey, a law may be passed by the States but it must be sanctioned by an Order of the Privy Council, registered in the Royal Court.

There are separate Courts of Appeal for Jersey and Guernsey. The judges are the Bailiffs of Jersey and Guernsey and their deputies, together with persons appointed by the Queen from those who have held judicial office in

---

[41]   Kilbrandon Report, part XI and HLE, vol 6, pp 381–7. And see *Re a Debtor, ex p Viscount of Royal Court of Jersey* [1981] Ch 384.

[42]   On criminal justice in the Channel Islands, see St J Robilliard [1979] Crim LR 566.

the Commonwealth or are senior practitioners at the bar in any part of the United Kingdom, the Isle of Man, Jersey or Guernsey. From a decision of the Courts of Appeal in civil matters, appeal lies to the Judicial Committee of the Privy Council.[43]

The Home Secretary is the United Kingdom minister responsible for relations with the Channel Islands. Formal legislative business is transacted by a Committee of the Privy Council for Channel Islands matters. By a long-standing practice, Orders in Council and Acts of Parliament which apply to the islands are registered in each Royal Court, but their legal effect does not derive from such registration. The Royal Courts may request reconsideration of an Order in Council but can in the last resort be compelled to register it.[44]

Since the UK government is responsible for the Channel Islands in international affairs, decisions may be taken in the course of Britain's relations with other states which directly affect the internal affairs of the Islands. Before the United Kingdom joined the European Communities, the Islands feared that British membership would prejudice their advantages as a tax haven and in other matters. In the event, special terms for the Islands were included in the Treaty of Accession, whereby the Islands are within the Community for the purposes of free movement of industrial and agricultural goods but are exempted from much of the EC Treaty, including provisions relating to the free movement of persons and tax harmonisation.[45] The United Kingdom's adherence to the European Convention on Human Rights extends to the Channel Islands.[46]

The Isle of Man[47]

The Isle of Man, an ancient kingdom, was until 1266 feudatory to the Kings of Norway: traces of this Norse heritage survive in Manx law and government. In the reign of Henry IV, the English claim to the island prevailed over that of Scotland and in 1405 the island was granted to the Earls of Derby with the title of King (later Lord) of Man. In 1765 the Lordship re-vested in the Crown. Tynwald, the ancient Manx legislature, consists of the Sovereign, represented by the Lieutenant-Governor (appointed by the Crown), the Legislative Council and the elected House of Keys. The powers of the Manx authorities now extend to all domestic matters. In particular, by a series of Isle of Man Acts passed at Westminster since 1866 (in particular those of 1958 and 1979) Tynwald may regulate the island's finances, customs, harbours, civil service and police. In 1981, an Order in Council was made delegating to the Lieutenant-Governor power to grant the royal assent to all internal legislation, except for particular measures that the Privy Council might reserve to itself. Executive power is divided between the Lieutenant-Governor and Tynwald, but since 1981 the chairman of the Executive Council has been elected by

---

[43]   Ch 18 A. See eg *Vaudin v Hamon* [1974] AC 569.
[44]   HLE, vol 6, p 382. Cf F de L Bois [1983] PL 385, 389–91.
[45]   Cmnd 4862–1 (1972), Protocol, No 3. And see Kilbrandon Report, part XI, chs 31, 32.
[46]   See ch 19 B and *Gillow v United Kingdom* (1986) 11 EHRR 335.
[47]   As well as the Kilbrandon Report, part XI, see Report of the Joint Working Party on the Constitutional Relationship between the Isle of Man and the UK, 1969; HLE, vol 6, pp 387–90; and Kermode, *Devolution at Work: a Case Study of the Isle of Man.*

Tynwald. A new Customs and Excise Agreement between the Manx authorities and the UK government took effect in 1980, replacing the former Common Purse Agreement. The Isle of Man has its own legal system and courts, from which an ultimate appeal lies to the Privy Council.[48]

The Westminster Parliament may legislate for the Isle of Man, either directly or by extending Acts of Parliament by Order in Council: in practice this power is exercised only after consultation with the island authorities and mainly in relation to obligations of the United Kingdom arising under international treaties. During the 1960s, there was a prolonged dispute between Tynwald and the UK government over the control of broadcasting in the island and off its coast; the Marine etc Broadcasting (Offences) Act 1967 was extended to the island by Order in Council against the wishes of Tynwald.[49]

The Isle of Man's position as regards the European Union is essentially the same as that of the Channel Islands. In relation to the European Convention on Human Rights, difficulties arose when in *Tyrer v United Kingdom*, the European Court of Human Rights held that judicial birching in the Isle of Man of a 15-year-old boy constituted degrading punishment contrary to art 3 of the Convention.[50] Subsequently, at the request of the Isle of Man government, the UK government did not renew the right of individuals in the Isle of Man to petition under the Convention.[51]

B.   Devolution of government – an outline

Although the United Kingdom is made up of four countries (England, Wales, Scotland and Northern Ireland) and contains three legal systems, the essential structure of the United Kingdom in 1997 was one of a unitary system of government. There was a single Parliament and a single central executive in the form of the Prime Minister and the Cabinet, and the machinery of government reflected this unitary character. During and after the 1960s there developed a movement to secure the devolution of government, particularly to Scotland and Wales.

Unlike federalism, devolution is not a term of art in constitutional law. It has been defined as 'the delegation of central government powers without the relinquishment of sovereignty'.[52] But while a narrow form of devolution may consist of nothing more than a decentralisation of some executive powers, devolution generally implies the transfer of legislative and executive powers from the centre to elected bodies who become responsible for exercising the devolved functions over a defined geographic area.[53] In the United Kingdom, devolution is seen to be a way of conferring a measure of 'home rule' on part

---

[48]   See eg *Frankland v R* [1987] AC 576 and *Davis v Radcliffe* [1990] 2 All ER 536.

[49]   Kilbrandon Report, pp 429–32.

[50]   (1978) 2 EHRR 1; ch 19 B.

[51]   HC Deb, 18 March 1981, col 98 (WA). And see *Teare v O'Callaghan* (1982) 4 EHRR 232.

[52]   Kilbrandon Report, para 543.

[53]   On aspects of devolution, see Bogdanor, *Devolution*; Calvert (ed), *Devolution*; Dalyell, *Devolution, The End of Britain?*; Grant (ed), *Independence and Devolution, the Legal Implications for Scotland*; Mackintosh, *The Devolution of Power*.

of the kingdom. Under a scheme of devolution, residual authority is retained at the centre, even if that authority need not be exercised so long as the scheme continues. But in a federal system, the powers of government at the central and regional levels are determined by the constitution, which regulates the formal relations between the two tiers of government.

In the late 19th and early 20th centuries, the burning issue of Ireland led to proposals for 'home rule all round'. Bills proposing home rule for Scotland and in some cases for Wales were introduced into Parliament before and after the First World War.[54] An inconclusive Speaker's Conference on devolution was held in 1919.[55] Thereafter, until the 1960s, the Labour and Conservative parties were interested primarily in controlling the British system of government from the centre; and Scotland and Wales were regarded as presenting administrative rather than political problems. The solution favoured by successive governments was to create the Scottish and Welsh Offices.

The Scottish Office system[56]

Since 1945, the Scottish Office has comprised four or five departments of central government, based in Edinburgh but headed by a Cabinet minister (the Secretary of State for Scotland, aided by a ministerial team) and expected to cooperate closely with their counterparts in Whitehall. The officials are all members of the British civil service. The Edinburgh system was reproduced on a smaller scale when in 1964 the Welsh Office was created in Cardiff, with its own Secretary of State.[57] Compared with the Scottish Office, the Welsh Office has a narrower range of functions and forms only one department.

Under this system many functions of domestic government are entrusted to the Scottish and Welsh Offices. Other functions, such as inland revenue, social security, employment and the control of immigration have been exercised in Scotland and Wales by British departments. In 1997, the functions of the Scottish departments included agriculture and fisheries, the arts, crofting, development, education, electricity, the environment, fire service, forestry, health, heritage policy, housing, local government, police, prisons, roads, social services, transport (except road freight and rail), tourism and town planning. As well as these direct responsibilities, the Secretary of State has an indirect interest in all matters affecting Scotland, and represents Scottish interests to other departments and in the Cabinet.

This system has some administrative advantages; thus it enables much Scottish and Welsh business to be dealt with by civil servants who are resident in and familiar with the two countries. On some matters, uniform social and economic standards are maintained throughout Great Britain, and there is also scope for administrative initiatives to be taken in Scotland and Wales. But while separate legislation may be enacted for Scotland (and to a lesser extent

---

[54] See Wolfe (ed), *Government and Nationalism in Scotland*, ch 1 (G Donaldson).
[55] Cmd 692, 1920.
[56] Drucker (ed), *Scottish Government Yearbook 1980*, ch 8 (M Macdonald and A Redpath); Keating and Midwinter, *The Government of Scotland*; Kellas, *The Scottish Political System*; Milne, *The Scottish Office*. And see Cmd 5563, 1937; and Cmd 9219, 1954.
[57] See Andrews (ed), *Welsh Studies in Public Law*, ch 4 (I L Gowan). And see HLE, vol 8(2), pp 50–4.

for Wales), this has to be fitted into Westminster's legislative programme.[58] The major drawback arises when as in 1970–74 and between 1979 and 1997, the majority of MPs from Wales and Scotland are in the Opposition at Westminster. Indeed, there was an acute shortage of Conservative MPs from both countries from 1979 until the 1997 election, at which no Conservative MPs were elected outside England. Yet despite the fact that only ten Conservative MPs out of 72 for Scotland were elected at the 1987 election, the Conservative government enacted bitterly unpopular legislation that abolished domestic rates as a means of financing local government in favour of the community charge (or poll tax), one year earlier in Scotland than in England and Wales.[59] The Scottish Office pattern therefore is not a form of 'home rule' but rather one, as in the recent experience of Northern Ireland, of 'direct rule' by the UK government in London.

The Stormont system[60]

Under the Government of Ireland Act 1920, Northern Ireland possessed its own executive (Governor, Prime Minister, Cabinet and departments) and a legislature of two houses (Senate and House of Commons) which sat at Stormont until 1972. Northern Ireland still elected MPs to sit at Westminster, although on a reduced scale, and was subject to the legislative supremacy of Westminster. By the 1920 Act, certain subjects were reserved for the United Kingdom, including the Crown, treaties and foreign relations, the armed forces and defence, nationality, postal services, customs and excise and income tax.

Subject to these matters, the Stormont Parliament had power 'to make laws for the peace, order and good government of Northern Ireland'.[61] Constitutional issues might be referred for decision to the Judicial Committee of the Privy Council,[62] but an Act of the Northern Ireland Parliament which exceeded its legal competence (for example, by legislating with respect to the armed forces)[63] could be held void by the ordinary courts. Stormont had some taxing powers, but in practice Northern Ireland became heavily dependent on the United Kingdom for financial support, for example in maintaining a social security system that offered the same benefits as in Great Britain. Westminster frequently found it convenient to legislate for Northern Ireland, even on matters that had been transferred to Stormont. The courts were rarely called on to interpret the Act of 1920, and when they were, they seemed reticent in matters of constitutional interpretation. Even in respect of religious matters, where the 1920 Act sought to exclude discrimination, little use was made of the courts.[64] Since the single-party Protestant majority was in power throughout the life of Stormont, the Catholic community was in a

---

58   Ch 10 A.
59   See C M G Himsworth and N C Walker [1987] PL 586 and, for a judicial sequel, *Pringle, Petitioner* 1991 SLT 330.
60   See note 22 above. Also Birrell and Murie, *Policy and Government in Northern Ireland*; Buckland, *The Factory of Grievances*; Lawrence, *The Government of Northern Ireland*, ch 10.
61   Government of Ireland Act 1920, s 4(1).
62   Ibid, s 51.
63   *R (Hume et al) v Londonderry Justices* [1972] NILR 91; Northern Ireland Act 1972.
64   Government of Ireland Act 1920, s 5; and *Londonderry CC v McGlade* [1925] NI 47.

permanent minority and their grievances accumulated over the years.[65] Eventually, the outbreak of protest and civil disturbances in 1968 forced the Unionist party to adopt a programme of reforms, but this came too late to save the system.

The relationship between the United Kingdom and Northern Ireland was sometimes described as quasi-federal, but it lacked the essential qualities of a federal relationship, since at any time Westminster could legislate despite the transfer of powers to Stormont.

Royal Commission on the Constitution 1969–73

Increased support for the Welsh and Scottish nationalist parties from the mid-1960s caused both the Conservative party[66] and the Labour government to reconsider the position of Scotland and Wales. In 1969, the government appointed a royal commission on the constitution, whose primary duty was 'to examine the present functions of the central legislature and government in relation to the several countries, nations and regions of the United Kingdom'. The Commission's report (the Kilbrandon report)[67] concentrated its attention on the position of Scotland, Wales and the English regions. For Scotland, eight of the 13 members of the Commission recommended a form of legislative devolution, by which Scotland would elect an assembly by proportional representation; executive powers in Scotland would be exercised by ministers drawn from the assembly. For Wales, six members of the Kilbrandon Commission (a minority) recommended a similar scheme. Under these proposals, the posts of Secretary of State for Scotland and for Wales would have ceased to exist. But there was much disagreement within the Commission. Two members signed a strong memorandum of dissent that adopted an altogether broader approach to constitutional reform. They recommended directly elected assemblies for Scotland, Wales and five English regions, responsible for the carrying out of social and economic policies within a framework of national laws.[68]

The Scotland Act and the Wales Act 1978

While not accepting all the Kilbrandon proposals, the Labour government committed itself to creating elected assemblies for Scotland and Wales. But its proposals arose as much from political expediency as from commitment to the principle of devolution. The proposals ran into much difficulty in Parliament, made worse by the fact that from 1976 the Labour government had lost its absolute majority in the Commons and depended on support from smaller parties. After protracted proceedings in two sessions of Parliament, the Scotland Act 1978 and the Wales Act 1978 were enacted.

The Scotland Act proposed to devolve legislative powers on many aspects of Scotland's domestic affairs to an elected assembly, and to vest executive powers in a Scottish executive. The single-chamber assembly was to consist of

---

[65]   See Cmnd 532, 1969 (the Cameron report).
[66]   *Scotland's Government*, 1970 (the Douglas-Home report).
[67]   Cmnd 5460, 1973, discussed by T C Daintith (1974) 37 MLR 544.
[68]   Cmnd 5460–I, 1973 (memorandum of dissent, Crowther-Hunt and Peacock).

about 150 members, elected every four years. The assembly's legislative powers were limited to matters devolved by the Act. The validity of assembly measures, both as Bills and after they were enacted, was made subject to judicial control to ensure that they came within the devolved powers. Twenty-five groups of powers were to be devolved in minutely detailed provisions, including education, housing, roads, local government, the courts and the legal profession, and aspects of civil and criminal law. The office of Secretary of State for Scotland was to continue, to exercise oversight of the Scottish assembly and executive (with power to override Scottish Acts when necessary to maintain essential UK interests) and to negotiate an annual block grant from London to pay for government in Scotland. One weakness of the scheme was that the assembly would have no power of its own for raising revenue by taxation. The Wales Act 1978 proposed a similar assembly for Wales, but with narrower legislative and executive functions.

Although these Acts passed through Parliament, the two assemblies were never created. The Labour government had intended that the assemblies should be set up only after an advisory referendum of the Scottish and Welsh electors. Against government wishes, the Commons included what came to be known as the 40% rule, intended to guard against a low turnout in either referendum.[69] This required not merely a simple majority of those voting in either country to be in favour of the assembly, but also that those voting 'Yes' had to be not less than 40% of those entitled to vote. When the two referendums were held on 1 March 1979, the result in Wales was a resounding defeat for devolution, 79% voting 'No'. In Scotland, a small majority was in favour of devolution (32.9% of the electorate voted 'Yes', and 30.8% voted 'No') but over one-third of the electorate did not vote and the 40% hurdle was far from being cleared. The Labour government's refusal to proceed with the two schemes led directly to a motion of no confidence in the government being carried by one vote. After the Conservative victory at the general election in May 1979, statutory orders repealing the Scotland and Wales Acts were approved by Parliament.

As was realised during the debates on home rule for Ireland in the late 19th century, proposals for devolution within the United Kingdom raise many difficult questions, including (a) the problem, once an elected assembly is created for part of the United Kingdom, of deciding what the future representation of that part should be at Westminster; (b) whether the subordinate assembly should have power to impose taxes; and (c) the relationship between the powers of an assembly and the legislative supremacy of the Westminster Parliament. The 1978 Acts did not provide adequate answers to these questions, the Labour government's policy being that it was possible to change the machinery of government in Scotland and Wales without changing 'the firm continuing framework of the United Kingdom'.[70]

Between 1979 and 1997, the Conservative government firmly opposed all proposals for devolution within Great Britain. In 1995, it did support minor changes in Scottish parliamentary business, extending the functions of the Scottish Grand Committee (comprising all MPs from Scottish constituencies),

---

[69]   Scotland Act 1978, s 85(2).
[70]   Cmnd 6348, 1975, p 1.

and enabling the Committee to sit in Scotland.[71] The Scottish National party continued to advocate independence for Scotland within the EC. The Labour and Liberal Democrat parties favoured a clearer scheme of devolution than was contained in the Scotland Act 1978,[72] and supported the Scottish Constitutional Convention, a self-appointed assembly representing many bodies in Scotland. In 1995, the Convention proposed a parliament of 112 members (including 40 elected by the additional member system), with legislative competence over all matters entrusted to the Scottish Office and able to adjust rates of tax within a defined range.[73] Early in 1997, an agreement on constitutional reform between Labour and Liberal Democrats promised an early referendum in Scotland on the Convention scheme. For Wales, the parties favoured an elected assembly to oversee Welsh affairs. For England, they gave cautious support to the creation of indirectly elected regional chambers on a step by step basis. One of the first measures proposed by the Labour government elected in May 1997 was legislation to authorize the holding of referendums on devolution in both Scotland and Wales.

---

[71] See H C Standing Orders, no 94A–94H (1995); HC Deb, 29 November 1995, col 1228, and 19 December 1995, col 1410.

[72] See eg Labour's Scotland Bill, November 1987, and HC Deb, 27 January 1988, col 321.

[73] *Scotland's Parliament; Scotland's Right* (1995); J McFadden [1995] PL 215 and D Millar (1997) 1 Edin LR 260. See also the Constitution Unit, *Scotland's Parliament: Fundamentals for a new Scotland* (1996).

CHAPTER 4

Parliamentary supremacy

A.   The growth of the legislative authority of Parliament

Before examining the legal meaning of the supremacy of Parliament today, we may consider briefly the main stages by which the legislative dominance of Parliament came to be established.

It was recognised in the middle ages that an Act of Parliament could change the common law. With the Reformation there disappeared the idea that there were certain ecclesiastical doctrines that Parliament could not touch. Henry VIII and Elizabeth I made the Crown of England supreme over all persons and causes and used the English Parliament to attain this end. Even in the 17th century it was contended that there were certain natural laws which were immutable,[1] but the common lawyers were the allies of Parliament in the struggle with the Crown and, to defeat the Crown's claim to rule by prerogative, conceded that the common law could be changed by Parliament.[2]

The struggle for supremacy

Legislative supremacy involves not only the right to change the law but also that no one else should have that right. In many spheres the King's prerogative at the beginning of the 17th century was undefined and the King exercised through the Council a residue of judicial power which enabled him to enforce his prerogative powers. Acts of Parliament which purported to take away any of the inseparable prerogatives of the Crown were considered invalid[3] but this view of the royal prerogative could not survive the political challenge from Parliament.

1 Ordinances and proclamations.   A clear distinction between the statutes of the English Parliament and the ordinances of the King in Council was lacking long after the establishment of the Model Parliament at the end of the 13th

---

[1]   *Bonham's* case (1610) 8 Co Rep 114a; Gough, *Fundamental Law in English Constitutional History.*

[2]   Dicey, *The Law of the Constitution*, Introduction by E C S Wade (at p c).

[3]   'No Act of Parliament can bar a King of his regality': *The Case of Ship Money* (1637) 3 St Tr 825, Finch CJ, at 1235. A valuable account of the leading 17th-century cases on prerogative is given in Keir and Lawson, *Cases in Constitutional Law*, ch II.

century. The Statute of Proclamations 1539 gave Henry VIII wide powers of legislating without reference to Parliament by proclamation, which had replaced the ordinance as a form of legislation. This statute did not give to the King and Council power to do anything that they pleased by royal ordinance, but was an attempt to deal with the obscure position of the authority possessed by proclamations. It safeguarded the common law, existing Acts of Parliament and rights of property, and prohibited the infliction of the death penalty for a breach of a proclamation.[4] 'Its chief practical purpose was undoubtedly to create machinery to enforce proclamations'.[5] Despite the repeal of this statute in 1547, Mary and Elizabeth continued to resort to proclamations. The judicial powers of the Council, and in particular of the Court of Star Chamber, were available to enforce proclamations. The scope of the royal prerogative to legislate remained undefined. James I made full use of this power, with the result that in 1611 Chief Justice Coke was consulted by the Council, along with three of his brother judges, about the legality of proclamations. The resulting opinion is to be found in the *Case of Proclamations*:

1 The King by his proclamation cannot create any offence which was not one before; for then he might alter the law of the land in a high point; for if he may create an offence where none is, upon that ensues fine and imprisonment.
2 The King hath no prerogative but what the law of the land allows him.
3 But the King for the prevention of offences may by proclamation admonish his subjects that they keep the laws and do not offend them upon punishment to be inflicted by law; the neglect of such proclamation aggravates the offence.
4 If an offence be not punishable in the Star Chamber, the prohibition of it by proclamation cannot make it so.[6]

A definite limit was thus put upon the prerogative, the full force of which was effective only when the Star Chamber and other conciliar tribunals were abolished in 1640. The gist of the *Case of Proclamations* is that the King's prerogative is under the law, and that Parliament alone can alter the law which the King is to administer.

2 Taxation. The imposition of taxes is a matter for legislation. Inevitably taxation was a major issue between the Stuart Kings and Parliament. If the Crown could not levy taxes without the consent of Parliament, the will of Parliament must in the long run prevail. It had been conceded by the time of Edward I that the consent of Parliament was necessary for direct taxation. The history of indirect taxation is more complicated, since the regulation of foreign trade was a part of the royal prerogative in relation to foreign affairs. There was no clear distinction between the imposition of taxes by way of customs duties and the prerogative powers in relation to foreign trade and defence of the realm.

In the *Case of Impositions (Bate's Case)*,[7] John Bate refused to pay a duty on imported

---

4   HEL, vol IV, pp 102–3.
5   G R Elton in Fryde and Miller, *Historical Studies of the English Parliament*, II, p 206.
6   (1611) 12 Co Rep 74. This case was applied by the Court of Session in *Grieve v Edinburgh and District Water Trustees* 1918 SC 700.
7   (1606) 2 St Tr 371; G D G Hall (1953) 69 LQR 200.

currants imposed by the Crown on the ground that its imposition was contrary to the statute 45 Edw 3 c 4 which prohibited indirect taxation without the consent of Parliament. The Court of Exchequer unanimously decided in favour of the Crown. The King could impose what duties he pleased for the purpose of regulating trade, and the court could not go behind the King's statement that the duty was in fact imposed for the regulation of trade.

In the *Case of Ship Money* (*R v Hampden*),[8] John Hampden refused to pay ship money, a tax levied by Charles I for the purpose of furnishing ships in time of national danger. Counsel for Hampden conceded that sometimes the existence of danger would justify taking the subject's goods without his consent, but only in actual as opposed to threatened emergency. The Crown conceded that the subject could not be taxed in normal circumstances without the consent of Parliament, but contended that the King was the sole judge of whether an emergency justified the exercise of his prerogative power to raise funds to meet a national danger. A majority of the Court of Exchequer Chamber gave judgment for the King.[9]

The decision was reversed by the Long Parliament,[10] and this aspect of the struggle for supremacy was concluded by the Bill of Rights, art 4, which declared that it was illegal for the Crown to seek to raise money without Parliamentary approval.[11]

3 Dispensing and suspending powers. The power of the Crown to dispense with the operation of statutes within certain limits may at one time have been necessary having regard to the form of ancient statutes and the irregular meetings of Parliament. So long, however, as the limits upon the dispensing power were not clearly defined, there was here a threat to the legislative supremacy of Parliament. In the leading case of *Thomas v Sorrell*,[12] the court took care to define the limits within which the royal power to dispense with laws was acceptable. But in *Godden v Hales* the court upheld a dispensation from James II to Sir Edward Hales excusing him from taking religious oaths and fulfilling other obligations imposed by the Test Act; it was held that it was an inseparable prerogative of the Kings of England to dispense with penal laws in particular cases and upon necessary reasons of which the King is sole judge.[13]

Thus encouraged, James II proceeded to set aside statutes as he pleased, granting a suspension of the penal laws relating to religion in the Declarations of Indulgence in 1687 and 1688. These acts of James were an immediate cause of the revolution of 1688. The Bill of Rights abolished the Crown's alleged power of suspending laws and also prohibited the Crown's power to dispense with the operation of statutes, except where this was authorised by Parliament.[14] Similar provision was made in the Scottish Claim of Right.[15]

---

8   (1637) 3 St Tr 825.
9   For a full analysis, see D L Keir (1936) 52 LQR 546.
10   Shipmoney Act 1640.
11   Page 15 above.
12   (1674) Vaughan 330.
13   (1686) 11 St Tr 1165.
14   Articles 1 and 2 of the Bill of Rights, p 15 above. The Bill of Rights did not curtail the prerogative of pardon nor the power to enter a nolle prosequi. Nor were all earlier dispensations declared invalid: Anson, *The Law and Custom of the Constitution*, vol 1, p 351. Cf the present practice of granting extra-statutory concessions in taxation, ch 17 C.
15   Page 16 above.

4 The independence of the judiciary. So long as the tenure of judicial office depended upon the royal pleasure, there was a risk of the subservience of judges to the Crown. To ensure that English judges should not hold office at pleasure of the Crown, the Act of Settlement 1700 provided that they should hold office *quamdiu se bene gesserint* (during good behaviour) but subject to a power of removal upon an address from both Houses of Parliament.[16]

Growth of ministerial responsibility

The Bill of Rights and the Act of Settlement established the legislative authority of the English Parliament vis-à-vis the Crown, while preserving the prerogatives of the Crown in matters which had not been called in question. But executive government was still conducted by and in the name of the monarch, and democratic government had yet to be established. The changed role of the Sovereign thereafter was summarised in this way:

The position of affairs has been reversed since 1714. Then the King or Queen governed through Ministers, now Ministers govern through the instrumentality of the Crown.[17]

The development after 1714 of Cabinet government and of ministerial responsibility to Parliament[18] was accompanied by changes in the electoral system, beginning in 1832 with the first parliamentary reform and continuing until the universal franchise for adults was achieved in 1929. The political authority of the House of Commons increased as it became more representative of the people and insisted that the executive must be responsive to the will of the electorate.

The result of the constitutional conflict between Commons and Lords in 1909–11 was to leave the House of Commons in a dominant position within Parliament. Thus the legislative authority of Parliament came to be based upon the political support of the electorate for the party with a majority of seats in the elected House.

B. Meaning of legislative supremacy

In this brief historical summary, we have examined the rise of Parliament to be at the centre of the constitutional system. We now consider the legal doctrine of the legislative supremacy of Parliament. This doctrine is referred to by many writers, notably by Dicey, as the sovereignty of Parliament. New constitutional developments are often debated in terms of their supposed effect on the sovereignty of Parliament. This was best seen in the debate about British membership of the EC; those opposed to British membership proposed, without success, an amendment to the Bill which became the European Communities Act 1972 declaring that British membership would not affect the sovereignty of Parliament.[19] In 1997, in the renewed debate about Britain's place in a changing Europe, reference was often made to the sovereignty of Parliament,

---

[16]   See now Supreme Court Act 1981, s 11(3). See also ch 18 A.
[17]   Anson, *Law and Custom of the Constitution*, vol II, p 41.
[18]   For an outline of this development, see ch 7.
[19]   HC Deb, 5 July 1972, cols 556–644; HL Deb, 7 August 1972, cols 893–914.

especially by those opposed to Britain's closer involvement in European integration. Such debates are often confused because of the wide variety of meanings attributable to the sovereignty of Parliament. In this chapter, the expression legislative supremacy will be used, partly because it is necessary to give it a specific content; partly because it is less likely to be confused with the notion of sovereignty in international law; and to avoid importing into constitutional law the jurisprudential doctrine of John Austin and his successors that in every legal system there must be a sovereign.[20]

By the legislative supremacy of Parliament is meant that there are no legal limitations upon the legislative competence of Parliament. Parliament here does not refer to the two Houses of Parliament individually, for neither House has authority to legislate on its own, but to the constitutional phenomenon known as the Queen in Parliament: namely the legislative process by which a Bill approved by Lords and Commons may receive the royal assent and thus become an Act of Parliament. Thus defined, Parliament, said Dicey, has 'under the English constitution, the right to make or unmake any law whatever; and further that no person or body is recognised by the law of England as having a right to override or set aside the legislation of Parliament'.[21] Now Dicey was writing at a time when England was often used as a loose synonym for Great Britain or the United Kingdom,[22] and today it is necessary to discuss whether the law on this matter is the same throughout the United Kingdom.[23] But the positive and negative aspects of the doctrine emerge clearly from Dicey's formulation, namely that power to legislate on any matter whatsoever is vested in Parliament and that there exists no competing authority with power either to legislate for the United Kingdom or to impose limits upon the legislative competence of Parliament.

British membership of the European Community since 1973 has given rise to the difficult issue of competing supremacies, the supremacy of Parliament on the one hand and the supremacy, or primacy, of Community law, on the other. This question will be considered below,[24] but we first examine the issue in terms of the law of the United Kingdom alone.

Legal nature of legislative supremacy

This doctrine consists essentially of a rule which governs the legal relationship between the courts and the legislature, namely that the courts are under a duty to apply the legislation made by Parliament and may not hold an Act of Parliament to be invalid or unconstitutional. 'All that a court of law can do with an Act of Parliament is to apply it.'[25] In *Madzimbamuto v Lardner-Burke*, which concerned the effect of the unilateral declaration of independence in 1965 by the Rhodesian government upon the Westminster Parliament's power to legislate for Rhodesia, Lord Reid said:

---

[20]   Austin, *The Province of Jurisprudence Determined*, Lecture 6. And see N MacCormick (1993) 56 MLR 1.

[21]   Dicey, *The Law of the Constitution*, pp 39–40.

[22]   Ch 3 A.

[23]   Section D below.

[24]   Page 75; and ch 8.

[25]   Keir and Lawson, *Cases in Constitutional Law*, p 1. For the power of the courts to disapply an Act of Parliament which conflicts with European Community law, see p 76 below.

It is often said that it would be unconstitutional for the UK Parliament to do certain things, meaning that the moral, political and other reasons against doing them are so strong that most people would regard it as highly improper if Parliament did these things. But that does not mean that it is beyond the power of Parliament to do such things. If Parliament chose to do any of them, the courts could not hold the Act of Parliament invalid.[26]

While the doctrine of legislative supremacy has great political significance, the legal rule is not to be confused with statements about the political dominance of the House of Commons or the Cabinet within the legislative process. Certainly, how Parliament exercises its legislative authority is of great importance in the debate about whether its supremacy should be retained or modified. Craig has argued that Dicey's exposition of sovereignty was advanced on the basis of assumptions about representative democracy which (in Craig's view) were flawed even in 1885, and cannot be made today.[27] However, in examining the legal effect which the courts at present assign to Acts of Parliament, we are concerned with a narrower issue than the question of how principles of constitutionalism may in future best be maintained in Britain.

Only an Act of Parliament is supreme

The courts ascribe to an Act of Parliament a legal force which they are not willing to ascribe to other instruments which for one reason or another fall short of being an Act of Parliament. Thus the courts do not attribute legislative supremacy to the following, and will if necessary decide whether or not they have legal effect:

(*a*) a resolution of the House of Commons;[28]
(*b*) a proclamation or other document issued by the Crown under prerogative powers for which the force of law is claimed;[29]
(*c*) a treaty entered into by the government under prerogative powers which seeks to change the law within territory subject to British jurisdiction;[30]
(*d*) an instrument of subordinate legislation which appears to be issued under the authority of an Act of Parliament by a minister or a government department,[31] even though this has been approved by resolution of each House of Parliament;[32]
(*e*) an act of a subordinate legislature within the United Kingdom;[33]
(*f*) byelaws made by a public corporation or local authority.[34]

---

[26]   [1969] 1 AC 645, 723. And see *Manuel v A-G* [1983] Ch 77.
[27]   In *Public Law and Democracy*, ch 2, Craig argues that Dicey's notion of sovereignty was 'firmly embedded within a conception of self-correcting majoritarian democracy' (p 15) since, in Dicey's words, 'The electors can in the long run always enforce their will'; further, that the British system 'became one dominated by the top, by the executive and the party hierarchy' (p 42), and that the danger has always been one of majoritarian tyranny.
[28]   *Stockdale v Hansard* (1839) 9 A & E 1; *Bowles v Bank of England* [1913] 1 Ch 57.
[29]   *Case of Proclamations* (p 55 above).
[30]   *The Parlement Belge* (1879) 4 PD 129, 154; *A-G for Canada v A-G for Ontario* [1937] AC 326. Cf *Malone v Metropolitan Police Commissioner* [1979] Ch 344. And ch 15 B.
[31]   Eg *Chester v Bateson* [1920] 1 KB 829; ch 27.
[32]   *Hoffmann-La Roche v Secretary for Trade & Industry* [1975] AC 295.
[33]   *Belfast Corpn v OD Cars Ltd* [1960] AC 490.
[34]   Eg *Kruse v Johnson* [1898] 2 QB 91.

In all such cases, the courts must consider whether the document for which legislative force is claimed is indeed legally binding. So too, when a party to litigation relies on an Act of Parliament, the court must if necessary decide whether the provision in question has been brought into force.

Position different under written constitution

The doctrine of legislative supremacy distinguishes the United Kingdom from those countries in which a written constitution imposes limits upon the legislature and entrusts the ordinary courts or a constitutional court with the function of deciding whether the acts of the legislature are in accordance with the constitution. In *Marbury v Madison*, the US Supreme Court held that the judicial function vested in the court necessarily carried with it the task of deciding whether an Act of Congress was or was not in conformity with the constitution.[35] In a constitutional system which accepts judicial review of legislation, legislation may be held invalid on a variety of grounds: for example, because it conflicts with the separation of powers where this is a feature of the constitution,[36] or infringes human rights guaranteed by the constitution,[37] or has not been passed in accordance with the procedure laid down in the constitution.[38] By contrast, in the United Kingdom the legislative supremacy of Parliament appears to be the fundamental rule of constitutional law and this supremacy includes power to legislate on constitutional matters. In so far as constitutional rules are contained in earlier Acts, there seems to be no Act which Parliament could not repeal or amend by passing a new Act. The Bill of Rights could in law be repealed or its effects varied by an ordinary Act of Parliament.

Legislative supremacy illustrated

The apparently unlimited powers of Parliament may be illustrated by many Acts of constitutional significance. The Tudor Kings used Parliament to legalise the separation of the English church from the church of Rome: Sir Thomas More was executed in 1535 for having denied the authority of Parliament to make Henry VIII supreme head of the Church. In 1715, Parliament passed the Septennial Act to extend the life of Parliament (including its own) from three to seven years, because it was desired to avoid an election so soon after the Hanoverian accession and the 1715 uprising in Scotland. In vain did opponents of the Act argue that the supreme legislature must be restrained 'from subverting the foundation on which it stands'.[39] Less controversially, the Parliament elected in December 1910 was dissolved in 1918, having five times extended its own existence, which had been limited to

---

[35] 1 Cranch 137 (1803).

[36] *Liyanage v R* [1967] 1 AC 259; *Hinds v R* [1977] AC 195, p 92 below.

[37] Eg *Aptheker v Secretary of State* 378 US 500 (1964) (Act of US Congress refusing passports to communists held an unconstitutional restriction on right to travel).

[38] *Harris v Minister of Interior* 1952 (2) SA 428. Generally see Brewer-Carias, *Judicial Review in Comparative Law*.

[39] Quoted in Marshall, *Parliamentary Sovereignty and the Commonwealth*, p 84.

five years by its own enactment, the Parliament Act 1911. So too did the Parliament elected in 1935 prolong its own existence until 1945.[40]

Parliament has altered the succession to the throne (in the Act of Settlement 1700 and His Majesty's Declaration of Abdication Act 1936); removed prerogative powers from the Crown; reformed the composition of both Houses of Parliament; dispensed with the approval of the House of Lords for certain Bills (the Parliament Acts 1911 and 1949); given effect to British membership of the EC (the European Communities Act 1972); given effect to the Scottish and Irish Treaties of Union and later departed from those treaties;[41] altered the territorial limits of the United Kingdom,[42] and so on. Parliament has even provided that certain provisions contained in an Act shall be subject to challenge in the courts as if they had merely been contained in subordinate legislation.[43]

Indemnity Acts and retrospective legislation

Moreover Parliament has exercised the power to legalise past illegalities and to alter the law retrospectively. This power has been used by an executive with a secure majority in Parliament to reverse inconvenient decisions of an impartial judiciary.[44] After the First World War, during which a number of illegal acts were committed in the interest of the prosecution of the war, two Indemnity Acts were passed; after the Second World War, more limited retrospective legislation was passed.[45] Retrospective laws are, however,

prima facie of questionable policy and contrary to the general principle that legislation by which the conduct of mankind is to be regulated ought ... to deal with future acts and ought not to change the character of past transactions carried on upon the faith of the then existing law ... Accordingly the court will not ascribe retrospective force to new laws affecting rights unless by express words or necessary implication it appears that such was the intention of the legislature.[46]

Retrospective laws may not only confirm irregular acts but may also authorise what was lawful when done to be punished, or subjected to other adverse action by the executive. The Immigration Act 1971 was held to have conferred powers on the Home Office to deport Commonwealth citizens who had entered in breach of earlier immigration laws but against whom no such action could have been taken under those laws at the time the 1971 Act came into effect:[47] but the Act did not make punishable by criminal sanctions conduct which had occurred before the Act was passed.[48] Although art 7 of the European Convention on Human Rights, to which the United Kingdom is

---

[40]   Eg Prolongation of Parliament Act 1944.
[41]   Ch 3 A, and section D below.
[42]   Island of Rockall Act 1972.
[43]   National Insurance Act 1965, s 116(2).
[44]   War Damage Act 1965 (*Burmah Oil Co v Lord Advocate* [1965] AC 75); Northern Ireland Act 1972 (*R (Hume* et al) *v Londonderry Justices* [1972] NILR 91); Education (Scotland) Act 1973 (*Malloch v Aberdeen Corpn* 1974 SLT 253); National Health Service (Invalid Direction) Act 1980 (*Lambeth BC v Secretary of State* (1980) 79 LGR 61).
[45]   Indemnity Act 1920 and War Charges Validity Act 1925; Enemy Property Act 1953, ss 1–3.
[46]   Per Willes J in *Phillips v Eyre* (1870) LR 6 QB 1, 23.
[47]   *Azam v Home Secretary* [1974] AC 18.
[48]   *Waddington v Miah* [1974] 2 All ER 377.

a party, provides that no one shall be held guilty of any criminal offence on account of conduct which did not constitute an offence at the time when it was committed,[49] Parliament has power to legislate retrospectively in breach of that provision: but, as Lord Reid said, 'it is hardly credible that any government department would promote or that Parliament would pass retrospective criminal legislation'.[50] Legislation which authorises payments to be made to individuals in respect of past events is also retrospective, but plainly less objectionable.[51]

Legislative supremacy and international law

So far as British courts are concerned, the legislative supremacy of Parliament is not limited by international law. The courts may not hold an Act void on the ground that it contravenes general principles of international law.

The Herring Fishery (Scotland) Act 1889 authorised a fishery board to make byelaws prohibiting certain forms of trawling within the Moray Firth, an area which included much sea that lay beyond British territorial waters. The Danish master of a Norwegian trawler was convicted in a Scottish court for breaking these byelaws. The High Court of Justiciary held that its function was confined to interpreting the Act and the byelaws, and that Parliament had intended to legislate for the conduct of all persons within the Moray Firth, whatever might be the position in international law. 'For us an Act of Parliament duly passed by Lords and Commons and assented to by the King is supreme, and we are bound to give effect to its terms.'[52]

Nor may the courts hold an Act invalid because it conflicts with a treaty to which the United Kingdom is a party.

An assessment to income tax was challenged on the ground that part of the tax raised was used for the manufacture of nuclear weapons, contrary to the Geneva Convention Act 1957. It was held that the unambiguous provisions of a statute must be followed even if they are contrary to international law. Regarding an argument that tax had been imposed for an improper purpose, the judge said: 'What the statute itself enacts cannot be unlawful, because what the statute says and provides is itself the law, and the highest form of law that is known to this country'.[53]

So far as the British courts are concerned, there are no territorial restrictions on the legislative competence of Parliament. Generally Parliament legislates only in respect of its own territory or in respect of the conduct of its own citizens when they are abroad, but occasionally legislation is intended to operate outside the United Kingdom: thus the Continental Shelf Act 1964 vested in the Queen the rights of exploration and exploitation of the continental shelf; the Act provided for the application of criminal and civil

---

49   Ch 19 B. On retrospection and the War Crimes Act 1991, see A T Richardson (1992) 55 MLR 73, 76–80; and S N McMurtrie (1992) 13 Statute Law Review 128.

50   [1974] 2 All ER 377, 379; and see *R v Home Secretary, ex p Bhajan Singh* [1976] QB 198.

51   Eg Employment Act 1982, s 2 and Sched 1.

52   Lord Dunedin in *Mortensen v Peters* (1906) 8 F(J) 93, 100. The Trawling in Prohibited Areas Prevention Act 1909 later made it an offence to land in the United Kingdom fish caught in prohibited areas of the sea, thus limiting the extra-territorial effect of the earlier ban.

53   Ungoed-Thomas J in *Cheney v Conn* [1968] 1 All ER 779, 782; and see *Inland Revenue Commissioners v Collco Dealings Ltd* [1962] AC 1.

law in respect of installations placed in the surface waters above the continental shelf.[54] A few serious crimes committed in a foreign state by UK citizens are justiciable in this country, such as treason, murder, manslaughter, bigamy and certain revenue offences.[55] But in general the United Kingdom makes very few of its criminal laws applicable to its citizens while abroad, and the courts apply a rule of interpretation that statutes will not be given extraterritorial effect, unless this is expressly provided or necessarily implied.[56] By general principles of international law, the United Kingdom may not exercise jurisdiction in territory belonging to a foreign state. Sir Ivor Jennings suggested that Parliament could make it an offence to smoke in the streets of Paris, while recognising that only courts in the United Kingdom would be bound to take note of the new offence.[57] In practice Parliament does not pass laws which would be contrary to the comity of nations. Yet on a particular matter the law in Britain may be inconsistent with Britain's international obligations. While the government under the royal prerogative may enter into treaties, treaties cannot themselves alter the law to be applied within the United Kingdom, and require to be approved or adopted by Act of Parliament if national law is to be altered.[58] While for some purposes international law may be part of national law, it yields to statute.[59]

British membership of the European Union raises questions as to the relationship between UK law and Community law which cannot be answered by reference to the general principles of international law.[60]

No legal limitations upon Parliament

Many illustrations may be given of the use which Parliament has made of its legislative supremacy in legislating on constitutional matters, retrospectively, in breach of international law, and so on. It does not follow from a recital of this kind that the powers of Parliament are unlimited. As Calvert has said:

No one doubts that the powers of the UK Parliament are extremely wide ... But that is not what is in issue. What is in issue is whether those powers are unlimited and one no more demonstrates this by pointing to a wide range of legislative objects than one demonstrates the contrary by pointing to matters on which Parliament has not, in fact, ever legislated.[61]

There is a great deal of evidence from the law reports that, at least since 1688, judges have been strongly inclined to accept the legislative omnicompetence of Parliament. Yet this has not always been the judicial attitude. In his note on *Dr Bonham's* case, Coke CJ said:

---

[54]   See also the Antarctic Act 1994. Contrast the Sexual Offences (Conspiracy and Incitement) Act 1996 (P Alldridge [1997] Crim LR 30).
[55]   Law Commission, Report No 91, 'Territorial and Extra-territorial Extent of Criminal Law', 1978, pp 36–41.
[56]   *Treacey v DPP* [1971] AC 537, 552. And see *R v Kelly* [1982] AC 665.
[57]   Jennings, *The Law and the Constitution*, pp 170–1.
[58]   Note 30 above.
[59]   See note 53 above; and ch 15 A.
[60]   Page 75 below and ch 8.
[61]   *Constitutional Law in Northern Ireland*, p 14.

In many cases, the common law will control Acts of Parliament, and sometimes adjudge them to be utterly void: for when an Act of Parliament is against common right and reason, or repugnant, or impossible to be performed, the common law will control it, and adjudge such Act to be void.[62]

While English judges made similar statements only rarely after 1688,[63] it is not possible by legal logic alone to demonstrate that they have utterly lost the power to 'control' an Act of Parliament – or to show that a judge who is confronted with a statute fundamentally repugnant to moral principle (for example, a law condemning all of a certain race to be executed) must either apply the statute or resign from office.[64] Support for this comes from New Zealand, where the former President of the Court of Appeal (Lord Cooke of Thorndon) has urged that within the common law the judges exercise an authority which extends to upholding fundamental values that might be at risk from certain forms of legislation.[65]

Short of such an extreme situation, it is very unlikely that the courts would of their volition exercise power derived solely from common law to review the validity of Acts of Parliament. Where in modern constitutional systems judicial review of legislation takes place, this is generally derived from a written constitution.[66] But in the United Kingdom, Parliament enjoys an unlimited power to legislate on constitutional matters. Is it therefore possible that, *on the initiative of Parliament itself*, the courts could begin to exercise a power of judicial review derived from constitutional legislation passed by Parliament? This possibility has often been dismissed out of hand by invocation of the principle that no Parliament may bind its successors. It has been said that the rule that the courts enforce without question all Acts of Parliament is the one rule of the common law which Parliament may not change.[67] But, it has been asked, 'Why cannot Parliament change that rule; since all other rules of the common law are subject to its sovereignty?'[68] It is to this difficult and fundamental question that we now turn.

C. The continuing nature of parliamentary supremacy

Within a modern legal system, enacted laws remain in force until they are repealed or amended, unless they are declared when enacted to have a

---

[62] (1610) 8 Co Rep 113b, 118a. And see S E Thorne (1938) 54 LQR 543.

[63] Eg Holt CJ, *City of London v Wood* (1702) 12 Mod 669, 687.

[64] Cf Jennings, *The Law and the Constitution*, pp 159–60. For the attitude that British courts should take to foreign legislation which infringes fundamental rights, see *Oppenheimer v Cattermole* [1976] AC 249 and F A Mann (1978) 94 LQR 512.

[65] See *Taylor v New Zealand Poultry Board* [1984] 1 NZLR 394, 398; also J L Caldwell [1984] NZLJ 357 and R Cooke [1988] NZLJ 158.

[66] Israel is an apparent exception: I Zamir [1991] PL 523, 529–30, and C Klein (1996) 2 European Public Law 225.

[67] H W R Wade [1955] CLJ 172, 187–9; and (1996) 112 LQR 568.

[68] E C S Wade, Introduction to Dicey, p lv; and see articles by Lord Hailsham, *The Times*, 12, 16, 19 and 20 May 1975.

limited life.[69] It is inherent in the nature of a legislature that it should continue to be free to make new laws. The fact that legislation about, say, divorce or slum-housing was enacted five or 50 years ago is no reason why fresh legislation on the same subject should not be enacted today: even if social conditions have not changed, a new legislature may favour a fresh approach. If the legislature wishes to alter a law previously enacted, it is convenient if the new Act expressly repeals the old law or states the extent to which the old law is amended. Suppose that this is not done, and a new Act is passed which conflicts with an older Act but does not expressly repeal it. There now appear to be two inconsistent statutes on the statute book. How is the apparent conflict to be resolved? And by whom?

The doctrine of implied repeal

It is for the courts to resolve this conflict because it is their duty to decide the law which applies to a given situation. Where two Acts conflict with each other, the courts apply the Act which is later in time, and any earlier Act inconsistent with the later Act is taken to have been repealed by implication.

> If two inconsistent Acts be passed at different times, the last must be obeyed, and if obedience cannot be observed without derogating from the first, it is the first which must give way ... Every Act is made either for the purpose of making a change in the law, or for the purpose of better declaring the law, and its operation is not to be impeded by the mere fact that it is inconsistent with some previous enactment.[70]

This doctrine is found in all legal systems, but in Britain its operation is sometimes considered to have special constitutional significance.

Before 1919, many public and private Acts of Parliament empowered public authorities to acquire land compulsorily and laid down many differing rules of compensation. In 1919, the Acquisition of Land (Assessment of Compensation) Act was passed to provide a uniform code of rules for assessing the compensation to be paid in future. Section 7(1) provided: 'The provisions of the Act or order by which the land is authorised to be acquired, or of any Act incorporated therewith, shall, in relation to the matters dealt with in this Act, have effect subject to this Act, and so far as inconsistent with this Act those provisions shall cease to have or shall not have effect.' The Housing Act 1925 sought to alter the 1919 rules of compensation by reducing the compensation payable in respect of slum-housing. In *Vauxhall Estates Ltd v Liverpool Corpn*,[71] it was held that the provisions of the 1925 Act must prevail over the 1919 Act so far as they were inconsistent with it. The court rejected the ingenious argument of counsel for the slum-owners that s 7(1) (and especially the words 'or shall not have effect') had tied the hands of future Parliaments so that the later Parliament could not (short of express repeal) legislate inconsistently with the 1919 Act. In a similar case, *Ellen Street Estates Ltd v Minister of Health*, Maugham LJ said: 'The Legislature cannot, according to our constitution, bind itself as to the form of subsequent legislation, and it is impossible for Parliament to enact that in a subsequent statute dealing with the

---

69   This has always been the position in English law (Edgar, *Craies on Statute Law*, pp 406–12). But in respect of Scottish Acts passed before 1707, by the doctrine of desuetude a statute may cease to be law through non-use and change of circumstances: see *M'Ara v Magistrates of Edinburgh* 1913 SC 1059 and Mitchell, *Constitutional Law*, pp 21–2. Even if the doctrine of desuetude applied to Acts of the UK Parliament, this would not materially affect legislative supremacy.

70   Lord Langdale, in *Dean of Ely v Bliss* (1842) 5 Beav 574, 582.

71   [1932] 1 KB 733.

same subject-matter there can be no implied repeal. If in a subsequent Act Parliament chooses to make it plain that the earlier statute is being to some extent repealed, effect must be given to that intention just because it is the will of Parliament.'[72]

The correctness of these two decisions is not in doubt, for there were very weak grounds for suggesting that in 1919 Parliament had been attempting to bind its successors. But Maugham LJ went far beyond the actual situation in saying that Parliament could not bind itself as to the *form* of subsequent legislation. He would have been closer to the facts of the case had he said that Parliament could not bind itself as to the *contents* of subsequent legislation.[73] However, these cases, which illustrate the doctrine of repeal by implication, have been used to support a broad constitutional argument that Parliament may never bind its successors.[74]

Can Parliament bind its successors?

The rule that Parliament may not bind its successors (and that no Parliament is bound by Acts of its predecessors) is often cited both as a limitation upon legislative supremacy and as an example of it. To adopt for a moment the language of sovereignty: if it is an essential attribute of a legal sovereign that there should be no legal restraints upon him or her, then by definition the rules laid down by a predecessor cannot bind the present sovereign, for otherwise the present holder of the post would not be sovereign. Dicey, outstanding exponent of the sovereignty of Parliament, accepted this point:

The logical reason why Parliament has failed in its endeavours to enact unchangeable enactments is that a sovereign power cannot, *while retaining its sovereign character*, restrict its own powers by any parliamentary enactment.[75] (italics supplied)

Thus to state that no Parliament may bind its successors is to assume that all future Parliaments must have the same attribute of sovereignty as the present Parliament. But why must this be so? The problem is less intractable than the comparable conundrum of whether an omnipotent deity can bind itself[76] for even sovereign Parliaments are human institutions; and there is nothing inherently impossible in the idea of a supreme Parliament having power to make fresh constitutional arrangements for the future. Merely to state that Parliament may not bind its successors leaves unclear both the nature of the obligation which a present Parliament is unable to impose on its successors, and also the meaning of 'successors'.[77] Indeed, it may be shown that the doctrine that Parliament may not bind its successors is an over-simplification.

(*a*) Some matters authorised by legislation are of such a kind that once done, they cannot be undone by further Act. Thus, over 60 years after Parliament approved the cession of Heligoland to Germany in 1890, Parliament repealed

---

[72]   [1934] KB 590, 597.
[73]   H R Gray (1953) 10 Univ of Toronto LJ 54, 67.
[74]   Cf H W R Wade [1955] CLJ 172, 187 and E C S Wade, Introduction to Dicey, *The Law of the Constitution*, p xlix.
[75]   Dicey, p 68.
[76]   Cf Hart, *The Concept of Law*, p 146; Marshall, *Parliamentary Sovereignty and the Commonwealth*, p 13; and H R Gray, note 73 above.
[77]   R Stone (1966) 26 Louisiana LR 753, 755.

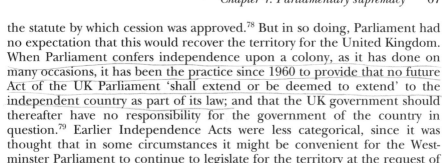

the statute by which cession was approved.[78] But in so doing, Parliament had no expectation that this would recover the territory for the United Kingdom. When Parliament confers independence upon a colony, as it has done on many occasions, it has been the practice since 1960 to provide that no future Act of the UK Parliament 'shall extend or be deemed to extend' to the independent country as part of its law; and that the UK government should thereafter have no responsibility for the government of the country in question.[79] Earlier Independence Acts were less categorical, since it was thought that in some circumstances it might be convenient for the West-minster Parliament to continue to legislate for the territory at the request of the territory concerned.[80] In earlier times it was suggested that provisions conferring legislative independence could be revoked by the Westminster Parliament;[81] but the truer position is that conferment of independence is an irreversible process; 'freedom once conferred cannot be revoked'.[82] Thus, by ceding territory or conferring independence, Parliament may restrict the geographical area of effective legislation by future Parliaments. In the Canada Act 1982, which conferred full power of constitutional amendment upon Canada, it was provided that no subsequent Act of the UK Parliament 'shall extend to Canada as part of its law'. If Westminster in future should seek to reverse the historical clock by attempting to legislate for Canada, the Canadian courts would ignore any such attempt, unless the Canadian Parliament had authorised them to give effect to the legislation from Westminster. But British courts would be bound to give effect to the Westminster legislation so far as it lay within their jurisdiction to do so.[83]

(*b*) In a different way, Parliament may bind future Parliaments by altering the rules for the composition of the two Houses of Parliament or the succession to the throne. Thus in 1832, when Parliament reformed the House of Commons to secure more democratic representation, later Parliaments were bound by that legislation inasmuch as the only lawful House of Commons was one elected in accordance with the 1832 Act. If it had been subsequently desired to revert to the pre-1832 composition of the House, this would have required the concurrence of the reformed House.[84] The same would be true of every occasion on which the composition of the Commons has been reformed since 1832. The same would also apply to legislative reform of the Lords (for example, the introduction of life peerages in 1958) subject only to the possibility that under the Parliament Acts 1911 and 1949 any such reform could be reversed without the approval of the reformed House of Lords.[85] In 1936, His Majesty's Declaration of Abdication Act altered

---

78 Anglo-German Agreement Act 1890, repealed by Statute Law Revision Act 1953, s 1, Sched 1.

79 Eg Kenya Independence Act 1963, s 1; and see Roberts-Wray, *Commonwealth and Colonial Law*, p 261.

80 Statute of Westminster 1931, s 4 and eg Ceylon Independence Act 1947, s 1; ch 15 C.

81 *British Coal Corpn v R* [1935] AC 500, 520.

82 *Ndlwana v Hofmeyr* 1937 AD 229, 237; *Ibralebbe v R* [1964] AC 900, 923; *Blackburn v A-G* [1971] 2 All ER 1380.

83 *Manuel v A-G* [1983] Ch 77, 88.

84 H R Gray note 73 above.

85 Ch 10 B.

the line of succession to the throne laid down by the Act of Settlement 1700, by removing Edward VIII and his issue from the succession: if a later Parliament had wished the throne to revert to Edward VIII, the assent of the Sovereign for the time being (ie George VI or his descendant) would have been required, just as Edward VIII's assent was needed for the Abdication Act itself. Thus, the supreme Parliament may alter the rules which determine who the successors of the component parts of Parliament are to be (and, it might be added, may abolish one of these component parts eg the House of Lords, though this issue deserves separate discussion below).

By contrast with these examples, an illustration may be given of the principle that a supreme Parliament may not bind its successors. Parliament may create subordinate legislatures, whether for parts of the United Kingdom or for colonies, without depriving itself of legislative authority for the territory concerned. Thus the Government of Ireland Act 1920, which established a legislature for the domestic affairs of Northern Ireland, did not (unlike earlier proposed schemes of home rule for Ireland[86]) affect the Westminster Parliament's continuing legislative authority for Northern Ireland. To avoid any doubt, whether legal or political, s 75 of the Act provided that the supreme authority of Parliament should remain undiminished in respect of Northern Ireland. The Westminster Parliament retained full authority to legislate for Northern Ireland and to abolish the legislature it had established:[87] this authority did not depend upon the inclusion of s 75 in the 1920 Act. As for British colonies, the legislative supremacy of the UK Parliament was not affected by the existence of a colonial legislature, even though its legislative authority would not normally be exercised. In the case of Rhodesia, the legislative authority of Westminster was exercised in 1965 after the unilateral declaration of independence by Ian Smith's government had caused a serious breach in the conventional relationship between Rhodesia and the United Kingdom, and again in 1979 when the Rhodesian question was settled.[88]

The rule that Parliament may not bind its successors presents difficulties for certain constitutional reforms (for example, the creation of an entrenched Bill of Rights, discussed below). But it presents no obstacle to the adoption of a wholly new constitutional structure for the United Kingdom. As was said about Gladstone's first Home Rule Bill for Ireland, 'if the Irish Government Bill had become law the Parliament of 1885 would have had no successors'.[89] The object of securing that no subsequent Parliament enjoyed the attribute of legislative supremacy could be achieved in a variety of ways, for example by creating a federal system in the United Kingdom under which England, Scotland, Wales and Northern Ireland would each have its own legislature and executive; these bodies, together with a federal legislature and executive, would all be subject to the constitution as interpreted by a federal

---

[86]   W R Anson (1886) 2 LQR 427.
[87]   Northern Ireland (Temporary Provisions) Act 1972 and Northern Ireland Assembly Act 1973.
[88]   Southern Rhodesia Act 1979; Zimbabwe Act 1979.
[89]   W R Anson, op cit, p 436.

court. The creation of such a system would be inconsistent with the continuance of the legislative supremacy of the present Parliament. The legislative ground for the new constitution would be laid by the supreme
Parliament before it ceased to exist.

With the possible exception of the Union between Scotland and England
in 1707 and the Union between Ireland and Great Britain in 1800,[90] no actual
constitutional reforms have been intended to go as far as this. Instead, as with
British accession to the European Communities,[91] problems have arisen only
where the clear intention of Parliament to divest itself of legislative supremacy
has not been manifested and where, therefore, it may be argued that the
overriding rule of supremacy has not been affected. The question is not, 'May
a supreme Parliament bind its successors?' but 'What must a supreme
Parliament do (a) to express the definite intention that future Parliaments
should not be supreme? and (b) to ensure (whether by positive direction or
structural changes) that the courts will in future give effect to that intention?'
The second part of the question is important: for if the matter were to rest
merely on the stated intention of the present Parliament, it is likely that the
courts would hold that a later Parliament would be free to depart from that
intention. Moreover, it is only by subsequent judicial decisions, taken in the
light of relevant political developments, that it would be known whether or
not the present (supreme) Parliament had successfully achieved its stated
objective. To avoid the period of uncertainty that would otherwise ensue, it
has been suggested as a simple form of entrenchment that the judges be
required to take a fresh oath to observe the new scheme.[92] But if anything less
than a completely new constitution were proposed, it would set an undesirable precedent for Parliament to require the judges to take an oath to be loyal
to a new piece of constitutional apparatus. Difficulties would arise if some
judges refused to cooperate.

Before these matters are considered further, one question which has
already been mentioned[93] needs to be more fully examined, namely the need
for legal rules identifying the measures which are judicially accepted as Acts of
Parliament.

What is an Act of Parliament?[94]

In an extremely simple community, where all powers within the human group
are exercised by one person recognised as sovereign, no legal problems of
identifying acts of the sovereign arise. But, as R T E Latham said:

Where the purported sovereign is anyone but a single actual person, the designation
of him must include the statement of rules for the ascertainment of his will, and these
rules, since their observance is a condition of the validity of his legislation, are rules of
law logically prior to him.[95]

---

90 Ch 3 A and section D below.
91 Ch 8.
92 Wade, *Constitutional Fundamentals*, pp 37–9.
93 Page 59 above.
94 R T E Latham (1939) King's Counsel 152 and G Marshall (1954) 2 Political Studies 193.
95 *The Law and the Commonwealth*, p 523; compare Hart's 'rule of recognition', *The Concept of
    Law* (pp 75, 245, and ch 6).

Latham pointed out that Parliament, regarded only as an assembly of human beings, was not sovereign. 'It can only be sovereign when acting in a certain way prescribed by law. At least some rudimentary "manner and form" is demanded of it: the simultaneous incoherent cry of a rabble, small or large, cannot be law, for it is unintelligible.'[96]

In the absence of a written constitution to guide the courts in identifying an Act of Parliament, the definition of an Act of Parliament is primarily a matter of common law.[97] The rule of English common law is that for a Bill to become law, it must have been approved by Lords and Commons and have received the royal assent. In the ordinary case, this simple test will be satisfied by a rapid inspection of the Queen's Printer's copy of an Act of Parliament which will bear at its head formal words of enactment.[98] When Acts of Parliament have been challenged on the ground of procedural defects during their passage through Parliament, the judges have laid down the 'enrolled Act' rule.

In *Edinburgh & Dalkeith Railway v Wauchope*, a private Act which adversely affected Wauchope's rights against a railway company was challenged by Wauchope on the ground that notice of its introduction as a Bill into Parliament had not been given to him, as required by standing orders of the House of Commons. The court rejected this challenge. Lord Campbell said: 'All that a court of justice can do is to look to the Parliament roll: if from that it should appear that a Bill has passed both Houses and received the Royal Assent, no court of justice can inquire into the mode in which it was introduced into Parliament, or into what was done previous to its introduction, or what passed in Parliament during its progress in its various stages through both Houses.'[99] And in *Lee v Bude & Torrington Railway Co* it was said: 'If an Act of Parliament has been obtained improperly, it is for the legislature to correct it by repealing it; but, so long as it exists as law, the courts are bound to obey it.'[100]

This principle was reaffirmed in 1974, when the House of Lords in *Pickin v British Railways Board* held that a local or private Act of Parliament was binding whether or not the standing orders of each House of Parliament had been complied with.

Private Acts of 1836 and 1845 authorised the taking of land for a railway and provided that, if the line were ever abandoned, the land should vest in the owners of the adjoining land. In 1968, another private Act was passed, promoted by the British Railways Board, which abolished this rule. In 1969, Pickin bought a small piece of adjoining land and, when the railway was discontinued, claimed a declaration that under the 1836 and 1845 Acts he was entitled to a strip of the old line. He alleged that the board had fraudulently misled Parliament when promoting the 1968 Act, and had not complied with the standing orders of each House requiring individual notice to be given to owners affected by private legislation. Although the Court of Appeal held that these allegations raised a triable issue,[101] the House of Lords held that the courts had no power to disregard an Act of Parliament, whether public or private, nor had they

---

[96]   (1939) King's Counsel, 153, quoted in Heuston, *Essays in Constitutional Law*, pp 7–8.
[97]   Sir Owen Dixon (1957) 31 ALJ 240. And see *Prince's Case* (1606) 8 Co Rep 1, 20b.
[98]   Interpretation Act 1978, s 3. And see *Manuel v A-G* [1983] Ch 77, 87.
[99]   (1842) 8 Cl and F 710, 725.
[100] (1871) LR 6 CP 577, 582 (Willes J).
[101] [1973] QB 219.

power to examine proceedings in Parliament to determine whether an Act had
n obtained by irregularity or fraud.[102]

[here are several reasons for this reluctance of the courts to inquire into
internal procedures of Parliament. One important reason is the privilege
each House to regulate its own proceedings.[103] There could be serious
·cedural difficulties if officers of Parliament were summoned before a
irt to give evidence about the internal proceedings of Parliament, as well as
anger of the courts infringing art 9 of the Bill of Rights.[104] On many
tters of parliamentary procedure, the courts have declined to intervene
ether or not alleged breaches of statute were involved.[105] The rule that a
  must be read three times in each House is not a requirement of the
nmon law but is part of the 'law and custom of Parliament' and upon this
standing orders of each House are based. If one House wished to alter the
uirement, say by abolishing the third reading, this change would not affect
validity of subsequent Acts.

But some comments must be made on the 'enrolled Act' rule. First, there is
ay no Parliament roll: in case of necessity, all that a court could inspect is
 two vellum prints of an Act which since 1849 have been signed by the
rk of Parliaments and preserved in the Public Record Office and the
use of Lords library.[106] Secondly, the rule is reinforced by the rule in the
erpretation Act 1978 that every Act passed after 1850 shall be a public Act
l judicially noticed as such, unless the contrary is expressly provided by the
.[107] Thirdly, if it should appear that a measure has not been approved by
e House, then (unless the Parliament Acts 1911–49 apply) the measure is
t an Act.[108] Fourthly, where there is a written constitution, this may lay down
: procedures which must be followed before a Bill can become an Act. Thus
South Africa, the former constitution provided that certain entrenched
hts could be revoked only by legislation adopted at a joint sitting of both
·uses of the South African Parliament, voting by a two-thirds majority:
ere this procedure was not followed, the court held that the result was not a
id Act of Parliament.[109]

Could the 'enrolled Act' rule be changed by Act of Parliament? To an
ent it has already been modified by statute. Thus the Regency Acts
37–53 make permanent provision for the infancy, incapacity or temporary
ence abroad of the Sovereign.[110] A regent appointed under these Acts may
ercise all royal functions, including assenting to Bills, except that he may
t assent to a Bill for changing the order of succession to the Crown or for
pealing or altering the Act of 1707 securing Presbyterian Church Govern-

[1974] AC 765.

Ch 11 A.

Page 16 above.

Bradlaugh v Gossett (1884) 12 QBD 271; *Bilston v Wolverhampton Corpn* [1942] Ch 391; *Harper v Home Secretary* [1955] Ch 238; *Rediffusion (Hong Kong) Ltd v A-G of Hong Kong* [1970] AC 1136 (see O Hood Phillips (1971) 87 LQR 321). And see B Beinart [1954] SALR 135.

Heuston, *Essays in Constitutional Law*, p 18; and Erskine May, *Parliamentary Practice*, p 535.

For an explanation of this rule, see *Craies on Statute Law*, pp 55–8.

The Prince's Case (1606) 8 Co Rep 1a; cf Erskine May, p 536.

Harris v Minister of Interior 1952 (2) SA 428. For a full account, see Marshall, *Parliamentary Sovereignty and the Commonwealth*, part 3.

Ch 12 A.

ment in Scotland. If, which is unlikely, a regent did assent to a Bill for on∎ these purposes, there seems no reason why the courts should regard resulting measures as an Act of Parliament.

Similarly, the Parliament Acts 1911–49[111] provide that in certain circ∎ stances a Bill may become an Act without having been approved by the Lo∎ The 1911 Act provides special words of enactment which refer to Parliament Acts (s 4(1)) and also provides that the Speaker's certificate ∎ the requirements of the Acts have been complied with shall be conclusive all purposes (s 3). But the Parliament Acts procedure does not apply eithe∎ a Bill to extend the life of Parliament or to private or local Bills. If it w∎ attempted to extend the life of Parliament by a measure which had not b∎ approved by the Lords, a court should decline to regard the result as an Ac∎ Parliament: the 'conclusiveness' of the Speaker's certificate would not ne∎ sarily bar such a decision by the court.[112]

In respect both of the Regency Acts and the Parliament Acts, it has b∎ argued that measures which become law thereunder are not Acts of supreme Parliament but are Acts of a subordinate legislature to which supreme Parliament has made a limited delegation of its powers; s∎ measures are thus no more than delegated legislation.[113] But in ot∎ contexts, courts have been reluctant to apply to a legislature the principle ∎ delegated power may not be sub-delegated (*delegatus non potest delegare*)[114] ∎ a preferable view is that, for all but the purposes excluded, Parliament provided a procedure for legislation which is alternative to the procedure legislation by the supreme Parliament recognised at common law.[115] On ∎ view, the legal definition of an Act of Parliament may already differ accord∎ to the circumstances, as it may where a written constitution requires spe∎ procedures or special majorities for certain purposes.[116]

There continues, however, to be doubt whether Parliament may by stat∎ alter the legal rules for identifying an Act of Parliament. In *Pickin's* case, L∎ Morris said:

It must surely be for Parliament to lay down the procedures which are to be follo∎ before a Bill can become an Act. It must be for Parliament to decide whether decreed procedures have in fact been followed.[117]

This statement needs to be read with great care. First, it was made in ∎ context of an alleged departure from the standing orders of the House Commons. Secondly, where there is a written constitution prescribing spe∎ legislative procedures for certain purposes, we have seen that the enfor∎ ment of these procedures may be a matter for the courts. Thirdly, L∎

---

[111]   Ch 10 B.
[112]   Section 3 of the 1911 Act requires that the Speaker's certificate shall be given 'under thi∎ Act'; in interpreting this section, a court might hold that the test of ultra vires had not been ousted: cf *Minister of Health v R* [1931] AC 494 and *Anisminic Ltd v Foreign Compensation Commission* [1969] 2 AC 147; ch 30.
[113]   H W R Wade [1955] CLJ 172, 193–4 and *Constitutional Fundamentals*, pp 27–8.
[114]   *R v Burah* (1878) 3 App Cas 889 and *Hodge v R* (1883) 9 App Cas 117 (power of colonial legislature to delegate).
[115]   P Mirfield (1979) 95 LQR 36, 47–50.
[116]   Note 109 above. And see J Jaconelli [1989] PL 587.
[117]   [1974] AC 765, 790.

Morris's use of 'Parliament' is ambiguous. Are the procedures for legislation to be laid down by the Queen in Parliament (ie by statute) or by each House of Parliament separately (ie by standing orders and resolutions)? If the procedures for legislation were to be laid down by statute, so that a new statutory definition of an Act of Parliament (for all or some purposes) replaced the former common law rule, why should the courts continue to observe the former common law rule rather than the new statutory definition? Finally, if the question whether a certain document was an Act of Parliament were to arise in the course of litigation between two parties, it would be for the court to decide whether the document satisfied the 'enrolled Act' rule or some other rule laid down in legislation. As Marshall CJ said in *Marbury v Madison*, 'It is emphatically the province and duty of the judicial department to say what the law is'.[118]

While it concerned a colonial legislature, the Judicial Committee's decision in *Attorney-General for New South Wales v Trethowan*[119] may be of some relevance.

Under the Colonial Laws Validity Act 1865, the legislature of New South Wales had power to make laws respecting its own constitution, powers and procedure, provided that these laws were passed 'in such manner and form' as might from time to time be required by an Act of Parliament or other law for the time being in force in the state. In 1929 an Act provided that the upper House of the legislature should not be abolished until a Bill approved by both Houses had been approved by a referendum of the electorate; the requirement of a referendum applied also to amendments of the 1929 Act. Following a change of government, a Bill passed through both Houses which sought to abolish both the upper House and the requirement of a referendum. The government did not intend to submit the Bill to a referendum. An injunction was granted by the New South Wales court to restrain the government of New South Wales from presenting the Bill for the royal assent unless and until a majority of the electors had approved it. On appeal, the Judicial Committee held that the requirement of a referendum was binding on the legislature until it had been abolished by a law passed in the 'manner and form' required by law for the time being, ie with the approval of a referendum.

Two views may be held of *Trethowan's* case. The first is that the decision depended on the fact that the New South Wales legislature was a subordinate legislature, subject to the Colonial Laws Validity Act 1865 of the UK Parliament which, as stated, expressly laid down the 'manner and form' rule. On this view, the decision is not relevant to the present discussion.[120] The opposing view is that there is at common law a rule that legislation may be enacted only in such manner and form as is laid down by law and that the decision is therefore applicable to the UK Parliament.[121] While this may be so, *Trethowan's* case has little authority on this more general issue, since the decision of the Judicial Committee was expressly based on the effect of s 5 of the Colonial Laws Validity Act. If a comparable question arose in a British

---

[118]   1 Cranch 137 (1803).
[119]   [1932] AC 526, discussed in Marshall, *Parliamentary Sovereignty and the Commonwealth*, ch 8, W Friedmann (1950) 24 ALJ 103, and Loveland, *Constitutional Law*, pp 46–57.
[120]   H W R Wade [1955] CLJ 172, 183; E C S Wade, Introduction to Dicey, *The Law of the Constitution*, pp lxxiii–v.
[121]   Eg Jennings, *The Law and the Constitution*, p 153; R T E Latham (1939) King's Counsel 152, 161; W G Friedmann (1950) 24 ALJ 103, 104; O Dixon (1935) 51 LQR 590, 603.

court, the court would first have to decide whether the issue was justiciable.[122] If so, and if grounds for relief existed, the court would be more likely to grant a declaration of law as a remedy than an injunction.[123] These matters apart, there is nothing in *Trethowan* which diminishes the force of the argument that some kind of 'manner and form' rule to identify the acts of the legislature is essential within a legal system.

Summary

The argument so far may be summarised as follows. In principle a legislature must remain free to enact new laws on matters within its competence: if a conflict occurs between the laws enacted by Parliament, the courts apply the later of the two laws. The authority of Parliament includes power to legislate on constitutional matters, including both the composition of Parliament and the 'manner and form' by which new legislation may be made. While the courts may not of their own accord review the validity of the internal proceedings of Parliament, the scope for judicial decision could be extended if Parliament by statute altered the common law rules according to which the courts recognise or identify an Act of Parliament. The doctrine of parliamentary supremacy is no bar to the adoption of a written constitution for the United Kingdom which imposes judicially enforceable limits upon a future legislature, at least if such structural changes are made that the new legislative process is radically different from the present process by Lords, Commons and royal assent. Greater difficulty would arise if changes were *not* made in the structure of the legislature but the attempt was made to impose limits or restrictions upon the present legislature; in this situation, the courts might not regard the purported limits or restrictions as being effective to oust the continuing legislative supremacy of Parliament. The matter remains open. While Parliament could alter the 'manner and form' of the legislative process, such an attempt would not be effective if the courts still gave allegiance to the supreme Parliament defined in common law.

These general principles will now be discussed briefly in relation to some current constitutional issues.

1 Constitutional guarantees for Northern Ireland.[124]   The United Kingdom of Great Britain and Ireland was established when the Irish Acts of Union took effect in 1801. An account is given elsewhere of the events by which Southern Ireland broke from the United Kingdom.[125] In the Ireland Act 1949, the UK Parliament recognised the republican status of Southern Ireland and its complete cessation from being part of the Crown's dominions. That Act also recognised the position of Northern Ireland within the United Kingdom by declaring in s 1(2):

that Northern Ireland remains part of His Majesty's dominions and of the United

---

122   Cf G Sawer (1944) 60 LQR 83; see also *Rediffusion (Hong Kong) Ltd v Attorney-General of Hong Kong* [1970] AC 1136.
123   Crown Proceedings Act 1947, s 21; and ch 31 C.
124   Calvert, *Constitutional Law in Northern Ireland*, pp 23–33; Heuston, *Essays in Constitutional Law*, ch 1; Hadfield, *Constitutional Law of Northern Ireland*, pp 104–5.
125   Ch 3 A.

Kingdom and it is hereby affirmed that in no event will Northern Ireland or any part thereof cease to be part of His Majesty's dominions and of the United Kingdom without consent of the Parliament of Northern Ireland.[126]

The 1949 Act gave no express guarantee of the continued existence of the Parliament of Northern Ireland. That Parliament was suspended in 1972 and abolished in 1973 by Westminster. This made it necessary for the guarantee of Northern Ireland's status to be given a new form. The Northern Ireland Constitution Act 1973, s 1, provides that Northern Ireland shall not cease to be part of the United Kingdom without the consent of the majority of the people of Northern Ireland voting in a border poll.[127] The guarantee is of great political significance. But has Parliament fettered itself from, say, ceding Londonderry to the Republic of Ireland without first obtaining the consent of the majority of the people of Northern Ireland? Or could Parliament at a future date merely repeal the 1973 Act and provide nothing in its place? The strongest legal argument for the proposition that Parliament could not in law breach the 1973 guarantee takes the form that for the purposes of legislating for the future status of Northern Ireland, Parliament has redefined itself so that an additional stage, namely approval by a border poll, is required. But would the courts hold that this intention had been clearly expressed in the 1973 Act, and that a subsequent Parliament had lost the legal capacity to repeal the 1973 Act, expressly or by implication? And would a court, whether in Northern Ireland or in Britain, assume jurisdiction in the matter? At one time, a court might have been reluctant to recognise an individual's standing (locus standi) to challenge action by Parliament[128] and to grant injunctive relief. However, standing to sue has presented few difficulties in recent public law cases, and a declaratory judgment would be an appropriate remedy.[129] It has been suggested that the Northern Ireland guarantee is an example of a limitation which Parliament may impose on itself but which does not incapacitate Parliament from acting.[130] On this basis, the 1973 Act is effective so long as it remains in force (in giving a continuing guarantee to the people of Northern Ireland, so far as executive action is concerned) but the guarantee, like that in the 1949 Act, might in law be withdrawn by Parliament.

2 British membership of the European Union. A later chapter will outline the structure of the European Union, and will discuss the relationship between national law and Community law. Community law has been held by the European Court of Justice to prevail over any inconsistent provisions of the national law of the member states:

the law stemming from the Treaty, an independent source of law, cannot because of its very nature be overridden by rules of national law, however framed ... without the legal basis of the Community being called into question.[131]

---

[126] For an analogous provision in Gladstone's first Home Rule Bill, see Marshall, *Parliamentary Sovereignty and the Commonwealth*, pp 63–6.
[127] See the Northern Ireland (Border Poll) Act 1972.
[128] Ch 30.
[129] See eg *R v Employment Secretary, ex p EOC* [1995] 1 AC 1.
[130] Mitchell, *Constitutional Law*, p 81.
[131] Case 11/70, *Internationale Handelsgesellschaft* case [1970] ECR 1125, 1134. And see ch 8 B.

By the European Communities Act 1972, legal effect was given within the United Kingdom to those provisions of Community law which were, according to the European Treaties, intended to have direct effect within member states. This applied both to existing treaties and regulations and also to any future Community treaties or regulations. The Community organs therefore may legislate for the United Kingdom, as they do for other member states. While Britain remains a member of the Community, the Westminster Parliament is not the sole body with power to make new law for the United Kingdom. Nor can Community law appropriately be described as delegated legislation.[132]

The extent to which Community law overrides inconsistent national law can best be seen in *R v Transport Secretary, ex p Factortame Ltd*:[133]

Spanish fishing interests that had formed companies registered under UK law challenged as contrary to Community law the Merchant Shipping Act 1988. This Act, by defining the term, British fishing vessels, in a restrictive way, sought to prevent non-British interests from having access to the British fishing quota. In interim proceedings to protect Spanish interests pending decision of the substantive case, the European Court of Justice held that a national court must set aside a rule of national law if this was the sole obstacle preventing it from granting temporary relief to protect Community rights. Thus the UK courts must disregard s 21 of the Crown Proceedings Act 1947 (no injunctions to be granted against the Crown)[134] and must also not apply the Merchant Shipping Act 1988. In the House of Lords, Lord Bridge challenged the view that 'this was a novel and dangerous invasion by a Community institution of the sovereignty of the United Kingdom Parliament'. He stated that long before the United Kingdom joined the Community, the supremacy of Community law over the laws of member states was well established. 'Thus whatever limitation of its sovereignty Parliament accepted when it enacted the European Communities Act 1972 was entirely voluntary'.[135]

In *R v Employment Secretary, ex p EOC*,[136] the House of Lords declared that provisions in the Employment Protection (Consolidation) Act 1978, making protection for part-time workers (who were mainly female) subject to conditions that did not apply to full-time workers (who were mainly male), were incompatible with the right of female workers under Community law to equal treatment with male workers.

These decisions establish that the British courts must not apply national legislation, whether enacted before or after the European Communities Act 1972, if to do so would conflict with Community law. In Sir William Wade's view, decisions such as *Factortame* have effected a 'constitutional revolution',

---

[132]   Cf Cmnd 3301, 1967, para 22.
[133]   [1990] 2 AC 85 and ibid (*No 2*) [1991] 1 AC 603. See also N Gravells [1989] PL 568 and [1991] PL 180; and ch 8 D.
[134]   See ch 31 C.
[135]   [1991] 1 AC at 659.
[136]   [1995] 1 AC 1. Cf *R v Social Security Secretary, ex p EOC* (Case C 9/91) [1992] 3 All ER 577 (upholding differential age in state pensions scheme).

by holding that Parliament in 1972 did bind its successors.[137] A narrower explanation is that the 1972 Act created a rule of construction requiring the courts to apply UK legislation consistently with Community law, except where an Act expressly overrides Community law.[138] Whichever explanation is preferred, the primacy of Community law is an inescapable, albeit indeterminate, consequence of membership of the European Union.

3 A new Bill of Rights for the United Kingdom. The doctrine that Parliament may not bind its successors presents a major obstacle in the way of a new Bill of Rights in so far as this is intended to have any controlling effect upon later Parliaments. No such problem would arise if the Bill of Rights were to apply solely to subordinate legislation and administrative decisions,[139] but some have argued that it is essential to limit the power of future Parliaments to infringe human rights.[140] If a completely new constitutional structure for the United Kingdom were to be created, protection for fundamental rights could be included within it. Short of that, are there ways by which fundamental rights could be entrenched against infringement by Parliament? A select committee of the House of Lords, appointed to consider a Bill of Rights proposed by a Liberal peer, Lord Wade, gave a negative answer to this question in 1978. The committee's view was that:

> there is no way in which a Bill of Rights could protect itself from encroachment, whether express or implied, by later Acts. The most that such a Bill could do would be to include an interpretation provision which ensured that the Bill of Rights was always taken into account in the construction of later Acts and that, so far as a later Act could be construed in a way that was compatible with a Bill of Rights, such a construction would be preferred to one that was not.[141]

It was on this basis that a Bill to incorporate the European Convention on Human Rights was approved by the House of Lords in 1979.[142] In brief, the Bill provided that the Convention should prevail over earlier enactments (cl 2); in the case of conflict between the Convention and any later enactment, the later Act was to be deemed to be subject to the Convention and must be so construed 'unless such subsequent enactment provides otherwise or does not admit of any construction compatible with' the Convention (cl 3). Clause 3 thus recognised the possibility of express repeal in the future, and also of implied repeal whenever a later Act could not be interpreted in a manner compatible with the Convention.

In 1977, the Northern Ireland Standing Advisory Commission on Human Rights had recommended legislation that went further than this, namely that no subsequent Act that was inconsistent with the European Convention should have effect unless the later Act expressly declared that it should apply

---

[137] (1996) 112 LQR 568.
[138] P Craig (1991) 11 YBEL 221, 251. And see ch 8 D.
[139] Ch 19 C.
[140] Eg Scarman, *English Law – the New Dimension*, p 15.
[141] HL 176 (1977–78), para 23.
[142] HL Deb, 6 December 1979, col 915. Government opposition in the Commons prevented the Bill becoming law. A similar fate met Lord Lester's Human Rights Bill in 1994–95.

notwithstanding the Convention.[143] On this basis, implied repeal would have been totally barred. But in 1978 the select committee of the House of Lords stated that this solution was excluded by the *Vauxhall Estates* and *Ellen Street Estates* cases considered above.[144] When political opinion moves in favour of creating a new Bill of Rights, an important choice will have to be made as to the legal form which it should take.[145] The problem of entrenchment raises fundamental questions about the future power of the courts to review legislation by Parliament; the range of options is wider than the select committee believed in 1978.[146]

4 Abolition of the House of Lords.   In chapter 10 B we examine the present role of the House of Lords under the Parliament Acts 1911 and 1949. Here we deal only with the issue of whether, as one of the component parts of the supreme legislature, the House of Lords can be abolished.[147] There would indeed be a significant change in fundamental legal doctrine if 'whatever the Queen, Lords and Commons enact is law' were to become 'whatever the Queen and Commons enact is law'. If, as argued above, the former proposition is ultimately grounded upon decisions of the courts, the latter proposition would be authoritatively established only when the courts accepted the legislative supremacy of the Queen and Commons in place of the former supreme legislature. Arguably this change could be regarded as a legal revolution or a breach in legal continuity,[148] but this would seem to be an overstatement if the courts had merely given effect to a constitutional change initiated and authorised by the former legislature.

Two issues of practical significance might arise. First, if the Act abolishing the House of Lords included a Bill of Rights which was declared to be incapable of amendment by the new legislature (Queen and Commons), the courts would then have a choice between whether (a) to give effect to the stated intention of the former legislature, by holding that the Bill of Rights must prevail over any Acts passed by the new legislature, or (b) to hold that the new legislature was as legislatively supreme as its predecessor. Since the courts might not wish to create a legislative vacuum (ie a situation in which certain legislation is totally impossible), the outcome might depend on whether any procedure was provided for use if it became necessary in an emergency to encroach upon the Bill of Rights.

Secondly, could the House of Lords be lawfully abolished against the wishes of the House, by use of the Parliament Acts 1911 and 1949? The answer depends essentially upon whether the legislative powers conferred by the Parliament Act 1911 on the House of Commons and the Queen are to be construed subject to implied limitations, over and above those that are

---

[143]   Cmnd 7009, 1977. Cf New Zealand Bill of Rights 1990, s 6: 'Wherever an enactment can be given a meaning that is consistent with [this Bill of Rights], that meaning shall be preferred to any other meaning.'

[144]   Page 65 above. And see the opinion given to the committee by D Rippengal QC (HL 81, 1977–78, pp 1–10).

[145]   See Jaconelli, *Enacting a Bill of Rights, the Legal Problems.*

[146]   See the Constitution Unit's report, *Human Rights Legislation* (1996).

[147]   For the main arguments, see P Mirfield (1979) 95 LQR 36 and G Winterton (1979) 95 LQR 386. And Dicey, *The Law of the Constitution*, pp 64–70.

[148]   Mirfield, op cit, pp 42–5.

expressed in the 1911 Act itself.[149] Since the analogy of delegated legislation does not seem a close one, it is submitted that an Act passed under the Parliament Act procedure could lawfully abolish the House of Lords; such a measure might be resisted on political grounds but not by challenge in the courts.[150]

D.   The Treaty of Union between England and Scotland

In Section C, we discussed the question whether the UK Parliament may impose legal limitations upon its successors. The Anglo-Scottish Union of 1707 raises the different question, 'was the UK Parliament born unfree?'[151] The main features of the Treaty of Union have already been outlined.[152] Now it is necessary to examine more closely provisions of the Treaty concerning the power to legislate after the Union.

The Treaty contemplated that the new Parliament of Great Britain would legislate both for England and Scotland; but no grant of general legislative competence to Parliament was made in the Treaty. Article 18 provided that the laws concerning regulation of trade, as well as customs and excise duties, should be uniform throughout Britain; subject to this, all other laws within Scotland were to remain in force,

but alterable by the Parliament of Great Britain, with this difference betwixt the laws concerning public right, policy, and civil government, and those which concern private right; that the laws which concern public right, policy and civil government may be made the same throughout the whole United Kingdom, but that no alteration be made in laws which concern private right except for evident utility of the subjects within Scotland.

By art 19, the Court of Session and the Court of Justiciary were to remain 'in all time coming' within Scotland as then constituted, and with the same authority and privileges as before the Union, 'subject nevertheless to such regulations for the better administration of justice as shall be made by the Parliament of Great Britain'. Other courts were to be subject to regulation and alteration by Parliament. No causes in Scotland were to be cognisable (ie capable of being heard) by the Courts of Chancery, Queen's Bench, Common Pleas (or any other court in Westminster Hall). An Act for securing the Protestant religion and Presbyterian Church government in Scotland was passed at the same time by the English and Scottish Parliaments and was declared to be a fundamental and essential condition of the Treaty of Union 'in all time coming'.

There is substantial evidence in the Treaty that, while the framers of the Union intended the new Parliament to be the sole legislature, they sought to distinguish between matters on which Parliament would be free to legislate, matters on which it would have a limited authority to legislate, and matters

---

149   Ibid, pp 45–6 and Winterton, op cit, pp 390–2. See also ch 10 B.
150   As suggested by Lord Denning in *What Next in the Law?*, p 320.
151   Mitchell, *Constitutional Law*, pp 69–74; T B Smith [1957] PL 99; D N MacCormick (1978) 29 NILQ 1. See also Munro, *Studies in Constitutional Law*, ch 4; M Upton (1989) 105 LQR 79; *Stair Encyclopedia: The Laws of Scotland*, vol 5, pp 137–62; and HLE, vol 8(2), pp 54–8.
152   Ch 3 A.

which were declared fundamental and unalterable. The Treaty made no provision for future amendment of itself, nor for future renegotiation of the terms of the Union. The former English and Scottish Parliaments ceased to exist. No machinery was provided for applying the distinction drawn in art 18 between the laws concerning 'public right, policy and civil government' and the laws concerning 'private right', nor, in the latter case, for ascertaining the changes in those laws that might be for 'evident utility' of the Scottish people.

The argument that the Union imposed limitations upon the new Parliament can be summarised as follows: the new Parliament entered upon its life by virtue of the Union; its powers were therefore limited by the guarantees in the Treaty, which guarantees had been enacted by the separate Parliaments before the united Parliament was born. The assertion that a sovereign Parliament may not bind its successors may be countered by the view that even if both the English and Scottish Parliaments were supreme before 1707,[153] they each committed suicide in favour of a common heir with limited powers. The Treaty of Union, concludes the argument, is a fundamental constitutional text which prevents the British Parliament from itself enjoying the attribute of legislative supremacy. When, as in *Cheney v Conn*, an English judge remarks, 'what the statute says and provides is the highest form of law that is known to this country',[154] a Scots lawyer might reply, 'Not so: the Treaty of Union is a higher form of law and may prevail over inconsistent Acts of Parliament.'

This viewpoint is subject to both theoretical and historical difficulties. First, no legislature other than the British Parliament was created. If circumstances changed, and amendments to the Union became desirable, how could they be made except by Act of Parliament? Thus in 1748, the heritable jurisdictions were abolished and, when Scottish local government was reformed in 1975, the royal burghs were abolished.[155] In 1853, the Universities (Scotland) Act abolished the requirement that the professors of the ancient Scottish universities should be confessing members of the Church of Scotland, thus repealing an 'unalterable' provision of the Act for securing the Presbyterian Church. Secondly, the distinction between laws concerning 'public right, policy and civil government' and laws concerning 'private right' is a very difficult one. For example, power to tax private property or to acquire land compulsorily for public purposes concerns both public and private right; and is the law of education or industrial relations a matter of public or private right? Thirdly, the test of 'evident utility' for changes in the law affecting private right is obscure: who is to decide – Scottish MPs, Scottish courts, public opinion or institutions such as the General Assembly of the Church of Scotland?[156] Fourthly, after the Union the Westminster Parliament continued to conduct its affairs exactly as before, subject only to its enlargement by

---

[153] On whether the Scottish Parliament was supreme before 1707, see Donaldson, *Scotland: James V–James VII*, ch 15; and Dicey and Rait, *Thoughts on the Union between England and Scotland*, pp 19–22, 242–4.
[154] Page 62 above.
[155] Cf arts 20 and 21 of the Treaty of Union.
[156] The court was prepared to find a statute to be of 'evident utility' in *Laughland v Wansborough Paper Co* 1921 1 SLT 341, but cf *Gibson v Lord Advocate* below.

members from Scotland.[157] As the dominant partners in the Union, the English assumed that continuity from pre-Union days was unbroken. On a matter left silent by the Treaty of Union, the House of Lords in its judicial capacity has heard appeals from Scotland in civil cases since the case of *Greenshields* in 1709 (the House of Lords was not a court within Westminster Hall within the meaning of art 19 of the Union) but it has no jurisdiction in Scottish criminal cases. Fifthly, even if the framers of the Union intended there to be legal limitations upon the British Parliament, this might not in itself be sufficient to vest jurisdiction in the courts to hold Acts of the UK Parliament invalid on the ground that they conflicted with the Treaty of Union. In Dicey's view, the subsequent history of the Union with Scotland 'affords the strongest proof of the futility inherent in every attempt of one sovereign legislature to restrain the action of another equally sovereign body'.[158]

These matters have been debated in several important Scottish cases.

In *MacCormick v Lord Advocate*,[159] the Rector of Glasgow University challenged the Queen's title as 'Elizabeth the Second', on the grounds that this was contrary to historical fact and contravened art 1 of the Treaty of Union. At first instance, Lord Guthrie dismissed the challenge for the reason, inter alia, that an Act of Parliament could not be challenged in any court as being in breach of the Treaty of Union or on any other ground. In the Inner House of the Court of Session, the First Division dismissed the appeal against Lord Guthrie's decision, but on narrower grounds. After holding that MacCormick had no legal title or interest to sue, that the royal numeral was not contrary to the Treaty, and that the Royal Titles Act 1953 was irrelevant, Lord President Cooper said: 'The principle of the unlimited sovereignty of Parliament is a distinctively English principle which has no counterpart in Scottish constitutional law'. He had difficulty in seeing why it should have been supposed that the Parliament of Great Britain must have inherited all the peculiar characteristics of the English Parliament but none of the Scottish Parliament. He could find in the Union legislation no provision that the Parliament of Great Britain should be 'absolutely sovereign' in the sense that it should be free to alter the Treaty at will. He reserved opinion on whether breach of such fundamental law as is contained in the Treaty of Union would raise an issue justiciable in the courts; in his view there was no precedent that the courts of Scotland or England had authority to determine 'whether a governmental act of the type here in controversy is or is not conform to the provisions of a Treaty, least of all when that Treaty is one under which both Scotland and England ceased to be independent States and merged their identity in an incorporating union'. Lord Russell, who concurred, stressed the limited functions of the courts in dealing with political matters, suggesting that a political remedy would be more suitable for MacCormick than a judicial remedy.

Although Lord Cooper's judgment went beyond what was necessary for decision of the case, the fundamental issues remain confused. In particular, the denial that the courts have jurisdiction to decide whether 'a governmental act of the type here in controversy' conformed to the Treaty must be read in

---

157   See eg the comment by Bryce, *Studies in History and Jurisprudence*, vol 1, p 194, that, by fusing herself with Scotland in 1707, England altered the constitution of the enlarged state no further than by the admission of additional members to Parliament and the suppression of certain offices in Scotland.

158   Dicey, *The Law of the Constitution*, p 65; and cf Dicey and Rait, op cit, p 252.

159   1953 SC 396.

relation to the disputed royal title. If the UK Parliament were to pass an Act which sought to deprive persons in Scotland of access to the Scottish courts in matters of private right, the courts would seem bound to decide whether to give effect to that Act.

In 1975, a Scottish fisherman unsuccessfully claimed in the Court of Session that British membership of the European Community was incompatible with the Treaty of Union.

In *Gibson v Lord Advocate*, Gibson claimed that an EC regulation granting EC nationals the right to fish in Scottish waters, and the European Communities Act 1972, which gave this legal effect in Britain, were contrary to art 18 of the Union, since this was a change in the law concerning a private right which was not for the 'evident utility' of the Scottish people. Lord Keith held that the control of fishing in territorial waters around Scotland was a branch of public law, which might be made the same throughout the United Kingdom and was not protected by art 18. Obiter, Lord Keith said that the question whether an Act of Parliament altering Scots private law was or was not for the 'evident utility' of the Scottish people was not a justiciable issue. 'The making of decisions upon what must essentially be a political matter is no part of the function of the court.'[160] He considered the question of title to sue (locus standi) to be of secondary importance.

Both in *MacCormick* and in *Gibson* the question was held open of the validity of legislation seeking to abolish the Court of Session or the Church of Scotland, both being institutions safeguarded by the Union. Short of such an extreme situation, the Scottish courts appear reluctant to claim a power to review the validity of Acts of Parliament. This attitude was maintained when the Court of Session declined to hold that the community charge (or poll tax) legislation, which applied to Scotland a year earlier than in England and Wales, was contrary to art 4 of the Treaty of Union.[161]

In 1872, an English court denied that it had any jurisdiction to determine the validity of an Act of Parliament, and rejected a challenge to the Irish Church Act 1869 on the ground that it was contrary to the Irish Acts of Union.[162] While the turbulent course of Irish history could make it difficult to base legal arguments upon the intended binding character of the Irish Union, the very different history of the Anglo-Scottish Union does not make the idea of a constitutional jurisdiction vested in the Court of Session with appeal to the House of Lords inherently absurd. If Scotland were to acquire its own legislative assembly, such a jurisdiction in respect of the measures passed by that assembly would almost certainly be necessary.[163]

E. Conclusions

This chapter has examined whether there are any legal limits upon the legislative supremacy of Parliament, in particular whether there are, or could be,

---

[160] 1975 SLT 134.
[161] *Pringle, Petitioner* 1991 SLT 330 and *Murray v Rogers* 1992 SLT 221. See also N C Walker and C M G Himsworth [1991] JR 45 and D J Edwards (1992) 12 Legal Studies 34. Cf *R v Lord Chancellor, ex p Law Society, The Times*, 25 June 1993.
[162] *Ex p Canon Selwyn* (1872) 36 JP 54.
[163] Ch 3 B. And see *Smith v Sillars* 1982 SLT 539.

any limits capable of being enforced judicially. While British tradition has been strongly against the courts having power to review the validity of primary legislation, the courts cannot escape the task of deciding whether a document for which legislative authority is claimed is in law an Act of Parliament. While the basic rule of legislative supremacy is a matter of common law, as well as being an important political fact, it cannot be demonstrated from existing precedents that under no circumstances could this rule be qualified by judicial decision – still less that the basic rule could not be changed by Act of Parliament. It is therefore not possible to assert dogmatically that the legislative supremacy of Parliament will continue for the future to be the primary rule of constitutional law in the United Kingdom. (Indeed, the advancing pace of European integration (through Community law) has already made extensive inroads into the Diceyan doctrine of legislative supremacy, and incorporation of the European Convention of Human Rights might do likewise, depending on the form of incorporation.[164] *V, L.*

Political significance of legislative supremacy

There are difficulties in attempting to assess the political significance of the legislative supremacy of Parliament. For one thing, constitutional and legal rules tend to reflect political facts, but sometimes only with a considerable time-lag. Moreover, the doctrine has always been affected by a tinge of political unreality since it would empower Parliament to do many unlikely, immoral or undesirable things which no one wishes it to do. Does Parliament really need power to condemn all red-haired males to death or to make attendance at public worship illegal? Or to create criminal offences retrospectively? Regarding legislative omnipotence, Sir Robert Megarry has emphasised that validity in law must not be confused with practical enforceability.[165]

Yet it would be wrong to ignore the strong political argument for retaining supremacy, particularly when the wishes of a newly elected House of Commons can be clearly identified with the will of the majority. Legislative supremacy is well suited to a centralised, unitary system of government in which the needs of the executive are closely linked with the dominant political voice in Parliament: and in which the judiciary exercise an important but subordinate role. Even in such a system, there are many factors which limit the use to which the executive can put Parliament's legislative powers. Dicey suggested that political sovereignty, as opposed to legislative sovereignty, lay in the electorate, and that ultimately the will of the electorate was sure to prevail on all subjects to be determined by the British government.[166] Certainly, the electoral system serves as a limitation upon the use of legislative powers, but the control which it provides is very generalised and sporadic in effect: and this effect depends in turn upon the political parties, on the media, on economic and social interest groups, and on other means by which public opinion is formed and expressed. Moreover, the voting system itself produces a House of Commons which is a distortion of the spread of views

---

[164] See A W Bradley, in Jowell and Oliver (eds), *The Changing Constitution*, ch 2.
[165] *Manuel v A-G* [1983] Ch 77, 89.
[166] Dicey, *The Law of the Constitution*, p 73. And see p 59 above.

amongst the electorate[167] and provides only weak protection for unpopular minorities.

Consultation of interests affected

The immense complexity of government often makes it expedient that Parliament should exercise its powers only after the major interests affected by proposed legislation have been consulted. In the case of delegated legislation, statute often requires there to be consultation with interest groups before the minister makes regulations.[168] In the case of legislation by Bill, there is no legal requirement of consultation but the government may consult with such bodies as the Confederation of British Industry, the British Medical Association and the National Farmers' Union. In any event, such bodies can make their views known to the government about proposed legislation. Even where consultation takes place, the bodies whose advice is sought cannot dictate the policy decisions taken by the government. Many social reforms would never have occurred if government had allowed interested organisations to veto changes made to protect other groups in society. During the 1980s, the Thatcher government saw little need to secure by persuasion the support of bodies such as local authority associations, the trade unions and the universities. Many legislative changes directly affecting such interests were made against their opposition.

Parliament and the electorate

Under the British system, the electorate takes no direct part in legislative decision-making, save by electing the House of Commons. In some constitutions, for example the Republic of Ireland and the Commonwealth of Australia,[169] constitutional amendments may take effect only with the consent of the electorate obtained by a referendum. In other constitutions (for example, Denmark and Switzerland) legislative proposals may be subject to a referendum. Until 1975, the United Kingdom found no place for the machinery of direct democracy, save in the case of the border poll in Northern Ireland.[170] Where major political issues are concerned, the outcome of a general election may indicate the degree of popular support for any changes. In 1910, two elections were held because of the legislative veto of the Lords and the necessity to establish popular support for the constitutional changes involved. In general, it is difficult to decide from the result of a general election the state of public opinion on particular issues. Since the party which wins a general election may be considered to have a mandate to implement its manifesto, a government can scarcely be criticised for seeking to carry out its election promises. Conversely, a government may be criticised for proposing major reforms, particularly of a constitutional nature, which have never been before the electorate. The Conservative government elected in 1970 was criticised by those opposed to British membership of the European Communities for having completed the negotiations for member-

---

167   Ch 9 B, part V.
168   Ch 27.
169   See Cmnd 5925, 1975, annex B.
170   Page 74 above.

ship, signed the Treaty of Accession and secured the passing of the European Communities Act 1972 without allowing the electorate the opportunity to vote on this issue. For these reasons, but mainly because of the internal division of opinion within the Labour party, a referendum on Britain's membership of the Communities was held in 1975. In 1979, referendums were held in Scotland and Wales on whether devolution under the Scotland Act and Wales Act 1978 should take effect.[171] It may be argued that the referendum should be used for deciding other constitutional issues, such as the future of the House of Lords, and the creation of a new Bill of Rights. While advisory referendums do not directly affect the legislative authority of Parliament, if referendums were to be mandatory for certain reforms, this would affect the position of Parliament and it would be essential to define in law the limits of their use. It has been argued that referendums should be used 'as an extra check against government, an additional protection to that given by Parliament'.[172] This would give a form of entrenchment to certain matters against action by the elected majority in the Commons. Without all-party agreement on the matter, the selection of those aspects of the constitution to be protected would be contentious. There is a case to be made for requiring a referendum whenever it is proposed to transfer the powers of Parliament;[173] as John Locke said, 'it being but a delegated power from the People, they who have it cannot pass it to others'.[174] However, it may be doubted whether greater use of referendums would be as significant as electoral reform.

Summary

The view taken in this chapter has been that Parliament's legislative authority includes power to make new arrangements under which future Parliaments would not enjoy legislative supremacy. The argument that the doctrine of legislative supremacy must be retained is strengthened if it can be shown that the political system provides adequate safeguards against legislation which would be contrary to fundamental constitutional principle or the individual's basic rights. It is, however, doubtful whether the present system, which relies so heavily on political controls, adequately protects individuals or minority groups who may be vulnerable to legislative oppression. Moreover, Parliament's importance within British government depends much less upon absolute legislative power, than upon its effectiveness as a political forum in expressing public opinion and in exercising control over government. In the case of the European Union, political necessity has brought about a situation, recognised by the judiciary, in which Community law prevails over inconsistent national legislation. A return of the United Kingdom to Diceyan orthodoxy would scarcely compensate for the disadvantages of an isolationist policy within Europe.

---

[171] Ch 3 B.
[172] Bogdanor, *The People and the Party System*, p 69.
[173] Ibid, p 77.
[174] *Second Treatise on Civil Government*, quoted in Bogdanor, p 77.

CHAPTER 5

The relationship between legislature, executive and judiciary

Emphasis on the legislative supremacy of Parliament as the basic doctrine of constitutional law may cause principles of constitutionalism to be undervalued. The separation of powers is found, in stronger or weaker form, in many modern constitutions; it is opposed to the concentration of state power in a single person or group, since that is a clear threat to democratic government. The need for a separation of powers arises not only in political decision-making but also in the legal system, where an independent judiciary is essential if the rule of law is to have any substance.[1]

For purposes of analysis, the functions of government are often divided into three broad classes – legislative, executive (or administrative) and judicial. It is not always easy, or indeed possible, to determine under which head a particular task of government falls, but the organs which mainly perform these functions are distinguishable. To give an example from one of the oldest tasks of government, that of taxation: to enact a law authorising a new tax is a legislative function; to operate machinery for assessing and collecting the tax payable by each taxpayer is an executive (or administrative) function; to determine disputes between the taxpayer and the tax-collector as to the tax due in a particular case is a judicial function, involving interpretation of the law and applying it to the facts. So too in criminal law: creation of a new offence is a matter for legislation, enforcement of the law is an executive function and the trial of alleged offenders is a judicial function. It is taken for granted in Britain that the imposition of a new tax and the creation of new offences are matters for Parliament, that enforcing the law is for the executive, and that determining the law in individual cases is for the courts. But the tasks of government today are complex. The simple model afforded by taxation and criminal law is not easily applicable to many of the more elaborate processes of government.

In this chapter, it is intended to examine the two questions:

(a) to what extent are the three functions (legislative, executive and judicial) distinguishable today?

---

[1] Vile, *Constitutionalism and the Separation of Powers*; Allan, *Law, Liberty and Justice*, chs 1, 3, 8. Also Mount, *The British Constitution Now*, pp 81–92; E Barendt [1995] PL 599.

(*b*) to what extent are these three functions exercisable separately by the institutions of Parliament, the executive and the courts to which they are often attributed?

The legislative function

The legislative function involves the enactment of general rules determining the structure and powers of public authorities and regulating the conduct of citizens and private organisations. In the United Kingdom, legislative authority is vested in the Queen in Parliament: new law is enacted when, usually on the proposal of the government, it has been approved by Commons and Lords and has received the royal assent. Under the Parliament Acts of 1911 and 1949, legislation may be enacted even though it has been rejected by the House of Lords.[2] While the House of Lords remains part of the legislature, its power to amend measures passed by the Commons is limited; and it is politically subordinate to the elected House of Commons.

While legislative authority is vested in the Queen in Parliament, several qualifications need to be borne in mind.

(*a*) By Act of Parliament, legislative powers may be conferred on executive bodies – for example on ministers, government departments and local authorities. While subordinate legislation of this kind is made under the authority of an Act, it is not directly made by Parliament.[3]

(*b*) In the European Communities Act 1972, Parliament recognised that the organs of the European Communities could legislate in respect of the United Kingdom. In Community matters, legislative powers for the United Kingdom are exercisable by the Council of Ministers and the Commission.[4]

(*c*) While one result of the 17th-century constitutional conflict was to impose very severe limits on the authority of the Crown to make new law without the approval of Parliament, certain legislative powers of the Crown have survived.[5]

(*d*) While primary legislative authority is vested in Parliament, the two Houses have much work to do which does not involve legislating. In fact the time devoted to the legislative programme seldom exceeds half the number of days in a session. The rest of Parliament's time is used in debating government policies and other national issues, and in scrutinising the work of government departments.[6]

(*e*) Government Bills predominate in Parliament, with ministers being responsible for supervising their passage through each House and for implementing new Acts once they have received the royal assent. The executive therefore participates actively, and often decisively, in the process of legislation. When the government has a working majority in the Commons, no new legislation can be enacted by Parliament without at least the tacit approval of the government.

(*f*) Once a new law has been enacted by Parliament, the authoritative

[2]   Ch 10 B.
[3]   Ch 27.
[4]   Ch 8.
[5]   Ch 12 D.
[6]   Ch 10 C and D.

interpretation of that law is a matter for the courts. The interpretation of statutes is in one sense a vital part of the law-making process, as it is only after such interpretation that it is known whether the intentions of those who framed the law have been carried into effect; in this task the judges must not challenge the political authority of the legislature.[7]

The executive function

It is more difficult to give a simple account of the executive function than of the legislative function. The executive function broadly comprises the whole corpus of authority to govern, other than that which is involved in the legislative functions of Parliament and the judicial functions of the courts. The general direction of policy includes the initiation of legislation, the maintenance of order, the promotion of social and economic welfare, administration of public services, and the conduct of the external relations of the state. The executive function has therefore a residual character, its techniques ranging from the formation of broad policy to the detailed management of routine services. Historically the executive was identified with the Sovereign, in whose name many acts are still performed by the Prime Minister, Cabinet and other ministers. Today, in a broad sense the executive comprises all officials and public authorities by which functions of government are exercised, including the civil service and armed forces. Executive functions are also performed by the police, local authorities and many statutory bodies, but these other bodies are not subject to the day-by-day control of central government. British membership of the European Union has meant that the Council and the Commission exercise executive functions in relation to the United Kingdom.[8]

The judicial function

The primary judicial function is to determine disputed questions of fact and law in accordance with the law laid down by Parliament and expounded by the courts. This function is exercised mainly in the civil and criminal courts by professional judges. Civil jurisdiction covers both private law issues (on such matters as tort, contract and property) and also questions of public law which arise in the process of judicial review. Lay magistrates exercise many powers of criminal justice in the lower courts and ordinary citizens contribute to the administration of justice by serving on juries at criminal trials. The civil and criminal courts do not have a monopoly of the judicial function. Many disputes which arise out of the conduct of government are entrusted to administrative tribunals. Today these tribunals are a recognised part of the machinery of justice; they operate subject to the supervision of the superior civil courts.[9]

As well as their primary function of settling legal disputes, the courts exercise certain minor legislative functions (for example, making rules governing court procedure) and administrative functions (for example,

---

[7]   *Stock v Frank Jones (Tipton) Ltd* [1978] 1 All ER 948; *Duport Steels Ltd v Sirs* [1980] 1 All ER 529.
[8]   Ch 8.
[9]   Ch 28 A.

administering the estates of deceased persons). In matters of Community law, judicial functions are exercised for the United Kingdom by the European Court of Justice and the Court of First Instance.

The doctrine of the separation of powers

Within a system of government based on law, there are legislative, executive and judicial functions to be performed; and the primary organs for discharging these functions are respectively the legislature, the executive and the courts. A legal historian has remarked:

This threefold division of labour, between a legislator, an administrative official, and an independent judge, is a necessary condition for the rule of law in modern society and therefore for democratic government itself.[10]

Admittedly there is no clear-cut demarcation between some aspects of these functions, nor is there always a neat correspondence between the functions and the institutions of government. As a matter of history, Parliament, the courts and central government in Britain owe their origin to the monarchy; before these institutions developed as distinct entities, the King governed through his Council, with a mixture of legislative, executive and judicial work. Today these tasks are all performed in the name of the Crown, but in a mature democracy it is important that judges are independent both of Parliament and government, and that Parliament is not merely a rubber stamp for the Cabinet. Indeed it may be argued that essential values of law, liberty and democracy are best protected if the three primary functions of a law-based government are discharged by distinct institutions. Robson described the separation of powers as 'that antique and rickety chariot . . ., so long the favourite vehicle of writers on political science and constitutional law for the conveyance of fallacious ideas'.[11] But this does not do justice to the contribution which the doctrine has made to the maintenance of liberty and the continuing need by constitutional means to restrain abuse of governmental power.[12] The rest of this chapter will examine the doctrine and how far it applies in Britain today.

Locke and Montesquieu

In 1690, the Englishman John Locke wrote in his *Second Treatise of Civil Government*:

It may be too great a temptation to humane frailty, apt to grasp at power, for the same persons who have the power of making laws, to have also in their hands the power to execute them, whereby they may exempt themselves from obedience to the laws they make, and suit the law, both in its making and execution, to their own private advantage.[13]

The doctrine of the separation of powers was developed further by the

---

[10] Henderson, *Foundations of English Administrative Law*, p 5.

[11] Robson, *Justice and Administrative Law*, p 14.

[12] See Vile, *Constitutionalism and the Separation of Powers*, for reassessment of the link between legal values and separation of powers; also Marshall, *Constitutional Theory*, ch 5, and Munro, *Studies in Constitutional Law*, ch 9.

[13] Ch XII, para 143, quoted in Vile, op cit, p 62.

French jurist, Montesquieu, who based his exposition on the British constitution of the early 18th century as he understood it. His division of power did not closely correspond except in name with the classification which has become traditional; for, although he followed the usual meaning of legislative and judicial powers, by executive power he meant only 'the power of executing matters falling within the law of nations', ie making war and peace, sending and receiving ambassadors, establishing order, preventing invasion.[14] He stated the essence of the doctrine thus:

> When the legislative and executive powers are united in the same person, or in the same body of magistrates, there can be no liberty ... Again, there is no liberty, if the judicial power be not separated from the legislative and executive. Were it joined with the legislative, the life and liberty of the subject would be exposed to arbitrary control; for the judge would then be the legislator. Were it joined to the executive however, the judge might behave with violence and oppression. There would be an end to everything, were the same man, or the same body, whether of the nobles or of the people, to exercise those three powers, that of enacting laws, that of executing the public resolutions, and of trying the causes of individuals.[15]

This statement emphasises that, within a system of government based upon law, the judicial function should be exercised by a body separate from legislature and executive. Montesquieu did not mean that legislature and executive ought to have no influence or control over the acts of each other, but only that neither should exercise the whole power of the other.[16]

In Montesquieu's observation of the British constitution in the 18th century, he saw that Parliament had achieved legislative dominance over the King with the passing of the Bill of Rights, and that the independence of the judiciary had been declared, but that the King still exercised executive power. Before the century was over, however, there had been established in Britain the Cabinet system, under which the King governed only through ministers who were members of Parliament and responsible to it. This system, with its emphatic link between Parliament and the executive, in a major respect ran contrary to Montesquieu's doctrine. It is in the United States constitution that his influence can best be seen.

Separation of powers in the US constitution

In the US constitution of 1787 the separation of powers formed one pillar of the new edifice.[17] The framers of the constitution intended that a balance of powers should be attained by vesting each primary function in a distinct organ. Possibly they were imitating the British constitution, but by that time in Britain executive power was passing from the Crown to the Cabinet. The US constitution vests legislative powers in Congress, consisting of a Senate and a House of Representatives (art 1), executive power in the President (art 2), and judicial power in the Supreme Court and such other federal courts as might be established by Congress (art 3). The President holds office for a fixed term of four years and is separately elected: he may therefore be of a

---

14   But cf Vile, op cit, p 87.
15   *De l'Esprit des Lois*, Book XI, ch 6, quoted in Vile, op cit, p 90.
16   Jennings, *The Law and the Constitution*, app 1.
17   For a classic defence of the US approach to separation, see *The Federalist*, XLVII (Madison).

different party from that which has a majority in either or both Houses of Congress. His powers, like those of Congress, are declared by the constitution. While the heads of the chief departments of state are known as the Cabinet, they are individually responsible to the President and not to Congress.

Neither the President nor members of his Cabinet sit or vote in Congress; they have no direct power of initiating Bills or securing their passage through Congress. The President may recommend legislation in his messages to Congress, but he cannot compel it to carry out his recommendations. While he has a power to veto legislation passed by Congress, this veto may be overridden by a two-thirds vote in each House of Congress. Treaties may be negotiated by the President, but must be approved by a two-thirds majority of the Senate. The President may nominate to key offices, including the justices of the Supreme Court, but the Senate must confirm these appointments and may refuse to do so. The President himself is not directly responsible to Congress for his conduct of affairs: in normal circumstances he is irremovable, but the constitution authorises the President to be removed from office by the process of impeachment at the hands of the Senate, 'for treason, bribery, or other high crimes and misdemeanours' (art 2(4)). (The prospect of impeachment was the immediate cause of President Nixon's resignation in 1974 following his complicity in the Watergate affair.) Once appointed, the judges of the Supreme Court are independent both of Congress and the President, although they too may be removed by impeachment. Early in its history, the Supreme Court assumed the power, expressed in the historic judgment of Chief Justice Marshall in *Marbury v Madison*,[18] to declare acts of the legislature and acts of the President to be unconstitutional should they conflict with the constitution.

Even in the US constitution, there is not a complete separation of powers between the executive, legislative and judicial functions, if by this is meant that each power can be exercised in isolation from the others. Having established the threefold allocation of functions as a basis, the constitution constructs an elaborate system of checks and balances to enable control and influence to be exercised by each branch upon the others. The Watergate affair showed not only the strong position of a President elected into office by popular vote: it also showed how a combination of powers exercised by Congress and the Supreme Court, as well as such forces as public opinion and the press, could combine to remove even the President from office.[19]

Separation of power in other constitutions

Many other constitutions have been influenced by the separation of powers. Written constitutions often contain distinct chapters dealing with legislative, judicial and executive powers, but display no uniformity in the extent to which these functions are separate. In France, the doctrine is of great importance but it has manifested itself very differently from the American version. Thus it is considered to flow from the separation of powers that the ordinary courts should have no jurisdiction to review the legality of acts of the

---

[18]   1 Cranch 137 (1803).
[19]   See *US v Nixon* 418 US 683 (1974). For separation of powers issues arising under the US constitution, see Tribe, *Constitutional Choices*, part II.

legislature or executive. In place of the courts the Conseil d'Etat, structurally part of the executive, has developed a jurisdiction over administrative agencies and officials which is exercised independently of the political arm of the executive; a more recent creation, the Conseil Constitutionnel, may review the constitutionality of new laws.[20]

The constitutions of member states of the Commonwealth have been influenced by the separation of powers in a variety of ways. Under the Australian constitution, for example, delegation of legislative powers to executive agencies has been accepted more readily than the delegation to them of judicial powers.[21] The former constitution of Sri Lanka was held to be based upon an implied separation of powers; legislation to provide special machinery for convicting and punishing the leaders of an unsuccessful coup was held to infringe the fundamental principle that judicial power was vested only in the judicature.[22] In countries with a written constitution based on an express or implied separation of powers, the courts may have to decide whether a particular statutory power should be classified as legislative, executive or judicial.[23] British courts do not have this task but have sometimes classified powers for such purposes as applying the law of contempt of court and the rules of natural justice.[24]

Meaning of separation of powers

As the contrast between the United States and France shows, the doctrine of separation of powers has a variety of meanings. The concept of 'separation' may mean at least three different things:

(a) that the same persons should not form part of more than one of the three organs of government, for example, that ministers should not sit in Parliament;

(b) that one organ of government should not control or interfere with the work of another, for example, that the executive should not interfere in judicial decisions;

(c) that one organ of government should not exercise the functions of another, for example, that ministers should not have legislative powers.

In considering these aspects of separation, it needs to be remembered that complete separation of powers is possible neither in theory nor in practice.

Legislature and executive

Writing in 1867, Bagehot described the 'efficient secret' of the constitution as 'the close union, the nearly complete fusion, of the legislative and executive powers'.[25] Bagehot's critics have rejected the concept of fusion, arguing that the close relationship between executive and legislature does not negate the constitutional distinction between the two. As Amery wrote:

---

[20]   See Brown and Bell, *French Administrative Law*, and Bell, *French Constitutional Law*.
[21]   Howard, *Australian Federal Constitutional Law*, ch 4 B.
[22]   *Liyanage v R* [1967] 1 AC 259.
[23]   *Hinds v R* [1977] AC 195 (appeal from Jamaica).
[24]   Chs 18 B and 26.
[25]   Bagehot, *The English Constitution*, p 65.

Government and Parliament, however closely intertwined and harmonized, are still separate and independent entities, fulfilling the two distinct functions of leadership, direction and command on the one hand, and of critical discussion and examination on the other. They start from separate historical origins, and each is perpetuated in accordance with its own methods and has its own continuity.[26]

The three meanings of separation mentioned above will be applied to the relationship between executive and legislature.

(*a*) Do the same persons or bodies form part of both the legislature and executive? Leaving aside the formal position of the Sovereign, there is a strong convention that ministers are members of one or other House of Parliament. Their presence in Parliament goes along with their responsibility to Parliament for their acts as ministers. However, there is a statutory limit on the number of ministers who may be members of the Commons.[27] Moreover, except for these ministers, most persons who hold positions within the executive are disqualified from the Commons, namely the civil service, the armed forces, the police and the holders of many public offices. The House of Commons Disqualification Act 1975 and the rules which forbid civil servants and the police from taking part in political activities are evidence of a strict separation of membership which is maintained between executive and legislature. Only ministers exercise a dual role as key figures in both institutions.

(*b*) Does the legislature control the executive or the executive control the legislature? This question goes to the heart of parliamentary government in Britain and no brief answer can be adequate. In one sense, the Commons ultimately controls the executive, since the Commons can oust a government which has lost the ability to command a majority on an issue of confidence. The Commons did this to Mr Callaghan's minority government in March 1979. But so long as the Cabinet retains the confidence of the Commons, it exercises a decisive voice in the work of the House. In 1978 the Select Committee on Procedure concluded that

the balance of advantage between Parliament and Government in the day to day working of the Constitution is now weighted in favour of the Government to a degree which arouses widespread anxiety and is inimical to the proper working of our parliamentary democracy.[28]

The period beginning with the Conservative government of 1970–74 has seen a developing willingness by MPs to use their voting power in the Commons to indicate when necessary their disapproval of particular government measures. This trend was at its height during the periods of minority government in 1974 and in 1976–79.[29] Although a government need not resign or call a general election whenever it is defeated on a policy issue, where a government is elected with a secure majority, its prospects of being defeated are slight.

---

[26] Amery, *Thoughts on the Constitution*, p 28: also Vile, *Constitutionalism and the Separation of Powers*, pp 224–30, and Mount, *The British Constitution Now*, pp 39–47.

[27] Ch 9 B IV.

[28] HC 588–1 (1977–78), p viii.

[29] See works by Norton: *Dissension in the House of Commons, 1945–74*; (same title) *1974–79*; *The Commons in Perspective*; and [1978] PL 360.

Between 1979 and 1990, during Mrs Thatcher's premiership, the continuing majority of the government in Parliament meant that Parliament could be used by government to make those changes in the law which it desired.

The close relationship between executive and legislature is not confined to legislation. It is also a function of the legislature to call the government to account for its administration of public policies. A variety of procedures exist for enabling Parliament to be informed of and to criticise the work of government departments. In the 1990s, these procedures appeared to fall short of achieving fully accountable government.[30]

(*c*) Do the legislature and the executive exercise each other's functions? The most substantial area in which the executive exercises legislative functions is in respect of delegated legislation. In Britain there is no formal limit on the power of Parliament to delegate legislative powers to the government. Provided that the main principles are laid down in an Act of Parliament, it is convenient for ministers and departments to be able to implement the Act by making regulations. But it is essential that parliamentary procedures should exist for scrutinising the use made of delegated power.[31]

Executive and judiciary

There must now be examined the relationship between the judiciary and the other two organs of government. Again the three questions may be asked:

(*a*) Do the same persons form part of the judiciary and the executive? The courts are the Queen's courts, but judicial functions are exercised by the judges. The Judicial Committee of the Privy Council is in form an executive organ, but in fact it is an independent court of law.[32] The Lord Chancellor, who is a member of the Cabinet, is also head of the judiciary and is entitled to preside over the Lords, which is the final court of appeal from the courts of the United Kingdom. In fact, he only occasionally sits to hear appeals today and does not hear appeals in which a government department is a party.

The law officers of the Crown (in particular the Attorney-General in England and the Lord Advocate in Scotland) have duties of enforcing the criminal law which are sometimes described as 'quasi-judicial'; it must be emphasised that the law officers are members of the executive, and are not judges.[33]

(*b*) Does the executive control the judiciary or the judiciary control the executive? Although judges are appointed by the executive, judicial independence of the executive is secured by law, by constitutional custom and by professional and public opinion.[34] Since the Act of Settlement 1700, judges of the superior English courts have held office during good behaviour and not at the pleasure of the executive. One essential function of the judiciary is to protect the citizen against unlawful acts of government agencies and officials. It is a duty of the courts, if proper application is made to them by an aggrieved

---

[30] Ch 7.
[31] Ch 27.
[32] Ch 18 A.
[33] Ch 18 C.
[34] Ch 18 A.

citizen, to check public authorities from exceeding their powers and to direct the performance of duties owed to private citizens.[35] In applying judicial review in administrative law, the judges must have regard to 'the peculiarly British conception of the separation of powers'.[36] Within the EC, it is the duty of the Court of Justice and the Court of First Instance to ensure that the acts of Community organs comply with the treaties on which the Community system is based.

(*c*) Do the executive and judiciary exercise each other's functions? The value of an independent judiciary would be reduced if essential judicial functions, for example the conduct of civil and criminal trials, were removed from the courts and entrusted to administrative authorities. But many disputes which arise out of public services today are not decided by litigation in the ordinary courts, but are entrusted to tribunals for decision. Tribunals such as industrial and social security tribunals form part of the machinery of justice and carry out their work independently of the departments concerned.[37] There are nonetheless many matters which are entrusted not to tribunals but to government departments and ministers for decision. Procedures like the public inquiry have been established to maintain standards of fairness and openness before a decision is made by the department concerned. It is because a decision is required in which full account may be taken of departmental policy, rather than a decision based on a judicial application of legal rules, that these matters remain subject to departmental or ministerial decision.[38]

It is not possible to draw a sharp distinction between decisions which should be entrusted to courts and tribunals on the one hand, and decisions which should be entrusted to administrative authorities on the other. When a new statutory scheme is introduced, a wide choice may be made between the different procedures available for deciding disputes likely to arise under the scheme. The separation of powers affords little direct guidance as to how particular categories of dispute should be settled, except to indicate that decisions which are to be made independently of political influence should be entrusted to courts or tribunals, and that decisions for which ministers are to be responsible to Parliament should be entrusted to government departments. At a local level, magistrates in England and the sheriffs in Scotland still have administrative duties surviving from the days when they were the principal agents of local administration, but this has for so long been a feature of local government that it causes less controversy than would a corresponding confusion of roles at the national level.

In *Gouriet v Union of Post Office Workers*, the House of Lords re-asserted the distinction between executive responsibility for enforcing the criminal law and the judicial function, and denied that the civil courts had any executive authority in criminal law.[39] In *M v Home Office*, the House held that ministers and civil servants were subject to the contempt jurisdiction of the courts, and

---

[35] Chs 29–31.
[36] *R v Home Secretary, ex p Fire Brigades Union* [1995] 2 AC 513, 567 (Lord Mustill).
[37] Ch 28 A.
[38] Ch 28 B.
[39] [1978] AC 435; ch 30.

that the Home Secretary was in contempt when he disobeyed a judge's order to return to London a Zairean teacher who had sought asylum in England.[40] A perceptive summary of the position was given by Nolan LJ:

The proper constitutional relationship of the executive with the courts is that the courts will respect all acts of the executive within its lawful province, and that the executive will respect all decisions of the courts as to what its lawful province is.[41]

Judiciary and legislature

Finally, the relationship between the judiciary and the legislature:

(*a*) Do the same persons exercise legislative and judicial functions? All full-time judicial appointments disqualify for membership of the Commons. In the House of Lords, the Lord Chancellor presides over the House in its legislative capacity; he is also entitled to preside over the Appellate Committee which discharges the judicial work of the House. The Lords of Appeal in Ordinary who sit as judges in the Appellate Committee take part in the legislative business of the House, but they do so as cross-benchers. Their place in the upper house of the legislature is a departure from the separation of powers, but it appears to be of practical benefit to the House of Lords. Lay peers by long-established convention do not take part in the hearing of appeals.[42]

(*b*) Is there any control by the legislature over the judiciary or by the judiciary over the legislature? By statute judges of the superior courts may be removed by the Crown on an address from both Houses, but only once since the Act of Settlement has Parliament exercised the power of removal.[43] The rules of debate in the Commons protect judges from certain forms of criticism. Apart from the lay magistracy in England, inferior judges have statutory protection against arbitrary dismissal by the executive. Under the Tribunals and Inquiries Act 1992, members of tribunals are protected against removal from office by the appointing government department.[44]

While the courts may examine acts of the executive to ensure that they conform with the law, the doctrine of legislative supremacy denies the courts the power to review the validity of legislation. The judges are under a duty to apply and interpret the laws enacted by Parliament.[45] The effect of their decisions may be altered by Parliament both prospectively and also, if necessary, retrospectively. In one sense, therefore, the courts are constitutionally subordinate to Parliament, but the courts are bound only by Acts of Parliament and not by resolutions of each House, which may have no legal force.[46] The European Communities Act 1972 provides an outstanding example of the control which the legislature may exercise over the judiciary: by s 3, the courts are required to follow the case-law of the European Court of Justice in dealing with matters of Community law and to take full account of

---

[40]   [1994] 1 AC 377; see G Marshall [1992] PL 7, M Gould [1993] PL 568.
[41]   *M v Home Office* [1992] QB 270, 314.
[42]   Ch 18 A.
[43]   Ibid.
[44]   Ch 28 A.
[45]   Note 7 above.
[46]   Eg *Bowles v Bank of England* [1913] 1 Ch 57; ch 4 B.

the reception of Community law into the United Kingdom. This duty may require the courts to disapply an Act of Parliament which clashes with rights in Community law.[47]

(*c*) Do the legislature and judiciary exercise each other's functions? The judicial functions of the House of Lords have already been discussed. Each House of Parliament has power to enforce its own privileges and to punish those who offend against them. This power might in some circumstances lead to a direct conflict with the courts.[48]

Because of the doctrine of precedent, the judicial function of declaring and applying the law has a quasi-legislative effect, whether in areas of common law or in statutory interpretation. The ability of the judges to create law by their decisions is narrower than the ability of Parliament to legislate, since Parliament may at will change established rules of law, whether contained in statutes or in decisions of the courts. However, there is much scope for judicial law-making in relation to individual liberties (notwithstanding the Police and Criminal Evidence Act 1984) and the principles of public law. Decisions that change the common law may be welcomed as bringing old law up to date (for example, the reversal of the rule that a married man cannot in law rape his wife)[49] or may be criticised for failing to do so.[50] The rules of precedent themselves are entirely judge-made, except where, as in the European Communities Act 1972, statute has intervened. In 1966 the House of Lords, sitting extra-judicially, announced that it would in future be prepared to depart from a former decision by the House when it appeared right to do so.[51] An important instance of this occurred when in *Conway v Rimmer*[52] the House held that the courts might overrule a minister's claim on grounds of public interest immunity to withhold evidence in civil litigation.

As *Conway v Rimmer* illustrates, judicial decision is important as a source of law on matters where the government is unwilling to ask Parliament to legislate.[53] The executive is understandably slow to propose new measures exposing itself to more effective judicial control. Some judicial decisions directly affect the formal relationship between the courts and Parliament.[54]

Summary

In the absence of a written constitution, there is no formal separation of powers in the United Kingdom. No Act of Parliament may be held unconstitutional on the ground that it seeks to confer powers in breach of the doctrine. The functions of legislature and executive are closely interrelated, and

---

[47] See the *Factortame* litigation, p 76 above, and *R v Employment Secretary, ex p EOC* [1995] 1 AC 1.
[48] Ch 11 A.
[49] *R v R (Rape: marital exemption)* [1992] 1 AC 599.
[50] *R v Lemon* [1979] AC 617 (offence of blasphemy), ch 22 D; *R v Brown* [1994] 1 AC 212 (criminal nature of consensual sado-masochistic acts).
[51] [1966] 3 All ER 77. Between 1898 and 1966, a contrary rule had prevailed: *London Street Tramways Co v LCC* [1898] AC 375.
[52] *Conway v Rimmer* [1968] AC 910; ch 31 C.
[53] See also *R v Home Secretary, ex p Brind* [1991] 1 AC 696, ch 19 B.
[54] Eg *R v Home Secretary, ex p Fire Brigades Union* [1995] 2 AC 513; and *Pepper v Hart* [1993] AC 593.

ministers are members of both. Yet '[it] is a feature of the peculiarly British conception of the separation of powers that Parliament, the executive and the courts each have their distinct and largely exclusive domain'.[55] The formal process of legislation is different from the day-to-day conduct of government, just as the legal effect of an Act of Parliament differs from that of an executive decision.[56] Practical necessity demands a large measure of delegation by Parliament to the executive of power to legislate. The independence of the judiciary is especially necessary given the role of the courts in judicial review of executive decisions. Although many disputes which arise out of public services are decided by tribunals, these tribunals must observe the essentials of fair judicial procedure.

The effect of British membership of the European Union is that the organs of the Community may now exercise legislative, executive and judicial powers in respect of the United Kingdom. While judicial powers are exercised by the European Court, whose independence is guaranteed, legislative authority is vested in the Council, representing the governments of the member states. In general this authority is exercised only after extensive preparatory work by the Commission, and after consultation with the European Parliament.[57] Experience at a national level suggests that the excessive concentration of power in any single organ of government is a greater danger to liberty than departures from a formal separation of powers.

While the classification of the powers of government into legislative, executive and judicial powers involves certain conceptual difficulties, within a system of government based on law it remains important to distinguish in constitutional structure between the primary functions of law-making, law-executing and law-adjudicating. If these distinctions are abandoned, the concept of law itself can scarcely survive.

---

[55] *R v Home Secretary, ex p Fire Brigades Union* [1995] 2 AC at 567 (Lord Mustill). The case concerned the 'separation' of legislative functions between Parliament and the Home Secretary. See E Barendt [1995] PL 357.

[56] It was the government's failure to observe this distinction which gave rise to the *Fire Brigades Union* case (above).

[57] Ch 8 A.

CHAPTER 6

The rule of law

During 1971, the IRA increased the ferocity of its campaign of violence in Northern Ireland, shooting soldiers and police and blowing up buildings. Early in August, the government of Northern Ireland, after consulting with the UK government, decided to exercise the power of internment available to it under the Civil Authorities (Special Powers) Act (Northern Ireland) 1922.[1] This power could be used against persons suspected of having acted or being about to act in a manner prejudicial to the preservation of peace or the maintenance of order. On 9 August, 342 men were arrested. By November 1971, when the total arrested had risen to 980, 299 of those arrested were being interned indefinitely; the remainder were held under temporary detention orders or had already been released.

The security forces saw in internment an opportunity of obtaining fresh intelligence about the IRA. In August 1971, 12 detainees and in October two more were interrogated in depth. The procedures of interrogation included keeping the detainees' heads covered with black hoods; subjecting them to continuous and monotonous noise; depriving them of sleep; depriving them of food and water, except for one slice of bread and one pint of water at six-hourly intervals; making them stand facing a wall with legs apart and hands raised. It was later held by a committee of inquiry that these procedures constituted physical ill-treatment.[2]

In November 1971, after these facts had been established, three Privy Councillors were asked to consider whether the procedures 'currently author-ised' for interrogating persons suspected of terrorism needed to be changed. They produced two reports.[3] Two members, a former Lord Chief Justice and a former Conservative Cabinet minister, recommended that the procedures could continue to be used subject to certain safeguards, including the express authority of a UK minister for their use, the presence of a doctor with psychiatric training at the interrogation centre, and a complaints procedure. This report did not express any view on the legality of the interrogation procedures, but stated that valuable information about the IRA had been discovered through the interrogation.

---

[1] See now Northern Ireland (Emergency Provisions) Act 1996, part IV and Sched 3; and ch 25 E. On the internments in 1971–76, see R J Spjut (1986) 49 MLR 712.
[2] Cmnd 4823, 1971 (Compton Report).
[3] Cmnd 4901, 1972 (Parker Report).

The minority report, by Lord Gardiner, a former Labour Lord Chancellor, held that the interrogation procedures had never been authorised:

If any document or minister had purported to authorise them, it would have been invalid because the procedures were and are illegal by the domestic law and may also have been illegal by international law.

Should legislation be introduced enabling a minister in time of emergency to fix in secret the limits of permissible ill-treatment to be used in interrogating suspects? Lord Gardiner viewed with abhorrence any proposal that a minister should be empowered to make secret laws. Nor could he agree that a minister should fix secret limits without the authority of Parliament, 'that is to say illegally', and then if found out ask Parliament for an Act of Indemnity: that, he said, would be a flagrant breach of the whole basis of the rule of law and of the principles of democratic government.

The government accepted Lord Gardiner's report and abandoned the interrogation procedures. When those who had been interrogated sued the government for damages for their unlawful treatment, liability was not contested and substantial awards of damages were made. The European Commission on Human Rights held that the interrogation procedures amounted to inhuman and degrading treatment and also torture, contrary to art 3 of the European Convention on Human Rights. When the Irish government referred the case to the European Court of Human Rights, the court held that the procedures were inhuman and degrading treatment but did not amount to torture.[4]

No clearer illustration could be given of the need to adhere to the rule of law if citizens are to be protected against arbitrary and harsh acts of government. However lawless may have been the acts of the IRA, and however seriously those acts infringed life and liberty, government must not retaliate with measures which are not only unlawful but are also of such a nature that it would be impossible on moral and political grounds to make them lawful. Controversial as the power of internment is, it was authorised by the legislature and its use was a matter of public knowledge and admitted political responsibility. But in law the power to intern does not include power to interrogate or to administer physical ill-treatment or torture.[5]

By similar reasoning, while the use of reasonable force is permitted in situations of self-defence or in the prevention of crime or the arrest of offenders, and in some circumstances the use of firearms may be justified,[6] the adoption of a 'shoot to kill' policy by the police or armed forces would be seriously objectionable. This was alleged to have occurred in 1988 when three IRA members were shot dead by British forces in Gibraltar while organising a terrorist attack. The European Court of Human Rights held that force resulting in the taking of life could be used only in 'absolute necessity' for purposes stated in the European Convention on Human Rights (art 2). Claims that the three deaths were premeditated were not upheld; but the Court held (by 10–9) that, on what was known of the arrest operation, the

---

[4]   *Ireland v UK* (1978) 2 EHRR 25; and see ch 19 B.
[5]   For the report of the Bennett committee of inquiry into police interrogation procedures in Northern Ireland in 1975–78, see Cmnd 7497, 1979.
[6]   See ch 25 A, B.

killings were not justified by 'absolute necessity'.[7] The British government was angered by this decision, but reluctantly complied with the Court's order to reimburse the dead terrorists' families for their legal costs.

These instances illustrate the complexity of the values associated with the 'rule of law', and the scope for disagreement about what they may require in concrete situations.

A.   Historical development

For many centuries it has been recognised that the possession by the state of coercive powers that may be used to oppress individuals presents a fundamental problem both for legal and political theory.[8] Since the days of the Greek philosophers there has been recourse to the notion of law as a primary means of subjecting governmental power to control. Aristotle argued that government by laws was superior to government by men.[9]

The legal basis of the state was developed further by Roman lawyers. In the middle ages, the theory was held that there was a universal law which ruled the world. Gierke wrote, 'Medieval doctrine, while it was truly medieval, never surrendered the thought that law is by its origin of equal rank with the state and does not depend on the state for its existence'.[10] Bracton, writing in the 13th century, maintained that rulers were subject to law: 'The King shall not be subject to men, but to God and the law: since law makes the King'.[11] Justice according to law was due both to ruler and subject. Magna Carta and its later confirmations expressed this principle in seeking to remedy the grievances of certain classes in the community. Renaissance and reformation in the 16th century weakened the idea of a universal natural law. Emphasis shifted to the national legal system as an aspect of the sovereignty of the state.[12] In Britain, the 17th-century contest between Crown and Parliament led to a rejection of the Divine Right of Kings and to an alliance between common lawyers and Parliament. The abolition in 1640 of the Court of Star Chamber ensured that the common law should apply to public as well as private acts, except as the common law was modified by Parliament.

The Bill of Rights in 1689 finally affirmed that the monarchy was subject to the law. Not only was the Crown thereby forced to govern through Parliament, but also the right of individuals to be free of unlawful interference in their private affairs was established.

In *Entick v Carrington*, two King's Messengers were sued for having unlawfully broken and entered the plaintiff's house and seized his papers: the defendants relied on a warrant issued by the Secretary of State ordering them to search for Entick and bring

---

7   *McCann v United Kingdom* (1995) 21 EHRR 97. And see Windlesham and Rampton, *Report on 'Death in the Rock'.*

8   See d'Entrèves, *The Notion of the State.* Also Heuston, *Essays in Constitutional Law,* ch 2.

9   d'Entrèves, p 71.

10   Quoted in d'Entrèves, p 83.

11   d'Entrèves, p 86; Maitland, *Constitutional History,* pp 100–4; McIlwain, *Constitutionalism Ancient and Modern,* ch 4.

12   For the rule of law in 16th-century England, see Elton, *Studies in Tudor and Stuart Politics and Government,* vol 1, p 260.

him with his books and papers before the Secretary of State for examination. The Secretary of State claimed that the power to issue such warrants was essential to government, 'the only means of quieting clamours and sedition'. The court held that, in the absence of a statute or a judicial precedent upholding the legality of such a warrant, the practice was illegal. Lord Camden said: 'what would the Parliament say if the judges should take upon themselves to mould an unlawful power into a convenient authority, by new restrictions? That would be, not judgement, but legislation ... And with respect to the argument of State necessity, or a distinction that has been aimed at between State offences and others, the common law does not understand that kind of reasoning, nor do our books take notice of any such distinction.'[13]

Such decisions stressed the value of personal liberty, and the necessity of protecting private property against official interference. At the same time, the remedy of habeas corpus was being developed. Formal adherence to the law was one of the public values of 18th-century Britain, though not all the people gained equally from it.[14] Economic and social developments since 1765 have qualified the forthright declaration of Lord Camden that in the absence of precedent no common law powers of search and seizure will be recognised,[15] but *Entick v Carrington* still exercises influence on judicial attitudes to the claims of government.

Dicey's exposition of the rule of law

One reason for this is to be found in the work of A V Dicey, whose lectures at Oxford were first published in 1885 under the title, *Introduction to the Study of the Law of the Constitution*.[16] Dicey's aim was to introduce students to 'two or three guiding principles' of the constitution, foremost among these being the rule of law. The spirit of *Entick v Carrington* seems to run through Dicey's arguments, but he expressed the general doctrine of the rule of law in the form of several detailed statements describing the English constitution, some of them derived from authors who immediately preceded him.[17] Dicey gave to the rule of law three meanings:

It means, in the first place, the absolute supremacy or predominance of regular law as opposed to the influence of arbitrary power, and excludes the existence of arbitrariness, of prerogative, or even of wide discretionary authority on the part of the government ...; a man may with us be punished for a breach of law, but he can be punished for nothing else.

Thus none could be made to suffer penalties except for a distinct breach of law established before the ordinary courts. In this sense Dicey contrasted the rule of law with systems of government based on the exercise by those in authority of wide or arbitrary powers of constraint, such as a power of detention without trial.

Secondly, the rule of law meant:

---

13   (1765) 19 St Tr 1030, 1067, 1073.
14   Thompson, *Whigs and Hunters: the Origin of the Black Act*, pp 258–69.
15   Ch 21 E. And see *Malone v Metropolitan Police Commissioner* [1979] Ch 344.
16   Dicey's text is reprinted in the 10th edn with introduction by E C S Wade. See also Cosgrove, *The Rule of Law: Albert Venn Dicey, Victorian Jurist*, and the symposium of articles at [1985] PL 587.
17   H W Arndt (1957) 31 ALJ 117.

equality before the law, or the equal subjection of all classes to the ordinary law of the land administered by the ordinary law courts.

This implied that no one was above the law; that officials like private citizens were under a duty to obey the same law; and that there were no administrative courts to decide claims by the citizens against the state or its officials.

Thirdly, the rule of law meant:

> that with us the law of the constitution, the rules which in foreign countries naturally form part of a constitutional code, are not the source but the consequence of the rights of individuals, as defined and enforced by the courts; that, in short, the principles of private law have with us been by the action of the courts and Parliament so extended as to determine the position of the Crown and of its servants; thus the constitution is the result of the ordinary law of the land.[18]

Therefore the rights of the individual were secured not by guarantees set down in a formal document but by the ordinary remedies of private law available against those who unlawfully interfered with his or her liberty, whether they were private citizens or officials.

Assessment of Dicey's views[19]

These three meanings of the rule of law raise considerable problems. In the first, for example, what is meant by 'regular law'? Does this include, for example, social security law, compulsory purchase of land or anti-discrimination law? Does 'arbitrary power' refer to powers of government which are so wide that they could be used for a wide variety of different purposes; powers which are capable of abuse if not subjected to proper control; or powers which directly infringe individual liberty (for example, power to detain a citizen without trial)?[20] If 'arbitrary power' and 'wide discretionary authority' alike are unacceptable, how are the limits of acceptable discretionary authority to be settled? If it is contrary to the rule of law that discretionary authority should be given to government departments or public officers, then the rule of law applies to no modern constitution. Today the state regulates national life in multifarious ways. Discretionary authority in most spheres of government is inevitable. While there are still certain powers which we are unwilling to trust to the executive (for example, the power to detain individuals without trial) except when national emergencies dictate otherwise,[21] attention has to be concentrated not so much on attacking the existence of discretionary powers as on establishing a system of legal and political safeguards by which the exercise of such powers may be controlled.[22] Doubtless Dicey would have regarded as arbitrary many of the powers of government on which social welfare and economic organisation now depend.

Dicey's second meaning stresses the equal subjection of all persons to the

---

[18]   Dicey, pp 202–3.
[19]   See Dicey, introduction by E C S Wade; Jennings, *The Law and the Constitution*, ch 2 and app 2; F H Lawson (1959) 7 Political Studies, 109, 207; H W Arthurs (1979) Osgoode Hall LJ 1; Craig, *Public Law and Democracy*, ch 2; Loughlin, *Public Law and Political Theory*, ch 7. For endorsement of Dicey's approach, see Allan, *Law, Liberty and Justice*, ch 2.
[20]   Cf Report of the Franks Committee, Cmnd 218, 1957, para 29.
[21]   Chs 21 C and 25.
[22]   Davis, *Discretionary Justice*.

ordinary law. Now the Fourteenth Amendment to the United States Constitution provides, inter alia, that no state shall 'deny to any person within its jurisdiction the equal protection of the laws', a provision which has been a fertile source of constitutional challenges to discriminatory state legislation.[23] Similar provisions are found in the constitutions of India, Germany and Canada.[24] In fact the legislature must frequently distinguish between categories of person by reference to economic or social considerations or legal status. Landlords and tenants, employers and employees, company directors and shareholders, British citizens and aliens, judges and tax officials – these and innumerable other categories are subject to differing legal rules. What a constitutional guarantee of equality before the law may achieve is to enable legislation to be invalidated which distinguishes between citizens on grounds which are considered irrelevant, unacceptable or offensive (for example, improper discrimination on grounds of sex, race, origin or colour).[25] Dicey had in mind no such jurisdiction. The specific meaning he attached to equality before the law was that all citizens (including officials) were subject to the jurisdiction of the ordinary courts should they transgress the law which applied to them, and that there should be no separate administrative courts, as in France, to hear complaints of unlawful conduct by officials.[26] He believed that *droit administratif* in France favoured the officials and that English law through decisions such as *Entick v Carrington* gave better protection to the citizens. Dicey's influence on administrative law in Britain was felt for many years, and Britain does not have administrative courts on the French model. But it is now widely accepted that individuals may be as well protected against unlawful official decisions by separate administrative courts as by the ordinary courts.

Dicey's third meaning of the rule of law, summarised in his conclusion that the constitution is the result of the ordinary law of the land, expressed a strong preference for the principles of common law declared by the judges as the basis of the citizen's rights and liberties. Dicey had in mind the fundamental political freedoms – freedom of the person, freedom of speech, freedom of association. The citizen whose freedoms were infringed could seek a remedy in the courts and did not need to rely on constitutional guarantees. Dicey believed that the common law gave better protection to the citizen than a written constitution. The Habeas Corpus Acts, which made effective a remedy by which persons unlawfully detained might obtain their freedom were, said Dicey, 'for practical purposes worth a hundred constitutional articles guaranteeing individual liberty'.[27] Today it is difficult to share Dicey's faith in the common law as the primary legal means of protecting the citizen's liberties against the state. In the first place, the common law is subject to modification by a supreme Parliament: fundamental liberties may be removed by statute. Secondly, the common law does not assure the citizen's economic or social well-being. Thirdly, while it remains essential that

---

[23]   Marshall, *Constitutional Theory*, ch 7; and Polyviou, *The Equal Protection of the Laws*.
[24]   India, 1949 Constitution, art 14; Federal Republic of Germany, Basic Law, art 3; Canadian Charter of Rights and Freedoms, s 15.
[25]   Ch 19 A; and Feldman, *Civil Liberties and Human Rights*, pp 858–73.
[26]   See Brown and Bell, *French Administrative Law*, and ch 26.
[27]   Dicey, p 199. And see ch 30.

legal remedies are effective, the experience of many countries is that there can be value in imposing legal limits upon the legislature's power to infringe human rights; and the European Convention on Human Rights has shown the value of supra-national remedies.[28]

Dicey's view of the rule of law, like his view of parliamentary sovereignty, is based on assumptions about the British system of government which in many respects no longer apply. Although he did not adequately resolve the potential conflict between the two notions of the rule of law and the supremacy of Parliament,[29] a recent formulation of the relationship implies equilibrium rather than conflict:

> The maintenance of the rule of law is in every way as important in a free society as the democratic franchise. In our society the rule of law rests upon twin foundations: the sovereignty of the Queen in Parliament in making the law and the sovereignty of the Queen's courts in interpreting and applying the law.[30]

While Dicey's views have greatly influenced attitudes to constitutional law in Britain, what follows in this chapter seeks to explore the main features of the rule of law in the British system of government today, a discussion which is not cast in the Diceyan mould.

B.   Rule of law and its implications today

Emphasis will be placed upon three related but separate ideas. First, the rule of law expresses a preference for law and order within a community rather than anarchy, warfare and constant strife. In this sense, the rule of law is a philosophical view of society which is linked with basic democratic notions. Secondly, the rule of law expresses a legal doctrine of fundamental importance, namely that government must be conducted according to law, and that in disputed cases what the law requires is declared by judicial decision. Thirdly, the rule of law refers to a body of political opinion about what the detailed rules of law should provide in matters both of substance (for example, whether the government should have power to detain citizens without trial) and of procedure (for example, the presumption of innocence in criminal trials, and the independence of the judiciary). While the second sense is founded on decisions of the courts, and expresses existing legal doctrine, the third sense is directly relevant to discussion in Parliament and elsewhere, when controversial events occur (like the Gibraltar shooting) or proposals for changing the law are examined. Supporters of the rule of law in this last sense are likely to favour protection for human rights by such means as a judicially enforceable Bill of Rights, so that legislation affecting fundamental rights may be subject to review in the courts.

---

[28]   Ch 19 B.
[29]   Dicey, ch 13. For an analysis that seeks to resolve the conflict, see T S R Allan [1985] CLJ 111; also his *Law, Liberty and Justice*, chs 3 and 11.
[30]   *X v Morgan-Grampian Ltd* [1991] AC 1, 48 (Lord Bridge).

Three aspects of the rule of law

1 Law and order better than anarchy.   In the limited sense of law and order, the rule of law may appear to be preserved by a dictatorship or a military occupation as well as by a democratic form of government. Under a government which is not freely elected, the courts of law may continue to function, settling disputes between private citizens and such disputes between a citizen and government officials as the regime permits to be so decided. Even in this restricted sense, the rule of law expresses preference for human disputes to be settled by peaceful means without recourse to armed force, terrorism or other forms of physical might. But undue stress on law and order as social values readily leads to the restriction or suppression of political liberty. Political groups opposed to a regime dependent on physical force rather than popular consent may readily turn to the adoption of violent means to overthrow it. Experience in Britain and other states has shown that the maintenance of law and order and the existence of political liberty are not mutually exclusive, but interdependent. As the Universal Declaration of Human Rights states, 'It is essential if man is not to be compelled to have recourse, as a last resort, to rebellion against tyranny and oppression, that human rights should be protected by the rule of law.'[31] In a democracy, it must be possible by the exercise of political rights to change a government without threatening the existence of the state. Unless this possibility exists, the state becomes identified with the sheer force of coercive might and the role of law within the state is virtually emptied of moral content: 'the State cannot be conceived in terms of force alone'.[32]

2 Government according to law.   It is a basic rule of constitutional law that the organs of government must operate through law. If the police need to detain a citizen, or if taxes are to be levied, the officials concerned must be able to show legal authority for their actions. In Britain, they may be challenged to do so before a court of law, as in *Entick v Carrington*. Acts of public authorities which are beyond their legal power may be declared ultra vires and invalid by the courts.[33] It is because of this fundamental principle of legality that legislation must be passed through Parliament if (for instance) the police are to have additional powers to combat terrorism. The rule of law serves as a buttress for the democratic principle, since new powers of government affecting individual liberty may be conferred only by Parliament.[34]

Moreover, a person directly affected by government action must be able, if necessary, to challenge the legality of that action before a court, and not merely to register a complaint with the department concerned. In the British tradition, it is from the ordinary courts that a remedy for unlawful acts of government is to be obtained. In other countries, the ordinary courts often do not exercise jurisdiction in administrative matters: thus in Germany this jurisdiction is assigned to the Federal Administrative Court, and in France to

---

[31]   Preamble, 3rd para.
[32]   d'Entrèves, *The Notion of the State*, p 69.
[33]   Ch 29.
[34]   For a broad analysis of the contribution that law can make to government, see J Jowell, in Jowell and Oliver (eds), *The Changing Constitution*, ch 3.

the Conseil d'Etat. Today both approaches are recognised to be ways of maintaining the rule of law. Nor is the existence of specialised tribunals (for example, for social security claims or immigration appeals) contrary to the rule of law, provided that the tribunals are subject to supervision by the superior courts, and are independent of the departments concerned.[35]

Public authorities and officials must also be subject to effective sanctions if they depart from the law. Often the sanction is that their acts are declared invalid by the courts. But another sanction is the duty to compensate citizens whose rights have been infringed. Today it is unlikely that the British Prime Minister would be sued for damages, not because he is immune from such action but because his political decisions do not normally have direct legal effect; but the Prime Minister of Quebec was in 1959 held liable in damages for having maliciously and without legal authority directed a liquor licensing authority to cancel the licence of a restaurant proprietor who had repeatedly provided bail for Jehovah's Witnesses accused of police offences.[36] In Britain, government departments came under a general liability to be sued for their wrongful acts only under the Crown Proceedings Act 1947.[37] That Act preserved the personal immunity of the Sovereign, an immunity which in other legal systems is enjoyed by the head of state. Thus in the USA, the President while in office is immune from liability for his unlawful acts. As the Watergate affair showed in 1974, when President Nixon resigned rather than face impeachment proceedings before a hostile Congress, the importance of impeachment is that it provides a constitutional means of removing a President, thus enabling him to be sued or prosecuted for unlawful acts which he may have committed while in office.[38] Even a President while in office is not at liberty to disregard the law.

In the course of criminal investigations into the Watergate affair, the special prosecutor appointed by the Attorney-General requested President Nixon to produce tape-recordings of discussions which the President had had with his advisers. When presidential privilege was claimed for the tapes, the US Supreme Court held that this claim had to be considered 'in the light of our historic commitment to the rule of law'. The court rejected the claim and ordered the tapes to be produced, since 'the generalised assertion of privilege must yield to the demonstrated, specific need for evidence in a pending criminal trial'.[39]

In 1993, the House of Lords held that the Home Secretary was liable for contempt of court, in that he decided not to require the return to the United Kingdom of a Zairean teacher who was claiming refugee status, despite an order by a High Court judge that this should be done.[40] This was the first time that the English courts had to decide whether a minister of the Crown could be guilty of contempt of court. Lord Templeman said: 'For the purpose of enforcing the law against all persons and institutions, ..., the courts are armed with coercive powers exercisable in proceedings for contempt of

---

[35] Ch 28 A.
[36] *Roncarelli v Duplessis* (1959) 16 DLR (2d) 689.
[37] Ch 31.
[38] Berger, *Impeachment.*
[39] *US v Nixon* 41 L Ed 2d 1039 (1974); for the power of the executive in Britain to withhold evidence, see ch 31 C.
[40] *M v Home Office* [1994] 1 AC 377.

court.' The Home Secretary's argument that the courts had no such powers against ministers 'would, if upheld, establish the proposition that the executive obey the law as a matter of grace and not as a matter of necessity, a proposition which would reverse the result of the Civil War.'[41]

The doctrine of government according to law stresses the importance of legal authority and form for the acts of government. In a system in which Parliament is supreme, and in which the Cabinet is supported by a majority in the Commons, executive decisions may readily be clothed with legality. In the absence of constitutional guarantees for individual rights, the need for legal authority does not protect these rights from legislative invasion. A political detainee's right to come to a court for a ruling on the legality of his or her detention is of little value if the government has taken care to obtain the requisite power to detain from a compliant legislature.

In the United Kingdom, Parliament may authorise the executive to exercise powers which drastically affect the liberty of the individual: for example, by authorising the detention of persons suspected of involvement in terrorist offences, on an order from the Secretary of State, for up to seven days without authority from a court.[42] If all that the rule of law means is that official acts must be clothed with legality, this gives no guarantee that more fundamental values are not infringed. It is this lack of a guarantee against abuse of Parliament's legislative authority that in part explains proposals for incorporating the European Convention on Human Rights in the law of the United Kingdom.

3 The rule of law as a broad political doctrine. If the law is not to be merely a means of achieving whatever ends a particular government may favour, the rule of law must go beyond the principle of legality. The experience and values of the legal system are relevant not only to the question, 'What legal authority *does* the government have for its acts?' but also to the question, 'What legal powers *ought* the government to have?' If, for example, the government is proposing to introduce criminal sanctions for conduct contrary to its economic or social policies, a lawyer will want the new legislation to respect accepted principles of fair criminal procedure. If a Bill seeks to depart from these principles (for example, by abolishing the presumption of innocence) arguments invoking the rule of law will be used in the debates on the Bill.

For a number of reasons the opinions of lawyers may not be unanimous in invoking the rule of law in a legislative context. What *are* the essential values which have emerged from centuries of legal experience? Are they absolute values, or may there be circumstances in which political necessity justifies the legislature in departing from them? For example, the rule of law requires that the power of interpreting statutes is vested in the courts, but is this power of the courts reduced if the courts look at the report of a government committee or a minister's speech in Parliament as an aid to interpreting a statute?[43]

---

41 [1994] 1 AC 377 at 395.
42 Ch 25 E. See the Prevention of Terrorism (Temporary Provisions) Act 1989 and *Brogan v UK* (1988) 11 EHRR 117.
43 *Black-Clawson International Ltd v Papierwerke AG* [1975] AC 591. And see *Pepper v Hart* [1993] AC 593 (Hansard permitted as aid in resolving statutory ambiguity).

Again, in the circumstances of Northern Ireland, physical liberty and trial by jury are two victims of the assault upon law and order.[44] Moreover, the legal system exists within a social and political context; a legislator's perception of legal values is likely to be affected by his or her outlook on other social and political questions.[45] Conservative, Labour and Liberal Democratic lawyers in Parliament often disagree as to the extent to which new legislation should protect or restrict the rights and interests of different social and economic groups; and like other politicians, lawyers may be influenced by electoral considerations.

Is the rule of law then in this broad sense too subjective and uncertain to be of any value? Would discussion of new legislation be clearer if the rule of law were excluded from the vocabulary of debate? One attempt to ascertain the values inherent in the system of law was made by Professor Lon Fuller, who argued that the enactment of secret laws would be contrary to the essential nature of a legal system, as would heavy reliance on retrospective legislation, or legislation imposing criminal sanctions for conduct which is not defined but may be deemed undesirable by an official.[46] However, these views have not found universal favour with all legal philosophers.[47] Amongst the judges there is an important vein of belief in certain values that should be upheld in a legal system. The nature of these values can be discovered not only from judicial decisions,[48] but also from the Law Lords' speeches in legislative debates, and the growing body of articles and lectures by judges.[49]

International movement to promote the rule of law

Since 1945, the rule of law, in parallel with the human rights movement, has been a matter of much international discussion. The Universal Declaration of Human Rights, adopted in 1948, was followed by the European Convention on Human Rights, signed at Rome in 1950. The Convention recognised that European countries have 'a common heritage of political traditions, ideals, freedom and the rule of law' and sought to create machinery for protecting certain human rights.[50] In *Golder's* case, which concerned the right of a convicted prisoner in the United Kingdom to have access to legal advice regarding a possible civil action against the prison authorities, the European Court of Human Rights referred to the rule of law and said: 'in civil matters one can scarcely conceive of the rule of law without there being a possibility of having access to the courts'.[51]

Further developments have been stimulated by the International Commis-

---

[44]   See eg Cmnd 5847, 1975 (Gardiner Report).

[45]   Cf Jennings, *The Law and the Constitution*, p 317: 'the "principles" of constitutional lawyers are always a dangerous foundation for the formation of policy'. But was not Lord Gardiner relying on constitutional principle in rejecting interrogation in depth (p 100 above)?

[46]   Fuller, *The Morality of Law*.

[47]   See H L A Hart (1958) 71 Harv LR 593; cf J Raz (1977) 93 LQR 195.

[48]   See eg D Feldman (1990) 106 LQR 246; and the judgments quoted at pp 102 and 105 above.

[49]   Examples include Lord Bingham (1993) 109 LQR 390; J Laws [1995] PL 72 and [1996] PL 622; R Scott [1996] PL 410 and 427; S Sedley (1994) 110 LQR 260; and Lord Woolf [1995] PL 57.

[50]   Ch 19 B.

[51]   *Golder v UK* (1975) 1 EHRR 524.

sion of Jurists, an international organisation of lawyers.[52] The aim has been to formulate the rule of law as a basic idea which can inspire lawyers of many backgrounds to work to improve their own national systems. At New Delhi in 1959, lawyers from 53 countries formally declared that the rule of law is a dynamic concept which should be employed to safeguard and advance the political and civil rights of the individual in a free society. The congress for the first time associated the concept with the establishment of social, economic, educational and cultural conditions under which the individual may realise his legitimate aspirations. On the one hand, the congress examined traditional safeguards required for the maintenance of the law: for example, the need for adequate controls against abuse of power by the executive, the essentials of fair criminal procedure and the maintenance of an independent judiciary. On the other, the congress stressed the need for an effective government capable of maintaining law and order and of ensuring adequate social and economic conditions.

Within the Commonwealth, the heads of government at their meetings have often expressed their support for the rule of law. In 1991 at Harare, they linked the rule of law, the independence of the judiciary and the protection of human rights, with 'democratic processes and institutions which reflect national circumstances' and 'just and honest government' as being among the fundamental political values of the Commonwealth association.[53]

Social and economic aspects of the rule of law

The rule of law movement has thus been broadened to include social and economic goals which lie far beyond the typical values associated with the legal profession and the practice of law. Such a broadening would be opposed by those critics of the mixed economy and the welfare state who wish to see a return to the restricted functions of government in the 19th century. Thus Hayek argued that economic planning in the sense of control of private enterprise by the state is inconsistent with the rule of law. In his view, government in all its actions must be 'bound by rules, fixed and announced beforehand – rules which make it possible to foresee with fair certainty how the authority will use its coercive powers in given circumstances, and to plan one's individual affairs on the basis of this knowledge'.[54] Now certainty and predictability are values often associated with law; in a different context, Lord Diplock said in 1975, 'The acceptance of the rule of law as a constitutional principle requires that a citizen, before committing himself to any course of action, should be able to know what are the legal consequences that will flow from it'.[55] But however desirable it may be that discretionary powers of government should be controlled by rules,[56] the certainty demanded by

---

52 N S Marsh, in Guest (ed), *Oxford Essays in Jurisprudence*, ch 9. International Commission of Jurists, *The Rule of Law and Human Rights – Principles and Definitions*, 1966. For the Declaration of Delhi see (1959) 2 Journal of the ICJ 7–43.

53 The Harare Communiqué, 1991; ch 15 C.

54 Hayek, *The Road to Serfdom*, p 54. Hayek, *The Constitution of Liberty*, makes a profound analysis of rule of law concepts; for a critique, see Loughlin, *Public Law and Political Theory*, pp 84–101.

55 *Black-Clawson International Ltd v Papierwerke AG* [1975] AC 591, 638.

56 Davis, *Discretionary Justice*, ch 3. And see page 103 above.

Hayek is not attainable so long as the state has responsibilities for economic and social affairs.

The welfare rights movement has sought since the 1960s to apply the legal concept of 'rights', traditionally associated with property and contracts, to the benefits received under social security and other welfare schemes. Why should less legal protection be given to these benefits, on which many citizens depend for subsistence, than to traditional rights of property?[57] During the 1980s and 1990s, in a different political climate, emphasis on the rights of the users of public services, as consumers and customers, was made in such areas as education, housing, transport and other services. In many areas of state power, the use of tribunals serves to subject government to the rule of law.[58] Indeed, the creation of immigration adjudicators and an immigration appeal tribunal to hear appeals from the decisions of immigration officials, was based on the principle that 'it is fundamentally wrong and inconsistent with the rule of law that power to take decisions affecting a man's whole future should be vested in officers of the Executive, from whose findings there is no appeal'.[59] Since the decisions of tribunals can be challenged by appeal or review in the higher courts, the judges determine the standards of due process which tribunals must maintain.

Conclusion

It is not possible to formulate a simple and clear-cut statement of the rule of law as a broad political doctrine. As society develops, and as the tasks of government change, lawyers, politicians and administrators must be prepared to adapt the received values of law to meet changing needs.[60] A government's changing programme must not lead it to suppose that new areas of public action which open up (such as the function of regulating the public utilities)[61] can be isolated from the scope of law and subjected only to administrative or political controls. Through membership of the European Union, the United Kingdom is part of a supra-national system which is intended (inter alia) to exercise control in legal form over important areas of economic activity. While the democratic base of the European Union needs to be strengthened, its organs are capable of enlarging the effective scope of the rule of law, for example by granting to the individual rights of legal protection against the governments of member states.[62]

There continues to be a wide variety of challenges to the regular legal system presented by phenomena such as hijacking, urban terrorism, direct action by militant groups, campaigns of civil disobedience, sit-ins, strikes, protests and demonstrations. All these are sometimes lumped together and described as a growing threat to the rule of law (by which may simply be

---

57   H W Jones (1958) 58 Col LR 143; C A Reich (1964) 73 Yale LJ 733; cf R M Titmuss (1971) 42 Political Quarterly 113.
58   Ch 28 A.
59   Report of Committee on Immigration Appeals, Cmnd 3387, 1967, p 23; ch 20 B.
60   Cf Scarman, *English Law – The New Dimension.*
61   See ch 14.
62   See Case 11/70, *Internationale Handelsgesellschaft* [1970] ECR 1125; Case 5/88, *Wachauf v Germany* [1989] ECR 2609. For a critical survey, see J Coppel and A O'Neill (1992) 12 LS 227. See further, ch 19 B.

meant the authority and stability of established institutions). There are many important distinctions to be drawn between these different forms of political or criminal action.[63] But, if we leave aside acts of criminal violence at one end of the scale and law-abiding political expression at the other end, do acts of non-violent civil disobedience endanger the legal system? In particular, does the rule of law require complete obedience to the law from all citizens and organisations?[64] It would be casting an impossible burden upon the courts to require them to base decisions as to whether certain conduct constitutes a criminal offence on the political motives of the accused.[65] It may be argued both that, in a democratic society, there are important reasons for obeying the law which do not exist in other forms of government, and also that there are some forms of principled disobedience which do not run counter to the democratic reasons for obedience, particularly those which are designed to improve the working of democratic procedures for political decisions.[66] Only rarely does the legislature recognise that citizens may feel compelled by their conscience to refuse to carry out a law, as in the provision made for conscientious objection to compulsory military service under the National Service Acts. What is the citizen to do if he or she believes that a certain law is unjust or immoral? H L A Hart wrote:

What surely is most needed in order to make men clear sighted in confronting the official abuse of power is that they should preserve the sense that the certification of something as legally valid is not conclusive of the question of obedience, and that, however great the aura of majesty or authority which the official system may have, its demands must in the end be submitted to a moral scrutiny.[67]

While this is so for the individual, there is a danger that decisions to disobey particular laws taken by organised groups (whether trade unions, local authorities or business corporations) might cumulatively suggest that there is no general obligation to obey the law, but only the law of which one approves. Our political system is not perfect and there are always many legislative reforms to be made. But the maintenance of life in modern society requires a willingness from most citizens for most of the time to observe the laws, even when individually they may not agree with them. Some writings on the subject tend to suggest that state power is the great antagonist against which the rule of law must for ever be addressed.[68] But it deserves to be remembered that law, like the democratic process, may be used to protect the weaker, underprivileged sections of society against those who can exercise physical, economic or industrial force.

---

63   Passive resistance is contrary to the rule of law: *R v Chief Constable of Devon, ex p Central Electricity Generating Board* [1982] QB 458, 473 (Lawton LJ).
64   Marshall, *Constitutional Theory*, ch 9; Dworkin, *Taking Rights Seriously*, ch 8; Allan, *Law, Liberty, and Justice*, ch 5.
65   Cf *Chandler v DPP* [1964] AC 763, and ch 24.
66   Singer, *Democracy and Disobedience*.
67   Hart, *The Concept of Law*, p 260.
68   H W Jones, cited in note 57.

Chapter 7

Responsible government

Within a democracy, those who govern must be accountable, or responsible, to those whom they govern. The power to govern derives from the votes of the electors, and may be taken away by their votes. Between general elections, one function of the elected representatives is to call the government to account for its acts and policies on a continuing basis. This both requires government to justify its decisions by giving the reasons for them, and enables decisions to be criticised that appear unjustified or mistaken. The process enables electors to make an informed appraisal of the government's record on their next opportunity to vote; until then it influences the formation of public opinion of the government.

In ordinary speech, the words 'responsible' and 'accountable' have several meanings; and the concept of responsible government takes several forms.[1] During the 1990s, possibly because of some serious failures of accountability, attempts were made to clarify the essential meaning of accountable government and to strengthen the procedures which apply it. In 1996, the Scott report on the 'arms for Iraq' affair contained penetrating criticism of numerous incomplete and misleading answers given in Parliament by ministers to questions about the government's policy.[2] Also in 1996, an influential report by the Public Service Committee of the House of Commons, while affirming that ministerial responsibility 'is a central principle of the British Constitution', examined the difficulties inherent in the principle.[3]

This chapter examines the political responsibility of government to Parliament, including both collective and individual responsibility. Another form of responsibility is the legal responsibility of ministers and officials for their acts. Whereas legal responsibility may be enforced in the courts, political responsibility is enforced through Parliament. A government's relationship with Parliament is too complex to be summarised in a code of precise rules, but the essential features of responsibility to Parliament give rise to obligations which are (or ought to be) observed in the regular practice of government. The debate on accountability has led to the publication of documents summarising these essential obligations, and recording official practice.[4]

---

[1]   See eg Birch, *Representative and Responsible Government*, pp 17–21.
[2]   HC 115 (1995–96), vol IV, section K.8, pp 1799–1806; and see R Scott [1996] PL 410.
[3]   HC 313–I (1995–96). For the government's response, see HC 67 (1996–97).
[4]   And see ch 2 B.

Early origins of responsible government

So long as government was carried on by the King, the nature of monarchy made it difficult to establish any responsibility for acts of government. In medieval times, the practice developed by which the royal will was signified in documents bearing a royal seal, which would be applied by one of the King's ministers. Maitland detected in this practice 'the foundation for our modern doctrine of ministerial responsibility – that for every exercise of the royal power some minister is answerable'.[5] With the responsibility of ministers came the rule that 'the King can do no wrong'. This meant not that everything done on behalf of the King was lawful, but that the King's advisers and ministers were liable for illegal measures that occurred in the course of government.[6] Today the use of the various seals or forms for recording decisions taken in the name of the Sovereign by ministers is regulated partly by statute and partly by custom.[7] These rules formerly ensured that, since the Sovereign could not be called personally to account, responsibility could be laid on those ministers who had carried out his decision.

For a period, this responsibility was enforced by the English Parliament through impeachment. Officers of state were liable to be impeached by the Commons at the bar of the House of Lords for the treason, high crimes and misdemeanours they were alleged to have committed in office. In the 17th century, impeachment became a political weapon wielded by Parliament for striking at unpopular royal policies.[8] Following the granting of a royal pardon to Danby in 1679 to forestall his impeachment, the Act of Settlement provided that a royal pardon could not be pleaded in bar of an impeachment. The last instance of a purely political impeachment came when the Tory ministers who in 1713 negotiated the Peace of Utrecht were later impeached by a Whig House of Commons. Thereafter only two impeachments occurred, of Warren Hastings between 1788 and 1795 for mis-government in India and of Lord Melville in 1806 for alleged corruption. The power of impeachment is still available to Parliament: but more modern means of achieving ministerial responsibility have rendered it an obsolete weapon.[9]

The legal responsibility of government

The principle that government must be conducted according to law has already been discussed.[10] The Sovereign may not personally be sued or prosecuted in the courts. But servants or officers of the Crown who commit crimes or civil wrongs are, and always have been, subject to the jurisdiction of the courts. This jurisdiction extends to contempt of court.[11] Superior orders

---

5   Maitland, *Constitutional History*, p 203. Cf art 64 of the Belgian Constitution of 1831.

6   Chitty, *Prerogatives of the Crown*, p 5.

7   Anson, vol II, part I, pp 62–72; HLE, vol 8(2), pp 233, 518–19.

8   Maitland, *Constitutional History*, pp 317–18; Taswell-Langmead, *English Constitutional History*, pp 164–5, 353–4, 529–38; Clayton Roberts, *The Growth of Responsible Government in Stuart England*; Berger, *Impeachment*, ch 1.

9   See A W Bradley, in Carnall and Nicholson (eds), *The Impeachment of Warren Hastings*, ch 7. Cf Dicey, *The Law of the Constitution*, p 499.

10   Ch 6.

11   *M v Home Office* [1994] 1 AC 377.

or the interest of the state are no defence to such proceedings.[12] Public authorities other than the Crown are at common law liable for the wrongful acts of their officials or servants.[13] The departments of central government became liable to be sued under the Crown Proceedings Act 1947, and their decisions are subject to control by means of judicial review.[14] It is with political responsibility that this chapter is concerned.

Development of collective responsibility

After 1688 the doctrine of collective responsibility developed in fits and starts as the Cabinet system came into being.[15] For much of the 18th century, the Cabinet was a body of holders of high office whose relationship with one another was ill-defined; the body as a whole was not responsible to Parliament. Although the King rarely attended Cabinet meetings after 1717, it was the King's government in fact as well as in name and the King could act on the advice of individual ministers. Under Walpole, ministries were relatively homogeneous. Other Cabinets in the century were less united. Parliament could force the dismissal of individual ministers who were disapproved, but could not dictate appointments to the King. The King sometimes consulted those who were out of office without the prior approval of his ministers. There was no clear dividing line between matters dealt with by individual ministers and matters dealt with in the Cabinet. As late as 1806, it was debated in the Commons whether ministers must accept collective responsibility for the general affairs of government or whether only those ministers who carried policies into execution were individually responsible.[16]

By the early 19th century, as the scope for personal government by the Sovereign sharply declined, so the tendencies towards the collective responsibility of the Cabinet became more marked. After 1832, it became evident that the Cabinet must retain the support of the majority in the House of Commons if it was to continue in office. Just as it had earlier been recognised that a single minister could not retain office against the will of Parliament, so it became clear that all ministers must stand or fall together in Parliament, if the Cabinet was to function effectively.

By the mid-19th century, ministerial responsibility was the accepted basis of parliamentary government in Britain.[17] As the Victorian foundations of the system were laid, critics of the rule of Cabinet unity were reminded that 'the various departments of the Administration are but parts of a single machine ... and that the various branches of the Government have a close connection and mutual dependence upon each other'.[18]

---

[12]   Smith and Hogan, *Criminal Law*, pp 270–1; Dicey, pp 302–6; *Entick v Carrington*, p 101 above.

[13]   *Mersey Docks and Harbour Board Trustees v Gibbs* (1866) LR 1 HL 93.

[14]   Chs 29–31.

[15]   Mackintosh, *British Cabinet*, ch 2.

[16]   Williams, *The 18th Century Constitution*, pp 123–5.

[17]   For a notable summary, see Grey, *Parliamentary Government*, p 4.

[18]   Grey, p 57.

The meaning of collective responsibility

The doctrine of collective responsibility was stated in absolute terms by Lord Salisbury in 1878:

For all that passes in Cabinet every member of it who does not resign is absolutely and irretrievably responsible and has no right afterwards to say that he agreed in one case to a compromise, while in another he was persuaded by his colleagues ... It is only on the principle that absolute responsibility is undertaken by every member of the Cabinet, who, after a decision is arrived at, remains a member of it, that the joint responsibility of Ministers to Parliament can be upheld and one of the most essential principles of parliamentary responsibility established.[19]

Over a century later, an official statement of the doctrine took this form:

Collective responsibility requires that Ministers should be able to express their views frankly in the expectation that they can argue freely in private while maintaining a united front when decisions have been reached. This in turn requires that the privacy of opinions expressed in Cabinet and Ministerial Committees should be maintained.[20]

Yet it is difficult to control political behaviour in absolute terms. In the 19th century, the degree of political cohesion was variable. Cabinet unity could not always be achieved when ministers held deeply divided opinions. Some subjects were regarded as 'open questions', for example women's suffrage between 1906 and 1914 and more recently capital punishment.[21] But it was a sign of political weakness if many issues were accepted as open questions. Except for open questions, ministers who did not wish to be publicly identified with Cabinet policies were expected to resign.

Today collective responsibility embodies a number of related aspects. Like other constitutional principles, it is neither static nor unchangeable and may give way before more pressing political forces.

1 The Prime Minister and other ministers are collectively responsible to Parliament, and to the Commons in particular, for the conduct of national affairs. In practice, so long as the governing party retains its majority in the House, the Prime Minister is unlikely to be forced to resign (although this was Mrs Thatcher's fate in 1990, after over 11 years in office) or seek a dissolution of Parliament. At a general election, the Cabinet is seeking renewed support for its policies.

2 When a Prime Minister dies or resigns office, then even if the same party continues in power, all ministerial offices are at the disposal of the new Prime Minister.

3 Although ministers are individually responsible to Parliament for the conduct of their departments, if members of the Commons seek to censure an individual minister, the government generally will rally to his or her defence: collective responsibility is a means of defending an incompetent or unpopular minister.

---

[19]   *Life of Robert, Marquis of Salisbury*, vol II, pp 219–20.
[20]   *Questions of Procedure for Ministers* (1992), para 18.
[21]   Jennings, *Cabinet Government*, pp 277–9; Hanham, *The 19th Century Constitution*, pp 79, 84–94; Grey, p 116.

4 Ministers while in office share in the collective responsibility of all ministers in the sense that they may not publicly criticise government policy. A Cabinet minister may however ask for dissent from a Cabinet decision to be recorded in the private minutes of Cabinet.[22] He or she is expected nonetheless to support the government by his or her vote in Parliament. Cabinet ministers who were also members of the National Executive of the Labour party were in 1974 told by the Prime Minister that they must observe the conventions of collective responsibility at Executive meetings.[23]

5 As a former Cabinet minister has said, an element of concealment is inherent in the concept of collective responsibility. 'Ministers must in the nature of things have differences, but they must outwardly appear to have none.'[24] In principle, secrecy attaches to Cabinet discussions, Cabinet documents and the proceedings of Cabinet committees, except where the Cabinet or the Prime Minister decides that disclosures shall be made.[25] Exceptionally, where a minister resigns because of a disagreement with the Cabinet, he or she may explain in detail the reasons for the resignation, both to Parliament and in the press.[26] Today leakages about controversial matters frequently occur and the principle of secrecy is under pressure to give way to a more open system of government.

6 Similarly, in principle secrecy attaches to communications between departments. Thus if a decision is taken to reject a proposal which would mean new expenditure it is often not known whether this was primarily because the spending department does not favour the proposal or because the Treasury is not prepared to approve the expenditure involved: nor whether the decision was taken by officials or at ministerial level. Thus collective responsibility reinforces the principle of the indivisibility of the executive.[27] Again an element of concealment is inherent in the principle: departments are apparently expected to agree with each other because their ministerial heads are members of the same Cabinet. In real life, serious disagreements between departments occur, and often cannot be kept secret.

7 The collective decisions of the Cabinet are communicated by or on behalf of the Prime Minister to the Sovereign. Certain exceptions exist to the principle of collective responsibility for advice to the Sovereign. Thus, in advising the Sovereign on the prerogative of mercy, the Home Secretary and the Secretary of State for Scotland act on their own responsibility.[28]

Collective responsibility thus serves a variety of political uses. As most governments are drawn from one party, it reinforces party unity and prevents back-bench MPs from inquiring too far into the processes of government. It helps to maintain the government's control over legislation and public

---

22 Mackintosh, *British Cabinet*, p 534, but cf *Questions of Procedure for Ministers*, paras 11–12.
23 Wilson, *The Governance of Britain*, pp 74–5, 191–3; and see D L Ellis [1980] PL 367, 379–83.
24 Gordon Walker, *The Cabinet*, pp 27–8.
25 Ch 13 B.
26 See R Brazier [1990] PL 300.
27 Heclo and Wildavsky, *The Private Government of Public Money*, p 116.
28 Ch 12 D.

expenditure and to contain public disagreement between departments. It reinforces the traditional secrecy of the decision-making process within government. It helps to maintain the authority of the Prime Minister.[29]

Some of the purposes for which the doctrine is maintained are controversial. Thus there is disagreement over the degree of protection which should be afforded to the secrecy of decision-making, to the authority of the Prime Minister and to the need for external unanimity. In some more open processes of government, especially public inquiries, it is now accepted that the separate views of government departments should be made public.[30] But there is an obvious political advantage in being able to maintain an outward appearance of unity, which is why some aspects of collective responsibility apply also to the 'shadow Cabinet' of the main opposition party in the Commons. The political authority of the Labour 'shadow Cabinet' was weakened when, in a Commons debate about denationalisation, two inconsistent policies were advocated by the leading speakers for the Opposition.[31]

An assessment of collective responsibility today must take account of the fact that not all important decisions of national policy are taken in full Cabinet. The decision to manufacture the British atomic bomb,[32] to mount the Suez operation in 1956, to raise the bank rate in 1957[33] and to devalue the pound in 1967[34] were effectively taken by a few ministers meeting with the Prime Minister. So was the decision to ban trade union membership for staff at Government Communications Headquarters, Cheltenham.[35] In such cases other members of the Cabinet are in little better position than ministers outside the Cabinet to influence the decision before it is taken. For much of the time, the size of modern Cabinets, as well as the departmental burden of most of its members, precludes active participation by each minister in decisions.

Whether decisions are taken by the Cabinet or are merely reported to it, a minister may at any time resign in protest against decisions with which he or she strongly disagrees. Such resignations may indicate a deep disagreement over the way in which the Prime Minister is conducting government. Sir Geoffrey Howe's resignation in November 1990 after a series of other Cabinet resignations set in train the events leading to Mrs Thatcher's own resignation on 23 November 1990. But by its nature a resignation does not affect decisions which have already been taken.[36]

Agreements to differ

In exceptional circumstances, it may be politically impossible for the Cabinet to maintain a united front. In 1932, the coalition or 'National' government,

29   See ch 13 A. Cf Crossman's comment that collective responsibility had come to mean collective obedience to the Prime Minister (Introduction to Bagehot, p 53). And see T Benn (1980) 33 Parliamentary Affairs 7.
30   Ch 28 B.
31   HC Deb, 10 November 1981, cols 438, 499.
32   Crossman, Introduction to Bagehot, pp 54–5. This was not an isolated event: Hennessy, *Cabinet*, ch 4.
33   Cmnd 350, 1957; and R A Chapman (1965) 43 Public Administration 199.
34   Wilson, *The Labour Government 1964–70*, ch 23.
35   See *CCSU v Minister for the Civil Service* [1985] AC 374.
36   Cf Alderman and Cross, *The Tactics of Resignation*.

formed in 1931 to deal with the economic crisis adopted an 'agreement to differ'. The majority of the Cabinet favoured the adoption of a general tariff of 10%, against the strong opposition of three Liberal ministers and one National Labour minister. It was announced that the dissenting ministers were to be free to oppose the proposals of the majority by speech and vote, both in Parliament and outside. When the Labour opposition criticised the government for violating 'the long-established constitutional principle of Cabinet responsibility', the motion of censure was defeated by an over-whelming majority.[37] Eight months later the dissenting ministers resigned on the related issue of imperial preference. This short-lived departure from the principle of unanimity in fact demonstrated the virtues of that principle and it was justifiable, if at all, only in the special circumstances of a coalition government formed to deal with a national crisis.

In 1975, the Labour Cabinet agreed to differ over Britain's continued membership of the EC. Many in the Labour party were opposed to British membership. Party unity was maintained in the two general elections in 1974 by an undertaking from Mr Wilson to re-negotiate the terms of British membership and to submit the outcome to the people for decision, either at a general election or by referendum. When in April 1975 the re-negotiation of terms was completed, the Cabinet by a majority of 16–7 decided to recom-mend continued membership to the electorate. It was agreed that ministers who opposed this policy should be free to speak and campaign against it, but only outside Parliament.[38] When a junior minister, Mr Eric Heffer, insisted on opposing Britain's membership in the Commons,[39] he had to resign from office. Other difficulties arose over the answering of parliamentary questions on European subjects by ministers opposed to British membership.[40]

In 1932 the agreement to differ occurred within a coalition between parties; in 1975, within the Labour party. Indeed, outside the Cabinet, majorities against Cabinet policy were recorded in the Parliamentary Labour Party, in the National Executive Committee and at a special party conference. Such agreements to differ on the part of the Cabinet give rise to many political difficulties, but neither in 1932 nor in 1975 did they lead to the downfall of the government. It is difficult to describe these rather desperate expedients as 'unconstitutional'. If conventions are observed because of the political difficulties which follow if they are not,[41] both in 1932 and 1975 it was less difficult to depart from Cabinet unanimity than to seek to enforce it. During a period of minority government, a free vote was allowed to the Labour party (including ministers) on the second reading of the European Assembly Elections Bill.[42] But there are other issues, notably capital punish-ment, on which ministers like other MPs are free to vote according to their conscience.[43]

---

[37] Jennings, *Cabinet Government*, pp 279–81.
[38] See Cmnd 6003, 1975; HC Deb, 23 January 1975, col 1745; HC Deb, 7 April 1975, col 351 (WA). And see Wilson, *The Governance of Britain*, pp 194–7.
[39] HC Deb, 9 April 1975, cols 1325–32.
[40] Eg HC Deb, 5 May 1975, cols 989–1015.
[41] Page 26 above.
[42] HC Deb, 23 March 1977, col 1307; and see D L Ellis [1980] PL 367, 388.
[43] Eg HC Deb, 13 July 1983, col 972.

Ministers not in the Cabinet

In any government there are more ministers outside the Cabinet than within it. Some have full departmental duties; others (for example, the parliamentary secretaries) merely assist in the work of their departments. These ministers are bound by Cabinet decisions and must refrain from criticising or opposing them in public. 'Ministers cannot speak publicly for themselves alone. In all cases they speak as Ministers; and the principle of collective responsibility applies.'[44]

Similar restraints apply to junior ministers. Thus, while in office they are barred from writing and publishing books relating to their ministerial experience. In 1969, a parliamentary secretary resigned to publish a book on the economy and the machinery of government. Refusing him permission to publish the book and remain a minister, the Prime Minister stated that he had no alternative 'but to uphold the principles which every Prime Minister must maintain in relation to the collective responsibility of the Administration'.[45] Collective responsibility is thus invoked to control the behaviour of ministers, and this control is exercised by the Prime Minister. The consequences of collective responsibility are thus in part what the Prime Minister of the day chooses to make them. The obligation to support government policy on important issues extends to the back-bench MPs who act as unpaid parliamentary secretaries to ministers and may be dismissed for stepping too far out of line.[46] They are not members of the government, but they must not vote against the government or embarrass it in other ways.

The later development of individual responsibility

While it was established in the 18th century that ministers were individually responsible to Parliament for their policies, the activities of the central executive were still minute compared with those of modern government. The foundations of the present structure of government were laid only in the period of reform after 1832, when it became necessary to settle the relationship between Parliament and the new agencies which administered statutory schemes. It was to be increasingly difficult for ministers to supervise in detail the work of these agencies. In the mid-19th century a new class of administrators developed, whose energy did much to make possible the achievements of Victorian government: men like Edwin Chadwick, in the field of poor law and local government, Sir James Stephen at the Colonial Office and Sir John Simon in public health. The formal powers of these administrators derived from Acts of Parliament. Was Parliament able to supervise the use made of these powers?

For a period after 1832, powers were often vested in appointed public boards which were not directly responsible to Parliament.[47] Thus the Poor

---

44   *Questions of Procedure for Ministers*, para 87. For the dismissal of a Defence minister for having publicly criticised naval cuts, see HC Deb, 19 May 1981, col 151.

45   *The Times*, 26 and 29 September 1969. *Questions of Procedure for Ministers*, para 90.

46   *Questions of Procedure for Ministers*, paras 45–8. And see P Norton [1989] PL 232.

47   F M G Willson (1955) 33 Public Administration 43, 44.

Law Commission between 1834 and 1847 consisted of three persons who were not answerable to Parliament for the manner in which they administered the reformed poor law. Dissatisfaction with such boards led to a strong parliamentary preference for administration to be conducted through a ministry, ie a department whose powers are vested in a single person who sits in Parliament and is responsible to Parliament for that department. Thus in 1847 the Poor Law Commission was replaced by a ministry responsible to Parliament.[48] Procedures such as the parliamentary question developed which enabled members to obtain information about matters within the responsibility of ministers.[49] As the civil service was reformed following the Northcote-Trevelyan report of 1854,[50] there developed as the corollary of ministerial responsibility the anonymity and permanence of the civil service. Nor was the scale of government too large for ministers to be able to supervise the work of their departments.[51]

The operation of individual responsibility today[52]

Ministerial responsibility remains important, both in the operation of government and in the executive's relations with Parliament. Structural changes have affected the application of the concept. During the 20th century, as the tasks of the state expanded and vast Whitehall departments were created, officials continued to act in their minister's name, but the ability of ministers to oversee their work declined. The state's economic and social functions led to the creation of non-departmental bodies, public corporations and other agencies. Many of these (especially the boards of the nationalised industries after 1945) were planned to operate beyond the reach of ministerial responsibility, at least for day-to-day decisions. By contrast, the executive agencies created since 1988 under the 'Next Steps' initiative were intended to achieve effective delegation of managerial power, without necessarily reducing overall ministerial control.[53]

By constitutional tradition, a minister answers to Parliament for his or her department. In the practice of Parliament, praise and blame are addressed to the minister, not civil servants. Ministers may not excuse the failure of policies by turning upon their expert advisers and administrators.[54] The corollary of the minister's responsibility is that civil servants are not directly responsible to Parliament for government policies or decisions, although they are respons-

---

[48] See Bagehot, *The English Constitution*, p 192.
[49] Chester and Bowring, *Questions in Parliament*, ch 2.
[50] Ch 13 D.
[51] Parris, *Constitutional Bureaucracy*, ch 3.
[52] Marshall, *Constitutional Conventions*, ch 4; C C Turpin, in Jowell and Oliver (eds), *The Changing Constitution*, ch 5; Woodhouse, *Ministers and Parliament*.
[53] See chs 13 D and 14.
[54] See eg *The Times*, 21 February 1949. In 1963, it was plainly exceptional when the Prime Minister named a former Secretary to the Cabinet as responsible for failing to inform him of a security warning given by the Secretary to a minister of Cabinet rank (HC Deb, 17 June 1963, col 59). In 1995, the Home Secretary, who had repeatedly intervened in the operation of the Prison Service, denied responsibility for defects in prison security and dismissed the Service's Director, saying that this came within his duty of 'accountability': see HC Deb, 16 October 1995, col 30 and 19 October 1995, col 502; and ch 13 D.

ible *to ministers* for their own actions and conduct. In 1996, the government defended 'the fundamental principle that civil servants are servants of the Crown, accountable to the duly constituted government of the day, and not servants of the House'.[55]

Much of the work of Parliament rests on this basis. Government Bills (drafted by civil servants on the instructions of ministers) are introduced by ministers, who are responsible for the proposals they contain. Question time emphasises the responsibility of ministers.[56] Although civil servants have no voice in most parliamentary proceedings, they appear before select committees to give evidence on departmental policies and decisions. In giving such evidence, they 'do so on behalf of their Ministers and under their directions' and their stated purpose 'is to contribute to the central process of Ministerial accountability, not to offer personal views or judgments on matters of political controversy, or to become involved in what would amount to disciplinary investigations . . .'.[57] Although officials must be as helpful as possible to select committees, the information which they provide is ultimately for ministers to decide.[58]

The sanctions for individual responsibility

What are the sanctions which underlie this general practice of Parliament? The system assumes that ministers will fulfil the parliamentary duties of their office, such as introducing legislation and answering questions. By a rota system, departments are assigned days for answering questions and a minister could not refuse to appear on the assigned day. But a minister may refuse to answer a question if he considers that it does not fall within his responsibility, that it would be contrary to the public interest to answer the question or that the expense of obtaining the information requested would be excessive.[59] If a minister persistently refused to provide information, and the Opposition moved a vote of censure upon him or her, the outcome would depend on whether the government could retain its majority in the House. It is most unlikely that the House could in this way force a Prime Minister to remove an individual minister from office, but situations may occur in which a Prime Minister is unable or unwilling to protect a minister from pressure to resign exerted in other ways. In 1986, the Westland affair caused the Trade and Industry Secretary (Mr Brittan) to resign for having improperly released to the press a confidential letter from the Solicitor-General. Mr Brittan refused to answer questions from the Commons Defence Committee about his role in the matter.[60]

---

[55] HC 67 (1996–7), app, para 10. And see ch 13 D.
[56] Ch 10 D. Chester and Bowring, note 49 above, pp 251–68, and app II; Franklin and Norton (eds), *Parliamentary Questions*.
[57] *Departmental Evidence and Response to Select Committees* (1997), para 38.
[58] Ibid, paras 48 and 53.
[59] Erskine May, *Parliamentary Practice*, pp 292–3. Since 1993, the practice of the House of Commons Table Office has been to reject questions only when a minister has refused to answer them in the same session: HC 313–I (1995–96), para 39; and R Scott [1996] PL 410, 416–17.
[60] HC (1985–86) 519; and see HC Deb, 29 October 1986, col 339; also A Tomkins (1996) 16 LS 63, 76-7.

Ministerial responsibility for departmental maladministration

Ministers are, or ought to be, responsible to Parliament for their own decisions and policies and the efficient administration of their departments. The position in respect of the errors of civil servants is less clear. Two questions arise: (*a*) to what extent is a minister responsible for acts of maladministration in the department? (*b*) if serious maladministration occurs, does such responsibility involve a duty to resign? For nearly 50 years, the Crichel Down affair has been the starting-point for discussion of these questions.

Farm land in Dorset known as Crichel Down had been acquired under compulsory powers from several owners by the Air Ministry in 1937. After the war, the land was transferred to the Ministry of Agriculture, for whom it was administered by a commission set up under the Agriculture Act 1947. While the future of the land was being considered, Lieutenant-Commander Marten, whose wife's family had previously owned much of the land, asked that it be sold back to the family. Misleading replies and false assurances were given when this and similar requests were refused, and a seriously inaccurate report was prepared by a junior civil servant which led the ministry to adhere to a scheme which it had prepared for letting all the land to a single tenant. Inadequate financial information was supplied to the headquarters of the ministry. When Conservative MPs took up Marten's case with the Minister of Agriculture, Sir Andrew Clark QC was appointed to hold an inquiry. His report established that there had been muddle, inefficiency, bias and bad faith on the part of some officials named in the report.[61] A subsequent inquiry to consider disciplinary action against the civil servants reported that some of the deficiencies were due as much to weak organisation within the ministry as to the faults of individuals.[62]

During a Commons debate on these reports, the Minister of Agriculture, Sir Thomas Dugdale, resigned. Speaking in the debate, the Home Secretary, Sir David Maxwell Fyfe, reaffirmed that a civil servant is wholly and directly responsible to his minister and can be dismissed at any time by the minister – a 'power none the less real because it is seldom used'. He went on to give a number of categories where differing considerations apply.

1 A minister must protect a civil servant who has carried out his explicit order.
2 Equally a minister must defend a civil servant who acts properly in accordance with the policy laid down by the minister.
3 'Where an official makes a mistake or causes some delay, but not on an important issue of policy and not where a claim to individual rights is seriously involved, the Minister acknowledges the mistake and he accepts the responsibility although he is not personally involved.' He states that he will take corrective action in the Department.'
4 Where action has been taken by a civil servant of which the minister disapproves and has no previous knowledge, and the conduct of the official is reprehensible, there is no obligation on a minister to endorse what he believes to be wrong or to defend what are clearly shown to be errors of his officers. He remains however, 'constitutionally responsible to Parliament for the fact that something has gone wrong', but this does not affect his power to control and discipline his staff.[63]

This statement and the implications of the Crichel Down affair have been

---

[61]   Cmd 9176, 1954.
[62]   Cmd 9220, 1954.
[63]   HC Deb, 20 July 1954, cols 1286–7.

much discussed.[64] Was the resignation due to the part which the minister had played, or was he accepting vicarious responsibility for the civil servants? There have been very few comparable resignations since 1954. In his analysis of the minister's duties, Maxwell Fyfe's four categories sought to identify situations in which a minister must 'accept responsibility' for the acts of civil servants. The analysis did not state that a minister's duty to accept responsibility carried with it a duty to resign.[65]

Subsequent events have confirmed that there is no duty upon a minister to resign when maladministration has occurred within his or her department. Whether a minister may resign depends on a variety of political factors, including the attitude of the Prime Minister, the mood of the party, the temperament of the minister and other political factors.[66] Rather different considerations apply where the personal conduct of a minister is in issue: inadvertent disclosure of a Budget secret led to the resignation of Hugh Dalton as Chancellor of the Exchequer in 1947;[67] and the resignation occurred in 1963 of the Secretary of State for War for having lied to the Commons in a personal statement[68] and of ministers in 1973 and subsequently because of personal improprieties.[69] Of the resignations since 1973, apart from those caused by disagreement on policy, many were brought about by personal misconduct which made it too difficult for the individuals to perform their duties in the face of continuing criticism in the media.[70] By contrast, there have been virtually no resignations because of departmental failures.

In 1964, when investigation by the Comptroller and Auditor-General revealed that there had been an overpayment of more than £4 million by the Ministry of Aviation to Ferranti Ltd in respect of work on defence contracts, and that this overpayment need not have occurred if two sections of the ministry had pooled their information, the minister, Julian Amery, explained to the House what had occurred and the steps taken to remedy the position, and displayed no intention of resigning: the Opposition motion of censure was defeated.[71] In 1968, when the first major investigation by the Parliamentary Commissioner for Administration (the Parliamentary Ombudsman) established that there had been maladministration within the Foreign Office in the Sachsenhausen affair[72] the Foreign Secretary, George Brown, assumed direct personal responsibility for the decisions of the Foreign Office, which he maintained were correct, while agreeing to provide compensation for the claimants. In the debate he said: 'We will breach a very serious constitutional position if we start holding officials responsible for things that are done wrong

---

64   See eg J A G Griffith (1955) 8 MLR 557; (1954) 32 Public Administration 385 (C J Hamson) and 389 (D N Chester). For a re-interpretation, see Nicolson, *The Mystery of Crichel Down*.
65   And see Sir R Scott [1996] PL 410 at 412–13.
66   S E Finer (1956) 34 Public Administration 377.
67   HC 20 (1947–48).
68   HC Deb, 22 March 1963, col 809; 17 June 1963, cols 34–170. And Cmnd 2152, 1963.
69   Cmnd 5367, 1973.
70   See D Woodhouse, *Ministers and Parliament*, and (1993) 46 Parliamentary Affairs 277; and R Brazier [1994] PL 431.
71   HC Deb, 30 July 1964, col 1801.
72   Ch 28 D, and see G K Fry [1970] PL 336.

... If things are wrongly done, then they are wrongly done by ministers'.[73] This statement did not take full account of the duties of the Parliamentary Ombudsman, whose investigation into departmental conduct must inevitably probe behind statements made for the department by the minister. But the creation of the Ombudsman did not mean a complete change in the relationship between minister and civil servant. As the Attorney-General, Sir Elwyn Jones, said in 1968:

> It is only in exceptional cases that blame should be attached to the individual civil servant and it follows from the principle that the minister alone has responsibility for the actions of his department that the individual civil servant who has contributed to the collective decision of the department should remain anonymous.[74]

In terms of this statement, an 'exceptional case' was provided by the investigation into the affairs of the Vehicle and General Insurance company.

In March 1971, the company collapsed, leaving a million policy holders uninsured. The Department of Trade and Industry had statutory powers of supervision and control of insurance companies but it had failed to exercise these powers. Following allegations of misconduct, the government appointed a tribunal of inquiry[75] to inquire, inter alia, whether there had been negligence or misconduct by persons in the service of the Crown 'directly or indirectly responsible' for the government's statutory functions. The tribunal reported that Mr C W Jardine, under-secretary, and two named assistant secretaries were responsible for the failure to deal with the risk of the company's insolvency before 1971, and that the under-secretary's conduct fell below the standard which could reasonably be expected of an official in that position, and constituted negligence. Under a scheme of delegation within the department, almost all the work allocated to a division was dealt with at the level of under-secretary or below. 'The responsibility for deciding whether or not to exercise the Department's powers lay with Mr Jardine as the Under-Secretary in charge of the Insurance and Companies Division.'[76]

The significance of the report lies in the fact that, after a full public examination into the affair, the tribunal held that a single official should bear the entire responsibility for the department's inactivity. While the tribunal may have correctly described the facts which they had found, did this resolve the question of political responsibility to Parliament? If so, what is left of the principle that a minister takes the praise for the successes of his or her department and the blame for its failures?[77] If a tribunal of inquiry had not been appointed in the Vehicle and General case, the Commons would not have accepted a statement from the Secretary for Trade and Industry pillorying the luckless Mr Jardine.

In April 1982, the Argentine invasion of the Falkland Islands led to the resignation of the Foreign Secretary, Lord Carrington, and two Foreign

---

73 HC Deb, 5 February 1968, col 112.
74 HC 350 (1967–68), para 24.
75 Under the Tribunals of Inquiry (Evidence) Act 1921: ch 28 C.
76 HL 80, HC 133 (1971–72), para 344.
77 See HC Deb, 1 May 1972, col 34; and R J S Baker (1972) 43 Political Quarterly 340. The collapse of the Barlow Clowes investment business in 1988 led to a detailed investigation of the role of the civil service in the affair by the Parliamentary Ombudsman: no ministers were implicated and no civil servants were named, although serious faults were found. See R Gregory and G Drewry [1991] PL 192, 408 and ch 28 D.

Office ministers. The ministers stated that they accepted responsibility for the conduct of policy on the Falkland Islands, and insisted against the express wishes of the Prime Minister that they should resign. The resignation of the Defence Secretary, Mr Nott, was offered but refused by the Prime Minister on the ground that his department was not responsible for policy on the Falkland Islands. A committee of privy councillors later reviewed the way in which government responsibilities had been discharged before the invasion, found that there had been a misjudgment of the situation within the Foreign Office and recommended changes in the intelligence organisation; but no blame was attached to any individual, nor did the committee consider that criticism for the circumstances leading to the invasion could be attached to the government.[78] The report thus cleared the ministers who had resigned of any culpability. The resignations may have served a political purpose at the time, but they set no precedent. Since Lord Carrington's resignation in 1982, ministers have been resolutely reluctant to resign for errors by civil servants; the resignation of Mr Brittan in 1986 was due to his own role in the Westland affair, not to the conduct of civil servants.

In 1996 Sir Richard Scott's report on the 'arms for Iraq' affair detailed numerous occasions on which ministers failed to inform Parliament adequately about their policy on exporting arms and machine tools to Iraq, and did not reveal changes they had made in the policy. Their answers to repeated questions had been misleading,[79] but ministers persuaded the inquiry that they had not intentionally misled Parliament. However, without the provision of full information it is not possible for Parliament

'to assess what consequences, in the form of attribution or blame, ought to follow ... A failure by Ministers to meet the obligations of Ministerial accountability by providing information about the activities of their departments undermines ... the democratic process'.[80]

When the report was debated in the Commons, the government survived by one vote. No ministers resigned.[81]

As the vote on the Scott report made clear, the relation between individual and collective responsibility is very close. If one or more ministers are attacked by the Opposition, the government will usually treat this as an attack on itself, except in the rare case when ministers lose the support of their back-bench MPs. The ultimate sanction for a failure of individual responsibility is a Commons vote, with the outcome depending on whether the government retains its majority. In fact, this often may be an appropriate sanction, since a minister's decisions may depend on the prior approval of other departments (for example, the Treasury) or a Cabinet committee. Many decisions announced by individual ministers are the result of collective decision-making.[82]

---

78   Cmnd 8787, 1983.
79   See eg the summary at HC 115 (1995–96), vol IV, pp 1799–1800.
80   HC 115 (1995–96), vol IV, p 1801.
81   HC Deb, 26 February 1996, col 589. For discussion of the Scott report, see articles at [1996] PL 357–507.
82   *Questions of Procedure for Ministers*, paras 3–8.

Ministerial responsibility and the courts

The responsibility of ministers to Parliament consists of a duty to account for what they and their departments are doing. The courts play no part in determining the extent of that duty, but the duty is so essential to British government that the courts have taken note of its existence. By legislative practice, administrative powers are usually vested in a specified minister. Does this mean in law that only the minister may exercise these powers?

In *Carltona Ltd v Commissioners of Works*, an order to requisition a factory was issued under defence regulations by an assistant secretary in the Ministry of Works, and it was challenged on the ground that the relevant minister had not personally considered the matter. The order was upheld by the court. Lord Greene MR said that government could not be carried on unless civil servants could take decisions on behalf of the minister. 'Constitutionally, the decision of such an official [ie the assistant secretary] is, of course, the decision of the minister. The minister is responsible. It is he who must answer before Parliament for anything that his officials have done under his authority.'[83]

While therefore a minister's powers may in law be exercised by civil servants, and it is not necessary to establish a formal delegation of authority to them (in the absence of a statutory provision requiring such delegation),[84] the courts have maintained that the minister remains responsible to Parliament. However, there may be cases where from the nature of the power or because of an express statutory provision the general principle does not apply and powers must be exercised personally by the minister.[85] Where a statutory duty is vested in one minister, he may not adopt a policy whereby decisions are effectively made by another minister.[86]

Judicial discussion of ministerial responsibility has generally occurred when a citizen has sought a legal remedy against central government. In the past, the courts sometimes held that the remedy through Parliament which ministerial responsibility may provide is better suited to the citizen's complaint than a legal remedy.[87] In *Local Government Board v Arlidge*, the House of Lords had to determine whether natural justice at common law bound a department in the procedure by which a decision was taken in the name of a minister following a public inquiry. In denying that the minister was bound to give a personal hearing to the citizen whose property was affected, the House stressed the minister's responsibility to Parliament, not only for his own acts but also for all that was done in his department.[88]

Earlier in the 20th century, before the procedure of judicial review became a widely used means of challenging government decisions, the judges' reliance on ministerial responsibility delayed the development of admin-

---

[83]   [1943] 2 All ER 560, 563. Also *Lewisham MB v Roberts* [1949] 2 KB 608; *R v Skinner* [1968] 2 QB 700; and *Re Golden Chemical Products Ltd* [1976] Ch 300.

[84]   *Commissioners of Customs and Excise v Cure & Deeley Ltd* [1962] 1 QB 340.

[85]   Eg Immigration Act 1971, in respect of exclusion or deportation orders: ss 13(5), 14(3) and 15(4). And see *R v Home Secretary, ex p Oladehinde* [1991] 1 AC 254.

[86]   *Lavender and Son Ltd v Minister of Housing* [1970] 3 All ER 871.

[87]   See eg *Rustomjee v R* (1876) 2 QBD 69.

[88]   [1915] AC 120; ch 29 B. In similar vein, see also *Johnson and Co (Builders) Ltd v Minister of Health* [1947] 2 All ER 395, 400 and *Liversidge v Anderson* [1942] AC 206.

istrative law.[89] While judicial review does not enable policy decisions by ministers to be decided afresh by the judges, and some executive decisions are less appropriate for judicial review than others,[90] it is now accepted that judicial review and ministerial responsibility serve complementary purposes and are not mutually exclusive.[91]

Responsibility and accountability re-stated?

A central theme in the Scott report was the tension between government power and democratic accountability. In 1986, during the Defence Committee's inquiry into the Westland affair, the head of the civil service re-stated the duties of ministers towards Parliament;[92] in revised form, the statement was presented to other Commons committees and the Scott inquiry.[93] The statement contrasts 'accountability' (in its non-financial sense) with 'responsibility'. A minister is '*accountable*' to Parliament for everything which occurs in a department: the duty, which may not be delegated, is to inform Parliament about policies and decisions of the department, except in rare cases where secrecy is an overriding necessity (as with currency devaluation or sensitive defence secrets). If something goes wrong, the minister owes it to Parliament to find out what has happened, ensure necessary disciplinary action, and take steps to avoid a recurrence.

By contrast, a minister is said to be '*responsible*' only for broad policies, the framework of administration, and issues in which he or she has been involved, not for all departmental affairs. The emphasis is on matters for which the minister may be personally praised or blamed. This form of 'responsibility' may be delegated, and the minister is not responsible for what is done by civil servants (for example, by the chief executive of a 'Next Steps' agency) within the authority assigned to them.

This distinction between accountability and responsibility requires close scrutiny, since it provides a means by which a minister may avoid personal liability for unpopular or mistaken decisions; and it opens up potential areas of government for which no one is 'responsible' to Parliament, even though a minister remains 'accountable'. The Public Service Committee of the Commons has insisted that no clear dividing line can be drawn between accountability and responsibility, and that the two main aspects of ministerial responsibility are (i) the duty to give an account, and (ii) the liability to be held to account.[94]

Certainly, the duty of ministers to inform Parliament is of primary importance, and includes the duty not to mislead Parliament by providing

---

[89]   See J D B Mitchell [1965] PL 95; and Dicey, *Law of the Constitution*, app 2.
[90]   Consider *R v Home Secretary, ex p Hosenball* [1977] 3 All ER 452; *Gouriet v Union of Post Office Workers* [1978] AC 435; and *R v Environment Secretary, ex p Notts CC* [1986] AC 240.
[91]   See *R v IRC, ex p National Federation of Self-Employed* [1982] AC 617, 644 and *R v Home Secretary, ex p Fire Brigades Union* [1995] 2 AC 513, 572–3 and 575.
[92]   HC 92–II (1985–86). And Cmnd 9916 (1986), para 40.
[93]   E.g. HC 390 (1992–93), para 25; HC 27 (1993–94), paras 118–20; Cm 2748 (1995), para 16; HC 313–I (1995-96), paras 15–18. See also the wealth of evidence in HC 313–II and 313–III (1995–96); and the Scott report, HC 115 (1995–96), vol IV, pp 1805–6.
[94]   HC 313 (1995–96), paras 21 and 32.

inaccurate or incomplete information. If a statement to Parliament is inadvertently misleading, the minister must correct it as soon as possible. For a minister knowingly to mislead Parliament is a contempt of Parliament;[95] it is now accepted that for such misconduct the minister must resign.[96] For other forms of maladministration, including general inefficiency, the Opposition may call for a minister to resign, but resignation in those circumstances is unlikely.

The emphasis on the duty of ministers to keep Parliament informed has had certain benefits. First, in answering MPs' questions, ministers are expected at least to observe the government's code of practice on access to information;[97] and clerks in the Commons have given up the practice of 'blocking' questions of a kind which a minister had refused to answer in a previous session of Parliament. Secondly, both the Cabinet Office booklet, *Questions of Procedure for Ministers*, and the guidance to civil servants on answering MPs' questions have been revised to emphasise the duty of ministers to keep Parliament informed.

But difficulties remain. One is the government's restrictive approach to the giving of evidence by civil servants (and retired civil servants) to select committees:[98] should ministers have power to censor evidence as to matters of fact which civil servants give to a committee? Another is the abusive manner in which the government controlled publication of the Scott report in 1996 and sought to dominate the initial response to it in the Commons and the media. The politicised use of executive power was criticised by the Scott report. Would it reduce the risk of such abuse if legislation permitted executive powers to be devolved to agencies outside ministerial control, subject to new parliamentary safeguards?

The British system has emphasised the need to place departments under the control of ministers, who are the link between executive and Parliament. But the ability of ministers to exercise control is limited and may be misused. An independent means of scrutinising administration is provided by the Parliamentary Ombudsman.[99] Remarkably, the doctrine of ministerial responsibility was used as an argument *against* creating both the Ombudsman in 1967, and the present select committees of the Commons in 1979 – fortunately on each occasion without success. In fact, at any given moment the boundaries of ministerial responsibility are not necessarily drawn in the right place.[100] The principle of accountable government is ultimately more important than ministerial responsibility. Thus, if there appears to be any conflict between the two, the former principle ought to prevail.

Finally, it must be recorded that shortly before the 1992–97 Parliament was dissolved, an agreement between the government and opposition parties enabled the House of Commons to adopt without debate a resolution on

---

95   See ch 11 A. Whether or not ministers had knowingly misled Parliament was a central issue in the Scott inquiry.
96   HC 313 (1995–96), para 34; HC 67 (1996–97), para 3; *Questions of Procedure for Ministers* (1992), revised para 1(iii), and see HC Deb, 18 July 1995, col 457.
97   A revised edition of the code of practice was issued in 1997; and see ch 13 E.
98   See *Departmental Evidence and Response to Select Committees* (1997), paras 37–75.
99   Ch 28 D.
100 Fulton Report on the Civil Service, Cmnd 3638, 1968, para 190.

ministerial accountability which stated that the following principles should govern the conduct of ministers in relation to Parliament:

(1) Ministers have a duty to Parliament to account, and be held to account, for the policies, decisions and actions of their Departments and Next Steps Agencies;

(2) It is of paramount importance that Ministers give accurate and truthful information to Parliament, correcting any inadvertent error at the earliest opportunity. Ministers who knowingly mislead Parliament will be expected to offer their resignation to the Prime Minister.

(3) Ministers should be as open as possible with Parliament, refusing to provide information only when disclosure would not be in the public interest, which should be decided in accordance with relevant statute and the Government's Code of Practice on Access to Government Information (second edition, January 1997);

(4) Similarly, Ministers should require civil servants who give evidence before Parliamentary Committees on their behalf and under their directions to be as helpful as possible in providing accurate, truthful and full information in accordance with the duties and responsibilities of civil servants as set out in the Civil Service Code (January 1996).[101]

---

[101]   HC Deb, 19 March 1997, col 1046. The same resolution was adopted by the Lords: HL Deb, 20 March 1997, col 1055.

CHAPTER 8

The United Kingdom and the European Community

The European Economic Community was created in 1957, the original six member states being West Germany, France, Italy, Belgium, Netherlands and Luxembourg. It was not until 1973 that Britain became a member, along with the Republic of Ireland and Denmark. There are now 15 member states of what is now the European Union with a combined population of some 370 million people.[1] From the earliest days membership has caused great constitutional anxiety to some in Britain, despite the fact that the United Kingdom allegedly has the most flexible and the only unwritten constitution among the member states. Nevertheless, attempts to challenge entry were made on the ground that it constituted an abuse of the prerogative treaty-making power to the extent that it would allegedly undermine the sovereignty of Parliament,[2] and on the ground also that the Treaty would breach art 18 of the Treaty of Union of 1707.[3] More recently the renegotiation of the Treaty at Maastricht in 1992 led to further challenges in the British courts, an unsuccessful attempt being made to prevent the government from ratifying it.[4] But if British membership has caused constitutional difficulties of a legal nature, this is as nothing when compared with the controversies of a political nature which it has generated. Thus political parties have been divided, constitutional conventions have been formally and informally suspended, and the only national referendum this century was held in 1975 on continued membership of what was then the EEC.[5]

Apart from enlargement, the EEC has undergone many significant changes since its formation in 1957. One of these was the Single European Act of 1986,[6] though this is now overshadowed by the changes wrought at Maastricht

---

[1] The full list of member states, apart from those already mentioned, includes Greece, Spain, Portugal, Sweden, Austria and Finland.
[2] *Blackburn v A-G* [1971] 2 All ER 1380. See ch 12.
[3] *Gibson v Lord Advocate* 1975 SLT 134. See ch 4 D.
[4] *R v Foreign Secretary, ex p Rees-Mogg* [1994] QB 552. See G Marshall [1993] PL 402, and also R Rawlings [1994] PL 254, 367.
[5] Referendum Act 1975. See also Cmnd 5925, 1975 and 6251, 1975.
[6] Cm 372, 1986. See European Communities (Amendment) Act 1986. The Single European Act increased the scope for decision-making by majority vote, dispensing with the unanimity rule in many areas.

in 1992 which led in the Treaty on European Union to substantial revisions of the EC Treaty and the creation of new structures and procedures.[7] The Maastricht Treaty provides a number of objectives for the EU, which include the strengthening of social and economic cohesion, the implementation of a common foreign and security policy, the introduction of a common citizenship,[8] and the development of close cooperation on matters relating to justice and home affairs.[9] The Treaty also provides that the EU shall respect the national identities of its member states, as well as fundamental rights as guaranteed by the European Convention on Human Rights and 'as they result from the constitutional traditions common to the member States'.[10] But the Treaty also contains a number of important amendments to the EC Treaty, which on the one hand increase the opportunity for law-making by majority or qualified majority voting by the Council, and on the other increase the power of the Parliament in the legislative process. It also adds a number of controversial Protocols to the EC Treaty, dealing with matters such as the establishment of the European System of Central Banks and the European Central Bank; European Monetary Union; and Social Policy, the last empowering the 14 member states without the United Kingdom to use the institutions, procedures and mechanisms of the EC Treaty for the purpose of developing social policy.[11]

EC law has now become a vast subject with an ever-expanding literature. It is calculated to grow even larger as the powers of the Community grow and as its institutions become more powerful. In this chapter we are concerned principally with the consequences of EC membership for the constitutional law of the United Kingdom, for as we shall see there is a distinctive EC constitutional law, the fundamentals of which were in place before Britain's accession in 1973, but which makes claims which are not easy for the British public lawyer, schooled in the traditions of Dicey and others, to embrace. Although the focus is thus on the European impact on the UK constitution, it is necessary to deal first with the institutions and law-making process of the Community, and with the relationship between the various sources of EC law and domestic law.[12] The most important constitutional questions clearly relate to the sovereignty of Parliament (politically as well as legally). Although the matter has been considered by the House of Lords on several occasions, it remains to be settled as a matter of English and Scottish constitutional law precisely where legal sovereignty ultimately resides, so long as the United Kingdom remains in membership of the European Community.

---

[7] See J C Piris (1994) 19 EL Rev 447, and J A Usher (1993) 14 Stat Law Rev 28. See also European Communities (Amendment) Act 1993.

[8] See esp EC Treaty, art 8b (every EU citizen residing in a member state of which he is not a national to have the right to vote and stand as a candidate at elections of the state in which he resides under the same conditions as nationals of that state). And ch 20 A.

[9] TEU, Title I, art B.

[10] TEU, Title I, art F. See J Weiler and N Lockhart (1995) 32 CML Rev 51; and ch 19.

[11] On the implications of the Protocol on Social Policy, see *ex p Rees-Mogg*, above.

[12] For fuller treatment of these matters, see esp Hartley, *The Foundations of EC Law*, Mathijsen, *A Guide to EC Law*; and Weatherill and Beaumont, *EC Law*. Also valuable are Craig and de Burca, *EC Law: Text, Cases and Materials*, and Ellis and Tridimas, *Public Law of the European Community: Text, Materials and Commentary*.

A. EC institutions

There are now five principal institutions of the EC, which is now said to constitute one of the three pillars of the EU (the others being (a) the common foreign and security policy, and (b) inter-governmental cooperation on home affairs and justice matters.[13] Art 4 of the EC Treaty provides that the tasks entrusted to the Community are to be carried out by the European Parliament, the Council, the Commission, the Court of Justice, and the Court of Auditors. The Council is not to be confused with the European Council, which consists of heads of state or government and meets at least twice a year to 'provide the Union with the necessary impetus for its development'.[14] Other institutions include the Economic and Social Committee and the Committee of the Regions,[15] while in the field of social policy law-making activity is, to an extent, delegated to the so-called social partners.[16] Although the Parliament is listed as the first Community institution, it is not the most powerful, though its role has become more prominent since 1957, particularly after the amendments to the EC Treaty in 1992.

The Commission

1 Composition. The Commission consists of 20 members,[17] appointed for renewable periods of five years.[18] There must be at least one Commissioner from each member state, with a maximum of two Commissioners with a common nationality. In practice two Commissioners are nominated by the larger states (France, Germany, Italy, Spain and the United Kingdom), with the remaining ten states nominating one Commissioner each. The practice in the UK (where nominations are made by the Prime Minister) is for Commissioners to be senior political figures, the convention being that one should have a record of service in the Conservative party and the other in the Labour party. Each Commissioner is responsible for one or more of the twenty-four departments, known as Directorates-General, such as Internal Market (DG III), Social Policy (DG V), Agriculture (DG VI), and Environment (DG XI). The President of the Commission is nominated by the member states, though 'by common accord' and only after consulting the Parliament. Once nominated both the President and the other members of the Commission are 'subject as a body to a vote of approval by the European Parliament', following which they are appointed again 'by common accord of the governments of the member states'.[19] The Parliament thus has no power to veto an individual nomination to the Commission, which must be accepted or rejected as a whole. But Commissioners may be removed from office by the Court of Justice on a reference by the Council or the Commission if they no longer fulfil the conditions re-

---

[13] HC 642–I (1992–93), para 25.
[14] TEU, Title I, art D,
[15] EC Treaty, art 4(2).
[16] EC Treaty, Protocol on Social Policy, Agreement on Social Policy, art 4. See Framework Agreement on Parental Leave, 1995 (*European Industrial Relations Review*, No 264, Jan 1996, p 35); discussed by Barnard, *EC Employment Law*, pp 513–20.
[17] EC Treaty, art 157.
[18] EC Treaty, art 158.
[19] EC Treaty, art 158(2).

quired for the performance of their duties or if guilty of serious misconduct.[20]

2 Functions. The Commission has two principal functions under the Treaty.[21] The first is to initiate proposals for legislation, to be considered by the Council and the Parliament. In this way the Commission plays a central role in the development of Community policy in the different areas of its competence, and in initiating legislative proposals to give effect to that policy. In doing so it consults widely with pressure groups, both at Community and national level.[22] However, Commission initiatives are not always endorsed by the Council, particularly where the unanimity of the Council is required.[23] The Commission's second main function is to ensure that the provisions of the Treaty, as well as Community law generally, are implemented and applied. This may mean initiating enforcement proceedings in the Court of Justice against any member state which is in breach of the EC Treaty or which has failed to implement directives or regulations.[24] So in case *C-382/92, Re Business Transfers: EC Commission v UK*[25] enforcement proceedings were initiated in respect of failure to implement directives protecting workers in the event of business restructuring; and in *Case C-222/94, EC Commission v UK*[26] proceedings were initiated in respect of a failure to implement correctly a directive on television broadcasting.[27] In exercising their functions, members of the Commission are required to act 'in the general interest of the Community' as a whole and to be 'completely independent in the performance of their duties'.[28] Specifically, they must 'neither seek nor take instructions from any government or from any other body'.[29]

The Council

1 Composition and functions. The Council consists of political representatives of the member states, each being represented by a minister who is 'authorised to commit the government of that member state'.[30] The representative at any particular session will depend on the subject of the meeting, so that for example on transport matters the UK representative will be the

---

20   EC Treaty, art 160.
21   For the main functions of the Commission, see EC Treaty, art 155; other powers are found elsewhere in the Treaty, eg art 48.
22   See A B Philip, 'Pressure Groups and Policy Making in the European Community', in Lodge (ed), *Institutions and Policies of the European Community*. On the role of advisory committees, see G J Buitendijk and M P C M Van Schendelen (1995) 20 EL Rev 37.
23   On voting procedures in the Council, see below, p 135.
24   EC Treaty, art 169. The Commission must first deliver a reasoned opinion on the matter and give the state in question an opportunity to respond by submitting its observations. Before one state commences proceedings against another, it must first bring the matter before the Commission, which shall deliver a reasoned opinion after each state concerned has been given the opportunity to submit its own case: EC Treaty, art 170; see also art 175.
25   [1995] 1 CMLR 345. For the sequel, see SI 1995 No 2587. See also *R v Trade and Industry Secretary, ex p UNISON* [1997] 1 CMLR 459. See further M Radford and A Kerr (1997) 60 MLR 23.
26   [1996] 3 CMLR 793.
27   See also *Case C-246/89, Commission v UK* [1991] ECR I–4585.
28   EC Treaty, art 157(2).
29   Ibid.
30   EC Treaty, art 146.

Secretary of State for Transport. In 1997 no fewer than 27 ministers represented the United Kingdom at different Council meetings. The Presidency of the Council rotates between member states every six months,[31] and the Council meets when convened by the President, or at the request of one of its members or the Commission.[32] The Council's functions include the co-ordination of general economic policies of member states. It also has a pivotal role in the legislative process, in the sense that it must approve Commission initiatives, and indeed is in a real sense the legislative authority within the Community,[33] though unusually for a 'legislative' body its deliberations are not in public. The Council is assisted by the Committee of Permanent Representatives (COREPER) which is responsible for preparing the work of the Council and carrying out tasks assigned to it.[34] In practice Commission proposals are referred to COREPER for consideration before they are formally considered by the Council itself. Indeed, although all decisions must be taken by ministers, on less important matters they may be taken without debate if they have been agreed to by COREPER. The Commission is represented at all meetings of both the Council and COREPER.[35]

2 Procedure and transparency. In performing its functions the Council may act by a majority of its members,[36] though in practice it may be required to act by a qualified majority vote or in some cases unanimously.[37] On a qualified majority vote (QMV), the votes of each country are weighted broadly by population, with France, Germany, Italy and the United Kingdom each having 10 out of a total of 87 votes. Where QMV is required acts of the Council require at least 62 votes before they may be adopted, which means that no one country can veto any Commission initiative. In some cases where QMV operates, the proposal must also be supported by 10 states. Although there has been an extension of the areas in which the Council can act by QMV, there remain important areas where unanimity is required and where one country does have a power of veto; this problem has arisen in the approximation of laws affecting social policy, where the unanimity of the Council continues to be required for measures which have as their object 'the establishment and functioning of the internal market'.[38] By Council Decision 93/731, the public have the right of access to Council documents,[39] subject to art 4(1), by which documents should not be disclosed where this could undermine considerations such as the public interest, personal privacy, commercial and industrial secrecy, and the Community's financial interests.

---

[31] EC Treaty, art 146.
[32] EC Treaty, art 147.
[33] D Curtin (1993) 30 CML Rev 17.
[34] EC Treaty, art 151.
[35] See generally Noel, *Working Together – The Institutions of the European Community*, p 38.
[36] But where majority voting is permitted, this is subject to an agreement (the Luxembourg Accord of 1966) which provides that where 'very important interests of one or more partners are at stake, the Members of the Council will endeavour, within a reasonable time, to reach solutions which can be adopted by all the Members of the Council while respecting their mutual interests and those of the Community'. On this agreement, see M Vasey (1988) 25 CML Rev 725 where it is said that it does not enable a state to 'hold up an unwelcome decision indefinitely or obtain complete satisfaction on specific requests'.
[37] EC Treaty, art 148.
[38] EC Treaty, art 100a(2).
[39] See J Michael [1996] PL 31.

Under art 4(2) disclosure may be refused to protect the confidentiality of Council proceedings, though in this case the Council must 'genuinely balance the interest of citizens in gaining access to its documents against any interest of its own in maintaining the confidentiality of its deliberations'.[40]

European Parliament

1 Composition. The status and powers of the European Parliament have greatly increased since its inception. In 1973 the Parliament was indirectly elected, Britain's delegation including members of both Houses of Parliament. Now it is elected for periods of five years by direct universal suffrage,[41] with the number of representatives elected in each state varying according to the population of the state in question. There are 626 seats in the unicameral Parliament, made up as follows: Austria, 21; Belgium, 25; Denmark, 16; Finland, 16; France, 87; Germany, 99; Greece, 25; Ireland, 15; Italy, 87; Luxembourg, 6; Netherlands, 31; Portugal, 25; Spain, 64; Sweden, 22; and United Kingdom, 87. The EC Treaty emphasises the importance of political parties as a factor for integration within the EU, on the ground that they 'contribute to forming a European awareness and to expressing the political will of the citizens of the Union'.[42] But there are no European political parties as such, though parties in the European Parliament are placed in nine political groupings, of which the Party of European Socialists is by far the largest with 221 members. It is this grouping to which the Labour party belongs along with other socialist and social democratic parties; the Conservative party forms part of the European People's Party (173 members in total); and the Liberal Democrats take part in the European Liberal Democratic and Reformist group (52 members in total). Election procedures are governed by the principles in Directive 93/103/EC regarding the right to vote and the right to stand as a candidate.[43] The directive does not prescribe a mandatory election procedure, and under the European Parliamentary Elections Act 1978 (as amended)[44] the 84 constituencies in Great Britain return members by simple majority vote, while in Northern Ireland (a single constituency) the three members are elected by single transferable vote.

2 Functions. The two most important functions of the European Parliament are its consultation by the Commission on legislative proposals and its powers in relation to the Community budget. So far as the former is concerned, we have seen that the Council is the principal legislative body of the Community; the focus in recent years has been not to substitute the Parliament for the Council but to develop a system which would enable the Parliament to participate in the law-making process.[45] Initially the Parliament enjoyed only a consultative status, and this remains the case in a number of areas. But a failure to consult could nevertheless lead to the annulment of an

---

40   *Case T-194/94, Carvel and Guardian Newspapers v EU Council* [1995] 3 CMLR 359. See
      K A Armstrong (1996) 59 MLR 582.
41   See European Parliamentary Elections Act 1978.
42   EC Treaty, art 138a.
43   See P Oliver (1996) 33 CML Rev 473. See also SI 1994 No 342, making the necessary
      amendments to the 1978 Act.
44   See esp European Parliamentary Elections Act 1993 and SI 1994 No 342.
45   D Curtin (1993) 30 CML Rev 17.

instrument,[46] and the Court of Justice has 'consistently held that the duty to consult the Parliament in the cases provided for by the Treaty includes a requirement that the Parliament be re-consulted on each occasion on which the text finally adopted, viewed as a whole, departs substantially from the text on which the Parliament has already been consulted'.[47] For example, under art 100 the Council acting unanimously on a proposal from the Commission and after consulting the Parliament may issue directives for the approximation of laws relating to the common market. After the amendments at Maastricht in 1992 a new 'negative assent procedure' has been introduced in a number of areas, effectively giving the Parliament a power of veto in a defined number of legislative areas,[48] this complementing earlier initiatives for a cooperation procedure introduced by the Single European Act in 1986.[49] So far as the budget is concerned, this must be adopted by the Parliament which, acting by a majority of its members and two-thirds of the votes cast, is empowered to reject it 'if there are important reasons'.[50] It can adopt amendments or propose modifications which it may ultimately insist on being carried. The Parliament has powers to question and censure the Commission,[51] though it has no power to censure individual Commissioners. It is required to appoint an Ombudsman to investigate maladministration by Community institutions.[52]

The European Court of Justice[53]

1 Composition and jurisdiction.   The function of the Court (ECJ) is to 'ensure that in the interpretation and application of [the] Treaty the law is observed'.[54] It consists of 15 judges who sit in plenary session,[55] and is assisted by eight Advocates-General, an office without parallel in the United Kingdom.[56] Under art 166, the duty of the Advocates-General is to make reasoned submissions on cases brought before the Court in order to assist the Court in the performance of its tasks. These submissions will include an assessment of the legal position in the matter referred for determination, an assessment which will often be endorsed by the Court. The submissions of the Advocates-General are reported along with the judgment of the Court. Both judges and Advocates-General are appointed from amongst people who are eligible for the highest judicial offices in their respective countries, and appointments are made 'by common accord of the Governments of the member states for a

---

[46]   *Case C-21/94, Re Road Taxes: European Parliament v EU Council* [1996] 1 CMLR 94.
[47]   *Case C-417/93, Re: Continuation of the Tacis Programme: European Parliament v EU Council* [1995] 2 CMLR 829, at p 853. See earlier *Case 138/79, S A Roquette Freres v EC Council* [1980] ECR 3333.
[48]   See EC Treaty, art 189b.
[49]   See now EC Treaty, art 189c.
[50]   EC Treaty, art 203(8).
[51]   EC Treaty, arts 140 and 144 respectively.
[52]   EC Treaty, art 138e.
[53]   For the work of the ECJ, see D Edward (1995) 20 EL Rev 539. For its jurisprudential approach, see T Tridimas (1996) 21 EL Rev 199. And see generally, Brown and Kennedy, *The Court of Justice of the European Communities.*
[54]   EC Treaty, art 164.
[55]   EC Treaty, art 165. It may, however, form chambers of 3 to 5 judges to deal with particular categories of case.
[56]   See A Dashwood (1982) 2 LS 202.

term of six years'.[57] Every three years there is a partial replacement of both the judges and the Advocates-General, though retiring judges and Advocates-General are eligible for re-appointment. The judges elect the President of the Court from among their number for a period of three years, a retiring President being eligible for re-election.[58] There is now a Court of First Instance attached to the ECJ to hear and determine a limited class of cases, the aim being to reduce the pressure of work on the ECJ itself, but to which there is a right of appeal on a point of law. The Court of First Instance deals with a 'wide and important' range of matters,[59] such as cases brought by natural or legal persons.[60]

Cases may be brought before the Court in a number of ways. First, as already suggested, proceedings may be brought by the Commission against a member state where it considers that the state has failed to comply with a Treaty obligation.[61] However, if the Commission considers that a member state has failed to fulfil a Treaty obligation, it must first deliver a reasoned opinion on the matter after giving the state concerned an opportunity to submit its observations. It is only if the state does not comply with the opinion that the Commission may bring the matter before the Court.[62] Secondly, one state may initiate proceedings against another where the former considers that the latter has failed to comply with a Treaty obligation.[63] Before doing so the matter must first be referred to the Commission, which will deliver a reasoned opinion in this situation too. Where the ECJ finds that a state has failed to comply with a Treaty obligation, 'the state shall be required to take the necessary measures to comply with the judgment of the Court',[64] and failure to do so could lead to subsequent proceedings before the Court initiated by the Commission with a view to imposing a financial penalty on the state.[65] Apart from actions brought against member states, it is possible for the ECJ 'to review the legality' of measures adopted by the different Community institutions,[66] in proceedings which may be commenced by 'a member state, the Council or the Commission on grounds of lack of competence, infringement of an essential procedural requirement, infringement of [the] Treaty or

---

57   EC Treaty, art 167.
58   Ibid.
59   L Neville Brown (1995) 32 CML Rev 743.
60   See EC Treaty, art 168a.
61   EC Treaty, art 169. Liability under art 169 arises whatever the agency of the state whose action or inaction is the cause of the failure to fulfil its obligations, even in the case of a constitutionally independent institution: *Case 77/69, EC Commission v Belgium* [1970] ECR 237 (difficulty in securing parliamentary approval because Parliament had been dissolved). See A C Evans (1979) 4 EL Rev 442, and A Dashwood and R White (1989) 14 EL Rev 388.
62   See *Case 293/85, EC Commission v Belgium* [1988] ECR 305, and *Case 74/82, EC Commission v Ireland* [1984] ECR 317.
63   See *Case 141/78, France v United Kingdom* [1979] ECR 2923.
64   EC Treaty, art 171(1). In the *Factortame* affair (note 99 below), secondary legislation was introduced to remove the discriminatory effect of the vessel registration scheme as set out in the Merchant Shipping Act 1988.
65   EC Treaty, art 171(2).
66   On the scope of reviewable acts, see *Case 22/70, EC Commission v EC Council* [1971] ECR 263, and *Case 34/86, EC Council v Parliament* [1986] ECR 2155. Cf *Cases C-181 and 248/91, Parliament v EC Council and Commission* [1993] ECR I–3685.

of any rule of law relating to its application, or misuse of powers'.[67] In the highly publicised *Case C-84/94, UK v EU Council*[68] the British government unsuccessfully argued that the Working Time Directive (93/104/EC) exceeded the power under art 118a to make by way of qualified majority measures designed to encourage improvements, especially in the working environment, as regards the health and safety of workers. If the action under art 173 is well founded the Court shall declare the act concerned to be void.[69]

2 Article 177. Apart from proceedings brought against member states or Community institutions, the Court also has jurisdiction under art 177 to give preliminary rulings concerning the interpretation of the Treaty, the validity and interpretation of acts of the institutions (and of the European Central Bank), as well as other matters.[70] A preliminary ruling may be sought by a national court or tribunal where the court or tribunal 'considers that a decision on the question is necessary to enable it to give judgment'.[71] In the case of a court or tribunal 'against whose decisions there is no judicial remedy under national law', the court or tribunal must bring before the ECJ for a ruling any question on a matter which is necessary for it to give judgment.[72] Where a ruling is sought, it is done on the basis of specific questions, the role of the ECJ being to answer these questions: it does not resolve the dispute between the parties, it being for the national court to apply the ruling to the facts of the case before it. Indeed, the Court 'has consistently held that under art 177 it has no jurisdiction to rule on the compatibility of national measures with Community law'.[73] Similarly, a national court or tribunal is not empowered to refer a matter unless it is pending before the court.[74] This means that the national case must be adjourned pending the ruling of the Court.

The leading case in English law on art 177 references is still *Bulmer Ltd v Bollinger SA*[75] in which Lord Denning gave detailed guidance first on when 'a decision on the question is necessary to enable it to give judgment', and secondly when in such a case the court should exercise its discretion to make

---

[67] EC Treaty, art 173. This includes a power to review acts of the Parliament. See *Case 294/83, Les Verts v Parliament* [1986] ECR 1339. Art 173 also provides that actions may be brought by the Parliament to protect its prerogatives, and in some cases also by natural or legal persons in respect of decisions addressed to or of concern to them.

[68] [1996] 3 CMLR 671.

[69] EC Treaty, art 175.

[70] EC Treaty, art 177(1).

[71] EC Treaty, art 177(2).

[72] EC Treaty, art 177(3). This would apply to the House of Lords (but see *R v Employment Secretary, ex p EOC* [1995] 1 AC 1), and possibly also to bodies whose decisions are protected by a privative clause.

[73] *Case C-458/93, Saddik* [1995] 3 CMLR 318.

[74] *Cases C-422-424/93, Zabala Erasun v Instituto Nacional de Empleo* [1995] All ER (EC) 758 (matter resolved by Spanish government amending the law to comply with a contested Council regulation).

[75] [1974] 1 Ch 401. See J D B Mitchell (1974) 11 CML Rev 351.

a reference.[76] As to the former, (i) the point must be conclusive of the case;[77] (ii) substantially the same point has not already been decided by the ECJ, unless there are reasons to believe that an earlier decision of the ECJ is wrong;[78] and (iii) if the point is reasonably clear or free from doubt (acte claire) there is no need to interpret the Treaty, but to apply it, and that is a task for the English court.[79] Lord Denning said that a reference should not be made until all the facts were determined, because it is only at that stage that it is possible to say whether it is necessary to resolve the matter. But even if a point of EC law is necessary to dispose of the case, there is no obligation to make a reference: 'the English court has a discretion either to decide the point itself or to refer it to the European court'.[80] In exercising that discretion it is to have regard to a number of factors, including (i) the length of time it may take to get a ruling, particularly where there is reason for expedition; (ii) the importance of not overwhelming or overloading the ECJ; (iii) the difficulty and importance of the point; (iv) the expense to the parties of getting a ruling from the ECJ; and (v) the wishes of the parties, particularly if one of the parties is resisting the making of a reference, in view of the expense and delay.

B.   EC law

The unique qualities of Community law were addressed by the ECJ in several ground-breaking early decisions, including *Case 26/62, Van Gend en Loos v Nederlandse Administratie der Belastingen*,[81] in which it was noted that the EEC Treaty 'is more than an agreement which merely creates mutual obligations between the contracting states'. The point was reinforced forcefully in *Case 6/64, Costa v ENEL*,[82] a case concerning the nationalisation of the Italian electricity industry, in which the Court asserted:

By contrast with ordinary international treaties, the EEC Treaty has created its own legal system which, on the entry into force of the Treaty, became an integral part of the legal systems of the member states and which their courts are bound to apply. By creating a Community of unlimited duration, having its own institutions, its own

---

[76]   These guidelines have been followed by the Scottish courts. See *Wither v Cowie*, 1990 SCCR 741. They continue to be applied by the English courts. See *Customs and Excise Commissioners v ALCS Samex* [1983] 1 All ER 1042, *R v Stock Exchange, ex p Else* [1993] QB 534, *BLP Group v Customs and Excise Commissioners* [1994] STC 41, and *Chiron Corp v Murex Diagnostics (No 8)* [1995] FSR 309.

[77]   See *Van Duyn v Home Office* [1974] 3 All ER 178, 186 (reference made because 'it would be quite impossible to give judgment without such a decision'). Also *Case C 169/91, Stoke-on-Trent City Council v B&Q plc* [1993] AC 900.

[78]   A reference may be particularly important where there is an existing decision but where the area in question is dynamic and fast-moving. See *Case C-13/95, Süzen v Zehnacker Gebäudereinigung GmbH Frankenhausservice* [1997] 1 CMLR 768.

[79]   Even though a matter is not acte claire, a reference may still be refused, for example where an appeal is likely. In such a case the House of Lords may decide that the matter is acte claire or that a reference should be made. See *R v Employment Secretary, ex p Seymour-Smith* [1995] IRLR 448.

[80]   *Bulmer Ltd v Bollinger SA* [1974] 1 Ch 401, at p 423.

[81]   [1963] ECR I.

[82]   [1964] ECR 1141.

personality, its own legal capacity and capacity of representation on the international plane and, more particularly, real powers stemming from a limitation of sovereignty or a transfer of powers from the states to the Community, the member states have limited their sovereign rights, albeit within limited fields, and have thus created a body of law which binds both their nationals and themselves.[83]

Various principles underpin the Community legal system. The first is the principle of legality, namely that the Community 'shall act within the limits of the powers conferred upon it' by the Treaty;[84] the second is the principle of subsidiarity, whereby, in areas falling within its exclusive competence, the Community shall take action 'only if and in so far' as its objectives 'cannot be sufficiently achieved by the member states';[85] the third is what has been referred to as the principle of solidarity,[86] whereby member states shall take all appropriate measures 'to ensure fulfilment of the obligations arising out of [the] Treaty';[87] and the fourth is the principle of non-discrimination, prohibiting discrimination on the ground of nationality.[88] In addition to these principles to be found in the Treaty, the ECJ has developed principles (such as legal certainty, proportionality, equal treatment, and the protection of human rights)[89] which it employs in determining points of Community law.[90]

The supremacy of Community law

1 The general principle. Within the Community legal order, EC law takes priority over national law. In *Case 6/64, Costa v ENEL,*[91] Mr Costa claimed that he was not obliged to pay for electricity supplied to him by ENEL on the ground that the supplier was an entity which had been nationalised in 1962 in breach of provisions of the EEC Treaty. The Italian court (the Giudice Conciliatore of Milan) referred to the ECJ for consideration whether Italian law violated the Treaty in the manner suggested, only to be faced with the argument by the Italian government that the reference was 'absolutely inadmissible' inasmuch as 'a national court which is obliged to apply a national law cannot avail itself of art 177'. In rejecting this argument, the ECJ held:

The integration into the laws of each member state of provisions which derive from the Community, and more generally the terms and the spirit of the Treaty, make it impossible for the states, as a corollary, to accord precedence to a unilateral and subsequent measure over a legal system accepted by them on a basis of reciprocity. Such a measure cannot therefore be inconsistent with that legal system. The executive force of Community law cannot vary from one state to another in deference to subsequent domestic laws, without jeopardising the attainment of the objectives of the Treaty.[92]

---

83   Ibid, p 593.
84   EC Treaty, art 3b.
85   Ibid. See A Toth (1992) 29 CMLR 1079.
86   See S Weatherill, *Law and Integration in the European Union*, pp 45–9.
87   EC Treaty, art 5.
88   EC Treaty, art 6.
89   See eg *Case C-331/88, Fedesa* [1990] ECR I–4023. And ch 19 below.
90   See Craig and de Burca, op cit, chs 7 and 8. See also E Szyszczak (1996) 21 EL Rev 351 on the effective protection of rights as an essential principle of Community law.
91   [1964] ECR 585.
92   Ibid, pp 593–4.

The ECJ further asserted that 'the laws stemming from the Treaty, an independent source of law, could not, because of its special and original nature, be overidden by domestic legal provisions, however framed, without being deprived of its character as Community law, and without the legal basis of the Community itself being called into question'.[93]

This case thus unequivocally declares the supremacy of Community law over inconsistent domestic law, including in particular domestic law introduced after accession.[94] Community law also takes priority over inconsistent provisions of national constitutional law. The leading case, *Case 11/70, Internationale Handelsgesellschaft v Einfuhr-und Vorratsstelle für Getreide und Futtermittel*,[95] was concerned with regulations which required applicants for export and import licences to pay a deposit which was forfeited if terms of the licence were violated. The German authorities were of the view that the system of licences violated certain principles of German constitutional law 'which must be protected within the framework of the German Basic Law'. But the ECJ disagreed and held:

Recourse to the legal rules or concepts of national law in order to judge the validity of measures adopted by the institutions of the Community would have an adverse effect on the uniformity and efficacy of Community law. The validity of such measures can only be judged in the light of Community law. In fact, the law stemming from the Treaty, an independent source of law, cannot because of its very nature be overridden by rules of national law, however framed, without being deprived of its character as Community law and without the legal basis of the Community itself being called into question.[96]

Further, 'the validity of a Community measure or its effect within a member state cannot be affected by allegations that it runs counter to either fundamental rights as formulated by the constitution of that state or the principles of a national constitutional structure'.[97] Although Community law thus prevails over even fundamental rights guaranteed by national constitutions, the ECJ did, nevertheless, hold that 'respect for fundamental rights forms an integral part of the general principles of law protected by the Court of Justice' and that 'protection of such rights, whilst inspired by the constitutional traditions common to the member states, must be ensured within the framework of the structure and objectives of the Community'.[98] On the facts it was held that the system of licences in question did not violate any such rights.

2 EC law and the United Kingdom.   The implications of this for the United Kingdom were revealed by the *Factortame* series of cases in which the company challenged the Merchant Shipping Act 1988 and regulations made there-

---

93   Ibid, p 594.
94   See also *Case 106/77, Amministrazione delle Finanze dello Stato v Simmenthal Sp A* [1978] ECR 629.
95   [1970] ECR 1125.
96   Ibid, p 1134.
97   See also *Case 44/79, Hauer v Land Rheinland-Pfalz* [1980] 3 CMLR 42.
98   [1970] ECR 1125, 1134.

under on the ground that they violated provisions of the EEC Treaty, including arts 7 and 52.[99] The Act had been introduced to prevent what was called 'quota hopping' and amended the rules relating to the licensing of fishing vessels by providing that only British-owned vessels could be registered, a requirement which excluded the Spanish-owned vessels of the applicants. In judicial review proceedings in *Factortame (No 1)* the Divisional Court made a reference under art 177 for a preliminary ruling on the issues of Community law raised by the proceedings, and ordered by way of interim relief that the application of the 1988 Act should be suspended as regards the applicants. This latter order was set aside by the Court of Appeal on the ground that the court had no power to suspend the application of an Act, since 'it is fundamental to our (unwritten) constitution that it is for Parliament to legislate and for the judiciary to interpret and apply the fruits of Parliament's labours'.[100] By the time the case reached the House of Lords, however, the question of parliamentary sovereignty had been diluted, though not completely displaced. Lord Bridge said:

If the applicants fail to establish the rights they claim before the ECJ, the effect of the interim relief granted would be to have conferred upon them rights directly contrary to Parliament's sovereign will and correspondingly to have deprived British fishing vessels, as defined by Parliament, of the enjoyment of a substantial proportion of the United Kingdom quota of stocks of fish protected by the common fisheries policy. I am clearly of the opinion that, as a matter of English law, the court has no power to make an order which has these consequences.[101]

It was also held that under English law it was not possible (at that time) to grant an interlocutory injunction against the Crown.

In the view of the ECJ, 'the full effectiveness' of Community law would be impaired 'if a rule of national law could prevent a court seised of a dispute governed by Community law from granting interim relief in order to ensure the full effectiveness of the judgment to be given on the existence of the rights claimed under community law'. It therefore followed that 'a court which in those circumstances would grant interim relief, if it were not for a rule of national law, is obliged to set aside that rule'. As a result EC law must take priority over domestic legislation, even if this means that the British courts are required to set aside a fundamental constitutional principle. However, there is nothing novel about such a conclusion, the ECJ holding on a number of occasions that the supremacy of Community law applies even in respect of provisions of national constitutional law. The position was reinforced by *Factortame (No 4)* which was concerned with whether the government was liable to the plaintiffs in damages for loss suffered as a result of the

[99] For the *Factortame* litigation, see *R v Transport Secretary, ex p Factortame Ltd (No 1)* [1989] 2 CMLR 353 (CA), [1990] 2 AC 85 (HL); *Case C 213/89, R v Transport Secretary, ex p Factortame Ltd (No 2)* [1991] AC 603 (ECJ and HL); *Case C-221/89, R v Transport Secretary, ex p Factortame Ltd (No 3)* [1992] QB 680 (ECJ); *Case C-48/93, R v Transport Secretary, ex p Factortame Ltd (No 4)* [1996] QB 404 (ECJ). For proceedings by the Commission under art 169 see *Case C-246/89, Commission v UK* [1991] ECR I–4585. For the sequel, see Merchant Shipping Act 1988 (Amendment) Order 1989, SI 1989 No 2006.

[100] [1989] 2 CMLR 353, 397 (Lord Donaldson MR).

[101] [1990] 2 AC 85, 143.

legislation.[102] It had already been held that failure to implement a directive could in some circumstances give rise to liability in damages on the part of a state to a citizen who suffered loss as a result.[103] In *Factortame (No 4)*, the ECJ held:

> The fact that, according to national rules, the breach complained of is attributable to the legislature cannot affect the requirements, inherent in the protection of the rights of individuals who rely on Community law and, in this instance, the right to obtain redress in the national courts for damages caused by the breach.[104]

So not only may an Act of Parliament be 'disapplied'; the courts may also be called upon to make an award of damages for losses suffered as a result of its terms where the conditions for state liability are met. It has been suggested that damages might best be based on principles analogous to breach of statutory duty.[105]

The sources of EC law

1 EC Treaty.   EC law takes a number of different forms. The highest form of law is the Treaty itself which not only sets out the constitution of the EC, but also deals with substantive matters, some of which give rise to rights which are directly effective in national courts. *Case 26/62, Van Gend en Loos v Nederlandse Administratie der Belastingen*[106] was concerned with the interpretation of art 12 of the EEC Treaty, this requiring member states to refrain from introducing between themselves new customs duties, or increasing those already in force, in trade with each other. The question referred by the Dutch tribunal to the ECJ was whether art 12 had direct effect in the domestic courts 'in the sense that nationals of member states may on the basis of [the] article lay claim to rights which the national court must protect'. The ECJ held:

> Independently of the legislation of member states, Community law ... not only imposes obligations on individuals but is also intended to confer upon them rights which become part of their legal heritage. These rights arise not only where they are expressly granted by the Treaty, but also by reason of obligations which the Treaty imposes in a clearly defined way upon individuals as well as upon the member states and upon the institutions of the Community.[107]

But not all terms of the Treaty will have direct effect in the sense that they will be enforceable by individuals in their own national courts.[108] Much will depend on the nature of the Treaty provision in question, it being stated in

---

102   [1996] QB 404. Although the government moved quickly to repair the legislation, losses were sustained from the time the 1988 Act came into force (31 March 1989) until the offending discrimination was removed (2 November 1989).

103   *Cases C-6&9/90, Francovich and Bonifaci v Italy* [1991] ECR I-5357. See below, pp 147–8.

104   [1996] QB 404, 497.

105   See T St J N Bates (1996) 17 Stat Law Rev 27 and N Gravells [1996] PL 567. Cf *Garden Cottage Foods v Milk Marketing Board* [1984] AC 130. Compare *Bourgoin SA v MAFF* [1986] QB 716. But see now *Kirklees Borough Council v Wickes Building Supplies* [1992] 2 CMLR 765.

106   [1963] ECR 1.

107   Ibid, p 12.

108   See eg *R v Home Secretary, ex p Flynn* [1995] 3 CMLR 397 (EC Treaty, art 7a held not to have direct effect).

Van Gend en Loos that art 12 contained 'a clear and unconditional prohibition' which was unqualified 'by any reservation on the part of states which would make its implementation conditional upon a positive legislative measure enacted under national law'.[109] This made it 'ideally adapted to produce direct effects in the legal relationship between member states and their subjects'.

Amongst the cases in which the ECJ has held that Treaty provisions have direct effect, *Case 43/75, Defrenne v Sabena*,[110] was concerned with art 119, which provides that 'each member state shall during the first stage ensure and subsequently maintain the application of the principle that men and women should receive equal pay for equal work'. The article was said to promote a double aim, one economic and the other social, the former seeking to eliminate unfair competition and the latter furthering social objectives of the Community 'which is not merely an economic union, but is at the same time intended, by common action, to ensure social progress and seek the constant improvement of living and working conditions'.[111] The principle of equal pay formed part of 'the foundations of the Community' and art 119 was held to have direct effect even though its complete implementation 'may in certain cases involve the elaboration of criteria whose implementation necessitates the taking of appropriate measures at Community and national level'. There were, however, forms of pay discrimination which could be addressed by a court, and it was appropriate at least in those circumstances for art 119 to have direct effect. Even though its full implementation of art 119 would require legislation, the ECJ held that direct effect would apply in particular to 'those types of discrimination arising directly from legislative provisions or collective labour agreements, as well as in cases where men and women receive unequal pay for equal work which is carried out in the same establishment or service, whether private or public'. In an important qualification of its decision, however, the ECJ ruled that the effect of the decision would not in the circumstances of the case be retrospective in the sense that it could not be relied upon to permit claims concerning pay periods prior to the date of the judgment.[112]

2 Community legislation. The Treaty also confers law-making powers on the Community institutions, these taking a number of different forms. By art 189 'the European Parliament, acting jointly with the Council, the Council and the Commission' are empowered to 'make regulations and issue directives, take decisions, make recommendations or deliver opinions'. These different measures have different legal consequences. Thus regulations have 'general application' in the sense that they are binding in their entirety and directly applicable in all member states. Like terms of the Treaty, regulations may have direct effect, a point established in *Case 93/71, Leonesio v Italian Ministry of Agri-*

---

[109]   [1963] ECR 1, p 13.
[110]   [1976] ECR 455.
[111]   Ibid, p 472.
[112]   See also on the temporal effect of art 119, *Case C-262/88, Barber v Guardian Royal Exchange Assurance Group* [1990] ECR I–1889. See too TEU, Protocol 2 (Protocol concerning art 119 of the Treaty establishing the European Community).

culture[113] which was concerned with regulation 2195/69/EEC providing a subsidy for those who slaughtered milk cows. The question for the ECJ was whether the regulation conferred on farmers a right to payment of the subsidy enforceable in national courts. In holding that it did, the Court held that, as a general principle 'because of its nature and its purpose within the system of sources of Community law', a regulation 'has direct effect and is, as such, capable of creating individual rights which national courts must protect'. It was no excuse in this case that the national Parliament had not allocated the necessary funds to meet the costs of the subsidy, for to hold otherwise would have the effect of placing Italian farmers in a less favourable position than their counterparts elsewhere 'in disregard of the fundamental rule requiring the uniform application of regulations throughout the Community'.[114] Directives generally require implementing legislation in each member state before they give rise to enforceable obligations, the EC Treaty providing that they are binding 'as to the result to be achieved', the national authorities being left 'the choice of form and methods'.[115] Decisions are binding in their entirety on those to whom they are addressed, while recommendations and opinions have no binding force.[116]

Directives also may have direct effect, the point having been established in *Case 41/74, Van Duyn v Home Office* where the ECJ said that it would be 'incompatible with the binding effect attributed to a directive by art 189 to exclude, in principle, the possibility that the obligation which it imposes may be invoked by those concerned'.[117] The jurisprudence has developed considerably since then so that 'a member state which has not adopted the implementing measures required by [a] directive in the prescribed periods may not rely, as against individuals, on its own failure to perform the obligations which the directive entails'.[118] Another line of authority concludes that 'wherever the provisions of a directive appear, as far as their subject-matter is concerned, to be unconditional and sufficiently precise, those provisions may be relied upon by an individual against the state where that state fails to implement the directive in national law by the end of the prescribed period or where it fails to implement the directive correctly'.[119] In *Case 152/84, Marshall v Southampton and South West Hampshire AHA*,[120] it was held that art 5(1) of the Equal Treatment Directive (76/207/EEC) was directly effective, thereby allowing a woman (who had been dismissed at the age of 62 in circumstances where men would not have been dismissed until the age of 65) to bring proceedings in domestic law for sex discrimination on an issue to which domestic legislation did not then apply. It was held,

---

113   [1972] ECR 287.
114   See also *Case 128/78, Re Tachographs: Commission v United Kingdom* [1979] 2 CMLR 45.
115   On the changing nature of the content of directives, see T St J N Bates (1996) 17 Stat Law Rev 27.
116   On decisions, see R Greaves (1996) 21 EL Rev 3.
117   [1974] ECR 1337.
118   *Case 148/78, Pubblico Ministero v Ratti* [1979] ECR 1629.
119   *Case 8/81, Becker v Finanzamt Münster-Innenstadt* [1982] ECR 53.
120   [1986] ECR 723. See A Arnull [1987] PL 383. See also *Case C-91/92, Faccini Dori v Recreb Srl* [1995] 1 CMLR 665; and see J Coppel (1994) 57 MLR 859.

however, that unlike art 119 of the Treaty, directives have only 'vertical' rather than 'horizontal' direct effect, which means that they can be enforced in national courts only against public authorities and not against individuals.[121] On the other hand, a directive may be relied upon against the state 'regardless of the capacity in which the latter is acting, whether employer or public authority'.[122]

3 State liability. Community law may be enforced in a number of ways. We have seen that enforcement proceedings may be brought against a member state by the Commission or by another state. Such proceedings could have the effect of requiring the state in question to legislate to give full effect to Community obligations. We have also seen that many provisions of Community law may have direct effect in domestic courts, though this is not true of all Community law. But where it does apply, direct effect may enable an individual to seek a remedy under Community law where none is presently provided by domestic law. A third way by which Community law may be enforced is by an action for damages for failure to implement a directive. This was established in *Cases C-6/90 and 9/90, Francovich and Bonifaci v Italy*[123] which were concerned with whether the applicants were entitled to compensation from the Italian government for its failure to implement Directive 80/987/EEC on the protection of employees in the event of insolvency by their employer. On a reference under art 177, the ECJ held:

> The full effectiveness of Community rules would be impaired and the protection of the rights which they grant would be weakened if individuals were unable to obtain redress when their rights are infringed by a breach of Community law for which a member state can be held responsible.[124]

The principle whereby a state must be liable for loss and damage caused to individuals as a result of breaches of Community law for which the state can be held responsible was stated to be 'inherent in the system of the Treaty'. But it is not every breach of a directive which will give rise to state liability. The ECJ prescribed three conditions as a pre-condition of liability:

> The first ... is that the result prescribed by the directive should entail the grant of rights to individuals. The second condition is that it should be possible to identify the content of those rights on the basis of the provisions of the directive. Finally, the third condition is the existence of a causal link between the breach of the state's obligation and the loss and damage suffered by the injured parties.[125]

In this case it was held that Italy was required to make good the loss and damage caused by the failure properly to implement the directive.

---

[121] The Area Health Authority was a public authority for this purpose. See further *Case C-222/84, Johnston v Chief Constable of the RUC* [1987] QB 129 (police authority); *Case 188/89, Foster v British Gas* [1991] 2 AC 306 (nationalised industry); and *Griffin v South West Water* [1995] IRLR 15 (privatised water company). See ch 14.

[122] *Marshall*, above, at p 749.

[123] [1991] ECR I–5357. See G Bebr (1992) 29 CML Rev, P P Craig (1993) 109 LQR 595, C Lewis and S Moore [1993] PL 157, M Ross (1993) 56 MLR 55, and J Steiner (1993) 18 E L Rev 3.

[124] *Francovich*, above, at p 5414.

[125] Ibid, at p 5415.

This is an important decision, for a number of reasons,[126] not the least of which is that it goes some way towards filling the gap left by the rule that directives do not have horizontal direct effect. For although a directive cannot be enforced against a private party, it could be enforced by way of 'a right of reparation' against the state in respect of losses suffered by the failure of the private party to comply with it, even though he or she may not be required to apply it in domestic law, and may indeed be prohibited from doing so by inconsistent national law.[127] The *Francovich* principle was developed further in *Factortame (No 4)*, where it was held that it may apply also in respect of obligations which have direct effect: according to the ECJ 'the right to reparation is the necessary corollary of the direct effect of the Community provision whose breach caused the damage sustained'.[128] As we have seen, it was also held that a state may be liable for the action (as well as the inaction) of its legislature. In these circumstances:

> where a breach of Community law by a member state is attributable to the national legislature acting in a field in which it has a wide discretion to make legislative choices, individuals suffering loss or injury thereby are entitled to reparation where the rule of Community law breached is intended to confer rights on them, the breach is sufficiently serious and there is a direct causal link between the breach and the damage sustained by the individuals.[129]

The state is required to make good the loss suffered by the individual 'in accordance with its national law on liability', though it is for the domestic law of each state to set the criteria for determining the extent of reparation. However, it is not possible to exclude damages for loss of profit, and it ought to be possible to award specific damages such as exemplary damages in claims founded on Community law where these may be awarded in proceedings founded on domestic law.

C.   EC law and British constitutional law[130]

We have seen so far that the EC Treaty has created a new legal order, that the ECJ has asserted the supremacy of EC law over national law, and that EC law may have direct effect in national legal systems. In each of these respects EC law presents a challenge to traditional English (though perhaps not Scottish) constitutional law, in so far as this is deeply rooted in parliamentary supremacy and in the obligation of the courts to give effect to legislation

---

[126]   For parallel developments in constitutional law, see *Simpson v A-G* [1994] 3 NZLR 667. Compare *Maharaj v A-G of Trinidad and Tobago (No 2)* [1979] AC 385.

[127]   However, such actions must be brought in the High Court and not (as in the case of Directive 80/987/EEC, the subject of the *Francovich* ruling) in an industrial tribunal. *Employment Secretary v Mann* [1996] IRLR 4. It has also been said that the A-G is the appropriate defendant in such cases: *EOC case*, note 72 above, at p 32 (Lord Keith).

[128]   [1996] QB 404, 497.

[129]   Ibid, at p 506. Note the requirement that the member state concerned 'manifestly and gravely disregarded the limits on its discretion' (p. 499). For what constitutes a 'serious' breach, see p 500. And see *Case C-392/93, R v HM Treasury, ex p BT plc* [1996] 2 CMLR 217, 244–5, where a certain reluctance in imposing liability in respect of legislation can be detected.

[130]   See A W Bradley, in Jowell and Oliver (eds), *The Changing Constitution*, ch 4.

passed by Parliament. Britain is not alone in experiencing difficulties in reconciling Community law with the principles of national constitutional law.[131] But the question of legislative supremacy is not the only potential flashpoint, with the courts being presented with difficulties of a more practical nature which some see as a challenge to their authority. Apart from the differences of style in the drafting of English and Community law,[132] there is the more serious point that British judges must determine questions of Community law in accordance with the principles laid down by and in accordance with any relevant decisions of the European Court of Justice.[133] Before considering the response of the courts, it is necessary to consider in some detail the constitutional issues presented by Community membership.

The constitutional implications of UK membership of the EC

The constitutional implications of EC membership were canvassed in a white paper published by the Labour government in 1967 which formed an important basis for the European Communities Act 1972.[134] It was pointed out that complex legislation would need to be introduced to implement measures which did not have direct effect, and that further legislation would be needed to give effect to subsequent Community instruments. Legislation would also be required in the case of those provisions of Community law which are 'intended to take direct internal effect within the member states':

This legislation would be needed, because, under our constitutional law, adherence to a treaty does not of itself have the effect of changing our internal law even where provisions of the treaty are intended to have direct internal effect as law within the participating states.[135]

The white paper further pointed out that 'the legislation would have to cover both provisions in force when we joined and those coming into force subsequently as a result of instruments issued by the Community institutions'. Although 'no new problem would be created by the provisions which were in force at the time we became a member of the Communities', a constitutional innovation would lie 'in the acceptance in advance as part of the law of the United Kingdom of provisions to be made in the future by instruments issued by the Community institutions – a situation for which there is no precedent in this country'. These instruments were said like ordinary delegated legislation to 'derive their force under the law of the United Kingdom from the original enactment passed by Parliament'.[136]

Quite whether this constitutional innovation could be successfully implemented is a question which was not resolved before the introduction of the 1972 Act. The 1967 white paper noted:

---

[131] In particular, for Germany, see V Everling (1994) 14 YBEL 1, N Foster [1994] PL 392, and M Zuleeg (1997) 22 EL Rev 19; for Ireland, see Kelly, *The Irish Constitution*, p 287, and B Wilkinson [1992] PL 20. See also ch 19 below.

[132] See *Bulmer v Bollinger SA* [1974] Ch 401, 425.

[133] European Communities Act 1972, s 3.

[134] Cmnd 3301, 1967.

[135] Para 22.

[136] Ibid. Today this analogy is seen to be badly misconceived. Ordinarily, delegated legislation (see ch 27) does not give rise to an autonomous body of law claiming supremacy over the source of its legal authority in domestic law.

The Community law having direct internal effect is designed to take precedence over the domestic law of the member states. From this it follows that the legislation of the Parliament of the United Kingdom giving effect to that law would have to do so in such a way as to override existing national law so far as inconsistent with it.[137]

But this merely rehearses rather than resolves the question: what happens if Parliament should legislate in a manner inconsistent with the directly effective terms of the Treaty? The answer it seems is that 'within the fields occupied by Community law Parliament would have to refrain from passing fresh legislation inconsistent with that law as for the time being in force', though this 'would not however involve any constitutional innovation', for 'many of our treaty obligations already impose such restraints – for example, the Charter of the United Nations, the European Convention on Human Rights and GATT'.[138] But this did not provide an answer either: what would be the position of a post-accession statute which is incompatible with a subsequently introduced regulation having direct effect, or a statute introduced to comply with the Treaty the terms of which are expanded in a novel and unpredictable way by the ECJ? In this context, the examples of the UN Charter or the ECHR are beside the point, for unlike the EC Treaty these provisions do not seek to create directly effective obligations but rely on implementing legislation for any obligations they generate.

The European Communities Act 1972

Britain's application for membership was made in 1967. The Treaty of Accession was signed on 22 January 1972 and was implemented by the European Communities Act 1972.[139] This deals with two central questions which were said to be 'fundamental to the structure and contents' of the Act,[140] the first being those provisions intended to embody in domestic law the provisions of Community law designed to have direct effect, and the second being the provisions which did not have direct effect but where action was necessary for their implementation. So far as the former is concerned, s 2(1) of the 1972 Act, said to be 'at the heart of the Bill',[141] provides:

All such rights, powers, liabilities, obligations and restrictions from time to time created or arising by or under the Treaties, and all such remedies and procedures from time to time provided for by or under the Treaties, as in accordance with the Treaties are without further enactment to be given legal effect or used in the United Kingdom shall be recognised and available in law, and be enforced, allowed and followed accordingly.

What this does is to provide that in so far as Community law has direct effect, it shall be enforceable in the UK courts. It is also designed to ensure that directly effective Community obligations take precedence over national law.

---

[137]   Para 23.
[138]   Ibid.
[139]   As amended by the European Communities (Amendment) Act 1986, and the European Communities (Amendment) Act 1993. Also important is the European Parliamentary Elections Act 1978, esp s 6. On the interaction of these measures, see *R v Foreign Secretary, ex p Rees-Mogg* [1994] QB 552.
[140]   HC Deb, 15 February 1972, col 271.
[141]   Ibid, col 650.

But it does not address the question of what should happen where there is a statute which is inconsistent with directly effective Community obligations. This, however, is addressed by s 2(4) which provides (*inter alia*):

any enactment passed or to be passed [ie by the Westminster Parliament], other than one contained in this part of this Act, shall be construed and have effect subject to the foregoing provisions of this section.

Together with s 2(1), this is expressly designed to mean that 'the directly applicable provisions ought to prevail over future Acts of Parliament in so far as they might be inconsistent with them'.[142] As such, s 2 is an attempt by one Parliament to fetter the continuing supremacy of Parliament by providing that, while future Parliaments may legislate in breach of Community law, the courts must (to the extent of any inconsistency) deny it any effect.[143]

The provisions of Community law which do not have direct effect were addressed in two ways by the 1972 Act. The first was by making a number of amendments to existing legislation to bring it into line with Community law; and the second was by introducing a general power to make subordinate legislation to cover future as well as some present Community instruments. Although there was concern about the new power to make subordinate legislation, the government did not expect the power to be frequently used,[144] an expectation which was clearly unfulfilled. By s 2(2) of the 1972 Act, regulations may be introduced by a designated minister for the purpose of implementing any Community obligation. This is subject to Sched 2 which provides that regulations may not be used for a number of purposes, these being (i) an imposition of or increase in taxation; (ii) a provision having retrospective effect; (iii) a power delegating legislative authority; and (iv) a measure creating a new criminal offence punishable with imprisonment for more than two years, or on summary conviction with imprisonment for more than three months, or with a fine of more than level 5 on the standard scale.[145] The power to make regulations under these provisions is exercisable by statutory instrument which, if not made following a draft being approved by resolution of each House of Parliament, is subject to annulment by either House.[146] Fresh obligations under Community law continue to be implemented by both primary and secondary legislation.[147] The power to make subordinate legislation has been widely construed to permit the procedure to be used to reduce rights from the level enacted initially by primary legislation where these exceeded the obligations imposed by Community law.[148]

Parliamentary scrutiny of EC legislation

In addition to the need to give effect to Community law, there was also a need to put in place procedures for ensuring the accountability of ministers who

---

[142]   Ibid, col 278.
[143]   See S A de Smith (1971) 34 MLR 597, H W R Wade (1972) 88 LQR 1, J D B Mitchell et al (1972) 9 CML Rev 134, F A Trindade (1972) 35 MLR 375, G Winterton (1976) 92 LQR 591.
[144]   HC Deb, 15 February 1972, col 282.
[145]   If the fine is calculated on a daily basis, not more than £100 per day.
[146]   For parliamentary scrutiny of delegated legislation, see ch 27.
[147]   See eg Trade Union Reform and Employment Rights Act 1993, and SI 1995 No 2587.
[148]   See *R v Trade and Industry Secretary, ex p UNISON* [1997] 1 CMLR 459.

were engaged in the making of new Community law, in particular where the Community instruments would have direct effect without the need for implementing legislation or other intervention by Parliament. The government expressed the view that 'Parliament should be informed about and have an opportunity to consider at the formative stage those Community instruments which, when made by the Council, will be binding in this country'.[149] Traditional parliamentary procedures, such as questions, adjournment debates and supply days, would continue to apply, and an undertaking was given that 'No Government would proceed on a matter of major policy in the Council unless they knew that they had the approval of the House'.[150]

Nevertheless, the government expressed the view that the traditional means of parliamentary accountability needed to be strengthened, and that 'special arrangements' should be made under which the House would be 'apprised of draft regulations and directives before they go to the Council of Ministers for decision'.[151] In 1974, special committees were set up by both Houses of Parliament, the Select Committee on European Legislation in the case of the Commons and the Select Committee on the European Communities in the case of the Lords. The Commons committee is empowered to consider European Community documents (a term defined to include proposed legislation) and to report its opinion on the legal and political implications (but not on the merits) of each.[152] The Lords Committee in contrast considers Community proposals and reports on those which raise important questions of policy or principle and on other questions to which the Committee thinks the attention of the House should be drawn. The Lords Committee has the power to appoint sub-committees, of which there are in fact five. Debates on matters identified by the Commons Scrutiny Committee now take place in one of two European Standing Committees which were established in 1991.[153]

The impact which these procedures have in the process of Community law-making is difficult to assess, though they no doubt ensure that at least some parliamentarians are well informed about European issues.[154] But in no sense do they provide effective scrutiny of EC legislation, as the Commons Procedure Committee pointed out as long ago as 1978:

the ability of the House to influence the legislative decisions of the Communities is inhibited by practical as well as legal and procedural obstacles. The practical obstacles stem from the sheer volume of EEC legislation, the complexity of the Communities' own decision-making structure, and the very limited time available for the consideration of many of the proposals, including some of the most important. The legal and

---

[149]   HC Deb, 15 February 1972, col 274.
[150]   Ibid.
[151]   Ibid, col 275.
[152]   It has 16 members and was chaired by a Labour back-bencher in 1996–97.
[153]   See HC Deb, 24 October 1990, col 399. Committee A deals with agriculture, fisheries and food, environment, and forestry; Committee B deals with trade and industry, and transport. See generally T St J N Bates (1991) 12 Stat Law Rev 109, and P Birkinshaw and D Ashiagbor (1996) 33 CML Rev 499. On the House of Lords see E Denza (1993) 14 Stat Law Rev 56.
[154]   It has been said that 'the nature of the Community is such that it is inherently difficult to make Community decision-makers accountable to any Parliament, national or European' (D Marquand (1981) 19 JCMS 223).

procedural obstacles include the fact that national parliaments have no right to be consulted, and the absence of direct control by national parliaments over legislation made by the Commission on its own authority. Moreover, the collective nature of decisions by the Council of Ministers necessarily weakens the responsibilities of the Government to Parliament for Council decisions to which they assent.[155]

Notwithstanding these difficulties, Parliament does purport to exercise some measure of accountability on the part of ministers who participate in the Community legislative process. By a Commons resolution of 1990, 'No Minister of the Crown should give agreement in the Council of Ministers to any proposal for European Community legislation (*a*) which is still subject to scrutiny (that is, on which the Select Committee on European Legislation has not completed its scrutiny); or (*b*) which is awaiting consideration by the House'.[156] However, these obligations may be waived in the case of a proposal which is confidential, routine, trivial, or substantially the same as a proposal on which scrutiny has been completed. The minister may also give agreement before scrutiny is complete with the agreement of the Committee, or if there are 'special reasons', though the minister should explain the reasons to the House or to the Scrutiny Committee. It is uncertain to what extent a minister is bound by a resolution of one of the European Standing Committees, and views predictably differ between government and Parliament. But ministers are unlikely to accept any formal constraint, and in many cases departure from a Committee resolution is a decision which is unlikely to be taken lightly without the involvement of other ministers, thereby raising the possibility that the matter would become one of collective rather than individual responsibility.[157]

D.   The response of the courts

As we have seen, the questions of parliamentary supremacy presented by Britain's membership were identified but not resolved in the pre-accession era. It would clearly be possible in principle for the United Kingdom to leave the Community, and to that extent the supremacy of Parliament is preserved. But this is a theoretical point which bears no relationship to contemporary reality, any more than do claims in another context that Parliament could legislate to regain sovereignty over former colonies.[158] The real problem is whether Parliament can legislate in a manner which is expressly in defiance of Community law. Should that happen, how should the United Kingdom courts respond? It is on this question that the politicians abdicated all responsibility in the pre-accession debates. The point was made by the Lord Chancellor in 1967:

There is in theory no constitutional means available to us to make it certain that no future Parliament would enact legislation in conflict with Community law. It would, however, be unprofitable to speculate on the academic possibility of a future

---

[155]   HC 588–I (1977–78), para 4.1.
[156]   HC Deb, 24 October 1990, col 399.
[157]   For further discussion, see 11th edn of this book, pp 150–2.
[158]   See ch 4.

Parliament enacting legislation expressly designed to have that effect. Some risk of inadvertent contradiction between United Kingdom legislation and Community law could not be ruled out.[159]

EC law and parliamentary supremacy

For the first decade after the passing of the 1972 Act, the courts vacillated between mutually conflicting positions. In *Felixstowe Dock and Railway Co v British Transport Docks Board*[160] Lord Denning commented that once a Bill 'is passed by Parliament and becomes a statute, that will dispose of all discussion about the Treaty. These courts will then have to abide by the statute without regard to the Treaty at all'.[161] Only three years later, Lord Denning appeared to change his mind. In *Macarthys Ltd v Smith*[162] the question was whether the Equal Pay Act 1970 permitted a woman to claim equal pay only with men currently in the employment of the employer, or whether she could use as a comparator her male predecessor. The Court of Appeal were divided on the question: the majority (Lawton and Cumming Bruce LJJ) were of the view that domestic law did not permit such claims, but that EC law was unclear. They were therefore minded to make a reference under art 177 to determine whether equal pay for equal work under art 119 was 'confined to situations in which men and women are contemporaneously doing equal work for their employer'. Lord Denning was of the view that EC law permitted the woman's claim and that domestic law should be construed accordingly, saying:

In construing our statute, we are entitled to look at the Treaty as an aid to its construction: and even more, not only as an aid but as an overriding force. If on close investigation it should appear that our legislation is deficient – or is inconsistent with Community law – by some oversight of our draftsmen – then it is our bounden duty to give priority to Community law. Such is the result of section 2(1) and (4) of the European Communities Act 1972.[163]

The ECJ confirmed the interpretation of art 119 which had been suggested by Lord Denning[164] following which the Court of Appeal sought to make it plain that the provisions of the Treaty 'take priority over anything in our English statute on equal pay which is inconsistent with art 119', this priority having been 'given by our own law'. According to Lord Denning:

Community law is now part of our law: and, whenever there is any inconsistency, Community law has priority. It is not supplanting English law. It is part of our law which overrides any other part which is inconsistent with it.[165]

Although Lord Denning appeared to have changed his mind, he also observed:

Thus far I have assumed that our Parliament, whenever it passes legislation, intends to fulfil its obligations under the Treaty. If the time should come when our Parliament deliberately passes an Act – with the intention of repudiating the Treaty or any

159 HL Deb, 8 May 1967, col 1203.
160 [1976] 2 LIL Rep 656.
161 Ibid, p 663.
162 [1979] ICR 785. See T R S Allan (1983) 3 OJLS 22.
163 Ibid, p 789.
164 *Case 129/79, Macarthys Ltd v Smith* [1980] ICR 672.
165 [1980] ICR 672, 692. See also Cumming Bruce LJ at p 693.

> provision in it – or intentionally of acting inconsistently with it – and says so in express terms – then I should have thought that it would be the duty of our courts to follow the statute of our Parliament.[166]

On this basis the European Communities Act 1972, s 2, effected only a limited form of entrenchment: it would have the effect that Community law will apply in preference to any post-1972 statute, and to that extent Parliament would have bound its successors. In these cases the courts would assume that Parliament had not intended to depart from Community obligations. But Lord Denning left open the possibility that Parliament might wish to assert its supremacy by stating clearly that a domestic statute is to apply notwithstanding Community law. In this case the domestic statute would displace to that extent s 2 of the 1972 Act. Further support in the early cases for the view that s 2 of the 1972 Act had only qualified the supremacy of Parliament was provided by *Case 12/81, Garland v British Rail Engineering Ltd.*[167] In an important passage which potentially goes further than Lord Denning in preserving the priority to be given to domestic legislation, Lord Diplock raised the question whether 'having regard to the express direction as to the construction of enactments "to be passed" … contained in section 2(4), anything short of an express positive statement in an Act of Parliament passed after January 1, 1973, that a particular provision is intended to be made in breach of an obligation assumed by the United Kingdom under a Community treaty, would justify an English court in construing that provision in a manner inconsistent with a Community treaty obligation of the United Kingdom'.[168]

Factortame

The most recent and authoritative view is that expressed in the *Factortame* series of cases.[169] In *Factortame (No 1)* it was said by Lord Bridge (in upholding the Court of Appeal's refusal to grant interim relief to restrain the operation of the Merchant Shipping Act 1988 pending the outcome of the art 177 reference) that s 2(4) was to be regarded as having

precisely the same effect as if a section were incorporated in Part II of the Act of 1988 which in terms enacted that the provisions with respect to registration of British fishing vessels were to be without prejudice to the directly enforceable Community rights of nationals of any member state of the EEC.[170]

As we have seen, however, the House of Lords held that they had no jurisdiction to grant the interim relief sought; on a reference under art 177, the ECJ ruled that a national court must set aside a rule of national law which precludes it from granting interim relief in a case concerning Community

---

166 [1979] ICR 785, 789.
167 [1982] ICR 420.
168 [1982] ICR 420, 438.
169 See note 99 above. On the question of parliamentary sovereignty, see P P Craig (1991) 11 YBEL 221; N Gravells [1989] PL 568, [1991] PL 180; and H W R Wade (1991) 107 LQR 1, (1996) 112 LQR 568.
170 [1990] 2 AC 85, 140.

law. When the matter returned to the House of Lords, relief was granted, thereby restraining the operation of the Merchant Shipping Act 1988 in relation to the plaintiffs pending the final resolution of the case.[171] In a much quoted passage in *Factortame (No 2)*, Lord Bridge said:

> Some public comments on the decision of the European Court of Justice, affirming the jurisdiction of the courts of member states to override national legislation if necessary to enable interim relief to be granted in protection of rights under Community law, have suggested that this was a novel and dangerous invasion by a Community institution of the sovereignty of the UK Parliament. But such comments are based on a misconception. If the supremacy ... of Community law over the national law of member states was not always inherent in the EEC Treaty it was certainly well established in the jurisprudence of the European Court of Justice long before the UK joined the Community. ... Thus, whatever limitation of its sovereignty Parliament accepted when it enacted the European Communities Act 1972 was entirely voluntary. Under the terms of the Act of 1972 it has always been clear that it was the duty of a UK court, when delivering final judgment, to override any rule of national law found to be in conflict with any directly enforceable rule of Community law. Similarly, when decisions of the European Court of Justice have exposed areas of UK statute law which failed to implement Council directives, Parliament has always loyally accepted the obligation to make appropriate and prompt amendments. Thus there is nothing in any way novel in according supremacy to rules of Community law in those areas to which they apply and to insist that, in the protection of rights under Community law, national courts must not be inhibited by rules of national law from granting interim relief in appropriate cases is no more than a logical recognition of that supremacy.[172]

In this way, the House of Lords appears to have effected a form of entrenchment of s 2(4) of the 1972 Act which thereby does what no statute has done before, namely fetter the continuing supremacy of Parliament.[173] Sir William Wade refers to this as a constitutional revolution; 'the Parliament of 1972 had succeeded in binding the Parliament of 1988 and restricting its sovereignty, something that was supposed to be constitutionally impossible'.[174] But although this may be necessary as a matter of European integration, it is unclear whether the House of Lords in *Factortame (Nos 1 and 2)* satisfactorily dealt with the issue as a matter of domestic constitutional law; nor is it clear that the decision answers all the questions which arise. Indeed, it is open to question whether the decisions advance the matter much beyond the Court of Appeal decision in *Macarthys Ltd v Smith*.[175] It is unfortunate that in a case of such constitutional significance, the full range of constitutional authorities were not addressed in the course of argument, even if it would have been difficult for the defendants to have mounted a full frontal attack on the

---

[171]   [1991] 1 AC 603.
[172]   Ibid, pp 658–9.
[173]   See also *R v Employment Secretary, ex p EOC* [1995] 1 AC 1 where declarations were made that provisions of the Employment Protection (Consolidation) Act 1978 were incompatible with art 119 of the EEC Treaty and Council Directive 75/117/EEC, and that other provisions of the Act were incompatible with the latter. For subsequent developments see D Nicol [1996] PL 579.
[174]   (1996) 112 LQR 568.
[175]   [1979] ICR 785.

constitutional implications of s 2(4). But in terms of unanswered questions, what would be the position in the (admittedly unlikely) event that Parliament should say expressly (or by clear implication) that a statutory provision should apply notwithstanding any Community obligation to the contrary? Wade has argued that 'If there had been any such provision in the Act of 1988 we can be sure that the European Court of Justice would hold that it was contrary to Community law to which by the Act of 1972 the Act of 1988 is held to be subject'.[176] But does it follow that in such a case national courts would be required to give effect to the 1972 Act rather than the 1988 Act? As a matter of British constitutional law (and regardless of what the ECJ might say), it would appear in such an eventuality that Parliament had repudiated the 'voluntary' 'limitation of its sovereignty' which it accepted when it enacted the 1972 Act (at least in so far as the 1988 Act is concerned).[177]

Parliamentary supremacy and the principle of indirect effect

Questions about parliamentary supremacy also arise, though rather less acutely, in the context of the interpretation of domestic legislation where questions are raised about its compatibility with directives. This presents problems of what is sometimes referred to as the indirect effect of directives, a matter which has given rise to a degree of inconsistency on the part of the ECJ and a degree of resistance on the part of the House of Lords. So far as the former is concerned, in one case (*Von Colson*),[178] a question arose about the relationship between German national law and the Equal Treatment Directive (76/207/EEC). In the view of the ECJ, 'in applying the national law and in particular the provisions of a national law specifically introduced in order to implement [a directive], national courts are required to interpret their national law in the light of the wording and the purpose of the directive'. But it is for the national court 'to interpret and apply the legislation adopted for the implementation of the directive in conformity with the requirements of Community law, in so far as it is given discretion to do so under national law'. In a more recent case (*Marleasing*),[179] the ECJ took a wider view of the application of directives, concluding now that 'in applying national law, whether the provisions in question were adopted before or after the directive, the national court called upon to interpret it is required to do so, as far as possible, in the light of the wording and the purpose of the directive in order to achieve the result pursued by the latter'. *Marleasing* thus involves an important reconsideration, with the domestic courts now being required to construe domestic law in line with the requirements of a directive, regardless of whether the legislation pre-dates or post-dates the directive. But it would appear that there is no overriding obligation to construe legislation in this

---

[176] (1996) 112 LQR 568, p 570.
[177] This is not to deny that such a decision would give rise to serious political and constitutional problems at Community level. But it would be for the Commission to take appropriate action by way of enforcement proceedings or otherwise, and it is perhaps in that way that any problems should be resolved, rather than in the British courts.
[178] *Case 14/83, Von Colson and Kamann v Land Nordrhein-Westfalen* [1984] ECR 1891.
[179] *Case 106/89, Marleasing SA v La Comercial Internacional de Alimentación SA* [1992] 1 CMLR 305. See also *Case C-334/92, Wagner Miret v Fondo de Garantia Salarial* [1993] ECR I–6911.

way: the obligation arises only where it is possible to do so.[180] In some instances this plainly may not be the case.

The issue first arose for consideration by the House of Lords in *Duke v Reliance Systems Ltd*[181] which was concerned with the differential retirement ages for men and women which were permitted by UK law but which were in breach of the Equal Treatment Directive. As we have seen, however, the directive does not have vertical direct effect and so could not be enforced in the domestic courts by someone who was not employed by a public authority. It was argued, nevertheless, that the Sex Discrimination Act 1975 should be construed so as to conform to the directive, a contention which drew the following response from Lord Templeman:

a British court will always be willing and anxious to conclude that United Kingdom law is consistent with Community law. Where an Act is passed for the purpose of giving effect to an obligation imposed by a directive or other instrument a British court will seldom encounter difficulty in concluding that the language of the Act is effective for the intended purpose.[182]

In the *Duke* Case, however, the Act in question was not passed to give effect to the directive. Indeed it was expressly intended to preserve discriminatory retirement ages, and was not reasonably capable of bearing any construction to the contrary. In these circumstances, it was held that s 2(4) of the 1972 Act does not 'enable or constrain a British court to distort the meaning of a British statute in order to enforce against an individual a Community directive which has no direct effect between individuals'. In more recent decisions, on the other hand, the House of Lords has adopted a radically different approach in cases where statutory instruments had been introduced quite clearly to give effect to a directive. Indeed, in two cases the House was prepared to take the extraordinary step of implying words into the legislation quite consciously to change its literal meaning,[183] for fear that the measures would otherwise have 'failed their object and the United Kingdom would have been in breach of its treaty obligations to give effect to directives'.[184] There is still some uncertainty about legislation (primary and secondary) which covers the field occupied by a directive but which was not passed necessarily in order to implement it.[185] In *Webb v EMO Air Cargo (UK) Ltd*,[186] however, it was accepted (following *Marleasing*) that an English court should construe a statute to comply with a directive regardless of whether the statute was passed before or after the directive was made. The requirement that the statute should have been passed to give effect to the directive was not mentioned, and the only condition was that the domestic law should be 'open to an interpretation consistent with the directive whether or not it is also open to an interpretation inconsistent with it'.[187]

---

[180]   See *Webb v EMO Air Cargo (UK) Ltd (No 2)* [1996] 2 CMLR 990.
[181]   [1988] AC 618.
[182]   Ibid, p 638.
[183]   *Pickstone v Freemans plc* [1989] AC 66 (see A W Bradley [1988] PL 485) and *Litster v Forth Dry Dock & Engineering Co Ltd* [1990] 1 AC 546.
[184]   *Litster*, ibid, at p 558.
[185]   See *Finnegan v Clowney Youth Training Programme Ltd* [1990] 2 AC 407.
[186]   [1992] 4 All ER 929. See N Gravells [1993] PL 44.
[187]   [1992] 4 All ER at 940.

E.   Conclusion

Whether or not Sir William Wade is correct in his assertion that a revolution has taken place,[188] British membership of the European Union continues to generate political controversy and legal uncertainty.[189] At least three issues of constitutional law are likely to continue to be of sustained interest. The first is the pressure towards ever closer political union in Europe and with it an enhancement of the role of the Community institutions. Constitutional law will have a role to play in this process, though whether the current arrangements are adequate to the task is open to argument. So far as they apply to extending the powers of the Community, these are to be found in the European Parliamentary Elections Act 1978, which simply requires by s 6 that no treaty which provides for the increase in the powers of the European Parliament shall be ratified by the United Kingdom unless it has been approved by an Act of Parliament.[190] Secondly there is the concern about what some refer to as the democratic deficit in the European Community, which takes a number of forms. But at the heart of the matter is a process of law-making by a legislative body (the Council) which is at best only indirectly elected and whose activities are in need of greater transparency. The challenge for constitutional lawyers and others will be to extend the principles of liberal democracy into this important arena, while at the same time ensuring a greater degree of parliamentary accountability on the part of those who represent the United Kingdom in the process. Thirdly, there is the matter of the constitutional base on which the whole enterprise is constructed. Although constitutional dogma has been shaken, the problem of sovereignty has not been adequately resolved, though it is unlikely that everyone would agree now with the view expressed in 1972 that 'the ultimate supremacy of Parliament will not be affected, and it will not be affected because it cannot be affected'.[191] Only time will tell whether this is a problem of any practical significance, and if so whether closer political union at Community level can be built on such foundations.

---

[188]   Cf J Eekelaar (1997) 113 LQR 185.
[189]   For stimulating accounts of some of the wider issues, see G de Burca (1996) 59 MLR 349, I Harden [1994] PL 609, N Walker [1996] PL 266, and Ward, *A Critical Introduction to European Law.* See also from a wider perspective C M G Himsworth [1996] PL 639 and N MacCormick (1993) 56 MLR 1.
[190]   See *R v Foreign Secretary, ex p Rees-Mogg,* above.
[191]   HC Deb, 5 July 1972, col 627. See also HL Deb, 7 August 1972, col 911.

PART II

The institutions of government

CHAPTER 9

Composition and meeting of Parliament

In this and the next two chapters, we examine the structure of Parliament, the functions of the two Houses and their privileges. Although both the House of Lords and the House of Commons meet in the palace of Westminster, they sit separately and are constituted on entirely different principles. The process of legislation is a matter in which both Houses take part and the two-chamber structure is an integral part of the parliamentary system. Within Parliament the House of Commons is the dominant House, as it is on the ability to command a majority in the Commons that a government depends for holding office. Under the Parliament Acts of 1911 and 1949, the formal power of the Lords in legislation is limited to imposing a temporary veto upon public Bills, a power which may sometimes be an effective check upon controversial legislation. The role of the Lords as a revising chamber is important, especially for securing amendments to Bills which have been subjected to closure in the Commons,[1] and the House serves other constitutional purposes.

The Queen is formally also part of Parliament. Thus she opens each session of Parliament, and the royal assent is necessary for primary legislation. These functions are performed on the advice of the government, but in very rare circumstances the Queen may have a personal discretion to exercise in relation to Parliament.

A. House of Lords

The most striking feature of the House of Lords is that its composition depends neither on methods of direct or indirect election nor on the principle of geographical representation. All members achieve their place either by the hereditary principle or on appointment by the Crown. The House consists of nearly 1,200 temporal, and 26 spiritual, Lords of Parliament. The temporal peers are:

(*a*) Hereditary peers and peeresses in their own right of the United Kingdom, who include holders of titles created in the peerage of England before the Union with Scotland in 1707 and in the peerage of Great Britain from 1707 to 1801 when the Union of Great Britain and Ireland took effect. In

---

[1] Ch 10 A.

October 1996, there were 755 peers who sat by succession and 12 hereditary peers of the first creation.[2]

(*b*) Hereditary peers of Scotland created before the Union of 1707 and not also members of the peerage of the United Kingdom.

(*c*) Not more than 12 Lords of Appeal in Ordinary appointed by the Crown on statutory authority to perform the judicial duties of the House and holding their seats for life.

(*d*) Life peers: by the Life Peerages Act 1958 the Crown may confer a life peerage upon a man or woman without limit as to the number of creations.

Creation of hereditary peers

Hereditary peerages may be created by the Queen on the advice of the Prime Minister; they are peerages of the United Kingdom and carry with them the right to a seat in the Lords. Between 1964 and 1983, all Prime Ministers pursued a policy of not advising the creation of hereditary peerages. Some of the oldest surviving hereditary peerages were created by the issue of a writ of summons to the House, followed by the taking of his seat by the recipient of the writ. In modern times, all peerages have been created by letters patent from the Sovereign.[3] A peerage created by letters patent descends according to the limitation expressed in the letters patent, which is almost always to the heirs male of the body of the grantee, ie to and through the male line in direct lineal descent from the grantee. A peerage created by writ of summons descends to the heirs general of the grantee, ie to his heirs male or female, lineal or collateral. Thus in the absence of a special limitation in the letters patent, it is only a peerage created by writ of summons which ever devolves upon a female. Where there is only one female heir, she becomes a peeress in her own right. Where, however, there are two or more female descendants of equal degree, the elder is not preferred to the younger, and both or all inherit as co-parceners. In such cases a peerage falls into abeyance. Such an abeyance may, on the advice of the Committee for Privileges of the House of Lords, which decides claims to existing peerages, be terminated by the Crown in favour of one co-heir, or in process of time may become vested in one descendant of the last holder of the peerage.[4] A dispute as to the right of a newly-created peer to sit is determined by the House itself, acting through the House's Committee for Privileges.

A peerage cannot be alienated nor, apart from disclaimer for life under the Peerage Act 1963, be surrendered,[5] nor has a peerage any connection with the tenure of land.[6] It was decided in 1856[7] that the Crown, although able to create a life peerage, could not create such a peerage carrying with it the right

---

[2] In this chapter statistics are from Griffith and Ryle, *Parliament* (ch 12), or, as here, from standard works of reference.

[3] For an example, see [1964] 2 QB 257, 271. And see the Crown Office Rules Orders of 1927 (SR and O No 425) and 1958 (SI No 1250).

[4] See HL 189 (1926) and HL Deb, 6 July 1927, col 222; 7 July 1927, col 285. Also HL 176 (1985–86) and HL Deb, 16 December 1986, col 105.

[5] *Re Parliamentary Election for Bristol South East* [1964] 2 QB 257.

[6] *Berkeley Peerage* case (1861) 8 HLC 21.

[7] *Wensleydale Peerage* case (1856) 5 HLC 958.

to a seat in the House. The conferment of life peerages upon those appointed to judicial office in the House had therefore to be authorised by statute.

Disqualification

An alien may not receive a writ of summons to the House of Lords nor may a writ of summons be issued to a bankrupt peer or to a person under 21 years of age.[8] It was decided in the case of *Viscountess Rhondda's Claim*[9] that the Sex Disqualification (Removal) Act 1919 did not enable a peeress in her own right to receive a writ of summons to Parliament. The Peerage Act 1963, s 6, now allows a peeress in her own right to take her seat. This change was not in fact of benefit to many women, since the great majority of hereditary peerages are restricted to male heirs. A peer who is a civil servant was formerly debarred by Treasury Minute from speaking or voting, but since 1973 such a peer is obliged only to exercise a general caution in entering any political controversy.

Creation of peers to coerce the Lords

The right of the Crown to create new peers without limit was in the past an important weapon to enable the Crown on the advice of the Prime Minister to compel the Lords to give way to the Commons in case of conflict. In 1712, Queen Anne appointed 12 new peers to secure a majority for the Tory administration. The Peerage Bill of 1719 attempted to limit the power of the Crown to create new peers, but the proposal was rejected. The passing of the Reform Bill in 1832 and the Parliament Bill in 1911 was procured by a statement that the King had consented to create peers in sufficient numbers to secure a majority for the government in the Lords. It seems improbable that this prerogative will again be invoked; the Parliament Act 1911 was intended to provide a more effective way of overcoming opposition in the Lords to new legislation.[10]

The peers of Scotland and Ireland

No new Scottish peerages have been created since the Union of 1707. The Peerage Act 1963, s 4, admitted all surviving peers of Scotland to the Lords. Formerly, when a new Parliament was summoned, the Scottish peers elected 16 of their number to represent them in the House.

Irish peers have fared differently. The Act of Union with Ireland in 1800 provided that the Irish peerage might be maintained to the number of 100. The last creation was in 1898. Formerly the peers of Ireland elected 28 of their number to represent Ireland in the House for life, but there has been no authority for an election to be held since the Irish Free State (now the Republic of Ireland) was created in 1922.[11] Holders of Irish peerages are, if

---

[8] HL Standing Order 2, which dates from 1685.
[9] [1922] 2 AC 339.
[10] Ch 10 B.
[11] *Earl of Antrim's Petition* [1967] 1 AC 691; Lord Dunboyne [1967] PL 314 and C E Lysaght (1967) 18 NILQ 277. See also (on the Barony of Farnham) HL Deb, 5 July 1995, col 1092, and HL (85) (1994–95).

otherwise qualified, entitled to be elected to the Commons and to vote at parliamentary elections.[12]

The Lords of Appeal in Ordinary

The 12 peers appointed under the Appellate Jurisdiction Act 1816 to perform the judicial functions of the House of Lords are styled Lords of Appeal in Ordinary. They may sit and vote for life, notwithstanding resignation or retirement from their judicial appointment. To be qualified for appointment, they must have held for two years high judicial office in the United Kingdom, or in England and Wales have had a right of audience in relation to all proceedings of the Supreme Court, in Scotland have been an advocate (or a solicitor entitled to appear in the Court of Session) or in Northern Ireland have been a practising barrister, in each case for at least 15 years.[13]

Life peers

The Life Peerages Act 1958 both strengthened the Lords and weakened the hereditary principle. The Act enabled the Queen, by letters patent, to confer a peerage for life with a seat in Parliament upon a man or woman. It did not restrict the power of the Crown to confer hereditary peerages, although it made it unnecessary for new hereditary peerages to be created. The object was to enable the Labour party's representation to be increased, and to bring in new members, particularly from outside the ranks of party politicians, without creating more hereditary titles. In October 1996, 320 peers and 70 peeresses appointed under the 1958 Act were in the House.

The Lords Spiritual

The Lords Spiritual are 26 bishops of the Church of England; they hold their seats in the Lords until they resign from their episcopal office. The Arch-bishops of Canterbury and York and the Bishops of London, Durham and Winchester have the right to a seat. The remaining spiritual lords are the 21 other diocesan bishops having seniority of date of appointment.[14] When such a bishop dies or resigns, his place in the House is taken by the next senior diocesan bishop. Since 1847, whenever a new diocesan bishopric has been created, it has been enacted that the number of bishops sitting in Parliament should not be increased.[15]

Disclaimer of titles

The Peerage Act 1963 enables hereditary peers other than those of the first creation to disclaim their titles for life. The primary purpose of granting this right was to enable hereditary peers to sit in the Commons. This reform was the direct result of the action of Mr Tony Benn, then Viscount Stansgate by succession, in challenging the existing law which disqualified members of the

---

[12] Peerage Act 1963, s 5.
[13] Appellate Jurisdiction Act 1876, s 6, as amended by the Courts and Legal Services Act 1990, s 71, and Sched 10; and see ch 18 A.
[14] The Bishop of Sodor and Man is excepted and cannot take a seat.
[15] Ecclesiastical Commissioners Act 1847, s 2; Bishoprics Act 1878, s 5.

Lords from standing for election to Parliament.[16] Under the 1963 Act, disclaimer is irrevocable and binds a wife, but the courtesy titles of children are not affected, nor has a disclaimer any effect on the succession of the heir. If a sitting member of the Commons succeeds to a title he has one month after the death of his predecessor in which to disclaim,[17] or, if the death occurs during an election campaign, one month from the declaration of the poll in favour of a successful peer. Existing peers were given 12 months from the royal assent to the Act, 31 July 1963, in which to exercise their power to disclaim; peers who succeed thereafter have 12 months from succession or their coming of age. These time limits are extended to cover any period when Parliament is not sitting or a peer is disabled by sickness from making the choice. After a disclaimer there can be no restoration of an hereditary peerage, but a peer who has disclaimed may subsequently be created a life peer under the Life Peerages Act 1958. One unforeseen sequel of the Peerage Act 1963 was that during the 12 months allowed for disclaimer by peers who were already members of the House, the Conservative Prime Minister (Macmillan) resigned because of ill-health and it was possible for the 14th Earl of Home to disclaim his title upon being appointed Prime Minister. Such a move from the Lords to the Commons has not been possible since the expiry in 1964 of the transitional period for disclaimer by existing peers.

Attendance

A summons to Parliament cannot be withheld from a peer who is entitled to it, and individual writs of summons are issued to both the temporal and spiritual lords for each new Parliament. In order to secure that only those peers interested in the work of Parliament shall in practice attend, the House adopted in June 1958 a standing order (now SO 20) relating to leave of absence. This order emphasises the obligation on peers to attend sittings in accordance with the writ of summons, but enables a peer to apply for leave of absence at any time during a Parliament for the remainder of that Parliament. A peer who has been granted leave of absence is expected not to attend sittings of the House during the period of leave. In this way it is hoped to eliminate the influence of the so-called 'backwoodsman'. Provision is made for a peer who wishes to terminate his leave of absence to give a month's notice. But the House has no power to prevent the attendance of a peer who, having received a writ of summons, does not observe the leave of absence rules.[18] In October 1996, 66 peers were on leave of absence and 80 peers did not receive a writ of summons.

Apart from the law lords, who receive a salary so long as they hold their judicial appointment, members of the House do not receive a salary, but since 1957, a daily attendance allowance has been paid and travel to the House is also paid for. Attending peers receive allowances for overnight stays away from home, and secretarial and research assistance. In the session 1995–96, the

---

16 Note 5 above.
17 Pending completion of the disclaimer, he may not sit or vote in the Commons : Peerage Act 1963, s 2; see D Shell [1995] PL 551.
18 See HL 7, 66–1, 67 (1955–56), paras 37–8.

average daily attendance was 372, compared with 95 in 1955, 140 in 1963, 292 in 1979 and 329 in 1987–88. In October 1996, there were 459 peers (of whom 318 were hereditary peers) in receipt of the Conservative whip, 111 Labour (15 hereditary) and 56 Liberal Democrats (24 hereditary). 319 peers (201 hereditary) belonged to the cross-bench group, ie peers without a party affiliation.

B.   House of Commons

The laws which govern the composition of the House of Commons are of fundamental political importance, for they provide the structure of the electoral system that determines which political party has the right to govern the country. Under a written constitution, the basic rules for electing the Commons would probably be contained in the constitution and possibly given some degree of entrenchment. But in the United Kingdom, these rules are contained in Acts of Parliament which may be amended by ordinary process of legislation. Whereas the composition of the Lords may be altered without upsetting the balance of political power, any change in the legal composition of the Commons is likely to benefit one or other of the political parties: constitutional arguments about proposed changes can be thin veils for the political calculations upon which the position of the parties is based. There is today general agreement over many essential rules of the electoral system, for example, the secret ballot. Other aspects of the electoral system are not universally accepted, for example, the 'first past the post' system of counting the votes, the distribution of constituencies, the financing of the parties and the use of broadcasting. Except for the controversy about proportional representation, these points of continuing controversy are less fundamental than the lengthy conflicts by which the unrepresentative House of Commons of the 18th century was transformed into the democratic assembly of today.

The composition of the House of Commons will be discussed under the following headings:

I.   The franchise
II.   Distribution of constituencies
III.   The conduct of elections
IV.   Membership of the House of Commons
V.   Electoral systems

I.   The franchise

Before 1918, the right to vote was largely dependent upon the ownership or occupation of property. It was also affected by the ancient distinction between counties and boroughs. For more than five centuries after Simon de Montfort's Parliament of 1265, the English people were represented in the Commons by two knights from every county and by two burgesses from every borough. Before the Reform Act of 1832, the franchise was exercisable in the counties by those men who owned freehold land worth 40 shillings per year. In the boroughs, the franchise varied according to the charter of the borough and to local custom. In fact many seats in the House before 1832 were controlled by members of the landowning aristocracy who had sufficient influence by purchasing votes or other means to nominate the successful candidates. Acts for widening the franchise were passed in 1832, 1867, 1884, 1918, 1928, 1948 and 1969 until today the total electorate is over 43 million. The details of the earlier Acts have passed into history. In 1918 a uniform franchise based on residence was established for county and borough constituencies.[19] Votes for women over 30 were introduced in 1918 and in 1928 for women over 21. After 1918, various categories of persons had the right to vote more than once either by reason of occupying land for business purposes or because of the right of graduates to vote in separate constituencies representing the universities. These elements of plural voting were abolished in 1948.

The present franchise

The law is now contained in part I of the Representation of the People Act 1983, which consolidated earlier legislation and which has itself been amended, for example in 1985 when the right to vote was extended to certain British citizens resident outside the United Kingdom.[20] By s 1 of the 1983 Act, the right to vote at parliamentary elections is exercisable by all Commonwealth citizens (which in law includes all British citizens and British subjects)[21] and citizens of the Republic of Ireland, who (*a*) are of full age, ie who have attained the age of 18 years by the date of the election; (*b*) are resident in a parliamentary constituency on the qualifying date; (*c*) are not subject to any legal incapacity to vote; and (*d*) whose names are in the official register of electors.

Except for certain categories of persons considered below, who may register to vote without satisfying the residence test, no person qualified by nationality may vote unless he or she is resident in a constituency on the qualifying date, 10 October, which each year serves as the basis on which the electoral register is prepared. Before 1948, a qualifying period of residence was required but this requirement now applies only to elections for the Westminster Parliament in Northern Ireland constituencies, where the elector must have been resident in Northern Ireland (not necessarily in a particular constituency) during the period of three months ending on the qualifying date, 15 September.

The meaning of residence for electoral purposes was considered in *Fox v Stirk*,[22] where university students were held to be resident on 10 October in their hall of residence and therefore entitled to register for those con-

---

19   See Butler, *The Electoral System in Britain since 1918*, and, for the law and practice today, Clayton (ed), *Parker's Law and Conduct of Elections*; also Blackburn, *The Electoral System in Britain* and Rawlings, *Law and the Electoral Process*.

20   Page 171 below.

21   See British Nationality Act 1981, s 37; and ch 20 A.

22   [1970] 2 QB 463, discussed by S Maidment in [1971] PL 25. And see *Hipperson v Newbury Registration Officer* [1985] QB 1060 (Greenham Common women resident in peace camp for electoral purposes).

stituencies. Applying the dictionary definition of 'reside' as meaning 'to dwell permanently or for a considerable time, to have one's settled or usual abode, to live in or at a particular place', the Court of Appeal held that the stay of the students at their university addresses displayed a considerable degree of permanence. A person's residence at their home address is not affected by temporary absence from that address, whether because of holidays, business duties[23] or other reasons. While a person may be resident at more than one address, and may therefore be registered in more than one constituency, no one may vote more than once at the same parliamentary election.[24] Ownership of a country cottage as a second home is not enough to make the owner resident there if on the facts the owner's use of it is incidental to the owner's main home.[25]

Special rules apply for determining the residence of mental patients, whose rights were widened in 1982.[26] In brief, a person detained under statutory powers because of mental disorder cannot be treated as resident in the hospital where he or she is detained. Voluntary patients resident in a mental hospital may complete a declaration entitling them to be registered as resident at an address elsewhere, for example their home; in this case they may vote by post in the relevant constituency.

The register of electors

It is a condition precedent to exercising the vote that the elector should be placed on the register of electors. The register is prepared once a year by the registration officer of each constituency, who in England and Wales is appointed by the council of each district or London borough.[27] A new register comes into force on 16 February each year.[28] The register is prepared after a house to house canvass or other inquiries have been made of all householders. It is first published in a provisional form on or before 28 November, to allow for claims and objections.

A separate register which is compiled on information obtained from service declarations contains the names of members of the forces, serving at home or abroad, and of other Crown servants and British Council staff who are employed abroad together with the names of their spouses resident with them. The principle of registration is that a service voter is registered as if he or she were living at the address at which but for Crown service he or she would normally be resident.[29]

If the registration officer's decision including or excluding someone from the register is disputed, an appeal lies to the county court (in Scotland to the

---

23   Representation of the People Act 1983, s 5(2)(a).
24   1983 Act, s 1(4) and s 61(2)(a).
25   *Scott v Phillips* 1974 SLT 32, following *Ferris v Wallace* 1936 SC 561: s 5(1) of the 1983 Act requires the courts to have regard to principles established by judicial decisions on the former qualifying period of residence.
26   1983 Act, s 7.
27   1983 Act, s 8(2)(a).
28   1983 Act, s 13.
29   1983 Act, ss 14–17. For members of the forces required to serve only in Northern Ireland, see Representation of the People Act 1993, s 1, amending s 59 of the 1983 Act.

sheriff) and thence on a point of law to the Court of Appeal (in Scotland to the Electoral Registration Court of three judges). The decision of the county court may also be reviewed on jurisdictional grounds.[30] Once placed upon the register, any person not suffering from a legal incapacity, such as infancy or insanity, is entitled to vote, the register being conclusive on such questions as whether a person was resident at the address shown on the qualifying date. But while a person registered cannot be excluded from voting he or she may incur penalties for recording a vote while subject to a legal incapacity.[31] Additions or alterations to the register may be ordered by the High Court[32] and may also be made by the registration officer.[33] Since 1985, the right to register and vote in a particular constituency as overseas voters has been given to British citizens who were formerly resident in the constituency and who may continue to be eligible to vote, initially for a period of only five years but now for 20 years.[34]

Disqualification for the franchise

The parliamentary franchise may not be exercised by:

(*a*)   aliens;[35]
(*b*)   persons who have not attained the age of 18 by the date of the poll;[36]
(*c*)   those who, for reasons such as mental illness, subnormality, drunkenness, and infirmity, lack the capacity at the moment of voting to understand what they are about to do. It is for the presiding officer at the poll to take the decision of refusing to allow such persons to vote;
(*d*)   peers and peeresses in their own right (but Irish peers may vote);[37]
(*e*)   convicted persons during the time that they are detained in a penal institution in pursuance of a sentence;[38]
(*f*)   persons convicted of corrupt or illegal practices at elections, the period and geographical extent of disqualification depending on the offence.[39]

Voting procedure

Responsibility for the official conduct of the election in each constituency rests upon the returning officer, who in England and Wales in the case of

---

30   *R v Hurst, ex p Smith* [1960] 2 QB 133.
31   1983 Act, ss 49 and 61(1).
32   Eg *R v Hammond, ex p Nottingham Council, The Times,* 10 October 1974. For Scotland, see *John Ferguson* 1965 SC 16.
33   1983 Act, s 11.
34   Representation of the People Act 1985, amended by Representation of the People Act 1989.
35   Citizens of the European Union resident in the UK may vote and stand in local government elections and in elections to the European Parliament: see respectively SI 1995/1948 and SI 1994/342.
36   1983 Act, s 1(1)(c).
37   *Beauchamp v Madresfield* (1872) 8 CP 245; Peerage Act 1963, ss 5 and 6. And see [1983] PL 393.
38   1983 Act, s 3.
39   1983 Act, s 160.

a county constituency wholly contained within the area of a county council is the sheriff, and in the case of a borough constituency wholly contained within a local government district is the chairman of the district council.[40] Most functions of the returning officer are however discharged by the registration officer or by an appointed deputy. Certain matters, for example the declaration of the poll, may be reserved to the returning officer. The official costs of an election, as distinct from the expenses of the candidates, are paid out of public funds in accordance with a scale prescribed by the Treasury.

Normally voting takes place in person at the polling station assigned to the area in which the elector is resident. Certain exceptions exist. Thus service voters may vote by proxy or by post. The right to vote by post may be claimed by an elector unable to vote in person on a number of grounds (for example, the general nature of his or her occupation, service or employment; employment on election duties; physical incapacity; no longer residing at an address in the same constituency). Those electors who satisfy the returning officer that they cannot reasonably be expected to vote in person may be granted a postal vote indefinitely or for a particular election, and overseas electors may also vote by post.[41]

The nomination of candidates, the form of the ballot paper, the secrecy of the ballot and the counting of votes are governed in detail by the Representation of the People Acts. It is only since 1969 that the ballot paper may include words describing the political affiliation of the candidates. The first proposal to Parliament was that a register of political descriptions should be created and maintained by the Registrar of Friendly Societies. This would have required political parties to register for electoral purposes. But the difficulties inherent in that proposal[42] led to a simpler solution being adopted by which each candidate may state his or her description in up to six words, which may include a statement of political allegiance.[43] There is a need for machinery to prevent a candidate from providing a description on the ballot paper which is intended to confuse voters as to the identity of genuine candidates.[44]

In the past, office-holders who conducted elections did not always exercise their functions impartially. In the great case of *Ashby v White*, the Mayor of Aylesbury as returning officer wrongfully refused to allow Ashby to vote and Ashby sued him for damages. The House of Lords upheld the view of Chief Justice Holt (dissenting in the Queen's Bench) that the remedy of damages should be given. In Holt's words, 'To allow this action will make public officers more careful to observe the constitution of cities and boroughs, and not to be so partial as they commonly are in all elections . . .'[45] Today, officials concerned with the conduct of elections are required to carry out their duties

---

40 1983 Act, s 24(1).
41 1983 Act, s 19(1), amended by the Representation of the People Acts 1989 and 1990.
42 Cf A P Herbert, *Uncommon Law*, ch 10 ('Which is the Liberal Party?').
43 1983 Act, Sched 1, r 6.
44 *Sanders v Chichester* (1994) SJ 225 ('Literal Democrat' candidate for European Parliament gaining over 10,000 votes and depriving Liberal Democrat candidate of victory). And see HL Deb, 25 May 1995, col 1099.
45 (1703) 2 Ld Raym 938, 956.

impartially and are subject to criminal penalties if they do not, but they cannot be sued for damages if breach of official duty is alleged.[46]

II. Distribution of constituencies

Before 1832, the unreformed House of Commons was composed on the general principle that every county and borough in England and Wales was entitled to be represented by two members. A similar principle applied to Scottish representation at Westminster, subject to the limit of numbers imposed in the Treaty of Union, which led to the grouping of certain shires and royal burghs for this purpose. Representation thus depended on the status of the unit of local government and bore no regard to population. Before 1832 counties such as Cornwall, which contained many tiny boroughs, were grossly over-represented by comparison with areas of rapidly growing industrial population. From the Reform Act 1832 onwards, successive measures of redistributing constituencies to remove glaring differences were undertaken, usually at the same time as reforms in the franchise were made.[47] Only since 1917 has there come to be general acceptance of the principle of broad mathematical equality in the size of constituencies,[48] and only since 1945 has there been permanent machinery to enable boundaries to be adjusted from time to time to take account of shifting population and to avoid excessive disparities developing between constituencies. The legislation has sought to establish impartial machinery, but in practice the system has not operated without controversy. The system does not try to achieve strict arithmetical equality between constituencies, but lays emphasis also on the territorial aspect of representation, on the link between elected member and his or her constituency and on the desirability of parliamentary boundaries not clashing with local government boundaries. The degree of discretion built into the system of electoral apportionment makes it particularly necessary to ensure that the machinery is impartial and charges of gerrymandering are avoided.

Machinery for determining constituency boundaries

By the Parliamentary Constituencies Act 1986, which consolidated the former House of Commons (Redistribution of Seats) Acts 1949 and 1958, there are four permanent boundary commissions, for England, Wales, Scotland and Northern Ireland. The Speaker is the chairman of each commission, but in practice does not sit, and a judge from the appropriate High Court (in Scotland, from the Court of Session) is appointed deputy chairman of each commission. Each commission includes two other members, those for England being appointed by the Home Secretary and the Secretary of State for the Environment. Each commission has two official assessors, those for England being the Registrar General and the Director General of Ordnance Survey. Each commission must undertake a general review of

---

[46]   1983 Act, s 63.
[47]   Butler, *The Electoral System in Britain since 1918*, app II.
[48]   Report of Speaker's Conference, Cd 8463, 1917; Report of Committee on Electoral Machinery, Cmd 6408, 1943.

constituencies in that part of the United Kingdom assigned to it, at intervals of not less than ten or more than 15 years (reduced in 1992 to an interval of from eight to 12 years);[49] changes in particular constituencies may be proposed from time to time when necessary. Notice must be given to the constituencies affected by any provisional recommendations. If objections are received from an interested local authority or from a body of at least 100 electors, a local inquiry must be held into the recommendations. Having received a report on the inquiries, a commission must submit its report to the Secretary of State. The 1986 Act, by s 3(5), imposes a duty on the Secretary of State, 'as soon as may be after a Boundary Commission have submitted a report', to lay the report before Parliament together with a draft Order in Council for giving effect, with or without modifications, to the recommendations in the report (reasons must be given to Parliament for any modifications). The draft Order must be approved by resolution of each House before the final Order can be made by the Queen in Council. The validity of any Order in Council which purports to be made under the 1986 Act and recites that approval was given by each House is not to be called into question in any legal proceedings.[50]

Rules for redistribution of seats

The 1986 Act contains the rules which the commissions must observe in redistributing seats. Scotland must be represented by not less than 71 seats, Wales by not less than 35, Northern Ireland by from 16 to 18 seats, and Great Britain by 'not substantially greater or less than 613'.[51] These rules are not easy to apply, particularly in the case of England, but their effect is that Scotland and Wales on a population basis are represented more generously than England. Thus in 1991 the average electorate in English constituencies was 69,279, compared with 58,086 in Wales and 54,369 in Scotland. Northern Ireland was formerly represented at Westminster by only 12 members, since until 1973 it had its own Parliament for devolved matters; but with direct rule continuing, increased representation was granted in 1979.

The legislation provides for the calculation of a separate electoral quota for each of the four countries (namely, the total electorate in each country divided by the number of constituencies existing when each commission starts on its general review). Each commission must secure that the electorate of a constituency shall be as near the relevant electoral quota as is practicable, having regard to certain other rules, for example, that parliamentary constituencies shall as far as practicable not cross certain local government boundaries. Strict application of these principles may be departed from if special geographical considerations make it desirable; and account must be taken of inconveniences that may follow the alteration of constituencies and of local ties that might be broken by alteration. The commissions thus have a broad discretion to decide how much priority should be given to achieving arithmetical equality between constituencies.[52]

---

49   Boundary Commissions Act 1992.
50   1986 Act, s 4(7).
51   1986 Act, Sched 2.
52   *R v Boundary Commission for England, ex p Foot* [1983] QB 600.

Boundary review in practice

General reviews were completed by the four commissions in 1954, 1969, 1982 and 1994. In 1954, the review resulted in the abolition of six constituencies and the creation of 11 new ones, all in England, to bring the membership of the House up to 630. As well as other difficulties experienced by the English commission,[53] the method of calculating the electoral quota for England under the 1949 Act resulted in the draft Orders in Council being challenged in the courts.

In *Harper v Home Secretary*, two electors in Manchester sought an injunction to restrain the Home Secretary from submitting the draft Order in Council, already approved by both Houses of Parliament, to the Queen in Council. The injunction was granted by Roxburgh J but was discharged by the Court of Appeal, which held that the English commission had not departed from the statutory rules which vested a wide discretion in them. 'In so far as the matter was not within the discretion of the commission, it was certainly to be a matter for Parliament to determine', said Evershed MR, who reserved his position on the power of the court where the commission had made recommendations which were manifestly in complete disregard of the Act.[54]

In 1954, the government gave effect without modification to the recommendations of the four commissions. But events took a different turn in 1969 when the next general review was completed. The commission for England proposed major changes to 271 constituencies and five new constituencies for England.

At the time the commissions submitted their reports, a radical reorganisation of local government in England (outside Greater London) and in Wales was in train and the Labour government decided that revision of parliamentary boundaries should wait until local government had been reorganised. The government therefore delayed laying the commissions' reports in Parliament and instead introduced a Bill which gave effect only to the changes affecting Greater London, and a few abnormally large constituencies elsewhere. The government thus sought by legislation to depart from its obligations under the Acts of 1949 and 1958. The Bill passed the Commons against severe criticism but was drastically amended by the Lords and was abandoned by the government when that House in October 1969 refused to give way to the Commons. An elector for the borough of Enfield then sought an order of mandamus from the High Court requiring the Home Secretary to perform his statutory duty of laying before Parliament the commission reports together with draft Orders in Council.[55] Thereupon the Home Secretary laid before Parliament the reports and the draft Orders in Council, but invited the Commons to reject them, using the government majority for this purpose.

---

53 D E Butler (1955) 33 Public Administration 125.
54 [1955] Ch 238, 251. See also Marshall and Moodie, *Some Problems of the Constitution*, ch 5; and S A de Smith (1955) 18 MLR 281.
55 *R v Home Secretary, ex p McWhirter, The Times*, 21 October 1969. The application was dismissed in view of the Home Secretary's action in October 1969 in laying the reports and draft Orders in Parliament. Previously on 19 June 1969 the reports alone had been laid in Parliament 'by Command' of the Crown rather than 'by Act', a distinction which it was difficult for the Home Secretary to sustain in view of the principle in *A-G v De Keyser's Royal Hotel Ltd* [1920] AC 508 (ch 12 E), and which was shown to be non-existent in *R v Immigration Appeals Tribunal, ex p Joyles* [1972] 3 All ER 213.

By this tangled course of events, the Labour government succeeded in postponing the much-needed adjustments of constituency boundaries until after the 1970 general election, following which the new Conservative government promptly secured parliamentary approval to the changes recommended in 1969. Some MPs complained that Parliament had fettered its hands by setting up the boundary commissions and argued that Parliament must retain the right to make the final decisions. But the Conservative Home Secretary considered it 'enormously important' that Parliament should comply with the impartial recommendations of the four commissions.[56] In 1983, the general review again led to extensive changes in constituencies, with seats in Great Britain being increased by ten, and the total in the House rising to 650. The Labour party leader challenged the English changes in the High Court, but with no success.[57] The review which was completed in 1994 increased the number of seats in England from 524 to 529, and the total in the Commons to 659.[58]

The boundary commission procedure, which derives from Act of Parliament, is liable to be set aside or modified by a later Act and this may tempt a government to do this if it should think that this will benefit its own electoral interests. But, as the late Aneurin Bevan said, 'I can think of nothing that could undermine the authority of Parliament more than that people outside should feel that the constitutional mechanism by which the House of Commons is elected has been framed so as to favour one party in the State'.[59] In the United States, the Supreme Court has acted to protect the value of the individual elector's vote in state elections, holding that the voter has a plain, direct and adequate interest in maintaining the effectiveness of his or her vote which falls within the 'equal protection of the laws' guaranteed in the US constitution.[60] In Britain the process of boundary reviews is more likely to be blocked in Parliament than to be set aside by the courts.

In a review of the system of boundary reviews, the Home Affairs Committee of the Commons recommended that a means should be found to check the tendency for every general review to lead to the creation of extra English constituencies, but this proposal has not been adopted.[61]

III.   The conduct of elections

The Representation of the People Act 1983 also regulates the behaviour of candidates and their supporters. The object of part II of the Act is to eliminate corrupt and illegal practices and other means by which one candidate could obtain an unfair advantage over another. The context within which the election is controlled is an individual candidate's campaign within the constituency. Every candidate must appoint an election agent, but a candidate

---

[56]   HC Deb, 28 October 1970, col 241 ff.
[57]   Note 52 above.
[58]   The boundary commission reports for England (HC 433–i, (1994–95), Scotland and Wales were implemented by SIs 1995/1626, 1037 and 1036, and took effect at the 1997 election.
[59]   HC Deb, 15 December 1954, col 1872.
[60]   *Baker v Carr* 369 US 186 (1962); *Reynolds v Sims* 377 US 533 (1964). See I Loveland [1994] PL 332.
[61]   See HC 97–1 (1986–87) and H F Rawlings [1987] PL 324.

may appoint himself to act in that capacity.[62] The most important control is a ban on expenditure being incurred with a view to promoting the election of a candidate on account of holding public meetings or issuing advertisements or circulars, or otherwise presenting the candidate or his views to the electorate, except with the authority of the candidate or the agent.[63] It is a corrupt practice to incur expenditure in breach of this ban. A maximum limit is imposed on the expenditure which may be incurred in respect of the conduct or management of the election on behalf of a candidate[64] and it is an illegal practice for a candidate or agent knowingly to exceed the limit. Certain forms of expenditure are prohibited, for example, payment to an elector for the display of posters unless payment is made in the ordinary course of the elector's business as an advertising agent; and payment to canvassers.[65] Corrupt practices include bribery, treating and undue influence, which includes the making of threats and attempts to intimidate an elector.[66]

The rules on election expenses are strictly enforced, and inadvertent departures from the rules require to be excused by the courts,[67] but the scope of the rules is limited. While they secure equality in many respects between candidates in their constituency campaigns, the rules are not designed to deal with the national expenditure of the parties before or during a general election, nor with national political advertising in the press.

In *R v Tronoh Mines Ltd,* just before a general election, the defendant company advertised in *The Times* urging the nation to save Britain from the perils of socialism. Both the company and the publishers of *The Times* were charged with unlawfully incurring expenses in the Westminster constituency in breach of s 63 of the 1949 Act (now s 75 of the 1983 Act). McNair J held that the section aimed at expenditure on advertisements which sought to promote the cause of a candidate at a particular election, and not at those which supported the interest of one party generally in all constituencies, 'even though that general political propaganda does incidentally assist a particular candidate amongst others'.[68]

The broad effect of this decision is that part II of the 1983 Act does not control expenditure on advertising in the national press during a general election. Particularly since the 1983 election, the Labour and Conservative parties have incurred considerable expenditure of this kind, the Conservative party having greater resources for this purpose. It is anomalous that national advertising escapes control while local expenditure is subject to strict limits. The problem of election material which is aimed against, rather than for, a candidate was reconsidered in 1976.

In *DPP v Luft,* in three constituencies an anti-fascist group had distributed pamphlets urging voters not to vote for the National Front candidate, there being at least three other candidates in each constituency. Members of the group were prosecuted under

---

62 1983 Act, s 67(2).
63 1983 Act, s 75(1): see *Grieve v Douglas-Home* 1965 SC 315 (below).
64 1983 Act, s 76, as varied subsequently by order of the Home Secretary.
65 1983 Act, ss 109 and 111.
66 1983 Act, s 115. And see *R v Rowe, ex p Mainwaring* [1992] 4 All ER 821 (fraudulent for party A to present leaflet as one issued by party B; but no evidence that voters impeded in free exercise of franchise).
67 1983 Act, s 167.
68 [1952] 1 All ER 697, 700.

what is now s 75 of the 1983 Act for incurring expenditure with a view to promoting the election of a candidate without authority from an election agent. The House of Lords held that the offence had been committed, since it was sufficient for the prosecution to establish an intention on the part of the accused to *prevent* the election of a candidate, and not necessary to prove an intention to promote the election of one particular candidate: a dictum to the contrary by McNair J in the *Tronoh Mines* case was disapproved.[69]

During local elections throughout Scotland, a national poster and newspaper campaign by a trade union which urged voters not to vote Conservative was held not to contravene s 75 of the 1983 Act.[70]

Broadcasting and elections

Political broadcasting at election times has also given rise to difficulties. It is an illegal practice for any person to procure the use of transmitting stations outside the United Kingdom with intent to influence voters at an election.[71] The Independent Television Commission is under a statutory duty to secure that news programmes are accurate and impartial and that due impartiality is preserved in political programmes.[72] Political advertising is banned on ITV and on local radio stations.[73]

Since 1945, time has been regularly provided both on radio and television for party political broadcasts. The allocation of time is made by agreement between the BBC, the ITC and the major parties acting through the committee on party political broadcasting; at general elections a special allocation of time is made. There is no statutory control of these allocations. Thus the Scottish National Party has complained about the arrangements without success, both in the Court of Session and to the Parliamentary Commissioner for Administration.[74] But once agreement on the broadcasts has been reached, the broadcasting authorities may be under a contractual liability to transmit the programme at the agreed time.[75] Do the costs of such broadcasts rank as election expenses?

In *Grieve v Douglas-Home*, an unsuccessful Communist candidate petitioned against the election of the Conservative leader, Sir Alec Douglas-Home, at the general election in 1964, on the ground that the expenses of the party broadcasts in which he had appeared fell within the then s 63 of the 1949 Act. The Election Court held that no election offence had been committed since the dominant motive of the broadcasting authorities had been the intention to transmit information of public importance and not to procure Douglas-Home's election. The court considered it inevitable that an allocation of times for party broadcasts must exclude some of the minor parties.[76]

---

69   [1977] AC 962.
70   *Walker v UNISON* 1995 SLT 1226.
71   1983 Act, s 92.
72   Broadcasting Act 1990, s 6(1)(b) and (c) and cf for radio, s 90(1)(b). The BBC, which exists under royal charter, seeks to maintain due impartiality although it is not subject to statutory restrictions. And see note 80 below.
73   Broadcasting Act 1990, s 8(2)(a).
74   *Scotsman*, 27 May 1970 (refusal of interdict by the Court of Session); Report of PCA for 1971, p 6 (investigation discontinued because complaint 'political'), HC 116 (1971–72).
75   *Evans v BBC and IBA, The Times*, 27 February 1974. See now Broadcasting Act 1990, s 36.
76   1965 SC 315.

Section 75 of the 1983 Act now makes it clear that the broadcasting authorities, like the press, are free to incur expenditure in disseminating matter relating to the election, other than advertisements.[77] Moreover, in 1969, the broadcasting of items about particular constituencies was also brought under control: in brief, if a candidate takes part in an item about a constituency election, the item may not be broadcast without his or her consent; and it is an offence for a candidate to take part in such an item for the purpose of promoting his or her election unless the broadcast has the consent of every other candidate for the constituency.[78] To 'take part' in a constituency item means to participate actively, for example in an interview or discussion; a candidate may not prevent the BBC from filming while he or she is campaigning in the streets.[79] The duty of the former Independent Broadcasting Authority to maintain a proper balance in its programmes was enforced by the Court of Session in 1979, when the IBA was barred before the devolution referendum in Scotland from transmitting a series of party political broadcasts, three in favour of devolution and one against.[80] In 1995, the BBC were barred in Scotland from transmitting a long interview with the Prime Minister only three days before local government elections.[81] The major parties are very quick to take up with the broadcasting authorities any breaches of their duty of impartiality.

In 1968, the Speaker's Conference on electoral law recommended that there should be a ban on broadcasting or publishing opinion polls and betting odds relating to an election within 72 hours before the holding of the poll, but this recommendation was not accepted.[82]

Funds of the political parties

While electoral law seeks to achieve equality between candidates in respect of constituency-based expenditure during the election campaign, the law does nothing to secure equality between national political expenditure nor to control constituency expenditure outside the election campaign. Political funds are not ranked as charitable and do not therefore receive the fiscal benefits which are enjoyed by charitable bodies.[83] Many but not all trade unions exercise their right to maintain political funds which are used to support the Labour party and other political activities, but individual members may 'contract out' of subscribing to the political fund. A member's complaint that the political fund rules have been broken may be heard by an impartial official, the Certification Officer.[84] For tax purposes, a company may

---

[77] 1983 Act, s 75(1)(c)(i).
[78] 1983 Act, s 93(1).
[79] *Marshall v BBC* [1979] 3 All ER 80. And see *McAliskey v BBC* [1980] NI 44.
[80] *Wilson v IBA* 1979 SC 351. Cf *R v Broadcasting Complaints Commission, ex p Owen* [1985] QB 1153; and see A E Boyle [1986] PL 562; and ch 22 A.
[81] *Houston v BBC* 1995 SLT 1305 and *The Times*, 9 May 1995.
[82] Cmnd 3550 and 3717, 1968.
[83] Cf *Conservative and Unionist Central Office v Burrell* [1982] 2 All ER 1; and *Re Grant's Will Trusts* [1979] 3 All ER 359.
[84] See now Trade Union and Labour Relations (Consolidation) Act 1992, ss 71–96. Also Ewing, *Trade Unions, the Labour Party and the Law* and *The Funding of Political Parties in Britain* ch 3.

deduct certain political contributions from its assessable profits[85] but companies must disclose details of their contributions for political purposes in excess of £200, including direct payments to political parties and indirect support of political activities.[86] Individual shareholders and company employees need not be consulted about such payments, and the former have no right to 'contract out'.

In 1975, when the parties were in financial difficulties caused by two general elections in 1974 and the effects of inflation, the government appointed the Houghton committee to consider whether support should be given to the parties out of public funds, as happens in Germany, Finland and Sweden. A majority of the committee recommended the introduction of a system of state aid for political parties, to take the form of annual Exchequer grants to the central organisations of the parties, the amounts to depend on the extent of each party's support at the previous general election, and, at local level, a limited reimbursement of the election expenses of candidates. The scheme was then estimated to cost about £2¼ million a year. Four members of the committee dissented, on the ground that direct state aid would breach the established British practice that organisation for political ends is a strictly voluntary activity.[87] The recommended scheme was not adopted. A non-governmental commission inquired into the financing of the parties in 1981: it concluded that the public interest justified support for the parties from public funds, in the form of matching payments being made to the headquarters of a party for every individual contribution of £2 made to a constituency party. This proposal opened up the issue of closer legal regulation of parties, and it was not adopted.[88] Public funds have been used since 1975 to assist opposition parties with their work in Parliament, since it is recognised that ministers enjoy an immense advantage at Westminster through being able to call on the resources of the civil service. The formula for calculating the payments takes account both of the seats won and the votes cast at the preceding general election for each party. The payments must be spent exclusively on the parliamentary expenses of each party.[89] The funding of parties was considered by the Home Affairs Committee in 1993.[90] But no major changes in the law have resulted, and the parties are still not obliged to disclose the source of their income.

Disputed elections

If elections are to be conducted according to law there must be effective machinery for investigating alleged breaches of the law and for imposing appropriate sanctions. Since the House of Commons has a direct interest in its own composition, it formerly claimed as a matter of privilege to determine questions of disputed elections. The Commons exercised the right to determine such questions from 1604 to 1868; and objected, not always with

---

[85] *Morgan v Tate and Lyle Ltd* [1955] AC 21.
[86] Companies Act 1985, Sched 7, paras 3–5.
[87] Cmnd 6601, 1976.
[88] Hansard Society, *Paying for Politics*; Ewing, *Funding of Political Parties*, above; Oliver, ch 8 in Blackburn (ed), *Constitutional Studies*.
[89] HC Deb, 24 May 1988, col 104 (WA); 21 June 1988, col 1075.
[90] HC 301 (1993–94); HL Deb, 7 June 1995, col 1356, and 5 February 1997, col 1675.

success, to breaches of election law being raised in the ordinary courts.[91] From 1672, election disputes were decided by the whole House but the growth of party government resulted in disputes being settled by purely party voting. In 1868, Parliament entrusted the duty of deciding disputed elections to the courts.

The procedure is now regulated by the Representation of the People Act 1983, part III. Within 21 days of the official return of the result of an election, an election petition complaining of an undue election may be presented by a registered elector for the constituency in question, by an unsuccessful candidate or by any person claiming to have been validly nominated as a candidate. The petition may raise a wide variety of issues, including the improper conduct of the election by officials,[92] the legal qualification of the successful candidate to be a member of the Commons,[93] and the commission of election offences such as unauthorised election expenditure.[94] The petition is heard by an Election Court consisting of two judges of the Queen's Bench Division in England or of the Court of Session in Scotland. The Election Court has a wide range of powers, including the power to order a recount or a scrutiny of the votes. The court determines whether the person whose election is complained of was duly elected and whether any corrupt or illegal practices at the election were proved. If the court finds the candidate to have been disqualified from membership of the House, the court may, if satisfied that the cause of the disqualification was known to the electorate, deem the votes cast for him or her to be void and declare the runner-up to have been elected.[95] If the election has not been conducted substantially in accordance with the law, or if there have been irregularities which have affected the result, the court must declare the election void and require a fresh election to be held.[96] The decision of the court is notified to the Speaker and is entered upon the journals of the House of Commons. The House must then give the necessary directions for confirming or altering the return or for issuing a writ for a new election, as the case may be.[97] In recent years there have been very few petitions in respect of parliamentary elections. The last instance of a successful candidate being unseated for election practices arose after the general election in December 1923.[98] Election petitions are more frequent in respect of local elections, where the procedure for challenging an irregular election is broadly the same.[99]

IV. Membership of the House of Commons

The following are the main categories of persons who are disqualified from sitting and voting in the House of Commons.[100]

---

[91] *Ashby v White* (1703) 2 Ld Raym 938; *R v Paty* (1704) 2 Ld Raym 1105. And Ch 11A.
[92] Eg *Re Kensington North Parliamentary Election* [1960] 2 All ER 150.
[93] Eg *Re Parliamentary Election for Bristol South East* [1964] 2 QB 257.
[94] Eg *Grieve v Douglas-Home* 1965 SC 315.
[95] As in the *Bristol South East* case.
[96] *Morgan v Simpson* [1975] QB 151; *Ruffle v Rogers* [1982] QB 1220 (local election cases).
[97] 1983 Act, s 144(7).
[98] Butler, *The Electoral System in Britain since 1918*, p 57.
[99] Note 96 above. And see *Sanders v Chichester* (above, p 172).
[100] For greater detail, see Erskine May, *Parliamentary Practice*, ch 3.

(a) Both by common law and by statute, aliens are disqualified; citizens of Commonwealth countries and the Republic of Ireland are not disqualified.[101]

(b) Persons under 21.[102]

(c) Mental patients. Under the Mental Health Act 1983, s 141, when a member is ordered to be detained on grounds of mental illness, the detention must be reported to the Speaker. The Speaker obtains a medical report from two medical specialists, followed by a second report after six months. If the member is still detained and suffering from mental illness, his or her seat is vacated.

(d) Peers and peeresses in their own right, other than those who have disclaimed under the Peerage Act 1963; peers of Ireland are eligible.

(e) Clergy who have been episcopally ordained (in the Church of England and Church of Ireland), ministers of the Church of Scotland,[103] and priests of the Roman Catholic Church.[104]

(f) Bankrupts. Under the Insolvency Act 1986, s 427, a debtor who is adjudged bankrupt is disqualified from election to the Commons (and from sitting in the House or on a committee). Where a sitting member is adjudged bankrupt, his or her seat becomes vacant when six months have elapsed without the judgment being annulled.

(g) Persons guilty of corrupt or illegal practices, under the Representation of the People Act 1983. Various forms of disqualification exist; depending on the offence the period may last from five to ten years, and the disqualification may be universal or limited to a particular constituency.[105]

(h) Under the Forfeiture Act 1870, a person convicted of treason is disqualified from membership until expiry of the sentence or receipt of a pardon. The effect of the Criminal Law Act 1967 was that other criminal convictions, even where a substantial prison sentence was imposed, did not disqualify from the House. Thus prisoners convicted of terrorist offences in Northern Ireland could be nominated and elected to the Commons, though they were unable to attend at Westminster.[106] Since 1981, a person convicted of an offence and sentenced to prison for more than a year by a court in the United Kingdom or elsewhere is, while detained in the British Isles or in the Republic of Ireland or is unlawfully at large, disqualified from being nominated and from being a member. If he or she is already a member, the seat is vacated.[107] It is within the disciplinary powers of the House to expel a member, but expulsion does not prevent him or her from being re-elected.[108]

---

[101] British Nationality Act 1981, Sched 7, first item.
[102] Parliamentary Elections Act 1695, s 7, was expressly preserved by the Family Law Reform Act 1969, Sched 2, para 2, when the age of majority was reduced to 18. And see P Norton [1980] PL 55.
[103] House of Commons (Clergy Disqualification) Act 1801; Re MacManaway [1951] AC 161; Report of Select Committee on Clergy Disqualification, HC 200 (1952–53).
[104] Roman Catholic Relief Act 1829, s 9. Under the Clerical Disabilities Act 1870, an Anglican clergyman may relinquish the rights and privileges of his office and become eligible for the Commons.
[105] 1983 Act, ss 159, 160, 173, 174.
[106] See G J Zellick [1977] PL 29.
[107] Representation of the People Act 1981; and see C P Walker [1982] PL 389.
[108] Page 240 below.

Formerly a person who held contracts with the Crown for the public service was disqualified from membership. But this disqualification was abolished in 1957 along with the disqualification of those who held pensions from the Crown. There continue to be rules and customs of the Commons regarding the declaration by members of their financial interests.[109]

Disqualification of office-holders

Until 1957, the law governing the disqualification which arose from the holding of public offices was 'archaic, confused and unsatisfactory'.[110] That law had grown out of ancient conflicts between Crown and Commons. During the early 17th century, the House secured recognition of the right to control its own composition. In particular, the House asserted the principle that a member could not continue to serve when appointed by the Crown to a position the duties of which entailed prolonged absence from Westminster. After 1660, the House feared that the Crown would exercise excessive influence over it by the use of patronage, and sought to avert a situation in which members held positions of profit at pleasure of the Crown. This fear led in 1700 to a provision in the Act of Settlement to the effect that no one who held an office or place of profit under the Crown should be capable of serving as a member of the House. This provision, which would have excluded ministers from the Commons, was repealed before it took effect. In its place, the Succession to the Crown Act 1707 enabled certain ministers to retain their seats in the House, subject to re-election after appointment, but excluded those who held office of a non-political character, for example in what today would be regarded as the civil service. But much legislation was necessary to establish the distinction between ministerial, or political, office-holders, who were eligible for membership, and non-political office-holders, who were excluded. Moreover, it was necessary to restrict the number appointed to ministerial office from the Commons, to avoid a situation in which the executive (now in the form of the Prime Minister) exercised excessive control by patronage over the House.

The House of Commons Disqualification Act 1957 (re-enacted in 1975) replaced disqualification for holding 'an office or place of profit under the Crown' by disqualification attached to the holding of specified offices. There are three broad reasons for disqualification: (1) the physical impossibility for certain office-holders of attendance at Westminster, (2) the risk of patronage and (3) the conflict of constitutional duties. Under s 1 of the 1975 Act, the disqualifying offices fall into six categories.

(*a*) A great variety of judicial offices, listed in Sched 1 of the Act, including judges in the High Court and the Court of Session, circuit judges in England and Wales, sheriffs in Scotland, resident magistrates in Northern Ireland and stipendiary magistrates. The principle is that no person may hold full-time judicial office and be a practising politician. Lay magistrates are not affected.
(*b*) Employment in the civil service of the Crown, whether in an established or temporary capacity, whole-time or part-time. The disqualification extends

---

[109] Ch 11 B.
[110] HC 120 (1940–41) and HC 349 (1955–56).

to members of the civil service of Northern Ireland and the diplomatic service. Civil servants who wish to stand for election to Parliament or to the European Parliament are required by civil service rules to resign before becoming candidates.[111]

(*c*) Membership of the regular armed forces of the Crown. Members of the reserve and auxiliary forces are not disqualified if recalled for active service. Members of the armed forces, like civil servants, must resign before becoming candidates for election to Parliament and they may apply for release to contest an election. A spate of such applications in 1962 led to the appointment of an advisory committee of seven members to examine the credentials of applicants and to test the sincerity of their desire to enter Parliament.[112]

(*d*) Membership of any police force maintained by a police authority.

(*e*) Membership of the legislature of any country or territory outside the Commonwealth. Except in the case of the Republic of Ireland, it is likely that members of such a legislature would be debarred by their status as aliens from membership of the Commons.

(*f*) A great variety of disqualifying offices arising from chairmanship or membership of commissions, boards, administrative tribunals, public authorities and undertakings; in a few cases the disqualification attaches only to particular constituencies (Sched 1, parts 2–4). As these offices cover such a wide range, each office is specified by name. The Schedule may be amended by Order in Council made following a resolution approved by the House of Commons.[113] This power obviates the need for amendment by statute as and when new offices are created (s 5). The Queen's Printer is authorised to print copies of the 1975 Act as it is amended by subsequent Orders in Council.

For one purpose alone acceptance of an office of profit continues to disqualify. From early times a member of the House was in law unable to resign his seat, and acceptance of an office of profit under the Crown was the only legal method of release from membership. The offices commonly used for the purpose were the office of Steward or Bailiff of the Chiltern Hundreds or of the Manor of Northstead. Under the Act of 1975 these offices are disqualifying offices (s 4). Appointment to them is made by the Chancellor of the Exchequer on the request of the member concerned.

Effects of disqualification

If any person is elected to the House while disqualified by the 1975 Act, the election is void (s 6(1)) and this could be so determined on an election petition. If a member becomes disqualified after election, his or her seat is vacated and the House may so resolve. Before 1957, Parliament might pass an Act of Indemnity in favour of members who had unwittingly become subject to disqualification. Today, the House may direct by order that a disqualification under the 1975 Act which existed at the material time be disregarded if it

---

[111]   Servants of the Crown (Parliamentary, European Assembly and Northern Ireland Assembly) Order 1987; and ch 13 D.

[112]   HC 111 and 262 (1962–63); HC Deb, 18 February 1963, col 163.

[113]   In 1993, an Order in Council made a net increase of 323 disqualifying offices and raised to £8,000 the level below which paid offices in the gift of the Crown do not normally disqualify; HC Deb, 16 June 1993, col 954; and SI 1993 No 1572.

has already been removed (for example, by the member's resignation from the office in question) (s 6(2)). Thus a new election is unnecessary where the House itself has dispensed with the consequences of the disqualification, but no such order can affect the proceedings on an election petition (s 6(3)).

Determination of claims

Disputed cases of disqualification are in general determined by the House after consideration by a select committee. Thus in 1961, the Committee of Privileges reported that Mr Tony Benn was disqualified because he had succeeded to his father's peerage while a member of the Commons.[114] While disputes under the 1975 Act as to disqualifying offices arise rarely, the Judicial Committee of the Privy Council has jurisdiction to declare whether a person has incurred a disqualification under that Act (s 7). Any person may apply to the Judicial Committee for a declaration of disqualification but must give security for costs. Issues of fact may on the direction of the Judicial Committee be tried by the High Court in England, the Court of Session in Scotland or the High Court in Northern Ireland (s 7(4)). A declaration may not be made if an election petition is pending or if one has been tried in which disqualification on the same grounds was in issue, nor where the House has given relief by order (s 7(5)). This jurisdiction replaces the former procedure by which a common informer could sue a disqualified member for financial penalties. Only in the case of members disqualified by the House of Commons (Clergy Disqualification) Act 1801 does the common informer procedure still survive. Another procedure open where there is a dispute over disqualification is for the Commons to petition the Crown to refer the matter to the Judicial Committee of the Privy Council for an advisory opinion on the law.[115]

Limitation of number of ministers in Commons

British practice requires that the holders of ministerial office should be members of either the Commons or the Lords and that the great majority should be drawn from the Commons. But it has long been necessary for limits to be imposed on the number of ministers who may sit in the Commons, lest excessive powers of patronage should be exercised by the Prime Minister over the House. The present law is found partly in the House of Commons Disqualification Act 1975 and partly in the Ministerial and other Salaries Act 1975. Section 2 of the former Act allows no more than 95 holders of ministerial office (whether paid or unpaid, it would seem) to sit and vote in the Commons; this limit had been raised from 70 to 91 in 1964[116] and to 95 in 1974.[117] If more members of the Commons are appointed to ministerial office than are allowed by law, those appointed in excess must not sit or vote in the House until the number has been reduced to the permitted figure (s 2(2)).

The Ministerial and other Salaries Act sets out the salaries payable to various categories of ministerial office, these salaries being subject to revision

---

[114]   HC 142 (1960–61).
[115]   Under the Judicial Committee Act 1833, s 4; and see *Re MacManaway* [1951] AC 161.
[116]   Ministers of the Crown Act 1964, noted by A E W Park (1965) 28 MLR 338.
[117]   Ministers of the Crown Act 1974.

by Order in Council (s 1(4)). Schedule 1 of the Act imposes limits upon the total number of such salaries payable at any one time to the various categories. Thus, in category 1 (holders of posts in the Cabinet apart from the Lord Chancellor) not more than 21 salaries are payable. Not more than 50 salaries are payable to posts in category 1 taken together with category 2 (ministers of state and departmental ministers outside the Cabinet). Not more than 83 salaries are payable to posts in categories 1, 2 and 3 (parliamentary secretaries) taken together. In addition, salaries are paid to the four law officers of the Crown, to five Junior Lords to the Treasury (government whips in the Commons) and to seven assistant whips in the Commons, as well as to various political posts in the royal household, some of which may be held only by members of the Lords.

The growth of the state has led to modern governments being larger than their predecessors. Statutory limits imposed on grounds of constitutional principle may seem irksome to a new Prime Minister, who may wish to by-pass these limits until they can be raised by legislation. Sometimes there are strong reasons for a particular increase to be made; thus the assumption of direct rule in Northern Ireland by the UK government made it necessary for extra ministers to be appointed. But the present limits are generous in relation to the size of the Commons, especially as there are also some 20 to 30 parliamentary private secretaries, who hold no statutory office but must support the government. The result is that the Prime Minister has at his or her disposal approximately 120 parliamentary appointments, most of which go to members of the Commons.[118]

V.   Electoral systems

Under the present electoral system in the United Kingdom, each constituency returns a single member. Each elector can vote for only one candidate and the successful candidate is the one who receives the highest number of valid votes. This system of 'first past the post' is known as the relative majority system since whenever there are more than two candidates in a constituency, the successful candidate may not have an absolute majority of votes but merely a majority relative to the vote of the runner-up.[119] This system is simple, but as a means of providing representation in Parliament it is very crude. It makes no provision for the representation of minority interests nor does it ensure that the distribution of seats in the Commons is at all proportionate to the national distribution of votes. In Britain, the general tendency of the system has been to exaggerate the representation of the two largest parties and to reduce that of the smaller parties; but even for the larger parties there is no consistent relation between the votes and the seats which they obtain. Thus in 1983, the Conservative party won 42% of the votes and 397 (61%) of the 650 seats; in 1992, 42% of the votes and 336 (52%) of the 651 seats. In 1983, the Labour party won 28% of the votes and 209 (32%) of the seats; in 1992, 34% of the votes and 271 (42%) of the seats. Ever since the Liberals became the third party in 1923, they have been regularly under-represented in relation to their national vote. Most strikingly,

---

[118]   See also ch 13 C on the position of ministers.
[119]   In the 1992 general election, 40% of the successful candidates lacked absolute majorities.

in 1983 the Liberal–Social Democratic alliance won 25.4% of the votes and only 23 (3.5%) of the seats; in 1992, the Liberal Democrat vote was 18%, electing 20 (3%); and in 1997 17% of the vote elected 46 (7%) of MPs. Similar anomalies occur for areas within the United Kingdom. Thus in Scotland in 1997, the Conservatives won 17% of the votes but none of the 72 seats. On this voting system, also used in Great Britain for election to the European Parliament and to local councils, the seats won by a party may bear no relation to the votes cast for that party.

The advantages claimed for the system include the simplicity of the voting method, the close links which develop between the member and his or her constituency, and its tendency to produce an absolute majority of seats in the House out of a large minority of votes. In defence of the system it is claimed that the function of a general election is to elect a government as well as a Parliament, and that the system produces strong government. This last claim needs to be examined with care, since a relatively small change of political support in a few constituencies may be exaggerated into an apparent change of mind from one party to the other by a majority of the electorate.

Other voting systems

Other electoral systems have long been devised with a view to securing better representation of minorities and a distribution of seats which bears a less haphazard relation to the votes cast. Many different systems are used in other countries.[120] One method, the alternative vote system, retains single-member constituencies but allows the elector to express a choice of candidates in order of preference. If no candidate has an absolute majority of first preferences, the lowest on the list is eliminated and his or her votes are distributed according to the second preference shown on the voting papers. The procedure continues until one candidate obtains an absolute majority. This system eliminates the return of a candidate on a minority vote when account is taken of second and later preferences, but it does not necessarily secure representation in the Commons proportional to the first preferences of the electorate on a national basis.

Other systems have been designed to secure representation in Parliament directly proportional to the national voting strengths of the parties. Thus by the list system, as used in Israel, voting for party lists of candidates takes place in a national constituency, with each party receiving that number of seats which comes closest to its national votes; this system does not provide for any local links between voters and their representatives. In Germany, a mixed system is used by which each elector has two votes, one to elect a candidate in a single-member constituency, the other to vote for a party list; the list seats are assigned to parties to compensate for disproportionate representation arising from the constituency elections, but a party must record 5% of the national vote or win three constituencies to gain any list seats.

The system which is likely to produce a reasonably close relationship between votes and seats while maintaining a local basis for representation is

---

[120] Bogdanor, *The People and the Party System*, parts III–V; and D Oliver [1983] PL 108. See also D Butler, in Jowell and Oliver (eds), *The Changing Constitution*, ch 13; and Turpin, *British Government and the Constitution*, ch 8(2).

that of the single transferable vote. This method has been used within the United Kingdom for several purposes.[121] It would require the country to be divided into multi-member constituencies, each returning between three and, say, seven members. Each elector would have a single vote but would vote for candidates in order of preference. Any candidate obtaining the quota of first preferences necessary to guarantee election would be immediately elected, the quota being calculated by a simple formula: in a five-member constituency, this quota would be one vote more than one-sixth of the total votes cast. The surplus votes of a successful candidate would be distributed to other candidates proportionately according to the second preference expressed; any candidate then obtaining the quota would be elected and a similar distribution of the surplus would follow. If at any count no candidate obtained the quota figure, the candidate with the lowest number of votes would be eliminated and all those votes distributed amongst the others.

Under this scheme, parties would both nationally and locally be likely to secure representation according to their true strength; minority parties and independent candidates would stand a better chance of election; and the number of ineffective votes would be reduced. Within the constituency, electors could in their order of preference choose between candidates from the same party and could base their choice of candidates on non-party considerations. Unless voting habits were to change, one party would be less likely to secure an absolute majority of seats in the Commons than at present; and Britain would become used to periods of minority or coalition government.[122] But this would not necessarily lead to instability nor to a proliferation of small parties. Nor would the quality of government be necessarily impaired. Existing MPs may resist the idea of multi-member constituencies. But it is not obvious why an elector is better represented in Parliament by a single member whose election he or she opposed rather than by a team of members the choice of which he or she has directly influenced, even if the first preference candidate has not been elected.

The case for proportional representation has been examined many times. A royal commission in 1910 rejected proportional representation but recommended the alternative vote.[123] In 1917, the Speaker's Conference on Electoral Reform recommended the adoption of proportional representation by the single transferable vote,[124] but Parliament after some vacillation refused to accept either this or the alternative vote. Following an all-party conference in 1929–30,[125] a Bill which sought to introduce the alternative vote passed the Commons but was abandoned when the Labour government fell in 1931. The Speaker's Conference on Electoral Reform in 1944 rejected by large majorities proposals for change, as did a similar conference in 1967.[126] But in 1973, the Royal Commission on the Constitution considered voting methods in

---

[121]   Eg for university constituencies between 1918 and 1948; in Northern Ireland for elections
         to Stormont in 1922–28, to the Assembly in 1973 and 1982, to the Constitutional
         Convention in 1975, and to the European Parliament.
[122]   Ch 2 D.
[123]   Cd 5163, 1910.
[124]   Cd 8463, 1917. And see Butler, *The Electoral System in Britain since 1918*, part I.
[125]   Cmd 3636, 1930.
[126]   Cmd 6534, 1944; and Cmnd 3202, 1967.

relation to elected assemblies for Scotland and Wales and recommended the adoption of the single transferable vote. The commission considered that an overriding requirement for the assemblies was to ensure the proper representation of minorities, but emphasised that it was not concerned with elections to the Westminster Parliament.[127] Nonetheless the Labour government supported by a majority in the Commons decided that the 'first past the post' system should be used for the assemblies that were to have been created under the Scotland Act and the Wales Act 1978.[128] The introduction of direct elections for the European Parliament at a time of minority government and the Callaghan–Steel pact gave an opportunity for the adoption of proportional representation in Great Britain, but the House of Commons defeated the proposal for a regional list system on a vote in which the Labour and Conservative parties were divided.[129]

In 1976, a non-governmental commission appointed by the Hansard Society (chairman, Lord Blake) recommended a system by which three-quarters of the Commons could be elected in single-member constituencies, the remainder to be allocated to parties within voting regions so that the seats won by parties might be brought closer to the proportion of votes. In 1982, a joint Liberal–Social Democratic commission on constitutional reform recommended a scheme of 'community proportional representation'; this was mainly based on the single transferable vote in multi-member constituencies but the alternative vote was also used in a few single-member constituencies retained for geographical reasons.[130] In 1995, a non-governmental body, the Scottish Constitutional Convention, recommended a mixed voting system for a Scottish parliament: each elector would vote for a constituency member and also for a regional party list.[131] In March 1997, before the general election in May, the Labour and Liberal Democratic parties agreed that an early referendum should be held on the system of national elections, that the regional list system be used for European elections, and that proportional systems should apply to the Scottish parliament and the Welsh assembly.

One device which has sometimes been used for facilitating reform of electoral law is a conference of party leaders meeting in private and chaired by the Speaker. The aim has been to secure all-party support for reforms in electoral law. However, the conference held in 1948 led to allegations of a private bargain being struck between party leaders and to subsequent recriminations; and the government was not bound by the conference's recommendations.[132] It is plainly desirable to secure as much cross-party support for electoral reform as possible, but today the purposes of a Speaker's conference may be better served by a royal commission or a select committee of the Commons. Changes in the electoral system must be made by Act of Parliament. However, if a referendum of the electorate were to become a

---

127   Kilbrandon Report, paras 779–88.
128   Cmnd 6348, 1975, p 9; and ch 3 B.
129   Cmnd 6768, 1977; HC Deb, 13 December 1977, col 417.
130   *Electoral Reform: Fairer Voting in Natural Communities*, 1982. And see [1982] PL 529.
131   *Scotland's Parliament, Scotland's Right*; and ch 3 B.
132   On the 1948 conference, see Butler, op cit, pp 109–22. Fewer difficulties arose in 1968 (Cmnd 3550 and 3717, 1968) and 1973 (Cmnd 5500, 1973). And see D Butler, in Butler and Halsey (eds), *Policy and Politics*, ch 2.

British constitutional practice, it could be argued that radical changes in electoral law should be the subject of a referendum.

C. Meeting of Parliament

Frequency and duration of Parliament

In law, a new Parliament is summoned by means of a royal proclamation. It is by the Sovereign that Parliament is prorogued, which occurs when a session of Parliament is terminated, and dissolved, which brings the life of one Parliament to an end. These powers of the Sovereign are prerogative powers, that is they are derived from the common law powers of the Crown, not from statutes.[133] They were used as political weapons by the Stuart kings during their struggles with Parliament in the 17th century; since then, they have been subjected to both legal and political controls, originally to ensure that the King could not govern without Parliament. In 1689, art 13 of the Bill of Rights provided that 'for redress of all grievances, and for the amending, strengthening and preserving of the laws, Parliament ought to be held frequently'.[134] In 1694, the Meeting of Parliament Act (formerly the Triennial Act) supplemented this rather vague demand by requiring that Parliament should meet at least once every three years, a requirement which still forms part of the law. Although there is no rule of law expressly requiring this, in practice Parliament has met annually ever since 1689. One reason for this is that since that time it has been the practice for some essential legislation, including authority for certain forms of taxation and expenditure, to be passed only for a year at a time; this legislation must therefore be renewed annually if lawful government is to be maintained. So too authority for the maintenance of the army has been continued in force annually, although this is now done by resolution of Parliament and not by Act.[135] Today the many pressures upon government to maintain a flow of legislation through Parliament and the expectation of all politicians that Parliament should meet regularly ensure that, subject to customary periods of holiday, Parliament is in constant session.

The Meeting of Parliament Act 1694 also regulated the life of a Parliament: no Parliament was to last for more than three years and, unless sooner dissolved, was then to expire by lapse of time. The Septennial Act 1715 extended the life of Parliament to seven years but the Parliament Act 1911 reduced the period to five years; the five-year period runs from the day which was appointed by writ of summons for Parliament to meet after a general election.[136] In practice, apart from the two world wars, when the life of Parliament was extended annually to avoid the holding of a general election during war-time, all modern Parliaments have been dissolved by the Sovereign, rather than expiring by lapse of time. The length of recent Parliaments has varied: that elected in February 1974 lasted only until October 1974; by

---

[133] Ch 12 D. And see Blackburn, *The Meeting of Parliament.*
[134] Ch 2 A.
[135] Ch 16.
[136] Septennial Act 1715 and Parliament Act 1911, s 5.

contrast, the Parliaments elected in 1987 and 1992 lasted for almost the full five years.

Modern practice is that the same proclamation both dissolves Parliament and summons a new one. Formerly Parliament would be dissolved only after it had first been prorogued, but dissolution may now occur while the two Houses are adjourned.[137] Between general elections, a session of Parliament usually runs from late October or early November for about one year. After the long summer adjournment of both Houses, there is usually a short resumption of the two Houses to complete necessary legislative business. Parliament is then prorogued, and a new session opens a few days later.

General elections and by-elections

After the summoning of Parliament by proclamation, individual writs are issued to the members of the Lords, and writs are issued to returning officers commanding an election of members of the Commons to be held.[138] When a vacancy occurs in the House during a Parliament, for example by the death of a member, the Speaker may by warrant authorise the issue of a writ for the holding of a by-election. When the House is sitting, the Speaker issues the warrant upon the order of the House.[139] By long-established custom of the House, the motion for the issue of a writ is moved by the Chief Whip of the party which held the seat before the vacancy occurred. There is no time-limit for filling the vacancy. In 1973, the Speaker's Conference on electoral law recommended that the writ for a by-election should normally be moved within three months of the vacancy occurring.[140]

Dissolution

Parliament continues for five years unless it is sooner dissolved by the Sovereign on the advice of the Prime Minister. Save in exceptional circumstances, the Sovereign must give effect to the Prime Minister's request. It is not necessary that the Cabinet should have decided in favour of dissolution, although the Prime Minister may have discussed the desirability of a dissolution with the Cabinet or with selected colleagues.[141] The opportunity to choose the timing of a general election is an important power at the disposal of the Prime Minister who may choose a time when there is a revival in the economy or when the government's popularity is rising. It is sometimes said that the right to request a dissolution is a powerful weapon in the hands of a Prime Minister to compel recalcitrant supporters in the Commons to conform. Where government policies are challenged by major national interests, the Prime Minister may take the dispute to the electorate in the hope of getting renewed support, as happened in February 1974 when Mr Heath called an election because the miners' strike challenged his economic policy.

---

137   See R Blackburn [1987] PL 533.
138   See section B above.
139   By the Recess Elections Act 1975, which re-enacted an Act of 1784, the Speaker may order the issue of a writ during a recess caused by prorogation or adjournment.
140   Cmnd 5500, 1973.
141   Jennings, *Cabinet Government*, pp 417–19; Mackintosh, *The British Cabinet*, pp 452–5; Marshall, *Constitutional Conventions*, ch 3; Brazier, *Constitutional Practice*, pp 90–2.

But dissolution is too ultimate a deterrent to be a convenient means of bringing pressure to bear on government members of the Commons, since an election at an unfavourable time may mean that the party goes out of office sooner than it otherwise would have done. Nevertheless, the possibility of a dissolution before the statutory life of a Parliament has run its course leaves the executive with a means of controlling Parliament which would not be available if the law required an election of a new Parliament at prescribed intervals (for example, once every four years). The personal role of the Sovereign in respect of a dissolution will be examined later.[142]

Since the Representation of the People Act 1867, the duration of Parliament has been independent of the life of the Sovereign. If Parliament should be prorogued or adjourned when the Sovereign dies, Parliament must reassemble at once without a summons.[143] Should the Sovereign die after a dissolution, but before the date fixed for the election, the former Parliament must meet immediately and polling day is postponed for two weeks.[144]

Prorogation and adjournment

Prorogation brings to an end a session of Parliament. Parliament is prorogued not by the Sovereign in person but by a royal commission, through whom the prorogation speech reviewing the work of the session is delivered to Parliament. Parliament may be recalled by proclamation at one day's notice during a prorogation, if this should be necessary.[145] Prorogation terminates all business pending in Parliament, with the exception of the judicial work of the House of Lords. Any public Bills which have not passed through all stages in both Houses lapse. In the case of private Bills a resolution may be passed before prorogation directing that a Bill be held over till the next session.

Each House may adjourn for such time as it pleases, but this does not end any uncompleted business. The Sovereign may call upon Parliament to meet before the conclusion of an adjournment intended to last for more than 14 days.[146] The standing orders of each House authorise an adjournment of either House to be terminated at short notice, should the Lord Chancellor or the Speaker be satisfied on the request of the government that the public interest requires it. Parliament must be recalled within five days if a state of emergency is declared or the reserve forces are called out during an adjournment or prorogation.[147]

Opening of Parliament

After a dissolution or a prorogation, Parliament is opened by the Sovereign in person or by royal commissioners. When a new Parliament meets, the House of Commons first elects a Speaker, for which purpose the MP who has the longest continuous period of membership and is not a minister of the Crown

---

[142] Ch 12 B.
[143] Succession to the Crown Act 1707, s 5.
[144] Representation of the People Act 1985, s 20, repealing the Meeting of Parliament Act 1797, ss 3–5.
[145] Parliament (Elections and Meetings) Act 1943, s 34.
[146] Meeting of Parliament Act 1870, amending the Meeting of Parliament Act 1799.
[147] Emergency Powers Act 1920 (ch 25 D); Reserve Forces Act 1966, s 5(2).

presides over the proceedings.[148] After this the House adjourns until the election of the Speaker has been announced to the Lord Chancellor in the House of Lords. The Lords take the oath of allegiance as soon as Parliament has been opened, and the Commons as soon as the Speaker has taken the oath.[149]

At the beginning of every session, the first business is the debate on the speech from the Throne. This speech announces in outline the government's plans for the principal business of the session. It is delivered in the House of Lords, to which the Commons are summoned to hear the speech read by the Sovereign or by the Lord Chancellor. In each House an address is moved in answer to the speech, and a general debate of national affairs takes place, lasting some four or five days.

Lord Chancellor

The Lord Chancellor presides over the House of Lords as its Speaker. He has important functions outside the House as a member of the Cabinet, responsible for many aspects of the machinery of justice.[150] In contrast with the impartial role of the Speaker in the Commons, the Lord Chancellor may take part in debates. He is often the principal spokesman for the government; while speaking, he vacates the Woolsack temporarily by stepping aside from it. That part of the Lord Chancellor's salary which is paid in respect of his duties as Speaker in the Lords is charged on the House of Lords vote.[151] In order that their official salaries may be paid, the Lord Chancellor must in cases of doubt decide which peers are the Leader of the Opposition and the Chief Opposition Whip in the Lords.[152] The duties of the Deputy Speaker are undertaken by the Lord Chairman of Committees. A member of the House is elected to this salaried office, which carries with it extensive duties relating to private Bills, as well as the duty to preside in committee of the whole House.

The Speaker

The chief officer of the House of Commons is the Speaker. Except when the House is in committee, she is its chairman and is responsible for the orderly conduct of debate. It is through the Speaker that the House communicates with the Sovereign. Today, the Speaker is expected to act with complete impartiality between the parties and to preserve the right of minorities in the House.[153] She determines whether a Bill is a money Bill within the meaning of the Parliament Act 1911.[154] The Speaker is nominal chairman of each of the four boundary commissions which review the distribution of seats.[155] She has many duties which affect the business of the House, for example to decide whether to accept for debate a question raised as an important matter that

---

[148] HC Standing Order 1(1), and see HC 111 (1971–72).
[149] Under the Oaths Act 1978, s 5, members may make a solemn affirmation in lieu of the oath.
[150] Ch 18 C.
[151] Ministerial and other Salaries Act 1975, s 1(2).
[152] Ibid, s 2(3).
[153] See Laundy, *The Office of Speaker*.
[154] Ch 10 B.
[155] Section B above.

should have urgent consideration by the House,[156] and has an important discretion to exercise in selecting amendments to Bills for debate.[157] The Speaker's rulings on procedure are an important source of Commons practice and if given in the House have always been recorded in Hansard. Since 1981, private rulings that are of general interest or likely to become precedents are also published in Hansard.[158]

A member of the House is elected to be Speaker at the beginning of each new Parliament and whenever a vacancy otherwise occurs. It is customary for the party with a majority in the House to select a candidate from amongst its own number, but that person will not necessarily be elected. In 1971, when Mr Selwyn Lloyd, a former Conservative minister, was elected Speaker, many members felt that there had been inadequate consultation; subsequently certain changes in procedure were made.[159] In 1992, the House elected its first woman Speaker, Miss Boothroyd, who came from the Opposition benches in a contested election to defeat a former Cabinet minister. If the Speaker in the previous Parliament is re-elected as an MP at the general election, it is customary for her to be re-elected as Speaker when the new Parliament meets. In such a case, she will have fought the election as Speaker, not as a member of her former party.

While the Speaker is unable to represent her constituency's interests in debate, she is able to take up the grievances of constituents privately with the departments concerned. The Speaker's salary is payable out of the Consolidated Fund. A retired Speaker receives a peerage and a statutory pension. If a Speaker dies in office, all business of the House comes to a halt until a successor is appointed.

Deputy Speaker

When the House of Commons is in committee, the chair is taken by the Chairman (or one of the two Deputy Chairmen) of Ways and Means, or by one of a chairmen's panel of not less than ten members nominated by the Speaker for the purpose of providing chairmen of standing committees. One of these officers will preside when a Bill is taken in committee by the whole House.[160] The Chairman of Ways and Means is the Deputy Speaker, but the duties of Deputy Speaker may also be performed by the two Deputy Chairmen of Ways and Means.[161] New appointments as Chairman of Ways and Means and Deputy Chairmen may be made on a change of government. By custom of the House the holders of these offices do not take an active part in debates but may resume their normal political activities after they have left these posts.

Officers of Parliament

The chief permanent officer of the House of Lords is the Clerk of the Parliaments, appointed by the Crown and removable only by the Crown on

---

[156]   HC Standing Order 20.
[157]   Ch 10 A.
[158]   HC Deb, 5 November 1981, col 113; and see eg HC Deb, 9 December 1981, col 970.
[159]   Note 148 above.
[160]   Ch 10 A.
[161]   Deputy Speaker Act 1855; HC Standing Orders 2–4.

address from the Lords. His duties include the endorsement of every Act of Parliament with the date on which it received the royal assent, and the custody of one copy of every Act printed on vellum. The Lord Chairman of Committees is assisted in his work on private legislation by Counsel to the Chairman of Committees.

The Clerk of the House of Commons is appointed by the Crown; two Clerk Assistants are appointed by the Crown on the nomination of the Speaker. These officers may be removed only upon an address from the House. The Clerk of the House is responsible for the records and journals of all proceedings in the Commons, endorsing all Bills sent to the Lords, and laying documents on the table of the House. He is the Accounting Officer for House of Commons expenditure. The Speaker's Counsel advises the Speaker and officers of the House on matters of law, and his duties include the oversight of private legislation and the scrutiny of statutory instruments. The Serjeant at Arms, appointed by the Crown, is responsible for enforcing the orders of the House. Before the Queen appoints a new Serjeant at Arms, she consults with the Speaker, who may take soundings in the House before the appointment is made.[162]

By the Parliamentary Corporate Bodies Act 1992, the Clerk of the Parliaments and the Clerk of the House of Commons were respectively designated as the Corporate Officers of the two Houses, each with capacity as a corporation sole to hold property, make contracts and so on for the House in question.

The administration of Parliament

The Palace of Westminster was formerly controlled on the Sovereign's behalf by the Lord Great Chamberlain but in 1965 control of the Palace (except for Westminster Hall) passed to the two Houses. Control of that part occupied by the House of Lords is vested in the Lord Chancellor, and is exercised by the House of Lords Offices Committee; and of that part occupied by the Commons in the Speaker. Administration of the Commons was reformed with the establishment of a House of Commons Commission under the House of Commons (Administration) Act 1978.[163] The commission consists of the Speaker, the Leader of the House, a member nominated by the Leader of the Opposition and three other members appointed by the House. The commission is responsible for the staff of the House, for preparing annual estimates of House expenditure, and for supervising the departments into which the work of the House is organised. Underlying these arrangements are such problems as how much should be paid to service the activities of the House, what these activities should be, and whether the government should control the House's expenditure. Acting on his own authority, the Speaker in 1987 directed that a BBC film on the Zircon defence project, alleged to have been made in breach of the Official Secrets Act 1911, should not be shown in a committee room at Westminster by back-bench MPs. This action was upheld by the Committee of Privileges.[164] Since 1992, after the Ibbs report on House

---

[162] HC Deb, 11 December 1962, cols 209–10.
[163] Largely based upon the Bottomley report (HC 624, 1974–75). And see Erskine May, ch 12.
[164] See HC 365 (1986–87); A W Bradley [1987] PL 1, 487.

of Commons services,[165] the House has appointed three select committees dealing respectively with accommodation and works, administration, and finance and services.

---

[165]   HC 38 (1990–91).

CHAPTER 10

Functions of Parliament

We have already examined the relationship between Parliament, the executive and the judiciary, and the principle of responsible government. In looking more closely at the functions of Parliament, we will focus attention upon the House of Commons, since it is the composition of this House that determines which party will form the government, it is from the Commons that most ministers are drawn, and it is the House of Commons that by withdrawing its support can cause the Prime Minister to resign or to seek a dissolution. But the work of the House of Commons must not be exaggerated beyond its context. First, the role of the House of Lords in Parliament, especially in legislation, is significant, although the political role of the House is secondary to that of the Commons. Secondly, the political authority of the House of Commons does not extend to its undertaking the work of government itself. Most members of the Commons are not members of the government. Nor could an elected assembly of 659 members itself take on the executive role in national affairs.

A classic statement of both the importance of parliamentary control of government and its limitations was made by the political philosopher, John Stuart Mill:

There is a radical distinction between controlling the business of government, and actually doing it. The same person or body may be able to control everything, but cannot possibly do everything; and in many cases its control over everything will be more perfect, the less it personally attempts to do ... It is one question, therefore, what a popular assembly should control, another what it should itself do ... Instead of the function of governing, for which it is radically unfit, the proper office of a representative assembly is to watch and control the government; to throw the light of publicity on its acts; to compel a full exposition and justification of all of them which anyone considers questionable; to censure them if found condemnable, and, if the men who compose the government abuse their trust, or fulfil it in a manner which conflicts with the deliberate sense of the nation, to expel them from office, and either expressly or virtually appoint their successors.[1]

Mill stressed that an important function of the Commons was also to be a sounding-board for the nation's grievances and opinions, 'an arena in which

---

[1] Mill, *Representative Government*, ch 5.

not only the general opinion of the nation, but that of every section of it . . . can produce itself in full light and challenge discussion'.[2]

This high-principled analysis is still of value, even though the strength of the executive power today, the present electoral and party system, and the fact that economic and industrial power is located outside the House of Commons, together present a formidable challenge to the political authority of the House. If it is a duty of the House to find out about, scrutinise and influence the many acts of government agencies, two consequences follow: first, the House needs procedures and resources that match the scale of the task; secondly, the members of the House who do not hold ministerial office need the political will to do more than simply sustain the government in office while voting through the measures laid before it. The creation by the Commons in 1979 of a system of specialist committees to scrutinise the main departments of government was a notable reform,[3] but the committees operate within a House which for many tasks still adopts an adversary approach to politics in its proceedings.[4]

Many writers have sought to list the principal functions of Parliament. Bagehot in *The English Constitution* included within the functions of the House of Commons the expressive function (expressing the opinion of the people), the teaching function, and the informing function ('it makes us hear what otherwise we should not'),[5] as well as the functions of legislation and finance. In 1978, the House's Select Committee on Procedure, whose report led to the reform of the committee system in 1979, considered that the major tasks of the Commons fell into four main categories: legislation, the scrutiny of the activities of the executive, the control of finance, and the redress of grievances.[6] Inevitably these categories overlap and the list does not include the broader political functions of the House that underly its more detailed tasks. Here the work of Parliament will be examined under four headings: (*a*) legislation; (*b*) conflict between the two Houses; (*c*) financial procedure; and (*d*) scrutiny of administration.[7] The redress of collective grievances is related to all these headings; the redress of individual grievances is an aspect of the scrutiny of administration, and also relevant is the Parliamentary Ombudsman, whose work will be considered in chapter 28 D.

A. Legislation

In chapter 4, we saw that the legislative supremacy of Parliament does not mean that the whole work of legislating is carried on within Parliament, nor that the parliamentary stage is the most formative stage in the process of legislation. In practice about half of the time of the Commons is devoted to

---

[2]   Ibid.
[3]   Section D below.
[4]   Cf Finer (ed), *Adversary Politics and Electoral Reform.*
[5]   Bagehot, p 153. And see Norton, *The Commons in Perspective,* ch 4.
[6]   HC 588–I (1977–78), p viii.
[7]   See also Ryle and Richards (eds), *The Commons Under Scrutiny;* Walkland (ed), *The House of Commons in the Twentieth Century;* Norton, *The Commons in Perspective;* Griffith and Ryle, *Parliament.*

legislative work. Many government policies can be achieved within the framework of existing legislation: for example, by the provision of more money for certain purposes or by the use of existing powers to direct local authorities. But other policies require legislation and most legislation is initiated by the government. The scope for legislative initiatives by individual MPs is severely limited, both because of restricted parliamentary time and of the tight hold which the government maintains over departmental action. The process by which government policies are turned into law falls into three broad stages:

(*a*) before publication of the Bill;
(*b*) the passage of the Bill through Parliament;
(*c*) after the Bill has received the royal assent.

In this section, emphasis is placed on the second of these stages. But stages (*a*) and (*c*) are both important to an understanding of the legislative process.[8]

The pre-Bill stage

The life-history of a Bill usually has begun long before it is laid before Parliament. The source of a Bill may be in a party's political programme or in the efforts of a pressure group to get the law reformed. Public authorities may have experienced difficulties in administering the existing law and may seek wider powers. A royal commission, a departmental committee or the Law Commissions may have published reports recommending reform. Economic problems or the action of terrorists may have made it necessary for government to take preventive measures. A decision of the courts, or a disaster such as the shooting of schoolchildren in Dunblane, may have shown the need for legislation. The government may have entered into a treaty which imposes an obligation to change the law of the United Kingdom. Whatever the circumstances which cause legislation to be seen as necessary, before a Bill can be introduced into Parliament by the minister of the sponsoring department, it must be adopted into the government's legislative programme. In 1995, it was the task of the Cabinet committee on the Queen's Speeches and Future Legislation to prepare proposals for the legislative programme in each session of Parliament; a second Cabinet committee (on Legislation) examined the text of all draft Bills and considered the parliamentary handling of Bills and European Community documents.[9]

Within the limits of Cabinet approval, it is for the department primarily concerned to decide what a Bill should contain and these instructions are conveyed to Parliamentary Counsel, who are responsible for drafting all government Bills. While a Bill is being drafted, extensive consultation may take place with other departments affected and successive revisions of the draft Bill are circulated confidentially within government. There may also be consultation with organisations outside government representing the interests primarily affected, but it is not usual for the draft Bill itself to be disclosed. If more open consultation is desired, the government may publish a con-

---

8 Cf the analysis made in *Making the Law* (Hansard Society report on the legislative process, 1993).
9 *Ministerial Committees of the Cabinet* (Cabinet Office, October 1995); and ch 13 B.

sultative document, for example a 'green paper', which states the government's provisional views, or a 'white paper', which while stating the government's decided position may leave certain matters open for further discussion. Where green or white papers are published, they are sometimes debated in Parliament, but the pre-Bill stage is essentially an administrative and political process which is carried on within government and behind the closed doors of Whitehall. More than once, committees of the Commons have recommended the wider use of pre-legislation committees of Parliament, so that MPs may be more closely associated with the stage when legislative policies are being settled. Occasionally select committees have been established for this purpose.[10] The system of select committees created in 1979 has enabled some committees to act as pre-legislation committees by receiving evidence from interested quarters and recommending changes in the law. Introduction of a Bill into Parliament by the responsible minister means that the form of the legislation has been settled. While lobbying and consultation may continue, subsequent changes to the Bill can be made only by formal amendment: this will involve persuading the government to admit publicly that it has had second thoughts.[11] Only rarely will a government Bill leave a choice between alternative proposals to be made by Parliament, but as a result of the Liberal/Labour pact in 1977, the choice of voting systems was left to the Commons in the Bill which became the European Assembly Elections Act 1978.

Public Bill procedure

The process of legislation, like most aspects of parliamentary procedure, is complicated.[12] A distinction must be drawn between public and private Bills. A public Bill seeks to alter the general law and is introduced into Parliament under the standing orders of the two Houses relating to public business. A private Bill is a Bill relating to a matter of individual, corporate or local interest and is subject to separate standing orders relating to private business.[13] A private Bill must not be confused with a public Bill introduced by a private member, which is known as a private member's Bill.[14] In the case of government Bills, the sponsoring minister presents the Bill to the Commons; it receives a formal first reading and is then printed and published. There follows the second reading of the Bill, when the House may debate the general proposals contained in the Bill. If the second reading is opposed, a division may take place on an opposition amendment to postpone the second reading for three or six months, or (more usually) on a reasoned amendment opposing the Bill. For a government Bill to be lost on second reading would be a serious political defeat. This setback has been avoided by most modern

---

[10]　See HC 538 (1970–71), paras 7–9 and app I, part IV, and HC 588–1 (1977–78), p xii.

[11]　*Making the Law*, op cit, ch 3, commented that many Bills reached Parliament in an unfinished state and that more open consultation would help the government to get Bills right before they were published.

[12]　See HC 538 (1970–71); Griffith, *Parliamentary Scrutiny of Government Bills*; Miers and Page, *Legislation*; Erskine May (especially ch 21); Griffith and Ryle, *Parliament*, chs 6–8; and *Making the Law* (above, note 8).

[13]　Page 210 below.

[14]　Page 205 below.

governments, but not by the government in 1986 when the Shops Bill, to reform the law on Sunday opening of shops, was defeated on second reading in the Commons by 296 votes to 282.[15] In the Commons, a whole day (ie from 3.30 pm to 10 pm) may be set aside for the second reading of a major Bill, but many Bills are debated for less than two hours and two or more days may be allotted to the debate of Bills of exceptional political importance.[16] Where a Bill involves new public expenditure or new taxation, the Commons must approve a financial resolution on the proposal of a minister before the clauses concerned may be considered in committee; the financial resolution is approved immediately after a Bill's second reading.[17]

Second reading committees

Some Bills may receive a second reading without any debate in the whole House. Where a Bill relates exclusively to Scotland, the Bill may, unless at least ten members object, be referred on the proposal of a minister to the Scottish Grand Committee, which consists of the 72 members for Scottish constituencies. The Scottish Grand Committee considers the principle of the Bill and, unless six or more MPs wish to divide the House, the Bill is deemed to have had a second reading.[18] In the case of other public Bills, a minister may propose that a Bill be referred to a second reading committee, subject to objection by at least 20 members. In this case a committee is appointed ad hoc to consider whether the Bill ought to be read a second time and to recommend accordingly to the House.[19] Where a second reading debate takes place in committee, the general merits of the Bill are debated, but any vote on the Bill is taken in the whole House. These procedures are not suitable for major or controversial Bills. Between 1965 and 1994, 139 Bills were referred to second reading committees, 105 of which had already passed through the House of Lords.[20]

Committee stage

After second reading, a Bill is normally referred for detailed consideration to a standing committee, consisting of between 16 and 50 members nominated by the Committee of Selection.[21] The Committee of Selection must have regard to the qualifications of the members and to the composition of the House, which means in practice that the parties are represented as nearly as possible in proportion to their representation in the House. If the government came into office with an overall majority over other parties and later loses that majority, it ceases to have a majority on standing committees.[22] Despite its name, a standing committee is constituted afresh for each Bill. The chairman of a standing committee is a member of the chairmen's panel

---

[15]   HC Deb, 14 April 1986, cols 584–702.
[16]   Griffith, op cit, ch 2; Griffith and Ryle, op cit, pp 322–9.
[17]   Page 220 below; Erskine May, ch 28; Griffith and Ryle, op cit, pp 231, 251–2, 330–1.
[18]   HC Standing Order (HC SO) 93. And see CMG Himsworth (1996) 1 Edin LR 79.
[19]   HC SO 90; Griffith, op cit, ch 2; Griffith and Ryle, op cit, pp 230, 312.
[20]   Hopkins, *Parliamentary Procedures and the Law Commission*, app 2.
[21]   HC SOs 84, 86; Griffith, op cit, ch 3.
[22]   HC Deb, 11 January 1995, col 158.

appointed by the Speaker. Not more than two standing committees may be appointed for the committee stage of Bills which relate exclusively to Scotland.[23]

Instead of referring a Bill to a standing committee, the House may commit the Bill to a committee of the whole House,[24] for which purpose the Speaker's place is taken by the Chairman of Ways and Means or one of the deputy chairmen. In practice this happens only on the proposal of the government, whether for minor Bills on which the committee stage is purely formal, for Bills of outstanding political or constitutional importance, or for Bills which the government wishes to see become law as soon as possible. Major Bills taken in committee of the whole House have included the Bills for the European Communities Act 1972, the Scotland Act and the Wales Act 1978, the Northern Ireland Act 1982, and the Representation of the People Act 1985, as well as the European Communities (Amendment) Act 1993, which approved the Treaty on European Union. Such Bills require a great deal of time if they are to be debated in detail by the whole House. Until 1967, the annual Finance Bill, which embodies the changes in taxation proposed in the Chancellor of the Exchequer's Budget speech, was referred to a committee of the whole House but the Bill is now divided, certain major clauses being taken before the whole House, the remainder being referred to a standing committee.[25]

Whether a Bill is considered in standing committee or in committee of the whole House, the object of the committee stage is to consider the individual clauses of the Bill and to enable amendments to be made. While general approval has been given to the Bill on second reading, members opposed to the Bill may use the committee stage to propose amendments narrowing the scope of the Bill or in other ways rendering it more acceptable to them. Members may be able to persuade the minister in charge of the Bill to reconsider a specific point, but the government expects to maintain its majority in committee and an amendment is not often made against the wishes of the government. As has been commented, 'The direct impact of the committee stage on the contents of Bills is very small: only rarely is an amendment successfully moved against the wishes of the government and only rarely does the government accept an amendment moved by the Opposition.'[26] The indirect impact is much greater than this, as the debate in committee often causes the government to propose amendments at a later stage. In committee, members may speak any number of times supporting or opposing amendments. After the amendments to a clause have been considered, there may take place a further debate on the motion that the clause, or the clause as amended, should stand part of the Bill. The chairman of the committee has wide powers of regulating proceedings: thus he must decide whether amendments are admissible or out of order and he exercises an

---

[23]   HC SO 95. For a public Bill relating exclusively to Wales, the standing committee includes all members for Welsh constituencies (SO 86(2)).

[24]   HC SO 61.

[25]   HC SO 61; Griffith, op cit, pp 34–7; Griffith and Ryle, op cit, pp 321–2.

[26]   Griffith and Ryle, op cit, p 317. For confirmation of this, see the fate of all amendments to government Bills in 1967–68, 1968–69, and 1970–71, recorded in Griffith, ch 3.

important discretion in selecting and grouping the amendments which are to be moved.[27] Civil servants are present, and assist ministers in dealing with points raised in debate, but they are not allowed to address the committee.

Exceptionally, when it is desired that a small number of members should investigate in detail the need for a Bill and the merits of its clauses, a Bill after second reading may be referred to a select committee of the Commons, or to a joint committee of Lords and Commons. Such a committee has power to take evidence from persons and organisations whether within government or outside at not more than three sittings.[28] While committees on procedure have recommended the more regular use of select committees, it has not been the practice to use select committees for Bills which are strongly supported by departments and which give effect to settled government policies. Between 1980 and 1984, 'special standing committees' were used for five Bills, including those which became the Criminal Attempts Act 1981 and the Mental Health (Amendment) Act 1982: before considering the Bills clause by clause, they took evidence from experts and interest groups. The procedure was not used after 1984, possibly because there was no obvious advantage to government in enabling members to form their own views on the contents of Bills.[29]

Report and third reading

When a Bill has completed its committee stage, it is reported as amended to the whole House. On the report stage, further amendments may be made to the Bill on the proposal of ministers, sometimes to give effect to undertakings which they have given in committee, sometimes to remove amendments made in committee but not accepted by the government. The Opposition may use the report stage to urge further amendments upon the government, although it is rare for these amendments to succeed and the Speaker has the discretion to select the amendments which will be debated.[30] A Bill committed to the whole House and not amended in committee is not considered by the House on report. Bills which were considered by a second reading committee or the Scottish Grand Committee may be referred to a standing committee or to the Scottish Grand Committee for the report stage, but there has been reluctance to deprive the whole House of its opportunity to consider Bills on report.[31]

After a Bill has been considered on report, it receives its third reading; only verbal amendments may be made to a Bill at this stage.[32] Such debates as there are tend to be brief and formal, although with a controversial Bill the Opposition may wish once more to vote against it.

---

[27]   HC SOs 31 and 89(3). By SOs 67 and 89(3), the chairman may refuse to allow debate of the motion that a clause 'stand part' of the Bill if he or she is of opinion that the principle of the clause has been adequately discussed in the debate on the amendments.

[28]   HC SO 91. See also HC 538 (1970–71), paras 27–9; HC 558–1 (1977–78), pp xv–xix; Griffith and Ryle, op cit, pp 317–18; and H J Beynon [1982] PL 193.

[29]   Hopkins, op cit, part III.

[30]   HC SO 3(1).

[31]   HC SO 92; HC 588–1 (1977–78), p xx; HC 350 (1986–87), p iv; Griffith and Ryle, op cit, pp 235–7.

[32]   HC SO 75.

Allocation of time

In the legislative work of the Commons, the time factor is always of importance both to the government, which wishes to see its Bills pass through Parliament without delay, and to the Opposition and back-bench MPs, who may seek to prolong proceedings as a means of persuading the government to make concessions. Exceptionally, as in the case of the Commonwealth Immigrants Act 1968 and the Prevention of Terrorism (Additional Powers) Act 1996, the government may see the passage of legislation as being of extreme urgency. But even in matters which are not themselves urgent, the more time which one Bill takes, the less time is available in the House for other legislation. As well as the power of the Speaker or chairman to require a member to discontinue speaking who persists in irrelevance or tedious repetition,[33] various methods of curtailing debates have been adopted by the House. The simplest method is that known as the closure, by which any member (in practice usually a government whip) may, either in the House or in Committee, move 'that the question be now put'. The chairman may refuse to put the motion on the ground that it is an abuse of the rules of the House or an infringement of the rights of the minority but, if the chairman does not so refuse, the closure motion must be put forthwith and it is voted upon without debate. It can be carried in the House only if not less than 100 members vote for the motion; if so carried, the debate cannot be resumed and the motion under discussion must then be voted upon.[34]

A second method, which has already been mentioned, is the power of the chairman at the committee stage and of the Speaker at the report stage to select those amendments which are to be discussed; this power is exercised more strictly at the report stage than in committee. A third and more drastic method is the 'guillotine', by which a minister may move an allocation of time order in the House to allot a specified number of days or portions of days to the consideration of a Bill in committee of the whole House or on report. The guillotine motion may be debated for no more than three hours. If it is carried it is the duty of the Business Committee, which consists of the Chairman of Ways and Means and up to eight other members nominated by the Speaker, to divide the Bill into parts and to allot to each part a specified period of time.[35] A similar procedure exists by which the House may allocate time for the proceedings of a standing committee on any Bill; the detailed allocation of time is then made by a Business sub-committee.[36] The effect of an allocation of time order is that at the end of each allotted period, the portion of the Bill in question is voted upon without further discussion. Compulsory timetabling of this kind can have the result that substantial parts of a Bill have not been considered at all by the Commons before it is sent to the Lords. In practice, the two sides in the House often agree through the usual channels (ie through the respective whips) on the voluntary timetabling of a Bill; where such informal

---

[33] HC SO 41.
[34] HC SOs 35, 36. In the 1993–94 session, 22 closures were claimed in the House; only two were refused by the chairman (HC 257 (1994–95)).
[35] HC SOs 80, 81. For the history, see Jennings, *Parliament*, pp 241–6; for recent practice, Griffith and Ryle, op cit, pp 302–7, and G Ganz [1990] PL 496.
[36] HC SO 103.

agreement is not available, an imposed timetable is necessary if the government wishes to maintain its legislative programme against pressure from the Opposition. The repeated proposal that a formal timetable should be established for all public Bills has not been favoured.[37] In the late 1980s, the practice of the Conservative government was to impose the guillotine on controversial Bills more frequently and at an earlier stage than any previous government had done, with the professed aim of ensuring 'proper, meaningful discussion of all parts of a Bill'.[38] But it is difficult to impose this on opposition MPs who are strenuously opposed to the government achieving any of its aims. In fact, for much of the 1992–97 Parliament, informal agreement was reached on the timetabling of many Bills.

Private members' Bills

Although the bulk of the legislative programme is taken up by government Bills, a small but significant part consists of Bills introduced by back-bench MPs. Standing orders generally give precedence to government business but they set aside ten Fridays in each session on which private members' Bills have priority. On the first six of these Fridays, precedence is given to the second reading of Bills presented by members who have secured the best places in the ballot for private members' Bills held at the beginning of each session. On the remaining four Fridays, precedence is given to the later stages of those Bills which received their second readings earlier in the session.[39] One of the standing committees is used primarily for the committee stage of private members' Bills, but these Bills may instead be referred to other standing committees which are not occupied with government Bills; the composition of a standing committee on a private member's Bill usually reflects the voting of the House on second reading, so that the supporters of the Bill form a majority. Private members' Bills are used for a variety of purposes[40] including matters of social reform (for example, abortion and divorce law reform) on which public opinion may be too sharply divided for the government to wish to take the initiative, matters of special interest to minority groups (for example, rights of disabled persons), and topics of law reform which may be useful but have too low a priority to find a place in the government's programme. A private member may not propose a Bill the main object of which is the creation of a charge on the public revenue;[41] where a Bill proposes charges on the revenue which are incidental to its main object, a financial resolution moved by a minister is needed before the financial clauses can be considered in committee. It is not the practice for the government to use its majority to defeat a private member's Bill by applying the whips.[42] Where a government supports a Bill, it may offer the services of a

---

[37] HC 538 (1970–71), part III; HC 588–1 (1977–78), pp xxii–xxv; HC 49 (1984–85); HC 324 (1985–86); *Making the Law*, op cit, ch 7.

[38] G Ganz [1990] PL at 497.

[39] HC SO 13(4), (5).

[40] See Richards, *Parliament and Conscience*, and (same author) in Walkland (ed), *The House of Commons in the Twentieth Century*, ch 6; Bromhead, *Private Members' Bills in the British Parliament*; Griffith and Ryle, op cit, pp 385–400.

[41] HC SO 48.

[42] Richards, *Parliament and Conscience*, p 27, describes this as a 'strong convention'.

draftsman to the member concerned and other assistance; the government may also provide extra time for the later stages of a Bill for which there is much parliamentary support. Such assistance may be vital but it may, as with the Disabled Persons (Services, Consultation and Representation) Act 1986, be offered only at a very late stage in the procedure.[43] Not all private members' Bills become law: many are talked out by their opponents. The guillotine is not applied and the closure of debate needs the support of 100 members, which may not be easy to achieve on a Friday. A Bill which has not become law by the end of the session lapses.

In addition to the ballot for Bills at the beginning of each session, there are two other procedures by which a private member's Bill may be introduced. A member may simply present a Bill for its first reading, after giving notice but without previously obtaining the leave of the House.[44] Under the 'ten-minute rule' procedure, on Tuesdays and Wednesdays a private member may seek leave to bring in a Bill; he or she may speak briefly in support of the Bill, an opponent may reply and the House may then divide on the issue.[45] Under each of these procedures the chances of a Bill proceeding further depend on whether it is completely unopposed or on whether some time can be found for a second reading debate and later stages, either by the government or on a Friday devoted to private members' business. While it is a hazardous business for a back-bencher to pilot the passage of a Bill through the House, private members' initiatives form a small but valuable part of the whole legislative work of Parliament.

Consolidation Bills

Where Parliament has legislated frequently on a particular subject (for example, education, social security or housing), the legislation may become very difficult to use, since numerous Acts must be consulted to discover the law on that subject. It is desirable that such legislation should be consolidated, that is, re-enacted in the form of a comprehensive Act, thus enabling all the earlier Acts on the subject to be repealed. As no new law is being made, consolidation Bills may become law with the minimum time being spent on them in Parliament. For this purpose a Joint Committee on Consolidation Bills is appointed each session, consisting of 12 members of each House; the purpose of the committee is to provide sufficient control to guard against abuse of the procedures by which consolidating Bills pass through the two Houses without full scrutiny. The main categories of Bill referred to the committee are (*a*) pure consolidation Bills; (*b*) Bills which, as well as consolidation, make corrections and minor improvements to the law under the Consolidation of Enactments (Procedure) Act 1949; (*c*) Bills which consolidate the law together with amendments recommmended by the English or Scottish Law Commissions under the Law Commissions Act 1965; (*d*) Bills which repeal obsolete enactments; and (*e*) draft Orders in Council under the

---

[43]   See Griffith and Ryle, op cit, p 387; cf HC 588 (1970–71), evidence of A Morris MP, pp 57–62.
[44]   HC SO 58(1).
[45]   HC SO 19.

Northern Ireland Act 1974 which consolidate the law in Northern Ireland.[46] Bills approved by the joint committee pass through curtailed proceedings thereafter and, in so far as they consolidate the existing law or make minor improvements under the 1949 Act, are immune from amendment. Thus consolidation is not delayed by the need for parliamentary time, only by such practical considerations as the shortage of draftsmen.

Procedure in the House of Lords[47]

Except under the Parliament Acts 1911 and 1949, which are considered below, a Bill may be presented for the royal assent only when it has been approved by both Houses. After a public Bill has had its third reading in the Commons, it will be introduced into the Lords. The various stages in the Lords are broadly similar to those in the Commons, although they are governed by separate standing orders. The main differences have been that standing committees are not used in the Lords and the committee stage of Bills is usually taken in committee of the whole House. In 1995 for the first time the 'committee of the whole House' sat in a separate room at Westminster to consider the Children (Scotland) Bill, enabling the House itself to deal with other business.[48] As recommended by the Jellicoe report on the committee work of the House,[49] the House in 1994 appointed a 'special standing committee' to receive evidence on proposals in a law reform Bill drafted by the Law Commission before considering the text.[50] In committee, there is no provision for the selection of amendments so that any amendments tabled may be moved. Even if no amendments are made in committee, there may be a Report stage; unlike the position in the Commons, there is no limitation on the amendments which may be moved at the third reading.

The distinctive procedures of the House, in contrast with those of the Commons, facilitate the submission and consideration of amendments.[51] While some Bills coming from the Commons are approved by the Lords unchanged and with little debate, it is more usual for Bills to be considered in detail by the Lords and amendments made. This is particularly valuable when the effect of the guillotine has been that only part of a Bill has been considered in detail by the Commons. The government itself tables many amendments in the Lords, some in response to undertakings given in the Commons. The passage of a Bill through the Lords thus enables the drafting of Bills to be improved as well as substantial amendments to be made and new material introduced. During the 1980s, the time spent by the Lords on legislation increased, and the House became more prepared to amend Bills

---

46   HC SO 123. Cmnd 6053, 1975, chs 4 and 14; Lord Simon of Glaisdale and J V D Webb [1975] PL 285.
47   Griffith and Ryle, op cit, pp 480–8, 503–11; Shell, *The House of Lords*, chs 5 and 6.
48   HL Deb, 6 June 1995, col CWH 1.
49   HL 35 (1991–92); HL Deb, 3 June 1992, col 899; 9 July 1992, col 1271.
50   Hopkins, op cit, part VIII; H Brooke [1995] PL 351. The procedure was later re-named 'special public Bill committee' (cf p 203 above). See also HL Deb, 21 January 1997, col 555. On the use of select committees on private members' Bills, see Griffith and Ryle, op cit, pp 486–7, and Shell, op cit, pp 236–9.
51   See D N Clarke and D Shell [1994] PL 409, 412.

against the government's wishes, often on issues of principle and policy.[52] In the 1996–97 session, the Lords played a notable part in criticising government proposals for extending police surveillance in private premises and for minimum sentences for repeated offences. In 1994, the Lords made permanent a committee to scrutinise proposals in Bills for delegating new legislative powers upon ministers and departments.[53]

Where a Bill approved by the Commons has been amended in the Lords, the Bill in its amended form goes back to the Commons so that the Lords' amendments may be approved or rejected. If all the amendments are approved, the House of Commons sends a message notifying the Lords of this. If not, the message will contain reasons for disagreement and possibly counter-amendments. It then is for the Lords to decide whether to persist in its earlier decisions or to give way to the views of the Commons. Usually the Lords give way; but if the House insists on maintaining its position, the disagreement between the two Houses must be resolved if the Bill is to receive the royal assent. The ultimate resolution of these conflicts is governed by the Parliament Acts 1911–49.[54]

Distribution of Bills between the Houses

While the foregoing account has assumed that Bills are always introduced in the Commons, in principle Bills may originate in either House. The major exception is that by ancient privilege of the Commons, Bills of 'aids and supplies', ie those which relate to national taxation and expenditure or to local rates and charges upon them, must begin in the Commons.[55] Moreover, the democratic character of the Commons and the fact that most ministers are MPs mean that Bills of major political importance start there.

These factors often mean that early in a session the Lords have too little legislative work, and have too much later in the session when a load of Bills approved by the Commons reaches them. In 1972, a standing order was adopted by the Commons which relaxed the extent of the Commons' financial privilege in the case of government Bills and made it easier for Bills with financial provisions to begin in the Lords.[56]

In the Lords, any peer may present a Bill without notice and without seeking leave to do so. In practice not many private members' Bills pass through the Lords before they have passed through the Commons, but Bills on controversial subjects are sometimes discussed in the Lords in one session before similar Bills are introduced into the Commons by private members in the following session.[57]

---

[52] Note 47 above. Also Brazier, *Constitutional Practice*, pp 243–8. Between 1970 and 1995, there were 603 government defeats in the Lords: HL Deb, 16 October 1995, col 90 (WA), and 27 November 1995, col 23 (WA). In 1992–96, out of 517 divisions, 430 government victories and 52 defeats were recorded (HL sessional business statistics, 1995–96).
[53] See C M G Himsworth [1995] PL 34; and ch 27.
[54] Section B below.
[55] Erskine May, ch 30; HC 538 (1970–71), paras 19–21. And see M Ryle, in Walkland (ed), *The House of Commons in the Twentieth Century*, pp 355–9.
[56] HC Deb, 8 August 1972, col 1656; Erskine May, p 745; HC SO 78.
[57] Shell, op cit, pp 151–6; Griffith and Ryle, op cit, pp 487–8. And see eg Lord Lester's Human Rights Bill, passed by the House in 1994–95 (HL Deb, 1 May 1995, col 1285) and re-introduced in 1996–97 (HL Deb, 5 February 1997, col 1725).

The royal assent

Parliament cannot legislate without the concurrence of all its parts, and therefore the assent of the Sovereign is required after a Bill has passed through both Houses. The Sovereign does not attend Parliament to assent in person, since an Act of 1541 authorised the giving of the assent by commissioners in the presence of Lords and Commons, and this became the invariable practice. Formerly the business of the Commons was interrupted to enable the Commons to attend the Lords for the purpose. But by the Royal Assent Act 1967, the assent, having been signified by letters patent under the Great Seal signed by the Sovereign, is notified separately to each House by its Speaker.[58] The traditional procedure has not, however, been abolished. In giving the royal assent ancient forms are used.[59] A public Bill, unless dealing with finance, as also a private Bill other than one of a personal nature, is accepted by the words '*La Reyne le veult*'. A financial Bill is assented to with the words '*La Reyne remercie ses bons sujets, accepte leur benevolence et ainsi le veult*'. The formula for the veto was '*La Reyne s'avisera*'. The right of veto has not been exercised since the reign of Queen Anne. The veto could now only be exercised on ministerial advice, and no government would wish to veto Bills for which it was responsible or for the passage of which it had afforded facilities through Parliament.[60]

The consent of the Sovereign is requested before legislation which affects any matter relating to the royal prerogative is debated. Although the seeking of such consent may today be no more than an act of courtesy so far as government Bills are concerned, the need for this consent presents an obstacle for a private member's Bill which seeks to abolish one of the Sovereign's prerogatives, since it enables the government to prevent the House considering any such proposals.[61]

After the royal assent

While the royal assent concludes the formal process by which Bills become law, it would be wrong to assume that the assent also marks the end of the legislative process. The royal assent may bring the Act into force immediately,[62] but the operation of all or part of an Act is often suspended by provisions in the Act itself. Thus the Act may specify a later date on which it is to come into force, or may give power to the government by Order in Council or to a minister by statutory instrument to specify when the Act, or different parts of it, will operate.[63] Moreover, many Acts confer powers on the government to regulate in detail topics which are indicated only in outline in

---

[58] See HL Deb, 2 March 1967, col 1181.
[59] See Crown Office Rules Order 1967, SI 1967 No 802.
[60] See ch 2 B above and p 268 below.
[61] Erskine May, pp 561–4.
[62] Acts of Parliament (Commencement) Act 1793 and Interpretation Act 1978, s 4: Acts deemed in force at beginning of day on which royal assent given, if no other provision made.
[63] Even if power to bring an Act into force has not been exercised, existence of the power may prevent the minister from acting under the prerogative to make provision inconsistent with the Act: *R v Home Secretary, ex p Fire Brigades Union* [1995] 2 AC 513; and E Barendt [1995] PL 357.

the Acts. While some Acts are complete in themselves, others, particularly those affecting complex social services, cannot take effect until the powers of delegated legislation which they confer are exercised. Exercise of these powers is primarily a matter for the executive, subject to scrutiny by Parliament.[64]

Parliamentary interest in what happens after a Bill becomes law is not confined to delegated legislation, but traditional procedures are not designed for enabling MPs to monitor the operation of legislation. In 1971, the Select Committee on Procedure recommended that use should be made of 'post-legislation' committees. These committees would examine the working of a statute within a short period of its enactment, and would consider whether there was a need for early amending legislation to deal with difficulties arising in the administration of the Act.[65] Select committees may be appointed to review the working of a particular Act (the Abortion Act of 1967 has been the subject of several reviews) and the select committees created in 1979 may also review the effects of legislation, but no scheme of post-legislation committees has been adopted.

Private Bills

A private Bill is a Bill to alter the law relating to a particular locality or to confer rights on or relieve from liability a particular person or body of persons (including local authorities and statutory undertakers, providing public utilities). The procedure is regulated by the standing orders of each House relating to private business.[66] When the objects of the Bill have been advertised and plans and other documents have been displayed in the locality concerned, a petition for the Bill together with the Bill itself must be deposited in Parliament by 27 November each year. Landowners and others whose interests are directly affected are separately notified by the promoters and they may petition against the Bill. The second reading of the Bill does not determine its desirability, as in the case of a public Bill, but merely that, assuming the facts stated in the preamble to the Bill to be true, it is unobjectionable from the point of view of national policy. If read a second time, the Bill is committed to a committee of four members in the Commons or of five members in the Lords.

The committee stage is usually the most important stage in the passage of a private Bill, particularly if there are many petitions of objection to the Bill. The promoters and opponents of the Bill are usually represented by counsel and call evidence in support of their arguments. The views of relevant government departments are made known to the committee. The committee first consider whether or not the facts stated in the preamble, which sets out the special reasons for the Bill, have been proved. If the preamble is accepted, the clauses are taken in order and may be amended. If the preamble is rejected, the Bill is dead. After the committee stage the Bill is reported to the House and its subsequent stages are similar to those of a public Bill. When a

---

[64]   Ch 27.
[65]   HC 538 (1970–71), pp vii–ix; and HC 588–1 (1977–78), p xxvii.
[66]   See Williams, *History of Private Bill Procedure*, vol I; and Erskine May, chs 33–7.

private Bill is opposed, the procedure is expensive, each side having to bear the fees of counsel, expert witnesses and parliamentary agents and the expense of preparing the necessary documents. Unopposed Bills are scrutinised closely by officers of each House. This method of obtaining special statutory powers is useful to local authorities who seek wider powers than are generally conferred or who have special needs for which the general law does not provide. One reason for the elaborate procedure is to ensure that Parliament does not inadvertently take away an individual's private rights.[67] But there are other means of obtaining statutory authority for the exercise of special powers, and ministerial orders are of more general importance today, for example by the provisional order procedure, a version of which is used in Scotland as a form of private legislation.[68] Another variant is 'special parliamentary procedure' under the Statutory Orders (Special Procedure) Act 1945: this must be observed if, for example, a government department wishes to acquire compulsorily certain types of land (such as land held inalienably by the National Trust).[69] The subject of private legislation was subject to a broad review by a joint committee of both Houses in 1988, and many detailed changes in the procedure were recommended, with the aim of reducing the need for private Bills.[70]

A hybrid Bill has been defined as 'a public Bill which affects a particular private interest in a manner different from the private interests of other persons or bodies of the same category or class'.[71] Thus a Bill to confer a general power on the Secretary of State to acquire land for the construction of railway tunnels is not a hybrid Bill since all landowners are potentially affected: but the Bill which became the Channel Tunnel Act 1987, after a protracted parliamentary battle, was a hybrid Bill since it sought to confer power to acquire specific land and construct specific works. After its second reading, a hybrid Bill is referred to a select committee and those whose rights are adversely affected by the Bill may petition against it and bring evidence in support of their objections. The Bill may then pass through committee and later stages as if it were an ordinary Bill.

Whether a public Bill is hybrid and therefore subject to the standing orders for private business is a matter decided initially by the Examiners of Petitions for Private Bills, usually before the second reading. In 1976, after a government Bill to nationalise the aircraft and shipbuilding industries had completed a lengthy committee stage in the Commons, the Speaker ruled that the Bill was prima facie a hybrid Bill: rather than submit the Bill to a select committee to enable petitions against the Bill to be considered and evidence received, the government proposed and the Commons resolved that the standing orders relative to private business should not be applied to the Bill, a reminder that the House is master of its own procedure.[72] When the Bill reached the Lords in the same form in the next session, the government

---

[67]   Cf *Pickin v British Railways Board* [1974] AC 765, ch 4 C.
[68]   Private Legislation Procedure (Scotland) Act 1936; Erskine May, ch 39.
[69]   Erskine May, ch 38; and see Acquisition of Land Act 1981, ss 17–20.
[70]   HL 625 (1987–88); and see Cm 1110, 1990.
[71]   Erskine May, p 519, and also pp 519–24, 793–4.
[72]   The complex saga may be followed at HC Deb, 25 May 1976 (col 299), 26 May (col 445), 27 May (col 632), 29 June (col 218) and 20 July (col 1527).

withdrew the hybrid clauses affecting ship-repairers rather than cause further delay to the Bill.

B.   Conflict between the two Houses

The background to the Parliament Acts 1911–49

No account has yet been given of the processes available for resolving disputes between the two Houses which cannot be settled by consultation and compromise while the Bill is passing to and fro between the Houses. Today it is generally accepted that the will of the elected House should ultimately prevail. In the 19th century, the only means of coercing the Lords available to a government was to advise the Sovereign to create enough new peers to obtain a majority for the government in the Lords. Thus in 1832 the Lords abandoned their opposition to the Reform Bill when William IV eventually agreed to accept Grey's advice to create peers. Thereafter a rather uncertain convention developed that the Lords should give way in the event of a deadlock between the two Houses, whenever the will of the people was clearly behind the Commons, as it had been in 1832. This proved unsatisfactory for the Liberal party, since it gave the Lords a virtual claim to decide when a general election should be held to find out the will of the people. More definite rules applied to Bills relating to public finance. Since the 17th century, the Commons had asserted privilege in proposals for taxation and public expenditure: it was clear that the Lords might not *amend* such Bills, for this would trespass upon the exclusive right of the Commons to grant or refuse supplies to the Crown. But, however contradictory to that exclusive right it seems to us today, it was still asserted by the Lords that they had the right to *reject* financial Bills.[73] With the widening of the electoral system, the growth of the Liberal party and the appearance of a perpetual Conservative majority in the Lords, the surviving powers of that House were bound to cause conflict. This conflict became an acute problem for the Liberal government after 1906. The Lords rejected measures of social reform which had been approved by the Commons; and in 1909 the Lords rejected the Finance Bill based on the budget which Lloyd George had presented to the Commons.

The Commons had in 1907 resolved that the powers of the Lords should be restricted by law to secure that within the limits of a single Parliament the final decision of the Commons should prevail. This principle of a suspensory veto became law in the Parliament Act 1911, passed after a prolonged constitutional crisis. This crisis was resolved only when, after two general elections in 1910, the Liberal government made known George V's willingness on the Prime Minister's advice to create over 400 new Liberal peers to coerce the Lords into giving way.[74]

---

[73]   In 1860 the Lords rejected the Bill to repeal the paper duty. The Commons challenged the propriety of this rejection and from 1861 all proposals for taxation were included in a single Finance Bill: Taswell-Langmead, *English Constitutional History*, pp 548–9.

[74]   See Jenkins, *Mr Balfour's Poodle*; Nicolson, *King George V*, chs 9 and 10; Jennings, *Cabinet Government*, pp 428–48. For an account of why the 1911 Act took the form it did, see J Jaconelli (1991) 10 Parliamentary History 277.

The 1911 Act, which did not alter the composition of the upper House, made three main changes: (*a*) it reduced the life of Parliament from seven to five years; (*b*) it removed the power of the Lords to veto or delay money Bills; and (*c*) in the case of other public Bills, apart from a Bill to prolong the life of Parliament, the veto of the Lords was abolished and there was substituted a power to delay legislation for two years. The Act enabled the Welsh Church Act 1914 and the Government of Ireland Act 1914 to become law. But the period of delay which the Lords could impose meant that in the fourth and fifth years of a Parliament the Lords could hold up a Bill knowing that it could not become law until after a general election. After 1945, faced with a massive programme of nationalisation which it wished to get through Parliament, the Labour government proposed to reduce the period of delay from two years to one year. After extensive discussions on the reform of the House of Lords, which broke down on the period of delay, the Parliament Act 1949 became law under the 1911 Act procedure.

The present law

Under the Parliament Acts 1911–49, Bills may in certain circumstances receive the royal assent after having been approved only by the Commons. There are two situations in which this may happen: (*a*) if the Lords fail within one month to pass a Bill which, having passed the Commons, is sent up at least one month before the end of the session and is endorsed by the Speaker as a money Bill;[75] or (*b*) if the Lords refuse in two successive sessions, whether of the same Parliament or not, to pass a public Bill (other than a Bill certified as a money Bill or a Bill to extend the maximum duration of Parliament beyond five years) which has been passed by the Commons in those two sessions, provided that one year has elapsed between the date of the Bill's second reading in the Commons in the first of those sessions and the date of its third reading in that House in the second of those sessions.[76]

A money Bill is a public Bill which, in the opinion of the Speaker, contains only provisions dealing with: the imposition, repeal, remission, alteration or regulation of taxation; the imposition of charges on the Consolidated Fund or the National Loans Fund, or on money provided by Parliament for the payment of debt or other financial purposes or the variation or repeal of such charges; supply; the appropriation, receipt, custody, issue or audit of public accounts; or the raising or guarantee or repayment of loans. Bills dealing with taxation, money or loans raised by local authorities or bodies for local purposes are not certifiable as money Bills.[77] Thus the controversial poll tax legislation (the Local Government Finance Bill 1988) was not a money Bill. It was debated at length and amended in the Lords, although the main challenge to the government (a proposal that the community charge should be banded according to the payer's income) was defeated by 317 to 183 votes.[78] The statutory definition has been so strictly interpreted that most

---

[75] 1911 Act, s 1.
[76] 1911 Act, s 2, as amended by the 1949 Act.
[77] 1911 Act, s 1, as amended by National Loans Act 1968.
[78] See R Brazier (1988) 17 Anglo-American LR 131.

annual Finance Bills have not been endorsed with the Speaker's certificate.[79] Before giving the certificate, the Speaker must, if practicable, consult two members appointed from the chairmen's panel each session by the Committee of Selection of the House of Commons.

Where a Bill is presented for the royal assent under s 2 of the 1911 Act, it must be endorsed with the Speaker's certificate that s 2 has been complied with. As the Speaker must certify that it is the same Bill which has been rejected in two successive sessions, there are strict limits on the alterations which may be made to a Bill between the first and second sessions. But the Bill in the second session may include amendments which have already been approved by the Lords and, in sending up the Bill in the second session, the Commons may accompany it with further suggested amendments without inserting them into the Bill.[80]

Any certificate of the Speaker given under the 1911 Act 'shall be conclusive for all purposes, and shall not be questioned in any court of law',[81] a formula which seeks to exclude any challenge to the validity of an Act passed under the Parliament Acts based on alleged defects in procedure.

The Parliament Acts do not apply to Bills which seek to extend the maximum duration of Parliament beyond five years, nor to local and private legislation, nor to public Bills which confirm provisional orders. Nor do they apply to delegated legislation: here the formal powers of the Lords will depend on whether the parent Act expressly empowers the Lords to approve or disapprove of the delegated legislation in question.[82]

Apart from the Welsh Church Act 1914 and the Government of Ireland Act 1914, only the Parliament Act 1949 became law under the Parliament Act procedure before 1991. Under Labour governments after 1945, it was the practice of the Lords to give way when Lords' amendments to government Bills were rejected by the Commons. Lord Salisbury, leader of the Conservative majority in the Lords during the Labour government of 1945–51, stated that the broad rule followed was that what had been in the Labour programme at the previous general election would be accepted as having been approved by the people; but that the Conservative peers 'reserved full liberty of action' as to measures that had not been in the election manifesto.[83] Direct confrontation between the Lords and the Commons was thus avoided, the general practice of the Lords being to allow a second reading to Bills coming from the Commons.

In the late 1960s the Lords, strengthened by the appointment of life peers, adopted a more resolute policy, causing the Labour government in 1969 to abandon the House of Commons (Redistribution of Seats) (No 2) Bill.[84] In the 1974–75 session, failure to reach agreement between the Commons and Lords meant that the Trade Union and Labour Relations (Amendment) Bill

[79] Erskine May, pp 751–3; and Jennings, *Parliament*, pp 416–19.
[80] 1911 Act, s 2(4). The procedure was used in relation to the Bill which became the Trade Union and Labour Relations (Amendment) Act 1976.
[81] 1911 Act, s 3.
[82] Ch 27.
[83] HL Deb, 4 November 1964, col 66; Griffith and Ryle, op cit, p 504; and see HL Deb, 19 May 1993, col 1780.
[84] Ch 9 B II.

did not become law. In the 1975–76 session, the Labour government invoked the Parliament Acts procedure but a much amended Bill was in March 1976 accepted by the Lords. The Aircraft and Shipbuilding Industries Act 1977 was similarly delayed by opposition from the Lords until the government abandoned the proposal to nationalise certain ship-repairing firms.[85]

In 1990–91, opposition from the Lords to the War Crimes Bill caused the Parliament Acts to be invoked for the first time by a Conservative government. The Bill retrospectively authorised prosecutions in Britain in respect of war crimes in Germany between 1939 and 1945 by persons who had become British citizens. It had not been part of the Conservative programme at the 1987 election and was carried on free votes in the Commons. It was however twice defeated on second reading in the Lords: following the second such defeat, the royal assent was given to it. The debates in the Lords were confused on the constitutional issues,[86] but those peers who voted against the Bill on the second occasion knew that their action would not prevent the Bill from becoming law.

Although the Parliament Acts applied in a clear way to the War Crimes Bill, the procedure under the Acts has potential difficulties (for example, at what stage has a Bill 'not been passed' by the Lords subsequently, once it has been given a second reading?). The statutory method of calculating the one year's delay means that the effective delay may be considerably less than twelve months.

It has been argued that the Parliament Act 1949 is invalid since the Parliament Act procedure was never intended to be used for amending the 1911 Act itself and since a delegate may not use delegated authority to increase the scope of his or her authority.[87] While there are indeed limits on the Bills which may become law under the Parliament Act procedure, the argument that the 1949 Act is invalid depends upon the view that measures passed by the Commons and the Crown alone should be regarded as delegated legislation: yet the interpretation of Commonwealth constitutions suggests that a legislature is not subject to the limitations implied by the maxim *delegatus non potest delegare*.[88] While the 1911 Act was not intended to provide a final solution to the House of Lords question, it is doubtful whether the scope of the Act should be subject to such implied limitations; if so, it would follow that, for example, a Bill to reform the Lords or to vary the succession to the throne could not become law under the Parliament Act procedure.[89]

House of Lords reform

The preamble to the 1911 Act looked forward to the creation of a new second chamber constituted on a popular instead of a hereditary basis and with its own powers, but this has never occurred. In 1918, an all-party conference chaired by Viscount Bryce agreed that the primary functions of the second

---

[85] Page 211 above.
[86] G Ganz (1992) 55 MLR 87.
[87] Hood Phillips and Jackson, *Constitutional and Administrative Law*, pp 90–1, 149; Hood Phillips, *Reform of the Constitution*, pp 18–19, 91–3. If it could be shown that the 1949 Act were invalid, would this also invalidate the War Crimes Act 1991?
[88] *R v Burah* (1878) 3 App Cas 889; *Hodge v R* (1883) 9 App Cas 117.
[89] And see ch 4 C.

chamber included (*a*) the examination and revision of Bills brought from the Commons; (*b*) the initiation and discussion of non-controversial Bills; (*c*) 'the interposition of so much delay (and no more) in the passing of a Bill into law as may be needed to enable the opinion of the nation to be adequately expressed upon it'; and (*d*) full and free discussion of current issues of policy which the Commons might not have time to consider. Yet the Bryce conference did not agree as to the composition of the House, although many members favoured indirect election of the second chamber by the House of Commons. Disputes between the Houses could, it was suggested, be settled by a joint conference of 60 members, chosen equally from each House, meeting in secret.[90]

At an inter-party conference in 1948, agreement was reached on broad questions such as the need for a second chamber which should complement and not rival the Commons; the need to secure that a permanent majority was not assured to any one party; the admission of women; and the ending of admission based solely on succession to an hereditary peerage. The conference broke down through disagreement over the Lords' delaying powers: the Labour government would have accepted a delay of 12 months from second reading in the Commons or nine months from third reading, whichever was the longer, but the Conservatives insisted upon 18 months from second reading or 12 months from third reading.[91] In the event the Parliament Act 1949 became law. No general reform of the House of Lords took place, although the Life Peerages Act 1958 and the Peerage Act 1963 modified its composition.[92]

Another all-party conference was convened by the Labour government in November 1967: this was very near the point of reaching complete agreement when the Lords in June 1968 rejected a government order continuing sanctions against the Rhodesian government.[93] This caused the government to break off the conference and to propose a comprehensive scheme for the reform of the House, which was embodied in the Parliament (No 2) Bill 1968–69.[94] This sought to eliminate hereditary membership, and to ensure that the House would not in future contain a permanent Conservative majority. It proposed two tiers of members. The 'voting' members, entitled to vote and speak, would comprise life peers and hereditary peers of first creation; but they would be expected to attend at least one-third of the sittings in each session and would retire at the end of the Parliament in which they became 72 years old; serving or retired law lords and a reduced number of Anglican bishops would also be voting members. The second tier of members, entitled to speak and take part in committees (except on legislation) but not to vote, would comprise created peers who were not able to attend the House regularly or had retired because of age from voting membership; and also, as a transitional measure, existing peers by succession who wished to stay in the House. Initially there would be about 250 voting members. New life peers

---

[90]   Cd 9038, 1918. See also Jennings, *Parliament*, ch 12, and Bromhead, *The House of Lords and Contemporary Politics 1911–1957*.

[91]   Cmd 7390, 1948.

[92]   Ch 9 A.

[93]   Ch 27; and see Morgan, *The House of Lords and the Labour Government 1964–70*.

[94]   Cmnd 3799, 1968; Morgan, op cit, chs 7 and 8.

would be created at the start of each new Parliament if this was necessary to give the government party approximately 10% more members than the other parties in the House. Thus the balance of power would be retained by those voting peers who sat on the cross-benches and were not allied to any party. The creation of peers was to remain in the hands of the Prime Minister without legal limits. But an advisory committee would review periodically the composition of the House, for example to consider how far the House included members with knowledge of Scotland, Wales, Northern Ireland and English regions.

Regarding the powers of the House, no change was proposed in respect of money Bills. In place of s 2 of the Parliament Act 1911, the reformed House was to have power to delay a Commons Bill for six months from the date on which the Lords had rejected the Bill, had insisted on maintaining amendments to which the Commons were opposed or had failed within 60 sitting days to make progress on a Bill sent up from the Commons. When the six months had elapsed, the Commons could then resolve that the Bill be submitted for the royal assent without the Bill needing to pass again through the Commons. The Bill could be sent for the royal assent in this way even though during the six months Parliament had been prorogued or dissolved. As regards delegated legislation, the Commons would have power to override any rejection of a statutory instrument by the Lords.

While this scheme had the support of Labour, Conservative and Liberal leaders, and of the House of Lords, it was not popular with back-benchers in the Commons and it moved so slowly through its committee stage in the House that the government abandoned the Bill. The objections raised to the scheme included the wide patronage left to the Prime Minister; the artificial arrangements for ensuring that the government had a majority over other parties after each general election (which assumed that the government would always have an absolute majority in the Commons); doubts about having a large number of non-voting members; failure to provide satisfactorily for representation of the parts and regions of the United Kingdom; and failure to declare what the essential functions of the Lords should be. But the scheme had some advantages and its failure has meant that, while a second chamber is needed to serve a number of legislative purposes, the present House is restricted by its composition from exercising its powers effectively.[95]

Within a federal system, the upper House normally has a role to play in representing the component parts of the federation, whereas the lower House may be elected on a population basis. In 1973 the majority report of the royal commission on the constitution rejected the idea of a regional structure for the Lords,[96] and in 1978 the Labour government's scheme of devolution to Scotland and Wales did not include reform of the Lords.

No political consensus on the House of Lords existed before 1997. The Labour party conference in 1977 had called for 'the total abolition of the House of Lords and the reform of Parliament into an efficient single chamber legislating body without delay'. In 1983, the party undertook to abolish the House as quickly as possible and in the interim to remove all its legislative

---

[95]   Cf Shell, op cit, ch 9.

[96]   Kilbrandon Report, p 322; cf vol II, Memorandum of Dissent, pp 116–19; ch 3 B.

powers, except for those relating to the life of Parliament. But in 1992, Labour declared that it would replace the Lords with an elected second chamber with power to delay for the lifetime of a Parliament 'change to designated legislation reducing individual or constitutional rights'. In 1978, a Conservative party committee considered a second chamber essential for the review of legislation and as a constitutional safeguard against an 'elected dictatorship'. It proposed a House of some 400 members, one-third appointed on the advice of the Prime Minister after consultation with a committee of Privy Councillors, two-thirds elected by proportional representation.[97] But this scheme was not adopted as Conservative policy. The Liberal Democrats in 1992 favoured an elected second chamber as a senate, representing the nations and regions of the United Kingdom, and with power to delay legislation other than money Bills for up to two years.

In March 1997, a joint committee from the Labour and Liberal Democrat parties agreed on a programme of constitutional reform, giving priority to the removal from hereditary peers of the right to sit and vote in the Lords. It was agreed that the cross-benchers should form about one-fifth of the House, that no one party should seek a majority, and that the party groups in the Lords should be proportional to the national vote for each party at the previous general election. A detailed scheme for the structure and functions of the House would be developed after the removal of the hereditary peers.

C.   Financial procedure[98]

No government can exist without raising and spending money. In the Bill of Rights 1689, art 4, the levying of money for the use of the Crown without grant of Parliament was declared illegal. Relying on the principle that the redress of grievances preceded supply, the Commons could after 1689 insist that the Crown pursued acceptable policies before granting the taxes or other revenue which the Crown needed. It has been said of the financial procedure of Parliament that the Crown demands money, the Commons grant it and the Lords assent to the grant.[99] Today, the assent of the Lords is only nominal, and it is generally regarded as vital to a government's existence that its financial proposals should be accepted by the Commons. It is unlikely that a government would accept that the Commons should modify its expenditure proposals. A government which failed to ensure supply would have to resign or to seek a general election.[100]

The requirement of statutory authority before a government can impose charges on the citizen is a fundamental principle which gives the citizen

---

97   *The House of Lords*: report of the Conservative review committee, chairman Lord Home. And see R Blackburn [1988] PL 187.
98   See also ch 17, with which this section must be read, and J F McEldowney, 'The Control of Public Expenditure', in Jowell and Oliver (eds), *The Changing Constitution*, ch 7.
99   Erskine May, p 684.
100 Hence the necessity for a general election after the Lords had rejected the Liberal government's Finance Bill in 1909. In 1975, the failure of the Prime Minister of Australia to ensure supply (because of opposition from the Australian Senate to two Appropriation Bills) was the reason given by the Governor-General for dismissing him; ch 12 B.

protection in the courts against unauthorised charges.[101] Another principle is that no payment out of the national Exchequer may be made without the authority of an Act, and then only for the purposes for which the statute has authorised the expenditure.[102] By contrast with the rule on taxation, this is less likely to give rise to litigation in the courts since the rights of individuals are not in issue if it is broken. Yet taxpayers and certain interest groups may have a sufficient interest in an expenditure decision to seek judicial review of its legality.[103]

The elaborate system of controlling expenditure which exists today still owes much to reforms linked with Gladstone's tenure of office as Chancellor of the Exchequer in the 1860s. While the formal controls ensure that legal and financial proprieties are observed, they were not designed to cope with the present scale of public expenditure; other procedures that seek to control public expenditure will be considered in chapter 17.

There are various roles which the Commons may play in respect of taxation and expenditure. First, since the level of public expenditure largely depends on the policies which governments pursue, the House may in principle influence the choices to be made between conflicting objectives (for example, improved social services as against lower taxation). Secondly, MPs who are not ministers can on behalf of the electorate scrutinise the performance of the departments, and find out whether they are effectively administered within the government's policies. Thirdly, in the watch-dog role, the Commons may scrutinise the government's activities to check that departments are observing the formal rules of public accounting. Fourthly, the Commons may scrutinise the details of tax legislation, as in the case of other legislation. Since not all these functions could be carried out by the whole House, the House makes considerable use of committees for various financial purposes.

Basic rules of financial procedure

The financial procedures of the Commons are intricate and can only be outlined here. According to Erskine May, three key rules govern present procedure.[104] For the purpose of these rules, the word 'charge' includes both charges upon the public revenue, ie expenditure, and charges upon the people, ie taxation.

1 A charge does not become fully valid until authorised by legislation; it must generally originate in the Commons, and money to meet authorised expenditure must be appropriated in the same session of Parliament as that in which the relevant estimate is laid before Parliament.

2 A charge may not be considered by the Commons unless it is proposed or recommended by the Crown. The financial initiative of the Crown is

---

[101] Ch 17. And see *Woolwich Building Society v IRC (No 2)* [1993] AC 70.

[102] *Auckland Harbour Board v R* [1924] AC 318. And see note 103 below.

[103] *R v Foreign and Commonwealth Secretary, ex p World Development Movement* [1995] 1 All ER 611: decision to finance Pergau Dam in Malaysia declared *ultra vires* the Overseas Development and Co-operation Act 1980. The government made up the money from other public funds: HC Deb, 13 December 1994, col 773.

[104] Erskine May, ch 26. For discussion of earlier forms of the rules, see Reid, *The Politics of Financial Control*, and M Ryle, in Walkland (ed), *The House of Commons in the Twentieth Century*, ch 7.

expressed in a standing order of the Commons which in part dates from 1713: 'This House will receive no petition for any sum relating to public service or proceed upon any motion for a grant or charge upon the public revenue ... unless recommended from the Crown.'[105] This rule gives the government formal control over almost all financial business in the Commons and severely restricts the ability of Opposition and back-benchers to propose additional expenditure or taxation.

3 A charge must first be considered in the form of a resolution which, when agreed to by the House, forms an essential preliminary to the Bill or clause by which the charge is authorised. Before 1967, these resolutions had to be passed by the whole House sitting as the Committee of Supply, in the case of expenditure, or as the Committee of Ways and Means, in the case of taxation. These committees no longer exist[106] and the resolutions are now passed by the House itself. Certain financial Bills must be preceded by a Commons resolution before they can be read a second time. But for most Bills, whether the main object or an incidental object is the creation of a public charge, the financial resolution normally follows the second reading and must be proposed by a minister.[107]

The work of the Commons is conducted on a sessional basis, each session usually running for a year from early November. However, the government's financial year begins on 1 April (the income tax year begins on 6 April). The result is a complex annual financial cycle, which will now be described – first in relation to the authorisation of expenditure (supply), second in relation to taxation.

Consideration of estimates

By a long-standing principle of financial procedure, the estimates of departmental expenditure must be approved by resolutions of the Commons to enable the necessary money to be appropriated from the Exchequer. Each year, generally during February or March, the estimates of expenditure for the year commencing in April are presented to Parliament and published. The estimates will have been prepared by the departments themselves in the previous autumn and will have been revised by and agreed with the Treasury, in accordance with current Cabinet policy.[108]

In the 19th century and until 1967, the estimates were considered by the House sitting in the Committee of Supply, which could reduce but not increase a departmental vote. In fact, by 1900 consideration of the estimates had become little more than a peg on which to hang a debate on some aspect of government policy. As was said in 1966, 'the forms of procedure by which the House considers and votes Supply have ... come to be mainly used not for truly financial purposes but as a means of controlling administration'.[109] By

---

[105] For the history of SO 46, see Reid, op cit, pp 35–45.
[106] See HC 122 (1965–66).
[107] HC SO 48. In 1995, the Select Committee on Procedure proposed that the money resolution should be put immediately after a Bill received its second reading and should not be debated: HC 491 (1994–95). And see HC Deb, 2 November 1995, col 405.
[108] Ch 17. For the supply estimates for 1996–97, see HC 261 (1995–96).
[109] HC 122 (1965–66). And see Reid, op cit, pp 69–70.

convention of the House, the subjects debated were chosen by the Opposition. The tradition of supply business for a time survived the abolition of the Committee of Supply. Between 1967 and 1982, 29 'supply days' were assigned for debate on topics chosen by the Opposition, taken during the session at times which enabled the various categories of estimates to be formally approved by certain fixed dates. In 1982, the House severed the connection between debates initiated by the Opposition and formal consideration of the estimates.[110] In each session, 20 days in the whole House are allotted for opposition business,[111] 17 at the disposal of the leader of the Opposition and three at the disposal of the second largest opposition party, out of which some time is made available to the smaller parties. By a separate standing order, three days each session are allotted for the consideration of estimates, and must be taken before 5 August.[112] The particular estimates to be debated are selected by the Liaison Committee, which comprises the chairmen of the House's select committees.[113] The estimates selected will usually have been the subject of reports by select committees; in 1990 the Select Committee on Procedure recommended that these three estimates days should become days on which reports by the departmentally related select committees should be considered.[114]

Standing orders specify the dates by which the House must approve (without debate) the winter supplementary estimates and votes on account (6 February), the spring supplementaries and excess votes (18 March), and all outstanding estimates (5 August).[115] Estimates for the Scottish departments are referred to the Scottish Grand Committee, with a limit of six days for debate.[116]

Consolidated Fund and Appropriation Acts

Once the formal supply resolutions have been approved by the Commons, they must be embodied in legislation. Where this authorises the issue of money from the Consolidated Fund, it is known as a Consolidated Fund Act; where it also gives authority for the appropriation of money to the purposes contained in the estimates, as with the main estimates that must be adopted in July or early August, it is known as an Appropriation Act. By custom of the House, debate on Consolidated Fund or Appropriation Bills had become an opportunity for back-bench MPs to debate subjects of their own choice. In 1982 the House decided that the various stages of these Bills should be taken formally and without debate; but on the day when such a Bill passes through the House, a series of private members' debates commences on a motion for the adjournment of the House that can continue through the night until 9 am on the next day.[117] The object of this strange procedure is to preserve for

---

[110] See HC 118 (1980–81) and HC Deb, 19 July 1982, col 117.
[111] HC SO 13(2).
[112] HC SO 52.
[113] HC SO 131.
[114] HC 19–1 (1989–90), p xii.
[115] HC SO 53.
[116] HC SO 96.
[117] HC SO 54.

private members opportunities for debate which they had previously exercised while essential financial legislation was passed.

Votes on account and supplementary estimates

Although no expenditure can be incurred without parliamentary authorisation, the Appropriation Act is not passed until July or early August. Since each financial year begins on 1 April, the government must have interim authority for its expenditure. For this purpose, in the preceding November, votes on account of the civil and defence departments are submitted, and are incorporated in one or more Consolidated Fund Bills passed before 1 April. The sum formally authorised by the Appropriation Act is the total expenditure for the year less the sum already authorised by Consolidated Fund Acts.

Where a department considers that it will need to exceed its estimated expenditure during the current financial year, whether because of unforeseen circumstances or new policy decisions, a supplementary estimate must be introduced. Supplementary estimates are submitted in June, November and February. The resolutions authorising the withdrawal from the Consolidated Fund of the sums so voted are embodied in the next Consolidated Fund Act to be passed or, in the case of the summer supplementary estimates, in the Appropriation Act.

Other forms of authorisation[118]

1 The need for an *excess vote* arises when a department has incurred expenditure beyond the amount granted to it but has not been able to present a supplementary estimate to cure the excess before the end of the financial year. The excess votes are examined each year by the Public Accounts Committee on a report from the Comptroller and Auditor General before they are granted in the March Consolidated Fund Bill.

2 In times of grave emergency there may be voted a lump sum not allocated to any particular object. Such votes are known as *votes of credit*. By this means the extraordinary expenditure in time of world war was in the main voted. The method involved relaxation of the usual methods of Treasury control.

3 The estimates for *appropriation in aid* appear side by side with the estimates of expenditure, though only the net amount of the latter is voted. Appropriations in aid are sums received by departments (usually in return for services provided) and retained to meet departmental expenditure.

4 Expenditure by a department may be needed for urgent purposes not covered by its existing legislation. In cases of urgent or temporary expenditure, the general provision made for the department in the Appropriation Act may be sufficient authority: but this is not acceptable if the Appropriation Act is thereby used to override limits imposed by existing legislation. Money may be spent in anticipation of express statutory authority when by a supplementary estimate expenditure is proposed for purposes to be authorised by a future Act. In 1967, the government was strongly criticised for paying the salaries of the Parliamentary Commissioner for Administration designate and his staff before the Bill to create this office had become law: the money had in

---

[118]   See further ch 17 C and D.

fact come out of the Civil Contingencies Fund, a statutory reserve fund to meet items of expenditure which could not have been foreseen.[119] The maximum capital in the Fund, now re-named the Contingencies Fund, is fixed at an amount equal to 2% of the authorised supply expenditure for the previous year:[120] it may not now be drawn upon for any purpose for which legislation is necessary until a second reading has been given to the Bill in question. The existence of the Fund, which has increased to over 2 billion pounds, is a striking exception to the principle that parliamentary authority should be obtained before expenditure is incurred; effective scrutiny of the Fund depends on the Treasury, backed up by the Comptroller and Auditor-General's powers of audit. The legality of payments from the Fund appears uncertain, but is not likely to arise for decision in the courts.[121]

Taxation

While many forms of revenue, such as customs and excise duties, are raised under Acts which continue in force from year to year, some taxes, notably income tax and corporation tax, are authorised from year to year. The machinery for the collection of these taxes is permanent but Parliament must approve each year the rates of tax. Until 1993, the traditional practice was that the Chancellor of the Exchequer presented his Budget early in April. The Budget speech is now combined with the annual statement on public expenditure and delivered in December, so that expenditure decisions are announced at the same time as the Chancellor appraises the economy and proposes tax changes.[122] The contents of the speech are kept secret until the speech is delivered. While the government is collectively responsible for the Budget speech and the Chancellor prepares it in close consultation with the Prime Minister, the contents are made known to the Cabinet only on the previous day, or even on the morning of the speech. 'The Budget is seen, not as a simple balancing of tax receipts against expenditure, but as a sophisticated process in which the instruments of taxation and expenditure are used to influence the course of the economy'.[123] The Chancellor may find it necessary to announce changes in indirect taxation and expenditure decisions at other times in the year.

Budget resolutions

As soon as the Chancellor's speech is completed, the House passes formal resolutions which enable immediate changes to be made in the rates of existing taxes and duties and give renewed authority for the collection of the annual taxes. These resolutions are confirmed by the House at the end of the Budget debate. The taxing resolutions are later embodied in the annual Finance Act. The effect of any changes made by the Finance Act may be made retrospective to the date of the Budget or any selected date.

---

[119] HC 257, 326 (1966–67); HC Deb, 7 February 1967, col 1357.
[120] Miscellaneous Financial Provisions Act 1946; Contingencies Fund Act 1974.
[121] HC 118–1 (1980–81), p xiv; HC 137 (1981–82), app 20; HC 24–1 (1982–83), p xliii. And see J F McEldowney [1988] PL 232.
[122] For the financial statement and Budget report for 1997–98, see HC 90 (1996–97).
[123] Plowden Report, Cmnd 1432, 1961, para 10.

It was for long the practice to begin at once to collect taxes under the authority of the Budget resolutions alone. But in *Bowles v Bank of England*,[124] Bowles successfully sued the Bank for a declaration that it was not entitled to deduct any sum by way of income tax from dividends, until such tax had been imposed by Act of Parliament. This decision illustrates the principle in *Stockdale v Hansard*[125] that no resolution of the House of Commons can alter the law of the land. The decision made it necessary to pass a law which has now been re-enacted in the Provisional Collection of Taxes Act 1968. This Act gives statutory force for a limited period to resolutions of the House varying an existing tax or renewing a tax imposed during the preceding year. Under the Act, the Finance Bill which embodies the resolutions must be read a second time within 25 sitting days of the resolutions having been approved by the House; and an Act confirming the resolutions must become law within four months from the date of the resolution or by 5 August in the same year if voted in March or April. As now amended, the Act applies to resolutions for the variation or renewal of income tax, value added tax, customs and excise duties and petroleum revenue tax.[126]

Because the Finance Bill must become law by 5 August, the government must ensure that the Bill has passed the Commons and is sent to the Lords as early in July as possible.[127] Although the House of Lords generally debates the Finance Bill on its second reading, its passage through the Lords is unopposed. Even if the Finance Bill is not certified as a 'money Bill' for the purposes of the Parliament Act 1911, it would be a serious breach of the financial privileges of the Commons for the Lords to seek to amend it as it comes within the hallowed class of 'Bills of Aids and Supplies'.[128] However, no such breach occurs if the Lords amend a Bill concerning the revenue-raising powers of local government.[129]

Parliamentary scrutiny of government expenditure

We have seen that the formal machinery for control of the government's estimates by the Commons has traditionally been used for broader political purposes. Before the creation of the present system of select committees in 1979,[130] the House appointed a succession of committees to examine government expenditure. After 1945, the House each year appointed a committee to examine such of the estimates presented to the House as it saw fit, 'and to report what, if any, economies consistent with the policy implied in those Estimates (might) be effected therein'. In fact, rather than making a detailed examination of estimates in order to propose economies, the committee inquired more broadly into the effectiveness of the work of departments; thus the Estimates Committee 'became an instrument of general administrative review and scrutiny, and a major source of information about how the

---

[124]   [1913] 1 Ch 57.
[125]   (1839) 9 A & E 1; p 239 below.
[126]   For details, see Erskine May, pp 735–6.
[127]   HC 276 (1970–71).
[128]   Erskine May, ch 30.
[129]   Ibid; and note 78 above.
[130]   Section D below.

departments operate'.[131] In 1965, the committee's sub-committees began to specialise in particular areas of activity as the demand was raised for the appointment of specialised investigatory committees. In 1971, the Estimates Committee gave way to a new Expenditure Committee of 49 members; its remit was 'to consider any papers on public expenditure presented to this House and such of the estimates as may seem fit to the Committee and in particular to consider how, if at all, the policies implied in the figures of expenditure and in the estimates may be carried out more economically'.[132]

The committee, composed of back-bench members, carried out its work through six sub-committees, concerned with such broad fields as defence and external affairs; the environment; trade and industry; social services and employment. Within these areas, each sub-committee inquired into a selected departmental activity. The aim of the committee was to inform the House about particular areas of the government's work so that they might be better debated in Parliament and outside. As with many committees of the Commons, the Expenditure Committee sought to avoid working in an atmosphere of party politics and to produce unanimous reports. The committee's work extended into matters that might have no financial implications, but this scrutiny of government derived directly from the constitutional function of the Commons in authorising expenditure. The Expenditure Committee was abolished in 1979, having prepared the way for the scheme of select committees described in the next section. Parliamentary scrutiny of expenditure as such is maintained through the audit procedures applied to departmental accounts by the Comptroller and Auditor-General and the Public Accounts Committee, and described in chapter 17.

D. Scrutiny of administration

In chapter 7, the principle of responsible government was discussed. We are now concerned with the procedures within the Commons by which the conduct of administration may be scrutinised by the House. The legislative and financial procedures of Parliament have strongly influenced the means by which Parliament finds out about the work of government. But certain procedures have an importance which is not related either to legislation or to finance.

Parliamentary questions[133]

At the start of each day that the House is sitting, except on Fridays, 45 to 55 minutes are set aside to enable members to question ministers. As well as receiving oral answers to written questions of which prior notice has been given, members may ask oral supplementary questions on matters arising out of the minister's reply to the written question. Members may ask questions for

---

[131] Johnson, *Parliament and Administration: the Estimates Committee 1945–65*, p 128.
[132] See Robinson, *Parliament and Public Spending: The Expenditure Committee 1970–76*.
[133] Chester and Bowring, *Questions in Parliament*; H Irwin, in Ryle and Richards (eds), *The Commons Under Scrutiny*, ch 5; Franklin and Norton (eds), *Parliamentary Questions*; Griffith and Ryle, *Parliament*, pp 254–62, 352–9, 366–76; HC 393 (1971–72); HC 379 (1989–90); HC 178 (1990–91); Erskine May, pp 281–97.

written answer at any time. According to Erskine May, 'the purpose of a question is to obtain information or press for action'; questions to ministers 'should relate to the public affairs with which they are officially connected, to proceedings pending in Parliament, or to matters of administration for which they are responsible'.[134] Because of the existence of question-time, matters concerning their constituencies may be raised by members in correspondence with ministers, who know that an unsatisfactory reply may lead to the tabling of a question. For this reason questions are used more for concentrating public attention on topics of current concern than for securing the redress of individual grievances. Civil servants are aware that action which they take may result in a parliamentary question. While ministers customarily answer those questions which have been accepted as being in order by the clerks of the House, acting under the Speaker's direction, it is for the minister to decide whether and how to reply to questions. There are a number of grounds on which the information sought may be withheld, for example, if the cost of obtaining the information would be excessive or if it would be contrary to the public interest for the information to be given (for example, matters relating to Cabinet proceedings or to the security services). 'An answer to a question cannot be insisted upon, if the answer be refused by a Minister'.[135] Question-time, it has been said, is 'pre-eminently a device for emphasizing the individual responsibility of ministers'.[136] Thus questions may be ruled out of order or refused an answer if they relate to matters for which ministers are not responsible: for example, decisions by local authorities, the BBC, courts and tribunals, the universities, trade unions and so on.

When a question to a minister concerns a matter which has been assigned to an executive agency set up under the 'next steps' initiative,[137] it is generally answered by a letter to the MP from the agency's chief executive to the MP (the minister may be consulted on what is said). MPs may require a ministerial response if they are dissatisfied with the chief executive's reply. The answers from chief executives to MPs have since 1992 (in an unusual departure from principle) been printed in Hansard.[138]

Departmental ministers attend for questioning by rota. In May 1997, the allocation for questions to the Prime Minister was changed from 15 minutes every Tuesday and Thursday to 30 minutes every Wednesday. Members may not ask more than two starred questions (ie questions for oral answer) on any day, and not more than one to a particular minister. Notice of starred questions cannot be given more than ten sitting days in advance.[139] Starred questions which are not reached during question-time receive a written answer. While question-time dramatises the personal responsibility of ministers for government policy and departmental action, its effectiveness as a means of securing information which the government does not wish to make available has often been limited. Since 1994, the government has operated a

---

[134]   Erskine May, pp 285–7.
[135]   Ibid, p 293.
[136]   Chester and Bowring, op cit, p 287.
[137]   Ch 13 D.
[138]   See P Evans, in Giddings (ed), *Parliamentary Accountability*, ch 7. Also HC 178 (1990–91) and HC 14 (1996–97).
[139]   HC SO 17.

code of practice on access to government information,[140] and expects ministers to comply with the code in answering MPs' questions. In 1996, the Scott report on 'arms for Iraq' extensively criticised attitudes within government to the answering of questions.[141] Civil servants are now instructed that in preparing answers they must be as open as possible with Parliament, although ministers are entitled to present government actions in a positive light; information should not be omitted merely because disclosure could lead to political embarrassment; and answers should be avoided 'which are literally true but likely to give rise to misleading inferences'.[142]

The regular questioning of the Prime Minister receives much attention in the media, and the use of 'open' questions to the Prime Minister (for example, asking him to list his engagements for the day) is permitted as a device for enabling a wide range of supplementary questions to be asked.[143] A member who is dissatisfied with a reply may take the matter further, for example by raising the matter in an adjournment debate. The marked increase in the number of questions asked for written answer, which is linked with the use by some MPs of research assistants, is not considered to make necessary any limit on the number of questions which MPs may ask.[144]

Debates

At the end of every day's public business, when the adjournment of the House is formally moved, half an hour is available for a private member to raise a particular issue and for a ministerial reply.[145] Members periodically ballot for the right to initiate an adjournment debate and advance notice of the subject is given so that the relevant minister may reply. While this gives more time for discussion of an issue than is possible in question-time, the minister's reply, which often consists of a reasoned defence of the department's decision, may not advance the matter very far. During the debate, incidental reference to the need for legislation may be permitted by the Speaker.[146] These brief debates are not followed by a vote of the House.

More substantial debates may be held at short notice on motions for the adjournment of the House for the purpose of discussing a specific and important matter that should have urgent consideration. The Speaker must be satisfied that the matter is proper to be discussed under the urgency procedure and either the request must be supported by at least 40 members, or leave for the debate must be given by the House, if necessary upon a division. In deciding whether the matter should be debated, the Speaker considers the extent to which it concerns the administrative responsibilities of ministers or could come within the scope of ministerial action, but she does not give reasons for her decision.[147] Only one or two requests for such debates

---

140   See Cm 2290, 1993; a revised version was issued in January 1997. And see ch 13 E.
141   HC 115 (1995–96), esp vol IV, section K.8.
142   See HC 671 (1996–97), annex C.
143   HC Deb, 3 February 1983, col 427; and HC 178 (1990–91).
144   HC 178 (1990–91), p xx.
145   HC SO 9(7).
146   HC SO 29.
147   HC SO 20.

are granted each year, requests from the Opposition front bench succeeding more often than those from back-bench MPs.[148]

Other occasions on which members may debate the administration of government departments include opposition days and debates on the Queen's Speech. All such debates are limited by the adversary framework in which they are held and individual members may have no means of probing behind the statements made by ministers. These limitations have given rise to demands for other procedures by which the House may inform itself more directly of the work of government. Where it is alleged that maladministration by a department has caused injustice to individual citizens, a member may refer the citizen's complaint for investigation to the Parliamentary Ombudsman.[149] Another method of investigating an issue is for the matter to be examined by a select committee.

Select committees

Select committees were much used to investigate social and administrative problems in the 19th century. A group of MPs would examine a topic of current concern, with power on behalf of the House to take evidence from witnesses with first-hand knowledge of the issues. Their report, published with the supporting evidence, might convince the House of the need for legislative reforms. The use of select committees declined as departments grew in strength and resources, as the primary initiative for legislation moved to the government, and as the party system established stricter control over back-bench MPs. The experience of the select committee on the Marconi scandal, when Liberal ministers were accused of reaping financial rewards through their prior knowledge of a government contract, showed that a select committee was not appropriate for investigations directly involving the reputation of Cabinet ministers.[150] However, the Public Accounts Committee has since 1861 had the task of reporting to the House on the financial and accounting practices of departments.[151] In the period after 1945, little use was made of committees for scrutinising administration, apart from the work of the Estimates Committee described in section C above, the technical scrutiny of delegated legislation by the committee on statutory instruments,[152] and (from 1956 to 1979) the work of the select committee on nationalised industries. One obstacle to the development of such committees was the fear that their investigations would interfere with the running of departments and conflict with ministerial responsibility. In 1959, the Select Committee on Procedure rejected a proposal for a committee on colonial affairs, on the ground that this was 'a radical constitutional innovation': 'there is little doubt that the activities of such a committee would be aimed at controlling rather than criticising the policy and actions of the department concerned. It would

---

[148] Griffith and Ryle, op cit, pp 264–5, 350–2, 377–9. For an outstanding example of such a debate, see that on the Westland affair on 27 January 1986.
[149] Ch 28 D.
[150] Donaldson, *The Marconi Scandal*; and ch 28 C.
[151] Ch 17.
[152] Ch 27.

be usurping a function which the House itself has never attempted to exercise.'[153]

By the mid-1960s, the mood of the Commons had changed. In 1965, the Committee on Procedure declared that lack of knowledge of how the executive worked was the main weakness of the House.[154] Some limited reforms were made in 1966–68 while Richard Crossman MP was leader of the House. Two specialised committees were created in 1966, one to consider the activities of a department (the Ministry of Agriculture, Fisheries and Food), the other to consider the subject of science and technology. The latter committee was regularly re-appointed, but the Committee on the Ministry of Agriculture survived only for two sessions. Other committees established piecemeal at this time included committees to examine the activities of two departments (Education and Science, and Overseas Development), race relations and immigration, and Scottish affairs. During the 1970s, such committees existed alongside the Expenditure Committee and its sub-committees (section C above).[155]

In 1978, an influential report by the Select Committee on Procedure recommended a complete reorganisation of the select committees to produce a more rational structure and to provide means by which MPs could regularly scrutinise the activities of the main departments.[156] The incoming Conservative government moved with notable speed to adopt these recommendations.[157]

Now embodied in the House's standing orders,[158] the system of select committees is directly related to the principal government departments. Seventeen committees are appointed for the life of a Parliament to examine the 'expenditure, administration and policy' of the main departments, the list in January 1997 being: agriculture; defence; education and employment; environment; foreign affairs; health; home affairs (including the Lord Chancellor's Department and the Attorney-General's Office); national heritage; Northern Ireland; public service; science and technology; Scottish affairs; social security; trade and industry; transport; Treasury; and Welsh affairs. Each committee has 11 members, except for two, the Education and Employment and the Northern Ireland Committees, with 13 members. Three committees have power to appoint a sub-committee: Education and Employment, Foreign Affairs (whose sub-committee has often dealt with overseas development) and Home Affairs (whose sub-committee, if appointed, has dealt with race relations and immigration).

As well as examining the work of the principal department specified for the committee, each committee has power to look at 'associated public bodies',

---

153 HC 92–1 (1958–59), para 47; Crick, *The Reform of Parliament*, ch 7.
154 HC 303 (1964–65).
155 See Morris (ed), *The Growth of Parliamentary Scrutiny by Committee*; and Mackintosh, *Specialist Committees in the House of Commons – have they failed?*
156 HC 588–1 (1977–78), chs 5–7; and see HC Deb, 19 and 20 February 1979, cols 44, 276.
157 HC Deb, 25 June 1979, col 33. The literature on the select committees includes Drewry (ed), *The New Select Committees*; Englefield (ed), *Commons Select Committees*; Griffith and Ryle, *Parliament*, ch 11; and N Johnson, in Ryle and Richards (eds), *The Commons under Scrutiny*, ch 9. For the Procedure Committee's review of the system in 1990, see HC 19–1 (1989–90).
158 HC SO 130.

that is, executive agencies, public corporations, boards and advisory bodies in the relevant field. The controversial work of the Child Support Agency has been examined more than once by the Social Security Committee.

Only back-bench MPs serve on the committees. Each committee has a majority of members from the government side of the House, but some committee chairmen are opposition members. The committees are serviced by House of Commons clerks, and they may appoint specialist advisers. Within its subject-area, each committee may choose the topics for investigation, subject only (through the Liaison Committee) to the avoidance of duplication with other committees. The topics investigated vary widely, ranging from major subjects that may take a year or longer to complete, to the latest departmental estimates and issues of topical concern which a committee may seek to influence by holding one or two hearings and publishing the evidence with a brief report. This freedom for a committee to decide for itself what to investigate is very important, and no government approval is needed. Thus the Foreign Affairs Committee explored the role of the Westminster Parliament in the Canadian constitutional controversy at a time when the government had indicated that its policy was to accept without question any proposals coming from the Canadian government in Ottawa; the committee came to a different conclusion, after studying the matter in much greater depth than the Foreign and Commonwealth Office had done.[159] Similarly, the Employment Committee chose to examine the government's decision banning trade union membership at GCHQ;[160] the Foreign Affairs Committee examined the sinking of the *General Belgrano* during the Falklands conflict;[161] the Treasury and Civil Service Committee examined the relations between ministers and civil servants following Clive Ponting's acquittal under the Official Secrets Act;[162] no less than three committees examined aspects of the Westland affair;[163] and the Foreign Affairs Committee examined the government's support for the Pergau Dam project in Malaysia.[164]

Such reports would be valueless if they merely reproduced the government's justification of its policies. The committees are aware that, even though they seldom change government decisions, as all-party committees they exercise an important critical function. Voting on party lines can occur when a committee is deciding the contents of its report, but this is exceptional and not the rule. For criticism of the government to be made, it must have been supported in the committee by one or more MPs from the government side of the House. The committee's report contains only the majority view; but the extent of unity or division is revealed in the minutes of proceedings that are published with the report.

In 1979, some MPs believed that such committees might detract from the adversary quality of parliamentary procedure, might develop consensus

159   HC 42 and 295 (1980–81); Cmnd 8450, 1981; HC 128 (1981–82).
160   HC 238 (1983–84).
161   HC 11 (1984–85).
162   HC 92 (1985–86).
163   Defence Committee, HC 518, 519 (1985–86); Trade and Industry Committee, HC 176 (1986–87); Treasury and Civil Service Committee, HC 92 (1985–86).
164   HC 271 (1993–94). So did the Public Accounts Committee: HC 155 (1993–94); see F White et al [1994] PL 526.

politics, might develop too close a relationship with the departments concerned, and so on. These fears have not been borne out. But the 1979 reform of committees did not transform the power-relationship between government and Parliament. The government has undertaken to cooperate fully with the committees[165] but it lays down the rules by which civil servants may give evidence; these rules seek to protect from investigation the process of decision-making within government.[166] The overriding but much criticised principle is: 'Officials who give evidence to Select Committees do so on behalf of their Ministers and under their directions'.[167] Despite the wishes of the Defence Committee, the government refused to allow the committee to examine five civil servants involved in the Westland affair.[168] Where civil servants are unable to answer a committee's questions, a minister may attend for questioning. While evidence is usually heard in public, departments may ask for private sittings and for sections of the evidence to be deleted from the published report, on grounds of public interest.

In 1990, the Select Committee on Procedure reported on the first ten years of the 'departmental' select committees. Between 1979 and 1990, they had published 591 reports and 231 special reports. Between 1979 and 1988, 116 reports (about 25% of the then total) had been debated in the Commons. In the committee's view, the committees 'provided a far more vigorous, systematic and comprehensive scrutiny of Ministers' actions and policies than anything which went before'.[169] The government accepted that select committees were an 'indispensable part of the work of the House of Commons' and repeated its pledge that where there was evidence of general concern in the House regarding a ministerial refusal to supply information to a committee, it would provide time to enable the House to express its view.[170]

Such an undertaking is worth little if the government is determined to resist a committee's requests for evidence on a sensitive matter. But, in general, it strengthens the Commons that for each major department of government there is a committee of MPs able to scrutinise its decisions and policies. In 1991, this was demonstrated when the Lord Chancellor's Department and the Law Officers' departments, which had been kept out of the committee system in 1979, were brought within the system.[171] The system of committees has not changed the power structure in British government: yet during the 1990s, the committees have made a positive contribution to the debate on accountability, the full fruits of which still lie ahead.[172]

---

[165]   HC Deb, 25 June 1979, col 45; and 16 January 1981, col 1697.
[166]   HC 588–1 (1977–78), app D. The Office of Public Service, *Departmental Evidence and Response to Select Committees* (1997), states the government's attitude towards the committees and the present rules for officials appearing before them.
[167]   *Departmental Evidence and Response*, para 37.
[168]   See ch 13 D. For the role of select committees in the affair, see Drewry, *The New Select Committees*, pp 411–17.
[169]   HC 19–1 (1989–90), p xxi.
[170]   Note 165 above.
[171]   Cm 1532, 1991.
[172]   See esp the Treasury and Civil Service Committee's report on the civil service (HC 27, 1993–94) and the Public Service Committee's report on ministerial accountability (HC 313, 1995–96).

This account has focused on the departmentally related select committees in the Commons. Of the other select committees appointed by the House,[173] the Public Accounts Committee, the Statutory Instruments Committee, and the Committee on the Parliamentary Commissioner for Administration are each concerned with the scrutiny of executive action.[174]

As well as the procedures of the House considered above, each MP's office provides a means by which individual grievances, particularly those emanating from his or her constituency, may be raised with the public body concerned.[175]

Despite the means that exist for enabling the Commons to scrutinise the actions of public bodies, there remains some concern that the balance of power is weighted in favour of the executive and that the House lacks the political will to secure due accountability. Thus the House appears to accept that ministers control the flow of information from departments to the select committees of the House.[176] The Scott report in 1996[177] delivered a challenge to traditional assumptions within Westminster and Whitehall which deserved a more positive response than it received.

---

[173]   See HC SOs 121–9.
[174]   See respectively chs 17, 27 and 28 D.
[175]   On the MP's 'complaints service', see R Rawlings (1990) 53 MLR 22, 149.
[176]   Ch 7.
[177]   Page 227 above.

CHAPTER 11

Privileges of Parliament

Parliamentary privilege does not exist for the personal benefit of members of Parliament. 'The sole justification for the present privileges of the House of Commons is that they are essential for the conduct of its business and maintenance of its authority.'[1] 'Their purpose is not to protect individual MPs but to provide the necessary framework in which the House in its corporate capacity and its Members as individuals can fulfil their responsibilities to the citizens whom they represent.'[2] The privileges of each House have both external and internal aspects: they restrain interference with the House from outside, restricting the freedom of speech and action which those outside the House would otherwise have; they also protect the House from internal attack, for example, from the conduct of members which is an abuse of their position.

Privilege is an important part of the law and custom of Parliament. In so far as privilege may affect the position of those outside the House, questions as to the existence and extent of privilege must be settled by the courts. Since neither House can separately exercise the legislative supremacy of Parliament, neither House can by its own resolution create new privileges. Where a dispute arises as to a matter of privilege, 'it is for the courts to decide whether a privilege exists and for the House to decide whether such privilege has been infringed'.[3] Today the most difficult disputes are likely to involve the issue of whether a particular application of privilege in a new set of circumstances is to be categorised (a) as the legitimate exercise of an existing privilege in changed circumstances or (b) as an attempt to create a new privilege; in the latter case, an Act of Parliament is needed if the law is to be changed.[4]

A. House of Commons

There have for centuries been attached both to the House and its members certain privileges and immunities. At the opening of each Parliament, the

---

[1] Memorandum by Sir Barnett Cocks, HC 34 (1966–67), p 12. See also Erskine May, chs 5–11; G Marshall, in Walkland (ed), *The House of Commons in the Twentieth Century*, ch 4; and Griffith and Ryle, *Parliament*, ch 3.

[2] HC 351–I (1994–95), p. vi.

[3] *Pepper v Hart* [1993] AC 593, 645 (Lord Browne-Wilkinson).

[4] Cocks, op cit, p 3: cf the position of prerogative powers, p 280 below.

Speaker formally claims from the Crown for the Commons 'their ancient and undoubted rights and privileges', and in particular: 'freedom of speech in debate, freedom from arrest, freedom of access to Her Majesty whenever occasion shall require; and that the most favourable construction should be placed upon all their proceedings'. The privileges of individual members are primarily freedom from arrest and freedom of speech.

Freedom from arrest[5]

This ancient privilege developed to enable individual members to attend meetings of the House. It protects a member from arrest in connection with civil proceedings for the customary period from 40 days before to 40 days after a session of Parliament. But MPs have no privilege from arrest in connection with criminal or quasi-criminal proceedings.

As regards civil arrest, the privilege has been of small importance since the virtual abolition of imprisonment for civil debt. A member is protected against committal for contempt of court where the imprisonment is sought to compel performance of a civil obligation.[6] Members have no general immunity from having civil actions brought against them,[7] but they retain certain privileges in regard to civil litigation. It is a contempt of the House for any person to seek to serve a writ or other legal process upon a member within the precincts of the House.[8] A subpoena addressed to a member to give evidence in a civil court probably cannot be enforced by the High Court while the House is in session, but the House may grant a member leave of absence to attend as a witness. Members are not protected against bankruptcy proceedings, but are exempt from jury service.[9]

As regards criminal law, members have no privilege from arrest. Nor are they protected in cases of refusal to give surety to keep the peace or security for good behaviour, nor against committal for contempt of court where contempt has a criminal character.[10] An MP was held in preventive detention under defence regulations during the Second World War,[11] although detention because of words spoken in Parliament would violate the privilege of freedom of speech. The House has always insisted on receiving immediate information of the imprisonment of a member, with reasons for the detention. In 1970, the Committee of Privileges inquired into the rights of members who were detained in prison whether awaiting trial or after conviction. The committee reported that a member awaiting trial could carry out many duties as a constituency representative, but that a member who had been convicted could do so only if granted exceptional concessions under

---

5   Erskine May, ch 7.
6   As in *Stourton v Stourton* [1963] P 302. As ministers are subject to the contempt jurisdiction (*M v Home Office* [1994] 1 AC 377, ch 31 C), would an MP who is a minister be protected by parliamentary privilege from committal for contempt of court? Cf Erskine May, pp 97–9.
7   *Re Parliamentary Privilege Act 1770* [1958] AC 331.
8   HC 221 (1969–70) and HC 144 (1972–73).
9   Insolvency Act 1986, s 427. For detention under the Mental Health Act 1983, see p 182 above. And see Juries Act 1974, s 9 and Sched 1.
10   Ch 18 B. And see note 6 above.
11   HC 164 (1939–40) (Captain Ramsay's case).

prison rules. The committee considered that no special advantages in the conditions of detention should be granted to members.[12]

Freedom of speech[13]

Freedom of speech is today the most substantial privilege of the House. Its essence is that no penal or coercive action should be taken against members for what is said or done in Parliament. Claims for the privilege were regularly made by the Speaker on behalf of the House from the end of the 16th century.[14] The right of the Commons to criticise the King's government was called in question in 1629 when Eliot, Holles and Valentine were convicted by the Court of King's Bench for seditious words spoken in the Commons and for tumult in the House.[15] This judgment was in 1668 reversed by the House of Lords on the ground that words spoken in Parliament could be judged only in Parliament. In art 9 of the Bill of Rights 1689 it was declared, 'that the freedom of speech and debates or proceedings in Parliament ought not to be impeached or questioned in any court or place out of Parliament'.[16]

The main effect of this declaration is that no member may be made liable in the courts for words spoken in the course of parliamentary proceedings. Thus members may speak in the House knowing that they are immune from the law of defamation.[17] Nor can what is said in Parliament be examined by a court for the purpose of deciding whether it supports a cause of action in defamation which has arisen outside Parliament: 'a member must have a complete right of free speech in the House without any fear that his motives or intentions or reasoning will be questioned or held against him thereafter'.[18] Since 1818, leave of the House has been required before clerks or officers of the House may give evidence in court of proceedings in the House. In 1980, the House relaxed its practice to the extent of permitting reference to be made in court to Hansard and to the published evidence and reports of committees, without special leave from the House.[19] This change did not diminish the continuing force of art 9 of the Bill of Rights, nor did it alter the rule that Hansard may not be used in court as an aid to statutory interpretation. In 1993, the House of Lords did change the rule, holding that courts may use ministerial statements in Hansard to resolve ambiguities in legislation; such use would not 'impeach or question' freedom of speech in the Commons.[20] And, it seems, a ministerial statement in the House explaining an executive decision may be used in court on an application for judicial review.[21]

---

[12]   HC 185 (1970–71). And see G J Zellick [1977] PL 29.
[13]   Erskine May, ch 6. And P M Leopold [1981] PL 30.
[14]   Erskine May, pp 71–4.
[15]   *Eliot's case* (1629) 3 St Tr 294.
[16]   And see *Re Parliamentary Privilege Act 1770*, note 7 above.
[17]   Eg *Dillon v Balfour* (1887) 20 LR Ir 600. And *Lake v King* (1667) 1 Saunders 131.
[18]   *Church of Scientology of California v Johnson-Smith* [1972] 1 QB 522, 530 (Browne J).
[19]   HC Deb, 3 December 1979, col 167, and 31 October 1980, col 879; HC 102 (1978–79); and P M Leopold [1981] PL 316.
[20]   *Pepper v Hart* [1993] AC 593; and ch 2 A.
[21]   Ibid, 639 (Lord Browne-Wilkinson). But could the litigant question the minister's good faith in making the statement without breaching art 9? Cf *Prebble v Television New Zealand Ltd* [1995] 1 AC 321, 333.

The protection of members for words spoken extends to criminal as well as civil liability. It seems that members could not be prosecuted for an alleged conspiracy to make untrue statements in Parliament to the injury of a third party[22] although such conduct might make the members liable to the disciplinary jurisdiction of the House. Again, subject to disciplinary action by the House, disclosures made in Parliament may not be made the subject of a prosecution under the Official Secrets Acts.[23] Speeches or questions in Parliament may be in breach of the House's own sub judice rule if they concern pending judicial proceedings, but may not be held to be in contempt of court.[24]

In protecting MPs from liability for speaking in Parliament, the Bill of Rights also restricted the ability of MPs to sue in defamation. If an MP sues a newspaper for a report alleging misconduct by him or her, and the newspaper seeks to justify the report by evidence of what the plaintiff has said in Parliament, the defence of justification is barred by art 9. The interests of justice may then require the whole case to be stopped.[25] In 1996, concern at 'cash for questions' allegations caused Parliament to amend the Bill of Rights to permit a plaintiff MP to waive privilege so that an action could proceed.[26]

The meaning of 'proceedings in Parliament'

Protection for members is not confined to debates in the House. It covers the asking of questions and giving written notice of questions, and also 'everything said or done by a member in the exercise of his functions as a member in a committee in either House, as well as everything said or done in either House in the transaction of parliamentary business'.[27] On this broad view, protection extends to officials of the House acting in course of their duties, as well as to witnesses giving evidence to committees of the House. It may be that privilege is not confined to words spoken or acts done within the precincts of the House and includes words spoken outside Parliament, for example, a conversation between a minister of the Crown and a member on parliamentary business in a minister's office. Conversely, it may not extend to a casual conversation within the House on private affairs. The posting by a citizen of alleged libels to members in the House on matters unconnected with proceedings in the House is not protected.[28]

The difficult question of whether a member's letter to a minister concerning a publicly owned industry is a 'proceeding in Parliament' arose in 1957.

G R Strauss MP had written to the minister responsible for the electricity industry (the Paymaster-General) complaining of the methods of disposal of scrap cable followed by

---

22   *Ex p Wason* (1869) LR 4 QB 573.
23   *Duncan Sandys* case, HC 101 (1938–39).
24   Eg the disclosure of Colonel B's identity on 20 April 1978; HC 667 (1977–78) and 222 (1978–79); and p 426 below.
25   *Prebble v Television New Zealand Ltd* (above); and see P M Leopold (1995) 15 LS 204.
26   Defamation Act 1996, s 13. See ch 22 F for full consideration.
27   HC 101 (1938–39).
28   *Rivlin v Bilainkin* [1953] 1 QB 485.

the London Electricity Board. The minister referred the letter to the board, who protested to Mr Strauss about its contents. Finally the solicitors to the board told him that they had instructions to sue for libel unless he withdrew and apologised. Mr Strauss drew the attention of the House to this threat, and the matter was referred to the Committee of Privileges. The most important question was whether the original letter from the member to the Paymaster-General was a 'proceeding in Parliament' within the meaning of the Bill of Rights. The committee concluded that Mr Strauss was engaged in a proceeding in Parliament; accordingly the threat by the board to sue for libel was a threat to impeach or question his freedom of speech in a court or place outside Parliament. Thus the board and their solicitors had acted in breach of privilege. On 8 July 1958, the House decided on a free vote (218 to 213) to disagree with the committee, and resolved (*a*) that the original letter was not a proceeding in Parliament and (*b*) that nothing in the subsequent correspondence constituted a breach of privilege.[29]

In support of the majority view, it was argued that members should not widen the scope of absolute parliamentary privilege and should be content to rely on the defence of qualified privilege in the law of defamation. There is no doubt that a complaint addressed by a member of Parliament to a minister on an issue of public concern in which the minister has an interest has the protection of qualified privilege.[30] But qualified privilege may be rebutted by proof of express malice and it might possibly be held to constitute malice if a member passed on to a minister without any inquiry a letter from a constituent containing defamatory allegations.

In support of the view that a member's letter to a minister should be regarded as a proceeding in Parliament, it is certain that if a member tabled a parliamentary question instead of writing to the minister, he or she would be absolutely protected. Today it is inevitable that many matters should be raised in correspondence with ministers and not immediately become the subject of questions.

One issue taken for granted in the parliamentary discussion was whether to commence proceedings for defamation against a member in respect of a proceeding in Parliament amounts in itself to a breach of privilege. For example, an action for libel based on remarks spoken in the course of a debate is bound to fail. It has been argued that members should leave it to the courts to reject such an action and that the House should not treat the action itself as a breach of privilege.[31]

While the resolution in the Strauss case binds neither the Commons nor the courts, there is a strong argument for legislation to define the meaning of 'proceedings in Parliament'[32] and to extend absolute privilege to letters written by an MP to a minister: 'such communications are today part of the

---

29 HC 305 (1956–57); *Re Parliamentary Privilege Act 1770* [1958] AC 331; HC 227 (1957–58). Also S A de Smith (1958) 21 MLR 465; D Thompson [1959] PL 10.
30 *Beach v Freeson* [1972] 1 QB 14 (MP forwarding constituent's complaint about solicitors to the Law Society and Lord Chancellor); and ch 22 D below.
31 S A de Smith (1958) 21 MLR 465, 468–75. Lord Denning's unpublished dissent in *Re Parliamentary Privilege Act 1770* (above) is at [1985] PL 80.
32 HC 261 (1969–70), pp 8–12; Cmnd 5909 (1975), p 51; HC 417 (1976–77), p v. Cf *Rost v Edwards* [1990] 2 QB 460 (register of members' interests not a proceeding in Parliament), doubted in *Prebble*'s case, [1995] 1 AC 321 at 337; P M Leopold [1990] PL 475.

ordinary way in which members perform their parliamentary duties or are inextricably mixed up with them'.[33]

Publication of parliamentary proceedings outside Parliament

The House has always maintained the right to secure privacy of its own debates. In wartime the House occasionally excluded the press and the public to enable matters to be discussed in secret for security reasons. The House formerly maintained the right to control publication of its debates outside Parliament. By resolution of 3 March 1762, any publication in the press of speeches made by members was declared a breach of privilege. In modern times this resolution bore no relation to reality. On 16 July 1971, the House resolved that in future it would entertain no complaint of contempt or breach of privilege in respect of the publication of debates in the House or its committees, except when the House or a committee sat in private session. The House thus retained the power to permit committees and sub-committees to meet in private.[34] While select committees generally take evidence in public, their deliberations, especially when a draft report is being considered, still take place in private. Premature reporting of these proceedings is a serious breach of privilege,[35] but the reporting of evidence taken at public sittings of committees is no longer restricted.[36]

The public interest in reports of parliamentary proceedings is recognised in the law of defamation; unless a defamed person can prove malice, a fair and accurate unofficial report of proceedings in Parliament is privileged, as is an article founded upon such proceedings, provided it is an honest and fair comment upon the facts.[37] The interest of the public in discovering what was said in Parliament outweighs the discomfort which may be caused to individuals mentioned in Parliament. The common law defence of qualified privilege protects a 'parliamentary sketch', that is an impressionistic and selective account of a debate,[38] but not reports of detached parts of speeches published with intent to injure individuals, nor the publication of a single speech which contains libellous matter. Thus a member who repeats outside Parliament what is said in Parliament is liable if the speech contains defamatory material.[39] It is doubtful if qualified privilege attaches to the publication of a member's speech for the information of constituents.[40]

After long discussion within Parliament, regular sound broadcasting of proceedings in both Houses began in 1978.[41] Debates in the Lords were first televised in 1985 and the Commons followed suit in 1989. The BBC and the ITC have full editorial control to select what is broadcast, but the use of extracts for light entertainment or political satire is excluded. It would seem

---

33   HC 34 (1966–67), para 91.
34   HC 34 (1966–77), paras 116–29.
35   Eg HC 357 (1967–68), debated on 24 July 1968; HC 185 (1969–70); HC 180 (1971–72); and HC 22 (1975–76), debated on 16 December 1975.
36   HC Deb, 31 October 1980, col 917; and HC SO 118.
37   *Wason v Walter* (1868) LR 4 QB 73.
38   *Cook v Alexander* [1974] QB 279.
39   *R v Creevey* (1813) 1 M & S 278.
40   Cf *Davison v Duncan* (1857) 7 E & B 229.
41   See HC 376 (1981–82) for an historical account of the broadcasting of debates.

that qualified privilege at common law protects the BBC and the ITC against liability for the broadcasting of speeches containing defamatory material, but it has been suggested that the BBC and the ITC should be granted absolute privilege in respect of live broadcasting.[42]

Parliamentary papers

A difficult question at common law concerned the authority of the House to publish accounts of debates and reports of committees outside Parliament. In 1839, after a protracted dispute between the House and the courts, it was established that at common law the authority of the House was no defence when defamatory material was published outside the House and, more fundamentally, that the House could not create a new privilege by its own resolution.

In *Stockdale v Hansard*,[43] Hansard had by order of the Commons printed and sold to the public a report by the inspectors of prisons which stated that an indecent book published by Stockdale was circulating in Newgate prison. The first action in defamation raised by Stockdale against Hansard was decided for Hansard on the ground that the statement in the report was true. When Stockdale brought a second action, after the report had been re-published, Hansard was ordered by the House to plead that he had acted under an order of the Commons, a court superior to any court of law; and further that the House had declared that the case was a case of privilege; that each House was the sole judge of its own privileges; and that a resolution of the House declaratory of its privileges could not be questioned in any court. The court rejected the defence, holding that only the Queen and both Houses of Parliament could make or unmake laws; that no resolution of either House could place anyone beyond the control of the law; and that, when it was necessary in order to decide the rights of private individuals outside Parliament, the courts should determine the nature and existence of privileges of the Commons. It was held further that the House had no privilege to permit the publication outside the House of defamatory matter.

One sequel to *Stockdale v Hansard* was the *Case of the Sheriff of Middlesex*, which will be considered below. The other sequel was the passing of the Parliamentary Papers Act 1840. By s 1, any civil or criminal proceedings arising out of the publication of papers, reports etc made by the authority of either House must be stayed on the production of a certificate of such authority from an officer of the House. Thus Parliament as a whole gave the protection of absolute privilege to parliamentary papers. The official report of debates in the House (Hansard) is covered by absolute privilege under the 1840 Act, and so are documents in the series of House of Commons papers. But Command papers as such are not considered to be covered; if the report of an inquiry may contain defamatory material, a minister will move an order calling for the report to be produced to Parliament, so bringing it within the 1840 Act.[44] Section 3 of the 1840 Act protects in the absence of malice the publication of fair and accurate extracts from, or abstracts of, papers published under the

---

[42]   HC 261 (1969–70); HC 376 (1981–82). See also P M Leopold [1987] PL 524 and (1989) 9 LS 53.

[43]   (1839) 9 A & E 1. For the background, see P and G Ford (eds), *Luke Graves Hansard's Diary 1814–1841*. And see E Stockdale [1990] PL 30.

[44]   HC 261 (1969–70); Cmnd 5909 (1975), p 55; Erskine May, pp 212–213; P M Leopold [1990] PL 183.

authority of Parliament: thus press reports of parliamentary papers are protected by qualified privilege, and the same privilege now applies to broadcast reports.[45] This defence of qualified privilege is unusually advantageous to the plaintiff, since the Act places upon the defendant the negative burden of proving that there has been no malice. But the 1840 Act does not apply to reports of debates appearing in the press which are based not on Hansard but on the reporter's own notes.

Right to control internal proceedings

The House has the right to control its own proceedings and to regulate its internal affairs without interference by the courts. This principle helps to explain why the courts refuse to investigate alleged defects of parliamentary procedure when the validity of an Act of Parliament is challenged on this ground.[46] The courts will not consider whether the report of a select committee of the House is invalid because of procedural defects[47] and will not issue an injunction to restrain a local authority from breaking a contractual obligation not to oppose in Parliament a Bill being promoted by another local authority.[48]

The House is considered to have the right to provide for its own proper constitution as established by law.[49] At one time this included the right to determine disputed elections; today election disputes are decided by the courts.[50] But the House retains (*a*) the right to regulate the filling of vacancies by ordering the issue of a warrant by the Speaker for a writ for a by-election;[51] (*b*) the right to determine whether a member is qualified to sit in the House and to declare a seat vacant if, for example, a member succeeded to an hereditary peerage and did not disclaim the title within the statutory month; and (*c*) the right to expel a member whom it considers unfit to continue as a member. When the House expels a member, he or she is not disqualified from re-election to the House. Subject to this, expulsion is the ultimate disciplinary sanction which the House can exercise over its members.

In 1947, Mr Allighan MP published an article which accused MPs of disclosing for reward or under the influence of drink the proceedings of confidential party meetings held in the precincts of the House but not forming any part of the formal business of Parliament. It was held by the House, after investigation by the Committee of Privileges, that the article was a gross contempt of the House; other grave contempts had been committed by Mr Allighan since he had corruptly accepted payment for disclosing information and, except for a single case, he had been unable to substantiate any of the charges against his fellow-members. The House voted to expel Mr Allighan.[52]

---

45   Defamation Act 1952, s 9(1).
46   *Pickin v British Railways Board* [1974] AC 765; cf *Harper v Home Secretary* [1955] Ch 238, p 175 above.
47   *Dingle v Associated Newspapers Ltd* [1961] 2 QB 162.
48   *Bilston Corpn v Wolverhampton Corpn* [1942] Ch 391.
49   Erskine May, pp 80–2.
50   Ch 9 B III.
51   Page 191 above.
52   HC 138 (1946–47).

By contrast with the position in the United States,[53] no court in Britain has jurisdiction to review the legality of a resolution of the House to exclude or expel a member. One safeguard against abuse of this power is that a constituency may re-elect an expelled member, as in the case of John Wilkes in the 18th century. Today, the House would generally prefer a member to resign rather than be expelled.[54] While the House has power to enforce the attendance of members at Westminster, this power is not now used.[55]

The right of the House to regulate its own proceedings includes the right to maintain order and discipline during debates. A member guilty of disorderly conduct who refuses to withdraw may, on being named by the Speaker, be suspended from the service of the House either for a specified time or for the remainder of the session.[56] While in *Eliot's* case[57] the question of whether the courts could deal with an assault on the Speaker committed in the House was left open when the judgment was declared illegal by resolutions of both Houses, in principle criminal acts in the Palace of Westminster may be dealt with in the ordinary courts. In the case of a statutory offence, it is necessary to show that the statute in question applies to the Palace of Westminster: an attempt to convict members of the Kitchen Committee of the House for breaches of licensing law failed, primarily on the ground of the right of the House to regulate its internal affairs.[58]

Breaches of privilege and contempt of the House

The House has inherent power to protect its privileges and to punish those who violate its privileges or commit contempt of the House. The penal powers of the House include power to order the offender to be reprimanded or admonished by the Speaker. Members may be suspended or expelled; officials of the House may be dismissed; and non-members such as lobby correspondents, who are granted certain facilities in the Palace of Westminster, may have those facilities withdrawn.[59] Although the House has no power to impose a fine, it has power to commit any person to the custody of its own officers or to prison for contempt of the House or breach of its privileges. Such commitment cannot last beyond the end of the session.

In parliamentary speech, the term 'breach of privilege' has often been used as synonymous with contempt of the House. However, while most breaches of privilege are likely to be contempts, a person may be adjudged to be guilty of a contempt who has not infringed any existing privilege of the House. Thus in *Allighan's* case[60] the unfounded allegation about the proceedings of party meetings held in private at Westminster involved an affront to the House: but information about such meetings was not in itself a breach of

---

53 *Powell v McCormack* 395 US 486 (1970).
54 For the case of the disappearing MP, John Stonehouse, who was eventually convicted of fraud and resigned, see HC 273, 357, 373, 414 (1974–75), and HC Deb, 11 June 1975, col 408.
55 Erskine May, pp 168–9.
56 HC SOs 42–4.
57 Page 235 above.
58 *R v Graham-Campbell, ex p Herbert* [1935] 1 KB 594.
59 Cf HC 22 (1975–76).
60 Page 240 above.

privilege. Contempt of the House, like contempt of court, is a very wide concept. In Erskine May's words:

any act or omission which obstructs or impedes either House of Parliament in the performance of its functions, or which obstructs or impedes any member or officer of such House in the discharge of his duty, or which has a tendency, directly or indirectly, to produce such results may be treated as a contempt even though there is no precedent of the offence.[61]

Contempt has been held by the House to include: disorderly conduct by members or strangers within the precincts of the House;[62] refusal of a person to give evidence to a committee of the House;[63] interference with the giving of evidence by others to a committee;[64] obstruction of a member in coming to and from the House;[65] inclusion by a member in a personal statement to the House of words which he knew to be untrue; bribery and corruption, or attempts thereat, in relation to the conduct of members as such;[66] molestation of a member on account of conduct in the House (for example, publication of a newspaper article inviting readers to telephone a member at his home to express their views about a question which he had tabled);[67] publication of material which is derogatory of the House (for example, an allegation of drunkenness amongst members);[68] an allegation that members 'have surrendered for money their freedom of action as parliamentarians';[69] the service of writs on members within the precincts of the House;[70] premature disclosure of the proceedings of a committee of the House;[71] obstructing or assaulting an officer of the House while in the execution of his duty; disruption of a meeting at Essex University of a sub-committee of the Select Committee on Education and Science;[72] and the secret recording by a journalist of his conversations with MPs at Westminster while trying to persuade them to accept cash for asking questions.[73] But it was held not to constitute a contempt for pressure to be brought to bear upon a citizen to withdraw a complaint which he had asked his MP to raise in Parliament.[74] The fact that certain action may be a contempt of the House does not mean that the House will take action against the offender. In 1978, it was agreed that the House should use its penal jurisdiction as sparingly as possible, and only when the House:

---

[61] Erskine May, p 115; and see HC 34 (1967–68), pp xi–xviii and 95–101.
[62] For the precedents and full references, see Erskine May, ch 9.
[63] On the power to compel evidence to be given to a select committee, see P M Leopold [1992] PL 516.
[64] The House resolved in 1688 that all witnesses summoned to the House should have the privilege of the House 'in coming, staying and returning'; and see the Witnesses (Public Inquiries) Protection Act 1892.
[65] Cf *Papworth v Coventry* [1967] 2 All ER 41.
[66] And see section B below.
[67] The *Daily Graphic* case, HC 27 (1956–57).
[68] *Duffy*'s case, HC 129 (1964–65) and see HC 302 (1974–75).
[69] *Ashton*'s case, HC 228 (1974).
[70] HC 221 (1969–70) and HC 144 (1972–73).
[71] See note 34 above.
[72] HC 308 (1968–69).
[73] HC 351–I (1994–95).
[74] *Stevenson*'s case, HC 112 (1954–55).

is satisfied that to do so is essential to provide reasonable protection for the House, its members or its officers, from such improper obstruction or attempt at or threat of obstruction as is causing or is liable to cause, substantial interference with the performance of their respective functions.[75]

The courts and contempt of the House

While the courts assert jurisdiction to decide the existence and extent of privileges of the House, what constitutes a contempt of the House is a matter which only the House can decide. If a contempt issue arises relating to the internal proceedings of the House, the courts will decline to interfere. The House has an undoubted power (but not exercised since 1880) to detain persons for contempt. There was in the past much debate as to whether the courts might review the House's decision to detain an individual.

In *Paty*'s case, which arose after five electors of Aylesbury had sued returning officers for the malicious refusal of their votes and thereby had annoyed the Commons, Chief Justice Holt in a dissenting judgment held that a writ of habeas corpus would go to release anyone committed for contempt by the House, where the cause of committal stated in the return to the writ was insufficient in law.[76] This view of the law is accepted today. But if only the bald statement of contempt of the House is shown in the return, the court will not make further inquiry into the reasons for the committal.[77] This principle was applied in the *Case of the Sheriff of Middlesex.*

As a sequel to *Stockdale v Hansard*, the sheriffs attempted to recover for Stockdale by execution on Hansard's property £600 damages awarded in the third action of the series. The money recovered from Hansard was in the hands of the sheriffs when a new parliamentary session opened. The House first committed Stockdale and then, on the sheriffs refusing to refund the money to Hansard, also committed the two sheriffs for contempt, without expressing the reason for the committal. In habeas corpus proceedings it was held that the court had to accept the statement by the House that the sheriffs had been committed for contempt.[78]

Thus the House of Commons has power to commit persons for contempt, and may not be required by the courts to state the nature of the contempt. If the House had power to impose fines for contempt, the power to imprison for contempt could be abolished.[79]

The courts and parliamentary privilege[80]

Questions of privilege used to be a potential source of conflict between the Commons and the courts. The House claimed to be the absolute and sole judge of its own privileges. But the court in *Stockdale v Hansard* resolutely maintained the right to determine the nature and limit of parliamentary privilege, should it be necessary to decide these questions in adjudicating upon the rights of individuals outside the House. Another illustration of the

---

[75] HC 34 (1967–68), para 15; HC Deb, 6 February 1978, cols 1155–98.
[76] (1704) 2 Lord Raymond 1105.
[77] *Burdett v Abbot* (1811) 14 East 1.
[78] (1840) 11 A & E 273. And see E Stockdale [1990] PL 30.
[79] HC 417 (1976–77).
[80] Erskine May, ch 11.

relationship between courts and Parliament is provided by the complex Bradlaugh affair in the 1880s.

Bradlaugh, an atheist, was elected as MP for Northampton on successive occasions. The House took the view that as an atheist he could not sit or vote, as he could not properly take the oath required by existing statute law. At one stage Bradlaugh was allowed by resolution of the House, subject to any legal penalties he might incur, to affirm instead of taking an oath. In an action brought against him by a common informer for penalties for sitting and voting without taking the oath, the Court of Appeal held that the Parliamentary Oaths Act 1866 and other statutes did not authorise him to affirm.[81]

Later, following his re-election to Parliament, Bradlaugh required the Speaker to call upon him to take the oath. The Speaker refused to do so. The House then authorised the Serjeant at Arms to exclude Bradlaugh from the House. Bradlaugh sought an injunction against the Serjeant at Arms to restrain him from carrying out this resolution. In *Bradlaugh v Gossett*, it was held that, this being a matter relating to the internal management of the procedure of the House, the court had no power to interfere. As Lord Coleridge CJ said, 'If injustice has been done, it is injustice for which the courts of law afford no remedy.'[82] The Act of 1866 permitted certain persons to affirm instead of taking an oath; any person making an affirmation otherwise than as authorised by the Act could be sued for certain penalties. Stephen J emphasised that, if the House had by resolution stated that Bradlaugh was entitled to make the affirmation, the resolution would not have protected him against an action for penalties: for the purpose of determining a right to be exercised within the House itself, only the House could interpret the statute; but 'as regarded rights to be exercised out of and independently of the House, such as a right of suing for a penalty for having sat and voted, the statute must be interpreted by this court independently of the House.'[83]

It has been said that 'there may be at any given moment two doctrines of privilege, the one held by the courts, the other by either House, the one to be found in the Law Reports, the other in Hansard'.[84] But this dualism must not be exaggerated. On the one hand, new privileges, for example, the absolute privilege which an MP has in forwarding a citizen's complaint to the Parliamentary Commissioner for Administration,[85] must be created by statute and not by resolution of the House. On the other hand, the courts recognise the control which the House has over its own proceedings. Today it is hardly conceivable that the House would use its power to commit for contempt so as indirectly to create a new privilege when it was not willing to do this by process of legislation.[86]

The expanding scope of judicial review[87] has caused some MPs to fear that the courts are trespassing into areas reserved for Parliament. In 1993, when the High Court was to hear an application for judicial review of the government's decision to ratify the Treaty on European Union, Speaker Boothroyd said that the House could expect that art 9 of the Bill of Rights

---

[81]   *Clarke v Bradlaugh* (1881) 7 QBD 38. And see Arnstein, *The Bradlaugh Case*.
[82]   (1884) 12 QBD 271, 277.
[83]   (1884) 12 QBD 271, 282.
[84]   Keir and Lawson, *Cases in Constitutional Law*, p 255.
[85]   Parliamentary Commissioner Act 1967, s 10(5); ch 28 D.
[86]   Cf the argument that use of the contempt power can never have the effect of creating a new privilege: HC 34 (1967–68), pp 97–8. And see G F Lock [1985] PL 64.
[87]   Chs 29–30 below.

would be fully respected by the parties to the case.[88] In its judgment, the court stated that the issues all concerned the legality of executive acts and were properly decided by judicial review.[89]

Procedure

How does the House exercise its power when a complaint of breach of privilege or contempt is raised? Before 1978, members were expected to raise a privilege complaint in the House at the earliest opportunity, whereupon the Speaker had 24 hours to consider whether there had been a prima facie breach of privilege. The procedure was changed in 1978, to enable complaints to be considered under less pressure and trivial complaints to receive less publicity.[90] A member must give written notice of a privilege complaint to the Speaker as soon as is reasonably practicable after the event in question. The Speaker has a discretion to decide if the complaint should have precedence over other Commons business. If not, she informs the member by letter, who may then if he or she wishes seek to bring the matter to the House by other means. If the Speaker decides that the complaint should have priority over other business, she announces this decision to the House, whereupon the member may table a motion for the next day proposing that the matter be referred to the Committee on Standards and Privileges or other appropriate action. The motion is then debated and voted upon by the House. The committee, which has 11 members, was created in 1995 in place of the former Committee of Privileges. One duty of the committee is to consider specific matters relating to privileges which are referred to it by the House. It is for the committee to decide on the procedure for investigating the complaint. It is not the practice of the House to authorise the person responsible for the alleged breach to be represented by counsel. After examining witnesses and being advised by the Clerk of the House on relevant precedents, and if necessary by the Attorney-General on matters of law, the committee reports to the House, and may recommend the action that the House should take. The House need accept neither the conclusions nor the recommendations. The party whips are not applied on privilege issues.[91]

This procedure has been criticised, in particular because the individual against whom the complaint is made has inadequate procedural safeguards: thus there is no right to be heard, to be legally represented, to have notice of the charge, to cross-examine witnesses and call evidence, nor to receive legal aid. In 1967, the Select Committee on Parliamentary Privilege recommended improvements in the procedure which went some way to meeting these criticisms but these proposals were not adopted.[92] It would only be possible to meet the major criticism, that the House is judge in its own cause, if power to decide questions of privilege were vested in a body outside the House. This the House has not been prepared to do, even in the wake of the 'cash for

---

88 HC Deb, 21 July 1993, col 353. See R Rawlings [1994] PL 367, 377–81.
89 *R v Foreign Secretary, ex p Rees-Mogg* [1994] QB 552.
90 HC 417 (1976–77); HC Deb, 6 February 1978, col 1155; and HC Deb, 29 April 1981, col 789.
91 In 1996, a junior whip had to resign his post for having sought to exercise improper pressure on the former Committee on Members' Interests: HC 88 (1996–97).
92 HC 34 (1967–68); and HC 417 (1976–77).

questions' affair in 1995–96. Today the House is likely to make restrained use of its powers, especially in the case of a minor breach of privilege. In 1975, when the Committee on Privileges had recommended that the editor of the *Economist* and a political correspondent should be denied access to the House for six months, the House voted that no further action be taken.[93] In 1986, when *The Times* had published a leaked version of a draft report of the Environment Committee on radioactive waste, the House resolved that it would be proper to punish a member of the committee who disclosed the draft report prematurely, but not to punish a journalist merely for doing his or her job.[94]

B.   The financial interests of members

It is one thing to assert the principle that MPs should have complete freedom of speech in Parliament, but another to ensure that they are in fact free of undue influence from financial and business interests outside the House, and do not abuse their public office for private gain.

This is not a new problem, and perceptions of what is acceptable behaviour by politicians are likely to change. In the 18th century, the use of patronage enabled control over the House to be maintained. One consequence of today's electoral system is that every MP is expected to take an active interest in questions which directly affect their constituency, such as the closure of a hospital or the building of a bypass, or issues which affect individuals or local businesses. At the national level, numerous interest groups (trade unions, professional associations, employers, manufacturers, environmental, charitable and social organisations) seek from widely varied motives to influence decisions and to win support in Parliament.[95]

Many such groups consider it necessary to obtain political advice from MPs, and to ensure that opportunities of promoting their cause in Parliament are taken. Where an MP gives time and effort to helping a constituent, no question of additional remuneration arises. But where an MP takes an interest in other matters, may he or she properly expect to be remunerated for such efforts? In 1994, after press allegations that some MPs would ask questions of ministers in return for payment, this issue was examined by the Nolan committee on standards in public life and by the House itself.

This was not the first time that concern about the conduct of MPs had arisen. After the business network associated with the architect John Poulson collapsed on his bankruptcy in 1972, it was found that his influence had extended to central and local government, police committees and health authorities, and also to three MPs, including a senior member of the shadow Cabinet, who had used their position as MPs to promote Poulson's business without disclosing benefits which they were receiving from him; the conduct

---

93   HC Deb, 16 December 1975, cols 1303–56.
94   HC Deb, 20 May 1986, cols 293–332. See Griffith and Ryle, *Parliament*, pp 98–104, for a review of privilege cases from 1977 to 1987.
95   There is an extensive literature on pressure groups; see eg Stewart, *British Pressure Groups*; Alderman, *Pressure Groups and Government in Great Britain*.

of one of those MPs, who had raised matters in the House for reward, was a contempt of the House.[96] This affair caused the House in 1975 to create the first register of members' interests.

During the 1980s, a commercialised form of political lobbying developed which proved very lucrative for some MPs. By 1994, it was evident that, despite earlier attempts to regulate members' interests, the services of some MPs were in fact available for hire in one form or another.

Payments and rewards to members of Parliament

It is only since 1911 that members not holding ministerial office have received a salary. Payment of salaries to members became essential after the House of Lords had held that the use of trade union funds for political purposes was ultra vires and illegal,[97] thus preventing unions from paying salaries to the Labour MPs whom they supported. Today, in addition to salary, members receive allowances for office costs, travel between Westminster and their constituencies, necessary overnight stays away from home, the benefit of a contributory pension scheme and an allowance when they cease to be members.[98] It is difficult to keep members' salaries and allowances fairly related to salaries outside the House; since 1987, these have been linked by means of a formula to civil service pay scales.[99] Since July 1996 these salaries are paid in full to members who also receive salaries under the Ministerial and other Salaries Act 1975.

Apart from public offices which disqualify from membership,[100] members may take paid employment outside the House, practise in their professions, and act as advisers or consultants to commercial or other organisations. Many members regard their public duties as occupying all their time, some regard them as the background to a successful career outside Parliament. Problems arise when payments or benefits from outside sources relate not to advice given outside the House but to acts of the member in Parliament.[101]

As long ago as 1695, the House resolved that 'the offer of any money, or other advantage, to any member of Parliament for the promoting of any matter whatsoever depending or to be transacted in Parliament is a high crime and misdemeanour'. In 1858, the House resolved that it was improper for a member to promote or advocate in the House any proceeding or measure in which he had acted or was acting for pecuniary reward. In 1945, it was considered that, in accordance with the resolution of 1695, it would be a breach of privilege for an offer of money or other advantage to be made to a

---

[96] See HC 490 (1976–77); HC Deb, 26 July 1977, col 332; and G J Zellick [1978] PL 133.

[97] *Osborne v Amalgamated Society of Railway Servants* [1910] AC 87. Under the Trade Union and Labour Relations (Consolidation) Act 1992, unions may pay the expenses of sponsored MPs from separate political funds, p 179 above.

[98] For the history of members' salaries, see Erskine May, ch 1.

[99] See HC Deb, 3 November 1993, col 455; 13 July 1994, col 1105; and 26 October 1995, col 1191. In 1996–97, the salary for MPs was £43,000 pa and the office cost allowance was £46,364 pa; and see HC Deb, 10 July 1996, cols 488–543.

[100] Ch 9 B IV.

[101] See generally Report from the Select Committee on Members' Interests (Declaration), HC 57 (1969–70); First Report of the (Nolan) Committee on Standards in Public Life, Cm 2850–I (1995); and Report of the Select Committee on Standards in Public Life, HC 637 (1994–95).

member, or to a local party or a charity, to induce him or her to take up a question with a minister.[102]

In 1947, the case of W J Brown MP, who had agreed with a civil service union to be their 'parliamentary general secretary', raised two questions: (1) Was the contract proper, or did it improperly restrict the MP's freedom of action in Parliament? (2) If it was proper, were the union improperly restricting Brown's freedom if they sought to terminate the contract?

The agreement, which provided Brown with lucrative benefits, stated that (*a*) he was entitled to engage in his political activities with complete freedom, and (*b*) he should deal with all questions relating to the work of the union which required parliamentary action. Political disagreements having arisen between Brown and the union, the union's executive proposed to end the appointment on terms to be agreed. The Committee of Privileges reported that (i) it would be improper for an MP to enter any arrangement fettering his independence as a member; and (ii) no organisation should seek to punish an MP pecuniarily because of his actions in Parliament. Further, Brown's contract was not improper; an MP who entered into such a contract must have accepted its termination as a matter which would not influence him in his parliamentary duties.

Accepting the committee's report, the House resolved that it was improper for an MP 'to enter into any contractual agreement with any outside body, controlling or limiting the Member's complete independence and freedom of action in Parliament or stipulating that he shall act in any way as the representative of such outside body in regard to any matters to be transacted in Parliament; the duty of a Member being to his constituents and to the country as a whole, rather than to any particular section thereof'.[103]

This is an important statement of principle, but why was the principle not breached by Brown's contract, which in return for payment envisaged action being taken by him in Parliament? The view taken in 1947 and later was that the contract did not in terms *require* Brown to take any specific action in Parliament – so that (in one sense) he was free to decide what issues to raise and what action to take. This view created uncertainty as to what was acceptable conduct, and left the door wide open for the growth of what are now termed 'parliamentary consultancies' – a door which in 1995 the Nolan committee recommended must be closed.[104] The register of members' interests in 1975 had compounded the uncertainty, since some MPs acted on the incorrect belief that registration of an interest was enough to legitimise it.[105]

The manner in which trade unions give support to Labour MPs in the House today bears no resemblance to the contract in the *Brown* case.[106] Such support is always public knowledge, and the MPs derive no personal financial benefit, union payments being made to the constituency funds. However, on

---

[102]   *Henderson*'s case, HC 63 (1944–45).
[103]   HC Deb, 15 July 1947, col 284; HC 118 (1946–47). See also *Robinson*'s case HC 85 (1943–44).
[104]   See report of the Nolan committee, Cm 2850–I, pp 24–32.
[105]   See the statement by Speaker Boothroyd in HC Deb, 12 July 1994, col 829.
[106]   Union sponsorship formerly conformed with the 'Hastings agreement', taking the form of financial support for an MP's constituency party: Ewing, *The Funding of Political Parties in Britain*, p 56. And see HC 57 (1969–70), app III.

several occasions in the past, questions of privilege were raised when branches of a union became dissatisfied with the political work of MPs whom they were sponsoring.[107]

Voting and declarations of interest

Members of local authorities are subject to statutory rules enforceable in the courts requiring the declaration of interests and excluding them from voting on matters which affect their interests.[108] No such statute applies to the Commons. By an old rule of the House, no member who has a direct pecuniary interest in a question may vote upon it. But this rule has been narrowly interpreted, Speaker Abbot declaring in 1811 that the rule applied only where the interest was a 'direct pecuniary interest and separately belonging to the persons ... and not in common with the rest of His Majesty's subjects, or on a matter of State policy'. The rule was applied only to private legislation, and a vote on a public Bill has never been disallowed.[109] By custom of the House, members had to declare their direct pecuniary interest when speaking in a debate, but the custom did not apply to question time, nor to letters which a member sent in his capacity as a member.[110] The duty to disclose private interests became a rule of the House, rather than custom, and its scope was extended on 25 May 1974, when the House resolved:

That in any debate or proceedings of the House or its committees or transactions or communications which a member may have with other members or with Ministers or servants of the Crown, he shall disclose any relevant pecuniary interest or benefit of whatever nature, whether direct or indirect, that he may have had, may have or may be expecting to have.

This resolution governs all parliamentary proceedings, but it does not in terms apply to dealings which MPs may have with local councils, public corporations or foreign governments.

Register of members' interests

A more systematic method of making members' interests public was required than the custom of the House. In 1969, a select committee recommended against a register, preferring to extend the traditional practice of the House. But in 1975, the Poulson affair caused the House to establish a compulsory register of members' interests.[111] The aim was to provide public information of any pecuniary interest or material benefit which might affect the conduct of members as such, or influence their actions, speeches or vote in Parliament. The register was maintained by a senior clerk of the House and supervised by a select committee. The initial criteria for registration were not always clear and led to some uninformative entries. In 1990, two complaints

---

[107] See eg HC 50 (1971–72), HC 634 (1974–75) and HC 512 (1976–77).
[108] Local Government Act 1972, ss 94–8.
[109] HC 57 (1969–70), p xii; Erskine May, pp 354–9.
[110] See *Boothby*'s case, HC 5 (1940–41).
[111] HC 57 (1969–70); and HC 102 (1974–75).

against Mr John Browne MP that he had failed to register financial interests were upheld; he was suspended for 20 days from the House.[112]

In 1995, the Committee of Privileges criticised two MPs who had been prepared to accept £1,000 from a *Sunday Times* reporter posing as a business-man, in return for asking a parliamentary question. The committee found that the reporter had committed a contempt of the House by secretly recording his conversations at Westminster with the MPs. The two MPs were suspended from the House, for 10 and 20 days respectively.[113]

The 'cash for questions' affair was one reason for the government's decision to appoint the Nolan committee on standards in public life.[114] In its first report,[115] the committee re-stated seven key principles of conduct in public life (stressing such qualities as integrity, accountability and openness) and examined their application to MPs. MPs could properly have employ-ment outside the House, but they should be barred from selling their services to firms engaged in lobbying on behalf of clients. The committee was deeply concerned by the nature of some parliamentary consultancies. The commit-tee was against placing the rules of conduct for MPs on a statutory basis, proposing new arrangements to enable the House to enforce the rules of conduct.

With the backing of a select committee on standards and conduct,[116] the House adopted the following measures.

(i) A new officer of the House was appointed, the Parliamentary Commis-sioner for Standards, to maintain the Register of Members' Interests, to advise MPs on what to register, and to receive and investigate specific complaints about registration and the propriety of MPs' conduct.

(ii) The Committee of Standards and Privileges was created, replacing the committees on registration of interests and on privileges, to oversee the work of the Commissioner for Standards, and to consider matters relating to the conduct of members referred to it by the Commissioner.

(iii) Stricter rules for the register were adopted. There are 10 categories of interest, including company directorships, employment, trade, profession and vocation; services to clients which arise from the member's position as MP; financial sponsorships, whether as a candidate (ie election expenses) or as a member; gifts, benefits and hospitality relating to membership; certain overseas visits; land and property of substantial value; certain shareholdings; and a residual category of any interest or benefit received which might reasonably be thought by others to influence the member's actions in Parliament.[117]

(iv) An MP who has entered into an employment agreement to provide services as a member must register a full copy of the agreement with the Commissioner and state the fees payable in specified bands.

---

112   See HC 135 (1989–90) and HC Deb, 7 March 1990, col 889. Also M Ryle [1990] PL 313; Griffith and Ryle, *Parliament*, pp 55–68.
113   HC 351–I (1994–95) and HC Deb, 20 April 1995, col 350.
114   See HC Deb, 25 October 1994, col 757.
115   Cm 2850–I, 1995.
116   HC 637 and 816 (1994–95); HC Deb, 18 May 1995, col 481.
117   HC 345 (1995–96) contains the first register of interests (as at 31 March 1996) prepared by the Parliamentary Commissioner for Standards.

(v) The 1947 resolution[118] was re-stated by the House, with the addition of the following:

in particular, no Member shall, in consideration of any remuneration, fee, payment, reward or benefit in kind, direct or indirect ...
(*a*) advocate or initiate any cause or matter on behalf of any outside body or individual, or
(*b*) urge any other Member of either House ... including Ministers, to do so,
by means of any speech, Question, Motion, introduction of a Bill or amendment to a Motion or Bill.[119]

(vi) A short code of conduct for members was prepared, together with a guide to the rules.[120]

It must be hoped that these measures will enable acceptable standards to be observed by all MPs. Should even a few MPs act improperly in providing their services in return for payment, legislation to make such conduct criminal could become necessary. In 1976, a royal commission on conduct in public life chaired by Lord Salmon considered that neither statute law nor the common law on corruption applied where an MP was involved, and recommended that the criminal law should be strengthened.[121] There is a strong argument that the existing common law is not as ineffective as the Salmon commission supposed,[122] but there should be no uncertainty in this area of the law.

Much will depend on the ability of the Parliamentary Commissioner for Standards to enforce the rules firmly and with integrity. The dissolution of Parliament in March 1997 put the Commissioner's activities into temporary abeyance, when he was still dealing with a series of allegations that certain MPs had broken the rules in the past.[123]

C. House of Lords

Questions of privilege very rarely arise in relation to the House of Lords. In outline, the privileges of the House and of peers are:

1 Freedom from civil arrest for peers. In *Stourton v Stourton*[124] a peer was held to be privileged from a writ of attachment for civil contempt following his failure to send his wife her property under a court order. The judge found that arrest was being sought to compel performance of a civil obligation. This privilege

---

[118] Above, n 103.
[119] HC Deb, 6 November 1995, cols 604, 661.
[120] HC 688 (1995–96); and HC Deb, 24 July 1996, col 392.
[121] Cmnd 6524, 1976.
[122] G J Zellick [1979] PL 31. The common law of corruption applies to MPs in Canada (*R v Bunting* (1885) 7 OR 524) and Australia (*R v Boston* (1923) 33 CLR 386). See also *A-G of Ceylon v de Livera* [1963] AC 103 and *US v Johnson* 383 US 169 (1966).
[123] See eg HC 460 (1994–95) (payment of bill at Ritz Hotel, Paris), HC 706 (1994–95) (working visit to Washington), HC 148 (1995–96) (offer to act as parliamentary consultant), HC 635 (1995–96) (banks' decision to allow insolvent MP time to pay), HC 636 (1995–96) (newspaper's donation to MP's research fund).
[124] [1963] P 302.

may be claimed by an individual peer at any time, but the House claims privilege only 'within the usual times of privilege of Parliament'.[125]

2 Freedom of speech. Article 9 of the Bill of Rights applies to the Lords as it does to the Commons; a speech made in the House is not privileged if published separately from the rest of the debate.[126]

3 The right to commit for contempt. The Lords can commit a person for a definite term, and the imprisonment is not terminated by prorogation of Parliament. The Lords also have power to impose fines and to order security to be given for good conduct.

4 The right to exclude disqualified persons from the proceedings of the House. The House itself decides, through the Committee for Privileges, the right of newly created peers to sit and vote. Claims to old peerages are referred by the Crown to the House, and are also decided by the Committee for Privileges.[127] That body is not bound by its own previous decisions.

Financial interests of peers

The House of Lords has not been under the same pressure as the Commons concerning the disclosure of interests. One view is that peers ought not to be required to account publicly for their interests in the same manner as elected MPs. Yet many peers take an influential part in the legislative process and have access to government, and they cannot expect to observe lower standards of public conduct than MPs. In 1995, the House resolved that its members should act always on their personal honour and should never accept a financial benefit in return for exercising parliamentary influence; peers who have a direct interest in lobbying ought not to speak, vote or otherwise use their office on behalf of clients. The House created a register of peers' consultancies and similar financial interests in lobbying for clients. The register is of much narrower scope than the Commons register, but peers may register other matters 'which they consider may affect public perception of the way in which they discharge their parliamentary duties'. The register is overseen by the House's Committee for Privileges, who may appoint a sub-committee including at least three law lords to investigate an alleged failure to register interests.[128]

---

[125]   HL SO 78. Regarding the Mental Health Act 1983, see HL 254 (1983–84). See also P M Leopold [1985] PL 9 (on the 1983 Act) and [1989] PL 398 (on peers' freedom from arrest generally).

[126]   *R v Lord Abingdon* (1795) 1 Esp 226.

[127]   See eg *The Ampthill Peerage* [1977] AC 547.

[128]   See HL 90 and 98 (1994–95); HL Deb, 1 November 1995, col 1428, and 7 November 1995, col 1631; and (for the 1996 register) HL 34 (1995–96).

CHAPTER 12

The Crown and the prerogative

Article II of the United States Constitution declares that, 'The executive power shall be vested in a President of the United States of America'. On this declaration is based the system of a presidential executive. By contrast, where the British system of cabinet government is practised, the formal statement that the executive power is vested in the Crown[1] corresponds much less closely with the reality of government. The Sovereign may reign, but it is the Prime Minister and other ministers who rule. Yet within the executive in Britain, it is not possible to dismiss the position of the Sovereign as an archaism since the Sovereign as head of state performs some essential functions. The fact that central government is carried on in the name of the Crown has left its mark on the law. Our law has never developed a notion of 'the state': the judges have been opposed to the idea of allowing interests of the state to override common law rights.[2] Although it is common to speak of state schools, state ownership and so on, legislation rarely refers to the state as such.[3] Instead, the Crown has developed as 'a convenient symbol for the State'.[4] It is usual to refer to 'the Sovereign' in matters concerning the personal conduct or decisions of the monarch, and to 'the Crown' as the collective entity which in law may stand for central government.

We have already seen that the functions of the executive are more diverse than those of the legislature and judiciary, having acquired a residual character after legislature and judiciary had become separated from the main work of governing.[5] The functions of the executive have been said to include 'the execution of law and policy, the maintenance of public order, the management of Crown property ..., the direction of foreign policy, the conduct of military operations, and the provision, regulation, financing, or supervision of such services as education, public health, transport and national insurance'.[6] Today such a catalogue is far from complete. To

---

[1] See eg for Canada, the Constitution Act 1867, s 9; for Australia, ch II of the Constitution; and cf Blackstone, *Commentaries*, vol 1, pp 249–50; HLE, vol 8(2), para 351.

[2] *Entick v Carrington* (1765) 19 St Tr 1030. Though cf *Council of Civil Service Unions* v *Minister of State for Civil Service* [1985] AC 374. See below, p 283.

[3] Cf *Chandler v DPP* [1964] AC 763.

[4] G Sawer's phrase, quoted in Hogg, *Liability of the Crown* (1st edn), p 10; and see Marshall, *Constitutional Theory*, ch 2.

[5] Ch 5.

[6] HLE, vol 8(2), para 9.

perform all the tasks of government the executive must comprise a wide array of officials and agencies. These include the Prime Minister and other ministers, government departments, the civil service, the armed forces, and also the police, who are outside the direct hierarchy of central government but exercise a vital executive function. Outside central government, but closely linked to it, are local authorities and many public boards and corporations, which may be considered to perform executive functions, albeit confined to one locality or one economic activity.

Unlike the work of Parliament and the courts, much of the work of the executive is carried on behind closed doors. British government still seeks to maintain secrecy on matters which it believes to affect its own vital interests.[7] This secrecy often masks a divergence between the legal form and the political substance. Thus in exercising some of the Crown's powers, the Sovereign may exercise a personal discretion; others are exercised by the Sovereign on the advice of ministers; and many powers are exercised directly by ministers and civil servants. Whether a statutory power is conferred upon the Queen in Council or directly in a named minister, the government is responsible to Parliament for the decisions taken. Since it is rare for statutory powers to be vested in the Cabinet or the Prime Minister,[8] decisions taken in Cabinet or by the Prime Minister usually have to be translated into the appropriate legal form before they can take full effect. In view of this interplay of legal form and conventional practice, study of the executive in the United Kingdom must begin with the legal position of the Sovereign.

A.   The Sovereign

Title to the Crown

In 1689, the Convention Parliament (that had been summoned by Prince William of Orange at the request of an improvised assembly of notables) filled the constitutional vacuum which arose on the departure of James II by declaring the throne vacant and inviting William of Orange and his wife Mary jointly to accept the throne.[9] These events finally confirmed the power of Parliament to regulate the succession to the Crown as it should think fit.[10] Today title to the Crown is derived from the Act of Settlement 1700, subsequently extended to Scotland in 1707 and to Ireland in 1800 by the Acts of Union. By the Act of Settlement, the Crown shall 'be remain and continue to the said most excellent Princess Sophia' (the Electress of Hanover, granddaughter of James I) 'and the heirs of her body being Protestant'.[11] The

---

7   Eg *A-G v Jonathan Cape Ltd* [1976] QB 752; ch 13 B. And see ch 13 E.
8   But see Interception of Communications Act 1985, and see ch 13 E. Security Service Act 1989, s 4, and Intelligence Services Act 1994, s 8.
9   Maitland, *Constitutional History*, pp 283–5; Taswell-Langmead, *English Constitutional History*, pp 443–8.
10   Taswell-Langmead, op cit, p 504.
11   See *A-G v Prince Ernest Augustus of Hanover* [1957] AC 436, for construction of Princess Sophia Naturalization Act 1705 (repealed by British Nationality Act 1948) which entitled to British nationality all non-Catholic lineal descendants of Princess Sophia.

limitation to the heirs of the body, which has been described as a parliamentary entail, means that the Crown descends in principle as did real property under the law of inheritance before 1926.[12] That law inter alia gave preference to males over females and recognised the right of primogeniture.

The major exception to the common law rules of inheritance is that for practical reasons the right of two or more sisters to succeed to real property as co-parceners does not apply: as between sisters, the Crown passes to the first-born.[13] The Act of Settlement disqualifies from the succession Roman Catholics and those who marry Roman Catholics; the Sovereign must swear to maintain the Churches of England and Scotland and must join in communion with the former Church. Since 1714, when the Hanoverian succession took effect under the Act of Settlement, the line of hereditary succession has been altered only once: it was provided by His Majesty's Declaration of Abdication Act 1936 that the declaration of abdication by Edward VIII should have effect; that the member of the royal family then next in succession to the throne should succeed (thus Edward VIII's brother became King George VI); and that Edward VIII, his issue, if any, and the descendants of that issue should not thereafter have any right to the succession.

The eldest son of a reigning monarch is the heir apparent to the throne; he is Duke of Cornwall by inheritance and is invariably created Prince of Wales.[14] When the Sovereign has no son, the person next in succession (for example, the eldest daughter of the Sovereign or, if the Sovereign is childless, his younger brother) is known as heir or heiress presumptive: his or her right to succeed may be displaced by the subsequent birth of a son to the Sovereign. It is probable that this principle applies even if the subsequent birth is posthumous. To take an extreme case, should a future King die leaving a daughter and a pregnant wife but no son, it would seem that the daughter as heiress presumptive succeeds to the Crown upon his death, but with a qualified title which is set aside if a son is posthumously born.[15]

Style and titles

The style and titles of the Crown are determined by royal proclamation under the great seal issued under statutory authority from time to time. The Royal Titles Act 1953 authorised the adoption by the Queen, for use in relation to the United Kingdom and all other territories for whose foreign relations the UK government is responsible, of such style and titles as the Queen may think fit. Under this Act in 1953 the present title was proclaimed:

Elizabeth II by the Grace of God of the United Kingdom of Great Britain and Northern Ireland and of Her other Realms and Territories Queen, Head of the Commonwealth, Defender of the Faith.

Before the 1953 Act, the royal style and titles had rested on the indivisibility of the Crown throughout the Commonwealth. The Preamble to the Statute of

---

12   On which, see Megarry and Wade, *The Law of Real Property*, pp 539–46.
13   Blackstone, *Commentaries*, I, p 193; Chitty, *Prerogatives of the Crown*, p 10.
14   On the constitutional role of the Prince of Wales, see R Brazier [1995] PL 401.
15   See Megarry and Wade, op cit, p 541, and eg *Richards v Richards* (1860) Johns 754. Cf Regency Act 1830, ss 3–5, and views of Lyndhurst LC at HL Deb, 15 November 1830, col 505; and 6 December 1830, col 764.

Westminster 1931 had declared that it would be in accord with the established constitutional position of the members of the Commonwealth in relation to one another that any alteration in the law or the succession to the throne or the royal style and titles should require the consent of the Parliaments of all the Dominions. By 1952, when the Commonwealth already included the Republic of India, a meeting of Prime Ministers agreed that in future it would be for each member state within the Commonwealth to enact its own form of title.[16] In the result the only description of the Sovereign common to all states within the Commonwealth is 'Head of the Commonwealth'. The Crown itself is no longer single and indivisible but 'separate and divisible' for each self-governing territory within the Commonwealth.[17]

In *MacCormick v Lord Advocate*[18] the proclamation of the Queen as Elizabeth II was challenged in Scotland on the ground that this contravened the Treaty of Union between England and Scotland (since there had never been an Elizabeth I of Scotland). The Court of Session considered that the royal numeral did not derive from the Royal Titles Act 1953 but from the proclamation of the Queen at her accession in 1952, and found nothing in the Treaty of Union which prohibited the adoption of the style 'Elizabeth II'. The court also held that no citizen had, under Scots law, title or interest to challenge the legality of the royal numeral.

Royal marriages

The archaic Royal Marriages Act 1772, by restricting the right of a descendant of George II to contract a valid marriage without the consent of the Sovereign, seeks to guard against undesirable marriages which might affect the succession to the throne. Until the age of twenty-five the Sovereign's assent is necessary, except in respect of the issue of princesses who have married into foreign families. After that age a marriage may take place without consent after a year's notice to the Privy Council, unless Parliament expressly disapproves.[19] In recent times no reigning monarch's marriage has been dissolved. When in 1992 it was announced that the Prince and Princess of Wales were to separate (with 'no plans to divorce'), it was said by the Prime Minister that this decision had no constitutional implications, and that the succession to the throne was unaffected.[20] Although this was thought to be 'perhaps rather unrealistic',[21] the problem has been resolved by the dissolution of the marriage in 1996, with the result that the Princess of Wales can no longer become Queen. But questions were raised about the Prince of Wales's possible future position as head of the Church of England.[22]

Accession and coronation

There are two ceremonies which mark the accession of the new Sovereign. Immediately on the death of his or her predecessor the Sovereign is proclaimed by the Accession Council, a body which comprises the Lords Spiritual and

---

[16]   Cmd 8748, 1953; and see S A de Smith (1953) 2 ICLQ 263.
[17]   *R v Foreign Secretary, ex p Indian Assn of Alberta* [1982] QB 892; and ch 15 C.
[18]   1953 SC 396; ch 4 D.
[19]   See C d'O Farran (1951) 15 MLR 53 and C Parry (1956) 5 ICLQ 61.
[20]   See HC Deb, 9 December 1992, col 845.
[21]   Bogdanor, *The Monarchy and the Constitution*, p 58.
[22]   On the relationship between the monarchy and the church, see Bogdanor, above, ch 9.

Temporal and other leading citizens, and is a survival of an old assemblage which met to choose and proclaim the King. The proclamation is afterwards approved at the first meeting of the new Sovereign's Privy Council. Later there follows the coronation, the ancient ceremony which, before the hereditary principle was established, gave religious sanction to title by election and brought to a close the interregnum between the death of one King and the election of his successor. Today there is no interregnum and the main legal significance of the coronation is the taking of the oath by the Sovereign of his or her duties towards his or her subjects. The form of the oath was prescribed by the Coronation Oath Act 1688 as amended by the Acts of Union.[23] In place of the declaration against transubstantiation required by the Bill of Rights and the Act of Settlement, the Accession Declaration Act 1910 substituted a modified declaration of adherence to the Protestant faith; this declaration is made when the new Sovereign first opens Parliament or at the coronation, whichever is earlier. The oath to preserve the Presbyterian Church in Scotland was taken by Elizabeth II at the first Privy Council held after her accession.

Minority and incapacity

The Regency Acts 1937–53 make standing provision for the Sovereign's minority, incapacity and temporary absence from the realm. Until the Sovereign attains the age of 18, the royal functions are to be exercised by a regent, who will also act in the event of total incapacity of an adult Sovereign. Normally the regent will be the next person in the line of succession who is not excluded by the Act of Settlement and is a British subject domiciled in the United Kingdom. If the heir apparent or heir presumptive is to be regent, he or she must have attained the age of 18; if another person, the age of 21.[24] Regency is automatic on the succession of a minor; but in the case of total incapacity a declaration has to be made by the wife or husband of the Sovereign, the Lord Chancellor, the Speaker, the Lord Chief Justice and the Master of the Rolls, or any three of them, that they are satisfied by evidence (including that of physicians) that the Sovereign is by reason of infirmity of mind or body incapable of performing the royal functions, or that for some definite cause he or she is not available for the performance of those functions. This declaration must be made to the Privy Council and communicated to the other governments of the Commonwealth. A regency on these grounds may be ended by a similar declaration. A regent may exercise all the royal functions, except that he or she may not assent to a Bill for changing the order of succession to the Crown or for repealing or altering the Scottish Act of 1706 for securing the Protestant religion and Presbyterian church government.[25]

Illness and temporary absence

In the event of illness which does not amount to total incapacity or of absence or intended absence from the United Kingdom, the Sovereign may appoint

---

[23]   For the oath taken by Elizabeth II, see HLE, vol 8(2), para 28.
[24]   The Regency Act 1953, s 1, provided for the Duke of Edinburgh to be regent in certain circumstances.
[25]   Regency Act 1937, s 4; ch 4 C above.

Counsellors of State to exercise such of the royal functions as may be conferred upon them by letters patent. There may not be delegated the power to dissolve Parliament otherwise than on the express instructions of the Sovereign (which may be conveyed by telegraph), or to grant any rank, title or dignity of the peerage. The Counsellors of State must be the wife or husband of the Sovereign, the four persons next in line of succession to the Crown (excluding any persons (*a*) disqualified from being regent, or (*b*) being absent or intending to be absent from the United Kingdom during the period of delegation) and Queen Elizabeth, the Queen Mother. The heir apparent or heir presumptive may be a Counsellor of State, if not under 18 years of age.[26] The functions of Counsellors of State during absence of the Sovereign from the United Kingdom do not extend to those functions which in relation to a Dominion are normally exercised by the Sovereign in person.

Demise of the Crown

Formerly the death of the Sovereign involved the dissolution of Parliament and the termination of the tenure of all offices under the Crown. The duration of Parliament is now independent of the death of the Sovereign.[27] The Demise of the Crown Act 1901 provided that the holding of any office should not be affected by the demise of the Crown and that no fresh appointment should be necessary. When in 1936 effect was given to Edward VIII's abdication by His Majesty's Declaration of Abdication Act 1936, it was enacted that there should be a demise of the Crown upon the Act receiving the royal assent. Before Edward VIII signed the declaration of abdication, the King's intention had been communicated informally to the Dominion governments by the Prime Minister. Upon signature the declaration was formally communicated to the Dominion governments.[28]

Financing the monarchy[29]

In the 17th century, when the Sovereign personally carried out the functions of government, the revenue from the taxes which Parliament authorised was paid over to the Sovereign and merged with the hereditary revenues already available to him. Today a separation is made between the expenses of government and the expenses of maintaining the monarchy. Since the time of George III, it has been customary at the beginning of each reign for the Sovereign to surrender to Parliament for his or her life the ancient hereditary revenues of the Crown, including the income from Crown lands.[30] Provision is then made by Parliament for meeting the salaries and other expenses of the royal household. This provision, known as the Civil List, was granted to the Queen for her reign and six months after, by the Civil List Act 1952. In 1952,

---

[26] Regency Act 1937, s 6.

[27] Ch 9 C.

[28] Different courses of action were taken by the Dominion governments and parliaments in assenting to the abdication: K H Bailey (1937–38) 3 *Politica* 1, 147.

[29] For a good account, see Bogdanor, above, ch 7.

[30] Under the Crown Estate Act 1961, the Crown Estate Commissioners are responsible for administering the Crown Estate: for the history, see HC 29 (1971–72), app 18. The Commissioners have wide powers under the Act. See *Walford v Crown Estate Commissioners* 1988 SLT 377.

the total annual amount paid was £475,000 but following an inquiry into the financial position of the monarchy by a select committee of the House of Commons,[31] the amount was raised to £980,000 by the Civil List Act 1972. The 1972 Act also provided that the annual sum might be increased by means of a Treasury Order subject to annulment by the House of Commons.

The idea behind the Civil List used to be that Parliament should not be asked to vote money for the expenses of the royal household each year, and the 1972 Act provided for a periodic report from the Royal Trustees on the state of the royal finances. But because of continuing inflation, the Civil List Act 1975 empowered the Treasury to make payments to the Royal Trustees for supplementing sums payable under the Queen's Civil List and abolished the procedure of periodic reports. The select committee of the Commons in 1971 had rejected a proposal that the royal household should be placed on the footing of a government department to receive an annual payment voted by normal budgetary procedures, but the 1975 Act was a step in that direction. In 1990, however, the Prime Minister announced that as from 1991 the arrangements would return to those provided for in the 1972 Act and that a fixed annual payment (equivalent to £7.9 million per annum) from the Consolidated Fund would be made for a period of ten years.[32] The Queen's official expenses thus reverted to a standing service on the Consolidated Fund, and the financial arrangements were such that it was hoped that the need for annual supplements voted by Parliament under the Civil List Act 1975 would cease. But the 1975 Act was left in place 'as a means of financing of last resort'.[33]

Since 1975, the Queen has reimbursed the Treasury for the annuities paid to three members of her extended family, and since 1993 she has reimbursed all but those paid to herself, the Duke of Edinburgh and the Queen Mother. So of the total of £10,417,000 paid under the Civil List, £1,515,000 is refunded. In practice, however, the Civil List, which is used 'to meet official expenditure necessarily incurred through [the Sovereign's] duties as head of state',[34] 'accounts for only a small percentage of government expenditure on the monarchy'.[35] Thus, certain expenses in connection with the royal household (such as the Royal Yacht, the Queen's Flight and the Royal Train) are met out of departmental allocations (in these cases the Ministry of Defence and the Department of Transport). In 1990–91, this accounted for £46.2 million, while another important source of government support, the grant-in-aid voted annually by Parliament to the Department of National Heritage used to maintain the royal palaces, accounted for another £25 million in 1995.[36] The Prince of Wales also enjoys separate provision out of the Duchy of Cornwall to meet official and personal expenses, though he receives no parliamentary annuity.

The Act of 1952, as amended in 1972, also makes provision for the Duke of Edinburgh, the Queen's younger children and other members of the royal family. The justification for this is stated to be that these members of the royal

---

[31]   HC 29 (1971–72).
[32]   Civil List (Increase of Financial Provision) Order 1990, SI 1990/2018.
[33]   HC Deb, 24 July 1990, cols 299–306. See Hall, *Royal Fortune: Tax, Money and the Monarchy.*
[34]   Bogdanor, above, p 186.
[35]   Ibid, p 187.
[36]   Ibid, pp 187–8.

family take a share in the burden of work placed on the Sovereign and are, by reason of their relationship to the Sovereign, unable to earn a living in ways open to the rest of the community.[37] The Sovereign also holds property in a personal capacity and derives income from this. In 1971, the Commons Select Committee were assured that suggestions that the Queen owned private funds in the region of £50 million were 'wildly exaggerated' but no estimate of their actual value was given to the committee. In 1996, the Press Complaints Commission upheld a complaint from the Press Secretary to the Queen about an article in *Business Age* magazine which claimed that the Queen was the wealthiest person in Britain with an estimated wealth of £2.2 billion. In the view of the Commission 'the article presented speculation as established fact', 'failed adequately to check its facts', and 'made a number of errors which were not properly addressed'.[38] One matter of concern was the failure to distinguish private wealth from that held in trust by the Queen as Sovereign and Head of State and not as an individual.

Unlike other members of the Royal family, however, the Queen benefits from the principle that the Crown is not liable to pay taxes unless Parliament says so either expressly or by necessary implication.[39] This is subject to the Crown Private Estates Act 1862 which provides that the Balmoral and Sandringham estates are liable to be taxed. The Prince of Wales also has an immunity from taxation, but only in respect of income derived from the Duchy of Cornwall. In 1992, however, it was announced that the Queen had undertaken to pay tax on her private income with effect from 1993,[40] the arrangements being subsequently explained in a report of the Royal Trustees. The Prince of Wales has also agreed to pay tax on income derived from the Duchy of Cornwall.[41]

Duties of the Sovereign

No attempt can be made to list the full duties which fall to the Sovereign to perform in person.[42] Many formal acts of government require her participation. Many state documents require her signature and she receives copies of all major government papers, including reports from ambassadors abroad and their instructions from the Foreign Office, and also minutes of Cabinet meetings and other Cabinet papers. 'There is therefore a continuing burden of unseen work involving some hours reading of papers each day in addition to Her Majesty's more public duties'.[43] She gives frequent audiences to the Prime Minister and visiting ministers from the Commonwealth, receives foreign diplomatic representatives, holds investitures and personally confers honours and decorations. She receives visits to this country by the heads of foreign states, and makes state visits overseas. She attends numerous state occasions, for example to deliver the Queen's Speech at the opening of each session of Parliament. Her formal

---

[37]   HC 29 (1971–72), para 31.
[38]   Press Complaints Commission, Report No 34 (1996), pp 5–8.
[39]   HC 29 (1971–72), app 12; and ch 13 C.
[40]   HC Deb, 26 November 1992, col 982.
[41]   HC 464 (1992–93).
[42]   See HC 29 (1971–72), paras 16–17, and evidence by the Queen's Private Secretary, pp 30–41 and app 13. See also generally Pimlott, *The Queen: A Biography of Elizabeth II.*
[43]   HC 29 (1971–72), para 17.

consent is needed for appointments made by the Crown on the advice of the Prime Minister, the Lord Chancellor and other ministers.

A catalogue of official duties does not reveal what influence, if any, the Sovereign has on the political direction of the country's affairs. In general, the Sovereign is bound to act on the advice of the Prime Minister or other appropriate minister, for example, the Home Secretary or the Secretary of State for Scotland in respect of the prerogative of mercy. The Sovereign cannot reject the final advice which ministers offer to her without the probable consequence of bringing about their resignation and their replacement by other ministers, thereby bringing the future of the monarchy into controversy. But to what extent may the Queen offer them guidance from her own fund of experience in public affairs? Bagehot described the Sovereign's rights as being the right to be consulted, the right to encourage and the right to warn.[44] While this may entitle the monarch to express personal views on political events to the Prime Minister, these views may have little influence over the whole range of the government's work.[45] This was so even in relation to the later years of Queen Victoria, whose attitude to Gladstone was, by the standards of her successors, not that of a constitutional monarch.

Much light was thrown upon the role of the Sovereign in the 20th century by Sir Harold Nicolson's biography of George V and by Sir John Wheeler-Bennett's biography of George VI. Thus it appears that the Sovereign, even before the days when Cabinet conclusions were regularly recorded by the Cabinet secretariat, could insist on the advice of the Cabinet being given in written form, if he felt that it was dangerous or opposed to the wishes of the people. This was so that the King could record in writing the misgivings and reluctance with which he followed the advice of his Cabinet.[46] The clear impression is given in these two biographies that the monarch is far from being a mere mouthpiece of his constitutional advisers. But it would be wrong to suppose that the right to be consulted, to encourage and to warn applies to all areas of policy-making, in many of which the Sovereign will have had no relevant experience. Such rights can be understood better in relation to those powers of the Sovereign where she may be required to exercise a personal discretion; they will be discussed below under the heading, the personal prerogatives of the Sovereign.

Private Secretary to the Sovereign

The Private Secretary to the Sovereign plays a significant role in conducting communications between the Sovereign and her ministers and, in exceptional circumstances where this is constitutionally proper, between the Sovereign and other political leaders. This office is filled on the personal selection of the Sovereign; usually it goes to a member of the royal household who has extensive experience in the service of the Court. It is through the Private Secretary that communications from the government to the Sovereign are sent. Inevitably, the secretarial function demands much discretion in selecting the information which should be brought to the personal notice of the

---

[44] *The English Constitution*, p 111. See also Brazier, *Constitutional Practice*, p 181.
[45] Jennings, *Cabinet Government*, ch 12; Mackintosh, *The British Cabinet*, chs 4, 9, 17 and 19.
[46] Nicolson, *George V*, p 115.

Sovereign, and in obtaining confidential advice for the Sovereign from independent sources should this be necessary.[47] The Private Secretary must belong to no political party. He is made a member of the Privy Council.

Occasionally, the Sovereign's Private Secretary may be drawn into public controversies. In 1950, Sir Alan Lascelles, Private Secretary to George VI, wrote to *The Times* under a pseudonym, to outline the circumstances in which he believed the monarch could properly refuse a dissolution when requested by the Prime Minister.[48] In 1986, Sir William Heseltine, the Queen's Private Secretary, wrote to *The Times* following alleged disagreements between the Prime Minister (Mrs Thatcher) and the Queen on policy matters. Sir William made three points which he considered axiomatic:

1 The Sovereign has the right – indeed the duty – to counsel, encourage and warn her government. She is thus entitled to have opinions on government policy and to express them to her chief minister.
2 Whatever personal opinions the Sovereign may hold or may have expressed to her government, she is bound to accept and act on the advice of her ministers.
3 The Sovereign is obliged to treat her communications with the Prime Minister as entirely confidential between the two of them.[49]

Sir William asserted that it was preposterous to suggest that the Queen would suddenly depart from these principles.

B.   Personal prerogatives of the Sovereign

The appointment of a Prime Minister[50]

In appointing a Prime Minister the Sovereign must appoint that person who is in the best position to receive the support of the majority in the House of Commons. This does not involve the Sovereign in making a personal assessment of leading politicians since no major party could fight a general election without a recognised leader. Where an election produces an absolute majority in the Commons for one party, the leader of that party will be invited to become Prime Minister or, if already Prime Minister, he or she will continue in office. In these circumstances, 'the Sovereign has no choice whom he or she should appoint as Prime Minister, and it is obvious who should be called to the Palace'.[51]

By modern practice, a defeated Prime Minister resigns from office as soon as a decisive result of the election is known. Where after an election no one party has an absolute majority in the House (as in 1923, 1929 and February 1974), the Prime Minister in office may decide to wait until Parliament resumes to see whether he can obtain a majority in the new House with

---

[47]   Wheeler-Bennett, *George VI*, app B; and HC 29 (1971–72), pp 30–41.
[48]   See p 266 below.
[49]   *The Times*, 29 July 1986. See G Marshall [1986] PL 505.
[50]   See Jennings, *Cabinet Government*, ch 2; Marshall and Moodie, ch 3; Brazier, *Constitutional Practice*, chs 2, 3; and Bogdanor, ch 6.
[51]   Bogdanor, above, p 84.

support from another party (as did Baldwin after the 1923 election, only to find that he could not) or he may resign without waiting for Parliament to meet (as did Baldwin in 1929 and Heath in 1974). When he has resigned, the Queen will send for the leader of the party with the largest number of seats (as in 1929 and 1974) or with the next largest number of seats (as in January 1924 after Baldwin had been defeated by combined Labour and Liberal votes).[52] Thus, where the election produces a clear majority for one party, the Sovereign has no discretion to exercise. Where an election does not produce a conclusive result, the Sovereign has no discretion except where the procedure described still fails to establish a government in office; in this case, the Sovereign would have to initiate discussions with and between the parties to discover, for example, whether a government could be formed by a politician who was not a party leader or whether a coalition government could be formed.[53]

Where a Prime Minister resigns because of ill-health or old age, or dies while in office, a new leader of the governing party must be found. Formerly, in the case of the Liberal and Conservative parties, this was a situation in which the Sovereign was required to exercise a discretion, namely to invite a person to be Prime Minister who would command general support within the governing party. Sometimes the successor might be clear (as in 1955 when Eden followed Churchill) and the retiring Prime Minister could advise the Sovereign of this fact, although he was not required to give advice to the Sovereign about his successor. Where there were two or more possible successors, the Sovereign was entitled to consult with senior members of the party concerned to discover which person would command most support within the party. In 1957, when Eden resigned because of illness, he left two possible successors, Butler and Macmillan; the Queen consulted with Sir Winston Churchill, a former Prime Minister, and with Lord Salisbury, to whom the views of the Cabinet ministers were known. This established that Macmillan commanded much the greater support, and he was invited by the Queen to be Prime Minister. In 1963, when Macmillan announced his imminent resignation because of ill-health, he organised rapid consultations with different sections of the Conservative party. On the basis of these consultations, he advised the Queen that the Earl of Home, as he then was, had the greatest support. The Queen then invited Home to see whether he could form a government, on the understanding that if successful he would disclaim his peerage.

After the events in 1957 and in 1963, it was realised that if the Sovereign was merely expected to invite as next Prime Minister the person whom the Conservative party wished to lead it, it would be better for the party to have its own procedure for electing a leader. This the Parliamentary Labour Party already had. The present position is that the Conservative party rules provide for a series of up to three secret ballots, in which only the MPs may vote. Consultation must take place with sections of the party outside the Commons.

---

[52] The precedents thus show a preference for 'minority government' rather than 'majority coalition' (Bogdanor, above, p 253).

[53] See Butler, *Governing without a Majority: Dilemmas for Hung Parliaments in Britain*, ch 5; and Bogdanor, *Multi-party Politics and the Constitution*, chs 5, 6.

New candidates may be nominated after the first ballot. In the first ballot, a candidate will be elected if he or she *both* (*a*) receives an overall majority of the votes of those entitled to vote, *and* (*b*) receives 15% more of the votes of those entitled to vote than any other candidate. If no candidate meets these requirements, the second ballot will be held a week later, in which new candidates may come forward. If no candidate receives an overall majority of the votes of those eligible to vote, a third ballot may be necessary. No new nominations are permitted at this stage, the ballot now being restricted to the three candidates who in the second ballot secured the highest number of votes. It was under these rules that Mr Major replaced Mrs Margaret Thatcher as leader of the Conservative party in 1990.[54] Although Mrs Thatcher won more votes in the first ballot in a challenge by Mr Michael Heseltine, she did not obtain enough to secure an outright victory. When she then withdrew from the contest, Mr Major and Mr Douglas Hurd put their names forward for the second ballot. Although Mr Major did not secure enough votes for an outright victory, the other two candidates withdrew after the second ballot, leaving Major to be elected without the need for a third ballot.

In the case of the Labour party, the right to vote in the election of leader was formerly confined to Labour MPs, but in 1981 the party changed its constitution and standing orders to provide for the leader and deputy leader to be elected at a party conference.[55] Candidates must be Labour MPs in contrast to the Conservative party's rules which do not expressly require that candidates are members of the Commons. The electoral college is in three sections, Labour MPs and constituency parties each having 33% of the votes, and affiliated organisations having 33%. Successive ballots with open voting are held until one candidate has more than half the votes so apportioned. When Labour is in opposition, an election shall be held at each annual conference. When Labour is in government and the party leader is Prime Minister, an election takes place only if required by a majority of the conference on a card vote. While both parties have used these procedures to elect leaders while in opposition (the Conservatives in 1965 and 1975; Labour in 1983, 1992 and 1994), new ground was broken in 1976, again in 1990, and yet again in 1995. In 1976, when Harold Wilson announced his intention of resigning as Prime Minister, he remained in office until (under the party's former rules) Labour MPs elected their new leader, Mr Callaghan. Mr Wilson then resigned and Mr Callaghan became Prime Minister. In 1990, as we have seen, the Conservative party removed Mrs Thatcher as party leader against her wishes while she was also Prime Minister. Although Mrs Thatcher's leadership had previously been challenged by using the leadership procedures, her replacement by Mr Major in 1990 represents the first time this century that a serving Prime Minister in peacetime has been forcibly removed

---

[54]   The rules were later modified 'to render an incumbent leader less vulnerable to challenge, to respond to complaints from the extra-parliamentary party and to remedy deficiencies in the rules ... detected during the 1990 contest' (R K Alderman [1992] PL 30). A leadership election may be held only if 10% of the party's MPs notify the chairman of the back-bench 1922 Committee that an election is necessary. After the second ballot only two rather than three candidates go through to a third ballot, which will be determined by a simple majority of the members. See Alderman, ibid.

[55]   The rules were revised again in 1993: see R K Alderman [1994] PL 24.

from office.[56] And in 1995, Mr Major resigned as leader of the Conservative party, thereby forcing an election for party leader, in which he was a candidate. He did not, however, resign as Prime Minister, though presumably he would have done so had he not succeeded in being re-elected as party leader.

Thus the Labour and Conservative parties have their own procedures for electing a new leader, as do the Liberal Democrats. Does this mean that the Sovereign has no residual discretion to exercise in appointing a Prime Minister? First, since the election of a new leader may take some weeks, the appointment of an acting Prime Minister might well be needed if, unlike the position in 1976, the outgoing Prime Minister had died or was too ill to continue in office. Presumably a senior member of the Cabinet would be so appointed.[57] Moreover, there could well be circumstances in which reliance on normal party procedures would not produce an immediate solution: for example, where a party holding office broke up after serious internal dissensions; or where no party had a majority in the House and there was a deadlock between the parties as to who should form a government; or where a coalition agreement had broken down.[58] In such situations, the Sovereign could not avoid taking initiatives to enable a new government to be formed, for example by initiating inter-party discussions. In 1931, when Ramsay MacDonald and the Labour Cabinet resigned because of serious disagreement within the Cabinet over the steps that should be taken to deal with the financial crisis, George V, after consulting with Conservative and Liberal leaders, invited MacDonald to form a 'National Government' with Liberal and Conservative support. The extreme bitterness which MacDonald's defection caused in the Labour party led to criticism of George V's conduct as unconstitutional, but such criticism seems unjustified.[59] While therefore under stable political conditions the Sovereign will not need to exercise a personal discretion in selecting a Prime Minister, circumstances could arise in which it might become necessary for the Sovereign to do so.

Dissolution of Parliament[60]

In the absence of a regular term for the life of Parliament fixed by statute, the Sovereign may by the prerogative dissolve Parliament and cause a general election to be held. The Sovereign normally accepts the advice of the Prime Minister and grants a dissolution when this is requested. Since 1918, it has become established practice that a Cabinet decision is not necessary before the Prime Minister may seek a dissolution, although members of the Cabinet

---

[56]   After that contest the Conservative party reviewed its election procedures. See note 54 above.
[57]   Cf Brazier, *Constitutional Practice*, p 12. By Labour party standing orders, when the party is in government and the leader becomes 'permanently unavailable', 'the Cabinet shall in consultation with the National Executive Committee appoint one of its members to serve as party leader until a ballot . . . can be carried out'.
[58]   See R Brazier [1986] PL 387.
[59]   A full account is in Bassett, *1931: Political Crisis*. See also Mackintosh, *British Cabinet*, pp 419–20, and Middlemas and Barnes, *Baldwin*, ch 23.
[60]   Forsey, *The Royal Power of Dissolution in the British Commonwealth*; Markesinis, *The Theory and Practice of Dissolution of Parliament*; Marshall, *Constitutional Conventions*, ch 3.

may be consulted before the Prime Minister makes a decision.[61] The refusal of a dissolution when the Prime Minister had requested it would probably be treated by him as tantamount to a dismissal. Are there circumstances in which the Sovereign would be justified in refusing a dissolution or is it automatic that the Sovereign should grant a dissolution when requested?

It is doubtful whether there can be grounds for the refusal of a dissolution to a Prime Minister who commands a clear majority in the Commons.[62] Political practice accepts that a Prime Minister may choose the time for a general election within the five-year life of Parliament prescribed by the Parliament Act 1911. If a Sovereign did refuse dissolution to a Prime Minister who commanded a majority in the House, and the Prime Minister then resigned from office with the other ministers, any other politician invited to be Prime Minister (for example, the leader of the Opposition) would presumably have no prospect of a majority at Westminster until an election had been held. The Sovereign would therefore be faced with an early request for a dissolution from the new Prime Minister and with inevitable criticism of political bias if the request was granted. Where a minority government holds office, the position is more complicated but here again it is essential for the Prime Minister to choose the time for an election. Much would depend on the circumstances in which the minority government had come about and on how recently a general election had been held. Thus a Prime Minister who had been granted one dissolution and failed to get a majority at the ensuing election could not request a second dissolution immediately. There would be a duty to resign and to give the leader of another party the opportunity of forming a government. Where a Prime Minister had been in office for a considerable period (for example, some months) since the previous election, and was then defeated on an issue of confidence in the House, he would then have a choice between resigning or, as MacDonald did in 1924, seeking a dissolution.

In 1950, during discussion of the problems caused by the Labour government's small majority after the 1950 election, it was submitted by the Private Secretary to George VI that the Sovereign could properly refuse a dissolution if he were satisfied that (*a*) the existing Parliament was still 'vital, viable, and capable of doing its job', (*b*) a general election would be detrimental to the national economy and (*c*) he could rely on finding another Prime Minister who could carry on his government for a reasonable period with a working majority.[63] It will be seldom that all these conditions can be satisfied, and it might be argued that these are eminently matters for the Prime Minister in office to decide. It might be particularly difficult for the Sovereign to be reasonably certain that another Prime Minister could command a working majority in the House. Yet the Sovereign would be strongly criticised if having

---

[61]   Jennings, *Cabinet Government*, pp 417–19; Mackintosh, op cit, pp 453–5; Markesinis, op cit, ch 5 A.

[62]   Markesinis, op cit, pp 84–6; Forsey, op cit, p 269. If an opportunist Prime Minister decided to take advantage of the death of the leader of the Opposition to seek an immediate dissolution, knowing that the rules of the opposition party required the election of a new leader to take a month, could the Sovereign insist on delaying the election so that the parties could campaign on more equal terms?

[63]   For his pseudonymous letter to *The Times*, see Markesinis, op cit, pp 87–8 and app 4.

refused a dissolution to one Prime Minister he or she was faced with an early request from the new Prime Minister for dissolution.

In the last 100 years there are no instances of the Sovereign having refused a dissolution in the United Kingdom, but there are two leading illustrations of the problem from the former Dominions where the prerogative was exercisable by the Governor-General. In 1939, the Governor-General of South Africa refused a dissolution to the Prime Minister, General Hertzog, whose proposal that South Africa should be neutral in the Second World War had been defeated in Parliament, and he invited General Smuts to form a government which remained in power thereafter. But in 1926, the Governor-General of Canada, Lord Byng, refused a dissolution to the Liberal leader, Mackenzie King, and instead invited Meighen, the Conservative leader, to form a government believing that Meighen would be supported by a third party which held the balance of power. When that support failed within a matter of days, Meighen sought a dissolution of Parliament which was granted by Lord Byng: the ensuing election was won by the Liberals and the Governor-General was much criticised for his decisions.[64]

The controversy between the 'automatic' and 'discretionary' views of the prerogative of dissolution arose again in 1969. Although Labour had a clear majority in the Commons, there were press reports of dissension within the party. The question was raised whether a Prime Minister could use the weapon of dissolution to defend his own position against attempts within the party to dislodge him.[65] In 1974, after the election in February 1974, when no party had an absolute majority, it was asked whether Mr Wilson as Prime Minister was entitled to a dissolution if his government were defeated in the Commons by a combined opposition vote. Certain Labour MPs, who feared that a Liberal–Conservative coalition might be formed to govern the country, urged that the Sovereign was both constitutionally and morally bound to grant dissolution whenever the Prime Minister requested it. In reply, the Lord President of the Council, Mr Short, told them: 'Constitutional lawyers of the highest authority are of the clear opinion that the Sovereign is not in all circumstances bound to grant a Prime Minister's request for dissolution'; it was impossible to define in advance the circumstances in which the Sovereign's discretion to refuse a request for a dissolution might be exercised.[66] The government refused to allow the matter to be debated in the Commons. In the event, when Mr Wilson sought a dissolution in September 1974, this was granted without question by the Sovereign.

That the Sovereign should not refuse a Prime Minister's request for dissolution except for very strong reason is obvious. In practice, the political significance of the Prime Minister's power to decide when Parliament should be dissolved is much greater than the possibility of the Sovereign's refusal of a dissolution. But the view that the Sovereign's reserve power may serve to restrain a Prime Minister who otherwise might be tempted to abuse his or her

---

[64] Forsey, op cit, gives a detailed commentary; and see Mallory, *The Structure of Canadian Government*, pp 50–2.

[65] Markesinis, op cit, app 4. Earlier in 1969, Captain O'Neill, Prime Minister of Northern Ireland, had been granted a dissolution of the Northern Ireland Parliament at a time when members of the Unionist party were growing restive at O'Neill's measures of reform.

[66] *The Times*, 11 May 1974.

position is an argument for maintaining the reserve power as a potential weapon, not for abolishing it.

The dismissal of ministers

The refusal of a Prime Minister's request for a dissolution is one aspect of a larger question, namely whether the Sovereign may ever reject the advice of the Prime Minister on a major issue, for example, by refusing to make an appointment to ministerial office which the Prime Minister had recommended, by refusing to give the royal assent to a Bill which has passed through both Houses or by insisting that a general election is held before the royal assent is given. In 1910, George V insisted that a general election be held on the Liberal proposal to remove the veto of the House of Lords, before he would create enough new Liberal peers to pass the Parliament Bill through the Lords against Conservative opposition; this decision was accepted by the Prime Minister, Asquith. But in other situations a refusal by the Sovereign to accept advice could be seen as a direct challenge to the authority of the Prime Minister and might mean his immediate resignation. The underlying question is whether the Sovereign is merely part of the formal apparatus of government, and thus incapable of taking an independent position on a point of constitutional principle, or whether the monarchy provides some kind of safeguard against potential abuses of power by the Prime Minister and Cabinet.

The last occasion on which it was seriously urged that the Sovereign should intervene to ensure that a general election should be held against the wishes of the government was during the crisis over Home Rule for Ireland between 1912 and 1914.[67] After the Parliament Act 1911 had become law, the Liberal government intended that the Government of Ireland Bill should be passed under the Parliament Act procedure. Opposition leaders regarded the relationship between the Liberal party and the Irish Nationalists as 'a corrupt Parliamentary bargain'. They urged George V to insist that an election be held before the Bill became law or to withhold the royal assent. Asquith, the Prime Minister, reminded George V of the constitutional limitations upon the Sovereign, of the principle of ministerial responsibility, and of the value for the Sovereign of having no personal responsibility for the acts of executive and Parliament. The King concluded that he should not adopt the extreme course of withholding the royal assent from the Bill 'unless there is convincing evidence that it would avert a national disaster, or at least have a tranquillizing effect on the distracting conditions of the time'.[68]

Where the question is that of assent to a Bill which has passed through Parliament, it would not be prudent for the Sovereign to challenge the wishes of a majority in the House of Commons. Yet the relationship between Sovereign and Prime Minister is bilateral in the sense that both persons hold office subject to some principles of constitutional behaviour, however vague these principles often appear to be. If the Prime Minister steps outside those principles (as, for example, Ian Smith, Prime Minister of Rhodesia, did in 1965 when with his Cabinet he unilaterally declared Rhodesia independent of

---

[67]   See Nicolson, *George V*, ch 14; Jennings, *Cabinet Government*, ch 13.
[68]   Draft letter by George V, 31 July 1914.

the United Kingdom), the Sovereign may respond by dismissing his or her ministers and by seeking to ensure the maintenance of constitutional government. In 1975, the Labour government of Australia was failing to get essential financial legislation through the Canberra Parliament because of opposition from the Senate, whose approval to the legislation was required. When Sir John Kerr, the Governor-General, had satisfied himself that Prime Minister Whitlam was not willing to hold a general election to resolve the deadlock, he dismissed Whitlam and invited the Opposition leader, Fraser, to form an interim government and hold an election. The election was won by Fraser, but the acts of the Governor-General gave rise to controversy of a kind which would be more damaging to a hereditary monarchy than to a Governor-General with a limited tenure of office.[69]

British government depends to a large extent upon implicit agreement between the parties and their leaders about the rules and understandings of the political contest. If in a particular situation it were clear that one party or its leader had seriously departed from the accepted rules, personal intervention by the Sovereign could be justified on constitutional grounds. But a plain instance of flagrant abuse is less likely than a situation which is not covered by existing rules and understandings, and in which it may be difficult to determine what are the constitutional requirements.[70] While the Sovereign may have a sensitive role to play in enabling a constitutional deadlock to be resolved, one lesson of British history is that personal government by the Sovereign is excluded. Indeed, the Sovereign needs the cooperation of ministers even for the purpose of dissolving Parliament and causing a new general election to be held.[71] The political impotence of a monarch who cannot find ministers willing to hold office explains why, as a 'far-sighted precaution' at an early stage of the abdication crisis in 1936, Prime Minister Baldwin ensured that other political leaders would not be willing to form a government if he were forced to resign.[72]

C. The Queen in Council

The Tudor monarchs governed mainly through the Privy Council, a select group of royal officials and advisers, having recourse to Parliament only when legislative authority was considered necessary for matters of taxation or to give effect to royal policies. The Privy Council survived the 17th-century conflicts, although its judicial arm, the Court of Star Chamber, was abolished in 1641. But in the 50 years after the restoration of the monarchy in 1660, the Privy Council lost its position as the main political executive and its numbers grew, many becoming members because of other offices which they held. As the Cabinet system developed, so did the English Privy Council lose its policy-making and deliberative role.[73] Soon after the union of England and Scotland

---

69   The literature includes Evans (ed), *Labour and the Constitution 1972–5*; Kerr, *Matters for Judgment*; Sawer, *Federation under Strain*; and Whitlam, *The Truth of the Matter*.
70   Ch 2 B.
71   Jennings, *Cabinet Government*, pp 412–17; Markesinis, op cit, p 56.
72   Middlemas and Barnes, *Baldwin*, p 999.
73   For the history of this period, see Mackintosh, *British Cabinet*, ch 2.

in 1707, the Scottish Privy Council was abolished and its functions were assumed by the Privy Council for Great Britain. In a formal sense the Council remained at the centre of the administrative machinery of government, but despite an attempt by Parliament in the Act of Settlement to insist that the Privy Council should exercise its former functions, the Council had lost its political authority. Significantly, politicians began to remain members of the Council after they had ceased to be ministers, a practice which has continued until today.

Office of Privy Councillor

Membership of the Privy Council is today a titular honour. Appointments are made by the Sovereign on ministerial advice. By convention all Cabinet ministers become Privy Councillors. Members of the royal family and holders of certain high offices of a non-political character such as Archbishops and Lords Justices of Appeal, are appointed members of the Council. So in recent years have the leaders of the Opposition parties 'so that they can be given classified information on "Privy Counsellor terms" should the need arise on a matter affecting national security'. In the 1970s, Len Murray, general secretary of the TUC, was made a Privy Councillor to facilitate consultation on government policy.[74] The office is a recognised reward for public and political service, and appointments to it figure in the honours lists. The Council now numbers about 400 members. Members are entitled to the prefix, 'Right Honourable'. They take an oath on appointment which binds them not to disclose anything said or done 'in Council' without the consent of the Sovereign. As all members of the Cabinet are also Privy Councillors, it has been considered that it is this oath which, in addition to their obligations under the Official Secrets Acts 1911–89, binds to secrecy all present and past Cabinet ministers, who may disclose Cabinet proceedings and other confidential discussions only if so authorised by the Sovereign; but little reliance was placed on this oath in the *Crossman Diaries* case[75] and its wording does not seem apt to include Cabinet proceedings. Aliens are disqualified, but on naturalisation an alien becomes qualified for membership.[76]

Functions of Privy Council

Despite the many powers conferred by statutes on individual ministers, the Order in Council remains a principal method of giving the force of law to acts of the government, especially the more important executive orders. A royal proclamation is issued when it is desired to give wide publicity to the action of the Queen in Council, as for the purpose of dissolving a Parliament and summoning its successor. Orders in Council are approved by the Sovereign at a meeting of the Council to which only four or five members are summoned. No discussion takes place and the acts of the Council are purely formal. Orders are made either under the prerogative, as for the dissolution of Parliament, or under an Act of Parliament, for example, orders which make regulations under the Emergency Powers Act 1920 after a state of emergency

[74]   Hennessy, *Whitehall*, pp 350–1.
[75]   *A-G v Jonathan Cape Ltd* [1976] QB 752; for the oath, see HLE, vol 8(2), p 523.
[76]   *R v Speyer* [1916] 2 KB 858.

has been proclaimed.[77] Statutory Orders in Council are generally subject to the Statutory Instruments Act 1946.[78]

A few traces remain of the Council's former advisory functions: the Committee for Channel Islands business is a survivor of the old standing committees appointed by the King at the beginning or in the course of his reign. Other committees are the Judicial Committee of the Privy Council,[79] a committee to consider grants of charters to universities, and the committee for the Scottish universities.[80] Issues of constitutional importance are sometimes referred to ad hoc committees of the Privy Council, as, for example, the legal basis of the practice of telephone tapping and matters affecting state security.[81] A committee of six Privy Councillors reviewed British policy towards the Falkland Islands leading up to Argentina's invasion in 1982; after the Prime Minister had consulted with five former Prime Ministers to secure their consent, the committee had access to the papers of previous governments and secret intelligence assessments.[82]

The functions of the Privy Council are quite distinct from those of the Cabinet. The first gives legal form to certain decisions of the government; the second exercises the policy-making function of the executive in major matters. The Cabinet is summoned by the Prime Minister; the Council is convened by the Clerk of the Council, whose office dates back to the 16th century. The Lord President of the Council is usually a senior member of the Cabinet. Being without onerous departmental duties, he or she often acts as chairman of Cabinet committees, and as Leader of the House of Commons supervises the government's legislative programme. Where Privy Council business concerns the activities of a department, responsibility for that business is borne by the minister of that department; thus the Secretary of State for Education is responsible for decisions of the Privy Council regarding university charters, although this responsibility is obscured by the dignified facade of Privy Council formality.

D. The royal prerogative

Both the Sovereign, as head of state, and the government, as personified for many purposes by the Crown, need powers to be able to perform their constitutional functions. The rule of law requires that these powers are grounded in law, and are not outside or above the system of law which the courts administer. In Britain the powers of the Sovereign and the Crown must either be derived from Act of Parliament or must be recognised as a matter of common law, for there is no written constitution to confer powers on the executive. In the 17th-century constitutional settlement, it was established that the powers of the Crown were subject to law and that there were no powers of the Crown which could not be taken away or controlled by statute.

---

[77] Ch 25 D.
[78] Ch 27.
[79] Ch 18 A.
[80] Universities (Scotland) Act 1889, s 9.
[81] Ch 24.
[82] HC Deb, 1 July 1982, col 1039, and 8 July 1982, col 469; Cmnd 8787, 1983; and ch 13 B.

Once that position had been achieved against the claims of the Stuarts, the courts thereafter accepted that the Sovereign and the Crown enjoyed certain powers, rights, immunities and privileges which were necessary to the maintenance of government and which were not shared with private citizens. The term prerogative is used as a collective description of these matters. Blackstone referred to prerogative as 'that special pre-eminence which the King hath, over and above all other persons, and out of the ordinary course of the common law, in right of his royal dignity'.[83] A modern definition would stress that the prerogative has been maintained not for the benefit of the Sovereign but to enable the government to function, and that prerogative is a matter of common law and does not derive from statute. Thus Parliament may not create a new prerogative, although it may confer on the Crown new rights or powers which may be very similar in character to prerogative power, for example, the statutory power to deport aliens from the United Kingdom whose further presence is considered undesirable,[84] or the statutory power to create life peerages.

History of the prerogative[85]

The mediaeval King was both feudal lord and head of the kingdom. He thus had all the rights of a feudal lord and certain exceptional rights above those of other lords. Like other lords the King could not be sued in his own courts; as there was no lord superior to the King, there was no court in which the King could be sued. In addition the King had powers accounted for by the need to preserve the realm against external foes and an 'undefined residue of power which he might use for the public good'.[86] We have already seen that mediaeval lawyers did not regard the King as being above the law.[87] Moreover certain royal functions could be exercised only in certain ways. The common law courts were the King's courts and only through them could the King decide questions of title to land and punish felonies. Yet the King possessed a residuary power of doing justice through his Council where the courts of common law were inadequate.

In the 17th century, the main disputes arose over the undefined residue of prerogative power claimed by the Stuart kings.[88] Those common lawyers who allied with Parliament in resisting the Stuart claims asserted that there was a fundamental distinction between what was called the ordinary as opposed to the absolute prerogative. The ordinary prerogative meant those royal functions which could only be exercised in defined ways and involved no element of royal discretion. Thus the King could not himself act as a judge; he must dispense justice through his judges.[89] And he could make laws only through Parliament.[90] By contrast, the absolute or extraordinary prerogative meant

---

[83]   Blackstone, *Commentaries*, I, p 239. Cf Wade, *Constitutional Fundamentals*, pp 45–53.
[84]   Ch 20 B.
[85]   A valuable account is in Keir and Lawson, *Cases in Constitutional Law*, part II. See also Heuston, *Essays*, ch 3.
[86]   Keir and Lawson, op cit, p 70.
[87]   Ch 6.
[88]   Ch 4 A.
[89]   *Prohibitions del Roy* (1607) 12 Co Rep 63; ch 18 A.
[90]   *The Case of Proclamations* (1611) 12 Co Rep 74; ch 4 A.

those powers which the King could exercise in his discretion. They included not only such powers as the right to pardon a criminal or grant a peerage, but also the King's undoubted powers to exercise discretion in the interest of the realm, especially in times of emergency. It was these powers on which Charles I relied in seeking to govern without Parliament. The conflict was resolved only after the execution of one King and the expulsion of another. But the particular disputes often gave rise to cases in the courts, in which the rival political theories were expressed in legal argument. Where the judges accepted the Crown's more extreme claims, their decisions had subsequently to be reversed by Parliament. As well as the cases on taxation and the dispensing power,[91] another outstanding case was *Darnel*'s or *The Five Knights* case,[92] where it was held that it was a sufficient answer to a writ of habeas corpus to state that a prisoner was detained *per speciale mandatum regis* (by special order of the King). Thus the King was entrusted with a power of preventive arrest which could not be questioned by the courts and which in *Darnel*'s case was used to enforce taxation levied without the consent of Parliament. This arbitrary power of committal was declared illegal by the Petition of Right 1628, and in 1640 the subject's right to habeas corpus against the King and his Council was guaranteed by statute.[93]

The problem of the prerogative was confronted in two stages. The first was that of the 17th-century struggle culminating in the Bill of Rights 1689, which declared illegal certain specific uses and abuses of the prerogative.[94] The second stage was the growth of responsible government and the establishment of a constitutional monarchy.[95] It became established that prerogative powers could be exercised only through and on the advice of ministers responsible to Parliament. Nonetheless, the ability of ministers to rely on prerogative powers gives rise to continuing problems of accountability.

The prerogative today

Today the greater part of government depends on statute. But certain powers, rights, immunities and privileges of the Sovereign and of the Crown, which vary widely in importance, continue to have their legal source in the common law. Where these powers or rights are common to all persons, including the Crown (for example, the power to own property or enter into contracts), they are not described as matters of prerogative;[96] but the term royal prerogative is properly applied to those legal attributes of the Crown which the common law recognises as differing significantly from those of private persons. Thus the legal relationship between the Crown and Crown servants is an aspect of the prerogative since it differs markedly from the normal contractual relationship between employer and employee; the same applies to the power of the Crown in certain circumstances to override contracts to which it is a party.[97]

Except in those special instances where prerogative powers involve the

---

91 Ch 4 A.
92 (1627) 3 St Tr 1.
93 Habeas Corpus Act 1640.
94 Ch 2 A.
95 Ch 7.
96 And see B V Harris (1992) 108 LQR 626.
97 Ch 31 B.

personal discretion of the Sovereign, prerogative powers are exercised by or on behalf of the government of the day. For their exercise, just as for the use of statutory powers, ministers are responsible to Parliament. Thus questions may be asked of ministers about the exercise of prerogative power. Where a matter does not fall within the province of a departmental minister, questions may be addressed to the Prime Minister. To this rule there are certain exceptions: thus the Prime Minister may not be questioned in the Commons as to the advice that may have been given to the Sovereign regarding the grant of honours or the ecclesiastical patronage of the Crown.[98] Nor could a question to the Home Secretary about the exercise of the prerogative of mercy in a sentence involving capital punishment be raised while the sentence was pending,[99] but questions are asked about the prerogative of mercy in non-capital cases.[100]

Although an Act of Parliament may abolish or curtail the prerogative, the prior authority of Parliament is not required for the exercise of a prerogative power. For example, the Crown may recognise a new foreign government or enter into a treaty without first informing Parliament. Parliament may criticise ministers for their action and for the consequences; but Parliament has no right to be consulted in advance, except to the extent that a conventional practice has developed of assuring the opportunity for such consultation.[101] Certain prerogatives could be exercised only if the government were assured of subsequent support from Parliament. The Crown may declare war, but Parliament alone may vote the supplies which enable war to be waged. Again, where a treaty envisages changes in our domestic law, Parliament could frustrate the treaty made by the Crown if it subsequently refused to pass the necessary legislation.

The extent of the prerogative today

Because of the diverse subjects covered by prerogative, and because of the uncertainty of the law in many instances where an ancient power has not been used in modern times, it is not possible to give a comprehensive catalogue of prerogative powers.[102] Instead the main areas where the prerogative is used today will be mentioned briefly; most of these are discussed more fully in other chapters.

1 Powers relating to the legislature. By virtue of the prerogative the Sovereign summons, prorogues and dissolves Parliament. The prerogative power to create hereditary peers could still be used on the advice of a government to ensure the passage of a Bill through the Lords, but the Parliament Acts 1911–49 and the Life Peerages Act 1958 make this unlikely. It is under the prerogative that the Sovereign assents to Bills. The Crown retains certain powers to legislate under the prerogative by Order in Council or by letters

---

[98]   Erskine May, p 288.
[99]   Cmd 8932, 1953, paras 37–41, and G Marshall [1961] PL 8. See also Erskine May, ibid.
[100]   A T H Smith [1983] PL 398, 436.
[101]   For the 'Ponsonby rule' in relation to treaties, see ch 15 B.
[102]   For a review of the scope of the prerogative, see HC Deb, 21 April 1993, col 490. For an account which was authoritative in its day, see Chitty, *Prerogatives of the Crown*; and see B S Markesinis [1973] CLJ 287 and C Walker [1987] PL 62.

patent. Formerly this was important in respect of the colonies,[103] but the power is still sometimes used in respect of the civil service.[104] While the Crown may not create new criminal offences or impose new obligations upon citizens,[105] it may under the prerogative create schemes for conferring benefits upon citizens provided that Parliament appropriates the necessary money to pay for these benefits; thus concerning the Criminal Injuries Compensation scheme, set up by means of a non-statutory document notified to Parliament, Diplock LJ said:

It may be a novel development in constitutional practice to govern by public statement of intention made by the executive government instead of by legislation. This is no more, however, than a reversion to the ancient practice of government by royal proclamation, although it is now subject to the limitations imposed on that practice by the development of constitutional law in the 17th century.[106]

2 Powers relating to the judicial system.[107] While the Crown may still have a prerogative power to establish courts to administer the common law[108] new courts are now established by statute. Through the Attorney-General in England and the Lord Advocate in Scotland, the Crown exercises many functions in relation to criminal justice. Thus in England prosecutions on indictment may be stopped by the Attorney-General entering a *nolle prosequi*, a power exercisable even in the case of those prosecutions over which he has no power of superintendence, as in the case of prosecutions by the Customs and Excise.[109] The Crown may pardon convicted offenders or remit or reduce a sentence on the advice of the Home Secretary or the Secretary of State for Scotland. It is under the prerogative that the Crown grants special leave to appeal from colonial courts to the Judicial Committee of the Privy Council, where the right of appeal to the Privy Council has not been abolished.[110] In civil matters the Attorney-General represents the Crown as '*parens patriae*' to enforce matters of public right.[111] In 1991, the Court of Appeal held that the Crown, unlike ministers and servants of the Crown, was not subject to the contempt jurisdiction vested in the courts.[112]

3 Powers relating to foreign affairs.[113] The conduct of foreign affairs by the

---

[103]   Roberts-Wray, *Commonwealth and Colonial Law*, ch 5. Cf Montserrat Constitution Order 1989, SI 1989 No 2401 and St Helena Constitution Order 1988, SI 1988 No 1842. The latter was made by Her Majesty in Council 'in exercise of the power conferred upon Her by section 112 of the Government of India Act 1833, the British Settlements Acts 1887 and 1945 *or otherwise in Her Majesty vested*'. Emphasis added.

[104]   Eg Civil Service Order in Council 1995. See p 283–4 below.

[105]   *The Case of Proclamations* (1611) 12 Co Rep 74.

[106]   *R v Criminal Injuries Compensation Board, ex p Lain* [1967] 2 QB 864, 886; cf Wade, *Constitutional Fundamentals*, pp 47–8. See also *R v Home Secretary, ex p Harrison* [1988] 3 All ER 86, and *R v Home Secretary, ex p Fire Brigades Union* [1995] 2 AC 513.

[107]   Ch 18.

[108]   Ch 18 A.

[109]   HC 115 (1995–96) (Scott Report), para C3.10.

[110]   Chs 15 C, 18 A.

[111]   *Gouriet v Union of Post Office Workers* [1978] AC 435.

[112]   *M v Home Office* [1992] QB 270. The House of Lords held the same, for other reasons: [1994] 1 AC 377.

[113]   Ch 15.

government is carried on mainly by reliance on the prerogative, for example, the making of treaties, the declaration of war and the making of peace. The prerogative includes power to acquire additional territory; thus by royal warrant in 1955, the Crown took possession of the island of Rockall, subsequently incorporated into the United Kingdom as part of Scotland by the Island of Rockall Act 1972. It is doubtful whether the Crown may by treaty cede British territory without the authority of Parliament and modern practice is to secure parliamentary approval,[114] but it seems that the prerogative includes power to declare or to alter the limits of British territorial waters.[115] The phrase 'act of state' is often used to refer to acts of the Crown in foreign affairs: while these acts would often fall within the scope of the prerogative, the concept of the prerogative is best confined to powers of the Crown exercised in relation to its own subjects and 'act of state' should apply only to a limited plea to the jurisdiction of the British courts, in respect of acts of the Crown performed in foreign territory in relation to aliens.[116]

The Crown has power under the prerogative to restrain aliens from entering the United Kingdom; but it is uncertain whether the Crown has a prerogative power to expel aliens who have been permitted to reside here. Today, powers over aliens are exercised under the Immigration Act 1971, although that Act expressly reserves such prerogative powers as the Crown may have (s 33(5)). The issue of passports to citizens is based on the prerogative.[117] At common law the Crown could restrain a person from leaving the realm when the interests of state demanded it by means of the writ *ne exeat regno*, but it is doubtful whether the power should today be exercised except in unusual circumstances in time of war the Crown may possibly under the prerogative restrain a British subject from leaving the realm or recall him from abroad, but during modern wars entry and exit have been controlled by statutory powers.

4 Powers relating to the armed forces.[118]   Both by prerogative and by statute the Sovereign is commander-in-chief of the armed forces of the Crown. The Bill of Rights 1689 prohibited the keeping of a standing army within the realm in time of peace without the consent of Parliament; thus the authority of Parliament is required for the maintenance of the army, the Royal Air Force and other forces serving on land. Although many matters regarding the armed forces are regulated by statute, their control, organisation and disposition are within the prerogative and cannot be questioned in a court.[119] But members of the armed forces and the Ministry of Defence may be held liable for unlawful acts which infringe the rights of individuals.[120]

---

[114]   Anson, *Law and Custom of the Constitution*, II, ii, pp 137–42; and Roberts-Wray, op cit, ch 4. The Hong Kong Act 1985 provides that 'As from 1st July 1997 Her Majesty shall no longer have sovereignty or jurisdiction over any part of Hong Kong' (s 1(1)).

[115]   *R v Kent JJ, ex p Lye* [1967] 2 QB 153; cf W R Edeson (1973) 89 LQR 364.

[116]   See the varying opinions on the application of prerogative abroad in *Nissan v A-G* [1970] AC 179; and ch 15 A.

[117]   Ch 20 A.

[118]   Ch 16.

[119]   *China Navigation Co Ltd v A-G* [1932] 2 KB 197; *Chandler v DPP* [1964] AC 763; Crown Proceedings Act 1947, s 11.

[120]   See ch 31 A.

5 Appointments and honours.[121]   On the advice of the Prime Minister or other ministers, the Sovereign appoints ministers, judges and many other holders of public office, including the members of royal commissions to inquire into matters of controversy. Appointments to the civil service are appointments to the service of the Crown. The Sovereign is the sole fountain of honour and alone can create peers, confer honours and decorations,[122] grant arms and regulate matters of precedence.[123] Honours are generally conferred by the Sovereign on the advice of the Prime Minister, who is advised by three Privy Councillors acting as a Political Honours Scrutiny Committee on the character and antecedents of those whom it is proposed to honour for political services.[124] Certain honours, namely the Order of the Garter, the Order of the Thistle, the Royal Victoria Order (for personal services to the Sovereign) and the Order of Merit are in the personal gift of the Sovereign. The system was revised in a number of ways in 1993.[125]

6 Immunities and privileges.   It is a principle of interpretation that statutes do not bind the Crown except by express statement or necessary implication.

In *Lord Advocate v Dumbarton Council*, the Ministry of Defence decided to erect an improved security fence at its submarine base at Faslane, Dumbartonshire. Part of the fence ran alongside the A814 road and when the roads authority (Strathclyde Council) discovered that the Ministry intended to place temporary works on part of the road, they notified the Ministry that it would require their consent under the Roads (Scotland) Act 1984. The Ministry replied that these provisions did not bind the Crown and contractors took possession of a one-mile stretch of part of the road by erecting a temporary fence. Thereupon the roads authority (Strathclyde) and the planning authority (Dumbarton) gave various notices under statutes to stop the work. The Lord Advocate sought judicial review of the councils' conduct, alleging that the statutes in question did not bind the Crown. Although the Crown's immunity was restricted by the Inner House of the Court of Session, the wider immunity was restored by the House of Lords. In the view of Lord Keith, 'the Crown is not bound by any statutory provision unless there can somehow be gathered from the terms of the relevant Act an intention to that effect. The Crown can be bound only by express words or necessary implication'. At the same time, Lord Keith rejected as no longer tenable the view that 'the Crown is in terms bound by general words in a statute but that the prerogative enables it to override the statute'.[126]

Tax is not payable on income received by the Sovereign as such, nor in respect of Crown property, nor on income received on behalf of the Crown by a servant of the Crown in the course of official duties.[127] But as we have seen, the Queen has undertaken to pay tax on her private income from 1993. Many of the immunities of the Crown in civil litigation were removed by the Crown

---

[121] Jennings, *Cabinet Government*, ch 14; Richards, *Patronage in British Government*, ch 10; Walker, *The Queen Has Been Pleased.*
[122] On which see Cm 1627 (1991) (the Gulf Medal); and Cm 2447 (1994) (the Accumulated Campaign Service Medal).
[123] A Wagner and G D Squibb (1973) 80 LQR 352.
[124] Cmd 1789, 1922; Honours (Prevention of Abuses) Act 1925. See Ewing, *The Funding of Political Parties in Britain*, pp 36–7.
[125] See HC Deb, 4 March 1993, col 455.
[126] [1990] 2 AC 580; and ch 31 C.
[127] *Bank voor Handel en Scheepvaart NV v Administrator of Hungarian Property* [1954] AC 584.

Proceedings Act 1947, but the Crown and government departments still have certain privileges. The 1947 Act preserved the personal immunity of the Sovereign from being sued.[128] The question has arisen whether the Crown enjoys immunity from criminal liability. During the Spycatcher affair, a retired MI5 officer, Mr Peter Wright, alleged that members of the Security Service had been engaged in surveillance operations which included burgling premises in London. The Home Secretary announced that the government had never asserted that actions 'could lawfully be done under the prerogative when they would otherwise be criminal offences'.[129]

7 The prerogative in time of emergency.   The extent of the prerogative in times of grave emergency cannot be precisely stated. That prerogative powers were wide was admitted by Hampden's counsel in the *Case of Ship Money.* Save in regard to taxation, they were not abridged by the Bill of Rights. In 1964, Lord Reid said: 'The prerogative certainly covers doing all those things in an emergency which are necessary for the conduct of war'; but he added that there was difficulty in relating the prerogative to modern conditions since no modern war had been waged without statutory powers.

The mobilisation of the industrial and financial resources of the country could not be done without statutory emergency powers. The prerogative is really a relic of a past age, not lost by disuse but only available for a case not covered by statute.[130]

According to the old law, in time of sudden invasion or insurrection, the King might demand personal service within the realm.[131] Either the Crown or a subject might invade the land of another to erect fortifications for the defence of the realm.[132] But it is not certain whether this should be regarded as an aspect of the prerogative since it was a duty shared by the Crown with all its subjects.

The difficulty of applying the old common law in modern circumstances was evident in *Burmah Oil Company v Lord Advocate.*[133]

In 1942 extensive oil installations were destroyed by British troops in Rangoon, not accidentally as a result of fighting but deliberately so as to prevent the installations falling into enemy hands. One day later, the Japanese army entered Rangoon. After receiving some £4 million from the British government as an ex gratia payment, the company sued the Lord Advocate representing the Crown in Scotland for over £31 million. It was agreed that the destruction had not been ordered under statutory authority and the company claimed compensation for the lawful exercise of prerogative power. The House of Lords held (*a*) that, as a general rule, compensation was payable by the Crown to the subject who was deprived of property for the benefit of the state, by prerogative act in relation to war and (*b*) that the destruction of the refineries did not fall within the 'battle damage' exception to the general rule. But the House left open the basis on which compensation should be assessed.

---

[128]   Ch 31 C.
[129]   HC Deb, 29 January 1988, col 397 (WA). Cf *A-G v Guardian Newspapers Ltd (No 2)* [1990] 1 AC 109, 190.
[130]   *Burmah Oil Co Ltd v Lord Advocate* [1965] AC 75, 101; and see ch 25 D.
[131]   Chitty, *Prerogatives of the Crown*, p 49.
[132]   *The Case of the King's Prerogative in Saltpetre* (1607) 12 Co Rep 12.
[133]   [1965] AC 75, discussed by A L Goodhart (1966) 82 LQR 97; T C Daintith (1965) 14 ICLQ 1000; and in (1966) 79 Harv LR 614.

This decision established that where private property was taken under the prerogative, the owner was entitled at common law to compensation from the Crown; but the War Damage Act 1965 retrospectively provided that no person should be entitled at common law to receive compensation in respect of damage to or destruction of property caused by lawful acts of the Crown 'during, or in contemplation of the outbreak of, a war in which the Sovereign is or was engaged'. This Act prevented the Burmah Oil Company's claim from succeeding but its effect was limited to acts of the Crown which destroyed property during or in contemplation of a war; the principle that the Crown is obliged to pay compensation for property taken under the prerogative for use of the armed forces still seems to apply.[134]

The principle that compensation may be payable for lawful acts of the prerogative was already known before the *Burmah Oil* case. Thus the Crown may under prerogative requisition British ships in time of urgent national necessity, but compensation is payable, as it was in 1982 when British ships were requisitioned for use in the recapture of the Falkland Islands.[135] By the right of angary, the Crown may in time of war appropriate the property of a neutral which is within the realm where necessity requires, but compensation must be paid.[136] In both World Wars, statutory powers of requisitioning property have been conferred on the Crown, and compensation has been paid. But if, for example, an emergency arose in which it was necessary for the armed forces to take immediate steps against terrorist action within the United Kingdom, it is possible both that private property needed for this purpose could be occupied under prerogative and that compensation would at common law be payable to the owners.

8 Miscellaneous prerogatives. Other historic prerogative powers, concerning matters which are today largely regulated by statute, relate to: the creation of corporations by royal charter; the right to mine precious metals; coinage; the grant of franchises, for example markets,[137] ferries and fisheries; the right to treasure trove;[138] the sole right of printing or licensing others to print the Authorised Version of the Bible,[139] the Book of Common Prayer and state papers;[140] and the guardianship of infants (a prerogative jurisdiction exercised through the High Court and not excluded by the statutory powers of local authorities).[141] It has been said that the courts may 'interfere for the protection of infants, qua infants, by virtue of the prerogative which belongs

---

[134]   Eg *Nissan v A-G* [1970] AC 179, 229 (Lord Pearce).
[135]   Requisitioning of Ships Order 1982. And see *Crown of Leon v Admiralty Commissioners* [1921] 1 KB 595; W S Holdsworth (1919) 35 LQR 12.
[136]   *Commercial and Estates Co of Egypt v Board of Trade* [1925] 1 KB 271. And see W I Jennings (1927) 3 CLJ 1.
[137]   Cf *Spook Erection Ltd v Environment Secretary* [1989] QB 300 (beneficiary of market franchise not entitled to Crown's exemption from planning control).
[138]   Treasure trove, ie gold or silver objects which have been hidden and of which no owner can be traced, is the property of the Crown; *A-G of Duchy of Lancaster v G E Overton (Farms) Ltd* [1982] Ch 277. See now Treasure Act 1996.
[139]   *Universities of Oxford and Cambridge v Eyre & Spottiswoode Ltd* [1964] Ch 736 (royal prerogative did not extend to New English Bible).
[140]   Copyright, Design and Patents Act 1988, s 163.
[141]   *Re M* [1961] Ch 328. But see now Children Act 1989, s 100.

to the Crown as parens patriae'.[142] When a court is exercising this paternal jurisdiction it is empowered to exclude the public where it is necessary to do so.[143] In *R v Central Television plc*,[144] however, it was held that the power could not be invoked to obscure the pictures of a man in a television programme imprisoned for indecency with young boys, on the ground that his identification would cause harm to his child: the programme had nothing to do with the care or upbringing of the child.

E.   The prerogative and the courts

Some prerogative acts are unlikely to give rise to the possibility of challenge in the courts, for example the conferment of an honour or the dissolution of Parliament. But where an act purporting to be done under the prerogative directly affects the rights of an individual, the courts may be asked to determine a number of issues:

1 The existence and extent of a prerogative power.   In principle the courts will not recognise the existence of new prerogative powers. In *Entick v Carrington*, in which the court held that the mere plea of state necessity would not protect anyone accused of an unlawful act, Lord Camden CJ said, 'If it is law, it will be found in our books. If it is not to be found there, it is not law.'[145] And in 1964 Diplock LJ said,

it is 350 years and a civil war too late for the Queen's courts to broaden the prerogative. The limits within which the executive government may impose obligations or restraints on citizens of the United Kingdom without any statutory authority are now well settled and incapable of extension.[146]

But some prerogative powers are very wide and difficulties arise when the courts are asked to decide whether an ancient power applies in a new situation; for example, whether the Crown's power to act in situations of grave national emergency justifies action to deal with a wholly new form of terrorist activity which threatens the nation, or whether the prerogative right to intercept postal communications justifies the tapping of telephones.[147] In these situations, it may be difficult to distinguish between creating a new prerogative and applying an old prerogative to new circumstances.

In *R v Home Secretary, ex p Northumbria Police Authority*,[148] the Home Secretary made available to police CS gas and baton rounds to deal with situations of serious public disorder, notwithstanding the objections of the local police authority. The police authority sought a declaration that the Home Secretary had no power to provide the equipment without their consent, save in a situation of grave emergency. The Court of

---

142   *Barnado v McHugh* [1891] AC 388, 395.
143   *Scott v Scott* [1913] AC 417.
144   [1994] Fam 192.
145   (1765) 19 St Tr 1030, 1066: ch 6 A. *Entick*'s case was distinguished in *Malone v Metropolitan Police Commissioner* [1979] Ch 344 (no evidence of unlawful act in tapping telephones); ch 24.
146   *BBC v Johns* [1965] Ch 32, 79.
147   Cf Cmd 283, 1957. In *Malone*'s case (above), no claim of prerogative power was made.
148   [1989] QB 26, criticised by A W Bradley [1988] PL 297.

Appeal held that the provision of the equipment was authorised by the Police Act 1964, but also by the royal prerogative. In so concluding, the court had first to determine that there did in fact exist a 'prerogative to enforce the keeping of what is popularly called the Queen's peace within the realm'. Although the court had difficulty in finding authority for such a power, Croom-Johnson LJ nevertheless concluded that such a general power is bound up with the Crown's 'undoubted right to see that crime is prevented and justice administered'. The supply of baton rounds and CS gas was held to fall within the scope of the prerogative, since it is open to the Home Secretary 'to supply equipment reasonably required by police forces to discharge their functions'.

A related question is whether the courts have power to rule that an ancient prerogative has become so unsuited to modern conditions that it can no longer be relied on by the Crown. In general, rules of common law do not lapse through desuetude.[149] But it is difficult to see why a court should be required to give new life to an archaic power which offends modern constitutional principles, merely because its existence had been recognised several centuries ago.

2 The effect of statutes upon prerogative powers. Parliament may abolish or restrict prerogative powers expressly or by necessary implication, whether or not coupling this with the grant of statutory powers in the same area of government. But often Parliament has not expressly abolished prerogative powers and has merely created a statutory scheme dealing with the same subject. Where this is the case, as a general principle must the Crown proceed under the statutory powers or may it rely instead upon the prerogative?

In *Attorney-General v De Keyser's Royal Hotel*[150] an hotel was required for housing the administrative staff of the Royal Flying Corps during the First World War. The Army Council offered to hire the hotel at a rent but, negotiations having broken down, a letter was sent on the instruction of the Army Council stating that possession was being taken under the Defence of the Realm Acts and Regulations. A petition of right was later brought against the Crown claiming compensation as of right for the use of the hotel by the authorities.

It was argued for the Crown that there was a prerogative power to take the land of the subject in case of emergency in time of war; that no compensation was payable as of right for land so taken; and that this power could be exercised, notwithstanding provisions of the Defence Act 1842 which had been incorporated into the Defence of the Realm Acts and provided for statutory compensation as of right to the owners. The argument for the owners of the hotel was that the Crown had taken possession under the statutes and so could not fall back on the prerogative.

The House of Lords rejected the argument of the Crown, holding that on the facts the Crown had taken possession under statutory powers. The House also held that the prerogative had been superseded for the time being by the statute. The Crown could not revert to prerogative powers when the legislature had given to the Crown statutory powers which covered all that could be necessary for the defence of the nation, and which were accompanied by important safeguards to the individual. Thus for the duration of the statutory powers, the prerogative was in abeyance. The House therefore did not have to decide whether the Crown had a prerogative power to

---

[149]   Maitland, *History*, p 418; cf *Nyali Ltd v A-G* [1956] 1 QB 1 and *McKendrick v Sinclair* 1972 SC (HL) 25, 60–1.

[150]   [1920] AC 508.

requisition land in time of war without paying compensation, but serious doubts were expressed about this claim.[151]

The principle in this case (that the 'executive cannot exercise the prerogative in a way which would derogate from the due fulfilment of a statutory duty')[152] may prevent the Crown from using prerogative powers which otherwise would have been available to it, is subject to a number of refinements. First, it applies only when Parliament has not given an express indication of its intention. Thus the Immigration Act 1971 provided that the powers which it conferred should be additional to any prerogative powers (s 33(5)), as did the Emergency Powers (Defence) Act 1939.[153] Secondly, there are suggestions that it may only apply where the statute confers rights or benefits on the citizen which would be undermined were the Crown to retain the right to use the prerogative power. In the *Northumbria Police* case, the Court of Appeal held that the supply of baton rounds and CS gas was authorised by the Police Act 1964, s 41, but also by the prerogative power to maintain the peace. Was the prerogative power displaced by the statute, or could both exist and operate contemporaneously? In opting for the latter position, Purchas LJ said:

It is well established that the courts will intervene to prevent executive action under prerogative powers in violation of property or other rights of the individual where this is inconsistent with statutory provisions providing for the same executive action. Where the executive action is directed towards the benefit or protection of the individual, it is unlikely that its use will attract the intervention of the courts ... [B]efore the courts will hold that such executive action is contrary to legislation, express and unequivocal terms must be found in the statute which deprive the individual from receiving the benefit or protection intended by the exercise of prerogative power.[154]

In the *Northumbria Police* case, even if the statute had not provided the necessary authority, the court was unable to find 'an express and unequivocal inhibition sufficient to abridge the prerogative powers, otherwise available to the Secretary of State, to do all that is reasonably necessary to preserve the peace of the realm'. Thirdly, where the statute restricting the prerogative is repealed, 'the prerogative power would apparently re-emerge as it existed before the statute'.[155] This is subject to 'words in the repealing statute which make it clear that the prerogative power is not intended by Parliament to be revived or again brought into use'.[156]

3 The manner of exercise of a prerogative power. Although the courts have long had the power to determine the existence and extent of a prerogative power, traditionally they have had no power to regulate the manner of its exercise. This contrasts with statutory powers of the executive, which the courts have held must generally be exercised in accordance with the rules of natural

[151] See the *Burmah Oil* case, p 278 above. See also *C O Williams Construction Ltd v Blackman* [1995] 1 WLR 102, 108; and *R v Home Secretary, ex p Fire Brigades Union* [1995] 2 AC 513.
[152] *R v Home Secretary, ex p Fire Brigades Union* [1995] 2 AC 513.
[153] Ch 25 D.
[154] [1989] QB 26, 53.
[155] *Burmah Oil Co Ltd v Lord Advocate* [1965] AC 75, Lord Pearce at 143.
[156] *R v Foreign Secretary, ex p CCSU* [1984] IRLR 309, at 321 (Glidewell J).

justice and in accordance with the so-called *Wednesbury* principles.[157] Thus, the courts have held that the courts cannot question whether the Crown has wisely exercised its discretionary power regarding the disposition of the armed forces;[158] nor could the courts say whether the government should enter into a particular treaty;[159] or whether the Home Secretary had properly advised the Sovereign regarding the prerogative of mercy.[160] In *Gouriet v Union of Post Office Workers*[161] the House of Lords held that the exercise of the Attorney-General's discretion in giving consent to the bringing of relator actions could not be reviewed by the courts. But even as this decision was being given, there were already some indications of a more flexible approach by the courts. In *Chandler v DPP*,[162] Lord Devlin said in the context of a discussion of the prerogative that 'The courts will not review the proper exercise of discretionary power but they will intervene to correct excess or abuse'. 'Excess' means action which exceeds the limits of the prerogative and although the point was never developed 'abuse' suggests the unreasonable use of an established power. Although it may not have been fully appreciated at the time,[163] *R v Criminal Injuries Compensation Board, ex p Lain*[164] was to prove an important breakthrough, where it was held that the High Court had the power to review the activities of the board, a body set up under the royal prerogative to administer benefits for the victims of criminal injury. Lord Parker CJ could see no reason why a body set up by prerogative rather than by statute should be any less amenable to judicial review for that reason alone. In *Laker Airways Ltd v Department of Trade and Industry*,[165] Lord Denning MR went further, saying that the use of prerogative power could be examined by the courts just as any other power that is vested in the executive. The position is now governed by the landmark decision of the House of Lords in *Council of Civil Service Unions v Minister of State for Civil Service*.[166]

In January 1984 the Foreign Secretary announced the government's decision to exclude trade unions from Government Communications' Headquarters (GCHQ). This would be done under an Order in Council of 1982 authorising the Minister for the Civil Service to give instructions regulating the terms and conditions of civil service employment. The instructions given directed that staff at GCHQ would no longer be permitted to be members of the civil service unions, but only to join an officially approved staff association. These steps had been taken because of earlier industrial action at GCHQ.

In deciding whether the government's decision was reviewable by the courts, a majority in the House of Lords held that the courts could review the manner of exercise of discretionary powers conferred by the prerogative just as they could review

---

[157]   See ch 29 A.
[158]   *China Navigation Co Ltd v A-G* [1932] 2 KB 197; *Chandler v DPP* [1964] AC 763; Crown Proceedings Act 1947, s 11.
[159]   *Blackburn v A-G* [1971] 2 All ER 1380. Also *R v Foreign Secretary, ex p Rees-Mogg* [1994] QB 552.
[160]   *Hanratty v Lord Butler* (1971) 115 SJ 386, discussed by A T H Smith [1983] PL 398, 432. Cf B V Harris [1991] PL 386.
[161]   [1978] AC 435.
[162]   [1964] AC 763, 810.
[163]   See C P Walker [1987] PL 62.
[164]   [1967] 2 QB 864.
[165]   [1977] QB 643.
[166]   [1985] AC 374. See H W R Wade (1985) 101 LQR 180.

the manner of exercise of discretionary powers conferred by statute. Lord Diplock could 'see no reason why simply because a decision-making power is derived from a common law and not a statutory source, it should for that reason only be immune from judicial review'. It does not follow, however, that all prerogative powers would be subject to review in this way. According to the House of Lords, it depends on the nature of the power, and in particular whether the power in question is justiciable, ie whether it gives rise to questions which are capable of adjudication in a court of law. It is not clear which powers are justiciable, though Lord Roskill gave many examples of those which are not, including the making of treaties, the disposition of the armed forces, the granting of honours and the dissolution of Parliament.

Where a prerogative power is justiciable and subject to review, it may be challenged on the same grounds as statutory powers.[167] There are suggestions in Lord Diplock's speech that so far as the prerogative is concerned, the scope for judicial review is limited to matters of illegality and procedural impropriety. However, the matter is not yet settled, despite a number of post GCHQ decisions. In this case there appeared to have been a procedural impropriety (the unions should have been consulted in advance) but nevertheless the unions failed on the ground that the government had acted in the interests of national security (the evidence of which was in an affidavit from the Cabinet Secretary). The scope of the *CCSU* decision remains very unclear,[168] particularly regarding the distinction between justiciable and non-justiciable powers. It may be presumed that the prerogative power to regulate terms of employment in the civil service is subject to review. However, a number of other challenges have been made to the exercise of powers conferred by the royal prerogative including *R v Home Secretary, ex p Bentley*,[169] where it was held that 'some aspects of the exercise of the Royal Prerogative [of mercy] are amenable to the judicial process', notwithstanding authority to the contrary[170] and the suggestion of Lord Roskill in the *CCSU* case that the exercise of the prerogative of mercy was not justiciable.[171] In other cases, largely unsuccessful challenges have been made to the exercise of powers conferred by the royal prerogative regarding the employment of civil servants, while the power to issue a passport is now subject to judicial review.[172] But the most important case since *CCSU* is *R v Home Secretary, ex p Fire Brigades Union*.[173]

The Criminal Justice Act 1988 provided for a new statutory scheme to compensate the victims of criminal injury, replacing the one which had been introduced in 1964 under the royal prerogative.[174] Under the Act the statutory scheme was to come into force on such day as the Secretary of State might by order appoint. But before bringing the Act into force, the government changed its mind and announced the introduction of a new tariff scheme; the 1988 Act would 'not now be implemented' but would be

---

[167]   See ch 29.
[168]   See C P Walker [1987] PL 62.
[169]   [1994] QB 349.
[170]   *Hanratty v Lord Butler* (1971) 115 SJ 386, and *de Freitas v Benny* [1976] AC 239.
[171]   [1985] AC at p 418.
[172]   *R v Foreign Secretary, ex p Everett* [1989] QB 811. Cf *R v Home Secretary, ex p Harrison* [1988] 3 All ER 86 where the court dismissed an application for judicial review of the Home Secretary's decision not to make an ex gratia payment of public funds from a non-statutory scheme to a person who had been improperly convicted and imprisoned.
[173]   [1995] 2 AC 513.
[174]   See above, p 275.

repealed 'when a suitable legislative opportunity occurs'. The effect of the new scheme was that 'particularly in relation to very serious injuries involving prolonged loss of earnings' the amount payable to the victim would be 'substantially less than the amount he would have received under the old scheme or the statutory scheme'.

The government's decision not to implement the statutory scheme and to introduce under prerogative the tariff scheme was challenged in an application for judicial review. The application succeeded in the House of Lords, which by a majority upheld what was in turn a majority decision of the Court of Appeal. *Held* that although under no duty to bring the statute into force, the Home Secretary could not 'lawfully surrender or release the power contained [in the Act] so as to purport to exclude its future exercise'. Nor could the Home Secretary lawfully use the prerogative power to replace the old scheme with the tariff scheme: by introducing the tariff scheme the Home Secretary had debarred himself from exercising his statutory power for the purposes and on the basis which Parliament intended. The decision to introduce the tariff scheme was an abuse of the prerogative, though not an application of the *De Keyser* principle: since 'the statutory provisions had not been brought into force, they had no legal significance of any kind'.

This decision confirms the present willingness of the courts to examine the legality and propriety of executive decisions, whether the powers in question are derived from statute or from the prerogative powers of the Crown.

CHAPTER 13

The Cabinet, government departments and the civil service

As organs of government, the Cabinet and the office of Prime Minister have evolved together since the 18th century. Their existence is recognised in occasional statutes (for example, the Ministerial and other Salaries Act 1975) but their powers of government derive neither from statute nor from common law administered in the courts. Parliament could confer powers directly upon the Prime Minister or upon the Cabinet. In practice this rarely happens, statutory powers being conferred either upon named ministers or upon the Queen in Council. Yet the Prime Minister and the Cabinet occupy key places at the heart of the political and governmental system.[1] As the Prime Minister provides the individual leadership of the majority party in the House of Commons, so the Cabinet provides the collective leadership of that party.[2] If national affairs are to be directed in any systematic way, if deliberate choices in government between competing political priorities are to be made, these decisions can be made only by the Prime Minister and the Cabinet. In the past, descriptions of the British system of government often labelled it Cabinet government. As L S Amery wrote:

> The central directing instrument of government, in legislation as well as in administration, is the Cabinet. It is in Cabinet that administrative action is co-ordinated and that legislative proposals are sanctioned. It is the Cabinet which controls Parliament and governs the country.[3]

Recently more emphasis has been placed on the role of the Prime Minister and less on the Cabinet itself. In 1963, when he had not yet served as a Cabinet minister, Richard Crossman wrote: 'The post-war epoch has seen the final transformation of Cabinet government into Prime Ministerial government', arguing that the Cabinet had joined the Crown and the House of

---

[1] Bagehot's celebrated description of the Cabinet in *The English Constitution*, pp 65–9, must still be read, though his definition of the Cabinet as 'a committee of the legislative body selected to be the executive body' is misleading. For general accounts, see Jennings, *Cabinet Government*; Mackintosh, *The British Cabinet*; Gordon Walker, *The Cabinet*; Wilson, *The Governance of Britain*; Hennessy, *Cabinet*; and James, *British Cabinet Government*.

[2] Gordon Walker, p 56.

[3] *Thoughts on the Constitution*, p 70.

Lords as one of the 'dignified' elements in the constitution.[4] This judgment appears to have been reinforced in the 1980s when it is claimed that 'members of Mrs Thatcher's Cabinets had allowed the usual forms of Cabinet government to be displaced by imperious prime ministerial rule'.[5] There is no doubt that the Prime Minister commands a formidable range of political and governmental powers, but it would be wrong to suppose that he or she can therefore govern without recourse to the Cabinet. Even in the earlier accounts of Cabinet government, the leader's role was stressed: thus Amery cited Morley's description of the Prime Minister as the 'keystone of the Cabinet Arch', and added:

It is his Cabinet and he has in large measure created it; he can at any time change its composition; his is the decisive voice in bringing it to an end by dissolution or resignation.[6]

Having served in the Cabinets of Eden and Macmillan, Lord Home said, 'if the Cabinet discusses anything it is the Prime Minister who decides what the collective view of the Cabinet is'.[7] Different styles of political leadership exist, but Cabinet and Prime Minister depend upon each other. Indeed any premature judgment about imperious prime ministerial rule in the 1980s may need to be revised in the light of Mrs Thatcher's removal from office by her party in 1990. As Brazier points out, this event demonstrated that 'there is clearly a point beyond which a Cabinet will not go in tolerating a Prime Minister who persists in clinging to electorally damaging policies and who sets the whole government's attitude on crucial questions in a fashion which is unsupported by the Cabinet and administration as a whole'.[8]

A.   The Prime Minister

The nature of the office

Like the Cabinet, the office of Prime Minister has evolved as a matter of political expediency and constitutional practice rather than of law. Though he did not recognise the title, Robert Walpole is now regarded as having been the first Prime Minister when he was First Lord of the Treasury, from 1721 to 1742. William Pitt the younger did much to create the modern office of Prime Minister in the years after 1784. In fact the post acquired its present form only with the advent of the modern party system and the creation of the present machinery of government. For most of its history, the office of Prime Minister has been held together with a recognised post, usually that of First Lord of the Treasury. Between 1895 and 1900 Lord Salisbury was both Prime Minister and Foreign Secretary, and between 1900 and 1902 he was Prime Minister and Lord Privy Seal; during these years A J Balfour was First Lord of the Treasury and Leader of the Commons. Since 1902, the offices of Prime Minister and

---

4   Introduction to Bagehot, pp 51, 54. See also Berkeley, *The Power of the Prime Minister*, and Mackintosh, op cit, ch 24; cf A H Brown [1968] PL 28, 96.
5   R Brazier (1991) 54 MLR 471, 476.
6   Amery, op cit, p 73.
7   Quoted in Mackintosh, op cit, p 628.
8   Brazier, op cit, 476. And see G Marshall [1991] PL 1.

First Lord of the Treasury have always been held together by a member of the Commons.

In 1905, by act of the prerogative, the Prime Minister was given precedence next after the Archbishop of York[9] and the existence of the office is recognised by occasional statutes.[10] Since 1937, statutory provision of a salary and a pension has assumed that the Prime Minister is also First Lord of the Treasury. In the latter capacity, the Prime Minister is one of the Treasury ministers, although the financial and economic duties of the Treasury are borne primarily by the Chancellor of the Exchequer. Exceptionally, the Prime Minister may decide also to hold another office: Ramsay MacDonald was both Prime Minister and Foreign Secretary in the first Labour government in 1924. During the Second World War, Churchill assumed the title of Minister of Defence, although without a separate ministry and without his duties being defined. When the Civil Service Department was established in 1968,[11] the Prime Minister became the minister for the department, although another Cabinet minister undertook the regular administration of the department on the Prime Minister's behalf.

The Prime Minister is responsible for the appointment of a Commissioner to oversee the work of the Security Service, and advises on the appointment of the Security Service Tribunal.[12] The approval of the Prime Minister is also required for appointment of the most senior civil servants, ie the permanent heads and deputy heads of departments and principal finance and establishment officers. The most important Crown appointments are filled on his or her nomination, for example, the senior judges, the bishops, the chairman of the BBC and the Parliamentary Ombudsman. The Prime Minister also advises the Sovereign on new peerages, on appointments to the Privy Council and the grant of honours,[13] and the filling of those chairs in English universities which are in the gift of the Crown. In these appointments, the Prime Minister's freedom of action may to a greater or lesser extent be restricted by conventions requiring prior consultation with the interests affected. Nonetheless, the Prime Minister's extensive patronage gives rise at least to the possibility that it could be used for political purposes.[14]

Powers of Prime Minister in relation to the Cabinet

Although each Prime Minister must adopt his or her own style of leadership, the Prime Minister is in a position to exercise a dominant influence over the Cabinet, having powers which other ministers do not have, however senior

---

9   *London Gazette,* 5 December 1905.
10   Eg Chequers Estate Act 1917; Chevening Estate Act 1959; Interception of Communications Act 1985; Security Service Act 1989; Ministerial and other Pensions and Salaries Act 1991; Intelligence Services Act 1994.
11   The Department was abolished in 1981 and its functions transferred: Section D below.
12   Security Service Act 1989. See also Intelligence Services Act 1994. For details, see ch 24.
13   Some honours are granted on the advice of other ministers, eg the Foreign Secretary and the Defence Secretary. Some appointments are made on the recommendation of other ministers, eg High Court judgeships on the recommendation of the Lord Chancellor.
14   Cf T Benn (1980) 33 Parliamentary Affairs 7. For a full account of Prime Ministerial patronage, see HC Deb, 19 May 1977, col 232 (WA). See also *Questions of Procedure for Ministers,* paras 49–58. On the role of political considerations in the exercise of patronage generally, see Cm 2850–I, 1995.

and experienced they may be. A sense of perspective is, however, needed for the point should not be exaggerated. As one commentator wrote following the removal of Mrs Thatcher, 'a Prime Minister's main political strength comes from the Cabinet and ... from the parliamentary party'.[15] A Prime Minister who loses the confidence of both will be in a very vulnerable position, even though he or she may be the choice of the electorate. On the other hand, however, we should not underestimate the political power of the Prime Minister where such confidence does exist.

1   The Prime Minister effectively makes all appointments to ministerial office, whether within or outside the Cabinet. He or she may ask ministers to resign, recommend the Sovereign to dismiss them or, with their consent, move them to other offices. In June 1962, in an attempt to regain popularity for his administration, Harold Macmillan removed from office seven ministers out of a Cabinet of 20 members. The Prime Minister settles the order of precedence in the Cabinet. He or she may name one of the Cabinet to be Deputy Prime Minister[16] or First Secretary of State as Mr Major did in 1995 with the appointment of Mr Heseltine to both positions.[17] These powers are exercised in a political context. In forming his or her first Cabinet, a new Prime Minister will be expected to appoint from the senior members of the party; and a leading politician may be able to stipulate the Cabinet post which he or she is prepared to accept. In the case of the Labour party the standing orders of the parliamentary party provide that on taking office as Prime Minister, the leader must appoint as members of his Cabinet those who were elected members of the Shadow Cabinet before the general election, provided that they have retained their seats in the new Parliament. Although there are no similar constraints on Conservative leaders, they too will normally rely on an established team when assuming the responsibilities of office.[18]

2   The Prime Minister controls the machinery of central government in that he or she decides how the tasks of government should be allocated to departments and whether departments should be created, amalgamated or abolished. Thus in 1981, Mrs Thatcher abolished the Civil Service Department and divided its duties between the Treasury and a new Management and Personnel Office.[19] In 1995, Mr Major abolished the Department of Employment and transferred its functions to the enlarged Department for Education and Employment and the Department of Trade and Industry. The Prime Minister may take interest in different areas of government from time to time and may indeed carry out policy through the agency of a minister whom he or she has appointed. Most Prime Ministers must take a special interest in foreign affairs, the economy and defence. The Prime Minister may intervene personally in major industrial disputes and other pressing issues. In consulta-

---

15   R Brazier (1991) 54 MLR 471, 477. For a recent assessment of the relationship between Prime Ministers and their Cabinets, see S James (1994) 47 Parliamentary Affairs 613.
16   In 1951, George VI refused to appoint Eden to this 'non-existent' office: Wheeler-Bennett, *King George VI*, p 797. But see R Brazier [1988] PL 176 for present practice.
17   See HC 265 (1995–96).
18   See Brazier, *Constitutional Practice*, pp 61–2.
19   The Management and Personnel Office was in turn abolished in 1987.

tion with individual ministers, he or she may take decisions or authorise them to be taken without waiting for a Cabinet meeting. When a Cabinet committee is dealing with a problem, the Prime Minister may take the chair and report on action taken to a later Cabinet meeting.

3   By presiding at Cabinet meetings, the Prime Minister is able to control Cabinet discussions and the process of decision-making by settling the order of business, deciding which items are to be discussed[20] and by taking the sense of the meeting rather than by counting the votes of Cabinet members. While the Cabinet Secretariat provides services for the whole Cabinet, it owes a special responsibility to the Prime Minister, who if necessary settles disputes over the minutes. Lord Wilson has said, 'the writing of the Conclusions is a unique responsibility of the Secretary of the Cabinet ... The Conclusions are circulated very promptly after Cabinet, and up to that time, no minister, certainly not the Prime Minister, asks to see them or conditions them in any way'.[21] On the other hand, Mr Michael Heseltine was concerned about the minutes of a Cabinet meeting before his resignation in 1986, in particular the failure to record his protest about the Prime Minister's refusal to allow discussion on competing plans to rescue Westland, a helicopter manufacturing company.[22]

4   The doctrine of collective responsibility helps to reinforce the powers of the Prime Minister. The effect of the doctrine is that ministers must not criticise government policy in public and if necessary must be prepared to defend it. This means that if the firm hand of the Prime Minister is guiding that policy, there will be no public criticism from the most influential and informed people in the government. The importance of the doctrine for silencing potential criticism is underlined by the fact that many decisions of government are not taken by the Cabinet as a whole, but by the Prime Minister in consultation with a few key colleagues. This was true, for example, of such controversial decisions as the banning of trade unions at Government Communications' Headquarters (GCHQ) and the selection of the American rather than the European rescue package for the Westland helicopter company. On one interpretation of the events, it was this attempt to control Cabinet colleagues by the doctrine of collective responsibility for decisions which had not been taken by the Cabinet which led to Mr Heseltine's resignation as Secretary of State for Defence in January 1986.[23]

5   Compared to other ministers, the Prime Minister has a more regular opportunity to present and defend the government's policies in Parliament and

---

[20]   Mackintosh, *The British Cabinet*, p 449, asserts that the Prime Minister can keep any item off the agenda indefinitely but the examples he gives do not support this. Cf Wilson, *The Governance of Britain*, p 47.

[21]   Wilson, *The Governance of Britain*, p 56.

[22]   Cf *Questions of Procedure for Ministers*, which provides that 'The Cabinet Office are instructed to avoid, so far as practicable, recording the opinions expressed by particular Ministers' (para 11).

[23]   Cf ibid: 'Decisions reached by the Cabinet or Ministerial committees are binding on all members of the Government' (para 17).

elsewhere.[24] He or she is available for questioning in the Commons on Wednesdays and may choose when to intervene in debates.[25] The Prime Minister is also in a position to control the government's communications to the press and to disclose information about government decisions and Cabinet business.[26] Alone among Cabinet ministers, he or she has regular meetings with the Sovereign and is responsible for keeping the Sovereign informed of the Cabinet's handling of affairs. In particular, he or she may recommend to the Sovereign that a general election be held, and in doing so is not required to discuss this first with the Cabinet.[27] It is sometimes argued that the threat of a dissolution is a device whereby a Prime Minister may exercise authority over colleagues in government and Parliament. But this may not always be an option. Why would a Prime Minister wish to recommend that a general election is called if the party was weakened by internal dissension, particularly when the dissidents may not be amongst those most likely to lose their seats?

B.   The Cabinet

Composition of the Cabinet

A modern Cabinet usually consists of between 18 members (Mr Heath's Cabinet in 1970) and 24 members (Mr Callaghan's in 1979). Mrs Thatcher's Cabinet usually consisted of 22 members, as did Mr Major's. No statute regulates the composition of the Cabinet, but there are both administrative and political constraints on the Prime Minister's freedom of choice. Thus in peacetime it is impossible to exclude certain offices, such as the Home Secretary, the Foreign Secretary, the Lord Chancellor and the Secretary of State for Scotland. In addition to the Secretaries of State and ministers in charge of the major departments, every Cabinet includes two or three members with few if any departmental responsibilities, for example, the Lord President of the Council, who is often also Leader of the House of Commons; the Lord Privy Seal, often also Leader of the House of Lords; and the Chancellor of the Duchy of Lancaster who may also be the Minister for Public Service. These ministers may assist the Prime Minister on special issues or coordinate different aspects of a single problem, and they often serve as chairmen of Cabinet committees. Since 1951, the government chief whip in the Commons, whose formal title is Parliamentary Secretary to the Treasury, has regularly attended Cabinet[28] but only rarely, as in 1975, has he been a member of it. The Law Officers of the Crown[29] are not appointed to the Cabinet but, like other ministers outside the Cabinet, the Attorney-General

---

[24]   But see P Dunleavy, G W Jones et al (1993) 23 British Journal of Political Science 267 on the declining accountability of the Prime Minister to Parliament.

[25]   Prime Ministers were previously available for questioning twice a week (Tuesdays and Thursdays). On Prime Minister's Question Time, see R K Alderman (1992) 45 Parliamentary Affairs 66. For proposals for its reform, especially to replace 'open' with 'substantive' questions, see HC 555 (1994–95).

[26]   See Margach, *The Abuse of Power*.

[27]   Ch 12 B.

[28]   Gordon Walker, p 104.

[29]   Ch 18 C.

and his Scottish counterpart, the Lord Advocate, may attend Cabinet meetings for particular matters.[30]

The size of the Cabinet is primarily determined by practical and political considerations. But the number of salaried Cabinet posts is limited by statute: apart from the Prime Minister and the Lord Chancellor, not more than 20 salaries may be paid to Cabinet ministers at one time.[31] Political necessity requires that all members of the Cabinet are members of the Commons or the Lords, unless a minister is actively seeking election to the Commons at a by-election or is to be created a life peer.[32] In practice at least two Cabinet offices (Lord Chancellor and Leader of the House of Lords) will be held by peers but more may be appointed. In all modern governments there have been some ministers with departmental responsibilities who are outside the Cabinet. They may serve on Cabinet committees, will see Cabinet papers relating to their departments and may be asked to attend Cabinet meetings. The amalgamation of departments to form larger departments which took place during the 1960s[33] meant that all major departments were placed under the supervision of a Cabinet minister. In wartime the normal Cabinet may be superseded by a small War Cabinet to take charge of the conduct of the war. In 1916 the War Cabinet consisted of five, later six, senior ministers, of whom only the Chancellor of the Exchequer had departmental duties. The War Cabinet of 1939–45 was larger, varying between seven and ten, including several senior departmental ministers.[34]

Cabinet committees[35]

The increase in the scale of government since 1900 has not been accompanied by a corresponding increase in the size of the Cabinet. Few problems of government can be solved by a single department acting on its own, if only because most policy decisions have expenditure and personnel implications (hence the interest of the Treasury in all new policies). The Cabinet could not have kept abreast of its work had there not developed under its umbrella a complicated structure of committees. In the 19th century, Cabinet committees were appointed for particular purposes (for example, to keep under review the conduct of the Crimean War). They were used much more frequently after 1918. Two main factors led to the appointment of a system of permanent committees. The first was the creation of the Committee of Imperial Defence in 1903, which showed the value of a permanent committee charged with a major policy area;[36] the second was the experience in two world wars of a system of specialised committees to deal with defined policy

---

[30]   Mr Major's Cabinet also included the Conservative party chairman as a minister without portfolio.

[31]   Ministerial and other Salaries Act 1975.

[32]   Ch 2 B.

[33]   Section C.

[34]   For the War Cabinet, see 8th edn of this book, 1970, pp 201, 203–7; Jennings, *Cabinet Government*, ch 10; and Mackintosh, op cit, ch 14 and pp 490–9.

[35]   Jennings, *Cabinet Government*, pp 255–61; Mackintosh, pp 521–9; Gordon Walker, pp 38–47; Wilson, *The Governance of Britain*, pp 62–8.

[36]   Jennings, op cit, ch 10.

areas which operated under the authority of a small War Cabinet. In 1945, the Labour government decided to adapt the wartime system to the problems of peace. Since then, a structure of standing committees has remained an important feature of the Cabinet system.

Successive governments have sought to keep secret the functions, composition and even the existence of most Cabinet committees. Various reasons have been advanced for this: that the existence of the committees is not intended to affect the collective responsibility of the whole Cabinet; that public knowledge of the existence and composition of committees would give rise to inconvenient public criticism and lobbying; and so on.[37] The existence of some committees was, however, made known from time to time, and a great deal of information was provided by unofficial sources.[38] Hennessy has claimed that in 1985–86 there were at least 160 committees,[39] including four acknowledged to exist by the Prime Minister.[40] This is said to compare with 461 while Attlee was Prime Minister and 246 under Churchill. In 1992, in a move to demystify Whitehall decision-making the government published details of 26 Cabinet committees and sub-committees. The information revealed the name, composition and terms of reference of the committees, but not when the committees met. In addition to the 26 named committees, another 140 ad hoc ministerial committees operated between 1987 and 1992, dealing with matters which included the poll tax. The government has not disclosed the list of inter-departmental committees of officials.[41] In 1995, the Prime Minister announced plans 'to streamline the current structure and rationalise the arrangements for discussion of policy issues into a smaller number of committees with wide terms of reference'. The details of 19 ministerial committees are now published, these dealing with matters such as economic and domestic policy, defence and overseas policy, nuclear defence policy, the intelligence services, public expenditure, and Northern Ireland.[42]

An account of the Cabinet committee system is provided in *Questions of Procedure for Ministers*, which contains the rules governing Cabinet ministers. Published in 1992,[43] it states that Cabinet committees have two purposes. The first is to relieve pressure on the Cabinet itself by settling as much business as possible at lower level; and the second is to 'support the principle of collective responsibility by ensuring that, even though an important question may never reach the Cabinet itself, the decision will be fully considered and the final judgment will be sufficiently authoritative to ensure that the Government as a

---

[37] For a personal minute by Mr Callaghan, when Prime Minister, see *New Statesman*, 10 November 1978. Cf *The Times*, 3 May 1973.

[38] Cmnd 2097, 1963 (Committee on Defence and Overseas Policy). See also Gordon Walker, pp 174–5; Crossman, *The Diaries of a Cabinet Minister*, vol 1, pp 198, 280.

[39] Hennessy, *Cabinet*, p 100.

[40] See HC Deb, 24 May 1979, col 179 (WA). See also HC Deb, 29 November 1979, col 540 (WA).

[41] *The Guardian*, 20 May 1992. Details of ad hoc committees newly wound up or newly created are to be found in *The Whitehall Companion 1996–97*, pp 385–6. The former include Refugees from former Yugoslavia, and the latter Smart Card Technology.

[42] HC Deb, 18 July 1995, col 1005 (WA).

[43] For the earlier disclosure of this document, see J M Lee (1986) 64 Public Administration 347.

whole can be properly expected to accept responsibility for it'.[44] It is thus clear that decisions reached by Cabinet committees are 'binding on all members of the Government', though they are 'normally announced and explained as the decision of the Minister concerned'. Because of the doctrine of collective responsibility, 'the privacy of opinions' expressed in Cabinet committee, as in the Cabinet itself, should be maintained.[45] Cabinet committees may be either standing committees – 'permanent for the duration of the Prime Minister's term of office' – or ad hoc committees – 'appointed to handle a single issue'. In terms of their personnel, Cabinet committees are said to be of three types: ministerial committees, in which only ministers participate; official committees, in which only officials participate; and mixed committees, in which both ministers and officials participate.[46]

The Cabinet Office[47]

Before 1917, there was no regular machinery for preparing the agenda for Cabinet meetings, circulating documents or recording decisions. Each Prime Minister sent his own accounts of Cabinet meetings to the Sovereign and members of the Cabinet took note of matters requiring action by their departments. On a major constitutional issue, for example, the creation of peers to coerce the House of Lords into approving the Parliament Bill in 1911, the Sovereign could require the Cabinet's advice to be recorded in writing. But in general there was often uncertainty about the actual decisions.

In 1917, to enable the War Cabinet and its system of committees to function efficiently, a Secretary to the Cabinet was appointed to be present at meetings of the Cabinet and its committees, to circulate minutes of the conclusions reached, to communicate decisions rapidly to those who had to act on them and also to circulate papers before meetings. The first Secretary was Sir Maurice Hankey, who applied to the Cabinet methods which he had developed as Secretary of the Committee of Imperial Defence. The secretariat has been maintained ever since, sometimes in an uneasy relationship with the Treasury. It is headed by the Secretary of the Cabinet, who is also Head of the Home Civil Service.

The conclusions prepared by the Secretary to the Cabinet and circulated to the Sovereign and Cabinet ministers are the only official record of Cabinet meetings. This account is designed to record agreement and not controversy. Differences of opinion in discussion are not attributed to individuals, although the arguments for and against a decision may be summarised: 'behind many of the decisions lay tensions and influences which are not reflected in the official records'.[48] However, if a minister expressly wishes his

---

[44]   *Questions of Procedure for Ministers*, paras 4–5.
[45]   Ibid, paras 17–19.
[46]   See Hennessy, *Cabinet*, pp 26–31.
[47]   Jennings, *Cabinet Government*, pp 242–5; Gordon Walker, pp 47–55; Mosley, *The Story of the Cabinet Office*; Wilson, *The Cabinet Office to 1945*; *The Times*, 8 March 1976; Wilson, *The Governance of Britain*, ch 4.
[48]   Wilson, *The Cabinet Office to 1945*, p 4. At p 142 are printed instructions on minute-taking current in 1936. Crossman's comment 30 years later was that the minutes 'do not pretend to be an account of what actually takes place in the Cabinet' (op cit, p 198).

or her dissent to be recorded, then this will be done. It was the alleged failure to follow this convention which added to the drama surrounding the resignation of Mr Michael Heseltine in the so-called Westland affair in 1986.

The Cabinet Office with staff of more than 1,000 has no executive functions like those of a department. It seeks to secure inter-departmental coordination by circulating documents before meetings and providing a formal record of decisions. While the Cabinet Office is responsible to the Prime Minister, it does not seek to operate as a 'Prime Minister's Department', although on one recent view, everything that a Prime Minister could create 'is already there to hand in the Cabinet Office'.[49] There are several different secretariats within the Cabinet Office, each with different areas of responsibility. These include the Economic and Domestic Secretariat; the Defence and Overseas Affairs Secretariat; the European Secretariat; the Telecommunications Secretariat; and the Joint Intelligence Organisation.[50] Within the Cabinet Office there are also the chief scientific adviser to the government and the Office of Public Service which has responsibility for the Citizen's Charter, the 'Next Steps' Initiative (see below), the policy on open government, public appointments and civil service recruitment.

In 1970, there was established within the Cabinet Office a small multi-disciplinary unit, known as the Central Policy Review Staff. Its task was to enable ministers collectively to work out the implications of their basic strategy in terms of policy in specific areas, to identify areas of policy in which new choices might be exercised and to ensure that the implications of alternative policies were fully analysed.[51] As well as advising ministers on more immediate issues, the CPRS produced studies in depth of issues requiring major policy decisions. Subjects included the organisation of government-sponsored research, the Concorde project, government support for a British-owned computer industry and the future of the British car industry; not all the reports were published. In 1983, Mrs Thatcher abolished the CPRS, though many of its functions were transferred to the Downing Street Policy Unit which had been created by Harold Wilson in 1974 but which had been retained by successive Prime Ministers and indeed expanded by Mrs Thatcher. Unlike the CPRS, the function of the No 10 Policy Unit is not to serve the Cabinet as a whole and with a staff of more than 100 it now operates as part of the Prime Minister's Office.[52]

Cabinet secrecy

The operation of the Cabinet system is surrounded by considerable secrecy.[53] Most Cabinet papers are made available for public inspection in the Public Record Office after 30 years or such other period as the Lord Chancellor may direct.[54] Many Cabinet decisions are notified to Parliament or otherwise made

---

49   Wilson, *The Governance of Britain*, p 82. Cf Clarke, *New Trends in Government*, ch 2.
50   *Civil Service Yearbook 1997*. See also Hennessy, *Whitehall*, pp 390–1.
51   Cmnd 4506, 1970, paras 44–8.
52   See D Willetts (1987) 65 Public Administration 443.
53   Williams, *Not in the Public Interest*, ch 2; Gordon Walker, pp 26–33, 164–8; Report on Section 2 of Official Secrets Act 1911, Cmnd 5104, 1972, ch 11; Report on Ministerial Memoirs, Cmnd 6386, 1976.
54   Public Records Act 1958, s 5, amended by Public Records Act 1967.

public, but the doctrine of collective responsibility throws a heavy veil over decision-making in Cabinet. It is inevitable that ministers often disagree as to the right course of action before a decision is made. One justification for Cabinet secrecy commonly supported by those with experience of the system is the view that anything which damages the collective unity and integrity of the Cabinet damages the good government of the country.[55] Certainly the public interest in national security requires that some information about defence and external relations must be kept secret by those in government. But the 'good government' argument goes very much further than national security since it seeks to preserve the process of decision-making within government from scrutiny by those outside. Some critics argue, to the contrary, that 'good government' in a democracy requires that more light should be thrown on political decision-making, and that government should be more open.[56] In fact newspapers frequently contain speculation about the Cabinet's deliberations, some of which may be based on unauthorised disclosures of Cabinet proceedings by ministers who wish to make their points of view known.

In law, Cabinet documents are protected to some extent from production as evidence in litigation by a rule which authorises non-disclosure of documents which it would be injurious to the public interest to disclose[57] and from examination by the Parliamentary Ombudsman;[58] they may also be protected by the Official Secrets Acts.[59] Political sanctions also operate: a serving Cabinet minister would be liable to lose office if he or she could be shown to have revealed the details of Cabinet discussions to the press. But is a former Cabinet minister, who may be subject to no political sanction, under a legal obligation not to reveal such secrets? The question arose for decision in *Attorney-General v Jonathan Cape Ltd*.[60]

Richard Crossman kept a political diary between 1964 and 1970 while a Labour Cabinet minister. After his death in 1974, his diary for 1964–66 was edited for publication and, as was customary, submitted to the Secretary to the Cabinet. He refused to consent to publication, since the diary contained detailed accounts of Cabinet discussions, reports of the advice given to ministers by civil servants and comments about the suitability of senior civil servants for promotion. When Crossman's literary executors decided to publish the diary, the Attorney-General sought an injunction to stop them. Lord Widgery CJ held that the court had power to restrain the improper publication of information which had been received by a Cabinet minister in confidence, and that the doctrine of collective responsibility justified the court in restraining the disclosures of Cabinet discussions; but that the court should act only where continuing confidentiality of the material could clearly be shown. On the facts, he held that publication in 1975 of Cabinet discussions during the period 1964–66

---

55   Cmnd 5104, 1972, p 68.
56   The evidence given to the Franks Committee on s 2 of the Official Secrets Act 1911 contained a wide range of opinions on the proper extent of Cabinet secrecy from senior civil servants, former ministers, academics and journalists.
57   Ch 31 C. On the relationship between the Cabinet and the courts, see M C Harris [1989] PL 251.
58   Parliamentary Commissioner Act 1967, s 8(4); ch 28 D.
59   Ch 24.
60   [1976] QB 752; Young, *The Crossman Affair*.

should not be restrained. In this decision, no reliance was placed either upon the Privy Councillor's oath of secrecy or upon the Official Secrets Acts.

This decision established the power of the court to restrain publication of Cabinet secrets but gave no clear guidance as to when the power should be exercised. The problems of memoirs of ex-Cabinet ministers were subsequently considered by a committee of Privy Councillors.[61] The committee distinguished between secret information relating to national security and international relations, on which an ex-minister must accept the decision of the Cabinet Secretary, and other confidential material about relationships between ministers or between ministers and civil servants. In the latter case there should be no publication within 15 years, except with clearance from the Cabinet Secretary, but in the event of a dispute it must in the last resort be for ex-ministers themselves to decide what to publish. Advice given by a civil servant to a minister should not be revealed while the adviser was still a civil servant. The committee recommended against legislation, preferring to suggest a clear working procedure which would be brought to the attention of every minister on assuming office. The committee's recommendations were accepted by the government in 1976 and have been maintained by subsequent governments. There has since been a spate of ministerial memoirs.[62]

One important practice is that the ministers in one government do not have access to the papers of an earlier government of a different political party. On a change of government the outgoing Prime Minister issues special instructions about the disposal of the Cabinet papers of the outgoing administration.[63] The practice applies to papers of the Cabinet and ministerial committees, as well as departmental papers that contain the private views of ministers and advice given by officials. The main reason for the practice is to prevent a minister from one party having access to 'matters that the previous Administration had been most anxious to keep quiet'.[64] Former ministers retain the right of access to documents which they saw in office. Before access to Cabinet papers or other ministerial documents of a former government can be given to third persons, the present Prime Minister must seek the agreement of the former Prime Minister concerned, or the current leader of his or her party. Thus, when a committee of privy councillors was appointed to review British policy towards the Falkland Islands before the Argentine invasion, five former Prime Ministers agreed to the relevant documents being seen by the committee.[65] Ministers relinquishing office without a change of government 'should hand over to their successors those Cabinet documents required for the current administration and should ensure that all others have been destroyed'.[66]

---

61   Cmnd 6386, 1976 (Radcliffe Report).
62   *Questions of Procedure for Ministers* requires former ministers to submit their manuscript to the Cabinet Secretary and to conform to the principles set out in the Radcliffe Report (note 61 above).
63   Ibid, para 15.
64   HC Deb, 8 July 1982, col 474 (Mr M Foot).
65   HC Deb, 1 July 1982, col 1039; 8 July 1982, col 469. See Lord Hunt [1982] PL 514.
66   *Questions of Procedure for Ministers*, para 14. And see R. Brazier [1996] CLJ 65, on the sale of the Churchill papers in 1995.

C.   Ministers and departments

Ministerial offices: the background

Some ministerial offices have a much longer history than the office of Prime Minister, others have been created more recently. The office of Lord Chancellor goes back to the reign of Edward the Confessor and was of great political and judicial significance for several centuries after the Norman conquest. The office of Lord Privy Seal dates from the 14th century and in a later period was often held by leading statesmen; but the historic duties in respect of the Privy Seal were abolished in 1884 and the office now carries no departmental responsibilities. The office of Lord President of the Council was created in 1497 and became important during the period of government through the Council under the Stuarts.

The office of Secretary of State has almost as long a history, acquiring its political significance in the Tudor period, particularly during the tenure of the Cecils under Elizabeth I. It came to be recognised as the means by which communications could take place between citizens and the Sovereign.[67] From the 17th century, two and sometimes three Secretaries of State were appointed, who divided national and foreign affairs between them. In 1782, a different division of functions vested in one Secretary of State responsibility for domestic affairs and the colonies, and in the other Secretary responsibility for foreign affairs. Thus were created the offices of Home Secretary and Foreign Secretary. In 1794, a Secretary of State for War was appointed, and thereafter from time to time additional Secretaryships (for example, for the colonies, for India, for Scotland) were created and abolished as need arose. In 1997, there were 14 Secretaries of State who between them headed nearly all the major departments. When statutory powers are conferred on a Secretary of State, it is usual for the statute to designate him or her as 'the Secretary of State' but it will be obvious from the context which Secretary of State is intended to exercise the new functions.[68] In law the duties of Secretaries of State are interchangeable, but in practice each Secretary's functions are limited to those related to his or her own department. One Secretary of State may be named by the Prime Minister as First Secretary; while this makes no legal difference to the office, it determines precedence in the Cabinet and the First Secretary may deputise for the Prime Minister in the latter's absence. In 1997, the position as First Secretary was combined with the office of Deputy Prime Minister.

Ministers of the Crown

According to one statutory definition, minister of the Crown means 'the holder of any office in Her Majesty's Government in the United Kingdom, and includes the Treasury, ... and the Defence Council'.[69] In a less technical

---

[67]   For the history of the Secretaries of State, see Anson, *The Law and Custom of the Constitution*, vol II, i, pp 172–84.

[68]   By the Interpretation Act 1978, unless the contrary intention appears, 'Secretary of State' means 'one of Her Majesty's Principal Secretaries of State'. See *Agee v Lord Advocate* 1977 SLT (Notes) 54.

[69]   Ministers of the Crown Act 1975, s 8(1).

sense, ministers are those members or supporters of the party in power who hold political office in the government. They are all appointed by the Crown on the advice of the Prime Minister and their offices are at the disposal of an incoming Prime Minister. They do not include members of the civil service or the armed forces, who continue in office despite a change of government; nor personal advisers of ministers, who may be paid salaries and are temporarily attached to departments but who lose their position when a minister leaves office; nor members of public boards, regulatory bodies and so on. Unlike many of these other office-holders, ministers are not disqualified from membership of the House of Commons.

There are various grades of ministerial appointment today, but they may be grouped into three broad categories: (*a*) Cabinet ministers, who may or may not have departmental responsibilities; (*b*) departmental ministers and ministers of state who are outside the Cabinet, the duty of a minister of state being to share in the administration of a department headed by a Cabinet minister;[70] and (*c*) parliamentary secretaries, whose duty it is to assist in the parliamentary work of a department and who may also have some administrative responsibility. The four Law Officers of the Crown are within category (*b*) but the government whips, who have no departmental responsibilities, may be allotted amongst the categories according to their status and seniority. By exercise of the prerogative, new posts in the Crown's service can be created, for example, extra Secretaries of State. But when a new ministry is formed, there is often secondary legislation to create the minister a corporation sole, thus giving him or her legal capacity, and providing in broad terms for his or her functions.[71] There are no legal limits on the number of ministers which the Crown may appoint, assuming that they are not to receive a salary and do not sit in the House of Commons, but there are statutory limits on the number of ministers who may be members of the Commons and on the number of salaries payable to holders of ministerial office.[72]

Ministerial salaries

The maximum salaries payable to the Prime Minister, other Cabinet ministers, ministers of state, parliamentary secretaries and the Law Officers of the Crown are prescribed by the Ministerial and other Salaries Act 1975, as varied by subsequent Orders in Council.[73] The making of such an Order in Council is subject to the prior approval of the Commons being given to the draft Order. Ministerial salaries are in practice increased only after their level has been considered by the Review Body on Top Salaries, at the same time as the salaries of MPs are reviewed.[74] In May 1997, the statutory salary of the Prime Minister was £100,000, of a Cabinet minister in the Commons £60,000 and of a parlia-

---

70 Cf House of Commons Disqualification Act 1975, s 9(1). Under-secretaries of State may perform a similar role.
71 Eg SI 1988 No 1843; and SI 1995 No 2985.
72 Ch 9 B.
73 The salary of the Lord Chancellor is governed by the Ministerial and other Pensions and Salaries Act 1991, by which his salary is '£2,000 a year more than the salary for the time being payable to the Lord Chief Justice' (s 3).
74 Eg Cmnd 8881, 1983; and Ch 11 B.

mentary secretary in the Commons £23,623.[75] All ministerial salaries are maximum salaries and less may be paid;[76] thus the House of Commons may exercise its traditional right to move the reduction of a minister's salary in order to call attention to a grievance or censure the conduct of a department.[77] Ministerial salaries are paid in addition to the salary received by all MPs.

While these are not ministerial salaries, the Act of 1975 also provides for the Speaker's salary and salary to the leader of the Opposition in the Commons, who is defined as being the leader of the party in opposition to the government having the greatest numerical strength in the House; the Speaker has power to resolve doubts as to who this is. Salaries are also paid under the Act to the chief opposition whip in the Commons and in the Lords to the leader of the Opposition and the chief opposition whip. The salaries of the Speaker and opposition officers are charged on the Consolidated Fund and are thus not subject to reduction by vote of the Commons. Under the Ministerial and other Pensions and Salaries Act 1991, severance payments are payable to ministers who are removed from office before reaching the age of 65 without being moved to another position in the government.

Ministers in Parliament

It is a convention that ministerial office-holders should be members of one or other House of Parliament. Such membership is essential to the maintenance of ministerial responsibility. There is, however, no law that a minister must be in Parliament. The statutory limit on the number of ministers receiving salaries who may sit at one time in the Commons ensures indirectly that there should be ministerial representation in the Lords. When a Prime Minister appoints to ministerial office someone who is not already in Parliament, a life peerage is usually conferred. Apart from the convention that ministers must be members of either the House of Commons or the House of Lords, they are also reminded by *Questions of Procedure for Ministers* (QPM) that they are 'accountable to Parliament for the policies, decisions and actions of their departments and agencies'.[78] This is now contained in para 1 of QPM following a recommendation of the Nolan committee that the ethical principles and rules which are to be found in QPM should form 'a free standing code of conduct or a separate section of a new QPM'.[79] The government has evidently adopted the latter course, with the new para 1 also providing that ministers 'must not knowingly mislead Parliament' and should 'correct any inadvertent errors at the earliest opportunity'.[80] There are those who feel that the word 'knowingly' should be deleted from the drafting, though it was not thought to make any 'material difference' by Sir Richard Scott.[81]

---

[75]   See SI 1996 No 1913 for maximum ministerial salaries payable in 1997.
[76]   Ministerial and other Salaries Act 1975, s 4.
[77]   In 1976, helped by a mix-up in voting, the Opposition carried a resolution calling for a reduction of £1,000 in the salary of the Secretary of State for Industry; this was overridden a week later (HC Deb, 11 and 17 February 1976).
[78]   *Questions of Procedure for Ministers* (as revised, 1995). See also HC Deb, 19 March 1997, cols 1046–47, and HL Deb, 20 March 1997, col 1057. See Ch 7 above.
[79]   Cm 2850–I, 1995.
[80]   See also HC Deb, 19 March 1997, cols 1046–47, and HL Deb, 20 March 1997, col 1057 where it is stated that ministers who knowingly mislead Parliament are expected to resign. See Ch 7 above.
[81]   HC 115 (1995–96), para K8.5. Cf A Tomkins [1996] PL 484.

Financial interests of ministers

Because of their office, many ministers take decisions which have a direct financial effect on particular businesses, sections of industry and land values. They also have access to confidential information about future decisions which could be put to financial profit. The Marconi affair of 1912 involved three leading members of the Liberal government who were alleged to have made use of secret information about an impending government contract to make an investment in Marconi shares: an inquiry by a parliamentary committee established that they had bought shares not in the company to which the contract was about to be awarded, but in a sister company.[82] In 1948 the Lynskey Tribunal of Inquiry reported on allegations that ministers and other public servants had been bribed in connection with the grant of licences by the Board of Trade; a junior minister, who later resigned from Parliament, was found to have received presents of wine and spirits and other gifts, knowing that they had been made to secure favourable treatment by the department of applications for licences.[83] While such conduct could give rise to criminal proceedings, additional safeguards are required if ministers are to avoid suspicion.

In 1952, the rules then in force were published in a parliamentary written answer.[84] They still remain in operation, though they have been amended and are now to be found in *Questions of Procedure for Ministers*.[85] The overriding principle is that ministers must ensure that no conflict arises, or appears to arise, between their private interests and their public duties. This conflict could arise if a minister took any active part or had a financial interest in any undertaking which had contractual or other relations (for example, receiving a licence or a subsidy) with his or her department. Under the current rules in force, ministers should on assuming office resign any directorships which they hold and should dispose of controlling interests in any company which could give rise to conflict of interest. In cases of doubt, for example as to the propriety of retaining certain shares in a company, the Prime Minister must be informed and is the final judge. In 1962, a junior minister in the Ministry of Aviation, Mr B de Ferranti, resigned a few months after accepting office as he had found it impossible to divest himself of his interests in a family business having extensive contractual relations with the Ministry.[86]

In 1982, the Secretary of State for Trade, Lord Cockfield, declined to take a decision on whether to approve a majority report of the Monopolies and Mergers Commission about a controversial takeover bid, since he had a small shareholding in the bidding company. The decision was instead taken by the minister of state in the same department. On becoming a minister, Lord Cockfield had in accordance with the rules on financial interests deposited the relevant share certificates with his bank, instructing the bank not to

---

[82]   See Donaldson, *The Marconi Scandal.*
[83]   Cmd 7616, 1949.
[84]   HC Deb, 25 February 1952, col 701; and 20 March 1980, col 293 (WA).
[85]   *Questions of Procedure for Ministers*, paras 103–27.
[86]   *The Times*, 31 October 1962.

deal in them so long as he held ministerial office.[87] Ministers are expected to disclose all relevant interests in the registers which are maintained by the House of Commons and House of Lords respectively.[88] There are no restrictions on ministers taking up employment when they leave office,[89] unlike senior civil servants who need government permission before taking up employment within two years of leaving the service.[90]

There are also rules which govern the conditions on which ministers may while in office contribute to the press or undertake other literary work. A minister may not become a regular columnist for a newspaper nor, as Dr Jeremy Bray discovered in 1969, may he or she publish a book on matters related to ministerial work.[91] Ministers may, however, contribute to a book, journal or newspaper for the purpose of supplementing other means of informing the public about the work of their department provided that publication will not be at variance with their obligations to Parliament and their duty to observe the principle of collective responsibility. In cases of doubt the Prime Minister should be consulted. No fee should be accepted for such writings, and ministers are advised not to engage in controversy in the correspondence columns of the press.[92]

Departments

While the term 'government department' has no precise meaning in law, it usually refers to those branches of the central administration which are staffed by civil servants, paid for out of exchequer funds and headed by a minister responsible to Parliament. A single minister may be responsible for more than one department: thus the Chancellor of the Exchequer is responsible for the Treasury and the two revenue departments (Inland Revenue; Customs and Excise), as well as for a group of executive departments closely associated with the Treasury, for example the Public Works Loan Board. Exceptionally, there are departments which for constitutional reasons do not have a ministerial head: thus the National Audit Office is headed by the Comptroller and Auditor General.[93] For the purposes of legal proceedings against the Crown, a list of departments is maintained under the Crown Proceedings Act 1947.[94] For the purposes of investigation by the Parliamentary Ombudsman, a statutory list of departments is maintained and this is revised as new departments are established.[95] There are many public bodies with governmental functions which are not regarded as government

---

[87] HC Deb, 21 December 1982, col 821, and 22 December 1982, col 955; and *R v Secretary of State for Trade, ex p Anderson Strathclyde plc* [1983] 2 All ER 233. Ministers are instructed to transfer any investments to a 'blind trust' (*Questions of Procedure for Ministers*, para 112).

[88] Ch 11 B. In practice, most ministers submit a nil return.

[89] R Brazier (1992) 43 NILQ 19. But ministers are asked to avoid 'any course which would reflect adversely on their or the government's reputation for integrity or the confidentiality of its proceedings' (*Questions of Procedure for Ministers*, para 105).

[90] See Section D below.

[91] *The Times*, 26–29 September 1969. See now *Questions of Procedure for Ministers*, para 98.

[92] *Questions of Procedure for Ministers*, paras 95–6.

[93] Ch 17 D.

[94] Ch 31 C.

[95] Ch 28 D.

departments. They include local authorities; regulatory bodies such as the Commission for Racial Equality and the Equal Opportunities Commission; grant-giving bodies such as the Arts Council and the research councils established under the Science and Technology Act 1965; advisory councils and committees, such as the Council on Tribunals, and other bodies which may report to ministers but are not directly controlled by them (for example, the English and Scottish Law Commissions).[96] Often such bodies are financed from central exchequer funds.[97]

Government departments are much affected by the principle of ministerial responsibility. In the 19th century, administrative tasks were often entrusted to boards which did not include a minister responsible to Parliament.[98] But strong emphasis was later laid on the principle of ministerial responsibility for government departments. In 1968, the report of the Fulton Committee on the Civil Service considered the effect of ministerial responsibility in relation to the variety of departments and other agencies which then existed, and said: 'we see no reason to believe that the dividing line between activities for which ministers are directly responsible and those for which they are not, is necessarily drawn in the right place today'.[99] The committee recommended that further consideration be given to the scope for 'hiving-off' areas of governmental work to autonomous or relatively autonomous agencies. One form of hiving-off was applied in 1969 when the Post Office Corporation was established; this took postal and telephone services away from a government department and entrusted them to a public corporation similar to those which ran the nationalised industries.[100] Other lesser forms of hiving-off have involved establishing agencies within government departments charged with specific managerial tasks: for example, the Procurement Executive within the Ministry of Defence, which obtains the weapons and equipment needed by the armed forces. Many tasks formerly performed by the Department of Employment are now entrusted to the Advisory Conciliation and Arbitration Service and to the Health and Safety Commission.[101] Further developments in this direction were implemented under the 'Next Steps' Initiative in the 1990s, which is discussed in section D below.

The organisation of central government

In 1918 was published the report of the Machinery of Government Committee presided over by Lord Haldane. This committee had been appointed to inquire into the responsibilities of central government departments and 'to advise in what manner the exercise and distribution by the Government of its functions should be improved'.[102] It recommended that the business of govern-

---

[96]   See the government publication, *Public Bodies*; and ch 14.
[97]   See also the peculiar position of the public utility regulators: ch 14 below.
[98]   F M G Willson (1955) 33 Public Administration 43; Parris, *Constitutional Bureaucracy*, ch 3.
[99]   Cmnd 3638, 1968, p 61.
[100] Ch 14.
[101] Trade Union and Labour Relations (Consolidation) Act 1992, ss 247–53; Health and Safety at Work etc Act 1974, s 10.
[102] Cd 9230, 1918. See also Daalder, *Cabinet Reform in Britain 1914–1963*, ch 17; and Brown and Steel, *The Administrative Process in Britain*, ch 10.

ment should be distributed into ten main divisions by reference to their functions: finance; national defence; external affairs; production; transport and commerce; employment; supplies; education; health; and justice. The report also favoured a small Cabinet of up to twelve members and the retention of a permanent Cabinet secretariat. Except for the last recommendation, the structure of central government after 1918 was not reorganised on the Haldane lines, although today the scope of some departments (for example, Ministry of Defence and Foreign Office) closely resembles the division of functions recommended in 1918. The Haldane report is notable for having been the only occasion in the 20th century on which the structure of government has been reviewed by an independent committee.

To enable changes in the structure of government to be carried out quickly, there have since 1946 been statutory powers by which new needs can be met without recourse to Acts of Parliament. The Ministers of the Crown Act 1975 now authorises the Crown, by Order in Council, to transfer to any minister functions previously exercised by another minister; to provide for the dissolution of a government department and for the transfer to other departments of the functions previously exercised by that department; and to direct that functions shall be exercised concurrently by two ministers. Consequential steps may also be authorised, such as the transfer of property from one department to another and changes in the title of ministers. Orders in Council under the 1975 Act are subject to parliamentary scrutiny. The powers conferred by the 1975 Act are in addition to the Crown's prerogative powers, which may still be exercised to make some governmental changes.[103] A significant use of the statutory powers occurred in 1988 when the Department of Health and Social Security was divided in two to form a Department of Health and a Department of Social Security.[104]

While the organisation of government often depends on short-term political factors, steps were taken during the 1960s for grouping related functions of government in larger departments. These steps led by 1970 to the emergence of five 'giant' departments, namely the Foreign and Commonwealth Office, Defence, Trade and Industry, Health and Social Security, and Environment,[105] each having been formed from an amalgamation of ministries. These large departments had certain advantages (for example, all departments could be represented in the Cabinet; and greater coordination between related activities could take place within the larger department) but also disadvantages in so far as a team of ministers had to be formed to lead each department. Nonetheless in 1997 the Foreign and Commonwealth Office and the Ministry of Defence still survived intact; but, without mentioning intervening changes, Transport was in 1997 separate from the Environment, and Social Security separate from Health; on the other hand the functions of Employment were allocated to Education and Employment, and Trade and Industry respectively. No final scheme for the allocation of tasks

---

[103] 1975 Act, s 5; SI 1988 No 1843; and SI 1995 No 2985. There have been several applications of this power.

[104] Transfer of Functions (Health and Social Security) Order 1988, SI 1988 No 1843. See also Transfer of Functions (Treasury and Minister for the Civil Service) Order 1995, SI 1995 No 269 and Transfer of Functions (Education and Employment) Order, SI 1995 No 2985.

[105] See Clarke, *New Trends in Government*; and Cmnd 4506, 1970.

between departments will ever emerge. The relevant political and administrative factors are often in conflict with each other. As R G S Brown remarked, 'there is no simple relationship between administrative functions and the focal points of ministerial responsibility'.[106]

D.   The civil service

What is a civil servant?

The departments of central government are staffed by administrative, professional, technical and other officials who constitute the civil service. It has been said to be 'common ground that the Civil Service defies an easy universally applicable definition' and that 'a civil servant has no specific legal status'. The Treasury defines a civil servant as 'a servant of the Crown working in a civil capacity who is not: the holder of a political (or judicial) office; the holder of certain other offices in respect of whose tenure of office special provision has been made; a servant of the Crown in a personal capacity paid from the Civil List'.[107] This definition excludes ministers of the Crown, members of the armed forces (who are Crown servants but are not employed in a civil capacity), the police, and those employed in local government and the National Health Service, even though they are all engaged in public services. A somewhat similar definition is contained in s 2(6) of the Crown Proceedings Act 1947, which limits proceedings against the Crown in tort (or in Scots law, delict) to the act, neglect or default of an officer who 'has been directly or indirectly appointed by the Crown and was at the material time paid in respect of his duties as an officer of the Crown' wholly out of the national exchequer.[108] Whatever the precise legal nature of the civil servant's relationship with the Crown, it is an important constitutional principle that those concerned with the administration of government departments should in fact enjoy a tenure of office by which they may serve successive ministers of different political parties. Particularly since 1979, the size and expense of the civil service have become a matter of political controversy. But without the service, the achievements of modern government would have been impossible.

The new structure of the civil service

The civil service has in the past been regulated by two government departments. The first is the Treasury, responsible for 'promoting improvements in the efficiency and effectiveness of civil service management and its pay and personnel structures'. In order to fulfil these obligations, the Treasury had powers under the Civil Service Order in Council 1991 to make regulations relating to various aspects of civil service management.[109] The other government department with responsibility for the civil service has been the Office of Public Service (previously the Office of Public Service and Science),

---

[106]   Op cit, p 214.
[107]   HC 390–II (1992–93), p 261.
[108]   Ch 31 A.
[109]   HC 390–II (1992–93), p 256.

established in 1992 as part of the Cabinet Office. As such the OPS brings together responsibilities of the Minister for the Civil Service with the units responsible for the Citizen's Charter, efficiency and market testing. It also incorporates the Office of Science and Technology, based previously in the Cabinet Office and the Department of Education and Science (as it then was).[110] There was clearly some overlap between the Treasury and the OPS in respect of their different functions, and in fact the responsibility of the Treasury for civil service functions was transferred in 1995 to the Minister for the Civil Service[111] (a position held by the Prime Minister) who exercises powers under the Civil Service Order in Council 1995.

The increasing role of the Treasury reflected the growing concern in the 1980s about the cost and efficiency of the civil service.[112] These concerns culminated with the publication in 1988 of a report to the Prime Minister drawn up by Sir Robin Ibbs, entitled *Improving Management in Government: The Next Steps*.[113] This is the most far-reaching and fundamental review of the civil service since 1968 and has led to the most radical changes since 1854.[114] The report expressed concern that the civil service (with over 600,000 staff) was too big and too diverse to be managed as a single organisation and that attempts should be made to establish a different way of conducting the business of government. It was suggested that the central civil service should consist of a relatively small core engaged in the function of servicing ministers and managing departments which would be the main sponsors of particular government policies and services. Responding to these departments would be a range of agencies employing their own staff, concentrating on the delivery of their particular service with responsibilities clearly defined between the Secretary of State and the permanent secretary on the one hand, and the chairman and chief executive of the agencies on the other.[115] These proposals reflected a perceived need to give greater priority to organising government so that its service delivery operations function effectively.

The proposals were largely accepted by the government, and by 1996 130 agencies had been created (this accounting for 67% of the civil service), with more (an estimated 34) on the way (covering another 84,000 civil servants). Spanning a wide range and diversity of functions, they vary enormously in size, from the National Weights and Measures Laboratory (45 staff) to the Employment Service (45,000 staff). Each agency has a defined task, or range of tasks, which are set out in its published framework document. In addition 'key performance targets – covering financial performance, efficiency and service to the customer – are set out by Ministers annually and announced to Parliament. Each Agency has a chief executive, normally directly accountable to Ministers and with personal responsibility for the success of the agency in

---

110   HC 390–II (1992–93), p 1.
111   See SI 1995 No 269.
112   For the changing structure, see Fredman and Morris, *The State as Employer*, pp 21–3.
113   HMSO (1988). The report had been commissioned in 1986. For the reaction to it, see Hennessy, *Whitehall*, pp 620–1, and Lawson, *The View from No 11*, pp 391–3.
114   See respectively Cmnd 3638 (Fulton Committee) and Northcote–Trevelyan Report (reprinted in app B of the Fulton Report).
115   For the previous consideration of this option with reference particularly to Sweden, see Cmnd 3638, 1968, paras 188–91. See above, section C.

meeting its targets.'[116] It is claimed that the agencies have led to a much stronger focus on performance in relation both to quality of service and to efficiency; the strengthening of accountability and greater openness; and new approaches to personnel management. The creation of the agencies has generally been approved, most notably by the Treasury and Civil Service Committee of the House of Commons, though a number of reservations have been made. These relate to the threat to the notion of a unified civil service which has prevailed since 1870; the accountability of ministers to Parliament for the work of the agencies; and to the manner by which such radical change has taken place without resort to legislation and the benefits (of scrutiny and accountability) which amendment by statute brings to the process of reform.

Tenure of appointment

Traditionally civil servants have been appointed under the royal prerogative, and as such had no contract of employment enforceable by the courts. The traditional rule has, however, been the subject of scrutiny by the courts. The view has been expressed that there would be 'nothing unconstitutional about civil servants being employed by the Crown pursuant to contracts of service'[117] and this position was established by the courts in 1991.[118] As it is, civil servants are deemed by statute for some limited but important purposes to be employed under contracts of employment;[119] the courts have already suggested that they have an action for salary due in respect of a period of service before dismissal;[120] and it has been said that the Crown has no power to alter the terms of service of any civil servants at will.[121] The Court of Appeal has recognised that a Crown servant may have terms of service 'which are contractually enforceable and in respect of which he can have a private law remedy'.[122] However, the courts still seem unwilling to challenge the other traditional rule that civil servants are employed at the pleasure of the Crown, which means that they may be dismissed at pleasure with no common law remedy for wrongful dismissal.[123] So if civil servants are to be regarded as being employed under a contract, its terms will be limited by the prerogative power of the Crown to dismiss without notice for any reason; a power which, it seems, cannot at common law be limited by an express term to the contrary in the terms of appointment.

The formal legal position at common law – one of great insecurity – is tempered by departmental rules laying down procedures which must be followed before adverse action is taken against a civil servant. They provide for notice to be given of what is alleged and grant the right to present his or her

---

[116]   Cm 2750, 1994, p ii.

[117]   *R v Civil Service Appeal Board, ex p Bruce* [1988] 3 All ER 686, 694.

[118]   See now *R v Lord Chancellor's Department, ex p Nangle* [1992] 1 All ER 897; S Fredman and G Morris [1991] PL 485 and Ch 31 B.

[119]   Trade Union and Labour Relations (Consolidation) Act 1992, s 245.

[120]   *Kodeeswaran v A-G of Ceylon* [1970] AC 1111.

[121]   *R v Civil Service Appeal Board, ex p Bruce* [1988] 3 All ER 686, 698. And see *Cresswell v Inland Revenue* [1984] 2 All ER 713.

[122]   *McLaren v Home Office* [1990] IRLR 338, 341.

[123]   *Dunn v R* [1896] 1 QB 116; *Riordan v War Office* [1959] 1 WLR 1046. And ch 31 B.

case and also to appeal, in cases of dismissal or premature retirement, to a Civil Service Appeals Board independent of the department concerned.[124] The Board consists of three persons: a permanent chairman, and two members, one drawn from a panel nominated by the government and another from a panel nominated by representatives of the staff. The purpose of the Board is to determine whether the decision to dismiss or prematurely retire is fair. If it does not, the Board may recommend that the decision be revoked or that compensation be paid to the civil servant. Its decisions are recommendations only, and the final authority whether to implement the recommendation rests with the appellant's head of department. Decisions of the Board – 'set up by an administrative act of the Minister for the Civil Service acting pursuant to [prerogative] power'[125] – are subject to judicial review, as it is 'a board or tribunal exercising functions of a judicial character and as such is a public or similar authority whose actions under its powers may call for the court's intervention'.[126] It must give reasons for its decisions.[127] Presumably a departmental head's refusal to implement a Board decision would be subject to judicial review, if it was exercised irrationally or without due regard to procedural fairness. Civil servants are protected against unfair dismissal by the employment protection legislation. But both this and other statutory employment rights may be withdrawn on the grounds of national security,[128] as happened to the staff at Government Communications' Headquarters in 1984. Personnel matters within the civil service may not be investigated by the Parliamentary Ombudsman, a restriction which has been maintained contrary to the view of the House of Commons Committee on the Parliamentary Ombudsman.[129]

Regulation of the civil service

While certain statutes affect the position of the civil servant, management of the civil service is conducted by reliance on the Crown's common law powers as employer, and where necessary on the royal prerogative, exercised through Orders in Council and supporting regulations. The Civil Service Order in Council 1995, which is a prerogative act, authorises the Minister for the Civil Service to make regulations and give instructions relating to, inter alia, 'the conditions of service of all persons employed in the Service'. Many of the standard conditions of service are drawn together in the comprehensive and detailed *Civil Service Management Code*, though the traditional view has been that many of the instruments which are gathered there would not be enforceable in the courts.[130] The code enjoys no formal legal status as such, but is binding on those to whom it is addressed. Indeed the customary

---

[124] For details of the Board, see *R v Civil Service Appeal Board, ex p Bruce* [1988] 3 All ER 686; [1989] 2 All ER 907.
[125] *R v Civil Service Appeal Board, ex p Bruce* [1988] 3 All ER 686, 699.
[126] Ibid, at 701.
[127] *R v Civil Service Appeal Board, ex p Cunningham* [1991] 4 All ER 310.
[128] Employment Rights Act 1996, s 193. Also Trade Union and Labour Relations (Consolidation) Act 1992, s 275.
[129] Parliamentary Commissioner Act 1967, Sched 3, para 10; ch 28 D.
[130] *Rodwell v Thomas* [1944] KB 596. Cf *Sutton v A-G* (1923) 39 TLR 294; L Blair [1958] PL 32 and (1958) 21 MLR 265.

approach of British government has been that the courts should be excluded from interfering in the internal management of the service.[131] But given the desire on the part of the government to confer a contractual status on civil servants, it may be increasingly difficult to exclude the provisions of the code from consideration by the courts. It may be open to argument in some cases that many of these measures will be incorporated (impliedly if not expressly) into the employment contracts of those to whom they are designed to apply.

In 1968, the Fulton committee had recommended that 'all civil servants should be organised in a single grading structure in which there are an appropriate number of different pay levels matching different levels of skill and responsibility'. The committee thought that it was neither practical nor desirable to allow each department to have autonomy over personnel matters, arguing instead that 'the Service must be a flexible, integrated whole; it must continue to be a unified service'. This view appears to have been accepted by the government as late as 1987 when in evidence to the Treasury and Civil Service Committee it was claimed that centralised pay and personnel regulation helped to ensure that 'staff can move easily between Departments and do any work for which their qualifications and experience suit them; machinery of government changes can be effected quickly and easily; Departments do not compete against each other for the same scarce skills'. The effect of these centralised arrangements was that the bulk of civil service staff were in grades which were common across the service: 'Centralised pay systems covered groups of staff whatever departments they worked in, with settlements negotiated nationally between the Treasury and the [trade] unions concerned.'[132] These arrangements have, however, been eroded, as the government has been seized of the benefits of delegation of responsibility for pay and personnel matters along with the delegation of function taking place, for example by the creation of the agencies: 'Managers had to have the freedom to organise their structures of pay and grading to suit the particular needs and objectives of their own organisation and to motivate their staff.'[133]

Major changes to the way in which the civil service is regulated have taken place following the major organisational changes which have already been discussed.[134] A key element of Treasury strategy 'for promoting improvements in the efficiency and effectiveness of Civil Service management' is to introduce greater delegation to departments and agencies. Delegation was in fact facilitated by the Civil Service (Management of Functions) Act 1992, following the enactment of which the Treasury delegated responsibility for pay and pay-related conditions of service to the Secretaries of State responsible for the agencies concerned in respect of the staff employed in these organisations. The delegation of power in this way imposed upon the individual agencies the responsibility for pay bargaining, within a framework of financial controls imposed by the Treasury. In the *Citizen's Charter: Second Report* it was pointed out that nearly 60% of all civil servants were employed in organisations (large agencies as well as the Inland Revenue and Customs and Excise) which were

---

[131]   Cf *R v Lord Chancellor's Department, ex p Nangle* [1992] 1 All ER 897.
[132]   *The Civil Service. Continuity and Change* (Cm 2627, 1994), pp 25–26.
[133]   HC 27–I (1993–94), para 255.
[134]   For an assessment, see R A Chapman (1994) 72 Public Administration 599.

'developing their own delegated pay schemes, all of which will be perform-ance based'.[135] In 1994, the government announced its intention to extend the programmes (supported by the Treasury and Civil Service Committee as responding 'to the needs and objectives of particular organisations within the Civil Service'[136]), so that by April 1996 'responsibility for the pay and grading of staff below senior levels should be delegated to all departments and the existing national pay arrangements replaced'.[137] Such developments reflect the move away from the Fulton vision of a unified service to what has become at best a unified but not a uniform service, and a 'federal structure of more autonomous units'.[138]

Civil service ethics and standards

A statement of the ethical standards by which the civil service should be bound, prepared by Sir Robert Armstrong, was first issued in 1985 in the wake of the Ponting case in which a senior civil servant leaked confidential information to an MP about conduct in the Ministry of Defence which led to allegations that ministers were seeking deliberately to mislead Parliament. The Treasury and Civil Service Committee questioned the adequacy of this statement,[139] and some revisions were made in 1987. The position was reviewed by the Treasury and Civil Service Committee in 1994 ('The Role of the Civil Service') which concluded that there was a need for 'a new Civil Service Code to 'enable civil servants themselves and those they serve' to know what was expected of them, and 'to make more tangible the values which civil servants hold in common'.[140] This recommendation was accepted by the government, which endorsed the need 'to set out with greater clarity and brevity than existing documents the constitutional framework within which civil servants work and the values which they are expected to uphold'. Further support was provided by the Nolan committee, which proposed a number of amendments to the draft which the government had by then prepared. The new Code was introduced under powers conferred by the royal prerogative, although the government left open the possibility of a new framework giving 'statutory backing to the rules in connection with the terms and conditions of employment of civil servants, including the new Code'.[141]

The new code was brought into operation in 1996, replacing the statement prepared by Sir Robert Armstrong.[142] Now formally incorporated into the Civil Service Management Code it declares that 'the constitutional and practical role of the Civil Service is, with integrity, honesty, impartiality and objectivity, to assist the duly constituted Government, of whatever political complexion, in formulating policies of Government, carrying out decisions of

---

[135]   Cm 2540, 1994, p 117.
[136]   HC 27–I (1993–94), para 262.
[137]   *The Civil Service. Continuity and Change* (above), p 26. For developments in civil service pay since 1979, see I Kessler (1993) 71 Public Administration 323.
[138]   HC 27–I (1993–94), para 63.
[139]   HC 92 (1985–86).
[140]   HC 27–I (1993–94).
[141]   Cm 2748, 1995, p 8.
[142]   See HC Deb, 30 October 1995, col 10 (WA).

the Government and in administering public services for which the Government is responsible'. As such civil servants are required to give 'honest and impartial advice to Ministers' and 'endeavour to deal with the affairs of the public sympathetically, effectively, promptly and without bias or maladministration'. They should endeavour to ensure the proper, effective and efficient use of public money. Civil servants are also required not to misuse their official position to further their own private interests (or those of others),[143] and they must conduct themselves in such a way as 'to deserve and retain the confidence of Ministers and to be able to establish the same relationship with those whom they may be required to serve in some future Administration'. So far as official information is concerned, this should not be disclosed without authority where it 'has been communicated in confidence within Government, or received in confidence from others'. Apart from reminding officials of their duty to be impartial, the code also provides that they 'should not seek to frustrate or influence the policies, decisions or actions of Government by the unauthorised, improper or premature disclosure outside the Government of any information to which they have had access as civil servants'. There is no qualification that such information should be confidential.

The emphasis of the code is on the responsibility of civil servants as servants of the Crown who 'owe their loyalty to the duly constituted government'. The extent to which the code recognises that civil servants may have other obligations is controversial, and at best constrained. Thus the duty to serve a 'duly constituted government' is qualified by a recognition that all public officials must 'discharge public functions reasonably and according to the law' and that there is a 'duty to comply with the law, including international law and treaty obligations, and to uphold the administration of justice'. But there is no right, far less any obligation, to bring wrongdoing to public notice.[144] At best the civil servant may in certain circumstances report any impropriety 'in accordance with procedures laid down in departmental guidance or rules of conduct'. This applies where the civil servant is being required to act in a way which is 'illegal, improper or unethical', in 'breach of a constitutional convention or a professional code', and may involve possible maladministration, or is otherwise inconsistent with the code.[145] Where a matter has been referred in this way and the civil servant is dissatisfied with the response, the matter may be taken further by way of a complaint to the Civil Service Commissioners, a body set up in 1870 with the rather different task of promoting competitive entry into the civil service on the principle of intellectual merit.[146] The code is silent on the powers of the Civil Service Commissioners in this new capacity, though the government did previously

---

143 See N Lewis and D Longley [1994] PL 596.
144 The issue was considered inconclusively by the Public Service Committee in HC 313–I (1995–96).
145 The Code also deals with the situation in which a civil servant, while not personally involved, is aware of the wrongdoing or maladministration, following recommendations in Cm 2850–I, 1995, para 3.51.
146 This gives effect to a recommendation of the Treasury and Civil Service Committee (HC 27–I (1993–94)) and replaces the procedure in the Armstrong memorandum which provided an appeal to the Head of the Home Civil Service. For discussion, see Cm 2850–I, 1995, para 3.53.

express the view that 'powers of enforcement would not be appropriate'. Rather, it was suggested that the Commissioners would have the 'power to report to Parliament which could be used in the event of the Government refusing to act on the Commissioners' recommendations'.[147] A civil servant who remains dissatisfied is expected either to carry out his or her duties or to resign, in which case he or she must observe any obligations of confidentiality.

The civil servant within the department

The senior civil servant within a department is the Permanent Secretary. According to the Fulton committee, he has four functions:

He is the Minister's most immediate adviser on policy; he is the managing director of the day-to-day operations of the department; he has the ultimate responsibility for questions of staff and organisation; as the Accounting Officer (in nearly every department), he also has the ultimate responsibility for all departmental expenditure.[148]

In the larger departments, a second Permanent Secretary may be appointed.[149] Beneath the Permanent Secretary, the affairs of the department will be handled by a number of divisions or branches, controlled (in descending order of seniority) by deputy secretaries, under-secretaries, and assistant secretaries. The work of these senior civil servants often brings them into close contact with ministers and Parliament. When the Fulton committee was established in 1966, the Prime Minister stated that the government was not intending to alter the basic relationship between ministers and civil servants. 'Civil servants, however eminent, remain the confidential advisers of Ministers, who alone are answerable to Parliament for policy'.[150] In fact the Fulton committee found that the constitutional framework of government had a strong influence over the way in which the work was transacted, and that much of the parliamentary work done by civil servants, for example, in preparing legislation and drafting answers to parliamentary questions, had no counterpart outside the government service.

Operating policies embodied in existing legislation and implementing policy decisions take up most of the time of most civil servants. There are taxes to be collected, employment and social security offices to be run. There is a mass of individual casework both in local offices and in the central departments of state. There are major programmes to be arranged and controlled, such as the planning and engineering of motorways from their initial location and design to the finished construction.[151]

The Fulton committee found that, while the position of a civil servant within the hierarchy was usually clear, departments did not find it easy to allocate to individual officers or units the authority to take decisions. The

---

[147]   The Nolan committee recommended that all successful appeals should be reported to Parliament: Cm 2850–I, 1995.
[148]   Cmnd 3638, p 58.
[149]   For a study of permanent secretaries, see K Theakston and G K Fry (1989) 67 Public Administration 129.
[150]   Cmnd 3638, app A.
[151]   Cmnd 3638, p 15.

principles of ministerial responsibility meant that decisions often had to be referred to a higher level than their difficulty or importance merited; and many decisions involved other departments. 'For these reasons clear delegation of authority is particularly difficult in the Civil Service'.[152] Since the Fulton committee reported in 1968, many measures designed to improve this position have been adopted. For example, in areas of mainly executive work where there is less need for detailed supervision by ministers, agencies have been set up within departments, managed by an executive head to whom authority is delegated and who has a degree of managerial independence from the department. The creation of the 'Next Steps' programme already described is an important development of this form of management.

Where schemes of delegation exist within a department, they do not generally affect the legal position of the department or of outsiders dealing with it. Where the power to make a discretionary decision affecting an individual is vested in a minister, an official within the department may in general take that decision on behalf of the minister (the *Carltona* principle),[153] unless there are express or implied limitations in the statute conferring the power.[154] In a criminal case in which it was claimed that the Home Secretary had never approved a breathalyser device as required by the Road Safety Act 1973, Widgery LJ said: 'The minister is not expected personally to take every decision entrusted to him by Parliament. If a decision is made on his behalf by one of his officials, then that constitutionally is the minister's decision'.[155] Except where the express delegation of authority is required by a particular statute, the civil servant's authority flows from the general nature of his or her administrative work and not from a formal delegation scheme.[156] Although a letter sent from a department may be signed by a particular civil servant, it cannot be assumed that that person made the decision expressed in the letter, since the matter may have been referred to a more senior official or to a minister for decision or approval. In regard to the Secretary of State's powers under the Immigration Act 1971, it was held that immigration officers (in whom certain functions are expressly vested by the Act) were also entitled by virtue of the *Carltona* principle to exercise decision-making powers in regard to deportation on behalf of the Secretary of State.[157]

New questions about departmental delegation arise following the introduction of the Next Steps agencies. Indeed, it has been suggested that the principle in the *Carltona* case is not strong enough to permit the delegation of ministerial authority to the agencies: 'the application of the *Carltona* principle was heavily contingent upon a certain structure of civil service administration which assumed and depended upon a very active notion of ministerial responsibility to Parliament, a principle which has been seriously eroded.' It has been argued further that there may therefore be no power for ministers to delegate to agencies, which 'cannot be seen as part of an integrated

---

[152]　Cmnd 3638, p 50.
[153]　*Carltona Ltd v Commissioners of Works* [1943] 2 All ER 560. See ch 7.
[154]　*R v Home Secretary, ex p Oladehinde* [1991] 1 AC 254, at p 282.
[155]　*R v Skinner* [1968] 2 QB 700, 707. See also *R v Home Secretary, ex p Doody* [1994] 1 AC 531, at p 566. And see ch 7.
[156]　Cf *Commissioners of Customs and Excise v Cure and Deeley Ltd* [1962] 1 QB 340.
[157]　*R v Home Secretary, ex p Oladehinde* [1991] 1 AC 254.

departmental structure, a departmental unity', such as the *Carltona* principle demands, and that as a result legislation is necessary if powers conferred on ministers are to be delegated by them to agencies.[158] It is thus far from clear whether the case-law which permits delegation by ministers to departmental officials for whom they are responsible would also permit delegation to members of executive agencies (even though they may be civil servants) for the operational activities of which the minister has disclaimed responsibility. It can hardly be said in these circumstances that the member of agency staff is a member of the minister's department 'for whom he accepts responsibility'. Nor is it clear whether it can be said that the minister must now 'answer before Parliament for anything that his officials have done under his authority'. At the very least it may be that the *Carltona* principle will require a degree of refinement and flexibility in operation if it is to facilitate delegation of the type required by the creation of the agencies, though legislation would be a more appropriate form of regulation.

Civil servants and ministerial responsibility

The principle of responsibility through ministers to Parliament is one of the most essential characteristics of the civil service. In a memorandum to the Treasury and Civil Service Committee, the Cabinet Office asserted that

The Minister in charge of a department is the only person who may be said to be ultimately accountable for the work of his department. It is usually on the Secretary of State as minister that Parliament has conferred powers, and Parliament calls on ministers to be accountable for the policy, actions and resources of their departments and the use of those powers. While ministers may delegate much of the day to day work of their departments, often now to agencies, they remain ultimately accountable to Parliament for all that is done under their power. Civil servants, except in those particular cases where statute confers powers on them directly, cannot take decisions or actions except insofar as they act on behalf of ministers. Civil servants are accountable to ministers, ministers are accountable to Parliament.[159]

According to the Cabinet Office, ministerial responsibility has often been used to describe this process. In recent years, however, there has been a significant refinement of the principle, the government taking the view that ministers are 'accountable' to Parliament for the work of their department, but are not 'responsible' for all the actions of civil servants in the sense of being blameworthy. There appears as a result to be a greater willingness to attribute responsibility for operational matters to individual civil servants. Although the distinction has been strenuously defended, there are those who remain sceptical, though it remains unclear how far the distinction expresses anything which is qualitatively different from what was expressed by Sir David Maxwell-Fyfe in the aftermath of the Crichel Down affair in the 1950s.[160]

1 Civil servants and select committees. According to the government guidance on departmental evidence to select committees (the so-called Osmotherly

---

[158]   M R Freedland [1996] PL 19.
[159]   HC 27–II (1993–94), p 188.
[160]   HC Deb, 20 July 1954, cols 1285–7. And see ch 7.

rules),[161] civil servants who give evidence to select committees do so on behalf of their ministers and under their directions.[162] One problem which has arisen is whether select committees can summon named individuals, a matter which has given rise to some controversy and which is not yet adequately resolved. During the Westland affair in 1985–86, the Defence Committee wished to examine five named officials, three from the Department of Trade and Industry and two from the Prime Minister's Office. The government took the view, however, that because these officials had participated in an internal departmental inquiry, it would be neither fair nor reasonable to expect them to submit to a second round of detailed questioning. The Defence Committee nevertheless asserted that 'its power to secure the attendance of an individual *named* civil servant is unqualified'[163] and that it was unacceptable for the government to prevent these officials from attending, a power which the same committee re-asserted in 1994.[164] Although such instances are rare, Westland is not unique: in 1992 the Ministry of Defence frustrated efforts by the Trade and Industry Committee's inquiry into arms to Iraq which had wished to take evidence from recently retired officials.[165] In a decision which was subsequently criticised by Sir Richard Scott, the Ministry refused to help contact the officials in question on the ground that 'retired officials are not normally given access to departmental papers'.[166] Sir Richard in fact proposed that in the interests of full and effective accountability select committees should not be hindered by the government in summoning named officials to appear before them, as did the Public Service Committee in 1996 which proposed that 'there should be a presumption that Ministers accept requests by Committees that named individual civil servants give evidence to them'.[167] The government has agreed that 'where a Select Committee has indicated that it wishes to hear evidence from named civil servants, Ministers should normally accept such a request', though not without important qualifications 'fundamental to the role of the Select Committees'.[168]

2 Civil servants and executive agencies. A second problem relating to the delegation of responsibilities concerns the Next Steps agencies and the responsibility of ministers for their activities, which it is claimed has given rise to an 'accountability gap' whereby ministers have distanced themselves from the

---

[161] Office of Public Service, *Departmental Evidence and Response to Select Committees* (1997).
[162] But see HC Deb, 19 March 1997, cols 1046–7, and HL Deb, 20 March 1997, col 1057. See ch 7.
[163] Westland plc: The Government's Decision-Making (HC 519 (1985–86)).
[164] HC 27–I (1993–94). But this was contested by the government which pointed out that it was ministers who were ultimately accountable to Parliament 'for the whole range of a department's business', even though this did not mean that 'Ministers must be expected to be personally responsible, in the sense of being creditworthy or blameworthy, for every act of their department' (Cm 2627, 1994, p 28).
[165] HC 86 (1991–92).
[166] HC 115 (1995–96), para F4.64.
[167] HC 313–I (1995–96), para 83.
[168] HC 67 (1996–97), p x. The Osmotherly rules have been amended accordingly. The government continues to be cautious about evidence by retired officials who 'cannot be said to represent the Minister and hence contribute directly to his accountability to the House'.

traditional full accountability for their departments.[169] These difficulties were brought sharply into focus following difficulties in the Prison Service which led to the dismissal in October 1995 of its chief executive, Mr Derek Lewis, by the Home Secretary, Mr Michael Howard. This followed the report of a review of security procedures in prisons by General Sir John Learmont, conducted after the escape of three prisoners from Parkhurst jail on the Isle of Wight. The report made a number of criticisms of Parkhurst and its security, but also claimed that some of the problems could be 'traced along the lines of communication to Prison Service headquarters'.[170] In the words of the Home Secretary, Learmont did not find that 'any policy decision of [his], directly or indirectly, caused the escape'.[171] Mr Lewis was dismissed, though not without complaining of ministerial interference in operational matters, and not without a substantial settlement being made in his favour for the premature termination of his appointment.[172] In the controversy which followed the dismissal of Mr Lewis, the Home Secretary declined to accept responsibility for the agency failures. In his view there was a distinction between policy and operations, a distinction said to be 'reflected in the framework document that established the Prison Service as an Executive Agency'.

The Director General of the Service 'is responsible for the day-to-day management of the Prison Service', and 'accountable directly to [the Home Secretary] for the Prison Service's performance and operations'. Although 'the Home Secretary will not normally become involved in the day-to-day management of the Prison Service, he will expect to be consulted on the handling of operational matters that could give rise to public or parliamentary concern'.[173] Although it is clear that a minister cannot be personally responsible for everything that goes on in the department, or within an agency, this distinction drawn by the Home Secretary has not been universally accepted, being described as a 'constitutional fiction' and on another occasion as meaning that 'the Home Secretary is not responsible for anything at all'. More seriously, it means that it is difficult to ensure effective parliamentary scrutiny for operational matters, particularly in light of the government's rejection of the Treasury and Civil Service Select Committee's proposal for greater direct and personal accountability of Agency chief executives to select committees, for example for matters relating to annual performance agreements.[174] In 1996, the Public Accounts Committee reported that while the government had been 'sympathetic to the aim of achieving greater clarity in the respective responsibilities of Minister and Chief Executive', at the same time 'it has been reluctant to surrender any rights over the agencies'.[175] The committee raised the interesting suggestion that in appropriate cases agencies should be converted into statutory bodies, an initiative which (depending on the content of the legislation) would make the obligations of the minister and chief executive more transparent while giving

---

[169]   HC 27–II (1993–94), p 189.
[170]   HC Deb, 16 October 1995, col 31.
[171]   Ibid.
[172]   *The Times*, 17 October 1995.
[173]   HC Deb, 19 October 1995, col 519.
[174]   For the government's position, see Cm 2748, 1995, p 31.
[175]   HC 313–I (1995–96), para 95.

more scope for operational autonomy and accountability to Parliament of the latter. The committee also raised the question of whether legislation is necessary for this purpose or whether it could be achieved by a 'contractual relationship' or more precise drafting of the framework agreements of the respective agencies.[176]

Anonymity of civil servants

Civil servants take part in a process of institutional decision-making in which, while their names may be known to the citizens primarily affected, they may not be identified with the policies or decisions which emerge. Indeed, the civil servant's anonymity is typically the corollary of ministerial responsibility. The Fulton committee found that the administrative process was surrounded by too much secrecy, criticising the convention that only ministers should explain departmental policies in public; the committee predicted that the traditional anonymity of civil servants would increasingly be eroded by the pressures of press and broadcasting.[177] In fact, while most departments employ press and public relations officers with responsibilities for the presentation of government policy, the major burden of defending publicly departmental policies and decisions is still borne by ministers. At public inquiries, for example into motorway proposals, civil servants may be required to give evidence about departmental policy but they may not be asked questions directly relating to the merits of government policy.[178] Senior civil servants frequently attend before parliamentary committees to give evidence about the work of their departments, but they may not be asked for their individual views on governmental policies.[179] Indeed under the Osmotherly rules it is expressly stated that officials who give evidence to select committees do so on behalf of their ministers and under their directions.[180]

The desirability of maintaining confidential relationships between ministers and civil servants has often been stressed, not least by the representatives of the officials themselves, who are sometimes placed in the invidious position of being identified by government or others without having a real opportunity to give a robust account of themselves and rebutting criticism.[181] It is unquestionably the case, however, that the veil of official anonymity is slowly being lifted, and is likely to be removed when a major inquiry is held into a piece of administration which has run into political criticism, as in the inquiries relating to Crichel Down and the Vehicle and General Insurance Company.[182] In these exceptional situations, it is right that the individual responsibility of officials should be made known but not without adequate procedural safeguards for the officials in question. The veil of official anonymity is likely also to be pierced when a civil servant is involved in ministerial conduct which may not be constitutionally proper. When in early 1986 parts of a confidential letter from the Solicitor-General to the Secretary

---

[176] Ibid, para 122. For the government's response, see HC 67 (1996–97).
[177] Cmnd 3638, pp 93–4.
[178] Ch 28 B.
[179] See HC 588–1 (1977–78), app D.
[180] Office of Public Service, *Departmental Evidence and Response to Select Committees* (1997), para 37.
[181] See Hennessy, *Whitehall*, p 306.
[182] Ch 7 above.

of State for Defence (Mr Michael Heseltine) were leaked by an official of the Department of Trade and Industry (acting under ministerial authority), her identity was soon revealed. The official in question had doubts about the propriety of her instructions but was unable to speak to the permanent head of her department.

There are, however, other ways by which the principle of civil service anonymity is being seriously eroded, not the least of these being the creation of the Next Steps agencies under the management of a named chief executive. Indeed, it has been suggested that the increased transparency in the relationship between ministers and agencies 'has done more than anything to reduce the coherence of the convention of Ministerial responsibility'.[183] The case of Mr Lewis referred to above highlights the real possibility of agency chief executives being identified and left to shoulder responsibility for operational lapses, a matter of some concern in view of the uncertainty of the demarcation boundaries between minister and agency. There is another sense too in which the practice of anonymity is breaking down, arising as a result of the greater degree of openness in government (reflected for example in the publication of the telephone numbers of civil servants[184]) and particularly as a result of the Citizen's Charter.[185] This provides, for example, that 'public servants should not be anonymous', and that 'save only where there is a real threat to their safety, all those who deal directly with the public should wear name badges and give their name on the telephone and in letters'.[186] It does not follow from this, however, that civil service anonymity has been fatally undermined or that it does not continue to play an important constitutional role. What these developments reveal is that while the principle has a role to play in the context of official advice to ministers, it is less easily justifiable in terms of operational failings or in terms of the delivery of services to the public. A balance has to be struck between the need for robust and uninhibited advice on the one hand and accountability on the other. It is far from clear whether that balance has tilted far enough in favour of accountability, particularly by those who occupy senior positions.

Financial interests of civil servants

We have seen that ministers are subject to rules enforced by the Prime Minister that are intended inter alia to ensure that they do not profit improperly from their public position.[187] Civil servants are fully subject to the criminal law, including the Prevention of Corruption Acts 1906 and 1916. Internal rules of the service provide that no civil servant may engage in any occupation which might conflict with the interests of his or her department or with his or her position as a public servant; nor must they put themselves in a position (for example, by dealing in shares or land) where their duty to the public service might conflict with their private interests. Moreover, there are strict rules about the acceptance of gifts or hospitality which might com-

---

[183]   HC 313–I (1995–96), para 89.
[184]   See *Civil Service Yearbook 1997.*
[185]   Cm 1599, 1991.
[186]   Cm 1599, 1991. See also Cm 2970, 1994, p 38.
[187]   Section C above.

promise the civil servant's judgment or integrity.[188] The integrity of the civil service is also protected by established procedures for the awarding of contracts and the disposal of surplus property, breaches of which are subject to investigation by the Comptroller and Auditor General.[189] Complaints of bias in the use of discretionary powers may be investigated by the Parliamentary Ombudsman.[190]

The public interest in integrity is not confined to what civil servants do while in post, but may extend to their actions after leaving the service. The rules that govern the taking up of private business appointments by former civil servants recognise the desirability of experienced administrators entering the private sector; but certain senior officials must obtain government approval if within two years of leaving the service they wish to accept employment with a public or private company or in the service of a foreign government. Permission must also be sought by less senior officials, depending on the nature of the employment proposed and in particular whether there are close relationships between the employer and the government. These rules are not statutory and may not be legally enforceable, having regard to the common law doctrine regarding contracts in restraint of trade.[191] A House of Commons committee in 1984 recommended that the rules should be tightened up, in response to senior personnel moving to the private sector from the Ministry of Defence. Among the recommendations of the Treasury and Civil Service Committee were an extension of the delay period from two to five years, and a ban on officials discussing jobs with prospective employers within the last 12 months of their service.[192] The recommendations were not accepted by the government. Further proposals for reform were made by the Defence Committee in 1988 which reported that the evidence before it relating to the Ministry of Defence did not demonstrate that the movement of Crown servants to industry was in the public interest, or that the rules ensured its propriety.[193]

Political activities of civil servants

Servants of the Crown are prohibited from parliamentary candidature and disqualified from membership of the Commons. But should civil servants be subject to additional limitations, to secure the political impartiality of the civil service as a whole? The Civil Service Management Code 'points out that from the nature of the work which a civil servant is required to do and the context in which he has to do it, there must be certain restrictions on the type of political activities in which a civil servant is allowed to participate and the extent to which he may do so will of course depend on his position and seniority'.[194] The present scheme, first brought into force in 1954,[195] recog-

---

188   *Civil Service Management Code*, para 4.1. Cf Cmd 3037, 1928.
189   Ch 17 D.
190   Ch 28 D.
191   On the contractual position of civil servants, see p 307 above.
192   HC 302 (1983–84).
193   HC 392 (1987–88). See also HC 622 (1987–88).
194   *R v Civil Service Appeal Board, ex p Bruce* [1988] 3 All ER 686, at 690 (May LJ). The arrangements are dealt with in *Civil Service Management Code*, ch 4.
195   See Cmd 7718, 1949, and Cmd 8783, 1953.

nises that the political neutrality of the civil service is fundamental, but that the rules need not be the same for all members of the service. The scheme was fully reviewed by the Armitage committee in 1978, in response to requests from the civil service unions for greater political freedom for civil servants. The committee re-asserted the constitutional importance of the political neutrality of the civil service. It recommended that the existing scheme should continue subject to substantial changes in its operation, the effect of which would be to reduce the number of civil servants in the 'restricted' category.[196] In 1984, these recommendations were adopted after extensive discussion between government and the civil service unions.[197]

Three categories exist. Participation in national political activities (for example, holding office in a political party; expressing public views on matters of national political controversy) is barred to the senior administrative grades and to those in executive or clerical grades whose work is associated with giving advice to ministers or who administer services directly to the public (for example, staff in social security offices); this 'restricted' category may with permission take part in local political activities (for example, candidature for local authorities) but must act with moderation and discretion, particularly in matters affecting their own departments. A second 'intermediate' category may with leave of their departments take part in all political activities, both local and national, except parliamentary candidature, subject to observing a code of discretion (for example, they may discuss national policies but should avoid personal attacks on ministers and should avoid causing embarrassment to their departments). The third 'politically free' category combines industrial staff and the non-industrial staff in minor and manipulative grades: they are free to engage in all political activities, national and local, except when on duty or on official premises or while wearing uniform. But like all civil servants they are subject to the rules of the Official Secrets Acts on unauthorised disclosure of information gained from official sources.[198]

The restrictions on political activity, especially in the first category, are severe. It has been argued that the restrictions on the intermediate category are still too wide. Apart from staff who (for instance) provide policy assistance to ministers or who regularly speak for the government, permission to participate in political activities may also be denied to people in this intermediate group where their 'official duties involve a significant amount of face-to-face contact with members of the public, and who make decisions affecting them, and whose political activities are likely to be known to those members of the public'.[199] However, there is a right of appeal to the Civil Service Appeal Board against a refusal to permit an official to participate in political activities. The procedure for such appeals 'is very much the same as the procedure adopted by the board on an appeal by a civil servant subject to a notice of dismissal'.[200] It has been estimated that about 20% of staff are in the politically restricted group, 50% are in the intermediate group, and 30%

---

[196] Cmnd 7057, 1978.
[197] HC Deb, 26 March 1981, col 1186; 4 March 1982, col 503; 19 July 1984, col 272 (WA).
[198] Ch 24.
[199] See Fredman and Morris, *The State as Employer*, p 218.
[200] *R v Civil Service Appeal Board, ex p Bruce* [1988] 3 All ER 686, at 690.

are in the politically free group.[201] Apart from personal involvement in political activities, civil servants may wish to participate in political action through their trade unions. Several civil service unions have established political funds under what is now the Trade Union and Labour Relations (Consolidation) Act 1992 to enable them more effectively to represent their members.[202] None is affiliated to any political party (though there are no legal restrictions on such affiliation), but several are affiliated to the TUC.

E. Open Government

Discussion of the new structure of the civil service leads directly to a consideration of the question of open government and the public right of access to official information. There is currently no such right in this country, in contrast to other parliamentary democracies based on the Westminster system of government. Not only is there no right; public officials may be under a duty not to disclose such information. The Official Secrets Act 1911, s 2, made it an offence for any servant of the Crown to communicate any official information, unless authorised to do so, breach of this measure being a criminal offence punishable by imprisonment. Although s 2 was repealed by the Official Secrets Act 1989, it cast a long shadow over the field for much of the 20th century, though it is true that it did not prevent the official release of a great deal of information. The repeal of s 2 did not remove the criminal law altogether, the 1989 Act retaining the criminal law, albeit for the protection of a narrower range of information. This relates, for example, to information dealing with intelligence, defence, foreign affairs, and so on. It is also the case that unauthorised disclosure of information by civil servants (or others) could fall foul of the equitable doctrine of breach of confidence, which in turn could lead to an injunction being obtained to restrain the publication of any such information unless it could be shown by the defence to be in the public interest. These are matters to which we return in chapter 24.

The pressure for reform

The process of facilitating access to information has been long and painful. In 1979, a green paper on 'Open Government' was published by the then Labour government in which it was claimed that 'openness of government' had a number of objectives: 'to secure more information to assist debate on national issues; to explain government decisions affecting groups of citizens; to assist interest groups in urging particular priorities within an area of policy; or to amplify the grounds on which decisions affecting individuals have been taken'. It was accepted that new measures were necessary 'to give further impetus to the process of making government more open', but that any such scheme 'should satisfy public demand so far as is reasonable and practicable; that it should be fully compatible with the constitutional and parliamentary

---

[201] Fredman and Morris, op cit, pp 217–18.
[202] Ch 9 B above.

systems of this country; and that the costs should be commensurate with the public benefit'. To this end it was proposed that a code of practice on access to official information would be 'a major step forward', with access to be given to official documents and information other than in fields which were specifically exempted from the operation of the code.[203] But these limited proposals for a non-statutory scheme were published shortly before the general election in 1979 and were not developed by the incoming administration, which also abandoned plans announced in the Queen's Speech in 1979 to reform s 2 of the Official Secrets Act 1911.

Although campaigners for open government were thus disappointed, important initiatives in the direction of reform were nevertheless taken in the 1980s and 1990s. In the first place, a number of statutes extended the right of individuals to have access to personal information held by others. This was true, for example, of local authority records, medical records and personal files, the legislation in each case being the product of private members' Bills.[204] The government has, however, been less willing to support private members' initiatives to extend the right of access to records held by government departments or agencies, though several such bills have been introduced. Secondly, there has been a gradual easing of the secrecy surrounding central government (with the publication (for example) of *Questions of Procedure for Ministers*), though it would be a mistake to exaggerate the extent to which this is taking place. On the other hand, various pressures in the 1990s have helped to promote a greater degree of openness in government. Among the most significant developments is the Citizen's Charter, which provides that every citizen is entitled to expect openness, and states unequivocally that there should be no secrecy about how public services are run, how much they cost, who is in charge, and whether or not they are meeting their standards.[205] But even more important is the white paper, *Open Government*, published in July 1993, proposing again that there would be introduced a Code of Practice on access to information held by central government and public bodies. It was also proposed that there would be 'a new and more comprehensive statutory right of access, by the subject, to personal records held by government and by other public sector authorities'. The former proposal was a recognition that 'open government is part of an effective democracy', while the latter was a response to the EC Data Protection Directive which requires more detailed regulation of the right of access to personal data than is provided by the Data Protection Act 1984.[206]

The Code of Practice

The Code of Practice on access to government information came into force in April 1994, with an amended second edition being issued in 1997. It is expressly stated that the code reinforces the government's policy under the

---

[203]   Cmnd 7520, 1979.
[204]   Access to Personal Files Act 1987; Access to Medical Reports Act 1988; and Access to Health Records Act 1990.
[205]   Cm 1599, 1991.
[206]   Cm 2290, 1993.

Citizen's Charter of extending access to official information, and responding to reasonable requests for information. As such its aims are threefold: first, 'to improve policy-making and the democratic process by extending access to the facts and analyses which provide the basis for the consideration of proposed policy'; secondly, 'to protect the interests of individuals and companies by ensuring that reasons are given for administrative decisions, except where there is statutory authority or established convention to the contrary'; and thirdly, 'to support and extend the principles of public service established under the Citizen's Charter'. These aims are balanced against the need to protect privacy and the confidentiality of personal and commercial information on the one hand, and to protect confidentiality where disclosure would not be in the public interest on the other. The code applies to all government departments and public bodies falling under the jurisdiction of the Ombudsman, which are required to give facts and analysis with major policy decisions; open up internal guidelines about departmental dealings with the public; give reasons for administrative decisions to those affected; provide information about public services (in terms of cost, performance, complaints and redress); and provide information in response to specific requests on policies, actions and decisions.

Although this was a welcome initiative, there are a number of features which in the eyes of some serve seriously to undermine the impact of the code. First and most obviously, it does not confer any legal right to information, though it does provide a complaint machinery by way of the Ombudsman, a creature of statute who has some legal powers. Complaints that information has not been provided or that unreasonable charges have been imposed, can be directed to the Ombudsman through a member of Parliament. Secondly, even in those areas to which the code applies, there is a right to information rather than a right of access to documents.[207] Moreover, a department is not required 'to acquire information they do not possess, to provide information which is already published, to provide material which the Government did not consider to be reliable information, or to provide information which is provided as part of an existing charged service' (for example, by the Stationery Office). Thirdly and most importantly, large categories of information are excluded from the commitment to disclose found in the code. There are 14 such categories, which include information relating to defence, security and international relations (where disclosure would be harmful); information the disclosure of which would 'harm the frankness and candour of internal discussion', including Cabinet proceedings, internal advice and confidential communications between departments; and information which if disclosed would prejudice the administration of justice. The exclusions also apply to information which if disclosed would harm the ability of the government to manage the economy; undermine effective management and operations of the public service; and personnel records and other confidential information relating to public appointments. More generally there are restrictions on disclosure which could constitute an

---

[207] Access to documents was recommended by the PCA Select Committee (HC 84 (1995–96), para 83) and by the Public Service Committee (HC 313–I (1995–96), para 160) but rejected by the government (HC 67 (1996–97)).

unwarranted invasion of privacy, as well as confidential information of different kinds.[208]

The role of the Ombudsman

The extension of the jurisdiction of the Ombudsman to deal with complaints about access to information was made without legislation to amend the Parliamentary Commissioner Act 1967, which simply authorises complaints to deal with claims by members of the public (filtered through MPs) that they 'have sustained injustice in consequence of maladministration'.[209] It was also made without extending or amending the powers of the Ombudsman, who is not authorised, for example, to require any person to furnish any information or answer any question relating to Cabinet proceedings or the proceedings of Cabinet committees. Under the code there is no absolute exclusion of such information, though admittedly in practice it is likely to be so excluded by virtue of the operation of the harm test (that is to say, disclosure would 'harm the frankness and candour of internal discussion'). Such information may of course be released by means otherwise than 'by virtue of' the 1967 Act. But this does reveal the rather unsatisfactory position, at least formally, of the absence of any legal underpinning of the Ombudsman's jurisdiction in this area. The mischief is compounded by the fact that there are several departments and agencies in respect of which the Ombudsman has no jurisdiction but which can reasonably be expected to be covered by any open government initiative.[210] In 1997, however, the government announced that it proposed to extend the Ombudman's jurisdiction to cover executive non-departmental public bodies not already in his remit,[211] the Nolan committee having already recommended that these bodies should develop their own codes of openness based on the government code.[212]

In 1995, the Ombudsman received only 44 complaints about alleged breaches of the Code of Practice. This compared with the 28 complaints received in the nine months from April 1994 when the code came into force. Although the Commissioner has been 'encouraged to see signs of a change in the attitude to the release of information' (especially with regard to the Treasury, the Inland Revenue and Social Security), he was also satisfied that the 'low level of complaints to [him] cannot be taken to show that there is a high level of satisfaction with regard to requests for the release of information'. This was simply 'a consequence of the fact that relatively few requests to departments are being made', while concern was also expressed about 'an unawareness' in some departments 'of the implications of the existence of the Code and an impermeability to its influence'. The Ombudsman has found

---

[208] The code was, however, amended (following a recommendation of the Public Service Committee in 1996 (HC 313–I (1995–96)) to make it clear that where information may be withheld on the ground of harm or prejudice, 'the presumption remains that information should be disclosed unless the harm likely to arise from disclosure would outweigh the public interest in making the information available' (HC 67 (1996–97)).

[209] See Ch 28 D.

[210] Separate codes have been introduced for the NHS and proposals have been made for a similar measure in local government.

[211] Cm 3557, 1997.

[212] Cm 2850–I, 1995. On NDPBs, see ch 14 below.

that knowledge of the Code's obligations can fall off 'quite rapidly as one moves away from those officials who have specific responsibilities in connection with information release'. There was also 'a tendency in some departments to use every argument that can be mounted, whether legally-based, Code-based or at times simply obstructive, to help justify a past decision that a particular document or piece of information should not be released instead of reappraising the matter in the light of the Code with an open mind'.[213] The practice of the Ombudsman is to publish details of each investigation when it is completed. The reports reveal that some of the most difficult cases relate to the operation of the exemptions, several of which feature relatively frequently as grounds for refusing a request.[214]

---

[213]   Cm 296, 1995–96.
[214]   For an account of some of the cases, see HC 606, 758 (1994–95), and HC 86 (1995–96).

CHAPTER 14

Public corporations, non-governmental agencies and advisory bodies

We have already considered the constitutional position of government departments, and have seen that they are staffed by civil servants and headed by ministers who are responsible to Parliament for their activities. When functions are entrusted to local authorities, the administrative structure is very different from that in central government, and political responsibility for the policies and decisions of local councils is borne by the elected councillors. Today many public tasks are entrusted not to central or local government, but to a wide variety of official boards, commissions and other agencies. Some are well known, such as the BBC, the Commission for Racial Equality and ACAS. Many of them operate in obscurity, known only to a few civil servants and specialists in the area concerned. It is difficult to generalise about such diversity, but these bodies have one feature in common, namely that the members of the boards and agencies are not publicly elected. Instead, these members have all been appointed to their posts, in the vast majority of cases by central government (that is, by the minister of the department concerned with the activity in question). Thus, while ministers do not directly administer the affairs of these bodies, ministers have an underlying but indirect responsibility to Parliament for their efficiency and effectiveness. Many of these bodies were created by legislation and many are wholly or mainly supported by public funds. If one of these bodies antagonises public opinion, overspends the funds available to it, is badly administered or has outlived its usefulness, then the minister can be asked in Parliament to introduce legislation abolishing the body or reforming its powers, to appoint a new governing body, or to take other steps for improving the position.[1] Moreover, because of the economic, financial and social significance of some agencies, strategic decisions concerning their activities are inevitably affected by government policies.

During the 1970s, the increasing scale and costs of government helped to bring these appointed bodies into public debate and controversy. Some critics objected to the fact that their functions were being undertaken by the

---

[1] For an outstanding example, see the ill-fated Crown Agents, whose affairs led to the Fay committee of inquiry (HC 48 (1977–78)), a judicial tribunal of inquiry (HC 364 (1981–82)), and the Crown Agents Act 1979; and see G Ganz [1980] PL 454.

state at all; others to their undemocratic nature and to the amount of patronage that ministers exercised in making appointments to them; and others to the lack of adequate accountability for their activities.[2] One problem was to find a generic name for such diverse bodies. Within government they were described by such terms as 'fringe bodies' and 'non-departmental public bodies' (NDPBs). One unofficial term applied to them was 'quangos', that originally stood for 'quasi non-governmental organisations',[3] though to confuse matters still more, it was used by the Nolan Committee on Standards in Public Life to refer to the narrower group of NDPBs.[4] After its election in 1979, the Conservative government's programme of cutting back the size and activities of the state included the pruning of quangos. A detailed survey by Sir Leo Pliatzky did much to clarify the various purposes served by many non-departmental public bodies and laid down principles to be observed in their creation and supervision.[5] Mainly because there is no single agreed definition of the bodies concerned, it is not possible to state accurately how many exist. According to one official but incomplete list,[6] there were in 1996 1,194 non-departmental public bodies. These were of three kinds: executive bodies, which normally employ staff and have their own budgets; advisory bodies, set up by the minister to advise on a particular area or issue; and tribunals, including licensing and appeal bodies. The figure of 1,194 (which compares with 2,167 in 1979) does not include other important public bodies such as the surviving nationalised industries, the utility regulators, national health service bodies or agencies set up under the 'Next Steps' Initiative. Other estimates suggest that there may be as many as 5,500 extra-governmental bodies of an executive nature.

A. Origins and purpose

History

The creation of specialised public agencies which are not government departments is not new. In the 18th century, there were innumerable bodies of commissioners created by private Acts, which exercised limited powers for such purposes as police, paving, lighting, turnpikes and local improvements. Through the curtailment of the powers of the Privy Council in the previous century, they were free from administrative control by central government, but in England they were subject to legal control by means of the prerogative writs issued by the Court of King's Bench. These bodies were essentially local in character.

In the period of social and administrative reform which followed the reform of Parliament in 1832, experiments were made in setting up national agencies with powers covering the whole country. One of the most notable experiments

---

2   See Cm 2850–I, 1995.
3   See Hague, Mackenzie and Barker (eds), *Public Policy and Private Interests*; and Barker (ed), *Quangos in Britain*.
4   Cm 2850–I, 1995, p 65. See also eg Holland, *The Governance of Quangos*, and G Drewry [1982] PL 384.
5   Cmnd 7797, 1980.
6   *Public Bodies* (Stationery Office, 1996).

occurred in 1834 when the English poor law was reformed. The Poor Law Commissioners enforced strict central control on the local administration of poor relief, by means of rules, orders and inspection. Yet no minister answered for the commissioners in Parliament, to defend them against political attack or to control their decisions. In 1847, the experiment gave way to a system based on a minister responsible to Parliament but similar experiments occurred, such as the General Board of Health in 1848. Administration by the board system was much used in Scotland and in Ireland. By the late 19th century, it was accepted that the vesting of public powers in departments of central government had the great constitutional advantage of securing political control through ministerial responsibility.[7] As Chester remarked, the House of Commons has never found a way of making anybody other than ministers accountable to it.[8]

In the 20th century, the state acquired vast new social and economic powers. Particularly as a result of the nationalisation programme followed by the Labour government from 1945 to 1951, the United Kingdom became a mixed economy, in which privately owned and publicly owned industrial enterprises co-existed. Moreover, extensive schemes of social regulation and welfare have been and continue to be accepted by all political parties, though there is now perhaps sharper disagreement about the nature and scope of these schemes. These developments not only meant an increase in the tasks entrusted to government departments. There was also a widespread creation of public boards and other agencies that are classifiable neither as government departments, nor as local authorities. Reacting to these trends, the Conservative government after 1979 sought both to abolish unnecessary public agencies and through privatisation to return profitable public undertakings to private ownership, either wholly or in part. By 1997, major and possibly irreversible changes in the boundary between the public and private sectors had occurred. Indeed, quite apart from any other consideration, because of the costs involved it is likely that future concerns will be confined to questions of regulation rather than the public ownership of the industries in question. It has been suggested that because of the policy of privatisation pursued by Conservative governments since 1979 (on which see below) Britain is no longer a mixed economy.[9] But there is still a considerable amount of regulation of social and economic affairs by the state, and indeed new agencies continue to be created.

Reasons for the creation of public corporations and non-governmental bodies[10]

In theory, the tasks entrusted to public boards and agencies could be undertaken directly by civil servants working in government departments, although this would mean a vast increase in the civil service and the adoption by it of new methods. Indeed, before the Post Office was established in 1969 as a public corporation, postal and telephone services had been for very many years

---

[7]   See also ch 7 and, for rise and fall of the board system, F M G Willson (1955) 33 Public Administration 43 and Parris, *Constitutional Bureaucracy*, ch 3.

[8]   D N Chester (1979) 57 Public Administration 51, 54.

[9]   D Marsh (1991) 69 Public Administration 459.

[10] The extensive literature includes: Chester, *The Nationalisation of British Industry 1945–51*; Robson, *Nationalised Industries and Public Ownership*; Friedmann and Garner (eds), *Government Enterprise*; Prosser, *Nationalised Industries and Public Control*.

provided by the Post Office as a government department.[11] But the existence of public corporations affords strong evidence for the view that departmental administration of major industries is likely to be less efficient and less flexible than management by a public board. The post-war nationalisation legislation sought to apply the concept of the public corporation associated with the late Herbert Morrison.[12] This aimed at a combination of vigorous and efficient business management with an appropriate measure of public control and accountability. Civil service methods, Treasury control, and complete accountability to Parliament were considered unsuited to the successful running of a large industry. In the 1945–51 period, when major public utilities, transport and energy undertakings were acquired by the state, they were entrusted not to departments but to new statutory boards. The relevant ministers were given important powers relating to the boards but were not expected to become concerned with day-to-day management of the industries. Similar reasoning led to the creation of public corporations to take over certain activities formerly performed by departments, for example the Atomic Energy Authority (1954) and the British Airports Authority (1965).

Another reason for establishing public corporations is to entrust an activity to an autonomous body and thereby reduce the scope for direct political control. The existence of the BBC and the Independent Television Commission separate from the government is necessary if ministers are not to be responsible for every programme broadcast. The same reason explains why many grant-giving bodies have been established to distribute funds provided by Parliament. The government is responsible for the total grants made to such bodies as the research councils, the arts councils and the Higher Education Funding Councils, but not for the detailed allocation of these funds. The aim of enabling discretionary decisions to be made by an agency without regard to short-term political considerations explains also the existence of the Commission for Racial Equality and the Equal Opportunities Commission, which enforce social legislation designed to reduce discrimination. However, ministers may not absolve themselves of broad responsibility for the existence, activities, funding and composition of such agencies. Nor have all attempts to take a sensitive area of administration 'out of politics' by entrusting it to an appointed board been successful.[13]

Privatisation[14]

After 1979 successive Conservative governments operated a policy of privatisation of public corporations, whereby the ownership of many state-controlled

---

[11] The Post Office remains as one of the few surviving public corporations. See Cm 2614, 1994.

[12] See his book, *Government and Parliament*, ch 12.

[13] As with financial relief for the unemployed in 1934: see Millett, *The Unemployment Assistance Board*.

[14] The growing literature on privatisation and public law includes Baldwin, *Regulation in Question*; Bishop, Kay and Mayer, *Privatisation and Economic Performance*, and *The Regulatory Challenge*; C Graham and T Prosser (1987) 50 MLR 16 and [1988] PL 413; D Marsh (1991) 69 Public Administration 459; T Prosser (1990) 53 MLR 304; T Prosser, 'Regulation, Markets and Legitimacy', in Jowell and Oliver (eds), *The Changing Constitution*, ch 9. For a valuable study of the social impact of utility privatisation, see Ernst, *Whose Utility?*

enterprises was returned to the private sector. There were a number of aims of this policy, not all of which were mutually consistent. They included a desire to reduce government involvement in industry, improve efficiency and competition in the supply of goods and services, reduce the Public Sector Borrowing Requirement by the revenue raised from asset sales, curb the power and influence of public sector trade unions, and widen share ownership, particularly amongst employees. But whatever the reasons, it has been said not only that the scale of privatisation has been 'immense' but also that the 'balance between the public sector and the private sector has been significantly changed and this appears to be a lasting legacy of the Thatcherite era'.[15] The programme between 1979 and 1997 took several forms, including the denationalisation of state corporations such as British Gas, British Telecom, British Airways, British Coal and British Rail;[16] the disposal of shares in companies previously owned by the government (such as Jaguar, Rolls-Royce, Amersham International, British Nuclear Fuels Ltd, and Cable and Wireless);[17] and the sale of government holdings in companies such as British Petroleum.[18] Two controversial privatisations, for different reasons, were of the water supply industry in England and Wales and the Trustee Savings Bank,[19] while two highly symbolic privatisations were those of the coal industry and the railways, both of which had been nationalised by the post-war Labour government.

But although public ownership retreated in this period, it would be premature to see this as the end of the public body, as that term is used generically in this chapter. New public bodies have been created to regulate the privatised utilities. Under the Gas Act 1986, for example, the Secretary of State must appoint a Director General of Gas Supply and a Gas Consumers Council, both of which are under a duty to supervise the performance by gas suppliers of their obligations under the Act.[20] Similar bodies have been created by the legislation privatising telecommunications, electricity and water.[21] Regulatory agencies have also been established in a number of other fields, sometimes to administer newly created statutory rights and sometimes to replace an existing agency. Examples include in broadcasting the Independent Television Commission, the Broadcasting Standards Commission, and the Radio Authority; in respect of the police and the security service, the Police Complaints Authority, the Interception Commissioner, the Security

---

[15] See D Marsh (1991) 69 Public Administration 459.
[16] See Gas Act 1986, Civil Aviation Act 1980, Telecommunications Act 1984, Railways Act 1993 and Coal Industry Act 1994. Other major privatisations included water (Water Act 1989) and electricity (Electricity Act 1989).
[17] See Atomic Energy (Miscellaneous Provisions) Act 1981 (Amersham, BNFL); British Telecommunications Act 1981, s 79 (Cable and Wireless). See now Atomic Energy Authority Act 1995. For the developments in the motor industry, see A A McLaughlin and W A Maloney (1996) 74 Public Administration 435.
[18] On this form of state intervention (the mixed enterprise), see pp 309–10 of the 10th edn of this book.
[19] See *Ross v Lord Advocate* [1986] 1 WLR 1077; and M Percival (1987) 50 MLR 231.
[20] For details of regulation of the gas industry, see below.
[21] See pp 339–340 and section D below.

Service Commissioner and the Intelligence Services Commissioner; and in legal services and the administration of justice, the Lord Chancellor's Advisory Committee on Legal Education and Conduct, the Legal Services Ombudsman, and the Authorised Conveyancing Practitioners' Board.[22] Other important public bodies created in the 1980s and 1990s include the Audit Commission, the Commissioner for the Rights of Trade Union Members, the Higher Education Funding Councils, the University Commissioners (charged with the duty of removing academic tenure), the Human Fertilisation and Embryology Authority, and the Occupational Pensions Regulatory Authority.[23] The Financial Services Act 1986 authorises the Secretary of State to transfer his regulatory functions (with parliamentary authority) to the Securities and Investments Board, 'a private company rather than a government agency',[24] though referred to judicially as a 'public authority'.[25] A number of self-regulatory bodies have also been created under government pressure or with government encouragement. These include the Press Complaints Commission and the City Panel on Take-Overs and Mergers, the latter being used by the government as the 'centrepiece' of its policy of regulation in the field.[26]

B.   The classification, status and composition of public bodies

Classification

The wide range of activities exercised by public bodies and the fact that they have nearly all been created under different Acts of Parliament make it difficult to classify them. One possible approach, that adopted by the government, is helpful, though not without its limitations.[27] According to the government's classification, there are four groups of public bodies.

1 The nationalised industries and similar commercial organisations, of which there are now very few. In 1996, the government identified 14 such bodies: British Waterways Board, Scottish Transport Group, Highlands and Islands Airports, Caledonian MacBrayne, British Shipbuilders, British Coal, British Nuclear Fuels, Magnox Electric, Post Office, British Railways Board, Civil Aviation Authority, London Regional Transport, Railtrack, European Passenger Services, and Union Railways.

2 Certain public corporations, which are subject to 'separate and specific arrangements of accountability and financial control'. There were 12 such bodies listed in 1996, these including the Covent Garden Market Authority at one end of the scale and the Bank of England at the other. Most of the other bodies in this group were those operating in the broadcasting sphere, and

---

[22]   See Broadcasting Act 1990, Police and Criminal Evidence Act 1984, Interception of Communications Act 1985, Security Service Act 1989, Courts and Legal Services Act 1990, Intelligence Services Act 1994, and Broadcasting Act 1996.

[23]   See National Audit Act 1983, Employment Act 1988 (now Trade Union and Labour Relations (Consolidation) Act 1992), Further and Higher Education Act 1992, Education Reform Act 1988, Human Fertilisation and Embryology Act 1990, and Pensions Act 1995.

[24]   Rider, Abrams and Ferran, *Guide to the Financial Services Act 1986*, para 304.

[25]   *Securities and Investment Board v FIMBRA* [1991] 4 All ER 398, at p 402.

[26]   *R v Panel on Take-Overs and Mergers, ex p Datafin* [1987] 2 QB 815, at p 838.

[27]   See *Public Bodies* (1996).

included the BBC (incorporated under Royal Charter and operating under a licence from the government), Channel Four Television Corporation, the Independent Television Commission, and the Radio Authority (the last three being established under the Broadcasting Act 1990).[28]

3 National Health Service bodies, including health authorities, special health authorities, and NHS trusts, of which there were 429 alone in April 1996.[29] These bodies are all established under the authority of the National Health Service Act 1977[30] and the National Health Service and Community Care Act 1990. Other NHS authorities include the National Blood Authority and the Microbiological Research Authority.

4 Non-departmental public bodies, a huge classification of 1,194 bodies in April 1996 which is in turn classified to include as follows.

(*a*) Executive bodies (of which there were 309) which 'normally employ staff and have their own budget', and in some cases may have regulatory or administrative functions. Examples of such bodies include the Advisory Conciliation and Arbitration Service (ACAS), the Commission for Racial Equality (CRE), the Equal Opportunities Commission (EOC), the Countryside Commission, the Higher Education Funding Council, and the Teacher Training Agency.

(*b*) Advisory bodies (of which there were 674), 'set up by Ministers to advise them and their departments on matters within their sphere of interest'. Such bodies 'generally do not employ staff or incur expenditure on their own account'. Included in this category are the Advisory Committee on Pesticides, the Advisory Committee on NHS Drugs, the Council on Tribunals, the Law Commission, the Arts Council, the Broadcasting Standards Council and the Football Licensing Authority.

(*c*) Tribunals (of which there were 75 species) with jurisdiction in specialist fields of law, generally serviced by staff from the sponsoring department. They include both standing tribunals (with a permanent membership) and those 'covered from panels so that the actual number of tribunals sitting varies'. Examples include the Dairy Produce Quota Tribunal, rent assessment panels, the Foreign Compensation Commission, the Mental Health Review Tribunal, social security appeal tribunals, and industrial tribunals.[31]

The category of NDPBs also includes other bodies, most notably boards of visitors to penal establishments, but it excludes a large number of other bodies, including central government departments, local authorities, and the civil and criminal courts (though it does include bodies like the Interception of Communications Tribunal whose membership includes senior members of the judiciary). More controversially, however, it also excludes what are referred to as non-ministerial government departments on the one hand and the Next Step agencies on the other.[32] The former includes the utility

---

[28] Ch 22 C.
[29] Regional health authorities, district health authorities and family health service authorities were abolished by the Health Authorities Act 1995.
[30] As amended by the Health Authorities Act 1995.
[31] Ch 28 A.
[32] Ch 13.

regulators, that is to say the Directors General of Telecommunications (OFTEL), Gas Supply (OFGAS), Water Supply (OFWAT), and Electricity Supply (OFFER) respectively.[33]

Legal status

Except where statutes provide otherwise, departments of central government share in the legal status of the Crown and may benefit from certain privileges and immunities which are peculiar to the Crown.[34] But local authorities, statutory bodies set up for local commercial purposes and privately owned companies do not benefit from Crown status.[35] Into which category do other public bodies fall?

In *Tamlin v Hannaford*, it had to be decided whether, after nationalisation of the railways, a dwelling-house owned by the British Transport Commission was subject to the Rent Restriction Acts or was exempted from them by virtue of being Crown property. After examining the Transport Act 1947, the Court of Appeal rejected the view that the Commission was the servant or agent of the Crown, even though the Ministry of Transport had wide statutory powers of control over the Commission. 'In the eye of the law, the corporation is its own master and is answerable as fully as any other person or corporation. It is not the Crown and has none of the immunities or privileges of the Crown. Its servants are not civil servants and its property is not Crown property ... It is, of course, a public authority and its purposes, no doubt, are public purposes, but it is not a government department nor do its powers fall within the province of government.'[36]

It would seem that this decision governs the status of other public corporations, unless they are expressly made to act by and on behalf of the Crown or are directly placed under a minister of the Crown. In *Pfizer Corpn v Ministry of Health*, it was held that, since a hospital board was acting on behalf of the then Minister of Health, the treatment of patients in NHS hospitals was a government function and thus the use of drugs was use 'for the services of the Crown'; the Crown could therefore make use of its special rights under patent law for importing drugs.[37] By contrast, in *BBC v Johns*, the BBC were held not to be entitled to benefit from the Crown's immunity from taxation since broadcasting had not become a function of the central government.[38] It was strange that financial considerations led the BBC in this case to argue its close dependence upon the Crown and central government, whereas usually the BBC is anxious to stress its independence. The immunities of many NHS bodies were later removed by the National Health Service and Community Care Act 1990.

It is today common for the statute which creates a new public corporation to make express provision for its status. Thus the Health and Safety Commission and the Health and Safety Executive, created in 1974 to exercise

---

[33]   See below.
[34]   Ch 12 D and 31 C.
[35]   *Mersey Docks and Harbour Trustees v Gibbs* (1866) LR 1 HL 93, ch 31 A below.
[36]   [1950] 1 KB 18, 24 (Denning LJ).
[37]   [1965] AC 512. Cf *BMA v Greater Glasgow Health Board* [1989] AC 1211, and from a different point of view *Norweb plc v Dixon* [1995] 3 All ER 952.
[38]   [1965] Ch 32.

functions previously exercised by departments, are stated to perform their functions on behalf of the Crown.[39] The National Audit Act 1983 provides that the staff of the National Audit Office are not to be regarded as holding office under Her Majesty or as discharging any functions on behalf of the Crown. The Gas Act 1986 provides that the Gas Consumers' Council shall not be regarded as a servant or agent of the Crown or as enjoying any status, immunity or privilege of the Crown (though it is curiously silent on the position of the regulator). A similar form of words is used, for example, in the case of the Commissioner for the Rights of Trade Union Members, the Higher Education Funding Councils, the National Rivers Authority and the Occupational Pensions Regulatory Authority.[40] Where a public corporation does not benefit from Crown immunities, it is subject to the criminal law.[41] For the purposes of the law relating to corruption, the boards of nationalised industries are 'public bodies', since they have public duties to perform which they carry out for the benefit of the public and not for private profit.[42]

Appointments to public bodies

The total number of appointments to NDPBs alone is over 40,000, of which some 10,000 are made annually. The 1,345 executive bodies in 1994 spent £15 billion of public money, a rise of expenditure in real terms of about 75% since 1979.[42a] Not surprisingly ministerial patronage on this scale has given rise to concern, and was fully addressed by the Committee on Standards in Public Life (the Nolan committee).[43] In its first report the committee found no evidence of political bias in public appointments and rejected calls for an impartial and independent body to be given the responsibility for making appointments, recommending that 'ultimate responsibility for appointments should remain with Ministers'. But it did not follow that ministers 'should act with unfettered discretion', and it was proposed that existing procedures should be 'substantially improved' in order to ensure that they were 'sufficiently robust'. The two safeguards proposed were first 'the establishment of clear published principles governing selections for appointment' and the second was more effective external scrutiny of appointments. So far as the former is concerned, this was to include the principle of appointment in merit; the principle that 'selection on merit should take account of the need to appoint boards which include a balance of skills and backgrounds'; and that appointments should be made only after advice from a panel or committee which includes independent members who should normally account for at least a third of the membership. So far as external scrutiny is concerned, this was to be achieved principally by the appointment of a

---

[39]   Health and Safety at Work etc Act 1974, s 10(7).

[40]   See Trade Union and Labour Relations (Consolidation) Act 1992, Further and Higher Education Act 1992, Water Act 1989, and Pensions Act 1995.

[41]   For the Scarcroft case, in which the Yorkshire Electricity Board was prosecuted, see Hanson, *Parliament and Public Ownership*, p 69.

[42]   *R v Manners* [1978] AC 43.

[42a] Cm 2850–I, 1995, p. 67.

[43]   Ibid. One complaint was that public bodies were ceasing to be representative, and were increasingly dominated by businessmen. On developments in the health service, see L Ashburner and L Cairncross (1993) 71 Public Administration 357.

Commissioner for Public Appointments to 'monitor, regulate and approve departmental appointments procedures', and to draw up a Code of Practice for public appointments procedures.

These recommendations were accepted by the government. Under the Public Appointments Order in Council 1995, a Commissioner for Public Appointments was appointed in November 1995 to oversee the way public appointments are made to the non-executive departmental bodies, a term defined to include 274 NDPBs and 760 NHS bodies specifically mentioned in an annex to the Order in Council. The Commissioner's juristiction is thus limited (though extensive) in the sense that it does not apply to the public utility regulators, the nationalised industries (such as they are) or the Next Steps Agencies, though it is expected that 'other bodies' will be able to seek his advice on their procedures. Under the Order in Council, the Commissioner is under a duty 'in the manner he considers best calculated to promote economy, efficiency and effectiveness in the procedures for making public appointments, [to] exercise his functions with the object of maintaining the principle of selection on merit in relation to public appointments'. The Commissioner is also required to 'prescribe and publish a code of practice on the interpretation and application' of the principle of appointment on merit, and is expressly empowered to adopt and publish from time to time such additional guidance to appointing authorities as he thinks fit. In order to ensure that any procedures are duly followed, the Commissioner is under a duty to 'audit appointment policies and practices pursued by appointing authorities to establish whether the code of practice is being observed', and may from time to time conduct an inquiry into the policies and practices followed by any authority in relation to any appointment or description of appointment. As well as the Code of Practice, the Commissioner is required to publish an annual report (though not to Parliament), which he has said (though this is not prescribed) 'will include appropriate statistical information and details of the monitoring of departments' appointments procedures'.[44]

Although not expressly provided for, the Commissioner has also indicated that he will deal with complaints and that the complaints process will have 'two sections'. The first consists of those complaints made directly to the Commissioner, and the second of those which are made to the department responsible for the contested appointment. In the case of the former the complaint will be forwarded to the department concerned, 'requesting an investigation and report', with a requirement of further investigation if necessary. In the case of the latter, the Commissioner expects to be 'copied in on the complaint and the response'. The information gathered from complaints will 'provide valuable additional information' on the operation of the public appointment process and will be summarised in an annual report. It is unclear, however, what executive authority the Commissioner has to deal with complaints (relying exclusively on the goodwill of the departments) or what steps he can take to remedy any failure properly to comply with the Code of Practice or accompanying procedures. There is no suggestion that people

---

[44]   Public Service Committee (The Code of Practice for Public Appointments) (HC 168 (1995–96)).

appointed in breach of the procedures could be required to re-apply in a manner consistently with the Code of Practice, a requirement which in any event could give rise to legal liability on the part of the department concerned for the breach of contract. The 'sanction' it seems would lie by virtue of the fact that 'the ultimate responsibility for appointments is with the Ministers', who ultimately will be accountable (but perhaps not personally responsible) to Parliament. The Public Accounts Committee (which generally endorsed the preliminary work of the Commissioner) has reported that it expects 'departments to follow closely the provisions of the new Code of Practice and the Commissioner's guidance', and moreover that it regards itself as the 'appropriate parliamentary body' to 'examine and, where necessary, report to Parliament on the Commissioner's annual reports'.[45]

C. Public utilities: the general framework

From public to private ownership

There was and is no uniform legislative framework for the nationalised industries.[46] The structure of the British Gas Corporation is, however, typical. The corporation was established after a re-organisation of the industry by the Gas Act 1972, replacing the Gas Council established by the Gas Act 1948. It 'provided a public service, the supply of gas, to citizens of the state generally under the control of the state which could dictate its policies and retain its surplus revenue'.[47] The chairman and between ten and twenty other members of the corporation were appointed by the Secretary of State (s 1(2)), and were paid salaries and allowances determined by the Secretary of State with the consent of the Minister for the Civil Service. It was the duty of the corporation, which had a 'special monopoly power for the supply of gas',[48] to develop and maintain an efficient, coordinated and economical system of gas supply and to satisfy so far as economical to do so all reasonable demands for gas (s 2). The minister was authorised to give to the corporation such directions as he considered appropriate for securing that it was managed efficiently (s 4), and was empowered to give 'directions of a general character as to the exercise and performance by the Corporation of their functions ... in relation to matters which appear to him to affect the national interest' (s 7).[49] Certain broad financial duties were laid upon the corporation (including a duty to ensure that revenues were 'not less than sufficient' to meet outgoings) (s 14), but many of its financial powers (for example to borrow money) required the consent of the minister given with the approval of the Treasury (s 17). The corporation was required to keep proper accounts which had to be audited by a person approved by the Secretary of State, to whom a copy of the accounts

---

45   HC 168 (1995–96). The committee also expressed the view that the Commissioner's jurisdiction should be extended to cover a wider range of public appointments, and that there are wider issues concerning public appointments which need to be examined, and to which it intended to return in due course.

46   For the Post Office, see Post Office Act 1969. See also Cm 2614, 1994.

47   *Foster v British Gas plc* [1991] 2 AC 306, 316.

48   *Foster v British Gas plc*, ibid. On the monopoly, see Gas Act 1972, s 29.

49   See SI 1981, No 1459.

had to be sent (s 23). The corporation was also required to give such information to the Secretary of State about its activities as he might require, and to report annually to the minister, the report being laid before Parliament.

The difficulty in privatising nationalised industries with this structure is that the corporations had no share capital which could be sold to private investors.[50] Although privatisation has been secured by a number of different techniques,[51] the difficulty was overcome in some cases by providing that on a day appointed by the Secretary of State all the property, rights and liabilities of the corporation would be transferred to a company nominated by the minister, the company in question being limited by shares wholly owned by the Crown. The government is empowered to retain a holding in this successor company, with the proceeds of the sale of the rest being paid into the Consolidated Fund. The Secretary of State may by order dissolve the old corporation as soon as he is satisfied that its affairs have been wound up and nothing remains to be done. This technique has been used in the case of British Aerospace, the British Transport Docks Board, British Airways, British Telecom, British Gas, and the water and electricity companies.[52] Each statute is 'very much a skeleton' with little provision being made with regard to the design of the privatised company.[53] These are matters dealt with in the articles of association of the companies, which are now governed by the Companies Act 1985 in terms of their legal structure, though the public utilities in particular are subject to specific regulation of their activities on a number of grounds discussed below.[54] It is not to be assumed from this transfer to private ownership that the government has relinquished any interest in the way these businesses are conducted. 'Indeed, in an economy as complex and interdependent as that of modern Britain, it should not surprise us that no government can stand aloof from strategic industrial decisions'.[55] The removal of the companies from the public sector has thus been accompanied by a degree of statutory regulation in which, as we shall see, the Secretary of State plays an important part.

The legal structure of the privatised utility

A study by the Comptroller and Auditor General in 1996 of the four main public utilities (water, gas, electricity and telecommunications) pointed out that they are 'large and economically significant', and together served some

---

[50] For a full account of the issues raised in this paragraph, see C Graham and T Prosser (1987) 50 MLR 16.

[51] See e.g. Coal Industry Act 1994, Atomic Energy Authority Act 1995, and in the case of HMSO see HC Deb, 18 December 1995, col 1272.

[52] See British Aerospace Act 1980, Transport Act 1984, Civil Aviation Act 1980, Telecommunications Act 1984, Gas Act 1986, Water Act 1989, and Electricity Act 1989. For an earlier approach, see Iron and Steel Act 1953.

[53] C Graham and T Prosser, 'The Privatisation of State Enterprises', in Graham and Prosser (eds), *Waiving the Rules: The Constitution under Thatcherism*, p 22.

[54] Competition and Service (Utilities) Act 1992. The aim is to extend competition, strengthen the powers of the regulators where monopoly remains and provide for compensation where standards are not met (HC Deb, 18 November 1991, col 37). And see A McHarg [1992] PL 385.

[55] Graham and Prosser, op cit, p 73, at 88. See pp 341–342 below.

25 million customers, in the process employing assets with a value of some £240 billion. Their total annual turnover of £51 billion represented roughly 8% of annual GDP of the UK.[56] These considerations alone make it inevitable that they should be subject to some form of regulation, as does the fact that each of the industries contains an important element of monopoly or dominance by a small number of firms. An example of the statutory model of regulation is found in the Gas Act 1986 which provides for the appointment by the Secretary of State of a regulator (the Director General of Gas Supply) (s 1) and for the abolition of the statutory monopoly of British Gas (s 3). The Act provides that both the minister and the regulator must exercise their respective statutory functions in a manner best calculated to satisfy all reasonable demands for gas, so far as it is economical to do so (s 4). But although the statutory monopoly of British Gas was abolished, under the new regime only a person authorised by the Secretary of State in consultation with the regulator could supply gas (s 5), which means that at least initially in the case of the supply of gas to domestic consumers, the monopoly of the public corporation was transferred to a private company for which there would be no direct ministerial responsibility. A number of duties were, however, imposed on public gas suppliers by the 1986 Act, including a duty to develop and maintain an efficient, coordinated and economical system of gas supply (s 9). The legislation also required 'fair treatment between customers' and ruled out 'undue preference for or discrimination against individual customers or classes of customer'; prices were to be set by a formula in the licence, with any changes to be made by reference to the retail price index and gas costs, with the regulator having the power to fix the maximum price.[57]

Under the Gas Act 1986 licences (or authorisations as they were then called) were issued for periods of 25 years. The terms of the licence could be varied only with the consent of the licence-holder (s 23), failing which a reference could be made by the regulator to the Monopolies and Mergers Commission (MMC) to investigate and report on whether any matter relating to the supply of gas by a public gas supplier to tariff customers operated against the public interest (s 24); if the MMC reaches adverse conclusions about the public interest, the regulator is required to make the necessary modifications to the licence conditions. In 1993, a major review of the gas industry by the MMC concluded that British Gas should be required to separate its transportation and storage business from its trading business, and that the tariff formula in the licence should be modified to permit a lower price increase.[58] It is expected that the role of the regulator in the fixing of prices will become much less important with the introduction of full competition for gas supply under the Gas Act 1995,[59] the other major feature of which is the formal division of the various components of the gas industry.[60] But although the 1986 Act was overhauled to give effect to the division of the

---

[56]   HC 645 (1995–96), p 2.
[57]   HC Deb, 10 December 1985, cols 769–71. See Gas Act 1986, ss 12–14.
[58]   Cm 2315, 1993.
[59]   See Gas Act 1995, s 6, and SI 1996 No 752. For background, see OFGAS, *Extension of Domestic Competition* (1996), and for details of competition in the domestic supply of gas, see OFGAS Press Releases 25/96 and 4/97.
[60]   HC Deb, 13 March 1995, col 581.

industry and new licensing functions, the principles of the 1986 Act remained intact. Indeed a number of new statutory duties were imposed on the minister and the regulator, including 'social obligations' in respect of the chronically sick, disabled and elderly (s 1).[61] There is now a new licensing regime for public gas transporters (those who operate the pipelines through which gas is delivered to premises), the gas supplier (those who contract with customers for the supply of gas), and the gas shipper (those who arrange with the transporters for the gas to be put in the pipes). It is, however, recognised that the first of these functions is a monopoly function and as such likely to be highly regulated. A licence for the supply of gas may not be issued to a company which is the holder of a gas transporter licence.

The role of the regulator

The key to the regulatory model which has been adopted is based on the idea of 'a single independent regulator for each industry, operating without undue bureaucracy and supported by a small staff', the government rejecting regulatory systems found overseas, particularly the United States, 'in favour of a quicker and less bureaucratic system of regulation'.[62] As such the regulators are a constitutional curiosity, a body sui generis, sometimes described as a 'non-ministerial government department',[63] a phrase which contrasts with other descriptions of regulators as being 'independent of Government', albeit with 'strong powers'.[64] One question relates to the uncertainty of their legal status, for unlike most modern legislation which creates regulatory or quasi-regulatory bodies, the Gas Act 1986 (for example) makes no provision for the status of the Director General, unlike (for example) the Trade Union and Labour Relations (Consolidation) Act 1992 which provides that ACAS is a body corporate whose functions are performed on behalf of the Crown but not so as to make it subject to directions from ministers. Nor does the 1986 Act provide one way or the other whether the Director General is to be regarded as a servant or agent of the Crown or is to enjoy any status, immunity or privilege of the Crown, though as we have seen such exclusions apply in the case of the Gas Consumers' Council.[65] But quite apart from matters of legal status, the position of the regulators raises important questions about their legal powers, which constitute a curious mixture of legislative, executive and judicial functions. In the case of the gas industry, for example, the regulator has the power to make statutory instruments (with the consent of the minister) (a legislative power);[66] to issue licences, vary the terms of the licences and regulate the activities of licence-holders[67] (an executive power);

[61]   HC Deb, 13 March 1995, col 578 (Mr Heseltine).
[62]   A Carlsberg (1992) 37 New York Law School Law Rev 285.
[63]   HL Deb, 5 July 1989, col 1201 (Baroness Hooper on OFFER).
[64]   HC Deb, 18 July 1983, col 36 (Mr Cecil Parkinson on OFTEL).
[65]   Page 334 above. Compare Trade Union and Labour Relations (Consolidation) Act 1992, s 247(4) which provides that the Crown Proceedings Act 1947 applies to ACAS as if it were a government department.
[66]   See SI 1996, No 439.
[67]   E.g. by investigating selective price cuts introduced by British Gas, on the ground that this could stifle the development of competition. See OFGAS Press Release 5/97.

and to deal with complaints from consumers (a judicial power).[68] Whether such a mingling of functions would be tolerated in a constitutional regime based upon a strict separation of powers is open to question, and this may be be a more serious problem in some cases than others.[69]

Serious disputes have arisen between regulator and regulated, especially in the early days of privatisation when the regulator was faced with a monopoly supplier before the emergence of competition. This was particularly true of the relationship between OFGAS and British Gas, the relationship being variously described as 'robust' and 'acrimonious', with the first Director General writing a notable introduction to his last annual report in 1992.[70] In its evidence to the MMC review in 1993, British Gas argued for an appeals procedure against determinations by the regulator and for greater procedural safeguards, but the Commission concluded that the regulatory system in the 1986 Act was 'fundamentally sound'.[71] Nevertheless, questions have been raised by the Comptroller and Auditor General about 'the over-concentration of power in one pair of hands', leading him to consider whether there might be a case for 'possible alternatives to the current system of industry specific regulation by single regulators'.[72] The case for reform is not unconnected with a perception that the regulator is not sufficiently accountable for his or her decisions, it being argued that 'A full MMC review (in most cases) is not an appropriate step for anything other than fundamental questions of industry structure or enquiries into widespread anti-competitive conduct', and that 'a quick appeals procedure' was necessary for 'the more "run of the mill" decisions' to enable the regulator and the regulated to 'test each others' arguments'.[73] Even more fundamental reforms of the regulatory system were proposed by the Trade and Industry Committee's examination of the electricity supply industry, which was 'not convinced that the accountability and structure of electricity regulation are satisfactory'.[74] It recommended that 'the Government consider the concept of a regulatory panel', thereby undermining one of the key features of the British regulatory model which is said to make it 'easier to establish a clear policy line', and in particular 'a very strong pro-competitive line to create the confidence that people need to enter the market-place'.[75] Concerns have also been expressed about the effectiveness of the regulator as consumer's champion.[76]

[68]   Gas Act 1986, s 27A (inserted by Gas Act 1995, Sched 3).
[69]   Somewhat similar problems have been raised in the case of the National Lottery (not a public utility but regulated in much the same way) where concern has been expressed that 'the appointment by the Act of the same organisation to choose the operator and regulate its activities could give rise to a conflict of interest' and that 'the Government should consider separating these two functions before the licence is due for renewal' (HC 240–I (1995–96), p xi). This has not been identified as a problem in the case of the utilities, where the concern has not been to license in hitherto virgin territory as much as to break the power of established monopolies.
[70]   *OFGAS Annual Report 1992*, pp 1–8.
[71]   Cm 2315, 1993.
[72]   HC 645 (1995–96), p 40.
[73]   HC 645 (1995–96). It is to be noted that there is a joint regulatory body in Northern Ireland (OFREG) for gas and electricity.
[74]   HC 170 (1994–95).
[75]   A Carlsberg, above, p 339.
[76]   See HC 37 (1996–97) (doubts about the effectiveness of the regulator in reducing price of gas).

D. The accountability of public utilities and public utility regulators

Accountability to government

1 Public corporations. Public ownership of an industry usually came about because of the need for greater public control than could be obtained by means of legal restrictions imposed on privately owned undertakings. If there is to be public control of a corporation, this must be achieved primarily through the relevant minister, who appoints the chairman and members of the board, who has power to call for information and give directions to the board, who approves the board's external financing limits, and who receives the board's accounts and annual report. This does not mean that ministers should be responsible for every act of day-to-day administration, but they must at least have power to intervene on strategic matters which by the legislation are subject to their approval. In turn, ministerial responsibility to Parliament requires that ministers should account to Parliament for the use that they make of their statutory powers.

Whatever the framers of the nationalisation Acts in 1945–50 may have intended, ministers in fact exercised very considerable control over the industries and often intervened in their affairs. One reason for this was that while for some periods some nationalised industries were financially profitable, many went through periods when they made heavy losses and needed financial support from the government. Another reason was that the industries played a substantial part in the national economy, as employers, as providers of basic means of communication and energy, and in their investment programmes: management of the industries became an aspect of the management of the economy. Many of the industries' decisions had widespread social and economic repercussions, for example the level of prices charged to the consumer, wage rates for their employees, purchasing decisions (for example, whether British Airways should buy British aeroplanes) and the closure of unprofitable activities (for example, railway lines and coal-mines). It was impossible to insulate such decisions from the political process, but it was extremely difficult to strike the right balance. A Commons select committee in 1968 advocated an 'arm's length' relationship between boards and ministers, with political intervention being confined to a few key points.[77]

2 Privatised utilities. Privatisation has not removed the scope for ministerial intervention in the activities of the former nationalised industries. As the Comptroller and Auditor General pointed out, 'the Government determined the initial position in which the industries would begin their life following privatisation. In particular they laid down the licences issued to companies, determined the capital structure of those companies that were formerly public owned, and set initial price controls for those which were monopolies or had a dominant position'.[78] The government also has a role in promoting competition, where the industry in question contains what is a 'natural

---

[77] HC 371–I (1967–68), p 3.
[78] HC 645 (1995–96), p 7.

monopoly', and for this purpose legislation may be necessary, as for example in the case of the Gas Act 1995 which extended competition in gas supply. On the other hand the government has a role to play in protecting consumers from the unfair practices of the utility companies, and to this end the legislation makes provision for the appointment by ministers of a regulator in each of the industries in question. The regulator thus becomes responsible for setting quality of service standards and for dealing with disputes about bills. It is anticipated that the need to cater for this responsibility will gradually diminish if and when effective competition is genuinely introduced in the provision of utilities, but this remains to be seen, even if effective competition is to become a reality in the delivery of all of the existing utilities. But apart from questions of structure and policy of this nature, there are also ministerial duties and powers under the legislation, of a wide and varied kind relating to the industry. It is the minister who issues the licences to the operators (except in the case of gas) and appoints the regulator (for fixed-term periods of up to 5 years).

Together with the regulator, ministers generally have prescribed statutory duties; thus the Gas Act 1995 requires the minister to exercise his or her responsibilities in a manner best calculated to ensure that all reasonable demand for gas is met, and that there is effective competition in the supply and transportation of gas. Ministers are also empowered in some cases to give directions to the regulator in determining the allocation of priorities in the performance of his or her duties. Otherwise, the legislation empowers the minister to make regulations, though in the case of the gas industry the effect of the Gas Act 1995 has been to transfer much of this power to the regulator. Nevertheless, even in gas the power to make regulations can generally be exercised only with the authority of the minister, who in any event retains some powers, for example in the case of public safety. Thus the Secretary of State may make regulations empowering an officer to (i) enter premises in which there is a gas service pipe for the purpose of inspecting gas fittings on the premises; (ii) examine and test any such fittings or other related equipment; and (iii) disconnect or seal off any gas fitting or gas supply to the premises, where 'in his opinion it is necessary to do so for the purpose of averting danger to life or property'. In the case of the last of these powers, the consumer may appeal to the minister on the ground that the defect did not constitute a danger so as to justify the action taken. These regulatory powers are typical of the different statutory provisions dealing with the public utilities, though in the case of the gas industry we see a formal retreat (though not exclusion) of the role of the minister as competition becomes more widespread in principle. Other ministerial powers relate to the possibility of intervention in the running of the industry where there are overriding public interest concerns.[79]

Select committees and accountability

1 Public corporations.   The difficulties encountered by MPs in obtaining information about the nationalised industries, together with the lack of adequate procedures for dealing with the reports and accounts laid annually before

[79]   See ch 25 below.

Parliament, led in the early 1950s to various attempts to use committees of the Commons to establish greater parliamentary control. In 1954–55, the House appointed a committee to inform Parliament about the current policy and practice of the industries, but excluded from its remit matters which involved a minister's responsibility to Parliament or were matters of day-to-day administration.[80] In 1956, there was set up a select committee with the duty of examining the reports and accounts of the nationalised industries.[81] The committee was regularly re-appointed until 1979. By then its terms of reference had been widened to include powers in respect of other public undertakings, such as the Independent Broadcasting Authority and the Bank of England, except for certain of the Bank's activities which were reserved from inquiry. Between 1956 and 1979 this all-party committee made a series of searching and sometimes highly critical inquiries into the industries and their relationships with the government. The inquiries started from the published reports and accounts of the industry under review but evidence was taken from the industry, the department concerned and other interested parties.

The committee sought to discover how far the industries were subject to informal ministerial control and to ensure that ministers were responsible to Parliament for the influence which they in fact exercised, especially when ministerial pressure had prevailed against the commercial judgment of the boards. The committee's reports on topics of general concern, for example, ministerial control of the industries (in 1968), contributed much to the development of policies relating to the nationalised industries. The success of the committee on a non-partisan basis also contributed to the spread of specialised parliamentary committees into other areas of governmental activity.[82] When in 1979 the present scheme of select committees was set up, each committee was empowered to examine the expenditure, administration and policy of the principal departments and their 'associated public bodies'.[83] This was considered to leave no place for the nationalised industries committee. Certain industries have been reviewed by the resulting committees such as the Treasury Committee, the Trade and Industry Committee and the Transport Committee.[84] Some aspects of the industries' finances have been considered by the Public Accounts Committee, but although the accounts of the industries were laid annually in Parliament, the Comptroller and Auditor General had no power to inspect the books of the industries themselves.[85] Although the National Audit Act 1983 extended the Auditor General's power to examine the economy, efficiency and effectiveness of government departments and related bodies, the nationalised industries and other public authorities, such as the BBC, were expressly excluded from the scope of the Act.[86]

2 Privatisation. Although privatisation has reduced the scope for scrutiny of

---

[80] HC 120 (1955–56).
[81] Coombes, *The Member of Parliament and the Administration.*
[82] Ch 10 D.
[83] HC SO 99(1); ch 10 D.
[84] See eg HC 597 (1988–89), HC 141 (1990–91).
[85] HC 115 (1980–81).
[86] National Audit Act 1983, s 7(4) and Sched 4; ch 17 D.

nationalised industries by the select committees, it has not yet disappeared altogether. In 1995, the Trade and Industry Committee rejected proposals for the privatisation of the Post Office, recommending instead that the government introduce legislation to convert the Post Office, 'for the time being at least', into a '100% government-owned plc (as has been done in other European countries), in the knowledge that the future sale of the government's shares in Post Office plc would be subject to parliamentary approval'.[87] The select committees have also examined a number of issues arising in connection with those privatisations which have already taken place, these inquiries generally taking one of a number of forms, including the way in which newly privatised utilities conduct their affairs. A notable example is the Employment Committee's inquiry on 'The Remuneration of Directors and Chief Executives of Privatised Utilities' in 1994,[88] following some controversial increases in executive pay which led even the Prime Minister to intervene and agree that they were distasteful and brought the system into disrepute. The committees have also examined the work of the regulators, with the Trade and Industry Committee, for example, examining OFGAS annual reports,[89] and on other occasions 'The Work of OFGAS'[90] and 'The Domestic Gas Market'.[91] Indeed in the first twenty months of her appointment the then gas regulator (Ms Spottiswoode) drew to the attention of the Trade and Industry Committee that she had been in front of six select committees in that time. Such occasions are potentially very important in view of the uncertain constitutional status of those regulators who perceive themselves as being 'independent of government,' in which case it will be difficult to attach any meaningful notion of ministerial responsibility for their actions.[92] Indeed it is open to question whether ministers are 'accountable' to Parliament for the work of the regulators even in the diluted sense which applies in the case of the Next Steps agencies.

If it is the case that 'regulators cannot be directly accountable to either ministers or to Parliament' [sed quaere],[93] and if it is the case that ministers are not responsible to Parliament for the work of the regulator, then the select committees provide the only effective channel for parliamentary scrutiny (if not necessarily direct accountability) of the regulator. This in turn raises questions about the adequacy of the current arrangements, with proposals having been made, for example by the gas regulator, for a select committee 'specifically for regulation and regulators' because their work 'cut across a whole series of committees', not all of which produced 'informed questions from people who understand the subject'.[94] The gas regulator is not alone in calling for such a committee, with similar proposals being made in evidence to the Trade and Industry Committee's investigation into the electricity supply industry. The Major Energy Users' Council proposed a 'well constructed Select Committee of expert MPs with their access to the best

---

[87]   HC 170 (1994–95) (Trade and Industry Committee), p x.
[88]   HC 159 (1994–95).
[89]   HC 646 (1994–95).
[90]   HC 185 (1993–94).
[91]   HC 681 (1993–94).
[92]   HC 646 (1994–95), p 1.
[93]   HC 646 (1994–95), p 1.
[94]   Ibid, pp 1–2.

advisers available', with each of the privatised utilities reporting to the House for an annual scrutiny.[95] The Trade and Industry Committee in fact considered a number of important proposals to reform the regulatory structure, the first being a need for a clearer separation of policy (the responsibility of the government) from its implementation (the responsibility of the regulator), with more precise duties and less discretion for the regulator. The second was the need to give reasons for decisions, said to be 'fundamental', with complaints being made about the lack of transparency in the regulatory process. Other complaints related to the absence of effective consultation by the regulator, who was said not to permit one participant in consultation exercises to comment on and challenge the evidence presented by others, even though they may have an interest and be affected by any decision which may be based upon contestable representations. The committee recommended that the government should impose a duty on all the regulators to give reasons for their decisions.[96]

Judicial review

1 Public corporations. As public corporations do not generally benefit from immunities of the Crown, in carrying out their operations they are fully subject to the law as are industrial enterprises in private ownership. In fact many corporations provide public utility services which were subject to statutory control long before the era of nationalisation. So far as the principal powers and duties of the nationalised corporations were concerned, these were usually expressed in such general terms in the parent Acts that it was doubtful whether they could be enforced by legal process.

In *Charles Roberts and Co Ltd v British Railways Board*[97] a company which manufactured railway tank wagons sought a declaration that the board were not authorised to manufacture such wagons for sale to an oil company for use on railways in Britain. *Held* that the court should not interfere with the board's bona fide decision that such manufacture was an efficient way of carrying out the board's business within its statutory powers and duties; the judge declined to consider the economic effect which the board's policies might have on private manufacturers.

It would similarly be difficult by action in the courts to enforce the general duties of a board, as this seems to be left by the statutes to the minister concerned.[98] But public corporations are subject to the jurisdiction of the courts if they commit a tort or a breach of contract, if they exceed their powers, or if they fail to observe statutory procedures or to perform specific statutory duties.[99] Questions have arisen as to the extent to which the BBC is subject to judicial review. Although it has been held that the corporation's duty of political impartiality is not enforceable in the courts,[100] it is not now possible to argue that judicial review does not apply at all on the ground that

---

95   HC 481–iii (1994–95).
96   HC 481 (1994–95).
97   [1964] 3 All ER 651.
98   Cf *British Oxygen Co v South of Scotland Electricity Board* 1956 SC (HL) 112, 1959 SC (HL) 17.
99   *Warwickshire CC v British Railways Board* [1969] 3 All ER 631; *Booth & Co (International) Ltd v National Enterprise Board* [1978] 3 All ER 624; *Grunwick Processing Laboratories Ltd v ACAS* [1978] AC 655; *Home Office v Commission for Racial Equality* [1982] QB 385.
100   *Lynch v BBC* [1983] NILR 193.

the BBC is a creature of prerogative.[101] Judicial review now casts a long shadow, and even regulatory bodies that do not exercise statutory functions may be subject to judicial review.[102]

2 Privatisation. So far as the privatised utilities are concerned, it is unlikely that the companies themselves would be subject to judicial review, though they would clearly be subject to the jurisdiction of the courts if they commit a tort or a breach of contract. They may, however, be regarded as authorities of the state for the purposes of the direct effect of EC directives, as were the nationalised industries after the House of Lords decision in *Foster v British Gas plc*.[103] In *Griffin v South West Water Services Ltd*[104] it was held that a privatised water company satisfied the test laid down in that case for the purposes of direct effect to the extent that it was a body which (i) provided a public service, (ii) under the control of the state, for the purposes of which (iii) it had special powers. It was the second of these three conditions which gave rise to most difficulty for the court, but the fact that it was prepared to acknowledge such a degree of state control is an interesting reflection on the public nature of the activities of the privatised companies. Indeed Blackburne J went so far as to say that the extent of control by the state under legislation and licence was 'at least as great' as that exercised in relation to the nationalised industries, though this alone is not enough to make these companies subject to judicial review. The fact that the water company operated in what was described as 'a business environment in compliance with legislation but driven by economic criteria' did not detract from the conclusion of the court, though on the facts the point was academic for it was also held that the directive in question (75/129/EC) was not sufficiently precise and unconditional to give rise to obligations which could be enforced directly in the domestic courts.

Different considerations apply in the case of the minister (exercising powers under the relevant regulatory legislation) and the regulators. There is perhaps more scope for review of the regulator than of anyone else in the process, either because of a failure to comply with ministerial directions, or because of decisions which have been taken under the authority of the Act.[105] But because judicial review may be available in principle, it does not follow that it is 'always appropriate' nor 'a substitute for proper political supervision and well-thought-out decision-making procedures'.[106] Indeed, it has been suggested that 'judicial review offers no meaningful protection to a party that feels it has been wronged by a regulator's decision', on the ground that the courts are unprepared 'to question the quality of the regulator's decision or require that the evidence underpinning the decision be examined'.[107] On the

---

[101] Cf *R v BBC, ex p Lavelle* [1983] ICR 99. See also *CCSU v Minister of State for the Civil Service* [1985] AC 374.
[102] *R v Panel on Take-Overs and Mergers, ex p Datafin plc* [1987] QB 815; ch 30.
[103] [1991] 2 AC 306.
[104] [1995] IRLR 15.
[105] *R v Director of Passenger Rail Franchising, ex p Save our Railways, The Times*, 18 December 1995.
[106] A McHarg [1995] PL 539, at p 550.
[107] HC 481–iii (1994–95), p 77 (memorandum submitted by National Power plc).

other hand, however, there is evidence that at least one regulator (OFGAS) has gone to considerable lengths to avoid judicial review by adopting a 'deliberate policy' of refusing to give reasons for decisions and by failing to keep adequate records of reasons for decisions (in this case relating to the adoption of a particular price control). This was strongly deprecated by the Public Accounts Committee, which considered it 'essential that public bodies keep adequate records of the reasons for their decisions, to help ensure the proper conduct of public business and accountability'.[108] Yet although judicial review under Order 53 of the Rules of the Supreme Court could be proper and important in some cases, there may also be cases where it is appropriate to seek declaratory relief by way of originating summons.[109]

Consumer consultation

The legislation has often provided formal machinery for consultation between the industries themselves and the consumers and users of their services. Consumer councils and consultative committees were created at different times for electricity, gas, coal, rail and air transport, and the Post Office. Thus the Post Office Act 1969 made provision for a Post Office Users' National Council (and also similar councils for Scotland, Wales and Northern Ireland) appointed by the minister. The National Council must consider any matters relating to Post Office services which are the subject of representation by any users of the services, or which are referred to it by the minister or by the Post Office, or which the Council itself thinks it ought to consider; and the Council must be consulted before the Post Office puts into effect any major proposals relating to its main services, for example, a general increase in postal charges.[110] Such consultative committees provide a means for the expression of the views of consumers, including opinions on the quality of services. They also provide a channel by which dissatisfied consumers may seek redress for grievances regarding the services they have received. But the existence of these consultative bodies is not widely known, and in 1976 it was suggested that an Ombudsman be established for the industries to be an impartial investigator of consumer complaints.[111] Privatisation has seen the abolition of the existing consultative committees and consumer councils, though somewhat similar bodies have been established in the newly privatised utilities. Under the Gas Act 1986, for example, the Gas Consumers' Council appointed by the Secretary of State is under a duty to investigate a number of matters arising under the Act (s 32) and generally to advise the regulator (s 40). It is also required to report annually on its activities under the Act (s 41).[112]

---

[108] HC 37 (1996–97).
[109] *Mercury Communications Ltd v Director General of Telecommunications* [1996] 1 All ER 575.
[110] Post Office Act 1969, ss 14, 15.
[111] Report by Justice, *The Citizen and Public Agencies: Remedying Grievances*. See also Robson, op cit, ch 10; HC 514 (1970–71) and Cmnd 5067, 1972; and HC 334 (1978–79).
[112] See also Electricity Act 1989, s 2; Water Act 1989, s 6.

E. Advisory bodies

While public boards may provide services or manage undertakings themselves, subject to a degree of control by ministers and departments, where a
department wishes to retain all decision-making and management in its own
hands, it may seek through advisory bodies to receive expert advice and
assistance from persons outside government. Such advisory bodies can take
many different forms. Some are primarily concerned with considering the
need for fresh legislation; others are concerned with the choice of policies
under existing laws. Some are appointed because an Act of Parliament says
that they must be; others are appointed simply because the government
wishes to seek information and advice from wherever it can find it. Some are
appointed for a particular purpose and have a temporary existence. We now
consider briefly some of the main kinds of advisory body.

Royal commissions and departmental committees

The appointment of a royal commission or a departmental committee is an
act of the executive which requires no specific parliamentary approval,
although often it may be a response to political demands. When an issue of
public policy or a possible change in the law requires thorough examination,
and the government is not already politically committed to a definite policy,
the task may be entrusted to an invited group of persons from outside the
relevant departments. A departmental committee is appointed by one minister or by several ministers acting jointly. For substantial matters where greater
formality is considered appropriate and where time is not of the essence, a
royal commission may be appointed instead. This requires a royal warrant to
be issued to the commissioners by the Sovereign on the advice of a Secretary
of State. Apart from the formality and greater prestige of a royal commission,
both commissions and departmental committees carry out their inquiries in a
similar manner. The commission or committee will usually call for evidence,
from individuals and organisations outside government as well as from public
authorities, and it may undertake its own programme of research. Usually a
royal commission hears the main evidence in public and copies of the oral
and written evidence received are published; the commission's report is
invariably published and laid before Parliament. A departmental committee is
more likely to receive evidence in private and it is less common for its
evidence to be published. But both the Committee on Ministers' Powers
(1929–32) and the Committee on Administrative Tribunals and Inquiries
(1955–57) took evidence in public and this was later published.[113] The reports
of departmental committees are usually but not always published.[114]

Neither royal commissions nor departmental committees have power to
compel the attendance of witnesses, unlike tribunals of inquiry appointed
under the Tribunals of Inquiry (Evidence) Act 1921 by authority of Parliament.[115] The choice of the chairperson to a commission or committee is

---

[113] Ch 26.
[114] For the use of commissions and committees in 1945–69, see Cartwright, *Royal Commissions
and Departmental Committees in Britain.*
[115] Ch 28 C; cf Cartwright, op cit, pp 142–5.

important since he or she must ensure that the commission or committee carries through its work efficiently and will seek to achieve a unanimous report where possible.[116] Usually the commission or committee disbands when it has reported but committees or commissions may be appointed on a more permanent basis and will produce a series of reports (for example, the Nolan committee on standards in public life, first appointed in 1994). When the investigating body has delivered its report, it is for the minister or the government to decide how far its recommendations are acceptable and if so in what form they should be carried out, for example by the preparation of a Bill to amend the law. In the 1980s, royal commissions and departmental committees were much less conspicuous than they had been in the 1970s when a number of important reports were published (on matters such as official secrecy, obscenity and film censorship, and financial aid to political parties).[117] However, these forms of advisory body are far from dead. A royal commission under the chairmanship of Lord Runciman was appointed in 1991 to investigate the criminal justice process in the wake of a number of highly publicised miscarriages of justice, while departmental committees have examined matters such as the ethics of gene therapy, and privacy and related matters.[118] A departmental committee should not be confused with a statutory public inquiry such as those held in connection with town planning appeals, where the department concerned is required to make a decision under existing law on the specific matters considered at the inquiry.[119] Nor should it be confused with the innumerable committees and working parties which exist within government and are usually staffed exclusively by ministers or civil servants.

Consultative committees

The practice of consultation between government departments and organisations outside government is a widespread phenomenon of British government even today. Consultation serves to meet the needs of the administrator for expert information and advice on scientific, technical or industrial matters. It also is an important means by which those in government seek to maintain the continuing consent of the governed, and it thus serves important political purposes. Where consultative committees and advisory councils exist, they enable the practice of consultation to be placed on a regular and structured footing. Consultative committees are used over the whole range of government. They have proved particularly useful in the process by which new delegated legislation is prepared, but their use is not confined to projected legislation. In some cases there is a statutory obligation on a minister to consult a standing committee or named association, though the advisory body may be unable to take the initiative in discussing a subject without the matter being referred to it by the minister. Many advisory bodies are appointed and consulted at the discretion of the minister or department

---

[116] Report of Balfour Committee on Procedure of Royal Commissions, Cd 5235, 1910; and see Lords Benson and Rothschild (1982) 60 Public Administration 339.

[117] Cmnd 5104, 1972; Cmnd 7772, 1979; Cmnd 6601, 1976.

[118] Cm 1788, 1992; Cm 1102, 1990.

[119] Ch 28 B.

concerned, and their discussions are often regarded as confidential, even where a more open approach to government would promote administrative fairness.[120]

An illustration of a statutory body which ministers must consult is the Police Negotiating Board for the United Kingdom. Regulations relating to the government, administration and conditions of service in police forces can be made under the Police Act 1996, and the equivalent Acts for Scotland and Northern Ireland, only after the Secretary of State has consulted the Board, on which sit representatives of local police authorities and of all ranks of the police.[121] The Social Security Advisory Committee gives advice and reports to the Secretary of State for Social Security on his or her functions under the Social Security Acts. In particular, where the Secretary of State proposes to make regulations about social security benefits the proposal must be referred to the committee; when the regulations are laid before Parliament, the Secretary of State must inform Parliament of the committee's views and, if effect is not to be given to the committee's recommendations, of the reasons for this.[122] The Council on Tribunals, appointed to oversee the operation of tribunals and inquiries, is essentially a body which advises and is consulted by government departments; like most advisory bodies it has no executive functions, but its watchdog role includes consideration of complaints about particular tribunals and inquiries.[123]

---

[120]   *R v Secretary of State for Health, ex p US Tobacco Inc* [1992] QB 353.
[121]   Police Act 1996, s 61.
[122]   See now Social Security Administration Act 1992, part XIII.
[123]   Ch 28 A.

CHAPTER 15

Foreign affairs and the Commonwealth

This chapter outlines the law relating to the conduct of the United Kingdom's foreign relations. International law has the primary function of regulating the relations of independent, sovereign states with one another.[1] For this purpose the United Kingdom of Great Britain and Northern Ireland is the state, with authority to act also for dependent possessions, such as the Channel Islands, the Isle of Man, and the surviving colonies, such as Gibraltar, none of which are states at international law. But political groupings and national boundaries seldom last for all time. Thus the Empire gave way to the Commonwealth, whose members are now all independent states. In the course of development of the European Union, organs of the Union have acquired capacity on behalf of the member states to conduct relations on economic matters between the Union and non-member states.[2]

This chapter considers (*a*) the executive's power to conduct foreign affairs; (*b*) aspects of the making of treaties; and (*c*) in outline, the development and nature of the Commonwealth. But it does not outline the whole of what can be called foreign relations law.[3]

A.   The foreign affairs prerogative, international law and the courts

In 1820, Chitty believed it to be essential for the conduct of foreign affairs that 'the exclusive power of managing and executing state measures' should be vested in one individual, as it was not practical for an assembly of people to decide what action should be taken by the state. The constitution, said Chitty, had vested in the King the supreme and exclusive power of managing the country's foreign affairs.[4] At common law, this power, like control of the armed forces,[5] is still vested in the Crown, although many aspects of foreign

---

[1] Page 11 above. And see Brownlie, *Principles of Public International Law*, and Jennings and Watts, *Oppenheim's International Law: the Law of Peace*.
[2] Ch 8 A, and p 361 below.
[3] See HLE, vol 18, title *Foreign Relations Law*.
[4] Chitty, *Prerogatives of the Crown*, ch 4.
[5] Ch 16.

relations law are the subject of legislation (for example, the Diplomatic Privileges Act 1964 and the State Immunity Act 1978).[6] As a prerogative power, the foreign affairs power is exercised on the authority of the Cabinet or of ministers, in particular the Prime Minister and the Secretary of State for Foreign and Commonwealth Affairs. While parliamentary approval is not generally needed before action is taken, ministers are responsible to Parliament for their policies and decisions.[7]

The Foreign Secretary is responsible for the Foreign and Commonwealth Office, which includes the diplomatic service that represents British interests abroad. Other ministers and departments deal as required with international aspects of their work. These include the Ministry of Defence, the Treasury, the Home Office (especially immigration control), the Department of Trade and Industry (international trade), and the departments of Inland Revenue and Social Security, concerned with British citizens who work abroad and foreigners who work in the United Kingdom.

The prerogative extends to the 'whole catalogue of relations with foreign nations',[8] such as making treaties, declaring war and making peace, instituting hostilities that fall short of war (as with the Falkland Islands and the Gulf campaigns), the recognition of foreign states, sending and receiving ambassadors, issuing passports[9] and granting diplomatic protection to British citizens abroad.[10]

But Crown prerogative does not include everything that is needed to carry out the government's foreign policies. Except in wartime, the prerogative does not extend to controlling trade between the United Kingdom and foreign countries. Thus import and export controls are authorised by statute.[11] Although some prerogative power exists to control the movement of aliens to and from the United Kingdom, immigration control is essentially derived from statute.[12] The prerogative does not include power to impose taxes for regulating foreign trade,[13] and the power to make treaties does not include power to change the law of the United Kingdom.[14]

The fact that the government may take action in foreign affairs without the prior consent of Parliament does not allow it to dispense with parliamentary support. Foreign affairs are the subject of debate and questions in Parliament; and the Foreign Affairs Committee of the House of Commons examines 'the expenditure, administration and policy of the Foreign and Commonwealth Office and of associated public bodies'.[15] Since 1979, the committee has reviewed many areas of foreign policy, sometimes in very critical terms.[16]

---

[6] Page 354 below.
[7] HLE, vol 8(2), pp 310–15.
[8] Mann, *Foreign Affairs in English Courts*, p 4.
[9] *R v Foreign Secretary, ex p Everett* [1989] QB 811; p 496 below.
[10] Cf *Mutasa v A-G* [1980] QB 114; *China Navigation Co Ltd v A-G* [1932] 2 KB 197.
[11] Import, Export and Customs Powers (Defence) Act 1939, made permanent by the Import and Export Control Act 1990: see (Scott Report) HC 115 (1995–96), vol I, pp 49–105; vol IV, pp 1759–66.
[12] Ch 20 B; cf Immigration Act 1971, s 33(5).
[13] Bill of Rights, art 4 (pp 15 and 55 above).
[14] Page 359 below.
[15] And see ch 10 D.
[16] C Y Carstairs, in Drewry (ed), *The New Select Committees*, ch 9.

The relationship between national and international law[17]

The relationship between national and international law raises difficult questions in both theory and practice. By art 25 of the German Constitution, the general rules of public international law are declared to be an integral part of German law; they take precedence over other German laws and create rights and duties for the people. By contrast with this instance of 'monism', English law in general favours 'dualism', that is, a position in which the two systems of law (national and international) co-exist, but function separately: each has distinct purposes and the subjects of international law are typically sovereign states, not individual persons. This co-existence does not guarantee harmony between the two systems. Thus an executive act in foreign affairs which is lawful in national law – under the prerogative or by statute – may be a breach of international law for which the United Kingdom is responsible.[18] Conversely, an executive act which seeks to perform an international obligation may be unlawful in national law.[19] This dualism is best seen in respect of treaties:

> It is axiomatic that municipal courts have not ... the competence to adjudicate upon or to enforce the rights arising out of transactions entered into by independent sovereign states between themselves on the plane of international law.[20]

When new obligations are created by treaty, legislation is needed for them to become rules of national law.[21]

In respect of customary international law (the 'common law' of interstate relations), English courts have sometimes stated that international law is part of the common law of England.[22] Blackstone declared: 'the law of nations (wherever any question arises which is properly the object of its jurisdiction) is here adopted to its full extent by the common law, and is held to be a part of the law of the land'.[23] On this approach, there is no need for any 'transformation': a national court may directly apply the customary international rule, provided that this would not be contrary to statute or a prior decision binding on the court.[24] For the courts to apply such a rule of international law, it must have 'attained the position of general acceptance by civilised nations as a rule of international conduct, evidenced by international treaties and conventions, authoritative textbooks, practice and judicial decision'.[25] Two decisions illustrate the potential difficulties.

In *R v Home Secretary, ex p Thakrar*,[26] arising from the expulsion of Asians from Uganda in 1972, the applicant, Thakrar (born in Uganda), claimed to be entitled to enter the United Kingdom on the basis of a rule of customary international law to the effect that a British protected person expelled from the country in which he was resident (here,

---

[17] Mann, op cit, chs 6–8; Brownlie, op cit, ch 2; Jennings and Watts, op cit, pp 56–63.
[18] Eg *Mortensen v Peters* (1908) 8 F(J) 93; p 62 above.
[19] Eg *Walker v Baird* [1892] AC 491; p 357 below.
[20] *Rayner (Mincing Lane) Ltd v Dept of Trade* [1990] 2 AC 418, at 499 (Lord Oliver).
[21] Section B below.
[22] Eg *Triquet v Bath* (1764) 3 Burr 1478.
[23] *Commentaries*, iv, 67.
[24] *Chung Chi Cheung v R* [1939] AC 160, at 168 (Lord Atkin).
[25] *The Christina* [1938] AC 485, at 497 (Lord Macmillan).
[26] [1974] QB 684, criticised by M B Akehurst (1975) 38 MLR 72.

Uganda) was entitled to enter British territory. The Court of Appeal held that no such rule of international law existed, nor (if it did) could it prevail against the Immigration Act 1971; in any event such a rule could not be enforced against the United Kingdom by a private individual, only by other states.

By contrast, in *Trendtex Trading Corpn v Central Bank of Nigeria*[27] a majority in the Court of Appeal held that because of changing practice in international law restricting sovereign immunity, the Central Bank of Nigeria was not immune from the jurisdiction of British courts. Since the rules of international law were changing to a narrower view of sovereign immunity, the court did not follow an earlier decision on the basis of which the Central Bank of Nigeria would have been immune from being sued in British courts.

In fact, the adoption of customary international law by national courts in this manner is limited, many matters relating to state and diplomatic immunity now being regulated by statute.[28] The State Immunity Act 1978, enacted in part to give effect to the European Convention on State Immunity,[29] takes a narrower view of sovereign immunity than did the common law. Immunity from the jurisdiction of UK courts is enjoyed only by foreign states, governments, and other entities exercising sovereign authority.[30] Exceptions from immunity arise in relation to commercial transactions, contracts to be performed in the United Kingdom, the ownership and possession of land in the United Kingdom, and death or personal injury arising from acts in the United Kingdom (ss 3–5). The Diplomatic Privileges Act 1964 gave effect within the United Kingdom to provisions of the Vienna Convention on Diplomatic Relations.[31] As well as categorising the diplomats and others entitled to claim immunity from legal process and the relevant immunities in each category, the Act authorises such immunities to be restricted by Order in Council for persons from a particular state if the privileges of the UK mission in that state are curtailed.[32]

Executive evidence and 'facts of state'[33]

One problem for the courts in dealing with disputes relating to international events is that these are often the subject of conflicting opinions and are particularly within the experience and knowledge of the executive; and it has been considered expedient that the judiciary and the executive should speak with one voice on these matters.[34] Rather than calling for proof of the relevant issues by evidence, the courts have evolved a practice by which certain matters are proved by a certificate from the Foreign Secretary or by a statement of the

---

[27]   [1977] QB 529, criticised by Mann, op cit, pp 124–5. See now State Immunity Act 1978, s 3.
[28]   See eg Consular Relations Act 1968 and International Organisations Act 1968.
[29]   Cmnd 5081, 1972.
[30]   See eg *Kuwait Airways Corpn v Iraqi Airways Co* [1995] 3 All ER 694. The 1978 Act does not apply to visiting forces in the UK: *Littrell v USA (No 2)* [1994] 4 All ER 203 (and p 387 below).
[31]   Cmnd 1368, 1964; s 2 of and Sched 1 to the 1964 Act.
[32]   1964 Act, s 3(1).
[33]   Mann, op cit, ch 2.
[34]   Eg *The Arantzazu Mendi* [1939] AC 256, at 264 (Lord Atkin); *Carl Zeiss Stiftung v Rayner & Keeler Ltd (No 2)* [1967] 1 AC 853, at 961 (Lord Wilberforce).

Attorney-General. These matters include such questions as whether the United Kingdom is still at war with another state,[35] the extent of British territorial jurisdiction,[36] whether the status of a person gives rise to immunity from jurisdiction,[37] and whether the existence of a state has been recognised.[38] An example of the last kind arose in *Carl Zeiss Stiftung v Rayner & Keeler Ltd*,[39] where the Foreign Office certificate stated that what was then East Germany was not an independent state but was subordinate to, and governed by, the Soviet Union. The court had therefore to determine the legal effect of decrees in East Germany upon this basis. Such certificates state what the Foreign Office recognises, not necessarily what other states or persons would accept.[40]

Before 1980, these certificates might state whether the United Kingdom had recognised the new government of a state (after a coup or other such change of government). In 1980, however, the Foreign Office abandoned its practice of recognising governments where a new regime came to power unconstitutionally; the Foreign Office now leaves it to be inferred from the actual dealings which the United Kingdom has with the country in question whether these are on a normal 'government to government' basis.[41] Even under this practice, there may be a need for a Foreign Office certificate as to the dealings that are taking place with a state whose status is in doubt.

By judicial practice, the statement of facts contained in such a certificate is conclusive: as Lord Reid said, 'no evidence is admissible to contradict that information'.[42] Several statutes now provide for certificates to be given on particular matters within the knowledge of the executive.[43] The effect of these statutory certificates depends on the statute. Thus a certificate issued under the State Immunity Act 1978 provides conclusive evidence of the facts that it states.[44] Despite the conclusive effect of such a certificate in national law, a litigant may be able to show that the certificate is in breach of an overriding rule of Community law.[45]

Moreover, a certificate stating the facts (as perceived by the Foreign Office) is not conclusive as to the legal inferences that may be drawn. It is for the court to decide the legal consequences of a certificate declaring that a state has been recognised.[46] The court should not seek an executive certificate

---

35 *R v Bottrill, ex p Kuechenmeister* [1947] KB 41; cf *Willcock v Muckle* [1951] 2 KB 844.
36 *The Fagernes* [1927] P 311, approved in *Post Office v Estuary Radio Ltd* [1968] 2 QB 740.
37 *Mighell v Sultan of Johore* [1894] 1 QB 149. Even without a certificate, material before a court may establish sovereign immunity: eg *Mellenger v New Brunswick Development Corpn* [1971] 2 All ER 593.
38 For such a certificate, see *Buttes Gas & Oil Co v Hammer* [1982] AC 888, 927–8.
39 [1967] 1 AC 853.
40 Mann, op cit, p 24.
41 Ibid, pp 42–6; Brownlie, op cit, pp 105–6. Also HL Deb, 28 April 1980, col 1121; 23 May 1980, col 1097; C R Symmons [1981] PL 249.
42 *Carl Zeiss Stiftung*, see note 34 above, at 901.
43 Eg Foreign Jurisdiction Act 1890, s 4 (extent of British jurisdiction in foreign country); Crown Proceedings Act 1947, s 40(3) (and see *Trawnik v Lennox* [1985] 2 All ER 368); Diplomatic Privileges Act 1964, s 4.
44 Section 21. And see *R v Foreign Secretary, ex p Trawnik*, *The Times*, 21 February 1986; Mann, op cit, p 19.
45 *Johnston v Chief Constable, RUC* [1987] QB 129.
46 *Carl Zeiss Stiftung*, see note 34 above, at 950 (Lord Upjohn).

as a means of obtaining guidance as to the principles of international law to be applied.[47]

Judicial review of decisions under the prerogative

As we have seen,[48] the House of Lords in *CCSU v Minister for the Civil Service* opened up the possibility that decisions under the prerogative are subject to judicial review. As Lord Scarman said, 'the controlling factor in deciding whether the exercise of prerogative power is subject to judicial review is not its source but its subject matter'.[49] However, in the *CCSU* case it was envisaged that many prerogative powers would not be justiciable; among these were mentioned powers relating to the making of treaties.[50] More generally, it has been stated that 'the conduct of foreign affairs cannot attract judicial review'.[51] Now, whether the government should make a treaty with country A[52] or take proceedings in an international court against country B[53] are plainly not matters for the judiciary to decide. But not all powers relating to foreign affairs are of the same kind. Even before *CCSU*, the Court of Appeal reviewed the legality of action taken by the government under a treaty with the United States concerning airline routes.[54] Since *CCSU*, a Foreign Office decision as to the issue of a passport has been held subject to review, on the basis that it 'is a matter of administrative decision, affecting the rights of individuals and their freedom of travel. It raises issues which are just as justiciable as ... the issues arising in immigration cases'.[55] The courts may also rule on questions directly affecting the legality of policies. In 1993, in rejecting an application for judicial review of the government's decision to ratify the Treaty on European Union, the court did so on the merits of the issues argued before it.[56] The court held (inter alia) that by entering the Union's common security and foreign policy the government was exercising prerogative power, not relinquishing it. In 1994, the court declared unlawful the government's decision to fund the Pergau Dam project, since the statutory conditions for granting foreign aid were not met by the project.[57]

Acts of state[58]

The Crown's prerogative in foreign affairs does not include power to change the law. But the Crown's actions may nonetheless have legal effects for individuals; for example, if war is declared against a state, British subjects may no longer trade with that state, and citizens of that state resident in the United

---

[47]   Cf *The Philippine Admiral* [1977] AC 373, 399.
[48]   Ch 12 E.
[49]   [1985] AC 374, at 407 (Lord Scarman).
[50]   Ibid, at 418 (Lord Roskill).
[51]   Mann, op cit, p 50.
[52]   *Rustomjee v R* (1876) 2 QBD 69; *Blackburn v A-G* [1971] 2 All ER 1380.
[53]   *R v Foreign Secretary, ex p Pirbai, The Times*, 17 October 1985; Mann, op cit, p 20.
[54]   *Laker Airways v Department of Trade* [1977] QB 643.
[55]   *R v Foreign Secretary, ex p Everett* [1989] QB 811, at 820 (Taylor LJ).
[56]   *R v Foreign Secretary, ex p Rees-Mogg* [1994] QB 552; see G Marshall [1993] PL 402; R Rawlings [1994] PL 254, 367.
[57]   *R v Foreign Secretary, ex p World Development Movement* [1995] 1 All ER 611.
[58]   See Harrison Moore, *Act of State in English Law*; J G Collier [1968] CLJ 102; D R Gilmour [1970] PL 120; Mann, op cit, chs 9, 10; P Wesley-Smith (1986) 6 LS 325.

Kingdom become enemy aliens, liable to detention or deportation. Those directly affected by the Crown's decisions may wish to seek a remedy in the courts, for example compensation in respect of any loss caused to them. For two reasons, the courts are unlikely to afford such relief. First, the acts of the Crown are likely to be within the prerogative; lawful acts in general do not give rise to a duty to compensate. (In exceptional cases there may be a duty to compensate if the prerogative act amounts to a taking of private property for public use.)[59] Secondly, the international element in a dispute may lead the court to conclude that, whether or not a claim is well founded in international law, it is outside the jurisdiction of national courts: if so, the court turns the plaintiff away without deciding the legal merits of the claim.

Although it is applied confusingly to different situations,[60] 'act of state' is often used in this context. One definition of act of state is that it is 'an act of the Executive as a matter of policy performed in the course of its relations with another state, including its relations with subjects of that state, unless they are temporarily within the allegiance of the Crown'.[61] This is not a wholly satisfactory definition,[62] and different legal inferences may be drawn from it. But some propositions may be stated briefly:

1 In general a plea of state necessity is not a justification for acts of the executive that are otherwise unlawful.[63]

2 The fact that the Crown has acquired territory or concluded a treaty does not in itself give rise to new rights enforceable against the Crown.[64]

3 In narrowly defined circumstances, a plea of act of state may be a reason why a claim for damages in tort or for compensation brought in the British courts may be held to be outside their jurisdiction. Such a plea is available to the Crown or an agent of the Crown when an alien who is resident abroad sues in respect of acts committed abroad.[65] In these circumstances, 'act of state' is a plea to the jurisdiction of the courts and is not to be confused with a defence that the Crown was acting lawfully under the prerogative. Whether such a defence is valid needs to be decided by the courts only if the claim is (apart from the plea) within their jurisdiction. It is, however, for a court to decide whether the executive acts in question are 'acts of state' for this purpose.

In *Nissan v Attorney-General*, a United Kingdom citizen who owned a hotel in Cyprus sued the Crown for compensation in respect of the occupation of the hotel by British troops; they had first entered Cyprus by agreement with the Cyprus government, and later remained there as part of a United Nations peace-keeping force. The House of Lords held that the Crown could not rely on the plea of 'act of state' as a bar to a claim based on these acts of the Crown. The House took the view that, while the agreement

---

[59]   *Burmah Oil Co v Lord Advocate* (p 278 above).

[60]   *Buttes Gas & Oil Co v Hammer* [1982] AC 888, at 930 (Lord Wilberforce).

[61]   E C S Wade (1934) 15 BYIL 98, 103.

[62]   *Nissan v A-G* [1970] AC 179, at 212 (Lord Reid); and cf P J Allott [1977] CLJ 255, 270.

[63]   *Entick v Carrington* (p 101 above).

[64]   *Rustomjee v R* (1876) 2 QBD 69; *Civilian War Claimants Association v R* [1932] AC 14.

[65]   *Buron v Denman* (1848) 2 Ex 167; *Walker v Baird* [1892] AC 491. Cf *Johnstone v Pedlar* [1921] 2 AC 262 (no act of state when US citizen arrested in the United Kingdom). And see 10th edn of this work, pp 316–20.

between the British and Cyprus governments might well have been an 'act of state', acts of the British forces in occupying the hotel did not constitute such an act of state: the plaintiff's claim was accordingly justiciable in the British courts.[66]

Amongst the difficult points of law left open by the House of Lords in *Nissan* was whether the plea of act of state can ever be raised to bar a claim brought against the Crown by a British citizen. Nor did the House resolve the question of whether prerogative power is being exercised by the Crown when its agents are carrying out its policy abroad.[67]

4 If war has been declared against a foreign state, citizens of that state who are within the United Kingdom are liable to be detained as enemy aliens and an attempt to secure their release in the British courts may be met by a plea of act of state (or, as seems more satisfactory, by the defence of lawful action under the prerogative).[68] Where war has not been declared by the United Kingdom against a foreign state, even if diplomatic relations are suspended, as was the case during the Gulf hostilities involving Iraq in 1991, nationals of that state resident in the United Kingdom are entitled to the protection of the courts against unlawful detention,[69] just as other friendly aliens within the jurisdiction are entitled to be protected against unlawful action, whether by public authorities or others.[70]

5 The plea of a 'foreign act of state' may arise where an action is brought in a British court in respect of the executive acts of foreign states, for example the making of a treaty; here too the court declines jurisdiction, giving as a reason that such an act between states cannot be adjudicated upon in municipal courts, or relying on the sovereign immunity of the defendant government.[71] British courts have no jurisdiction to rule on the validity of the constitution of a foreign state.[72]

The term 'act of state' is evidently not a far-reaching bar to legal claims arising from government action with a foreign element. The term came into use in a period when the doctrine of national sovereignty was at its most absolute. Today, its use is diminishing since, at least in Europe, the barriers between international and national law are being eroded. The claim that acts of 'foreign policy' affecting individuals should be beyond judicial scrutiny is

---

[66]   *Nissan v A-G* [1970] AC 179.
[67]   Ibid, at 213 (Lord Reid), 236 (Lord Wilberforce) and cf 227 (Lord Pearce). If a British citizen resident in Kuwait had been injured through action by British forces during the Gulf hostilities and sued the soldiers and the Crown in a British court, the best analysis would seem to be that (*a*) no act of state can be pleaded against a British citizen; (*b*) the soldiers were acting under the prerogative (preserved by the Crown Proceedings Act 1947, s 11; ch 31 A); (*c*) no duty to compensate arises for battle damage (cf *Burmah Oil Co v Lord Advocate*, p 278 above). If a Kuwait or Iraq citizen sued in a British court, the plea of act of state would succeed.
[68]   *R v Vine Street Police Station, ex p Liebmann* [1916] 1 KB 268; *Netz v Ede* [1946] Ch 224.
[69]   See eg *R v Home Secretary, ex p Cheblak* [1991] 2 All ER 319; also I Leigh [1991] PL 331 and F Hampson [1991] PL 507.
[70]   *Johnstone v Pedlar* [1921] 2 AC 262.
[71]   Eg *Cook v Sprigg* [1899] AC 572. And see *Buttes Gas & Oil Co v Hammer* [1982] AC 888, at 931–4. Note the distinction in the law of sovereign immunity between acts 'jure imperii' (which attract immunity) and acts 'jure gestionis' (which do not): *I Congreso del Partido* [1983] 1 AC 244; *Kuwait Airways Corpn v Iraqi Airways Co* [1995] 3 All ER 694.
[72]   *Buck v A-G* [1965] Ch 745.

unlikely to be welcomed today, whether in administrative law, Community law,[73] or in European human rights law.

B. Treaties[74]

By the Vienna Convention on the Law of Treaties, a treaty is defined as an international agreement concluded between states in written form and governed by international law, whether embodied in a single instrument or in two or more related instruments and whatever its particular designation.[75] Whatever name may be given to it (convention, covenant, protocol, charter, exchange of notes etc), a treaty is an agreement between two or more sovereign states which creates rights and obligations for the parties. A country's constitutional law determines who can exercise the treaty-making power. By the US Constitution, this power is vested in the President, 'by and with the advice of the Senate', provided that two-thirds of the Senate concur; treaties so approved have a status equal to that of legislation by Congress.[76] By contrast, in the United Kingdom there is no direct parliamentary involvement in the making of treaties. To this, three qualifications must be made. First, under the so-called Ponsonby rule, which applies to treaties that have been negotiated and signed but have not come into effect because they have not (in international law) been ratified by the parties, the government notifies Parliament of the treaty and must not ratify it (save in cases of urgency) until 21 parliamentary days have elapsed.[77] This both informs Parliament of the treaty and enables it to be debated. Secondly, Parliament may restrict the ability of the executive to conclude or ratify treaties by imposing an express requirement of parliamentary consent.[78] Thirdly, a treaty which is entered into by the government does not alter the law in the United Kingdom: 'the making of a treaty is an executive act, while the performance of its obligations, if they entail alteration of the existing domestic law, requires legislative action'.[79] 'Except to the extent that a treaty becomes incorporated into the laws of the United Kingdom by statute, the courts ... have no power to enforce treaty rights and obligations at the behest of a sovereign government or at the behest of a private individual.'[80] If the objects of a treaty require national law to be changed, this must be done by legislation. Often an Act of Parliament is necessary, but a minister may be able to make the required changes in national law by exercising existing powers of delegated legisla- tion.[81] To avoid a situation in which a treaty has become binding but the

---

[73] *Bourgoin SA v Ministry of Agriculture* [1986] QB 716; *Van Duyn v Home Office* [1975] Ch 358.
[74] See McNair, *Law of Treaties*; Brownlie, op cit, ch 25; Jennings and Watts, op cit, ch 14.
[75] Cmnd 4848, 1969, art 2, para 1.
[76] US Constitution, art II(2), art VI; *Whitney v Robertson* 124 US 190 (1888).
[77] HC Deb, 1 April 1924, cols 2001–4; Erskine May, pp 215, 549–50; HLE, vol 8(2), pp 465–9.
[78] See European Parliamentary Elections Act 1978, s 6(1) (no treaty increasing powers of European Parliament to be ratified unless approved by Act); and *R v Foreign Secretary, ex p Rees-Mogg* [1994] QB 552.
[79] *A-G for Canada v A-G for Ontario* [1937] AC 326, at 347 (Lord Atkin).
[80] *Rayner (Mincing Lane) Ltd v Department of Trade* [1990] 2 AC 418, at 477 (Lord Templeman); *Littrell v USA (No 2)* [1994] 4 All ER 203.
[81] See ch 27.

necessary changes in national law have not been made, the implementing legislation may need to be enacted before the government ratifies the treaty. In general a state cannot rely on defects in its own law as a defence to a claim in international law.[82]

Where a treaty has not been incorporated in national law by legislation, the courts may not directly enforce the treaty. The European Convention on Human Rights is one such treaty. In 1991, the House of Lords held that the Convention, not having been incorporated in English law, could not be a source of rights and obligations.[83] In 1995, the High Court of Australia held that an unincorporated treaty could give rise to a 'legitimate expectation' that executive decision-makers would act in accordance with the treaty.[84] The Australian government promptly issued a statement to prevent such an expectation arising. It is doubtful whether a British court would follow the Australian precedent.

Even where a treaty seeks to benefit a definite class of persons (for example, where a foreign government provides funds to compensate British citizens who have suffered at that government's hands), such persons do not acquire rights of enforcing the treaty against the British government.[85] Often the money received under such treaties is distributed in accordance with a statutory scheme by the Foreign Compensation Commission, whose decisions are now subject to an appeal to the courts.[86] In the Sachsenhausen case, this procedure was not followed: a short cut taken by the Foreign Office proved unsatisfactory, mainly because of an erroneous view that the Office had formed of the so-called Butler rules.[87] Were this to occur today, someone who claimed that the Foreign Office was not correctly applying the rules of distribution could seek judicial review.[88] Such an application might be strengthened if the treaty in question declared that the UK government was acting as agent or trustee for its subjects.[89] But this would not necessarily be decisive, since not all governmental obligations in the nature of a trust are justiciable.[90]

Interpretation of legislation giving effect to treaties

The methods by which Parliament may give effect in national law to obligations arising under a treaty include the following.[91] First, the statute may enact the substance of the treaty in its own words without referring to the treaty.[92] Secondly, the statute may name the treaty (for example, in the title of the Act)

---

[82]   Brownlie, op cit, p 35.
[83]   *R v Home Secretary, ex p Brind* [1991] 1 AC 696. See ch 19 B.
[84]   *Minister of State for Immigration v Teoh* (1995) 128 ALR 353. See R Piotrowicz [1996] PL 190 and Lord Lester [1996] PL 187.
[85]   *Civilian War Claimants Association v R* [1932] AC 14; *Lonrho Exports Ltd v Export Credits Guarantee Dept* [1996] 4 All ER 673, 687–9.
[86]   Foreign Compensation Act 1969, s 3 (enacted after *Anisminic Ltd v Foreign Compensation Commission*, ch 29 below).
[87]   Ch 28 D.
[88]   *R v Criminal Injuries Compensation Board, ex p Lain* [1967] 2 QB 864; pp 275, 283 above.
[89]   *Civilian War Claimants Association* (note 85 above) at 26–7 (Lord Atkin).
[90]   *Tito v Waddell (No 2)* [1977] Ch 106; cf *Mutasa v A-G* [1980] QB 114.
[91]   Mann, *Foreign Affairs in English Courts*, pp 97–102.
[92]   Eg Evidence (Proceedings in other Jurisdictions) Act 1975, considered in *Re Westinghouse* [1978] AC 547.

and then either enact all or part of the substance of the treaty in its own words.[93] Thirdly, the statute may set out the text of the treaty in a schedule, while giving legal effect either to part of the treaty[94] or to the whole text.[95]

The choice between these various methods might be thought to affect the manner in which the courts should seek to resolve problems of interpretation that arise, for example from a discrepancy between the statutory words and the treaty. However, the courts' approach does not turn on the precise method of incorporation, provided it appears, if necessary from extrinsic evidence, that a statute was enacted in pursuance of an international obligation. If Parliament uses express and unambiguous language, this must be given effect by the courts even if the result of so doing departs from what was intended by the treaty.[96] However,

it is a principle of construction of United Kingdom statutes, now too well established to call for citation of authority, that the words of a statute passed after the treaty has been signed and dealing with the subject matter of the international obligation of the United Kingdom, are to be construed, if they are reasonably capable of bearing such a meaning, as intended to carry out the obligation and not to be inconsistent with it.[97]

The law may be developing even beyond this so that, whether the court is construing statutory words or resolving a disputed question of common law in an area where the United Kingdom has international obligations, the court may have regard to the treaty 'as part of the full content or background of the law'.[98] The application of this doctrine to the European Convention on Human Rights is especially significant.[99]

When a court does look at the text of a treaty, further questions may arise as to how that text should be interpreted. According to Lord Wilberforce, the approach 'must be appropriate for the interpretation of an international convention, unconstrained by technical rules of English law, or by English legal precedent, but on broad principles of general acceptance'.[100]

The European Union and the law on treaties

The European Union, and the Communities within the Union, were created and enlarged by successive treaties.[101] The new legal order brought about by those treaties, as interpreted by the European Court of Justice, has consequences that go far beyond the general law of treaties. First, in giving effect within the United Kingdom to Community law, the European Communities Act 1972 provides a further variant to the methods of treaty implementation described above. The existing European Treaties were listed in a schedule to

---

[93] Eg Arbitration Act 1975.
[94] Eg Geneva Conventions Act 1957 (F Hampson [1991] PL 507); and Diplomatic Privileges Act 1964.
[95] Eg Carriage of Goods by Road Act 1965; and see *Buchanan & Co v Babco Ltd* [1978] AC 141.
[96] *Salomon v Commissioners of Customs & Excise* [1967] 2 QB 116.
[97] *Garland v British Rail Engineering Ltd* [1983] 2 AC 751, at 771 (Lord Diplock).
[98] *Pan-American World Airways v Department of Trade* [1976] 1 Lloyd's Rep 257.
[99] *Derbyshire CC v Times Newspapers Ltd* [1993] AC 534.
[100] *Buchanan & Co v Babco Ltd* (note 95 above) at 152 (Lord Wilberforce). Also Brownlie, op cit, pp 626–32.
[101] Ch 8 A.

the Act but their texts were not set out. Those rights, obligations and other matters arising from the treaties that were to have legal effect without further enactment within the United Kingdom were declared to have that effect (s 2(1)).[102] Future European Treaties may be designated by Order in Council and thus brought within the scope of the Act (s 1(3)). While such an Order in Council is delegated legislation, and could be challenged as ultra vires if the treaty which it named could not properly be regarded as a European Treaty,[103] such a challenge would be unlikely to succeed. The Treaty on European Union was designated a European Treaty not by Order in Council, but by the European Communities (Amendment) Act 1993. Through the doctrines of direct applicability and direct effect, no transformation or re-enactment is needed before many Community measures are enforceable in national courts.[104]

The European Community's powers include the making of international agreements with states outside the Union and with other international organisations.[105] New treaties are negotiated by the Commission in consultation with special committees appointed by the Council of Ministers and are concluded by the Council, generally after consulting the European Parliament (art 228). They are binding upon all member states and may contain provisions that are directly effective.[106] One consequence is that 'each time the Community, with a view to implementing a common policy envisaged by the Treaty, adopts provisions laying down common rules, ... the Member States no longer have the right, acting individually or even collectively, to undertake obligations with third countries which affect those rules'.[107] Thus in these situations there is a transfer of treaty-making power from member states to the Community. Unlike treaties made by the British government, treaties concluded by the Communities may have direct domestic effect without legislative implementation.[108] The competence of the Community to enter into treaties does not include power to subscribe to the European Convention on Human Rights in its own right; in the opinion of the European Court of Justice, this would require an amendment to the EC Treaty.[109]

C.   The United Kingdom and the Commonwealth[110]

In the heyday of empire, the imperial Crown, government and Parliament were at the apex of an impressive network of power that extended to many

---

[102] Ch 8 C.
[103] *R v HM Treasury, ex p Smedley* [1985] QB 657.
[104] Ch 8 B.
[105] EC Treaty, arts 113 (trade and commercial agreements), 238 (association agreements with states and international organisations) and 229–31 (relations with international organisations).
[106] Eg *Case 104/81, Hauptzollamt Mainz v Kupferberg & cie KG* [1982] ECR 3641, cited in Mann, op cit, p 118.
[107] *Case 22/70*, the ERTA case [1971] ECR 263, 274.
[108] See generally Hartley, *The Foundations of European Community Law*, ch 6; Mann, op cit, pp 113–19.
[109] *Re the Accession of the Community to the European Human Rights Convention* (*Opinion 2/94*) [1996] 2 CMLR 265; P Beaumont (1997) 1 Edin LR 235; and ch 19 B.
[110] See Roberts-Wray, *Commonwealth and Colonial Law*, and Dale, *The Modern Commonwealth*. Also Wheare, *The Constitutional Structure of the Commonwealth*, and de Smith, *The New Commonwealth and its Constitutions*.

countries. Legal power was exercised through legislation and executive decision in London; and the Judicial Committee of the Privy Council heard appeals from national courts across the world.[111] Imperial rule was often indirect rule, since many territories within the sovereignty or protection of the Crown had their own forms of government, possibly involving elected assemblies; other territories kept in place rulers already in power when they came within British influence.[112] Within a territory, the form of government might be laid down in a constitutional instrument, enacted by the imperial Parliament or issued by the Crown, whether under prerogative powers or under powers delegated by statute (for example, the Foreign Jurisdiction Acts 1890 and 1913). For some countries that had been settled from Britain, democratic forms developed by or during the 19th century: the need for responsible government in Canada was recognised in 1838.[113] While government within a territory might be subject to a constitution, the imperial authorities could always override this, if not by executive action then by recourse to the sovereignty of the Westminster Parliament; no written constitution restricted the imperial powers.[114]

Today, the former constitutional law of the colonies and the Empire is primarily of historic interest, except in the case of the few surviving overseas possessions of the United Kingdom.[115] The structure of the Commonwealth is scarcely a matter of law at all: the informality of the Commonwealth contrasts with the emphasis on law and legal form in the European Union. For the Commonwealth, there is no written constitution, nor, unlike most international organisations, was it created by treaty; it is 'a community of states in which the absence of a rigid legal basis of association is compensated by the bonds of common origin, history and legal tradition'.[116]

Dependence and independence[117]

The evolution of the Commonwealth involved a protracted process in which the United Kingdom's colonies and other dependent territories first received some kind of representative legislature; then acquired responsible self-government in domestic affairs while still being subject to imperial control in matters of defence and external relations; and later achieved full independence. By this last step, the territory became a separate state in international law, having its own organs of government and power to determine its own policies. Where British influence was felt, the English common law was often received into the legal system; and colonial government generated its own body of law relating to the powers and duties of colonial authorities. A notable response to the legal problems that arose from the existence of colonial

---

[111] Pages 370–2 and Ch 18 A below.
[112] Morris and Read, *Indirect Rule and the Search for Justice.*
[113] See the Earl of Durham's *Report on the Affairs of British North America.*
[114] In the leading case on colonial law, *Campbell v Hall* (1774) 1 Cowp 204, the dispute involved the Crown's power to legislate, not the authority of the British Parliament.
[115] In 1997, these included Anguilla, Bermuda, the British Indian Ocean Territory, the Cayman Islands, the Falkland Islands, Gibraltar, Hong Kong (until 30 June), the Turks and Caicos Islands and the (British) Virgin Islands.
[116] Jennings and Watts, op cit, p 266.
[117] See Roberts-Wray, op cit, chs 5, 6.

legislatures was the Colonial Laws Validity Act 1865.[118] The Act was passed to confirm, subject to certain limits, the authority of colonial legislatures to make laws that departed from the English common law or from imperial statutes of general application. The Act also authorised a colonial legislature, at least half of whose members were democratically elected in the colony, to make laws respecting its own constitution, powers and procedure, provided that such laws were passed in such manner and form as might be required by any Act of Parliament, other imperial legislation or colonial law applying to the colony.[119] This Act reinforced the ability of colonial legislatures to act within their devolved powers, but confirmed that their powers were limited and subject to imperial control. What became known as Dominion status developed in the late 19th century as certain colonies (particularly Canada, Australia, New Zealand and South Africa) moved towards full statehood.[120] By the mid 1920s, the Dominions had full internal autonomy in accordance with their constitutions (contained in Acts of the imperial Parliament: for example, the British North America Act 1867 in the case of Canada, and the Commonwealth of Australia Act 1900) and had acquired the right to conduct their own foreign relations. The imperial conference in 1926 declared that Great Britain and the Dominions were:

autonomous Communities within the British Empire, equal in status, in no way subordinate to another in any aspect of their domestic or external status, though united by a common allegiance to the Crown, and freely associated as members of the British Commonwealth of Nations.[121]

This important statement of equal status and free association reflected the changing conventional relationship between the United Kingdom and the Dominions, but in law the Dominions still had the status of colonies and were subject to the Colonial Laws Validity Act 1865. Thus in 1926 it was held that the Canadian Parliament had no power to abolish certain criminal appeals from Canadian courts to the Privy Council.[122]

To deal with these limitations on Dominion authority, and to implement resolutions of imperial conferences in 1926, 1929 and 1930,[123] the Statute of Westminster was enacted by the UK Parliament in 1931.[124] The lengthy preamble to the Statute described the Crown as the symbol of the free association of the members of the British Commonwealth of Nations, united by a common allegiance to the Crown; and referred to the 'established constitutional position' that changes in the law relating to the succession to the throne and the royal style and titles should receive the assent of the

---

118   Roberts-Wray, op cit, pp 396–409. For the background to the Act, see O'Connell and Riordan, *Opinions on Imperial Constitutional Law*, pp 60–74.
119   This was the background to *A-G for New South Wales v Trethowan* [1932] AC 526; p 73 above.
120   The older meaning of 'dominion' in the phrase, 'Her Majesty's dominions', denotes all territories belonging to the Crown, including the UK and colonies: Roberts-Wray, op cit, pp 23–9.
121   Cmd 2768, 1926, p 14; Dale, op cit, p 21.
122   *Nadan v R* [1926] AC 482; and see p 371 below.
123   Cmd 2768, 1926; Cmd 3479, 1930; and Cmd 3717, 1930.
124   Wheare, *The Statute of Westminster and Dominion Status*; Marshall, *Parliamentary Sovereignty and the Commonwealth*; Dale, op cit, part 1.

Dominion parliaments as well as of the UK Parliament.[125] The Statute broadened the powers of the Dominion legislatures by, for instance, authorising them to amend or repeal Acts of the UK Parliament applying to the Dominion (s 2). However, this did not authorise a legislature to ignore limits on its powers laid down in the Act containing the country's constitution.[126]

Section 4 of the Statute stated that no future act of the UK Parliament would extend to the Dominion as part of its law 'unless it is expressly declared in that Act that that Dominion has requested, and consented, to the enactment thereof'. The effect of this on the sovereignty of the Westminster Parliament was often discussed. In the *British Coal Corporation* case, Lord Sankey said that the power of the imperial Parliament to legislate for Canada on its own initiative remained unimpaired, adding 'But that is theory and has no relation to realities'.[127] A more decisive note was struck by the Supreme Court of South Africa: 'freedom once conferred cannot be revoked'.[128] It is unlikely that the UK Parliament would ever have wished to disregard s 4 of the Statute of Westminster. Had it done so, the Australian, Canadian or New Zealand courts would have acted properly if they had taken no notice of the attempt to legislate. But British courts would have been bound by the legislation.[129]

The ability of Westminster to legislate for Canada remained important in Canada long after the Statute of Westminster. This was because the British North America Act 1867, which contained Canada's constitution, included no amendment power: therefore legislation at Westminster was required to amend the Canadian constitution. This anomaly was removed when the Canada Act 1982 was enacted at Westminster to bring about the 'patriation' of the Canadian constitution to Canada. The 1982 Act, whose text had been prepared in Canada after a most controversial process,[130] gave the force of law to a Constitution Act which provided for its own future amendment; and it was declared that no future Act of the UK Parliament should extend to Canada as part of its law.[131] When the validity of the Canada Act 1982 was challenged by groups of indigenous Indians in Canada who claimed that their consent was needed to the legislation, the English Court of Appeal held that it was sufficient compliance with the Statute of Westminster that the 1982 Act declared that 'Canada' had requested and consented to its enactment; the court could not go behind this declaration.[132]

A similar but less controversial change took place in 1986 with the passing of the Australia Act at Westminster, together with related legislation by the

---

125   See p 255 above; also, on the abdication of Edward VIII, K H Bailey (1937–38) 3 *Politica* 1, 147, and, on the accession of Elizabeth II, Wheare, *Constitutional Structure of the Commonwealth*, pp 164–8.

126   See s 7(1) (Canada) and ss 8, 9(1) (Australia). For South Africa, see *Harris v Minister of the Interior* 1952(2) SA 428 and also D V Cowan (1952) 15 MLR 282, (1953) 16 MLR 273.

127   *British Coal Corporation v R* [1935] AC 500, 520.

128   *Ndlwana v Hofmeyr* 1937 AD 229, 237. And see *Blackburn v A-G* [1971] 2 All ER 1380.

129   See ch 4 B.

130   See *Re Amendment of the Constitution of Canada* (1981) 125 DLR (3d) 1; and Marshall, *Constitutional Conventions*, ch 11 (and app A, 10th edn of this work).

131   Canada Act 1982, s 2.

132   *Manuel v A-G* [1983] Ch 77 (and Marshall, *Constitutional Conventions*, ch 12); also *R v Foreign Secretary, ex p Indian Association of Alberta* [1982] QB 892.

parliaments of the Commonwealth of Australia and the Australian States. One effect was to sever the remaining legislative links between the United Kingdom and Australia; another was to terminate appeals to the Privy Council from any Australian court.[133]

In 1931, as we have seen, it was envisaged that there might be subjects on which the United Kingdom would continue to legislate on behalf of one or more Dominions. When after 1945 independence was granted to India, Pakistan, Ceylon, Ghana and many other countries, it was seen to be anomalous for the Westminster Parliament to retain any power to legislate for independent states, even with their consent. Thus it would be provided for a country at independence that the UK government should thereafter have no responsibility for the country's government; that the Colonial Laws Validity Act 1865 should cease to apply; and that no future Act of the UK Parliament should extend or be deemed to extend to the country in question as part of its law.[134]

During colonial government in a country there was often an active nationalist movement campaigning for early independence, with resulting strains on public order. But for the most part the actual conferring of independence took place in a lawful manner. One exception to this occurred in 1965 when Mr Ian Smith and other Cabinet ministers of the self-governing colony of Rhodesia, impatient with waiting for independence, unilaterally declared Rhodesia to be independent of the United Kingdom. The consequences of this unlawful declaration were complex[135] and for some years it seemed that this revolution had been successful. But internal and international pressure continued and in 1979 a constitutional conference in London laid the basis for a return to legality. In April 1980, under the authority of the Westminster Parliament, independence was conferred on the new state of Zimbabwe.[136]

The divisibility of the Crown

At one time the British Crown was considered to be a single, ubiquitous entity in the many territories under British sovereignty. Thus in 1919 the Privy Council referred to the Crown as 'one and indivisible throughout the Empire'.[137] But if, as we have seen,[138] the Crown was the legal embodiment of government, this unity could not be maintained in the light of responsible government in many colonies, the creation of federal constitutions in Canada and Australia (each having two levels of government), and (later) with the conferment of independence on former colonies. As separate governments came into being, the Crown in one sense comprehended them all; in reality the legal concept began to fragment. Moreover, when independence was conferred, obligations which the UK government had in relation to a

---

[133]   See J Goldring [1986] PL 192.
[134]   See eg Nigeria Independence Act 1960, s 1(2) and Sched 1.
[135]   They included the Southern Rhodesia Act 1965 and, in the Privy Council, *Madzimbamuto v Lardner-Burke* [1969] 1 AC 645; in the Rhodesian courts, *Dhlamini v Carter* 1968 (2) SA 464 and *R v Ndhlovu* 1968 (4) SA 515. (And see the 10th edn of this work, pp 430–2.)
[136]   See the Southern Rhodesia Act 1979, the Zimbabwe Act 1979 and SI 1979 No 1600.
[137]   *Theodore v Duncan* [1919] AC 696, at 706 (Lord Haldane).
[138]   Ch 12.

particular territory passed by succession to that country's government.[139] Thus the Crown 'in right of the United Kingdom' (ie the UK government) was held to have no continuing liability in respect of a royal proclamation of 1763 that reserved certain land in Canada for the Indian peoples; any liability arising from that proclamation was enforceable, if at all, against the Crown in right of Canada (ie the Canadian government).[140] While the transfer of responsibilities is an inevitable consequence of a country's independence, the divisibility of the Crown could arise at an earlier stage of colonial development.[141] Thus the Court of Appeal held that a passport issued to citizens of Mauritius by the governor of the colony was not a UK passport, even though the holders of such passports were 'citizens of the United Kingdom and Colonies'.[142] However, this decision did not take full account of the fact that the UK government *was* responsible for a colony's international relations; and it was 'the Crown in right of the Government of the United Kingdom'[143] which had full control over the actions of such a subordinate government.[144]

Membership of the Commonwealth

Independence of the United Kingdom and membership of the Commonwealth are not the same. The granting of independence to a dependent territory of the United Kingdom is a matter for the UK government and the territory concerned. But the admission of a new member to the Commonwealth requires the agreement of existing members. In 1971, it was declared by the heads of Commonwealth governments meeting at Singapore that the Commonwealth:

is a voluntary association of independent sovereign states, each responsible for its own policies, consulting and co-operating in the common interests of their peoples and in the promotion of international understanding and world peace.[145]

There are no written rules of membership.[146] Probably the most significant change in the basis of membership occurred in 1949 when India announced its intention of becoming a republic. Before then, all members owed a common allegiance to the Crown. In 1949, the response of other governments was, in the Declaration of London, to note India's desire to continue its full membership of the Commonwealth and its acceptance of the British Sovereign 'as the symbol of the free association of its independent member nations and as such the Head of the Commonwealth'. Since 1949, while some states have adopted republican status after becoming independent, others have become republics at the moment of independence or have become monarchies with their own royal head of state. In 1997, only a minority of

---

[139]   Cf *A-G v Great Southern and Western Rly* [1925] AC 754.
[140]   *R v Foreign Secretary, ex p Indian Association of Alberta* [1982] QB 892.
[141]   The judgments in *Ex p Indian Association* offer three different explanations of the date of the 'division' of the Crown.
[142]   *R v Home Secretary, ex p Bhurosah* [1968] 1 QB 266.
[143]   Crown Proceedings Act 1947, s 40(2)(b) and (c).
[144]   But cf *Tito v Waddell (No 2)* [1977] Ch 106, 254; and *Trawnik v Lennox* [1985] 2 All ER 368, at 375 (Browne-Wilkinson LJ).
[145]   Commonwealth Declaration, 22 January 1971 (Dale, op cit, p 41).
[146]   For the practice, see Dale, op cit, ch 3.

Commonwealth states owed allegiance to the Crown, but all states recognised the British Sovereign in the symbolic role of Head of the Commonwealth, a role that involves the Queen in no specific governmental functions.

Most states which have become independent of the United Kingdom since 1945 have considered it worthwhile to become members of the Commonwealth. In 1961, when South Africa had decided to become a republic, the government withdrew its application to remain in membership rather than have it rejected; with the ending of apartheid-based government 30 years later, South Africa was welcomed back to membership.[147] When a coup in Fiji in 1986 brought the republic of Fiji into existence, Fiji's membership of the Commonwealth lapsed.[148] A member state may decide to leave the Commonwealth at any time (secession is too strong a word for the act of withdrawal) and it seems likely that a member could be expelled against its wishes; in 1995, because of the lack of democracy and disregard for human rights, the membership of Nigeria was suspended. The category of Special Member has been devised for certain very small territories (including Nauru, a former dependent territory of Australia, and Tuvalu) which have the right to participate in activities of the Commonwealth but not to attend meetings of heads of Commonwealth governments.[149] Membership is reserved for independent states. Thus Bermuda and Gibraltar are within the Commonwealth since they are colonies of the United Kingdom, which is a member; but they are not members of the Commonwealth in their own right. In 1995, membership was extended to Mozambique, although this country had never been a dependency of the United Kingdom.

Meetings of heads of Commonwealth governments

After 1944, meetings of Commonwealth Prime Ministers were held in London and were presided over by the British Prime Minister; the secretariat for the meetings was provided by the British government. These meetings gave way to what are now biennial meetings of heads of Commonwealth governments, over which the head of government of the host country has presided. In 1965, it was agreed to establish a Commonwealth Secretariat, headed by a Secretary-General. The headquarters are in London, but the secretariat is responsible for servicing Commonwealth conferences wherever they may be held. The secretariat is a clearing house for information on questions of common concern and has oversight of many forms of practical Commonwealth cooperation. The Secretary-General has an important diplomatic role on international issues that directly affect the Commonwealth. Under the Commonwealth Secretariat Act 1966, an Act of the Westminster Parliament, the secretariat is a body corporate and its members, from many Commonwealth countries, are entitled to diplomatic immunities and privileges.

Since the enlargement of the Commonwealth, the nature of the heads of government meetings has changed. While they provide an umbrella for various forms of practical cooperation, the meetings themselves are mainly

---

[147]   And see the South Africa Act 1995.
[148]   And see page 518 below, note 229.
[149]   Dale, op cit, p 62.

concerned with contentious issues of world politics, such as economic development and the global environment. In 1971, the Singapore conference produced the Commonwealth Declaration, which defined the nature of the Commonwealth, stressed the diversity of its membership and stated the principles which were held in common by the members. In 1977, the heads of governments meeting in Britain issued a statement of a common policy on apartheid in sport, known as the Gleneagles Agreement. In 1991, the meeting at Harare re-affirmed the Singapore Declaration and renewed its support for the 'fundamental political values' of the Commonwealth (including democracy and the rule of law) and for the promotion of sustainable economic development within a framework of respect for human rights and the protection of the global environment.[150]

Other aspects of Commonwealth membership

As independent sovereign states, members of the Commonwealth do not observe any uniform constitutional pattern in their own systems of government. While most of them entered on independence with constitutions drafted under the guiding influence of Westminster and Whitehall, many of these gave way to new constitutions after independence or were pushed aside by political or military coups and civil war. In the case of members which are monarchies and owe allegiance to the Queen, a Governor-General is appointed by the Queen, on the advice of the government of the state in question, to carry out the functions of head of state. There was formerly uncertainty as to whether the constitutional powers of a Governor-General were the same as those of the Sovereign in the United Kingdom. After the controversial action in 1926 of Lord Byng, Governor-General of Canada, in refusing a dissolution to one Prime Minister and granting one to the next, the imperial conference in 1926 laid down that the Governor-General held the same position in relation to the affairs of the Dominion as the Sovereign did in the United Kingdom and that he was not the representative or agent of the UK government.[151] However, depending on the constitution of the country concerned, the Governor-General may be required to exercise a personal discretion which could not arise in the same form in the United Kingdom.[152] Where a Governor-General is appointed by the Queen on the advice of the government concerned, questions may arise as to her duties if thereafter she receives advice from that government to dismiss the Governor-General.[153] Answers to these questions depend on the constitution of the country in question: the UK Prime Minister has no standing to advise the Queen in the matter.

The United Kingdom's relations with other Commonwealth members are carried on by the Secretary of State for Foreign and Commonwealth Affairs. Members are represented in other member states by high commissioners;

---

[150]   And see A W Bradley [1991] PL 477.
[151]   Cmd 2768, 1926, p 7. And see Evatt, *The King and his Dominion Governors.*
[152]   As in Australia in 1975, when the Governor-General, Sir John Kerr, dismissed the Labor Prime Minister; ch 12 B.
[153]   V Bogdanor and G Marshall [1996] PL 205.

they do not have the title of ambassador but are members of the diplomatic service of their own state and are equal in rank and status to ambassadors. Members of the Commonwealth conduct their own defence and foreign policies and have their own treaty-making capacity. The UK government may conclude an international treaty on behalf of the United Kingdom and its own dependent territories, but it has no power to bind other member states. By comparison with the European Community, which exists as an entity in international law, the position of the Commonwealth in international law is uncertain.[154] Some areas of UK law are still affected by the history of the Commonwealth. Citizens of other Commonwealth countries were formerly under UK law regarded as British subjects but are now described as 'Commonwealth citizens'.[155] This allows them to exercise political rights if they are resident in the United Kingdom, but does not entitle them to enter the United Kingdom.

Appeals to the Privy Council

In deciding appeals from the courts of the dependent territories of the United Kingdom, the Judicial Committee of the Privy Council exercises the ancient jurisdiction of the King in Council to hear appeals from the overseas dependencies of the Crown.[156] This jurisdiction was based on 'the inherent prerogative right and, on all proper occasions, the duty of the King in Council to exercise an appellate jurisdiction, with a view not only to ensure ... the due administration of justice in the individual case, but also to preserve the due course of procedure generally'.[157] This jurisdiction was given statutory form by the Judicial Committee Acts of 1833 and 1844.

Where the jurisdiction survives, appeals may be brought without special leave of the Privy Council or with special leave. Appeals without special leave, available mainly in civil cases, are regulated by legislation applying to the territory in question. This legislation lays down the conditions for appeal and states whether the local court may exercise a discretion in deciding whether a question is in issue which ought to be decided by the Privy Council. In such cases, an intending appellant must apply to the local appellate court for a decision on whether the statutory requirements are satisfied. The Judicial Committee may interpret legislation regulating the right of appeal.[158]

Appeals with special leave of the Privy Council apply mainly in criminal cases: special leave may be granted by the Judicial Committee where the local court has no power to grant an appeal or, exceptionally, has in the exercise of its discretion decided not to grant it.[159] The Judicial Committee is not a court of criminal appeal in the usual sense of the term. Appeals are allowed with special leave only where there has been a clear departure from the requirements of justice and it is shown that by a disregard of the forms of legal

---

[154]   Fawcett, *The British Commonwealth in International Law*; Dale, op cit, ch 6; Jennings and Watts, op cit, pp 263–5.
[155]   British Nationality Act 1981, s 37; ch 20 A.
[156]   Ch 18 A; Roberts-Wray, op cit, pp 433–63; Dale, op cit, p 128.
[157]   *R v Bertrand* (1867) LR 1 PC 520, 530.
[158]   *Davis v Shaughnessy* [1932] AC 106.
[159]   Cf *Thomas v R* [1980] AC 125.

process or by some violation of the principles of natural justice, or otherwise, substantial and grave injustice has been done.[160]

In the colonies and other dependent territories, the local legislature may under its constitution have power to regulate the conditions on which appeals lie to the Privy Council; it will not have power to legislate contrary to the provisions of a UK Act applying to the territory.[161] Thus it cannot abolish the power of the Judicial Committee to grant special leave to appeal. When independence has been conferred, any state may legislate to abolish or curtail appeals to the Privy Council.[162] Most Commonwealth states have in fact abolished appeals to the Privy Council, but jurisdiction continues in respect of certain appeals from the Bahamas, Barbados, Belize, the Gambia, Jamaica, Malaysia, Mauritius, New Zealand, Singapore and from Trinidad and Tobago. In the case of Australia, surviving rights of appeal were abolished under the authority of the Australia Act 1986.[163] In Singapore, the right to appeal to the Judicial Committee (except by consent of both parties) was taken away in 1989, the evident aim of the government being to prevent an appeal to London about freedom of the press.[164]

It is evident that the legal link between Commonwealth states which arises from appeals to the Judicial Committee is less substantial than in the past. At one time, the Committee played an important if controversial role as a constitutional court, especially in regard to Canada; it helped to develop the common law in jurisdictions outside the British Isles, but without excluding autonomous developments in the law;[165] and it sought to preserve certain fundamentals of criminal justice.[166] From time to time proposals were made for re-constituting the Judicial Committee as a travelling Commonwealth court of appeal, but these never attracted much support.[167] The Committee's role is now of special significance in relation to those constitutions which include protection for fundamental human rights, but the degree of protection which the Committee has given in this role has been very uneven. In particular, the Committee has fluctuated between adopting a strict and legalistic approach to fundamental rights provisions and a broader, more purposive approach that recognises the constitution as a living instrument.[168]

---

[160] *Ibrahim v R* [1914] AC 599; *Prasad v R* [1981] 1 All ER 319. And see eg *Knowles v R* [1930] AC 366.

[161] Colonial Laws Validity Act 1865, s 2.

[162] *Moore v A-G of Irish Free State* [1935] AC 484; *British Coal Corporation v R* [1935] AC 500; *A-G for Ontario v A-G for Canada* [1947] AC 127.

[163] Page 366 above. And see G Nettheim (1965) 39 ALJ 39.

[164] See *Dow Jones Publishing Co (Asia) Inc v A-G of Singapore* [1989] 1 WLR 1308 (and [1990] PL 453).

[165] See eg *Invercargill City Council v Hamlin* [1996] 1 All ER 756.

[166] Eg *Dunkley v R* [1995] 1 AC 419 (withdrawal of counsel during murder trial); *Burut v Public Prosecutor* [1995] 2 AC 579 (confession obtained by oppression).

[167] Roberts-Wray, op cit, pp 461–3; J E S Fawcett, in Miller (ed), *Survey of Commonwealth Affairs: Problems of Expansion and Attrition 1953–1969*, p 429. And see Swinfen, *Imperial Appeal*, for an excellent historical account; and Stevens, *The Independence of the Judiciary*, chs 4 and 8.

[168] See K D Ewing, in Finnie, Himsworth and Walker (eds), *Edinburgh Essays in Public Law*, at 231. For the broader approach, see *Minister of Home Affairs v Fisher* [1980] AC 319 and *A-G of Trinidad and Tobago v Whiteman* [1991] 2 AC 240; and (compensation for breach of fundamental right) *Maharaj v A-G of Trinidad and Tobago (No 2)* [1979] AC 385. See also note 169 below.

Not surprisingly, the resulting case-law on issues such as freedom of expression and the death penalty is not wholly satisfactory.[169] Yet it still provides an ultimate court of appeal for the smaller jurisdictions in the Commonwealth, and the demise of its jurisdiction over Hong Kong during 1997 is not merely symbolic.

---

[169]   See (press freedom) *A-G v Antigua Times Ltd* [1976] AC 16 and *Hector v A-G of Antigua* [1990] 2 AC 312; (death penalty) *Runyowa v R* [1967] 1 AC 26, *Ong Ah Chuan v Public Prosecutor* [1981] AC 648 (criticised in Pannick, *Judicial Review of the Death Penalty*), *Riley v A-G of Jamaica* [1983] 1 AC 719, reversed in *Pratt v A-G of Jamaica* [1994] 2 AC 1 (excessive delay on death row), and *Reckley v Minister of Public Safety (No 2)* [1996] 2 WLR 281.

CHAPTER 16

The armed forces

In the interests of constitutional government and the rule of law, the exercise of the physical might of the modern state must be subject to democratic control. Experience of government at the hands of Cromwell's army led after the restoration of the monarchy in 1660 to a declaration by Parliament in the Militia Act 1661 that:

the sole supreme government, command and disposition of the militia and of all forces by sea and land is, and by the laws of England ever was, the undoubted right of the Crown.

Subsequent attempts by Charles II and James II against parliamentary opposition to maintain their own armies led to the declaration in the Bill of Rights that:

the raising or keeping of a standing army within the Kingdom in time of peace, unless it be with consent of Parliament, is against law.

This declaration remains important not because there is now any possibility that Parliament would withdraw authority for the continued maintenance of an army but because it asserts that the armed forces are constitutionally subordinate to Parliament.

Legislative authority for the armed forces[1]

The armed forces of the Crown include the army, the Royal Navy, the Royal Air Force, and the reserve forces. Since the Bill of Rights, authority for the maintenance of the armed forces on land during peacetime has never been granted on a permanent basis but only for limited periods. Statutory authority has been needed for three reasons: to overcome the Bill of Rights provision; to provide funds to pay for the armed forces; and to authorise discipline within the armed forces to be enforced by rules which differ from the common law. Statutory authority was not needed to authorise the maintenance of the navy, which had not aroused the suspicion of Parliament and was not included in the prohibition in the Bill of Rights against a standing armed

---

[1] For the history of the legal position of the armed forces, see Maitland, *Constitutional History*, pp 275–80, 324–9, 447–62; Anson, *Law and Custom of the Constitution*, vol II(2), ch 10. For the current position, see Rowe, *Defence: The Legal Implications*, and Rowe, *The Gulf War 1990–91*.

force. But naval discipline was from 1661 authorised by statute and the appropriation of funds by Parliament to maintain the navy has long been authorised annually as for the other armed forces.

After the Bill of Rights, it became the custom of Parliament each year to pass a Mutiny Act, giving authority for one year to the Crown to maintain armed forces up to the limit of manpower stated in the Act and to enforce rules of discipline. Eventually what had become a lengthy and detailed collection of rules of military law was codified in the Army Act 1881. This code was until 1955 continued in force from year to year by the passing of an Act known after 1917 as the Army and Air Force (Annual) Act. Amendments to the 1881 Act were made when necessary by the annual Act. When a separate Air Force was constituted in 1917, its discipline was governed by the Army Act 1881 with modifications.

By 1955, it had come to be accepted that approval of the size of the armed forces was granted through parliamentary consideration of the defence estimates and the formal procedure for appropriating supply to the armed forces. Following a series of reports from select committees of the Commons,[2] there was enacted the Army Act 1955 and the Air Force Act 1955. Each Act was in the first instance limited to a duration of 12 months, but for a period of five years it could be continued in force from year to year by resolution of each House of Parliament. At the end of the five years a further Act would be needed.[3]

The effect of this has been to use the requirement for regular approval of the armed forces as a device whereby the Commons may scrutinise periodically the rules and procedures of service discipline. Thus the Armed Forces Acts of 1966, 1971, 1976, 1981, 1986, 1991 and 1996 have revised the disciplinary codes of the forces and related legislation. One feature of the procedure has been that each Armed Forces Bill has after second reading been referred to a select committee of the Commons, which has examined the Bill thoroughly, a process which is now a procedural rarity.[4] In 1971, the Naval Discipline Act 1957 was brought within the same system. There has been a tendency to make similar provision for the main matters of discipline in each of the armed forces.

Legislative authority for maintaining the armed forces does not confer power on the executive to conscript citizens into the forces. Recruitment for the navy by impressment under the prerogative is now only a matter of history. In both world wars conscription was authorised by Parliament. After the Second World War, conscription was continued under the National Service Act 1948 until its operation was brought to an end in 1960. Like earlier legislation, the 1948 Act made provision for conscientious objectors to military service.[5]

---

2   HC 244 and 331 (1951–52), 289 (1952–53) and 223 (1953–54).
3   For an argument that these arrangements do not overcome the Bill of Rights prohibition on a standing army, see (1981) 4 State Research 149; cf *The Times*, 17 June 1981.
4   See eg HC 170 (1985–86), HC 179 (1990–91), and HC 143 (1995–96).
5   For details, see 8th edn of this work, pp 394–6. See also Loveland (ed), *Frontiers of Criminality*, ch 3, where it is pointed out that in the First World War in particular objectors found themselves exposed to punishment 'without receiving the benefit of the procedural due process protection traditionally associated with the criminal trial'.

As well as the full-time regular forces of the Crown, the reserve forces are maintained under statutory authority. The legislation makes provision for the recall of the reserve forces, in some circumstances by notice from the Secretary of State for Defence, but in the case of imminent national danger or great emergency by an order of the Sovereign, signified by the Secretary of State and notified to Parliament; if Parliament is not sitting at the time, it must meet within five days.[6] It is an offence for a member of the reserve forces to fail to respond to a call out, unless he or she has leave or reasonable excuse. The power to recall was used (selectively) during the Gulf hostilities when those with 'medical qualifications were called out to supplement volunteers with relevant military and medical experience'.[7] Under the Reserve Forces (Safeguarding of Employment) Act 1985, an employer must reinstate a reservist at the end of his or her period of service.[8]

Central organisation for defence

Like other branches of central government, the armed forces are placed under the control of ministers of the Crown, who are in turn responsible to Parliament. Formerly each of the main services had its own ministerial head. Today the responsibility for a unified defence policy rests upon the Secretary of State for Defence, whose office has undergone several changes since the post of Minister of Defence was created and occupied by Winston Churchill in the Second World War. In 1964, the Ministry of Defence became a unified ministry for the three services and absorbed the Admiralty, the War Office and the Air Ministry.[9] The present ministerial structure dates from May 1981, when the junior minister for the navy was dismissed after publicly criticising proposed reductions in Britain's naval strength. The Prime Minister promptly abolished the separate junior ministerial posts for the three services. The Ministry was in 1997 headed by the Secretary of State for Defence, with (*a*) a minister of state responsible for all the armed forces, (*b*) a minister of state and a parliamentary under-secretary responsible for defence procurement and equipment, and (*c*) a parliamentary under-secretary responsible for a range of matters.

All statutory powers for the defence of the realm which formerly were vested in the separate service ministers were in 1964 vested in the Secretary of State.[10] The creation of a unified Ministry of Defence was necessary because it had been found inadequate for a Minister of Defence to seek to control defence policy by coordinating the policies of three departments responsible to separate ministers. A unified ministry was also essential if the defence budget was to strike a proper balance between the commitments, resources and roles of the three services. Within the Ministry of Defence, there is a Defence Council, whose members include the defence ministers, the Chief of the Defence Staff, the three service chiefs of staff and the Vice Chief of the Defence Staff. Beneath the Defence Council there are separate boards for the

---

6   Reserve Forces Act 1996, ss 52–4.
7   P Rowe [1991] PL 170, 173.
8   See *Slaven v Thermo Engineers Ltd* [1992] ICR 295.
9   Cmnd 2097, 1963.
10   Defence (Transfer of Functions) Act 1964.

navy, the army and the air force, to whom is delegated management of the three services, including formal powers in relation to the regulation and discipline of each service.[11] The chiefs of staff are the professional heads of the armed forces; they give professional advice to the government on strategy and military operations and on the military implications of defence policy.

The collective responsibility of the government for defence is exercised primarily through the Cabinet's Committee on Defence and Overseas Policy under the chairmanship of the Prime Minister. In 1997, the members of the committee were the Deputy Prime Minister, the Foreign Secretary, the Chancellor of the Exchequer, the Home Secretary, the Secretary of State for Defence, the President of the Board of Trade and the Attorney-General. In attendance on this committee are the Chief of the Defence Staff and the chiefs of staff of each of the three services if the business so requires.[12] Major questions of defence policy cannot be decided in purely military terms without reference to the government's financial and economic policies, which affect the size, disposition and equipment of the armed forces.

Parliamentary control of the armed forces

As we shall see in chapter 21, the chain of command within the police stops with the chief constable and neither local police authorities nor central government may give him instructions on the operational use of the police. This is not the case with the armed forces. In the case of the army, for example, the line of command runs upwards from the private soldier, through his commanding officer and higher levels of command to the Chief of the Defence Staff and the Secretary of State for Defence. During active operations many immediate decisions have to be taken by soldiers in the field. But the tasks which are undertaken by the armed forces, the objectives which they are set, and the manner in which they carry out these tasks are matters for which the government is accountable to Parliament – whether it be the activities of the troops in Northern Ireland, the use of the army to empty dustbins during a prolonged strike by local authority workers (as in Glasgow in 1975), the making of a controversial public speech by a high-ranking army officer, the sinking of the Argentinian ship *General Belgrano* during the Falklands conflict in 1982, or the conduct of the armed forces during the Gulf hostilities or while performing peace-keeping duties in what was once Yugoslavia. The full range of parliamentary procedures which are available in respect of other branches of central government may be used in respect of defence and the armed forces. Thus the Public Accounts Committee has often investigated cases of excessive spending by the services.

Since 1979, the Defence Committee of the House of Commons has regularly examined the Ministry of Defence's annual statement on the defence estimates. It has also conducted major inquiries into strategic nuclear weapons policy, the handling of press and public information during the

---

[11]   The boards also deal with grievances of service personnel. See Army Act 1955, s 180, and Armed Forces Act 1996, s 20.

[12]   Others, including the British Ambassador to Peking, may be invited to attend as appropriate.

Falklands conflict, and the future defence of the Falkland Islands.[13] The committee played an important part in the Westland affair and in the process did much to raise the profile and highlight the value of select committees generally.[14] More recently the committee has examined ethnic monitoring and the armed forces,[15] and business appointments taken by service personnel and Ministry of Defence officials.[16] In 1988–89, the committee expressed concern about the lack of availability of merchant shipping for defence purposes,[17] and in 1994–95 it delivered a strong rebuke to the Ministry of Defence for its response to allegations of a 'Gulf War syndrome' afflicting those who had served in the conflict, as well as their families. The Ministry was said to have been 'reactive rather than proactive', and to have behaved with 'scepticism, defensiveness and general torpor'.[18]

Defence policies and expenditure are often matters of keen political debate in the House. As mentioned earlier, military law has received close scrutiny from select committees appointed to consider the Armed Forces Bills. Members of the forces are entitled under service regulations to communicate with MPs on all matters, including service matters, so long as they do not disclose secret information, but it is the policy of the Ministry of Defence that wherever possible servicemen should pursue the normal channels of complaint open to them through superior officers.[19] While allegations of maladministration on the part of the Ministry of Defence may be referred by MPs for investigation by the Parliamentary Ombudsman, it is outside his jurisdiction to investigate action relating to appointments, pay, discipline, pensions, or other personnel matters affecting service in the armed forces; nor may he investigate complaints relating to the conduct of judicial proceedings under military law.[20] A proposal for a military ombudsman has not received very much support.[21]

The nature of military law[22]

Military law is the internal law of the armed forces, administered by officers with appropriate authority, by courts-martial and on appeal by the Courts-Martial Appeal Court. It is made by Parliament and, under the authority of Parliament, by the defence authorities by means of Queen's Regulations. There is also power to make rules of procedure for the administration of military law. Military law must be distinguished from 'martial law', a term used to describe the situation which arises when the normal processes of law and justice have broken down and the military exercise de facto authority over the public at large.[23] Strictly speaking, military law applies to the army alone. Air

---

13   See respectively HC 35, 130 (1980–81), HC 17–I (1982–83) and HC 154 (1982–83).
14   See HC 518 and 519 (1985–86). Also ch 10 D above.
15   HC 391 (1987–88).
16   HC 392 (1987–88).
17   HC 495 (1988–89).
18   HC 197 (1994–95), para 60.
19   Army Act 1955, ss 180 and 181. Cf the Stevenson case, HC 112 (1954–55).
20   Parliamentary Commissioner Act 1967, Sched 3, paras 6, 10.
21   Cmnd 4509, 1971, app 5.
22   See the Manual of Military Law for a complete account, and J Stuart-Smith (1969) 85 LQR 478 for a lucid introduction.
23   Ch 25 C.

force law was founded upon the army's scheme of discipline and closely resembles it. Discipline within the navy derived from separate statutes but is today being brought closer to army and air force law.

Military law is the basis of discipline in the armed forces, for a disciplined force could not be run with reliance on the ordinary law applicable to civilians. For example, an employee's misconduct in private employment may lead to his being dismissed. Misconduct by a soldier may eventually lead to his discharge, but a citizen who has agreed to enter the armed forces necessarily gives up the freedom to walk out on the job which a private employee has. In the case of a conscript, his freedom of decision has been taken from him by the legislator.

The Army Act 1955, and its counterparts for the air force and the navy, create a large number of offences, including mutiny, insubordination, disobedience to orders, desertion, absence without leave, malingering, and, by s 69 (as amended by the Armed Forces Act 1986), a residual offence of any act or omission to 'the prejudice of good order and military discipline'. It is also an offence against the Army Act, s 70, for any person subject to military law to commit, whether in the United Kingdom or elsewhere, a civil offence ie an offence punishable by English criminal law or which, if committed in England, would be so punishable. Because of the loss of freedom involved in military service, it is important that, in the absence of conscription, enlistments into the forces are voluntary. The formal process of enlistment is laid down by the Army Act. The terms of engagement upon which members of the forces are enlisted are governed by regulations made by the Defence Council; it is provided that the statutory rights of existing members of the forces are not to be varied or revoked by a change of regulations except with their consent.[24]

Military law and human rights

Military law is the basis of discipline in the armed forces, for a disciplined force could not be run on the ordinary law applicable to civilians. But it does not follow from this that those who join the armed forces should be required to surrender the right to be treated fairly or that they should be expected to waive their human rights. In 1994 (as a result of the requirements of EC law), the Sex Discrimination Act 1975 was extended to members of the forces,[25] and there have been many cases, some highly controversial, involving servicewomen who were discharged because of their pregnancy and who have been able successfully to seek compensation as a result.[26] Less successful were the men and women who challenged their administrative discharge from the armed forces on account of their homosexual orientation. Although homosexual acts in the armed forces are no longer a criminal offence, this does not prevent such conduct from constituting a ground for discharge, and it continues to be the policy that homosexual activity or orientation should be an absolute bar to membership of the forces.[27] Yet although 'there has been a

---

[24] Armed Forces Act 1966, s 2.
[25] SI 1994 No 3276.
[26] For background to this issue, see *Ministry of Defence v Cannock* [1994] ICR 918.
[27] Criminal Justice and Public Order Act 1994, s 146.

progressive development and refinement of public and professional opinion at home and abroad', it was held by the Court of Appeal that the policy was not irrational in 1994, though the view was expressed by Simon Brown LJ that 'so far as this country's international obligations are concerned, the days of this policy are numbered'.[28] Concern about human rights failings in the armed forces was also addressed by the Commission for Racial Equality in 1996, with the publication of its report on racial discrimination in the Household Cavalry and the army, following 'years of concern by the CRE at the effective colour bar operated by the Guards Regiments'. The CRE is said to have 'come within a hair's breadth of serving a non-discrimination notice' and was only persuaded not to do so by an undertaking from the army 'to beef up recruitment from ethnic minorities and a programme to increase racial awareness'.[29]

The Race Relations Act 1976 expressly applied to the armed forces, though enforcement was by way of a complaint to the Defence Council under the Army Act 1955.[30] The Sex Discrimination Act 1975 was extended to members of the forces only in 1994, in order to comply with Council Directive 76/207/EEC. In so extending the Act the regulations provide that nothing is to render unlawful an act done for the purpose of ensuring the combat effectiveness of the naval, military or air forces of the Crown. Further reforms in this area were made by the Armed Forces Act 1996 'as part of an overall adoption of a more consistent approach to access to industrial tribunals across the range of existing and proposed employment protection legislation'.[31] Thus under the Act complaints relating to race discrimination, sex discrimination and equal pay may now be made to industrial tribunals, though in all cases complainants are required to submit their case for consideration under the services' internal grievance procedures, a qualification which at least in sex discrimination complaints involves a qualification rather than an extension of an existing right. Nevertheless these arrangements were approved by the Defence Select Committee, despite objections from both the CRE and the EOC, on the ground that in 'most circumstances internal redress procedures will be the most satisfactory means' for resolving complaints. The committee did, however, propose that there should be an opportunity in some cases for the simultaneous pursuit of complaints internally and before industrial tribunals. Further rights of application to industrial tribunals were made in 1993 in respect of a broad range of employment protection measures.

Courts-martial

The constitution and proceedings of the military courts are regulated by the Army Act 1955, the Rules of Procedure (Army) 1972, and the Queen's Regulations. There has been some concern about the procedures, leading to

---

28 *R v Ministry of Defence, ex p Smith* [1996] QB 517. The Defence Committee did not recommend any change to current policy (HC 143 (1995–96), para 34).
29 See J Mackenzie, *New Law Journal*, 14 June 1996. For an account of racial discrimination in the armed forces, see HC 143 (1995–96), pp 209–15 (extracts from memorandum submitted by Commission for Racial Equality on the Armed Forces Bill).
30 See *R v Army Board, ex p Anderson* [1992] 2 QB 169.
31 HC 143 (1995–96), p 154.

a number of significant reforms in the Armed Forces Act 1996, which were said to constitute 'the most important part' of the Act.[32] These reforms follow a decision of the European Commission on Human Rights and may have the effect of bringing the law and practice in this area more fully into line with art 6 of the European Convention on Human Rights which provides that in the determination of any criminal charge against him 'everyone is entitled to a fair and public hearing within a reasonable time by an independent and impartial tribunal established by law'. In *Findlay v United Kingdom*,[33] in holding admissible an application by a British soldier who had been convicted by a court-martial, the Commission called into question the 'independence and impartiality of the court-martial procedure', referring to the jurisprudence of the court which has established criteria for assessing the independence of tribunals, these including 'the manner of appointment of members, the duration of their terms of office, the guarantees afforded by the procedure against outside pressures and whether the body presents an appearance of independence'. The main concerns about the court-martial procedures before the 1996 reforms related to the independence of the members of the court-martial from the prosecuting authority, arising in particular from their manner of appointment.

Charges against any law can be tried by district, field or general court-martial, the court consisting of a President and four army officers. A general court-martial is convened by a Convening Officer who would normally be a major-general in the army. According to the European Commission of Human Rights:

the Convening Officer is empowered to direct upon what charges the accused is to be tried, to decide the wording of these charges, to decide on the type of court-martial required and to convene the court-martial. He appoints the members of the court-martial and appoints, or directs, a commanding officer to appoint, the Prosecuting Officer.[34]

The Convening Officer is thus not only 'central to the prosecution of a case' but also the person responsible for the tribunal to hear it. In the *Findlay* case all five members of the court-martial were serving army officers, not only subordinate in rank to the Convening Officer but, as members of units in the London District, were under his overall command. One of the members moreover had the Convening Officer as his second superior reporting officer while the President was on the Convening Officer's staff. The Convening Officer's role does not, however, end there for the finding of guilt and the sentence of a court-martial do not take effect until confirmed by a higher military authority, referred to as the Confirming Officer, who may 'withhold confirmation, commute a punishment for one or more lesser punishments and postpone the carrying out of the sentence'. The fact that the Convening Officer normally acted as Confirming Officer gave 'further cause to doubt the independence of the court-martial from the prosecuting authority'.[35] A person sentenced by a court-martial may also petition higher authority for a

---

[32] HC Deb, 13 December 1995, col 1027.
[33] (1996) 21 EHRR CD 7.
[34] Ibid, at p CD 18.
[35] Ibid.

review of the sentence. The sentencing powers of courts-martial were refined by the Armed Forces Acts 1986 and 1991, reflecting developments in sentencing law in the civil jurisdiction.

The other key actor in the court-martial procedure is the Judge Advocate-General, who must be a person who has a ten-year general qualification within the meaning of the Courts and Legal Services Act 1990, s 71, appointed by the Crown on the recommendation of the Lord Chancellor. He may be removed from office only for inability or misbehaviour.[36] Amongst his duties, which do not include the task of prosecuting, is to provide a legally qualified judge advocate to attend the more important courts-martial. The Judge Advocate's function at a court-martial is to give expert and independent advice to the court on the law and to summarise the evidence; although he must act judicially, he is not a member of the court and does not retire with the court when it is considering its findings. The Judge Advocate-General's office also plays a role in the confirming and reviewing stages of the court-martial process. Thus the Confirming Officer must consult the office for advice which will be given by a judge advocate other than the one who assisted the tribunal. The reviewing authorities may also consult the Judge Advocate-General's office, though it appears that the applicant is not entitled to be informed of 'the fact or nature of the advice obtained from the Judge Advocate-General's office'. It was held by the European Commission on Human Rights in the *Findlay* case that this involvement of the Judge Advocate-General's office (which otherwise has duties of legal adviser to the Ministry of Defence) 'is not sufficient to dispel any doubt as to the court-martial's independence'.[37] Where a person has been convicted by a court-martial and the conviction has been reversed because new evidence reveals beyond reasonable doubt that there has been a miscarriage of justice, the Secretary of State must now compensate the victim of the miscarriage.[38]

Even apart from the decision of the European Court of Human Rights in the *Findlay* case,[39] there is a strong argument for the reform of the court-martial procedures in order to give the appearance of a fair trial and in order to 'remove the impression, however mistaken, that the chain of command can have an undue influence over court martial proceedings'.[40] Two initiatives were in fact taken by the government, the first administrative and the second statutory. So far as the former is concerned, it was announced that the role of the Convening Officer in the form described above would cease and the duties be divided, with many functions being transferred to new bodies independent of the chain of command. In particular, new prosecuting authorities would be established, staffed by legal officers, with the responsibility to decide whether to prosecute and what charges should be brought, and to conduct the prosecution. Moreover '[t]he administrative arrangements for courts-martial will be in the hands of cells independent of both higher authorities and the prosecuting

---

[36] Courts-Martial (Appeals) Act 1951, ss 29–32 (as amended by the Courts and Legal Services Act 1990, Sched 10). See ch 18 below. For the history of the Judge Advocate-General, see Stuart-Smith, op cit.

[37] For developments in Canada, see *R v Genereaux* (1992) 88 DLR (4th) 110.

[38] Armed Forces Act 1991, s 10 and Sched 1.

[39] On 25 February 1997, the Court upheld the complaint under art 6(1) ECHR for lack of due independence and impartiality.

[40] HC Deb, 13 December 1995, col 1028.

authorities. These cells will be responsible for selecting court-martial members, who will be officers who are not in the same command as the accused'.[41] So far as statutory initiatives are concerned, these were taken principally in the form of a number of amendments to the Army Act 1955 which, inter alia, remove the provisions for findings of courts-martial to be the subject of confirmation and revision at the direction of the Confirming Officer. This means that court-martial decisions will take immediate effect, as was already the case in the Royal Navy. The Armed Forces Act 1996 also introduced a new simplified one-stage procedure (in place of the previous two-stage procedure) for the review by the Defence Council or its delegate of findings of guilt and sentence by court-martial. These changes were fully supported by the Select Committee on the Armed Forces Bill.[42]

Courts-Martial Appeal Court

An important link between military courts and the ordinary judicial system is provided by the Courts-Martial Appeal Court, which is governed by the Courts-Martial (Appeals) Act 1968. The judges of the court are the Lord Chief Justice, the judges of the Court of Appeal, and such of the judges of the Queen's Bench Division of the High Court and corresponding judges for Scotland and Northern Ireland as may be nominated, together with such other persons of legal experience as the Lord Chancellor may appoint. A person convicted by a court-martial may appeal to the court against both conviction and sentence, which means that all court-martial decisions are subject to scrutiny by a civilian court. But leave to appeal must be obtained from the court itself, and only one application for leave to appeal may be made.[43] Before he can apply for leave to appeal, a convicted person must first await confirmation of the sentence and, unless he is under sentence of death, must petition the Defence Council for the quashing of his conviction. In deciding whether to grant leave to appeal, the court must have regard to any opinion of the Judge Advocate-General on whether the case is a fit one for appeal. In deciding an appeal, the court must consider whether a conviction is in all the circumstances unsafe; otherwise the appeal must be dismissed.[44] A further appeal to the House of Lords lies by leave of the court or of the House on a point of law of general public importance.[45]

Judicial control of military jurisdiction

Courts-martial are limited to the powers conferred on them by statute. The prerogative orders of certiorari or prohibition lie, at the discretion of the Queen's Bench Divisional Court, to control the limits of jurisdiction of a court-martial, just as they lie to control all inferior courts or tribunals on jurisdictional matters.[46] Where as a result of a decision by a court-martial a person is detained in prison, he or she may recover freedom by habeas corpus

---

41   Ibid.
42   HC 143 (1995–96), para 12.
43   *R v Grantham* [1969] 2 QB 574.
44   Courts-Martial (Appeals) Act 1968, s 12 (as amended by the Criminal Appeal Act 1995, Sched 2, para 5).
45   Eg *Cox v Army Council* [1963] AC 48 and *R v Warn* [1970] AC 394.
46   *Grant v Gould* (1792) 2 HBL 69.

if it can be shown that the decision was outside the jurisdiction of the court-martial, for example, because he or she was not a person subject to military law.[47] These remedies were especially important before the creation of the Courts-Martial Appeal Court. In fact the Divisional Court had come to take a narrow view of the extent to which it could intervene in imposing proper standards of justice upon courts-martial and was inclined to intervene only when there was a clear excess of jurisdiction and not when serious procedural errors had occurred.[48]

This disinclination to intervene may have stemmed from a wider reluctance on the part of the courts to become involved in disciplinary grievances for which military channels of redress exist. This reluctance was seen at work in cases in which former soldiers sought to recover damages from the military authorities or from individual officers who had been concerned with disciplinary proceedings against them. In one such case, *Heddon v Evans*,[49] a distinction was drawn between liability (*a*) for an act done in excess of or without jurisdiction by the military tribunal, which amounts to an assault, false imprisonment or other common law wrong, and (*b*) for an act which, though within jurisdiction and in the course of military discipline, is alleged to have been done maliciously and without reasonable or probable cause. Only in the former case would the military officers be held liable. The problem resembles that which arises in relation to the individual liability of magistrates and the members of other inferior tribunals.[50] In the present context, it seems that it is still open to the House of Lords to decide whether an action will lie for the malicious abuse of military authority without reasonable and probable cause.[51] Probably the major obstacle which faces a former soldier in seeking to recover damages in respect of his dismissal from the service of the Crown is that at common law a soldier serves at the pleasure of the Crown.[52]

Who is subject to military law?

It is not only serving members of the armed forces and reservists undergoing training who are subject to military law. Various classes of civilians are also subject to military law. As well as civilian employees of the Ministry of Defence who accompany the armed forces when they are on active service, the Army Act 1955 makes subject to military law, albeit with modifications, civilians who are employed outside the United Kingdom within the limits of the command of any officer commanding a body of the regular forces. Also subject to military law are the families of members of the armed forces who are residing with them outside the United Kingdom, and even relatives merely staying with a service family on holiday.[53] The main effect of this is to make the families of British servicemen in Germany and elsewhere subject to be tried under

---

47   *R v Governor of Wormwood Scrubs, ex p Boydell* [1948] 2 KB 193.
48   Eg *R v Secretary of State for War, ex p Martyn* [1949] 2 All ER 242, and see D C Holland [1950] CLP 173; de Smith, Woolf and Jowell, *Judicial Review of Administrative Action*, p 270.
49   (1919) 35 TLR 642. And see *Dawkins v Paulet* (1869) LR 5 QBD 94.
50   Ch 18 A.
51   Eg *Fraser v Balfour* (1918) 34 TLR 502.
52   Ch 31 B.
53   Army Act 1955, s 209 and Sched 5. See also Armed Forces Act 1986, s 80. And see G J Borrie (1969) 32 MLR 35.

military law for 'civil offences', defined by s 70 of the 1955 Act as acts or omissions punishable under English law or which, if committed in England, would be so punishable. In *Cox v Army Council*,[54] it was held that a 'civil offence' for this purpose included the offence of careless driving on a public road in Germany.[55] In view of difficulties encountered in entrusting such extensive jurisdiction over civilians to courts-martial, the Armed Forces Act 1976 authorised the Secretary of State for Defence with the approval of the Lord Chancellor to specify areas abroad to be served by a Standing Civilian Court. The court deals with the less serious offences committed by civilians in the area concerned. It consists of a legally qualified magistrate, appointed by the Lord Chancellor to the staff of the Judge Advocate General; for dealing with juvenile offenders, he sits with two other persons. As in the case of courts-martial, the sentencing powers of the Standing Civilian Court were extended by the Armed Forces Acts 1986 and 1991.

Dual jurisdiction

A person subject to military law continues to be subject to the ordinary criminal law and to the jurisdiction of the criminal courts in the United Kingdom. In the context of military law, by a somewhat confusing usage which will be followed here, the ordinary criminal courts are referred to as 'civil courts' to distinguish them from military courts. Except so far as Parliament provides otherwise, the soldier's obligations under the Army Act and Queen's Regulations are in addition to his or her duties as a citizen.

As we have seen, s 70 of the Army Act provides that a civil offence committed by a person subject to military law may be dealt with as an offence against military law; but certain serious crimes (including treason, murder, manslaughter and rape) must, if committed in the United Kingdom, be tried by the competent civil court. In practice, most criminal offences committed by members of the armed forces in the United Kingdom are dealt with in peacetime by the civil courts. The decision rests with the civil prosecutor: offences affecting the person or property of a civilian will usually be prosecuted in the civil courts.[56] But even alleged breaches of the Official Secrets Acts may be dealt with in civil rather than military courts, as with the prosecution of eight signals personnel based in Cyprus who were prosecuted unsuccessfully in 1986 under the 1911 Act for allegedly passing intelligence information to enemy agents in return for sexual favours.[57]

Where a person subject to military law has been tried for an offence by court-martial or has been dealt with summarily by his or her commanding officer, a civil court may not try him or her subsequently for an offence which is sub-

---

54   [1963] AC 48.
55   See also HC 143 (1995–96), p 169.
56   Stuart-Smith, op cit, p 492.
57   A subsequent inquiry found the pre-trial detention and questioning of the suspects to be unlawful, in the sense that the 'procedures in RAF and military law intended to protect individuals against oppressive treatment and arbitrary detention had been honoured more in the breach than in the observance'. The government undertook to make ex gratia payments to those involved. See Cmnd 9781, 1986 (Calcutt Report); A W Bradley [1986] PL 363.

stantially the same as that offence.[58] Apart from this there is no restriction on a civil court trying a member of the armed forces for an offence under criminal law. A person tried by a civil court in the United Kingdom or elsewhere is not liable to be tried again under military law in respect of the same or substantially the same offence.[59] In general, a person who is no longer subject to military law is liable to be tried under military law for offences committed while he or she was so subject, but only within prescribed time limits after he or she ceased to be subject to military law (three months in the case of summary proceedings and six months in the case of trial by court-martial).[60]

Conflict of duty

Does the dual jurisdiction of the military and civil courts lead to a possible conflict of duty for the soldier? In theory there is no conflict since military law is part of the law of the land and a soldier is only required to obey orders which are lawful.[61] If an order involves a breach of the general law, a soldier is not only under no obligation to obey it but is under an obligation not to obey it. But in practice, particularly when troops are operating in a peace-keeping role within the United Kingdom at a time when the civil courts are functioning, as now in Northern Ireland, soldiers may be placed in an awkward position. They are not trained, nor may they have time, to assess the legality of an order. But if, for example, unlawful injuries are inflicted on a citizen as the result of compliance, the soldier may be liable to an action for damages or to a criminal prosecution. In principle, the defence of obedience to the order of a superior is not accepted by the civil courts if the order is unlawful. But if a soldier disobeys an order claiming that it is unlawful, a court-martial may hold that it was lawful. The practical difficulty for the soldier is only partially eased by the possibility of an appeal to the Courts-Martial Appeal Court, whose judges are in a position to ensure that military law and the ordinary law do not conflict; indeed, their duty is to use their powers 'so far as they think it necessary or expedient in the interests of justice'.[62] But it may be better to leave the soldier in a position of some difficulty, and for the circumstances to be relied on in mitigation of a criminal offence, than to place him or her and thus the army outside the ordinary law.

There is little direct authority on the matter. In *Keighley v Bell*, Willes J expressed the opinion that if a prosecution results from obedience to an order, the soldier who obeys it is not criminally liable unless the order was necessarily or manifestly illegal.[63] This opinion was followed during the Boer War by a special court in South Africa which acquitted of murder a soldier who had shot a civilian in obedience to an unlawful order given to him by his officer,[64] a decision which today seems an alarming one in view of the facts. It

---

58   Armed Forces Act 1966, s 25.
59   Army Act 1955, s 134, as amended by Armed Forces Act 1991, s 26.
60   Army Act 1955, s 132(3), amended by Armed Forces Act 1981, s 6, and Armed Forces Act 1986, s 8. The time-limit does not apply to mutiny, desertion nor, with the consent of the Attorney-General, offences committed outside the UK.
61   Army Act 1955, s 34.
62   Courts-Martial (Appeals) Act 1968, s 1(3).
63   (1866) 4 F & F 763, 790.
64   *R v Smith* (1900) 17 Cape of Good Hope SCR 561.

would seem that for the defence to succeed the mistaken belief in the legality of the order must be reasonable, and this would be a matter for the jury to decide. In a Scottish case, *Her Majesty's Advocate v Hawton and Parker*, when a naval officer and a marine were charged with killing a fisherman on a trawler which was being intercepted by a naval vessel, Lord Justice General McNeill said: 'it was the duty of the subordinate to obey his superior officer, unless the order given by his superior was so flagrantly and violently wrong that no citizen could be expected to obey it'.[65] This test is materially different from that proposed by Willes J but there was in the Scottish case no order to kill. In the circumstances in which British troops have been used in Northern Ireland, the question of criminal liability for the death or injury of a civilian will normally depend not on the legality of army orders but on whether a soldier's use of firearms is reasonably justifiable in the immediate circumstances.[66] It was held in *R v Clegg*[67] that a soldier who killed a person by discharging a firearm in self-defence was guilty of murder rather than manslaughter where the force used was excessive and unreasonable.

Civil liability

Questions arise as to whether the Crown can be vicariously liable for the acts or omissions of members of the armed forces. The problem could arise in a number of ways: by a member of the armed forces negligently causing damage to another member of the services, or to a third party; and in each case it could arise either in wartime or in peace. Before the Crown Proceedings Act 1947 difficulties would have been faced by some plaintiffs (particularly those who were themselves members of the armed forces) by virtue of the Crown's immunity from liability. But even with the passing of the Act difficulties would still be encountered by a member of the armed forces who was injured by the negligence of another, if the Secretary of State issued a certificate under s 10 of the 1947 Act that the (death or) injury of the plaintiff was attributable to service for the purposes of a war pension. However, s 10 was repealed in 1987[67a] though the 1987 Act provides a complex provision for the revival of s 10 of the 1947 Act in response to any 'imminent national danger or of any great emergency' or 'for the purposes of any warlike operations in any part of the world outside the United Kingdom'. The order must be made by the Secretary of State, the power being exercisable by statutory instrument which is subject to annulment by Parliament. As a result of the 1987 Act, it is thus possible that a member of the armed forces might sue the Ministry of Defence, not only in respect of injuries sustained by the negligence of another as a result of military operations in times of peace (as in Northern Ireland), but also in times of war or other hostilities (as in the case of the Gulf campaign in 1991).

For reasons explained this is a matter about which there is not a great deal of authority. There is, however, authority for the view that the Crown could be

---

[65]   (1861) 4 Irvine 58, 69.
[66]   The case of Marine Bek, *The Times*, 31 March 1971; *A-G for Northern Ireland's Reference (No 1 of 1975)* [1977] AC 105; *Farrell v Secretary of State for Defence* [1980] 1 All ER 166; *R v Thain* (1985) 11 NIJB 31. And see ch 25.
[67]   [1995] 1 AC 482. See Cm 2706, 1995, p 52.
[67a]   See Crown Proceedings (Armed Forces) Act 1987; and ch 31 A.

vicariously liable for injuries sustained by a member of the armed forces as a result of the negligence of another in peacetime,[68] and by third parties as a result of negligence by a member of the armed forces who was not engaged at the time in operations against the enemy.[69] But there is also authority for the view that there is no liability to a third party where the injury is sustained by the negligence of a member of the armed forces while in the course of an actual engagement with the enemy.[70]

In *Mulcahy v Ministry of Defence*[71] a soldier deployed in Saudia Arabia during the Gulf conflict was injured as a result of a fellow soldier negligently causing a howitzer to fire while the plaintiff was fetching water from the front of the gun. An action for damages for negligence, claiming that the Ministry was vicariously liable, was struck out by the Court of Appeal on the ground that it disclosed no cause of action. Although no order had been made under s 2 of the 1987 Act to revive s 10 of the Crown Proceedings Act 1947, it was nevertheless held that (adopting a dictum of the High Court of Australia)[72] there is no civil liability for injury caused by the negligence of persons in the course of an actual engagement with the enemy, in accordance with 'common sense and sound policy'. In the view of Sir Iain Glidewell, 'it could be highly detrimental to the conduct of military operations if each soldier had to be conscious that, even in the heart of battle, he owed [a duty of care] to his comrade'.

Visiting Forces Act 1952

Just as it is necessary for British military jurisdiction to be exercised when British forces are stationed abroad, so it is necessary that foreign troops stationed in the United Kingdom should be able to enforce their own military law. This would be unlawful without the authority of Parliament. The Visiting Forces Act 1952 gave effect to an agreement reached between parties to the North Atlantic Treaty on the legal status of the armed forces of one state when stationed in the territory of another.[73] It also applies to forces from member states of the Commonwealth which are stationed in the United Kingdom, and it may be extended to forces from other countries by Order in Council. The Act was extended by the Armed Forces Act 1996 to apply also to countries with which this country has 'arrangements for defence cooperation', to accommodate the possibility of military personnel from the countries of central and eastern Europe exercising in the UK.

Under part I of the Act, the service courts and service authorities of visiting forces may exercise in the United Kingdom all the jurisdiction given to them by their own national law over all persons (including civilians accompanying the visiting forces) who may be subject to their jurisdiction; the death penalty may not, however, be carried out in the United Kingdom unless under United Kingdom law the death sentence could have been passed (s 2). The Act excludes the jurisdiction of criminal courts in the United Kingdom over

---

68 *Groves v Commonwealth of Australia* (1982) 150 CLR 113. See also *Barrett v Ministry of Defence* [1995] 3 All ER 87 (scope of liability where a soldier off duty dies because of over-indulgence in alcohol).

69 *Shaw, Savill and Albion Co Ltd v The Commonwealth* (1940) 66 CLR 344.

70 *Shaw, Savill and Albion*, above.

71 [1996] QB 732.

72 *Groves v Commonwealth of Australia*, above.

73 Cmd 8279, 1951.

members of visiting forces only if the alleged offence (*a*) arises out of and in the course of military duty; or (*b*) is one against the person or a member of the same or another visiting force, for example, murder or assault; or (*c*) is committed against property of the visiting force or of a member thereof (s 3). The service authorities of the visiting force may however waive jurisdiction over such an offence. A member of a visiting force who has been tried by his or her own service court cannot be put on trial in a United Kingdom court for the same offence (s 4). Police powers of arrest and search in respect of offences against United Kingdom law may still be exercised notwithstanding the jurisdiction of the visiting service authorities, but the police may deliver an arrested member of a visiting force into the custody of that force (s 5). The 1952 Act also makes provision for the settlement by the Secretary of State for Defence of certain civil claims in respect of acts or omissions of members of visiting forces (s 9).

In part II of the 1952 Act, s 13 confers important powers on the police and on United Kingdom courts to arrest and hand over into the custody of the appropriate visiting force persons who are deserters or absentees without leave from the forces of any country to which the Act applies. In *R v Thames Justices, ex p Brindle*,[74] the Court of Appeal held that this power could be exercised in respect of any person who had deserted from any of the forces of a country to which the Act applied, and was not restricted to persons who had deserted from visiting forces while they were serving in the United Kingdom; thus a United States citizen who deserted from a unit of the US army in Germany and came to England could be handed over to the US authorities in England, who might then return him in custody to the USA. Difficulties of a different kind arose in relation to the community charge; although visiting forces were exempt, British wives of US service personnel were not.[75]

---

[74]   [1975] 3 All ER 941. And see *R v Tottenham Magistrates' Court, ex p Williams* [1982] 2 All ER 705.
[75]   *Tatum v Cherwell DC* [1992] 1 WLR 1261 and *Earl v Huntingdonshire DC* [1994] CLYB 2936.

CHAPTER 17

Public finance, taxation and the economy

Government policies for taxation and public expenditure have long been liable to give rise to legal and constitutional disputes. In the 20th century, the responsibilities of central government widened to include not just raising and spending the proceeds of taxation to meet the costs of government but also the tasks of overseeing the national economy, maintaining policies on employment and the social services, and securing a sound external balance of payments. In chapter 10 C, an account was given of the financial procedures of Parliament. The present chapter deals in outline with the main financial procedures of government. These matters are mostly the responsibility of the Treasury which, with the Cabinet Office, is at the centre of government.

A. The Treasury[1]

Treasury ministers

Since 1714, the ancient office of Lord High Treasurer has been in commission; that is, its duties have been entrusted to a board of commissioners. Today the commissioners are the First Lord of the Treasury, an office held by the Prime Minister; the Chancellor of the Exchequer; and the Junior Lords of the Treasury, who are the assistant government whips in the House of Commons. The Treasury Board never meets, individual members of the board being responsible for the Treasury's business. Treasury warrants are usually signed by two of the Junior Lords. The Chancellor of the Exchequer's responsibilities cover the whole range of Treasury business, including the control of public expenditure and the direction of economic and financial policy. He or she is invariably a member of the Commons.

The other Treasury ministers include the Chief Secretary to the Treasury, who is often a member of the Cabinet and deals with public expenditure planning control, public sector pay, export credit, and value for money in the public services, including the Next Steps Agencies. The Financial Secretary to the Treasury is responsible for oversight of the Inland Revenue, privatisation, civil service pay and industrial relations, competition and deregulation policy

---

[1] See Bridges, *The Treasury;* Roseveare, *The Treasury;* Barnett, *Inside the Treasury;* Pliatzky, *The Treasury under Mrs Thatcher,* and Lawson, *The View from No 11.*

and parliamentary financial business. The Economic Secretary to the Treasury deals with monetary policy as well as matters such as Treasury responsibility for the financial system (including banks and building societies), European monetary union and procurement policy. The Parliamentary Secretary to the Treasury acts as the government's chief whip in the Commons and has had no connection with Treasury business since political patronage in the civil service disappeared in the 19th century. The duties of Paymaster-General are purely formal: payments on account of the public service are made to the Paymaster-General by the Bank of England and the money is then paid out in his or her name to the departments and other persons authorised to receive it. In practice the Paymaster-General may serve as a minister without portfolio, or may be assigned ministerial duties in the Treasury or in another department.

Functions of the Treasury

The Treasury's functions were formerly concerned primarily with financial matters, including the imposition and regulation of taxation, the control of expenditure and the management of the government's funds and accounts. But in the 20th century, except for two periods when a separate department for economic affairs was established (for some months in 1947 and between 1964 and 1969), the Treasury also became an economic policy department. After a review of senior management structure in 1995, its work is organised into seven principal directorates dealing with macro-economic policy; international finance; budget and financial services; spending; financial management, reporting and audit; finance regulation and industry; and personnel and support. We have already seen that with the abolition of the Civil Service Department in 1981 the Treasury again became responsible for civil service pay, personnel management, and industrial relations.[2]

The Treasury has a strong complement of the most senior civil servants, who include the Permanent Secretary to the Treasury. There are also a number of executive agencies within the Treasury, including the Office for National Statistics and the Royal Mint. Moreover, both the Inland Revenue and Customs and Excise operate fully on agency lines. The former was established in 1849[3] and the latter in 1909 following a merger of the separate boards of customs and excise, each of which was founded in the 17th century. The Inland Revenue (with a staff of 57,600) is responsible for the administration of income and corporation tax, collecting just under £100 billion in 1995–96, while the Customs and Excise (with a staff of 25,000) is responsible for VAT and excise duty as well as the problem of drug trafficking. Both come under the general direction of the Chancellor of the Exchequer, who is responsible to Parliament for their work. Although Customs and Excise have a number of responsibilities unrelated to fiscal matters (such as enforcing export controls) it is their traditional role of collecting customs dues on imported goods which explains why departmentally they fall within the aegis of the Treasury.[4]

---

[2]   Ch 13 D.
[3]   Inland Revenue Board Act 1849.
[4]   HC 115 (1995–96) (Scott Report), para C3.3.

B.   The Bank of England

Origins and functions of the Bank

The Bank of England was first established in 1694, mainly to provide loans to meet the needs of the Crown; it eventually became the government's bankers for all purposes. It was taken into public ownership under the Bank of England Act 1946, although the Treasury had for many years been able to control its policies. Under the 1946 Act, the Bank of England remains a separate institution from the Treasury and it is not a government department, though the Governor and directors of the Bank are appointed by the Crown,[5] and the Treasury may issue formal directions to the Bank.[6] But it has been pointed out that 'unlike the detailed constitutions of some of the other central banks', the 1946 Act 'did not accord the Bank stated duties and responsibilities'.[7] Instead it was an 'apparently simple Act by which the Treasury merely acquired stock from the Bank's proprietors, made arrangements for the Crown to appoint the Governors and directors, and gave legal support firstly to the ultimate authority of the Treasury over the Bank in matters of policy and secondly to the authority of the Bank over the banks'.[8]

Although the 1946 Act describes how the Bank will be governed, it 'does not describe what it may do'.[9] In practice, however, the Bank has a number of responsibilities which have evolved over its long history: these include acting as banker to the government and to the clearing banks; the implementation of monetary policy; the issue of currency; the management of government debt and the official reserves; and the supervision of other banks and financial institutions. Only the last of these responsibilities is regulated by statute, with the Exchequer Equalisation Act 1979[10] providing for the implementation of exchange rate policy on behalf of the Treasury, and the Banking Act 1987 providing for the supervision of deposit-taking institutions. Under the latter a bank may not engage in 'deposit-taking business' unless it is authorised by the Bank of England, and an authorisation shall not be granted unless a number of statutory criteria are met, these addressing the qualifications of the directors and the assets of the institution. The Bank may revoke or restrict an authorisation, in the latter case by 'imposing such conditions as it thinks desirable for the protection of the institution's depositors or potential depositors' (s 12(2)(b)). It must also agree to any change of control of an authorised institution and may object (and may be directed by the Treasury to object) to anyone becoming a controller unless satisfied that he or she is a fit and proper person to become a controller. An appeal lies to the Banking Appeal Tribunal with regard to both (*a*) the refusal, revocation or restriction of an authorisation, and (*b*) the issuing of a notice of objection to anyone acquiring a controlling interest in an authorised institution. The legally qualified chairman of the tribunal is appointed by the Lord Chancellor, the

---

5   The Governor, Deputy Governor and directors are known as the Court of Directors: 1946 Act, s 2.
6   Bank of England Act 1946, s 4.
7   HC 98–I (1993–94), para 13.
8   Fforde, *The Bank of England and Public Policy 1941–1958*, p 5.
9   HC 98–I (1993–94), para 14.
10   As amended by the Finance Act 1986.

other two members (with experience of banking and accountancy respectively) being appointed by the Chancellor of the Exchequer. An appeal lies to the High Court.

Accountability

Between 1969 and 1979, the Bank was in some of its activities subject to investigation by the select committee on nationalised industries of the House of Commons.[11] Since 1979, the Bank has come within the sphere of the Treasury and Civil Service Committee, and now the Treasury Committee, of the Commons, as one of the 'associated public bodies' related to the Treasury.[12] A major study of the Bank was conducted by the Treasury and Civil Service Committee in 1993 which considered a number of questions including relations between the Bank, the executive and Parliament, and the arguments for and against establishing the Bank as an agent independent of both government and Parliament, as well as its role as supervisor of other banking institutions. The committee noted that for a number of reasons the Bank's role and influence in monetary policy had strengthened, particularly as a result of the production of a quarterly inflation report which gave a greater transparency to the Bank's position and which was said to represent 'a move in the direction of greater independence'. But at the same time concern was expressed about the lack of accountability of the Bank to Parliament, the committee reporting that under the present system for determining monetary policy 'it remains unknown whether the Chancellor is acting in strict accordance with the bank's advice or not, and neither the Chancellor nor the Governor will answer questions about the content of their discussions with each other on interest rate decisions'. In any case, the government's responsibility to Parliament for monetary policy is 'diffused with its accountability to Parliament for the general management of the economy'.[13] In the view of the committee, the transfer of authority from the Treasury to the Bank would provide a clear focus for parliamentary accountability, with the government responsible for setting targets and the Bank having to account to Parliament on progress in achieving these targets. It was also proposed that the 1946 Act should be amended to specify that the primary objective of the Bank should be 'to achieve and maintain stability in the general level of prices', in the promotion of which the Bank would be responsible to Parliament. These changes would require the creation of a strong and independent monetary policy committee of the Bank.[14]

So far as the Bank's supervisory function is concerned, the main issues here were the adequacy of the current arrangements and in particular whether this function should be performed by a new agency separate from the Bank itself. The 1987 Act was a direct response to the failure of the earlier supervisory machinery in the Banking Act 1979 to prevent the collapse of the Johnson Matthey Bank, and was itself unable to prevent the collapse of the Bank of

---

[11]   Ch 14 and see HC 258 (1969–70).
[12]   Ch 10 D.
[13]   HC 98–I (1993–94), para 79.
[14]   And see HC 338 (1993–94). In May 1997, the new government proposed to give the Bank of England operational responsibility for setting interest rates under the guidance of a new monetary policy committee.

Commerce and Credit International in 1991.[15] However, an inquiry by Bingham LJ concluded that no radical restructuring of the supervisory arrangements was necessary, though proposing that the Bank should adopt new strategies in the way in which existing powers were employed.[16] The Bank has powers of investigation under the 1987 Act which may be ordered where it appears to be desirable in the interests of depositors, with investigators being armed with wide powers in some cases. These include a power to order the production of documents, to require an individual to answer questions, and to enter premises. In some cases the investigator may obtain a warrant authorising him to enter and search premises with a police officer, and to seize or make copies of documents.[17] Since the BCCI case, the Bank of England has adopted a more 'proactive and penetrating approach' to investigation and supervision, and has made more use of on-site methods, developments which were welcomed by the Treasury and Civil Service Committee, which was concerned that the traditional restrained approach which had been adopted was no longer appropriate.[18] Although the committee rejected arguments for a separate and autonomous supervisory agency, it is already the case that the Banking Act 1987 provides for the appointment of a Board of Banking Supervision to include the Governor, Deputy Governor and executive director of the Bank of England, as well as six independent members to be appointed jointly by the Governor and the Chancellor of the Exchequer. The function of the Board is to advise the Bank in the performance of its duties under the Act, and its presence is a recognition of the need to introduce 'an element of independent advice and judgement into the process'.[19] But concern about the effectiveness of supervision by the Bank was heard again after the collapse of Barings Bank with the Treasury Select Committee reporting that the Bank 'needs to demonstrate that it is able to separate supervisory activities from other functions'.[20]

Transparency

A great deal of secrecy has traditionally surrounded matters of national finance. Indeed, under the Bank of England Act 1946 the Treasury has powers to issue formal directions to the Bank, and it is a measure of the close relations between the Treasury and the Bank that these powers have never been used. It was, however, provided that any such directions would be covered by the Official Secrets Act 1911, s 2, a measure subsequently repealed by the Official Secrets Act 1989, with attendant consequences for the 1946 Act. Yet it remains the case that there are still restrictions on access to banking and financial information. Under the Code of Practice on Access to Government Information, the categories of excluded information include information whose disclosure would harm the ability of the government to manage the economy, prejudice the

---

15   For an attempt to hold the Bank liable, see *Three Rivers DC v Bank of England (No 3)* [1996] 3 All ER 558.
16   HC 198 (1992–93). See also HC 250 (1992–93).
17   Banking Act 1987, s 43.
18   HC 98–I (1993–94), para 89.
19   HC Deb, 28 November 1986, col 545.
20   HC 65 (1996–97). On 20 May 1997, the new government announced that a new regulatory body would be created, stripping the Bank of its watchdog role.

conduct of official market operations, or lead to improper gain or advantage. It also excludes information the disclosure of which would prejudice the assessment or collection of tax. A greater degree of transparency was, however, promoted, not only by the publication of the Bank's quarterly inflation report but also by the publication of the minutes of the monthly meetings between the Governor and the Chancellor of the Exchequer; these record the views of them both, but the advice of officials remained private. In May 1997, the government's transfer to the Bank of operational responsibility for setting interest rates was said to be 'within a framework of enhanced accountability', a change which may involve a greater role for the Treasury Select Committee. Although public interest immunity applies to documents 'which cover discussions and communications between the Bank and the government', the courts can order their disclosure in appropriate cases.[21] In *Burmah Oil Co v Bank of England*, public interest immunity was also held to apply to financial information communicated to the government and to the Bank by major businesses.[22]

C. Public finance

The annual cycle of revenue and expenditure that was established in the 19th century depended on a highly centralised system of financial procedure built up by a combination of statutory and parliamentary rules, Cabinet conventions and administrative practices. In chapter 10 C we saw that without the formal authority of Parliament the Crown could neither raise money by taxation nor incur expenditure. While permanent authority was given by statute for some forms of expenditure and revenue, authority for much expenditure and taxation was given by Parliament strictly on an annual basis. This led to the system by which each year the Treasury coordinated the expenditure needs of the departments. While the annual cycle ensured that Parliament should regularly approve the government's financial proposals, the government in fact retained a firm control over the House; thus by a standing order of the House dating from 1713, the House could not consider new charges on the public revenue or new taxes except on the recommendation of the Crown signified by a minister.[23] This emphasised that the government bore responsibility for all taxation and expenditure.

Authority for taxation

Permanent authority for tax collection is contained in such Acts as the Income and Corporation Taxes Act 1988 and the Taxation of Chargeable Gains Act 1992. These Acts provide for the appointment of the Commissioners of Inland Revenue,[24] who are all civil servants: under their direction, a citizen's liability to tax is assessed by inspectors of taxes and the assessed tax is collected by collectors of taxes. In performing their duties, the Commissioners of Inland Revenue are subject to the authority, direction and control of the Treasury.[25] Where a taxpayer does not accept that he or she has been

21   *Burmah Oil Co v Bank of England* [1980] AC 1090.
22   Ibid. See further ch 31 C below.
23   Ch 10 C.
24   See Johnston, *The Inland Revenue*, and annual reports of the Commissioners.
25   Inland Revenue Regulation Act 1890, s 2. Cf *IRC v Nuttal* [1990] 1 WLR 631.

correctly assessed for income tax, he or she has a right of appeal to an independent tribunal which may be either the General Commissioners of Income Tax or the Special Commissioners of Income Tax. From these tribunals, appeals on points of law lie to the High Court in England or to the Court of Session in Scotland; further appeals may reach the House of Lords.

The principal forms of indirect taxation, such as value added tax, customs and excise duties, and gaming and betting duties, are administered by the second revenue department, the Commissioners of Customs and Excise,[26] whose position closely resembles that of the Inland Revenue Commissioners. As with income tax, VAT and customs and excise duties must be collected in accordance with the law and assessments are subject to an appeal to the VAT and Duties Tribunal and thence to the court. The detailed rules of these forms of taxation are contained in continuing Acts of Parliament, but the rates of duty may be subject to variation from time to time by the Treasury or by a Secretary of State under statutory authority.[27] Many duties administered by the Commissioners of Customs and Excise are directly affected by obligations which arise from British membership of the EU.

Taxation and the courts

Whenever a department demands payment of a tax or other charge from the citizen, the citizen may challenge the legality of the demand in the courts but he may first be required to appeal to the relevant tribunal. When such a dispute reaches the court, the court may take into account the ancient principle in the Bill of Rights that the authority of Parliament must be shown to exist if any charge on the citizen is to be lawful.[28] Thus a tax may not be imposed in reliance on a resolution of the House of Commons alone, in the absence of a statute giving legal effect to the resolution.[29] Subordinate legislation which infringes the Bill of Rights principle may be declared invalid by the courts.[30] When in 1975 the television licence fee was increased, it was held unlawful for the Home Office to use a discretionary power to revoke licences so as to prevent viewers from receiving the benefit of an overlapping licence bought at the lower rate just before the increased fee became operative.[31] The courts control the legality not only of the taxes which may be demanded but also of administrative steps leading to a tax assessment: thus in *Dyson v Attorney-General*[32] the court declared that certain information demanded by the Commissioners of Inland Revenue on threat of a £50 penalty could not lawfully be required. Money which has been paid to a public

---

[26] Customs and Excise Management Act 1979; Value Added Tax Act 1994. Crombie, *Her Majesty's Customs and Excise*. See HC 115 (1995–96) (Scott Report), C3.11–3.65, for an account of the work of customs and excise on matters relating to export control.

[27] Eg Excise Duties (Surcharge or Rebates) Act 1979.

[28] Ch 2 A.

[29] *Bowles v Bank of England* [1913] 1 ch 57; ch 10 C.

[30] *Commissioners of Customs and Excise v Cure and Deeley Ltd* [1962] 1 QB 340; *Woolwich Building Society v IRC* [1991] 4 All ER 92; and ch 27.

[31] *Congreve v Home Office* [1976] QB 629. Cf *R v Richmond upon Thames LBC, ex p McCarthy and Stone Developments* [1992] 2 AC 48; and ch 29 A.

[32] [1912] 1 Ch 158.

authority under tax regulations which are ultra vires is recoverable by the taxpayer as of right and with interest.[33]

Although the assessment of tax is governed by law, some areas of tax administration tend to escape judicial control. Thus the revenue authorities may exercise their discretion not to enforce payment against an individual taxpayer or a class of taxpayers; only in very exceptional circumstances could another taxpayer complain of such a decision to the courts.[34] Although they have been criticised for doing so, the revenue authorities may also issue extra-statutory concessions by which they announce that tax due will be waived in certain circumstances,[35] and in other cases may agree a settlement which is not a true estimate of liability, a feature of the investigation of wealthy tax avoiders carried out by the Inland Revenue which was exposed by the prosecution of a senior tax inspector for corruption in 1997.[36] These concessions may come under the scrutiny of the Comptroller and Auditor General. An individual's complaint about the refusal of a concession in his or her case may be investigated by the Parliamentary Ombudsman on a complaint of maladministration causing injustice to the citizen.[37] The Inland Revenue Commissioners are subject to judicial review. Although it would not normally be proper for the Commissioners to absolve a taxpayer from an undisclosed tax liability of which the Commissioners were unaware, in principle it may be possible successfully to challenge a decision by the Commissioners assessing liability to pay tax if it is unfair to the taxpayer because the later conduct of the Commissioners is similar to a breach of contract or a breach of a representation in view of earlier events.[38] This principle does not enable a taxpayer to avoid payment of tax where a full disclosure of the facts has not been made to the Inland Revenue.[39]

Consolidated Fund and other funds

With certain exceptions, all revenue derived from taxation is paid into the Consolidated Fund.[40] In the case of receipts which arise in the course of a department's business (for example, sales or fees for services provided) these may be appropriated in aid of the department's estimate of the money which it will need, thereby reducing the provision which would otherwise have to be made by Parliament; but any surplus over the estimated figure must be paid

---

[33]   *Woolwich Building Society v IRC (No 2)* [1993] AC 70. See J Beatson (1993) 109 LQR 401; and Ch 31 A.

[34]   *R v IRC, ex p National Federation of Self-Employed* [1982] AC 617; and ch 30.

[35]   *Vestey v IRC* [1980] AC 1148; ch 27.

[36]   *Guardian*, 19, 20 February 1997.

[37]   Ch 28 D.

[38]   *R v IRC, ex p Preston* [1985] AC 835; and ch 29 C.

[39]   *R v IRC, ex p Matrix-Securities Ltd* [1994] 1 All ER 769.

[40]   Consolidated Fund Act 1816 and Exchequer and Audit Departments Act 1866, s 10. Certain payments are made to special funds eg the National Insurance Fund in the case of social security contributions (Social Security Administration Act 1992, s 162).

into the Consolidated Fund.[41] Formerly all money lent by the government came from the Consolidated Fund but in 1968 a separate account with the Bank of England was established, named the National Loans Fund, through which all borrowing by central government and most domestic lending transactions now pass. The operations of the two funds are very closely linked: thus sums needed to meet charges on the National Loans Fund must be paid into it from the Consolidated Fund and a process of daily balancing takes place between the funds.[42]

The annual cycle of financial provision by Parliament proved unsuitable as a means of financing activities of government which were in the nature of trading or business undertakings. In 1973, it was provided that certain services (for example, the Royal Mint and Her Majesty's Stationery Office)[43] could be financed by means of a trading fund established with public money, instead of by means of annual votes and appropriations from Parliament.[44] The enabling powers in the Act were extended in the Government Trading Act 1990 as part of civil service management changes. If it appears to a minister that any operations of a department are suitable to be financed by a trading fund, and that such a fund would be in the interests of improved efficiency and effectiveness of the management of these operations, he may by order, with Treasury concurrence, establish such a fund.[45] The order may designate a person other than the minister to control and manage the fund, and it should also designate either the National Loans Fund or the minister as the source of loans to the trading fund, which in the first instance must come from money provided by Parliament.

These initiatives were designed to encourage the civil service to take a more business-like approach to the efficiency and quality of the delivery of government services by introducing greater financial discipline akin to that under which private sector organisations operate.[46] They have been introduced at the same time as other measures, such as the Financial Management Initiative (FMI) which are also designed to promote greater efficiency in government. Most trading funds are likely to be established in agencies created under the 'Next Steps' programme which is considered more fully in chapter 13 D, though agencies which are not trading funds can now be required by the Treasury to produce commercial style accounts to be audited by the Comptroller and Auditor General and laid before Parliament.[47] Where a fund is established the staff remain members of the civil service. But agency status is not a method of financing an activity: 'it simply provides a way of organising, managing and reporting on the work of all or part of a Govern-

---

[41]   Public Accounts and Charges Act 1891.
[42]   National Loans Act 1968, s 18.
[43]   HMSO was privatised in 1996 and most of its functions were transferred to the Stationery Office Ltd. The Royal Mint became a Next Steps Agency in 1990. And see ch 13 D.
[44]   Government Trading Funds Act 1973.
[45]   See SI 1991 No 773, SI 1991 No 857, SI 1993 No 380, SI 1993 No 751, SI 1993 No 938, SI 1993 No 948, SI 1994 No 1192, SI 1995, No 650, SI 1995 No 1665.
[46]   See HC Deb, 8 January 1990, col 726–9.
[47]   Government Trading Act 1990, s 3, amending Exchequer and Audit Departments Act 1921, s 5.

ment department within a structured environment',[48] and they must be financed either as a supply service or by means of a trading fund. An example of many such funds is the Land Registry Trading Fund, which was established in 1993 under the control and management of the Chief Land Registrar with designated assets, liabilities and public dividend capital. Assets include freehold and leasehold land used or allocated for use in the funded operations as well as plant and equipment and computer hardware and software. The fund is empowered to borrow up to a limit of £130m, with the National Loans Fund being designated as the authorised lender.[49]

Consolidated Fund and supply services

The expenditure of central departments may be classified under two heads, namely Consolidated Fund services and supply services. The Consolidated Fund services are payments under statutes which provide continuing authority for the payments in question: the customary statutory phrase is that such payments 'shall be charged on and paid out of the Consolidated Fund'. As this authority continues from year to year, it is not necessary for the payments to be voted each year by the Commons. The principal expenditure under this heading is the provision which is made *via* the National Loans Fund for paying the interest on the national debt.

There are also charged on the Consolidated Fund other payments which for constitutional reasons are considered inappropriate for annual authorisation by Parliament. These include the Civil List,[50] and the salaries of the Speaker, the judiciary, the Comptroller and Auditor General and the Parliamentary Ombudsman. This means that there is no regular annual opportunity of discussing in Parliament the work of these officers. This practice tends purposely to preserve their independence, but the justification for it loses some of its force during rapid inflation when the Civil List and public salaries may need to be increased or supplemented annually. A different example of a charge on the Consolidated Fund was created by the European Communities Act 1972: s 2(3) gives continuing authority for payment from the Consolidated Fund or National Loans Fund of any amounts required to meet Community obligations.[51] While it was argued by the government in 1972 that such continuing authority was an essential feature of British membership of EEC,[52] it is politically convenient for the government to have continuing authority to pay over the sums concerned, without seeking fresh approval from Parliament each year.

By contrast, supply services involve charges for purposes stated by the statutes which authorise them to be payable 'out of money to be provided by Parliament.' This phrase means that an estimate must be presented to Parliament in each year that the expenditure is to be incurred and payment appropriated to it by an Appropriation Act. The great bulk of departmental expenditure is voted annually on this basis, through the procedure of supply

---

[48]   HM Treasury, *Government Accounting*, paras 1.3.7–8.
[49]   SI 1993 No 938.
[50]   Ch 12 A.
[51]   See *Monckton v Lord Advocate* 1995 SLT 1201.
[52]   HC Deb, 22 February 1972, col 1137, and 8 June 1972, col 813. Cf *R v HM Treasury, ex p Smedley* [1985] QB 657.

already described.[53] Questions arise, however, as to the purposes for which voted expenditure may be used, it being pointed out that while the Appropriation Act is 'the sole legal authority for voted expenditure, it may not in itself be sufficient to establish the propriety of that expenditure'.[54] It has been an accepted principle since 1932 that the continuing functions of government should be defined by statute, particularly where they involve financial constraints: in other words, there should be both statutory authority for the expenditure and a vote of supply to meet it. Similarly the Appropriation Act should not be used to override any statutory limits in the amount of grants or conditions for their payment, though there are exceptions from these principles for continuing expenditure resulting from the exercise of prerogative powers of the Crown, such as obligations under international treaties. Specific legislation is unnecessary in such cases, which may therefore rest on the authority of the Appropriation Act. It may thus be important to determine precisely the scope and extent of the prerogative, even if it is difficult to see what legal remedy would be available in the event of a breach of the foregoing principles, which rest on a concordat between the Treasury and the Public Accounts Committee.[55]

D. Public expenditure control and accountability

Control of public expenditure[56]

The annual cycle of estimates and supply backed up by public accounting provided a structure within which Treasury control of expenditure was formerly exercised.[57] In addition to the approval of a department's estimates, Treasury consent was needed for new services and for any new policies which involved an increase in expenditure.[58] Another aspect of the system has been the rule laid down by successive Prime Ministers that, except in cases of extreme urgency, no memorandum involving any financial issue may be circulated to the Cabinet or a Cabinet committee unless it has been seen and discussed by the Treasury. The system of Treasury control depended ultimately on the Chancellor's political authority within the Cabinet. Significantly, three Treasury ministers resigned in January 1958 when they had failed to persuade Mr Macmillan's Cabinet to restrict expenditure.[59]

One limitation of the system was that individual policy decisions could be taken on a piecemeal basis, commitments being accepted for political reasons without regard for the implications for total government spending. Another

---

[53] Ch 10 C.
[54] *Government Accounting*, op cit, para 2.2.6.
[55] *Government Accounting*, op cit, annex 2.1.
[56] See Cabinet Office and HM Treasury, *Public Expenditure Management* (1989).
[57] For the system as it used to be, see Beer, *Treasury Control*, and Chubb, *The Control of Public Expenditure*.
[58] See HC 251–1 (1957–58), p 3.
[59] For the relationship between Chancellor and Cabinet, see Heclo and Wildavsky, *The Private Government of Public Money*, ch 4.

limitation was that decisions were made within a system related to cash provision for one financial year at a time, whereas many modern programmes (for example, hospital building and defence procurement) may take many years to be planned and brought into operation. Moreover, the supply procedure applied only to a part of total public expenditure (namely the supply services) and not to the Consolidated Fund services, nor to such matters as the payment of social security benefits from the National Insurance Fund, nor to expenditure by local authorities and nationalised industries.

In 1961, the Plowden report recommended that regular surveys should be made of public expenditure as a whole, over a period of years ahead and in relation to prospective resources; and that decisions involving substantial future expenditure should be taken in the light of those surveys.[60] This influential report led to the creation of a new system of public expenditure control,[61] but changes in that system became necessary in the 1970s as economic growth declined and the control of expenditure broke down during the period of rapid inflation in 1973–75. Further changes were made in the 1980s to accommodate the new policy of government to reduce public expenditure in real terms.[62] Under the present arrangements (which have no statutory basis[63]) the government annually reviews its existing public expenditure plans for the next two financial years (years 1 and 2) and formulates plans for the following year (year 3). This review is known as the Public Expenditure Survey and takes place within the context of the Medium Term Financial Strategy.

The most significant change made during the 1970s was probably the introduction of cash limits in 1976.[64] Before then, public expenditure was essentially planned in 'volume terms'; that is, it was based on the volume of approved programmes (for example, so many new miles of motorway). As wages and prices of material increased with inflation, the programmes were not themselves affected and the cash requirement was automatically increased. In 1976, cash limits were applied by the Labour government to counter this automatic increase in cash provision. The method was extended by the Conservative government after 1979 as a primary means of restraining public expenditure and of managing the economy. Thus, cash limits have been used to limit pay-increases within the public sector and to control the numbers of those so employed.[65] Cash limits are applied to as many spending

[60] Cmnd 1432, 1961.
[61] For early accounts of PESC, see Cmnd 4071, 1969, and HC 549 (1970–71); Clarke, *New Trends in Government*, ch 2; and Heclo and Wildavsky, op cit, ch 5.
[62] See generally, Harrison, *The Control of Public Expenditure 1979–89*. See *Autumn Statement 1992* (Cm 2096, 1992), para 2.01–02. It was also announced that new ways would be found to mobilise 'the private sector to meet needs which have traditionally been met only by the public sector'. See also HC 508 (1992–93).
[63] Pliatzky, *The Treasury under Mrs Thatcher*, p 41.
[64] Cmnd 6440, 1976; HC 274 (1977–78); M Elliott (1977) 40 MLR 569; and Likierman, *Cash Limits and External Financing Limits*.
[65] See P K Else and G P Marshall (1981) 59 Public Administration 253, and G Bevan, K Sisson and P Way (1981) 59 Public Administration 379.

programmes as possible, including the revenue support grant paid to local authorities, but they do not apply to programmes which are 'demand determined', such as social security payments, which must be paid to every person who becomes entitled to them (though from 1988 cash limits were imposed on payments from the Social Fund).[66] Since 1979, cash limits have been related directly to the supply estimates, and as such are approved by Parliament.

In 1992, new arrangements were introduced for the distribution of public expenditure. Concern had been expressed about earlier arrangements and the dominant role played by bilateral discussions between the Chief Secretary and individual ministers, it being argued that this arrangement left insufficient room for consideration of priorities in the government's overall spending plans.[67] Limits were set on each department rather than particular programmes being considered on their merits. The drawbacks of this arrangement led to reforms and in particular to 'a more explicitly top-down approach'[68] to the distribution of public expenditure, with the government agreeing to what is referred to as the New Control Total (NCT) for each of the three planning years. Under the new arrangements expenditure is measured against a new spending aggregate (the NCT), which is to be constrained to a rate that ensures that total public spending grows by less than the economy as a whole over the economic cycle.[69] A new Cabinet committee ('EDX') prepares options for particular programmes for the Cabinet to consider. This is followed by the bilateral discussions between the Chief Secretary and the individual ministers in which the Chief Secretary's role is similar to that in the past, except that there is now no need for him to reach an agreement with the ministers in question. Rather, he reports back to the Cabinet committee which is able to make an informed decision on the basis of the Chief Secretary's discussions. These reforms were generally welcomed by the Treasury and Civil Service Committee, which added the caveat that Cabinet ministers should have sufficient information to consider the efficiency and effectiveness as well as the political merits of individual programmes.[70]

Departmental accountability for public expenditure

For each department the Treasury appoints an Accounting Officer (AO) who by long-standing practice approved by the Public Accounts Committee is the permanent secretary of the department, though in the case of the Executive Agencies the chief executive may be designated the AO. According to a Treasury Memorandum of 1991, the AO has the personal duty of signing the

---

[66] See Social Security Contributions and Benefits Act 1992; and eg *R v Social Fund Inspector, ex p Stitt* [1990] COD 288.
[67] HC 20 (1989–90).
[68] HC 201 (1992–93), para 174.
[69] *Autumn Statement 1992* (Cm 2096, 1992), para 2.02.
[70] HC 201 (1992–93), paras 174–8. Cf J F McEldowney in Jowell and Oliver (eds), *The Changing Constitution*, ch 7.

accounts described in his or her letter of appointment and of being a witness to the Public Accounts Committee to deal with questions arising from the accounts or from reports made to Parliament by the Comptroller and Auditor General under the National Audit Act 1983. Officials are expected to combine their role as AO with their 'duty to serve the Minister in charge of their Department, to whom they are responsible, and from whom they derive authority' (para 2). Under the terms of the memorandum, the AO must 'ensure that there is a high standard of financial management in the department as a whole; that financial systems and procedures promote the efficient and economical conduct of business and safeguard financial propriety and regularity in the department; and that financial considerations are fully taken into account in decisions on policy proposals' (para 5). The AO has particular responsibility for ensuring compliance with parliamentary requirements in the control of expenditure and in particular to ensure that funds for which he is responsible are used 'only to the extent and for the purposes authorised by Parliament' (para 10). He or she must also ensure that appropriate advice is tendered to ministers on all matters of financial propriety and regularity, and more broadly as to all considerations of 'prudent and economical administration, efficiency and effectiveness' (para 12).[71]

But what happens if the minister is 'contemplating a course of action involving a transaction which an AO considers would infringe the requirements of propriety or regularity'? In these cases the Treasury Memorandum provides that the AO should set out in writing his or her objection to the proposals, the reasons for the objection, and his or her duty to notify the Comptroller and Auditor General (C&AG) should the AO's advice be overruled. If the minister proceeds, the AO should seek written instructions to make the payment, and must then comply, but should also inform the Treasury of what has happened and pass the papers to the C&AG 'without delay', in which case the AO will bear no 'personal responsibility' for what happens (para 13). Following an important case in 1991 (when the Foreign Secretary overruled the AO in the Overseas Development Administration about expenditure of £234 million on the Pergau Dam project in Malaysia) the AO must now send the C&AG 'without undue delay' the papers relating to all cases where the AO has been overruled on matters relating to economy, efficiency and effectiveness, as well as impropriety or irregularity.[72] It has been said that the 'incidence of ministers overruling their accounting officers on matters of value for money appears to be on the increase, but remains rare'.[73] These arrangements have implications for appearances before the Public Accounts Committee where 'in general, the rules and conventions governing appearances of officials before parliamentary committees apply' (para 27).

---

[71]   The foregoing is drawn from the Treasury Memorandum of 1991, which is reproduced in *Government Accounting*, op cit, ch 6.

[72]   See HC 271 (1993–94), Cm 2602, 1993–94. See also F White, I Harden and K Donnelly [1994] PL 526. See further *R v Foreign Secretary, ex p World Development Movement* [1995] 1 All ER 611.

[73]   White et al, op cit, where 15 such instances since 1979 are noted.

Comptroller and Auditor General[74]

An essential aspect of parliamentary control of expenditure is that the House of Commons should be able to ensure that public money is used for the purposes for which it has been voted. The Comptroller and Auditor General is head of the National Audit Office, known before 1984 as the Exchequer and Audit Department. Like senior judges, he holds office during good behaviour, subject to a power of removal by the Crown on an address from both Houses of Parliament. His duties are twofold. First, as Comptroller, he ensures that all revenue is duly paid into the Consolidated Fund and the National Loans Fund, and his authority to the Bank of England is required before the Treasury may withdraw money from the Funds; in this capacity, he must see that the total limits of expenditure authorised by Parliament are not exceeded. Secondly, as Auditor General, he is responsible for examining the accounts of departments annually. The purpose was originally to ensure that money had been spent only for the purpose intended by Parliament and, when required, with the authority of the Treasury.[75] In practice, from the 19th century the audit also sought to discover instances of waste and extravagance. Express authority for 'value for money' and 'efficiency' auditing was given by the National Audit Act 1983.[76] The Comptroller and Auditor General may under that Act carry out examinations into the economy, efficiency and effectiveness with which a department has used its resources in discharging its functions; but he may not question the merits of the policy objectives set for a department. His powers extend not only to central departments but also the National Health Service and to other bodies or institutions (such as the universities) which are wholly or mainly supported from public funds and to whose records and accounts he has access for inspection purposes.[77] Since 1994, the Comptroller and Auditor General may examine records relating to expenditure by the Security Service under the Intelligence vote. The Public Accounts Commission examines the annual accounts of the National Audit Office.[78]

The Comptroller and Auditor General reports on his investigations to the Public Accounts Committee of the Commons, said to be the 'doyen' of select committees,[79] with no other select committee having the 'same authority,

---

[74] Exchequer and Audit Departments Acts 1866–1957; National Audit Act 1983; Normanton, *The Accountability and Audit of Governments*; Henley (and others), *Public Sector Accounting and Financial Control*, chs 2, 7.

[75] Exchequer and Audit Departments Act 1921, s 1.

[76] For the background, see Cmnd 7845, 1980; HC 115 (1980–81), discussed by G Drewry [1981] PL 304; and Cmnd 8323, 1981. See McEldowney, op cit, pp 196–203. Also I Harden (1993) 13 LS 16, at pp 23–4.

[77] National Audit Act 1983, ss 6–8. See also Education Act 1996, s 310 (accounts of a governing body of a grant-maintained school are open to inspection by the Comptroller and Auditor General).

[78] National Audit Act 1983, s 2. The Commission consists of the chairman of the Commons Public Accounts Committee, the Leader of the House, and seven other MPs appointed by the House, none of whom is a minister.

[79] J F McEldowney, op cit.

clarity of remit and breadth and depth of advice available to it'.[80] This committee has 15 members and its chairman by tradition is always a senior opposition MP.[81] The practice of the committee is to follow up selected audit reports by calling the departmental accounting officer before it to explain publicly the actions of the department. In exceptional circumstances, as described above, the minister may have to account to the committee for a particular item of expenditure. The committee's work depends essentially on the investigations made by the staff of the Comptroller and Auditor General. This may reveal misuse of funds that was unknown to the department concerned, as in 1963 when serious overcharging by contractors in the Bloodhound missile contracts was discovered.[82]

In 1994–95 matters examined by the committee included the Sports Council; the Merseyside Development Corporation; Wolds Remand Prison; improving social services in London; protecting and managing sites of special scientific interest; management of telephones in the Ministry of Defence; the privatisation of Northern Ireland Electricity; NHS day hospitals for the elderly; the financial health of higher education institutions; the administration of the Crown Court; the administration of retirement pensions; and fraud in defence procurement.[83]

The reports made to the Commons by the Public Accounts Committee are debated annually by the House. The government is expected to reply to criticisms and to act on them. The published rulings made by the committee and the related Treasury Minutes are an authoritative guide to the main rules of financial accountability.[84]

Important changes in the status of the Comptroller and Auditor General were made by the National Audit Act 1983. Appointments to the office are no longer made by the Crown on the advice of the Prime Minister, but by the Crown upon a resolution of the House of Commons, moved by the Prime Minister with the approval of the chairman of the Public Accounts Committee (s 1(1)). The Comptroller and Auditor General is declared to be an officer of the House of Commons (s 1(2)), a statutory change which confirmed the assumption made since 1866 that he exercises his powers on behalf of the House. While he has complete discretion in exercising his functions, he must take into account proposals regarding his investigations that may be made by the Public Accounts Committee (s 1(3)). The staff of the Comptroller are no longer civil servants: they are appointed by and are answerable to him.[85] The

---

[80]   A Robinson, 'The Financial Work of the Select Committees', in Drewry (ed), *The New Select Committees*.
[81]   Erskine May, p 660. On the Public Accounts Committee, see also Griffith and Ryle, *Parliament*, pp 441–4; St J Bates, in Ryle and Richards (eds), *The Commons under Scrutiny*, pp 187–93.
[82]   HC 183 (1963–64) and HC Deb, 19 April 1964, col 408.
[83]   See HC 93, 94, 138, 145, 375, 188, 24, 95, 139, 173, 415, 365 (1994–95).
[84]   Epitome of Reports from the Committee of Public Accounts 1857–1937 and 1938–69, HC 154 (1937–38) and 187 (1969–70).
[85]   See I Harden (1993) 13 LS 16, at p 23.

aim behind these reforms was to strengthen still further the authority and independence of the audit system, and to improve the ability of the Commons to ensure the proper use of public funds. But no system of public audit can guarantee that controversial political decisions involving heavy expenditure will not be made (for example, the costly development of the Concorde aircraft)[86] and economies for their own sake are not always popular, either with politicians or civil servants.[87]

E. Management of the economy

Power to control public expenditure and the imposition of taxes are only two of the means by which governments seek to manage the economy. In a vast area of governmental power, which public lawyers have begun to explore,[88] other means include monetary policy and control of borrowing, control over consumer transactions, prices and incomes, and financial assistance to business and industry. These techniques of economic management have been accompanied by the emergence of new structures and methods of government. So far as the former is concerned, perhaps the most significant development in the post-war period was the emergence of systematic consultation between government and the leaders of the trade union and business communities. Important symbols of this phenomenon (which is common practice in other European countries and which was not confined to Labour governments) were the wage restraint bargain of 1948, the creation of the National Economic Development Council in 1962, and the 'social contract' of 1974–76. The first two initiatives were tripartite, and in terms of institutional innovation the creation of the NEDC is perhaps the most significant. Designed to be a national planning body which 'established a permanent niche for itself in the machinery of economic policy-making', it did not, however, have any executive power, and hardly evolved beyond 'a useful framework for the exchange of different views'.[89] It was, however, chaired by the Chancellor of the Exchequer and included senior trade and industry ministers as well as senior representatives of the trade union and business communities.[90] Yet despite its symbolic and practical importance, the NEDC was not the creature of statute, but a product of the relative informality of much of the British administrative state, which could easily be sidelined and eventually abolished (in 1992) when it no

---

86   See HC 335 (1972–73) and generally, Turpin, *Government Procurement and Contracts.*
87   Cf Chapman, *Your Disobedient Servant.* For the cautionary tale of the Crown Agents, see G Ganz [1980] PL 454.
88   Eg V Korah (1976) 92 LQR 42; T C Daintith (1976) 92 LQR 62, (1979) 32 CLP 41, (1982) 9 Jl of Law and Society 191 and in Jowell and Oliver, *The Changing Constitution*, ch 8; and A C Page (1982) 9 Jl of Law and Society 225.
89   Grant and Marsh, *The Confederation of British Industry*, p 141.
90   See National Economic Development Council, Annual Report 1978–79, for an account of membership and terms of reference, as well as the activities of the NEDC.

longer suited government strategy in terms of the content or method of economic policy-making.[91]

The special powers which economic difficulties during the 1970s forced governments to take to deal with inflation were usually limited in duration; they enabled governments to intervene more extensively in private economic transactions than had previously been possible in peacetime. This legislation (long since repealed) had a number of novel aspects. Thus the Price Commission, a regulatory body set up under the Counter-Inflation Act 1973, could issue orders or notices to employers and businesses. Breach of these could create criminal liability, yet the orders or notices themselves might define expressions used in the Act under which they were issued.[92] The Remuneration, Charges and Grants Act 1975 was notable for the manner in which the 'social contract' approved by the trade unions as a basis for voluntary wage restraint was given a measure of statutory effect and provision made for a new policy document to take its place.[93] One consequence of the need to continue an incomes policy after the 1975 'social contract' expired came in the Chancellor of the Exchequer's 1976 Budget: certain increases in personal tax allowances were made conditional upon the agreement of the trade unions being obtained to an incomes policy. This agreement was duly obtained and the allowances were included in the Finance Act 1976, but some considered that this development diminished the authority of both government and Parliament.[94]

Between 1979 and 1997, Conservative governments adopted a wholly different approach to economic management, emphasising the importance of a market economy and the need to remove perceived barriers to the free functioning of the market. Financial and economic policy was directed mainly at the control of inflation, the restraining of public expenditure, and the lifting of bureaucratic controls on pay, prices, dividends, credit and foreign exchange. Industrial policy was directed mainly at the encouragement of small firms, the break up of monopolies, the fostering of competition, and the releasing of business from public sector constraints. In the labour market, policy was directed at encouraging flexibility, a goal reflected in the spate of legislation since 1980 designed to limit the power of trade unions and reduce the scope of employment protection legislation.[95] One consequence of viewing trade unions as an obstacle to the free functioning of the market was to deny them any role in economic policy-making.[96] Whilst in the 1970s trade unions reached the zenith of their power in a quasi-corporatist state, by 1997 they had little if any political influence on a government which repudiated

---

[91]   See Davies and Freedland, *Labour Legislation and Public Policy*, p 439.
[92]   Counter-Inflation Act 1973, Sched 3, para 1(1), discussed by Korah, op cit, p. 44.
[93]   Remuneration, Charges and Grants Act 1975, s 1.
[94]   Eg *The Times*, 7 April 1976 (editorial). See also the Labour government's efforts to enforce non-statutory guidelines on pay by means that included the boycotting of companies which breached the guidelines. See R B Ferguson and A C Page (1978) 128 NLJ 515; G Ganz [1978] PL 333; HC Deb, 13 December 1978, col 673, and 14 December 1978, col 920.
[95]   See Cmnd 9474, 1985.
[96]   See K D Ewing, 'Trade Unions and the Constitution: the Impact of the New Conservatives', in Graham and Prosser (eds), *Waiving the Rules: The Constitution under Thatcherism.*

the very idea that they had a role to play in the formulation of economic policy.

Trade unions which had been drawn into the process of economic management were now pushed to the margins of government, there being no doubt that until 1979 trade unions had an important constitutional role. It is true that, as already indicated, this did not crystallise in any formal legal sense, but this did not make it any less real, for as Beer has pointed out in relation to the wage restraint bargain of 1948 (which was not embodied in any legislative instrument), it 'achieved a regulation of an important aspect of the British economy that no such legislative instrument by itself could have done. Indeed, one may think of it as a kind of extra-governmental legislation'.[97] With the abolition of the NEDC and the retreat of dialogue between government and the social partners, it is seriously open to question how much of the 'constitutional architecture of the Keynesian State', built with 'no formal constitutional changes', remains intact, as has been suggested.[98] It could, however, be rebuilt just as quickly as it has been demolished. Although regulatory informality has not been removed altogether with the re-shuffling of the pack of constitutional players, there is a sense in which it is in retreat having been displaced to some extent by a greater emphasis on regulatory instruments, including contracts and licences.[99]

---

[97]   Beer, *Modern British History*, p 205.
[98]   I Harden [1994] PL 609, at p 616.
[99]   See N Deakin and K Walsh (1996) 74 Public Administration 33.

CHAPTER 18

The courts and the machinery of justice

In chapter 5 the broad relationship between the judiciary, the legislature and the executive was examined. This chapter will consider the major constitutional aspects of the courts and the machinery of justice. After the barest catalogue of the civil and criminal courts, the House of Lords, the Privy Council and certain specialised courts will be briefly discussed.[1] It must be stressed that there are in the United Kingdom three distinct court systems: in England and Wales, in Scotland, and in Northern Ireland. The judiciaries in the three systems are separate from each other, except that judges and senior practitioners in each system are eligible for appointment to the House of Lords as Lords of Appeal in Ordinary. They are also eligible for appointment to the Court of Justice and to the Court of First Instance of the European Communities and to those specialised courts and tribunals (such as the Restrictive Practices Court) which have jurisdiction throughout the United Kingdom.

A. The courts and the judiciary

The courts of civil and criminal jurisdiction

In England and Wales, civil jurisdiction is exercised by the High Court, the judges of which sit in three divisions (Queen's Bench, Chancery and Family) and, on appeal, by the Court of Appeal, Civil Division. Together the High Court, the Court of Appeal and the Crown Court form the Supreme Court. From the Court of Appeal, and in some cases direct from the High Court, appeals lie with leave to the House of Lords, sitting as a court. A limited civil jurisdiction is exercised by the county courts and on a few subjects (for example, certain matrimonial disputes) by the magistrates' courts, though the jurisdiction of the former may be extended by powers of the Lord Chancellor contained in the Courts and Legal Services Act 1990, which authorises the transfer of business from the High Court to the county courts. Criminal

---

[1] For accounts of the English legal system, see Spencer, *Jackson's Machinery of Justice*; Zander, *Cases and Materials on the English Legal System.* For Scotland, Walker, *The Scottish Legal System*, and Paterson and Bates, *The Legal System of Scotland: Cases and Materials.*

jurisdiction is exercised at first instance in summary trials by the magistrates' courts and in jury trials by the Crown Court, created by the Courts Act 1971, which sits in London and in over 80 provincial centres. In the Crown Court the judge may be a High Court judge, a circuit judge or a part-time recorder. Criminal appeals lie, depending on the nature and grounds of the appeal, to the Queen's Bench Divisional Court of the High Court (composed of two or three judges sitting together) or to the Court of Appeal, Criminal Division. A further appeal in criminal cases on matters of law may lie, with leave, to the House of Lords.

In Scotland, civil jurisdiction is exercised by the ancient Court of Session.[2] Single judges sit in the Outer House for trials at first instance; eight senior judges form the Inner House, sitting in two divisions for mainly appellate purposes.[3] A wide civil jurisdiction is exercised by the sheriff court, from which appeals may lie to the Inner House of the Court of Session. Criminal jurisdiction, for jury trials and appeals, is exercised by the High Court of Justiciary, which comprises the same judges as sit in the Court of Session; and also by the sheriff court, both for summary trials and jury trials. The district courts, established by the District Courts (Scotland) Act 1975, have a summary criminal jurisdiction which is less extensive than magistrates' courts in England. Appeals from Scotland in civil cases, but not in criminal cases, lie to the House of Lords.

In Northern Ireland, jurisdiction is exercised by the High Court, the Crown Court and the Court of Appeal, forming the Supreme Court of Northern Ireland. Civil jurisdiction is exercised by the High Court (with Queen's Bench, Chancery and Family divisions) and the Court of Appeal. Criminal jurisdiction is exercised by the Crown Court (in which sit the judges of the High Court and the county court judges), by the Queen's Bench side of the High Court, and by the Court of Appeal. Criminal cases are heard by judge and jury, except in cases where the Northern Ireland (Emergency Provisions) Act 1996 applies, in which case there is no right to trial by jury.[4] At an intermediate level, civil jurisdiction is exercised by the county courts. At a local level, civil and criminal jurisdiction is exercised by magistrates' courts, presided over by resident magistrates who are legally qualified. Civil and criminal appeals from the Court of Appeal and, in specified cases, from the High Court lie to the House of Lords.

The House of Lords

For practical purposes, the House of Lords sitting as the final court of appeal is distinct from the House in its legislative capacity, although judicial business is governed by standing orders of the House. The sittings of the House for judicial business used to be ordinary sittings of the House. After *O'Connell's*

---

[2] The constitution and administration of the Court of Session are now governed by the Court of Session Act 1988.

[3] The maximum number of judges in Scotland was increased in 1993 from 25 to 27 (see SI 1993 No 3154, and HL Deb, 9 December 1993, col 1079).

[4] See ch 25 E.

case,[5] in which the presence of lay peers was ignored by the Lord Chancellor, it was a conventional rule that no lay peer should take part in appellate work. Because of a shortage of peers who held judicial office, the Appellate Jurisdiction Act 1876 provided for the appointment of two Lords of Appeal in Ordinary, for whom the statutory qualification was to have held high judicial office in the United Kingdom or to have been a practising barrister (or advocate in Scotland) for 15 years. The Act declared that appeals should not be heard unless there were present at least three from the following, the Lord Chancellor, the Lords of Appeal in Ordinary, and such peers as held or had previously held high judicial office (ie in a superior court in the United Kingdom). The Lords of Appeal in Ordinary, of whom up to 12 may now be appointed,[6] are salaried and under an obligation to sit for appellate work; the other qualified peers serve voluntarily. There is a convention, but no more than a convention, that an ex-Lord Chancellor in receipt of a pension should serve when requested to do so by the Lord Chancellor. Usually appeals are heard by five judges but in exceptional cases seven judges may sit.[7]

In 1948, as a temporary measure, the House of Lords authorised the hearing of appeals by an appellate committee. This practice became permanent: appeals are now heard by the Law Lords sitting as one or two appellate committees of the House. Judgment is still delivered by members of a committee in the full Chamber, but the speeches of the individual members are not delivered orally but are handed to the parties and their counsel already printed. As the sittings of the appellate committees often clash with those of the whole House, the Lord Chancellor rarely sits for judicial business: he is entitled to preside when he does so. The appellate committees may sit to hear appeals when Parliament has been prorogued or dissolved or during an adjournment of the House. Standing orders also provide for two appeals committees which consider and report to the House on petitions for leave to appeal.

Being at the apex of the hierarchy of courts in the United Kingdom, except that it has no jurisdiction in Scottish criminal cases, the House of Lords has great authority in influencing the development of the law through the system of precedent.[8] For many years the House regarded itself as bound by its own previous decisions[9] but in 1966 the Lords of Appeal in Ordinary made through the Lord Chancellor a statement modifying that doctrine and accepting that too rigid adherence to precedent might lead to injustice in a particular case and unduly restrict the proper development of the law.[10] The House of Lords now treats its former decisions as normally binding but is prepared to depart from a previous decision when it appears right to do so.[11]

---

5   *O'Connell v R* (1844) 11 Cl & Fin 155, 421–6.
6   Maximum Number of Judges Order 1994, SI 1994 No 3217.
7   Eg *Murphy v Brentwood DC* [1991] 1 AC 398; and *Pepper v Hart* [1993] AC 593.
8   For studies of its work, see Blom-Cooper and Drewry, *Final Appeal*; Paterson, *The Law Lords*; Stevens, *Law and Politics*; A Paterson (1988) 33 JR 235.
9   *London Street Tramways Co v LCC* [1898] AC 375.
10 Practice Statement [1966] 3 All ER 177; and see Paterson, *The Law Lords*, ch 6.
11 For use made of this freedom in public law cases, see eg *Conway v Rimmer* [1968] AC 910, *Knuller Ltd v DPP* [1973] AC 435, *R v Home Secretary, ex p Khawaja* [1984] AC 74 and *Murphy v Brentwood DC* [1991] 1 AC 398. For exercise of the power in criminal law, see *R v Shivpuri* [1987] AC 1.

Judicial Committee of the Privy Council

Although in 1640 the Long Parliament abolished the jurisdiction of the King in Council at home, the power of the Council to receive petitions from the Channel Islands and the Isle of Man survived. From the late 17th century onwards, an increasing number of petitions by way of appeal were brought from the colonies and other overseas possessions of the Crown. In 1833, the Judicial Committee of the Privy Council was set up by statute to exercise the jurisdiction of the Council in deciding appeals from colonial, ecclesiastical and admiralty courts. In the heyday of the British Empire, the Judicial Committee was indeed an imperial court exercising what was potentially a vast jurisdiction over much of the globe. Today its role as an appeal court within the Commonwealth has much declined.[12]

Apart from this, it has a miscellany of judicial functions. The Judicial Committee is still the final court of appeal from the Channel Islands and the Isle of Man. It lost much of its appellate jurisdiction in Church of England matters when in 1963 new appellate courts were created within the church, but appeals may still be taken to it in faculty cases from the consistory courts. An appeal lies to the Judicial Committee from various professional disciplinary boards, including the disciplinary committees of the General Medical Council and the Dental Council.[13] By s 4 of the Judicial Committee Act 1833, the Crown may refer any matter to the committee for an advisory opinion: this unusual power has been used infrequently, to obtain advisory opinions on matters of some public concern and legal difficulty which cannot otherwise be brought conveniently before the courts, including matters relating to disqualification from the House of Commons and parliamentary privilege.[14] Under s 5 of the Government of Ireland Act 1920, which formed the constitution for Northern Ireland until 1972, the government was empowered to refer to the Judicial Committee questions as to the interpretation of the Act; while this provided a procedure for obtaining a judicial decision on whether measures passed by the Northern Ireland Parliament were within their legislative competence, only one reference under this procedure was made to the Judicial Committee in 50 years.[15]

The composition of the Judicial Committee is governed by the 1833 Act: usually three or five Lords of Appeal in Ordinary sit but the committee also includes the Lord Chancellor, the Lord Justices of Appeal, such members of the Privy Council as hold or have held high judicial office in the United Kingdom or have been judges in the superior courts of the Commonwealth states from which appeals still lie to the Committee, or of any colony that may be determined by Order in Council. In theory the Judicial Committee does not deliver judgment, but merely advises the government, which by conven-

---

12   Ch 15 C. For the background, see L P Beth [1975] PL 219. See also Swinfen, *Imperial Appeal.*
13   Medical Act 1983, s 40; Dentists Act 1984, s 29. For the scope of the appeal, see eg *Libman v General Medical Council* [1972] AC 217. See also Osteopaths Act 1993, s 31, and Chiropractors Act 1994, s 31.
14   In *Re MacManaway* [1951] AC 161; *Re Parliamentary Privilege Act 1770* [1958] AC 331; and see HLE, vol 10, pp 362–3.
15   *Reference under the Government of Ireland Act 1920* [1936] AC 352; Calvert, *Constitutional Law in Northern Ireland,* pp 298–301. Compare Scotland Act 1978, s 19 and Sched 12.

tion acts on its report and issues an Order in Council to give effect to the advice. Until 1966, the opinion of the majority alone was given but dissenting opinions are now permissible.[16] Although the committee in form gives advice to the Crown, 'in substance, what takes place is a strictly judicial proceeding'.[17]

Courts of specialised jurisdiction

The judicial system is not confined to the courts of general civil and criminal jurisdiction.[18] The numerous administrative tribunals, in whose proceedings judges of the civil and criminal courts rarely play a part, will be examined in chapter 28 A. Rather than creating such tribunals, Parliament has sometimes created specialised courts which are solely composed of judges of the superior courts (for example, the election court[19] or the Patent (Appellate Section) Court) or which include both judges and lay members. The Restrictive Practices Court was established in 1956 and its jurisdiction has been subsequently enlarged.[20] As a superior court of record, it has a status coordinate with that of other superior courts in the United Kingdom. The court consists of five judges and not more than ten other members, being persons who appear to the Lord Chancellor to have knowledge or experience of industry, commerce or public affairs. Of the five judges, three come from the English High Court, one from the Court of Session and one from the Supreme Court of Northern Ireland. The court is concerned with the enforcement of the legislation against restrictive trade practices, which may be brought before the court by the Director-General of Fair Trading; they are deemed to be contrary to the public interest unless the court is satisfied that one or more of the statutory circumstances which may justify an agreement are proved to exist.

The short-lived National Industrial Relations Court from 1971 to 1974 had a similar form to that of the Restrictive Practices Court. As well as its controversial powers in relation to industrial disputes, appeals could be brought to it from industrial tribunals. In its place in 1975 was created the Employment Appeal Tribunal to hear appeals on points of law from industrial tribunals, for example on claims by employees against employers for unfair dismissal. The tribunal is composed of one or more judges from the English Supreme Court nominated by the Lord Chancellor and at least one judge from the Court of Session nominated by the Lord President, who sit together with persons having special knowledge of industrial relations as representatives of employers and of workers. Despite its name, the tribunal is a superior court of record. It may sit anywhere in Great Britain. Parties to appeals may be represented by counsel, solicitors, trade union officials or any other person. Appeals from the tribunal lie on points of law, with leave to the Court of Appeal or to the Inner House of the Court of Session.[21]

---

[16]   Judicial Committee (Dissenting Opinions) Order 1966 (*Statutory Instruments 1966*, part I, 1100).
[17]   *Hull v McKenna* [1926] IR 402.
[18]   *R v Home Secretary, ex p Cheblak* [1991] 2 All ER 319, at 333 (Lord Donaldson MR).
[19]   Ch 9 B.
[20]   Restrictive Trade Practices Act 1976, Restrictive Practices Court Act 1976.
[21]   Industrial Tribunals Act 1996, s 37. For industrial tribunals, see ch 28 A.

The Sovereign and the courts

According to Blackstone, 'All jurisdiction of courts are either indirectly or immediately derived from the Crown. Their proceedings are generally in the King's name; they pass under his seal, and are executed by his office', but it is 'impossible as well as improper that the King personally should carry into execution this great and extensive trust'.[22] The notion of the Sovereign as the fountain of justice was important in feudal times in helping to ensure that a single system of justice prevailed over competing jurisdictions. The early kings delivered justice in their own courts. But the delegation of this duty to judges was an inevitable result of the growth of the business of government and the development of a system of law requiring specialised knowledge. In England, it was enacted in 1328 by the Statute of Northampton that the royal command should not disturb or delay common justice and that, although such commands had been given, the judges were not therefore to cease to do right in any point.

In Scotland, the Court of Session, which was placed on a permanent basis in 1532, more than once had to resist royal interference in the course of justice and issued a notable rebuff to King James VI in 1599.[23] In 1607, James, who had by then also become King James I of England, claimed the right in England to determine judicially a dispute between the common law courts and the ecclesiastical courts. In the case of *Prohibitions del Roy*, it was decided by all the common law judges headed by Coke that the right of the King to administer justice no longer existed.[24] In a famous passage, Coke declared:

> that the King in his own person cannot adjudge any case, either criminal, as treason, felony, etc, or betwixt a party and party, concerning his inheritance, chattels or goods, etc, but this ought to be determined and adjudged in some Court of Justice, according to the law and custom of England; ... true it was, that God had endowed His Majesty with excellent science, and great endowments of nature; but His Majesty was not learned in the laws of his realm of England, and causes which concern the life, or inheritance, or goods, or fortunes of his subjects, are not to be decided by natural reason, but by the artificial reason and judgment of law, which law is an act which requires long study and experience, before that a man can attain to the cognizance of it: that the law was the golden met-wand and measure to try the causes of the subjects; and which protected His Majesty in safety and peace.

This declaration may not have been supported by all Coke's precedents[25] but it served to establish a fundamental constitutional principle. This principle was reinforced by provisions in the Bill of Rights 1689 and the Scottish Claim of Right which restricted royal interference in the course of justice. Certain prerogative powers in relation to the administration of justice have survived and will be examined later in this chapter. But the Crown can no longer by the prerogative create courts to administer any system of law other than the common law.[26] This restriction had its roots in the common lawyers' distrust of the prerogative courts of the Star Chamber and the High

---

22   I *Commentaries*, Book 1, ch VII.
23   *Bruce v Hamilton*, recounted in (1946) 58 JR 83; and see *Earl of Morton v Fleming* (1569) Morison 7325.
24   (1607) 12 Co Rep 63.
25   Cf Dicey, *The Law of the Constitution*, p 18.
26   *Re Lord Bishop of Natal* (1864) 3 Moo PC (NS) 115.

Commission. Its effect today is that new courts and tribunals may be created only by Act of Parliament, but this does not prevent the Crown under prerogative power from establishing a body to administer a scheme for conferring financial benefits upon individuals.[27]

Judicial independence[28]

The primary judicial function is to determine disputes, whether between private persons or between a private person and a public authority. Judges must apply the law and are bound to follow the decisions of the legislature as expressed in statutes. In interpreting statutes and applying decided cases they do however make, as well as apply, law. In countries where there is a written constitution which cannot be overridden by ordinary legislation (for example, the United States of America), the judges are guardians of the constitution and may declare a statute to be unconstitutional and invalid. In the United Kingdom, the chief constitutional function of the judiciary is to ensure that government is conducted according to law and thus to help secure the observance of the rule of law.[29] If this function is to be adequately performed, independence of the judiciary must be maintained. Like other constitutional principles, judicial independence has many facets, only some of which are expressed in definite legal rules. Clearly a judge must be able to decide a case without fear of reprisals, whether from the executive or a wealthy corporation. But there is no reason why judges should be immune from public opinion and the discussion of current issues in the media. Judicial independence does not mean isolation of the judge from society.

Appointment of judges

Judicial appointments in the United Kingdom are a matter for the executive. The Queen's judges are appointed on the advice of the Queen's ministers. There is no formal machinery, such as a Judicial Service Commission, to insulate judicial appointments from executive control. Nor is there, as in the United States, any requirement that the executive's nominees should be subject to scrutiny and confirmation by the legislature. Appointments to the House of Lords and to the most senior judicial posts in England (including Lord Justice of Appeal, Master of the Rolls, President of the Family Division and Lord Chief Justice) are made by the Crown on the advice of the Prime Minister. High Court judges, circuit judges and recorders are appointed by the Crown on the advice of the Lord Chancellor.[30] Magistrates, who except for stipendiary magistrates are not required to be legally qualified, are appointed to the commission of the peace by the Lord Chancellor. Judges of the Court of Session are appointed by the Crown on the advice of the Secretary of State for Scotland, who forwards to the Crown nominations submitted by the Lord Advocate after the latter has consulted with the Lord President of the Court of Session and the Dean of the Faculty of Advocates.[31]

---

[27]   *R v Criminal Injuries Compensation Board, ex p Lain* [1967] 2 QB 864: Ch 12 E.
[28]   See N Browne-Wilkinson [1988] PL 44.
[29]   Ch 6.
[30]   Supreme Court Act 1981, s 10.
[31]   HC Deb, 19 June 1996, col 500 (WA). For a study of Scots judges, see S Styles (1988) 33 JR 41.

By statute, minimum qualifications for appointments must be observed. Thus before the Courts and Legal Services Act 1990 judges of the High Court had to be of at least ten years' standing as a barrister. Since the 1990 Act, however, it is now possible for solicitors with rights of audience in the High Court and for circuit judges of at least two years' standing to be appointed.[32] So far as the Court of Appeal is concerned, candidates for appointment as a Lord Justice of Appeal had previously to be of at least 15 years' standing as a barrister or already have been a High Court judge.[33] Since the 1990 Act, however, this has been reduced to ten years and extended to include solicitors with rights of audience in the High Court, as well as anyone who is already a member of the High Court[34] (which in principle would allow someone appointed to the Circuit Bench to move quickly through the system). In Scotland, membership of the Court of Session is regulated by a rule of five years' standing as a member of the Faculty of Advocates.[35] In 1990, however, the rules were liberalised, with eligibility being extended to sheriffs principal and sheriffs (who must have held office for at least five years) and solicitors, who must have had a right of audience in the Court of Session for at least five years.[36] There are also rules of standing for members of the inferior judiciary. After the 1990 reforms the general rule is that candidates should have at least ten years' experience as a barrister or advocate or as a solicitor with appropriate rights of audience.

In practice appointments to the superior courts are made only from successful practitioners, and the average experience of those appointed is well above the legal minimum. It is said to be the 'cardinal principle' of the Lord Chancellor that appointments are made on 'merit': 'Subject to the statutory requirements in relation to eligibility, the Lord Chancellor appoints or recommends for appointment to each judicial post the candidate who appears to him to be best qualified to fill it without regard to ethnic origin, gender, marital status, sexual orientation, political affiliations, religion, or (subject to the physical requirements of the office) disability'. It has also been said that the Lord Chancellor 'seeks to appoint candidates of the highest integrity and judicial quality, looking in particular for the good judgement once described by Lord Devlin as the first quality of a good judge'.[37] So far as senior judicial appointments are concerned, these are made by invitation to fill particular vacancies, and although those interested in appointment may make this known to the Lord Chancellor or his officials in the Judicial Appointments Group, 'invitation is not dependent on application'.[38] When a vacancy arises at the level of the High Court or Court of Appeal, the Lord Chancellor 'personally reviews suitable candidates' with Heads of Division (the Lord Chief Justice, the Master of the Rolls and the President of the Family Division) at a meeting of them all, taking into account the nature of the expertise and experience required of a successful appointee, before making his recommendations to the Queen or the Prime Minister as

---

32 Courts and Legal Services Act 1990, s 71.
33 Supreme Court Act 1981, s 10(3).
34 Courts and Legal Services Act 1990, s 71.
35 Treaty of Union 1706, art 19.
36 Law Reform (Miscellaneous Provisions) (Scotland) Act 1990, s 35.
37 HC 52–II (1995–96), p 129.
38 Ibid, p 133.

appropriate'. According to the Lord Chancellor's department an 'on-going programme of consultation with all judges of the Supreme Court and above assists the Lord Chancellor to identify potential candidates among leading practitioners and Circuit Judges'.[39] The Permanent Secretary at the Lord Chancellor's department has referred to this as a 'structured, organised, rolling programme of quite extensive consultations', and objected to the use of the term 'soundings' to describe the exercise, 'a term which suggested to him a "casual old-boy network" which he believed to be an inaccurate representation'.[40]

In the case of appointments to the circuit and district benches, important administrative reforms have been introduced, these being based on the publication of a statement of more explicit criteria, as well as open and advertised appointments, a step welcomed by the Home Affairs Committee in 1996 as representing a distinct advance upon the previous system of appointments which had been described as recently as 1992 as being 'a closed system of selection by peers and supervisors which is free from scrutiny and largely free from challenge or redress'.[41] It is less clear whether these criticisms cease to be relevant in the case of senior appointments, though in a largely complacent and uncritical report the Home Affairs Committee rejected proposals for a Judicial Appointments Commission which would have the effect of transferring responsibility for the appointment of judges from the executive to an independent body. There is no evidence to suggest that in recent years judicial appointments have been made by the government in power as a reward for political services. But equally there is nothing formally to prevent this, and it is not beyond the realms of possibility that senior appointments could be influenced by political considerations. If the process is to be entirely beyond criticism, a greater degree of transparency and accountability in the appointment procedures is required.

The composition of the judiciary

Should the judiciary be 'representative', and if so what does this mean? The idea that the judiciary should be 'representative of the community' was repudiated by the Home Affairs Committee, and by the Lord Chancellor's department on behalf of which it was asserted that:

It is not the function of the judiciary to reflect particular sections of the community, as it is of the democratically elected legislature. The judges' role is to administer justice in accordance with the laws of England and Wales. This requires above all professional legal knowledge and competence. Any litigant or defendant will usually appear before a single judge and it is of paramount importance that the judge is fully qualified for the office he or she holds, and is able to discharge his or her functions to the highest standards. Social or other considerations are not relevant for this purpose; the Lord Chancellor accordingly seeks to appoint, or recommend for appointment, those who are the best qualified candidates available and willing to serve at the time.[42]

---

[39]   Ibid.
[40]   HC 52–I (1995–96), para 36.
[41]   Ibid, para 45.
[42]   HC 52–II (1995–96), p 130.

On the other hand, however, there is recognition of the principle that the judiciary should 'more closely' reflect the make-up of society as a whole, which should tend over time to emerge by 'ensuring the fullest possible equality of opportunity for persons in all sections of society who wish to enter the legal profession and who aspire to sit judicially'. But, as was pointed out, this will require 'equality of opportunity at all levels of the educational system and the legal system as well as in the appointments system itself', a sentiment which it is perhaps easier to identify than implement.[43]

Neither the Sex Discrimination Act 1975 nor the Race Relations Act 1976 apply to judicial appointments, though they have been extended to apply to the legal profession in the sense that it is unlawful for a barrister or a barrister's clerk to discriminate on grounds of race or sex in relation to pupillage or tenancy.[44] This is clearly important if there is to be a pool of eligible candidates for appointment to the highest positions, though it is open to question whether unequal representation can be promoted by anti-discrimination measures alone, particularly if the goal is to draw more women in particular into the legal profession at the highest levels. It remains the case that women and members of the ethnic minority communities are under-represented on the bench. The Home Affairs Committee stated in June 1996 that none of the 12 Lords of Appeal in Ordinary were women; only one member of the Court of Appeal was a woman; and only seven out of 96 High Court judges were women. Yet although women are thus poorly represented, the same is true of the ethnic minority communities: there is none in the High Court, Court of Appeal or House of Lords, though 5 (out of 517) circuit judges, 12 (out of 891) recorders, 9 (out of 354) assistant recorders, and 2 (out of 322) district judges were thought to be of ethnic minority origin. The Home Affairs Committee rejected the suggestion that positive discrimination should be introduced and encouraged initiatives taken by the Lord Chancellor in May 1994 with the announcement of measures designed to promote equality of opportunity in judicial appointments for women and ethnic minority practitioners. Although committed to the principle of appointment on merit and opposed to any form of positive discrimination, the Lord Chancellor is nevertheless 'prepared to take affirmative action to ensure that all applicants or potential applicants are given appropriate encouragement and are treated fairly on their merits'. And although appointments are not governed by the anti-discrimination legislation, it is accepted that 'appointment practices should be fully consistent with appropriate current principles in the general field of appointment'.[45]

---

[43] Contrast the policy as to the representativeness of the magistracy which should 'broadly [reflect] the communities which they serve' (HC 52–II (1995–96)) and the view that 'the aim of balancing the bench to take account of the age, employment background and political leanings of magistrates has not, as yet, been achieved' (HC 52–I (1995–96)).

[44] Courts and Legal Services Act 1990, s 64, amending the Sex Discrimination Act 1975 and the Race Relations Act 1976.

[45] HL Deb, 23 May 1994, col 27. While confirming the principle of selection on merit from suitably qualified candidates, the Lord Chancellor also confirmed his support for the principle of equality of opportunity and that steps would be taken to encourage women and ethnic minority practitioners to apply for judicial appointments by promoting awareness of opportunities (by inviting judges and others to encourage women and people

Tenure of judges

1 England and Wales. Judges of the High Court and Court of Appeal hold office during good behaviour, subject to a power of removal by the Queen on an address presented by both Houses of Parliament.[46] A similar provision applies to Lords of Appeal in Ordinary.[47] These statutory rules clearly prevent a judge being removed at the pleasure of the Crown, but their meaning is not wholly certain. The wording of the provision in the Act of Settlement from which these rules derived[48] suggests that the intention of Parliament was that, while a judge should hold office during good behaviour, Parliament itself should enjoy an unqualified power of removal. Assuming that there was no intention to alter the effect of the Act of Settlement by the revised wording now contained in the Supreme Court Act 1981, it is theoretically possible for a judge to be dismissed not only for misconduct but for any other reason which might induce both Houses to pass the necessary address to the Crown. It is, however, extremely unlikely that Parliament would be willing to pass an address from any motive other than to remove a judge who had been guilty of misconduct.

But what would constitute misconduct sufficient to justify removal? It is not the case that any conviction for a criminal offence will lead to the removal of a judge, although arguably any conviction is misconduct. In 1975, a High Court judge pleaded guilty to driving with more than the permitted degree of alcohol in his blood;[49] and he continued in office. Since the Act of Settlement, only one judge has been removed from office by means of an address to the Crown from both Houses: in 1830, Jonah Barrington, an Irish judge, was found to have misappropriated money belonging to litigants and to have ceased to perform his judicial duties many years previously.[50] It would seem that the address to the Crown must originate in the Commons. The accused judge is entitled to be heard at the bar of the House or before a select committee; if the facts of misconduct are disputed, witnesses may be called to give evidence. But although the removal of a judge is now unlikely, a judge who steps out of line may be publicly rebuked by the Lord Chancellor, as in a case in 1978 when the Lord Chancellor 'strongly deprecated' remarks made by Melford Stevenson J about the Sexual Offences Act 1967.[51] Where legislation (or in other contexts the constitution) 'provides a procedure and an exclusive procedure for such suspension and termination ... if judicial

---

of ethnic minority to apply) and by publicising the opportunity for all to apply. Other steps in a nine-point procedure include the application of age limits for judicial appointments flexibly in the case of practitioners who take a career break, ensuring that women and ethnic minority candidates are included, wherever possible, among those under consideration for particular posts, and taking account of the domestic circumstances of individuals concerned wherever possible when making appointments to particular geographical locations.

[46]   Supreme Court Act 1981, s 11(3).
[47]   Appellate Jurisdiction Act 1876, s 6.
[48]   Ch 2 A.
[49]   *The Times*, 2 September 1975.
[50]   D M R Esson 1972 JR 50.
[51]   *The Times*, 6 July 1978.

independence is to mean anything, a judge cannot be suspended nor can his appointment be terminated by others or in other ways'.[52]

Before 1959, judicial appointments were made for life, but statutory ages for retirement were then introduced (until 1993, 75 for a High Court judge, 72 for a circuit judge). Although Parliament could by passing an Act alter the tenure of existing judges, in 1959 judges already in office who wished to remain on tenure for life were permitted to do so.[53] The Judicial Pensions and Retirement Act 1993 introduced a new retirement age of 70 with the possibility of this being extended to the age of 75 where it is desirable in the public interest to retain an individual in office for a further period. It also sought to standardise the pension entitlement of judges and to allow judges to retire on full pension at 65. In 1973, a statutory procedure for the compulsory retirement of judges was introduced to deal with the difficult but unusual situation where a judge is permanently incapacitated from carrying out his judicial duties and is also incapacitated from resigning. In this situation, the Lord Chancellor may declare the judge's post to be vacant, subject to medical evidence and to the approval of the relevant senior judge.[54]

Inferior judges receive a lesser degree of protection. Circuit judges may be removed from office by the Lord Chancellor, if he thinks fit, for incapacity or misbehaviour.[55] Lay magistrates may be removed from the commission of the peace at the discretion of the Lord Chancellor, though in practice a magistrate is not removed unless he or she has been arrested for a criminal offence of some gravity or for persistent minor offences, or has in some other way ceased to uphold the law, for example, by taking part in a civil disobedience campaign.[56] It appears that behaviour which cannot be tolerated and which leads to removal of a lay magistrate 'includes conviction of an offence involving moral turpitude, refusal to apply a law with which he disagrees, breaking his undertakings given as a condition precedent to appointment, and bringing the law into disrepute'.[57] It has also been stated that 'From time to time Magistrates may become involved in civil or criminal proceedings or in a personal relationship which may bring discredit on the magistracy as a whole'. There are 'clear Directives from the Lord Chancellor as to the kind of conduct' which will require some form of intervention on his part, including the suspension or removal of a magistrate from office. A magistrate will be interviewed before being removed.[58]

2 Scotland. In Scotland, the historic tenure on which judges hold office is *ad*

---

[52] *Rees v Crane* [1994] 2 AC 173, at p 187.
[53] See now Judicial Pensions Act 1981, Sched 2, para 1(1), and Judicial Pensions and Retirement Act 1993, s 26(7).
[54] See now Supreme Court Act 1981, s 11(8), (9).
[55] Courts Act 1971, s 17(4). And see *Ex p Ramshay* (1852) 18 QB 173. In 1983, a circuit judge was dismissed for misbehaviour after a conviction for smuggling quantities of whisky and cigarettes from the Channel Islands to England.
[56] Cf Spencer, *Jackson's Machinery of Justice*, pp 411–12; also Brazier, *Constitutional Practice*, pp 287–96.
[57] Brazier, op cit, p 292.
[58] HC 52–II (1995–96).

vitam aut culpam, ie they cannot be removed except on grounds of miscon-duct.[59] Judges of the Court of Session still hold office on this basis, subject to the retiring age of 75 for appointments made after 1959. The Act of Settlement procedure involving a resolution from both Houses of Parliament does not apply to them. Should the need arise, a procedure for removal by the Crown for misconduct would have to be devised: it might well be prudent for the Crown to seek the support of the two Houses for its action. Sheriffs have greater protection than do circuit judges in England: a sheriff may be removed from his office only after an inquiry, conducted jointly by the Lord President of the Court of Session and the Lord Justice-Clerk, has established unfitness for office by reason of inability, neglect of duty or misbehaviour, and only by means of an order of removal made by the Secretary of State for Scotland and laid before Parliament.[60]

This procedure was used in 1977 to dismiss Sheriff Peter Thomson who despite a warning had persisted in using his judicial position to promote political activities, namely a campaign for government by plebiscite. An attempt by some MPs to persuade the House of Commons to grant the judge a hearing was unsuccessful; he had earlier declined to make use of the statutory rules entitling him to a hearing.[61] The procedure was also used in 1992 to remove Sheriff Ewan Stewart,[62] on the ground of his inability due to 'an underlying defect in character, which manifests itself in various ways to the severe prejudice of the Sheriff's function as a Judge'. It was said that he '[carried] with him to the Bench a wealth of private knowledge culled from various sources, which he employs with no sense of self-restraint whenever he likes to decide cases in his own way irrespective of the issues which he has been asked to decide'. In judicial review proceedings it was noted that the 1971 Act was silent as to the procedure to be followed and that the senior judges 'were the masters of their own procedure, subject only to the requirement to act fairly'. It was held, however, that the senior judges were not required to provide the petitioner with witness statements or with a statement of their preliminary conclusions before they completed their investigations.[63]

Judicial salaries

Salaries are an aspect of tenure. The Act of Settlement provided that judicial salaries should be 'ascertained and established'. This was interpreted as requiring that judicial salaries should be fixed by Act of Parliament and not left to the discretion of the executive. By long-standing practice, judicial salaries are charged on the Consolidated Fund, which means that the authority for payment is permanent and does not have to be reviewed by Parliament each year.[64] In 1931, consternation was caused to some English

59   Claim of Right 1689, art 13; *Mackay and Esslemont v Lord Advocate* 1937 SC 860.
60   Sheriff Courts (Scotland) Act 1971, s 12.
61   HC Deb, 25 November 1977, col 922 (WA), 30 November 1977, col 245 (WA), and 6 December 1977, col 1288.
62   Sheriff (Removal from Office) Order 1992.
63   *Stewart v Secretary of State for Scotland* 1995 SLT 895. Compare *Rees v Crane* [1994] 2 AC 173.
64   Supreme Court Act 1981, s 12(5); and see ch 17 C.

judges when the National Economy Act 1931 authorised the Crown by Order in Council to make economies in the remuneration of persons in the service of the Crown, and an Order in Council was made reducing the salaries of judges (which had been £5,000 per annum since 1832) by 20%. A deputation of judges complained to the Lord Chancellor but a petition of right against the cuts which MacNaghten J threatened to bring never materialised, even though the judges had some strong legal arguments on their side.[65]

In a period of rapid inflation, the need is not so much to guard against reductions in the statutory salaries as to provide machinery to enable salaries to be increased to keep pace with other public salaries. The Judges' Remuneration Act 1965 gave authority for judicial salaries to be increased, but not reduced, by means of Order in Council, subject to the approval of both Houses of Parliament. A further step was taken in 1973 when the Lord Chancellor (or, in the case of the Court of Session, the Secretary of State for Scotland) was authorised to increase judicial salaries, acting with the approval of the Prime Minister.[66] There is now no requirement of express parliamentary approval but, at the request of the government, judicial salaries may be examined by the advisory Senior Salaries Review Body.[67] The highest paid judge in the United Kingdom is the Lord Chief Justice, whose salary in 1996 was £132,178; in the second highest bracket come the Lords of Appeal in Ordinary, the Master of the Rolls and the Lord President of the Court of Session (£122,231). Judges of the High Court in England were then paid £104,431.[68]

Use of judges for extrajudicial purposes

Judges have often been called on by the government to preside over royal commissions, departmental committees and inquiries conducted under the Tribunals of Inquiry (Evidence) Act 1921. From 1953 to 1973, not including judges who served on permanent committees for law reform, 79 such appointments were made.[69] More recent figures are not easily available, though in the 1980s and 1990s judges continued to be used by government for a wide range of extra-judicial purposes, including safety at sports grounds, prison riots, the collapse of an international bank, the so-called Arms for Iraq affair, and the future of legislation against terrorism. An emerging theme of some significance is the appointment of senior judges as Commissioners to oversee and to report annually to the Prime Minister about the operation of surveillance powers created by legislation such as the Interception of Communications Act 1985, the Security Service Act 1989, and the Intelligence Services Act 1994. This is based on the earlier arrangements which saw Lord Diplock accept appointment as a commissioner to review the operation of the

---

[65]   Heuston, *Lives of the Lord Chancellors 1885–1940*, pp 513–19, and see W S Holdsworth (1932) 48 LQR 25.

[66]   See now Supreme Court Act 1981, s 12.

[67]   See eg Cm 3094, 1996; 3330, 1996 (Reports No 37 and No 38).

[68]   The Vice Chancellor, the President of the Family Division and Lord Justices of Appeal were each paid £117,190. By virtue of the Ministerial and other Pensions and Salaries Act 1991, the Lord Chancellor is paid £2,000 a year more than the Lord Chief Justice (s 3).

[69]   HC Deb, 7 December 1973, col 478 (WA). And see Griffith, *Politics of the Judiciary*, and G Zellick [1972] PL 1.

practice of telephone tapping before it was placed on a statutory basis.[70] Also important is the appointment of Lord Nolan in 1994 to examine concerns about standards of conduct in public life.[71]

Many judges are well suited to this work but there are potential dangers to judicial independence in the practice, particularly when matters of acute political controversy are referred to a judge for an impartial opinion. Examples may be found in the inquiries by Lord Wilberforce in 1970 and 1972 into industrial disputes and in the regular use of judges (including Lords Diplock, Bridge and Griffiths) to chair the Security Commission which investigates shortcomings in the work of British intelligence services.[72] Particularly controversial references were the investigations conducted by Lord Denning on the request of the Prime Minister into the security aspects arising out of the resignation of a minister (J Profumo) in 1963; by the Lord Chief Justice, Lord Widgery, in 1972 into deaths in Londonderry; and by Lord Bridge in 1985 into allegations of improper telephone tapping of trade unionists and peace activists by members of the security service.[73] Such references may give rise to allegations that the government is using the judiciary for its own ends; and they may expose the judge in question, particularly if he or she is the sole member of the inquiry, to political criticism by those who disagree with his or her report. It needs to be stressed that such work is not the primary task of the judges, and that the government cannot assume that the services of a judge will be available whenever an awkward political situation might be eased by an impartial inquiry. There may also be concerns about judges being too intimately involved with the operation and needs of government, particularly in cases where they are drawn upon to give advice on a matter about which they are subsequently called upon to adjudicate, albeit in a different context.

While the government may invite judges to take part in inquiries into current problems, the political parties are not entitled to ask judges to assist them in the preparation of their policies.

In 1968, the leader of the Opposition, Mr Heath, appointed a committee to consider possible changes in the constitutional position of Scotland. Included in the committee, which was chaired by a former Conservative Prime Minister, Sir Alec Douglas-Home, was a judge of the Court of Session, Lord Avonside, nominated at the request of Mr Heath by the Lord President of the Court of Session. In the ensuing controversy, the Lord Advocate maintained that the nomination of a judge to this committee was in breach of 'a longstanding constitutional convention' by which the judiciary did not participate in the activities of a political party. When the Scottish National Party asked the Lord President to nominate a judge to serve on that party's constitutional committee, the Lord President declined. Lord Avonside thereupon resigned from the Douglas-Home committee, while denying that a judge in Scotland could be bound against his will to eschew party politics.[74]

Despite the judge's assertions to the contrary, these unusual events reinforced

70   See ch 24.
71   HC Deb, 25 October 1994, col 757. Lord Nolan is also the Commissioner under the Interception of Communications Act 1985. And see ch 24.
72   Ch 24.
73   See respectively Cmnd 2152, 1963; HC 220 (1971–72); and *The Times*, 7 March 1985.
74   *The Times* and *The Scotsman*, 26 July–6 August 1968.

the strong constitutional convention that a judge should not become involved in party political activities. All salaried judges are disqualified from membership of the Commons. While the Lords of Appeal in Ordinary and other senior judges are members of the House of Lords, they sit on the cross-benches and do not take part in the legislative work of the House as party supporters, though they may, and do, participate in the legislative and scrutiny work of the House.

Parliamentary criticism of the judiciary

The work of the courts should not be outside the scope of political discussion. There is however a convention that members of the executive, whether ministers or civil servants, do not criticise the judiciary or judicial decisions. The government may say that a judicial decision differs from the legal advice upon which it had acted or that it proposes to bring in amending legislation, but ministers are not expected to state that a court's decision is wrong. Nonetheless in 1977 Mr Michael Foot, while holding a senior Cabinet post, told a trade union rally that the British people, especially trade unionists, would have 'precious few' freedoms if these had been left to the good sense and fair-mindedness of the judges.[75] In 1982, the Prime Minister stated that she found the decision of a judge to impose a suspended prison sentence for rape of a six-year-old girl incomprehensible, and informed the House of Commons of action taken by the Lord Chancellor requiring trials for rape to be conducted by senior judges.[76] In 1987, when the Prime Minister said at question-time that she was unable to comment on a particular sentence, the Speaker subsequently ruled, 'It is perfectly in order to criticise or to question a sentence: but it is not in order to criticise a judge. That has to be done by motion'.[77]

As individuals, back-bench MPs are also subject to restraints in their criticism of judges, though not to the same degree as are members of the executive. There is a long-standing rule of the House that unless the discussion is based on a substantive motion, reflections must not be cast upon the conduct of judges, nor upon judges generally.[78] The effect of these rules was seen in 1973 when the National Industrial Relations Court and its president, Sir John Donaldson, became the subject of acute controversy.

The court had been set up under the Conservative government's Industrial Relations Act 1971, and its jurisdiction in industrial disputes was bitterly opposed by trade unions. The Amalgamated Union of Engineering Workers disregarded an order of the court and were fined £100,000 for contempt. The court directed that funds of the union be sequestrated to pay the fine, action which was later defended by Sir John Donaldson in the course of an after-dinner speech. Over 180 Labour MPs signed a motion calling for Sir John's dismissal as High Court judge, but this was not supported by opposition leaders. When the Commons debated a motion calling for the repeal of the 1971 Act, and regretting the involvement of the court in matters of political controversy, the Speaker ruled that it could be argued in debate that a judge's decision was wrong, and the reasons for this view could be given. But no reflections on a judge's

---

75   *The Times*, 16 May 1977.
76   HC Deb, 14 December 1982, col 123; 15 December 1982, col 285.
77   HC Deb, 2 July 1987, col 641.
78   Erskine May, pp 325 and 379–80.

character or motives could be raised except on a motion for his dismissal.[79] In the event, the motion calling for the judge's dismissal was never debated, since neither the government nor the Opposition wished to provide time for the purpose. The Speaker ruled that the ancient Article of Charge procedure, if it were still available, could not be given precedence over the ordinary business of the House.[80]

On subsequent occasions, when judges have made controversial remarks or decisions, MPs have been quick to raise these matters in the Commons and to show their disapproval. Thus in January 1978, Judge McKinnon conducted a trial at the Old Bailey of charges of incitement to racial hatred and in his summing-up called into question the policy behind the race relations legislation. After these remarks had been criticised in Parliament, the Lord Chancellor discussed the criticisms with the judge, who indicated that he did not wish to conduct further trials for similar offences.[81] Concern was also expressed over remarks by Judge King-Hamilton criticising a jury's decision to acquit defendants at an 'anarchist' trial.[82] In 1977, motions were tabled for the dismissal of three judges who in the Court of Appeal had reduced a sentence for rape.[83] A judge who described a victim of rape as having been guilty of 'contributory negligence' was also criticised.[84] Instant political reaction to events such as these may sometimes be ill-informed or exaggerated, but a corrective is needed when judges are seriously insensitive to changing social opinion.

Another parliamentary rule seeks to protect the principle of a fair trial rather than the status of the judges: by the sub judice rule, matters awaiting the adjudication of a court may not be raised in debate. The rule applies to matters pending decision both in criminal and civil cases; but in regard to civil cases, the Speaker has a discretion to permit reference to matters awaiting adjudication where they relate to ministerial decisions which can be challenged in court only on grounds of misdirection or bad faith, or to issues of national importance, such as the national economy, the essentials of life or public order.[85] The reason for this relaxation is to permit some parliamentary discussion of ministerial decisions or other major issues of public concern, notwithstanding the fact that a civil action may have been instituted.[86] The operation of the rule arose for consideration in 1987 when the British government was seeking to restrain the publication of Mr Peter Wright's book, *Spycatcher*. At a time when proceedings had been instituted against the publishers in Australia, the Speaker ruled that 'it is legitimate to raise anything that has come out in the Australian courts, but what should not be raised under our sub judice rule is the action that is pending before the British courts ... anything that has come out in the Australian courts is fair

[79]   HC Deb, 4 December 1973, col 1092. And see HC Deb, 19 July 1977, col 1381.
[80]   HC Deb, 10 December 1973, col 42.
[81]   *The Times*, 7 and 14 January 1978.
[82]   *The Times*, 20 and 21 December 1979, 17 January and 1 February 1980.
[83]   HC Deb, 23 June 1977, col 1748.
[84]   *The Times*, 6 and 12 January 1982.
[85]   Erskine May, p 378; HC Deb, 23 July 1963, col 1417; 28 June 1972, col 1589.
[86]   See eg debate on the thalidomide cases, HC Deb, 29 November 1972, col 432.

game'.[87] The sub judice rule has been described as a self-denying ordinance, created by the Commons so that Parliament should not influence or seem to be influencing the administration of justice.[88] It does not affect the power of Parliament to legislate: thus the War Damage Act 1965 altered the law retrospectively while litigation against the government was in process.

Judicial immunity from civil action

Just as the public interest in free debate in Parliament justifies the rule of absolute privilege for things said in the course of parliamentary debates, so the public interest in the administration of justice justifies similar protection for judicial proceedings. At common law no action will lie against a judge for any acts done or words spoken in his or her judicial capacity in a court of justice.

It is essential in all courts that the judges who are appointed to administer the law should be permitted to administer it under the protection of the law independently and freely, without favour and without fear. This provision of the law is not for the protection or benefit of a malicious or corrupt judge, but for the benefit of the public, whose interest it is that the judges should be at liberty to exercise their functions with independence and without fear of consequences.[89]

The judge of a superior court is not liable for anything done or said in the exercise of judicial functions, however malicious, corrupt or oppressive are the acts or words complained of.[90] A similar immunity attaches to the verdict of juries,[91] and to words spoken by parties, counsel and witnesses in the course of judicial proceedings.[92] In *Rondel v Worsley*, it was held that a barrister is not liable to be sued for the negligent conduct of a client's case in court.[93] The immunity of judges is reinforced by the Crown Proceedings Act 1947, s 2(5), which absolves the Crown from liability for any person 'while discharging or purporting to discharge any responsibilities of a judicial nature vested in him' or in the execution of judicial process. But immunity does not extend to the acts or words of a judge in his or her private capacity.

Judicial immunity also applies to the work of inferior courts, for example county courts and magistrates' courts. But the immunity is narrower than in the case of the superior courts. In *Sirros v Moore*[94] the Court of Appeal appeared to assimilate the position of judges in inferior courts to that of judges in superior courts when it held that a circuit court judge was immune from liability for damages after he had by a wholly erroneous procedure ordered a Turkish citizen to be detained by the police. The Court of Appeal considered that no distinction should be drawn in principle between the protection given to superior court judges and that given to inferior courts. According to Lord Denning and Ormrod L J, every judge, including a justice

---

[87]   HC Deb, 13 July 1987, col 710. And see ch 22 G.
[88]   HC Deb, 29 July 1976, col 882; and see HC 222 (1978–79).
[89]   *Scott v Stansfield* (1868) LR 3 Ex 220, 223 per Kelly CB.
[90]   *Anderson v Gorrie* [1895] 1 QB 668. And see generally Olowofoyeku, *Suing Judges*.
[91]   *Bushell's* case (1670) 6 St Tr 999.
[92]   *Munster v Lamb* (1883) 11 QBD 588.
[93]   [1969] 1 AC 191. But see *Saif Ali v Sydney Mitchell & Co* [1980] AC 198, and *Ridehalgh v Horsefield* [1994] Ch 205.
[94]   [1975] QB 118, discussed by M Brazier [1976] PL 397.

of the peace, was entitled to be protected from liability in respect of what he did while acting judicially and in the honest belief that his acts were within jurisdiction. But the scope of this decision was doubted, at least so far as justices of the peace are concerned. It was subsequently pointed out in the House of Lords that a magistrate is personally liable where an innocent error of law or fact results in an unlawful sentence of imprisonment imposed without jurisdiction. The fact that the magistrate thought that he or she was acting within jurisdiction appears to be irrelevant, though the absence of bad faith would affect the quantum of damages.[95] As if to acknowledge Lord Templeman's claim in *Re McC (a minor)* that 'the time is ripe for the legislature to reconsider the liability of a magistrate',[96] a greater measure of protection was introduced by the Courts and Legal Services Act 1990. By s 108, a magistrate will not be liable for any acts within his or her jurisdiction, nor for any acts outside jurisdiction unless in the latter case the plaintiff can show bad faith.

To what extent does judicial immunity extend to the members of administrative tribunals, some of whose duties may be judicial, others of which may be administrative or 'ministerial'? Here there may be immunity for judicial acts, but liability for 'ministerial' acts, such as refusal to perform a definite duty, which permits of no discretion.[97] When a licensing body does not have the attributes of a court, even though for some purposes it may be required to act judicially, words spoken in the course of its proceedings are privileged only in the absence of malice.[98] But where a statutory inquiry was held in Scotland into a teacher's dismissal, by an adversary procedure modelled on that of a court and conducted before a lawyer appointed by the Secretary of State, the witnesses were held to be protected by absolute privilege.[99]

Other safeguards

Despite their immunities, it would be wrong to suppose that professional judges are uncontrolled despots. For one thing, laypersons make a significant contribution to the administration of justice: the role of the jury in major criminal trials is an important constitutional safeguard against an oppressive judiciary; removal of the right to trial by jury is a matter of grave concern.[100] So too is interference with the freedom of the jury, whether it takes the form of criminal conduct or 'jury-vetting'.[101] Lay magistrates in England and Wales discharge a heavy burden of adjudication. Non-lawyers have a significant role to play in courts of specialised jurisdiction and in tribunals.

There are also many legal rules which serve to maintain the quality of justice in the courts. The law of contempt of court is considered in the next section. The written rules of court procedure as well as the unwritten rules of

---

[95]   *Re McC* [1985] AC 528. See *R v Waltham Forest JJ, ex p Solanke*, [1986] QB 383.
[96]   [1985] AC 528, at 559.
[97]   *Ferguson v Earl of Kinnoull* (1842) 9 Cl & F 251.
[98]   *Royal Aquarian Society Ltd v Parkinson* [1892] 1 QB 431.
[99]   *Trapp v Mackie* [1979] 1 All ER 489; N Y Lowe and H F Rawlings [1982] PL 418, 431–40.
[100] 'The constitutional law of England requires that a man accused of a serious crime should be tried by Judge and Jury' (Lord Denning [1990] Crim LR 536). See Cmnd 5185, 1972; and Northern Ireland (Emergency Provisions) Act 1996, s 11(1); ch 25 E.
[101] See ch 24.

natural justice seek for each litigant a fair and orderly hearing before an unbiased judge.[102] The statutory schemes for legal aid from public funds help to ensure that it is not only the wealthy who benefit from legal representation in the courts. The rules of evidence, particularly in criminal trials before a jury, exclude material which might be unfairly prejudicial to the accused. Most judges carry on their work knowing that their decisions may be subject to scrutiny and criticism by a higher court on appeal.

In principle all trials are conducted in open court and may be fully reported in the press. It has been said that 'If the way the courts behave cannot be hidden from the public ear and eye this provides a safeguard against judicial arbitrariness or idiosyncracy and maintains the public confidence in the administration of justice'.[103] In a few exceptional cases, the court may sit in camera, and press and public are then excluded.[104] These exceptions include cases in which the court is asked to preserve the secrecy of an industrial process or invention; proceedings brought under the Official Secrets Acts 1911–89, for example for spying, where the public interest so requires; certain domestic and juvenile court hearings; and proceedings for an offence against morality or decency when evidence is being given by children or young persons.[105] But the court may not hear a case in camera merely in the interests of decency.[106] In *R v Murphy*[107] it was held that although contrary to principle, a judge could permit the evidence of media witnesses in a terrorist trial to be given anonymously and from behind screens, following experience in such trials that 'even prosecution witnesses whose evidence is merely formal, unchallenged by the defence, but a necessary link in the narrative of the prosecution case, suffer considerable anxiety for their safety as a result'. The rule of public hearing does not apply when a judge sits in chambers,[108] nor in cases concerning wards of court or mentally disordered persons.

Where judicial proceedings take place in open court in the United Kingdom, the press may be present and may publish reports of the proceedings which, if fair and accurate reports, are privileged in the law of defamation.[109] But Parliament has imposed various restrictions on reporting of judicial proceedings. Newspapers may not publish details of the evidence in matrimonial cases, but may only publish the names of parties, a statement of the issues, submissions on points of law and the judgment.[110] Industrial tribunals have the power to order restrictions on publicity in cases involving alleged sexual misconduct;[111] and there are also reporting restrictions relating

---

[102] Ch 29 B.
[103] *A-G v Leveller Magazine Ltd* [1979] AC 440, 449 (Lord Diplock).
[104] Both by statute and by judicial discretion, reporters may sometimes be present when the public are excluded: eg Children and Young Persons Act 1933, s 47(2), and *R v Waterfield* [1975] 2 All ER 40. Cf Official Secrets Act 1920, s 8(4).
[105] Children and Young Persons Act 1933, s 37.
[106] *Scott v Scott* [1913] AC 417.
[107] [1990] NI 306.
[108] See *Re Crook* [1992] 2 All ER 687.
[109] Defamation Act 1996, ss 14, 15.
[110] Judicial Proceedings (Regulation of Reports) Act 1926; Magistrates' Courts Act 1980, s 71 (amended by Broadcasting Act 1990).
[111] Industrial Tribunals Act 1996, s 11 (also s 31).

to the identity of children and young persons.[112] The law relating to committal proceedings, at which magistrates in England determine whether or not an accused person shall be tried on indictment before judge and jury, was amended in 1981: if full committal proceedings take place, the evidence is heard in open court, but reporting restrictions prevent publication of the evidence unless the accused asks for the restrictions to be lifted.[113] Apart from the requirements that judicial proceedings should be held in public and that they may be reported in the press, the principle of open justice also requires that the judges who hear cases between parties should be known to the public. So the power of magistrates to control their own proceedings does not permit them to sit anonymously or to withhold their identity from the public or the press.[114] Additional powers of restricting press reporting were conferred on courts in 1981.[115]

B.   Contempt of court[116]

The law on contempt of court was developed by the judges as a means whereby the courts may prevent or punish conduct that tends to obstruct, prejudice or abuse the administration of justice, whether in a particular case or generally.[117] This branch of the law operates in the interests of all who take part in court proceedings, as judges, counsel, parties or witnesses. But it also imposes restraints upon many persons, particularly on the press, whose freedom to report news about the administration of justice is sometimes severely limited by the law of contempt. Significant reforms were made by the Contempt of Court Act 1981, which sought to strike a fresh balance between the need of the judicial system to be protected against improper attack, and the public interest in maintaining freedom of speech and discussion.

Contempt of court may broadly take two forms. Civil contempt is the failure to obey the order of a superior court of record which prescribes certain conduct upon a party to a civil action. A civil judge may commit to prison anyone who disregards an order addressed to him or her. In this way, decrees of specific performance and injunctions, as well as the writ of habeas corpus and other judicial orders, may be enforced by the High Court. The power of courts to enforce their orders against litigants is not available against the Crown but ministers of the Crown and civil servants are liable to be

---

[112]   Children and Young Persons Act 1933, s 39. See *R v Lee* [1993] 2 All ER 170, *Re R (A Minor)* [1994] Fam 254 and *R v Cambridge Health Authority, ex p B (No 2), The Times*, 27 October 1995 (restriction revoked to enable a newspaper to carry the identity of a child for which it was proposing to pay the costs of private medical care, though regret was expressed by the court about the need to exploit 'the medical problems of the child for financial gain').

[113]   Magistrates' Courts Act 1980, s 8 (amended by Broadcasting Act 1990). For the position where there are two or more accused, see Criminal Justice (Amendment) Act 1981, s 2. For reporting restrictions in relation to the new preparatory hearing procedure under the Criminal Procedure and Investigations Act 1996, see ss 37–8.

[114]   *R v Felixstowe Justices, ex p Leigh* [1987] QB 582.

[115]   Contempt of Court Act 1981, s 4(2).

[116]   See Lowe and Sufrin, *Borrie and Lowe's Law of Contempt*; Miller, *Contempt of Court*; Arlidge and Eady, *The Law of Contempt*; Report of the Phillimore Committee on Contempt of Court, Cmnd 5794, 1974.

[117]   Phillimore Report, p 2.

proceeded against for contempt of court in respect of acts or omissions by them personally and it is no defence that what would otherwise constitute a contempt of court was committed in the discharge or purported discharge of official duties.[118] Where a civil contempt is committed, the court may commit the wrongdoer to prison for a fixed period, may fine him or her or may order his or her property to be sequestrated. The Official Solicitor to the Supreme Court is required to review all cases of persons committed to prison for contempt and may intervene to secure their release.[119] The Crown may not grant a pardon in cases of civil contempt since this would be to intervene in litigation between parties.

Conduct which is calculated to interfere with the due administration of justice or to bring the courts into disrepute gives rise to proceedings which are in the nature of criminal proceedings, although both civil and criminal courts may exercise the jurisdiction. Although criminal contempt takes various forms and although it is necessary to protect the workings of the courts, nevertheless judges should seek to ensure, in the words of Lord President Normand

that the greatest restraint and discrimination should be used by the court in dealing with contempt of court, lest a process, the purpose of which is to prevent interference with the administration of justice, should degenerate into an oppressive or vindictive abuse of the court's powers.[120]

The need for restraint is all the greater since one of the implications of contempt of court is to restrict freedom of expression. The main categories of contempt will now be outlined.

1 Scandalising the court.[121]   The law protects courts and judges from criticism which might undermine public confidence in the judiciary, in particular scurrilous abuse and attacks upon the integrity or impartiality of a judge. Proceedings on this ground are rare: 'More than fifty years have passed since the last successful prosecution in England and Wales for scandalising the court'.[122] Nevertheless, criticism of a court's decision may be a contempt if it imputes unfairness and partiality to a judge in the discharge of his duties.

In 1928, the *New Statesman*, commenting on a judgment in a libel action against Dr Marie Stopes, a known advocate of birth control, concluded, 'an individual owning to such views as those of Dr Stopes cannot apparently hope for a fair hearing in a court presided over by Mr Justice Avory and there are so many Avorys'. Three colleagues of the judge in question, though they imposed no fine on the editor, adjudged him guilty of contempt.[123]

---

[118]   *M v Home Office* [1994] 1 AC 377.
[119]   *Churchman v Joint Shop Stewards' Committee* [1972] 3 All ER 603; *Enfield BC v Mahoney* [1983] 2 All ER 901.
[120]   *Milburn, Petitioner* 1946 SC 301, 315.
[121]   See D Hay (1987) 25 Osgoode Hall LJ 431.
[122]   C Walker (1985) 101 LQR 359.
[123]   *R v New Statesman (Editor), ex p DPP* (1928) 44 TLR 301.

Yet it is clearly in the public interest that there should be public discussion and criticism of judicial decisions and the work of the courts. When a colonial newspaper had discussed a variation in sentence in two apparently similar cases, suggesting that this was due to the personal attitudes of the judge, the Privy Council set aside the conviction for contempt. The judgment of the Judicial Committee was given by Lord Atkin, who said:

> But whether the authority and position of an individual judge, or the due administration of justice, is concerned, no wrong is committed by any member of the public who exercises the ordinary right of criticising, in good faith, in private or public, the public act done in the seat of justice. The path of criticism is a public way: the wrongheaded are permitted to err therein: provided that members of the public abstain from imputing improper motives to those taking part in the administration of justice, and are genuinely exercising a right of criticism, and not acting in malice or attempting to impair the administration of justice, they are immune. Justice is not a cloistered virtue: she must be allowed to suffer the scrutiny and respectful, even though outspoken, comments of ordinary men.[124]

Discussion of the legal merits or social implications of judicial decisions is therefore not contempt, even where a Queen's Counsel chooses to make sweeping and inaccurate criticism of the Court of Appeal in the columns of *Punch*.[125] Potentially this aspect of the law might deter a critic who sought to show that the judges were biased politically or socially or that a particular court was failing to administer justice. But today the scope of permissible criticism has widened, to judge by the sharp controversy over the National Industrial Relations Court between 1971 and 1974, by the attacks made on some of Lord Denning's decisions before his retirement in 1982, and by some of the criticisms of the Law Lords after the first *Spycatcher* case in 1987. The Phillimore committee recommended that this branch of contempt should be replaced by an offence of publishing matter which imputes improper judicial conduct with the intention of impairing confidence in the adminstration of justice,[126] but this recommendation has wisely not been adopted.

2 Contempt in the face of the court.   All superior courts have power to punish summarily by fine or imprisonment violence committed or threats uttered in face of the court. Thus the judge may punish an attack on anyone in court, or restrain the use of threatening words or scurrilous abuse. The issue whether an act constitutes a contempt is for the judge alone. If the act is committed in court, the judge is in a sense prosecutor, chief witness, judge and jury.

In *Morris v Crown Office*,[127] a group of students demonstrated in support of the Welsh language by interrupting a sitting of the High Court in London, where they sang, shouted slogans and scattered pamphlets. After order was restored, the trial judge sentenced some of the students to prison for three months and fined others £50 each. On appeal, the Court of Appeal, Civil Division, held that a High Court judge still had

---

[124]   *Ambard v A-G for Trinidad and Tobago* [1936] AC 322, 335.
[125]   *R v Metropolitan Police Commissioner, ex p Blackburn (No 2)* [1968] 2 QB 150. Probably the most savage criticism of a British court ever published was N J D Kennedy, *The Second Division's Progress* (1896) 8 JR 268.
[126]   Phillimore Report, pp 69–71.
[127]   [1970] 2 QB 114.

power at common law to commit instantly to prison for criminal contempt; and that the requirement under the Criminal Justice Act 1967 that prison sentences under six months be suspended did not apply to committal for contempt. The court did not consider the prison sentences to be excessive, but, having regard to all the circumstances, allowed the appeal against sentence and bound over the appellants to be of good behaviour for one year.

Contempt in the face of the court includes insulting behaviour,[128] disregard of a judge's ruling and refusal by a witness to give evidence or to answer questions which he or she is required to answer.[129]

In *Attorney-General v Mulholland and Foster*,[130] two journalists refused to disclose their sources of information to a tribunal of inquiry appointed after an Admiralty clerk, Vassall, had been convicted of espionage. The tribunal had by statute the powers of the High Court in examining witnesses.[131] On appeal against a prison sentence imposed by the High Court, to whom the tribunal had reported the journalists, it was held that journalists had no legal privilege to refuse to disclose sources of information given to them in confidence, where the information was relevant and necessary to the trial or inquiry.

So too, in *British Steel Corpn v Granada Television Ltd*,[132] the House of Lords ordered the Granada company to reveal the name of an employee of the corporation who had passed secret documents to Granada that were then used in a programme about the corporation. Although failure by Granada to comply with this order would have constituted contempt, the matter was resolved when the employee concerned made his identity known. In 1981, the power of the court to demand information was limited by Parliament. The court may not now request a person to disclose the source of information contained in a publication for which he or she is responsible, unless the court is satisfied that disclosure is necessary in the interests of justice or national security or for the prevention of disorder or crime.[133] If cases such as *Mulholland* and *British Steel Corpn* were to occur today, the statutory test of necessity would have to be applied before the court decided to require disclosure, but the outcome might still be the same.[134]

In *Secretary of State for Defence v Guardian Newspapers Ltd*[135] a junior civil servant delivered anonymously to the *Guardian* newspaper confidential documents addressed to Cabinet ministers by the Secretary of State for Defence. The documents related to the arrival of

---

128 See *R v Powell, The Times*, 3 June 1993.
129 *R v Montgomery, The Times*, 19 July 1994.
130 [1963] 2 QB 477. And see *Senior v Holdsworth* [1976] QB 23.
131 Ch 28 C.
132 [1981] AC 1096.
133 Contempt of Court Act 1981, s 10.
134 But cf *Broadmoor Hospital v Hyde, The Independent*, 4 March 1994 (court refused to order defendant to reveal source of confidential inquiry reports on escape of convicted murderers from the hospital. Although it was in the interests of justice that it should find the source, it had not been shown that it was 'necessary' for the court to so order, as the plaintiff had not made any other efforts to find the source).
135 [1985] AC 359. Other cases under s 10 include *Maxwell v Pressdram Ltd* [1987] 1 All ER 621; *Re an Inquiry under the Company Securities (Insider Dealing) Act 1985* [1988] AC 660; and *X Ltd v Morgan-Grampian (Publishers) Ltd* [1991] 1 AC 1. See T R S Allan [1991] CLJ 131; S Palmer [1992] PL 61. See also *Goodwin v UK* (1996) 22 EHRR 123.

US cruise missiles at Greenham Common airbase. The Ministry of Defence sought to recover the documents to help them to identify the person responsible for the leak. The House of Lords held that s 10 of the 1981 Act was a valid defence not only where a journalist was asked a direct question in court, but also in an action for recovery of property where the property once recovered would help to reveal the newspaper's source. But the House also held (Lords Fraser and Scarman dissenting) that it was necessary to recover the documents and identify the source of the leak in the interests of national security. The minister had expressed concern that a significant document relating to the defence of Britain had found its way to a national newspaper. This was of grave importance for national security, since Britain's allies could not be expected to continue to entrust the government with secret information if it was liable to unauthorised disclosure.

3 Publications prejudicing the course of justice.   Until the Contempt of Court Act 1981 this matter was governed by the common law, which imposed penalties on those whose publications were prejudicial to a fair trial or to civil proceedings.[136] The law was reformed in 1981, following recommendations of the Phillimore committee[137] and the decision of the European Court of Human Rights in the *Sunday Times* case.

Nearly 400 claims against Distillers Ltd, the manufacturers of thalidomide, were pending when the *Sunday Times* published an article which inter alia urged the company to make a generous settlement. Later it proposed to publish an article examining the precautions taken by the company before the drug was sold. On the Attorney-General's request, the Divisional Court granted an injunction to restrain publication of the article, holding that it would create a serious risk of interference with the company's freedom of action in the litigation. The Court of Appeal discharged the injunction, on the grounds that the article commented in good faith on matters of outstanding public importance and did not prejudice pending litigation since the litigation had been dormant for some years.

The House of Lords restored the injunction, holding that it was a contempt to publish an article prejudging the merits of an issue before the court where this created a real risk that a fair trial of the action would be prejudiced; the thalidomide actions were not dormant, since active negotiations for a settlement were going on. It was a contempt to use improper pressure to induce a litigant to settle a case on terms to which he did not wish to agree, or to hold a litigant up to public obloquy for exercising his rights in the courts.[138] Thereafter the *Sunday Times* claimed that the decision of the House of Lords infringed the freedom of expression protected by art 10 of the European Convention on Human Rights. Before the European Court of Human Rights, the main issue was whether, under art 10, the ban on publication was 'necessary in a democratic society . . . for maintaining the authority and impartiality of the judiciary'. By 11 to 9 votes, the court held that the ban had not been shown to be necessary for this purpose.[139]

The Contempt of Court Act 1981 was designed to bring British law into line with the requirements of the *Sunday Times* decision, though there is much scope for argument about whether it does so fully.[140]

---

[136]   Leading cases arising out of criminal litigation before 1981 include *R v Bolam, ex p Haigh* (1949) 93 SJ 220; *R v Evening Standard Co Ltd* [1954] 1 QB 578; *R v Thomson Newspapers, ex p A-G* [1968] 1 All ER 268; and *Stirling v Associated Newspapers Ltd* 1960 JC 5. And in relation to civil litigation, see *Vine Products Ltd v Green* [1966] Ch 484.
[137]   Cmnd 5794, 1974.
[138]   *A-G v Times Newspapers Ltd* [1974] AC 273.
[139]   *Sunday Times v UK* (1979) 2 EHRR 245.
[140]   See S Bailey (1982) 45 MLR 301.

Liability for contempt under the 1981 Act is based on the strict liability rule, defined to mean 'the rule of law whereby conduct may be treated as a contempt of court as tending to interfere with the course of justice in particular legal proceedings regardless of intent to do so' (s 1). By s 2, the strict liability rule applies to any publication which creates 'a substantial risk that the course of justice in the proceedings in question will be seriously impeded or prejudiced'. This applies to both civil and criminal proceedings. The other requirement of s 2 is that the proceedings in question must be 'active', governed by Sched 1, which lays down in detail when civil or criminal proceedings begin to be active. Criminal proceedings become active when an individual is arrested or orally charged, or when an arrest warrant is issued (whereas at common law liability for contempt could arise where legal proceedings were imminent).[141] Civil proceedings become active not when the writ is served but when the action is set down for trial. In some cases, proceedings may be instituted at common law to deal with publications which are likely to prejudice the outcome of proceedings not yet active within the statutory definition.[142] Proceedings remain active in criminal cases until concluded by acquittal, sentence or discontinuance, and in other cases until the proceedings are disposed of, discontinued or withdrawn.[143]

The question whether the course of justice in particular legal proceedings will be impeded or prejudiced is ultimately one of fact; this will depend primarily on whether the publication will bring influence to bear which is likely to direct the proceedings in some way from the course which they would otherwise have followed.[144] Many of the cases on contempt of court, both before and after 1981, are concerned with pre-trial publicity which may influence the jury. Thus *Attorney-General v Times Newspapers Ltd*[145] concerned reports carried by newspapers about a man who had intruded into the Queen's bedroom at Buckingham Palace. The man in question was awaiting trial on a number of counts, including the theft of a bottle of wine. It was held that a newspaper report that he had admitted the theft was a contempt, since it was difficult to see how an assertion that an accused person had admitted the very fact which was in issue could do otherwise than cause a very substantial risk that the trial might be prejudiced. The leading case on s 2(2) is *Re Lonrho plc*,[146] an extraordinary case which arose out of a battle for control of the London department store, Harrods.

---

[141] *R v Savundranayagan* [1968] 3 All ER 439; *R v Beaverbrook Newspapers Ltd* [1962] NI 15.

[142] *A-G v News Group Newspapers* [1989] QB 110. Cf *A-G v Sport Newspapers Ltd* [1992] 1 All ER 503.

[143] On the question of appeals against sentence and 'misguided' press campaigns, see *R v Vano, The Times*, 29 December 1994.

[144] *Re Lonrho* [1990] 2 AC 154.

[145] *The Times*, 12 February 1983. See also *R v Wood, The Times*, 11 July 1995, and *A-G v BBC* [1997] EMLR 76. But compare *A-G v ITN News, The Times*, 12 May 1994; adverse publicity at the time of arrest not contempt of court (by creating a risk that jurors might be influenced) when trial did not take place for nine months: 'That was a long time to retain a story, however startling, even allowing that the murder of a police officer might prompt recall of matters related'. But although the court was not satisfied that the trial had been prejudiced, it censured ITN and newspapers for a broadcast and articles which 'should never have been made'.

[146] Note 144 above.

In 1987 the Secretary of State for Trade and Industry appointed inspectors to investigate the affairs of the company which owned the store. The inspectors submitted their report in 1988, but the Secretary of State refused to publish it and he also refused to refer the matter to the Monopolies and Mergers Commission. Lonrho instituted two applications for judicial review, designed to compel the minister to publish the inspectors' report and to refer the matter to the Commission. While appeals on both applications were pending before the House of Lords, Lonrho acquired a copy of the inspectors' report, which the *Observer* agreed to publish in a special issue of the newspaper. Some copies of the issue were sent to persons on a mailing list to whom Lonrho had been regularly sending propaganda literature. These people included four of the five Lords of Appeal in Ordinary who were to hear the appeals. These circumstances were referred to three other members of the House of Lords. They held that the special issue (which contained extensive extracts from the inspectors' report as well as editorial comment accusing the Secretary of State of bad faith) did not create a substantial risk that the course of justice in Lonrho's appeals would be seriously impeded or prejudiced. 'So far as the appellate tribunal is concerned, it is difficult to visualise circumstances in which any court in the United Kingdom exercising appellate jurisdiction would be in the least likely to be influenced by public discussion of the merits of a decision appealed against or of the parties' conduct in the proceedings'.

A number of defences are provided in the 1981 Act. The first of these is the defence of innocent publication (s 3), where the person responsible for the publication can prove that, having taken all reasonable care, he or she did not know that relevant legal proceedings were active. The second is the contemporary reporting of legal proceedings in respect of 'a fair and accurate report of legal proceedings held in public, published contemporaneously and in good faith' (s 4(1)). However, a court may order that publication of reports be delayed where necessary to avoid a substantial risk of prejudice to the administration of justice (s 4(2)).[147] 'In forming a view whether it is necessary to make an order for avoiding such a risk a court will inevitably have regard to the competing public interest considerations of ensuring a fair trial and of open justice.'[148] The power was used at the trial of Clive Ponting under the Official Secrets Act 1911 to prevent a television company from recreating the court proceedings as a drama documentary at the end of each day.[149] Before granting an order under s 4(2), the magistrates are entitled to hear representations from the press that the order should not be granted.[150] The third defence is where the publication contains a good faith discussion of public affairs if the risk of prejudice to particular legal proceedings is merely incidental to the discussion (s 5). In *Attorney-General v English* Lord Diplock noted that s 5 does not take the form of an exception to s 2, but stands on an equal footing with it: 'It does not set out exculpatory matter. Like s 2(2) it states what publications shall *not* amount to contempt of court despite their

---

[147] The exercise of this power is governed by the *Practice Note* [1983] 1 All ER 64, on the importance of which see *Re Central Television plc* [1991] 1 All ER 347. For the approach which the courts should adopt in such cases, see *MGN Pension Trustees Ltd v Bank of America* [1995] 2 All ER 355. On the right of appeal against an order issued under s 4(2) see Criminal Justice Act 1988, s 159.

[148] *Ex p The Telegraph plc* [1993] 2 All ER 971. See *R v Horsham Justices, ex p Farquharson* [1982] QB 762; M J Beloff [1992] PL 92.

[149] Ewing and Gearty, *Freedom under Thatcher*, p 145.

[150] *R v Clerkenwell Metropolitan Magistrate, ex p The Telegraph plc* [1993] QB 462.

tendency to interfere with the course of justice in particular legal proceedings'.[151]

In *Attorney-General v English* the *Daily Mail* published an article in support of a woman standing for election to Parliament as an independent pro-life candidate, one of her aims being to stop the alleged practice in hospitals whereby newly-born handicapped babies are allowed to die. At the time the article was published a well-known paediatrician was standing trial, accused of murdering a three-day-old boy with Down's syndrome, by allowing him to die of starvation. The House of Lords held that this did not amount to a contempt of court; although the publication of the article on the third day of the trial was capable of prejudicing the jury, the publication was a discussion in good faith on a matter of wide public interest and the risk of prejudice was incidental to the discussion. To hold otherwise 'would have prevented [the candidate] from ... obtaining publicity for what was a main plank in her election programme and would have stifled all discussion in the press ... about mercy killing from the time that [the doctor] was charged in the magistrates' court in February 1981 until the date of his acquittal [in] November of that year'.[152]

4 Other acts interfering with the course of justice. Nothing in the Contempt of Court Act 1981 is designed to restrict liability for contempt of court in respect of conduct intended to impede or prejudice the administration of justice (s 6(2)). Many other acts are punishable as contempts, some of them also being criminal offences in their own right, for example, attempts to pervert the course of justice or interference with witnesses.[153] A prison governor who, acting under prison rules, obstructed a prisoner's communication with the High Court was held to be in contempt.[154] It is a contempt to punish or victimise a witness for evidence which has already been given, even in proceedings which have concluded, since this might deter potential witnesses in future cases.[155] It may be a contempt of court for a solicitor to disclose to a journalist documents relating to litigation.

A prisoner challenged the legality of a Home Office decision to set up a 'control unit' for prisoners considered to be troublemakers. An order for discovery of documents being made against the Home Office, a large number of official documents were made available to the prisoner's solicitor. She undertook that the documents would be used only for the case in hand, but she later allowed a journalist to see documents which had been read out in open court. The journalist published an article based on these documents. The House of Lords held (by three to two) that although the documents had been read in court, and could have been reported by journalists present, the solicitor was guilty of contempt since she had used the documents for a purpose which was not necessary for the conduct of her client's case, and had broken her implied undertaking to the court that had ordered discovery.[156]

Interference with the work of a jury may constitute contempt, whether before,

---

[151] [1983] 1 AC 116, 141.
[152] [1983] 1 AC 116, at 144 (Lord Diplock).
[153] See *Peach Grey & Co v Sommers* [1995] 2 All ER 513.
[154] *Raymond v Honey* [1983] AC 1.
[155] *A-G v Butterworth* [1963] 1 QB 696; *Moore v Clerk of Assize, Bristol* [1972] 1 All ER 58.
[156] *Home Office v Harman* [1983] AC 280. Subsequent proceedings under the European Convention on Human Rights were the subject of a friendly settlement. In 1987, the decision was largely reversed by an amendment to the Rules of the Supreme Court: Ord 24, r 14A, releases parties from any undertaking once the material has been read in open court. See now *Apple Corp v Apple Computer Inc, The Times*, 10 April 1991.

during or after a trial. By s 8 of the Contempt of Court Act 1981, it is a contempt of court to solicit, obtain or disclose details of any statements made or votes cast by jurors during their deliberations in any legal proceedings. This reversed a decision in 1980 that a magazine article disclosing aspects of the jury's deliberations during the trial of Mr Jeremy Thorpe was not a contempt of court.[157] It is an offence under s 8 for a newspaper to publish information disclosed to it by a jury member.[158]

The dynamic nature of the law of contempt has been well demonstrated by decisions arising out of important disputes between the courts and the press. It is a contempt for a newspaper to disregard a judge's directions that the names of prosecution witnesses in blackmail cases should not be published.[159] But the power to issue such directions is not limited to blackmail cases.

In *Attorney-General v Leveller Magazine Ltd* a magazine published the name of a prosecution witness at an official secrets trial, who had been described in court as Colonel B. The House of Lords held that it was contempt of court to publish a witness's name if this interfered with the administration of justice. But on the facts no contempt had occurred, since inter alia no clear direction against publication had been given by the magistrates; and Colonel B's identity could have been discovered from evidence given in open court.[160]

The uncertainties left by this decision were lessened by the Contempt of Court Act 1981. By s 11, where a court has the power to withhold evidence from the public (although the court is sitting in public) and allows the name of a witness or other matter to be withheld, it may restrict publication accordingly.[161] Thus it would be a contempt of court to publish such information, even though the identity of the witness could be discovered from evidence given in open court, as in the *Leveller Magazine* case. However, a court cannot prohibit the press from reporting names which are mentioned in court unless there has first been a direction that these names should be withheld from the public.[162] And it has been said that the courts should be careful about exercising this power, which should not be used simply to protect privacy or avoid embarrassment.[163]

It may also be contempt to publish material which has been the subject of an injunction against another party.[164] A third party who knowingly acts in breach of the terms of the injunction may be in contempt even though he or she is not a party to the proceedings and indeed may not have had an opportunity to make representations in these proceedings.

In 1986 interlocutory injunctions were granted against two newspapers, the *Guardian* and the *Observer*, restraining them from publishing material from the book *Spycatcher*, by Mr Peter Wright, pending a full trial of the action in which the Attorney-General sought permanent injunctions on the ground that the information was confidential.

---

[157]   *A-G v New Statesman Publishing Co* [1981] QB 1.
[158]   *A-G v Associated Newspapers* [1994] 2 AC 238.
[159]   *R v Socialist Worker Ltd, ex p A-G* [1975] QB 637.
[160]   [1979] AC 440.
[161]   The exercise of this power is also governed by the *Practice Note* [1983] 1 All ER 64.
[162]   *R v Arundel Justices, ex p Westminster Press* [1985] 2 All ER 390.
[163]   *R v Westminster City Council, ex p Castelli*, The Times, 14 August 1995.
[164]   *A-G v Times Newspapers Ltd* [1992] 1 AC 191. See also *A-G v Observer* [1988] 1 All ER 385.

While interlocutory injunctions were still in force, extensive extracts from the book were published in other newspapers, including the *Sunday Times*. The House of Lords held that these publications amounted to a contempt of court, even though the injunctions had not been issued against these newspapers in the first place. In the view of the House, where a party (C) knowingly does something which would if done by B be a breach of an injunction obtained by A against B, C is guilty of contempt of court if this conduct interferes with the administration of justice between A and B. In this case the publication by C (the *Sunday Times*) did interfere with proceedings between A (the Attorney-General) and B (the *Guardian* and the *Observer*). The consequence of the publication by the *Sunday Times* before the main *Spycatcher* trial was to nullify, in part at least, the purpose of such trial, because it put into the public domain part of the material which the Attorney-General claimed should remain confidential.

The scope of contempt of court

Many legal disputes are determined not by the civil and criminal courts but by administrative tribunals.[165] These bodies have no inherent power to deal with conduct which prejudices their proceedings, but the High Court has power to punish conduct that is in contempt of inferior courts.[166] Are tribunals to be classified as inferior courts for this purpose? In 1980, the House of Lords held that, despite its name, a local valuation court that hears appeals against rating valuations was not a court, since its functions were essentially administrative; it was thus not protected by the law of contempt.[167] The government's response to this decision was to propose that contempt of court be extended to all tribunals, but neither this nor a proposal to list tribunals for this purpose was accepted in Parliament.[168] The Contempt of Court Act 1981 thus does not deal with the matter, although s 19 defines 'court' as including 'any tribunal or body exercising the judicial power of the State'. The effect of this definition in the framework of the Act is far from clear, though it has been held that a mental health review tribunal is a court for this purpose and as a result its proceedings are subject to the law of contempt.[169] The same is true of industrial tribunals which have 'many of the characteristics to which the authorities refer as being those of a court of law'.[170] Tribunals within the definition now appear to have power under s 9 to control the use of tape recorders in proceedings before them, and possibly under s 11 to direct that certain matters be not published.

Procedure in contempt cases

In English law contempt is treated as a common law misdemeanour. Unlike other crimes it may be dealt with by a superior court in summary proceedings and without a jury. An indictment before judge and jury is possible but unusual. Criminal contempts may be punished by a fine or by a prison

---

[165]   Ch 28 A.
[166]   RSC Ord 52, r 1.
[167]   *A-G v BBC* [1981] AC 303. See *Badry v DPP of Mauritius* [1982] 3 All ER 973, and N V Lowe and H F Rawlings [1982] PL 418.
[168]   HL Deb, 9 February 1981, col 163; HC Deb, 16 June 1981, col 917. Cf Tribunals and Inquiries Act 1992, Sched 1.
[169]   *Pickering v Liverpool Daily Post plc* [1991] 2 AC 370.
[170]   *Peach Grey and Co v Sommers* [1995] 2 All ER 513, at p 519.

sentence. A two-year prison sentence is now the maximum that may be imposed by a superior court.[171] Inferior courts may imprison for up to one month or impose a fine. All orders for committal must now be for a fixed term, but the court may order release at an earlier date.[172] While the superior courts need to be able to exercise summary powers, the normal safeguards of criminal process should not be absent from contempt proceedings. In 1960, a general right of appeal was provided in cases of criminal contempt[173] and legal aid became available in 1981.[174] In appropriate cases it may also be possible to obtain an injunction to restrain a publication which creates a substantial risk of serious prejudice to the trial of the action.[175] For although the courts are rightly concerned to protect freedom of expression, they are equally anxious to protect the right to a fair trial.

Prejudicial publicity may also lead to a conviction being quashed, as in *R v Cullen*[176] where three Irish nationals (the Winchester Three) were found guilty of conspiracy to murder the then Secretary of State for Northern Ireland. During their trial, in the course of which the accused refused to give evidence, the Home Secretary announced plans to change the law on the right to silence. This was widely reported in the media, which also carried interviews by the Secretary of State for Northern Ireland (who said that those who stood on the right to silence in terrorist cases did so to conceal their guilt) and by Lord Denning (who said that too many people had been acquitted when they were guilty and that the right to silence should be abolished, particularly in Northern Ireland).[177] But it does not follow that a conviction for contempt for prejudicing a fair trial will lead to the acquittal of the accused.[178]

After a press campaign about a dubious insurance company, its prime mover Savundra was interviewed on television by David Frost. Soon after, charges of fraud were brought against Savundra. When he appealed against his conviction claiming that this interview had prevented him from receiving a fair trial, the Court of Appeal considered that the object of the interview had been to establish Savundra's guilt at a time when 'it must surely have been obvious to everyone' that fraud charges were about to be brought. Yet the court rejected an appeal against the conviction on the grounds that the trial did not take place until 11 months after the interview, that the judge warned the jury not to take into account any pre-trial publicity, and that the case for the Crown was so overwhelming that no jury could conceivably have returned any different verdict against Savundra.

---

[171]   The county court ranks as a superior court for this purpose: County Courts (Penalties for Contempt) Act 1983, overruling *Peart v Stewart* [1983] 2 AC 109. On the principles applicable to sentencing, see *R v Montgomery, The Times*, 19 July 1994. There is no power to place on probation for contempt: *R v Palmer* [1992] 3 All ER 289.

[172]   See eg *Enfield BC v Mahoney* [1983] 2 All ER 901.

[173]   Administration of Justice Act 1960, s 13. See *A-G v Hislop* [1991] 1 QB 514.

[174]   Contempt of Court Act 1981, s 13.

[175]   See *A-G v News Group Newspapers* [1987] QB 1.

[176]   (1990) NLJ 629 (4 May). See also *R v Wood, The Times*, 11 July 1995 (conviction quashed and re-trial ordered).

[177]   For comment, see Lord Denning [1990] Crim LR 535.

[178]   *R v Savundranayagan* [1968] 3 All ER 439. See also *Stuurman v HM Advocate* 1980 JC 111 (a sequel to *HM Advocate v George Outram & Co Ltd* 1980 JC 51). Cf *Atkins v London Weekend Television Ltd* 1978 SLT 76.

Scots law

The law of contempt of court serves the same broad purposes both in England and Scotland. But the law is distinct and there are many procedural differences. Thus Scots law does not recognise the distinction between civil and criminal contempts and the law of contempt is regarded as 'sui generis'.[179] The contempt jurisdiction may be exercised by the Court of Session, the High Court of Justiciary and the sheriff court. Reliance is placed for some purposes upon the residual authority, or nobile officium, of the Court of Session and the High Court, to whom a petition and complaint alleging a contempt may be presented with the consent of the Lord Advocate. Appeal lies either by normal channels of appeal or through a petition to the nobile officium. In some instances the law has been more strictly applied in Scotland than in England.[180] The Phillimore committee considered that the law applying to the press and broadcasting should be the same in the two jurisdictions; consequently the Contempt of Court Act 1981 for the most part applies both in England and Scotland, including the reforms in the strict liability rule discussed above.

As in England and Wales it is possible for an interested party to seek to restrain a publication or broadcast which may tend to prejudice a pending trial.[181] But unlike in England and Wales (where the Attorney-General's consent is required for proceedings under the strict liability rule), it is possible for any interested party (including the party against whom criminal proceedings had been instituted) to bring a contempt to the attention of the court.[182]

In *HM Advocate v Caledonian Newspapers Ltd*[183] the *Evening Times* published an article about the escape of a man from custody where he had been on remand for armed robbery. The article claimed that he was dangerous and that he had been freed twice in the past after standing trial for murder. The article was accompanied by a photograph of the man. It was held that the article did not breach the strict liability rule because the proceedings were at an early stage and there was likely to be a long interval before the trial so that a jury was not likely to be affected. But the position was different with the photograph which could be discounted in the case of possible prejudice of jurors, but not witnesses. In the view of the court, newspapers should publish photographs of untried prisoners only with the consent of the Lord Advocate, which would remove the risk of a finding of contempt against the publisher. In this case consent had not been secured, and although there were mitigating factors the publishers and the editor were fined £2,500 and £250 respectively.

---

[179] Gordon, *Criminal Law*, ch 51.
[180] Eg *Stirling v Associated Newspapers Ltd* 1960 JC 5; and consider *Wylie v HM Advocate* 1966 SLT 149; *Royle v Gray* 1973 SLT 31; and *Cordiner v Cordiner* 1973 SLT 125.
[181] *Atkins v London Weekend Television Ltd* 1978 SLT 76; *Muir v BBC* 1996 SCCR 584.
[182] *Robb v Caledonian Newspapers Ltd* 1994 SCCR 659.
[183] 1995 SCCR 330.

C.   The executive and the machinery of justice[184]

The court system is part of the framework by which our society is governed
and it cannot be totally separated from the executive. Such questions as what
courts we should have, in what buildings they should be housed, and how the
court system should be paid for, are questions which cannot be decided by the
judges and the legal profession. Many countries have a Ministry of Justice to
administer the court system. This was proposed for the United Kingdom in
1918 by the Haldane committee on the machinery of government[185] but a
Ministry of Justice by that name has never been established. Instead the duties
that would fall to such a ministry are in England and Wales exercised
principally by the Lord Chancellor and the Home Secretary, and in Scotland
by the Secretary of State for Scotland and the Lord Advocate. The conflicting
responsibilities of the Lord Chancellor sometimes cause difficulties, as we
shall see below. But it has been said that although the office is 'a difficult one',
it is not easy 'to work out, against the background of our system, a good
alternative that would protect ... the independence of the judiciary'. The
presence of the head of the judiciary accountable to Parliament for the
administration of the courts is said by one Lord Chancellor to be 'probably as
good an arrangement as we can achieve'.[186]

Lord Chancellor[187]

The Lord Chancellor is concerned with virtually all judicial appointments in
England and Wales, appointing to the magistracy himself, formally advising
the Crown on new circuit and High Court judges, and informally advising the
Prime Minister on the most senior judicial appointments. He is entitled to
preside over the House of Lords in its judicial work and the Judicial
Committee of the Privy Council; although today Lord Chancellors do not sit
frequently: Lord Mackay sat on 67 occasions (House of Lords and Privy
Council) between 1987 and 1994 while Lord Hailsham sat 68 times as Lord
Chancellor between 1979 and 1987.[188] He is titular head of the Supreme
Court; within the High Court, he is president of the Chancery Division,
although the duties of this office are performed by the Vice-Chancellor.
   The administrative business of the Supreme Court and the appointment of
court officials are in the hands partly of the Lord Chancellor and partly of the
judges, primarily the presidents of the various divisions of the court. Rules of
the Supreme Court are made by the Rule Committee, consisting of the Lord
Chancellor and other judges together with practising barristers and solicitors.
The secretariat comes from the Lord Chancellor's department. The Lord
Chancellor is responsible for the administration of the county court system;
thus he may alter the boundaries of county court districts and the groupings

---

[184]   R Brazier [1989] PL 64. And see Brazier, *Constitutional Practice*, pp 264–99, and G Drewry
        (1983) 61 Public Administration 396; [1987] PL 502.
[185]   Cd 9230, 1918.
[186]   HL Deb, 27 April 1994, col 804 (Lord Mackay).
[187]   See Haldane Report, Cd 9320, ch 10; Lord Schuster (1949) 10 CLJ 175; Heuston, *Lives of
        the Lord Chancellors 1885–1940*; Spencer, *Jackson's Machinery of Justice*, pp 497–9. See also R
        Stevens, *The Independence of the Judiciary, The View from the Lord Chancellor's Office*.
[188]   HL Deb, 24 October 1994, col 395 (WA). See also HL Deb, 20 October 1992, col 82 (WA).

of county courts into circuits. He appoints the County Court Rule Committee and may alter or disallow the rules which it prepares. By the Courts Act 1971, the Lord Chancellor assumed responsibility for setting up a unified service to administer the courts and acquired power to issue directions regarding sittings of the High Court outside London. Rules for the Crown Court are made by the Lord Chancellor together with the Crown Court Rule Committee. Additional powers were conferred on the Lord Chancellor by the Courts and Legal Services Act 1990. These include the allocation and transfer of business between the High Court and county courts; the appointment of members to the Lord Chancellor's advisory committee to maintain and develop standards in the education, training and conduct of those offering legal services; and the authorisation of professional bodies which can grant rights of audience before the courts. In April 1992, responsibility for the organisation and management of magistrates' courts was transferred from the Home Secretary to the Lord Chancellor.

The Lord Chancellor's department has a growing responsibility for administrative tribunals, especially since the Tribunals and Inquiries Act 1958. The Council on Tribunals is appointed jointly by the Lord Chancellor and the Lord Advocate and reports to these ministers. The Lord Chancellor appoints the chairmen of many tribunals; dismissal of a chairman or member of a tribunal usually requires the approval of the Lord Chancellor. The Lord Chancellor has also important duties in connection with the solicitors' profession, for example, power to regulate the rates of remuneration.[189] He is the minister responsible for legal aid; and it is through his department that central funds are provided for neighbourhood law centres. The Lord Chancellor also has broad responsibility for the Land Registry and the Public Trust Office (both of which are 'Next Steps' executive agencies). The Public Record Office was placed under his direction by the Public Records Act 1958; there is an advisory council on public records of which the Master of the Rolls is chairman. Under the Courts and Legal Services Act 1990, s 21, the Lord Chancellor is responsible for the appointment of the Legal Services Ombudsman, an office created by that Act.

The Lord Chancellor is also Speaker of the House of Lords (on which 'he spends a significant proportion of his time' and for which 14% of his salary is paid by the House of Lords)[190] and a member of the Cabinet (which together with his duties as head of the judiciary consumes most of his time). He has no greater security of tenure than any other minister, although the post is in fact less vulnerable to Cabinet re-shuffles and Lord Chancellors tend to remain in post longer than other Cabinet ministers. The office is a bridge between the judicial and the political worlds. Despite its judicial responsibilities, the office must be classed as political. A previous political career is not an essential qualification, but (until the appointment of Lord Mackay of Clashfern in 1987) all modern Lord Chancellors have had extensive and successful experience of practice at the English bar; some before becoming Lord Chancellor have already held judicial appointments, others have been law officers of the Crown. Despite the heavy departmental duties of the Lord

---

189   See eg *Bates v Lord Hailsham* [1972] 3 All ER 1019.
190   HL Deb, 20 October 1992, col 82 (WA).

Chancellor it was only in 1992 that a junior minister was appointed to his department, able to act for him if required in the House of Commons. When in 1979 the present scheme of select committees related to government departments was created by the Commons, neither the Lord Chancellor's department nor the Law Officers' departments were brought within it, although this would have been a valuable means of informing MPs about the problems of administering the system of justice.[191] In 1991, the government agreed to extend the select committee system to include the Lord Chancellor's and Law Officers' departments, but excluding individual cases and judicial appointments, the advice of the Law Officers to the government, and prosecution policy.[192]

The Lord Chancellor and judicial independence

In his Holdsworth Club address in 1950, Lord Justice Denning, as he then was, stoutly defended the independence of the judiciary, reminding his audience that 'No member of the Government, no member of Parliament, and no official of any Government department has any right whatever to direct or influence or to interfere with the decisions of any of the judges'.[193] In a speech which repays reading to this day, he went on to say that the critical test which judges must pass 'if they are to receive the confidence of the people' is that 'they must be independent of the executive'. The difficulty, however, is that government criticism is unlikely to be publicly expressed (though this may happen), but is more likely to take more insidious forms of pressure which are unlikely to come to public attention. One such case, however, involved an exchange of correspondence between the President of the Employment Appeal Tribunal (Mr Justice Wood) and the Lord Chancellor in 1994. The details were disclosed in the *Observer*[194] newspaper and the matter was the subject of a robust article in the *New Law Journal*[195] by Sir Francis Purchas, who had recently retired from the Court of Appeal. The correspondence, which was deposited in the House of Lords library, tended to show that the Lord Chancellor had put pressure on the President to speed up the backlog of appeals and 'to ensure that public money is not wasted on preliminary hearings in cases where there is no point of law shown in the notice of appeal'. After consulting senior judicial colleagues, Sir John Wood replied in terms which Lord Mackay thought 'frankly disappointing'. Lord Mackay sought in turn an 'immediate assurance' that preliminary hearings would not be used where 'no jurisdiction is shown in a notice of appeal', the letter concluding 'If you do not feel that you can give me that assurance, I must ask you to consider your position'. The matter was raised in a House of Lords debate,[196] in the course of which several speakers not only defended the

---

[191]   See ch 10 D; HC 588–1 (1977–78), p lv; and HC Deb, 25 June 1979, cols 118, 230. See also A W Bradley [1988] PL 163.

[192]   HC Deb, 1 May 1991, col 183 (WA). See HC 52 (1995–96).

[193]   Denning, 'The Independence of the Judges', in Harvey (ed), *The Lawyer and Justice*, p 53, at p 57.

[194]   6 March 1994.

[195]   'The Constitution, Lord Mackay and the Judges', 22 April 1994.

[196]   HL Deb, 27 April 1994, cols 751–804.

propriety of Sir John Wood's interpretation of his legal responsibilities, but also criticised the Lord Chancellor for the manner of his intervention.

The debate in the House of Lords raised important questions about the relationship between the executive (in the form of the Lord Chancellor) and the judges, and indeed also about the relationship between judges. In the first place, it highlights the practical problems caused by the anomalous position occupied by the office of Lord Chancellor ('a standing violation of the pure constitutional doctrine of the separation of public powers'). Thus as Lord Lester of Herne Hill pointed out, the Lord Chancellor will command the confidence of his judicial colleagues only if he 'will protect the judges' independence from any improper interference'; but he will enjoy the confidence of his political colleagues only by giving effect to 'the government's political programme while remaining democratically responsible to Parliament, administratively as well as financially, for the proper functioning of the courts and the proper performance by the judges of their duties'. There can be no doubt, however, that in the hierarchy of obligations it is the former which must prevail, and must be defended if government is to be conducted according to the law. In this affair a number of senior judges expressed strongly the view that the Lord Chancellor had applied pressure to a judge in an 'unconstitutional way'. Lord Oliver thought the matter to be one of 'very grave public concern', on the ground that 'the pressure which was applied in this case, for whatever reason, constituted an attempt by the Executive – no doubt in the praiseworthy interests of economy and expedition – to overbear the conscience of a judge in the way in which he was to exercise his judicial duty and his judicial discretion'. For his part, however, the Lord Chancellor denied that his conduct was in any way 'prejudicial to the proper independence of the judge', though he regretted not having expressed himself more plainly.

Responsibilities for law reform

As well as his responsibility for the judicial system, the Lord Chancellor has a general responsibility for law reform in England and Wales. Many branches of law are the responsibility of particular departments (thus town planning law is a matter for the Department of the Environment; company law for the Department of Trade and Industry) and the Home Secretary has the primary responsibility for reform of the criminal law. The Lord Chancellor is therefore mainly concerned with those areas of civil law which are not looked after by particular departments. The Law Commissions Act 1965 was essentially the work of Lord Gardiner, then Lord Chancellor; this established the Law Commission (for England) and the Scottish Law Commission to keep under review all the law with which each is concerned 'with a view to its systematic development and reform', including codification and generally the simplification and modernisation of the law.[197] Members of the Law Commission in England are appointed by the Lord Chancellor for terms not exceeding five years. They are qualified for appointment through holding judicial office (the chairman of the Commission is always a judge seconded

---

[197] Law Commissions Act 1965, s 3. See also Cmnd 2573, 1965; and Farrar, *Law Reform and the Law Commission.*

from the High Court) or having professional or academic experience of the law. Programmes of work prepared by the Commission and approved by the Lord Chancellor are laid before Parliament; the Lord Chancellor may ask the Commission to report on particular topics. While the Law Commissions consult widely with the legal profession, government departments and other interested parties, they exercise an independent judgment in preparing recommendations for reform. The two Law Commissions must consult with each other and they may produce joint reports. Very many Law Commission reports have been followed by legislation, but pressure on parliamentary time and a lack of political interest may still be obstacles to reform.

The Law Officers of the Crown[198]

The Law Officers of the Crown in respect of England and Wales are the Attorney-General and Solicitor-General. Their historic role is to represent the Crown in the courts. They now act as legal advisers to the government on important matters which cannot be left to the lawyers in the civil service who advise the departments on day-to-day matters. The English Law Officers are today invariably members of the House of Commons and of the English bar; as ministers they support the government of the day. Their duties require them to fill a wide variety of roles, which include leading for the Crown in major prosecutions (especially in trials involving state security) or in major civil actions to which the Crown is a party. They are assisted by junior counsel to the Treasury, who are practising barristers and hold no political office. Representing the Crown, the Law Officers take part in many judicial or quasi-judicial proceedings relating to the public interest, such as statutory tribunals of inquiry[199] and contempt of court proceedings.[200] The Attorney-General's consent is needed for relator actions: his decisions granting or refusing consent are not subject to review by the courts.[201] They also have parliamentary responsibilities, helping to see legal and fiscal Bills through the Commons and giving advice to the Committee on Privileges and Standards.

The Attorney-General is responsible for the work of the Treasury Solicitor, and for the parliamentary counsel who draft most government Bills; but Bills that relate exclusively to Scotland or Northern Ireland are prepared by parliamentary draftsmen for Scotland and Northern Ireland respectively. The Attorney-General is leader of the English bar. He has sometimes been a member of the Cabinet but in view of his duties in connection with prosecutions, it is regarded as preferable that he should remain outside the Cabinet as the government's chief legal adviser, attending particular Cabinet meetings only when summoned. Many Law Officers receive further advancement to judicial or political posts, but today the Attorney-General has no claim to become Lord Chief Justice when a vacancy in that office occurs: the development of any such claim was effectively stifled by the disastrous elevation of Sir Gordon Hewart as Lord Chief Justice in 1922.[202] In 1974, the

---

[198]   Edwards, *The Law Officers of the Crown* and *The Attorney-General, Politics and the Public Interest*.
[199]   Ch 28 C.
[200]   Section B above.
[201]   *Gouriet v Union of Post Office Workers* [1978] AC 435; chs 12 E and 30.
[202]   Edwards, *The Law Officers of the Crown*, ch 15.

Labour Law Officers declined the knighthoods that have customarily gone with their jobs.[203] Where a Law Officer has given advice to a minister on a matter upon which the minister has subsequently acted, the opinion is treated as confidential and not laid before Parliament or quoted from in debate; but if a minister considers it expedient to do so, he or she may make the advice known to Parliament and there is no absolute rule of confidentiality.[204]

The machinery of justice in Scotland

Except for his membership of the House of Lords and for his part in nominating the two Lords of Appeal in Ordinary who by custom are appointed from Scotland, the Lord Chancellor has no jurisdiction in Scotland. The Secretary of State for Scotland has a wide responsibility for Scotland's internal affairs, under whom the Scottish Office Home Department is responsible for the police and the penal system. The department also has many responsibilities for the legal system, including legal aid. In 1971, the Secretary of State was placed under a general duty to secure the efficient organisation of the sheriff courts, and was equipped with ample powers of issuing administrative directions, re-organising the sheriffdoms, providing court-houses and so on.[205] His duties are discharged through the Scottish Courts Administration. The Secretary of State appoints the justices of the peace who sit in the district courts. In respect of law reform the Secretary of State has general oversight of all branches of the law which are not the specific responsibility of other departments or of the Lord Advocate.[206]

The law officers for Scotland are the Lord Advocate and the Solicitor-General for Scotland. They represent the Crown's interests before the Scottish courts and they advise the government on matters of Scots law. But their position is not identical with their English counterparts. It has not always been possible to fill these offices from the House of Commons[207] and a life peerage may be conferred on the Lord Advocate if he is not an MP. The head of the Scottish bar is the elected Dean of the Faculty of Advocates, not the Lord Advocate. One important function of the Lord Advocate is that, assisted by the Solicitor-General, he controls the system of public prosecutions throughout Scotland. The Lord Advocate discharges machinery of justice and law reform functions which in England are performed by the Lord Chancellor. These now include the appointment of the Scottish Law Commission, and responsibility for the reform of branches of the law relating to evidence and civil procedure.[208] The Lord Advocate is responsible for the parliamentary draftsmen who draft Bills applying to Scotland. Functions which in England are performed by the Lord Chancellor as head of the judiciary are in Scotland entrusted to the Lord President of the Court of Session: these

---

[203] Cf Edwards, ibid, pp 282–5.

[204] Edwards, ibid, pp 256–61. In the Westland affair in 1985–86, a Cabinet minister resigned because he had authorised civil servants to leak a confidential letter of advice from the Solicitor-General to other ministers.

[205] Sheriff Courts (Scotland) Act 1971; cf I D MacPhail 1971 SLT 80, 104. And see HLE, vol 8(2) pp 65–71.

[206] HC Deb, 21 December 1972, col 456 (WA).

[207] For the difficulties of the first Labour government, see J P Casey (1975) 26 NILQ 18.

[208] Note 197 above.

include the making of rules of court procedure and the appointment and removal of tribunal personnel.

Control of prosecutions in England and Wales[209]

In principle, private persons may institute prosecutions in English law for any criminal offence unless by statute this has been excluded.[210] In practice the great majority of criminal prosecutions are initiated by the police; others are instituted by government departments (for example, revenue departments for evasion of tax) or local authorities (for example, for breach of byelaws). Certain prosecutions may by statute be instituted only with the consent of the Attorney-General, for example, for certain offences against the state or public order, under the Official Secrets Acts 1911–89 or the Public Order Act 1986, and for obscenity in dramatic productions under the Theatres Act 1968. The position regarding criminal prosecutions in England and Wales was over-hauled by the Prosecution of Offences Act 1985 which introduced a public prosecution service. The philosophy of the Act was 'to separate the functions of the investigation of crime, that being the responsibility of the police, and the prosecution of offences, that being the prosecution of a single national prosecution service'.[211]

1 The Crown Prosecution Service

The Crown Prosecution Service, 'an autonomous and independent agency', though 'not a body corporate but a collection of individuals with statutory functions to perform',[212] is under the central direction of the Director of Public Prosecutions, an office created in 1897. Until 1983, the DPP, a barrister or solicitor of not less than ten years' standing, was appointed by the Home Secretary, but is now appointed by the Attorney-General to work under his general supervision. Apart from the DPP, other key personnel in the Crown Prosecution Service are the Chief Crown Prosecutors (appointed by the DPP to supervise the work of the CPS in geographical areas) and Crown Prosecutors (barristers or solicitors who conduct proceedings under the direction of the DPP). Surprisingly perhaps, the dismissal of a Crown Prosecutor from his or her employment is not subject to judicial review. In *R v Crown Prosecution Service, ex p Hogg,*[213] the Court of Appeal applied the emerging principle that 'in the ordinary way the relationship between the Crown as employer and Crown servant as employee was a private law relationship and not one which brought in public law principles'. This was heavily qualified, however, by the recognition that the 'principle of the prosecutor's independence was much more than a term to be implied into the contract between the prosecutor and the CPS and amounted to a constitutional principle' which 'fell within the area of public law'. Sir Thomas Bingham continued by making it 'abundantly clear' that

---

[209] See Report of Royal Commission on Criminal Procedure, Cmnd 8092, 1981, part II.
[210] For the procedural rights of a private prosecutor, see *R v George Maxwell (Developments) Ltd* [1980] 2 All ER 99; *R v DPP, ex p Hallas* (1988) 87 Cr App Rep 340.
[211] *Elguzouli-Daf v Metropolitan Police Commissioner* [1995] QB 335, at p 346.
[212] *Elguzouli-Daf,* above at pp 346, 351. On the work of the CPS, see HC 193–i (1993–94). See also HC 425 (1995–96).
[213] *The Times,* 14 April 1997.

judicial review could apply in any case where 'there was a plausible suggestion that action taken against a Crown Prosecutor was in any way attributable to any exercise of discretion, whether as to the charge being preferred or the plea to be accepted or the course to be adopted in the course of any prosecution'.[214]

The CPS reviews police decisions to prosecute and conducts prosecutions on behalf of the Crown. The Service also institutes proceedings in difficult or important cases, and gives advice to the police on all matters relating to criminal offences. Although the CPS is under a duty to take over all legal proceedings instituted by the police, it is not required to but may take over proceedings begun by others (such as private prosecutions). Having taken over such proceedings the CPS may discontinue them if the evidence is insufficient, or if the proceedings would be contrary to the public interest, or to avoid duplication, or for any other good reason. If it is too late to discontinue, the prosecutor may offer no evidence, so that an acquittal automatically follows. The Attorney-General may however exercise the prerogative power to stop a prosecution on indictment by issuing a nolle prosequi.[215] This power is rarely used today: abuse of the power would be subject to criticism in Parliament, but may not be reviewed by the courts. The Attorney-General, and through him the DPP, are accountable to Parliament for what they do in relation to criminal proceedings. However, despite the reforms in the 1985 Act, the right to bring a private prosecution remains intact. It has been said that the 1985 Act creates 'a coherent and consistent framework in which the right of the private citizen to bring a prosecution is preserved but subject always to the Director's right to intervene at any stage'. The Act thereby 'provides a useful and effective safeguard' against the danger of any 'improper inaction'.[216]

2 The Attorney-General

The decision whether to prosecute or not may involve difficult questions of law and proof.[217] It may also involve questions of prosecuting policy. Prosecuting is not a judicial function but an executive function; it has been called a quasi-judicial function, said to mean that the Attorney-General 'is expected to act as guardian of the general public interest and to put out of his mind any party political advantage or disadvantage.'[218] The Attorney-General has powers of superintendence over the Crown Prosecution Service and the Serious Fraud Office,[219] and after the Scott Report, powers of 'increased supervision of Customs and Excise prosecutions in relation to export control matters.'[220] Most difficult for the prosecutor may be to decide when the public interest requires that a case which would probably lead to a conviction should nonetheless not be prosecuted.[221] In the case of prosecutions instituted by the

---

214   *Elguzouli-Daf*, above at p 346.
215   For examples of its use in relation to customs prosecutions (where the Attorney-General had no duty of superintendence), see HC 115 (1995–96) (Scott Report), para C 3.10.
216   *R v Bow Street Magistrate, ex p South Coast Shipping* [1993] 1 All ER 219, at p 222.
217   For a review which echoes many of the points in this paragraph, see HC 115 (1995–96) (Scott Report), paras C3.8–3.9.
218   HC 115 (1995–96), para C3.9.
219   See Prosecution of Offences Act 1985.
220   HC Deb, 17 June 1996, col 331 (WA). Cf HC 115 (1995–96) (Scott Report), para K4.11.
221   See Cmnd 8092, 1981, pp 128–9.

DPP or the Attorney-General, what political control is there over the discretion that may have been exercised? Can the Prime Minister or the Cabinet control or influence the Attorney-General's decision? What is the Attorney-General's responsibility to Parliament for prosecution decisions? These questions were raised by the Campbell case in 1924, which brought down the first Labour government.[222] In brief, the Attorney-General, Sir Patrick Hastings, who was experienced in advocacy but not in ministerial work, authorised the prosecution of J R Campbell, acting editor of a Communist weekly, for having published an article which apparently sought to seduce members of the armed forces from their allegiance to the Crown. A few days later, the prosecution was withdrawn in circumstances which suggested that improper political pressure had been brought to bear on the Attorney-General. The true facts are not easy to establish but the Cabinet minutes record a decision by the Cabinet on 6 August 1924 that '*no public prosecution of a political character should be undertaken without the prior sanction of the Cabinet being obtained*'; the Cabinet also agreed to adopt the course indicated by the Attorney-General ie to withdraw the Campbell prosecution.[223]

Whatever the faults of the different actors in the Campbell affair, and the precedents were less clear than the critics of the Labour government stated, there can be no doubt that the Cabinet decision in the words italicised was asserting a right to interfere in prosecuting decisions which was constitutionally improper, as well as being seriously vague.[224] The decision was promptly rescinded by the next Cabinet. The present doctrine is something like this: the Attorney-General is required to take his own prosecuting decisions, and must not receive directions from the Cabinet or any ministerial colleague; in his decisions he must not be influenced by considerations of party advantage or disadvantage; but if he considers that a particular case involves wider questions of public interest or state policy, he may seek information from ministerial colleagues and also their opinions.[225] It is not possible to know whether it is present-day practice for such information or opinions to be sought at meetings of the Cabinet, but this seems unlikely. Since current practice emphasises that the Attorney-General must make his decisions personally, it follows that he bears personal responsibility to Parliament for these decisions; and that there is no collective responsibility for his decisions,

---

[222]   Edwards, *Law Officers of the Crown*, chs 10 and 11; Edwards, *The Attorney-General, Politics and the Public Interest*, pp 310–17; F H Newark (1969) 20 NILQ 19. For the censure debate, see HC Deb, 8 October 1924, col 581.

[223]   Newark, op cit, p 35.

[224]   What *is* a public prosecution of a political character? It might refer to (*a*) prosecution of a politician for an ordinary criminal offence, (*b*) prosecution of a politician for offences related to political activities eg corruption or election offences, (*c*) prosecution of an individual for political beliefs, (*d*) prosecution for criminal conduct committed in the course of a strike or political demonstration, (*e*) prosecution for offences against the security of the state, etc.

[225]   See the Shawcross statement in the debate on the gas strikers, HC Deb, 29 January 1951, col 681; and HC Deb, 16 February 1959, col 31.

except to the extent that the Prime Minister could be criticised for allowing an incompetent Attorney-General to remain in office. It is in order for questions to be asked in the Commons about particular decisions made by the Attorney-General: how much information the Attorney-General gives in reply is a matter for his own discretion.[226]

3 Accountability

The creation of the Crown Prosecution Service in 1988 brought into prominence both the scope for central influence over the criminal justice system, which had previously been exercised without publicity,[227] and the question of accountability for the abuse of power by public prosecutors. It is true that 'by convention the Attorney-General is answerable to Parliament for general prosecution policy and for specific cases where the Attorney-General and the Director of Public Prosecutions intervenes'. But, as has been pointed out, 'Parliament can usually only call the Attorney-General to account after a prosecution has run its course.'[228] And Parliament will not give directions to the Attorney-General. The House of Commons thus has no effective machinery for ensuring due accountability to the House for the Attorney-General's decisions, the assumption being that both he and the DPP should be free from extraneous political interference in their work. So far as accountability to the courts is concerned, the scope for judicial review appears to be very limited, though there may be remedies in private law for malicious prosecution or misfeasance in public office, leading to the surprising conclusion that 'a citizen, who is aggrieved by a prosecutor's decision, has in our system potentially extensive private law remedies for a deliberate abuse of power.' The CPS will not, however, normally be liable in negligence, as in one case where the plaintiff had been detained for 85 days before proceedings were discontinued, the plaintiff alleging that it should not have taken this long to conclude that the case against him was bound to fail. Although it was 'always tempting to yield to an argument based on the protection of civil liberties', the Court of Appeal concluded on contestable grounds that 'the interests of the whole community are better served by not imposing a duty of care on the CPS'.[229]

However it may not always be possible for prosecutors to escape detailed scrutiny. The role of the Attorney-General in the Matrix Churchill affair was closely reviewed and sharply criticised by Sir Richard Scott's inquiry into the export of arms for Iraq. Sir Richard found in his report that the decision to prosecute three executives of the company was taken by the Commissioners of

---

226 Cf Edwards, *Law Officers of the Crown*, p 261.
227 See the controversy over jury-vetting in 1978–80: HC Deb, 1 August 1980, col 1929; M D A Freeman [1981] CLP 650; Harman and Griffith, *Justice Deserted*. See also *Practice Note* [1980] 3 All ER 785.
228 *Elguzouli-Daf v Metropolitan Police Commissioner* [1995] QB 335, at p 349.
229 Ibid at p 346.

Customs and Excise following the advice of Treasury counsel. In this decision the Attorney-General was not consulted, and indeed he was not necessarily or usually kept informed of important Customs prosecutions, having no duty of superintendence of such prosecutions, though he did have 'an overall purview of prosecutions brought by the Crown by any authority'. His position was called into question nevertheless, as a result of his conduct in relation to public interest immunity (PII) certificates dealing with the development of government policies over exports to Iraq, the granting of export licences to Matrix Churchill and other companies and certain security operations. Although a number of ministers had signed such certificates, the President of the Board of Trade (Mr Heseltine) refused to do so on the ground that the interests of justice required the disclosure of many of the documents in question. Yet although he had not read them, the Attorney-General effectively informed Mr Heseltine that he was under a duty to sign the certificates (as a result of the case-law) [230] but that his reservations could be put to the judge. In the event Mr Heseltine's reservations were not even disclosed to the prosecution legal team, despite the fact that Mr Heseltine's position was well known in government, an omission which drew a strong rebuke from Sir Richard Scott. Sir Richard also repudiated the belief of the Attorney-General that he was personally as opposed to constitutionally blameless for the inadequacy of the instructions sent to prosecuting counsel, in relation particularly to the position of Mr Heseltine. [231]

Control of prosecutions in Scotland

While in England the Attorney-General has traditionally been concerned only with a few exceptionally difficult or sensitive prosecutions, in Scotland, the Lord Advocate is responsible for virtually all criminal proceedings, assisted by the Solicitor-General for Scotland and a number of Advocates-Depute, who are practising advocates retained to act for the Crown. The work is conducted through the Crown Office in Edinburgh and by procurators-fiscal who serve in every part of Scotland. The police make no prosecuting decisions, reporting every case to the procurator-fiscal, who may decide whether to prosecute or may refer a case to the Crown Office for the decision of an Advocate-Depute or a Law Officer. Prosecution policies are laid down by the Lord Advocate and are binding on all procurators-fiscal. Some of these policies are publicly known: thus it was at first considered unnecessary for the Sexual Offences Act 1967, which in England legalised homosexual conduct between consenting adult males in private, to be extended to Scotland since it

---

[230] *Makanjuola v Metropolitan Police Commissioner* [1992] 3 All ER 617. On the law of public interest immunity, see below, ch 31 C and especially *R v Chief Constable of the West Midlands Police, ex p Wiley* [1995] 1 AC 274, where the House of Lords over-ruled *Makanjuola*. Compare HC 115 (1995–96) (Scott Report), para G 59.

[231] See further A W Bradley [1996] PL 373.

was already Crown Office policy not to prosecute in such cases.[232] In Scotland private prosecutions are virtually unknown, although in law a private citizen may prosecute if he or she has a personal and peculiar interest in the case and gets the permission of the High Court of Justiciary.[233] Such permission was given in a much-publicised Glasgow rape case in 1982, in which prosecution by the Crown was barred because of an earlier statement on behalf of the Lord Advocate that no further proceedings would be taken.[234] What has been said earlier about the personal responsibility of the Attorney-General and his freedom from political direction applies equally to the Lord Advocate, but is of even greater significance under the Scottish system than in England. In 1982, a judicial inquiry into events related to the Meehan case held inter alia that mistakes had been made by the Crown Office, particularly in failing to coordinate the extensive investigations involved; but such an inquiry is a very rare event.[235]

Miscarriages of justice

One of the most regrettable features of the criminal justice system in the 1970s and 1980s was the number of miscarriages of justice, particularly the number of people who were wrongly convicted for offences which they did not commit.[236] Some of these cases arose out of terrorist incidents, most notably the pub bombings at Guildford and Birmingham in 1974,[237] though there were many other cases unrelated to acts of terrorism, including that of the so-called 'Bridgewater 3'.[238] A number of different factors were responsible for these events, not the least significant of which were the serious shortcomings of the police and the prosecuting authorities.[239] The matter was reviewed by the Royal Commission on Criminal Justice which was appointed in 1991 with terms of reference which included 'whether changes were needed in the arrangements for considering and investigating allegations of miscarriages of justice when appeal rights have been exhausted'.[240] The procedures then in force were governed by the Criminal Appeal Act 1968, s 17, which authorised a reference to the Court of Appeal by the Home Secretary. Although this provided 'the mechanism for unlocking the door back to the criminal justice system',[241] the royal commission pointed out that the Home Secretary and the civil servants advising him operated within 'strict self-imposed limits', which rested 'both upon constitutional considerations and upon the approach of the Court of Appeal itself to its own powers'. The Home Secretary would not refer cases to

---

232 The law on homosexuality in Scotland was changed in Criminal Justice (Scotland) Act 1980, s 80, and Criminal Justice and Public Order Act 1994, s 145(2).

233 *J & P Coats Ltd v Brown* 1909 SC (J) 29; *McBain v Crichton* 1961 JC 25.

234 *H v Sweeney* 1983 SLT 48. And see HC Deb, 21 January 1982, col 423.

235 HC 444 (1981–82), pp 1257–63.

236 For a wider definition of the term, see HC 419 (1993–94).

237 See *R v Richardson, The Times*, 20 October 1989; *R v McIlkenny* [1992] 2 All ER 417; *R v Maguire* [1992] QB 936. And note the case of Judith Ward: *R v Ward* [1993] 2 All ER 577.

238 See *The Times*, 21–22 February 1997.

239 See on specific aspects, I H Dennis [1993] PL 291.

240 Cm 2263, 1993.

241 *R v Home Secretary, ex p Hickey (No 2)* [1995] 1 All ER 490, at p 494.

the Court of Appeal merely to enable it to reconsider matters that it had already considered, but would 'normally only refer a conviction if there is new evidence or some other consideration of substance which was not before the trial court'. The Home Office adopted this approach 'not only because they have thought that it would be wrong for Ministers to suggest to the Court of Appeal that a different decision should have been reached by the courts on the same facts', but also because there was 'no purpose' in referring a case where there was 'no real possibility of the Court of Appeal taking a different view than it did on the original appeal because of the lack of fresh evidence or some other new consideration of substance'.[242]

These arrangements were criticised both by Sir John May (who had been asked to inquire into the cases of the Guildford Four and the Maguire Seven)[243] and by the Royal Commission on Criminal Justice,[244] and a new procedure was proposed for the referral of cases. This would require the creation of a new body, independent of both the government and the courts, for dealing with allegations that a miscarriage of justice had occurred, reflecting concern that the Home Secretary should not be 'directly responsible for the consideration and investigation of alleged miscarriages of justice as well as being responsible for law and order and for the police'.[245] The Criminal Appeal Act 1995 addresses the incompatibility of these procedures 'with the constitutional separation of powers as between the courts and the executive'[246] and makes provision for the appointment by the Queen (on the advice of the Prime Minister) of a Criminal Cases Review Commission (s 9) with the power to refer to the Court of Appeal (following the conviction of an offence on indictment) any conviction or sentence where it considers that 'there is a real possibility that the conviction, verdict, finding or sentence would not be upheld were the reference to be made' (s 13). The power is not, however, undiluted, though nothing is to be taken to prevent the Commission from making a reference where there appear to be exceptional circumstances. The Act also introduces for the first time a power (on the part of the Commission) to refer convictions or sentences arising from cases tried summarily (s 11), in this case to the Crown Court, subject to the same conditions as apply in the case of references to the Court of Appeal following a conviction on indictment. The Commission has wide powers to obtain documents and to appoint investigating officers to carry out inquiries in relation to a case under review, though these will generally be carried out by the police rather than by the Commission's own officers (ss 17–20).[247]

---

242   Cm 2263, 1993, pp 181–2. The propriety of this approach was called into question in *R v Home Secretary, ex p Hickey (No 2)* [1995] 1 All ER 490 where it was suggested that the Secretary of State should ask another question: could the new material reasonably cause the Court of Appeal to regard the verdict as unsafe? If it could, the matter should then have been referred without more ado.

243   HC 296 (1992), pp 93–4.

244   Cm 2263, 1993, pp 181–2.

245   Ibid, p 182.

246   Ibid. And see HC Deb, 6 March 1995, col 32.

247   It was held in *Ex p Hickey (No 2)* above that under the procedures in the 1968 Act the applicant was entitled, on grounds of fairness, to be given an opportunity to make effective representations to the Home Secretary upon whatever material had been revealed by his inquiries before the decision to refer a case to the Court of Appeal was made.

It has been said that a miscarriage of justice by which a man or woman has lost his or her liberty is one of the gravest matters which can occupy the attention of a civilised society. Although it is important that a procedure should be in place to enable such miscarriages to be rectified when they do occur (and Mr Kenneth Baker referred no fewer than 14 cases involving 19 people when he was Home Secretary),[248] it is also important that they do not happen in the first place. The government hopes that the many changes of police procedure introduced since the Police and Criminal Evidence Act 1984 will go a long way towards preventing such incidents,[249] though it is to be noted that not all of the cases which gave rise to concern, including that of Stefan Kiszko,[250] occurred before the implementation of the Act and its related codes of practice. It is also the case that 'a number of safeguards provided by PACE [ie the 1984 Act] in the interests of fairness are denied in terrorist cases',[251] which, as already noted, have contributed significantly to the number of miscarriages of justice.[252] Yet apart from seeking to prevent miscarriages of justice, it is clearly important to ensure that victims are properly compensated, to the extent that this is possible, for their loss of liberty. Before 1988, it had been the practice of the Home Secretary, in exceptional circumstances, to authorise ex gratia payments from public funds to persons who had been detained in custody as a result of a wrongful conviction.[253] Since 1957, it had been the practice for the amount of compensation to be fixed on the advice of an independent assessor who, in considering claims, applied principles analogous to those in which claims for damages in civil wrongs are settled.[254] The procedures were given statutory force in the Criminal Justice Act 1988, s 133, which applies where a conviction has been reversed on a reference under the Criminal Appeal Act 1995 or a convicted person has been pardoned 'on the ground that a new or newly discovered fact shows beyond reasonable doubt that there has been a miscarriage of justice'.[255] In such cases the Home Secretary must pay compensation to the person concerned or his or her personal representative, the amount to be determined by an assessor appointed by the minister.[256]

The prerogative of pardon[257]

The royal prerogative of pardon is exercised by the Crown on the advice of the Home Secretary in cases from England and Wales and, in cases from Scotland, by the Secretary of State for Scotland. Each minister acts on his

---

248   HC Deb, 6 March 1995, col 39.
249   See also HC 449 (1993–94).
250   HC Deb, 30 June 1994, cols 650–1 (WA).
251   HC 449 (1993–94), p 300.
252   'If all the safeguards of PACE are necessary to avoid miscarriages of justice then it must be recognised that in terrorist cases greater risks of injustice are accepted than in the ordinary course of criminal cases'. (HC 449 (1993–94), p 300).
253   HC Deb, 29 November 1985, cols 689–90 (WA).
254   For the amount of compensation paid out, see HC Deb, 15 April 1991, col 6 (WA).
255   Cf *Maharaj v A-G of Trinidad (No 2)* [1979] AC 385 (right to compensation for judicial error derived from constitutional guarantee of remedy for infringement of fundamental rights).
256   See now Criminal Appeal Act 1995, s 28.
257   See A T H Smith [1983] PL 398; also the report 'Miscarriages of Justice', HC 421 (1981–82), and, for the position in Scots law, C H W Gane 1980 JR 18.

individual responsibility in giving his advice to the Crown. A royal pardon could in law be used as a bar to criminal prosecution being brought (as was the effect of the blanket pardon given by President Ford to ex-President Nixon in 1974). But in British practice, a pardon is granted only after conviction when there is some special reason why a sentence should not be carried out or why the effects of a conviction should be expunged. Now that the right of an appeal in criminal cases is recognised, a pardon is not normally granted in respect of matters that could be raised on an appeal. Pardons under the prerogative are of three kinds: (*a*) an absolute or free pardon, which sets aside the sentence but not the conviction;[258] (*b*) a conditional pardon, which substitutes one form of punishment for another (for example, the substitution of life imprisonment for the death penalty, which occurred when the prerogative of mercy was exercised in the days of capital punishment);[259] and (*c*) a remission, which reduces the amount of a sentence without changing its character, and has been used to enable a convicted spy to be exchanged for a British subject imprisoned abroad, or to reward prisoners who have given exceptional assistance to prison staff, the police or the prosecuting authorities.

The prerogative power of pardon may not be used to vary the judgment of the court in matters of civil dispute between citizens. Under the Act of Settlement 1700, a pardon may not be pleaded in bar of an impeachment by the Commons, nor under the Habeas Corpus Act 1679 may the unlawful committal of any person to prison outside the realm be pardoned. Extensive use of the power of pardon could come close to being an attempt to exercise the royal power to dispense with laws which was declared illegal in the Bill of Rights 1689. The Home Secretary is answerable to Parliament for the advice which he or she gives to the Queen. Before the abolition of the death penalty, questions could not be raised in the House of Commons regarding a case while it was still pending.[260] The question arises whether the power of pardon is now necessary following the reforms introduced by the Criminal Appeal Act 1995. In the view of the government, however, it is thought still to be necessary but only for 'the very exceptional case' where there is new evidence which for some reason is inadmissible.[261] In these cases the Home Secretary may refer to the Criminal Cases Review Commission 'any matter which arises in the consideration of whether to recommend the exercise of Her Majesty's prerogative of mercy in relation to the conviction' (s 16). The Commission is required to give reasons where it is of the opinion that the minister should recommend the exercise of the prerogative, but strangely is not required to do so where it makes no such recommendation, even though it is in the latter type of case that the need for judicial review is likely to be greater.[262]

---

[258]   *R v Foster* [1985] QB 115.
[259]   P Brett (1957) 20 MLR 131.
[260]   G Marshall [1961] PL 8.
[261]   HC Deb, 6 March 1995, col 26.
[262]   See *R v Home Secretary, ex p Bentley* [1994] QB 349. See further, ch 12 E above.

The Treasury Solicitor

The Treasury Solicitor is the head of the government legal service.[263] His department carries out legal work for the Treasury and for all government departments which do not have their own solicitors or, as in the case of the Foreign Office, their own legal advisers. The department undertakes most of the litigation to which the Crown or a department is a party in the superior courts; it also provides legal advice to government on European Union law and conducts litigation before the European Court of Justice. The Treasury Solicitor's department became an executive agency in 1996. The Solicitor to the Secretary of State for Scotland serves a similar function in relation to the Scottish departments.

---

[263]   See Sir R Andrew, *Review of the Government Legal Service* (Cabinet Office, 1989); also [1989] PL 374.

The citizen and the state

CHAPTER 19

The nature and protection of civil liberties

This part is concerned with the legal regulation of civil liberties. The first question is to determine what is meant by civil liberties. There is a great deal of terminological inconsistency in this area, with a number of terms frequently used – human rights, civil liberties, fundamental rights – often referring to the same thing. To add to the confusion, many of these so-called rights or liberties are neither rights nor liberties at all, but are merely aspirations or standards to be applied and followed. In the absence of a firm constitutional, statutory or common law basis, they can be identified as rights only by the natural lawyer, but not by the positivist. The rights and liberties under discussion essentially divide into two kinds. On the one hand, there are social and economic rights – the right to employment, health care, housing and income maintenance during periods of ill-health, unemployment or old age. On the other hand, there are the classical civil and political rights – the right to liberty of the person, the right to form political parties and to participate in elections, and the rights to freedom of conscience, religion and expression. Traditionally the realm of civil liberties has been confined to this latter group, to the exclusion of the former even though social and economic security are indispensable to effective participation in the civil and political life of the community. Yet, although there are several international treaties promoting social and economic security,[1] the boldness of their aspirations is generally matched only by the difficulties in their enforcement, while few democracies in the common law tradition take them seriously as fundamental rights. The position is different with regard to so-called civil and political rights. One international treaty in particular – the European Convention on Human Rights[2] – has had a significant influence on British law and practice, with the British government having been held in violation of its terms over 35 times and having introduced legislation on several occasions to give effect to

---

[1] These include the Convention of the International Labour Organisation, a United Nations agency based in Geneva, set up to promote the interests of working people. Also important is the Council of Europe's Social Charter of 1961, while the EC Charter of the Fundamental Social Rights of Workers of 1989 has also contributed to the development of social law. On the former, see Harris, *The European Social Charter*. On the latter, see Bercusson, *European Labour Law*.

[2] Cmd 8969, 1953.

rulings of the European Court of Human Rights.[3] Many western countries give constitutional protection to civil and political rights, often in a Bill of Rights with which all executive and legislative measures must comply, failing which they may be struck down by the courts. Britain is one of only a few western nations (the others being Israel and until recently New Zealand) which do not have a Bill of Rights enshrining and protecting civil and political liberties in this way.[4]

A.   The British approach

The common law

The traditional British approach to the protection of civil liberties has been greatly influenced by Dicey.[5] For him there was no need for any statement of fundamental principles operating as a kind of higher law because political freedom was adequately protected by the common law and by an independent Parliament acting as a watchdog against any excess of zeal by the executive.[6] Under the common law, a wide measure of individual liberty was guaranteed by the principle that citizens are free to do as they like unless expressly prohibited by law. So people already enjoy the freedom of religion, the freedom of expression, and the freedom of assembly, and may be restrained from exercising these freedoms only if there are clear common law or statutory restrictions. This approach is illustrated by a number of classical decisions, the first of which is *Entick v Carrington*[7] where the Secretary of State issued a warrant to search the premises of John Entick and to seize any seditious literature. When the legality of the conduct was challenged, the minister claimed that the existence and exercise of such a power were necessary in the interests of the state. But the court upheld the challenge on the ground that there was no authority in the common law or in statute for warrants to be issued in this way. A second example is *Beatty v Gillbanks*[8] where members of the Salvation Army in Weston-super-Mare were forbidden to march on Sundays because their presence attracted a large hostile crowd of people, thereby causing a breach of the peace. When the Salvationists ignored the order not to assemble, they were bound over to keep the peace for having committed the crime of unlawful assembly. The order binding them over was set aside on appeal because they had done nothing wrong. In the view of the court, they could not be prohibited from assembling merely because their lawful conduct might induce others to act unlawfully.

Although there are thus important illustrations of the principle, it is open

---

[3]   See A W Bradley, 'The United Kingdom before the Strasbourg Court 1975–1990', in Finnie, Himsworth and Walker (eds), *Edinburgh Essays in Public Law*.

[4]   See S Levine (1991) 44 Parliamentary Affairs 337.

[5]   Dicey, *The Law of the Constitution*. And see ch 6.

[6]   For a vivid expression of this view, see *Wheeler v Leicester City Council* [1985] AC 1054, at 1065 (Browne-Wilkinson LJ). For a powerful critique, see Craig, *Public Law and Democracy*.

[7]   (1765) 19 St Tr 1030; ch 6.

[8]   (1882) 9 QBD 308.

to question whether this approach is an adequate basis for the protection of liberty. In the first place, the common law rule that people are free to do anything which is not prohibited by law applies (it would seem) equally to the government. As a result, the government may violate individual freedom even though it is not formally empowered to do so, on the ground that it is doing nothing which is prohibited by law. So in *Malone v Metropolitan Police Commissioner*[9] the practice of telephone tapping was exposed as being done by the executive without any clear lawful authority. But when Mr Malone sought a declaration that the tapping of his telephone was unlawful, he failed because he could not point to any legal right of his which it was the duty of the government not to invade. There was no violation of his property rights, no breach of confidence, and no invasion of any right to privacy recognised by the law. A second difficulty with the British approach is that liberty is particularly vulnerable to erosion. The common law merely recognises that people are free to do anything which is not unlawful, but is powerless to prevent new restrictions from being enacted by the legislature. Paradoxically, many restrictions upon liberty are imposed by the common law, for it is sometimes convenient for the executive to avoid seeking new powers from Parliament.[10] In this way the authorities may seek a decision of the courts which will develop the law restrictively and create a precedent of general application. As a source of restraint of individual liberty, rules of this kind can be as effective as legislation by Parliament. Thus in *Moss v McLachlan*[11] the Divisional Court created, from the common law powers of the police to control and regulate public assemblies, an extended right to prevent people from assembling in the first place. And in the *Spycatcher* and other cases, it was held that injunctions could be granted to the Attorney-General to restrain the publication of confidential government secrets.[12]

The role of Parliament

Another weakness of the traditional British approach relates to the decline in the power of Parliament. The late 19th century, when Dicey was writing, was in many ways the high-water mark of an independent Parliament acting as a watchdog of the executive.[13] This was the time when Parliament was 'a body which chose the government, maintained it and could reject it' and which 'operated as an intermediary between the electorate and the executive'.[14] Since then, however, the inexorable growth of the party system and its attendant discipline has seen the executive increasingly gain control of the House of Commons. As a result, the government in the 1990s, unlike the position in the 1890s, can now expect its Bills to be passed by a largely quiescent House of Commons. To put the matter into perspective, in the 1980s only one government Bill was defeated on its second reading in the

---

9   [1979] Ch 344.
10 Cf Lord Browne-Wilkinson [1992] PL 397 and Sir J Laws [1993] PL 59.
11 [1985] IRLR 76. See ch 23 below.
12 *A-G v Guardian Newspapers Ltd* [1987] 1 WLR 1248; [1990] 1 AC 109.
13 See Mackintosh, *The British Cabinet.*
14 Mackintosh, *The Government and Politics of Britain.*

House, the first time this had occurred since at least 1945.[15] Modern governments have tended to take advantage of this development, resulting in statutory initiatives which it is said are corrosive of individual freedom.[16] These measures having been passed by Parliament, there is little that the courts can do to deny effect to these measures. As a result the residue of liberty, the freedom to do that which is not unlawful, becomes conspicuously less extensive. Such measures include the Police and Criminal Evidence Act 1984 (extending police powers of arrest and detention), the Public Order Act 1986 and the Criminal Justice and Public Order Act 1994 (extending police powers to prohibit and regulate public meetings and assemblies) and the Security Service Act 1989 (extending the legal powers of the security service, particularly in relation to the surveillance of individuals).

These critical views are not uncontroversial. Seeking to defend the government's position, ministers often claim that government is now more open than in the past, citing the Data Protection Act 1984 (giving individuals right of access to information held about them on computers), the Local Government (Access to Information) Act 1985 (giving rights of access to local authority meetings and to documents and records) and the Access to Personal Files Act 1987 (giving individuals the right of access to manual records containing personal information for the purposes of housing and social services). Legislation has also strengthened the rights of those who have grievances against agencies of the state. Thus, a new Police Complaints Authority has been set up, and new tribunals have been created for those who claim that a warrant has been improperly issued to intercept their communications or gain access to their home for the purposes of surveillance. The Public Order Act 1986, although restricting freedom of assembly, also strengthened the law on incitement to racial hatred, thereby promoting the rights of racial minorities in particular.[17] And partly as a result of EC initiatives, the statutory rights for women at work have been extended in a number of directions, while the Disability Discrimination Act 1995 was an important 'concession of the facts of social exclusion and marginalisation of a sizeable minority' of British citizens.[18]

Race Relations Act 1976

The British principle of liberty – that people are free to do anything which is not prohibited by law – is open to criticism because it fails to acknowledge that unrestrained liberty, particularly of private as opposed to public power, can be the antithesis of the liberty of others. For that reason Parliament may need to intervene to restrain that power and to regulate competing interests of liberty and freedom. Thus in the fields of race and sex discrimination,

---

15   However, governments in the 1960s and 1970s often suffered setbacks of other kinds on the floor of the House. Indeed, in the 1974–79 Parliament the government is said to have suffered 42 defeats. Even the government in the 1980s had to be more responsive to the wishes of Parliament than a single defeat in a second reading debate might otherwise indicate. See Brazier, *Constitutional Practice*, pp 204–13. See also ch 10 A.

16   See e.g., Ewing and Gearty, *Freedom under Thatcher*.

17   Patten, *Political Culture, Conservatism and Rolling Constitutional Change*.

18   B Doyle (1997) 60 MLR 64, at p 64. See also Doyle, *Disability, Discrimination and Equal Opportunities*.

common law rules relating to freedom of contract permitted the most egregious forms of racist and sexist behaviour by those in positions of power and authority – employers, landlords and traders – over others.[19] If a policy commitment to equality of opportunity was to be implemented, this could be done only by legislation. So in this way Parliament needs to act as a watchdog, not only to restrain the possibility of abuse by the executive, but also to initiate measures to revise common law rules which in a changing social climate are seen to be oppressive.

In the field of race relations Parliament first intervened with the Race Relations Act 1965, strengthened and extended by the Race Relations Act 1968.[20] The law is now found in the Race Relations Act 1976 which, although it goes further than its predecessors, is thought by some to be not as effective as it should be.[21] The 1976 Act applies to discrimination on grounds of race, defined to mean colour, race, nationality or ethnic or national origins.[22] It seeks to outlaw both direct and indirect discrimination. The former occurs where the discriminator treats one person less favourably on racial grounds than he or she would treat another.[23] The latter – introduced in 1976 and based on US case-law[24] – occurs where a person acts in a manner not in itself overtly discriminatory but where the effect of that action, intentional or not, is to discriminate. Thus, in terms of the 1976 Act, a person may apply to another a requirement or condition[25] which he or she applies or would apply equally to persons of different racial groups (defined by reference to colour, race, nationality or ethnic or national origins) and which therefore does not directly or overtly discriminate. Such action becomes discrimination, however, when the condition imposed is such that the proportion of persons of the same racial group who can comply with it is considerably smaller than the proportion of other persons who can comply; and when the condition is not justifiable irrespective of racial considerations[26] and has a detrimental effect on those who cannot comply. *Mandla v Dowell Lee* concerned the question whether the

---

[19]   Only exceptionally did the common law provide protection for members of minority racial groups: *Constantine v Imperial Hotels Ltd* [1944] KB 693; *Scala Ballroom v Ratcliffe* [1958] 3 All ER 220.

[20]   For good accounts of these measures, see Lester and Bindman, *Race and Law*, and Hepple, *Race, Jobs and the Law in Britain*. See also Lester [1994] PL 224.

[21]   See N Lacey [1984] PL 186.

[22]   Problems have arisen as to whether Jews (*Seide v Gillette Industries* [1980] IRLR 427), Sikhs (*Mandla v Dowell Lee* [1983] 2 AC 548), gypsies (*CRE v Dutton* [1989] IRLR 8) and Rastafarians (*Crown Suppliers PSA v Dawkins* [1993] ICR 517) are covered by the Act.

[23]   The fact that less favourable treatment took place without a racial motive is irrelevant: *R v CRE, ex p Westminster City Council* [1984] ICR 770 and *James v Eastleigh BC* [1990] 2 AC 751. See also *Dhatt v McDonalds Hamburgers Ltd* [1991] IRLR 130.

[24]   *Griggs v Duke Power Co* 401 US 424 (1971). See Lustgarten, *Legal Control of Racial Discrimination.*

[25]   On the meaning of 'requirement or condition', see *Perera v Civil Service Commission* [1983] ICR 428 and *Meer v London Borough of Tower Hamlets* [1988] IRLR 399.

[26]   For the suggestion that justification may be based on reasons acceptable to right-thinking people as sound and tolerable, see *Ojutiku v Manpower Services Commission* [1982] ICR 661. This has been rejected in favour of an approach which 'requires an objective balance between the discriminatory effect of the condition and the reasonable needs of the party who applies the condition'. See *Hampson v Department of Education and Science* [1991] 1 AC 171. See also *Webb v EMO Air Cargo* [1992] 4 All ER 929, and *St Matthias School v Crizzle* [1993] ICR 401.

headmaster of a private school discriminated against a Sikh boy by enforcing rules on school uniform which forbade the wearing of headgear. This was a requirement with which the plaintiff could not comply because of the practice of his religion. Holding the rules to be discriminatory, the House of Lords interpreted the words 'can comply' to mean not 'can physically comply', but 'can in practice comply' or 'can consistently with the customs and cultural conditions of the racial group comply'.[27]

Discrimination is unlawful in the field of employment, except where being of a particular racial group is a genuine qualification for stated jobs (for example, the theatre) and except for employment in a private household (ss 4, 5).[28] It is unlawful to dismiss an employee for refusal to carry out racially discriminatory instructions.[29] It is, further, unlawful to discriminate in the choice of partners for partnerships of six or more persons, admission to trade unions and professional organisations, granting of licences and qualifications for trades or vocations, vocational training and employment agency services (ss 10–14). Discrimination is also unlawful in education and in the provision of goods, services and facilities to the public or a section of the public.[30] There are exceptions for residential accommodation in small premises and for the fostering or care of children in a person's home (s 23(2)). Associations which have more than 25 members may not discriminate as respects admission to membership or the treatment of associate members (s 25)[31] but an association whose main aim is to provide benefits to persons of a particular racial group may discriminate on grounds of race, nationality or ethnic or national origin but not as regards colour (s 26). Advertising in terms which suggest an intention to discriminate is unlawful, but it is permissible to state that a job requires a member of a particular racial group (for example, a Chinese waiter for a Chinese restaurant) (s 29). Other conduct declared unlawful includes the adoption of discriminatory requirements or conditions (s 28), and instructing, inducing or aiding persons to commit unlawful discrimination (ss 30, 31, 33).

The Commission for Racial Equality replaced both the former Race Relations Board and the Community Relations Commission. Its chair and members are appointed by the Home Secretary and its annual report is laid before Parliament.[32] Unlike the former Board, the Commission has power on its own initiative or when directed by the Home Secretary to carry out formal investigations, and for this purpose it may require evidence to be given to it (ss 48–52). Such investigations must not, however, be lightly undertaken. The Commission may not embark upon an investigation unless it has a reasonable

---

27   [1983] 2 AC 548, at 565–6 (Lord Fraser). This test was derived from that applied in the sex discrimination case, *Price v Civil Service Commission* [1978] 1 All ER 1228.
28   See *Lambeth London Borough Council v CRE* [1990] ICR 768.
29   *Zarczynska v Levy* [1979] 1 All ER 864; *Showboat Entertainment Centre Ltd v Owens* [1984] 1 All ER 836.
30   For advice from the Inland Revenue being treated as a service, see *Savjani v Inland Revenue Commissioners* [1981] QB 458. On the liability of the police under s 20, as providers of a public service, see *Farah v Metropolitan Police Commissioner* [1997] 1 All ER 289.
31   On the law before 1976, see *Race Relations Board v Charter* [1973] AC 868 and *Race Relations Board v Dockers' Labour Club* [1976] AC 285.
32   The Commission also conducts valuable periodic reviews of the legislation. See most recently CRE, *Second Review of the Race Relations Act 1976* (1992).

suspicion that acts of discrimination have occurred.[33] If discrimination is established, the Commission has power to issue a non-discrimination notice (against which there is a right of appeal)[34] and may within five years follow up such a notice by seeking an injunction from the county court or, in Scotland, an interdict from the sheriff court (ss 57–61). Enforcement in the employment field by individuals takes the form of a complaint by the victim of discrimination to an industrial tribunal, from whom an appeal on a point of law lies to the Employment Appeal Tribunal.[35] When such a complaint is brought to a tribunal, the services of a conciliation officer are available. The tribunal may declare the rights of the parties in regard to the alleged discrimination, or order compensation to be paid, or recommend other steps to be taken by way of a remedy (ss 53–5).[36] Complaints of discrimination outside employment may be brought by the victim before designated county courts. The court may award damages,[37] including compensation for injury to feelings, but it is a defence to an action for damages based on indirect discrimination if the alleged discriminator proves that he or she did not intend to discriminate against the claimant on racial grounds (s 57(3)).[38] By virtue of the Race Relations (Remedies) Act 1994 there is no limit on the amount of compensation which may be awarded.[39] The Commission for Racial Equality has power to assist complainants in pursuing their remedies in difficult or important cases (s 66).[40] The Act applies to service under the Crown (including the armed forces)[41] and to the police. Government departments and ministers are required not to make discriminatory appointments to offices or posts which are not covered by the general rules against discrimination in the employment field (s 76). Local authorities are under a duty to make appropriate arrangements with a view to securing the elimination of unlawful racial discrimination and to promoting equality of opportunity and good relations between persons of different racial groups (s 71).[42]

---

[33] *R v Commission for Racial Equality, ex p Hillingdon Council* [1982] AC 779, applied in *Re Prestige Group* [1984] 1 WLR 335; and see *Home Office v CRE* [1982] QB 385.

[34] *CRE v Amari Plastics Ltd* [1982] QB 265.

[35] Ch 28 A.

[36] Problems may arise in discrimination cases in relation to the discovery of confidential documents. See *Science Research Council v Nassé* [1980] AC 1028 and, as to public interest immunity, *Halford v Sharples* [1992] 3 All ER 624 (see also ch 31 C).

[37] On damages, see *Alexander v Home Office* [1988] 2 All ER 118. On exemplary damages, see *AB v South West Water Services Ltd* [1993] QB 507. See further *Deane v Ealing LBC* [1993] ICR 329.

[38] See *J H Walker Ltd v Hussain* [1996] ICR 291.

[39] This follows amendments to the comparable terms of the Sex Discrimination Act 1975 (SI 1993 No 2798) which were driven by the need to comply with the Equal Treatment Directive 76/207/EEC, following the decision in *Case C-271/91, Marshall v Southampton and South West Hampshire Health Authority (No 2)* [1994] QB 126.

[40] As it did in *Mandla v Dowell Lee* [1983] 2 AC 548.

[41] See *R v Army Board of Defence Council, ex p Anderson* [1992] QB 169; Armed Forces Act 1996, s 23.

[42] See *Wheeler v Leicester City Council* [1985] AC 1054; *R v Lewisham London BC, ex p Shell UK Ltd* [1988] 1 All ER 938; *R v London Borough of Tower Hamlets, ex p Mohib Ali* (1993) 25 HLR 218. See also Local Government Act 1988, s 18.

B.   European Convention on Human Rights[43]

The protection of human rights, which is primarily a matter for the state in whose territory the rights may be enjoyed, cannot today be confined within national boundaries. The European Convention on Human Rights was signed at Rome in 1950, was ratified by the United Kingdom in 1951 and came into force amongst those states which had ratified it in 1953. The Convention is a treaty under international law and its authority derives solely from the consent of those states who have become parties to it. It was a direct result of the movement for cooperation in Western Europe which in 1949 created the Council of Europe. Inspiration for the Convention came from the wide principles declared in the United Nations Universal Declaration of Human Rights in 1948.[44] The Convention declares certain human rights which are or should be protected by law in each state. It also provides political and judicial procedures by which alleged infringements of these rights may be examined at an international level. In particular, the acts of public authorities may be challenged even though they are in accordance with national law. The Convention thus provides a constraint upon the legislative authority of national parliaments, including that at Westminster.[45]

The scope of the Convention

The Convention does not cover the whole field of human rights. It omits economic and social rights, and is confined to certain basic rights and liberties which the framers of the Convention considered would be generally accepted in the liberal democracies of Western Europe. These rights and liberties include:

the right to life (art 2);

freedom from torture or inhuman or degrading treatment or punishment (art 3);

freedom from slavery or forced labour (art 4);

the right to liberty and security of person (art 5), including the right of one who is arrested to be informed promptly of the reasons for his arrest and of any charge against him;

the right to a fair trial by an impartial tribunal of a person's civil rights and obligations and of criminal charges against him (art 6), including the right to be presumed innocent of a criminal charge until proved guilty and the right to be defended by a lawyer and to have free legal assistance 'when the interests of justice so require';

the prohibition of retroactive criminal laws (art 7);

---

[43]   The extensive literature includes Beddard, *Human Rights and Europe*; Fawcett, *The Application of the European Convention on Human Rights*; Jacobs and White, *The European Convention on Human Rights*; Harris, O'Boyle and Warbrick, *Law of the European Convention on Human Rights*; Janis, Kay and Bradley, *European Human Rights Law: Text and Materials*; Van Dijk and Van Hoof, *Theory and Practice of the European Convention on Human Rights*; Robertson and Merrills, *Human Rights in Europe*. For a valuable comparative study of the operation of the Convention in a number of jurisdictions, see Gearty (ed), *European Civil Liberties*.

[44]   See Brownlie, *Basic Documents on Human Rights*.

[45]   Ch 4 C.

the right to respect for a person's private and family life, his home and correspondence (art 8);

freedom of thought, conscience and religion (art 9) and freedom of expression (art 10);

freedom of peaceful assembly and of association with others, including the right to form and join trade unions (art 11);

the right to marry and found a family (art 12).

By art 14, the rights declared in the Convention are to be enjoyed

without discrimination on any ground such as sex, race, colour, language, religion, political or other opinion, national or social origin, association with a national minority, property, birth or other status.

All persons within the jurisdiction of the member states benefit from the Convention regardless of citizenship, though a state may restrict the political activities of aliens.

Many of these rights are subject to exceptions or qualifications. Thus art 5 sets out the grounds on which a person may lawfully be deprived of his liberty; these include the lawful arrest of a person to prevent his entering the country without authority, and the lawful detention 'of persons of unsound mind, alcoholics or drug addicts or vagrants' (art 5(1)(f)). So too the right to respect for private and family life under art 8 is protected from interference by a public authority

except such interference as is in accordance with the law and is necessary in a democratic society in the interests of national security, public safety or the economic well-being of the country, for the prevention of disorder or crime, for the protection of health or morals, or for the protection of the rights and freedoms of others.

Clearly it is essential that such restrictions should not be interpreted so widely that the protected right becomes illusory. Member states may derogate from most but not all of their obligations under the Convention in time of war or other public emergency (and the United Kingdom has done so in respect of Northern Ireland), but they must inform the Secretary-General of the Council of Europe of the measures taken and the reasons (art 15).[46]

The scope of the Convention was extended by the first protocol concluded as an addendum to the Convention in 1952, and ratified by the United Kingdom. By this protocol, every person is entitled to the peaceful enjoyment of his possessions (art 1); the right to education is protected and states must respect the right of parents to ensure education of their children in conformity with their own religious and philosophical convictions (art 2);[47] and the right to take part in free elections by secret ballot is declared (art 3).[48] The fourth protocol to the Convention, concluded in 1963, guarantees freedom of movement within a state and freedom to leave any country; it also precludes a state from expelling or refusing to admit its own nationals. This

---

[46]   See *Lawless v Ireland* (1961) 1 EHRR 15.

[47]   The United Kingdom accepted this principle 'only so far as is compatible with provision of efficient instruction and training, and the avoidance of unreasonable public expenditure'; see *Campbell and Cosans v United Kingdom* (1980) 4 EHRR 293.

[48]   See *Liberal Party v United Kingdom* (1982) 4 EHRR 106 (simple majority electoral system not a breach of Convention).

protocol has not been ratified by the United Kingdom because our citizenship and immigration laws do not guarantee to all citizens the right to enter the United Kingdom.[49] The sixth protocol provides for the abolition of the death penalty thereby qualifying the terms of art 2 of the Convention itself. Under the terms of the protocol, which is not ratified by the UK, no one is to be condemned to death or executed, with the only exception being made for times of war when the penalty could be imposed only 'in the instances laid down in the law and in accordance with its provisions'. The seventh protocol (again not ratified by the UK) deals mainly with appeals procedures in criminal cases, though it also provides (in art 5) for 'equality of rights and responsibilities of a private law character' between spouses. Of the remaining protocols, the eleventh is by far the most significant, and is dealt with fully below.

Institutions and procedure

One novel feature of the Convention was the right which it gave to individuals to complain of breaches of the Convention by the states party to it. The enforcement procedure makes use both of the Committee of Ministers of the Council of Europe (a committee of political representatives of the member states) and of two institutions created by the Convention: (*a*) the European *Commission* of Human Rights, which in 1996 comprised 30 individual members, elected by the Committee of Ministers but in office acting independently; and (*b*) the European *Court* of Human Rights, comprising judges elected by the Consultative Assembly of the Council of Europe. No two members of the Commission or the Court respectively may be citizens of the same state. In 1996, the Council of Europe had 39 member states, most (but not all) of whom had ratified the Convention. They included Austria, Cyprus, Iceland, Malta, Norway, Sweden, Switzerland, Turkey, Hungary and the Czech Republic, as well as the 15 members of the EU.

The function of the *Commission* is to receive and inquire into alleged breaches of the Convention either (*a*) at the request of any state party to the Convention which alleges that another state has breached the Convention (art 24) (these are known as inter-state cases); or (*b*) where a state has recognised the competence of the Commission to receive such petitions, on the receipt of a petition from an individual or a non-governmental organisation alleging a violation of rights by the state in question (art 25). Although not all states have recognised the right of individuals to petition to the Commission, very many more petitions come to the Commission than inter-state cases. Thus between 1955 and 1991, only 11 inter-state cases had been considered by the Commission yet no fewer than 17,116 complaints had been considered by the Commission as to their admissibility. By 1995 more than 27,000 applications had been submitted.

When an individual petition is received, the Commission must first decide whether it is admissible under the Convention: thus the Commission may deal with a matter only after the applicant has exhausted all available domestic remedies and only if the petition is brought within six months of the final

---

[49]   Ch 20.

national decision (art 26). The Commission must also reject as inadmissible any petition which it considers incompatible with the Convention, manifestly ill-founded or an abuse of the right of petition (art 27). In fact the vast majority of the petitions considered since 1955 have been declared inadmissible. When a petition clears the hurdle of admissibility, the Commission must then investigate the facts fully and must offer its services to the parties with a view to securing a friendly settlement of the dispute (art 28). If such a settlement is not arranged, a secret report on the dispute is sent by the Commission to the state or states concerned and to the Committee of Ministers (art 31). Thereafter the matter may be dealt with finally by the Committee of Ministers, deciding by a two-thirds majority, or it may be brought within three months before the European Court of Human Rights.

A case may be brought before the *Court* only where the states concerned have accepted the compulsory jurisdiction of the Court (art 46) or expressly consent to the case coming to the Court (art 48). Only the Commission or a state concerned may refer a case to the Court: the individual applicant formerly had no such right, although since 1983 he or she has had the right to be represented in proceedings before the Court. But an amendment to art 48 made by the ninth protocol gives applicants a limited right to refer their cases to the Court.[50] The decision of the Court is final. If the Court finds that action taken on behalf of a state has conflicted with the Convention, and if the domestic law of the state does not allow full reparation to be made, the Court 'shall, if necessary, afford just satisfaction to the injured party' (art 50), for example, by an award of compensation.[51]

Protocol 11

Important new procedures for dealing with complaints are provided for in protocol 11 which creates a new full-time court. Although it has the same title as the existing court, 'it is an entirely different body with new functions, powers and composition'.[52] The protocol will come into force only after all parties to the Convention consent to be bound by it; and then only when a year has elapsed thereafter. When it does come into force the terms of office of the existing judges and members of the Commission will expire and new judges will be appointed. The new court will consist of a number of judges equal to the number of states which are party to the Convention (art 20), with a judge from each country, though they are to be elected by the Parliamentary Assembly of the Council of Europe by a majority of the votes cast from a list of three candidates nominated by the country in question (art 22). The judges are to serve for renewable periods of 6 years, though the terms of office of one half of the first group of judges are to expire after three years (art 23). The protocol has the effect of radically pruning the existing text of the Convention, replacing arts 19–56 with new arts 19–51. The main effect of the changes is to enable applicants complaining of a breach of the Convention to proceed

---

50   See A R Mowbray [1991] PL 353. See also Harris, Boyle and Warbrick, above, pp 661–3.
51   For a valuable review of the work of the court, see C A Gearty [1993] 45 CLJ 89.
52   A R Mowbray [1994] PL 540 (and [1993] PL 419). See also Harris, Boyle and Warbrick, ch 26; Janis, Kay and Bradley, above, ch 4 and app D; H Schermers (1994) 19 Eur Law Rev 367.

directly to the Court, and to remove the role of the Commission in dealing with complaints. For this purpose 'the new court will operate through a number of constituent bodies', these being committees, chambers and the Grand Chamber (art 27). Applications may continue to be made by one state against another (art 33), or by 'any person, non-governmental organisation or group of individuals claiming to be the victim of a violation' (art 34).

There is still a requirement that an applicant should have exhausted all domestic remedies, and have brought the complaint within six months of the final decision of the domestic authorities. There is no jurisdiction to deal with complaints which are anonymous or substantially the same as any already examined by the Court, which is required to declare inadmissible any application submitted under art 34 considered to be incompatible with the terms of the Convention, manifestly ill-founded or an abuse of the right to petition (art 35). Under the new procedures, cases will be dealt with initially by a committee of three judges who will determine whether the complaint is admissible. A complaint may be ruled inadmissible only by a unanimous vote (art 28) failing which the decision on admissibility must be taken by a chamber of seven judges (who must also decide on the admissibility of inter-state applications), which also deals with the merits of the case (art 29). In some cases, however, the chamber may relinquish jurisdiction in favour of a Grand Chamber of 17 judges, an option which is available where the case 'raises a serious question affecting the interpretation of the Convention or the protocols thereto or where the resolution of a question before it might have a result inconsistent with a judgment previously delivered by the Court' (art 30). Provision is made for disposing of an application by means of a friendly settlement, where it has been ruled admissible, for which purpose the Court will place itself at the disposal of the parties (art 38). Decisions of committees are final (art 29), as are decisions of chambers and grand chambers (art 44). The revised text retains the power of the Court to afford just satisfaction to the injured party (art 41).

Cases involving the United Kingdom[53]

It will be seen that enforcement of the Convention depends essentially upon a state recognising both the right of individual petition to the Commission and also the compulsory jurisdiction of the Court.[54] It was in 1966 that the British government first made the two declarations necessary under arts 25 and 46; these declarations have since been renewed at intervals.[55] Since 1966, a wide variety of individual petitions have been brought against the UK government, and there have also been inter-state references to the Commission by the Republic of Ireland. In addition to the innumerable decisions and opinions being given by the Commission, the Court between 1975 and April 1990 decided 30 cases involving the United Kingdom, with a number of others awaiting decision. In 21 of the 30 cases the Court found breaches of the

---

[53] The account draws heavily on A W Bradley, note 3 above. See also R R Churchill and J R Young [1991] BY IL 283.

[54] For an account of the British attitude to the Convention, see A Lester [1984] PL 46.

[55] See most recently HC Deb, 13 December 1995, col 647 (renewed with effect from 13 January 1996).

Convention, whereas the other nine were dismissed. This ratio of 70:30 in the success rate for cases brought against the United Kingdom is very nearly the same as for the Court's record as a whole between 1960 and 1987. During that period 108 principal decisions of the Court were made, and breaches were found to have occurred in 75 cases, a 'success' ratio of 69:31.[56] More recent information shows that as of 3 April 1995, the Court had found at least one breach of the Convention on 35 occasions in the case of the UK. This compared with 82 in the case of Italy, 29 in the case of France, 27 in the case of Austria, 23 in the case of the Netherlands, 21 in the case of Sweden, and 11 in the case of Germany.[57] Many countries recognised the right of individual petition more recently than Britain, so it is not possible to conclude from these statistics that the requirements of the Convention are (in relation to population) more liable to be infringed in the UK than in any other country. Indeed it has been suggested that Britain comes 14th out of 30 Council of Europe states (the first being Italy with the poorest record) in a comparison based on population and the number of years the right of individual petition has been recognised.[58]

The first British case to reach the Court,[59] *Golder v United Kingdom*,[60] concerned a refusal by the prison authorities to permit a convicted prisoner access to legal advice about a possible action in defamation against a prison officer. The Court held unanimously that this refusal infringed art 8 of the Convention (respect for private life and correspondence) and by a majority of nine judges to three that the guarantee of a fair hearing in the determination of a person's civil rights (art 6(1)) included the right of access to a lawyer for advice about possible proceedings. The British cases before the Court in fact span a wide range of subjects. In *McCann v United Kingdom*[61] it was held that art 2 (protecting the right to life) had been violated following the use of lethal force by members of the security forces in Gibraltar. Questions concerning the interpretation of art 3 (protection against torture and inhuman or degrading treatment or punishment) arose in *Republic of Ireland v United Kingdom*[62] in relation to the interrogation of IRA suspects, in *Tyrer v United Kingdom*[63] in relation to the corporal punishment of juveniles in the Isle of Man, and in *Soering v United Kingdom*[64] in relation to the request for the extradition of a German citizen to the USA to stand trial for murder with the risk of being sentenced to capital punishment and being kept on death row. In *X v United Kingdom*[65] the Court held certain procedures for the compulsory detention of mental patients to infringe art 5, a similar conclusion being reached in *Brogan v United Kingdom*[66] in relation to the provisions of the Prevention of Terrorism Act authorising the detention of suspects for up to

---

[56] Bradley, note 3 above, at p 188.
[57] HL Deb, 18 April 1995, col 44 (WA).
[58] HL Deb, 5 June 1995, col 86 (WA).
[59] For a full account of the case-law, see C Gearty, in Gearty (ed), *European Civil Liberties*, ch 2.
[60] (1975) 1 EHRR 524.
[61] (1996) 21 EHRR 97.
[62] (1978) 2 EHRR 25.
[63] (1978) 2 EHRR 1. See also *Costello-Roberts v UK* (1995) 19 EHRR 112.
[64] (1989) 11 EHRR 439.
[65] (1981) 4 EHRR 188.
[66] (1988) 11 EHRR 117; and see ch 25 E.

seven days without judicial authority. Article 6 has been found to have been violated in a number of cases, including *Murray v United Kingdom*[67] where the applicant was denied access to a solicitor for 48 hours while in police detention. Similarly in *Benham v United Kingdom*[68] a complaint was upheld in a case brought by a person denied legal aid and imprisoned for failure to pay the community charge (poll tax) without the benefit of legal representation. In *McMichael v United Kingdom*[69] a breach was found to have taken place where the natural parents of a child were denied access to relevant confidential reports in child-care proceedings. Decisions under art 7 have been no less important, it being held in *SW and CR v United Kingdom*,[70] for example, that convictions for rape did not constitute a breach despite claims that at the time the offence was committed, it was covered by the long-standing marital immunity which had been effectively removed by the House of Lords in *R v R*.[71]

In *Dudgeon v United Kingdom*,[72] legislation in Northern Ireland making homosexual conduct between adult males a crime was held to infringe the individual's right to respect for his private life under art 8. The practice of telephone tapping was held to infringe art 8 in *Malone v United Kingdom*.[73] The law of contempt of court was held to infringe freedom of expression under art 10 in *Sunday Times Ltd v United Kingdom*,[74] but the English law on obscene publications survived scrutiny in *Handyside v United Kingdom*.[75] In three other important cases it was held that art 10 had been violated by (i) restraints on the publication by newspapers (the *Observer, Guardian* and *Sunday Times*) of the contents of a book (*Spycatcher*) by a retired security service officer;[76] (ii) a requirement imposed by a court that a journalist should disclose the confidential sources of an article he had written, publication of which had been restrained by the courts;[77] and (iii) the award of £1.5 million damages to Lord Aldington for defamatory remarks contained in a pamphlet written by a historian.[78] In *Young, James and Webster v United Kingdom*[79] three former employees of British Railways, dismissed for refusing to join a trade union, established that their freedom of association had been infringed as a result of legislation on the closed shop initiated by a Labour government in 1974 and 1976: they were awarded substantial compensation.[80] But in *Lithgow v United Kingdom*[81] it was held that the compensation arrangements following the nationalisation of the shipbuilding industry did not breach the protection for

---

[67]   (1996) 22 EHRR 29.
[68]   (1996) 22 EHRR 293.
[69]   (1995) 20 EHRR 205.
[70]   (1996) 21 EHRR 363.
[71]   [1992] 1 AC 599.
[72]   (1981) 4 EHRR 149.
[73]   (1984) 7 EHRR 14.
[74]   (1979) 2 EHRR 245; and see ch 18 B above.
[75]   (1976) 1 EHRR 737.
[76]   (1991) 14 EHRR 153, 229.
[77]   *Goodwin v United Kingdom* (1996) 22 EHRR 123.
[78]   *Tolstoy Miloslavsky v United Kingdom* (1995) 20 EHRR 442.
[79]   (1981) 4 EHRR 38.
[80]   See K D Ewing and W M Rees (1983) 12 ILJ 148.
[81]   (1986) 8 EHRR 329.

private property in art 1 of the first protocol. And in *Air Canada v United Kingdom* it was held that there was no breach of art 1 of the first protocol where an aeroplane was seized by customs officers after it was found to be carrying cannabis.[82]

These decisions have often led to changes in the law intended to prevent future infringements of the Convention. Such legislative changes include the Contempt of Court Act 1981 (regulating more clearly the circumstances in which pre-trial publicity is unlawful), the Interception of Communications Act 1985 (regulating the circumstances in which telephone tapping may take place, and giving individuals a right of redress against improper use) and the Homosexual Offences (Northern Ireland) Order 1982 (changing the law on homosexual conduct in Northern Ireland). Other significant consequences of Court decisions include the introduction of amendments to the procedures for detention and release of mental patients following the decision in *X v United Kingdom*[83] and the issuing of new Prison Rules and changing practices in prisons following decisions on prisoners' correspondence. In at least two cases, however, the government has been unwilling to give effect to decisions of the European Court and has taken steps to avoid doing so. In *Abdulaziz v United Kingdom*[84] the Court held that British immigration rules discriminated against women permanently settled in the United Kingdom because their husbands and fiancées were not entitled to enter, whereas the wives and fiancées of men settled here were entitled to enter. The government responded to this decision by amending the Immigration Rules to remove the entitlement of wives and fiancées to enter, thereby removing the source of discrimination. More recently, in *Brogan v United Kingdom*[85] the government responded to the Court's decision, that the detention powers of the Prevention of Terrorism (Temporary Provisions) Act 1984 violated art 5, by declaring that the power was necessary on security grounds and by depositing at Strasbourg a limited derogation from the Convention to the extent that the legislation violated art 5. Although the practice of birching offenders on the Isle of Man was held to violate art 3,[86] the law on the island was not altered to give effect to the Court's ruling.

The Convention in domestic law[87]

By art 1 of the Convention, states who are parties to it must secure to all within their jurisdiction the rights declared. Article 13 declares that everyone whose rights are violated 'shall have an effective remedy before a national authority, notwithstanding that the violation has been committed by persons acting in an official capacity'. While these articles undoubtedly impose an obligation on every state to ensure that its domestic law conforms to the Convention, a state is under no duty to incorporate the Convention itself within its domestic

---

[82]   (1995) 20 EHRR 150.
[83]   (1981) 4 EHRR 188.
[84]   (1985) 7 EHRR 471.
[85]   (1988) 11 EHRR 117.
[86]   *Tyrer v United Kingdom* (1978) 2 EHRR 1.
[87]   For a full account, see C Gearty, in Gearty (ed), *European Civil Liberties*, ch 2.

law.[88] In practice it is for each state to decide whether this should be done and, subject to review by the Convention institutions, how to provide an effective remedy for breaches of the Convention. In most of the states who are parties to the Convention (including Austria, Belgium, Germany, Italy, Luxembourg, the Netherlands and Sweden) the Convention has been incorporated within the domestic law, but for this purpose incorporation may take one of several forms.[89] Successive British governments have maintained that human rights are already adequately protected by law in the United Kingdom. Indeed, in the Court of Appeal in 1990 Lord Donaldson concurred in the view that 'you have to look long and hard before you can detect any difference between the English common law and the principles set out in the Convention, at least if the Convention is viewed through English judicial eyes'.[90] Not everyone would agree with this view and there is strong support for the formal incorporation of the Convention into domestic law, thereby empowering the courts to strike down or to refuse to apply legislation or executive action which breaches its terms. But the case for taking this step is not irrefutable. We return to this matter in section C.

The Convention has been considered by the courts on a number of occasions in both England and Scotland. Clearly, the courts may not rely on the Convention in preference to an Act of Parliament and may not rely on it to invalidate an Act of Parliament.

The Convention which is contained in an international treaty to which the United Kingdom is a party has not yet been incorporated into English domestic law. The appellants accept that it is a constitutional principle that if Parliament has legislated and the words of the statute are clear, the statute must be applied, even if its application is in breach of international law.[91]

It is accepted, however, that the Convention may be used as an aid to clear up any ambiguity or uncertainty in a statute, as in *Waddington v Miah*[92] where the House of Lords referred to art 7 of the Convention to support its view that s 34 of the Immigration Act 1971 could not be construed to have retrospective effect. Apart from statutory interpretation, the question has also arisen as to whether those who exercise discretionary powers conferred by statute are bound to take the Convention into account.

In *Brind v Home Secretary*,[93] the defendant had issued directives to the IBA under the Broadcasting Act 1981 and to the BBC under its Licence and Agreement of 1964. Their effect was to prevent the broadcasting of material by representatives or

[88]   *Swedish Engine Drivers' Union v Sweden* (1975) 1 EHRR 617.
[89]   Drzemczewski, *European Human Rights Convention in Domestic Law.*
[90]   *R v Home Secretary, ex p Brind* [1991] 1 AC 696, at 717.
[91]   *R v Home Secretary, ex p Brind* [1991] 1 AC 696, at 760. See also *Kaur v Lord Advocate* [1980] 3 CMLR 79 and *Moore v Secretary of State for Scotland* 1985 SLT 38. Cf J L Murdoch [1991] PL 40.
[92]   [1974] 1 WLR 683. See also *R v Chief Immigration Officer, Heathrow Airport, ex p Salamat Bibi* [1976] 1 WLR 979. But see *R v Brown* [1994] 1 AC 212 where there are suggestions (by Lord Lowry) that the ECHR could be used only in the construction of statutes passed after it was ratified. Cf Sir John Laws [1993] PL 59 arguing for a greater role for the Convention in the interpretation of statutes and in the development of the common law. For the position in Scotland, see A Brown (1996) SLT (News) 267.
[93]   [1991] 1 AC 696. See now *NALGO v Secretary of State, The Times,* 2 December 1992. Cf *UKAPE v ACAS* [1980] ICR 201.

supporters of proscribed terrorist organisations, as well as Sinn Fein, Republican Sinn Fein and the Ulster Defence Association. The Home Secretary was challenged in the courts on a number of grounds, one of which was that the directives violated art 10 of the Convention and that in exercising his discretion the minister was required not only to have taken it into account, but also to have 'properly construed it and correctly taken it into consideration'. The argument failed, with Lord Ackner in the House of Lords concluding that 'not having been incorporated in English law', the Convention 'cannot be a source of rights and obligations'. The House of Lords indicated that short of proper incorporation of the Convention into domestic law by Parliament, it would be inappropriate for the domestic courts 'to police the operation of the Convention and to ask [themselves] in each case, where there was a challenge, whether the restrictions were "necessary in a democratic society ..." applying the principles enunciated in the decisions of the European Court of Human Rights'.

So far as the common law is concerned, the courts are unwilling to rely on the Convention to create new common law rights and duties where none exist, but where there may be an obvious gap which needs to be filled. So in *Malone v Metropolitan Police Commissioner*,[94] the Vice-Chancellor (Sir Robert Megarry) preferred not to fashion a new common law right to privacy from art 8 of the Convention in a case involving the tapping of a private telephone by police officers on the authority of a Home Secretary's warrant, issued without statutory authority. On the other hand, the courts may refer to the Convention to help develop and clarify existing common law rules. So in *Attorney-General v BBC*[95] Lord Fraser said that the courts should have regard to the Convention and to the decisions of the European Court in cases where 'domestic law is not firmly settled'. One such case is *Derbyshire County Council v Times Newspapers Ltd*[96] where the Court of Appeal (but not the House of Lords) relied heavily on art 10 of the Convention in deciding that a local authority could not sue in libel. In the view of the court, to allow a local authority to sue for libel would impose a substantial restriction on freedom of expression. The Convention has also been instrumental in reducing the size of damages awards which may be made by juries in libel trials. In *Rantzen v Mirror Group Newspapers Ltd*,[97] the Court of Appeal held that 'the common law if properly understood requires the courts to subject large awards of damages to a more searching scrutiny than has been customary in the past', having regard 'to the guidance given by the court in Strasbourg'.[98]

Finally, it appears that the courts may properly have regard to the Convention in exercising their discretion in the law relating to remedies on the one hand, and the admissibility of evidence on the other.

In *Attorney-General v Guardian Newspapers Ltd*[99] interim injunctions had been granted to restrain two newspapers from publishing information contained in *Spycatcher*, the memoirs of a retired security service official, Mr Peter Wright. When copies of the

---

94   [1979] Ch 344. See also *Gleaves v Deakin* [1980] AC 477.
95   [1981] AC 303.
96   [1992] 1 QB 770 (CA); [1993] AC 534.
97   [1994] QB 670.
98   The court reduced a jury award from £250,000 to £110,000. Compare *John v Mirror Group Newspapers* [1996] 3 WLR 593.
99   [1987] 3 All ER 316. See also *Broome v Cassell & Co Ltd* [1972] AC 1027.

book became freely available in Britain, the newspapers applied to the courts to have the injunctions discharged. In deciding whether to continue the injunctions until the full trial or to discharge them, Lord Templeman in the House of Lords (with the express support of Lord Ackner) clearly thought it appropriate to take into account art 10 of the Convention. However, after referring to art 10(2) he decided to continue the injunctions, along with the majority of his colleagues. Article 10(2) allows restrictions on freedom of expression where these are prescribed by law and 'necessary in a democratic society, in the interests of national security, territorial integrity or public safety, for the prevention of disorder or crime, for the protection of health or morals, for the protection of the reputation or rights of others, for preventing the disclosure of information received in confidence, or for maintaining the authority and impartiality of the judiciary'. In Lord Templeman's view, the continuation of the injunctions until the trial was necessary on several of these grounds.

It has also been held that an apparent breach of the Convention is relevant to the exercise by a court of its discretion under the Police and Criminal Evidence Act 1984, s 78. This provides that the court may refuse to allow evidence for the prosecution which would have such an adverse effect on the fairness of the proceedings that it ought not to be admitted.

In *R v Khan*[100] the question arose about the admissibility of evidence obtained by the placing of a surveillance device on the appellant's property. It was accepted that the conduct of the police was unlawful in the sense that it amounted to a trespass, and it was argued that it violated the right to privacy as protected by art 8 of the Convention. The House of Lords accepted that if evidence had been obtained in circumstances which involved 'an apparent breach' of the Convention, then 'that is a matter which may be relevant to the exercise of the s 78 power'. An apparent breach will not, however, necessarily mean that the evidence would be ruled inadmissible, for much depends on the significance of the irregularity and its effect on 'the fairness or unfairness of the proceedings'. In this case the House of Lords dismissed the appeal, holding that the evidence was admissible.

The European Convention on Human Rights and the EC

For practical purposes, the European Convention on Human Rights is separate from the system of Community law. The Commission and Court of Human Rights both sit at Strasbourg under the Council of Europe umbrella and must not be confused with the EC Commission at Brussels or the European Court of Justice at Luxembourg. The European Convention does not rank as a 'European Treaty' for the purposes of the European Communities Act 1972 and thus s 2(1) of the Act does not give it direct effect within United Kingdom law.[101] Indeed, the EC Treaty made no express provision for the protection of human rights, although it created certain new rights in the economic and social field and provided machinery by which these rights could be enforced. But the lack of express protection for human rights has caused difficulties, particularly in German courts, which have been reluctant to accept that Community law should prevail over the protection for human

---

[100]   [1996] 3 All ER 289. Cf *R v Saunders, The Times*, 28 November 1995.
[101]   *Kaur v Lord Advocate* [1980] 3 CMLR 79.

rights which is a fundamental aspect of the German constitution.[102] Moreover, the absence of a formal protection of human rights means that they
tend to play a subordinate role to the economic rights such as freedom of
movement of goods which are to be found expressly in the Treaty.[103]
Nevertheless it has been held that the EC does not have the competency to
accede to the European Convention on Human Rights, with the result that
an amendment to the EC Treaty would be necessary before such a step could
be taken.[104] It is true that by art F(2), the Treaty on European Union of 1992
requires the EU to respect fundamental rights as guaranteed by the ECHR
and 'as they result from the constitutional traditions common to Member
States, as general principles of Community law'. But it has been pointed out
that 'this provision is not part of Community Law and is not justiciable by the
European Court'.[105]

It does not follow from this, however, that the Convention has no role to
play in the development of EC law.[106] By art 164 of the EC Treaty the
European Court of Justice must ensure the observance of the general
principles of law in the interpretation and application of the Treaty. In a
developing line of cases, that court has stated that respect for human rights
forms part of the common legal traditions shared by members of the EC.[107] As
evidence of these general principles of law, the Court of Justice may look to
the European Convention on Human Rights (and other international treaties, such as the Council of Europe's Social Charter of 1961).[108] There is now a
body of case-law where 'the Convention has been employed by the ECJ as an
aid to the construction of Community provisions or as a yardstick for
determining the validity of Community acts'.[109]

In *Case C-13/94, P v S and Cornwall County Council*[110] the applicant brought an action
for unfair dismissal after having been dismissed following her 'gender re-assignment'.

---

[102]   See the decision of the German Constitutional Court in the *Internationale Handelsgesellschaft*
case [1974] 2 CMLR 540; and U Scheuner (1975) 12 CML Rev 171. A different view was
taken by the German Constitutional Court in the *Wünsche Handelsgesellschaft* case [1987] 3
CMLR 225. See subsequently *Brunner v European Union Treaty* [1994] 1 CMLR 57. For a
review, see M Zuleeg (1997) 22 Eur Law Rev 19. For similar problems in Ireland, see *A-G v
X* [1992] 2 CMLR 277.

[103]   See *R v Coventry City Council, ex p Phoenix Aviation* [1995] 3 All ER 37 and *R v Chief Constable
of Sussex, ex p International Trader's Ferry* [1997] 2 All ER 65.

[104]   *Op 2/94, Re the Accession of the Community to the European Human Rights Convention* [1996] 2
CMLR 265. For an earlier consideration of this issue, see HL Deb, 26 November 1992, col
1087.

[105]   Weatherill and Beaumont, *EC Law*, p 257.

[106]   The literature on the role of the ECHR in EC law is vast. A good account is Craig and De
Burca, *EC Law*, ch 7.

[107]   See *Case 11/70, Internationale Handelsgesellschaft* [1972] CMLR 255; *Case 4/73, Nold v EC
Commission* [1974] CMLR 338; *Case 36/75, Rutili v French Minister of Interior* [1976] 1 CMLR
140; and *Case 5/88, Wachauf v Germany* [1989] ECR 2609.

[108]   *Case 149/77, Defrenne v Sabena* [1978] ECR 1365.

[109]   N Grief [1991] PL 555, at 556. See eg *Case 222/84, Johnston v Chief Constable of the RUC*
[1987] QB 129; *Cases 46/87* and *227/88, Hoechst AG v Commission* [1989] ECR 2859; *Case
374/87, Orkem v EC Commission* [1989] ECR 3283; *Case 331/88, R v Ministry of Agriculture, ex
p Fédération Européenne de la Santé Animale* [1991] 1 CMLR 507.

[110]   [1996] 2 CMLR 247.

She began to dress and behave as a woman before undergoing surgery to give her the physical attributes of a woman. The situation was not covered by the Sex Discrimination Act 1975 and the question arose whether it was unlawful under the Equal Treatment Directive of 1976. On a reference to the ECJ, the court referred to the jurisprudence of the European Court of Human Rights (although in the case which was cited approvingly the applicant was unsuccessful)[111] and held that 'the right not to be discriminated against on grounds of sex is one of the fundamental human rights whose observance the [ECJ] has a duty to ensure'. Accordingly, it continued, 'the scope of the directive cannot be confined simply to discrimination based on the fact that a person is of one or other sex. In view of its purpose and the nature of the rights which it seeks to safeguard, the scope of the Directive is also such as to apply to discrimination arising, as in this case, from the gender re-assignment of the person concerned.'

When considering the application of Treaty provisions, domestic courts as well as the ECJ are as a result of this line of authority bound to 'apprise the application of these provisions having regard to all the rules of Community law, including freedom of expression, as embodied in art 10 of the European Convention on Human Rights, as a general principle of law the observance of which is ensured by the Court'.[112] This developing jurisprudence has had important implications for domestic constitutional law.

In *T Petitioner*[113] the question was whether the homosexual father could adopt his child under the Adoption (Scotland) Act 1978. In reversing the Lord Ordinary, the Inner House of the Court of Session held that he could and in so doing reversed the earlier decisions of the Scottish courts that the Convention could not be used as an aid to the construction of statutes.[114] It was held that the Scottish courts should adopt the same position as their counterparts in England, namely that 'when legislation is found to be ambiguous in the sense that it is capable of a meaning which either conforms to or conflicts with the Convention, Parliament is to be presumed to have legislated in conformity with the Convention, not in conflict with it'. This re-positioning was adopted at least partly by reference to EC law under which it is an 'integral part of the general principles' of law 'that fundamental human rights must be protected, and that one of the sources to which regard may be had for an expression of these rights is international treaties for the protection of human rights on which member states have collaborated or of which they are signatories'.

This is a bold decision, particularly in view of the fact that the dispute before the court did not appear to deal with a matter of EC law, and that the ECJ has held that it has no power to examine the compatibility with the ECHR of national rules which do not fall within the scope of community law.[115]

---

[111]   *Rees v United Kingdom* (1987) 9 EHRR 56.
[112]   *Case C-260/89, ERT* [1991] ECR I-2925.
[113]   (1996) SCLR 897. See A Brown (1996) SLT (News) 267.
[114]   See J L Murdoch [1991] PL 40.
[115]   *Case C-159/90, SPUC v Grogan* [1991] ECR I-4685. And see on this point *R v MAFF, ex p First City Trading, The Times*, 20 December 1996.

C.   A Bill of Rights for the United Kingdom?

The unwritten constitution lays emphasis on the virtues of the common law and the legislative supremacy of Parliament. It relies on the political process to secure that Parliament does not override the basic rights and liberties of the individual, nor remove from the courts the adjudication of disputes between the citizen and the state arising out of the exercise of public powers. In the mid-1970s, a growing number of critics doubted the continuing effectiveness of the traditional British approach to individual liberties and advocated the creation of a new Bill of Rights.[116] These proposals were taken up and examined in governmental and parliamentary circles. Thus in 1977, the Standing Advisory Commission on Human Rights in Northern Ireland published a full study, recommending that the protection of rights in Northern Ireland would be best advanced by the creation of a Bill of Rights for the whole United Kingdom.[117] In 1978, a select committee of the House of Lords considered whether a Bill of Rights was desirable and, if so, what form it should take.[118] The committee was unanimous that if there were to be a Bill of Rights, it should be a Bill to incorporate the European Convention on Human Rights in UK law, but the committee was divided on whether a Bill of Rights was desirable. The House of Lords later approved a Bill that sought to incorporate the Convention in UK law.[119] However, the Conservative government after 1979 was not persuaded that a Bill of Rights was necessary or desirable. A similar Bill passed by the Lords in the 1985–86 session also failed in the Commons, as have other measures.[120]

In the 1980s, the call for a Bill of Rights became more vocal, fuelled by the British record at Strasbourg and also by a number of highly publicised incidents which included the banning of trade unions at Government Communications Headquarters (GCHQ),[121] the (ultimately unsuccessful) attempts to ban the publication of *Spycatcher* (a book of memoirs of Mr Peter Wright, a retired security service agent),[122] and the enthusiastic use of the Official Secrets Act 1911 to prosecute civil servants (such as Sarah Tisdall and Clive Ponting)[123] who leaked official information which they believed ought to have been in the public domain. The campaign in favour of a Bill of Rights was given a considerable boost by Charter 88, a group pressing for a wide range of constitutional reform, as well as by the Institute for Public Policy Research (which published their own detailed proposals for a written constitution in 1991) and by Liberty whose proposals for *A People's Charter*

---

[116]   See Scarman, *English Law – the New Dimension*; Hailsham, *The Dilemma of Democracy*; Joseph, *Freedom under the Law*; Zander, *A Bill of Rights?*; Wallington and McBride, *Civil Liberties and a Bill of Rights*; Campbell (ed), *Do We Need a Bill of Rights?*; Wade, *Constitutional Fundamentals*.

[117]   Cmnd 7009, 1977.

[118]   HL 176 (1977–78). And see *Legislation on Human Rights, A Discussion Document*, 1976 (Home Office).

[119]   HL Bill 54 (1980–81); HL Deb, 5 December 1980, col 533; 3 February 1981, col 1102; and see HC Deb, 8 May 1981, col 419.

[120]   See HC Bill 39 (1990–91).

[121]   See ch 24 below.

[122]   See ch 22 below.

[123]   See ch 24 below.

(including a Bill of Rights) were also published in 1991.[124] But some public lawyers have expressed concern about the desirability of any constitutional change likely to give greater political power to the judiciary.[125] So far as the political parties are concerned, the Liberal Democrats are unequivocally in favour of a Bill of Rights,[126] and a Bill to incorporate the ECHR was introduced in the House of Lords by the Liberal Democrat peer, Lord Lester of Herne Hill.[127] The Conservatives prefer 'rolling constitutional change' as 'a more certain recipe for a relaxed democracy than the tumult of speculative and radical constitutional upheaval'.[128] The Labour party expressed concern that the purpose of a Bill of Rights would be 'principally declaratory', which 'would need constant and detailed interpretation by the courts, with no certainty that its general provisions would protect the most vulnerable members of the community'.[129] Subsequently, however, successive party leaders endorsed the campaign for the incorporation of the European Convention on Human Rights into domestic law, and in 1996 a consultation paper was issued by the party proposing the incorporation of the Convention to 'enable British people to enforce their rights in UK courts and enable our own judges to apply the ECHR in their jurisdictions'.[130]

A Bill of Rights is often understood as an entrenched provision with which all legislation and executive action must comply or else be struck down by the courts. In the words of Lord Scarman, a Bill of Rights would be 'a constitutional law which it is the duty of the courts to protect even against the power of Parliament'.[131] The difficulty with entrenching a Bill of Rights in this way has traditionally been the doctrine of parliamentary supremacy. In other words, the principle which has led to calls for such a device has itself been thought to be a major obstacle to its effective implementation. Conventional wisdom teaches that if legislation passed after the enactment of the Bill of Rights was inconsistent with the Bill of Rights, the courts would be bound to give effect to the most recent expression of Parliament's wishes, so that the Bill of Rights would be easily overridden.[132] But as we have already suggested, the rules relating to parliamentary sovereignty may be changing, particularly since the House of Lords in the *Factortame* case appeared to accept at least a limited entrenchment of EC law.[133] It may thus be possible to adopt a similar device in the case of a Bill of Rights. Indeed, such a precedent already exists in

---

[124]   On Liberty's proposals, see [1993] PL 579. See also Constitution Unit, *Human Rights Legislation* (1996). For a different perspective, see S Palmer, 'Critical Perspectives on Women's Rights', in Bottomley (ed), *Feminist Perspectives on the Foundational Subjects of Law*.

[125]   See J A G Griffith (1979) 42 MLR 1; K D Ewing, 'The Bill of Rights Debate: Democracy or Juristocracy in Britain?', in Ewing, Gearty and Hepple, *Human Rights and Labour Law*, ch 7; Ewing and Gearty, *Democracy or a Bill of Rights*; and T G Ison (1985) 10 Adelaide LR 1.

[126]   Liberal Democrats, *We, The People . . . Towards a Written Constitution* (1990).

[127]   See Lord Lester [1995] PL 198. This was the fourth such Bill to have been passed by the House of Lords.

[128]   Patten, *Political Culture, Conservatism and Rolling Constitutional Change*.

[129]   Labour party, *Meet the Challenge, Make the Change. A New Agenda for Britain*.

[130]   J Straw and P Boateng, *Bringing Rights Home* (1996). For a critique, see K D Ewing and C A Gearty [1997] EHRLR 146.

[131]   *English Law – the New Dimension*, p 20.

[132]   See ch 4 C, D above.

[133]   *Factortame v Secretary of State for Transport (No 2)* [1991] 1 AC 603. Although this decision appears to allow the courts not to apply post-1972 legislation in favour of an obligation

the shape of the Canadian Bill of Rights of 1960[134] which is significant in that the doctrine of parliamentary sovereignty was exported to Canada by the British North America Act 1867.[135] Section 1 of the Bill of Rights declared that certain human rights and fundamental freedoms had existed and should continue to exist in Canada 'without discrimination by reason of race, national origin, colour, religion or sex'. Those rights and freedoms included:

(*a*) the right of the individual to life, liberty, security of the person and enjoyment of property, and the right not to be deprived thereof except by due process of law;

(*b*) the right of the individual to equality before the law and the protection of the law.

By s 2, unless it was expressly declared by an Act of the Canadian Parliament that a law should operate notwithstanding the Bill of Rights, every law of Canada had to be construed and applied so as not to abrogate, abridge or infringe the rights or freedoms protected in the Bill of Rights. Crucially, in s 5 the term 'law of Canada' was defined to include federal statutes passed before and after the introduction of the Bill of Rights. But although the Bill of Rights was used in *R v Drybones*[136] to override an incompatible provision of an earlier Act of Parliament, it was never once used to trump a provision passed in a subsequent statute, at least until the rather different circumstances following the introduction of the Canadian Charter of Rights and Freedoms in 1982.[137]

The introduction of a Bill or a Charter of Rights could be done in one of several ways; indeed, there is a great variety of legal forms which a Bill of Rights could adopt. These include:

(*a*) a completely new written constitution for the United Kingdom, to include entrenched clauses devoted to fundamental rights and not liable to be overthrown by ordinary process of legislation;

(*b*) a Bill of Rights passed by Parliament intended to prevail over all earlier Acts of Parliament and judicial decisions, and which might also seek to entrench the rights declared in the Bill against subsequent Acts of Parliament;

(*c*) a Bill to incorporate within national law the European Convention on Human Rights and to empower British courts to give relief against breaches of the Convention;

(*d*) a Bill to declare certain principles which must be observed in the exercise of their powers by subordinate bodies (such as government departments and local authorities), but not applying to Parliament itself;

---

arising under EC law, it is not authority for the proposition that the courts must apply EC law even where the domestic statute states expressly that it shall apply in the event of conflict with EC law. See above, ch 8.

[134] For a full account, see Tarnopolsky, *The Canadian Bill of Rights*.

[135] See especially *Re Alberta Reference* [1938] SCR 100.

[136] [1970] SCR 282, discussed in Tarnopolsky, op cit, ch 4; V S MacKinnon [1973] PL 295; J G Sinclair (1970) 8 Osgoode Hall LJ 549; Weiler, *In the Last Resort*, ch 7.

[137] The continuing importance of the Bill of Rights is demonstrated by *Singh v Minister of Employment and Immigration* [1985] 1 SCR 177.

(*e*) a procedure to ensure that all proposed legislation is subject to parliamentary scrutiny, specifically with reference to the European Convention on Human Rights.

Of these possibilities, (*a*) is the most innovatory: in a wholly new constitution, the powers of the legislature could clearly be limited by the constitution, as most recently illustrated by developments in South Africa where a new constitution including a Bill of Rights has been introduced in the post-apartheid era.[138] Examples of Bills of Rights proposed as part of a new constitutional settlement in this country include Mr Tony Benn's Commonwealth of Britain Bill presented to the House of Commons in 1991,[139] and the Institute for Public Policy Research's proposed new constitution, also published in 1991.[140] Apart from the introduction of a Bill of Rights which would allow the courts to strike down legislation inconsistent with it, the latter proposes other reforms, including devolution, an elected second chamber and freedom of information. As a device specifically to introduce a Bill of Rights, however, this method seems unnecessary, particularly as the initiative could as easily be introduced by adopting either solutions (*b*) or (*c*) above.

A model for scheme (*b*) is to be found in the influential Canadian Charter of Rights and Freedoms of 1982 which, confusingly, operates alongside the Bill of Rights of 1960.[141] The terms of the Charter may be read in the Canada Act 1982. The Charter seeks to guarantee certain fundamental freedoms (freedom of conscience and religion, freedom of thought and expression, freedom of peaceful assembly, freedom of association), democratic rights (related to the right of citizens to vote and the holding of elections), mobility rights (the right of citizens to enter, remain in and leave Canada), rights in relation to the system of law and justice (for example, the right not to be arbitrarily detained or imprisoned), rights to the equal protection and equal benefit of the law without discrimination, and rights in respect of the two official languages of Canada. By s 24 of the Charter, anyone whose guaranteed rights or freedoms have been infringed may apply to a Canadian court 'for such remedy as the court considers appropriate and just in the circumstances'. By s 26, the guarantee in the Charter of certain rights and freedoms must not be taken as denying the existence of other rights or freedoms that exist in Canada. Two important limitations on the effect of the Charter must be noted. First, by s 1, the Charter guarantees the rights and freedoms specified 'subject only to such reasonable limits prescribed by law as can be demonstrably justified in a free and democratic society'. This appears to authorise legislative limits to be imposed on the guaranteed rights and freedoms, subject to review by the courts of the justification for such limits.[142]

---

138   See H Corder [1996] PL 291, and S Kentridge (1996) 112 LQR 257. See also Busson, *South Africa's Interim Constitution*.

139   HC Bill 161 (1990–91).

140   Institute for Public Policy Research, *The Constitution of the United Kingdom*.

141   The literature on the Charter is vast. For a general account, see Hogg, *Constitutional Law of Canada* and [1988] PL 347–401. For a recent review for a British audience, see R Penner [1996] PL 104.

142   This section reproduces in a looser and more general form qualifying provisions that are found in arts 8–11 of the European Convention on Human Rights.

Secondly, by s 33, the Charter is not entrenched against either the Federal Parliament or provincial legislatures, whenever in new federal or provincial legislation it is expressly declared that the legislation shall operate notwithstanding a named right or freedom. This power of 'express legislative override' does not apply to the rights guaranteed in respect of the two official languages of Canada. However, s 33 is in practice rarely if ever used by the Federal Parliament. The need for such a measure is perhaps most acute in emergency situations, in war or peace. But in these situations the courts are usually sensitive to the burdens of government and are generally unwilling to obstruct temporary restrictions on freedom.[143] At other times it may be very difficult politically to sponsor a Bill which contains a clause suggesting that the government is less than wholly committed to civil liberties or human rights.

A model for scheme (*c*) is to be found in the several Bills which have been introduced to incorporate the European Convention on Human Rights into domestic law. As originally introduced by Lord Lester of Herne Hill the Human Rights Bill 1995 provided by cl 1(2) that the Convention and the first protocol were to be 'incorporated in the law of the United Kingdom', and to be 'given full legal effect', to apply 'notwithstanding any rule of law to the contrary'. In a frontal challenge to what remains of Parliament's supremacy, it was further provided that:

An Act of Parliament or any instrument made by or under an Act of Parliament or an Order in Council (whether passed or made before or after the passing of this Act) shall not be enforced and may not be relied upon in any legal proceedings (including those commenced before the Act comes into force) if and to the extent to do so would deprive a person of any of the rights and freedoms defined [in the ECHR or the first protocol].

Unlike earlier Bills there was no power of legislative override of the kind contained in s 33 of the Canadian Charter requiring the Convention to give way in domestic legal proceedings to legislation which stated expressly that it is to apply notwithstanding any provision of the ECHR to the contrary. It is unclear what would be the effect if, despite the omission of such a provision, Parliament expressly stated that a particular measure was to apply notwithstanding the terms of a Human Rights Act to the contrary, though the conventional view would be that the obligation to apply the Convention would be displaced.[144] Lord Lester's Bill was not, however, passed in the form in which it was introduced, and after amendment the Bill became a candidate for inclusion in category (*d*) rather than category (*c*).[145] Before considering category (*c*) it is to be noted that one difficulty with incorporating the Convention in the manner proposed here is that in giving the domestic courts the power to refuse to apply legislation, under the Convention the body with authority to interpret the Convention is the European Court of Human Rights. If the domestic courts were to interpret it wrongly against the

---

143   The classic British example being *Liversidge v Anderson* [1942] AC 206. For the US, see Walker, *In Defense of American Liberties*.

144   Cf *Garland v BREL* [1983] 2 AC 751.

145   For an account, see Lord Lester [1995] PL 198.

government, there would be no way by which this mistake could be rectified for only individuals have a right of direct petition to Strasbourg.

A model for scheme (*d*) is to be found in the New Zealand Bill of Rights 1990.[146] This affirms the usual rights and freedoms (life, thought, conscience and religion, expression, assembly and association) but also some unusual ones (the right not to be subjected to medical or scientific experimentation and the right to refuse to undergo medical treatment). Although it purports to apply to the legislative, executive and judicial branches of the government of New Zealand, the Bill of Rights also expressly provides that no court shall in relation to any enactment (whether passed before or after the Bill of Rights), hold any provision of the enactment to be impliedly repealed or revoked or to be in any way invalid or ineffective. Thus all a court may do is to interpret an enactment in a manner consistent with the Bill of Rights (wherever such an interpretation can be given) and also use it as an additional basis for the review of administrative action.[147] It is unclear what difference this would make in English law in view of the fact that in judicial review cases the courts have regard to human rights considerations anyway. In *Brind v Home Secretary*,[148] Lord Bridge asserted that although the courts could not have regard to the Convention as a restraint on the exercise of ministerial discretion, this did not mean that they 'are not perfectly entitled to start from the premise that any restriction of the right to freedom of expression requires to be justified and that nothing less than a competing public interest will be required to justify it'. On the other hand, the Court of Appeal in *R v Ministry of Defence, ex p Smith*[149] indicated strongly that incorporation of the Convention would have the effect of introducing a higher standard of scrutiny than is permitted by the principles of judicial review, even to the extent that these permit the courts to have regard to human rights considerations. Thus although it was held that the practice of discharging homosexual men and women from the armed forces was not irrational, it does not follow that the practice would satisfy the requirements of the Convention. By art 8 this requires that any violation of the right to privacy should be shown to be 'necessary in a democratic society' on one of a number of grounds, thereby imposing a potentially much higher standard of scrutiny which embraces considerations of proportionality, as well as rationality.

The fifth scheme (*e*) is concerned to reinforce the power of Parliament rather than the courts in the protection of human rights. As such it is preferred by some on the ground that there are 'very real obstacles' to enforcement through the courts 'not least the limitations it would impose on the sovereignty of Parliament and the minimisation of democratic accountability inherent in judge-made law'. It is also argued as a practical matter that 'Reliance on redress of wrongs by the courts means that human rights are being established and protected after their infringement, not before', and that 'from the point of view of the citizen whose human rights are threatened,

---

[146] See S Levine (1991) 44 Parliamentary Affairs 337. On the operation of the New Zealand measure, see Joseph (1996) 7 Public Law Review 162. Support for this model is to be found in Woolf [1995] PL 57, at p 70.

[147] Cf A Lester and J Jowell [1987] PL 368.

[148] [1991] 1 AC 696.

[149] [1996] QB 517.

it is much better to prevent any infringement of those rights being included in legislation in the first place'.[150] Considerations of this nature have led to proposals for more effective forms of scrutiny by Parliament,[151] to prevent the enactment of legislation which is thought to violate human rights standards, which could include treaties such as the ECHR but also others which are equally important, such as the Council of Europe's Social Charter. The proposals for greater parliamentary scrutiny include (i) the creation of a new constitutional committee,[152] (ii) the formation of specialist legislative commit-tees,[153] and (iii) the use of existing committees, particularly the House of Lords Committee on the Scrutiny of Delegated Powers.[154] Most of the proposals are for a joint committee, though fuller consideration needs to be given to the question of the composition and powers of any such body, for it would be critical that it had a sufficient degree of independence from the government whose activities were the subject of scrutiny.[155] The other question relates to the powers of any such committee, with current proposals varying from those which would give it simply an advisory role,[156] to those which would give it the power to delay the passage of legislation.[157] Although there is much to be said for the greater institutionalisation of human rights considerations as part of the parliamentary process, there is no reason in principle why this could not be in combination with a strategy which gave a residual role for the courts. Parliamentary scrutiny may not be effective, for example, where the breach of human rights standards is the responsibility of the administration in a particular case rather than the legislature.[158]

Conclusion

At the time of writing there is support for new structures for the better protection of human rights and in particular for the incorporation of the European Convention on Human Rights into domestic law, though it is clear that there is no single way by which this could best be achieved. Few people it seems have confidence in Parliament's ability to restrain the illiberal tenden-cies of the executive, or in its ability adequately to attend to civil liberties issues by initiating discrete legislation to create or extend certain funda-mental rights. The reformers can point to an impressive array of supporters,

---

[150]   M Ryle [1994] PL 192. Under *Questions of Procedure for Ministers* (See ch 13 B), ministers are already required to consider the impact of the ECHR in preparing business for Cabinet (para 8).

[151]   For Labour party proposals to this effect which no longer appear to be in favour, see the 11th edn of this work, at p 430.

[152]   See K D Ewing, 'Human Rights, Social Democracy and Constitutional Reform', in Gearty and Tomkins, *Understanding Human Rights*, ch 3, and Ewing and Gearty, *Democracy or a Bill of Rights.*

[153]   Kinley, *The European Convention on Human Rights.* See also Liberty, *A People's Charter,* and Klug and Wadham [1993] PL 579.

[154]   M Ryle [1994] PL 192. See also Constitution Unit, *Human Rights Legislation* (1996). On the work of the committee, see C Himsworth [1995] PL 34.

[155]   Klug and Wadham, above.

[156]   See Kinley, above, and Ryle, above.

[157]   See Ewing, above, and Ewing and Gearty, above.

[158]   As Klug and Wadham, above, point out, experience suggests that violations are most likely to take place in the context of administrative rather than legislative action.

not only political, but also many of the senior members of the judiciary.[159] Whether in law review articles or in the course of House of Lords debates both the Lord Chief Justice (and his predecessor) and the Master of the Rolls are on record as supporting incorporation (in one form or another), as are a number of Law Lords and prominent High Court judges.[160] Their case has been undoubtedly helped by a more progressive approach to adjudication of human rights cases by the Privy Council[161] and by developments elsewhere in the Commonwealth,[162] particularly Canada, New Zealand, and now South Africa, while Australia appears also to be moving in the direction of judicial enforcement of human rights following the decision of the High Court to imply freedom of expression restrictions into the federal constitution.[163]

If the European Convention is to be incorporated into domestic law, options (*d*) and (*e*) above would provide a good basis for doing so, though it is unclear whether it would be appropriate to go further without delivering a fatal blow to the ebbing legal principle to parliamentary supremacy and the political principle of popular sovereignty which it sustains. The merit of option (*e*) is that it would be possible to combine the better protection of human rights with an enhanced role and responsibility for Parliament which in the modern constitution appears to be the weakest (when in fact it should the strongest) of our political institutions. But even a step this far in the direction of judicial review may produce what an American scholar has referred to in a study of the Canadian Charter as 'empty promises' in the absence of 'adequate resources for legal mobilisation'. In his view, 'interpreting and developing the often ambiguous provisions of a Bill of Rights depends on mobilisation of the law by individuals, but they typically lack the resources to take cases to a country's highest court'.[164] These are issues which are no less likely to arise in the context of the ECHR which is drafted in very ambiguous and often equivocal terms, though the problem could be overcome by public money being made available for litigation under the Convention. Whether this would be a prudent use of resources is a question beyond the scope of this work, and on which views will vary.

---

[159] But *quaere* whether it is desirable for judges to declare themselves on an important constitutional question which could give rise to litigation. See also Lord Hoffmann, *A Sense of Proportion* (Kelly Memorial Lecture, 1996) p 4.

[160] See HL Deb, 25 January 1995, col 1136 (Lord Chief Justice Taylor, Lord Browne Wilkinson, Lord Lloyd of Berwick, and Lord Woolf (by proxy)). See also Sir Thomas Bingham (1993) 109 LQR 390, Lord Woolf [1995] PL 57, J Laws [1993] PL 59 and [1995] PL 72. See also S Sedley [1995] PL 386. Compare Lord Irvine of Lairg [1996] PL 5.

[161] For recent cases on the death penalty in particular, see *Guerra v Baptiste* [1996] AC 397, and *Pratt v Jamaica* [1994] 2 AC 1. For an earlier unfavourable account of the work of the Privy Council, see K D Ewing, 'The Bill of Rights Debate: Lessons from the Privy Council', in Finnie, Himsworth and Walker, *Edinburgh Essays in Public Law*. See now Zander, *A Bill of Rights?*

[162] See S Kentridge [1997] PL 96.

[163] See esp *Australian Capital Television Pty v Commonwealth of Australia* (1992) 66 AJLR 695. See K D Ewing [1993] PL 256, and H P Lee [1993] PL 606. The case has spawned a voluminous literature in the Australian Law Reviews. See e.g. the special issue of the (1994) 16 Sydney Law Review 145–304 in which the piece by T D Campbell, p 195, is particularly valuable for a British audience.

[164] C R Epp (1996) 90 Am Pol Sc Rev 764.

CHAPTER 20

Citizenship, immigration and extradition

A. Citizenship

Nationality in international law

It is impossible to use a passport in travelling from one country to another without being aware of the significance of the national status which the passport attributes to its holder. Both in international and national law, the nationality or citizenship of an individual determines many aspects of the relationship which a person has with the state of which he or she is a national, and with other states. As has been said,

To the extent to which individuals are not directly subjects of international law, nationality is the link between them and international law. It is through the medium of their nationality that individuals can normally enjoy benefits from international law.[1]

By an established principle of international law, each state is entitled (subject to treaty obligations which it may have) to determine, through its constitution and other laws, who are its subjects or nationals.[2] The fact that states enact their own rules on nationality may cause some persons to have dual or multiple nationality, or (more seriously) may cause others to have no nationality, ie to be stateless.

Upon an individual's nationality, other rights and duties may depend – not only the right to hold a passport, but also liability to military service, political rights, and possibly the right to seek employment, own land, or enter the civil service. In general, most national law (the ordinary civil and criminal law, access to the legal system) applies to all those within a country, regardless of nationality. Where a state is party to the European Convention on Human Rights, it must respect the human rights of all persons within its jurisdiction, whatever their nationality.[3] But some areas of national law, notably freedom of movement and its control by immigration law, may depend crucially on one's national status.

In general, and in the absence of treaty obligations to the contrary, a state is under no duty in international law to admit citizens of foreign states

---

[1]   Jennings and Watts, *Oppenheim's International Law*, p 849.
[2]   Ibid, p 852; and Brownlie, *Principles of Public International Law*, ch XVIII, esp pp 381–6.
[3]   Ch 19 B. By customary international law, every state must observe minimum standards of treatment in respect of aliens in its territory: Jennings and Watts, op cit, p 903.

(aliens) to its territory. A state's immigration law lays down admission procedures, determines whether aliens will be admitted, regulates their status after entry and when they may be required to leave the country. Usually immigration law does not regulate the admission and removal of the state's own citizens, for the reason that a state has a duty in international law to admit to its territory such of its nationals as are not allowed to remain in the territory of other states, and no other state is obliged to admit them.[4]

Because of the importance of nationality for the individual and the state, the basic rules which determine who are citizens are often in the constitution,[5] amplified if necessary by other legislation. In the United Kingdom, nationality developed from the allegiance to the King which subjects owed at common law; and powers under the prerogative could be exercised over aliens who wished to enter or leave the jurisdiction. Only in the 20th century were nationality and immigration control placed on a statutory basis.

Today, these matters are governed primarily by the British Nationality Act 1981 (taken with the continuing effects of the British Nationality Act 1948) and the Immigration Act 1971 (as amended subsequently). These Acts must be read together for the reason that, particularly between 1962 and 1982, the legal categories of citizenship did not fit the public policies considered necessary for controlling entry to the United Kingdom from Commonwealth countries. During these years, immigration law was used to prevent certain classes of British subject from exercising their right at common law to enter the United Kingdom. To distinguish between British subjects who had the right of abode and those who did not, the Immigration Act 1971 created the concept of 'patriality'.[6] The Act of 1981 re-cast the law of nationality to take account of immigration policy, converting the criteria for 'patriality' into the criteria for citizenship. This enabled 'patriality' as such to disappear from immigration law, but its influence lives on in the new rules of nationality.

In this chapter, this section mentions the main features of nationality law; section B describes the system of immigration control; section C outlines the law of extradition, which (inter alia) enables those in the United Kingdom who are charged with, or convicted of, serious crimes in another country to be removed there in the interests of justice.

The rules of nationality and immigration law are complex. Technicalities abound, and may have crucial significance for individuals they affect. It must be emphasized that the present account is not comprehensive, and detailed exceptions are not always mentioned.

The development of nationality law[7]

The development of nationality from the common law to the British Nationality Act 1981 has been shaped by the growth of the United Kingdom, by the

---

4   Jennings and Watts, op cit, p 857.
5   See eg Constitution of the USA, 14th Amendment (1868), s 1: 'All persons born or naturalized in the US . . . are citizens of the US and of the State wherein they reside.'
6   See section B below.
7   For the current law, see Fransman, *British Nationality Law*; Macdonald and Blake, *Immigration Law and Practice in the United Kingdom*, ch 6. For the history, see Dummett and Nicol, *Subjects, Citizens, Aliens and Others*; also Jones, *British Nationality Law*, and Parry, *Nationality and Citizenship Laws of the Commonwealth*.

transition from the Empire to today's Commonwealth,[8] and most recently by European integration. The subjects of the English king were at first all those who owed allegiance to the Crown. The primary means of becoming a subject was by the 'ius soli': a person born within the King's dominions became a subject regardless of the status of the parents.[9] As early as 1350, the English statute *De natis ultra mare* applied the 'ius sanguinis' (ie birth by descent, regardless of the place of birth) so that certain persons born abroad whose fathers (or in some cases both parents) were subjects would also be subjects. In *Calvin's* case,[10] those born in Scotland after James VI of Scotland had become James I of England were held not to be aliens in England, since they owed allegiance to the same king. In 1707, English and Scottish citizens became British subjects by reason of the Treaty of Union; and they were joined by the Irish in 1800. Although citizenship was generally acquired on birth, it could also be conferred by law, when individuals or defined classes were 'naturalised' by Parliament; from 1870, the power of naturalisation was exercised by the executive.[11]

As the Empire grew, the status of 'British subject' became a common citizenship throughout most of the Empire. The British Nationality and Status of Aliens Act 1914 declared that all persons born within the King's dominions were British subjects.[12] Some territories (mainly in Africa and India) under British control were never possessions of the Crown, but were only in the protection of the Crown: persons born there became 'British protected persons', not British subjects.

At common law, those who were not British subjects were regarded as aliens. Aliens within the King's territory owed local allegiance to the monarch, and were entitled to protection of their person and property in the courts.[13] However, in the event of war being declared upon a foreign state, citizens of that state became enemy aliens; if they were in Britain, they lost their right to protection by the courts.[14] In 1698, Parliament had declared that aliens were not to be permitted to vote,[15] but it was not until 1905 that legislation restricted the entry of some aliens into the United Kingdom. In 1914, further measures for controlling the entry and presence of aliens were authorised.[16]

Until 1948, the status of British subject applied across the Commonwealth. The entry by British subjects into the United Kingdom was not restricted by

---

[8]   Ch 15 C.
[9]   An early exception to the 'ius soli' was made for those born within the territory to a foreign envoy or diplomat, or to enemy aliens.
[10] (1608) 7 Co Rep 1a. And see *Stair Memorial Encyclopedia: the Laws of Scotland*, vol 14, pp 743–4.
[11] See eg Dummett and Nicol, op cit, pp 71–7.
[12] Subject to the exception of those born to foreign diplomats and to enemy aliens.
[13] On the concept of allegiance, see the 11th edn of this work, pp 437–8. A person who owes allegiance to the Crown is subject to the law of treason (*R v Casement* [1917] 1 KB 98; *Joyce v DPP* [1946] AC 347). The Crown's duty to provide protection in return for allegiance is not enforceable by judicial process: *China Navigation Co v A-G* [1932] 2 KB 197; *Mutasa v A-G* [1980] QB 114.
[14] See p 495 below.
[15] See Will 3 c 7.
[16] British Nationality and Status of Aliens Act 1914, under which the Aliens Order 1953 was later issued.

law. Nor was there power for the executive to distinguish between British subjects present in the United Kingdom according to their place of origin. However, the dominion and colonial legislatures often restricted entry to their territories;[17] and there was no universal freedom of movement throughout the Commonwealth.

The British Nationality Act 1948

The desire of countries such as Canada and Australia to have their own citizenship laws led to the British Nationality Act 1948, enacted after a Commonwealth conference.[18] The 1948 Act assumed that each independent state would provide its own scheme of citizenship,[19] and on this basis created a common citizenship for the Commonwealth. The 1948 Act used the terms *British subject* and *Commonwealth citizen* with the same meaning, namely a person who was a citizen of the United Kingdom and colonies or of an independent state in the Commonwealth.

For the United Kingdom and its dependencies, the 1948 Act created the term *Citizen of the United Kingdom and Colonies* (CUKC). The 1948 Act did not change the common law right of all British subjects (both CUKCs and citizens of other Commonwealth states) to enter and reside in the United Kingdom; no distinction was made for this purpose between persons having a close connection with the United Kingdom, those whose home was in a colony, and those who were citizens of independent Commonwealth states.

After 1948, when a dependent territory gained independence, the legislation conferring independence generally provided that the population of the territory would cease to be CUKCs and become citizens of the new state. By virtue of that new citizenship, they would remain 'Commonwealth citizens' under the 1948 Act.[20] However, some resident in the territory might be permitted to remain as CUKCs rather than take up the new state's citizenship, as were the Asian minorities in the East African countries.[21] The independence legislation also sought to ensure that no one became stateless by losing one citizenship and gaining nothing in its place.[22]

The 1948 Act provided for a residual category of *British subjects without any other citizenship*. It also recognised the status of *British protected persons*. Irish citizens as such did not qualify to be Commonwealth citizens (Ireland left the Commonwealth on becoming a republic in 1949). However, the Ireland Act 1949 declared that they were not aliens and that Ireland was not a foreign country; while in the United Kingdom, Irish citizens may, like British subjects, exercise political rights.

---

17   Dummett and Nicol, pp 115–25.
18   See Cmd 7326, 1948.
19   Hence in the 1948 Act, s 32(7). And see *R v Foreign Secretary, ex p Ross-Clunis* [1991] 2 AC 439.
20   They would however owe allegiance to the British Crown only if their state recognised the Queen as head of state; most Commonwealth states are republics and recognise the Queen only as titular head of the Commonwealth; ch 15 C.
21   See below, section B.
22   The United Kingdom is a party to the UN Convention on the Reduction of Statelessness, 1961. See now the British Nationality Act 1981, s 36 and Sched 2.

The British Nationality Act 1981

Section B will describe how British subjects under the 1948 Act were affected by immigration policy between 1962 and 1982. The British Nationality Act 1981 created categories of citizenship which were narrower than under the 1948 Act and were intended to fit the United Kingdom's immigration policies. The Act also changed the old rule conferring citizenship on all those born in the United Kingdom, to a more complex rule by which a child born in the United Kingdom during or after 1983 becomes a British citizen only if his or her parents satisfy conditions as regards their immigration status.

Categories of citizenship

Under the 1981 Act, which came into effect on 1 January 1983, as modified subsequently,[23] there are, including Irish citizens and aliens, nine main categories of citizenship:

(1) Virtually all those who before 1983 were citizens of the United Kingdom and Colonies (CUKCs) and were patrials under the Immigration Act 1971 became *British citizens.*[24]

(2) Those who before 1983 were CUKCs by reason of their connection with a dependent territory but did not have a sufficient connection with the United Kingdom to be patrials became *British Dependent Territories citizens.*[25]

(3) Those who before 1983 were CUKCs and did not come within the first two previous categories formed a residual category, *British Overseas citizens.*[26]

(4) Because of the ending of British rule over Hong Kong in 1997, a new form of British nationality, *British Nationals (Overseas)*, was created by the Hong Kong Act 1985. British Dependent Territories citizens whose local connection was with Hong Kong could between 1987 and 1997 apply for registration as British Nationals (Overseas).[27]

(5) The term *British subject* lost the meaning which it had under the 1948 Act. It now denotes only persons who under the 1948 Act were 'British subjects without citizenship'; this included persons who were born in an independent Commonwealth country before 1949 and who neither had citizenship of that country nor became CUKCs. Some older citizens of Ireland are also British subjects.[28]

(6) The term *Commonwealth citizen* retains the broad meaning that it had under the 1948 Act. It comprises citizens of the 50 or so states of the Commonwealth, as well as all persons with British citizenship or nationality (ie categories 1–5 above).[29]

---

[23] By the British Nationality (Falkland Islands) Act 1983; the British Nationality (Hong Kong) Act 1985; and the British Nationality (Hong Kong) Act 1990.

[24] See Immigration Act 1971, s 1(1) (section B below); British Nationality Act 1981, s 11(1). And see s 11(2), (3).

[25] 1981 Act, s 23. Under the 1981 Act, those with an appropriate connection with the Falkland Islands became British Dependent Territories citizens on 1 January 1983. The British Nationality (Falkland Islands) Act 1983 provided retrospectively that the Falkland Islanders became *British citizens* on that day.

[26] 1981 Act, s 26.

[27] Hong Kong (British Nationality) Order 1986, SI 1986 No 948.

[28] 1981 Act, ss 30–31. And see Macdonald and Blake, op cit, pp 126–7.

[29] 1981 Act, s 37 and Sched 3.

(7) *British protected persons* continue under the 1981 Act with no material change from their status under the 1948 Act.[30]

(8) *Citizens of the Republic of Ireland* (unless they have a second nationality) are neither Commonwealth citizens nor aliens.

(9) The status of *alien* denotes a person who is outside categories 1–8.[31]

Under the Treaty on European Union, those who for this purpose are nationals of one of the 15 member states of the Union enjoy the status of *citizen of the Union*, and thus the rights conferred by arts 8–8e of the European Community Treaty.[32] This class comprises British citizens (category 1), British Dependent Territories citizens from Gibraltar,[33] Irish citizens (category 8) as well as the citizens of all other EU states (who, unless they have dual nationality, are aliens in UK law). Except for the Gibraltarians, those in categories 2–7 above are not European Union citizens.

We can see that the major change in categories made by the 1981 Act was to divide the former citizens of the UK and Colonies (CUKCs) into categories 1–3, to which has been added category 4 in the case of Hong Kong. Only British citizens (category 1) have the right of abode in the United Kingdom. However, by the British Nationality (Hong Kong) Act 1990, the Home Secretary was empowered to register as British citizens up to 50,000 Hong Kong residents (with their spouses and children under 18), nominated by the Governor of Hong Kong on the basis of a statutory scheme.[34]

Acquisition of British citizenship after 1 January 1983

Under the 1981 Act, there are five ways by which British citizenship may be acquired where this did not occur by operation of law on 1 January 1983.

1 Birth in the United Kingdom. A person born in the United Kingdom (in which the 1981 Act includes the Channel Islands and the Isle of Man)[35] on or after 1 January 1983 acquires British citizenship only (*a*) if his or her parents are married, and at least one of them is a British citizen or is settled in the United Kingdom; or (*b*) if his or her parents are not married, and the mother is a British citizen or is settled in the United Kingdom. To be 'settled' in the United Kingdom, a parent must be 'ordinarily resident' there without being subject under the Immigration Act 1971 to any restriction on the period for which one may remain.[36] No one is 'ordinarily resident' who is in the United Kingdom 'in breach of the immigration laws'.[37] A woman is taken to be the

---

[30] Ibid, ss 38 and 50(1). And see SI 1982 No 1070, as amended. Under the 1948 Act, a person could be both a British protected person and a CUKC: *Motala v A-G* [1992] 1 AC 281.

[31] 1981 Act, s 50(1).

[32] Such rights include the right to move and reside freely in the territory of member states, subject to limitations deriving from the EC Treaty; and the right to vote and stand in local and European elections in other member states. See ch 8; and section B below.

[33] Gibraltar is the only British dependent territory within Europe. On the UK declaration for EU purposes, see p 515 below.

[34] British Nationality (Hong Kong) (Selection Scheme) Order 1990, SI 1990 No 14.

[35] 1981 Act, s 50(1).

[36] Ibid, s 50(2); see also s 50(3), (4); and section B below.

[37] 1981 Act, s 50(5).

mother of any child born to her; a man is taken to be the father only of a legitimate child born to him.[38]

2 Adoption in the United Kingdom. A minor (ie under 18) who is not a British citizen and is adopted in the United Kingdom on or after 1 January 1983 becomes a British citizen on adoption if the adopter or one of joint adopters is a British citizen.[39]

3 Citizenship by descent. A person born outside the United Kingdom on or after 1 January 1983 acquires British citizenship by descent if at least one of the parents (*a*) is a British citizen otherwise than by descent;[40] or (*b*) is abroad in Crown service under the UK government or (on certain conditions) is working for the European Community or for certain public services.[41]

4 Registration. There are various grounds on which one who does not qualify under the above rules may be registered by the Home Secretary as a British citizen. Registration is an entitlement for someone born in the United Kingdom who did not become a British citizen at birth (*a*) if, while he or she is still a minor, a parent becomes a British citizen or settled in the United Kingdom, and an application is made for registration;[42] or (*b*) if he or she, during the first ten years of his or her life, has not been absent from the United Kingdom for more than 90 days each year.[43] The Home Secretary also has a general power to register any minor as a British citizen.[44] Registration as a British citizen is an entitlement for British Dependent Territories citizens and other categories, including British protected persons, who meet certain requirements as to being settled or present in the United Kingdom.[45]

5 Naturalisation. The Home Secretary has power to grant naturalisation as a British citizen to any person who is of full age and capacity and satisfies certain requirements as to residence, character, language and future intentions.[46]

The departure made by the 1981 Act from the rule that birth in the United

---

[38] Ibid, s 50(9). The father's position is subject to the legitimation of the child by subsequent marriage: s 47. For citizenship of a new-born infant found abandoned, see s 1(2), and for birth on ships or aircraft outside the United Kingdom, s 50(7).

[39] 1981 Act, s 1(5).

[40] For the meaning of British citizen by descent, see 1981 Act, s 14.

[41] Ibid, s 2.

[42] Ibid, s 1(3).

[43] Ibid, s 1(4). The Home Secretary has discretion to dispense with the 90-day rule: s 1(7). Under s 3, certain minors born abroad to a British citizen by descent are entitled to be registered as British citizens.

[44] Ibid, s 3(1).

[45] Ibid, s 4. There is discretion to waive most of these requirements: s 4(4). British Dependent Territories citizens from Gibraltar have an absolute right to be registered as British citizens: s 5.

[46] Ibid, s 6 and Sched 1. The requirements are less onerous where the applicant is married to a British citizen: s 6(2).

Kingdom qualifies the child for British citizenship means that a child's citizenship depends on the citizenship or immigration status of the parents. The complex rules as to registration mitigate some of the adverse effects of the new rule.

Where the Home Secretary has discretion in registration or naturalisation, it must be exercised without regard to the race, colour or religion of persons affected.[47] The Home Secretary is not required to assign any reason for granting or refusing applications which are at his or her discretion, nor are these decisions 'subject to appeal to, or review in, any court'.[48] Yet the 1981 Act also states that the court has jurisdiction concerning the rights of any person under the Act; accordingly, where an individual claims to be entitled to be registered as a British citizen, he or she may seek judicial review of a decision rejecting such an entitlement.[49] However, since the relief obtained by judicial review is itself discretionary, the court may refuse relief on public policy grounds to an applicant guilty of criminal deception in obtaining citizenship.[50] In 1996, the Court of Appeal held that, although the Home Secretary was under no duty to give reasons for refusing naturalisation, he must act fairly; he must give sufficient indication about the subject-matter of his concern as to whether the criteria for naturalisation are met, to enable the applicant to make submissions to him.[51]

Termination of British citizenship

A British citizen may renounce that citizenship to acquire another nationality, but the renunciation does not take effect until it has been registered by the Home Secretary, who may on various grounds withhold registration.[52] The Home Secretary may deprive a British citizen of citizenship acquired by registration or naturalisation,[53] but only on certain grounds, including the use of fraud, false statements or concealment to obtain citizenship,[54] disloyalty or disaffection towards the Queen, trading or communicating with the enemy and (within 5 years of becoming a British citizen) receiving a sentence of imprisonment for not less than 12 months. The Home Secretary must also be satisfied that it is 'not conducive to the public good' that the person should continue to be a British citizen.[55] Notice of the grounds must be given, and the citizen may apply for a formal inquiry to be held.[56]

---

[47]   Ibid, s 44(1).
[48]   Ibid, s 44(2).
[49]   Ibid, s 44(3).
[50]   *R v Home Secretary, ex p Puttick* [1981] QB 767.
[51]   *R v Home Secretary, ex p Fayed* [1997] 1 All ER 228, applying *A-G v Ryan* [1980] AC 718. For earlier comment on s 44, see T St J N Bates [1982] PL 179.
[52]   The Home Secretary must be satisfied that the individual will acquire some other nationality, and may refuse to register a renunciation in time of war: 1981 Act, s 12. For resumption of citizenship after renunciation, see s 13.
[53]   1981 Act, s 40.
[54]   This is the sole ground for deprivation in respect of citizens who became CUKCs by registration or naturalisation before 1983: 1981 Act, s 40(2)(b), (c). And see *R v Home Secretary, ex p Parvaz Akhtar* [1981] QB 46.
[55]   1981 Act, s 40(5)(a). Cf the 'not conducive' ground for deportation, section B below.
[56]   See also 1981 Act, s 40(6)–(8).

Aliens

The class of aliens was defined by the British Nationality Act 1981.[57]Aliens present in the United Kingdom are subject to the general law and are entitled to the protection of the courts.[58] They are also subject to common law and statutory rules affecting aliens except, in the case of European citizens, where those rules are inconsistent with EC law. Another exception applies to members of foreign armed forces visiting the United Kingdom.[59] Aliens are subject to some political disabilities: they have no right to vote (European citizens may vote in local and European elections);[60] they may not be members of the Privy Council or either House of Parliament;[61] and certain restrictions exist as to their appointment to civil or military office under the Crown.[62] Other restrictions affect the ownership by aliens of British ships and of aircraft registered in the United Kingdom.[63] Aliens benefit from the European Convention on Human Rights, the rights under which extend to all persons within UK jurisdiction,[64] and from the Race Relations Act 1976, which outlaws discrimination on grounds (inter alia) of nationality and national origin.[65] The EC Treaty excludes discrimination against nationals of member states.[66] If aliens are ill-treated while in the United Kingdom, they may seek consular or diplomatic protection from their own state.

In the event of war being declared between the United Kingdom and a foreign state, they may be interned or expelled by the Crown,[67] and are subject to other disabilities.[68] In neither the Falkland Islands campaign in 1982 nor the Gulf hostilities in 1991 was there a formal declaration of war; thus citizens of Argentina and Iraq did not become enemy aliens. In 1991, when the government detained certain Iraqi citizens in Britain, the power used was that of detention with a view to deportation under the Immigration Act 1971, a power that was not wholly appropriate.[69]

The right to travel

Under art 12(2) of the International Covenant on Civil and Political Rights, to which the United Kingdom is a party, 'Everyone shall be free to leave any

---

[57]   P 492 above.
[58]   See eg *Kuchenmeister v Home Office* [1958] 1 QB 496 and *R v Home Secretary, ex p Cheblak* [1991] 2 All ER 319.
[59]   See the Visiting Forces Act 1952; ch 16.
[60]   Ch 9 B, 1.
[61]   Act of Settlement, s 3.
[62]   Aliens Employment Act 1955, s 1, modifying the Aliens Restriction (Amendment) Act 1919, and modified by the EC (Employment in the Civil Service) Order, SI 1991 No 1221; Army Act 1955, s 21; Macdonald and Blake, op cit, pp 192–3.
[63]   Status of Aliens Act 1914, s 17; UK (Air Navigation) Order 1980, SI 1980 No 1965.
[64]   Eg *Soering v UK* (1989) 11 EHRR 439; and ch 19 B.
[65]   Ch 19 A.
[66]   EC Treaty, art 6 (formerly art 7). And see *Case C-221/89, R v Transport Secretary, ex p Factortame Ltd (No 3)* [1992] QB 680.
[67]   See *Netz v Ede* [1946] Ch 244; *R v Bottrill, ex p Kuechenmeister* [1947] KB 41.
[68]   See Jennings and Watts, op cit, pp 904–910; McNair and Watts, *The Legal Effects of War*, chs 2, 3; and 11th edn of this work, p 437.
[69]   *R v Home Secretary, ex p Cheblak* [1991] 2 All ER 319; I Leigh [1991] PL 331 and F Hampson [1991] PL 507.

country, including his own'. Since Magna Carta in 1215, it has been recognised that citizens ought to be free to enter and leave the realm. But the right to travel abroad is not protected in law as it is under the US and Irish Constitutions.[70] The old common law writ *ne exeat regno* originally enabled the Crown for reasons of state to prevent a subject from leaving the realm; it now merely prevents a wealthy defendant from leaving the jurisdiction to frustrate a lawful claim before the court, and does not enable the government to prevent a citizen from travelling abroad.[71] Despite the virtual necessity today of having a passport if one wishes to travel abroad, the issue of passports is a matter for the Crown, acting through the UK Passport Agency under authority emanating from the royal prerogative, not from an Act of Parliament. Decisions to refuse or revoke a passport are subject not to appeal but to judicial review; while the Foreign Secretary may have a policy for refusing a passport abroad to someone accused of serious crime in the United Kingdom, reasons must be given for the refusal and the citizen must have a chance to show that an exception should be made.[72] In practice, the power to refuse a passport is rarely exercised.[73]

The rights of British citizens (as European citizens) to travel within European Union states may require national courts to protect them against improper refusal of a passport. The Immigration (European Economic Area) Order 1994[74] sought to incorporate in national law free movement directives issued under the EC Treaty, but did not deal with a British citizen's right under EC law to be issued with a travel document to facilitate movement within Europe. There is certainly a case to be made for placing the system of passports upon a firm legislative base, but until that is done the freedom of movement within Europe could if necessary be protected by means of judicial review.

B.   Immigration and deportation[75]

Background to the Immigration Act 1971

In section A, we saw that at international law, and apart from any treaty obligations, a state is entitled to control entry into its territory by citizens of another state. At common law, the Crown had power under the prerogative to

---

[70]   See respectively *Kent v Dulles* 357 US 116 (1958) and *A-G v X* [1992] 2 CMLR 277, 303 (Finlay CJ).

[71]   See *Felton v Callis* [1969] 1 QB 200 and *Al Nahkakel for Contracting Ltd v Lowe* [1986] QB 235.

[72]   *R v Foreign Secretary, ex p Everett* [1989] QB 811. Passports are also withheld (*a*) to prevent a minor going abroad contrary to a court order or the wishes of the parent with custody; (*b*) until a citizen repays the cost of repatriation to the United Kingdom at public expense; and (*c*) most rarely, to protect the public interest against travel by a person whose activities are demonstrably undesirable.

[73]   See *Going Abroad: a Report on Passports* (Justice, 1974); HC Deb, 15 November 1974, col 265 (WA); HL Deb, 22 January 1981, col 558.

[74]   SI 1994 No 1895. Below, p 515.

[75]   The leading text is Macdonald and Blake, *Immigration Law and Practice*. See also Dummett and Nicol, *Subjects, Citizens, Aliens and Others*; Evans, *Immigration Law*; Harlow and Rawlings, *Law and Administration*, chs 16, 17; Legomsky, *Immigration and the Judiciary*.

prevent aliens from entering the United Kingdom.[76] As Widgery LJ said in *Schmidt v Home Secretary*:

when an alien approaching this country is refused leave to land, he has no right capable of being infringed in such a way as to enable him to come to this court for the purpose of assistance ... In such a situation the alien's desire to land can be rejected for good reason or bad, for sensible reason or fanciful or for no reason at all.[77]

At common law, though no definite authority existed, it was possible that the Crown had power to expel friendly aliens who had been previously admitted into the United Kingdom.[78] Such prerogative powers as the Crown may have in respect of aliens have been expressly preserved in being.[79] But for most of the 20th century, the executive has relied upon statutory powers for controlling the entry of aliens and for enabling aliens here to be deported.

By contrast with aliens, British subjects before and after the British Nationality Act 1948 were entitled to enter and remain in the United Kingdom without restriction and the Crown had no power to prevent their admission, to deport them or to prevent their departure.[80] These rights were in law available to the citizens of all member states of the Commonwealth.

The right of British subjects (within the meaning of the 1948 Act) to enter the United Kingdom was severely restricted by the Commonwealth Immigrants Acts of 1962 and 1968. The 1962 Act, passed to check immigration from the Caribbean, India and Pakistan, subjected all British subjects to immigration control, except for those born in the United Kingdom and those who were citizens of the United Kingdom and Colonies (CUKCs) and held passports issued by the UK government.[81] The 1962 Act also authorised the deportation of Commonwealth citizens (but not holders of UK passports) who had been convicted of offences punishable with imprisonment and recommended by a court for deportation.

The Commonwealth Immigrants Act 1968 was passed in great haste to forestall what was feared might be a mass exodus to Britain from Kenya of persons of Asian origin who, when Kenya had become independent in 1963, had chosen to continue as CUKCs rather than become citizens of Kenya. Since they held passports issued by the UK government, they were not subject to the controls established by the 1962 Act.[82] The 1968 Act was notable because it took away from a non-resident CUKC the right of entry into the United Kingdom unless he or she, or at least one of his or her parents or grandparents, had a prior UK connection (for example, through having been born, adopted or naturalised in the United Kingdom). The 1968 Act thereby

---

[76] *Musgrove v Chun Teeong Toy* [1891] AC 272; cf *Poll v Lord Advocate* (1899) 1 F 823.

[77] [1969] 2 Ch 149, 172.

[78] See Parry (ed), *British Digest of International Law*, vol 6, pp 83–98; *A-G for Canada v Cain* [1906] AC 542, 547; Dicey, *Law of the Constitution*, pp 224–7; and C L Vincenzi [1985] PL 93.

[79] Immigration Act 1971, s 33(5), which ousts the principle in *A-G v De Keyser's Royal Hotel Ltd* [1920] AC 208 (ch 12 E).

[80] Cf D W Williams (1974) 23 ICLQ 642.

[81] Passports issued by colonial governments did not entitle holders to enter the United Kingdom: *R v Home Secretary, ex p Bhurosah* [1968] 1 QB 266.

[82] For the controversy over the UK government's intentions towards the Kenyan Asians in 1963, see HC Deb, 27–28 February 1968; HL Deb, 29 February 1968; Steel, *No Entry*; Dummett and Nicol, op cit, ch 11; and Evans, *Immigration Law*, pp 64–8.

prevented CUKCs from entering the United Kingdom, even though they were subject to expulsion from the state in which they had been residing and were entitled to enter no other country. The UK government subsequently came under great pressure to admit other UK citizens in similar circumstances and, notwithstanding the 1968 Act, did admit many of the Asians expelled from Uganda in 1972.[83]

The Immigration Act 1971 and after

The 1971 Act provided a new and extensive code for the control of immigration. On 1 January 1973, when it came into operation, the legal distinction between aliens and Commonwealth citizens lost much of its significance for purposes of immigration control, but this did not mean a relaxation in the system of control. Since it was in 1973 that the United Kingdom joined the European Communities, a new distinction arose between citizens of Community countries and those from non-Community countries.

Under the 1971 Act, the most important distinction drawn was between those who had the right of abode in the United Kingdom and those (whether aliens or Commonwealth immigrants) who were subject to immigration control and needed permission to enter and reside in the United Kingdom. The fact that an intending immigrant might be a CUKC or a citizen of a Commonwealth country did not confer the right of entry. The 1971 Act created the concept of patriality to identify those British subjects who (under the new scheme) had a sufficient connection with the United Kingdom to entitle them to the right of abode there. Under the 1971 Act, s 2, the class of patrials included (i) those who were CUKCs by reason of birth, adoption, naturalisation or registration in the United Kingdom or in the Islands (ie the Isle of Man and the Channel Islands); (ii) CUKCs who had been settled and ordinarily resident in the United Kingdom or Islands for 5 years or more without being in breach of immigration law; (iii) citizens of other Commonwealth countries who were born to or adopted by a parent who at the time of the birth or adoption was a UK citizen by virtue of his or her birth in the United Kingdom or Islands; and (iv) women who were Commonwealth citizens and married to patrials. Those claiming to be patrial and wishing to enter the United Kingdom could prove their status by obtaining a certificate of patriality (s 3(9)). In *R v Home Secretary, ex p Phansopkar*, the court ordered the Home Secretary to hear and determine an application for such a certificate made by an Indian woman, married to a man who had become a UK citizen by registration; the woman's right to a certificate could not be withheld by arbitrary delay on the part of the Home Office.[84]

The elaborate concept of patriality was subject to much criticism. Foremost was the criticism that patriality did not extend to persons who, like the East African Asians, were CUKCs but had no country to which they might go other than the United Kingdom. For this reason the UK government was unable to ratify the fourth protocol to the European Convention on Human Rights,

---

[83]   Cf *R v Home Secretary, ex p Thakrar* [1974] QB 684.
[84]   [1976] QB 606; cf *R v Home Secretary, ex p Akhtar* [1975] 3 All ER 1087. See now Immigration Act 1971, s 3(9)(b), as amended in 1988 (certificate of entitlement to right of abode).

which declares that 'no-one shall be denied the right to enter the territory of which he is a national'.[85] Patriality was also criticised for including citizens of other Commonwealth countries at least one of whose parents had been born in the United Kingdom; this rule favoured those from countries such as Australia, Canada and New Zealand who were of British origin, exposing the 1971 Act to the charge that it was racially motivated.

The desire to bring the law of nationality into conformity with immigration policy and to take account of changes in the Commonwealth since 1948 was the main reason for the British Nationality Act 1981. As we saw in section A, the 1981 Act created a new category of British citizen, the rules defining which were derived from the rules of patriality. Some criticisms of the 1971 scheme remain applicable to the 1981 Act.

The Immigration Act 1988 tightened up aspects of the law, repealing the assurance given in the 1971 Act (s 1(5)) to Commonwealth immigrants resident in the United Kingdom in 1971, cutting down rights of appeal against decisions to make deportation orders, and making it a continuing offence to overstay one's leave to enter. Since 1988, the most pressing problems in immigration control have arisen in relation to the large number of claims by those from very diverse countries for admission as refugees.[86] Those problems have led to two further Acts, the Asylum and Immigration Appeals Act 1993 and the Asylum and Immigration Act 1996, making provision for dealing with claims for asylum and modifying the appeal procedures which apply to them and other visitors. What follows is an outline of the present structure of immigration control, founded on the 1971 and later Acts. As in section A, many detailed rules of practical importance are not mentioned.

Immigration control

In broad terms, the following are the main categories for purposes of immigration control. They mostly derive from the British Nationality Act 1981 and were explained in section A.

(*a*) *British citizens.* They have the right of abode in the United Kingdom and do not need leave to enter or reside there.

(*b*) *British dependent territories citizens, British overseas citizens, British subjects and citizens of other Commonwealth countries.* In general, they do not have the right of abode in the United Kingdom and are subject to immigration control. But some Commonwealth citizens, who as patrials under the 1971 Act had the right of abode in the United Kingdom, continue to have that right and are treated as if they were British citizens.[87]

(*c*) *Citizens of the Republic of Ireland.* They benefit from the 'common travel area' for immigration purposes formed by the United Kingdom, the Isle of Man, the Channel Islands and the Republic of Ireland, travel within which is in principle not subject to immigration control.[88] Irish residents enter the

---

[85] See ch 19 B and cf *R v Home Secretary, ex p Thakrar* (above).
[86] Pages 505–7 below.
[87] 1971 Act, s 2(1)(b) and (2), as amended by British Nationality Act 1981.
[88] 1971 Act, s 1(3). And see s 9 and Sched 4.

United Kingdom from Ireland without passing through immigration control, but they are subject to deportation from the United Kingdom under the 1971 Act and to exclusion under the Prevention of Terrorism (Temporary Provisions) Act 1989.[89]

(*d*) *Aliens who are nationals of other EU countries.* They benefit from the right to freedom of movement within the EU conferred by Community law, which necessarily restricts the powers of the UK authorities over them. When such persons are exercising an enforceable Community right to enter or remain in the United Kingdom, they do not require leave under the 1971 Act to do so.[90] To this category may be added the nationals of those European countries (in 1995, Norway and Liechtenstein) that, while not members of the EU, are parties to the Agreement on the European Economic Area. The area comprises all EU states together with the additional countries. The agreement, providing freedom of movement within the area for all qualified nationals of the states concerned, came into effect in 1994.[91]

(*e*) *Other aliens* (ie those outside category (*d*)). As nationals of non-EC countries, they are subject to immigration control. Similarly placed are British protected persons, who do not come within category (*b*) above.

An important practical distinction is between visa nationals (ie those from countries requiring a visa to enter the United Kingdom, which includes several Commonwealth countries) and nationals of other countries.[92]

Under the 1971 Act, as amended, those who have the right of abode in the United Kingdom 'shall be free to live in, and to come and go into and from, the United Kingdom without let or hindrance', except such as may be required under the Act to enable their right to be established (s 1(1)). Those who are not British citizens and do not have the right of abode may not enter or remain in the United Kingdom unless leave is given to them in accordance with the Act. Such leave may be given for a limited or an indefinite period. Where a person is given a limited leave to enter or remain, this leave may be given subject to conditions restricting employment or occupation in the United Kingdom, or requiring him or her to register with the police, or both (s 3(1)); where indefinite leave to remain is given, no such conditions may be imposed (s 3(3)). Even though a person has indefinite leave to remain, he or she may be deported where this would be 'conducive to the public good'.[93] A person's leave to enter or remain may lapse when he or she goes outside the common travel area and fresh leave will be needed on return (s 3(4)).

The 1971 Act exempts certain groups of non-British citizens from the need to get individual leave to enter and remain. These groups include non-British citizens who were settled in the United Kingdom on 1 January 1983; that is, they were ordinarily resident in the country and were not subject to any restriction on the period for which they might remain.[94] Formerly, Com-

---

89   Ch 25 E. See Sched 5 to the 1989 Act for travel controls within the common travel area.
90   Immigration Act 1988, s 7; and p 514 below.
91   And see the Immigration (European Economic Area) Order 1994, SI 1994 No 1895.
92   Immigration Rules, rr 24–30 and appendix. Visa requirements were first applied to Commonwealth countries in 1985 and 1986: R M White [1987] PL 350.
93   Page 508 below.
94   1971 Act, ss 1(2) and 33(2A); *R v Home Secretary, ex p Mughal* [1974] QB 313.

monwealth citizens settled in the United Kingdom when the Act came into force were assured by s 1(5) that their freedom of movement would not be restricted by rules made under the Act. The assurance was withdrawn by the Immigration Act 1988. It had not prevented powers of removal under the 1971 Act from being exercised retroactively against those who had unlawfully entered the United Kingdom in breach of earlier legislation.[95]

Other groups exempted from the need to get individual leave to enter and remain include crew members of a ship or aircraft coming temporarily to the United Kingdom, diplomats and others entitled to diplomatic privilege, and members of certain military forces.[96]

The 1971 Act equipped the Home Secretary and immigration officers with a wide variety of powers, including power to examine persons arriving or leaving the United Kingdom, to remove persons who are refused leave to enter, have entered unlawfully or have outstayed a limited leave to remain, and to detain persons pending examination or removal. Many powers of control on entry are vested directly in immigration officers. Other powers (for example, the decision to deport someone without the right of abode) are vested in the Home Secretary. Some of these powers must be exercised by the Home Secretary personally,[97] but most of them may be exercised on his or her behalf by officials in the Home Office (including members of the immigration service).[98]

Part III of the Act created many criminal offences including illegal entry,[99] overstaying a limited leave to enter or remain, failure to observe a condition of a limited leave, assisting or harbouring illegal entrants, failure without reasonable excuse to submit to examination on arrival into the United Kingdom, and securing or facilitating the entry of illegal entrants or the obtaining of leave to remain by deception.[100] Before the 1971 Act, Commonwealth citizens who managed to avoid immigration control when they entered the United Kingdom did not commit criminal offences by remaining here.[101] The offence of remaining in the United Kingdom beyond the time limit for which leave to enter was granted is a continuing offence, but not more than one prosecution may be brought in respect of the same limited leave.[102] The 1971 Act authorises the Home Secretary to meet the expenses of repatriation for a non-British citizen (and his or her family or household) who wishes to leave for a country where he or she intends to reside permanently, when it is shown that it is in that person's interest to leave the United Kingdom (s 29).

---

[95] *Azam v Home Secretary* [1974] AC 18. In 1974, the government granted an amnesty from removal to those in the *Azam* category: HC Deb, 11 April 1974, col 637.
[96] 1971 Act, s 8; Macdonald and Blake, op cit, ch 7.
[97] Eg 1971 Act, ss 13(5), 14(3) and 15(4).
[98] *R v Home Secretary, ex p Oladehinde* [1991] 1 AC 254, applying the so-called *Carltona* principle, ch 13 D above.
[99] See *R v Naillie* [1994] AC 674 and *R v Immigration Officer, ex p Chan* [1992] 2 All ER 738.
[100] It is now an offence to facilitate the entry of asylum claimants, but this does not apply to acts done otherwise than for gain, or in the course of employment by a bona fide organisation to assist refugees: Asylum and Immigration Act 1996, s 5(1), (2).
[101] *DPP v Bhagwan* [1972] AC 60.
[102] 1971 Act, s 24(1)(b), (1A); cf ss 24(3) and 28.

Immigration rules[103]

The policies of the immigration authorities may derive from primary legislation, but they are mainly contained in immigration rules which the Home Secretary lays down as the practice to be followed in the administration of the Act (1971 Act, s 3(2)). Statements of the rules must be laid before Parliament. If such a statement is disapproved by resolution of either House passed within 40 days, the Home Secretary shall 'as soon as may be' make such changes in the rules as appear to him to be required.[104] The status of the rules is difficult to define. They are not statutory instruments[105] but, as they are binding on those who decide immigration appeals, they are akin to delegated legislation, and they are far from being mere circulars or guidance.[106] They must be interpreted sensibly, according to the natural meaning of the words used,[107] and may be declared ultra vires if they conflict with a statutory provision or on other grounds.[108] The present rules, which took effect in October 1994,[109] are much fuller than earlier versions of the rules. Some passages merely refer to requirements in the parent legislation; some contain procedural rules; many state the policies which are to be applied or list the factors to be taken into account in the exercise of discretion. As we shall see, the rules have a crucial effect when appeals are brought.[110]

The 1994 rules provide that immigration control is to be exercised without regard to a person's race, colour or religion (r 2). The rules do not apply to those who are entitled to enter the United Kingdom as EU nationals (r 5). So far as entry is concerned, a person arriving in the United Kingdom must produce a valid passport or other document establishing his or her identity and nationality (r 11) and also, if this is claimed, the right of abode (r 12); prior entry clearance is required of many persons wishing to enter, in the form of a visa or an entry certificate (rr 24, 25). Certain persons are admitted for short-term visits or other temporary purposes, for example as students (rr 57–87) or for au pair placements (rr 88–94). A person arriving for employment must normally hold a work permit issued by the Department of Employment (r 128), but work permits are not needed for certain occupations, for example ministers of religion (rr 171–7) and overseas journalists (rr 136–43). Subject to conditions, admission is granted to persons intending to establish themselves in business (rr 200–23) or, if they own at least £1 million, as investors (rr 224–31). A Commonwealth citizen who can show that one grandparent was born in the United Kingdom does not need a work permit and will be admitted for four years (rr 186–93). Children born in the

---

103   See Macdonald and Blake, op cit, pp 38–41; Legomsky, op cit, pp 50–72.
104   New rules made by the government were disapproved by the Commons on 22 November 1972 and again on 15 December 1982; in each case revised rules were later approved by the Commons. And see ch 27 below.
105   Ch 27.
106   *R v Chief Immigration Officer, ex p Salamat Bibi* [1976] 3 All ER 843, 848; *R v Home Secretary, ex p Hosenball* [1977] 3 All ER 452, 459, 463; *Pearson v Immigration Appeal Tribunal* [1978] Imm AR 212, 224.
107   *Alexander v IAT* [1982] 2 All ER 766.
108   Eg *R v IAT, ex p Begum* [1986] Imm AR 385.
109   HC 395 (1994–95) (as amended); and see Macdonald and Blake, op cit, pp 699–779.
110   Below, p 505.

United Kingdom who are not British citizens because of the status of their parents,[111] have left the country and later wish to return, will in general be given leave to return on the same basis as their parents (rr 304–9). The rules apply to the granting of leave to enter or remain and to the variation of such leave (rr 31–3), for example where a person admitted as a visitor seeks leave to remain in another capacity.

One controversial policy contained in the rules applies to the spouse or fiancé(e) of a person who is settled in the United Kingdom. Among the requirements to be satisfied are that the parties to the marriage (or intended marriage) have met, that they intend to live permanently with each other, and that the primary purpose of the marriage was (or is) not 'to obtain admission to the United Kingdom'. The need to prove negatively the 'primary purpose' of a marriage presents real difficulties in practice, particularly for arranged marriages involving men coming from South Asia.[112] But there is no 'primary purpose' test in Community law and the UK rule cannot be applied to a marriage where this would deter the couple from exercising their freedom of movement under Community law.[113]

Important changes of policy can be made by alteration of the immigration rules, subject only to the parent legislation or (where applicable) to Community law. The Acts and the rules leave many difficult decisions of law, fact and discretion to be made by the immigration authorities. The rights of individuals thus depend a great deal upon the scope for appealing against decisions by immigration officials.

Immigration appeals[114]

Before 1969, there was no right of appeal against decisions refusing admission to the United Kingdom, although they were subject to review by the courts on grounds of legality. The Immigration Act 1971 provides a two-tier system of appeals.[115] The lower tier consists of adjudicators, who since 1987 have been appointed by the Lord Chancellor; some, designated special adjudicators, hear appeals concerning claims for asylum.[116] The upper tier is the Immigration Appeal Tribunal, appointed by the Lord Chancellor, whose president must be a lawyer of not less than 7 years' standing. Both adjudicators and the tribunal are subject to the supervision of the Council on Tribunals. In 1995–96, some 28 full-time adjudicators and 108 part-time adjudicators heard nearly 21,000 cases. The tribunal, sitting in two divisions of three members each, decided over 9,900 appeals,[117] but the volume of appeals continued to place the system under great pressure.

The 1971 Act did not confer a general right of appeal against every

---

[111] Section A above.

[112] See eg *R v IAT, ex p Hoque and Singh* [1988] Imm AR 216.

[113] *Case C-370/90, R v IAT, ex p Home Secretary* (ECJ) [1992] 3 All ER 798 (applying arts 48 and 52 EC Treaty).

[114] Macdonald and Blake, op cit, ch 18; Evans, op cit, ch 7.

[115] The system had been created by the Immigration Appeals Act 1969, implementing the Wilson report on immigration appeals (Cmnd 3387, 1967).

[116] Below, p 505.

[117] Annual Report of Council on Tribunals, 1995–96, p 105; and ch 28 A below.

decision that affects an immigrant, and subsequent Acts (in 1988, 1993 and 1996) both added to and took from rights of appeal under the 1971 Act. In general, and with certain exceptions, an appeal lies in respect of (*a*) the refusal of entry, entry clearance and other exclusions from the United Kingdom; (*b*) refusals to extend leave, the imposition of conditions on admission and curtailment of leave[118] (except curtailment following the refusal of an asylum claim); (*c*) refusals of asylum;[119] and (*d*) decisions on deportation and removal.[120] The list of matters in which there is no right of appeal was lengthened by the Asylum and Immigration Appeals Act 1993 (ss 10–11), and includes (i) refusal of entry clearance or leave to enter as a visitor, for short-term study, or as a potential student (there is a right of appeal only where the individual held a current entry clearance); (ii) refusal of entry because the individual does not have the required passport, entry clearance or work permit, or does not satisfy a requirement of the immigration rules as to age or nationality; (iii) a variation of leave or refusal to vary leave if the application to vary was made after the expiry of the existing limited leave;[121] (iv) curtailment of an asylum-seeker's leave after rejection by the Home Secretary of the asylum claim;[122] (v) refusal of a work permit or a special entry voucher;[123] and (vi) refusal of leave to enter where the Home Secretary has personally directed that a person's exclusion is conducive to the public good.[124]

Written notice to the individual must be given of any decision that may be appealed against, together with the reasons for it.[125] Even where there are rights of appeal, important restrictions apply. In general, a person may not appeal against a refusal of leave to enter while in the United Kingdom, unless he or she is claiming asylum[126] or was refused such leave at a port of entry when holding a current entry clearance or work permit.[127] Thus many appeals can be brought only after the appellant has left the United Kingdom. Where a person who has a limited leave to remain in the United Kingdom applies before the expiry of that leave for an extension in the time limit, that leave to remain is deemed to be extended until 28 days after the Home Secretary's decision on the application. If he or she appeals against that decision, he or she cannot be required to leave the United Kingdom so long as the appeal is pending.[128] The rule that an appeal can be brought only if the appellant first leaves the United Kingdom is in itself no reason why the individual should

---

[118]   Immigration Act 1971, ss 13–14. And see *R v IAT, ex p Coomasaru* [1983] 1 All ER 208.
[119]   See p 505 below.
[120]   See below, p 508.
[121]   Immigration Act 1971, s 14(1); and *Suthendran v IAT* [1977] AC 359. The effect of *Suthendran* was modified by SI 1976 No 1752, as amended by SI 1989 No 1005 and SI 1993 No 1657.
[122]   1993 Act, s 7(2).
[123]   *Pearson v IAT* [1978] Imm AR 212; *Amin v Entry Clearance Officer, Bombay* [1983] 2 All ER 864.
[124]   Immigration Act 1971, s 13(5).
[125]   For appeals procedure, see SI 1984 No 2040, and SI 1984 No 2041 and (for asylum appeals) SI 1993 No 1661.
[126]   1993 Act, s 8, subject to Asylum and Immigration Act 1996, s 3(2).
[127]   1971 Act, s 13(3).
[128]   See n 121 above.

seek judicial review rather than use the right of appeal, but in exceptional circumstances recourse to judicial review may be justified.[129]

Where an individual exercises a right of appeal, what are the powers of the adjudicators over the decision appealed against? By s 19 of the 1971 Act, an adjudicator must allow an appeal in two situations: (i) if he or she considers that the decision was not in accordance with the law[130] or with the relevant immigration rules (for this purpose he may review questions of fact); (ii) if he or she considers, where the decision involved the exercise of discretion, that the discretion should have been exercised differently. Otherwise the appeal must be dismissed. No decision in accordance with the immigration rules is to be treated as having involved the exercise of discretion merely because the Home Secretary was asked to depart from the rules and refused to do so (s 19(2)). These rules also bind the Immigration Appeal Tribunal, to whom an appeal may lie with leave from the adjudicator's decision. A refusal of leave to appeal is subject to judicial review. Selected decisions by the tribunal are published and bind adjudicators. Given this framework of rules and an independent hierarchy to administer them, decisions that involve the exercise of discretion may be reviewed by adjudicators without, from the Home Office point of view, creating too great a risk of decisions on appeal that cut across the regular pattern of administration. The system has at times been criticised for being unduly influenced by the Home Office[131] and in some areas of law (notably claims for asylum and the primary purpose rule regarding marriage) the decisions of some adjudicators reflect a 'culture of disbelief'. However, effective steps to foster the independence of the appeals system have been taken since 1987, and the right to appeal continues to be a vital aspect of immigration control.

Before 1993 there was no further appeal from decisions of the Immigration Appeal Tribunal, but these were subject to judicial review in the High Court.[132] Since 1993, there has been an appeal on law (from final determinations made by the tribunal) with leave to the Court of Appeal or (where the adjudicator's decision was made in Scotland) to the Court of Session.[133]

Apart from the appeal process, the Home Office can always be asked to make a different decision. In practice, the Home Secretary exercises an exceptional discretion[134] to permit individuals to enter or remain in the United Kingdom even though the adjudication authorities cannot do so. In asylum cases, exceptional leave to remain may be granted on humanitarian or other grounds where the case for asylum status is not made out.

Refugees and asylum status

A refugee is defined for purposes of immigration law as one who 'owing to a well-founded fear of being persecuted for reasons of race, religion, nation-

[129] *R v Home Secretary, ex p Swati* [1986] 1 All ER 717; *R v Chief Immigration Officer, ex p Kharrazi* [1980] 3 All ER 373.
[130] Which includes the principles of administrative law: *Singh v IAT* [1986] 2 All ER 721, 728. Cf *R v IAT, ex p Home Secretary* [1992] IAR 554; and Macdonald and Blake, op cit, pp 577–80.
[131] E.g. Evans, op cit, pp 362–74 (written in 1983).
[132] Page 511 below, and chs 29, 30.
[133] Asylum and Immigration Appeals Act 1993, s 9.
[134] The legal basis for which is uncertain: C Vincenzi [1992] PL 300.

ality, membership of a particular social group or political opinion' is outside his or her country of nationality and because of such fear is unwilling to return to it.[135] By customary international law, it is for each state to decide whether to grant asylum to those who seek it. Long before the Geneva Convention of 1951, the British government admitted political and other refugees when it chose to do so, taking into account the national interest.[136] By ratifying that Convention, the government undertook (inter alia) not to expel or return refugees in any manner whatsoever to the frontiers of a territory where their lives or freedom would be threatened for one of the Convention reasons quoted above: this is the duty of 'non-refoulement'.[137] The duty is not breached if, instead of being returned to the country where they fear persecution, asylum-seekers are sent to a safe third country; whether this can be done is often a very contentious issue.[138]

While immigration rules have long included procedure for dealing with asylum claims, only in 1993 did Parliament recognise the 1951 Convention by declaring that nothing in the immigration rules 'shall lay down any practice which would be contrary to the Convention'.[139]

Under the 1994 immigration rules,[140] all claims to asylum are to be determined by the Home Secretary, acting through authorised officials,[141] not by immigration officers at the ports of entry. Asylum decisions were formerly subject only to judicial review on grounds of legality, and the House of Lords explained why they should be closely scrutinised:

The most fundamental of all human rights is the individual's right to life and, when an administrative decision under challenge is said to be one which may put the applicant's life at risk, the basis of the decision must surely call for the most anxious scrutiny.[142]

To decide whether someone's fear of persecution for a Convention reason is established, the Home Secretary must on the basis of objective facts consider if there is a real risk or likelihood of that person being persecuted.[143] An applicant for asylum is not protected by the Convention where there are serious reasons indicating that he or she has committed a crime against

---

[135]   Geneva Convention relating to the Status of Refugees, 1951, art 1(A), applied by Asylum and Immigration Appeals Act 1993, s 1. And see Macdonald and Blake, op cit, ch 12.

[136]   See Dummett and Nicol, op cit, ch 8.

[137]   Art 33, Geneva Convention of 1951. Under the European Convention on Human Rights, art 3, the UK must not return an individual to a country where he or she is likely to suffer torture or inhuman treatment: eg *Chahal v UK*, note 145 below.

[138]   See eg *R v Home Secretary, ex p Abdi* [1996] 1 All ER 641 (HL) (return of Somalis to Spain, where they had stayed briefly before reaching the UK; evidence necessary to decide whether the Spanish government could be relied on to comply with the Convention).

[139]   Asylum and Immigration Appeals Act 1993, s 2. And the 1994 Immigration Rules, part 11 (Asylum).

[140]   Part 11, rr 327–52.

[141]   In accordance with *Oladehinde's* case, note 98 above.

[142]   *R v Home Secretary, ex p Bugdaycay* [1987] AC 514, 531 (whether Home Secretary had properly decided whether Ugandan would be at risk of being sent on to Uganda if he were returned to Kenya).

[143]   *R v Home Secretary, ex p Sivakumaran* [1988] AC 958. The applicant must prove that there is a real risk of persecution, not that persecution is more probable than not.

humanity, a war crime or a serious non-political crime.[144] Although the Home Secretary may consider that a person's presence in the United Kingdom is on security grounds not 'conducive to the public good', the person's claim to asylum must still be considered on its facts and a balancing exercise may be necessary.[145]

Since 1993, an asylum-seeker whose claim is refused by the Home Secretary has had a right of appeal to a special adjudicator on the ground that removal would be contrary to the Convention.[146] There is a further appeal on law (with leave) to the Immigration Appeal Tribunal.[147] If the Home Secretary certifies that an individual's Convention claim is 'without foundation', a much speedier procedure is used, and there is no appeal from the special adjudicator. Under the 1993 Act, the fast-track procedure was available where the certificate was based on the fact that the applicant could be sent to a safe third country.[148] In 1996, the law was changed to enable many more claims for asylum to be dealt with as being 'without foundation'; a claim may not be disposed of in this way where there is a reasonable likelihood that an applicant had been tortured.[149] The 1996 Act restricted other rights of appeal open to claimants for asylum, and prevents claimants sent to certain third countries designated by the Home Secretary from appealing so long as they are in the United Kingdom.[150] The 1996 Act validated social security regulations which deprived asylum-seekers of the right to receive various social benefits if they had claimed asylum after entering the country and not at the port of entry.[151] The Act sought generally to reduce the numbers of those making asylum claims.

In an earlier attempt to reduce the numbers of claimants arriving in the United Kingdom, the Immigration (Carriers' Liability) Act 1987 imposed onerous obligations on airlines and shipping companies to ensure that they bring to the United Kingdom only passengers with the necessary documents to establish their identity, nationality and entry clearance.[152] However, under the 1951 Convention, art 31, refugees coming directly from a country in which they are persecuted may not be penalised for using false documents if on arrival they report themselves to the authorities promptly.

Under the Treaty of European Union, as we see below, asylum policy is one of the matters stated to be of common interest to member states in relation to cooperation in the fields of justice and home affairs.[153]

---

[144] *T v Home Secretary* [1996] AC 742 (airport explosion killing innocent civilians); and section C below.

[145] *R v Home Secretary, ex p Chahal* [1995] 1 All ER 658. The European Court of Human Rights decided differently: *Chahal v UK, The Times,* 28 November 1996.

[146] Asylum and Immigration Appeals Act 1993, s 8. For the procedure, see SI 1993 No 1661.

[147] 1993 Act, s 9.

[148] See *R v Home Secretary, ex p Mehari* [1994] QB 474.

[149] Asylum and Immigration Act 1996, s 1.

[150] 1996 Act, ss 2 and 3.

[151] Ibid, s 11 and Sched 1, reversing the Court of Appeal's decision that the regulations were ultra vires: *R v Social Security Secretary, ex p JCWI* [1996] 4 All ER 385. See also *R v Kensington Council, ex p Kihara* (1997) 9 Admin LR 25.

[152] See A Ruff [1989] PL 222. And Macdonald and Blake, op cit, pp 28–32.

[153] See ch 8; and p 516 below.

Deportation and removal from the United Kingdom[154]

The power to deport a person is a drastic power which must be subject to political and judicial safeguards. Under the law before 1971, aliens could be deported *either* where a court recommended deportation of an alien convicted for a criminal offence punishable with imprisonment *or* if the Home Secretary deemed it 'conducive to the public good' that an alien should be deported. The latter power proved highly resistant to attempts to control it through recourse to the courts.[155] Indeed, the deportation power could be used as 'disguised extradition' since, although the Home Secretary could not name the country to which the alien must go, he could achieve the same result by placing the alien on a specified ship or aircraft.[156]

Under the Immigration Act 1971 and the British Nationality Act 1981, there is no power to deport British citizens; all those who are not British citizens are in principle subject to the same powers of deportation. A non-British citizen may be deported in five situations: (*a*) if, having only limited leave to remain, he or she broke a condition of the leave or overstayed the limit;[157] (*b*) if he or she obtained leave to remain by deception;[158] (*c*) 'if the Secretary of State deems his deportation to be conducive to the public good';[159] (*d*) if another person to whose family he or she belongs is ordered to be deported;[160] or (*e*) if, aged 17 or more, he or she is convicted of an offence punishable with imprisonment and is recommended for deportation by the court.[161] If a deportation order is made, it requires the person named to leave the United Kingdom and prohibits him or her from returning until the order is revoked; it ceases to have effect if he or she becomes a British citizen or, in case (*d*) above, ceases to belong to the family of the original deportee (for example, on becoming 18).[162]

Certain exemptions from deportation were given to Commonwealth citizens and citizens of Ireland who were ordinarily resident in the United Kingdom on 1 January 1973.[163] EU citizens are not as such exempt from deportation, but exercise of the power must have regard to their rights under Community law.[164]

Three procedural matters may be mentioned. First, before a deportation

---

154 Macdonald and Blake, op cit, ch 15; Immigration Rules 1994, part 13.
155 See eg *R v Leman Street Police Inspector, ex p Venicoff* [1920] 3 KB 72 and *R v Governor of Brixton Prison, ex p Soblen* [1963] 2 QB 243, criticised by P O'Higgins (1964) 27 MLR 521.
156 *R v Home Secretary, ex p Chateau Thierry* [1917] 1 KB 922. For extradition, see section C below.
157 Immigration Act 1971, s 3(5).
158 Asylum and Immigration Act 1996, Sched 2, para 1(2).
159 This power may be used against a person who obtained entry by deception: *R v IAT, ex p Patel* [1988] AC 910.
160 For this purpose, a person's family means (*a*) his or her spouse and (*b*) the children under 18 of either of them: Immigration Act 1971, s 5(4), amended by Asylum and Immigration Act 1996, Sched 2. And see 1971 Act, s 15(6).
161 Immigration Act 1971, s 3(6); see s 6 for the procedure, including the individual's right of appeal (s 5(5)), and Sched 3.
162 Immigration Act 1971, s 5(2), (3).
163 Immigration Act 1971, s 7.
164 See eg *R v Home Secretary, ex p Santillo* [1981] QB 778 (timing of court's recommendation); *R v Home Secretary, ex p Dannenberg* [1984] QB 766 (reasons); and text at notes 208–19 below.

order is made, a 'decision to deport' must have been taken and it is then that a right of appeal may arise.[165] Secondly, power to detain an individual pending deportation arises when the decision to deport is made, when a court has recommended deportation and when the deportation order is signed.[166] In each case, the detainee may be granted bail or released on temporary admission subject to conditions. Thirdly, a person liable to deportation may always make a voluntary or supervised departure.

Under the 1971 Act, there are powers for summary removal of illegal entrants and others refused entry that may be exercised without a deportation order.[167] These powers are of increased importance since the courts have held that illegal entry is not confined to clandestine entry (that is, complete avoidance of immigration control) but also includes entry by deception through the use of false documents, the making of false representations and even non-disclosure of material facts.[168]

Appeals against deportation

The decision as to whether an individual should be deported may involve the exercise of a broad discretion,[169] especially if the issue is whether deportation would be 'conducive to the public good'. Circumstances affecting individuals vary widely and rights of appeal also vary. Under the Immigration Appeals Act 1969, there was a full right of appeal to an adjudicator and then to the Immigration Appeal Tribunal against deportation decisions. This applied to decisions made on 'conducive to the public good' grounds, but such decisions taken on grounds of national security were subject only to an appeal to an advisory panel, which had power to hear evidence in the absence of the appellant.[170]

The Immigration Act 1971 made a different attempt to reconcile the conflicting interests of justice, political discretion and national security. The complicated provisions for appeals against deportation decisions may be outlined as follows:

(*a*) Where a criminal court after recording a conviction has recommended deportation, appeal against the recommendation lies to a higher criminal court, not to the immigration appeals system. If the Home Secretary accepts the recommendation, there is no further appeal.[171]

(*b*) Where the Home Secretary decides to deport a person for breach of an entry condition or for overstaying, appeal lies to an adjudicator and thence to the Immigration Appeal Tribunal,[172] subject to (*c*) and (*d*) below.

---

[165] See Immigration Act 1971, s 15(2).
[166] The power of an immigration officer to detain for examination those suspected of being illegal entrants applies to a claimant for asylum, *R v Home Secretary, ex p Khan* [1995] 2 All ER 540.
[167] Immigration Act 1971, Sched 2, paras 8–10.
[168] Macdonald and Blake, op cit, ch 16; *R v Home Secretary, ex p Zamir* [1980] AC 930; and *R v Home Secretary, ex p Khawaja* [1984] AC 74; p 512 below.
[169] See the Immigration Rules, paras 364–7.
[170] This procedure was used only once, in the case of a German student leader who wished to do research at Cambridge: see B A Hepple (1971) 34 MLR 501.
[171] Immigration Act 1971, s 6(5).
[172] Ibid, s 15(1).

(*c*)   Where a person is to be deported because he or she belongs to the family of a person who is being deported, the appeal lies direct to the tribunal; where such an appeal is related to an appeal against deportation within (*b*) above, both appeals go direct to the tribunal.[173]

(*d*) Appeals under (*b*) and (*c*) are subject to the restriction that where the deportee was last given leave to enter the United Kingdom less than 7 years before the deportation decision, the adjudicator and the tribunal may consider only whether there is in law the power to deport for the reasons stated in the notice of the decision.[174]

(*e*)   Where the ground of the decision is that the deportation is conducive to the public good, appeal lies direct to the tribunal. There is, however, no right of appeal if the decision is that deportation is conducive to the public good 'as being in the interests of national security or of the relations between the United Kingdom and any other country or for other reasons of a political nature'.[175] In this case, in lieu of an appeal, the individual may be given a private hearing before a panel of three advisers of the Home Secretary. The reason for this non-statutory procedure was stated by the Home Secretary in 1971 to be that deportation decisions based on national security 'are decisions of a political and executive character which should be subject to Parliament and not subject to courts, arbitrators and so on'.[176] The procedure was tested in 1977.

Deportation orders in the interests of national security were made against two American journalists, Agee and Hosenball. It was claimed that they had sought to obtain and publish information harmful to the security services. At a hearing before the panel of three advisers, the Home Office gave no further particulars of the allegations or of the evidence, nor was the panel's report on the appeal seen by the deportees. When Hosenball sought judicial review of his deportation, the Court of Appeal upheld the decision, holding that natural justice must give way to the interests of state security; the Home Secretary was responsible to Parliament for the decision and for holding the balance between national security and individual freedom.[177]

This procedure was utilised in 1990, when Iraqis in Britain were detained during the Gulf hostilities: the Court of Appeal refused to intervene.[178] If an EU citizen were subjected to deportation on 'not conducive to the public good' grounds which were such as to prevent there being an appeal to the Immigration Appeal Tribunal,[179] questions as to the compatibility of UK law with Community law would arise as regards both substance and procedure.[180]

---

[173]   Ibid, s 15(7).
[174]   Immigration Act 1988, s 5; *R v Home Secretary, ex p Oladehinde* [1991] 1 AC 254, approving *R v Home Secretary, ex p Malhi* [1991] 1 QB 194; S S Juss (1992) 12 LS 364. For those exempt from the restriction, see 1988 Act, s 5(2) and SI 1993 No 1656.
[175]   Immigration Act 1971, s 15(3).
[176]   HC Deb, 15 June 1971, col 375. However, the grounds on which there is no right of appeal go much wider than national security.
[177]   *R v Home Secretary, ex p Hosenball* [1977] 3 All ER 452.
[178]   *R v Home Secretary, ex p Cheblak* [1991] 2 All ER 319. See also I Leigh [1991] PL 331 and F Hampson [1991] PL 506.
[179]   Which is envisaged in such a situation by the Immigration (European Economic Area) Order 1994, art 20(2)(d).
[180]   Cf *R v Home Secretary, ex p Adams* [1995] All ER (EC) 177; *R v Home Secretary, ex p McQuillan* [1995] 4 All ER 400.

The Immigration Act 1971 made one improvement in the law of deportation. Formerly a deportee had no right to challenge the choice by the Home Secretary of the country to which he or she was to be sent. Yet the essence of the power to deport is to ensure that someone leaves this country, not that he or she is sent to another. Under the 1971 Act, s 17, where directions are given for removal following the making of a deportation order, the individual may appeal to an adjudicator against the directions on the ground that he or she ought to be removed to a different country from that named. Subject to such an appeal, the Home Secretary may direct removal either to a country of which the deportee is a citizen or to one where there is reason to believe that he or she will be admitted.[181] The deportee has no absolute right to go to the country of his or her choice, but the right of appeal reduces the risk of deportation being used as 'disguised extradition'.

Judicial review of immigration decisions[182]

In principle, decisions under the 1971 Act are subject to judicial review. However, if the decision of an immigration officer or the Home Secretary is subject to an appeal to an adjudicator or to the Immigration Appeal Tribunal, an individual will normally be expected to appeal rather than to have direct recourse to the courts.[183] The remedies obtainable on judicial review, which are discretionary, are available where either there is no right of appeal or the applicant can show that there are exceptional grounds on which, despite the right of appeal, the court should intervene to assist the applicant.[184] Those decisions of adjudicators which are not subject to appeal (for example, the decision of a special adjudicator upholding the Home Secretary's certificate that an asylum claim is 'without foundation') are subject to judicial review. Since 1993, the decisions of the Immigration Appeal Tribunal have been subject to an appeal on law to the Court of Appeal;[185] this will generally cause the High Court to refrain from granting leave for judicial review. Habeas corpus, which is not a discretionary remedy, is available to enable the legality of a person's detention to be reviewed,[186] but it is not the primary means of challenging a decision to detain an immigrant pending his removal.[187]

The grounds on which immigration decisions may be reviewed include a breach of duty by the Home Office,[188] failure to take account of relevant considerations[189] and abuse of power. For example, if it could be shown that a deportation order was made for an improper purpose, the order could be

---

181 Immigration Act 1971, Sched 3, para 1.
182 Macdonald and Blake, op cit, pp 620–5; Legomsky, op cit, ch 1. For judicial review, see chs 29, 30.
183 *R v Home Secretary, ex p Swati* [1986] 1 All ER 717.
184 As in *R v Chief Immigration Officer, ex p Kharrazi* [1980] 3 All ER 373.
185 Asylum and Immigration Appeals Act 1993, s 9.
186 As in *R v Governor of Durham Prison, ex p Hardial Singh* [1984] 1 All ER 983 and *R v Home Secretary, ex p Khan* [1995] 2 All ER 540.
187 *R v Home Secretary, ex p Muboyayi* [1992] QB 244. See A P Le Sueur [1992] PL 13 and M Shrimpton [1993] PL 24.
188 E.g. *Phansopkar's* case, note 84 above.
189 *R v Home Secretary, ex p Bugdaycay* [1987] AC 514.

quashed by the courts, but the burden of establishing this is a heavy one.[190] The interpretation of a statutory provision may be reviewed by the courts and so may interpretation of the immigration rules.[191] Although an immigration officer must give an intending visitor the reasons why entry is refused, in *R v Home Secretary, ex p Swati* a bare statement that the applicant had not shown that he was a genuine visitor was held to be sufficient.[192]

Difficult questions may arise as to whether findings made by the immigration authorities are supported by the evidence. Under the 1971 Act, s 3(8), the burden of proving that a person is a British citizen or is entitled to any exemption under the Act is placed on the person asserting it. But it may be difficult to determine the truth of past events, particularly where an intending immigrant has not always told the same story,[193] or to decide a person's future intentions.[194] The approach of the courts in reviewing findings made by the immigration authorities has fluctuated. Some courts have been willing to intervene only when there are no grounds upon which the authorities could reasonably have come to a particular conclusion, a test derived from *Associated Provincial Picture Houses Ltd v Wednesbury Corpn*.[195] In 1980, the House of Lords applied this test in upholding a decision that a Pakistani citizen, Zamir, should be deported as an illegal entrant, who on entry had not revealed that he had married after receiving an entry certificate.[196] In 1983, the House adopted a different approach in *Khawaja*'s case, holding that the question whether an individual is an illegal entrant is a 'precedent fact', which has to be established to the satisfaction of the court.[197] Only when this fact can be established on the available evidence, does the power to remove the individual arise. The approach adopted in *Khawaja*'s case in relation to such a key issue enables the courts to protect the individual against executive decisions that affect his or her liberty. Thus, if the Home Secretary decided to deport someone wrongly believing him or her not to be a British citizen, the question of citizenship must be decided by the court itself; the court should not confine itself to deciding whether the Home Secretary's belief was in the circumstances reasonable.

To what extent can immigration decisions be challenged on grounds of natural justice?[198] Under the former law, the Home Secretary was not required to give a hearing before deciding to deport an alien or deciding that he or she should leave the United Kingdom.[199] The extension of immigration control to all non-British citizens and the creation of an appeals system has broadened the scope for the application of natural justice. In *Re H K*, which concerned the investigation by an immigration officer into the question of whether an intending immigrant was under 16 and the son of a Commonwealth citizen

---

190   *Soblen*'s case, note 155 above.
191   Eg *Kharrazi*'s case, note 184 above.
192   [1986] 1 All ER 717.
193   *R v Home Secretary, ex p Mughal* [1974] QB 313.
194   *R v Immigration Appeals Adjudicator, ex p Khan* [1972] 3 All ER 297.
195   [1948] 1 KB 233; ch 29 A.
196   *R v Home Secretary, ex p Zamir* [1980] AC 930.
197   *R v Home Secretary, ex p Khawaja* [1984] AC 74; and Macdonald and Blake, op cit, p 525.
198   Ch 29 B.
199   Note 155 above; *Schmidt v Home Secretary* [1969] 2 Ch 149.

settled in England, the court held that the officer was bound to act impartially and fairly; to that extent he or she must observe the rules of natural justice, but he or she need not hold any full-scale inquiry nor adopt judicial procedure.[200] In the case of citizens from EC countries, the United Kingdom is not free to adopt whatever procedure it likes. In *R v Home Secretary, ex p Santillo*, the deportation of an Italian citizen, who had been convicted of serious sexual offences and recommended for deportation by a British court, was challenged unsuccessfully on grounds of natural justice. However, in its judgment the European Court of Justice established that Community law, on which Santillo could rely, may impose procedural requirements (including the right of representation and defence before an independent authority) greater than those imposed by national law.[201] As we shall see below, the immigration authorities are required to observe Community law in decisions applying to citizens of EC countries. But, despite an earlier difference of judicial opinion, immigration officers are not required to have regard to the European Convention on Human Rights.[202]

The European Court of Human Rights in 1991 held that judicial review provides effective control over immigration decisions in the case of refugees seeking asylum, even though such review is confined to aspects of illegality, irrationality and procedural propriety.[203]

Parliamentary oversight of executive decisions

There is wide political interest in immigration. The practice and policies of the immigration authorities are often controversial. When changes are made to the immigration rules, a statement of the changes must be laid before Parliament and either House may resolve to disapprove the statement within 40 days of the laying.[204] Immigration statistics are published annually to Parliament. Individual decisions, particularly in deportation cases, may give rise to questioning or debate in Parliament. Despite the system of appeals, MPs are often anxious to raise with the Home Secretary the personal circumstances of individuals who are refused permission to stay in the United Kingdom. Political pressure may be exercised to persuade the Home Secretary to depart from the immigration rules in favour of an individual, a matter that is beyond the powers of the adjudicator or the Immigration Appeal Tribunal.[205] Such political intervention seems essential to mitigate distress and hardship caused by over-rigid administration of the law. Complaints of maladministration in immigration matters may be sent by MPs to the Parliamentary Ombudsman, although he or she may not investigate a complaint where it was reasonable for the individual to exercise a right of

---

[200] [1967] 2 QB 617. See also, as to claims for refugee status, *ex p Bugdaycay* (note 189 above) and *Gaima v Home Secretary* [1989] Imm AR 205.

[201] *Case 131/79, R v Home Secretary, ex p Santillo* [1981] QB 778.

[202] *R v Chief Immigration Officer, Heathrow, ex p Salamat Bibi* [1976] 3 All ER 843, now approved in *R v Home Secretary, ex p Brind* [1991] 1 AC 696. See Macdonald and Blake, op cit, pp 455–62; and ch 19 B.

[203] *Vilvarajah v UK* (1991) 14 EHRR 248.

[204] Immigration Act 1971, s 3(2). And see note 104 above.

[205] Ibid, s 19(2). And see p 505 above.

appeal to an adjudicator or tribunal.[206] It was formerly the practice of the Home Office not to remove a person from the United Kingdom when representations on the case by an MP were being considered, but such representations do not now necessarily prevent a removal or deportation from taking place.[207] Aspects of immigration policy and administration are examined from time to time by the Home Affairs Committee of the House of Commons.

Immigration law and the European Union

One aim of the Treaty of Rome 1957 in establishing the European Community was to abolish, as between member states, 'obstacles to the free movement of persons, services and capital'.[208] The Treaty was amended by the Single European Act 1986 and the Treaty on European Union 1992, but the aim is still to protect freedom of movement for workers and also freedom of establishment, namely the right of individuals and companies to set up undertakings and to supply services within member states (arts 48, 52 and 59, EC Treaty). By art 6 of the Treaty, discrimination on grounds of nationality is prohibited. By art 48, discrimination based on nationality between workers of member states as regards employment, remuneration and other labour conditions is prohibited. Subject to 'limitations justified on grounds of public policy, public security or public health', workers of member states may accept offers of employment made within a member state, move freely for this purpose, stay in a member state for employment, and remain after being employed there. Detailed provision is made by EC regulations and directives for the freedom of movement for workers and their families, and for their equal treatment by national authorities without discrimination as regards nationality.[209] A worker's right of entry extends to the spouse, children who are under 21 or dependent on the worker, grandchildren, and the dependent parents or grandparents of the wage-earner and spouse.[210]

As we saw in section A, the Treaty on European Union provided for every national of a member state to be a citizen of the Union, having the right to move and reside freely within member states, subject to limitations and conditions in the Treaty and in implementing measures. Although by three directives in 1990 the right of residence was extended to categories of persons other than workers, European citizens who are outside the category of worker do not enjoy directly the rights of members of that category.

It is not possible here to summarise the measures and decisions which give effect to these Community rights.[211] The immigration rules formerly made

---

[206] Ch 28 D.
[207] Macdonald and Blake, op cit, p 42.
[208] Art 3(c) EC Treaty. And see Macdonald and Blake, op cit, ch 8.
[209] Including EC Regulations 1612/68 and 1251/70, Directives 64/221, 1612/68, 68/360, 73/1148, 75/34, 77/86, 90/364, 90/365 and 93/96.
[210] EC Regulation 1612/68, art 10.
[211] See eg Craig and de Burca, *EC Law*, ch 15; Wyatt and Dashwood, *European Community Law*, ch 9; F Burrows, *Free Movement in Community Law*. Also Macdonald and Blake, op cit, ch 8 and materials at pp 849–99.

some provision for EC nationals and their families to enter the United Kingdom to take up employment, set up homes and so on, but these rules did not fully recognise the free movement rights of Community nationals. Since 1994, persons who are exercising their Community rights do not require leave under the 1971 Act to enter and remain in the United Kingdom;[212] their position is governed by the Immigration (European Economic Area) Order 1994.[213]

Some other matters may be briefly noted. First, Community law leaves it to each member state to decide who are its nationals for EC purposes. In 1972, the government's declaration, annexed to the final Act of the Treaty of Accession, defined UK nationals for Community purposes as (*a*) citizens of the United Kingdom and Colonies (CUKCs), and also British subjects who were not citizens of a Commonwealth country, who in either case had the right of abode in the United Kingdom; and (*b*) persons who were CUKCs by birth, naturalisation or registration in Gibraltar (or whose fathers were). This declaration omitted (i) citizens of Commonwealth countries other than the United Kingdom (even if they were patrial); and (ii) CUKCs and Commonwealth citizens who were settled in the United Kingdom, but not patrial. For special reasons, those who held UK citizenship by virtue of a connection with the Channel Islands or the Isle of Man were excluded from freedom of movement in Community law.[214] When the British Nationality Act 1981 came into effect in 1983, the government made a new declaration, placing UK nationals in three categories for purposes of EC law: (*a*) British citizens, (*b*) British subjects with the right of abode in the United Kingdom, and (*c*) British Dependent Territory citizens from Gibraltar.[215]

Secondly, the provisions of Community law which provide for the free movement of persons are directly effective within national law,[216] thereby restricting powers which could otherwise be exercised under the Immigration Act 1971. For example, the power of the Home Secretary to exclude or deport an alien on the ground that his or her presence would not be conducive to the public good is limited by EC Directive 64/221 which by art 3(1) provides: 'Measures taken on grounds of public policy or of public security shall be based exclusively on the personal conduct of the individual concerned' and by art 3(2): 'Previous criminal convictions shall not in themselves constitute grounds for the taking of such measures.'

In *Case 41/74, Van Duyn v Home Office*, a Dutch scientologist offered employment at a college of scientology in England, was denied entry, the Home Secretary having decided that it was undesirable to grant anyone leave to enter the United Kingdom for such employment. On a reference under art 177, EC Treaty, the European Court of Justice held that the provision in the directive quoted above was directly effective and that the voluntary act of an individual in associating with a particular organisation could be regarded 'as a matter of personal conduct'. The ban on persons entering the

---

[212]   Immigration Act 1988, s 7, brought into force by SI 1994 No 1923.
[213]   Above, note 91. The Order is examined by C Vincenzi [1995] PL 259.
[214]   Treaty of Accession, protocol 3, arts 2, 6.
[215]   And notes 32, 33 above.
[216]   See ch 8 B.

United Kingdom to take employment with the college did not therefore conflict with the directive.[217]

These restrictions on the Home Secretary's powers in respect of EC nationals are enforced through the British courts. The directly effective provisions of Community law are binding on adjudicators and the Immigration Appeal Tribunal.[218]

Thirdly, the Treaty on European Union marked a new stage in closer European integration by providing in Title 6 for member states to cooperate (outside the Community structure) in justice and home affairs on such matters as asylum policy, control over the external borders of states, immigration policy and policy regarding nationals of third countries. Such cooperation is to be in compliance with the European Convention on Human Rights and the 1951 Convention on the Status of Refugees, but not so far as to affect the responsibility of states for law and order and internal security.[219]

C. Extradition

The statutory background[220]

The object of extradition is to ensure that those accused or convicted of serious crime do not escape from justice by crossing international boundaries. Extradition is the procedure by which a person present in state A may be arrested by the authorities of that state and surrendered to state B, for the reason either that he or she is wanted to stand trial for a criminal offence in state B, or that he or she has been convicted in state B of an offence and is wanted back to serve the lawful punishment. This procedure gives rise to questions both of international and national law, and requests for extradition may raise issues which are politically sensitive within a state or internationally. Sometimes an alternative to extradition is for state A, where the requested person is found, to place that person on trial in its own courts rather than return him or her to stand trial in state B. This is possible where the law of state A permits extraterritorial jurisdiction to be exercised over the alleged offences.[221]

In the United Kingdom, extradition procedures are statutory, and the police have no common law powers to arrest anyone with a view to his or her extradition.[222] Before the Extradition Act 1989, the law on extradition comprised three main forms. First, extradition to and from some 50 foreign states (not including Ireland, nor states in the Commonwealth) was governed

---

217   [1975] Ch 358. See *Case 30/77, R v Bouchereau* [1978] QB 732 (deportation after criminal offence); and *Case C-370/90, R v IAT, ex p Home Secretary* [1992] 3 All ER 798 (primary purpose rule).
218   See eg *R v IAT, ex p Antonissen* [1992] Imm AR 196.
219   Treaty on European Union, arts K.1, K.2.
220   Jones, *Extradition*, provides a guide to the law and reproduces relevant texts. See also Gilbert, *Aspects of Extradition Law*.
221   See eg Suppression of Terrorism Act 1978, s 4; Aviation and Maritime Security Act 1990, s 1. Certain offences committed in the Republic of Ireland may be tried in Northern Ireland, and vice versa: Criminal Jurisdiction Act 1975 and (in the Republic) Criminal Law (Jurisdiction) Act 1976.
222   *Diamond v Winter* [1941] 1 KB 656.

by the Extradition Acts 1870–35 and by bilateral treaties entered into between the United Kingdom and each of the states. Secondly, extradition between Commonwealth states was governed by the Fugitive Offenders Act 1967 (replacing an Act of 1881 with the same name). Thirdly, and not directly affected by the 1989 Act, the return of escaping wrongdoers between the United Kingdom and the Republic of Ireland was (and continues to be) undertaken not by extradition but by a simple procedure authorised in UK law by the Backing of Warrants (Republic of Ireland) Act 1965. In brief, arrest warrants issued in the Republic may be endorsed by a justice of the peace in the United Kingdom; if the named person is arrested by the British police, the justice may be required to order his delivery to the Irish authorities. Some of the same safeguards that exist in extradition law apply to the procedure; in particular, offences of a political character are excluded.[223]

During the 1980s, it became evident that aspects of the first two forms of extradition made it too difficult for criminals to be extradited from the United Kingdom, and extensive changes were made by the Criminal Justice Act 1988.[224] The Extradition Act 1989 was then enacted to consolidate the earlier legislation, as amended in 1988. One aim of the new law was to harmonise the procedures for extradition to and from foreign states with those for extradition to and from Commonwealth countries. Its enactment enabled the United Kingdom to ratify the European Convention on Extradition,[225] so that extradition to and from some 24 European states (including Cyprus) is now conducted on the basis of that Convention.

So far as extradition to and from non-European foreign states is concerned, the United Kingdom could not by its own act alter the treaties with those states which had effect under the former Extradition Acts. Accordingly, those treaties remain in force, and the machinery by which they apply, derived from the 1870 Act, is now found in Sched 1 of the 1989 Act.[226] However, all new treaties will operate under the 1989 Act, and existing bilateral treaties will be re-negotiated for this purpose.

So far as Commonwealth countries are concerned, the Fugitive Offenders Act 1967 had operated by the mutual agreement of Commonwealth states and without a structure of formal treaties; in 1990, an amended scheme for dealing with fugitive offenders was adopted by Commonwealth states and this enabled the Extradition Act 1989 to be applied.[227]

In the outline which follows, emphasis is given to the law enacted in the 1989 Act (section references in the text are to that Act). Some reference will be made to case-law under the earlier legislation, much of which is still relevant. It must not be assumed, however, in any particular instance that the

---

[223] The UK case-law includes *Keane v Governor of Brixton Prison* [1972] AC 204 and *R v Governor of Winson Green Prison, ex p Littlejohn* [1975] 3 All ER 208. The equivalent law in the Republic is in the Extradition Act 1965 (No 17), as amended. For the Irish case-law, see H Delany and G Hogan [1993] PL 93. See also the 11th edn of this work, pp 465–7.

[224] See *A Review of the Law and Practice of Extradition in the United Kingdom* (Home Office, 1982); Cmnd 9421, 1985; and Cmnd 9658, 1986. Also C Warbrick [1989] Crim LR 4.

[225] SI 1990 No 1507.

[226] Two notable instances in 1995 were Belgium (which had not ratified the European Convention on Extradition) and the USA: Jones, op cit.

[227] Commonwealth Scheme for the Rendition of Fugitive Offenders, as amended in 1990. For designation of the states, see SI 1991 No 1700.

general provisions in the 1989 Act necessarily apply, since (except within the Commonwealth) the procedure may still be governed by Sched 1 to the Act.

Availability of extradition procedures

For extradition between the United Kingdom and a foreign state to occur, there must usually be in place 'general extradition arrangements'. These will often take the form of a bilateral treaty between the two states made in accordance with the Act of 1989 (or the Extradition Acts 1870–1935), and to which the relevant legislation has been applied, with any necessary exceptions or qualifications, by Order in Council (1989 Act, ss 3, 4). Such 'general extradition arrangements' may also be created by a multilateral treaty such as the European Convention on Extradition 1957, which the United Kingdom ratified in 1990.[228]

In the absence of general extradition arrangements with a foreign state, the United Kingdom and that state may agree to operate 'special extradition arrangements' in the case of a particular individual (ss 3(3)(b), 15). The existence of general extradition arrangements is proved conclusively by the relevant Order in Council, and the existence of special extradition arrangements by a certificate from the Foreign Secretary (ss 4(3), 15(2)).

In the case of extradition to and from Commonwealth states, the 1989 Act applies to every such state which has been designated for the purpose by Order in Council, and it also applies generally in relation to every colony (ss 1(2), 5).[229]

Definition of extradition crime

Formerly, under the Extradition Acts 1870–1935, a crime giving rise to extradition existed where the conduct charged if committed within English jurisdiction would have been within the classes of crimes listed in Sched 1 to the 1870 Act. This list has been added to and varied from time to time: for example, the Criminal Justice (International Cooperation) Act 1990 provided that offences contrary to the Drug Trafficking Offences Act 1986 are to be extraditable offences. However, an extradition treaty might contain a list of offences narrower than that in the 1870 Act, or impose restrictions on the 1870 Act list, or might expressly impose a rule of double criminality ie requiring exact equivalence between the definition of the crime in the two states concerned. After many years in which a different view of the law was taken, it was held by the House of Lords that, apart from specific treaty provisions to the contrary, there was no general rule of double criminality.[230] The House also held that the English magistrate considering a request for extradition ought not to hear evidence as to foreign law nor consider the terms of the treaty, and should consider only whether the conduct alleged was

---

228   Note 225 above.
229   See also ss 32–4 (special provision for colonies) and *R v Governor of Brixton Prison, ex p Kahan* [1989] QB 716 (Fiji's designation not affected by departure from Commonwealth).
230   *Re Nielsen* [1984] AC 606, disapproving *Re Arton* [1896] 1 QB 108; see also *United States of America v McCaffery* [1984] 2 All ER 570.

an offence in English law.[231] In respect of Commonwealth states, a double criminality test was imposed under the Fugitive Offenders Act 1967.[232]

Under the 1989 Act, there is no list of extradition offences. Instead, an extradition crime means primarily conduct in the territory of the requesting state which is punishable under the law of that state with imprisonment for a term of 12 months or more, and which would be so punishable if it occurred in the United Kingdom (s 2(1)(a)). The effect of this change is to bring more offences within the scope of extradition. Extra-territorial offences may under similar conditions be extradition crimes (s 2(1)(b)), and conduct on a vessel, aircraft or hovercraft of a state is treated as if it were conduct within that state's territory (s 2(4)(b)).

The Extradition Act 1989 extends the purposes of extradition to include a number of offences (such as unlawful seizure of aircraft, the taking of hostages, and unlawful acts in relation to nuclear material) which are the subject of international multilateral conventions. Such offences may be the basis of requests for extradition from states that are parties to those conventions but do not have general extradition arrangements with the United Kingdom (s 22).

Offsetting the wider scope of extraditable offences, there continue to be many restrictions on the return of individuals, and an elaborate procedure must be observed before extradition takes effect.

General restrictions on return of individuals

Under the 1989 Act, part II, the same general restrictions on the return of individuals apply whether the requesting state is a foreign state or a member of the Commonwealth. However, in the case of a particular foreign state, additional restrictions can be imposed by conditions in the extradition treaty.

Of primary importance is the rule that no person shall be returned if it appears 'that the offence of which that person is accused or was convicted is an offence of a political character' (s 6(1)(a)). Since a similar rule has applied to extradition since 1870, the earlier case-law may still be relevant. In regard to those who seek asylum, as we have already seen, the 1951 Convention does not apply to a person where there are reasons for considering that he or she 'has committed a serious non-political crime' before seeking admission as a refugee.[233] Thus someone who has committed a 'serious non-political crime' is denied refugee status and may be subject to extradition; but someone who has committed an 'offence of a political nature' is not subject to extradition for that act and may claim asylum.

The phrase 'offence of a political character', used in the Extradition Act 1870 and now in the 1989 Act, has been found difficult to interpret. In 1996, the English decisions were reviewed by the House of Lords in a case arising from a claim for asylum.

---

[231] *R v Governor of Pentonville Prison, ex p Sinclair* [1991] 2 AC 64.
[232] *Government of Canada v Aronson* [1990] 1 AC 579. And see Cmnd 3008, 1966, para 10, cited in [1990] 1 AC at 592.
[233] Convention relating to the Status of Refugees, 1951, art 1F(b); and see note 144 above.

In *T v Home Secretary*, the asylum-seeker was an Algerian who belonged to a revolutionary fundamentalist movement in Algeria and had been involved in two terrorist incidents: the more serious one was the planting of a bomb at a civilian airport in which 10 members of the public were killed; the other was an attempt to steal arms from army barracks, during which one person was killed.

Lord Lloyd (Lords Keith and Browne-Wilkinson concurring) defined a crime as a 'political crime' for the purposes of the 1951 Convention if: '(1) it is committed for a political purpose, ie, with the object of overthrowing or subverting or changing the government of a state or inducing it to change its policy; and (2) there is a sufficiently close and direct link between the crime and the alleged political purpose. In determining whether such a link exists, the court will bear in mind the means used to achieve the political end, and will have particular regard to whether the crime was aimed at a military or governmental target, on the one hand, or a civilian target on the other, and in either event whether it was likely to involve the indiscriminate killing or injuring of members of the public'.[234] On the facts, the two crimes in which T was involved satisfied condition (1) but not condition (2) and could not be regarded as political. The Home Secretary's decision not to grant T asylum was upheld.

Lord Mustill agreed with the result, but not with the test of 'sufficiently close and direct link' between the crime and the alleged purpose. He preferred to exclude from the concept of political crimes acts of terrorism, which he held to be criminal acts directed against a state ('depersonalised and abstract violence') and intended to create terror in the minds of a group of persons or the general public.[235] Lord Slynn took a similar approach, holding that 'serious non-political crime' included acts of violence which were intended or likely to create a state of terror in the minds of individuals or the public and which caused, or were likely to cause, injury to persons who had no connection with the government of the state.[236]

Since the House in this case accepted that the same basis for defining political offences would apply both to asylum and extradition, it is not necessary here to review the earlier extradition decisions in any detail. However, they are generally consistent with the new definition.[237] Thus, in 1891, the alleged killing of a municipal guard in the course of an armed uprising against the cantonal government in Switzerland was held to be an offence of a political character.[238] In 1894, anarchist explosions in Paris were held to be directed against the public at large, not against the government, and were not political offences.[239] In *Schtraks v Government of Israel*,[240] offences of child stealing and perjury were committed in the course of a family dispute over the religious upbringing of a young boy. The subject of the dispute was a matter of political controversy in Israel, but the offences were held not to be of a political character: the fugitive was (in Lord Radcliffe's words) not at odds with the Israeli government on some issue connected with the political control or government of the country;[241] moreover, the Israeli government was con-

---

[234]   [1996] AC 742, 786–7. And see *R v Home Secretary, ex p Fininvest SpA* [1997] 1 All ER 942 (applying *T v Home Secretary*, offences related to political corruption in Italy were not political in character).

[235]   [1996] AC at 773.

[236]   Ibid at 776.

[237]   The decisions are summarised in Jones, op cit, ch 6.

[238]   *Re Castioni* [1891] QB 149.

[239]   *Re Meunier* [1894] 2 QB 415. And see *Re Arton (No 1)* [1896] 1 QB 108.

[240]   [1964] AC 556.

[241]   Cf *R v Governor of Brixton Prison, ex p Kolczynski* [1955] 1 QB 540.

cerned only to enforce the criminal law and did not have ulterior political motives for seeking Schtraks' extradition. The requirement of a political conflict between the fugitive and the state requesting extradition was applied by the House of Lords when a Taiwanese citizen, while in the USA, took part in the attempted murder of a Taiwanese political leader hoping to bring about a change in the Taiwan government. The US government obtained the fugitive's return to serve his sentence in the USA. Lord Diplock confined the 'political offence' exception to offences in which the offender's political purpose was directed against the government of the state requesting his surrender, and not against a third state.[242]

The decision in *T v Home Secretary* must be seen against the background of increasing concern about terrorism and the necessity for securing international cooperation to deal with terrorists[243] and for outlawing such crimes against humanity as genocide.[244] Within the Commonwealth, offences against the life or person of the head of the Commonwealth (ie the Queen) are declared not to be offences of a political character.[245]

The return of offenders is subject to other general restrictions imposed by the 1989 Act. Thus, a person may not be extradited if the request for the return is in fact made 'for the purpose of prosecuting or punishing him on account of his race, religion, nationality or political opinions' or, if returned, he or she might be prejudiced at the trial or be punished, detained or restricted by reason of such opinions (s 6(1)(c), (d)). This restriction broadly corresponds to the test applied under immigration law to claims for refugee status.[246]

A convicted person may not be extradited if the conviction was obtained in his or her absence and it would not be in the interests of justice to return him or her because of the conviction (s 6(2)). Nor may someone be returned to stand trial who, if tried in the United Kingdom, would be discharged under the 'double jeopardy' rule because he or she has previously been tried for the offence (s 6(3)). The Act seeks to prevent abuse of the procedure by requiring that before an individual is extradited, arrangements must exist to ensure that after the return he or she will be tried only for the offences for which the extradition was sought and that he or she must be given an opportunity to leave the country again before being tried for other offences, save with the consent of the Secretary of State (s 6(4)–(7)). That consent can be given only if the additional offences were themselves extraditable (s 6(6)).

Extradition procedure[247]

In general, proceedings under part III of the 1989 Act are commenced by a request being made to the UK government by a diplomatic or consular representative of a foreign state, or by a Commonwealth government (s 7(1)).

---

242   *Cheng v Governor of Pentonville Prison* [1973] AC 931.
243   See especially the Suppression of Terrorism Act 1978, s 1 (certain offences not to be regarded as of a political character when requesting state is a party to the European Convention on the Suppression of Terrorism), and Extradition Act 1989, s 24.
244   See Extradition Act 1989, s 23(1).
245   Ibid, s 6(8).
246   Note 135 above.
247   This account deals only with procedure on extradition under part III of the Act, not on extradition under Sched 1.

On receiving a request containing the requisite information (s 7(2)), the Home Secretary[248] may issue an authority to proceed, unless it appears that an order for extradition could not lawfully be made or would in fact not be made (s 7(4)). When authority to proceed is given, a warrant for the arrest of the individual to be extradited may be issued by the chief metropolitan magistrate (in Scotland, by the sheriff of Lothian and Borders) (s 8(1)(a)). In case of urgency, a provisional warrant may be issued by any magistrate, justice of the peace or sheriff in the absence of authority to proceed (s 8(1)(b); notice of the warrant has to be given to the Home Secretary, who may then issue an authority to proceed or may cancel the provisional warrant (s 8(4)).

When an individual is arrested on a warrant issued under the Act, he or she must be brought before either a metropolitan magistrate (in London) or the sheriff of Lothian and Borders (in Edinburgh), sitting as a court of committal (s 9(1)).[249] The court of committal must in every case be satisfied that the offence in question is an extradition crime and may in some cases need to decide whether there is sufficient evidence to make a case requiring an answer by the individual if the proceedings had been a summary trial of an information against him or her.[250] In a significant change from the procedure under the Extradition Acts 1870–1935, the court of committal is not required to consider the sufficiency of the evidence if the request is made by a foreign state and the general extradition arrangements with the state provide for this (s 9(4)).[251]

If the court refuses to commit the individual to custody or on bail, the requesting state may challenge the refusal in law by requiring the court to state a case for the opinion of the High Court (in Scotland, the High Court of Justiciary) on the question of law involved (s 10). This procedure was not available before the 1989 Act.[252]

If the court makes a committal order, the individual has the right to apply to the High Court for a writ of habeas corpus within a period of 15 days: he or she cannot be extradited during that time and until the habeas corpus proceedings are settled (s 11).[253] On such an application, the High Court may order discharge if it seems to the court (by reason of the trivial nature of the offence, or of the passage of time since it was committed,[254] or because the accusation is not made in good faith in the interests of justice) that in all the circumstances it would be unjust or oppressive to extradite him or her (s 11(3)).[255] The High Court on a habeas corpus application will consider matters such as whether the magistrate had jurisdiction to order the committal or whether there was material on which the order could properly have been made. But the High Court will not re-examine facts which were before

---

248 Or a Minister of State or an Under-Secretary of State: s 28(1).
249 On the duties of the magistrate as court of committal, see *In re Evans* [1994] 3 All ER 449.
250 1989 Act, s 9(8), amended by Criminal Justice and Public Order Act 1994, s 148(5).
251 For difficulties caused by the rule that the court of committal must be satisfied of the sufficiency of evidence, see eg *R v Governor of Ashford Remand Centre, ex p Postlethwaite* [1988] AC 924. The duty to consider if the evidence is enough to justify committal still applies under the 1989 Act, Sched 1: *R v Governor of Pentonville Prison, ex p Alves* [1993] AC 284.
252 *Atkinson v United States* [1971] AC 197.
253 An equivalent to habeas corpus is available in Scotland: s 11(6).
254 On delay, see eg *Oskar v Government of Australia* [1988] AC 366.
255 See *Re Schmidt* [1995] 1 AC 339.

the magistrate nor generally admit fresh evidence. However, the 1989 Act permits additional evidence to be received that is relevant to the court's power to decide whether it would be unjust or oppressive to extradite the applicant, or that relates to the power of the court to apply the general restrictions on return (including the exception for offences of a political character) already summarised.[256] There is an appeal, with leave, to the House of Lords from the High Court.[257]

If the application for habeas corpus does not succeed, the Home Secretary may by warrant order the individual to be returned to the requesting state, unless that return is prohibited by the Act or the Home Secretary decides to make no such order (s 12(1)). The Home Secretary has a general discretion as to whether to make an order (s 12(2)), but no order must be made if, having regard to the same grounds as the High Court could consider on habeas corpus, it would be unjust or oppressive to do so. He may also decide not to order the return if the person could be or has been sentenced to death for the offence for which return is sought (s 12(2)(b)).[258] No order may be made for return of a person who is serving a prison sentence, or is facing charges for an offence, in the United Kingdom (s 12(3)). Moreover, the Home Secretary must at this stage consider whether any of the general restrictions on return[259] are applicable.

If the Home Secretary is minded to order extradition, notice of this must be given (s 13(1)) and the individual then has 15 days in which to make representations as to why he or she should not be extradited (s 13(2)). When the Home Secretary orders the return to take place, it is not to be implemented for at least 7 days. During this time, the individual may seek judicial review of the Home Secretary's decision to make the order (s 13(6)).[260] If the individual does so, no return may take place so long as proceedings for judicial review are pending (s 13(7)).

This elaborate scheme provides time limits within which the warrant for an individual's extradition has to be carried out, after which the court may order his or her discharge (s 16). A much simpler procedure may be applied if the individual decides not to challenge the decision to remove him or her (s 14).

The general restrictions on return which were described earlier apply at almost every stage of this procedure, since they must be taken into account by the Home Secretary, the court of committal and the High Court (in Scotland, High Court of Justiciary), whether on an application for habeas corpus or for review of an order of committal (s 6(1), (9)).

Wider benefit from the reformed law enacted in the Extradition Act 1989 will be felt when the United Kingdom concludes new bilateral treaties bringing it into effect in respect of those foreign states not yet within its scope. Before then, conditions in Europe and beyond may lead to proposals for a simpler approach to the problem of escaping criminals that would reduce the

---

256 Text at notes 233–46 above.
257 Administration of Justice Act 1960, s 15.
258 Cf *Soering v United Kingdom* (1989) 11 EHRR 439.
259 Text at notes 233–46 above.
260 For judicial review, see chs 29, 30.

temptation (to which the United States has unhappily succumbed)[261] for states to resort to self-help by kidnapping wanted offenders who have taken refuge abroad. Within Europe, such events would be in breach of the European Convention on Human Rights, which permits the lawful exercise of powers of extradition.[262] In 1993, the House of Lords held that the power of the High Court to stay a prosecution on the grounds of abuse of process could be exercised where an accused person had been brought to England from South Africa by an irregular procedure.[263] Some requests for extradition made by governments may be groundless or even abusive, but many are not. It must be remembered that the ease with which state boundaries can be crossed today presents an evident advantage to those who wish for their own reasons to escape from the law, or at least wish to delay the normal machinery of criminal justice.

---

[261]   *US v Alvarez-Machain* 119 L Ed 2d 441 (1992).
[262]   See European Convention on Human Rights art 5(1)(f) and eg *Bozano v France* (1987) 9 EHRR 297 (disguised extradition held to be unlawful deportation).
[263]   *R v Horseferry Road Magistrates' Court, ex p Bennett* [1994] 1 AC 42. Cf *In re Schmidt* (note 255 above).

CHAPTER 21

The police and personal liberty

The preservation of law and order and the prevention and detection of crime are matters of great importance to the maintenance of organised government. But it is equally important that these concerns should not be used to justify equipping the police with more power than is absolutely necessary, for every power conferred on police officers inevitably means a corresponding reduction in the liberty of the individual. It is difficult to exaggerate the central importance of personal liberty in a free and democratic society. As the European Court of Human Rights reminded us, protection from arbitrary interference by the state with an individual's liberty is 'a fundamental human right'.[1] There is thus a need to ensure that the police have adequate measures to protect the public without at the same time conferring powers that undermine the very freedom which the police are employed to defend. This chapter considers how this problem of modern democracy is resolved in English law. Sections A and B are concerned with the organisation, structure and accountability of the police, and provide the background to the issues considered in sections C to F, namely the statutory and common law powers of the police to interfere with personal liberty, powers such as the power of arrest and the powers of search and seizure.

A. Organisation of the police[2]

While the executive has a strong interest in maintaining an effective police system, the central government does not itself undertake the policing of the country. In 1962, a royal commission which inquired into the constitutional position of the police in Great Britain examined the arguments for and against establishing a national police force. The commission rejected the view that a national force would lead to a totalitarian 'police state', considering that a national force in Britain would be subject to the law and to the authority of Parliament. But, except for an incisive dissenting opinion from Dr A L Goodhart, the commission concluded that the police should not be brought under the direct central control of the government and that the

---

[1] *Brogan v United Kingdom* (1989) 11 EHRR 117, at 134.
[2] For a stimulating account of the issues, see Lustgarten, *The Governance of Police.*

police should continue to be linked with local government; provided that the responsibilities of central government and the controls from the centre were made more explicit, a system of local police forces should be continued.[3] The commission's report led to the Police Act 1964 which, as amended subsequently, contained the main legal framework of the police system in England and Wales until 1994. As such it provided a structure of the police which is 'sui generis': while police forces have connections with local government, the police system is not a typical local government service; nor is it in form a central government service, although its operation is supervised by central government.

Yet within this framework there are signs of a growing centralisation of policing activity and a tendency towards the concentration of power in the hands of the Home Office. As we shall see, the Home Secretary has always had extensive supervisory powers in respect of local policing, and indeed could on occasion assert some degree of supervision over operational matters. A major step in this direction was taken in the Police and Magistrates Courts Act 1994 which conferred a number of additional powers on the Home Secretary and indeed gave him powers in respect of the membership of local police authorities, though the latter proved much less directly intrusive than had originally been proposed. Part II of the consolidating Police Act 1996 (headed 'Central Supervision, Direction and Facilities') gives the Home Secretary powers to set objectives for police authorities and to direct police authorities to set performance targets, as well as powers to give directions as to minimum budgets. A further step in the direction of the greater centralisation of police activity is to be seen in the Police Act 1997, and the provision which it makes in Part I for the National Criminal Intelligence Service, and in Part II for the National Crime Squad. The function of the former is to acquire and provide criminal intelligence for police forces (s 2), while the function of the latter is to prevent and detect serious crime which is of relevance to more than one police area in England and Wales (s 48). According to the government 'the arrangements for both services will be firmly rooted in our structure of local policing.'[4]

Local police authorities

Under the Police Act 1996, England and Wales are divided into police areas, of which there are three kinds: the Metropolitan Police district, the City of London police, and those listed in Sched 1 of the Act. The Metropolitan Police was created in 1829 as the first modern British force: it is the only police force for which the Home Secretary is directly responsible as the police authority. It is subject to the Metropolitan Police Acts which have been passed since 1829 and to some provisions of the Police Act 1996. The chief officer is the Commissioner of Police for the Metropolis, who is appointed by the Crown on the advice of the Home Secretary, together with Assistant Commissioners. The Commissioner appoints constables and has powers of suspension

---

3   Cmnd 1728, 1962, ch 5; cf memorandum of dissent by A L Goodhart. And see Marshall, *Police and Government*, and J Hart [1963] PL 283.
4   HC Deb, 12 February 1997, col 345.

and dismissal; he has power to make orders for the general government of the force, subject to the Home Secretary's approval. The City of London Police are a separate force; the chief officer, the Commissioner, is appointed by the police authority, the Court of Common Council, subject to the approval of the Home Secretary. Outside London there are 41 police areas listed in the Schedule, giving a total of 43, the same number as before the 1994 reforms. In the white paper preceding the 1994 Act, the government did announce, however, that it intended to implement a programme of police force amalgamation in the future, and powers to alter police areas are now to be found in s 32 of the Police Act 1996, to be exercised by the Home Secretary where it appears expedient 'in the interests of efficiency or effectiveness'. The Act also provides that for each police area there shall be a police authority (which in turn shall be a body corporate), but as a result of controversial measures introduced in 1994, the composition of these authorities has changed, most notably by the reduction in the number of local authority councillors. Although local authority representatives will still be in the majority (with 9 out of the standard membership of 17), 5 of the members are to be appointed from a short-list prepared by the Home Secretary. The remaining members are appointed by local magistrates from amongst their number, whereas before the 1994 changes, one-third of the membership of the committee was appointed in this way.

The 1996 Act retains the duty whereby each police authority must secure the maintenance of an effective and efficient police force for its area (s 6). But in discharging this duty police authorities are required to have regard to any objectives which may be set by the Home Secretary; the local policing objectives and performance targets set by the police authority; and any local policing plan, local policing authorities now being required to issue such plans on an annual basis (s 6). Subject to the approval of the Home Secretary, the police authority appoints the chief constable, as well as assistant chief constables (though in this latter case after consultation with both the chief constable and the Home Secretary). But a police force is under the direction and control of the chief constable, who must have regard to the local policing plan. It is true that the police authority has powers to require the chief constable and any assistant chief constable to retire in the interests of efficiency or effectiveness (ss 11, 12). But in exercising this power the police authority must act with the approval of the Home Secretary, who may himself take the initiative by requiring the police authority to retire the chief constable (s 42). The chief constable must be given an opportunity to make representations to the police authority or the Home Secretary before he or she can be required to retire (ss 11, 42). The police authority may institute disciplinary proceedings against the chief constable.[5] The police authority is the paymaster for local police expenditure, though salaries are fixed according to national scales.

---

[5] Cf *Ridge v Baldwin* [1964] AC 40, ch 29 B below, which concerned the dismissal of a chief constable under the pre-1964 legislation. The arrangements for disciplining senior officers were reviewed in 1987, 'in the light of concern expressed about the investigation of allegations against the former deputy chief constable of Greater Manchester, Mr John Stalker', HC Deb, 22 July 1987, col 200 (WA). Cf Stalker, *Stalker*.

Chief constables

Before the Police Act 1964, there was much uncertainty about the legal position of the chief constable, which for historical reasons differed between county and borough forces.[6] The importance of his or her position is that the hierarchy of command within a police force runs from the police constable on the beat to the chief constable, and no further. The royal commission in 1962 went so far as to say, 'The problem of controlling the police can ... be restated as the problem of controlling chief constables'.[7] The Police Act 1996 places each police force under the chief constable's direction and control (s 10). Subject to the powers of the police authority already mentioned (for example, in regard to finance), all appointments and promotions to ranks below that of assistant chief constable are made by the chief constable (s 13). He or she is also the disciplinary authority for these ranks and, subject to an appeal to the Home Secretary (not, it should be noted, to the police authority), may impose disciplinary penalties, including dismissal or suspension.

The chief constable also appoints special constables (s 27)[8] and may provide on request special police services (for example, to a football club for policing on match days) in return for payments to the police authority.[9] Certain duties are imposed on the chief constable by the 1996 Act, for example, to report annually to the Home Secretary and the police authority, to make special reports when requested by either, and to submit criminal statistics as required by the Home Secretary (ss 22, 44, 45). He or she may be required to enter into collaboration agreements with other police forces or to provide extra constables or other assistance in aid of another force (ss 23, 24). The chief constable has important duties in regard to complaints against the police.[10] He or she personally must observe police discipline and may be dismissed for misconduct or required to resign in the interests of efficiency; but it seems that neither the police authority nor the Home Office may direct him or her as to the use of the police force.

Functions of the Home Secretary

Within the Metropolitan area, the Home Secretary is the police authority. While some of his powers in this capacity derive from the Police Act 1964, he has a long-standing and close relationship with the Metropolitan Police Commissioner which is not governed solely by that Act. In the past, Home Secretaries accepted a wide responsibility for the general policies followed by the Metropolitan Police, while not directing the detailed operations of the force.[11] More recently, the official Home Office view, which convinced the Parliamentary Ombudsman in 1967, is that the Home Secretary as police authority has no power to give instructions to members of the Metropolitan

---

6   Cmnd 1728, pp 25–8; Marshall, op cit, chs 4 and 5.
7   Cmnd 1728, p 34.
8   See *Sheikh v Chief Constable of Greater Manchester Police* [1990] 1 QB 637.
9   1996 Act, s 25; Cf *Harris v Sheffield United Football Club Ltd* [1988] QB 77; and S Weatherill [1988] PL 106.
10 See Section F below.
11 Critchley, *A History of the Police in England and Wales*, p 268; Marshall, op cit, pp 29–32.

Police as to the manner in which they should carry out their duties as constables.[12] In 1968, Salmon LJ said: 'Constitutionally it is clearly impermissible for the Home Secretary to issue any order to the police in respect of law enforcement',[13] but this forthright view is not in full accord with the history of the Metropolitan Police.

Apart from the special position of the Metropolitan Police, the Home Secretary has very many statutory powers affecting the police. As we have seen, these were extended in 1994 so that he may (by order) determine policy objectives for police authorities, after consultation with persons representative of the police authorities as well as chief constables (s 37). Where objectives have been set in this way, the Home Secretary may direct police authorities to establish performance targets, the minister having a wide discretion to issue a direction to one or more or to all police authorities, and a power to impose different conditions on different authorities (s 38). He may also issue codes of practice relating to the discharge by police authorities of any of their functions (s 39). Otherwise the Home Secretary may require a police authority to report on any matter relating to the discharge of its functions (s 43) and may require chief constables to do the same (s 44). Still further powers enable the Home Secretary to cause a local inquiry to be held into any matter connected with the policing of any area (s 49), and to provide and maintain 'such organisations, facilities and services as he considers necessary or expedient for promoting the efficiency and effectiveness of the police' (s 57). This extends powers previously contained in the Police Act 1964, s 41, which were nevertheless held to be wide enough to enable the Home Secretary to make available from a central store baton rounds and CS gas to be used in the event of serious public disorder.[14] By s 50 of the 1996 Act, the Home Secretary may make regulations for the government, administration and conditions of service of police forces, in particular with respect to ranks, qualifications for appointment and promotion, probationary service, voluntary retirement, discipline, duties, pay, allowances, clothing and equipment.

In addition to these wide statutory powers, the Home Secretary has always exercised considerable financial control. Since 1856, a grant has been made from the exchequer towards the police expenses of local authorities. Payment of the grant, formerly 51% of all approved expenses, is now determined annually by the Home Secretary with the approval of the Treasury. In determining how much any one authority receives, the Home Secretary 'may exercise his discretion by applying such formulae or other rules as he considers appropriate' (s 46). Both the Metropolitan and City of London Police also receive grants, the balance of expenditure in the case of the former being contributed by the councils who are within the Metropolitan Police district. Her Majesty's Inspectors of Constabulary have proved powerful instruments in maintaining the efficiency and effectiveness of police forces: they are appointed by and report to the Home Secretary (s 54). The

---

[12]   HC 6 (1967–68), p 25; HC 350 (1967–68), pp xiii, 56–68.
[13]   *R v Metropolitan Police Commissioner, ex p Blackburn* [1968] 2 QB 118.
[14]   See *R v Home Secretary, ex p Northumbria Police Authority* [1989] QB 26; and see A W Bradley [1988] PL 298.

Inspectorate of Constabulary must submit an annual report to the Home Secretary (s 54) and may be directed by him to carry out an inspection of any force. Where a report states that the force is not efficient or not effective, or will cease to be efficient or effective unless remedial measures are taken, the Home Secretary may direct the police authority to take prescribed measures (s 40), a power which further reinforces the power of central government. This includes a power specifically to give directions as to the minimum level of the annual budget to be provided by the authority (s 41).

Legal status of a police officer

The courts have not always found it easy to define the precise status of a police officer. There is no doubt at common law that a constable is personally liable to be sued for damages in respect of wrongful or unlawful acts which he or she commits while a constable. 'The powers of a constable *qua* peace officer, whether conferred by common or statute law, are exercised by him by virtue of his office, and cannot be exercised on the responsibility of any person but himself'.[15] Indeed, in the past it was found necessary to protect constables by statute against certain risks of liability, as was done in the Constables' Protection Act 1750. The individual liability of the constable continues today and it is no defence to an action for trespass or false imprisonment that the constable had been ordered by a superior officer to act.

As modern police forces grew in professionalism, organisation and resources, citizens who suffered from improper police action sought to make the local police authority vicariously liable for the wrongful acts of the constables. These attempts were unsuccessful. In *Fisher v Oldham Corporation*, a borough council which maintained a police force was held not to be the employer of a constable sued for wrongful arrest, though the council's committee was at that time responsible for appointing, paying and dismissing the constables.[16] The court explained that in making an arrest, a police officer was 'a servant of the State, a ministerial officer of the central power'; and that in the absence of power to control his acts, the local authority could not be held vicariously liable for them. When first appointed, a police officer swears to serve the Sovereign as a constable. In *Lewis v Cattle*, which concerned the unauthorised publication of confidential police information, a police officer was held to be 'a person holding office under His Majesty' for the purpose of the Official Secrets Acts.[17] But in relation to vicarious liability, at common law a constable was not in the employment of the Crown since he was neither appointed nor paid by the Crown, and this was not affected by the Crown Proceedings Act 1947. In the absence of legal liability, police authorities might decide to stand behind individual constables and to pay any damages and costs awarded against them. But this remained a matter for their discretion until Parliament changed the law.

---

[15] *Enever v R* (1906) 3 CLR 969, 977.
[16] [1930] 2 KB 364. See also *Sheikh v Chief Constable of Greater Manchester* [1990] 1 QB 637. For Scotland see eg *Muir v Hamilton Magistrates* 1910 1 SLT 164. On a related issue, see *Metropolitan Police Receiver v Croydon Corporation* [1957] 2 QB 154.
[17] [1938] 2 KB 454, criticised by Sir Ivor Jennings in (1938) 2 MLR 73. See now Official Secrets Act 1989, s 12(1)(c).

By s 88 of the Police Act 1996, liability for the wrongful acts of constables is placed upon the chief constable in respect of torts committed in the performance of their functions by constables under his or her direction and control, in the same way as a master is liable for torts committed by servants in the course of their employment. Any damages and costs awarded against the chief constable for vicarious liability are paid out of the local police fund, as is any sum required to settle a claim against the chief constable where the police authority approves the settlement. The police authority has also a statutory discretion to pay damages or costs awarded against a constable, whether or not the chief constable has been sued.[18] The Race Relations Act 1976 has provided that for the provisions of that Act dealing with employment, the office of constable is to be treated as employment by the chief officer of police or the police authority respectively in respect of any acts done by him or them in relation to a constable.[19] These provisions apply to special constables[20] as well as to regular members of a police force: 'when one looks at the "deeming" section 16 one can see no reason why the part-time constable should have been left out'.[21] Nevertheless it is 'ingrained in the law of the Constitution that police officers are office-holders; there is no relationship of employer and employee'.[22] It has been held that the chief constable is not vicariously liable for the discriminatory conduct of individual police officers contrary to the Race Relations Act 1976, for which the latter may be personally liable.[23]

Notwithstanding these developments, there are still legal contexts in which it is important to appreciate that the police constable holds a public office and is not employed under a contract of employment. The constable's tenure of office is essentially statutory and can be terminated only in accordance with regulations which create a disciplinary code and contain an elaborate procedure for dealing with offences against discipline. These offences include discreditable conduct, neglect of duty, disobedience to orders, improper disclosure of information, corrupt or improper practices, abuse of authority, and racially discriminatory behaviour.[24] Indeed, legislation restricts the freedom of a police officer in a way in which no employer could by a contract of employment. Thus police officers are not allowed to be members of a trade union or of any association which seeks to control or influence the pay or conditions of service of any police force; instead, there are Police Federations for England and Wales and for Scotland which represent police officers in all matters of welfare and efficiency, other than questions of promotion affecting

---

[18] For similar liability in Scotland, see *Wilson v Chief Constable of Lothians and Borders Constabulary* 1989 SLT 97.
[19] 1976 Act, s 16. Cf Sex Discrimination Act 1975, s 17.
[20] For the law relating to special constables, see *Sheikh*, above.
[21] *Sheikh v Chief Constable of Greater Manchester Police* [1990] 1 QB 637, at 648.
[22] *Farah v Metropolitan Police Commissioner* [1997] 1 All ER 289, at 305 (Otton LJ).
[23] *Farah*, ibid.
[24] See SI 1985 No 518 and Police and Criminal Evidence Act 1984, part IX. For senior officers, see SI 1985 No 519. See *Calveley v Chief Constable of the Merseyside Police* [1989] AC 1228 (no action for breach of statutory duty or for negligence available to police officer who has been the subject of disciplinary proceedings). At the time of writing new arrangements under the Police Act 1996, part IV, have yet to be settled.

individuals, and with limited powers in relation to discipline.[25] Police regulations impose a great many restrictions upon the private life of serving police
officers, including one of constitutional importance, namely that a police
officer 'shall at all times abstain from any activity which is likely to interfere
with the impartial discharge of his duties or which is likely to give rise to the
impression amongst members of the public that it may so interfere; and in
particular [he] shall not take any active part in politics'.[26] It has been
suggested that still further restrictions should be introduced following unease
in some quarters over allegations that membership of a police force is
incompatible with freemasonry.[27]

B.   Accountability and control of the police[28]

Whether in the field of maintaining public order or in the work of detecting
and prosecuting crime, police decisions constantly involve the exercise of
discretion, choice between alternative courses of action and the setting of
priorities for the use of limited resources. In a stable society it is easier for the
police to seek to play an impartial and a non-political role, but even this role
has latent political significance. In less stable conditions, issues of law and
order acquire a more immediate political content. In the sometimes troubled
1980s, questions were often raised about the procedures for police accountability. Problems about police reaction to racial violence, to public demonstrations and to the events surrounding the miners' strike in particular all
contributed to the concern. A complicating dimension is what some see as the
movement towards greater centralisation of police work.[29] There are many
forms of cooperation between forces, but there is also now the potential for
the development of common policies, informally through the activities of
bodies such as the Association of Chief Police Officers (ACPO), and indeed of
central control and organisation of police strategy through bodies such as the
National Reporting Centre, renamed as the Mutual Aid Coordination Centre.[30] This is a unit which operates from Scotland Yard in times of crisis, as
during the miners' strike of 1984/85. Its purpose is to coordinate policing
strategy and the deployment of officers on a national basis in consultation
with the Home Office, which is not a disinterested observer.[31] This emerging

---

25   Police Act 1996, s 59.
26   Police Regulations 1995, SI 1995 No 215. See *Champion v Chief Constable of Gwent* [1990] 1
     All ER 116 (membership of appointments sub-committee of school governors not
     prohibited by these regulations).
27   HC Deb, 28 June 1988, cols 198–202. See also HC Deb, 18 November 1994, col 281. See
     also HC 269 (1995–96), p 35 (call by Police Complaints Authority for police officers to
     declare membership of freemasons or similar organisations).
28   On police accountability see Baldwin and Kinsey, *Police Powers and Politics*; Jefferson and
     Grimshaw, *Controlling the Constable*; G Marshall and B Loveday, 'The Police: Independence
     and Accountability', in Jowell and Oliver (eds), *The Changing Constitution*, ch 11; Reiner,
     The Politics of the Police; Spencer, *Called to Account*; Uglow, *Policing Liberal Society*.
29   Cf Lustgarten, note 2 above.
30   Bailey, Harris and Jones, *Civil Liberties Cases and Materials*, p 175.
31   For details, see M Kettle, in Fine and Miller (eds), *Policing the Miners' Strike*; see now
     provisions for a National Criminal Intelligence Service and National Crime Squad in Police
     Act 1997 (Section A above).

centralisation raises new questions about police accountability which the existing institutional structure may not be well suited to answer.

Local police authorities

As we have seen, the police authority is responsible for ensuring an efficient and effective force (s 6), and it exercises a measure of supervision over the chief constable. In practice, however, the changes introduced by the Police and Magistrates' Courts Act 1994 have gone some way to diminish further the already limited scope for local control of the police. As we have seen, the objectives for police authorities are set by the Home Secretary,[32] while the representation of elected representatives on police authorities has been reduced, with each authority now containing members appointed by the Home Secretary, their legitimacy and authority perhaps being no more than the fact that they are 'people with management or financial experience'.[33] The police authority has no power to give instructions to the chief constable about the deployment of the police or to interfere with the chief officer's overall operational control. A measure of the diminishing role of police authorities as agents of accountability is reflected in rather startling terms in the white paper, *Police Reform*, which preceded the changes introduced by the 1994 Act. There it is said that in future police authorities would 'act on behalf of local people as the "customer" of the service which the police force provides',[34] a role which not all will find unexceptionable. It is true that police authorities are now required to determine local policing objectives on an annual basis and that in doing so they must not only consult the chief constable, but also consider any views obtained in accordance with arrangements made under s 96 of the 1996 Act. This requires the police authority to make arrangements to obtain the views of the local population about local policing arrangements. But the Act does not prescribe what arrangements should be made for this purpose, and so far as it gives any guidance the white paper suggested that the duty might be discharged through the medium of local consultative groups (not necessarily elected), and by canvassing local views in a variety of ways, for example by public opinion surveys.[35]

In addition to the statement of policing objectives, the police authority is required to produce an annual policing plan, which must give particulars, inter alia, of local policing objectives (s 7). The plan is in fact drafted by the chief constable and submitted for consideration by the police authority, which in turn must consult with the chief constable before any amendments are made to his draft (s 8). Even then the chief constable is not bound by the plan, but is required in the discharge of his or her duties simply to 'have regard to it' (s 10). Chief constables are, however, required to report annually to the police authority, and (subject to a power of the chief constable with the support of the Home Secretary to withhold information which in the public interest ought not to be disclosed), the authority may require the chief constable to report on specific matters connected with the policing of the

---

[32]   Police Act 1996, s 37.
[33]   Cm 2281, 1994, p 21.
[34]   Ibid, p 20.
[35]   Ibid.

area (s 22). This is a power (previously contained in the Police Act 1964) to which Lord Scarman attached some importance in his inquiry into the Brixton riots in 1981. The breakdown of order in the social, and particularly racial, conditions of Brixton led Lord Scarman to make substantial criticisms of the police and their relations with the community. He recommended that, without the sacrifice of independence, police accountability should be improved, and argued that police authorities should take more seriously their existing powers under the Police Act 1964 to require reports from the chief constable and to ensure close cooperation between police authority and chief officer.[36] Questions continue to arise about the political accountability of the police authority, which is advanced only by the terms of s 20 of the 1996 Act that arrangements should be made by local authorities to enable questions on the discharge of the functions of a police authority to be put by members of the local council.[37]

Parliamentary control of the police

It is both inevitable and desirable that there should be parliamentary interest in the work of the police. One problem which has often faced MPs wishing to raise police subjects in Parliament has been that there is no direct ministerial responsibility either for the acts of the police or for the decisions of police authorities. The position of London has always been exceptional since it has long been recognised in the Commons that the Home Secretary accepts what has been described as an extremely wide and detailed responsibility for the Metropolitan Police.[38] The royal commission in 1962 proposed additional powers for the central government which, the commission considered, would make the Secretaries of State accountable to Parliament for the efficient policing of the whole country. The Police Act 1964 did not go as far as the royal commission recommended, but the extent of ministerial responsibility for police outside London was undoubtedly widened by the Act.

Thus MPs who wish to raise a matter of local policing may now ask the appropriate Secretary of State whether he or she proposes to call for a report on the matter from the chief constable, institute an inquiry into the matter, to require the chief constable to resign in the interests of efficiency, and so on. But the fact that such a question may be asked does not mean that as full an answer will be given as the MP would like. The Home Secretary will not give to Parliament details of police work which he or she considers should not be publicly disclosed. Nor does the jurisdiction of the Parliamentary Ombudsman include power to investigate complaints against the police.[39] On specific matters of great political concern, however, the Secretary of State may be willing to order an inquiry to be held[40] or to lay before Parliament the report received from a chief officer of police.[41] More general police subjects are

---

36 Cmnd 8427, 1981.
37 Cf *R v Lancashire Police Authority, ex p Hook* [1980] QB 603.
38 Marshall, note 3 above.
39 See ch 28 D.
40 See the reports by Lord Scarman into the Red Lion Square disorders, Cmnd 5919, 1975, and into the Brixton disorders, Cmnd 8427, 1981.
41 Eg HC 351 (1974), report from Metropolitan Police Commissioner on the Lennon case.

suitable for examination by the Home Affairs Committee of the House of Commons.[42]

Judicial control of police policies

Relying on the time-worn but inaccurate sentiment that a policeman possesses few powers not enjoyed by the ordinary citizen, and is only 'a person paid to perform, as a matter of duty, acts which if he were so minded he might have done voluntarily', the royal commission in 1962 came to an astonishing conclusion: 'The relation of the police to the courts is not ... of any greater constitutional significance than the relation of any other citizen to the courts'.[43] The corrective was supplied in *R v Metropolitan Police Commissioner, ex p Blackburn*.[44]

Under the Betting, Gaming and Lotteries Act 1963, certain forms of gaming were unlawful, and gaming clubs in London sought to avoid the Act. After legal difficulties in enforcing the Act had arisen, the Commissioner issued a secret circular to senior officers giving effect to a policy decision that no proceedings were to be taken against a gaming club for breach of the law, unless there were complaints of cheating or it had become the haunt of criminals. Blackburn sought an order of mandamus against the Commissioner which in effect ordered him to reverse that policy decision. The circular was withdrawn before the case was concluded, but the Court of Appeal held that every chief constable owed a duty to the public to enforce the law. That duty could if necessary be enforced by the courts. Although chief officers had a wide discretion with which the courts would not interfere, the courts would control a policy decision which amounted to a failure of duty to enforce the law. The court in this case left open whether Blackburn had a sufficient interest in the matter to ask for mandamus. In a later case brought by Blackburn to enforce the obscenity laws, the court held on the merits that the Commissioner was doing what he could to enforce the existing laws with the available manpower and no more could reasonably be expected.[45]

Further consideration was given to the 'clear legal duty'[46] which the police owe to the public to enforce the law in *Hill v Chief Constable of West Yorkshire*, where it was held that the existence of a general duty in the police to suppress crime does not carry with it a liability to individuals for damage caused to them by criminals whom the police have failed to apprehend in circumstances when it was possible to do so.[47] Obvious difficulties are presented by the proposal that a court should direct a chief constable in the performance of his

---

[42]   Eg Race relations and the 'sus' law (HC 559 (1979–80)); Deaths in police custody (HC 631 (1979–80)); Police complaints procedures (HC 98 (1981–82)); Special Branch (HC 71 (1984–85)); Police Cooperation in Europe (HC 363 (1989–90)); Police cell accommodation costs (HC 524 (1992–93)); and Metropolitan Police Service responding to calls from the public (HC 33 (1995–96)).

[43]   Cmnd 1728, p 34.

[44]   [1968] 2 QB 118.

[45]   *R v Metropolitan Police Commissioner, ex p Blackburn (No 3)* [1973] QB 241. See also *R v Chief Constable of Devon and Cornwall, ex p CEGB* [1982] QB 458 and *R v Oxford, ex p Levey, The Times*, 1 November 1986.

[46]   *R v Metropolitan Police Commissioner, ex p Blackburn* [1968] 2 QB 118, at 138 (Salmon LJ).

[47]   [1989] AC 53 (unsuccessful action in negligence brought by mother of a victim of Sutcliffe, the Yorkshire Ripper). See also *Osman v Ferguson* [1993] 4 All ER 344 ([1994] PL 4), and *Ancell v McDermott, The Times*, 4 February 1993.

or her duties at the instance of a member of the public. It is one thing for a court to strike down instructions by a chief constable which are plainly illegal; it is another for the court to impose its own views on the priorities for the use of police resources.[48] Given that the courts must allow the police discretion in carrying out their work, a capable chief constable with some appreciation of the law should have little difficulty in keeping within the permissible bounds. Rather than relying to the extent that we have come to do upon the autonomy and professional judgment of the chief officer to solve difficult questions of social policy for us, and then looking to the courts to control their decisions, it might be better to re-assess the proper scope for political direction and parliamentary discussion of police policies.

C.   Personal liberty and police powers

In 1929, a royal commission on police powers and procedure, reviewing the practice of the police in searching the dwelling of a person for whose arrest a warrant had been issued, expressed the concern that police 'in the discharge of their essential duties, should have to rely on powers of which the legality seems doubtful'.[49] But the law was not reformed and in 1960 an eminent judge wrote: 'The police power of search under English law is haphazard and ill-defined'.[50] The comment was almost equally true of the law of arrest. In 1978, a royal commission was set up by the Labour government to review the powers and duties of the police in the investigation of offences and the process of the prosecution of crime. The commission was required to have regard 'both to the interests of the community in bringing offenders to justice and to the rights and liberties of persons suspected or accused of crime'. Its report sought within the criminal justice system 'to define a balance between the rights of individuals and the security of society and the state'. Many of the changes recommended by the report were controversial, but there could be little disagreement with the commission's main finding that there was a strong need to bring the law up to date. Existing police powers were 'found in (or extracted with difficulty from) a mixture of statute law, common law, evidential law, and guidance to the police from the judges and the Home Office'; the law regulating police investigation needed 'to be reformulated and restated in clear and coherent terms that have regard to contemporary circumstances'.[51]

This broad conclusion was accepted by the Conservative government, which introduced what was to become the Police and Criminal Evidence Act 1984, 'an important reforming statute'[52] usually referred to by its acronym

---

[48]   See *R v Chief Constable of Sussex, ex p International Trader's Ferry Ltd* [1997] 2 All ER 65.
[49]   Cmd 3297, 1929, p 45.
[50]   Devlin, *The Criminal Prosecution in England*, p 53.
[51]   Cmnd 8092, 1981 (the Philips report on criminal procedure), pp 8 and 110. For comment, see M Inman [1981] Crim LR 469; K W Lidstone [1981] Crim LR 454; D McBarnet [1981] Crim LR 445; and B Smythe [1981] PL 184, 481.
[52]   *Vince v Chief Constable of Dorset* [1993] 2 All ER 321, at 335.

PACE.[53] Together with codes of practice[54] issued under the authority of the Act,[55] this measure provides a very extensive (although not comprehensive) code of police powers, which both confers new powers on the police and introduces new safeguards for the citizen. However, the Act tilts the scales of justice very firmly in favour of the police, and it is seriously open to question whether the safeguards for individual liberty are adequate. Before turning to these questions, we may note that deprivation of personal liberty may take place by means other than arrest and detention by police officers in the exercise of their duties to investigate and prevent crime. One important measure relates to the compulsory admission to hospital of those suffering from acute mental disorder.[56] Under statute, compulsory admission generally requires an application to have been made by the nearest relative of the patient or an approved social worker, and to be supported by the recommendation of two medical practitioners, one of whom must have had special experience in the diagnosis or treatment of mental disorder. In an acute emergency, admission for up to 72 hours may be based upon only one medical recommendation. Voluntary patients already in hospital may be detained from leaving for up to six hours on the decision of a mental nurse, and for up to 72 hours on the decision of a hospital doctor.[57] The criminal courts may make hospital and restriction orders for the compulsory admission of those suffering from mental disorder who have been convicted of, or in some cases merely charged with, criminal offences.[58] Since 1959, compulsorily detained patients have been able to seek release by applying to mental health review tribunals, which exist for each hospital area.[59]

Police powers short of arrest

Most police powers affecting the individual's liberty depend upon an arrest having been made. At common law, the pre-arrest powers of the police are very limited, a point illustrated in different ways by three cases. In *Jackson v Stevenson*,[60] it was held to be contrary to constitutional principle and illegal to search someone to establish whether there are grounds for an arrest. In *Kenlin v Gardner*,[61] it was held that the police had no right physically to detain someone for questioning without first arresting the person concerned.

---

[53] The leading work is Zander, *The Police and Criminal Evidence Act 1984.* See also articles at [1985] PL 388 and (1989) 40 NILQ 319.

[54] There are five codes of practice: Code A: Code of Practice for the Exercise by Police Officers of Statutory Powers of Stop and Search; Code B: Code of Practice for the Searching of Premises by Police Officers and the Seizure of Property found by Police Officers on Persons or Premises; Code C: Code of Practice for the Detention, Treatment and Questioning of Persons by Police Officers; Code D: Code of Practice for the Identification of Persons by Police Officers; and Code E: Code of Practice on Tape Recording of Interviews with Suspects. The codes as revised in 1995 may be found in Zander, op cit.

[55] Police and Criminal Evidence Act 1984, ss 66, 67.

[56] For full accounts, see Hoggett, *Mental Health Law,* and Jones, *Mental Health Act Manual.* See also Unsworth, *The Politics of Mental Health Legislation.*

[57] Mental Health Act 1983, part II.

[58] Mental Health Act 1983, part III. Separate legislation exists for Scotland.

[59] Now constituted under Mental Health Act 1983, s 65.

[60] (1879) 2 Adam 255. Cf *Lodwick v Sanders* [1985] 1 All ER 577.

[61] [1967] 2 QB 510.

Anyone who resists such detention cannot be guilty of obstructing a police officer in the execution of his duty. And in *R v Lemsatef*[62] it was held that the police cannot require individuals to accompany them to the police station in order to help the police with their inquiries. In a forceful judgment, Lawton LJ said that if the idea 'is getting around' that the police could detain suspects for this purpose, the sooner people disabuse themselves of the idea, the better. But although the police have no common law right to stop and search, no right to detain for questioning and no right to require assistance with their inquiries, these common law rules may be modified by statute. An early example is the Metropolitan Police Act 1839, which by s 66 gave to the police in London the power to stop and search persons and vehicles reasonably suspected of having stolen property on them. The same power was adopted in local Acts applying to urban areas outside London. There are clearly potential dangers in granting wide stop and search powers to the police for there is a possibility that the power will be abused,[63] with harassment of ethnic minority groups being a particular concern. Nevertheless, in his report on the Brixton disorders, Lord Scarman thought such powers necessary to combat street crime, provided that the safeguard of 'reasonable suspicion' was properly and objectively applied.[64]

Stop and search powers are now found in a number of statutes. By s 23 of the Misuse of Drugs Act 1971, a constable may search (and detain for the purpose of the search) anyone who is suspected on reasonable grounds to be in unlawful possession of a controlled drug.[65] Similar powers apply in relation to vehicles. Powers to stop and search are also found in part I of PACE.[66] Thus a constable may search a person or vehicle, or anything which is in or on the vehicle, for stolen or prohibited articles, a term defined to include an offensive weapon or an article used for the purpose of burglary or related crimes (s 1). The power may be so exercised only if the constable 'has reasonable grounds for suspecting that he will find stolen or prohibited articles' (s 1(3)). Code of Practice A (on the exercise by police officers of statutory powers of stop and search) gives some guidance as to reasonable grounds for suspicion. Paragraph 1.7 provides:

Reasonable suspicion can never be supported on the basis of personal factors alone. For example, a person's colour, age, hairstyle or manner of dress, or the fact that he is known to have a previous conviction for possession of an unlawful article, cannot be used alone or in combination with each other as the sole basis on which to search that person. Nor may it be founded on the basis of stereotyped images of certain persons or groups as more likely to be committing offences.

If during a search a constable discovers stolen or prohibited articles, they may be seized (s 1(6)). But before exercising these powers, a constable must (inter alia) inform the person to be searched of his or her name and police station

---

[62]   [1977] 2 All ER 835.
[63]   See Home Office Advisory Committee on Drug Dependence, Powers of Arrest and Search in Relation to Drug Offences, 1970.
[64]   Cmnd 8427, 1981, para 7.2.
[65]   See *Wither v Reid* 1979 SLT 192 (on the distinction between (*a*) arrest, and (*b*) detention for search).
[66]   Note that they are powers of 'stop and search' not 'stop and question'. See Zander, above, p 10.

and of the grounds for the search. The Act also requires a police officer to provide documentary evidence that he or she is a police officer if he or she is not in uniform (s 2). Details of the search must be recorded, and if requested a copy must be supplied to the person searched (s 3). Reasonable force may be used by the police (s 117) but during any search made before an arrest a person may not be required to remove any clothing in public except for an outer coat, jacket or gloves (s 2(9)).[67] Stop and search powers were extended in 1988 to knives,[68] and again in the Criminal Justice and Public Order Act 1994 (s 60) to prevent prospective incidents of serious violence which it is reasonably anticipated may take place.

Under the Road Traffic Act 1988, s 163, a constable in uniform may require a person driving a vehicle, or a cyclist to stop. Failure to do so is an offence. It has been held that in exercising this power the police may immobilise a vehicle by removing the keys. Where a police officer has required a vehicle to stop, he 'is entitled to take reasonable steps to detain it for such reasonable time as will enable him, if he suspects it to have been stolen, to effect an arrest and to explain to the driver the reason for the arrest'.[69] In some circumstances, a police officer can require the driver to produce his or her driving licence and his or her name, address and date of birth.[70] But otherwise the driver is under no duty to answer any questions which the police may ask: 'the right to silence in such a circumstance is predominant'.[71] In addition to powers conferred by the Road Traffic Act 1988, s 4 of PACE authorises the police to set up road checks when it is believed that there is or about to be in the locality during the period of the check someone who has committed or witnessed a serious arrestable offence, someone who is intending to commit such an offence, or an escaped prisoner. In view of the wide definition of serious arrestable offence (which includes serious harm to public order)[72] this is a wide power, though it can be used only for the purpose of determining whether the vehicle is carrying any of the categories of person referred to. It confers no power on the police to question the driver or occupants of a vehicle and imposes no duty on such people to respond to police questions. According to Zander 'the number of road checks fluctuated for the first six years', from a low of 222 in 1991 to a high of 445 in 1992. But in 1993 the numbers rose sharply to 3,560, with no less than 3,200 being conducted in the City of London in response to terrorist activity.'The number of arrests was, however, small, and it has been questioned whether the powers in s 4 of PACE were wide enough to sanction this particular police action. Additional powers are found in the Prevention of Terrorism (Temporary Provisions) Act 1989.[73] In addition to these statutory provisions, a common law power to stop vehicles

---

[67] See further Code of Practice A, para 3. On the use of the s 1 power, see Zander, above, p 17, noting 'a consistent annual increase in the number of recorded stops and searches – from 109,800 in 1986 to 442,800 in 1993'. There has, however, been a decline in the annual 'success rate' to 13%.

[68] Criminal Justice Act 1988, s 140.

[69] *Lodwick v Sanders* [1985] 1 All ER 577.

[70] Road Traffic Act 1988, s 163.

[71] *Lodwick v Sanders* [1985] 1 All ER 577, 581. But see below on the 'right to silence'.

[72] Police and Criminal Evidence Act 1984, s 116.

[73] See ch 25 E below.

appears to have been recognised by the Divisional Court in *Moss v Mc-Lachlan*.[74] We consider this case more fully in chapter 23.

Police powers of arrest

1 The grounds for arrest. Powers of arrest are not exclusive to the police and some may be exercised by any person. But today the very great majority of arrests are undertaken by the police. The significance of the act of arrest is that it is at that moment that an individual loses his or her liberty and, if the arrest is lawful, becomes subject to lawful detention. Arrests are of two kinds: (*a*) with a warrant and (*b*) without a warrant.

(a) Arrest with a warrant. Most arrests relate to the initiation of proceedings in the criminal courts. Under the Magistrates' Courts Act 1980, s 1, proceedings may be initiated either by the issue of a summons, requiring the accused to attend court on a certain day, or in more serious cases by a warrant of arrest, naming the accused and the offence with which he or she is charged. A warrant is obtained from a magistrate after a written application (information) has been substantiated on oath.[75] In issuing a warrant for arrest, the magistrate may endorse it for bail.[76] A warrant may be executed anywhere in England or Wales by a police constable.[77] If the warrant is to arrest a person charged with an offence, it may be executed even when a constable does not have it in his or her possession, but the warrant must be shown, on demand, to the arrested person as soon as possible.[78] Despite judicial dicta to the contrary[79] a person arrested would seem entitled to know that he or she is being arrested under a warrant (for if not, how can he or she demand to see it?). Where a constable in good faith executes a warrant that seems valid on its face, he or she is protected from liability for the arrest by the Constables' Protection Act 1750 if it should turn out that the warrant was beyond the jurisdiction of the magistrate who issued it. The requirement that the warrant be issued by a magistrate is thus as much a safeguard for the police as it is for the person named on it. When an arrest warrant has been issued, a constable may enter and search premises to make the arrest, using such reasonable force as is necessary.[80]

(b) Arrest without a warrant under PACE. The law on arrest without a warrant has hitherto been a complicated mixture of common law and statutory powers.[81] The Police and Criminal Evidence Act 1984 makes further reform of the law which was begun when the Criminal Law Act 1967, s 2, abolished the distinction between felonies and misdemeanours, and creates a new category of arrestable offences. This initially comprised: (*a*) all offences for which the

---

74   [1985] IRLR 76. See G S Morris (1985) 14 ILJ 109.

75   The exercise of the power may not be delegated: *R v Manchester Stipendiary Magistrate, ex p Hill* [1983] 1 AC 328.

76   Magistrates' Courts Act 1980, s 17.

77   They may now be executed in Scotland: Criminal Justice and Public Order Act 1994, s 136. For the cross border execution of warrants in the UK, see C Walker [1997] 56 CLJ 114.

78   Ibid, s 125(3); and cf *R v Purdy* [1975] QB 288. And see Police and Criminal Evidence Act 1984, s 33.

79   *R v Kulynycz* [1971] 1 QB 367, 372.

80   Police and Criminal Evidence Act 1984, ss 17, 117.

81   For the position in Scots law, see Brown, *Criminal Evidence and Procedure*.

sentence is fixed by law (for example, life imprisonment in the case of murder); (*b*) all offences for which a first offender over 21 may be sentenced to five years' imprisonment or more; and (*c*) certain other specified offences (under such legislation as the Official Secrets Acts 1911–89, the Sexual Offences Act 1956, and the Theft Act 1968), even though they may not carry prison sentences of five years or longer.[82] Other offences (dealing, for example, with obscene publications and publications intended or likely to stir up racial hatred) have been added by subsequent legislation.[83]

Any person (whether a constable or not) may arrest without a warrant anyone who is, or whom he or she reasonably suspects to be, in the act of committing an arrestable offence. Where such an offence has actually been committed, any person may arrest anyone who is with reasonable cause suspected to be guilty of the offence, or is guilty of it. Where there is merely reasonable cause to suspect that an arrestable offence has been committed, a constable has the additional power of arresting any person whom he or she reasonably suspects of having committed it: but a private person does not have this additional power and may be liable in damages to the person arrested if it should turn out that no arrestable offence has been committed by anyone.[84] A constable may also arrest any person whom with reasonable cause he or she suspects to be about to commit an arrestable offence.

In *O'Hara v Chief Constable of the RUC*[85] the appellant had been arrested under the Prevention of Terrorism (Temporary Provisions) Act 1984, which provided by s 12 that a constable may arrest without a warrant anyone whom 'he has reasonable grounds for suspecting' to be involved with acts of terrorism, a form of words similar to that used in PACE, s 24. At issue was whether the police officer could arrest a suspect (who in this case was detained for 15 days without any explanation, before being released without charge) after a briefing from other colleagues, in the course of which he was told that the appellant had been involved in a murder. It was held by the House of Lords that in order to have a reasonable suspicion 'the information which causes the constable to be suspicious of the individual must be in existence to the knowledge of the police officer at the time he makes the arrest'. The power is vested in the constable, and cannot be exercised simply on the request or instructions of another officer, though the information which causes the arresting officer to be suspicious of the individual 'may come from other officers'. On the facts of this case, however, the appeal failed and the arrest was held to have been lawful, even though the trial court had 'scanty evidence' of the matters disclosed to the arresting officer at the briefing.

In addition to the power to arrest without a warrant for an arrestable offence, s 25 of PACE applies to any other offence which has been or is being committed or attempted, and it seems to a constable impracticable or inappropriate to rely on the service of a summons at a later date. Such an arrest may be made when any of the 'general arrest conditions' is satisfied. These conditions include situations in which the constable does not know and

---

82   Police and Criminal Evidence Act 1984, s 24, replacing Criminal Law Act 1967, s 2.
83   See Football (Offences) Act 1991, s 5(1) and Criminal Justice and Public Order Act 1994, ss 85(2), 155, 166(4), and 167(7).
84   Police and Criminal Evidence Act 1984, s 24(4)–(6), which maintains the rule in *Walters v W H Smith & Son Ltd* [1914] 1 KB 595. See *R v Self* (1992) 95 Cr App Rep 42.
85   [1997] 1 All ER 129.

cannot ascertain the name of the relevant person; where the constable reasonably doubts whether the name given by the person is his or her real name; where the person has not provided a satisfactory address for the service of a summons; and where the constable reasonably believes that arrest is necessary to prevent the person causing physical harm to another, damage to property, an offence against public decency or obstruction of the highway.[86]

(c) Other powers of arrest without warrant.   In addition to the powers of arrest without a warrant under ss 24 and 25 of PACE, other specific statutory powers of arrest continue in force, while there remain some residual common law powers. The former include the power to arrest someone apparently driving a car while unfit through drink or drugs, and persons reasonably suspected of various offences including absence without leave from the armed forces, entering and remaining on property under the Criminal Law Act 1977, illegal entry under the Immigration Act 1971, and offences under the Public Order Act 1936. The police may also arrest and detain prisoners who are unlawfully at large, children who are neglected, exposed to moral danger or absent without authority from a place of safety, and persons liable to be examined or removed from the United Kingdom under the Immigration Act 1971. New specific statutory powers of arrest without a warrant have also been introduced since 1984. For example, under the Public Order Act 1986, a police officer may arrest without warrant anyone he or she reasonably suspects is committing an affray or who is reasonably suspected of using threatening, abusive or insulting words or behaviour towards another person with intent to cause that person to believe that immediate unlawful violence will be used against him or her or another. The same Act also confers a power to arrest a person without a warrant for disorderly conduct which a constable has warned the person in question to stop and he or she fails to do so.[87]

At common law, a police officer has a power to arrest without warrant anyone who commits a breach of the peace. The important decision in *R v Howell*[88] established that there is a power of arrest where a breach of the peace was committed in the presence of the person making the arrest; or if the person making the arrest reasonably believed that such a breach would be committed in the immediate future by the person arrested, even though at the time of the arrest he or she had not committed the breach; or if a breach of the peace has been committed and it is reasonably believed that a renewal of it is threatened. *Howell* also established that there can be no breach of the peace unless an act was done or threatened to be done which actually either harmed a person or his or her property, or was likely to cause such harm, or put someone in fear of such harm being done.[89] An apprehended breach of

---

[86]   The general arrest conditions are not satisfied where the arresting officer doubts the veracity of the arrested person's name and address, and these doubts are 'based solely on his experience that people who commit offences did not give their correct name and address': *G v DPP* [1989] Crim LR 150. Failure to give a name and address is not in itself a ground for arrest. See *Nicholas v Parsonage* [1987] RTR 199.

[87]   See Public Order Act 1986, s 5.

[88]   [1982] QB 416. See also *Albert v Lavin* [1982] AC 546.

[89]   A breach of the peace may occur in private premises: *McConnell v Chief Constable of Greater Manchester* [1990] 1 All ER 423.

the peace is an essential ingredient in the power to arrest without a warrant for obstructing a police officer in the execution of his duty.

In *Wershof v Metropolitan Police Commissioner*[90] a young solicitor was telephoned by his brother and asked to come to the family jewellery shop where the brother was engaged in a dispute with a police officer about a ring which the officer thought had been stolen. When the solicitor arrived, he told the police officer that he could take the ring only if he produced a receipt for it. The officer refused to provide a receipt, the solicitor refused to let him have the ring and after an argument the solicitor was arrested for obstructing a police officer in the execution of his duty. The police officer thereupon put a tight and painful grip on the solicitor's right arm and frog-marched him down the road. In a successful action by the solicitor for damages for assault, the court held that a police officer has power to arrest without a warrant a person who wilfully obstructs him in the execution of his duty only if the obstruction was such that an offender actually caused or was likely to cause a breach of the peace. In this case the solicitor would not have physically resisted a seizure of the ring by force and this should have been apparent to the police officer.

2 The manner of arrest. Although the first ingredient of a proper arrest is the existence of lawful authority to make the arrest, it is not the only one. The arrest must also be executed in a proper manner, which means that the arrested person must be told of the fact of arrest (ie that he or she is under arrest) and also of the reasons for the arrest (PACE, s 28), measures 'laid down by Parliament to protect the individual against the excess or abuse of the power of arrest'.[91] The origin of the latter rule (requiring reasons to be given for the arrest) may be found in *Christie v Leachinsky*,[92] where the Liverpool police had purported to exercise a power of arrest contained in a local Act when they knew that the conditions for this were not met. When the officers concerned were later sued for wrongful arrest and false imprisonment, it was argued that the arrest was lawful because at the time they had information about Leachinsky which would have justified his arrest for another offence. The House of Lords held that the arrest was unlawful, since it was a condition of a lawful arrest that the person arrested should be entitled to know the reason for it. An actual charge need not be formulated at the time of arrest, but 'the arrested man is entitled to be told what is the act for which he is arrested'. Indeed it has been said that 'giving the correct information of the reasons for an arrest was of the utmost constitutional significance'.[93]

This information must be given at the time of arrest, or as soon as practicable thereafter.[94] Otherwise the arrest is unlawful (PACE, s 28(1), (3)) though there is nothing laid down in the Act specifying how the information should be communicated to an arrested person.[95] A duty to inform people of

---

[90] [1978] 3 All ER 540.

[91] *Hill v Chief Constable of South Yorkshire* [1990] 1 All ER 1046.

[92] [1947] AC 573, 593 (Lord Simonds). And see *Pedro v Diss* [1981] 2 All ER 59. But note that the 1984 Act goes beyond the common law position: see *Hill v Chief Constable of South Yorkshire*, above.

[93] *Edwards v DPP* (1993) 97 Cr App Rep 301. In the case of someone arrested under s 14(1)(b) of the Prevention of Terrorism (Temporary Provisions) Act 1989 (power to arrest on reasonable suspicion of involvement in terrorism rather a specific crime), it is not necessary to specify the crime alleged: *Oscar v Chief Constable of RUC* (1993) 2 BNIL 52.

[94] See *Dawes v DPP, The Times*, 2 March 1994.

[95] See *Nicholas v Parsonage* [1987] RTR 199.

the fact of arrest is also recognised by the common law. In *Alderson v Booth*,[96] the accused had given a positive breathalyser test to a police officer who then said to the accused: 'I shall have to ask you to come to the police station for further tests'. He went and subsequently was acquitted at his trial for drunk driving on the ground that he had not been arrested before going to the police station, a lawful arrest being a condition precedent to a conviction under the drink/driving legislation. On appeal the acquittal was upheld, the court taking the view that compulsion is a necessary element of arrest and that police officers should use clear words to bring home to a person that he or she is under arrest, such as the words 'I arrest you'. However, in *R v Inwood*,[97] it was made clear that there is no single magic formula for this purpose and that different procedures may have to be followed with different people, depending on age, ethnic origins, knowledge of English, intellectual qualities and mental disabilities.[98] The common law may be relevant in other respects too. Unlike the police stop and search powers, there is no statutory duty on police officers (even if not in uniform) to identify themselves as such to an arrested person. *Abbassy v Metropolitan Police Commissioner*[99] suggests, however, that there may be a common law obligation to this effect.

In relation to the requirements of s 28 of PACE, two interesting questions have arisen. The first is, what happens if the police are unable to inform the arrested person of the fact and reasons at the time of arrest and then fail to do so as soon as it becomes practicable? Does this subsequent failure mean that the earlier arrest is unlawful? In *DPP v Hawkins*,[100] the court's answer was no:

When a police officer makes an arrest which he is lawfully entitled to make but is unable at the time to state the ground because it is impracticable to do so, ... it is his duty to maintain the arrest until it is practicable to inform the arrested person of that ground. If, when it does become practicable, he fails to do so, then the arrest is unlawful, but that does not mean that acts, which were previously done and were, when done, done in the execution of duty, become, retrospectively, acts which were not done in the execution of duty.[101]

The second question relates to the position where the police have no reason to delay informing an arrested person of the fact and reasons for the arrest. Does this initial failure, rendering the arrest therefore unlawful, vitiate all the subsequent proceedings? Again, it seems not.

In *Lewis v Chief Constable of South Wales*[102] two women were arrested for burglary but were not told why they were being arrested. They were then taken to a police station where they were informed of the reasons for the arrest, within (respectively) 10 minutes and 23 minutes after the time of arrest. Some five hours later both were released. They subsequently sued for wrongful arrest and false imprisonment and the question which arose was whether they were entitled to be compensated for 10 and 23 minutes respectively or for the entire five-hour period. The Court of Appeal agreed

---

96   [1969] 2 QB 216. Cf *Nichols v Bulman* [1985] RTR 236.
97   [1973] 2 All ER 645.
98   On the continuing importance of *Booth* and *Inwood*, see *R v Brosch* [1988] Crim LR 743.
99   [1990] 1 All ER 193, 202 (citing Burn's *Justice of the Peace*, 1755).
100   [1988] 3 All ER 673.
101   At 674.
102   [1991] 1 All ER 206.

with the first instance decision that, although the initial arrest had been unlawful because the women had not been given the reasons for it, it ceased being unlawful when this was done. The court did not consider this result to be inconsistent with s 28(3) of PACE.

While a police officer may use reasonable force to make the arrest,[103] the use of unreasonable force does not necessarily make the arrest unlawful.[104]

3 Invoking the power of arrest.   Although the police must thus have grounds for arrest, and must exercise these powers in a proper manner, it does not follow that an arrest will necessarily be lawful where these conditions have been met. The power of arrest is a discretionary power, and like other discretionary powers of public officials, it is subject to review by the courts to ensure that it is not exercised improperly.

In *Holgate-Mohammed v Duke*[105] the appellant was arrested without a warrant and taken to a police station where she was questioned in connection with the theft of jewellery. The arrest was made under the Criminal Law Act 1967, s 2(4) (now PACE, s 24(6)) which permitted a constable to arrest without warrant anyone whom he, with reasonable cause, suspected to be guilty of an offence which he, with reasonable cause, suspected to have been committed. The appellant was later released without charge, whereupon she brought proceedings for wrongful imprisonment. In dismissing her appeal, the House of Lords held that the statutory power of arrest must be exercised in accordance with the so-called *Wednesbury* principles, meaning in essence that the discretion so conferred should not be abused. There was no such abuse in this case when the police officer arrested the appellant in the belief that she would be more likely to respond truthfully to his questions if she were questioned under arrest at the police station than if she were questioned at her own home, 'from which she could peremptorily order him to depart at any moment'.

Although this decision establishes a crucially important point of principle, in practice the courts are unlikely very often to say that the power of arrest has been unreasonably exercised in the *Wednesbury* sense. Although the court stressed that this was likely to happen only exceptionally, nevertheless *Plange v Chief Constable of South Humberside*[106] is one such case.

The plaintiff had allegedly assaulted a third party, who had reported it to the police. Knowing that the complaint had subsequently been withdrawn and having no intention of charging the plaintiff, a police officer nevertheless proceeded to arrest him and detained him for four hours. It was conceded for the plaintiff that at the time of arrest there were reasonable grounds for suspecting that an arrestable offence had been committed by the person arrested. But it was held albeit on the 'special facts' of the case that 'there was sufficient evidence to go to the jury that notwithstanding that the condition precedent in section 24(6) [of PACE] was satisfied the arrest was nevertheless unlawful'.

---

[103]   Police and Criminal Evidence Act 1984, s 117.
[104]   *Simpson v Chief Constable of South Yorkshire Police, The Times*, 7 March 1991. Cf *Hill v Chief Constable of South Yorkshire*, above.
[105]   [1984] AC 437.
[106]   *The Times*, 23 March 1992.

D.   Police powers of detention and questioning of suspects

The detention of suspects

Apart from powers given by anti-terrorist legislation,[107] the police in England and Wales did not before 1984 have express power to detain suspects for further investigations to be carried out, nor did they have a general power to detain individuals for questioning, whether as suspects or potential witnesses.[108] In practice the police sometimes acted as if they had such powers.[109] The royal commission on criminal procedure recommended in 1981 that extra powers to detain suspects for questioning should be given to the police, with safeguards to ensure that those powers were not abused.[110] These extra powers were granted by PACE, which provides that an arrested person must be brought to a police station as soon as practicable after the arrest (s 30), though this may be delayed if his or her presence elsewhere is necessary for immediate investigation (s 30(10)). At every police station that is designated for such detention,[111] there must be a custody officer of the rank of sergeant or above (s 36).[112] It is the duty of the custody officer to authorise the detention of suspects if this is necessary to secure or preserve evidence relating to an offence or 'to obtain such evidence by questioning' the suspect (s 37). The custody officer is required to ensure that the detention is carried out in accordance with the 1984 Act and the Code of Practice on the Detention, Treatment and Questioning of Persons by Police Officers (Code C) (s 39).[113] In addition to the custody officer, the other intermediary between the arrested person and the investigating team is the review officer, who in the case of someone who has not been charged is an officer of the rank of inspector or above who has not been involved in the investigation. The review officer is required by the Act to conduct regular reviews of detention. The first review should take place not later than six hours after the detention was first authorised, and subsequent reviews should take place at intervals of no more than nine hours. The review may be postponed if the review officer is not available or if it would prejudice the investigation, though in either case it should be carried out as soon as practicable (s 40).

At common law someone arrested on the authority of a warrant had to be brought before the magistrates immediately, while someone arrested without a warrant had to be brought before the magistrates as soon as possible. In practice, however, people were detained for questioning, often euphemistically 'helping the police with their enquiries'. In *R v Holmes, ex p Sherman*,[114] it was held that 48 hours was the maximum period someone could be

---

[107]   See ch 25 E.
[108]   Though cf *Holgate-Mohammed v Duke* [1984] AC 437.
[109]   See the condemnation of this practice by Lawton LJ in *R v Lemsatef* [1977] 2 All ER 835.
[110]   Cmnd 8092, 1981, ch 4.
[111]   See 1984 Act, s 35.
[112]   On the limitations of this crucial measure designed 'to ensure that the welfare and interests of detained subjects are properly protected', see *Vince v Chief Constable of Dorset*, above.
[113]   For the duties of the custody officer in respect of arrested juveniles, see Criminal Justice Act 1991, s 59.
[114]   [1981] 2 All ER 612.

detained without being brought before magistrates. Detention for police questioning was first authorised by the Prevention of Terrorism (Temporary Provisions) Act 1974[115] which permitted detention for up to seven days. It was introduced as a general power in Scotland by the Criminal Justice (Scotland) Act 1980, which authorised detention (without arrest) for up to six hours.[116] PACE now allows the police to detain people who have been arrested for up to 24 hours without being released or charged in the first instance (s 41). This may be extended to 36 hours by an officer of the rank of superintendent or above where the offence is a 'serious arrestable offence' (s 42), a term defined to include murder, manslaughter, rape, kidnapping, and other arrestable offences which are likely to have consequences such as serious harm to state security or public order, or death, serious injury or serious financial loss to any person.[117] When serious arrestable offences are concerned, the period of 36 hours may be extended for up to 96 hours in total, if a magistrates' court (defined as a court of *two or more* justices of the peace, a potentially important safeguard) on application by the police is satisfied that further detention is justified to secure or preserve evidence by questioning the detainee (s 43). The detainee must be notified of the application to the magistrates and may be legally represented at the hearing. If the court does not authorise further detention, the detainee must be released or charged. Thus, from the time an arrested person reaches the police station, he or she may be detained for questioning by the police in connection with a serious arrestable offence for no less than 96 hours.

Arrested persons brought to a designated police station may be searched, fingerprinted and have samples taken of an intimate and non-intimate nature.[118] The search of arrested persons is authorised by s 54 of PACE which requires the custody officer to ascertain and record everything which the person has in his or her possession.[119] Any item may be seized and retained except for clothing and personal effects, which may be seized only if the custody officer has reasonable grounds to believe the item is evidence relating to the offence; or believes that the arrested person may use the items in question to cause physical injury personally or to another, damage property, interfere with evidence, or assist him or her to escape. Section 55 authorises intimate searches, ie the physical examination of a person's body orifices other than the mouth.[120] But this may be done only if it has been authorised by an officer of the rank of superintendent or above and there are reasonable grounds for believing that the person may have concealed on him or her

---

115 See ch 25 E.
116 Now Criminal Procedure (Scotland) Act 1995, s 14. See Brown, *Criminal Procedure and Evidence*, pp 22–6.
117 For the definition of a serious arrestable offence, see 1984 Act, s 116.
118 Suspects (and others) may also be photographed (with or without their consent), though unlike searches, fingerprints and samples, the practice is not regulated by statute. The practice is authorised by Code D.
119 For the position at common law, see *Lindley v Rutter* [1981] QB 128; *Brazil v Chief Constable of Surrey* [1983] 3 All ER 537.
120 See *R v Hughes* [1994] 1 WLR 876 (an intimate search requires physical intrusion, not visual examination).

either a Class A drug or an article which could be used to cause physical injury to himself or herself or others. In the course of such an examination, the police may 'seize' any material where there is cause to believe that it could be used to cause physical injury, damage property, interfere with evidence or assist an escape. An intimate search for drugs should be conducted by a medical practitioner or nurse at a hospital or surgery. Otherwise the search may be conducted at a police station and the requirement that it should normally be by a doctor can be dispensed with if none is available. If anything is seized, the person is to be told of this unless incapable of understanding what is said to him or her. Both a non-intimate and an intimate search must be carried out by a police officer of the same sex as the detainee (ss 54(9), 55(7)). These are formidable powers which invite abuse and which require a great deal of integrity on the part of all police officers if they are not to be misused. It is open to question whether these powers should be exercisable at the discretion of the police alone or whether magistrates or some other third party should be required to authorise what could be a monstrous invasion of privacy, particularly in the case of an innocent person.[121]

It was formerly the law that fingerprints could be taken only with the consent of the arrested person. Otherwise a magistrates' court order was required, and even this could be granted only in the case of a person who was not less than 14 years old and who had been charged with a criminal offence.[122] So there was no power to fingerprint anyone without their consent before charge. The position was different in Scotland,[123] and it has changed in England and Wales as a result of PACE. Section 61 allows fingerprints to be taken without consent with the authority of a police superintendent if there are reasonable grounds both to suspect the individual's involvement in a recordable offence and to believe that the prints will tend to prove or disprove guilt.[124] By s 62, intimate samples may be required for the same reasons,[125] an intimate sample being defined to include various bodily fluids, including blood and swabs from intimate parts of the anatomy (s 65) but not now swabs taken from the mouth.[126] Apart from urine and saliva, such samples must be taken by a doctor or a nurse and dental impressions by a dentist. Unlike fingerprints, however, intimate samples may be taken only with the consent of the detainee. It is indeed difficult to imagine how some such samples could be taken without consent. However, a refusal without good cause to consent may lead a court to 'draw such inferences from the refusal as appear proper' (s 62(10)). A non-intimate sample (eg hair, a sample from under a nail, or a

---

[121]   See further Code C: Code of of Practice for the Detention, Treatment and Questioning of Persons by Police Officers, especially para 4 and annex A.

[122]   Magistrates' Courts Act 1980, s 49.

[123]   *Adair v McGarry* 1933 SLT 482.

[124]   The definition of 'recordable' offence is wider than 'arrestable' offence and includes any offence punishable with imprisonment as well as others: see SI 1985 No 1941; SI 1989 No 694; SI 1997 No 566.

[125]   They may be used in the investigation of other offences: see *R v Kelt* [1994] 2 All ER 780 ('the public interest would not be served if a sample lawfully obtained in connection with one investigation could not be compared with blood left at the scene of another serious crime').

[126]   Criminal Justice and Public Order Act 1994, s 58, amending PACE, s 65.

swab taken from the mouth) may in contrast be taken without consent, if authorised by an officer of the rank of superintendent or above, if the offence for which the arrested person is being detained is a recordable offence (s 63). A non-intimate sample may also be taken without consent from a person who has been charged with or convicted of a recordable offence.[127] Where prints and samples are taken and the accused is later cleared of the offence, they must be destroyed as soon as practicable (s 64).[128]

An important question which has arisen in the light of scientific developments relates to the possibility that information obtained from samples (intimate and non-intimate) can be used by the police to compile a DNA register of individuals, on a national scale. Indeed one of the aims of the 1994 reforms to PACE was to allow samples to be taken for DNA testing, a process which is to be a major weapon of the police, the intention being that this country would have the most comprehensive DNA database in the world.[129] The implications of this for personal privacy are obvious, and although the prevention and detection of crime are important counterweights, there is clearly the need for safeguards in the way in which any information may be used by the police. It is for consideration whether any such information should be stored by the police rather than by an independent public agency,[130] and it is open to question whether the existing legal framework strikes the appropriate balance between two competing public interest concerns. The Police and Criminal Evidence Act 1984 expressly authorises the police to check information derived from samples obtained under the Act against 'information derived from other samples lawfully obtained by the police' (s 63A).[131] Secondly, as already suggested, the Act authorises the police to take samples inter alia from persons who have been charged with a recordable offence (or informed that they are to be reported for such an offence) or convicted of such an offence, even though it is not necessary for the purpose of securing a conviction (s 63). There is no need for the sample or the information derived therefrom to be destroyed. Thirdly, although prints and samples must be destroyed where the accused is cleared of the offence, this principle has been modified, though admittedly there are restrictions on the purposes for which the samples may be used.[132]

---

127 PACE, ss 3A, 3B, inserted by Criminal Justice and Public Order Act 1994, s 55. See now Criminal Evidence (Amendment) Act 1997.

128 So far as photographs are concerned, Code D requires the destruction of photographs and negatives if the suspect is prosecuted and cleared, or is not prosecuted (unless he or she admits the offence and is cautioned). But destruction is not required where someone has been convicted. In such cases the use of a photograph taken without consent may be protected by the law of confidence, though this does not prevent the release of a photograph (in the public interest, for the purposes of identification) by the police to shopkeepers who had been subjected to a 'sustained campaign of harassment, vile language and general mayhem': *Hellewell v Chief Constable of Derbyshire* [1995] 4 All ER 473 (Laws J).

129 Home Office Press Release 220/94, quoted by Morton, *Criminal Justice and Public Order Act 1994*, p 4. According to Zander, above, p 150, the police anticipate that the database will eventually hold some 5 million records.

130 See Royal Commission on Criminal Justice (Cm 2263, 1993), pp 14–16.

131 As amended by the Criminal Procedure and Investigations Act 1996, s 63.

132 Criminal Justice and Public Order Act 1994, s 57. For further details, see Zander, above, pp 153–6.

The rights of suspects

(a) The right to silence.[133]   An important principle in criminal procedure is the right of a suspected or accused person to remain silent; it is for the police to obtain evidence of guilt, not for a suspect to clear himself or herself. The main control over abuse at the stage of questioning is exercised by the criminal courts. It has long been established that a confession or statement by an accused person is not admissible in evidence at the trial unless it is voluntary, in the sense that it has not been obtained by fear of prejudice or hope of advantage, exercised or held out by a person in authority, or by oppression.[134] Moreover in 1912 and again in 1964,[135] the judges of the Queen's Bench Division drew up rules to govern the taking of statements from those being questioned by the police. The Judges' Rules did not have the force of law, but voluntary statements taken in accordance with the rules were usually admitted in evidence at a trial, and statements taken in serious breach of the rules might be excluded.[136] The 1964 Judges' Rules required that a person being questioned should be cautioned as soon as a police officer had evidence which afforded reasonable grounds for suspecting that he or she had committed an offence. When a person was charged with an offence, he or she had again to be cautioned; thereafter only for special reasons might further questions be put to him or her. In issuing the rules, the judges emphasised that the rules were not to affect certain principles, including the principle that every person at any state of an investigation should be able to consult privately with a solicitor (provided that no unreasonable hindrance was thereby caused to the investigation); and that a person should be charged with an offence as soon as there was enough evidence to do this.[137]

The 1984 Act did not directly affect the right to silence. From time immemorial it has been accepted that the burden is on the police to obtain evidence of guilt, not on the suspect to prove innocence. As we have seen, however, the principle was eroded by the provisions of the 1984 Act which permit negative inferences to be drawn from an accused's failure to provide an intimate sample. More seriously, this was extended by the Criminal Justice and Public Order Act 1994, which permits the court in criminal proceedings to draw such inferences as appear to it to be proper where the accused failed to mention 'any fact relied on in his defence in these proceedings' when questioned by the police or on being charged with an offence, where the fact was one which in the circumstances 'the accused could reasonably have been expected to mention' (s 34).[138] The Act also permits a court or jury 'to draw such inferences as appear proper' from the failure of the accused to give evidence at his or her trial, or without good cause to answer any question. The

---

[133]   On the different meanings of the right to silence, see *R v Smith* [1993] AC 1, per Lord Roskill. See generally Zander, pp 303–23. See also Cmnd 4991, 1972; and S Greer (1990) 53 MLR 709.

[134]   *Ibrahim v R* [1914] AC 599.

[135]   *Judges' Rules and Administrative Directions to the Police.* Home Office Circular No 89/1978. Cmnd 8092–1, app 12.

[136]   See eg *R v Prager* [1972] 1 All ER 1114.

[137]   See *R v Holmes, ex p Sherman* [1981] 2 All ER 612.

[138]   For background to the changes, see Royal Commission on Criminal Justice, note 130 above, which argued in favour of the right to silence.

court or jury may, moreover, draw such inferences as appear proper in such circumstances in determining whether the accused is guilty of the offence charged. The accused is not, however, required to give evidence on his or her own behalf, and is not guilty of contempt of court for failing to do so (s 35).[139] More specifically, inferences are permitted to be drawn where an accused person refuses to answer questions about incriminating objects, substances or marks which may be on his or her person, clothing or in his or her possession (s 36), or about his or her presence at a place at or about a time an offence for which he or she has been arrested was alleged to have been committed (s 37). But it is not yet an offence to refuse to answer questions put by the police.[140] Indeed, in *Lodwick v Sanders*[141] Watkins LJ emphasised that 'A constable may ask a question of a person, but he cannot ... demand an answer to any question; the right to silence in such a circumstance is predominant'.

(b) Detention and questioning. Nevertheless, PACE does allow people to be detained for questioning, in extreme cases for up to 96 hours. In order to help reduce the risk of this power being abused, the detention and questioning of suspects should be carried out in accordance with the safeguards laid down in the Act and in Code of Practice C. The Act itself provides two safeguards. The first is the right not to be held incommunicado. A person who has been arrested and is held in custody in a police station is entitled on request to have a friend or relative (or some other person who is known to him or her) informed of the arrest, as soon as reasonably practicable (s 56).[142] The other safeguard provided by the Act is that arrested persons held in custody in a police station are entitled on request to consult a solicitor privately at any time (s 58).[143] In some cases the exercise of these rights may be delayed for up to 36 hours, where the arrest is for a serious arrestable offence and where the delay has been authorised by an officer at least of the rank of superintendent. This applies particularly where there is a risk of danger to evidence or witnesses; or where the detained person has benefited from drug trafficking; or where there is a danger of interference with the gathering of information about acts of terrorism. In terrorist cases, the right to consult a solicitor may be subject to the condition that it is conducted within 'the sight and hearing' of a uniformed officer (s 58(15)). This applies where there is a risk of interference with the gathering of information about acts of terrorism, or where there is a risk that people may be alerted thereby making it more difficult to prevent acts of terrorism or to secure the arrest or prosecution of anyone in connection with an act of terrorism.

The statutory rights not to be held incommunicado and to consult privately with a solicitor are supplemented by the Code of Practice for the Detention,

---

139 See *R v Cowan* [1996] QB 373.
140 But see *R v Saunders, The Times,* 28 November 1995. See also *Bishopsgate Investment Management Ltd v Maxwell* [1992] 2 All ER 856.
141 [1985] 1 All ER 577, at 580–1.
142 See *R v Kerawalla* [1991] Crim LR 451. See previously the Criminal Law Act 1977, s 62.
143 See *R v Samuel* [1988] QB 615; *R v Alladice* (1988) 87 Cr App Rep 380. In *R v South Wales Chief Constable, ex p Merrick* [1994] 2 All ER 560 it was held that s 58 does not apply to give the accused the right of access to a solicitor where he is in custody in a magistrates' court following the denial of bail. But it was also held that there is a common law right to this

Treatment and Questioning of Persons by Police Officers (Code C).[144] So far as the right not to be held incommunicado is concerned, detained persons may receive visits at the custody officer's discretion and may speak on the telephone for a reasonable time to one person, though the call (other than to a solicitor) may be listened to and anything said used in evidence in any subsequent criminal proceedings (para 5). So far as the right to legal advice is concerned, a person must be permitted to have his or her solicitor present while being questioned by the police. The solicitor may be required to leave the interview only if his or her conduct is such that the investigating officer is unable properly to put questions to the suspect (para 6). The code also deals with such matters as the conditions of detention (para 8), the giving of cautions to detained persons (para 10) and the conduct of interviews (para 11). Regarding cautions, a suspected person 'must be cautioned before any questions about [the suspected offence] ... are put to him'. The effect of the 1994 Act is that the caution should be in the following terms: 'You do not have to say anything. But it may harm your defence if you do not mention when questioned something which you later rely on in court. Anything you do say may be given in evidence.' In conducting interviews, officers should not try 'to obtain answers to questions or to elicit a statement by the use of oppression', nor 'shall indicate, except in answer to a direct question, what action will be taken on the part of the police if the person being interviewed answers questions, makes a statement or refuses to do either' (para 11). In any period of 24 hours, a detained person normally should be allowed a continuous period of at least 8 hours for rest, free from questioning, travel or other interruption arising out of the investigation (para 12).

(c) Miscarriages of justice.   Despite these safeguards, concern continues to be expressed about miscarriages of justice arising largely from convictions based on evidence given by suspects in police stations.[145] Apart from the cases of the Bridgewater Three, the Guildford Four and the Birmingham Six, who were convicted before the 1984 Act came into operation, the most notorious is the case of the Tottenham Three. Three men were convicted for offences in connection with the murder of a police officer during a riot at Broadwater Farm, North London, in 1985. The men's convictions were overturned by the Court of Appeal in 1991[146] (following a Home Secretary's reference under the Criminal Appeal Act 1968, s 17)[147] when it became clear that the confession evidence which led to their convictions had been fabricated. Regulations have since been introduced requiring the tape-recording of interviews at police stations,[148] though remarkably these do not apply to terrorist offences or to offences under the Official Secrets Act 1911, s 1. Had these regulations been in force in the 1970s there would have been no obligation to tape-record the

---

effect 'which preceded the Act of 1984 and which [was] not abrogated by that Act' (p 572). This common law right does not appear to extend to having the solicitor present during police interviews: *Begley* (1996) 5 BNIL 39, and *Russell* (1996) 9 BNIL 33. On the role of the solicitor, see *R v Paris* (1993) 97 Cr App Rep 99.

[144] See D Wolchover and A Heaton-Armstrong [1991] Crim LR 232.
[145] See Walker and Starmer, *Justice in Error.*
[146] *R v Silcott, Braithwaite and Raghip, The Times,* 9 December 1991.
[147] See ch 18 C.
[148] SI 1991 No 2687; SI 1992 No 2803.

interviews of the Birmingham Six, the injustice visited upon whom by false confession evidence is one of the greatest ever perpetrated in Britain. In 1992, however, the practice was extended to terrorist cases on a trial basis,[149] though it remains the case that many of the other safeguards in PACE are expressly excluded from offences under the Prevention of Terrorism (Temporary Provisions) Act 1989.

E.   Police powers of entry, search and seizure[150]

Police powers of entry

'By the law of England', said Lord Camden in *Entick v Carrington*,[151] 'every invasion of private property, be it ever so minute, is a trespass. No man can set foot upon my ground without my licence, but he is liable to an action though the damage be nothing'. This principle was applied in *Davis v Lisle*[152] where it was held that two police officers, who had entered a garage to make inquiries about a lorry which had been obstructing the highway, became trespassers when the occupier told them to leave. There are, however, three circumstances in which the police may lawfully enter private property. The first, as Lord Camden suggests, is with the consent of the owner or occupier.[153] Indeed, in *Robson v Hallett*[154] it was held that a police officer, like other members of the public coming to a house on lawful business, has an implied licence from the householder to walk to the front door and to ask whether he can come inside; and that he must be allowed a reasonable time to leave the premises before he becomes a trespasser. Secondly, the police may have statutory authority to enter private property even without the consent of the owner. Under the Police and Criminal Evidence Act 1984, a police officer may enter private premises to execute a search warrant (s 8) and to execute an arrest warrant; arrest a person for an arrestable offence;[155] arrest a person for certain public order offences; recapture a person who is unlawfully at large;[156] save life and limb, or prevent serious damage to property (s 17).[157]

These powers under s 17 are generally exercisable only if the officer has reasonable grounds for believing that the person whom he or she is seeking is on the premises. There is a power to search the premises entered, but only a search that is reasonably required for the purpose for which the power to enter was exercised. So if the officer enters premises under s 17 to arrest a person, he or she may search the premises to find that person, but may not under s 17 search for evidence relating to the offence. Other provisions of

---

[149]   Cm 2263, 1993.
[150]   See Stone, *Entry, Search and Seizure: A Guide to Civil and Criminal Powers of Entry*. Also Polyviou, *Entry, Search and Seizure: Constitutional and Common Law*.
[151]   (1765) 19 St Tr 1030, 1066; ch 6 above.
[152]   [1936] 2 KB 434.
[153]   See Code of Practice B, para 4.
[154]   [1967] 2 QB 939.
[155]   *Chapman v DPP* [1988] Crim LR 842.
[156]   See *D'Souza v DPP* [1992] 4 All ER 545 (no right of entry unless *in pursuit* of someone unlawfully at large).
[157]   As amended by the Prisoners (Return to Custody) Act 1995.

PACE confer this power.[158] Additional powers of entry were conferred by the Police Act 1997, Part III, which empowers senior police officers to authorise the entry to and interference with property, mainly for the purposes of surveillance, as in the placing of listening devices. These controversial provisions were heavily amended as a result of opposition in the House of Lords to the government's proposals, so that in many instances (for example, in respect of domestic or office premises) the authorisation will not take effect until approved by a judicial commissioner.[159]

Thirdly, apart from entry with consent or under statutory authority, a power of entry may arise from common law. Although s 17(5) abolishes all common law rules authorising the entry of private premises by the police, it is expressly provided that this does not affect any power of entry to deal with or prevent a breach of the peace. The existence of such a power appears to have been recognised in *Thomas v Sawkins*,[160] though the ratio of that case is controversial.[161]

Police powers of search

1 Search with a warrant. The effect of decisions such as *Entick v Carrington* was that, except for the power to search for stolen goods, for which a warrant could be obtained at common law from a magistrate,[162] statutory powers were needed if the police were lawfully to search private premises. Before the Police and Criminal Evidence Act 1984, the law was haphazard and irrational. Although there were about 50 statutes conferring the power to issue search warrants, as Lord Denning pointed out in *Ghani v Jones*,[163] none gave power to a magistrate or a judge to issue a search warrant for evidence of murder. Included amongst these statutes are powers conferred upon Inland Revenue officials to obtain a search warrant from a circuit judge if there is reasonable ground to suspect that a serious tax fraud is being, has been or is about to be committed, and evidence of it is to be found on the premises specified in the application.[164] These powers were described by Lord Scarman as 'a breath-taking inroad on the individual's right of privacy and right of property',[165] before they were modified in 1989. By the Misuse of Drugs Act 1971, s 23(3), a search warrant may be obtained if a constable satisfies a magistrate that there are reasonable grounds for suspecting that controlled drugs are in the

---

[158]   Police and Criminal Evidence Act 1984, s 32(2)(b). For an example of other powers of entry without a warrant, see *Whitelaw v Haining* 1992 SLT 956.

[159]   For discussion of the Police Bill, see K D Ewing and C A Gearty, London Review of Books, 6 February 1997.

[160]   [1935] 2 KB 249; and see ch 23.

[161]   See A L Goodhart (1936) 6 CLJ 22. The power is not confined to meetings. See *McLeod v Metropolitan Police Commissioner* [1994] 4 All ER 553.

[162]   See now Theft Act 1968, s 26.

[163]   [1970] 1 QB 693.

[164]   Taxes Management Act 1970, s 20C, inserted by Finance Act 1976, amended by Finance Act 1989, s 146.

[165]   *R v IRC, ex p Rossminster Ltd* [1980] AC 952, 1022; and see Cmnd 8822, 1983. Customs officers have long exercised similar powers without warrants in respect of smuggled goods under the so-called 'writ of assistance'. See Customs and Excise Management Act 1979, s 161; and [1983] PL 345.

unlawful possession of a person on any premises. Very wide powers of search are conferred by the Official Secrets Act 1911, s 9: a magistrate may issue a warrant authorising the search of named premises and persons found there, and the 'seizure of anything which is evidence of an offence under this Act having been or about to be committed'; where the interests of the state require immediate action, a police superintendent may authorise such a search. These powers were used to search the premises of BBC Scotland in Glasgow following government concern about the proposed broadcast of a television programme about a British spy satellite.[166] Under the Incitement to Disaffection Act 1934, s 2, there are similar powers, but the warrant must be issued by a High Court judge.

General powers for the granting of search warrants are now found in s 8 of PACE.[167] A search warrant may be granted by a justice of the peace on an application by a police constable where there are reasonable grounds for believing that a serious arrestable offence has been committed and that there is material on the premises which is likely to be of substantial value in the police investigation.[168] This power of magistrates to grant a warrant does not apply, however, to material which consists of or includes items subject to legal privilege, 'excluded material' or 'special procedure material'. Items subject to legal privilege include communications between a lawyer and his or her client (s 10),[169] while excluded material is defined to cover confidential personal records,[170] human tissue or tissue fluid taken for purposes of medical treatment and held in confidence, and journalistic material which is held in confidence (s 11).[171] Special procedure material refers to other forms of journalistic material,[172] and also other material that is held in confidence or subject to an obligation of secrecy and has been acquired in the course of any business, profession or other occupation (s 14). No warrant can be issued in relation to material subject to legal privilege, but orders may be issued by a circuit judge under Sched 1, para 4, following an *inter partes* hearing requiring excluded material or special procedure material to be delivered to a police constable within seven days.[173] If this is not complied with, a circuit judge may issue a warrant authorising a police officer to enter and search premises and seize the material in question (Sched 1, para 12). In some circumstances, a warrant may be secured under para 12 without first seeking an order under

---

[166]   See Ewing and Gearty, *Freedom under Thatcher*, pp 147–52.
[167]   K W Lidstone (1989) 40 NILQ 333. See also Code of Practice B, esp paras 2 and 5.
[168]   See also PACE 1984, s 8(3), and *R v Reading JJ, ex p South West Meat Ltd* [1992] Crim LR 672.
[169]   Cf *R v Central Criminal Court, ex p Francis and Francis* [1989] AC 346. See *R v R* [1994] 4 All ER 260.
[170]   On confidential material, see Zuckerman [1990] Crim LR 472.
[171]   Hospital records of patient admission and discharge are excluded material: see *R v Cardiff Crown Court, ex p Kellam, The Times*, 3 May 1995.
[172]   On journalistic material, see s 13. Also *R v Bristol Crown Court, ex p Bristol Press Agency Ltd* (1987) 85 Cr App Rep 190; *R v Middlesex Crown Court, ex p Salinger* [1993] QB 564.
[173]   The material may be surrendered voluntarily by the person who holds it without the consent of the person to whom it relates: *R v Singleton* (1995) 1 Cr App Rep 431. Powers of circuit judges to grant production orders are also in the Criminal Justice Act 1988, s 93H, and the Drug Trafficking Act 1994. On the relationship between these measures and PACE, see *R v Crown Court at Guildford, ex p DPP* [1996] 4 All ER 961.

para 4. This practice was, however, strongly deprecated in *R v Maidstone Crown Court, ex p Waitt*,[174] where it was said:

The special procedure under section 9 and schedule 1 is a serious inroad upon the liberty of the subject. The responsibility for ensuring that the procedure is not abused lies with circuit judges ... The responsibility is greatest when the circuit judge is asked to issue a search warrant under paragraph 12. It is essential that the reason for authorising the seizure is made clear. The preferred method of obtaining material for a police investigation should always be by way of an *inter partes* order under paragraph 4, after notice of application has been served under paragraph 8. An *ex parte* application under paragraph 12 must never become a matter of common form and satisfaction as to the fulfilment of the conditions is an important matter of substance.

Apart from thus extending the grounds for granting search warrants, the 1984 Act also introduced new safeguards.[175] These are found in ss 15 and 16, and they apply not only to search warrants issued under PACE, but also to warrants issued to a constable 'under any enactment, including an enactment contained in an Act passed after this Act'.[176] An application, which is made ex parte, must be in writing and must explain the grounds for the application and the premises to be searched. The constable must answer on oath any question put by the justice of the peace or the circuit judge. The warrant authorises only one search, and unlike an arrest warrant must be executed within one month from the date of its issue. Entry and search must be at a reasonable hour. Where the occupier of the premises is present, the police officers must identify themselves, produce the warrant, and supply a copy to the occupier.[177] If there is no person present, a copy of the warrant should be left in a prominent place on the premises. A search under the warrant does not authorise a general search of the premises, but only a search to the extent required for the purpose for which the warrant was issued (s 16).

In *R v Longman*,[178] police officers with a search warrant effected entry to a house by deception, as a result of difficulties they had encountered in the past. A woman police officer in plain clothes pretended to deliver flowers. When the door was opened to her, other officers in plain clothes immediately entered the house, with one shouting 'Police, got a warrant' which he held in his hand. The Court of Appeal held that this procedure complied with ss 15 and 16 of PACE. The court rejected the contention that '*before entering* the premises a police officer must not only identify himself but must produce his warrant card and ... also the search warrant and serve a copy of the search warrant on the householder'. It is enough that these things are done *after entry* to the premises. To hold otherwise, said Lord Lane CJ, would mean that the whole object of the more important type of search would be stultified.

2 Search without a warrant.   Police powers to search without a warrant arise in three circumstances. The first is the power to search a person following arrest. At common law such a power was recognised, as also was the power of the police to take possession of articles which might be evidence connected with

---

174   [1988] Crim LR 384.
175   Further safeguards are in Code of Practice B, paras 2 and 5.
176   Police and Criminal Evidence Act 1984, s 15(1).
177   See *R v Chief Constable of Lancashire, ex p Parker* [1993] QB 577 (the warrant and any schedule must be shown; an uncertified photocopy is impermissible rendering the search unlawful and requiring the return of any seized documents).
178   [1988] 1 WLR 619.

the offence or which might help the arrested person to escape or cause harm.[179] However, the police had a discretion to exercise and could not apply an automatic rule of searching every arrested person.[180] These powers are extended by PACE. Section 32 allows a constable to search an arrested person, at a place other than a police station, 'if the constable has reasonable grounds for believing that the arrested person may present a danger to himself or others'. A constable may search an arrested person for anything which might be used to escape from lawful custody, or for anything which might be evidence relating to an offence (s 32(2)), though in both these cases the power to search is a power to search only to the extent that is reasonably required for the purpose of discovering 'any such thing or any such evidence' (s 32(3)). Moreover, the power to search does not authorise the police to require a person to remove any clothing in public, except an outer coat, jacket or gloves (s 32(4)) but it does authorise the search of a person's mouth.[181] A police officer conducting such a search may seize any item which may cause physical injury, might assist in an escape from lawful custody, or is evidence relating to any offence (s 32(8)). The only items which cannot be seized in this way are those which are subject to legal privilege (though no such exception applies to excluded material or to special procedure material) (s 32(9)). An arrested person should be taken directly to a police station (s 30). Once there he or she may be searched again. Depending on the circumstances, this may be a strip search and/or an intimate search of body orifices.[182]

The second power of search without a warrant is a power to search premises ancillary to arrest. In the Irish case, *Dillon v O'Brien*,[183] the existence of a common law power to search property following an arrest was recognised in order to preserve material evidence of guilt. Not only was the right to take evidence admitted, but there was a right to take it by force if necessary. This position was confirmed by *Ghani v Jones*:[184] where police officers arrest a man lawfully, with or without a warrant, for a serious offence, they are entitled to take away goods which they find in his possession or in his house which they reasonably believe to be material evidence. The position is governed now by PACE, s 32, whereby following the arrest of a person, a constable may enter any premises in which the person was when arrested or immediately before he or she was arrested. The constable may search the premises for evidence relating to the offence for which the person was arrested (s 32(2)(b)). At common law, the power to search premises incidental to arrest was a power to search at the time of the arrest. So in *McLorie v Oxford*[185] it was held that after having arrested a suspect and detained him in custody, the police had no right to return to the house to search for the instruments of crime, even of serious crime; that is to say, no right to do so unless they could get a search warrant, though (as we have seen) that would not have been available in all

---

[179]   *Dillon v O'Brien* (1887) 16 Cox CC 245.
[180]   *Lindley v Rutter* [1981] QB 128; *Brazil v Chief Constable of Surrey* [1983] 3 All ER 537.
[181]   Criminal Justice and Public Order Act 1994, s 59.
[182]   See Section D above.
[183]   (1887) 16 Cox CC 245.
[184]   [1970] 1 QB 693.
[185]   [1982] QB 1290.

circumstances where it might have been necessary. Yet although the police powers to secure search warrants are now much wider, so too are their powers of search ancillary to arrest without a warrant. Section 32 is at least open to the interpretation that the power to search the premises where the person was when arrested may be, but need not be, contemporaneous with the arrest. The only safeguard is that the power can be used only if the police officer has reasonable grounds for believing that there is evidence on the premises for which a search is permitted.[186]

The third power of search without a warrant is a power to search the home of the arrested person, even though he or she was not arrested there and even though he or she was not there immediately before arrest. At common law, the courts seemed reluctant to recognise any such power.

In *Jeffrey v Black*,[187] the accused was arrested for stealing a sandwich from a public house. He was taken to a police station and charged and was told that police officers intended to search his house. The accused went to the house in the presence of officers, who did not have a search warrant, and let them in, though he did not consent to the search; cannabis being found, charges were brought under the Misuse of Drugs Act 1971. It was held that the search was unlawful, the court refusing to accept that there was a common law right to search a person's premises without a warrant in circumstances where the person was arrested elsewhere.[188]

There were suggestions, however, that such a search might be permitted where the house search was concerned with securing evidence relating to the offence for which the person had been arrested. But that was not the case in *Jeffrey v Black*, with the police using the alleged theft of a sandwich as an excuse to look for drugs. Section 18 of PACE now permits a constable to enter and search any premises occupied or controlled by any person who is under arrest for an arrestable offence if there are reasonable grounds to suspect that there is on the premises evidence (other than items subject to legal privilege) that relates to that offence or to a related arrestable offence. So *Jeffrey v Black* should be decided the same way today, though s 18 removes the doubt about the existence of the power in appropriate cases. The exercise of the power should normally be authorised in writing by an inspector or an officer of a higher rank, though the power can be used without first taking a suspect to the police station and securing authorisation, if this is necessary for the effective investigation of the offence.

Police powers of seizure

The powers of search which we have discussed are generally also associated with a power of seizure. However, the nature of that power varies from case to case. In the case of entry to search for an escaped person or to make an arrest (s 17), there is no power to seize and retain property. In the case of search with a search warrant (s 8), there is a power only to seize and retain 'anything for which a search has been authorised'. The same is true of the power to enter and search an arrested person's premises after arrest (s 18). In the case of a search of premises where the arrested person was at or immediately

---

[186]   See further, Code of Practice B, para 3.
[187]   [1978] QB 490.
[188]   But the cannabis found at the flat was held to be admissible as evidence. See Section F.

before the arrest (s 32), there is no power of seizure in the section itself, though in the case of a personal search there is a right to retain anything reasonably believed to be evidence of any offence, including an offence unrelated to the grounds for the arrest. What is the position if the police are on property for any of these purposes, or if they are present with the consent of the owner or occupier, and they stumble across something which may suggest that an offence has been committed? In what circumstances, if any, can the police seize that evidence? Clearly they can do so if they are present with a search warrant and the material relates to the offence for which the warrant was granted. But what if it relates to some wholly unconnected offence? Similarly, what is the position if the police enter under s 17 to make an arrest and stumble across incriminating evidence? Difficult questions arose at common law as to the police power to seize and retain private property.

In *Elias v Pasmore*[189] the police raided the premises of the National Unemployed Workers' Movement to execute a warrant for the arrest of Wal Hannington for sedition. The police arrested Hannington and also took away a large quantity of documents, though they did not have a search warrant. The documents were later used as evidence in proceedings against Syd Elias for inciting Hannington to commit the sedition. Horridge J held that the 'interests of the State' justified the police in seizing material that was relevant to the prosecution for any crime of any person, not only of the person being arrested.

In this poorly reasoned judgment, Horridge J argued that although it may at the time have been improper to seize the material, its later use as evidence justified the seizure. These views were disapproved by the Court of Appeal in *Ghani v Jones*,[190] a case arising out of an investigation of a suspected murder in the course of which police officers wished to retain the passports of the victim's close relatives and some letters belonging to them. The Court of Appeal ordered the police to return the passports and letters to the relatives, since it had not been shown that they were material evidence to prove the commission of the murder nor that the police had reasonable grounds for believing that the relatives were in any way implicated in a crime. The court laid down certain principles which it considered to apply when the police need to take private property in the course of an investigation: the police must have reasonable grounds for believing (*a*) that a serious crime has been committed, (*b*) that the article is the instrument by which the crime was committed or is material evidence to prove commission of the crime, and (*c*) that the person in possession of the article is implicated in the crime 'or at any rate his refusal (of consent to the police) must be quite unreasonable'; moreover (*d*) the police must not keep the article longer than is reasonably necessary; and (*e*) the lawfulness of the conduct of the police must be judged at the time and not (as in *Elias v Pasmore*) by what happens afterwards.[191]

Additional powers of seizure and retention are in PACE, ss 19–22. These powers supplement but do not replace the common law powers (s 19(5)). So to the extent that the statute is less extensive, the police may continue to rely

---

189   [1934] 2 KB 164. See E C S Wade (1934) 50 LQR 354.
190   [1970] 1 QB 693.
191   Cf *Frank Truman (Export) Ltd v Metropolitan Police Commissioner* [1977] QB 952; *Wershof v Metropolitan Police Commissioner* [1978] 3 All ER 540.

on their common law powers as recognised by *Ghani v Jones*[192] and in subsequent cases.[193] The powers conferred by s 19 apply where a constable is lawfully on any premises, whether by invitation, to make an arrest, or to conduct a search with or without a warrant. In such circumstances material may be seized where the constable has reasonable grounds to believe *either* that it has been obtained as a result of the commission of any offence (s 19(2)); *or* that it is evidence in relation to an offence which he or she is investigating or any other offence (s 19(3)). In either case, seizure is permitted only where this is necessary to prevent the items from being concealed, lost, damaged, altered or destroyed. The only restriction on what may be seized relates to items reasonably believed to be subject to legal privilege (s 19(6)). This power to seize articles is subject to the safeguards laid down in ss 21 and 22. By s 21, a constable who seizes anything is required, if requested, to provide a record of what is seized to the occupier of the premises or the person who had custody of it immediately before the seizure. In addition, the person who had custody or control of the item seized has a right of access to it under the supervision of a police officer, though this may be refused if the officer in charge of the investigation reasonably believes that this would prejudice the investigation. By s 22, anything seized may be retained for so long as is necessary in all the circumstances. In particular, it may be retained for use as evidence at a trial or for forensic examination. Also, anything may be retained in order to establish its lawful owner where there are reasonable grounds for believing that it has been obtained in consequence of an offence. Nothing is to be retained for use as evidence or for investigation if a photograph or a copy would be sufficient.[194] But where material is unlawfully seized, it must be returned, the police having no right to retain it for use as evidence.[195]

F.   Remedies for abuse of police powers

Having examined the rights and duties of the police in respect of the citizen, we now turn to consider the remedies available when the police overstep the mark. We consider five possible remedies or consequences of unlawful police conduct:

1. The right to resist the police in self-defence.
2. The writ of habeas corpus.
3. The right to initiate legal proceedings to recover damages for any loss suffered.
4. The right to complain to the Police Complaints Authority.
5. In the event of criminal proceedings being brought against the victim of police misconduct, the possibility that evidence improperly obtained may be excluded.

---

[192] [1970] 1 QB 693.
[193] See eg *Garfunkel v Metropolitan Police Commissioner* [1972] Crim LR 44.
[194] See further, Code of Practice B, para 6.
[195] *R v Chief Constable of Lancashire, ex p Parker* [1993] QB 577.

Self-defence[196]

At the time of interference with person or property, the citizen may have some right of self-defence, and this can affect both civil and criminal liability. The point is acknowledged in the leading case, *Christie v Leachinsky*,[197] the ratio of which (as we have seen) forms the basis of what is now s 28 of PACE. There Lord Simonds said that 'it is the corollary of the right of every citizen to be thus free from arrest that he should be entitled to resist arrest unless that arrest is lawful'.[198] In *Abbassy v Metropolitan Police Commissioner*,[199] Woolf LJ acknowledged that one of the reasons for the rule that a person is to be told the reason for his arrest is so that if what he is told is not a reason which justifies his arrest he can exercise 'his right to resist arrest'.[200] On the other hand, however, under the Police Act 1996, s 89, it is an offence to assault, resist or wilfully obstruct a constable in the execution of his or her duty. There are therefore hazards in the way of a citizen who uses force to resist what he or she believes to be an unlawful arrest by police, whether of himself or herself, or of a close relation.[201] 'The law does not encourage the subject to resist the authority of one whom he knows to be an officer of the law'.[202] Although in *Kenlin v Gardiner* two boys were entitled to use reasonable force to escape from two constables who were seeking to question them,[203] in general it is inexpedient by self-defence to resist arrest by a police officer: if the arrest is lawful, the assault on the constable is aggravated because he or she is in execution of duty. On the other hand, if a defendant 'applies force to a police or court officer which would be reasonable if that person were not a police or court officer, and the defendant believes that he is not, then even if his belief is unreasonable he has a good plea of self-defence'.[204] The offence of obstructing a constable in execution of his duty has been widely interpreted in English law;[205] the equivalent offence in Scotland has been interpreted as limited to some physical interference with the police.[206]

Habeas corpus[207]

If an individual is wrongfully deprived of liberty, it is not sufficient that he or she should be able to sue the gaoler for damages under the ordinary civil law. Whether detained by an official or by a private individual, it would be wrong that the detention should continue while the process of civil litigation takes its normal lengthy course. English law provides in the writ of habeas corpus a means by which a person detained without legal justification may secure

---

[196] See C Harlow [1974] Crim LR 528.
[197] [1947] AC 573.
[198] At 591.
[199] [1990] 1 All ER 193.
[200] And see *Edwards v DPP*, *The Times*, 29 March 1993.
[201] *R v Fennell* [1971] QB 428.
[202] *Christie v Leachinsky* [1947] AC 573, 599 (Lord du Parcq).
[203] [1967] 2 QB 510. And see *Lindley v Rutter* [1981] QB 128; *Pedro v Diss* [1981] 2 All ER 59.
[204] *Blackburn v Bowering* [1994] 3 All ER 380, at 384.
[205] R C Austin [1982] CLP 187; Smith and Hogan, pp 413–22.
[206] *Curlett v McKechnie* 1938 JC 176.
[207] And see ch 30 below.

prompt release. The person responsible for the detention is not thereby punished, but the person imprisoned is set free and may pursue such further remedies for compensation or punishment as may be available. Habeas corpus may be sought by convicted prisoners, those detained in custody pending trial, and those held by the police during criminal investigations;[208] those awaiting deportation or otherwise detained under the Immigration Act 1971; those awaiting extradition; and mental patients.[209] The writ may be used as a means of determining disputes over the custody of children, but these cases are dealt with by the Family Division of the High Court and because of other procedures recourse to habeas corpus is seldom necessary. We have seen that the Bill of Rights declared that excessive bail ought not to be required: legislation today encourages the magistrates to give bail to persons awaiting trial whenever possible,[210] though this presumption has been seriously eroded by the Criminal Justice and Public Order Act 1994 in respect of serious offences (s 25) and offences committed while on bail (s 26).

Habeas corpus has often been described as 'the most important writ known to the constitutional law of England, affording as it does a swift and imperative remedy in all cases of illegal restraint or confinement'.[211] Its scope is potentially very wide. Suffice to say for present purposes that it is available to anyone who is illegally detained by the police. In 1981, Donaldson LJ pointed out that 'all should know that the writ of habeas corpus has not fallen into disuse, but is ... a real and available remedy'.[212] On that occasion, before the passing of PACE, the writ was issued in the case of a man who had been in police detention for two days without being charged or brought before magistrates. However, now that 'strict time limits apply to detention, with provision for magistrates' court warrants to extend detention periods, there should be very little scope for habeas corpus applications in relation to suspects in police custody'.[213] But an action would lie if someone were detained for more than 36 hours without a warrant or, as shown in *Re Gillen's Application*,[214] where there is evidence that the police are physically maltreating a suspect. It has been said that:

Habeas corpus is probably the oldest of the prerogative writs. Authorising its issue in appropriate cases is regarded by all judges as their first duty, because we have all been brought up to believe, and do believe, that the liberty of the citizen under the law is the most fundamental of all freedoms. Consistently with this, an application for a writ of habeas corpus has virtually absolute priority over all other court business.[215]

The duty to make the remedy available as a means of testing the legality of any

---

208   See eg *R v Holmes, ex p Sherman* [1981] 2 All ER 612.
209   See *X v United Kingdom* (1982) 4 EHRR 188. See *Re S-C (Mental Patient)* [1996] QB 599.
210   Bail Act 1976.
211   *Home Secretary v O'Brien* [1923] AC 603, 609 (Lord Birkenhead). And see ch 30.
212   *R v Holmes, ex p Sherman* [1981] 2 All ER 612, 616.
213   Robertson, *Freedom, the Individual and the Law*, p 43. But cf *Re Maychell, The Independent*, 26 February 1993 (territorial army officer detained under close arrest by military authorities for 75 days following a charge under the Official Secrets Act 1911, s 1. Habeas corpus refused because delay was not excessive in the circumstances).
214   [1988] NILR 40.
215   *R v Home Secretary, ex p Cheblak* [1991] 2 All ER 319, 322.

contested detention is imposed on the United Kingdom by the European Convention on Human Rights, art 5(4).[216]

Legal proceedings against the police

A person who claims to be the victim of unlawful police conduct may be able to bring an action for damages against the officers in question and/or against the chief constable, who is vicariously liable for the torts committed by his or her officers.[217] An action may be for assault, wrongful arrest, false imprisonment, trespass to property or goods, public misfeasance[218] or may take the form of an action for the return of property which has been improperly seized. An action for malicious prosecution may be maintained by any person who is prosecuted for a criminal offence maliciously and without reasonable and probable cause; but it is difficult to win such an action against the police.[219] In principle, public officials are personally liable for their own wrongful acts. But special protection is given to some officials against certain liabilities.[220] Many of the cases discussed earlier in this chapter relate to civil proceedings brought by aggrieved individuals. So in *Wershof v Metropolitan Police Commissioner*[221] the plaintiff was awarded £1,000 for his wrongful arrest. Exemplary damages may be awarded against the police, even though there has been no oppressive behaviour or other aggravating circumstances.[222]

Civil liability may also arise even where an arrest is lawful, for subsequent detention as well as the initial arrest must be in accordance with law.[223] In *Kirkham v Chief Constable of Greater Manchester*[224] it was held that the police owe a duty of care towards prisoners in their custody and that the widow of a man who had committed suicide while in police custody was entitled to damages in circumstances where there had been negligence by the police. And in *Treadway v Chief Constable of West Midlands*,[225] £2,500, £7,500 aggravated, and £40,000 exemplary damages were awarded to a plaintiff who had signed a confession 'only after he had been handcuffed behind his back and a succession of plastic bags had been placed over his head with the ends bunched up behind his neck causing him to struggle and pass out'. Many of the actions which are initiated against the police are settled before they reach the court. One of the most widely publicised was the settlement by the South Yorkshire police in favour of 39 former striking miners in connection with incidents arising from clashes between police and demonstrators at Orgreave

---

[216] On the continuing significance of habeas corpus, see *R v Oldham Justices, ex p Cawley* [1996] 1 All ER 464. See also R Epstein (1996) NLJ, 8 November 1996 (on its application to people under 21 who are unlawfully imprisoned for fine default), and Sir William Wade (1997) 113 LQR 55.

[217] Police Act 1996, s 88. See Lustgarten, *The Governance of Police*, pp 136–8. See also Clayton and Tomlinson, *Civil Actions against the Police*.

[218] But see *Bennett v Metropolitan Police Commissioner*, *The Times*, 28 December 1994.

[219] See *Glinski v McIver* [1962] AC 726; *Wershof v Metropolitan Police Commissioner* [1978] 3 All ER 540. Cf *Hunter v Chief Constable of West Midlands Police* [1982] AC 529.

[220] See eg Constables' Protection Act 1750.

[221] [1978] 3 All ER 540.

[222] See also *Reynolds v Metropolitan Police Commissioner* [1982] Crim LR 600.

[223] *Re Gillen's Application* [1988] NILR 40.

[224] [1990] 2 QB 283. See also Code of Practice C, esp paras 8.10 and 9.

[225] *The Times*, 25 October 1994.

coking plant in June 1984. The police force is reported to have paid a total of £425,000 in favour of the plaintiffs who had sued for assault, wrongful arrest, malicious prosecution and false imprisonment.[226]

In 1997, concern about the size of damages awards in civil actions against the police led to the Court of Appeal issuing guidelines for juries on the level of exemplary damages in which an 'absolute maximum' of £50,000 should be awarded for particularly bad conduct by officers of at least the rank of superintendent.[227] This followed two cases in which awards of £302,000 and £220,000 respectively had been awarded to victims of police brutality.[228] Quite apart from civil proceedings, a criminal prosecution may be instituted against the police for unlawful conduct such as an assault. In England, the possibility of a private prosecution of a police officer is sometimes a valuable means of legal protection: in 1963, it was a private prosecution of police officers in Sheffield which led to an official inquiry into the 'rhino tail' assaults.[229] There are, however, serious difficulties in practice with private prosecutions, or indeed any criminal prosecution against the police even in cases following serious miscarriages of justice to which the actions of the police were alleged to contribute.[230]

Complaints against the police

Under the 1984 Act, complaints made by or on behalf of a member of the public against a police officer are submitted to the chief officer of the force concerned.[231] It is his or her first duty to take steps to obtain or preserve relevant evidence.[232] The procedure thereafter depends on whether or not the complaint concerns a senior officer (that is, above the rank of chief superintendent). The main difference is that investigation of complaints about senior officers is the duty of the police authority, while other complaints are handled by the chief officer.[233] What follows outlines the procedure to be adopted by a chief officer.[234] Having established that he or she rather than the police authority is responsible, the chief officer must record the complaint. Thereafter three levels of complaint are distinguished and treated differently.

(*a*) At the lowest level is a category of complaint suitable for informal resolution: it is the chief officer's duty to decide, with the help of an inquiry by a chief inspector if necessary, whether a complaint falls into this category. The

---

226   *The Guardian*, 20 June 1991.
227   *Thompson v Metropolitan Police Commissioner* [1997] 2 All ER 762; and see ch 31 A.
228   *The Guardian*, 20 February 1997.
229   Cmnd 2176, 1963.
230   Cf *R v Bow Street Magistrates, ex p DPP* (1992) 95 Cr App Rep 9.
231   1984 Act, s 83 and Sched 4. For the background, see Cmnd 8681, 1982; and Cmnd 9072, 1983. For an account of the procedures, see G Marshall [1985] PL 448 and Zander, *The Police and Criminal Evidence Act 1984*, pp 254–87. The arrangements apply only in England and Wales. New procedures are contained in the Police Act 1996, but at the time of writing these had not been implemented.
232   On the question of public interest immunity for material obtained in the course of police complaints proceedings, see *R v Chief Constable of West Midlands, ex p Wiley* [1995] 1 AC 274, on which see ch 31 C. See also Cm 396, 1994, p 13.
233   On senior officers, see SI 1985 No 519.
234   See SI 1985 No 520, SI 1985 No 671, SI 1985 No 672, SI 1985 No 673, SI 1991 No 1673.

complaint cannot be dealt with informally unless the complainant consents and the chief officer is satisfied that the conduct complained of, even if proved, would not justify a criminal or disciplinary charge.[235] The actual arrangements for informal resolution may vary but will include discussion with the complainant and, in some cases, a meeting between the complainant and the accused officer. Most recorded complaints are informally resolved, withdrawn or not proceeded with.[236]

(*b*) If a complaint is not suitable for informal resolution, the chief officer must arrange for it to be investigated either by an officer (of at least chief inspector rank) from his or her own force or from another area. When the report of the investigation is received, the chief officer must send a copy to the Director of Public Prosecutions in all cases where there is an indication that a criminal offence may have been committed and the officer ought to be charged with it. The Director then decides whether criminal proceedings should be taken against the officer concerned.[237] If there is a criminal prosecution, whether it ends in conviction or acquittal, there can be no disciplinary charge for an offence which is in substance the same.[238] Different considerations apply where the Director decides against prosecution, in which case disciplinary proceedings may be brought, although the Home Office advises that special care be taken in cases where the Director's decision is based on the insufficiency of evidence.

Disciplinary proceedings are conducted by the chief constable and must allow a fair hearing. If an officer is found guilty of an offence, penalties range from dismissal to a caution. The more serious penalties of dismissal, requirement to resign or reduction in rank may not however be awarded unless the officer has been given the prior opportunity of electing to be legally represented at the hearing.[239] There is a right of appeal to the Home Secretary, who must refer most appeals for consideration by a three-person inquiry. An officer may be legally represented at this stage.[240] This procedure for handling of complaints is subject to some supervision by the Police Complaints Authority. Reports on investigations must be sent by chief officers to the Authority, which may require a report to be referred to the Director of Public Prosecutions. It may also recommend, and in the last resort direct, that disciplinary charges be brought. In exceptional circumstances, the Authority may require that a charge shall be heard not by the chief constable alone but by a disciplinary tribunal consisting of the chief constable and two members of the Authority.[241] In the exercise of their powers, both chief officers and the Complaints Authority must have regard to guidance given to them by the Home Secretary.[242]

---

[235] 1984 Act, s 85. See SI 1985 No 671.
[236] HC 351 (1990–91).
[237] 1984 Act, s 90.
[238] Ibid, s 104. See Cm 2263, 1993, pp 47–48.
[239] Ibid, s 102. For the previous exclusion of legal representation, see *Maynard v Osmond* [1977] QB 240.
[240] 1984 Act, s 103.
[241] Ibid, ss 90–4.
[242] Ibid, s 105. Cf *R v Police Complaints Board, ex p Madden* [1983] 2 All ER 353.

(*c*)   The Authority's role is much stronger in relation to the third category of complaint. If a complainant alleges that the conduct of a police officer has been the cause of a death or serious injury, the complaint must be referred to the Authority before investigation begins (s 87). Similarly, if the complaint alleges conduct which would constitute assault occasioning serious bodily harm, corruption, or a serious arrestable offence under the 1984 Act, s 116, this too must be referred.[243] In addition, the Authority may call in any other complaint. A chief officer may refer to the Authority other complaints, and other matters which are not the subject of a complaint but which indicate a criminal or disciplinary offence and, by reason of their gravity or exceptional circumstances, ought to be so referred (s 88). In all these cases the Authority does not merely monitor the outcome of an investigation but supervises the investigation itself. The Authority has to approve the appointment of the investigating officer and it may thereafter give instructions on the conduct of the investigations. Once the investigation is complete, however, the outcome is processed as in other cases.[244]

In 1990, 5,078 cases were referred to the Authority under ss 87 and 88 to determine whether an investigation should be supervised, of which supervision was undertaken in 836 cases.[245] By 1995–96, this had fallen to 2,761 of which 1,142 were accepted for supervision.[246] Many investigations have related to matters of public interest, including policing of the miners' strike of 1984/85; a demonstration at Manchester University in 1985; demonstrations outside the Wapping printing works in 1987; a number of firearms incidents; the falsification of crime statistics by officers in Kent; the disorders at Broadwater Farm in 1985; the conduct of the West Midlands Serious Crime Squad between 1986 and 1989; deaths in police custody; allegations of corruption, and the policing of demonstrations against live animal exports. Lack of resources have prevented the supervision of several other investigations.[247] Yet a considerable amount of time has been spent in at least some of these investigations. The Manchester case was concluded with a lengthy report, for the purposes of which 700 witnesses were examined and 220 police officers interviewed. The report also covered subsequent allegations of burglary, harassment and assault made by two students against the police.

The admissibility of evidence

If the police act unlawfully by denying a citizen any rights provided by PACE; or if they secure evidence by unlawful means, as by an illegal search; or if they extract a confession from a suspect in breach of the code of practice, what is the position regarding the evidence which has been obtained in this way? Can it be used in legal proceedings against the accused? In the United States, unlawfully obtained evidence has been excluded by the Supreme Court, which has argued that constitutional rights to liberty and privacy should not

---

[243]   SI 1985 No 673.
[244]   1984 Act, ss 87–9.
[245]   HC 351 (1990–91).
[246]   HC 469 (1995–96).
[247]   The annual reports of the PCA include HC 307 (1988–89); HC 365 (1989–90); HC 351 (1990–91); HC 15, 611 (1992–93); HC 305 (1993–94); HC 469 (1995–96).

be 'revocable at the whim of any police officer who, in the name of law enforcement itself, chooses to suspend [their] enjoyment'.[248] But in truth this is not an easy matter to resolve, for a difficult conflict of principle arises. On the one hand, there is a clear public interest in protecting the citizen against the unlawful invasion of his or her liberties by the police; on the other hand, there is an equally clear public interest in ensuring that those who commit serious criminal offences should not escape the consequences of their actions on what may be merely formal or technical grounds.[249] At common law in Scotland, irregularity in the obtaining of evidence does not necessarily render it inadmissible, but it may do so; and whether unlawfully obtained evidence is admitted is a matter for the trial judge, who may deem it inadmissible if it has been obtained in circumstances of unfairness to the accused.[250]

At common law in England and Wales, it was necessary to distinguish between statements and other forms of evidence. Statements were governed by the Judges' Rules[251] which provided, inter alia, that statements should be made voluntarily in the sense of being made without fear of prejudice or hope of advantage. The courts would not admit statements which had been obtained by oppression or by other means which suggested that they had been involuntary.[252] So far as evidence other than statements is concerned, English common law was rather confused. In *Kuruma v R*,[253] Lord Goddard CJ said that evidence is admissible if it is relevant, and that the court is not concerned with how it was obtained. However, he said that in a criminal case the judge always has a discretion to disallow evidence in the interests of fairness to the accused, and that if a piece of physical evidence has been obtained by a trick, a judge might properly rule it out. In *Jeffrey v Black*,[254] Lord Widgery CJ said that judges have a general discretion to decline to allow any evidence if they think it has been obtained unfairly or oppressively. However, that discretion was to be exercised only in exceptional circumstances, and in *Jeffrey v Black* the evidence obtained by the illegal search was held to be admissible. The only reported case where evidence appears to have been excluded is *R v Payne*:[255] the defendant who had been charged with drunk driving had been asked to submit himself to a medical examination to see if he was suffering from any illness or disability, on the understanding that the doctor would not examine him to determine whether he was fit to drive. The doctor then gave evidence at the defendant's trial that he was unfit to drive because of alcohol. The conviction was quashed on appeal on the ground that the evidence ought to have been excluded. So it was only in very rare and unusual circumstances that this power would be used. Indeed in *R v Sang*,[256]

---

248 *Mapp v Ohio* 367 US 643 (1961) (Clark J). See also *Cross and Tapper on Evidence*, pp 532–42, and W J Stuntz [1989] Crim LR 117.
249 See *Lawrie v Muir* 1950 JC 19, 26 (Lord Cooper).
250 *HM Advocate v Turnbull* 1951 JC 96; *Fairley v Fishmongers of London* 1951 JC 14; *HM Advocate v Hepper* 1958 JC 39; *Leckie v Miln* 1982 SLT 177; *HM Advocate v Graham* 1991 SLT 416; *Drummond v HM Advocate* 1994 SCCR 789; and *Wilson v Brown* 1996 SCCR 470.
251 See Section D above.
252 See *Ibrahim v R* [1914] AC 599; *DPP v Ping* [1976] AC 574; *R v Prager* [1972] 1 All ER 1114.
253 [1955] AC 197, 203. See also *King v R* [1969] 1 AC 304.
254 [1978] QB 490. And see *Callis v Gunn* [1964] 1 QB 495.
255 [1963] 1 All ER 848.
256 [1980] AC 402. See J Heydon [1980] Crim LR 129. See also *R v Fox* [1986] AC 281.

the House of Lords appeared to deny the possibility that some illegally obtained evidence could ever be excluded. Although the House held that a trial judge in a criminal trial has always a discretion to refuse to admit evidence if its prejudicial effect outweighs its probative value, it was also held that except in the case of confession and other evidence obtained from the accused after the commission of the offence, the judge 'has no discretion to refuse to admit relevant admissible evidence on the ground that it was obtained by improper or unfair means'. In the view of Lord Diplock, 'It is no part of a judge's function to exercise disciplinary powers over the police or prosecution as respects the way in which evidence to be used at the trial is obtained by them'.[257]

The position is now governed by ss 76 and 78 of PACE.[258] Section 76 provides that a confession made by an accused person may be given in evidence against him or her so far as it is relevant and is not excluded by the court exercising powers contained in s 76(2). This requires the court to exclude evidence obtained by oppression of the person who made it[259] or 'in consequence of anything said or done which was likely, in the circumstances existing at the time, to render unreliable any confession which might be made in consequence thereof'.[260] Where a representation has been made to the court that a confession may have been secured in either of these ways, the onus is on the prosecution to establish otherwise (s 76(1)). The term oppression is defined 'to include torture, inhuman or degrading treatment, and the use or threat of violence (whether or not amounting to torture)' (s 76(8)).[261] In *R v Fulling*[262] the court said that otherwise 'oppression' should be given its ordinary meaning, that is to say, the exercise of authority or power in a burdensome, harsh or wrongful manner or giving rise to unjust or cruel treatment. In that case it was held that there was no oppression where a confession had been made by a woman after being told by police of her lover's affair with another woman.[263] But although oppressive conduct by the police is thus discouraged by s 76, much of the impact of this is lost by s 76(4), which provides that the exclusion of a confession does not affect the admissibility in evidence of any facts discovered as a result of the confession, or 'where the confession is relevant as showing that the accused speaks, writes or expresses himself in a particular way, of so much of the confession as is necessary to show that he does so'. The fruit of the poison tree thus appears to be edible in English law.

---

257 [1980] AC 402, at 436.
258 For background, see Cmnd 8092, 1981, pp 112–18. Section 78 is qualified by the Criminal Procedure and Investigations Act 1996, Sched 1, para 26, in respect of proceedings before examining magistrates.
259 On oppression, see *R v Fulling* [1987] QB 426. See also *R v Ismail* [1990] Crim LR 109.
260 On unreliability, see *R v Goldenberg* (1988) 88 Cr App Rep 285.
261 Confession evidence may also be excluded under s 78 (see below). See *R v Mason* [1987] 3 All ER 481.
262 [1987] QB 426.
263 For a disturbing example of oppression which 'horrified' the Court of Appeal, and in which the accused was 'bullied and hectored', see *R v Paris* (1993) 97 Cr App Rep 99 ('The officers ... were not questioning him so much as shouting at him what they wanted him to say. Short of physical violence, it is difficult to conceive of a more hostile and intimidatory approach by officers to a suspect').

Section 78, introduced as a result of pressure in the Lords from Lord Scarman and others, provides that in any proceedings the court may refuse to allow evidence on which the prosecution proposes to rely 'if it appears to the court that, having regard to all the circumstances, including the circumstances in which the evidence was obtained, the admission of the evidence would have such an adverse effect on the fairness of the proceedings that the court ought not to admit it'. Despite the lack of clarity in its drafting, there is evidence to suggest that together with s 76, this provision has helped to induce the judges to take a more assertive approach when faced with improper police practice. Thus in *R v Canale*,[264] the Court of Appeal held that the trial judge should not have admitted evidence of interviews which had not been contemporaneously recorded by the police officers conducting the interviews: they had been written up afterwards.[265] These breaches of Code of Practice C, as it was then drafted, were described as 'flagrant', 'deliberate' and 'cynical'. In so holding the Lord Chief Justice sharply observed:

This case is the latest of a number of decisions emphasising the importance of the 1984 Act. If, which we find it hard to believe, police officers still do not appreciate the importance of that Act and the accompanying Codes, then it is time that they did.[266]

Another area where s 78 has been invoked successfully by defendants relates to the denial of access to a solicitor.[267]

In *R v Samuel*[268] the appellant was arrested on suspicion of armed robbery. He was taken to a police station at 2 pm on 5 August and shortly after 8 pm asked for a solicitor to be present. The request was refused on the grounds that this was a serious arrestable offence and there was a likelihood of other suspects being inadvertently warned. The appellant was interviewed again later that evening and during the following morning, 6 August. He again denied being implicated in the armed robbery but admitted two burglaries. At this time his mother was informed of his arrest and she in turn instructed a 'highly respected' solicitor to attend him. At 4.45 pm on 6 August the solicitor was refused access to his client, and this was denied until 7.25 pm. Before then Samuel had been interviewed again about the robbery, to which he confessed.

The Court of Appeal concluded that the decision to deny access at 4.45 pm 'was very probably motivated by a desire to have one last chance of interviewing the appellant in the absence of a solicitor'. At the trial, the judge had concluded that the denial of access to a solicitor was justified and that the evidence of an interview at which the appellant confessed was admissible. The Court of Appeal, in contrast, held that the denial of access to the solicitor at 4.45 pm on 6 August was unjustified, being a breach of s 58 of PACE and the code of practice. The court then held the evidence inadmissible under s 78 of PACE, noting that 'this appellant was denied improperly one of the most important and fundamental rights of a citizen'.

More generally, the Court of Appeal said:

It is undesirable to attempt any general guidance as to the way in which a judge's discretion under section 78 or his inherent powers should be exercised. Circumstances vary infinitely. [Prosecuting counsel] has made the extreme submission that, in the

---

[264] [1990] 2 All ER 187.
[265] See also *R v Keenan* [1990] 2 QB 54.
[266] [1990] 2 All ER 187, 190 (Lord Lane CJ).
[267] *R v Samuel* [1988] QB 615; *R v Absolam* (1989) 88 Cr App Rep 332; *R v Beylan* [1990] Crim LR 185. Cf *R v Alladice* (1988) 87 Cr App Rep 380.
[268] [1988] QB 615.

absence of impropriety, the discretion should never be exercised to exclude admissible evidence. We have no hesitation in rejecting that submission, although the propriety or otherwise of the way in which the evidence was obtained is something which a court is, in terms, enjoined by the section to take into account.[269]

Although there are now many cases in which evidence has been excluded, it has been said not to be possible 'to give general guidance as to how a judge should exercise his discretion under section 78' on the ground that 'each case had to be determined on its own facts'.[270] The courts have, however, rejected the submission that 'in the absence of impropriety, the discretion should never be exercised to exclude admissible evidence'.[271] But it does not follow that evidence obtained in breach of the codes of practice or in breach of the defendant's statutory rights (for example to legal representation), will always be held inadmissible. Particular difficulties have arisen with police undercover work, it having been held that 'the fact that the evidence had been obtained by entrapment or by an agent provocateur or by a trick did not of itself require the judge to exclude it', though it may be excluded if the circumstances so require.[272] Nor have the courts been prepared to exclude evidence obtained from surveillance devices, use of which has been governed by a Home Office circular of 1984 and not (unlike the interception of communications or the surveillance work of the Security Service) by legislation. In *R v Khan*[273] the House of Lords rejected the claim that evidence obtained in this way should be excluded, though it was accepted that the placing of the device involved a trespass on the part of the police for which there was no legal excuse. But although it was also argued that the police conduct violated the accused's right to privacy as protected by art 8 of the ECHR, the question whether police conduct amounted to an apparent or probable breach of some relevant law or convention was in the view of the House of Lords simply 'a consideration which may be taken into account for what it is worth'. Its significance, however, 'will normally be determined not so much by its apparent unlawfulness or irregularity, as upon its effect, taken as a whole, upon the fairness or unfairness of the proceedings'.

---

269   Ibid, at 630.
270   *R v Smurthwaite, The Times*, 5 October 1993.
271   *Samuel*, op cit.
272   *R v Smurthwaite*, op cit. See also *R v Latif* [1996] 1 WLR 104.
273   [1996] 3 All ER 289. See now Police Act 1997, Part III.

CHAPTER 22

Freedom of expression

The right to freedom of expression in the words of art 10 of the European Convention on Human Rights, includes freedom to hold opinions, 'and to receive and impart information and ideas without interference by public authority and regardless of frontiers'. This freedom is fundamental to the individual's life in a democratic society. In the first place, it has a specific political content. The freedom to receive and express political opinions, both publicly and privately, is linked closely with the freedom to organise for political purposes and to take part in free elections.

Without free elections the people cannot make a choice of policies. Without freedom of speech the appeal to reason which is the basis of democracy cannot be made. Without freedom of association, electors and elected representatives cannot bind themselves into parties for the formulation of common policies and the attainment of common ends.[1]

So does freedom of expression closely affect freedom of religion. Lawyers remember *Bushell's* case in 1670 as having established the right of the jury to acquit an accused 'against full and manifest evidence', and against the direction of the judge: they should also remember that Bushell was foreman of the jury which acquitted the Quakers William Penn and William Mead on charges of having preached to a large crowd in a London street contrary to the Conventicle Act.[2] Moreover, liberty of expression is an integral part of artistic, cultural and intellectual freedom – the freedom to publish books or produce works of art, however disconcerting they may be to the prevailing orthodoxy.

In this broad field, as with other freedoms of the individual, English law has relied 'on the principle that what is not prohibited is permitted and ... therefore on keeping within acceptable limits, and providing precise definitions of, the restrictions imposed by the civil and criminal law' on the individual's freedom.[3] Several comments may be made on this view. First, the freedom to express political or religious opinions may have to be restrained if social harmony is to be maintained. The bold assertion of freedom of expression in the European Convention on Human Rights, art 10, is subject

---

[1]   Jennings, *Cabinet Government*, p 14. See also Laski, *A Grammar of Politics*, ch 3.
[2]   *R v Penn and Mead* (1670) 6 St Tr 951.
[3]   Report of Committee on Privacy, Cmnd 5012, 1972, p 10.

to such formalities, restrictions or penalties as are prescribed by law and are necessary in a democratic society, in the interests of national security, territorial integrity or public safety, for the prevention of disorder or crime, for the protection of health or morals, for the protection of the reputation or rights of others, for preventing the disclosure of information received in confidence, or of maintaining the authority and impartiality of the judiciary (art 10(2)).[4]

Secondly, the restrictions on freedom of expression have often been imprecise and entrusted to the subjective judgment of those administering the law. As Dicey remarked, 'Freedom of discussion is, then, in England little else than the right to write or say anything which a jury, consisting of twelve shopkeepers, think it expedient should be said or done.'[5] Today juries are composed rather differently but in several areas of the law, such as obscenity, they retain power to decide contested cases. Thirdly, the principle that what is not prohibited is permitted may suggest that freedom of expression is no more than the residue left when all restrictions have taken effect. Yet in many situations of legal restriction, a process of balancing occurs to weigh the public interest in freedom of expression against public interests such as the administration of justice or the protection of confidentiality.[6]

In this chapter an account will be given of the principal restrictions on freedom of expression, which has been said to be 'a sinew of the common law'.[7] Restrictions are of two kinds: the first is censorship of material by state authorities before it is published or displayed, and the second is the imposition of penalties, or the granting of redress in the case of someone specifically harmed by the material, after the event. Restrictions of the first kind have often been viewed with great suspicion and have been strongly deprecated by the US Supreme Court in cases arising under the free speech guarantee in the First Amendment. Yet despite Blackstone's insistence that free speech meant 'laying no previous restraints upon publication',[8] there is still some censorship in Britain, particularly of films and video recordings, though there are also restrictions imposed by Parliament and by governments on what may be broadcast on television and radio.[9] Thus in 1988, the Home Secretary instructed the BBC and the IBA not to broadcast interviews with members or supporters of named organisations which included terrorist groups and also Sinn Fein, a lawful political party.[10] Although there is now no prior censorship of the press, there are important rules on newspaper ownership which are designed to ensure that transfers operate in the public interest. So far as other restrictions are concerned, there is a wide range of criminal offences which restrict free speech. These offences exist to protect the security of the state and public order; to protect public morality by punishing the publication of obscene material; and by virtue of the law on

---

[4]   For interpretation of these provisions, see *Sunday Times v UK* (1979) 2 EHRR 245 and *Handyside v UK* (1976) 1 EHRR 737.

[5]   Dicey, *The Law of the Constitution*, p 246.

[6]   An approach perceptively explored in A Boyle [1982] PL 574.

[7]   *R v Advertising Standards Authority, ex p Vernons* [1993] 2 All ER 202 (Laws J). See also *R v Central Independent Television plc* [1994] Fam 192 (Hoffman L J at p 203).

[8]   *Commentaries*, 9th edn, IV, p 151.

[9]   The classic legal study of censorship is O'Higgins, *Censorship in Britain*.

[10] See *R v Home Secretary, ex p Brind* [1991] 1 AC 696.

contempt of court, to maintain the authority and impartiality of the judiciary. Restrictions imposed by the law of defamation exist to protect the rights and reputations of others, while the developing law on breach of confidence may help to prevent the disclosure of information received in confidence.[11] These different restrictions will now be examined in turn, with the exception of the law relating to contempt of court which was dealt with in chapter 18 B. Limits on free speech which relate to public meetings and demonstrations will be considered in chapter 23, and the Official Secrets Acts and other national security restraints in chapter 24.

A. Censorship and prior restraints

Theatres[12]

For many years dramatic and operatic performances in Great Britain were subject to the prior censorship of the Lord Chamberlain, an officer of the royal household. The Theatres Act 1968 abolished the requirement that plays should receive a licence before being performed.[13] Theatres are now licensed by local authorities but only in regard to such matters as public health and safety. In place of censorship, rules against obscenity similar to those in the Obscene Publications Act 1959 are applied to the performance of plays, subject to a defence of public good. Other criminal restraints placed upon theatrical performances are in respect of the use of threatening, abusive or insulting words or behaviour intended or likely to stir up racial hatred[14] or occasion a breach of the peace.[15] Prosecutions for these various offences, including obscenity, require the consent of the Attorney-General in England and Wales. There may be no prosecution at common law for any offence the essence of which is that a performance of a play is 'obscene, indecent, offensive, disgusting or injurious to morality' nor may there be prosecutions under various statutes relating to indecency (1968 Act, s 2(4)), an important safeguard against moral censorship. However, in 1982 a private prosecution of the director of the National Theatre's production of *The Romans in Britain* was withdrawn after the judge had decided that the Sexual Offences Act 1956, s 13 (relating to gross indecency between males) could apply to simulated homosexual acts on stage.[16]

Cinemas[17]

Censorship of films originated unintentionally with the Cinematograph Act 1909, which authorised local authorities to license cinemas in the interests of

---

[11] It is important also not to lose sight of the possible limits arising under the law of copyright: see *Home Secretary v Central Broadcasting Ltd*, *The Times*, 28 January 1993.
[12] On theatrical censorship, see Findlater, *Banned!*
[13] For the background, see HC 503 (1966–67).
[14] Public Order Act 1986, s 20.
[15] Theatres Act 1968, s 6.
[16] *The Times*, 19 March 1982.
[17] Hunnings, *Film Censors and the Law*; Williams report on obscenity and film censorship, Cmnd 7772, 1979; Robertson, *Freedom, the Individual and the Law*, pp 238–41.

public safety, mainly against fire. In fact, with the approval of the courts,[18] local authorities extended the scope of licensing to other matters including power to approve the films shown in licensed cinemas. In the Cinematograph Act 1952, and more recently in the Cinemas Act 1985, Parliament confirmed the power of licensing the films shown and required licensing authorities to impose conditions restricting children from seeing unsuitable films. Licensing authorities are now the district councils and the London borough councils: they may delegate their powers to a committee or to the local magistrates. The main work of censorship of films is undertaken by the British Board of Film Classification (previously the British Board of Film Censors), a non-statutory body set up, with the approval of central and local government, by the film industry. The board is responsible for the classification of films with special reference to the admission of young children and others under 18. Although a licensing authority normally allows the showing of films which have been classified by the board, the authority may not transfer its functions to the board and must retain power to review decisions of the board.[19] Thus it may refuse a local showing to a film classified by the board; it may vary the board's classification; or it may grant permission to a film refused a certificate by the board. Powers of local censorship are not popular with the film industry, and were not supported by the Williams committee in 1979, but a case can be made for maintaining some local option in issues of public morality.

The relationship between the system of film censorship and the law of obscenity and public indecency has caused many difficulties. Before 1977, the Obscene Publications Act 1959 did not apply to the public showing of films,[20] but the Cinematograph Acts did not protect licensed films against prosecution at common law.[21] In 1976, the Court of Appeal held the licensing policy followed by the Greater London Council to be unlawful since it applied only a test of obscenity (that is, whether a film would tend to deprave and corrupt those likely to see it) and excluded from consideration issues of public decency.[22] By the Criminal Law Act 1977, s 53, the public showing of films was brought within the Obscene Publications Act, subject to a defence that showing a film is for the public good in the interests of drama, opera, ballet or any other art, or of literature or learning. The consent of the Director of Public Prosecutions is required for prosecution and forfeiture of films of not less than 16 millimetres in width. The Video Recordings Act 1984 (amended by the Video Recordings Act 1993) established a scheme for the censorship of video recordings, under which it is an offence to supply (whether or not for reward) any recording for which no classification certificate has been issued. Certain recordings are exempt from this requirement (such as those concerned with sport, religion or music and those designed to be educational) and so are certain kinds of supply. A video work may not, however, be an exempted work if to any extent it depicts or is designed to encourage such matters as 'human sexual activity or acts of force or restraint' (s 2(2)(a)).[23]

---

[18]   Eg *LCC v Bermondsey Bioscope Ltd* [1911] 1 KB 445.
[19]   *Ellis v Dubowski* [1921] 3 KB 621; *Mills v LCC* [1925] 1 KB 213.
[20]   Section 1(3) and *A-G's Reference (No 2 of 1975)* [1976] 2 All ER 753.
[21]   G Zellick [1971] Crim LR 126; and HC 176 (1975–76), pp 84–103.
[22]   *R v Greater London Council, ex p Blackburn* [1976] 3 All ER 184.
[23]   See *Kent CC v Multi Media Marketing, The Times*, 9 May 1995 (need not be 'hard core').

Nor is it exempt if to any extent it depicts criminal activity which is likely to any significant extent to stimulate or encourage the commission of an offence.[24] Classification is conducted by the British Board of Film Classification, which may certify that a video work is suitable for general viewing, or suitable only for persons over the age of 18, or that it is to be supplied only in a licensed sex shop.[25]

B. The press: ownership and self restraint

Ownership

The historic freedom of the press means that, subject to the civil and criminal restraints upon publication which will be considered below, any person or company may publish a newspaper or magazine without getting official approval in advance. For economic reasons, this liberty is unlikely to be exercised effectively on a national scale except by a very few newspaper publishers. Fears of a movement towards monopoly conditions in sectors of the press led, after an inquiry by a royal commission,[26] to the enactment in what is now the Fair Trading Act 1973, ss 57–62, of provisions to ensure that newspaper mergers above a certain scale do not take place in a manner contrary to the public interest. By s 58, it is an offence for one newspaper to be transferred to the proprietor of another without the consent of the Secretary of State for Trade and Industry where the joint circulation of the two newspapers is 500,000 or more. Consent should not normally be given until the matter has been investigated by the Monopolies and Mergers Commission following a reference to it by the minister. The duty of the Commission is to consider 'whether the transfer in question may be expected to operate against the public interest, taking into account all matters which appear in the circumstances to be relevant and, in particular, the need for accurate presentation of news and free expression of opinion'.[27] One case which was opposed on these grounds was the proposed transfer of the *Bristol Evening Post* to Mr David Sullivan who held a 50% interest in the company publishing the *Sunday Sport* and *The Sport*, both of which are said to operate at the lower end of the tabloid market.[28] In some cases the Trade and Industry Secretary may approve a transfer without first referring the matter to the Commission; but in such cases he or she must be satisfied that the newspaper which is the subject of the proposed transfer is not economic as a going concern and that the transfer is urgent if the newspaper is to survive.[29] One controversial acquisition which was not referred for investigation took place in 1981 when Rupert Murdoch bought *The Times* and *Sunday Times*, thereby giving him 30% of the

---

[24] Criminal Justice and Public Order Act 1994, s 89. And see s 88, increasing the penalties for breach.

[25] For the procedures adopted by the Board, see *Wingrove v UK* (1997) 1 BHRC 509.

[26] Cmnd 1811, 1962.

[27] See Cm 2373, 1993 (Argus Press Ltd and Trinity International Holdings plc); Cm 2374, 1993 (Trinity International Holdings plc and Joseph Woodhead and Sons Ltd).

[28] Cm 1083, 1990.

[29] Fair Trading Act 1973, s 58(3). See now SI 1995 No 1351.

national daily circulation and 36% of the national Sunday circulation.[30] Even where a reference has been made, the Trade and Industry Secretary is probably not bound by the report of the Monopolies and Mergers Commission and could thus reject the recommendations, though he or she would clearly be required to take them into account in reaching a decision.[31] These measures appear to have done little to prevent the growing concentration of newspaper titles in the hands of a few proprietors. Indeed, in 1995–96 the four principal newspaper publishers – News International, Mirror Group, United Newspapers, and Associated Newspapers – controlled between them 85% of the national daily and 88.7% of national Sunday circulation.[32]

Press Council

Freedom of expression is capable of being abused: 'Newspapers are sometimes irresponsible and their motives in a market economy cannot be expected to be unalloyed by considerations of commercial advantage'.[33] Sensational reporting, intrusive investigations and careless editing may cause unjustified distress to private individuals. The Press Council was established in 1953 by the newspaper industry: it was reconstituted in 1963, and again in 1973 and 1978. Before its replacement by the Press Complaints Commission in 1991, in addition to the chairman, who was always an eminent lawyer, the Press Council had 36 members, half nominated by sections of the press, and half appointed from outside the industry. The council sought to preserve the freedom of the British press, to maintain the highest professional and commercial standards and to consider complaints about the conduct of the press. Before it would accept a complaint, the individual must first have tried to obtain redress from the editor of the newspaper. No complaint would be accepted for consideration if the complainant was also bringing legal proceedings against the newspaper, for example, for defamation. The Press Council had no power to impose sanctions: when it upheld a complaint, the newspaper was expected to publish a statement of the complaint and the council's ruling. The published decisions of the council built up an extensive system of precedent,[34] and in 1977 a royal commission on the press recommended that a code of press conduct should be prepared. Declarations of principle had been issued on cheque-book journalism and on privacy but, in the Commission's view, the council needed to be more vigilant in protecting the public 'against the danger of partisan opinion exacerbated by factual inaccuracy'.[35] Criticism of the Press Council challenged its effectiveness as an adjudicating body. 'It has been said that the Council's existence is not widely known, that it does little to promote itself and that the number of complaints it receives in a year bears little relation to the level of dissatisfaction with the press'.[36] Questions were raised about its independence (it relied on the press

---

[30]   Curran and Seaton, *Power without Responsibility*, pp 293–4.
[31]   Cf *R v Trade and Industry Secretary, ex p Anderson Strathclyde plc* [1983] 2 All ER 233.
[32]   Williams, *Media Ownership and Democracy*, p 39. And see T Gibbons [1992] PL 279.
[33]   *R v Central Independent Television plc*, above note 7, at p 203.
[34]   For which, see Levy, *The Press Council*.
[35]   Cmnd 4810, 1977; and cf Robertson, *The People Against the Press*.
[36]   Cm 1102, 1990. See C Reid (1992) 43 NILQ 99.

industry for funding); the time taken to deal with complaints; and the lack of any effective sanctions. An internal review was conducted in 1989 under its chairman, Louis Blom-Cooper QC, the outcome of which addressed some of these concerns. It was argued, however, that these proposals did not go anything like far enough and that the Press Council should be abolished because of its limited impact and the lack of full commitment by the industry to its aims.

Press Complaints Commission

The recommendation to abolish the Press Council was made by the Calcutt committee on privacy and related matters which was set up on 1989 'following a number of striking instances in which sections of the press had been severely criticised for intruding upon accident victims and other patients in hospital, for using stolen private correspondence or photographs and for publishing scurrilous (and sometimes false) details of individuals' private lives'.[37] One notorious case led to judicial calls for a right to privacy when the common law proved unable to provide a remedy to the actor, Gorden Kaye, 'for a monstrous invasion of his privacy'.[38] But Calcutt recommended against the introduction of such a tort[39] for a number of reasons, including 'arguments of principle, practical concerns and the availability of other options, for tackling the problems'.[40] The committee also proposed that the press should be given one last chance to prove that voluntary self-regulation could work. To replace the Press Council, the committee proposed the introduction of a new Press Complaints Commission (PCC), modelled on the Broadcasting Complaints Commission,[41] 'generously funded by the newspaper and magazine publishing industry'[42] by means of a levy on the entire industry.[43] There are 14 members of the commission: apart from the independent chair, there are 8 independent members with no press connections and 5 senior editors drawn from the national and regional newspapers and magazines. Its primary responsibilities include the handling of complaints of alleged violations of the code of practice which was drafted in 1990 (by the newspaper industry) to regulate its conduct on a range of matters dealing mainly with accuracy and privacy. The code is kept under scrutiny and has been amended on a number of occasions since, as in 1993 when a new clause was inserted on the use of listening devices. Where there is a breach of the code leading to a formal adjudication by the commission, 'the publication concerned must publish the critical adjudication in full and with due prominence', but the commission 'does not award compensation to successful [complainants] and nor does it fine publications'. The commission received 2,508 complaints in 1995, an

---

[37] Ibid.
[38] *Kaye v Robertson* [1991] FSR 62 (B Markesinis (1992) 55 MLR 118).
[39] Cf the classic study by S D Warren and L D Brandeis (1890) 4 Harv LR 193.
[40] See also Cmnd 5012, 1972. For the case against a right to privacy, see Wacks, *The Protection of Privacy*. For general accounts, see Bailey, Harris and Jones, *Civil Liberties Cases and Materials*, ch 8; and Robertson, *Freedom, the Individual and the Law*, ch 3.
[41] See Section D. On the possibility of judicial review of the PCC, see G Crown (1997) NLJ 8.
[42] Press Complaints Commission, Annual Report 1995, p 1.
[43] The expenditure of the PCC in 1994 was just over £1 million.

increase of nearly 30% on the previous year, leading to the conclusion that this reflects 'a welcome sign of growing public awareness of the PCC and the service it offers',[44] though another conclusion might also be drawn. Most of the complaints which raise issues which fall within the jurisdiction of the commission (and the vast majority do not) are resolved informally – usually by the publication of an apology or correction, or an opportunity being given to the complainant to reply. In 1995, only 63 complaints led to an adjudication being made, of which 28 were upheld.[45] In 1996, 'the unjustified reporting of the private lives of public individuals' led the chairman of the commission (Lord Wakeham) to express concern that this could 'cast into doubt the system of self-regulation', which in his view had achieved 'notable successes'.[46]

In 1992, Sir David Calcutt was asked to conduct an assessment of the system of press self-regulation which had been set up in the wake of his earlier report. He concluded that the practice under the Press Complaints Commission had not been effective and that a statutory press complaints tribunal should be established. He repeated the earlier recommendation for the introduction of a number of offences (such as the unauthorised entry onto private property with intent to obtain personal information with a view to its publication) subject to a number of public interest defences, and that the government should give full consideration to the introduction of a new tort of infringement of privacy.[47] Further support for a statutory right to privacy was provided by the National Heritage Committee of the House of Commons, which accepted that 'a free society requires the freedom to say or print things that are inconvenient to those in authority', but argued forcefully that 'in a democratic society there must be a right to privacy as well', a right which must not be 'ignored by those who claim that everything that everybody does is fair game, so long as it provides a saucy story'.[48] The committee rejected Calcutt's recommendation for a statutory press complaints tribunal,[49] on the ground that it was against legislation that would apply to the media exclusively and in practice to the press alone. Instead the committee proposed that 'a Protection of Privacy Bill, which will provide protection for all citizens and whose provisions similarly will apply to all citizens, should now be introduced, containing both a new tort of infringement of privacy and criminal offences resulting from unauthorised use of invasive technology and harassment'. Continuing concerns about the activities of the press led the committee to repeat its calls for a 'comprehensive' Protection of Privacy Bill, together with a Press Ombudsman appointed by statute.[50] Yet as late as July 1995 the

---

[44]   Press Complaints Commission, *Annual Report 1995*, p 6.
[45]   Ibid, pp 6–7.
[46]   *The Times*, 10 October 1996.
[47]   Cm 2135, 1993.
[48]   HC 294–I (1992–93).
[49]   Though it was later to deliver a stinging rebuke to the PCC on the ground that 'time and time again' its 'reaction to criticism is to offer half measures when radical change is called for' (HC 86 (1996–97)). As a result of the failures of the PCC Code of Practice, the National Heritage Committee recommended the introduction of legislation to forbid the payment to witnesses.
[50]   HC 38 (1993–94).

government was continuing to place its faith in self-regulation, though conceding it still has 'a case to prove'.[51]

C. Regulation of television and radio

The BBC

In the case of broadcasting, technical reasons have so far prevented access to the medium being open to all-comers as in the case of the press. Even if all broadcasting were to be provided by privately owned companies, it would still be necessary for a regulatory agency to allocate channels and wavelengths to them. Until 1954, the British Broadcasting Corporation enjoyed a public monopoly of all broadcasting in the United Kingdom, and it still provides a large share of broadcasting services. The BBC is a corporation set up by royal charter, and its chairman and governors are appointed by the Crown on the advice of the Prime Minister. It transmits broadcasts throughout the United Kingdom under licence from the government issued under the Wireless Telegraphy Acts.[52] Although the BBC is mainly financed by a grant from the exchequer, equivalent to the net revenue of television licence fees, the structure of the BBC seeks to maintain its independence of the government of the day. The BBC's charter was renewed in 1996 for a period of 10 years,[53] together with a new agreement between the corporation and the government whereby the broadcaster is subject to a number of duties. These are similar in terms to those imposed on the commercial broadcasters by legislation. Questions have been raised whether the BBC should be regulated by legislation rather than royal prerogative, but this was rejected by the National Heritage Committee in 1993 on the ground that the present arrangements 'gave the BBC flexibility and that it helped its independence'.[54] But although the charter is debated by both Houses of Parliament before it is granted by the Queen in Council,[55] this is a poor substitute for legislation which would give MPs 'the opportunity to debate the substance of the statutes and to move detailed amendments'.[56]

Certain duties are imposed on the BBC: it must broadcast a daily account of the proceedings in Parliament and any minister of the Crown may require announcements to be broadcast. The minister responsible for broadcasting (in 1997 the National Heritage Secretary) may require the BBC not to broadcast certain matters. The BBC may not broadcast its own opinions about current affairs or matters of public policy, being under a duty to do all it can to treat controversial subjects with due accuracy and impartiality, 'both in the Corporation's news services and in the more general field of programmes dealing with matters of public policy or of political or industrial controversy'.

---

[51] HC Deb, 17 July 1995, col 1323. See also Cm 2918, 1995.
[52] For the charter, see Cm 3248, 1996, and for the licence and agreement, Cm 3152, 1996. And see *BBC v Johns* [1965] Ch 32.
[53] Cm 3248, 1996. See HL Deb, 9 January 1996, col 13.
[54] HC 77–I (1993–94), para 51.
[55] *The Future of the BBC*, Cm 2621, 1994, p 53.
[56] HC 77–I (1993–94), para 50.

But 'due impartiality does not require absolute neutrality on every issue or detachment from fundamental democratic principles', the meaning of which is not specified. The BBC should also seek to ensure that programmes do not include 'anything which offends against good taste or decency or is likely to encourage or incite to crime or lead to disorder or to be offensive to public feeling'.[57] In an emergency the government may take over the BBC's broadcasting facilities. Apart from these specific powers, the government may not control the BBC's programmes, though it may bring great pressure to bear, particularly at a time of emergency such as the Falklands campaign,[58] or in respect of terrorism in Northern Ireland.[59] The government is responsible for the structure of broadcasting as well as for financing the BBC, which continues to be a matter of political controversy. In 1993, the National Heritage Committee of the House of Commons 'after considering the various funding options', concluded 'with the greatest reluctance' that 'the present flat rate licence system has the fewest objections to it'.[60]

Commercial television and radio

Television and radio services financed by advertising are now regulated by the Broadcasting Acts 1990 and 1996, the latter responding to demands presented by new technology in the form of digital television. The Independent Television Commission is a body corporate, whose members are appointed by the Secretary of State to regulate the provision of television services which are provided within the UK other than by the BBC and by the Welsh Fourth Channel Authority. By virtue of amendments introduced in 1996, its regulatory duties extend to what are referred to as 'multiplex services' and 'digital additional services'. The Commission is under a duty to provide both a wide range of services and fair and effective competition in the provision of services, a duty which applies also in respect of their licensing activities under part I of the 1996 Act. Provided that certain quality threshholds laid down in the 1990 Act are met, the licences for Channel 3 television must be awarded to the highest bidder, though there are several restrictions as to who may be a licence-holder (political organisations are barred). Restrictions also apply to newspaper proprietors, though these were amended by the 1996 Act to 'prevent those groups having 20% or more of national newspaper circulation from acquiring Channel 3 [and Channel 5] licences'.[61] Controversially, however, 'this restriction does not apply to the emerging markets of cable, satellite and digital terrestrial broadcasting'.[62] Licences issued under the 1996 Act are not issued to the highest cash bidders, but by having regard to the extent to which 'the award of the licence to each applicant would be

---

57 Cm 3152, 1996.
58 On the handling of press and public information during the Falklands conflict, see HC 17 (1982–83) and Cmnd 8820, 1983. On the protection of military information in general, see Cmnd 9112, 1983.
59 See Windlesham and Rampton, *Report on 'Death on the Rock'* (government pressure on the Independent Broadcasting Authority).
60 HC 77–I (1993–94), para 78.
61 HL Deb, 16 January 1996, col 473.
62 Ibid.

calculated to promote the development of digital television broadcasting in the United Kingdom otherwise than by satellite'.[63]

Important restrictions on what may be broadcast are contained in s 6 of the 1990 Act. This requires the ITC to be satisfied that (*a*) nothing is included in the programmes which offends against good taste or decency or is likely to encourage or incite to crime or to lead to disorder or be offensive to public feeling; (*b*) all news is presented with due accuracy and impartiality; (*c*) due impartiality is preserved in respect of matters of political or industrial controversy or relating to current public policy; and (*d*) due responsibility is exercised with respect to the content of any religious programmes and in particular that any such programmes do not involve any improper exploitation of any susceptibilities of those watching the programmes.[64] Regarding (*c*) (due impartiality), the ITC is to draw up a code giving guidance as to the rules to be observed. The code will indicate to such extent as the commission considers appropriate what due impartiality does and does not require, as well as ways in which due impartiality may be achieved in connection with particular kinds of programmes. The rules are also to specify that due impartiality does not require absolute neutrality on every issue or detachment from fundamental democratic principles (whatever that may mean). Presumably this is designed to ensure that due impartiality is not used to prevent controversial programmes about extremist organisations. The 1990 Act also contains strict rules on advertising: no advertisements may be directed to political ends or relate to any industrial dispute. In the latter case an exception is made if the advertisement is by the government. One effect of these rules is that there can be no television advertising by political parties during general election campaigns, as in many other countries.

The Broadcasting Standards Commission

The Broadcasting Act 1996 established the Broadcasting Standards Commission (BSC) which replaced two different bodies which had been regulated by the Broadcasting Act 1990, these being the Broadcasting Complaints Commission (BCC) and the Broadcasting Standards Council. Appointed by the National Heritage Secretary, the Commission has two principal tasks, the first of which is regulatory or standard-setting, the second being the adjudication of complaints. So far as the first is concerned, the Commission is required to draw up a code for dealing with unjust or unfair treatment in programmes as well as the unwarranted infringement of privacy in, or in connection with, the obtaining of material included in such programmes. It is also under a duty to draw up a Code of Practice giving guidance on practices to be followed in connection with the portrayal of sex and violence, and on standards of taste and decency generally. So far as the Commission's second task is concerned, it must consider and adjudicate on complaints which relate either to unjust or unfair treatment on the one hand,[65] or to the unwarranted invasion of privacy

---

63 Broadcasting Act 1996, s 8.
64 Cf Broadcasting Act 1990, s 47(4), (5).
65 Cf *R v Broadcasting Complaints Commission, ex p BBC, The Times,* 26 May 1994 (a complaint could not be made by a researcher on a programme complaining of unfair treatment. The complainant's interest had to be in the subject-matter of the programme).

on the other.[66] It may also deal with complaints about the portrayal of sex and violence, or alleged failures of programmes to attain standards of taste and decency. The former are referred to in the Act as 'fairness complaints', and the latter as 'standards complaints'.[67]

The Commission is authorised to deal with fairness complaints only if made by the individual affected or by someone authorised by him or her, and it may refuse to entertain a fairness complaint relating to unjust or unfair treatment 'if the person named as the person affected was not himself the subject of the treatment complained of and it appears to the BSC that he did not have a sufficiently direct interest in the subject-matter of that treatment to justify the making of a complaint with him as the person affected'.[68] A fairness complaint may also be refused if it is not made in good time, while a standards complaint must normally be made within two weeks in the case of a television programme and three weeks in the case of radio. Other restrictions on complaints mean that they cannot be considered where the matter complained of is the subject of court proceedings, while in the case of a fairness complaint jurisdiction may be denied if it appears to the Commission that the person affected has a remedy by way of legal action in a court of law. The Commission sits in private to hear complaints, though it has a discretion in the case of standards complaints to hear these in public. It may direct the broadcasting authority to publish a summary of the complaint together with the Commission's findings or observations. The Commission does not, however, have the power to order any compensation to be paid to the victim of unfair or unjust treatment, though its intervention may help to prevent any continuation or recurrence of the offending conduct. At least one half of the

[66]   Cf *R v Broadcasting Complaints Commission, ex p BBC, The Times*, 16 October 1992 (the right to complain about invasion of privacy applies not only to the broadcast itself but also to the techniques used to collect information for a programme). Cf also *R v Broadcasting Complaints Commission, ex p Granada Television Ltd, The Times*, 31 May 1993: a broadcast may invade privacy even though the matter had previously been reported and the matter was already in the public domain: 'Privacy was different from confidentiality and went well beyond it. It was not confined to secrets. The Act was designed to prevent hurt and anguish by intruding into the lives of people about matters which everyone would recognise as being private' (Popplewell J, upheld by the Court of Appeal, *The Times*, 16 December 1994).

[67]   As was pointed out in relation to one of the Commission's predecessor bodies (the Broadcasting Standards Council) this is 'an extremely interesting body from the public perspective' in that it performs 'the legislative power to make a binding Code of Practice, the executive power to monitor programmes and make complaints concerning them and the judicial power to hold hearings and make findings on complaints about breaches of the Code' (F Coleman [1993] PL 488, at p 512). But as we saw in ch 14 it is not the only regulatory body of this kind.

[68]   Cf *R v Broadcasting Complaints Commission, ex p Channel Four Television, The Times*, 6 January 1995 (the term 'direct interest' had to be broadly construed, even if did mean that 'too many complaints' would be made). But cf *R v Broadcasting Complaints Commission, ex p BBC, The Times*, 24 February 1995 (complaint by National Council for One Parent Families refused on the ground that it did not have a sufficiently direct interest in a *Panorama* programme which was said to build up a false picture of lone parents by using misleading and false information. According to Brooke J, 'it was hard to conceive that any parliamentary language, consistent with this country's obligations under the European Convention on Human Rights, could embrace the legitimate bringing of complaints on behalf of over a million individuals who were unidentifiable save that they were one-parent families, other than in the most exceptional circumstances'.

costs of the Commission are met by the industry itself, which is under a duty to arrange for the publication of regular announcements publicising the BSC. Although its powers are limited, the Commission may nevertheless find that its activities are subject to judicial review, as was the BCC which took a generous view of its own powers to hear complaints.

The role of the courts

A few attempts have been made to challenge broadcasting content. A difficulty with the BBC, however, is that it was established under the prerogative, and at least until the *CCSU* case[69] it was unclear to what extent those exercising power under the prerogative were subject to judicial review. As late as 1983 the High Court in Northern Ireland was unwilling to enforce the BBC's policy of political impartiality in an action brought by the Workers' Party contesting election broadcasting.[70] It now appears to be accepted, however, that the BBC is subject to judicial review.[71] So in *Houston v BBC*,[72] an interim interdict was granted to restrain the corporation from broadcasting in Scotland an extended interview with the Prime Minister three days before the local government elections in Scotland. It was accepted that the pursuers had established a prima facie case that the broadcast would violate the BBC's duty, under the terms of its licence, to treat controversial subjects with due impartiality, and that the balance of convenience favoured the granting of relief to prevent the programme being broadcast until after the close of the poll.

The former IBA, a statutory body, was thus until recently an easier target in legal proceedings.

In *Attorney-General, ex rel McWhirter v IBA*, McWhirter, a member of the public, sought an injunction against the IBA to stop a film being shown about Andy Warhol which according to press reports contained matter offending against good taste and decency. An interim injunction was granted by the Court of Appeal at a time when members of the IBA had not seen the film. Some days later, the injunction was lifted since the court was then satisfied that the IBA had performed its statutory duty and there were no grounds on which the court should interfere with the IBA's decision. Lawton LJ said, 'In the realm of good taste and decency, whose frontiers are ill-defined, I find it impossible to say that the (IBA) have crossed from the permissible into the unlawful.' Although the interim injunction had been sought by McWhirter in his own name, the court ruled that such proceedings required the consent of the Attorney-General, since the individual had no locus standi to apply for the injunction himself.[73]

While this case lays down the admirable principle that the IBA like everyone else is required to observe the law, and that the IBA's decisions are subject to judicial review, the court did not show a desire to assume the role of censor, nor indeed would such a role be desirable. A similar restraint has been shown in the cases which have been brought to challenge party election broadcasts (more fully explained in chapter 9 B) and now the operation of the statutory

---

69   *Council of Civil Service Unions v Minister for the Civil Service* [1985] AC 374.
70   *Lynch v BBC* [1983] NILR 193.
71   See C Munro (1995) NLJ 518, (1996) NLJ 1433.
72   1995 SLT 1305. See also *R v BBC, ex p Lavelle* [1983] ICR 99.
73   [1973] QB 629.

restrictions on political advertising,[74] though there are exceptions.[75] There are also cases where the television or radio company itself may be the subject of legal proceedings.

In *R v Central Independent Television plc*[76] the respondents were due to broadcast a programme on the work of the obscene publications squad of Scotland Yard and in particular about the work of detectives engaged in the tracing, arrest and conviction of a man who was imprisoned on two charges of indecency. The man had previously been married to Mrs R who was the mother of his child and there was concern that the programme contained scenes which would identify the mother and the child, causing the latter distress. Invoking the parental jurisdiction of the court, the mother moved successfully to have the moving pictures of the father obscured, a decision reversed by the Court of Appeal which held that the press and broadcasters were entitled to publish the results of criminal proceedings, even though 'the families of those convicted had a heavy burden to bear and the effect of publicity on small children might be very serious'.

In a robust defence of freedom of expression, in a case where it was perhaps unnecessary, Hoffman LJ said:

'Publication may cause needless pain, distress and damage to individuals or harm to other aspects of the public interest. But a freedom which is restricted to what judges think to be responsible or in the public interest is no freedom. Freedom means the right to publish things which government and judges, however well motivated, think should not be published. It means the right to say things which 'right-thinking people' regard as dangerous or irresponsible. This freedom is subject only to clearly defined exceptions laid down by common law or statute.'

It is to a consideration of some of these exceptions that we now turn.

D.   Offences against the state and public order

Sedition

It is an offence at common law to publish a seditious libel or to utter seditious words. In 1886, at a trial of Socialist leaders for speeches made at a demonstration in Trafalgar Square which had been followed by disorder, a seditious intention was defined very widely as:

an intention to bring into hatred or contempt, or to excite disaffection against the person of, Her Majesty ... or the government and constitution of the United Kingdom, as by law established, or either House of Parliament, or the administration of justice, or to excite Her Majesty's subjects to attempt, otherwise than by lawful means, the alteration of any matter in Church or State by law established, or to raise discontent or disaffection amongst Her Majesty's subjects, or to promote feelings of ill-will and hostility between different classes of such subjects.[77]

But at the same time it was explained that it is not seditious to point out errors

---

[74]   *R v Radio Authority, ex p Bull* [1997] 2 All ER 561.
[75]   *Wilson v Independent Broadcasting Authority* 1979 SLT 279. Cf *Wilson v Independent Broadcasting Authority* 1988 SLT 276.
[76]   [1994] Fam 192.
[77]   *R v Burns* (1886) 16 Cox CC 355, citing Stephen's *Digest of Criminal Law*. And see Williams, *Keeping the Peace*, ch 8.

or defects in the government or constitution of the United Kingdom, or to seek to bring about changes in church or state by lawful means or, with a view to their removal, to draw attention to matters which were tending to produce ill-will or hostility between classes of Her Majesty's subjects.

In prosecutions for seditious libel, the element of incitement to violence was stressed. In *R v Aldred*, a journal advocating independence for India published articles which commended political assassination soon after an assassination by an Indian nationalist had occurred in London; Coleridge J told the jury that sedition implied violence or lawlessness in some form, and said, 'the test is this: was the language used calculated, or was it not, to promote public disorder or physical force or violence in a matter of state?' Aldred, editor of the journal, was convicted.[78] The test of whether the words were *calculated* (that is, likely) to promote violence was not followed in *R v Caunt*, where Birkett J directed the jury that proof of *intention* to promote violence was an essential part of the offence.

At a time shortly before the creation of the state of Israel, when British troops in Palestine were being subjected to terrorist atrocities and soldiers had been murdered, the editor of the *Morecambe and Heysham Visitor* published a leading article attacking British Jews in virulent terms and calling for Jews to be ostracised. The article ended with a suggestion that violence might be the only way to bring British Jews to the sense of their responsibility to the country in which they lived. Notwithstanding these words, the jury acquitted the editor of having published a seditious libel.[79]

Such a case provided a severe test for the principle of free speech. A possible comment on the outcome is that the jury shared the editor's views, or at least did not find his anti-Semitism so abhorrent to them that he should be punished for having published them. On the other hand, given the judge's direction on the law of seditious libel, the jury may not have been satisfied beyond reasonable doubt that the editor was intending to incite his readers to violence: in evidence he had denied any such intention, while adhering to the words of his article. It is fundamental in such a case that a jury does not give reasons for its verdict nor need the jurors each come to their decision by the same route. Nevertheless, the scope of sedition has appeared to change in the sense that the prosecution must now show an intention to promote violence and disorder over and above the strong criticism of public affairs.[80] Further developments took place in *R v Chief Metropolitan Stipendiary Magistrate, ex p Choudhury*.[81]

This case concerned an attempt to bring criminal charges against Mr Salman Rushdie, author of *The Satanic Verses*. It was alleged that publication constituted seditious libel on the ground that 'it raised widespread discontent and disaffection among her Majesty's subjects, contrary to common law'. When the magistrate refused to issue the summonses, the applicants sought judicial review of his decision, thereby providing an opportunity for reconsideration of the scope of seditious libel. Agreeing with the magistrate, the Divisional Court followed the Supreme Court of Canada in *Boucher v R*,[82] where it was held that 'the seditious intention on which a prosecution for seditious libel must be founded is an intention to incite to violence or to create public

---

78   (1909) 22 Cox CC 1.
79   See *An Editor on Trial*, 1948; and E C S Wade (1948) 64 LQR 203.
80   Smith and Hogan, p 759; cf *Boucher v R* [1951] SCR 265.
81   [1991] 1 QB 429.
82   [1951] SCR 265.

disturbance or disorder against His Majesty or the institutions of government'. Apart from thus reinforcing the requirement of an intention to promote violence, this indicates a further qualification: namely that sedition can no longer be constituted by an intention to promote feelings of ill-will and hostility between different classes of subjects. According to Watkins LJ, not only must there be proof of an incitement to violence in such cases, 'but it must be violence or resistance or defiance for the purpose of disturbing constituted authority'. In this case, given the absence of any element of attacking, obstructing, or undermining public authority, the court held that the magistrate was bound not to issue the summonses.

It would thus appear that there is no basis in the future for prosecution for sedition in cases such as *Caunt*.

Incitement to disaffection[83]

Parliament has on several occasions legislated to prevent the spread of disaffection, mainly to protect members of the armed forces, who might otherwise be exposed to attempts to persuade them to disobey their orders. The Incitement to Mutiny Act 1797, passed following the Nore mutiny, made it a felony maliciously and advisedly to endeavour to seduce members of the armed forces from their duty and allegiance to the Crown, or to incite members to commit any act of mutiny. The Aliens Restriction (Amendment) Act 1919, s 3, prohibits an alien from causing sedition or disaffection among the civil population as well as among the armed forces; and it is an offence for any alien to promote or interfere in an industrial dispute in any industry in which he or she has not been bona fide engaged in the United Kingdom for at least two years preceding an alleged offence. The Police Act 1996, s 91, replacing legislation first passed in 1919 at a time of serious unrest within the police, prohibits acts calculated to cause disaffection among police officers or to induce them to withhold their services or commit breaches of discipline. The Incitement to Disaffection Act 1934, which passed through Parliament against severe criticism from a variety of quarters,[84] sought without repealing the 1797 Act to provide a modern version of it. Under the 1934 Act, it is an offence maliciously and advisedly to endeavour to seduce a member of the armed forces from his duty or allegiance. The Act contains stringent provisions for the prevention and detection of the offence, including wide powers of search on reasonable suspicion, but a warrant may be issued only by a High Court judge. Moreover, it is an offence for any person, with intent to commit or to aid, counsel or procure commission of the main offence, to have in his possession or under his control any document of such a nature that the distribution of copies among members of the forces would constitute that offence. Notwithstanding the safeguards in the Act, it does restrain certain forms of political propaganda; and it could be used to suppress or interfere with the distribution of pacifist literature. Prosecutions under the Act in England require the consent of the Director of Public Prosecutions. This consent was given between 1973 and 1975 for prosecution of members of a campaign for the withdrawal of British troops from Northern Ireland in

---

[83]   Williams, op cit, ch 8; Young, *Incitement to Disaffection*; Bunyan, *The Political Police in Britain*, pp 28–36.

[84]   See eg Jennings, *The Sedition Bill Explained*.

respect of leaflets which they had prepared. One conviction was upheld by the Court of Appeal.[85] The accused has a right to jury-trial: it would be a matter for the jury to decide whether a leaflet which gave information to a soldier about procedures for leaving the army and his or her rights as a soldier was an attempt to seduce him or her from duty or allegiance to the Crown.

Blasphemy

While it continues to be a common law offence to utter or publish blasphemous words and writings, the old precedents which held that it is blasphemy to deny the truth of the Christian religion or the existence of God have ceased to be helpful. 'If the decencies of controversy are observed, even the fundamentals of religion may be attacked without the writer being guilty of blasphemy'.[86] In the absence of modern authorities, it became unclear what the essentials of the offence were. But in *R v Lemon*, the publishers of *Gay News* were in 1977 convicted by a jury of publishing a blasphemous libel, in the form of a poem by James Kirkup that linked homosexual practices with the life and crucifixion of Christ. The House of Lords held by three to two that it was sufficient for the prosecution to prove that blasphemous material had been published, and not necessary to prove that the defendants intended to blaspheme. In the view of the House, a blasphemous libel was material calculated to outrage and insult a Christian's religious feelings; it is not an element of the offence that the publication must tend to lead to a breach of the peace.[87] More recently, in *Ex p Choudhury*,[88] a Divisional Court confirmed that the offence is limited to Christianity, and does not extend to other religions, in this case Islam. In 1985, the Law Commission proposed (by a majority) that the crime of blasphemy should be abolished, concluding that the arguments were quite evenly balanced, but that 'while the presence of a pressing social need might justify the imposition of penalties for incitement to racial hatred, there was no corresponding need in the context of religion which might justify an offence of blasphemy'.[89] But in 1995 the government announced that it had no plans to change the law,[90] which in 1997 the European Court of Human Rights found did not violate the Convention.[91]

Incitement to racial hatred

It has long been recognised that the preservation of public order justifies the imposition of criminal sanctions on those who utter threats, abuse or insults

---

85   *R v Arrowsmith* [1975] QB 678; and see *Arrowsmith v UK* (1978) 3 EHRR 218 (no infringement of European Convention on Human Rights).

86   *R v Ramsay and Foote* (1883) 15 Cox CC 231, 238 (Coleridge CJ). See also *Bowman v Secular Society* [1917] AC 406; and *R v Gott* (1922) 16 Cr App Rep 87.

87   *R v Lemon* [1979] AC 617. And see *Gay News Ltd v UK* (1982) 5 EHRR 123.

88   [1991] 1 QB 429.

89   Law Commission Report No 145 (HC 442 (1985)). See also the Law Commission's 1981 Working Paper No 79, Offences Against Religion and Public Worship. See further St J Robilliard (1981) 44 MLR 556.

90   HC Deb, 10 May 1995, col 478 (WA).

91   *Wingrove v UK* 1997 1 BHRC 509.

in public places which are likely to give rise to a breach of the peace.[92] In 1965, when Parliament first created machinery to deal with racial discrimination,[93] an offence of incitement to racial hatred was created which was not dependent on proof of an immediate threat to public order. The reason for this was the belief that racial hatred itself contains the seeds of violence.[94] The position is now governed by the Public Order Act 1986, which deals specifically with 'racial hatred', defined to mean 'hatred against a group of persons in Great Britain defined by reference to colour, race, nationality (including citizenship) or ethnic or national origins' (s 17).[95] This replaces measures enacted in the Race Relations Act 1976 and previously in the Race Relations Act 1965.[96] By s 18 of the 1986 Act, it is an offence for a person to use threatening, abusive or insulting words or behaviour or to display any material which is threatening, abusive or insulting if he does so with intent to stir up racial hatred, or if in the circumstances racial hatred is likely to be stirred up.[97] The Act applies to publicising or distributing such material (s 19),[98] theatrical performances (s 20), the distribution, showing or playing of a recording of visual images or sounds (s 21), and television and radio broadcasts (s 22). A new offence in s 23 of the Act relates to the possession of material which if published or displayed would amount to an offence under the Act. Where there are reasonable grounds for suspecting that a person has possession of such material, a justice of the peace may grant a warrant to a police constable authorising the entry and search of premises for such material. It is not an offence to publish a fair and accurate report of proceedings in Parliament or of proceedings publicly heard before a tribunal or court where the report is published contemporaneously with the proceedings (s 26). No prosecution in England and Wales may occur without the consent of the Attorney-General (s 27). Although these are wide-ranging restrictions, they are justifiable primarily because a serious threat to personal security and dignity, not to mention public order, is inherent in certain forms of political and social expression. Sadly, legislation of this kind will not in itself necessarily reduce the occurrence of racial violence and harassment in the streets. But it may help,[99] as in a more specific context may the Football (Offences) Act 1991, which by s 3 makes indecent or 'racialist' chanting at football matches a criminal offence.

---

92   Ch 23.

93   Ch 19 B.

94   See D G T Williams [1966] Crim LR 320; Lester and Bindman, *Race and Law*, ch 10; and P M Leopold [1977] PL 389.

95   Religion is not mentioned, but Sikhs in Britain form an ethnic group under the Act: *Mandla v Dowell Lee* [1983] 2 AC 548. See also *King-Ansell v Police* [1979] 2 NZLR 531.

96   *R v Britton* [1967] 2 QB 51; *R v Malik* [1968] 1 All ER 582. See also A Dickey [1968] Crim LR 48.

97   It is not now necessary, as it was under the 1965 Act, to prove that the accused intended to stir up racial hatred: in practice, such proof had been too stringent a requirement for the law to be an effective restraint upon racist propaganda. See also W J Wolffe [1987] PL 85 and S Poulter [1991] PL 371.

98   The offence under s 19 is an arrestable offence for the purposes of the Police and Criminal Evidence Act 1984 (Criminal Justice and Public Order Act 1994, s 155).

99   For important proposals to amend the law, see Commission for Racial Equality, *Second Review of the Race Relations Act 1976* (1992). On racial violence, see HC 71 (1993–94).

E.   Obscene publications

Before the Act of 1959

It resulted from the development of the law concerning the printing of books that, as with seditious, blasphemous and other libels, it became an offence punishable by the common law courts to publish obscene material. This jurisdiction was exercised for the first time in *Curll*'s case when the court held that it was an offence to publish a book which tended to corrupt morals and was against the King's peace.[100] The flourishing business of pornography in the Victorian underworld led to the Obscene Publications Act 1857. This Act gave the police power to search premises, seize obscene publications kept for sale and bring them before a magistrates' court for destruction. The Act did not define 'obscene' but its sponsor, Lord Campbell, stated that it was to apply 'exclusively to works written for the single purpose of corrupting the morals of youth, and of a nature calculated to shock the common feelings of decency in any well regulated mind.'[101]

In 1868, in *R v Hicklin*, Cockburn CJ declared the test for obscenity to be

whether the tendency of the matter charged as obscenity is to deprave and corrupt those whose minds are open to such immoral influences and into whose hands a publication of this sort may fall.[102]

This test came to dominate the English law of obscenity. It required account to be taken of the circumstances of publication: in *Hicklin*'s case Cockburn CJ said that immunity for a medical treatise depended upon the circumstances, since the publication of some medical details would not be fit for boys and girls to see. But the test did not permit the author's intention to be taken into account. Although the tendency to deprave and corrupt was often assumed from the character of a book, who might the potential readers be? In 1954, in *R v Reiter*, the Court of Criminal Appeal took the view that a jury should direct their attention to the result of a book falling into the hands of young people.[103] But a few months later, in *R v Secker Warburg Ltd*, Stable J asked: 'Are we to take our literary standards as being the level of something that is suitable for the decently brought up young female aged 14?' He continued:

A mass of literature, great literature from many angles, is wholly unsuitable for reading by the adolescent, but that does not mean that the publisher is guilty of a criminal offence for making those works available to the general public.[104]

Other difficulties in the law included the lack of authority establishing that the publication of matter prima facie obscene might nonetheless be for the public good; the use of the 1857 Act against serious literature; the failure of the 1857 Act to enable a publisher or author to defend a work against destruction; and the tendency of prosecutors to take selected passages of a

---

[100]   (1727) 17 St Tr 153; Robertson, *Obscenity*, ch 2.
[101]   HL Deb, 25 June 1857, col 329.
[102]   (1868) LR 3 QB 360, 371.
[103]   [1954] 2 QB 16.
[104]   [1954] 2 All ER 683, 686 (Kauffman's *The Philanderer*).

book out of context. A lengthy campaign by publishers and authors led to the Obscene Publications Act 1959.[105]

The Obscene Publications Acts 1959 and 1964

The 1959 Act, which does not apply to Scotland, sought both to provide for the protection of literature and to strengthen the law against pornography. For the purposes of the 1959 Act (but not of other Acts in which the word 'obscene' is used),[106]

an article shall be deemed to be obscene if its effect or (where the article comprises two or more distinct items) the effect of any one of its items[107] is, if taken as a whole, such as to tend to deprave and corrupt persons who are likely, having regard to all relevant circumstances, to read, see or hear the matter contained or embodied in it (s 1(1)).

A wide definition of 'article' (s 1(2)) includes books, pictures, films, records and such things as film negatives used in producing obscene articles,[108] and video cassettes.[109] It is an offence to publish an obscene article, whether for gain or not, or to have obscene articles in one's possession, ownership or control for the purpose of publication for gain or with a view to such publication,[110] whether for sale within Britain or abroad.[111] The definition of 'publishing' includes distributing, circulating, selling, hiring and, for example, showing pictures or playing records; since 1991 it includes television and sound broadcasting.[112] No person may be prosecuted for an offence at common law consisting of the publication of an article when the essence of the offence is that the matter is obscene.[113] It is a defence to prove that publication of an obscene article is justified 'as being for the public good on the ground that it is in the interests of science, literature, art or learning or other objects of general concern'. Expert evidence on the literary, artistic, scientific or other merits of an article is admissible to establish or negative the defence of public good.[114]

The 1959 Act, s 3, confers search, seizure and forfeiture powers similar to those in the 1857 Act. A warrant may be obtained by a constable or the Director of Public Prosecutions[115] from a magistrate for the search of specified premises, stalls or vehicles, where there is reasonable suspicion that obscene articles are kept for publication for gain. When a search is made, articles believed to be obscene and also documents relating to a trade or business may be seized. The seized articles must be brought before a magistrate. When

---

[105] See HC 123 (1957–58); and Robertson, op cit, pp 40–4.
[106] *R v Anderson* [1972] 1 QB 304, 317 (*Oz, School Kids Issue*).
[107] On the item by item test, see *R v Anderson*, at 312.
[108] 1964 Act, s 2, the sequel to *Straker v DPP* [1963] 1 QB 926.
[109] *A-G's Reference (No 5 of 1980)* [1980] 3 All ER 816.
[110] 1959 Act, s 2(1), as amended in 1964. See *R v Taylor* [1995] 1 Cr App Rep 131 (publication where films depicting obscene acts are developed, printed and returned to the owner).
[111] *Gold Star Publications Ltd v DPP* [1981] 2 All ER 257; and see (1983) 5 EHRR 591.
[112] Broadcasting Act 1990, s 162, amending 1959 Act, s 1(3).
[113] 1959 Act, s 2(4). This does not prevent a prosecution for conspiracy to corrupt public morals: see below. In the case of cinema performances, such prosecution is excluded by 1959 Act, s 2(4A), inserted by Criminal Law Act 1977, s 53.
[114] 1959 Act, s 4.
[115] Criminal Justice Act 1967, s 25. See *Darbo v DPP, The Times*, 11 July 1991.

notice has been given to the occupier of the premises to show cause why the articles should not be forfeited, the magistrates' court may order forfeiture if satisfied that the articles are obscene and were kept for publication for gain. The owner, author or maker of the articles may also appear to defend them against forfeiture. The defence that publication is for the public good is available, and expert evidence relating to the merits of the articles may be called. In these proceedings there is no right to the decision of a jury, but there are rights of appeal to the Crown Court or by case stated to the High Court. Because of certain defects in the 1959 Act, the Act of 1964 was passed to strengthen the law against publishing obscene matter. Inter alia, the Act made it an offence to have an obscene article for publication for the purposes of gain,[116] and authorised a forfeiture order to be made following a conviction under the 1959 Act.

The best-known outcome of the 1959 Act was the trial and acquittal of Penguin Books Ltd for publishing *Lady Chatterley's Lover* in 1960.[117] The verdict did not reveal whether the jurors considered the book not to be obscene, or considered the book to be obscene but its publication to be for the public good in the interests of literature, art or learning. But the Act had clearly achieved one of its main objects. Since then many difficulties have arisen out of the legislation. The confusion and perplexities were discussed in *R v Metropolitan Police Commissioner, ex p Blackburn:*[118] the Court of Appeal was satisfied that, despite the powers of the police, hard-core pornography was freely on sale in central London and that 'moderately obscene' publications were generally available. The court considered that the cause of the ineffectiveness of police efforts lay largely with the legal framework in which the police had to operate. In fact some of the difficulties are inherent in the legal problem of defining obscenity; others are attributable to features of the 1959 Act; and some were due to police corruption.

One difficulty is the 1959 Act's definition of obscenity as 'a tendency to deprave and corrupt'. The definition makes it impossible to rely on such synonyms as 'repulsive', 'filthy', 'loathsome' or 'lewd'[119] and requires the jury to consider whether the effect of a book is to tend to deprave and corrupt a significant proportion of those likely to read it. 'What is a significant proportion is entirely for the jury to decide'.[120] Lord Wilberforce has said, 'An article cannot be considered as obscene in itself: it can only be so in relation to its likely readers'.[121] Experienced police officers may for practical purposes not be susceptible to being depraved and corrupted[122] but it seems that a man may be corrupted more than once.[123] Although the circumstances in which articles are sold are relevant, it is no defence for booksellers to prove that

---

[116]   Cf *Mella v Monahan* [1961] Crim LR 175.

[117]   See Rolph, *The Trial of Lady Chatterley*.

[118]   [1973] QB 241.

[119]   *R v Anderson* [1972] 1 QB 304; cf the perceptive analysis by Windeyer J in *Crowe v Grahame* (1968) 41 AJLR 402, 409.

[120]   *R v Calder & Boyars Ltd* [1969] 1 QB 151, 168. But it is 'more than a negligible number' (*R v O'Sullivan* [1995] 1 Cr App Rep 445).

[121]   *DPP v Whyte* [1972] AC 849, 860.

[122]   *R v Clayton and Halsey* [1963] 1 QB 163.

[123]   *Shaw v DPP* [1962] AC 220, 228 (CCA).

most of their sales are made to middle-aged men who are already addicted to pornography; articles may 'deprave and corrupt' the mind without any overt sexual activity by the reader resulting.[124] Obscenity is not confined to sexual matters: a book dealing with the effects of drug taking may be obscene[125] and so may cards depicting scenes of violence when sold with chewing gum to children.[126]

Other difficulties have been caused by the defence of public good. Expert evidence relating to literary and other merits may not deal with the issue of whether the article is obscene,[127] except when the jury needs to be informed of the likely effect of an article upon children, and is not admissible to establish that obscene articles may have a therapeutic effect on some individuals.[128] The jury must be directed to balance the number of readers who would tend to be corrupted by a book, and the nature of that corruption, against the literary or other merits of the book, and then decide whether on balance publication is for the public good. The need for such a balancing act springs from the structure of the 1959 Act. As Geoffrey Robertson has said, 'Instead of one clause enabling a court to weigh all aspects of the publication in one decision, the two-tier approach set up an illogical and unworkable dichotomy between "obscenity" and "artistic merit"'.[129]

Other legislation on indecency and pornography

Fewer legal difficulties arise in the exercise of other powers of restriction on moral grounds. Under the Customs Consolidation Act 1876, s 42, and the Customs and Excise Management Act 1979, s 49, customs officers may seize and destroy 'indecent or obscene' books and other articles being imported into the United Kingdom;[130] and the Post Office Act 1953, s 11, seeks to prevent the postal service being used for the dispatch of 'indecent or obscene' articles. These statutes do not provide a defence of publication for the public good, and the test appears to be whether an article offends current standards of propriety.[131] The concept of indecency is no doubt as subjective as obscenity, but implies a less serious judgment and in practice is easier to apply than obscenity.[132] A difficulty with the customs restrictions has arisen in the context of EC law. Article 30 of the Treaty of Rome facilitates the free movement of goods by prohibiting restrictions on imports from other EC countries. Although art 36 allows import restrictions on the grounds of public morality, in Case 121/85 *Conegate Ltd v Customs and Excise Commissioners*[133] it was held that this cannot be used to restrict the import of indecent material which may be manufactured and sold in Britain, but it can be used to restrict

---

[124] *DPP v Whyte* [1972] AC 849, 867.
[125] *Calder (Publications) Ltd v Powell* [1965] 1 QB 509; *R v Skirving* [1985] QB 819.
[126] *DPP v A & BC Chewing Gum Ltd* [1968] 1 QB 159.
[127] *R v Anderson* (above). And see *R v Stamford* [1972] 2 QB 391.
[128] *DPP v Jordan* [1977] AC 699; and see *A-G's Reference (No 3 of 1977)* [1978] 3 All ER 1166.
[129] *Obscenity*, p 163.
[130] See *Derrick v Commissioners of Customs and Excise* [1972] 2 QB 28; *C Manchester* [1981] Crim LR 531, [1983] Crim LR 64.
[131] *R v Stamford* [1972] 2 QB 391.
[132] See *McGowan v Langmuir* 1931 JC 10 (Lord Sands).
[133] [1987] QB 254.

the import of obscene material. So the customs legislation applies only to restrict the import of obscene material from the EC, but obscene and indecent material from other countries.[134]

The Protection of Children Act 1978[135] tightened up the law with regard to indecent photographs (including films and video recordings) involving children under 16. Offences under the Act include the taking and distribution of indecent photographs (or pseudo-photographs) of children, and the distribution, showing or advertisement of such photographs. Prosecutions require the consent of the Director of Public Prosecutions.[136] By the Criminal Justice Act 1988,[137] it is an offence for a person to have any indecent photograph (or pseudo-photograph) of a child in his possession. The Indecent Displays (Control) Act 1981 deals with the public nuisance aspects of pornography, making it an offence to display publicly any indecent matter, where the display is visible from a public place.[138] A public place is a place to which the public have access except either on payment for the display or within a shop where the public have passed a warning notice, provided in each case that entry is limited to persons over 18. The exceptions to the Act include television broadcasts, displays in art galleries or museums that are not visible from outside the premises, and matter contained within the performance of plays and films. Since the Act contains no definition of indecency, 'indecent' will probably receive the same interpretation as in the customs and post office legislation.[139] In 1982, district councils were authorised to license sex shops and sex cinemas, by resolving to introduce a licensing scheme.[140] The grounds on which a council may refuse a licence include the reason that the existing number of such establishments in the area is equal to or exceeds the number which the council considers to be appropriate.

Common law offences

The specific objectives of these recent Acts prevent them from being a grave restriction upon the liberty of expression. The same cannot be said of the common law offence of conspiracy to corrupt public morals.

In *Shaw v DPP*, the appellant had published the *Ladies' Directory*, an illustrated magazine containing names, addresses and other details of prostitutes and their services. The House of Lords upheld Shaw's conviction for the offence of conspiracy to corrupt public morals. Lord Simonds accepted that the law must be related to the changing standards of life, having regard to fundamental human values and the

---

[134] Cf *R v Bow Street Metropolitan Stipendiary Magistrate, ex p Noncyp Ltd* [1990] 1 QB 123 (obscene articles imported from EC countries may be seized under customs legislation even though publication under the 1959 Act would not be an offence because of the public good defence in s 4). *R v Uxbridge Justices, ex p Webb* [1994] COD 24.

[135] As amended by the Criminal Justice and Public Order Act 1994.

[136] See *R v Graham-Kerr* [1988] 1 WLR 1098 (photograph of boy taken at naturist swimming session not an offence).

[137] Section 84(4).

[138] See K D Ewing (1982) SLT (News) 55.

[139] See J L Lambert [1982] PL 226 and R T H Stone (1982) 45 MLR 62.

[140] Local Government (Miscellaneous Provisions) Act 1982, s 2 and Sched 3. The numerous cases include *McMonagle v Westminster City Council* [1990] 2 AC 716; *Quietlynn Ltd v Plymouth City Council* [1988] QB 114; *Quietlynn Ltd v Southend-on-Sea BC* [1991] 1 QB 454; and *Willocell Ltd v Westminster City Council* (1995) 94 LGR 83.

purposes of society; he said that 'there remains in the courts of law a residual power to enforce the supreme and fundamental purpose of the law, to conserve not only the safety and order but also the moral welfare of the State'.[141] It was the jury which provided a safeguard against the launching of prosecutions to suppress unpopular or unorthodox views. Lord Reid, dissenting, rejected the view that the court was guardian of public morals.

This controversial decision derived in part from the supposed offence of conspiracy to effect a public mischief, which was later held not to be part of criminal law.[142] Although Shaw was also convicted for having published an obscene book, contrary to the 1959 Act, *Shaw's* case enabled prosecutions to be brought at common law for conspiracy rather than for breaches of the 1959 Act. Thereafter the Law Officers assured the House of Commons that a conspiracy to corrupt public morals would not be charged so as to circumvent the 'public good' defence in the 1959 Act.[143]

In *Knuller Ltd v DPP*, the House of Lords reaffirmed the decision in *Shaw's* case. The appellants had published a magazine which contained advertisements by male homosexuals seeking to meet other homosexuals. The Lords upheld a conviction of the appellants for conspiracy to corrupt public morals, rejecting a defence based on the Sexual Offences Act 1967 by which homosexual acts between adult males in private had ceased to be an offence. A second conviction for conspiracy 'to outrage public decency' was quashed on the ground of misdirection, but a majority of the House held that at common law it was an offence to outrage public decency and also to conspire to outrage public decency; and that such a conspiracy could take the form of an agreement to insert outrageously indecent matter on the inside pages of a magazine sold in public.[144] Lords Reid and Diplock did not agree that 'outraging public decency' was an offence; Lord Reid said, 'To recognise this new crime would go contrary to the whole trend of public policy followed by Parliament in recent times'.[145]

The common law of conspiracy was reformed by the Criminal Law Act 1977, which created a new statutory offence of conspiracy. But the abolition of common law conspiracy is not to affect conspiracy that involves an agreement to engage in conduct which tends to corrupt public morals or outrages public decency.[146] However, few prosecutions for conspiracy to corrupt public morals or to outrage public decency have been brought since *Knuller* though one such case is *R v Gibson*,[147] in which both the owner of an art gallery and an artist were convicted for exhibiting a model's head to the ears of which were attached earrings made out of a freeze-dried human foetus of three or four months' gestation. The case raised the question whether a prosecution at common law to outrage public decency was precluded by s 2(4) of the Obscene Publications Act 1959 whereby common law proceedings are not to

---

141   [1962] AC 220, 268. See D Seaborne Davies (1962) 6 JSPTL 104, J E Hall Williams (1961) 24 MLR 626, and Robertson, *Obscenity*, ch 8.
142   *DPP v Withers* [1975] AC 842.
143   HC Deb, 3 June 1964, col 1212.
144   See now *R v Walker* [1996] Cr App Rep 111.
145   *Knuller Ltd v DPP* [1973] AC 435, 459.
146   Criminal Law Act 1977, s 5(3); cf s 53(3).
147   [1990] 2 QB 619; M Childs [1991] PL 20.

be brought where 'it is of the essence of the offence that the matter is obscene'. The Court of Appeal held that there are two broad types of offence involving obscenity and that the 1959 Act applied only in respect of one (those involving the corruption of public morals) but not the other (those which involve an outrage on public decency, whether or not public morals are involved). This decision may make it easier for the Crown to bring prosecutions at common law, thereby circumventing the defences which would otherwise be available in a prosecution brought under the Act. Of these, the most important is undoubtedly the public good defence in s 4.

Reform of the law

The law of obscenity and indecency was reviewed by a Home Office committee (chairman, Professor Bernard Williams) which reported in 1979.[148] The committee analysed the purposes for which regulation of obscenity was justified. It considered that the existing law should be scrapped and a fresh start made with a comprehensive new statute. In particular, terms such as 'obscene', 'indecency', 'deprave and corrupt' should be abandoned as having outlived their usefulness. The government did not accept these recommendations and developing technology has subsequently presented new challenges for the legislation.[149] Since 1979, as we have seen, Parliament has legislated in a piecemeal manner that in important respects runs contrary to the Williams report. Further evidence of the tendency towards greater restriction rather than restraint is reflected by the provisions of the Criminal Justice and Public Order Act 1994 whereby offences under the Obscene Publications Acts 1959–64 are deemed to be serious arrestable offences for the purposes of the Police and Criminal Evidence Act 1984. It may be reflected also in the expressions of frustration by the courts in whose judgment 'the only way of stamping out this filthy trade is by imposing sentences of imprisonment on first offenders and all connected with the commercial exploitation of pornography'.[150] Although judges continue to express difficulty with the complexity of the legislation of 1959 and 1964,[151] there was in 1997 no prospect of another governmental attempt to review the law with a view to its reform.

F. Defamation

Criminal libel[152]

To publish defamatory material in writing became a criminal offence punishable by the common law courts after the abolition of Star Chamber in 1640. The justification for treating libel as a criminal offence was considered to be

---

[148] Cmnd 7772, 1979. See Simpson, *Pornography and Politics – the Williams Report in Retrospect.*
[149] On computer pornography, see HC 126 (1994).
[150] *R v Holloway* (1982) 4 Cr App Rep (S) 128. The Court of Appeal expressly repudiated the Williams committee: 'There is an evil in this kind of pornography. It is an evil which in our opinion has to be stopped.' But for evidence of serious problems in the enforcement of the law, see *New Law Journal*, 9 August 1996, p 1179.
[151] *R v O'Sullivan*, note 120 above.
[152] J R Spencer [1977] Crim LR 383 and [1979] CLJ 60.

the threat to the preservation of the peace which some libels presented. Today criminal proceedings are rarely instituted for libel. If they are, it is not necessary to prove that the libel was likely to cause a breach of the peace,[153] but a criminal libel must be a serious libel to justify invoking the criminal law. At common law, truth was no defence to a prosecution for libel but by the Libel Act 1843, truth is a defence if the accused also proves that the publication was for the public benefit. By the Law of Libel Amendment Act 1888, s 8, no prosecution may be commenced in respect of a libel in a newspaper without the order of a High Court judge. Prosecutions are rare but in 1976, Wien J gave an order enabling a private prosecution to be brought by Sir James Goldsmith against the publishers of *Private Eye* in respect of repeated allegations that Goldsmith was the ringleader of a conspiracy to obstruct the course of justice; the judge said that the press does not have licence to publish scandalous or scurrilous matter which is wholly without foundation.[154] In 1982, the Law Commission's provisional view was that criminal libel at common law should be abolished and replaced by a much narrower statutory offence, aimed at a person who publishes a deliberately defamatory statement, which he or she knows or believes to be untrue, and is likely to cause the victim significant harm.[155] But it has been argued that the criminal law should be excluded from the area of defamation.[156]

Civil liability

The law of defamation seeks to resolve the conflict between the freedom of speech and publication, and the right of the individual to maintain his or her reputation against improper attack.[157] Possibly because of this, defamation law is one of the most complex branches of civil liability. In principle the law provides a remedy for false statements which expose a person to 'hatred, ridicule or contempt' or which tend to lower him or her 'in the estimation of right-thinking members of society generally'.[158] Defamation takes two main forms: (*a*) slander (defamation in a transitory form by spoken word or gesture) and (*b*) libel (defamation in a permanent form such as the written or printed word). By statute, words used in the course of broadcasting and of public performances in a theatre are treated as publication in permanent form.[159] With certain exceptions, slander is actionable only when the plaintiff can prove special damage as a result of the slander, whereas libel is actionable without such proof. Actions for defamation are one of the few surviving forms

---

153 *R v Wicks* [1936] 1 All ER 384; *Gleaves v Deakin* [1980] AC 477.
154 *Goldsmith v Pressdram Ltd* [1977] QB 83. And see *Desmond v Thorne* [1982] 3 All ER 268.
155 Law Commission, Working Paper No 84, Criminal Libel. See also J R Spencer [1983] Crim LR 524 and Cmnd 5909, 1975, ch 16.
156 G Robertson [1983] PL 208.
157 For fuller accounts of the law of defamation, see textbooks on the law of tort and also Robertson, *Freedom, the Individual and the Law*, ch 7, and Report of Committee on Defamation, Cmnd 5909, 1975.
158 *Sim v Stretch* (1936) 52 TLR 669, 671 (Lord Atkin). In order to succeed the publication must be read as a whole, rather than concentrate on an isolated passage. See *Charleston v News Group Newspapers Ltd* [1995] 2 AC 65.
159 Broadcasting Act 1990, s 166; and Theatres Act 1968, s 4.

of civil action where either party has a right to insist on trial by jury.[160] When the judge rules that a statement is capable of being regarded as defamatory, it is the jury which decides whether the plaintiff has been defamed and if so the damages that he or she should recover. Substantial damages may be awarded for injury to reputation and may include exemplary damages.[161] In fact many claims are settled out of court and newspapers often publish notes of correction or apology to persons whom they have unintentionally defamed.

The law of libel has undergone a number of important changes in recent years, with major revisions being made both by statute and the courts. So far as legislation is concerned, the major source of change has been the Defamation Act 1996 which follows a working party established under Lord Justice Neill to examine various aspects of the law, and the publication in 1990 of the Lord Chancellor's department consultation paper on 'The Defence of Innocent Dissemination'. The 1996 Act expands the defences available in defamation cases; reduces the limitation period for actions to be brought to one year; introduces measures to eradicate delaying tactics by the parties; introduces a new 'fast track' procedure to provide a prompt and inexpensive remedy for less serious cases; and amends the law relating to absolute and qualified privilege. The Act also contains controversial measures designed to overcome obstacles presented by the 1689 Bill of Rights to actions for defamation brought by members of Parliament. But in addition to these wide-ranging statutory reforms, important initiatives have been taken by the Court of Appeal, reflecting public concern about the amount of damages which were being awarded by libel juries. So in *John v Mirror Group Newspapers*,[162] steps were taken in an important judgment to propose that judges give greater guidance to libel juries, this following the decision of the European Court of Human Rights in the *Tolstoy* case in which it was held that a libel award of £1.5 million in favour of Lord Aldington was a violation of the applicant's right to freedom of expression under art 10 of the ECHR.[163] The applicant had written a pamphlet accusing Aldington of war crimes, and although the award was held to be in accordance with the law, it was disproportionately large and therefore not necessary in a democratic society for the purposes of art 10(2).[164]

Absolute and qualified privilege

Publication of statements that would otherwise be defamatory may be protected if made in circumstances of absolute or qualified privilege. Absolute privilege applies to, inter alia, (*a*) statements made during parliamentary proceedings and statements in the official reports of debates or in other papers published by order of either House of Parliament;[165] (*b*) statements

---

[160] Supreme Court Act 1981, s 69, and RSC, Order 33(5). There are exceptions, for example where the court is of the opinion that the trial will require a prolonged examination of documents.

[161] *Broome v Cassell and Co Ltd* [1972] AC 1027; *Riches v News Group Newspapers Ltd* [1986] QB 256. Cf *John v Mirror Group Newspapers* [1996] 3 WLR 593.

[162] [1996] 3 WLR 593.

[163] *Tolstoy Miloslavsky v UK* (1995) 20 EHRR 442.

[164] See also *Rantzen v Mirror Group Newspapers* [1994] QB 670.

[165] Ch 11 A.

made by one officer of state to another in the course of his official duty, a privilege which in absolute form applies only to certain communications at a high level;[166] (*c*) reports by and statements to the Parliamentary Ombudsman;[167] (*d*) the internal documents of a foreign embassy;[168] and (*e*) the fair and accurate report of proceedings in public before a court in the UK if published contemporaneously with the proceedings. For this purpose a court includes any tribunal or body exercising the judicial power of the state.[169] Absolute privilege also applies to the fair and accurate report of public proceedings of the European Court of Justice and the European Court of Human Rights.[170]

Qualified privilege, unlike absolute privilege, is destroyed as a defence if the plaintiff proves malice on the part of the defendant.[171] Such privilege arises in two types of case. The first comprises reports privileged without 'explanation or contradiction', a category which applies to the fair and accurate report of public proceedings by a legislature or international organisation anywhere in the world;[172] a court anywhere in the world;[173] or a person appointed to hold a public inquiry by a government or legislature anywhere in the world.[174] It also applies to the fair and accurate report of any public document and of any material published by or on the authority of a government or legislature anywhere in the world, as well as to any matter published anywhere in the world by an international organisation or conference. The second category comprises reports privileged subject to explanation or contradiction, in the sense that there is no defence if the plaintiff shows that the defendant failed following a request, 'to publish in a suitable manner a reasonable letter or statement by way of explanation or contradiction'. This category includes 'a notice or other matter issued for the information of the public' by the legislature, government or any authority carrying out governmental functions (expressly defined to include police functions) of any member state of the EU; and a fair and accurate report of proceedings at any public meeting in the UK of (*a*) a local authority or local authority committee; (*b*) a justice of the peace acting otherwise than as a court exercising judicial functions; (*c*) a commission or tribunal; (*d*) a local authority inquiry; or (*e*) any other statutory tribunal, board or inquiry. The second category also includes the fair and accurate reports or copies of (*a*) public meetings, (*b*) a general meeting of a UK public company, (*c*) documents circulated to members of UK public companies, (*d*) the findings of one of a number of regulatory bodies of a voluntary nature, and (*e*) any adjudication or report by a body or person designated by the Lord

---

[166]   Eg *Chatterton v Secretary of State of India* [1895] 2 QB 189.
[167]   Parliamentary Commissioner Act 1967, s 10(5); ch 28 D.
[168]   *Al-Fayed v Al-Tajir* [1988] QB 712.
[169]   Defamation Act 1996, s 14(3)(a). And see *Trapp v Mackie* [1979] 1 All ER 489, and *A–G v BBC* [1981] AC 303.
[170]   Defamation Act 1996, s 14(3)(b)–(d).
[171]   Ibid, s 15(1). But carelessness, impulsiveness or irrationality do not amount to malice: *Horrocks v Lowe* [1975] AC 135.
[172]   See also ch 11 A.
[173]   See also ch 18 B, and *Webb v Times Publishing Co* [1960] 2 QB 535.
[174]   See *Tsikata v Newspaper Publishing plc* [1997] 1 All ER 655 (report need not be a contemporary report).

Chancellor.[175] Defamatory statements at an election meeting are not covered by qualified privilege, though fair and accurate reports of them by a newspaper may be.[176]

Other defences in defamation law

Certain other defences are also available. The defendant may seek to justify the defamatory statement, that is, to prove at the trial that what he or she said was true. Not every detail of the statement need be shown to be literally true, provided that the defendant shows it to be true in substance.[177] By the Defamation Act 1952, s 5, where an action contains a number of distinct charges against the plaintiff, a defence of justification does not fail because the truth of every charge is not proved, provided that the words not proved to be true do not materially injure the plaintiff's reputation having regard to the truth that has been established.[178]

The defence of 'fair comment' protects expressions of opinion on matters of public interest. The comment itself can be quite outspoken, and even unfair, provided that the comment could have been made by an honest man holding strong, exaggerated or even prejudiced views. It is also important that the comment does not contain any incorrect allegations of fact,[179] that the subject of the comment is a matter of public interest, and that malice on the part of the defendant is not shown.[180] The policies and acts of politicians are clearly of public interest. In *Silkin v Beaverbook Newspapers Ltd*, described by Diplock J as an important case since it concerned 'the right to discuss and criticise the utterances and actions of public men', a former Cabinet minister sued the *Sunday Express* over remarks by a political columnist which pointed to inconsistencies between the plaintiff's speeches in Parliament and his business interests: the jury decided that the defence of fair comment had been established.[181] In *Slim v Daily Telegraph Ltd*, fair comment was a defence to an action brought concerning two letters which criticised a company and its legal adviser over the use for cars of a riverside footpath; Lord Denning MR said, 'When a citizen is troubled by things going wrong, he should be free to "write to the newspaper": and the newspaper should be free to publish his letter. It is often the only way to get things put right'.[182] In both these cases, the court stressed that the facts on which the comment was based were correctly stated.

Two other defences are to be found in the Defamation Act 1996. The first,

---

175   Defamation Act 1996, s 15 and Sched 1. The protection does not apply to the publication of a matter which is not of public concern or the publication of which is not for the public benefit (s 15(3)): see *Kingshott v Associated Kent Newspapers* [1991] 1 QB 88.

176   Defamation Act 1952, s 10, reversing *Braddock v Bevins* [1948] 1 KB 580.

177   See *Polly Peck (Holdings) plc v Trelford* [1986] QB 1000; *Prager v Times Newspapers* [1988] 1 All ER 300; *Bookbinder v Tebbit* [1989] 1 All ER 1169.

178   But the value of s 5 is limited: see eg *Speidel v Plato Films Ltd* [1961] AC 1090 and *Polly Peck (Holdings) Ltd v Trelford* [1986] QB 1000. The Rehabilitation of Offenders Act 1974, s 8 restricts the use of justification as a defence in respect of statements imputing spent convictions to ex-offenders. See *Herbage v Pressdram* [1984] 2 All ER 769.

179   See Defamation Act 1952, s 6.

180   See *Telnikoff v Matusevitch* [1992] 2 AC 343.

181   [1958] 2 All ER 516.

182   [1968] 2 QB 157.

in s 1, is a defence of 'innocent dissemination' which is intended to supersede the common law defence which was thought to be too uncertain. The statutory defence applies to anyone other than the author, editor or publisher of the statement complained of; it is available where he or she took 'reasonable care' in relation to the publication, and 'did not know, and had no reason to believe, that what he or she did caused or contributed to the publication of a defamatory statement'. The other defence is the defence of 'unintentional defamation' which replaces the more complex (and consequently little used) provision of the Defamation Act 1952, s 4, a step recommended on a number of occasions, but most recently in the review conducted by Lord Justice Neill referred to above. Under s 2 of the 1996 Act a person who has published a statement alleged to be defamatory may offer to make amends, either generally or 'in relation to a specific defamatory meaning which the person making the offer accepts that the statement conveys' ('a qualified offer'). An offer to make amends is an offer to make a suitable correction and apology, and to pay to the aggrieved party agreed compensation and costs. The failure of the plaintiff to accept an offer which has not been withdrawn is a defence, either generally or in the case of a qualified offer 'in respect of the meaning to which the offer related'. The defence does not, however, apply where the statement complained (*a*) refers to the aggrieved party or was likely to be understood as so referring, and (*b*) was both false and defamatory of that party. However, the onus is on the plaintiff to show that the defendant knew that the statement referred to him or her, and also that the defendant knew it to be both false and defamatory. The offer may be relied upon in mitigation of damages whether or not it was relied on as a defence.

The press and the law of defamation

There is no doubt that the press and the broadcasting authorities have constantly to be aware of the law of defamation. The important role of the press in reporting on current events of public interest has been recognised more than once by Parliament. The Law of Libel Amendment Act 1888 and the Defamation Act 1952 extended the protection of privilege to various classes of report published in a newspaper or broadcast. But since the Defamation Act 1996 the law now applies to any fair and accurate report with the result that the law of defamation makes little special provision for the press,[183] although by the so-called 'newspaper rule', a newspaper which is pleading privilege or fair comment in defence of an action for libel is not required on discovery to disclose the source of its information. This rule is confined to defamation proceedings and does not confer on the press and broadcasting authorities a general immunity from disclosure of their sources.[184]

The position of the press is very different in the United States, where, by the First Amendment to the Constitution, 'Congress shall make no law ... abridging the freedom of speech, or of the press' and, by the Fourteenth Amendment, 'No State shall make or enforce any law which shall abridge the

---

[183]   But see the Law of Libel Amendment Act 1888, s 8.
[184]   *British Steel Corpn v Granada Television Ltd* [1981] AC 1096. But see ch 18 B above.

privileges or immunities of citizens of the United States'. The effect of Supreme Court decisions on the freedom of the press, particularly *New York Times v Sullivan*,[185] has been to create a new law of libel concerning matters of public or general interest under which the press has much greater freedom to publish information and comment than under English law. Thus in an action brought by a public figure, the plaintiff must prove that the publication was false and that it was published either with knowledge of its falsity or with serious doubts as to its truth.[186] It has been said in the High Court of Australia that the great virtue of the American approach is that 'it offers some protection to the reputation of the individual who is defamed and at the same time offers a large measure of protection to the publisher'.[187]

The leading US authorities were referred to by the House of Lords in *Derbyshire County Council v Times Newspapers Ltd*[188] in holding that local authorities (and by inference government departments) cannot sue in libel. But despite this development, English law still falls far short of the more relaxed standards in the United States, and it has been suggested in Britain that there should be no liability for statements made on matters of public interest when the publisher believes the statement of fact to be true and has exercised all reasonable care in relation to the facts.[189] What underlies such a proposal is the view that British newspapers are inhibited by the law of defamation from publishing reports (for example, exposing corruption in high places) which should be available to the public. But in the absence of legislation steps in this direction have been rejected by the courts: 'The public figure defence had its origins in the United States but the culture of the USA was not the same as in other countries, including the United Kingdom and what was appropriate in the USA was not necessarily appropriate else-where'.[190]

The press, the law of defamation and parliamentary privilege

A rather paradoxical and unanticipated protection for the press emerged as a result of the operation of art 9 of the Bill of Rights of 1689 which precludes any court from impeaching or questioning the freedom of speech and debates or proceedings in Parliament. In the decision of the Privy Council in *Prebble v Television New Zealand Ltd*[191] the plaintiff was a Cabinet minister in the New Zealand government who claimed that he had been defamed by the television company. The defendants wished to demonstrate the truth of

---

[185] 376 US 254 (1964). See Lewis, *Make No Law*, where it is argued that without this decision it is questionable whether the press could have done as much as it has to penetrate the power and secrecy of modern government, or to inform the public of the reality of policy issues. Some may see this as unduly hyperbolic: just how effective is the American press in penetrating power? And just how ineffective is its British counterpart? But compare Lester [1995] PL 1.

[186] Cmnd 5909, 1975, ch 23, and see *New York Times v Sullivan* 376 US 254 (1964).

[187] *Theophanos v Herald and Weekly Times* (1994) 68 ALJR 713 (I Loveland [1996] PL 126).

[188] [1993] 1 All ER 1011. See also *Guardian*, 29 June 1996 (libel action brought by British Coal against the National Union of Mineworkers thrown out by French J on the ground that public bodies should be open to criticism in the interests of freedom of speech).

[189] Report by Justice, *The Law and the Press*, 1965; cf Cmnd 5909, above, pp 53–5.

[190] *Bennett v Guardian Newspapers Ltd*, *The Times*, 28 December 1995.

[191] [1995] 1 AC 321.

the allegations by relying on things said or done in Parliament, but were confronted by the Bill of Rights. In upholding the lower courts on the first point to arise the Privy Council held that 'parties to litigation, by whomsoever commenced, cannot bring into question anything said or done in the House (whether by direct evidence, cross-examination, inference or submission) that the actions or words were inspired by improper motives or were untrue or misleading'. But on a second point the Privy Council reversed a decision of the lower court to stay the proceedings in the light of the disability under which the defendant laboured, on the ground that although there 'may be cases in which the exclusion of material on the grounds of Parliamentary privilege makes it quite impossible fairly to determine the issues between the parties', on the facts this was not one of them. Where, however, 'the whole subject matter of the alleged libel relates to the plaintiff's conduct in the House so that the effect of Parliamentary privilege is to exclude virtually all the evidence necessary to justify the libel', the proceedings should be stayed not only to prevent an injustice to the defendant, but also to avoid the 'real danger' that 'the media would be forced to abstain from the truthful disclosure of a member's misbehaviour in Parliament'.

Although the plaintiff was permitted to proceed with his action on the facts, the impact of the *Prebble* decision was immediately felt in this country by two Conservative members of Parliament. In the case of Rupert Allason,[192] an action against *Today* newspaper was stayed, the defendant seeking to show that which was prohibited, namely that 'early day motions were at least inspired by improper motives'. To enforce parliamentary privilege but to refuse a stay would be unjust to the defendant who would be deprived of their only defence 'while allowing the plaintiff to continue on an unsatisfactory and unfair basis'. In the view of Owen J, MPs 'had to take the ill consequences together with the good consequences' of parliamentary privilege. In the case of Neil Hamilton, it was claimed by the plaintiff that he had been libelled by the *Guardian* which alleged that he had received money from a businessman in return for asking ministers questions which were intended to further that businessman's interests. In this case it was ruled by May J that the case could not proceed as the evidence directly involved proceedings in Parliament.[193]

The *Prebble* case and its progeny were thought to create a real injustice, and in the House of Lords an amendment to the Defamation Bill was introduced by Lord Hoffman, moved by 'an injustice which needs a remedy'.[194] It was also pointed out, however, that it would be unfortunate if the amendment 'were seen in some way to be especially for the protection of the rights of Mr Hamilton or any other MP currently engaged in legal proceedings'. The matter was therefore dealt with as a 'matter of principle', and as such it was enacted that a member of Parliament might waive the protection of any rule of law which prevented proceedings in Parliament being impeached or questioned in any court or place out of Parliament. This allows the MP to overcome the problem presented by art 9 of the Bill of Rights in the following way: an MP may bring an action in defamation to vindicate his or

---

192   *Allason v Haines, The Times*, 25 July 1995.
193   For details, see HL Deb, 7 May 1996, cols 24–25. See also cols 42–43 (regarding Mr Ian Greer).
194   Ibid, col 24.

her reputation provided he or she is willing to permit the defence to refer to proceedings in Parliament in order to justify what it had written. On the other hand, if the MP is not prepared to waive the protection of art 9 then *Prebble* will continue to apply and the action may be stayed, on the ground that the newspaper must be allowed in defamation proceedings to prove that what it said was true. Newspapers would otherwise be 'extremely reluctant to criticise what anyone said in Parliament if it meant that they could be sued while they had to stand with their hand tied behind their backs'.[195] An interesting question which was raised in the course of the parliamentary debates is whether the report of proceedings in Parliament in respect of which the protection is waived is covered by qualified privilege. By virtue of s 15 of the Defamation Act 1996 this would be true only of 'a fair and accurate report of proceedings in public'. To the extent that this falls short of what is required, it will be for the courts to develop the common law rules of qualified privilege (expressly retained by the Defamation Act 1996), though its boundaries are not widely drawn.[196]

G. Breach of confidence

In the law of defamation, the courts are reluctant to ban publication of a book or article before trial of the action; in particular, the courts do not restrain publication of a work, even though it is defamatory, when the defendant intends to plead justification or fair comment on a matter of public interest and it is not manifest that such a defence is bound to fail.[197] According to Griffiths LJ in *Herbage v Pressdram Ltd* this is because of 'the value the court has placed on freedom of speech and ... also on freedom of the press, when balancing it against the reputation of a single individual, who ... can be compensated in damages'.[198] In actions for breach of confidence, however, damages may be recovered but emphasis is laid on the power of the court by an injunction to prohibit publication which would be in breach of confidence. Breach of confidence is a rapidly developing branch of the law, and there is uncertainty as to its legal basis.[199] The law has been much influenced by the equitable doctrine that a person should not knowingly take unfair advantage of the plaintiff's confidence, for example, by publishing information received in confidence. Thus in the early case of *Prince Albert v Strange*, the defendant was prohibited from publishing etchings made by Prince Albert and Queen Victoria and a catalogue describing the etchings based on information which had been obtained in breach of confidence.[200] The action

---

[195] Ibid, col 251.
[196] See *Blackshaw v Lord* [1984] QB 1 (no qualified privilege at common law for newspaper report about 'inefficient' civil servant).
[197] *Fraser v Evans* [1969] 1 QB 349.
[198] [1984] 2 All ER 769, 771. See also *Khashoggi v IPC Magazines Ltd* [1986] 3 All ER 577 and *R v Advertising Standards Authority, ex p Vernons* [1992] 1 WLR 1289. Cf *Gulf Oil (Great Britain) v Page* [1987] Ch 327.
[199] For a full analysis, see Law Commission, Cmnd 8388, 1981. See also Gurry, *Breach of Confidence*.
[200] (1849) 1 Mac & G 25.

has been used mainly to protect commercial and industrial secrets but in *Argyll v Argyll*, the Duke of Argyll and a Sunday newspaper were barred by injunction from publishing articles which sought to reveal marital confidences entrusted to the Duke by his wife during a former marriage.[201] The same action was invoked in 1975 by the Attorney-General in his attempt to restrain publication of the Crossman diaries. While in that case an injunction was not granted, Lord Widgery CJ ruled that publication of information received by a Cabinet minister prejudicial to the collective responsibility of the Cabinet would be restrained if the public interest clearly required this.[202] It must be emphasised that the label of 'confidential' applied to a document, whether by a public authority or not, does not mean that the court will restrain publication of it should a copy reach a newspaper. In *Fraser v Evans*, the court refused to ban publication of a confidential report which Fraser, a public relations consultant, had prepared for the Greek government, when the *Sunday Times* had obtained a copy of it from Greek sources: Fraser's contract with the Greek government required him but not the government to keep it confidential.[203]

The action for breach of confidence may not be used to suppress disclosure of material that should in the public interest be made known, such as dishonest trading practices[204] or defects in equipment used as evidence in criminal prosecutions.[205] But severe difficulties are encountered in defining the relationship between a private duty of confidence, the public interest in the protection of confidence and the public interest in information being made known.[206] The most sensational case to raise these difficulties is the so-called *Spycatcher* case.

Mr Peter Wright, a retired security service officer, wrote a book, *Spycatcher*, in which he claimed to reveal secrets relating to activities of the British security service. The book was due to be published initially in Australia, which the British government sought an injunction to restrain. Two British newspapers (the *Guardian* and the *Observer*) carried accounts of what the book was said to contain, at which point the Attorney-General moved for an injunction to restrain the newspapers from carrying any such reports. An interim injunction was granted on the ground that publication would be a breach of confidence. Legal proceedings to restrain publication in Australia failed,[207] and the book was also published in the United States. When copies of the book began freely to enter the United Kingdom, the *Guardian* and the *Observer* moved to have the interim injunctions discharged on the ground that there was now no public interest in maintaining the injunctions in view of the fact that the contents of the book were widely known and freely available throughout the world. The House of Lords (by a majority of three to two) refused the application on the ground that the restrictions

---

201   [1967] Ch 302. See also *Stephens v Avery* [1988] Ch 449.
202   *A-G v Jonathan Cape Ltd* [1976] QB 752. See also *Commonwealth of Australia v John Fairfax and Sons Ltd* (1980) 147 CLR 39.
203   [1969] 1 QB 349.
204   *Initial Services Ltd v Putterill* [1968] 1 QB 396; and see Cmnd 8388, 1981, pp 41–51.
205   *Lion Laboratories Ltd v Evans* [1985] QB 526.
206   *X v Y* [1988] 2 All ER 648. Other difficult cases include *Schering Chemicals v Falkman Ltd* [1982] QB 1. And see Cripps, *The Legal Implications of Disclosure in the Public Interest*.
207   (1987) 8 NSWLR 341 (Powell J); (1987) 75 ALR 353 (NSW Court of Appeal); (1988) 78 ALR 449 (High Court of Australia). See Turnbull, *The Spycatcher Trial*.

remained necessary in the public interest, for reasons that were neither clear nor convincing.[208]

However, the Attorney-General's application for permanent injunctions against the newspapers failed.[209] The House of Lords agreed that security service personnel owe a life-long duty of confidence and that they may be restrained by injunction from disclosing any information which they obtain in the service of the Crown, as may any third party to whom such information is improperly conveyed. However, the availability of the book in the United States fatally undermined the government's claim that the maintenance of the injunctions was necessary in the public interest. In the opinion of Lord Keith, 'general publication in this country would not bring about any significant damage to the public interest beyond what has already been done. All such secrets as the book may contain have been revealed to any intelligence service whose interests are opposed to those of the United Kingdom'.[210] But although the actions for permanent injunctions failed, the conviction of several newspapers for contempt of court was subsequently upheld by the House of Lords. The appellants had published material which breached the terms of the injunctions against the *Observer* and the *Guardian*, and it was held that in their conduct they had interfered with the administration of justice.[211]

It was subsequently held by the European Court of Human Rights that the refusal of the House of Lords in 1987 to discharge the injunctions violated art 10 of the European Convention on Human Rights on the ground that after publication of the book in the United States, the material in question was no longer confidential.[212] Nevertheless, breach of confidence featured in other cases involving press and television reporting and comment on matters relating to the security services. In *Spycatcher*'s Scottish sequel, the House of Lords upheld the Scottish court's decision refusing to restrain *The Scotsman* from publishing material from a privately published book by a retired MI6 officer.[213] It was held that the public interest did not require *The Scotsman* to be restrained from publishing this material in view of a concession made by the government that nothing in the book was capable of damaging national security. The willingness of the government to use the equitable doctrine of confidentiality to gag the press renews concern about the scope of the doctrine. The English Law Commission in 1981 recommended legislation to abolish the present action for breach of confidence, to replace it by a new tort of breach of confidence, to define the circumstances in which a duty of confidence would arise, and to provide for the public interest in confidentiality to be balanced against the public interest in disclosure of information.[214] While such legislation would clarify the doctrinal basis of breach of confidence, the judges would still have to make difficult and far-reaching choices in exercising their discretionary powers of control. But although the boundaries of the present law give rise to concerns in terms of its

208   *A-G v Guardian Newspapers Ltd* [1987] 3 All ER 316.
209   *(The same)(No 2)* [1990] 1 AC 109.
210   For a fuller treatment of this intricate affair, see Ewing and Gearty, *Freedom under Thatcher*, pp 152–69. See also Bailey, Harris and Jones, *Civil Liberties Cases and Materials*, pp 474–87; D G T Williams (1989) 12 Dalhousie LJ 209; and A W Bradley [1988] All ER Rev 55.
211   *A-G v Times Newspapers Ltd* [1992] 1 AC 191.
212   *The Observer v United Kingdom* (1992) 14 EHRR 153. And see I Leigh [1992] PL 200.
213   *Lord Advocate v Scotsman Publications Ltd* [1990] 1 AC 812. See N Walker [1990] PL 354.
214   Cmnd 8388, 1981. See M W Bryan [1982] PL 188.

effect on freedom of expression, it may on the other hand play a valuable role in protecting people from the unwarranted invasion of their privacy in the absence of more direct forms of protection.[215]

---

215   H Fenwick and G Phillipson [1996] 55 CLJ 447. Cf Wilson (1990) 53 MLR 43.

CHAPTER 23

Freedom of association and assembly

This chapter examines the principal features of the law relating to freedom of association and assembly.[1] If there were for the United Kingdom a written constitution guaranteeing fundamental rights, it is likely that it would include protection for freedom of association and assembly, although as in the case of the European Convention on Human Rights, it is likely that the protection would be subject to extensive qualifications.[2] In the absence of such constitutional protection, these freedoms are protected in the same way as other freedoms and liberties in English law. That is to say, people are free to associate and assemble to the extent that their conduct is not otherwise unlawful. The principle is best illustrated in this context, in the case of freedom of assembly, by the seminal decision in *Beatty v Gillbanks*,[3] one of the few cases in this area where the court appeared sensitive to the constitutional significance of the issues raised.

The case arose out of opposition to the Salvation Army in its early days, members of which insisted in marching through the streets of Weston-super-Mare despite violent opposition from the 'Skeleton Army' and despite an order from the magistrates that they should not march. In an attempt to stop the Salvationist marches, the police sought to have their leaders bound over to keep the peace on the ground that they had committed an unlawful assembly. If the Salvationists had not marched there would clearly have been no disturbance of the peace. As previous processions had led to disorder, the Salvationists knew that similar consequences were likely to ensue. The Divisional Court held that the acts of the Salvation Army were lawful and that it was not a necessary and natural consequence of these acts that disorder should have occurred.

---

[1] See Supperstone, *Brownlie's Law of Public Order and National Security;* Bailey, Harris and Jones, *Civil Liberties Cases and Materials,* ch 3; Robertson, *Freedom, the Individual and the Law,* ch 2; Ewing and Gearty, *Freedom under Thatcher,* ch 4; Feldman, *Civil Liberties and Human Rights,* ch 17; and C A Gearty, 'Freedom of Assembly and Public Order', in McCrudden and Chambers (eds), *Individual Rights and the Law in Britain,* ch 2. An earlier account of value is Williams, *Keeping the Peace.* See also Morgan, *Conflict and Order,* and Townshend, *Making the Peace.*
[2] See European Convention on Human Rights, art 11(2).
[3] (1882) 9 QBD 308. And see Hart and Honoré, *Causation in the Law,* pp 333–5. Cf *Deakin v Milne* (1882) 10 R(J) 22.

The court did not accept that a man might be punished for acting lawfully if he knew that his doing so might lead another man to act unlawfully.

This approach does not recognise a guaranteed right of collective protest, but it does ensure that civil or criminal restrictions on the freedom of people to meet together must be shown to derive from existing law. It may be debated, however, whether the approach provides a firm enough foundation for such freedom, at a time when it is under heavy pressure from competing interests, and is subject now to a wide range of statutory and common law restrictions which make it very difficult to argue that there is an effective right of peaceful assembly in English law.[4] Indeed, it is possible that on similar facts to those in *Beatty v Gillbanks*, the police could today lawfully arrest those taking part in the procession. As we shall see, the subsequent decision in *Duncan v Jones*[5] did much damage to the principle in *Beatty v Gillbanks*.

The first major statutory regulation of this area was the Public Order Act 1936, which was a direct response to the activities of the Communist Party of Great Britain and the rise of fascism.[6] Section 1 prohibited the wearing of political uniforms in a public place or at a public meeting; section 2 made it an offence to organise paramilitary organisations;[7] and ss 3, 4 and 5 gave powers to the police to regulate public processions and counter-demonstrations. These last three sections of the 1936 Act gave way to the more detailed powers of the police in the Public Order Act 1986, a direct response to the growing levels of street protest in the 1970s and 1980s.[8] The 1986 Act is a wide-ranging measure which not only extends the power of the police to deal with public processions and public assemblies, but also replaces the common law offences of riot, unlawful assembly and rout with new and clearer statutory measures.[9] Even though significantly amended by the wider-ranging Criminal Justice and Public Order Act 1994 (conferring more powers on the police),[10] the 1986 Act does not provide an exhaustive code of regulation. Other measures, such as the Highways Act 1980, s 137, and the Police Act 1996, s 89, continue to be an important source of restraint on freedom of assembly, even though it is unlikely that this was intended to be the main purpose of these measures. Nor is it to be assumed that with the passing of the 1986 Act the common law has been completely removed from this area. As we shall see, the common law concept of breach of the peace remains important while, as the miners' strike of 1984/85 reminded us, the dynamic nature of the common law should never be underestimated.

---

4   For a consideration of the different issues which arise in this area, see Cmnd 5919, 1974 and Report of the independent review of parades and marches (chairman: Dr P North) (1997).

5   [1936] 1 KB 218.

6   See Morgan, *Conflict and Order*.

7   See below.

8   For the background to the 1986 Act, see Cmnd 7891, 1980; HC 756 (1978–80); Cmnd 9510, 1985. Also Law Commission, Criminal Law: Offences Relating to Public Order (1983).

9   The works on the 1986 Act include Card, *Public Order: the New Law*; and Smith, *Offences against Public Order*.

10   On the 1994 Act, see M J Allen and S Cooper (1995) 59 MLR 364.

Freedom of association[11]

In principle, the law imposes no restrictions upon the freedom of individuals to associate together for political purposes. Thus people are free to form themselves into political parties, action groups, campaign committees and so on without any official approval or registration. In a number of circumstances, however, restrictions have been imposed. The first of these relates to considerations of public order. As we have seen, under the Public Order Act 1936, s 1, it is an offence for any person in a public place or at a public meeting to wear a uniform signifying association with a political organisation or with the promotion of any political object.[12] Section 2 of the same Act made it an offence (*a*) to organise or train the members or supporters of any association for the purpose of enabling them to be used in usurping the functions of the police or the armed forces, or (*b*) to organise and train (or equip) them, either for enabling them to be employed for the use or display of physical force in promoting any political object, 'or in such manner as to arouse reasonable apprehension that they are organised and either trained or equipped for that purpose'. In 1963, the leaders of a movement known as Spearhead, whose members wore uniforms and exchanged Nazi salutes, were convicted under this section, even though there was no evidence of specific training for attacks on opponents.[13] The organisers of a volunteer force intended to be available for maintaining order in emergencies would run some risk of contravening this section, even if their avowed aim was to lend support when needed to the police or armed forces.[14] In 1974, several organisations of this kind started by former army officers were severely criticised on such grounds. More recently, the Prevention of Terrorism (Temporary Provisions) Act 1989 enacted wide-ranging restrictions on membership and participation in the activities of terrorist organisations.[15] This Act contains what appears to be the only example of British legislation which makes it an offence simply to be a member of a specific organisation,[16] namely the Irish Republican Army and the Irish National Liberation Army.[17]

A second reason for restricting freedom of association is the threat of subversion and fears for external security, concerns which were especially acute before the ending of the Cold War. Two measures in particular were directed to this end. The first is the purge procedure introduced in 1948 and designed to ensure the removal of communist and fascist sympathisers from key civil service positions. The other measure directed at the threat of subversion is the positive vetting procedure, which seeks to exclude the members or supporters of disapproved organisations from entry to 'all posts

---

11 See K D Ewing, 'Freedom of Association', in McCrudden and Chambers (eds), *Individual Rights and the Law in Britain.*

12 See *O'Moran v DPP* [1975] QB 864. See now Prevention of Terrorism (Temporary Provisions) Act 1989, s 3.

13 *R v Jordan and Tyndall* [1963] Crim LR 124; D G T Williams [1970] CLJ 96, 102–4.

14 Supperstone, op cit, p 185.

15 Prevention of Terrorism (Temporary Provisions) Act 1989, s 2. And see ch 25 E.

16 K D Ewing, op cit.

17 In Northern Ireland the authorities have had for many years power to ban organisations with unlawful or seditious objectives. See *McEldowney v Forde* [1971] AC 632. See now Northern Ireland (Emergency Provisions) Act 1996, s 30. See further, ch 25 E.

which are considered to be vital to the security of the state, and is invoked when the reliability of a public servant is thought to be in doubt on security grounds'.[18] The concern about external security led to the controversial banning of trade union membership at Government Communications' Headquarters (GCHQ). This was not done because of fear of communist, fascist or other infiltration, but because of the dangers to national security associated with industrial action organised by trade unions. With the end of the Cold War, many of these restrictions have become redundant, though there is a case for some regulation of entry to the civil service to avoid infiltration by members or supporters of terrorist organisations.[19] It is not only in the area of external security that restrictions on freedom of association have been extended. A third justification for such limits – the need to secure a politically neutral public service – has led to the extension of restrictions on the freedom of association of civil servants and police officers to include also local government officers. The position of civil servants is dealt with in chapter 13 D. Police officers may not take any active part in politics,[20] a rule designed 'to prevent a police officer doing anything which affects his impartiality or his appearance of impartiality'.[21] Local government officers in politically restricted posts may not actively engage in party politics, though there appears to be no restriction on membership of a political party.[22]

Freedom of assembly

This freedom arises essentially from the fact that no permission is needed from any public authority before a group of individuals meets to discuss a matter of common concern. Such meetings or assemblies may be in private and restricted to invited individuals or be open to the public or a section of the public (for example, all students), and be advertised publicly. The so-called right of public meeting is often applied to meetings held in the open air in places to which members of the public have free access. Here, however, it is usually necessary to get the prior consent of the owners of the land. Many local authorities have made byelaws governing the use of parks, beaches etc for various purposes, including public meetings; breach of these byelaws is a criminal offence, unless the court is prepared to hold the byelaw to be ultra vires,[23] and a civil remedy may also be available to restrain persistent breach of the law.[24] In the case of Trafalgar Square in London, statutory regulations have been made under which application for the holding of public rallies must be made to the Department of the Environment; while permission is a

---

[18] Fredman and Morris, *The State as Employer*, p 23.
[19] For a full account, see ch 24.
[20] Police Regulations 1995, SI 1995 No 215, Sched 2. See also Police Act 1996, s 64(1) – restrictions on freedom of police officers to join trade unions.
[21] *Champion v Chief Constable of Gwent* [1990] 1 All ER 116.
[22] Local Government and Housing Act 1989, ss 1, 2: Local Government Officers (Political Restrictions) Regulations 1990, SI 1990 No 851. Also SI 1990 No 1447. See K D Ewing (1990) 19 ILJ 111, 192; *NALGO v Environment Secretary, The Times*, 2 December 1992; and *Darroch v Strathclyde Regional Council* 1993 SLT 1111.
[23] *De Morgan v Metropolitan Board of Works* (1880) 5 QBD 155; *Aldred v Miller* 1925 JC 21. And see *R v Barnet Council, ex p Johnson* (1991) 89 LGR 581 (condition excluding 'political activity' at community festival held invalid).
[24] Cf *Llandudno UDC v Woods* [1899] 2 Ch 705.

matter of discretion, the Secretary of State for the Environment is responsible to Parliament for the decisions taken.[25] Similarly in the case of Hyde Park, no meetings may be held as of right[26] although Speaker's Corner is available for any who wish to speak there.

For meetings, rallies or assemblies which are not held in the open air, a major practical restriction is the need to find premises for them, to say nothing of the cost of hiring a hall and dealing with security.[27] The organisers of an unpopular cause may find it difficult to hire suitable halls, whether these are owned by private individuals or by public authorities such as a local council. However, candidates at local and parliamentary elections are entitled to the use of schools and other public rooms for the purpose of holding election meetings.[28] Otherwise local authorities appear to have a wide discretion in deciding to whom to let their halls, though this discretion is subject to law and could be challenged if the refusal to let a hall was unreasonable in the *Wednesbury* sense.[29] But recent developments in administrative law have not fully met the argument that local authorities in particular should be under a general duty to make their halls available to all groups, whether popular or unpopular, without discriminating between them on political or other grounds.[30] Indeed, such a duty applies to universities, polytechnics and colleges under the Education (No 2) Act 1986. By s 43, the governing bodies of such establishments must 'take such steps as are reasonably practicable to ensure that freedom of speech within the law is secured for members, students and employees of the establishment and for visiting speakers'. This includes an obligation 'to ensure, so far as it is reasonably practicable, that the use of any premises of the establishment is not denied to any individual or body of persons on any ground connected with (*a*) the beliefs or views of that individual or of any member of that body, or (*b*) the policy or objectives of that body'. Governing bodies must issue and keep up to date a code of practice to facilitate the discharge of these duties.[31]

In *R v University of Liverpool, ex p Caesar-Gordon*,[32] the university authorities refused permission for a meeting at the university to be addressed by two first secretaries from the South African Embassy. This was done because of fear that in the event of the meeting taking place public violence would erupt in Toxteth, the residential area adjacent to the university. In an application for judicial review by the chairman of the student Conservative Association, the Divisional Court held that, on a true construction of s 43(1), the duty imposed on the university is local to the members of the university and its premises. Its duty is to ensure, so far as is reasonably practical, that

---

25   SI 1952 No 776. See *Ex p Lewis* (1888) 21 QBD 191. See further Bailey, Harris and Jones, op cit, pp 189–90.
26   *Bailey v Williamson* (1873) 8 QBD 118; Royal and Other Parks and Gardens Regulations 1977, SI 1977 No 217.
27   Under the Criminal Justice and Public Order Act 1994, s 170, the security costs of political party conferences may be met by the Treasury.
28   Representation of the People Act 1983, ss 95, 96. See *Webster v Southwark Council* [1983] QB 698; *Ettridge v Morrell* (1986) 85 LGR 100.
29   *Wheeler v Leicester City Council* [1985] AC 1054. Cf *Verrall v Great Yarmouth BC* [1981] QB 202.
30   Street, *Freedom, the Individual and the Law* (5th edn), p 56.
31   See E Barendt [1987] PL 344.
32   [1991] 1 QB 124.

those whom it may control, that is to say its members, students and employees, do not prevent the exercise of freedom of speech within the law by other members, students and employees and by visiting speakers in places under its control. But under s 43(1), the university was not entitled to take into account threats of 'public disorder' outside the confines of the university by persons not within its control. A declaration was granted that the university acted ultra vires in denying permission to hold the meeting. The court suggested, however, that had the university authorities confined their reasons when refusing permission 'to the risk of disorder on university premises and among university members', then no objection could have been taken to their decisions.

Public processions

By contrast with static meetings on the highway, at common law a procession in the streets is prima facie lawful, being no more than the collective exercise of the public right to use the highway for its primary purpose.[33] This does not mean that it would be a reasonable use of the highway for a dozen demonstrators to link arms and proceed down a street so as to interfere with the right of others to use the highway or for a large group of demonstrators to decide to obstruct a street: a procession would become a nuisance 'if the right was exercised unreasonably or with reckless regard of the rights of others'.[34] Because processions were prima facie lawful, statutory powers were needed if the police were to control them. General powers were contained in the Public Order Act 1936, passed at a time when fascist marches in the East End of London were a serious threat to order. By s 3 of the Act, if a chief officer of police, having regard to the time, place and route of an actual or proposed procession, had reasonable ground for apprehending that the procession might occasion serious public disorder, he could issue directions imposing on the persons organising or taking part in the procession such conditions as appeared to him to be necessary for the preservation of public order, including conditions prescribing the route of the procession and prohibiting it from entering any public place specified; but he could not restrict the display of flags, banners or emblems unless this was reasonably necessary to prevent risk of a breach of the peace. Breach of the conditions was an offence against the 1936 Act.[35] If these powers were insufficient to prevent serious public disorder being occasioned by the holding of processions in any urban area, the chief officer of police could apply to the local authority for an order prohibiting all or any class of public processions for a period not exceeding three months; such an order could be made by the council only with the approval of the Secretary of State. In the case of London, the Commissioner of Metropolitan Police could himself, with the approval of the Home Secretary, issue a prohibition order. The need for the approval of the Secretary of State made it likely that the matter would be raised in Parliament if MPs disagreed with the ban.

These powers were extended by the Public Order Act 1986. The first major change is the introduction of a requirement that the organisers of a public procession should give advance notice to the police (s 11). The duty applies in

---

[33]   A Goodhart (1937) 6 CLJ 161, 169.
[34]   *Lowdens v Keaveney* [1903] 2 IR 82, 90 (Gibson J); and see *R v Clark (No 2)* [1964] 2 QB 315.
[35]   See *Flockhart v Robinson* [1950] 2 KB 498.

respect of processions designed (*a*) to demonstrate support for or opposition to the views or actions of any person or body of persons; (*b*) to publicise a cause or campaign; or (*c*) to mark or commemorate an event. There are a few exclusions from the duty to notify,[36] but most processions for political purposes will be caught by these requirements. The notice, which must specify the proposed time, date and route, must be delivered to a police station (in the area where the procession is to start) at least six clear days in advance. In addition to this notice requirement, the 1986 Act extends the grounds for which conditions can be imposed on public processions as well as the circumstances whereby such processions may be banned. So even if serious public disorder is not likely, a senior police officer may impose conditions where he or she reasonably believes that the procession may result in serious damage to property or serious disruption to the life of the community. He or she may also impose conditions where the purpose of the organisers of the procession is to intimidate others (s 12). The directions may be such as appear necessary to prevent disorder, damage, disruption or intimidation, including conditions prescribing the route and prohibiting entry to a specified public place. Unlike the 1936 Act, there is now no restriction on the giving of directions relating to the display of flags, banners or emblems. If these powers to impose conditions are not enough to prevent serious public disorder, the chief officer of police may apply for a banning order under what is now s 13 of the 1986 Act. The procedure here is similar to that in s 3(2) of the 1936 Act, and the power to apply for a banning order is restricted to serious public disorder; the section does not permit a banning order to be made on the wider grounds on which conditions may now be imposed.

Similar powers in Scotland are in the Civic Government (Scotland) Act 1982 (as amended by the Local Government etc (Scotland) Act 1994).[37] By s 62, the organisers of a public procession must notify (at least seven days in advance) both the police and the local authority in whose area the procession is to be held. After consulting the chief constable, the local authority may then prohibit the holding of the procession or impose conditions upon it. These powers are expressly made subject to the Public Order Act 1986, so that the power to issue directions may be only for the grounds specified in that Act.[38] It nevertheless appears that a local authority in Scotland could ban a specific march whereas in England and Wales the ban must be on the holding of all public processions, or of any class of public processions specified in the order. Another important difference between Scots law and English law is the appeal procedure in s 64 of the Civic Government (Scotland) Act. A person who has given notice of a procession under s 62 may appeal within fourteen days to the sheriff against an order prohibiting or imposing conditions on the procession. The grounds of appeal are limited by the statute to error of law, mistake of fact, unreasonable exercise of discretion, or that the local authority

---

36   By s 11(2), there is no duty to notify where 'the procession is one commonly or customarily held in the police area (or areas) in which it is proposed to be held or is a funeral procession organised by a funeral director acting in the normal course of his business'.

37   See Ewing and Finnie, *Civil Liberties in Scotland: Cases and Materials*, ch 8. See also W Finnie, in Finnie, Himsworth and Walker (eds), *Edinburgh Essays in Public Law*, pp 251–77.

38   Civic Government (Scotland) Act 1982, s 62.

have 'otherwise acted beyond their powers'. There is no comparable provision in the Public Order Act 1986. It is true that the organiser of a procession could seek judicial review of a banning order or of an order to impose conditions.[39] But, unlike in Scotland, this would be review and not an appeal; it would be in the High Court under the Order 53 procedure and not in the local sheriff court; and in any event the Court of Appeal has made it clear in a case involving a banning order under s 3(2) of the 1936 Act that it is not willing to encourage such applications.[40] There is also the practical problem of securing judicial review in enough time before the procession is due to be held. There is no duty on the police to give notice of the conditions 'as early as possible', as there is on the local authority in Scotland.[41] If the police exercise their powers unreasonably, it may be possible for anyone arrested for violating the conditions to challenge their legality as a defence in criminal proceedings. But this will not restore their right to participate in the procession, nor will it restore the right to conduct the procession as initially conceived.

Public assemblies

Police powers specifically to regulate public assemblies were introduced in the Public Order Act 1986 (s 14). The senior police officer present at an assembly (or the chief constable in the case of an assembly intended to be held) may impose conditions as to its location and duration, as well as the number of people who may be present. These conditions may be issued where it is reasonably believed (*a*) that the assembly may result in serious public disorder, serious damage to property, or serious disruption to the life of the community; or (*b*) that the purpose of organising the assembly is to intimidate others. A public assembly is defined to mean an assembly of 20 or more people in a public place which is wholly or partly open to the air (s 16). (In imposing conditions, could the police limit the presence to a smaller number than 20?) There is no procedure in the Act for challenging instructions issued under this power, though if they are issued long enough in advance, judicial review is available in principle, subject to the reluctance of the courts to encourage review of such decisions.[42] The only other means of challenging any directions would be collaterally, as a defence in criminal proceedings for violating a direction given under the Act. It could be argued that the police had exceeded their powers, for example because the purpose of an assembly was to cause inconvenience and embarrassment to third parties, rather than to intimidate them.[43] Nevertheless, the section gives the police wide powers to control public assemblies and by the power to issue directions to frustrate the purpose of the assembly.

The Criminal Justice and Public Order Act 1994 added new powers in

---

[39] Judicial review was also available in principle to challenge banning orders under s 3(2) of the Public Order Act 1936. See *Kent v Metropolitan Police Commissioner, The Times*, 15 May 1981. For the position under the European Convention on Human Rights, see *Plattform 'Ärzte Für Das Leben' v Austria* (1991) 13 EHRR 204.

[40] *Kent v Metropolitan Police Commissioner*, above.

[41] Civic Government (Scotland) Act 1982, s 63.

[42] See ch 29 A.

[43] *Police v Lorna Reid* [1987] Crim LR 702.

respect of public assemblies, corresponding to the powers relating to public processions in s 13 of the 1986 Act. This applies to 'trespassory assemblies', that is to say an assembly 'on land to which the public has no right of access or only a limited right of access', a definition wide enough to include the public highway. The power of the police is activated where a chief officer 'reasonably believes' that such an assembly (*a*) is likely to be held without the permission of the occupier of the land and (*b*) may result in serious disruption to the life of the community, or significant damage to land, a building, or monument of historical, architectural, archeological or scientific importance. If these conditions are met the chief officer of police may apply to the district council for an order prohibiting all 'trespassory assemblies' in the district or part of it, for a specified period of up to four days to an area within five miles radius of a specified centre. The order, which may be varied or revoked before it expires, may be made after consulting the Secretary of State who must give consent, and the order may be made as requested, or with modifications, which must be approved by the Secretary of State. In Scotland there is no need for ministerial approval to the making of the order (or in granting it with varied terms) while in London the order may be issued by the Metropolitan Police Commissioner with the consent of the Home Secretary. It is an offence to organise or take part in an assembly which is known to be prohibited, and a constable in uniform may (*a*) arrest without a warrant anyone committing an offence, and (*b*) stop any person reasonably believed to be on the way to an assembly 'likely to be an assembly which is prohibited' and 'direct him [or her] not to proceed in the direction of the assembly'. It is an offence to fail to comply with a direction.

In *DPP v Jones*[44] an order had been made prohibiting the holding of assemblies within a four mile radius of Stonehenge from 29 May to 1 June 1995. While the order was in force, a peaceful assembly was held within the area covered by the order. When those present refused to disperse, they were arrested and convicted of trespassory assembly. The conviction was overturned by the Crown Court and on an appeal by way of case stated it was held that conduct could constitute a trespassory assembly even though the conduct complained of was peaceful and did not obstruct the highway. The question was whether the assembly exceeded the public's right of access to the highway for the purposes of the definition of a 'trespassory assembly': if the public had the right to use the highway in this way, there would be no 'trespass' under the 1986 Act as amended. The High Court, however, emphasised the view that the rights of the public in respect of the highway are limited to the use of it for passing and repassing. In an important passage, Collins J said that 'The holding of a meeting, a demonstration or a vigil on the highway, however peaceable, has nothing to do with the right of passage. Such activities may, if they do not cause an obstruction, be tolerated, but there is no legal right to pursue them. A right to do something only exists if it cannot be stopped: the fact that it would not be stopped does not create a right to do it.'[45]

Although s 14 of the Public Order Act 1986 appears to be the first police power specifically to regulate public assemblies, there are a number of

---

[44]   [1997] 2 All ER 119.
[45]   Cf *Hirst v Chief Constable of West Yorkshire* (1986) 85 Cr App Rep 143. According to Collins J (in *Jones*) 'there is no case which ... suggests that there is a right to hold an assembly on the highway, although there are cases which establish that the holding of an assembly may not constitute an offence of obstructing the highway'.

general police powers which have been available for this purpose. The first of these is the statutory offence of obstructing a police officer in the execution of his or her duty.[46] We deal with this later, but in practice this would give to the police powers perhaps as great as those to be found in s 14 of the 1986 Act, but which may be used even when the assembly does not exceed 20. This offence remains unaffected by the 1986 Act and it is strongly arguable that in practice s 14 adds little to the existing law. The other general offence available to the police is obstruction of the highway, though the utility of this is restricted to assemblies held on the highway.[47] Under the Highways Act 1980, s 137, it is an offence 'if a person without lawful authority or excuse in any way wilfully obstructs the free passage along a highway'. An obstruction in this sense is caused when a meeting or assembly is held on the highway (which for this purpose includes the pavement or sidewalk as well as the road). It is no defence that the obstruction affected only part of the highway leaving the other part clear.[48] Nor that the arrested person was only one of a number of people causing the obstruction.[49] Nor indeed that the defendant believed that she was entitled to hold meetings at the place in question or that other meetings had been held there.[50] The offence thus gives wide powers to the police effectively to disperse what may be a peaceful assembly,[51] and it has been widely used. Apart from the Highways Act 1980, s 137, obstruction of the highway is a public nuisance, which may be prosecuted as an indictable offence at common law.[52]

Picketing

The purpose of picketing is to enable pickets to impart information or opinions to those entering or leaving premises, or in some cases to seek to persuade them not to enter in the first place. Those who picket may be subject to directions issued by the police under s 14 of the Public Order Act 1986 if their number exceeds 20. The police may also issue directions to prevent a breach of the peace; failure to comply with such directions may lead to an arrest for obstructing a police officer.[53] But even if a picket is perfectly peaceful and is not subject to regulation by the police in these ways, those who participate may in law be committing offences for which they can be arrested without a warrant. Under the Trade Union and Labour Relations (Consolidation) Act 1992, s 241, it is an offence for a person 'wrongfully and without legal authority' to 'watch and beset' premises where a person works or happens to be with a view to compelling him or her to abstain from doing something which he or she is entitled to do. Although this offence had fallen into disuse, it was revived during the miners' strike of 1984/85 as one of the weapons in the police armoury for dealing with the large-scale picketing

---

[46]   Police Act 1996, s 89(2).
[47]   See P Wallington [1976] CLJ 82.
[48]   *Homer v Cadman* (1886) 16 Cox CC 51.
[49]   *Arrowsmith v Jenkins* [1963] 2 QB 561.
[50]   Ibid. Cf *Cambs CC v Rust* [1972] 2 QB 426.
[51]   Though cf *Hirst v Chief Constable of West Yorkshire* (1986) 85 Cr App Rep 143. See S Bailey [1987] PL 495.
[52]   *R v Clark (No 2)* [1964] 2 QB 315.
[53]   Police Act 1996, s 89(2). See below.

which then took place.[54] More usually perhaps, picketing may lead to an arrest for obstructing the highway under the Highways Act 1980, s 137. A picket is no more a lawful use of the highway than is any other kind of assembly.[55]

Apart from a possible criminal liability, those who organise a picket may also face civil liability. There is authority for the view that picketing premises may constitute a private nuisance against the owner or occupier of these premises. At least the law is sufficiently unclear that an interlocutory injunction is likely to be granted in an application by such a plaintiff.

In *Hubbard v Pitt*, a community action group organised a peaceful picket outside the offices of estate agents in Islington, distributing leaflets and displaying placards to protest against the firm's part in improving property at the expense of working-class residents. On the issue of whether an interim injunction should be issued to the firm against the pickets, Forbes J held that the picketing was unlawful since it was not in contemplation or furtherance of a trade dispute (on the significance of which, see below) and was inconsistent with the public right to use the highway for passage and repassage. But in the Court of Appeal, the majority upheld the interim injunction on quite different grounds, holding only that the plaintiffs had a real prospect of establishing at the eventual trial that the protesters were committing a private nuisance against them and that the balance of convenience lay in favour of the picketing being stopped until the main hearing of the action. Lord Denning MR dissented, holding that the use of the highway for the picket was not unreasonable and did not constitute a nuisance at common law; he considered that picketing other than for trade disputes was lawful so long as it was done merely to obtain or communicate information or for peaceful persuasion.[56]

During the miners' strike of 1984/85 an attempt was made – successfully in the short term – to extend the tort of private nuisance. So in *Thomas v NUM (South Wales Area)*,[57] Scott J held that pickets would be liable not only to the owner or occupier of the premises being picketed, but also to workers (and presumably others) who were 'unreasonably harassed' in entering the premises. This extension of tortious liability was subsequently disapproved by Stuart-Smith J, in relation to an industrial dispute at Wapping in 1985/86.[58]

Special rules govern picketing in the case of trade disputes. As now provided by statute:

It shall be lawful for a person in contemplation or furtherance of a trade dispute[59] to attend
  (*a*) at or near his own place of work; or
  (*b*) if he is an official of a trade union, at or near the place of work of a member of that union whom he is accompanying and whom he represents

---

[54] See P Wallington (1985) 14 ILJ 145.
[55] See *DPP v Broome* [1974] AC 587; *Kavanagh v Hiscock* [1974] QB 600; and *Hirst v Chief Constable of West Yorkshire* (1986) 85 Cr App Rep 143.
[56] [1976] QB 142. See P Wallington [1976] CLJ 82. But picketing is not necessarily a nuisance: see K Miller and C Woolfson (1994) 23 ILJ 209, at pp 216–17.
[57] [1986] Ch 20. See K D Ewing [1985] CLJ 374. See now *Khorasandjian v Bush* [1993] QB 727.
[58] *News Group Newspapers Ltd v SOGAT 1982 (No 2)* [1987] ICR 181.
[59] For the meaning of the term 'trade dispute', see now Trade Union and Labour Relations (Consolidation) Act 1992, s 244.

for the purpose only of peacefully obtaining or communicating information or peacefully persuading any person to work or abstain from working.[60]

This provision, unlike its predecessors, restricts the freedom to picket in a trade dispute to one's own place of work. Secondary picketing – the picketing of other workplaces – is thus excluded.[61] There is no restriction in the Act on the number of people who may picket in this way, but a Code of Practice on Picketing issued by the Department of Employment (with parliamentary approval)[62] recommends no more than six people at any particular site, though this could be reduced if the police are of the view that, to prevent a breach of the peace, a smaller number is necessary.[63] Even if these requirements are met, there is no right on the part of pickets to stop vehicles and to compel drivers and their occupants to listen to what they have to say. In *Broome v DPP*,[64] the House of Lords refused to read such a right into a statutory predecessor of the current law on the ground that it would involve reading into the Act words which would seriously diminish the liberty of the subject. Everyone has the right to use the highway free from the risk of being compulsorily stopped by any private citizen and compelled to listen to what he or she does not want to hear.[65] Pickets thus have a right to seek to communicate information or to seek peacefully to persuade, but not to stop persons or vehicles.

The purpose of these provisions is to give workers and trade union officials a limited protection from both criminal and civil liability. So far as the criminal law is concerned, those who picket peacefully for the permitted purposes will not be liable under either the Highways Act 1980, s 137, or the Trade Union and Labour Relations (Consolidation) Act 1992, s 241. This is because the latter, by s 220 (providing that picketing 'shall be lawful'), gives legal authority to obstruct the highway and to watch and beset. If, however, the purpose of the picket is deemed to be the causing of an obstruction rather than the peaceful communication of information, then s 220 of the 1992 Act will not prevent those involved from being arrested and convicted. So when an organiser had directed 40 pickets to walk in a circle in the highway near a factory entrance, this was held to be an obstruction of the highway and not protected by statute.[66] So far as civil liability is concerned, s 220 provides an immunity from liability for private nuisance where the pickets are acting peacefully.[67] But it does not provide immunity where the purpose of the picket is adjudged to be to harass others, as in *Thomas v NUM (South Wales Area)*.[68] Together with s 219 of the 1992 Act, s 220 also gives pickets immunity

---

[60]   Trade Union and Labour Relations (Consolidation) Act 1992, s 220. And see the Code of Practice on Picketing issued under the 1992 Act.

[61]   As to secondary action under the old law, see *Duport Steels Ltd v Sirs* [1980] 1 All ER 529.

[62]   SI 1992 No 476. Failure to comply with the code does not render any person liable to proceedings, but it may be taken into account by a court or tribunal. See eg *Thomas v NUM (South Wales Area)* above.

[63]   Code of Practice on Picketing, para 51.

[64]   [1974] AC 587. Also *Kavanagh v Hiscock* [1974] QB 600.

[65]   [1974] AC 587, 603.

[66]   *Tynan v Balmer* [1967] 1 QB 91.

[67]   *Hubbard v Pitt* [1976] QB 142.

[68]   Note 57 above.

in tort for conspiracy, inducing breach of contract and intimidation.[69] In this case, however, the protection is of qualified value, for it applies only where the increasingly tight restrictions on the conduct of industrial action have been complied with, including the holding of a secret ballot and the giving of appropriate notice to employers. But there may be circumstances where picketing in the course of a trade dispute does not involve the commission of a tort and where as a result the immunity is unnecessary. Although such cases are rare, they are not unknown.

In *Middlebrook Mushrooms Ltd v Transport and General Workers' Union*[70] the plaintiff employers were in dispute with some of their employees who went on strike and were subsequently dismissed. The employees then organised a campaign to distribute leaflets outside supermarkets to persuade shoppers not to buy the plaintiffs' mushrooms. An injunction was granted at first instance to restrain the defendants from directly interfering with the employers' contracts, but was discharged on appeal. Neither party relied on the 1992 Act and it was held that in order for the defendants' action to be tortious, the persuasion had to be directed at one of the parties to the contracts allegedly interfered with (in this case between the supermarket and the employers). Here the 'suggested influence was exerted, if at all, through the actions or the anticipated actions of third parties who were free to make up their own minds'. The leaflets were directed at customers and contained no message which was directed at the supermarket managers.

But for all practical purposes the freedom conferred by the 1992 Act is very narrow and does not address the crucial problem of the extraordinarily wide discretionary powers vested in the police to regulate the competing claims of pickets and others.

Riot and violent disorder

As well as the rules relating to assemblies and processions, there are several ways in which breaches of public order constitute offences. Such offences were initially developed through the common law, but following Law Commission recommendations in 1983[71] these common law offences were abolished and replaced with new offences in the Public Order Act 1986.[72] The first of these is *riot*, now defined by s 1 of the 1986 Act to apply where 12 or more persons who are present together use or threaten unlawful violence for a common purpose in circumstances where their conduct 'would cause a person of reasonable firmness present at the scene to fear for his personal safety'.[73] The scope of the offence is widened considerably since no person of reasonable firmness need actually be present at the scene, and since, unlike at common law, a riot may be committed in private as well as in a public place.[74]

---

69 For full consideration of these questions, reference should be made to the labour law texts, eg Deakin and Morris, *Labour Law*; Smith and Wood, *Industrial Law*.
70 [1993] ICR 612.
71 Criminal Law: Offences Relating to Public Order (Law Commission 123).
72 1986 Act, part I.
73 For the common law definition, see *Field v Metropolitan Police Receiver* [1907] 2 KB 853. At common law riot could be committed by three or more people.
74 Public Order Act 1986, s 1(5).

Although charges of riot are unusual today,[75] they were brought during the miners' strike of 1984/85 though many of the prosecutions collapsed in controversial circumstances.[76] When a riot is in progress, the police and other citizens may use such force as is reasonable in the circumstances to suppress it.[77] Anyone convicted of riot is liable to imprisonment of up to ten years or a fine, or both,[78] while anyone who suffers property damage in a riot may bring a claim for compensation against the police authority under the Riot (Damages) Act 1886.[79] Compensation has been paid for damage done by those celebrating the end of the First World War[80] and by football fans seeking to climb into Stamford Bridge football ground to watch Chelsea play Moscow Dynamo during their post-war British tour.[81]

Section 2 of the Public Order Act 1986 replaces the old common law offence of unlawful assembly with a new offence of *violent disorder*. The history of unlawful assembly is an important part of the history of the law of public order. After the lapse of the Seditious Meetings Act 1817, it fell to the courts to develop the definition of an unlawful assembly, upon which depended the powers of the police to control and disperse such assemblies.[82] The new statutory offence clears up some of the confusion of the old law.[83] Violent disorder is committed where three or more persons who are present together use or threaten unlawful violence and their conduct (taken together) is such as would cause a person of reasonable firmness present at the scene to fear for his or her personal safety. As with riot, no person of reasonable firmness need actually be present and the offence may be committed in private as well as in public places. As with the old common law rules, a meeting which begins as a lawful gathering may become an unlawful assembly if disorder takes place, weapons are produced, or if language inciting an offence is used by speakers. But unlike the common law, under the new statutory offence, when this transformation occurs persons present who do not share the unlawful purpose are not guilty of violent disorder. A person is guilty of violent disorder only if he or she intends to use or threaten violence or is aware that his or her conduct may be violent or threaten violence.[84] Such a person is liable on conviction on indictment to imprisonment of up to five years and on summary conviction to imprisonment of up to six months.[85] In both cases a

---

75 Charges of mobbing and rioting were unsuccessfully brought in Scotland during the miners' strike in 1972, when strikers used force to prevent supplies of coal reaching a power station. See P Wallington (1972) 1 ILJ 219.

76 See McCabe and Wallington, *The Police, Public Order and Civil Liberties*, p 163.

77 Criminal Law Act 1967, s 3. The Riot Act 1714 has now been repealed, both for England and Wales, and Scotland.

78 Public Order Act 1986, s 1(6).

79 *Field v Metropolitan Police Receiver* above: *Munday v Metropolitan Police Receiver* [1949] 1 All ER 337. In Scotland, compensation is payable under the Riotous Assemblies (Scotland) Act 1822, s 10 (as amended by the Local Government etc (Scotland) Act 1994).

80 *Ford v Metropolitan Police Receiver* [1921] 2 KB 344.

81 *Munday v Metropolitan Police Receiver* [1949] 1 All ER 337.

82 Leading cases included *R v Vincent* (1839) 9 C & P 91, and *R v Fursey* (1833) 6 C & P 80. See also Hawkins, *Pleas of the Crown*, c 63, s 9.

83 See *R v Chief Constable of Devon and Cornwall, ex p CEGB* [1982] QB 458. See also HC 85 (1983–84), p 38.

84 Public Order Act 1986, s 6(2). The same is true for riot, see s 6(1).

85 Ibid, s 2(5).

fine may be imposed rather than or as well as imprisonment. At common law when an unlawful assembly was in progress, it was the duty of every citizen to assist in restoring order, for example by dispersing or by going to the assistance of the police.[86] Presumably the duty survives the abolition of the common law offence and its replacement with violent disorder.[87]

Prosecutions for unlawful assembly and violent disorder are not unknown in modern times. When serious disorder occurred at a demonstration protesting against a Greek dinner at the Garden House Hotel in Cambridge (at a time when the Greek government was unpopular in radical circles) students in the forefront of the disorder were convicted of riot and unlawful assembly.[88] In *Kamara v DPP*,[89] students from Sierra Leone occupied the Sierra Leone High Commission in London, locking the staff in a room and threatening them with an imitation gun. Their conviction for, inter alia, unlawful assembly was upheld by the House of Lords, which ruled that it was not necessary to show that an unlawful assembly had occurred in a public place. As we have seen, this ruling has been given statutory force for the purposes of violent disorder.[90] Unlawful assembly charges were brought during the miners' strike of 1984/85, reflecting 'a specific prosecution policy intended to have a deterrent effect even before charges were proved and sentence pronounced'. However, many charges were dropped before the first hearing, and of those which did proceed, only 'a few indictments for unlawful assembly resulted in conviction'.[91] A few charges of affray were also brought during the strike. This ancient offence consists of unlawful fighting or a display of force by one or more persons in a public place or on private premises, involving a degree of violence calculated to terrify persons present who are of reasonably firm character.[92] The Public Order Act 1986 placed this offence on a statutory footing (s 3).[93]

Threatening, abusive and insulting behaviour

Apart from riot, violent disorder and affray, the other category of offences dealt with by the Public Order Act 1986 relates to threatening, abusive and insulting behaviour. This offence – which appears to correspond with the Scottish common law offence of breach of the peace – was originally enacted in the Public Order Act 1936, s 5. This provided that it was an offence to use threatening, abusive or insulting words or behaviour with intent to provoke a breach of the peace or whereby a breach of the peace was likely to be

---

86 Charge to the Bristol Grand Jury (1832) 5 C & P 261; *R v Brown* (1841) Car & M 314. And see *Devlin v Armstrong* [1971] NILR 13.

87 Cf *A-G for Northern Ireland's Reference (No 1 of 1975)* [1977] AC 105.

88 *R v Caird* (1970) 54 Cr App Rep 499. And see *The Listener*, 8 October (S Sedley) and 26 November 1970 (A W Bradley).

89 [1974] AC 104. For unlawful assembly during an industrial dispute, see *R v Jones* (1974) 59 Cr App Rep 120.

90 Public Order Act 1986, s 2(4).

91 McCabe and Wallington, *The Police, Public Order and Civil Liberties*, pp 99–100.

92 *Button v DPP* [1966] AC 591; *Taylor v DPP* [1973] AC 964.

93 By s 3 of the 1986 Act, a person is guilty of *affray* if he uses or threatens unlawful violence towards another and his conduct is such as would cause a person of reasonable firmness present at the scene to fear for his personal safety. Where two or more persons use or threaten the unlawful violence, it is their conduct taken together that must be considered.

occasioned. If the purpose of ss 1–4 of the 1936 Act was to regulate the conduct of fascist demonstrators in the 1930s, the purpose of s 5 was, it seems, to deal with communist counter-demonstrators who would disrupt fascist rallies. Section 5 of the 1936 Act has been replaced by ss 4 and 5 of the Public Order Act 1986. By s 4:

A person is guilty of an offence if he –
    (*a*) uses towards another person threatening, abusive or insulting words or behaviour, or
    (*b*) distributes or displays to another person any writing, sign or other visible representation which is threatening, abusive or insulting,
with intent to cause that person to believe that immediate unlawful violence will be used against him or another by any person, or to provoke the immediate use of unlawful violence by that person or another, or whereby that person is likely to believe that such violence will be used or it is likely that such violence will be provoked.

This provision of the 1986 Act was supplemented by a new s 4A inserted by the Criminal Justice and Public Order Act 1994. This provides that it is an offence for a person with intent to cause a person harassment, alarm or distress to (*a*) use 'threatening, abusive or insulting words or behaviour, or disorderly behaviour', or (*b*) display any writing, sign or other visible representation which is threatening, abusive or insulting, thereby causing that person or another person (who need not be the intended target of the conduct) 'harassment, alarm or distress'. This complements s 5 of the 1986 Act by which it is an offence for any person to use the words or behaviour in (*a*) or display material referred to in (*b*) within the hearing of any person 'likely to be caused harassment, alarm or distress thereby'.[94] All three offences may be committed in a public or private place, though no offence is committed in a private place where the words or behaviour are used by a person within a dwelling and the person harassed, alarmed or distressed is also inside the dwelling. It is a defence under ss 4A and 5 that the accused's conduct took place inside a dwelling and that he or she had no reason to believe that it would be seen or heard outside. It is also a defence under ss 4A and 5 that the accused's conduct was reasonable and additionally under s 5 that he or she had no reason to believe that there was any person within hearing or sight who was likely to be caused harassment, alarm or distress.[95] Moreover, a person is guilty of an offence under ss 4 and 5 only if he or she intends or is aware that the conduct is threatening, abusive, insulting or disorderly.[96] A constable may arrest without a warrant under ss 4 and 4A, but may do so under s 5 only after the person to be arrested fails to heed a warning to stop the offending conduct.

---

[94]   The threat of violence is not a requirement of s 5 (nor indeed s 4A), and 'a police officer can be a person who is likely to be caused harassment and so on' (*DPP v Orum* [1988] 3 All ER 449).

[95]   See *Morrow, Geach and Thomas v DPP* [1994] Crim LR 58 (defence not made out in a case of a protest outside an abortion clinic – 'shouting slogans, waving banners, and preventing staff and patients from entering' thereby causing distress to patients).

[96]   See *DPP v Clarke* (1992) 94 Cr App R 359 (defendants displaying pictures outside an abortion clinic: even though the defendants must have been aware that pictures might cause alarm or distress, it did not follow that they intended them to be threatening, abusive or insulting or were aware that they might be so).

As with s 5 of the 1936 Act, the crucial words 'threatening, abusive or insulting' are not defined, though a person is guilty of an offence under ss 4 and 5 (but not under s 4A) only if he or she intends the conduct to be threatening, abusive or insulting, or in the case of s 5 only, disorderly (s 6). Decisions under s 5 of the 1936 Act may thus be helpful in the construction of ss 4, 4A and 5 of the 1986 Act. On what is meant by insulting, the leading case is *Brutus v Cozens.*[97]

During a Wimbledon tennis match, Brutus and other anti-apartheid protesters went on to the court, distributed leaflets and sat down. The spectators strongly resented the interruption of play. Brutus was prosecuted for using insulting behaviour whereby a breach of the peace was likely to be occasioned. The justices dismissed the charge, finding that the conduct was not insulting. On appeal by the prosecutor, the Divisional Court directed the justices that behaviour was insulting if it affronted other people and evidenced a disrespect or contempt for their rights, and thereby was likely to cause the resentment which the spectators had expressed at Wimbledon. The House of Lords unanimously allowed an appeal by Brutus against this direction, holding that 'insulting' was to be given its ordinary meaning and that the question of whether certain behaviour had been insulting was one of fact for the justices to determine. Lord Reid pointed out that s 5 of the 1936 Act did not prohibit *all* speech or conduct likely to occasion a breach of the peace. Vigorous, distasteful and unmannerly speech was not prohibited. There could be no definition of insult: 'an ordinary sensible man knows an insult when he sees or hears it'.

It is not enough that the accused's conduct is insulting. Under the Act it must, for example in the case of s 4, be likely to provoke violence. This corresponds with the requirement in s 5 of the 1936 Act that the accused's conduct be likely to provoke a breach of the peace. In *Jordan v Burgoyne*[98] the accused was convicted under s 5 because a speech he made in Trafalgar Square was provocative 'beyond endurance' to Jews, blacks and ex-servicemen in the crowd. It was held that the words used were insulting, but the Divisional Court rejected the interpretation of the court below that the words used by the defendant were not likely to lead ordinary, reasonable persons to commit breaches of the peace. In the view of the court the defendant must 'take his audience as he finds them, and if those words to that audience or that part of the audience are likely to provoke a breach of the peace, then the speaker is guilty of an offence'.[99] A similar conclusion would be reached under the 1986 Act.

An important issue under s 4 of the 1986 Act relates to the question of how soon after insulting conduct must the violence be likely to take place. Section 5 of the 1936 Act 'did not require that the breach of the peace which was either intended or likely to be occasioned should follow immediately upon the actions of the defendant.' The question whether such a requirement now exists was considered in *R v Horseferry Road Magistrate, ex p Siadatan.*[100]

The applicant laid an information against Penguin Books and Mr Salman Rushdie, the publishers and author of *The Satanic Verses*, which many devout Muslims found offensive. It was alleged that the respondents had distributed copies contrary to s 4(1)

---

[97] [1973] AC 854.
[98] [1963] 2 QB 744.
[99] Ibid, at 749.
[100] [1991] 1 QB 260.

of the 1986 Act on the ground that the book contained abusive and insulting writing whereby it was likely that unlawful violence would be provoked. On a strict construction of the Act, the Divisional Court held that the magistrate was correct in refusing to issue a summons. In the view of the court, the requirement in the Act that the insulted person should be 'likely to believe that such violence will be used' means that the insulted person is likely to believe that the violence will be used immediately. Watkins LJ observed: 'A consequence of construing the words "such violence" in s 4(1) as meaning "immediate unlawful violence" will be that leaders of an extremist movement who prepare pamphlets or banners to be distributed or carried in public places by adherents to that movement will not be committing any offence under s 4(1) albeit that they intend the words in the pamphlet or on the banners to be threatening, abusive and insulting and it is likely that unlawful violence will be provoked by the words in the pamphlet or on the banner'.

Although s 4 of the 1986 Act thus appears to be narrower than the corresponding provisions of the 1936 Act, the police have other powers which may go some way towards closing any 'gap in the law which did not exist under the 1936 Act'.[101] These include the powers conferred by the Police Act 1996, s 89(2).

Breach of the peace

The apprehension of a breach of the peace is important in the law of arrest and for the purpose of binding over, but the concept of breach of the peace at common law is not clear-cut.[102] English law does not recognise a substantive offence of breach of the peace. By contrast, in Scots law there is a very broad common law offence of breach of the peace,[103] which includes the use of violent and threatening language in public, breaches of public order and decorum, and even the making of indecent suggestions in private to young persons, but not the peaceful singing of hymns at a prayer meeting in the street.[104] The offence has more recently been adapted for use against excited football fans[105] and against an individual selling a National Front newspaper outside a football ground.[106] The broad nature of this offence probably explains why, on facts very similar to those in *Beatty v Gillbanks*, the Scottish courts convicted the local leaders of a Salvation Army procession of breach of the peace.[107] Breach of the peace is commonly used by the police in public order situations. During the miners' strike of 1984/85, of the 1,046 charges brought in Scotland, no fewer than 648 of these were for breach of the peace.[108] Although used to deal with a wide range of anti-social behaviour, this offence may serve as a flexible and adaptable restraint on different forms of public protest.

---

[101] Ibid, at 266.
[102] See *R v Howell* [1982] QB 416; *R v Chief Constable of Devon and Cornwall, ex p CEGB* [1982] QB 458; *McConnell v Chief Constable of Greater Manchester* [1990] 1 All ER 423.
[103] See Christie, *Breach of the Peace*.
[104] *Ferguson v Carnochan* (1880) 2 White 278; *Dougall v Dykes* (1861) 4 Irv 101; *Young v Heatly* 1959 JC 66.
[105] *McGivern v Jessop* 1988 SCCR 511.
[106] *Alexander v Smith* 1984 SLT 176.
[107] *Deakin v Milne* (1882) 10 R(J) 22.
[108] McCabe and Wallington, *The Police, Public Order and Civil Liberties*, p 164.

Colhoun v Friel[109] concerned the protest against the M77 motorway, in the course of which the appellant sat astride a felled tree which a workman was cutting up with a chainsaw and played a flute. When he refused to comply with a request to move, the appellant was arrested for breach of the peace and convicted, the conviction being upheld on appeal on the ground that 'it is well settled that the test to be applied is whether the proved conduct may reasonably expect to cause any person who observed it to be alarmed, upset or annoyed or to provoke a disturbance'. The appellant had 'placed himself and the workman in a position of danger by his refusal to move as the workman proceeded in the task of cutting the tree up with the power-operated saw. This was disorderly conduct which might reasonably have caused a person to be alarmed by virtue of what might ensue if the appellant was to remain in that position as the work proceeded.'

Preventive powers of the police and courts

1 Binding over to keep the peace.[110] Magistrates in England and Wales have a wide power to order any person to enter into a recognisance (undertaking), with or without sureties, to keep the peace or to be of good behaviour, either in general or towards a particular person.

At a time of suffragette militancy, when many acts of damage to property were being committed, George Lansbury made speeches encouraging the militants to continue. The magistrate required him to give undertakings to be of good behaviour in the sum of £1,000 and to find sureties for his good behaviour, or in default to go to prison for three months. The Divisional Court upheld the order, holding that a person could be bound over for inciting breaches of the peace even though no particular person was threatened.[111]

The origin of this power is obscure: it may rest upon the Justices of the Peace Act 1361 or it may be inherent in the commission of the peace held by magistrates.

A magistrate may bind a person over when it is apprehended that he or she is likely to commit a breach of the peace or do something contrary to law, a wider power still.[112] But in the case of breach of the peace it may now be necessary to show that something has been done calculated to lead to acts of personal violence.[113] In *Percy v DPP*[114] it was held, in a successful appeal against a binding-over order, that a non-violent protest in an RAF base could not constitute a breach of the peace. 'A civil trespass itself cannot amount to a breach of the peace', and 'although circumstances can easily be imagined in which trespass may produce violence as its natural consequence', it was highly improbable that non-violent acts of trespass 'would provoke trained personnel to violent reaction'. Moreover, it has been held that conduct capable of provoking violence (so as to be a breach of the peace) must also be unreasonable, which would exclude cases where 'the defendant was properly exercising his own basic rights, whether of assembly, demonstration or free

---

[109] 1996 SCCR 497.

[110] Williams, *Keeping the Peace*, ch 4, and [1977] Crim LR 703; A D Grunis [1976] PL 16; D Feldman [1988] CLJ 101.

[111] *Lansbury v Riley* [1914] 3 KB 229. See also *Wise v Dunning* [1902] 1 KB 167.

[112] *Hughes v Holley* (1986) 86 Cr App Reps 130.

[113] *R v Sandbach, ex p Williams* [1935] 2 KB 192; cf *R v Aubrey-Fletcher, ex p Thompson* [1969] 2 All ER 846.

[114] [1995] 3 All ER 124.

speech'.[115] Where an order is made by the magistrates, a person who refuses to give an undertaking to be of good behaviour may be committed to prison for a term not exceeding six months.[116] There is a right of appeal to the Crown Court against an order binding a person over, though the making of an order does not constitute a conviction.[117] Natural justice requires that a person may not be bound over until he or she has been at least told what is passing through the magistrate's mind and given a chance of answering.[118] Nevertheless it has been argued that the power is 'open to serious objection when one considers the principles which ought to underpin sound modern domestic English law'.[119]

Binding-over orders were used extensively during the miners' strike of 1984/85,[120] and they are in fact routinely used on a surprisingly extensive scale.[121] The strike also saw the emergence of a new and closely related preventive power, the use of bail conditions as a means of keeping people away from picket lines or other areas of protest. In some areas striking miners charged with public order offences were routinely remanded on bail by the justices subject to the conditions that they should not 'visit any premises or place for the purpose of picketing or demonstrating in connection with the current trade dispute between the NUM and NCB other than peacefully to picket or demonstrate at their usual place of employment'. The conditions were imposed under the Bail Act 1976, which by s 3(6) provides that a person granted bail must comply 'with such requirements as appear to the court to be necessary to secure that ... he does not commit an offence while on bail'. In *R v Mansfield Justices, ex p Sharkey*,[122] the imposition of such conditions was upheld to prevent defendants from resuming intimidatory picketing, which in the view of Lord Lane would almost certainly have been an offence under s 5 of the Public Order Act 1936. The decision has, however, been strongly criticised for authorising what was merely a pretext to stop secondary picketing, which was not then and is not now per se a criminal offence.[123]

2 Entry into meetings. In a public place like Trafalgar Square, there can be no doubt of the power of the police to be present and to deal with outbreaks of disorder if they occur. Where a public meeting is held on private premises, the power of the police to attend is less certain. At one time the official view of the Home Office was that except when the promoters of a meeting asked the

---

[115] *Nicol v DPP, The Times*, 22 November 1995.
[116] Magistrates' Courts Act 1980, s 115.
[117] Magistrates' Courts (Appeals from Binding Over Orders) Act 1956 (amended by Courts Act 1971); *Shaw v Hamilton* [1982] 2 All ER 718. See Law Commission, Working Paper 103, pp 26–8 which also deals with the possibility of judicial review. In *Percy* it was thought that the proceedings were criminal rather than civil.
[118] *Sheldon v Bromfield JJ* [1964] 2 QB 573. Also *R v South Molton JJ, ex p Ankerson* [1988] 3 All ER 989.
[119] Law Commission Report 222, Binding Over, Cm 2439, 1994, para 4.34. The Law Commission recommended the abolition of the power.
[120] P Wallington (1985) 14 ILJ 145.
[121] Cm 2439, 1994, para 2.19 ('A crude extrapolation of a month's returns produced an annual figure of 34,000 binding over orders made in magistrates' courts' alone').
[122] [1984] IRLR 496.
[123] Wallington, above, p 156. For the use of bail conditions in this way during the Timex dispute in Dundee in 1994, see Miller and Woolfson, note 56 above.

police to be present in the meeting, they could not go in, unless they had reason to believe that an actual breach of the peace was being committed in the meeting.[124] This view was stated after disorder occurred at a fascist meeting at Olympia in London, when the stewards inflicted physical violence on dissentients in the audience. No police were stationed on the premises, though large numbers had been assembled in nearby streets. Within a year, the court disapproved of the Home Office view of the law.

In *Thomas v Sawkins*[125] a meeting had been advertised in a Welsh town (*a*) to protest against the Incitement to Disaffection Bill which was then before Parliament and (*b*) to demand the dismissal of the Chief Constable of Glamorgan. The meeting was open to the public without payment, and the police arranged for some of their number to attend. The promoter requested the police officers to leave. A constable committed a technical assault on the promoter thinking that the promoter was on the point of employing force to remove a police officer from the room. There was no allegation that any criminal offence had been committed at the meeting or that any breach of the peace had occurred. When the promoter prosecuted the constable for assault, the magistrates' court found that the police had reasonable grounds for believing that if they were not present there would be seditious speeches and other incitement to violence and that breaches of the peace would occur; that the police were entitled to enter and remain in the hall throughout the meeting; and that consequently the constable did not unlawfully assault the promoter. In the Divisional Court these findings were upheld. Lord Hewart CJ was of opinion that the police have powers to enter and to remain on private premises when they have reasonable grounds for believing that an offence is imminent or likely to be committed; nor did he limit this statement to offences involving a breach of the peace. In the opinion of Avory J, 'the justices had before them material on which they could probably hold that the police officers in question had reasonable grounds for believing that, if they were not present, seditious speeches would be made and/or that a breach of the peace would take place. To prevent any such offence or a breach of the peace the police were entitled to enter and remain on the premises'.[126]

Although the second objective of the meeting in *Thomas v Sawkins* was admittedly provocative to the local police, it did not suggest an incitement to violence, which is a necessary element in the offence of sedition. Nor does protest against a Bill involve a breach of the peace. It is unclear whether Lord Hewart's opinion is confined to public meetings on private premises or whether it also applies to private meetings and other activities on private premises. May the police enter any private premises if they reasonably believe that any offence is imminent or is likely to be committed? The judgments in the case gave scant consideration to the argument that as soon as the promoter asked the police to withdraw from the premises, this rescinded the open invitation given to the public (including the police) to attend. Did this not make the officers trespassers on private premises from that point onwards?[127] It may be that it is in the public interest that the police should be entitled to enter and remain in any public meeting: but why should a similar right apply to private meetings? Doubts as to the width of *Thomas v Sawkins* are

---

124   HC Deb, 14 June 1934, col 1968.
125   [1935] 2 KB 249. See A L Goodhart (1936) 6 CLJ 22. See also D G T Williams (1985) Cambrian LR 116.
126   [1935] 2 KB 249, at 256.
127   *Davis v Lisle* [1936] 2 KB 434, *Robson v Hallett* [1967] 2 QB 939.

resolved by the Police and Criminal Evidence Act 1984, which preserves the power of the police to enter premises to deal with or prevent a breach of the peace, but otherwise abolishes all common law powers of the police to enter premises without a warrant.[128]

3 Obstruction of the police.   The statutory offence of obstructing the police in the execution of their duty has already been considered in relation to the law of arrest.[129] It is no less important in the law of public order. The leading case is *Duncan v Jones*[130] in 1936, which gave rise to fears about the uses to which the offence could be put.

Mrs Duncan was forbidden by Jones, a police officer, to hold a street meeting at a place opposite a training centre for the unemployed. She refused to hold the meeting in another street 175 yards away. Fourteen months previously Mrs Duncan had held a meeting at the same spot, which had been followed by a disturbance in the centre attributed by the superintendent of the centre to the meeting. Mrs Duncan mounted a box on the highway to start the meeting but was arrested and charged with obstructing a police officer in the execution of his duty. There was no allegation of obstruction of the highway or of inciting any breach of the peace. The lower court found (*a*) that Mrs Duncan must have known of the probable consequences of her holding the meeting, viz, a disturbance and possibly a breach of the peace, and was not unwilling that such consequences should ensue, (*b*) that Jones reasonably apprehended a breach of the peace, (*c*) that in law it therefore became his duty to prevent the holding of the meeting, (*d*) that by attempting to hold the meeting Mrs Duncan obstructed Jones when in the execution of his duty. The Divisional Court upheld the conviction. Humphreys J remarked that on the facts as found, Jones reasonably apprehended a breach of the peace: it then became his duty 'to prevent anything which in his view would cause that breach of the peace.'

The decision has been strongly criticised on several grounds. First, for reasons of principle. Goodhart remarked:

At first sight it may seem unreasonable to say that a police officer cannot take steps to prevent an act which, when committed becomes a punishable offence. But it is on this distinction between prevention and punishment that freedom of speech, freedom of public meeting and freedom of the press are founded.[131]

Secondly, the decision gave rise to concern about the nature of the power extended to police officers. On one view, it would give a police officer power to prevent the holding of a lawful meeting if he or she suspected not that the meeting itself might be disorderly but that breaches of the peace might occur as a result of the meeting, whether committed by supporters or opponents of the speakers at the meeting. The reasoning of Humphreys J brings forward in time and widens the preventative powers of the police to a degree that could lead to intolerable restrictions upon the liberty of meeting. On this basis the police could forbid a meeting in the students' union of a college from taking place merely because a 'disturbance' had previously occurred in the college after a similar meeting.

Yet despite this criticism and concern, the offence of obstructing a police

---

[128]   1984 Act, s 17(5), (6); ch 21 E.
[129]   Police Act 1996, s 89(2). See ch 21 F.
[130]   [1936] 1 KB 218; E C S Wade (1937) 6 CLJ 175; T C Daintith [1966] PL 248.
[131]   (1937) 6 CLJ 22, 30.

officer is now an important weapon in the armoury of police powers for controlling public protest. It would appear to give to the police much wider powers than those contained in the Public Order Act 1986, s 14. Thus, it applies to all public order policing situations, not just assemblies, and the power to issue directions can be exercised even though fewer than 20 people may be present. For although *Duncan v Jones* illustrates the power to issue directions as to location where this is considered necessary to maintain the peace, other cases illustrate that the power may be used to issue directions as to numbers. In *Piddington v Bates*,[132] a police officer gave instructions that during a trade dispute at a factory in North London only two pickets would be permitted outside each entrance. When the appellant insisted on joining the pickets, despite a police officer's instructions not to do so, he was arrested for obstruction. The Divisional Court dismissed his appeal against the conviction, in which it was argued that a restriction to two pickets was arbitrary and unlawful. In the view of Lord Parker CJ, 'a police officer charged with the duty of preserving the Queen's peace must be left to take such steps as, on the evidence before him, he thinks are proper'.[133] But apart from this wide power to give directions as to how a demonstration or picket is conducted, recent developments indicate that the power permits the police to give directions not only to disperse a demonstration but effectively to ban or to prevent one from being held in the first place.

In *Moss v McLachlan*[134] the defendants were stopped during the miners' strike at a motorway exit by police officers who suspected that they were travelling to attend a picket line at one of a number of collieries several miles away. When they refused to turn back, they were arrested for obstructing a police officer in the execution of his duty. Their appeals against conviction were dismissed, with Skinner J observing that 'The situation has to be assessed by the senior police officers present. Provided they honestly and reasonably form the opinion that there is a real risk of a breach of the peace in the sense that it is in close proximity both in place and time, then the conditions exist for reasonable preventive action including, if necessary, the measures taken in this case'.[135]

This is therefore a very wide power, the exercise of which the courts seem reluctant to scrutinise closely. A great deal of discretion is left to the police officer on the spot. If the facts in *Beatty v Gillbanks*[136] were to occur again now, the police could certainly give directions to and if necessary arrest the counter-demonstrators. But it would also be possible for the police to direct the Salvationists as to their route, numbers, and methods of expression. If necessary the police could require the Salvationists to disperse and indeed could prevent them from assembling at all. This illustrates how very fragile is the freedom of assembly in English law.

---

132 [1960] 3 All ER 660.
133 Ibid, at 663.
134 [1985] IRLR 76. See G S Morris (1983) 14 ILJ 109. Also *O'Kelly v Harvey* (1883) 15 Cox CC 435.
135 [1985] IRLR 76, at 78. For evidence of the practice being adopted by the Scottish police (though inevitably on a different legal base, possibly breach of the peace), see Miller and Woolfson, above, at pp 220–1.
136 (1882) 9 QBD 308 (note 3 above).

Sit-ins, squatting and forcible entry

In recent years the expression of protest has often taken the form of entry onto private land, most notably by animal rights protesters and environmental activists, the former protesting about field sports in particular and the latter about the building of new motorways which in the process spoil or destroy the natural or built environment. Other groups to engage in this type of activity in the past were workers protesting about the threat of job losses and peace campaigners anxious about nuclear weapons. This form of protest action may fall foul of some of the measures already discussed, though there are others which may be relevant in this area. So in *Chandler v DPP*,[137] an attempt by nuclear disarmers to enter and sit down on an RAF base was held to be a conspiracy to commit a breach of the Official Secrets Act 1911, s 1(1), which makes it an offence for any purpose prejudicial to the safety of the state to approach or enter 'any prohibited place'. In *Galt v Philp*,[138] a sit-in at a hospital laboratory by scientific officers was held to be a breach of s 7 of the Conspiracy and Protection of Property Act 1875 (now s 241 of the Trade Union and Labour Relations (Consolidation) Act 1992).

Action of this type is also governed to some extent by the Criminal Law Act 1977, which extensively reformed the law following the recommendation of the Law Commission.[139] The old offences of forcible entry and forcible detainer were abolished and conspiracy to commit a civil trespass, as in *Kamara v DPP*,[140] ceased to be a criminal offence (ss 1(1), 5(1), 13). Part II of the 1977 Act created various offences relating to entering and remaining on property. These include (*a*) without lawful authority, to use or threaten violence for the purpose of securing entry into any premises on which another person is present, and against the will of that person (s 6); (*b*) to remain on residential premises as a trespasser after being required to leave by or on behalf of a displaced residential occupier of the premises (s 7); (*c*) without lawful authority, to have offensive weapons on premises after having entered them as a trespasser (s 8); (*d*) to enter as a trespasser any foreign embassies and other diplomatic premises (s 9); and (*e*) to resist or obstruct a sheriff or bailiff seeking to enforce a court order for possession (s 10). Additional measures directed at trespassing on private land 'with the common purpose of residing there for any period' were introduced by the Public Order Act 1986.[141]

Yet further restrictions were introduced by the Criminal Justice and Public Order Act 1994. Indeed, part V of the Act is entitled 'Public Order: Collective Trespass or Nuisance on Land', but deals with a wide range of different issues, not all of which are concerned with freedom of assembly. This part of the Act deals, for example, with people trespassing on land, 'with the common purpose of residing there for any period' (s 61), gatherings on land in the open air of 100 or more persons (whether or not trespassers) at which

---

[137]   [1964] AC 763.
[138]   [1984] IRLR 156. See K Miller (1984) 13 ILJ 111. For the offence under the 1992 Act, see page 616 above.
[139]   Report on Conspiracy and Criminal Reform, HC 176 (1975–76).
[140]   [1974] AC 104.
[141]   See *Krumpa v DPP* [1989] Crim LR 295.

amplified music is played during the night (so-called raves) (s 63), the removal of squatters (ss 75–6), and unauthorised campers residing on land without the consent of the occupier (s 77). The Act does, however, deal expressly with questions of freedom of assembly and public protest, not least in the provision which it makes for 'trespassory assemblies', the terms of which we have already encountered. Otherwise s 68 deals with what are referred to as 'disruptive trespassors', the main targets being apparently animal rights activists who trespass on land to disrupt fox-hunting events in particular. But s 68 is not confined to such activity, the government declining to accept an Opposition amendment to limit its scope to country sports, on the ground that there is no reason why events such as church fêtes, public race meetings, or open-air political meetings 'should suffer the invasion of others who intend to intimidate, obstruct or disrupt these proceedings'.[142] Thus it is an offence (of aggravated trespass) for any person to trespass on land in the open air to intimidate persons taking part in lawful activities, or to obstruct or disrupt such activity. Anyone suspected of committing such an offence may be arrested without a warrant by a constable in uniform, and the senior police officer present at the scene is empowered to require anyone committing or participating in aggravated trespass to leave the land in question; failure to do so is also an offence.

As in the case of picketing,[143] liability in civil law has an important role to play here too. In *Department of Transport v Williams*,[144] an application was made for injunctions to restrain protesters from action designed to disrupt the building of the M3 extension over Twyford Down. Interim injunctions were granted by Alliott J to restrain the defendants from (i) entering upon land specified in the order, (ii) interfering with the use of the highway specified in the order, and (iii) restraining them from interfering with the carrying on of work authorised by the M3 Motorway Scheme (SI 1990 No 463). In the case of the first injunctions, it was held that these could be granted on the ground of trespass, but that the second should be set aside because they added nothing to the first. The third required there to be a basis in law for holding that it was tortious to prevent or interfere with the department's carrying out of works under the authorisation in the statutory instrument. It was held that in such a case an injunction could be founded on the tort of wrongful interference with business; the unlawful means for the purposes of establishing this was found in the Highways Act 1980, which provides by s 303 that it is an offence wilfully to obstruct any person carrying out his lawful duties under the Act.[145] The risk of civil liability is particularly serious in view of the principle in *American Cyanamid Co v Ethicon Ltd*[146] that an interim injunction may be granted on the ground that there is a serious issue to be tried and that the balance of convenience is in favour of relief, pending the trial of the action. The defendant thus need not be acting unlawfully to be restrained, it being possible and indeed likely that the balance of convenience will lie in favour of

---

142   Official Report, Standing Committee B, 8 February 1994, col 614.
143   *Hubbard v Pitt* [1976] QB 142.
144   *The Times*, 7 December 1993.
145   See also *CIN Properties Ltd v Rawlins*, *The Times*, 9 February 1995.
146   [1975] AC 396.

the plaintiff where disorder is threatened. On the other hand, it has been held that *American Cyanamid Co* does not deal with the situation where the granting or otherwise of the interim injunction is likely to dispose finally of the matter,[147] as in the case of a protest, the cause of which may well have passed before the matter comes to trial. In these cases, it has been held that 'the degree of likelihood the plaintiff would have succeeded in establishing his right to an injunction if the action had gone to trial, is a factor to be brought into the balance'.[148] It has also been held, however, that interim proceedings are not the place to decide difficult questions of fact and law.[149]

---

[147] *NWL Ltd v Woods* [1979] ICR 867 (a trade dispute case, where the *American Cyanamid Co* rule was modified by statute).

[148] Ibid, at p 881 (Lord Diplock).

[149] See *Series 5 Software Ltd v Clarke* [1996] 1 All ER 853. See also *Department of Transport v Williams*, above.

CHAPTER 24

State security and official secrets

The maintenance of the security of the state is a primary duty of the government. But in performing this duty, it is important that governments do so without trespassing on individual liberty any more than is reasonably necessary. Today state security, or more commonly national security, is mentioned in a large number of statutes, nearly always in provisions which exclude security issues from public knowledge or scrutiny. Thus the Parliamentary Ombudsman may not investigate action taken with the authority of the Secretary of State for the purposes of protecting the security of the state[1] and under the Immigration Act 1971, s 15(3), an alien who is deported on the ground that the deportation is in the interests of national security has not the usual right to appeal to a tribunal against the deportation order.[2] Under such legislation, a minister commonly has conclusive power to determine whether action was taken on grounds of national security.[3] The common law may at first sight appear to take little account of state necessity.[4] However, national security is a matter to which the courts in fact attach considerable importance.[5] This does not mean that the judges should abandon all their power to decide at the mere mention by an official of national security,[6] and indeed it has been said extra-judicially that 'the courts should be less awe-struck by the mantra of national security'.[7]

There is also the problem of how to secure effective political accountability for security measures. There has, however, been in recent years a welcome lifting of the veil of secrecy which has for so long surrounded the security and intelligence services. This is reflected most notably in the greater role of legislation in regulating their affairs and in particular by the extension of the principle of judicial oversight and with it the publication of annual reports by

---

[1] Parliamentary Commissioner Act 1967, Sched 3, para 5. And see eg Contempt of Court Act 1981, s 10 and Employment Rights Act 1996, s 193.

[2] Ch 20 B. On deportations during the Gulf hostilities, see B Walsh, in Rowe, *The Gulf War 1990–91*, ch 15.

[3] Eg Race Relations Act 1976, ss 42, 69(2).

[4] *Entick v Carrington* (1765) 19 St Tr 1030.

[5] Eg *Conway v Rimmer* [1968] AC 910, at 955, 993; *A-G v Jonathan Cape Ltd* [1976] QB 752, 768.

[6] *Chandler v DPP* [1964] AC 763, 811. Cf *R v Home Secretary, ex p Hosenball* [1977] 3 All ER 452.

[7] Sir Simon Brown [1994] PL 579, at pp 589–90.

the judicial commissioners. But it is reflected also in the slightly greater degree of openness and accountability in terms of their finances. Although there is still some way to go, since 1994 the government has brought forward in a single published vote the aggregate expenditure of all three agencies, this being 'fully open to scrutiny by the Comptroller and Auditor General, apart from limited restrictions to protect the identities of certain sources of information and the details of particularly sensitive operations'.[8] Perhaps less seriously the lifting of the veil of secrecy is reflected further by steps such as the announcement of the names of the heads of the various security and intelligence services, and by the publication in 1993 of a booklet by MI5 outlining its activities, together with the delivery of the Dimbleby lecture by the Director-General of the Security Service in the following year.[9]

The Security Service

The Security Service was created in the War Office in 1909 to deal with the fears about German espionage in the period immediately before the First World War. The unit was called MO5, and later MI5. In 1935, MI5 was amalgamated with the section of the Metropolitan police dealing with counter-subversion and in that year it changed its name to the Security Service.[10] The domestic security service is, however, still referred to as MI5. A remarkable feature of these developments is that they took place without statutory authority. The Service was set up by executive decision (presumably under the royal prerogative) with functions determined by the executive, and accountable only to the executive. In his report on the Security Service following the Profumo scandal in 1963, Lord Denning wrote:

> The Security Service in this country is not established by Statute nor is it recognised by Common Law. Even the Official Secrets Acts do not acknowledge its existence. The members of the Service are, in the eye of the law, ordinary citizens with no powers greater than anyone else. They have no special powers of arrest such as the police have. No special powers of search are given to them. They cannot enter premises without the consent of the householder, even though they may suspect a spy is there. If a spy is fleeing the country, they cannot tap him on the shoulder and say he is not to go. They have, in short, no executive powers. They have managed very well without them. We would rather have it so, than have anything in the nature of a 'secret police'.[11]

According to Lord Denning, this absence of legal powers was made up for by the close cooperation between the Security Service and the police, particularly the Special Branch.[12] The Security Service would make all the initial investigations relying on its technical resources and specialised field force.

---

[8]   HC Deb, 24 November 1993, col 52 (WA). The vote for 1996–97 was £751,058,000: Appropriation Act 1996.

[9]   See respectively *MI5, The Security Service* (2nd edn, 1996), and S Rimington, *Security and Democracy – Is there a Conflict?* (1994).

[10]   For a full account of its origins, see Andrew, *Secret Service*. See also West, *MI5: British Security Service Operations 1909–45*; and *A Matter of Trust: MI5. 1945–72*. For further analyses, see Gill, *Policing Politics*; Lustgarten and Leigh, *In From the Cold*; Williams, *Not in the Public Interest*, part 2; and Bunyan, *The Political Police in Britain*, chs 3, 4.

[11]   Cmnd 2152, 1963.

[12]   See p 644 below.

But as soon as an arrest was possible, the police were called into consultation and from that point onwards both forces worked as a team. Because of the lack of executive power of the Security Service, an arrest would be made by the police and if a search warrant was sought, this too would be done by the police.[13]

Before the Security Service Act 1989 (see below), the operation of the Service was governed by a directive issued by the Home Secretary in 1952 (Sir David Maxwell Fyffe) to the Director-General.[14] This provided that, although the Security Service was not a part of the Home Office, the Director-General would be responsible to the Home Secretary personally, with a right on appropriate occasions of direct access to the Prime Minister. The directive also stated that the Service 'is part of the Defence Forces of the country' and that 'its task is the Defence of the Realm as a whole, from external and internal dangers arising from attempts at espionage and sabotage, or from actions of persons and organisations whether directed from within or without the country, which may be judged to be subversive of the State'. The work of the Service was to be strictly limited to what is necessary for these purposes and was expressly required to be kept absolutely free from any political bias or influence. Questions of political responsibilities of the Service were clarified by Lord Denning in his 1963 report.[15] Although the function of the Service is the defence of the realm, political responsibility does not lie with the Secretary of State for Defence, but with the Home Secretary and the Prime Minister, who is advised on security matters by the Cabinet Secretary.[16] This confused chain of responsibility is reinforced by the Security Service Act 1989. It is, however, an open question just what degree of political responsibility does exist, particularly in view of the convention that ministers 'do not concern themselves with the detailed information which may be obtained by the Security Services in particular cases, but are furnished with such information only as may be necessary for the determination of any issue on which guidance is sought'.[17]

Since 1989, the work of the Service has changed in response to the new international position. During the Cold War the Service was concerned to a large extent with counter-subversion and counter-espionage. So far as the former is concerned, it was reported in 1995 that the threat from subversive organisations had decreased to the point where it was assessed as being 'low'. The Communist Party of Great Britain (CPGB) no longer exists, while the main surviving organisation (the Communist Party of Britain) was assessed to be only about 1,100 strong, compared to 25,000–30,000 in the CPGB in the 1970s and 56,000 at its peak in 1942.[18] According to the Security Commission, it had been agreed inter-departmentally that the investigation of subversive organisations should be reduced,[19] and in 1992 the service assumed a new

---

13   Cmnd 2152, 1963, para 273.
14   Reproduced in *R v Home Secretary, ex p Hosenball* [1977] 3 All ER 452 in the judgment of Lord Denning MR.
15   See also Wilson, *The Labour Government 1964–70*, p 481.
16   Cmnd 2152, 1963, para 238.
17   Ibid.
18   Pelling, *The British Communist Party*, p 192.
19   Cm 2930, 1995.

responsibility in the form of 'Irish republican terrorism' which was transferred from the Special Branch. Although this step seems clearly to have been inspired by the need to fill the gap in the work of the Service caused by the end of the Cold War, it was explained in Parliament that the Service already had responsibility for Irish loyalist and international terrorism, and for Irish republican terrorism overseas.[20] Indeed it was only the accident of history which had given the police the leading responsibility for Irish republican terrorism, a decision which had been taken in 1883 when the Special Irish Branch was formed to track down Sinn Feiners who at the time were placing bombs in London. The Home Affairs Committee of the House of Commons expressed anxiety in 1992 that 'intelligence gathering in terrorism will be followed by work in other areas previously within the control of the police', in which case there was a need for 'effective scrutiny'.[21] The role of the Service has in fact been extended by the Security Service Act 1996 so that it now has duties in respect of serious crime.

The Secret Intelligence Service, GCHQ, and the Defence Intelligence Staff

The existence of the Secret Intelligence staff (SIS or MI6 as it is more commonly known) was first officially acknowledged in May 1992, though it is thought to have been founded in 1909, but not in its modern form. Despite the ending of the Cold War the government is nevertheless of the view that there is a role for the security and intelligence services 'alongside the armed services and diplomatic services in protecting and furthering the interests of Britain and its citizens at home and abroad'.[22] The threats which are said to make the continued existence of these agencies necessary 'include nuclear, chemical, biological and conventional proliferation of weapons', as well as 'terrorism and the threat to our armed forces in times of conflict, serious crime, espionage and sabotage'.[23] Officially, MI6 produces secret intelligence in support of the government's security, defence, foreign and economic policies as laid down by the Joint Intelligence Committee, an official committee chaired by a Deputy Secretary in the Ministry of Defence who is also head of the Defence and Overseas Secretariat. The members of the committee include senior officials in the Foreign Office, Ministry of Defence and the Treasury, as well as the heads of the three security and intelligence agencies. Its responsibilities include giving directions to and keeping under review the organisation and working of British intelligence activity at home and overseas. It also submits requirements and priorities for intelligence gathering, and coordinates inter-departmental plans for intelligence activity.

Although it had been operating at least since 1947, Government Communications' Headquarters (GCHQ) was not publicly acknowledged to exist until the trial of Geoffrey Prime, an official who was convicted under s 1 of the Official Secrets Act 1911 in 1982 for passing information to the Soviet Union. This was followed by a report of the Security Commission which not only revealed the existence of the centre but also gave an account of the security

---

[20]   HC Deb, 8 May 1992, cols 297–306.
[21]   HC 265 (1992–93).
[22]   HC Deb, 22 February 1994, col 155 (Mr Douglas Hurd).
[23]   Ibid (giving examples of the work of MI6 in the contemporary world).

procedures in operation there, including those for physical and document security.[24] It came more prominently to the fore in 1984 when controversially the government announced a trade union ban,[25] one irony of which is that as a result GCHQ 'has become as well known in political circles as MI5 and MI6'.[26] Officially the centre provides government departments and military commands with signals intelligence in support of the government's security, defence, foreign and economic policies, again in accordance with requirements laid down by the Joint Intelligence Committee. It also produces advice and assistance to government departments and the armed forces on the security of their communications and information technology systems, a task undertaken by the Communication Electronics Security Group. The Director of GCHQ, like the Chief of SIS, is personally responsible to the Foreign Secretary, subject to the overall responsibility of the Prime Minister for intelligence and security matters. Both GCHQ and SIS have been placed on a statutory footing by the Intelligence Services Act 1994 (see below): like the Security Service before them, they have come in from the cold.

Although not formally a security and intelligence agency, mention might nevertheless be made of the Defence Intelligence Staff. Established in 1964, it is run by the Chief of Defence Intelligence, under whom there are three directors-general who deal respectively with intelligence assessments, scientific and technical intelligence, and the management and support of intelligence. Much of its work is said to be devoted exclusively to military subjects, and it is also concerned with weapons proliferation, arms sales and control, as well as defence industries.[27] It serves the Ministry of Defence, the armed forces and other government departments, and analyses information from a wide variety of sources, both overt and covert. The Chief of Defence Intelligence is responsible to the Secretary of State for Defence, subject to the overall responsibility of the Prime Minister. But although it appears in official accounts of the security and intelligence services, the work of DIS is not subject to any statutory regulation or independent oversight in the manner of the other agencies. Nor is the DIS the only part of the Ministry of Defence intelligence activity, which includes 'intelligence elements throughout the armed forces and within the single Service Commands'.[28] Indeed in 1994–95 the £60 million budget for DIS accounted for only one-third of the budget of the Chief of Defence Intelligence, the coordinator of all intelligence activity.[29]

The Security Service Act 1989[30]

The Security Service is now governed to some extent by the Security Service Act 1989. In providing for the continuation of the Service, the Act defines its function to be 'the protection of national security and, in particular, its

---

24   Cmnd 8876, 1983.
25   See pp 647–8 below.
26   Official Report, Standing Committee E, 15 March 1994, col 115.
27   See HC 115 (1995–96) (Scott Report), para C2.26.
28   Defence Estimates 1994, Cm 2550, 1994, p 41.
29   For further details, see *Defence Estimates*, ibid, pp 41–2.
30   See I Leigh and L Lustgarten (1989) 52 MLR 801; also Ewing and Gearty, *Freedom under Thatcher*, pp 175–88.

protection against threats from espionage, terrorism and sabotage, from the activities of agents of foreign powers and from actions intended to overthrow or undermine parliamentary democracy by political, industrial or violent means' (s 1(2)). The term 'national security' is not defined, although it has been said to be wider than the particular heads specified in the Act.[31] The Service also has the task of safeguarding the economic well-being of the country against threats posed by the actions or intentions of persons outside the United Kingdom (s 1(3)). By an amendment to the 1989 Act introduced by the Security Service Act 1996, it is now also the function of the Service 'to act in support of the activities of police forces and other law enforcement agencies in the prevention and detection of serious crime'. According to the government this last provision reflects 'the firm intention' that the Service 'should be deployed against organised crime', and that the 'drug traffickers, the money launderers and the racketeers' are to become the Service's new targets. The role of the Service is to be 'a supporting one' in this capacity, the legislation reflecting fully 'the principle that the public and the law enforcement agencies will retain the primary responsibility'.[32] Nevertheless, these provisions are extremely controversial and gave rise to concern in Parliament and elsewhere. There is no definition of 'serious crime' and no guarantee that the work of the Service will be confined to organised crime, the search for a definition of which was dismissed as it would 'distract us from our task' and could create 'loopholes that could be exploited by unscrupulous defence lawyers to challenge the legality of the Security Service's involvement in a case'.[33] Admittedly the executive powers of the Service are restricted by a definition of serious crime which restrains the circumstances in which a warrant may be issued to interfere with property, but even this is extremely wide, as was pointed out during the committee stage in the House of Lords.[34] Apart from the absence of effective legal boundaries, concerns were also expressed about the lack of accountability of the Service when performing its new function in assisting the police: there will be no accountability to local police authorities and no supervision by the Police Complaints Authority.[35]

In exercising these wide powers, the Service continues to be under the operational control of the Director-General, who is appointed by the Home Secretary (s 2(4)). The duties of the Director-General, who must make an annual report to the Prime Minister and the Home Secretary (s 2), include taking steps to ensure that the Service does not take any action to further the interests of any political party (s 2(2)(b)). This is narrower than the rule contained in the Maxwell Fyffe directive which required the Service to be kept free from 'any political bias or influence', a rule which allegedly did not prevent the surveillance of the Campaign for Nuclear Disarmament or trade

---

[31]   Cm 1480, 1991. Although not 'easily defined', it 'includes the defence of the realm and the government's defence and foreign policies involving the protection of vital national interests at home and abroad'. What is a vital national interest is 'a question of fact and degree', more 'easily recognised when being considered than defined in advance'.

[32]   HL Deb, 14 May 1996, cols 398–9 (Baroness Blatch).

[33]   Ibid.

[34]   HL Deb, 10 June 1996, col 1495 (Lord Williams of Mostyn).

[35]   This point is considered in some detail at HL Deb, 10 June 1996, cols 1500–20. For a particularly powerful critique, see the *Guardian*, 10 June 1996 (editorial).

unions involved in pay disputes.[36] The 1989 Act also conferred a new power on the Service. This is the power to apply to the Home Secretary for a warrant authorising 'entry on or interference with property' (s 3).[37] Hitherto there was no power to grant any warrant, but it appears that the Service may not have been unduly impeded in the absence of such power. Indeed, in *Attorney-General v Guardian Newspapers (No 2)* Lord Donaldson MR appeared willing to turn a blind eye to the unauthorised entry of private property by the security services, referring to it as a 'covert invasion of privacy' which might be considered excusable in the defence of the realm.[38] Section 3 has been replaced by ss 5 and 6 of the Intelligence Services Act 1994 (see below), but was not repealed, though it ceases to have effect.[39]

The 1989 Act is significant also for having introduced new procedures for the supervision of the Service. These are modelled on procedures introduced in the Interception of Communications Act 1985, which is discussed later in this chapter. It would have made sense to have had a single statute dealing with all these matters.[40] However, the 1989 Act provides for the appointment of a Security Service Commissioner, being someone who holds or has held high judicial office (s 4). The Commissioner must keep under review the exercise by the Home Secretary of the power to issue warrants to the Service,[41] and reports annually to the Prime Minister, who lays a copy of the report before each House of Parliament, though sensitive parts of the report may be withheld. In addition to the supervisory role of the Commissioner, the Act provides for a tribunal to investigate complaints from any person who is aggrieved by anything which he or she believes the Service has done in relation to him or his property (s 5). However, the powers of the tribunal are very limited. The tribunal may investigate whether the complainant has been the subject of inquiries by the Service and, if so, whether the Service had reasonable grounds for deciding to institute such inquiries. But if he or she has been under surveillance because he or she belongs to a category of persons regarded by the Service as requiring investigation, the tribunal cannot act if the Service had reasonable grounds to believe that the complainant belonged to that category of persons.[42] Similarly, where the complaint relates to the disclosure of information about a complainant to a potential employer (as in the case of positive vetting), the tribunal may investigate only to determine whether the Service had reasonable grounds to believe the information to be true. It has no power to determine whether the information has been misused.[43] If a complaint is upheld the tribunal may order any inquiries to be discontinued, any records to be destroyed, and compensation

---

[36] Allegations to this effect were made by a retired MI5 officer, Cathy Massiter, in a Channel 4 television programme. For the unsuccessful challenge to the legality of this activity, see *R v Home Secretary, ex p Ruddock* [1987] 2 All ER 518.

[37] On the way this power is exercised, see Cm 1480, 1991, para 3.

[38] [1990] AC 109, at 190. Cf *Entick v Carrington* (1765) 19 St Tr 1030.

[39] See Cm 3253, 1996.

[40] For arrangements in other countries, see S Farson [1992] PL 377 (Canada), and Lee, Hanks and Morabito, *In the Name of National Security* (Australia). See also Lustgarten and Leigh, op cit, which is strong on Australian and Canadian developments.

[41] On the standard applied by the Commissioner, see Cm 1480, 1991.

[42] 1989 Act, Sched 1, para 2(4).

[43] Ibid, para 3.

to be paid.[44] But complainants have no right to be told if the Service has a file on them or to be informed of its contents. The decisions of the tribunal and the Commissioner (including decisions as to their jurisdiction) are not subject to appeal nor are liable to be questioned in any court (s 5(4)).

The Commissioner appointed under the Act is Lord Justice Stuart-Smith, who was re-appointed for a further period of two years until 14 December 1997. Unlike the Commissioner appointed under the Interception of Communications Act 1985, the Security Service Commissioner does not provide details of the number of warrants issued under s 3 in any one year, explaining that this is because of the 'comparatively small number of warrants issued under the 1989 Act and the fact that the purpose for which they can be granted is more restricted than under the 1985 Act'.[45] On the other hand, the number of warrants granted in any one year is sufficiently voluminous to preclude the Commissioner examining them all and questioning all those involved.[46] In all six annual reports published at the time of writing, the Commissioner has expressed himself satisfied that ministers had properly exercised their powers under the Act and that satisfactory arrangements were in place for ensuring that no information is disclosed by the Service except as far as necessary for the discharge of its functions. A total of 205 complaints had been made to the tribunal between 18 December 1989 (when the Act came into force) and 31 December 1995, though in none of these cases did the tribunal find in favour of the complainant. But this does not mean that the Service 'does not fulfil a useful function', the Commissioner concluding that 'the very existence of the Tribunal as a body empowered to investigate complaints provides the Security Service with a strong additional incentive to ensure that its procedures are designed to eliminate the chance of a complaint being found to be justified'.[47] Despite their shortcomings, the procedures established by the 1989 Act have been found by the European Commission of Human Rights not to raise an admissible issue that they breach art 8 of the ECHR.[48]

The Intelligence Services Act 1994

So far as the Secret Intelligence Service is concerned, its activities are governed by the Intelligence Services Act 1994, which also applies to GCHQ. The functions of SIS are stated by s 1(1) to be first the obtaining and providing information relating to the actions or intentions of persons outside the British Islands, and secondly the performing of 'other tasks relating to the actions or intentions of such persons'. These extraordinarily wide provisions are constrained by s 1(2) which provides that the statutory functions are exercisable only (*a*) in the interests of national security (with 'particular reference to the defence and foreign policies of Her Majesty's Government'), (*b*) in the interests of the economic well-being of the United Kingdom, or (*c*) in support of the prevention or detection of serious crime. The 'interests of

---

[44]   Ibid, para 6.
[45]   Cm 1480, 1991. And see Cm 3253, 1996.
[46]   Cm 1480, 1991, para 13.
[47]   Cm 1946, 1992.
[48]   Cm 2523, 1994.

national security' are not otherwise defined, nor (more surprisingly) is what constitutes 'serious crime'.[49] And although 'a well worn provision', it was acknowledged that a power to take action 'in the interests of the economic well-being' of the UK 'sometimes causes puzzlement as to what it can mean'.[50] It was explained, however, that the power 'might be useful' where 'substantial British economic interests were at stake, or where there was a crisis or a huge difficulty about the continued supply of a commodity on which our economy depended'.[51] Under the Act the agencies are not permitted to become involved in domestic economic, commercial or financial affairs, though they may acquire information which has a bearing on domestic issues.[52]

The Act also places GCHQ on a statutory footing, under the authority of the Foreign Secretary. By virtue of s 3, its functions are twofold, the first being 'to monitor or interfere with electromagnetic, acoustic and other emissions and any equipment producing such emissions' (and 'to obtain and provide information derived from or related to such emissions or equipment'). The second duty is to provide advice and assistance about language and cryptology, this information to be provided to the armed forces, government departments, or any other organisation approved by the Prime Minister. As in the case of SIS these functions are exercisable only in the interests of national security (with particular reference to the defence and foreign policies of the government); or the interests of the economic well-being of the UK 'in relation to the actions or intentions of persons outside the British Islands; or in support of the prevention and detection of serious crime'. These measures were strongly criticised in standing committee as providing a mandate which is 'wide and sweeping', inadequately constrained by the 'partial stricture' that it be exercised in the interests of national security.[53] It was pointed out in reply, however, that there were a number of safeguards in the Act to prevent the abuse of power (according to the minister there were 11 in total). So far as the duty of GCHQ to assist in the prevention and detection of crime is concerned, this was said not to be new, but had been going on for 'decades'. It appears that GCHQ intervenes when criminals use 'sophisticated communications devices to commit a crime' and assist in the deciphering of diaries and notebooks kept by criminals in sophisticated codes.[54]

The Act authorises 'entry on or interference with property or with wireless telegraphy' by each of the three security and intelligence agencies, provided that any such action is taken with the authority of a warrant issued by the Secretary of State; otherwise the action is 'unlawful', though unlike the unauthorised interception of communications it is not an offence. A warrant may be issued only if the Secretary of State 'thinks it necessary' for the action to be taken 'on the ground that it is likely to be of substantial value' in assisting the agency making the application in carrying out any of its functions, and that the action sought to be achieved cannot reasonably be secured by other means (s 5). A warrant issued on the application of either

---

[49]   See Cm 3288, 1996, para 8.
[50]   HC Deb, 22 February 1994, col 157 (Mr Hurd).
[51]   Ibid.
[52]   See HC 115 (1995–96) (Scott Report).
[53]   Official Report, Standing Committee E, 15 March 1994, col 117.
[54]   Ibid, col 132.

the SIS or GCHQ may not relate to British property, unlike warrants issued to the Security Service which may be issued for two such purposes. The first relates to the traditional functions of the Service, as defined in s 1(2) and (3) of the Security Service Act 1989, in which case it may relate to property in Britain, without further qualification. The second relates to the new function of the Service, added by the Security Service Act 1996, namely to act in support of the police and law enforcement agencies in the prevention and detection of serious crime. In this case the warrant may authorise action in respect of property in Britain, but only if the action is to be taken in relation to offences that involve violence, result in substantial financial gain or constitute conduct by a large number of persons in pursuit of a common purpose; or if the offence is one which carries a term of three years' imprisonment on conviction for the first time.[55] Warrants are normally to be issued by a Secretary of State and are valid for up to six months, though they may (but need not) be cancelled before the period of six months expires (s 6).

Apart from the power to interfere with property (albeit with the authority of a warrant), the 1994 Act also contains a remarkable power for the Secretary of State to authorise a person to commit an act 'outside the British Islands' which would be unlawful 'under the criminal or civil law of any part of the United Kingdom' (s 7). The effect of such authorisation is to give the individual committing an offence (or other unlawful act) immunity from legal liability in this country (but not in the country in which the crime or unlawful act may be committed), though authorisation should only be given where the acts to be done by the authorisation are 'necessary for the proper discharge of a function of the Intelligence service'. Understandably these powers gave rise to some concern in Parliament, with one Opposition member pointing out that they grant 'the Secretary of State complete power to authorise activities that violate the law of other States as well as that of the United Kingdom. There is no limit on what can be authorised. In extreme cases the use of lethal force will be allowed'.[56] Ministers were, however, rather coy about the way in which these powers would be used and appeared to think it enough to re-assure the House that 'certain actions can be undertaken by the agencies under the specific authority of Ministers only',[57] and were unwilling to contemplate even an obligation to report annually to the Intelligence and Security Committee (see below) on the number and general description of all acts authorised under this section on the ground that provision was made for the appointment of a judicial commissioner to ensure that the ministers' powers were exercised properly.[58]

Political responsibility for the agencies was said to be 'primarily' that of the Foreign Secretary 'under the Prime Minister'.[59] Under the Act, however, the operations of the SIS continue to be under the control of the Chief of the Intelligence Service (s 2), while the operations of GCHQ continue to be

---

55   1994 Act, s 5, as amended by Security Service Act 1996.
56   Official Report, Standing Committee E, 17 March 1994, col 174.
57   HC Deb, 22 February 1994, col 160.
58   Official Report, Standing Committee E, 17 March 1994, col 175.
59   HC Deb, 22 February 1994, col 154.

under the control of the Director (s 4). Each is responsible for ensuring the efficiency of the respective services and that no information is obtained by their organisations except so far as is necessary for the proper discharge of their functions. They must also ensure that information is not disclosed by their organisations except 'so far as necessary' for the proper discharge of their functions, and that the respective agencies do not take 'any action to further the interests of any United Kingdom political party' (ss 2(2)(b), 4(2)(b)). By a strange quirk of drafting (though it may not be unintended) either Service may disclose information even though it is not necessary for it to do so in 'the proper discharge of its functions'. Thus the SIS may disclose (without violating the duty of the Chief of the Intelligence Service) material on the additional (but not necessarily consequential) ground that it is in the interests of national security, for the prevention or detection of serious crime, or for the purpose of any criminal proceedings (s 2(2)(a)). GCHQ may disclose information falling into the last of these three categories, even though again disclosure is not necessary for the proper discharge of its functions, a much narrower incidental power than that possessed by SIS. Both the Chief of Intelligence Service and the Director of GCHQ are required to make an annual report to the Prime Minister and the Foreign Secretary, and they may report to either 'at any time' on any matter relating to the work of their respective services (ss 2(4) and 4(4)).

Following the precedents established in 1985 and 1989, the 1994 Act makes provision for the creation of an Intelligence Services Commissioner (appointed by the Prime Minister and to be a person who holds or has held high judicial office) and a tribunal for the investigation of complaints about the SIS or GCHQ (the first president of which is Lord Justice Simon Brown). The decisions of both the Commissioner and the tribunal (including decisions as to jurisdiction) are not subject to appeal and are not liable to be questioned in any court of law. The first Commissioner under the Act is Lord Justice Stuart-Smith, who as we have seen is also the Security Service Commissioner. In his first report under the 1994 Act he expressed satisfaction that the Secretary of State had properly exercised his powers under the Act,[60] having examined all warrants issued under s 5 on the application of SIS and GCHQ, and all authorisations issued under s 7. He did not, however, consider it to be in the public interest to disclose the number of warrants or authorisations which had been issued, though he did draw attention to the different types of authorisation which may be made. Thus authorisations may be given for (i) particular acts, (ii) acts of a description specified in the authorisation (class authorisations) or (iii) acts carried out in the course of a specified operation. He also revealed an intention that 'class authorisations would be sought only for relatively minor infractions of the law, not involving significant risks to persons or property'. Twenty-one complaints were referred to the tribunal during the first year of its operation (of which, as required by the Act, five were referred to the Commissioner as relating to property), compared with 21 complaints made to the Security Service Tribunal in the same year, of which 13 were referred to the Commissioner. In no case did either tribunal or Commissioner uphold a complaint.

---

[60] Cm 3288, 1996.

The Special Branch[61]

Another agency engaged in work related to state security is the police Special Branch, which as we have seen was formed in 1883 in response to a Sinn Fein bombing campaign in London. After three years the word 'Irish' was dropped from the Branch's title and it was expanded to deal with other security problems. After 1945 provincial police forces established their own permanent Special Branch and today each police force has a Special Branch under the direction of its chief constable. According to *Home Office Guidelines*, 'each Special Branch remains an integral part of the local police force, accountable to individual Chief Officers and available for them to deploy on any duties flowing from their responsibility for the preservation of the Queen's Peace, including the prevention and detection of crime'.[62] The size of each Branch, and the rank of its Head, depends on the size of the force as a whole, and the nature and extent of the responsibilities given to the Branch in the force area.[63] There is no national Special Branch force though 'the small size of most Special Branches, the specialised nature of their work and the potential for exceptional demands to arise from time to time in a particular locality have necessitated more extensive arrangements for cooperation between Special Branches within regions than was once the case'.[64] There are, moreover, a number of 'national policing arrangements' which affect Special Branch work, in the sense that much Special Branch activity is coordinated by the Metropolitan Police Special Branch (said to exercise a 'national role') which together with the Security Service also has responsibility for 'initial and continuation training'. Special Branch officers are bound by the same disciplinary code as other police officers and have no additional powers by virtue of their employment in the Special Branch.

Although the organisation and functions of the Special Branches are neither prescribed nor directly regulated by statute, the *Home Office Guidelines* describe their role as being:

primarily to acquire intelligence, to assess its potential operational value, and to contribute more generally to its interpretation. They do so both to meet local policing needs and also to assist the Security Service in carrying out its statutory duty under the Security Service Act 1989 – namely the protection of national security and, in particular, protection against threats from espionage, terrorism, and sabotage, from the activities of agents of foreign powers and from actions intended to overthrow or undermine parliamentary democracy by political, industrial or violent means.[65]

In practice, however, it is countering the threat of terrorism which is said to be the most important single function of the Special Branch, with any intelligence acquired being passed on to the Security Service, now the 'lead agency' since responsibility was transferred in 1992. As part of their counter-terrorist role, Special Branches provide armed personal protection for people

---

[61]   See Bunyan, *The Political Police in Britain*, and Allason, *The Branch: A History of The Metropolitan Police Special Branch 1883–1983*.
[62]   *Home Office Guidelines on Special Branch Work in Great Britain* (1994), para 2.
[63]   Ibid, para 16.
[64]   Ibid, para 17. This is said to occur informally and on the basis of the mutual aid provisions in what is now the Police Act 1996.
[65]   Ibid, para 3.

at risk and keep watch at airports and seaports. So far as counter-subversion is concerned, this has been reduced in recent years, though the Special Branch continues to gather information about the public order implications of events such as marches and demonstrations,[66] particularly in cases where there is a possibility of 'politically motivated violence or subversive influence'; in other cases the police 'routinely look to other parts of their organisations to provide information on public order events'.[67] This enables measures to be taken to ensure the physical safety of participants and the public, and that proportionate and cost-effective policing arrangements are made to deal with any likely disorder or violence. Although not referred to in the revised *Home Office Guidelines*, Special Branches in the past have assisted in jury vetting in cases involving national security or terrorism, to exclude jurors with 'political beliefs so biased as to go beyond normally reflecting the broad spectrum of views and interests in the community to reflect the extreme views of sectarian interest or pressure group to a degree which might interfere with his fair assessment of the facts of the case or lead him to exert improper influence on his fellow jurors'.[68] In 1984, the Home Affairs Committee concluded that there was no cause for anxiety about the work of the Special Branches and that they were adequately controlled through chief constables.[69]

Security procedures in the civil service[70]

Since 1948, procedures have been in place to seek to exclude from sensitive positions in the civil service those who are perceived to be a threat to national security. The first of these, the so-called purge procedure, was thought to have been introduced (in 1948) as a result of American pressure following major spy scandals in the immediate post-war period. The aim was to ensure that 'no one who is known to be a member of the Communist Party, or to be associated with it in such a way as to raise legitimate doubts about his or her reliability, is employed in connection with work, the nature of which is vital to the security of the State'.[71] This was followed by the introduction of positive vetting in 1952 which had been on the agenda at least since the arrest and conviction of Klaus Fuchs in 1950 for communicating atomic secrets to the Soviet Union, for which he was sentenced to 14 years' imprisonment. Its implementation was a direct consequence of the defection of Donald MacLean and Guy Burgess to Moscow, in the aftermath of which the Foreign Secretary set up a committee under the chairmanship of Sir Alexander Cadogan to examine all aspects of the security arrangements in the Foreign Office. The committee reported in November 1951 approving plans for positive vetting which had already been prepared, and recommending that it should apply widely within the Foreign Service. The committee proposed that vetting should cover not only 'political unreliability' but also 'the problem of character defects, which

---

66   It would also include picketing in the course of trade disputes: HC 71 (1984–85).
67   *Home Office Guidelines on Special Branch Work*, para 14.
68   [1988] 3 All ER 1086, 1087 (Attorney-General's guidelines).
69   HC 71 (1984–85).
70   See Fredman and Morris, *The State as Employer*, pp 232–6; Robertson, *Freedom, the Individual and the Law*, pp 148–52.
71   HC Deb, 25 March 1948, cols 3417–26. See M L Joelson [1963] PL 51. The procedure was applied also to fascists, though communists were the real target.

might lay an officer open to blackmail, or otherwise undermine his loyalty and sense of responsibility'. The practice of positive vetting was thus introduced as a 'regular system' at the beginning of 1952, but without recourse to legislation, or without even informing or seeking the approval of Parliament.[72] It has since been extended well beyond the Foreign Service.

The procedures were revised in 1985, again in 1990, and most recently in 1994. In a statement on vetting policy[73] it was announced that 'In the interests of national security, safeguarding Parliamentary democracy and maintaining the proper security of the Government's essential activities, it is the policy of HMG that no one should be employed in connection with work the nature of which is vital to the interests of the State' who fell within one of five categories. The first of these relates to those who are or who have been involved in, or associated with espionage, terrorism, sabotage, or actions intended to overthrow or undermine parliamentary democracy by political, industrial or violent means. The second category applies to anyone who is or has recently been a member of an organisation which has advocated such activities, or associated with any such organisation or its members 'in such a way as to raise reasonable doubts about his or her reliability'. The third and fourth categories apply to those who are 'susceptible to pressure or improper influence', and to those who have shown 'dishonesty or lack of integrity which throws doubt upon their reliability', while the fifth applies in respect of those who have 'demonstrated behaviour' or are 'subject to circumstances which may otherwise indicate unreliability'. Less rigorous inquiries are made in the case of those who have frequent and uncontrolled access to SECRET information than in the case of those who deal with TOP SECRET information. In the former case individuals are subjected to a Security Check (SC), whereas in the latter case the level of clearance to which the person is submitted is known as Developed Vetting (DV) and will involve inquiries being made of people familiar with the person concerned. Counter Terrorist Checks (CTC) are also made in respect of a number of sensitive posts.

Both the positive vetting and the purge procedures have been introduced without statutory authority. Although both procedures involve matters which vitally affect the reputation and livelihood of the individuals in question, the administrative safeguards fall far short of being judicial or quasi-judicial procedures. Where positive vetting is refused because of character defect, an appeal lies to the permanent head of the individual's department.[74] In all other cases, the appeal is to the 'Three Advisers' who also deal with appeals by victims of the purge procedure.[75] As has been pointed out:

Details of the charges are ... not made available if this might involve the disclosure of sources; there is no right to know of the evidence nor to lead witnesses in defence and 'prosecution' witnesses are not available for cross examination. The employee is not entitled to any representation, although, as a concession to the trade unions, a friend is allowed to be present during the accused's opening statement, and may remain to

---

[72] 'Not surprisingly the purge procedure has been regarded as of dwindling importance since Positive Vetting has been applied to new entrants to sensitive posts in the civil service for more than thirty years': Lustgarten and Leigh, *In From the Cold*, p 131.

[73] HC Deb, 15 December 1994, col 765 (WA).

[74] Bailey, Harris and Jones, *Civil Liberties: Cases and Materials*, p 498.

[75] See Fredman and Morris, *The State as Employer*, p 233.

assist the person for as much of the proceedings as the advisers consider appropriate.[76]

Such a procedure falls far short of what the rules of natural justice normally require.[77] Although the court might insist that the Three Advisers must comply with the duty to act fairly, they are unlikely to require much more than is presently done. As Lord Denning said in *R v Home Secretary, ex p Hosenball*,[78] 'Great as is the public interest in the freedom of the individual and the doing of justice to him, nevertheless in the last resort it must take second place to the security of the country itself'. The reluctance of the courts to become involved in this area is illustrated by *R v Director of GCHQ, ex p Hodges*[79] where positive vetting clearance was withdrawn from a staff member at GCHQ when he announced that he was homosexual. His application for judicial review failed, Glidewell J holding that the decision had been neither unreasonable, nor procedurally unfair, but that in any event the court was unable to examine the matter on the ground that it had been taken in the interests of national security.[80]

Trade unionism at GCHQ[81]

The concern about security in the civil service assumed a new dimension with the banning of trade unions at Government Communications' Headquarters (GCHQ), 'a branch of the public service under the Foreign and Commonwealth Office, the main functions of which are to ensure the security of the United Kingdom military and official communications and to provide signals intelligence for the Government. These functions ... involve handling secret information which is vital to the national security'.[82] Over 4,000 people were employed at the main establishment in Cheltenham. Since the establishment was created in 1947, staff had been 'permitted, and indeed encouraged, to belong to national trade unions, and most of them did so'.[83] The government was concerned however by events between 1979 and 1981 when industrial action was taken at GCHQ on seven occasions, leading to a loss of some 10,000 working days and on one occasion to the virtual shutting down of operations, causing 'some interruption of the constant day and night monitoring of foreign signals communications'.[84] The government responded by deciding on 22 December 1983 to introduce new terms of service for staff at GCHQ whereby they would be no longer permitted to join national trade unions but would be free to belong only to an officially approved departmental staff association.[85] This decision, taken without consultation with the trade unions, was implemented in two ways. First, by virtue of powers delegated to

---

[76] Ibid.
[77] The requirements of procedural fairness are dealt with in ch 29 B.
[78] [1977] 3 All ER 452, 460.
[79] *The Times*, 26 July 1988.
[80] Cf *Council of Civil Service Unions v Minister for the Civil Service* [1985] AC 374.
[81] And see Fredman and Morris, op cit, pp 98–102.
[82] *Council of Civil Service Unions v Minister for the Civil Service* [1985] AC 374, at 394 (Lord Fraser).
[83] Ibid.
[84] Ibid, at 395.
[85] See *Government Communications Staff Federation v Certification Officer* [1993] ICR 163.

her by the royal prerogative, the Prime Minister (acting as Minister of the Civil Service) issued appropriate instructions under art 4 of the Civil Service Order in Council 1982. Secondly, the Foreign Secretary signed certificates under s 121(4) of the Employment Protection Act 1975 and s 138(4) of the Employment Protection (Consolidation) Act 1978 withdrawing certain statutory rights from staff at GCHQ.[86] These included the right not to be discriminated against or dismissed because of trade union membership or activities. This power, which had been exercised previously in respect of MI5 and MI6, may be invoked for the purpose of safeguarding national security.

These measures, announced by the Foreign Secretary on 25 January 1984,[87] were widely criticised and challenged both in international law and in domestic law. It was concluded by agencies of the International Labour Organisation that the government's conduct violated ILO Convention 87 on Freedom of Association and Protection of the Right to Organise.[88] But the government refused to accept this view, arguing that the matter was governed not by Convention 87 but by Convention 151 on the Right to Organise in the Public Sector, which does not apply to employees engaged in work of a 'highly confidential nature'.[89] The unions also complained of a violation under art 11 of the European Convention on Human Rights. Although this protects the right to freedom of association, including the right to join trade unions, it is subject to a proviso in art 11(2) which permits lawful restrictions to be imposed on the exercise of the right 'by members of the armed forces, of the police or of the administration of the state'. The government convinced the Commission at Strasbourg that the staff at GCHQ fell into this last category, and the complaint was ruled inadmissible.[90] The Commission held that 'States must be given a wide discretion when ensuring the protection of their national security'.[91]

The challenge under domestic law also ultimately failed, after an initial success before Glidewell J in the High Court.[92] In these proceedings the unions chose mainly to attack the instructions issued by the government under the Civil Service Order in Council rather than the certificates issued by the Foreign Secretary under the employment protection legislation. But as we saw in chapter 12, the instructions were issued using powers delegated under the royal prerogative. The House of Lords swept away centuries of learning, with a majority holding that the exercise of prerogative powers may be subject to judicial review, just as the exercise of statutory powers may be.[93] Of the different grounds of review, the one most relevant here was procedural impropriety, in the sense that the government had taken action against a

---

[86] See now Trade Union and Labour Relations (Consolidation) Act 1992, s 275, and Employment Rights Act 1996, s 193. The power has also been exercised in respect of the Security Service.

[87] HC Deb, 25 January 1984, col 917.

[88] For a full account, see Ewing, *Britain and the ILO*.

[89] The government also refused to accept an amendment to the Intelligence Services Bill requiring GCHQ to respect the trade union rights of staff under ILO Convention 87. See Official Report, Standing Committee E, 29 March 1994, col 295.

[90] (1988) 10 EHRR 269. See S Fredman and G S Morris (1988) 17 ILJ 105.

[91] (1988) 10 EHRR 269, at 290.

[92] [1984] IRLR 309.

[93] The Court of Appeal had taken a very conventional approach: see [1984] IRLR 353.

party which should have been consulted in advance, not because it had a legal right to be consulted, but because it had a legitimate expectation of consultation 'when conditions of service were to be significantly altered'. But although the unions were thus able to surmount two difficult hurdles, they stumbled at a third, namely the government's defence that its decisions (including the decision that there should be no prior consultation) had been taken in the interests of national security. On this issue, Lord Fraser said:

> The decision on whether the requirements of national security outweigh the duty of fairness in any particular case is for the government and not for the courts; the government alone has access to the necessary information, and in any event the judicial process is unsuitable for reaching decisions on national security.[94]

It is not enough for the government merely to assert after the event that a decision was taken for reasons of national security. It must produce evidence (considered here by the Lords to be sufficient) to show that this was in fact a reason for the decision. But the government does not have to show that its measures were necessary or even reasonably necessary in the interests of national security.[95]

The Official Secrets Acts 1911–89[96]

The Official Secrets Acts 1911–89 serve two distinct but related purposes:

(*a*) to protect the interests of the state against espionage and other activities which might be useful to an enemy and therefore injurious to state security;
(*b*) to guard against the unauthorised disclosure of information which is held by servants of the state in their official capacity, whether or not the information has any direct reference to state security as such.

The legal sanctions under (*b*) help to support the sanctions against espionage, since it may in a particular case be possible to prove unauthorised disclosure of information without being able to prove elements of espionage. But they may also serve to protect the corridors of power against disclosure of information and publicity which a government might find politically embarrassing or inconvenient. The Official Secrets Act 1911, on which later Acts have been built, was passed rapidly through Parliament in circumstances in which ministers emphasised purpose (*a*) as the primary object of the Act and did not mention purpose (*b*). In 1972, the Franks committee on s 2 of the 1911 Act commented that new legislation should be introduced to separate the espionage laws from the general protection of official information.[97]

Section 1(1) of the 1911 Act creates a group of offences, mainly connected with espionage. It is an offence, punishable with 14 years' imprisonment,

if any person *for any purpose prejudicial to the safety of the State* –
(*a*) approaches, inspects, passes over or is in the neighbourhood of, or enters any prohibited place within the meaning of this Act; or

---

94   [1985] AC 374, at 402.
95   And see G S Morris [1985] PL 177; S Lee [1985] PL 186.
96   Williams, *Not in the Public Interest*, part 1; Bailey, Harris and Jones, *Civil Liberties: Cases and Materials*, ch 7; Andrew, *Secret Service*.
97   Cmnd 5104, 1972.

(*b*) makes any sketch, plan, model, or note which ... might be or is intended to be directly or indirectly useful to an enemy; or

(*c*) obtains, collects, records, or publishes or communicates to any other person any secret official code word or any sketch, plan, model, article, or note, or other document or information which ... might be or is intended to be directly or indirectly useful to an enemy.

The italicised phrase caused difficulties when charges under s 1 were brought following a non-violent political demonstration against an RAF base, in *Chandler v DPP*.[98]

Anti-nuclear demonstrators sought to immobilise an RAF bomber base by sitting down on the runway. They were arrested as they approached the base and charged with conspiring to enter a prohibited place for a purpose prejudicial to the safety or interests of the state, contrary to s 1 of the 1911 Act. The trial judge refused to allow the accused to bring evidence to show that it would be beneficial to the United Kingdom if the government's nuclear policy were abandoned. For a variety of interlocking reasons, the House of Lords unanimously upheld the conviction. The demonstrators admittedly wished to obstruct the use of the airbase and it was immaterial that they believed that such obstruction would ultimately benefit the country. The offences created by the 1911 Act, s 1 were not confined to spying but included sabotage and other acts of physical interference.

This decision was criticised,[99] but it seems impossible to argue that Parliament intended a spy who had passed military secrets to a foreign power to be able to establish as a defence that his or her purpose in so doing was to force the British government to change its policies. The outcome in *Chandler's* case would have been different if the demonstrators' intention had merely been to hold a protest meeting on the road outside the air-base, since the prosecution would have to establish that to protest about nuclear policy was itself an act prejudicial to the interests of the state. In *Chandler's* case, Lord Devlin alone stressed that it was for the jury to decide all questions of fact, including the issue of the accused's purpose and its likely effect on the interests of the state. During an official secrets trial in 1978, Mars-Jones J indicated that the use of s 1 in situations that fell short of spying and sabotage could be oppressive.[100] Cases since then have been concerned mainly with spying, these including the convictions of Geoffrey Prime in 1983,[101] Michael Bettaney in 1984,[102] and Michael Smith in 1993,[103] all of whom had communicated secret information to the USSR. The other celebrated s 1 prosecution in the 1980s was that of eight signals intelligence officers based in Cyprus.[104] But unlike the cases of Prime, Bettaney and Smith, the prosecution failed. A subsequent inquiry by David Calcutt QC revealed that the accused had been unlawfully and oppressively detained while investigations were being conducted by the police and security service.[105]

---

[98]   [1964] AC 763.
[99]   D Thompson [1963] PL 201.
[100]   A Nicol [1979] Crim LR 284; Aubrey, *Who's Watching You?*
[101]   *R v Prime* (1983) 5 Cr App Rep 127.
[102]   *R v Bettaney* [1985] Crim LR 104.
[103]   Cm 2930, 1995.
[104]   See A W Bradley [1986] PL 363. See also Cmnd 9923, 1986.
[105]   Cmnd 9781, 1986.

Section 2 of the 1911 Act created a plethora of over 2,000 different offences related to the misuse of official information.[106] In particular, by s 2(1) it was an offence punishable by two years' imprisonment

if any person having in his possession or control ... any document or information ... which has been entrusted in confidence to him by any person holding office under Her Majesty ... communicates the ... document or information to any person, other than a person to whom he is authorised to communicate it or a person to whom it is in the interests of the State his duty to communicate it.[107]

Other offences included the unauthorised retention of documents and failure to take reasonable care of documents. Section 2 plainly extended to the disclosure of information which bore no relation to national security.[108] An offence could be committed even though the information was not secret[109] and even though it was disclosed in order to promote rather than undermine British interests abroad.[110] The scope of the section – well described as a 'catch all'[111] – was, however, mitigated in two ways. First, as with all offences under the Official Secrets Acts, the consent of the Attorney-General in England (or the Lord Advocate in Scotland) was necessary before any prosecution could be brought.[112] Secondly, the authorisation which prevented disclosure of information being an offence could be wholly informal and could be implicit in the circumstances of disclosure. Ministers and many senior civil servants, by what was known as the practice of self-authorisation, were able to decide for themselves how much information to disclose, at least in matters relating to their own duties.[113] Thus, when an off the record briefing was given to a journalist (for example, to enable him to 'leak' the contents of a Bill before it is published in Parliament) no breach of the Official Secrets Acts would have occurred. More than once it had been stressed that s 2 of the 1911 Act was not to be blamed for secrecy in government, since at any time ministers could adopt a more open approach.[114] Nonetheless the form of the 1911 Act often presented journalists with a real difficulty in knowing what they might safely publish.

Other provisions of the Official Secrets Acts include s 7 of the 1920 Act, under which it is an offence to attempt to commit any offence under the Acts or to endeavour to persuade another person to commit such an offence, or to aid and abet or to do *any act preparatory* to the commission of such an offence. Under the 1920 Act, s 8, a court may exclude the public from the trial of an offence under the Acts if the prosecution applies for this on the ground that the publication of evidence would be prejudicial to national safety. This measure, which is employed in s 1 prosecutions[115] and which has also been

---

[106] Cmnd 5104, 1972, para 16.
[107] In *R v Ponting* [1985] Crim LR 318 it was held that the interests of the state are the interests of the state as determined by the government of the day.
[108] See *Loat v James* [1986] Crim LR 744.
[109] *R v Crisp* ((1919) 83 JP 121.
[110] *R v Fell* [1963] Crim LR 207.
[111] Cmnd 5104, 1972, para 17.
[112] Official Secrets Act 1911, s 8.
[113] Cmnd 5104, 1972, para 18.
[114] Eg Cmnd 4089, 1969, p 11; Cmnd 5104, 1972, ch 5.
[115] Eg in the cases of *Bettaney* and the Cyprus intelligence personnel, above.

employed in s 2 cases,[116] is an important departure from the general rule of 'the English system of administering justice' that 'it be done in public'.[117] For if 'the way the courts behave cannot be hidden from the public ear and eye this provides a safeguard against judicial arbitrariness or idiosyncrasy and maintains the public confidence in the administration of justice'.[118] Even if a prosecution is held behind closed doors, the accused and his or her lawyer may not be excluded and sentence must be delivered in open court.[119] Section 6 of the 1920 Act effectively removes a suspect's right of silence in a case brought under s 1 of the 1911 Act by providing that a Secretary of State may authorise the police to call a prospective witness for questioning about a s 1 offence, and in this event refusal to attend or to give information constitutes an offence.[120] Moreover, s 9 of the 1911 Act confers wide powers of search and seizure, authorising a magistrate to grant a search warrant permitting the police to enter and search premises 'and every person found therein', and to seize anything which is evidence of an offence under the Act 'having been or being about to be committed'. In cases of 'great emergency' where in the interests of the state immediate action is necessary, written authority for such a search may be granted by a superintendent of police.

In January 1987 it was reported that the BBC had decided not to broadcast a programme about the Zircon spy satellite in the interests of national security. In so doing the Corporation denied that there had been any government pressure. Two days later, an injunction was obtained by the Attorney-General restraining the journalist responsible for the programme, Duncan Campbell, from talking or writing about the contents of the film. He could not be found, however, to be served with the injunction whereupon the *New Statesman* published details about the contents of the film. This was followed by a Special Branch raid of the *New Statesman*'s offices, and subsequently of the BBC's premises in Glasgow. The latter raid – which lasted for 28 hours – was conducted under the authority of a warrant granted under s 9 of the 1911 Act.[121] The police filled several police vans with documents, discarded film clips and over 200 containers of film. It was never entirely clear what the police were looking for, and no prosecutions followed. The episode illustrates the extent to which the 1911 Act may be used oppressively even without a prosecution taking place.[122]

The Official Secrets Act 1989

The operation of the Official Secrets Act 1911, s 2, was examined closely by a committee chaired by Lord Franks which reported in 1972.[123] The committee had been appointed after an unsuccessful prosecution of the *Sunday Telegraph* for publishing Foreign Office documents relating to the Labour govern-

---

116   Eg in the *Ponting* case; see below.
117   *A-G v Leveller Magazine Ltd* [1979] AC 440, at 449–50.
118   Ibid, at 450.
119   Official Secrets Act 1920, s 8(2).
120   Before the Official Secrets Act 1939 amended the 1920 Act, s 6, refusal on demand by a police inspector to disclose the source of information obtained in breach of the Acts was itself an offence (*Lewis v Cattle* [1938] 2 KB 454).
121   The warrant was arguably unlawful, having been issued by a sheriff, not by a justice of the peace: R Black (1987) J of the Law Society of Scotland 138.
122   For fuller details, see Ewing and Gearty, *Freedom under Thatcher*, pp 147–52. See also A W Bradley [1987] PL 1, 488.
123   Cmnd 5104, 1972.

ment's policy towards the Nigerian civil war.[124] The committee reported that the present law was unsatisfactory and that there should be a new Official Information Act, to protect only certain forms of information, namely:

(*a*) classified information relating to defence or internal security, or to foreign relations, or to the currency or to the reserves, the unauthorised disclosure of which would cause serious injury to the interests of the nation;
(*b*) information likely to assist criminal activities or to impede law enforcement;
(*c*) Cabinet documents (in the interests of collective responsibility);[125]
(*d*) information which has been entrusted to the government by a private individual or concern (for example, for tax or social security purposes or in a census).

The requirement that information of the kind specified in (*a*) must be classified would make necessary a new system of classifying documents which, unlike the existing system, would have legal consequences. Offences under the new Act were proposed to include the communication by a Crown servant, contrary to his or her official duty, of information subject to the Act; the communication by any person of information of the kinds set out in (*a*), (*b*), and (*c*) which he or she reasonably believes has reached him or her as a result of a breach of the Act; and the use of official information of any kind for purposes of private gain.

The Franks committee therefore recommended that protection of official information by criminal sanctions should continue only where the public interest clearly required this. But no reform of the Official Secrets Acts was forthcoming, although other weaknesses in the law became evident during the so-called ABC trial in 1978.[126] In 1979, the Conservative government introduced not a Freedom of Information Bill but a Protection of Official Information Bill. This sought to give absolute protection to information regarding security and intelligence, regardless of whether that information was already available to the public.[127] But the Bill was abandoned by the government because of the severe political reaction to the disclosure that Anthony Blunt had been a Russian spy, a disclosure which could have been criminal if the Bill had been enacted. Pressure for reform was maintained in the 1980s, with interest fuelled by some controversial prosecutions. These included the cases of Sarah Tisdall, a Foreign Office clerk, who leaked to the *Guardian* a secret document relating to the delivery of cruise missiles to Greenham Common;[128] and Clive Ponting, a senior official in the Ministry of Defence, who leaked to an MP documents relating to the sinking of the Argentine vessel, the *General Belgrano*, during the Falklands war.[129] Tisdall was

---

[124]   See Aitken, *Officially Secret.*
[125]   Cf ch 13 B.
[126]   A Nicol [1979] Crim LR 284.
[127]   HL Deb, 5 November 1979, col 612; cf Cmnd 7285, 1978, para 31.
[128]   For the circumstances, see *Secretary of State for Defence v Guardian Newspapers Ltd* [1985] AC 339.
[129]   See Ponting, *The Right to Know: The Inside Story of the Belgrano Affair.* Also R Thomas [1986] Crim LR 318.

convicted and Ponting was found not guilty, a verdict which ran counter to McCowan J's direction to the jury.[130]

The pressure for reform culminated in the Official Secrets Act 1989, which many would argue does not go far enough.[131] While repealing s 2 of the 1911 Act, the 1989 Act introduced new restrictions on the unauthorised disclosure of an admittedly narrower range of information. One category of information protected from disclosure relates to security and intelligence in that s 1 of the Act distinguishes between disclosures without lawful authority by security and intelligence staff on the one hand, and civil servants and government contractors on the other.[132] So far as the former are concerned, it is an offence for any such person to disclose any information obtained in the course of employment in the Service; in the case of the latter, the unauthorised disclosure is unlawful only if 'damaging' to the work of the security and intelligence services. Sections 2 and 3 make it an offence for a civil servant or government contractor, without lawful authority, to disclose any information relating to defence or international affairs if the disclosure is damaging. In the case of defence, disclosure is defined as being damaging if it damages the capability of the armed forces to carry out their tasks, while in both cases disclosure is damaging if it endangers the interests of the United Kingdom abroad or endangers the safety of British citizens abroad (s 2(2)). It is an offence by s 4 for a civil servant or a government contractor to disclose without lawful authority any information if this results in the commission of an offence, facilitates an escape from legal custody, or impedes the prevention or detection of offences or the apprehension or prosecution of suspects. Section 4 further provides that it is an offence to disclose information 'relating to the obtaining of information' (as well as any information obtained) as a result of warrants issued under the Interception of Communications Act 1985 (phone tapping), the Security Services Act 1989 (interference with private property), or the Intelligence Services Act 1994 (interference with property or unlawful acts done outside the UK). It is thus not an offence under s 4 to disclose information obtained unlawfully without a warrant, though it might be an offence under s 1.

The offences under the Act are committed only where disclosure is made without lawful authority. This corresponds with the former s 2 of the 1911 Act, whereby the offence was committed only if the disclosure was unauthorised. The question of when a Crown servant was authorised to disclose information is, as we have seen, one which gave rise to considerable difficulty, particularly in the case of Cabinet ministers and senior officials.[133] By s 7 of the 1989 Act, a disclosure is authorised if it is made in accordance with the official duty of the minister or civil servant concerned. An offence may be committed not only by the official disclosing the information, but also by a third party, such as a newspaper, which reports it. Although it is no longer an offence to receive

---

[130]   *R v Ponting* [1985] Crim LR 318.
[131]   For background, see Cm 408, 1988. For analyses, see S Palmer [1990] PL 243; Birkinshaw, *Reforming the Secret State*.
[132]   See s 12 on the scope of the Act. See also SI 1990 No 200, and SI 1993 No 847.
[133]   See Cmnd 5104, 1972, para 18. See also Bailey, Harris and Jones, *Civil Liberties: Cases and Materials*, who contrast the prosecution of Tisdall and Ponting with the failure to prosecute two Cabinet ministers (p 464).

information protected against disclosure (as it was under s 2 of the 1911 Act), it is an offence for the recipient to disclose the information without lawful authority knowing or having reasonable cause to believe that it is protected from disclosure (s 5). In effect, it is an offence for a newspaper to publish protected information which has been leaked without authority. Controversially, there is no public interest defence available in this or indeed in other cases, the government having rejected such a measure.[134] However, in these circumstances, a newspaper is liable only if the disclosure is damaging and is made knowing or having reasonable cause to believe that it is damaging. There was no proposal to introduce such a defence or otherwise amend the 1989 Act in the government's white paper on Open Government.[135]

Defence advisory notices

The Official Secrets Acts impose important restrictions on press freedom in the sense that they effectively control the information which might be made available. And as we saw in chapter 22 E, the action in equity for breach of confidence has the capacity to do much the same. Indeed, it was this which formed the basis for controlling the press during the so-called Spycatcher affair in 1987. But there are other restrictions and fetters on press freedom which have been introduced in the interests of national security. One of these is the system of 'DA' notices (known previously as 'D' notices')[136] a form of extra-legal censorship in which the press cooperates with the government. A DA notice is a means of providing advice and guidance to the media about defence and counter-terrorist information the publication of which would be damaging to national security. DA notices are issued by the Defence, Press and Broadcasting Advisory Committee (DPBAC), an advisory body composed of senior civil servants and editors from national and regional newspapers, periodicals, news agencies, television and radio. The committee is chaired by the Permanent Under-Secretary of State for Defence and although membership may be varied by agreement, in 1996 there were three members representing government departments (Home Office, Ministry of Defence, and Foreign Office), and 13 members nominated by the media (only the Publishers Association declined to nominate a representative). The committee normally meets twice a year to review the contents of existing notices and the advice and guidance given by its Secretary over the course of the year.

The system was overhauled in 1993 (following a review by the committee itself)[137] in the light of international changes (in particular the break-up of the Soviet Union and Warsaw Pact) and the increased emphasis on openness in government. As a result the number of standing notices was reduced from 8 to 6 (though it is possible that it may be found necessary to issue a DA notice on a particular subject), and their content and style revised to make them

---

[134]   Cm 408, 1988.
[135]   Cm 2290, 1993. See ch 13 E above.
[136]   D Fairley (1990) 10 OJLS 430; Williams, *Not in the Public Interest*, ch 4.
[137]   For an earlier parliamentary review, see HC 773 (1979–80); J Jaconelli [1982] PL 37.

'more relevant and user-friendly'. It was as a result of this review that the name of the notices was changed from D to DA notices and that of the committee to Defence, Press and Broadcasting Advisory Committee, 'better to reflect the voluntary and advisory nature of the system'.[138] The six standing notices are now published, and deal in the case of DA notice 1 with highly classified military information dealing with future operations, the state of readiness and operational capability of individual units, and counter-terrorist measures. DA notice 2 deals with highly classified information about defence equipment and equipment used to counter terrorist threats, while DA notice 3 deals with highly classified information about nuclear weapon installations. DA notice 4 applies to highly classified government codes and ciphers and related communications facilities, DA notice 5 with details, illustrations or photographs or illustrations of headquarters sites for use of government in time of crisis, and DA notice 6 deals with information about the security and intelligence services. This applies particularly to the 'specific operations, sources and methods, the identities, whereabouts and tasks of staff employed by these services or engaged on such work', and the addresses and telephone numbers used by these services, 'other than those which have been the subject of an official announcement'.[139]

The secretary of the committee plays a key role in advising the media on the interpretation of notices. He is normally a retired two-star general from the armed forces, employed as a civil servant on the budget of the Ministry of Defence. According to the Ministry of Defence review, the secretary 'is available at all times to Government departments and the media to give advice on the system, taking into account the general guidance given to him by the Committee'. It is a problem that DA notices are inevitably drafted in general terms, though it is 'the application of a DA notice to a particular set of circumstances on which the secretary is expected to give guidance, consulting as necessary with appropriate departmental officials'. The Ministry of Defence takes the opportunity to point out that the secretary is not 'invested with the authority to give rulings nor to advise on considerations other than national security', and on the other hand that 'compliance with the DA notice system does not relieve the editor of responsibilities under the Official Secrets Acts'; nor indeed will it necessarily prevent legal proceedings being brought to restrain any publication or broadcast.[140] The importance of the secretary's role was shown in 1967 when the *Daily Express* published a report that copies of private cables and telegrams sent overseas from the United Kingdom were regularly made available to the security authorities, a practice authorised by the Official Secrets Act 1920, s 4. The Prime Minister, Mr Wilson, claimed that this article was a breach of a 'D' notice. An investigation by three Privy Councillors established that this was not the case but that there had been misunderstandings to which the secretary of the committee had contrib-

---

[138]   HC Deb, 23 July 1993, col 454 (WA).
[139]   The DA notices are reproduced in *The Defence Advisory Notices. A Review of the D Notice System* (Ministry of Defence Open Government Document No 93/06), from which much of the foregoing is drawn.
[140]   See *A-G v BBC*, *The Times*, 18 December 1987 regarding the broadcast by the BBC of a radio series ('My Country Right or Wrong') about the Security Service.

uted.[141] The Defence Committee of the House of Commons reviewed the 'D' notice system in 1980, and concluded (with reservations) that 'D' notices should be maintained, despite sharp divisions within the press about the value of the scheme which, judged in legal terms, is manifestly imperfect and imprecise.[142]

Interception of communications

In 1957, controversy arose over the practice of telephone tapping when it was revealed that the Home Secretary had disclosed to the chairman of the Bar Council information obtained by police tapping of telephones in the course of investigations relating to the association of a barrister (Marrinan) with a known criminal (Billy Hill). A committee of Privy Councillors, the Birkett committee, was appointed to inquire into the powers and practice of the executive in intercepting communications.[143] The committee's conclusions on the law were accepted as the basis for official practice thereafter, but growing disquiet about telephone tapping led in 1979 to a judicial ruling on the matter and to subsequent proceedings under the European Convention on Human Rights.

1 The Birkett committee. The Crown's monopoly of the postal service derives from the prerogative, but for many years a series of Post Office Acts has regulated the service. As far back as 1663, a royal proclamation forbade the opening of any letters or packets except with the direct warrant of the Secretary of State. Since at least that date, the Secretary of State (now the Home Secretary) has from time to time authorised the interception of letters. The Birkett committee reported that at no time had it been suggested with any authority that the exercise of the power to intercept postal packets was unlawful, the power being used mainly to assist in the detection of certain crimes and the serious evasion of customs duty. It was exceptionally used on the request of the Security Service where there was a major subversive or espionage activity that was likely to injure the national interest and the material likely to be obtained by interception would be of direct use in providing necessary information for the Security Service. Warrants were issued on the personal authority of the Home Secretary and were subject to regular review.

As regards telephone tapping, the Birkett committee's verdict was unpersuasive. The committee found that messages had been intercepted by the Post Office as controllers of the telephone service ever since the introduction of the telephone. Before 1937, the Post Office had acted on the view that the practice was not contrary to law and did not require the authority of the Secretary of State. In 1937, the Home Office expressed the opinion that power to authorise the interception of letters and telegrams by warrant of a Secretary of State was wide enough to include the interception of telephone

---

141 Cmnd 3309 and 3312, 1967; Hedley and Aynsley, *The D-notice Affair.* In 1967, Prime Minister Wilson rejected the finding that no breach of a 'D' notice had occurred but he later admitted that his handling of the affair was wrong: *The Labour Government 1964–70*, pp 478–82, 530–4.

142 HC 773 (1979–80); J Jaconelli [1982] PL 37.

143 Cmnd 283, 1957.

messages. After 1937, telephones were tapped only when expressly authorised by warrant of the Home Secretary, by analogy with the interception of mail. But the legal basis of telephone tapping remained obscure: was the power derived from the application of Crown prerogative to a new technology, or had the power been obliquely recognised by statute?[144] The Birkett report in 1957 reached a feeble conclusion: 'it is difficult to resist the view that if there is a lawful power to intercept communications in the form of letters and telegrams, then it is wide enough to cover telephone communications as well'.[145]

2 The 1985 Act. It was only in 1979 that the law on telephone tapping was reviewed by a court.

Malone, a London antique dealer who had been accused of handling stolen goods, sued the police for a declaration that the police acted unlawfully in tapping his telephone on the authority of a warrant from the Home Secretary. Malone claimed that the tapping had infringed his rights of property, privacy and confidentiality and also the right to respect 'for his private and family life, his home and his correspondence' (European Convention on Human Rights, art 8). Megarry V-C dismissed the action, holding that Malone's rights under common law had not been infringed; there was in English law no right of privacy and no user of a telephone could assume that his conversations were confidential. Tapping by the Post Office could be carried out for the police without any breach of the law, and no statutory or common law power was required to justify it. Malone could not rely on the European Convention on Human Rights since, as it had not been given domestic effect by legislation, the Convention was not justiciable in English courts. However, the judge examined a decision of the European Court of Human Rights on telephone tapping in Germany,[146] and concluded that telephone tapping 'is a subject which cries out for legislation'.[147]

Malone subsequently took his complaint to Strasbourg, alleging that the practice of telephone tapping in Britain violated art 8 of the European Convention on Human Rights. Article 8(2) of the Convention appears to leave some scope for the practice of interception, by providing that restrictions on the right to privacy can be imposed, where these are in accordance with law, and necessary in a democratic society on a number of grounds which include national security and the detection of crime. In the *Malone* case, the European Court of Human Rights held that telephone tapping violated the privacy rights in art 8(1), and that the British arrangements could not be justified under art 8(2). This latter decision was taken on the narrow ground that the administrative procedures for Home Office warrants were not in 'accordance with law', because it was not sufficiently clear to members of the public in what circumstances their telephones were liable to be tapped.[148] The court did not comment on the substance of the procedures,[149] but in effect

---

[144] See *A-G v Edison Telephone Co* (1880) 6 QBD 244.

[145] Cmd 283, 1957, p 15.

[146] *Klass v Federal Republic of Germany* (1978) 2 EHRR 214.

[147] *Malone v Metropolitan Police Commissioner* [1979] Ch 344; C P Walker [1980] PL 184, V Bevan [1980] PL 431.

[148] *Malone v UK* (1985) 7 EHRR 14.

[149] In *Klass v Federal Republic of Germany* (above) the European Court had previously rejected a complaint that the German law in substance violated the Convention.

merely invited the British government to introduce legislation to give them statutory force. This is largely what has happened, with the Interception of Communications Act 1985 making lawful the existing arrangements, with a few important modifications intended to safeguard the individual from abuse of the procedures.

The passing of the Act was all the more timely in view of allegations made by a retired MI5 officer concerning the misuse of interception, and in particular its use to acquire information from trade unionists and peace campaigners for political reasons unrelated to national security.[150] It remains to be seen whether the 1985 Act will stop possible abuses of this kind in the future, though it does promise much by providing that it is an offence to intercept a communication system (whether transmitted by post or by means of a public telecommunication system) with conviction on indictment leading to the possibility of a two-year prison sentence and/or a fine (s 1). However, no offence is committed where the interception is carried out under the authority of a warrant issued by a Secretary of State; in England and Wales this will usually be the Home Secretary and in Scotland the Secretary of State for Scotland (s 2). A warrant may be issued where the appropriate minister considers that it is necessary in the interests of national security; for preventing or detecting serious crime; or for safeguarding the economic well-being of the United Kingdom (s 2(2)). The term national security is not defined in the Act, and the government refused to accept an opposition amendment which would have restricted the power to issue warrants on national security grounds to reasons connected with subversion, terrorism, or espionage. According to the government, there is more to national security than this. Indeed, warrants have been issued under the Act for unspecified reasons of national security, but unrelated to subversion, terrorism or espionage.

3 Safeguards against abuse. Although wide powers of interception are provided in the 1985 Act, they are accompanied by safeguards. One is the creation of a tribunal appointed by the Prime Minister to which complaints may be made by people who believe that their communications have been intercepted (s 7). But the tribunal has very limited powers: it may investigate cases only where a warrant has been issued to establish whether the grounds and procedures for the issuing of such warrants have been followed. The 1985 Act also established the office of Commissioner, a senior judicial figure appointed by the Prime Minister to keep under review the carrying out by ministers of their functions under the Act and to give the tribunal all the assistance which it may require (s 8). This effectively continues arrangements which began in 1980 with the appointment of Lord Diplock to monitor the procedures for interception of communications carried out by the police, the Customs and Excise and the Security Service. The present Commissioner must make an annual report to the Prime Minister, who must then lay a copy of it before each House of Parliament, though parts of it may be withheld. There is, however, little scope for judicial review of the procedure. Despite its

---

[150] See *R v Home Secretary, ex p Ruddock* [1987] 2 All ER 518. Also Ewing and Gearty, *Freedom under Thatcher*, p 54.

shortcomings the procedures established under the 1985 Act have been found by the European Commission of Human Rights to meet the requirements of the Convention.[151]

The first Commissioner under the Act was Lord Justice Lloyd, to be succeeded in 1992 by Sir Thomas Bingham, who was succeeded in turn by Lord Nolan. The reports generally express satisfaction with the operation of the procedures under the 1985 Act, though in doing so they shed some light on the nature and scale of the operation. It appears that there are now very few warrants in force relating to counter-subversion: indeed in 1993 there were 'no warrants currently in force against individual subversives on the ground that they represent a threat to parliamentary democracy and so to national security', while only 'a very few organisations are currently the subject of interception on that ground'.[152] Yet there has been a remarkable increase in the number of warrants issued, from a total of 519 to the Home Secretary and the Secretary of State for Scotland in 1988 to 1,135 in 1995 (with a steady increase in between).[153] No figures are given for the warrants issued by the Foreign Secretary or the Secretary of State for Northern Ireland, though it is said that while the numbers have declined in the former case (but from what to what?), in the latter case they have 'increased substantially', though the Commissioner found no instance where the issue of a warrant had not been fully justified.[154] One reason for the increase in the number of Home Office and Scottish Office warrants is the revocation in 1992 of the quota system which had been in operation for many years whereby a restriction was imposed on the number of warrants issued to the Customs and Excise on the one hand and the police on the other. The quota system was considered by the Commissioner (Sir Thomas Bingham) who questioned whether 'the Secretary of State should circumscribe his discretion to authorise the issue of warrants by reference to an arithmetical norm'. In his view there was 'much to be said for dealing with applications ... very strictly on their merits and without reference to numerical constraints beyond those necessarily imposed by the existence of limited facilities'.[155]

4 The role of the courts. Although the Commissioner is thus a senior judge, there is little role for the courts in the operation of the Act. Both the tribunal and the Commissioner are protected by a statutory provision which precludes judicial review of their decisions, including decisions as to jurisdiction (s 7). Moreover, no evidence may be adduced in legal proceedings which tends to suggest that a warrant has been issued under the Act or that an offence has been committed by a servant of the Crown, a Post Office employee or a public telecommunications operator (s 9). This is designed to prevent 'the asking of questions suggesting that a warrant to intercept material has been or is to be issued',[156] and the combined effect of the 'impenetrable' s 9 and s 6 is that

---

[151]   Cm 2828, 1995, para 5.
[152]   Cm 2522, 1994.
[153]   Cm 3254, 1996.
[154]   Cm 2522, 1994.
[155]   Cm 2173, 1993, paras 14–16.
[156]   *R v Preston* [1994] 2 AC 130, at p 144 (Lord Jauncey).

'neither the existence of a telephone intercept under warrant nor the result thereof are to be disclosed in evidence'. As such the position compares with evidence obtained from listening devices under the 1994 Act: 'information obtained by the secret intelligence service or the security service through the use of listening devices may be disclosed, not only for the purpose of preventing or detecting serious crime, but also for the purpose of criminal proceedings'.[157] It also compares with the position with regard to the use of surveillance equipment by the police which has been held by the House of Lords to be admissible in criminal proceedings, even though there was at the time no statutory authorisation for the practice and even though the police may have acted unlawfully in planting the listening devices.[158] It is not surprising that calls have been made in some quarters for the repeal of s 9 of the Interception of Communications Act 1985.

As it stands, s 9 could normally be expected to benefit the defence for it could be expected that if telephone intercepts 'revealed anything material it would favour a conviction, so that counsel for the Crown would argue for, and counsel for the defendant against, the retention of the material and its deployment at the trial'.[159] In *R v Effik*,[160] however, the House of Lords held that the contents of material from a cordless telephone were admissible on the ground that this particular technology was not covered by the Act which applies only to public telecommunications systems. This was deemed to be a private system, even though the 'apparatus consists of a base unit which is connected to the mains electricity and also, by means of a wire and jack, to a telephone socket within the house'. On the other hand, in the leading case of *R v Preston*[161] it was held by the House of Lords that the accused were not entitled to be supplied with details of telephone interceptions to help rebut a prosecution submission of conspiracy based on the number of telephone calls made by defendants. Although it was accepted in a strong speech by Lord Mustill that the evidence was relevant (even though perhaps inadmissible) and in principle should therefore have been disclosed, it was also accepted that the object of the Act (which did not include the securing of material for the prosecution as opposed to the prevention and detection of crime) was to promote the early destruction of intercepted material.[162]

The Security Commission[163]

An initiative taken in 1964 as a result of the Profumo affair is designed to respond to breaches of security as they arise. The creation of the Security Commission was announced by the Prime Minister, Sir Alec Douglas-Home, on 23 January 1964 with the following terms of reference:

---

157 *R v Khan* [1996] 3 All ER 289, at p 296 (Lord Nolan).
158 *R v Khan*, above. See now Police Act 1997, Part III.
159 *R v Preston*, above, at p 165 (Lord Mustill).
160 [1995] 1 AC 309. See also *R v Governor of Belmarsh Prison, ex p Martin* [1995] 2 All ER 548.
161 Above, n 156.
162 Consider now Criminal Procedure and Investigations Act 1996, part I (duty of prosecutor to disclose 'any prosecution material which has not previously been disclosed to the accused' (s 3(1)(a)).
163 For a full account, see Lustgarten and Leigh, above, pp 476–92.

If so requested by the Prime Minister, to investigate and report upon the circumstances in which a breach of security is known to have occurred in the public service, and upon any related failure of departmental security arrangements or neglect of duty; and, in the light of any such investigation, to advise whether any change in security arrangements is desirable.

The Prime Minister also stated that before asking the Security Commission to investigate a particular case, he would consult the Leader of the Opposition.[164] Normally the Commission sits in private and it is left to the Commission to determine whether legal representation of witnesses is necessary for the protection of their interests. The chairman of the Security Commission is a judge and it may also include retired members of the civil service, the armed forces and the diplomatic service. Recent chairmen have included Lord Diplock, Lord Bridge, Lord Griffiths and Lord Lloyd.[165]

The Commission may be called upon to investigate in a wide range of circumstances. So, for example, after two ministers (Earl Jellicoe and Lord Lambton) resigned in 1973 because of sexual impropriety, the Commission considered whether security had been endangered by their conduct.[166] In 1982, the Commission completed a full review of security procedures in the civil service[167] and in 1983 it reported on the security implications of the conviction for spying of Geoffrey Prime, a member of staff at GCHQ.[168] Since then it has reported on the security implications of the conviction under s 1 of the Official Secrets Act 1911 of Michael Bettaney, a member of the Security Services;[169] on security in signals intelligence following the (unsuccessful) prosecution of the 'Cyprus 8';[170] and the security implications of the case of Michael Smith, also convicted (in 1993) under s 1 of the 1911 Act.[171] The last mentioned report gives a remarkable and disarmingly frank assessment of the work of the Security Service, it being reported that 'Michael John Smith first came to the notice of the Security Service in November 1971 when a Michael Smith living in Birmingham applied to join the Communist Party of Great Britain (CPGB). Efforts were made at that stage by the Security Service and the police, at the former's request, to identify Smith but without result.' The Security Commission 'is not an oversight body, an inspectorate, nor an appeal tribunal. It does not sit continuously, is not pro-active, has no links with any department or ministry, and has no adjudicative function'. On the other hand, it 'may venture on any terrain where security may be said to be involved' and it may go wherever the Prime Minister directs.[172] But it is no substitute for effective parliamentary oversight of the security and intelligence services.

---

[164]   HC Deb, 23 January 1964, cols 1271–5. The terms of reference were subsequently modified. The chairman of the Commission's view is also considered before any matter is referred to it.
[165]   For details of composition and procedure, see Lustgarten and Leigh, op cit, pp 476–87.
[166]   Cmnd 5367, 1973.
[167]   Cmnd 8540, 1982.
[168]   Cmnd 8876, 1983.
[169]   Cmnd 9514, 1985.
[170]   Cmnd 9923, 1986.
[171]   Cm 2930, 1995.
[172]   Lustgarten and Leigh, op cit, p 477.

Parliamentary scrutiny

1 The Home Affairs Committee. Since 1979, the Defence Committee of the House of Commons has reviewed aspects of state security, but parliamentary committees have been advised by the government not to inquire into the Security Service.[173] In 1989, the government rejected proposals for parliamentary scrutiny of the Security Service by specially created select committees.[174] In 1992, the Home Affairs Committee invited the Director-General of the Security Service to appear before them, possibly in private. In a series of remarkable exchanges, the invitation was declined after consultation with the Home Secretary, who later said that he would consider whether the committee might meet her informally, 'perhaps over lunch'. This stance was adopted following the convention 'under which information on matters of security and intelligence is not placed before Parliament' which the Home Secretary regarded 'as binding in relation to Departmental Select Committees no less than in relation to Parliament itself'. In his view the Security Service was not to be regarded as falling within the ambit of any select committee, though this need not 'prevent the Director-General from having a meeting with [the Chairman of the Committee] and one or two senior members on an informal basis to discuss the work of the Security service in general terms providing that the Government's position is understood'. Mrs Rimington (the then Director-General) was said to share this view and would 'accordingly be in touch with [the Chairman] to invite [him] and a couple of [his] senior colleagues to lunch'. As the committee said, however, an informal lunch with Mrs Rimington (who was 'permitted to lunch with the press'), 'while a welcome move towards openness', was 'no substitute for formal parliamentary scrutiny of the Security Service'.

The Home Affairs Committee was of the view that the Service fell within its terms of reference and that 'the value-for-money of the security service and its general policy are proper subjects for parliamentary scrutiny as long as such scrutiny does not damage the effectiveness of the Service'. The committee then reviewed the various options for enhanced accountability of the Service by means of parliamentary scrutiny which in its view would meet 'an important public interest and help to protect against any possible future abuse of power'.[175] For its part, however, the government responded by saying that in 1989 Parliament had considered very carefully the question of oversight.[176] It had concluded in favour of preserving the existing approach to accountability, by which the Director-General of the Security Service is responsible to the Home Secretary of the day, who is himself accountable to Parliament for the work of the Security Service. (It is, however, a strange kind of accountability which labours under a convention which prevents matters relating to security and intelligence from being placed before Parliament.) The government also referred to the procedures for judicial oversight of the Service by means of a Commissioner and a tribunal under the Security Service Act 1989. In the government's view this system had worked well in the three

---

[173]   See HC 773 (1979–80); HC 242 (1982–83); HC Deb, 12 May 1983, col 444 (WA).
[174]   See HC Deb, 16 January 1989, col 36.
[175]   HC 265 (1992–93).
[176]   Cm 2197, 1993.

and a half years since the 1989 Act had come into force, though again it is a strange kind of oversight which examines only the exercise of specific statutory powers rather than the work of the Service as a whole, and more importantly which has no base in Parliament itself. The government accepted that the position should be examined afresh, and an opportunity to do so was in fact provided by the Intelligence Services Act 1994 where important concessions in the direction of democratic accountability were made, though it is open to question whether they go far enough.

2 *The Intelligence and Security Committee.*[177]   The 1994 Act introduced an 'entirely new form of oversight of all three security and intelligence agencies' in the form of a committee of parliamentarians, though not a parliamentary committee. It is not altogether clear why the government relented even to this extent and why as a result the 'ring of secrecy' has been extended, though it is to be noted that the committee has no powers in relation to operational matters. Under the Act the committee is charged with the responsibility of examining 'the expenditure, administration and policy' of the Security Service, the Intelligence Service and GCHQ (s 10(1)). It consists of nine members drawn from both the House of Commons and the House of Lords (though none may be a minister of the Crown), and is appointed by the Prime Minister after consulting the Leader of the Opposition. In 1996 the committee was chaired by a former member of Mrs Thatcher's and Mr Major's Cabinet, and included among its other eight members one member of the House of Lords (the former Foreign Secretary, Lord Howe), five Conservative MPs (three of whom were former ministers in defence departments), and one Labour and one Liberal MP. Under the Act the committee is required to make an annual report on the discharge of its functions to the Prime Minister, which must then be laid before Parliament, though parts of the report may be held back, after consultation with the committee, if it appears to the Prime Minister that the publication of any matter would be prejudicial to any of the agencies.

In its first report the committee commented that because of the nature of its work 'it must have access to national security information', with the result that committee members 'have all been notified under the Official Secrets Act 1989'. The constitutional position was that the committee was 'now operating within the "ring of secrecy"', reporting directly to the Prime Minister on its work, and through him to Parliament. But because 'the necessary security' must be observed in its work, there could be no 'regular reporting' of its procedures. The committee pointed out that it had been briefed on the work of the different agencies, and that it had taken evidence from senior Whitehall officials, including those in 'two key "customer" departments for intelligence, the Foreign Office and the Department of Trade and Industry'. An important priority was to address how the agencies had adapted to 'the new situations in the post-Cold War' era, and in particular 'how tasks and the priorities attached to them have altered, and whether the resources now provided are appropriate to those tasks and used in a cost

---

effective way'.[178] In its second report, the committee examined the government's proposal to bring the Security Service into the fight against organised crime, and concluded that the Service could 'bring a distinct package of skills to this arena', but that a number of issues needed to be resolved, these relating to 'the tasking (sic), command, integration and accountability of the Service, particularly where its work extends into the operational field'. More specifically, it was concluded that if the Service was to be given a new role in countering 'conventional' criminal activity 'the legislation needs to make very clear that it will be working *in support* of the law enforcement organisations'. It was also pointed out, usefully, that accountability issues would need to be resolved as would 'the differing systems under which authorisation is given for the interception of communications and for the entry on, or interference with, property'.[179]

These points were repeated in the committee's first annual report, though as we have seen the functions of the Security Service were extended by the Security Service Act 1996. Nevertheless the value of the committee was revealed when it expressed concern in its second annual report that ministers were not always 'fully and promptly briefed on relevant intelligence and security issues'. Three other points of interest emerged from the report, the first being that there had been significant shifts in the response of the SIS in the light of the break-up of the Soviet Union, having reduced by about two-thirds its operational efforts on Russia and other former Soviet Union states. By the same token, the Security Service had reduced its effort on the intelligence threat posed by the former Warsaw Pact states, and although Russian espionage was on the increase, it intended to deploy about half of its operational resources against 'Irish terrorism'. Secondly, it was anticipated that the Security Service could make a serious contribution to the work against serious organised crime, though in addition to repeating concerns expressed in the interim report, the committee expressed concern about the fact that surveillance by the Service involving interference with property required a warrant whereas the police acted only on the authority of Home Office guidelines.[180] In the view of the committee there would be 'clear problems if these different systems are being operated side by side'. And thirdly, reference was made to the 'less traditional' areas of activity carried out by the agencies, including that relating to the interests of the economic well-being of the UK. According to the committee this 'whole area is one where there is a need for clear policy guidance on the practical uses to which intelligence may be put'.[181]

---

[178] Interim report of the Intelligence and Security Committee (Cm 2873, 1995).
[179] Intelligence and Security Committee: Report on Security Service work against organised crime (Cm 3065, 1995).
[180] See now Police Act 1997, Part III.
[181] Cm 3198, 1996.

CHAPTER 25

Emergency powers

In times of grave national emergency, normal constitutional principles may have to give way to the overriding need to deal with the emergency. In Lord Pearce's words, 'the flame of individual right and justice must burn more palely when it is ringed by the more dramatic light of bombed buildings'.[1] The European Convention on Human Rights, art 15, permits a member state to take measures derogating from its obligations under the Convention 'in time of war or other public emergency threatening the life of the nation'. The UK government has exercised the right of derogation in respect of events in Northern Ireland. But even under such circumstances no derogation is permitted from art 2 (which protects the right to life) except in the case of deaths resulting from lawful acts of war, art 3 (which prohibits the use of torture), art 4(1) (which prohibits slavery) and art 7 (which bars retrospective criminal laws). Thus even in grave emergencies there are limits beyond which a state may not go, and it is open to question whether and how far 'the desirability of an effective remedy for judicial review must yield to the higher interests of the State'.[2] This chapter examines the role of the armed forces and the use of statutory emergency powers during war and peace, and includes an account of recent anti-terrorist legislation. Emphasis will be both on the increased powers of the state in emergencies and on the continuing limits on state action.

A. Use of the troops in assisting the police

In chapter 23 we examined the main powers available to the police in maintaining public order. In the 20th century in Great Britain, the police, with greater or less difficulty depending on the circumstances, have been able to control and contain public protest. For most of the century (with the notable exception of the period of strikes in South Wales in 1911), the armed forces have not been used to suppress unrest,[3] although they have been

---

[1] *Conway v Rimmer* [1968] AC 910, 982.

[2] *R v Home Secretary, ex p Adams* [1995] All ER (EC) 177, at p 185 (Steyn LJ). See *R v Home Secretary, ex p Cheblak* [1991] 2 All ER 319 where judicial review yielded rather too easily. Compare the thoughtful discussion of this issue by Sedley J in *R v Home Secretary, ex p McQuillan* [1995] 4 All ER 400, at pp 420–1.

[3] See Williams, *Keeping the Peace*, pp 32–5.

required to maintain essential services during strikes and on occasion to deal with extreme terrorist action (for example, the occupation of the Iranian embassy in London in May 1980). But in the 19th century and earlier, when there was less political freedom and police forces were weaker, the local magistrates were expected to call in detachments of soldiers to restore order when necessary. Today in Great Britain, conditions would indeed have the character of an emergency if it became necessary to call on the armed forces for this purpose.

As the events of the miners' strike of 1984/85 emphasised, it is increasingly unlikely that the military will be called upon to maintain order. Despite large-scale public disturbances, national coordination of policing together with new training and operational methods meant that it was unnecessary to deploy the army.[4] A decision to call in the troops to restore order was, in the past at least, a decision enabling firearms to be used to repress the disturbances. This use of the troops may be illustrated by a rather late example, the Featherstone riots in 1893.[5] When the police were engaged elsewhere, a small detachment of soldiers was summoned to protect a colliery against a riotous crowd which broke windows and set buildings on fire. As darkness was falling, a magistrate called on the crowd to disperse and he read the proclamation from the Riot Act. When the crowd did not disperse, the magistrate authorised the soldiers to fire and their officer decided that the only way to protect the colliery was to fire on the crowd. Two members of the crowd were killed. A committee of inquiry held that the action of the troops was justified in law.

When troops are thus used, what is the basis of their authority? Whatever may be the rules today that govern the decision that the armed forces should be called in,[6] their legal authority to act in a situation of riot seems to rest upon no statutory or prerogative powers of the Crown but simply on the duty of all citizens to aid in the suppression of riot and on the duty of the armed forces to come to the aid of the civil authorities.[7] In place of the common law rules on the use of force in the prevention of crime, s 3 of the Criminal Law Act 1967 now provides:

A person may use such force as is reasonable in the circumstances in the prevention of crime, or in effecting or assisting in the lawful arrest of offenders or suspected offenders or of persons unlawfully at large.

Thus, the use of firearms must be justified by the necessity of the situation and does not become legal by reason of the decision to call in the troops. Indeed, the use of excessive force or the premature use of firearms would render the officer in command and the individual soldiers personally responsible for death or injuries caused. Issues of liability are decided by the criminal or civil courts after the event.[8]

By contrast with 19th-century practice, the 'civil power' that may call in the armed forces appears no longer to be the local magistracy, but the Home

---

[4]   See McCabe and Wallington, *The Police, Public Order and Civil Liberties*, pp 49–50.
[5]   Report of the Committee on the Disturbances at Featherstone, C 7234, 1893. And see HC 236 (1908).
[6]   See authorities cited in note 39 below.
[7]   *Charge to Bristol Grand Jury* (1832) 5 C & P 261.
[8]   See *R v Clegg* [1995] 1 AC 482.

Secretary, acting on a request from a chief officer of police.[9] It is then for the Secretary of State for Defence to respond to the call. In such a situation, conventions of individual and collective responsibility of ministers must merge. It may be assumed that the decisions of both Cabinet ministers would be taken through machinery authorised by the Cabinet for dealing with civil emergencies, machinery serviced in previous cases by what was the Civil Contingencies Unit of the Cabinet Office. In themselves, these arrangements for joint operations between police and army give no additional legal authority to police or army for interfering with the rights of citizens. In modern conditions, the proposition that to call in the troops makes possible the use of firearms needs to be qualified in two ways. First, the police have already had to train and equip themselves with firearms 'to deal with armed criminals and political terrorists not posing any extraordinary problem or capable of posing a limited threat'.[10] The occasions on which firearms may be carried are governed by police rules, but in 1976 Sir Robert Mark argued that the discretion of the individual constable extended to cover the use of firearms: 'A jury or a police disciplinary inquiry may examine his actions but his use of a firearm does not differ in law from his use of a truncheon'.[11] Second, it is no longer correct, as was said in 1893, that a soldier can act only by using deadly weapons.[12] To call in the army to deal with civil unrest would indeed be of incalculable political significance. But the British army's experience in Northern Ireland suggests that there are many other ways of dealing with hostile crowds which are more effective and less deadly than firing into them – batons, riot shields, water cannon, rubber bullets and even CS gas[13] – and the armed forces do not have a monopoly of the use of CS gas.[14]

B. Use of troops in Northern Ireland

The nature and scale of military involvement

The use of troops in Northern Ireland and their potential use against political terrorists are of the kind which have been described by a military writer as low-intensity operations.[15] Such use gives rise to formidable political and constitutional problems, not least in the identification of political groups whose

---

9   HC Deb, 8 April 1976, col 617. See also E Bramall (1980) 128 Jl of Royal Society of Arts 480; S C Greer [1983] PL 573; and Evelegh, *Peace Keeping in a Democratic Society*, pp 11–21, 91–4.

10 Cmnd 6496, 1976, p 95.

11 Ibid. Incidents involving the discharge of firearms by the police are supervised by the Police Complaints Authority. See HC 469 (1995–96), p 27, where it is reported that a police officer would be charged with murder as a result of a firearms incident.

12 C 7234, pp 10, 12.

13 See Reports on medical and toxicological aspects of CS gas, Cmnd 4173, 1969; Cmnd 4775, 1975. On the use of CS incapacitants, see HC 469 (1995–96), p 39.

14 On the power to make it available to the police, see *R v Home Secretary, ex p Northumbria Police Authority* [1989] QB 26. Also HC 469 (1995–96), p 39.

15 Kitson, *Low Intensity Operations*.

activities may be described as subversive.[16] In 1975, the Home Office defined subversion as comprising activities 'which threaten the safety or well-being of the State, and are intended to undermine or overthrow parliamentary democracy by political, industrial or violent means'.[17] On this basis, since 1969 the scale of subversive activities in Northern Ireland has required the armed forces to share with the police a difficult and unenviable role in maintaining internal security.[18] Reference has been made already to the grave errors made in the adoption of interrogation in depth against selected internees.[19] In 1972, the Northern Ireland Court of Appeal decided that the Northern Ireland Parliament under the Government of Ireland Act 1920 had no legal authority to confer powers of arrest upon the armed forces; this decision led instantly to legislation which retrospectively conferred this power upon the Stormont parliament.[20]

The nature and scale of military involvement in Northern Ireland are outlined in some detail in the annual defence estimates. The General Officer Commanding Northern Ireland is responsible to the Secretary of State for Northern Ireland and the Chief Constable of the Royal Ulster Constabulary for directing the military contribution to security policy and counter-terrorist operations, and is responsible to the Ministry of Defence for the conduct of operations by all elements of the armed forces in Northern Ireland.[21] In 1969, the normal peacetime garrison in Northern Ireland was about 3,000, but since then the number of military personnel has fluctuated from a high of over 30,000 in 1972 to 17,000 in 1983–85; in the 1990s, the military presence was typically in the region of 19,000. But despite this heavy presence, it is said that the RUC takes the lead in maintaining law and order, and that the role of the army is 'to support the RUC in combatting terrorism'.[22] Moreover,

Armed forces' operations are carried out to meet the requirements set by the RUC, and are agreed in advance with them. Most of these operations are carried out jointly. There is very close cooperation between RUC and military commanders, who often meet on a daily basis to plan operations, with the RUC chairing the meetings. At the highest operational level, the Province Executive Committee, which assists in the overall co-ordination of the counter-terrorist effort, is chaired by a Deputy Chief Constable.[23]

When first deployed in Northern Ireland in 1969, the army was used primarily to maintain public order. But since then the role has changed, with military operations now being intended to (i) deter terrorist activity, (ii) reassure the community by providing a visible armed presence, and (iii) reduce terrorist capability through the arrest of terrorists and the seizure of arms, explosives

---

[16]   See eg Kitson's definition at p 3 of subversion as 'all illegal measures short of the use of armed force taken by one section of the people ... to overthrow those governing the country ... or to force them to do things which they do not want to do'; and note the reference to the role of the law at pp 69–70.
[17]   HC Deb, 6 April 1978, col 618.
[18]   See eg the critical study by Evelegh, *Peace Keeping in a Democratic Society.*
[19]   Ch 6.
[20]   *R (Hume et al) v Londonderry Justices* [1972] NILR 91; Northern Ireland Act 1972.
[21]   Defence Estimates 1994 (Cm 2550, 1994), p 38.
[22]   Ibid, p 36.
[23]   Ibid.

and other terrorist equipment.[24] Operations include patrolling on foot and in vehicles; the maintaining of vehicle check-points; and the searches of property for arms and explosives. The announcement of the republican and loyalist ceasefires in August 1994 enabled the military presence to be reduced in a 'cautious and carefully planned way',[25] with measures being taken to reduce the military profile and to extend the areas in Northern Ireland where the RUC operated without routine military support. Although the republican ceasefire came to an end with the Canary Wharf bombing on 9 February 1996, it is nevertheless accepted by the Ministry of Defence that there is no military solution to the current problems in Northern Ireland, which are said to require 'a combination of political, social, economic and security measures to resolve'.[26]

Legal position of the soldier

The legal position of the soldier called to assist the civil authorities in Northern Ireland to contain terrorist or political violence may not be the same as that of his or her counterpart called to assist the civil authorities elsewhere for other purposes:

There is little authority in English law concerning the rights and duties of a member of the armed forces of the Crown when acting in aid of the civil power; and what little authority there is relates almost entirely to the duties of soldiers when troops are called upon to assist in controlling a riotous assembly. Where used for such temporary purposes it may not be accurate to describe the legal rights and duties of a soldier as being no more than those of an ordinary citizen in uniform. But such a description is in my view misleading in the circumstances in which the army is currently employed in aid of the civil power in Northern Ireland ... In theory it may be the duty of every citizen when an arrestable offence is about to be committed in his presence to take whatever reasonable measures are available to him to prevent the commission of the crime; but the duty is one of imperfect obligation and does not place him under any obligation to do anything by which he would expose himself to the risk of personal injury ... In contrast to this a soldier who is employed in aid of the civil power in Northern Ireland is under a duty, enforceable under military law, to search for criminals if so ordered by his superior officer and to risk his own life should this be necessary in preventing terrorist acts. For the performance of this duty he is armed with a firearm, a self-loading rifle, from which a bullet, if it hits the human body, is almost certain to cause serious injury if not death.[27]

It has been said by the government, however, that 'service personnel are given certain specific powers under the law (for example, to make arrests and carry out searches) in order to enable them to carry out effective support to the RUC. In exercising these powers and in seeking to uphold the law, service personnel remain accountable to the law at all times. They have no immunity, nor do they receive special treatment. If service personnel breach the law, they are liable to arrest and prosecution under the law. This applies equally to the use of force, including lethal force'.[28]

---

24 Ibid, p 37.
25 Defence Estimates 1995 (Cm 2800, 1995), p 42.
26 Ibid, p 38.
27 *A-G for Northern Ireland's Reference (No 1 of 1975)* [1977] AC 105, at 136–7 (Lord Diplock).
28 Defence Estimates 1994 (Cm 2550, 1994), p 36.

Considerable controversy has, nevertheless, arisen from time to time as a result of the use of firearms by the military, most notably on 30 January 1972 when thirteen civilians were killed 'when the army opened fire during a demonstration in Derry'.[29] Between 1969 and 1994 the security forces are said to have been responsible for 357 deaths in Northern Ireland, of which 141 were republican 'military activists', 13 were loyalist equivalents, and 194 were civilians. Eighteen of these deaths led to criminal charges, with a total of six convictions being secured, one for attempted murder, one for manslaughter, and four for murder.[30]

In *Attorney-General for Northern Ireland's Reference (No 1 of 1975)*[31] the accused was a soldier on foot patrol who shot and killed a young man in an open field in a country area in daylight. The shot had not been preceded by a warning shot and the rifle was fired after the deceased ran off after having been told to halt. The area was one in which troops had been attacked and killed by the IRA and where a surprise attack was a real threat. When the accused fired, he believed that he was dealing with a member of the IRA, but he had no belief at all as to whether the deceased had been involved or was likely to be involved in any act of terrorism. In fact, the deceased was an 'entirely innocent person who was in no way involved in terrorist activity'. After the soldier's acquittal for murder, the House of Lords held that the stated circumstances (where 'he fires to kill or seriously wound an unarmed person because he honestly and reasonably believes that person is a member of a prescribed organisation (in this case the Provisional IRA) who is seeking to run away, and the soldier's shot kills that person') raised an issue for the tribunal of fact as to whether the Crown had established beyond reasonable doubt that the shooting constituted unreasonable force. According to Lord Diplock, (at p 138) 'there is material upon which a jury might take the view that the accused had reasonable grounds for apprehension of imminent danger to himself and other members of the patrol if the deceased were allowed to get away . . ., and that the time available to the accused to make up his mind was so short that even a reasonable man could only act intuitively'.

On the other hand, in *R v Clegg*[32] it was held that a soldier who used excessive force in self-defence leading to the death of the victim was guilty of murder rather than manslaughter. The use of firearms earlier gave rise to allegations of a shoot-to-kill policy, these being directed at both the RUC and the armed forces.[33] The allegations were sufficiently serious that an inquiry was appointed under the chairmanship of Mr John Stalker, the deputy chief constable of Greater Manchester.[34] Following Mr Stalker's removal from the inquiry in controversial circumstances, it was completed by Mr Sampson, the chief constable of West Yorkshire. No evidence was published to substantiate the allegations,[35] though the controversy was revived following the decision of the

---

[29]   C A Gearty (1994) 47 CLP 19, at p 33. See HC 220 (1971–72) (Widgery Report).

[30]   Gearty and Kimbell, *Terrorism and the Rule of Law*, pp 57–8.

[31]   [1977] AC 105. See also *Farrell v Defence Secretary* [1980] 1 All ER 166; *R v Bohan and Temperley* (1979) 5 BNIL; *R v Robinson* (1984) 4 BNIL 34; *R v McAuley* (1985) 10 BNIL 14. See also R J Spjut [1986] PL 38 and [1987] PL 35.

[32]   [1995] 1 AC 482.

[33]   For suggestions that such an alleged policy conflicts with the ECHR, see *Farrell v United Kingdom* (1983) 5 EHRR 466.

[34]   See Stalker, *Stalker*.

[35]   See HC Deb, 25 January 1988, cols 21–35.

European Court of Human Rights in *McCann v United Kingdom*,[36] which concerned the fatal shooting of three IRA activists in Gibraltar in 1987.

Three known IRA personnel were shot by four SAS officers while it was thought that they were about to detonate a bomb, to the danger of life on Gibraltar. It transpired that this belief was erroneous and that the suspects were not only unarmed, but that they also were not in possession of bomb equipment at the time of their deaths. They were nevertheless shot 29 times (one suspect being shot 16 times) in highly controversial circumstances. By a majority of 10 to 9, the Court held that there had been a breach of article 2 which in protecting the right to life was said to rank as 'one of the most fundamental provisions in the Convention'.[37] There was no evidence of 'an execution plot at the highest level of command in the Ministry of Defence or in the Government'; although 'all four soldiers shot to kill', on the facts and in the circumstances the actions of the soldiers did not in themselves give rise to a violation of article 2. But it was held that the operation as a whole was controlled and organised in a manner which failed to respect article 2, and that the information and instructions given to the soldiers rendered inevitable the use of lethal force in a manner which failed to take adequately into consideration the right to life of the three suspects. Having regard 'to the decision not to prevent the suspects from travelling into Gibraltar, to the failure of the authorities to make sufficient allowances for the possibility that their intelligence assessments might in some respects, at least, be erroneous and to the automatic recourse to lethal force when the soldiers opened fire', the Court was not persuaded that 'the killing of the three terrorists constituted the force which was no more than absolutely necessary in defence of persons from unlawful violence.'[38]

C. Martial law

The meaning of martial law

The term martial law may be given a variety of meanings. In former times martial law included what is now called military law.[39] In international law, martial law refers to the powers exercised by a military commander in occupation of foreign territory. In the present context, martial law refers to an emergency amounting to a state of war when the military may impose restrictions and regulations upon citizens in their own country.[40] In such a situation of civil war or insurrection, the ordinary functioning of the courts gives way before the tasks of the military in restoring the conditions which make normal government possible. Unlike the use of armed forces for restoring order during riots, when the military are subject to direction by the civil authorities and to control by the courts if excessive force is used, under

---

[36] (1995) 21 EHRR 97.
[37] Art 2(1) provides that 'Everyone's life shall be protected by law', while art 2(2) provides by way of qualification that 'Deprivation of life shall not be regarded as inflicted in contravention of this Article when it results from the use of force which is no more than absolutely necessary: (a) in defence of any person from unlawful violence ... '
[38] The political reaction to the decision was very critical of the Court: see eg HL Deb, 29 January 1996, col 1225. Compare C Gearty, 'After Gibraltar', *London Review of Books*, 16 November 1995.
[39] Ch 16.
[40] Keir and Lawson, *Cases in Constitutional Law*, ch III C; Heuston, *Essays in Constitutional Law*, pp 150–62.

martial law the military authorities are (for the time being) the sole judges of the steps that should be taken. These steps might involve taking drastic steps against civilians, for example, the removal of life, liberty or property without due process of law, but possibly accompanied by the creation of military tribunals to administer summary justice. Such tribunals are not to be confused with the courts-martial which regularly administer military law.

It would be wrong to state the principal aspects of martial law as if they were part of present-day law, if only for the reason that within Great Britain occasions for the exercise of martial law have not arisen since at least 1800. Moreover, the Petition of Right 1628 contains a prohibition against the issue by the Crown of commissions of martial law giving the army powers over civilians, at least in time of peace, and the meaning of this prohibition is far from clear today.[41] In times of national emergency today, Parliament prefers to give the civil and military authorities wide powers of governing by means of temporary legislation. It is submitted, therefore, that any discussion of the possible operation of martial law in Great Britain must assume that Parliament itself is prevented by the urgency of events from giving the necessary powers to the military authorities. If Parliament is sitting but refuses to pass emergency legislation, there would seem to be great difficulty, from a constitutional standpoint, in accepting that extraordinary powers of the military arise by process of common law.[42] Moreover, short of a military coup, or an extreme emergency in which human survival becomes the only criterion, it must be assumed that the government continues to control the armed forces and to be responsible for their use to Parliament. In Northern Ireland since 1969, at no time has the British government invoked the doctrine of martial law as a justification for exempting the actions of the forces from scrutiny in the courts; instead there has been reliance on statutory powers, or on the use of common law powers falling far short of a martial law situation.

An attempt to describe the doctrine of martial law must be based upon case-law arising out of the Boer War, the civil war in Ireland early in the 1920s, and incidents in the earlier history of British colonies. But it would take an alarming deterioration in political stability for it to be necessary to determine whether this mingled case-law is applicable in Great Britain.[43] During the two world wars, the civil and criminal courts continued to function in Great Britain although their operation was subject to statutory restrictions. No state of martial law was declared. The Defence of the Realm Act 1914 authorised for a few months the trial of civilians by court-martial for offences against defence regulations. The Emergency Powers (Defence) (No 2) Act 1940, passed under the threat of imminent invasion, gave authority for special war zone courts to exercise criminal jurisdiction if, on account of military action, criminal justice had to be more speedily administered than in the ordinary courts. Such courts were never required to sit. In Northern Ireland since 1968, the ordinary civil and criminal courts have continued to function,

---

[41]   Cf *Marais v General Officer Commanding* [1902] AC 109, 115.

[42]   Cf *Egan v Macready* [1921] 1 IR 265, 274.

[43]   Cf the argument in Dicey, *The Law of the Constitution*, ch 8, that martial law is unknown to the law of England.

although in dealing with terrorist offences the powers and procedures of the criminal courts have been much amended.[44]

Position of the courts during martial law

If in a state of civil war or insurrection the administration of justice breaks down because the courts are unable to function, it follows as a matter of fact that the acts of the military in seeking to restore order cannot be called into question in the courts so long as this situation lasts. As the English Law Officers said in 1838 in relation to the power of the governor of Lower Canada to proclaim martial law, martial law 'can only be tolerated because, by reason of open rebellion, the enforcing of any other law has become impossible'.[45] If in such a situation the executive proclaims martial law, the proclamation does not increase the powers of the military but merely gives notice to the people of the course which the government must adopt to restore order. In 1838, the Law Officers considered that, when the regular courts were in operation, any persons arrested by the military must be delivered to the courts to be dealt with according to law: 'there is not, as we conceive, any right in the Crown to adopt any other course of proceeding'.[46]

In 1902, in the *Marais* case, the Privy Council significantly extended the doctrine of martial law by holding that a situation of martial law might exist though the civil courts were still sitting. During the Boer War martial law had been proclaimed over certain areas of Cape Colony: Marais, a civilian, sought in the Supreme Court at Cape Town to challenge the legality of his arrest and detention for breach of military rules in an area subject to martial law. Lord Halsbury, on behalf of the Judicial Committee, declared that where war actually exists, the ordinary courts have no jurisdiction over the military authorities, although there might often be doubt as to whether a situation of war existed, as opposed to a mere riot or other disturbance.[47] Once a war situation had been recognised to exist, the military would presumably be able to deal with the inhabitants of an area under martial law on the same footing as the population of a foreign territory occupied during a war between states, subject only to the possibility of being called to account for their acts in civil courts after the resumption of normal government at a later date.

Advantage of the *Marais* case was taken by the UK government during the serious disturbances in Ireland in 1920–21. Early in 1920, the Westminster Parliament passed the Restoration of Order in Ireland Act, which gave exceptional powers to the executive, created new offences, provided for civilians to be tried and sentenced by properly convened courts-martial and prescribed the maximum penalties that could be imposed. Yet in December 1920, martial law was proclaimed in areas of Ireland and the General Officer Commanding the army declared inter alia that any unauthorised person found in possession of arms would be subject to the death penalty. The General also established informal military courts for administering summary

---

44   Northern Ireland (Emergency Provisions) Act 1996. See Section E below.
45   Opinion of J Campbell and R M Rolfe, 16 January 1838; Keir and Lawson, op cit, p 231.
46   Ibid.
47   *Marais v General Officer Commanding* [1902] AC 109. And see *Tilonko v A-G of Natal* [1907] AC 93.

justice to those alleged to have committed the prohibited acts. In *R v Allen*, the King's Bench Division in Ireland refused to intervene in the case of a death sentence imposed by such a military court on a civilian for possession of arms. The court held that a state of war existed in the area in question; that military acts could not therefore be questioned in the civil courts even though the latter were still operating; and that the army authorities could take the lives of civilians if they deemed it to be absolutely essential. It was immaterial that Parliament had not authorised the death penalty for unauthorised possession of arms.[48]

The decisions of other Irish courts were not all so favourable to the army. In *Egan v Macready*, O'Connor MR distinguished the *Marais* case, holding that the Restoration of Order in Ireland Act 1920 created a complete code for military control of the situation which excluded the power of the army to impose the death penalty where Parliament had not granted this; he ordered the prisoner to be released by issuing habeas corpus.[49] In *R (Garde) v Strickland*, the court in strong terms asserted its power and duty to decide whether or not a state of war existed which justified the application of martial law, holding also that, so long as that state existed, no court had jurisdiction to inquire into the conduct of the army commander in repressing rebellion.[50] In *Higgins v Willis*, in which an action was brought for wrongful destruction of a civilian's house, the court declared that the plaintiff had a right to have his case against the military decided by the courts as soon as the state of war had ceased.[51] In the only decision by the House of Lords, *Re Clifford and O'Sullivan*, on facts similar to those in *R v Allen* it was held that the courts could not by issuing a writ of prohibition review the proceedings of a military tribunal set up under a proclamation of martial law.[52] This decision turned on the technical scope of the writ of prohibition, at that time considered to be available only against inferior bodies exercising judicial functions.[53] The House of Lords regarded the military tribunal in question, which was not a regularly constituted court-martial, as merely an advisory committee of officers to assist the commander-in-chief; moreover its duties had already been completed. The House expressly refrained from discussing the merits of other remedies that might be available, for example, a writ of habeas corpus. It followed that the army's decision to take the life of a citizen did not become subject to judicial control merely because an informal hearing had been given to the civilian by a military tribunal.

Position of the courts after martial law ends

After termination of the state of martial law, the courts have jurisdiction to review the legality of acts committed during the period of martial law. It is not possible to state with any certainty what standards will be applied by the courts in respect either of criminal or civil liability. First, there is no doubt that at

---

[48]   [1921] 2 IR 241. See Campbell, *Emergency Law in Ireland 1918–1925*. For Cabinet discussion of martial law in Ireland, see Jones, *Whitehall Diary*, vol 3, part I.
[49]   [1921] 1 IR 265, criticised in Heuston, *Essays in Constitutional Law*, p 158.
[50]   [1921] 2 IR 317.
[51]   [1921] 2 IR 386.
[52]   [1921] 2 AC 570.
[53]   Ch 30.

common law many acts of the army which are necessary for dealing with civil war and insurrection will be justified; nor would there be liability at common law for damage to person or property inflicted accidentally in the course of actual fighting.[54] But what is not clear is whether the test should be that of strict necessity or merely bona fide belief in the necessity of the action, nor whether a stricter standard may be required in the case of some acts than others, nor where the burden of proof should lie. Secondly, there is some uncertainty as to the legal effect of superior orders.[55] Thirdly, in the past it was usual after martial law for an Act of Indemnity to be passed giving retrospective protection to the armed forces. On the basis of *Wright v Fitzgerald*[56] it would seem that in interpreting an Indemnity Act, the courts presume that Parliament does not intend to indemnify a defendant for merely wanton or cruel acts not justified by the necessities of the situation, but the extent of protection depends on the terms of the Indemnity Act, which may be both explicit and very wide.[57]

D. Emergency powers in peace and war

While the Crown has some emergency powers under the prerogative, particularly in time of war or invasion, these powers are generally too uncertain for the government to rely on them.[58] During the two world wars, Parliament conferred exceptional powers for the conduct of the war and the maintenance of civilian life. During time of peace there is permanent statutory authority by which a state of emergency may be declared, and in the recent past machinery existed in what was the Civil Contingencies Unit of the Cabinet Office for enabling the government to respond rapidly in emergency situations, if necessary by the activation of regional emergency committees throughout the country.[59]

Emergency powers in peacetime

By the Emergency Powers Act 1920, as amended in 1964, a wide power to govern in emergency by means of statutory regulations is conferred on the executive, subject to parliamentary control. This power arises only when a state of emergency has been declared by royal proclamation. A proclamation of emergency may be issued if at any time it appears to the Crown that there have occurred, or are about to occur, events of such a nature as to be calculated to deprive the community, or any substantial part of it, of the essentials of life by interfering with the supply and distribution of food, water, fuel or light, or with the means of locomotion. Such events might in principle include include a strike in one or more major public utilities or industries, natural disasters or a serious nuclear accident.[60] A proclamation can remain

---

[54]   *Burmah Oil Co v Lord Advocate* [1965] AC 75; and ch 12 E.
[55]   Ch 16.
[56]   (1798) 27 St Tr 765, discussed by P O'Higgins (1962) 25 MLR 413.
[57]   See the notorious example in *Phillips v Eyre* (1870) LR 6 QB 1 and cf Indemnity Act 1920.
[58]   Ch 12 D.
[59]   HC Deb, 15 January 1979, col 1318.
[60]   But see HC Deb, 14 February 1996, col 629 (WA).

in force only for one month, though the emergency may be prolonged by the issue of a fresh proclamation. The proclamation must be forthwith communicated to Parliament. If Parliament is not sitting, it must be summoned to meet within five days.

So long as a proclamation is in force, regulations may be made by Order in Council for securing the essentials of life to the community. Such powers may be conferred on government departments, the armed forces and the police as may be deemed necessary for preserving peace or for securing and regulating the supply and distribution of necessities for maintaining the means of transport, 'and for any other purposes essential to the public safety and the life of the community' (1920 Act, s 2(1)). But the regulations may not impose compulsory military service or industrial conscription, nor make it an offence for anyone to take part in a strike or peacefully persuade others to do so. Regulations may provide for the trial, by courts of summary jurisdiction, of persons guilty of offences against the regulations, subject to maximum penalties; but existing procedure in criminal cases may not be altered and no right to punish by fine or imprisonment without trial may be conferred. The regulations must be laid before Parliament and expire after seven days unless a resolution is passed by both Houses providing for their continuance.

The 1920 Act has been used 12 times, to deal with strikes by coal-miners, dockers, power workers as well as others. Indeed, no fewer than five states of emergency were declared by the Conservative government between 1970 and 1974. However, the Act has not been used since then despite the fact that there have been major public-sector strikes, including the so-called winter of discontent of 1978/79 and the miners' strike of 1984/85. The Act thus appears to have fallen into disuse, with governments preferring to rely on other powers when faced with major conflict in the public services.[61] These include the Emergency Powers Act 1964, s 2 of which gave permanent force to defence regulations originating in the Second World War that enable members of the armed forces, by order of the Defence Council, to be temporarily employed in agriculture or in 'urgent work of national importance'.[62] This has enabled troops to be used to maintain essential services and utilities which have been interrupted by strikes, notably during the firemen's strike in 1977/78 and the prison officers' strike in 1980.[63]

Also potentially important in the context of some industrial action are the emergency powers provisions in the privatisation statutes. For example, the Electricity Act 1989 authorises the Secretary of State to give 'such directions of a general character as appear to the Secretary of State to be requisite or expedient for . . . mitigating the effects of any civil emergency which may occur' (s 96(1)). A civil emergency means 'any natural disaster or other emergency which, in the opinion of the Secretary of State, is or may be likely to disrupt electricity supplies' (s 96(7)). It has been claimed that an unpublished direc-

---

[61]   For a full account, see Morris, *Strikes in Essential Services*; also G S Morris [1980] PL 317 and C Whelan (1979) 8 ILJ 222.

[62]   As the Manual of Military Law points out, it is by virtue of this measure that 'troops may be used to maintain essential supplies and public services which become threatened by strikes and industrial disputes', part 2, section 5, para 28.

[63]   Note also the possibility of the police being used to maintain essential supplies during a strike: see G S Morris (1980) 9 ILJ 1.

tive was issued by the Energy Secretary in 1990 to the electricity generating companies to hold £1 billion of coal stocks as insurance against a miners' strike.[64] The stockpiling of coal may have been a major factor in determining the outcome of the 1984/85 miners' strike.[65] Under the Railways Act 1993, s 118, powers are given to the Secretary of State to control the railways in times of hostility, severe international tension or great national emergency, the last being defined to mean 'any national disaster or other emergency which, in the opinion of the Secretary of State, is or may be likely to give rise to such disruption of the means of transport that the population, or a substantial part of the population, of Great Britain is or may be likely to be deprived of essential goods or services'. Owners or operators of services who suffer loss as a result of ministerial intervention are entitled to compensation, the amount to be determined by arbitration in default of an agreement.[66]

Emergency powers in time of war

Before the mid-19th century, it was the practice in times of national danger to pass what were often known as Habeas Corpus Suspension Acts.[67] Such Acts took various forms. Some prevented the use of habeas corpus for securing speedy trial or the right to bail in the case of persons charged with treason or other offences. Others conferred wide powers of arrest and detention which would not normally have been acceptable. After the danger was over, it was often the practice to pass an Indemnity Act to protect officials retrospectively from liability for illegal acts which they might have committed. During the two world wars, habeas corpus was not suspended but extremely wide powers were conferred on the executive. The Defence of the Realm Acts 1914–15 empowered the Crown to make regulations by Order in Council for securing public safety or for the defence of the realm.[68] In *R v Halliday, ex p Zadig* the House of Lords held that this general power was wide enough to support a regulation authorising the Secretary of State to detain persons without trial on the grounds of their hostile origins or associations.[69] In a powerful and memorable dissent, Lord Shaw of Dunfermline declined to infer from the delegation of a general power to make regulations for public safety and defence that a man could be detained without trial and without being accused of any offence.

Although the powers of the executive were wide, it was still possible to challenge defence regulations in the courts.

In *Attorney-General v Wilts United Dairies Ltd*[70] an attempt by the Food Controller to impose a charge of two pence a gallon as a condition of issuing licences for the supply of milk was held invalid, on the ground that the Food Controller's power under defence regulations to regulate the supply of milk did not confer power to impose

---

[64] See G S Morris (1991) 20 ILJ 89, at p 98.
[65] For other strategies, see eg Imprisonment (Temporary Provisions) Act 1980.
[66] For further details of the emergency powers and industrial disputes, see Deakin and Morris, *Labour Law*, pp 823–7.
[67] Dicey, *The Law of the Constitution*, pp 229–37.
[68] For a fascinating account of these powers and their operation, see Rubin, *Private Property, Government Requisition and the Constitution, 1914–1927*.
[69] [1917] AC 260.
[70] (1921) 37 TLR 884.

charges upon the subject. Doubt was also expressed whether a regulation conferring such a power would have been within the general power to make regulations for the public safety or the defence of the realm.

In *Chester v Bateson*[71] a defence regulation empowered the Minister of Munitions to declare an area in which munitions were manufactured to be a special area. The intended effect of such a declaration was to prevent any person without the consent of the minister from taking proceedings to recover possession of any dwelling-house in the area, if a munitions worker was living in it and duly paying rent. It was held that Parliament had not deliberately deprived the citizen of access to the courts and that the regulation was invalid, since it could not be shown to be a necessary or even reasonable way of securing the public safety or the defence of the realm.

Such decisions explain the passing after the war of the wide Indemnity Act 1920 and a separate Act relating to illegal charges, the War Charges Validity Act 1925.

When war was declared in 1939, the Emergency Powers (Defence) Act 1939 empowered the making of regulations by Order in Council which appeared necessary or expedient for the public safety, the defence of the realm, the maintenance of public order, the efficient prosecution of any war in which His Majesty might be engaged and the maintenance of supplies and services essential for the life of the community. There followed a list of particular purposes for which regulations could be made, including the detention of persons in the interests of public safety or the defence of the realm. To avoid another *Wilts United Dairies* case, the Treasury was empowered to impose charges in connection with any scheme of control under Defence Regulations. Treasury regulations imposing charges required confirmation by an affirmative resolution of the House of Commons. Other regulations had to be laid before Parliament after they were made and could be annulled by negative resolution within 28 days.[72] Compulsory military service was imposed by separate National Service Acts and compulsory direction of labour to essential war work was authorised by the Emergency Powers (Defence) (No 2) Act 1940.

Although access to the courts was not barred, the scope for judicial review of executive action was limited. Thus the courts could not consider whether a particular regulation was necessary or expedient for the purposes of the Act which authorised it.[73] The courts could, however, hold an act to be illegal as being not authorised by the regulation relied upon to justify it.[74] Special problems of judicial control arose in relation to the power of the executive to authorise detention without trial in the interests of public safety or the defence of the realm. Under Defence Regulation 18 B, the Home Secretary was empowered to detain those whom he had reasonable cause to believe came within specified categories (including persons of hostile origin or association) and over whom it was necessary to exercise control. Persons detained could make objections to an advisory committee appointed by the Home Secretary. The Home Secretary had to report monthly to Parliament

---

[71]   [1920] 1 KB 829.
[72]   Ch 27.
[73]   *R v Comptroller-General of Patents, ex p Bayer Products* [1941] 2 KB 306. See also *Pollok School v Glasgow Town Clerk* 1946 SC 373.
[74]   Eg *Fowler & Co (Leeds) Ltd v Duncan* [1941] Ch 450.

on the number of persons detained and the number of cases in which he had not followed the advice of the committee. It was open to a detainee to apply for habeas corpus, but such applications had little chance of success in view of the decision of the House of Lords in *Liversidge v Anderson*.[75] In spite of a powerful dissenting judgment by Lord Atkin, the House took the view that the power to detain could not be controlled by the courts, if only because considerations of security forbade proof of the evidence upon which detention was ordered. The words 'had reasonable cause to believe' only meant that the Home Secretary must have a belief which in his mind was reasonable. The courts would not inquire into the grounds for his belief, although apparently they might examine positive evidence of mala fides or mistaken identity.[76] Stress was laid upon the responsibility of the Home Secretary to Parliament. In only one case did a person who had been detained under the regulation secure his release by habeas corpus proceedings. His detention having been ordered on the ground that he was connected with a fascist organisation, he was wrongly informed that the order had been made on the ground of his being of hostile origins and association. The Divisional Court ordered his release, but the Home Secretary thereupon made a new order for his detention.[77]

E. Emergency powers and political violence

For the past 20 years the population of Northern Ireland which totals 1.5 million people, has been subjected to a campaign of terrorism. More than 2,750 people, including almost 800 members of the security forces, have been killed and 31,900 more have been maimed or injured. The campaign of terror has extended to the rest of the United Kingdom and to the mainland of Europe.[78]

Special powers to deal with threats to security have long been known in Northern Ireland. It was under the Civil Authorities (Special Powers) Act 1922 passed at Stormont that internment of suspected terrorists was introduced in 1971.[79] That Act was eventually replaced by the Northern Ireland (Emergency Provisions) Act passed at Westminster in 1973, amended in 1975 and 1977 and re-enacted in 1978.[80] Following a review of the legislation by Sir George Baker[81] further re-enactment occurred in 1987, again in 1991

---

[75] [1942] AC 206; and see C K Allen (1942) 58 LQR 232 and R F V Heuston (1970) 86 LQR 33.

[76] Lord Wright at 261. The majority decision in *Liversidge v Anderson* cannot now be relied on as an authority, either on the point of construction or in its declaration of legal principle: *R v Home Secretary, ex p Khawaja* [1984] AC 74, 110 (Lord Scarman), and see eg *Ridge v Baldwin* [1964] AC 40, 73 (Lord Reid).

[77] *R v Home Secretary, ex p Budd* [1942] 2 KB 14; *The Times*, 28 May 1941. On Regulation 18 B generally, see Simpson, *In the Highest Degree Odious*.

[78] *Fox v United Kingdom* (1991) 13 EHRR 157, at 160.

[79] For criticism of the 1922 Act, see report of a commission of inquiry appointed by the National Council for Civil Liberties, 1936. See also Calvert, *Constitutional Law in Northern Ireland*, ch 20, and *Emergency Powers: A Fresh Start* (Fabian Tract 416), 1972.

[80] The 1973 Act was preceded by the Diplock report, Cmnd 5185, 1972, and the Northern Ireland (Emergency Provisions) Amendment Act 1975 by the Gardiner report, Cmnd 5847, 1975.

[81] Cmnd 9222, 1984.

following an extensive review by Viscount Colville,[82] and most recently in 1996 following a review by J J Rowe QC.[83] So far as Britain is concerned, it was only when serious bomb attacks were made by the IRA in Birmingham in 1974 that Parliament within a few hours passed the Prevention of Terrorism (Temporary Provisions) Act 1974 to give additional powers to the police and the government for dealing in Great Britain with suspected terrorists. The 1974 Act was re-enacted in 1976, after fuller consideration from Parliament than had been given to it in 1974. A detailed review of the 1976 Act was undertaken in 1978 by Lord Shackleton and again in 1983 by Lord Jellicoe,[84] and the Act was re-enacted with modifications in 1984.[85] Like its predecessors, the 1984 Act had a life of only five years, subject to annual renewal. In 1987, a review by Viscount Colville concluded that legislation of this kind continued to be necessary,[86] thus leading to the Prevention of Terrorism (Temporary Provisions) Act 1989. Unlike its two predecessors, this measure has not been enacted for a period of five years only, though like its predecessors it is subject to annual renewal by Parliament.[87] The same is true of parts of the Northern Ireland (Emergency Provisions) Act 1996.

Prevention of Terrorism (Temporary Provisions) Act 1989[88]

Part I of the 1989 Act restricts freedom of association in Great Britain by proscribing specified organisations. These are respectively the IRA and the Irish National Liberation Army, though the Secretary of State may by order add to Sched 1 'any organisation that appears to him to be concerned in, or in promoting or encouraging, terrorism occurring in the United Kingdom and connected with the affairs of Northern Ireland' (s 1(2)(a)).[89] In cases of urgency, such orders may be made without being approved by a resolution of each House (s 1(3)). By s 2 it is an offence to belong to a proscribed organisation; to solicit or invite support for such an organisation; or to organise a meeting (whether in public or private) in support of such an organisation. Breach of these provisions may lead to imprisonment on conviction on indictment for up to ten years or a fine or both. It is an offence under s 3 for any person in a public place to wear any item of dress or to wear, carry or display any article 'in such a way or in such circumstances as to arouse reasonable apprehension that he is a member or supporter of a proscribed organisation'. For this purpose a public place includes any highway or any premises to which at the material time the public have or are permitted to have access (s 3(3)). Conduct violating s 3 may also be unlawful under s 1 of

---

[82] See Cm 1115, 1990.
[83] Cm 2706, 1995.
[84] Cmnd 7324, 1978; Cmnd 8803, 1983.
[85] Prevention of Terrorism (Temporary Provisions) Act 1984.
[86] Cm 264, 1987.
[87] See HC Deb, 14 March 1996, col 1124.
[88] See Bonner, *Emergency Powers in Peacetime*; Walker, *The Prevention of Terrorism in British Law*. On the 1989 Act, see D Bonner [1989] PL 440; B Dickson (1989) 40 NILQ 250. See also Gearty, *Terror*, and Vercher, *Terrorism in Europe*.
[89] Terrorism is defined throughout to mean 'the use of violence for political ends, and includes any use of violence for the purpose of putting the public or any section of the public in fear' (s 20(1)).

the Public Order Act 1936, which makes it an offence to wear a political uniform in public.[90] Although this was designed initially for use against fascists, the provision was revived in 1975 when it was employed successfully against IRA members who led funeral processions in England, dressed in dark pullovers, dark berets and dark glasses.[91] The restrictions in the 1989 Act are wider, there being no need to show that the demonstration of support amounts to the wearing of a uniform as such.

Part II restricts the freedom of movement within the United Kingdom by authorising the Secretary of State to issue exclusion orders where it 'appears to him expedient to prevent acts of terrorism'[92] connected with the affairs of Northern Ireland (s 4). These 'particularly controversial'[93] powers have been strongly and widely criticised,[94] with freedom of movement having been described as 'a fundamental value of the common law', which is undermined by the 'draconic power' to make an exclusion order which effectively con-demns 'a citizen of this country to what has been known in other parts of the world as internal exile or banishment'.[95] An exclusion order may be made against a person whom the Secretary of State is satisfied has been concerned in the commission, preparation or instigation of terrorist acts. An exclusion order may (a) prohibit persons from being in or entering Great Britain (but such an order may not be made against a British citizen who at the time is ordinarily resident in Great Britain and has been so resident for the preceding three years) (s 5); (b) prohibit persons from being in or entering Northern Ireland (subject to a restriction similar to that in (a) in the case of British citizens ordinarily resident in Northern Ireland) (s 6); or (c) prohibit any person who is not a British citizen from being in or entering the United Kingdom (s 7). Where the Secretary of State is considering making an exclusion order, since 1996 he or she must serve notice in writing on the person concerned, and give the individual an opportunity to make repre-sentations and seek a personal interview with a person nominated by the minister. The individual may be detained pending the final decision of the minister to make the exclusion order. There is no right to be told of the reasons for an exclusion order, and no right to be told the identity of the minister's nominated adviser.[96]

Part III of the 1989 Act makes it an offence to solicit, receive or make

---

[90] See ch 23 above.

[91] *O'Moran v DPP* [1975] QB 864.

[92] For the definition of terrorism, see note 89 above.

[93] *Inquiry into Legislation Against Terrorism*, by Lord Lloyd of Berwick (Cm 3420, 1996), para 16.3.

[94] Lord Colville recommended in his 1987 review of the Act that the power should be allowed to lapse (Cm 264, 1987, para 11.6.1).

[95] *R v Home Secretary, ex p Adams* [1995] All ER (EC) 177. They are, however, defended by the government on the ground that they 'deter people from carrying out terrorist acts and deprive the groups to which they belong of some of their experienced operators'. HC Deb, 14 March 1996, cols 1127–8.

[96] See *R v Home Secretary, ex p Gallacher* [1994] 3 CMLR 295. See also *R v Home Secretary, ex p Adams* above, and *R v Home Secretary, ex p MacQuillan* [1995] 4 All ER 400. In *Adams*, a reference was made for a preliminary ruling under art 177 of the EC Treaty to determine whether art 8a(1) of the Treaty gave rise to directly effective rights and whether it was inapplicable to statutes wholly internal to a particular member state.

financial contributions for the support of 'acts of terrorism', which until 1989 meant acts of terrorism connected with the affairs of Northern Ireland, but which has been defined since 1989 to include international terrorism (s 9).[97] Part III contains new powers to regulate financial assistance for proscribed organisations,[98] reflecting the belief of the government that the existing measures were insufficient 'to strike at the financial roots of terrorism'.[99] During debate in the Commons, the Home Secretary expressed concern that the IRA had devoted effort to fund-raising, its annual income being estimated at between £3 million and £4 million. This was generated partly by armed robbery and extortion, but also by apparently legitimate business activity which gives it 'an assured income and a firmer base'.[100] So apart from the direct financing of terrorism, it is also an offence to give financial support to a terrorist organisation, or to enter into, or otherwise be concerned in, an arrangement whereby money or other property is made available to a person for terrorist purposes.[101] This is intended to cover, for example, banking transactions involving payments to a customer's order, and also 'an arrangement whereby money or other property is made available to a lawful business and either that money, or the profits of that activity, is intended to be used for terrorist purposes'.[102] Section 11 creates the so-called laundering offence, making it unlawful to enter into an arrangement 'whereby the retention or control by or on behalf of another person of terrorist funds is facilitated, whether by concealment, removal from the jurisdiction, transfer to nominees or otherwise'. The Act provides for the forfeiture of money or property destined for terrorist use or which was the subject of an arrangement for handling or laundering terrorist funds. This power applies in respect of international terrorism, as well as terrorism in connection with the affairs of Northern Ireland.[103]

Part IV of the 1989 Act deals with police powers of stop and search, and arrest and detention. By s 13A (inserted by the Criminal Justice and Public Order Act 1994, s 81), powers are conferred on the police to stop and search vehicles where it is expedient to do so to prevent acts of terrorism. Authorisation may be given by a senior police officer (as defined in the Act), and is valid for a renewable period of up to 28 days. The power applies in respect of acts of terrorism connected with the affairs of Northern Ireland, and acts of terrorism of any other description (except those connected solely with the affairs of the UK other than Northern Ireland). Where an authorisation has been given, a police officer in uniform may stop and search any vehicle (as well as its driver and passengers), for articles which could be used for terrorist purposes. By virtue of s 13B (inserted by the Prevention of Terrorism

---

[97]   For the definition of terrorism, see note 89 above.
[98]   For this purpose a proscribed organisation includes an organisation proscribed for the purposes of the Northern Ireland (Emergency Provisions) Act 1996, s 30.
[99]   HC Deb, 6 December 1988, col 212 (Mr Douglas Hurd).
[100] Ibid, at col 213.
[101] Prevention of Terrorism (Temporary Provisions) Act 1989, s 10(1)(c).
[102] HC Deb, 6 December 1988, col 213.
[103] See also Proceeds of Crime (Northern Ireland) Order 1996, containing measures previously to be found in Northern Ireland (Emergency Provisions) Act 1991, part VII. See Cm 2706, 1995.

(Additional Powers) Act 1996), a constable in uniform may stop and search pedestrians for similar purposes, whether or not he or she has any grounds for suspecting that they may be carrying offending articles. In other words, the Act authorises random stopping and searching provided that the necessary authorisation has been given by a police officer. An authorisation under s 13B, but not under s 13A, must be notified to the Home Secretary as soon as reasonably practicable thereafter, and must then be confirmed or cancelled by the minister, and ceases to have effect if not confirmed within 48 hours from the time it was given. If confirmed it may remain in force for up to 28 days, though a lesser period may be authorised, or directed by the Home Secretary. It is an offence punishable by imprisonment to fail to stop as directed, or unlawfully to obstruct a police officer in the exercise of his or her powers. But unlike PACE, there is no duty on the part of chief constables to report annually on the exercise of these powers.[104]

By s 14, a constable may arrest without a warrant a person whom he or she has reasonable grounds for suspecting to be guilty of an offence under the Act; to be subject to an exclusion order; or to be concerned in the commission, preparation or instigation of acts of terrorism, again defined to mean international terrorism as well as terrorism connected with the affairs of Northern Ireland.[105] A person so arrested may be detained for up to 48 hours, in contrast to the normal 24 hours (or 36 hours in the case of a serious arrestable offence) permitted by PACE.[106] After 48 hours, the detention may be extended by the Secretary of State,[107] but any such extensions may not exceed five days in all. These provisions (previously contained in s 12 of the 1984 Act) were held to violate art 5(3) of the European Convention on Human Rights, by which arrested or detained persons 'shall be brought promptly before a judge or other officer authorised by law to exercise judicial power and shall be entitled to trial within a reasonable time or to release pending trial'.[108] In the view of the European Court of Human Rights in *Brogan v United Kingdom*, to hold otherwise 'would import into Article 5(3) a serious weakening of a procedural guarantee to the detriment of the individual and would entail consequences impairing the very essence of the right protected by this provision'. The Court pointed out that the 'facts that

---

[104] For details of the frequency of the use of these powers, see the Lloyd Report (Cm 3420, 1996), p 57. Between February and August 1996 the police in London carried out searches under ss 13A and 13B of 9,700 drivers and passengers, and of 270 pedestrians.

[105] See *O'Hara v Chief Constable of the RUC* [1997] 1 All ER 129. For a trenchant criticism of this provision, see Gearty and Kimbell, above, n 30, pp 18–19; which also gives an account of the frequency of its use, and indicates that in the vast majority of cases no one is prosecuted. It is also stated '"Terrorism" is not and has never been in itself a criminal offence' (p 19). Compare the *Inquiry into Legislation Against Terrorism* (Lord Lloyd) (Cm 3420, 1996), where sympathy is expressed for the view that s 14(1)(b) contravenes a 'fundamental principle that a person should be liable to arrest only when he is suspected of having committed (or of being about to commit) a specific crime' (p 40). It was proposed, however, that there should be a new offence of 'being concerned in the preparation of a terrorist act' (p 42) so that if s 14(1)(b) is repealed, it would still be possible to arrest those to whom the provision currently applies.

[106] See ch 21 D.

[107] See *HM Advocate v Copeland* 1988 SLT 249. See also Prevention of Terrorism (Temporary Provisions) Act 1989, s 19.

[108] *Brogan v United Kingdom* (1989) 11 EHRR 117. See S Livingstone (1989) 40 NILQ 288.

the arrest and detention of the applicants were inspired by the legitimate aim of protecting the community as a whole from terrorism is not on its own sufficient to ensure compliance with the specific requirements of Article 5(3)'.[109] The government, however, was unwilling to accept the constraints imposed by the Convention, claiming that a facility to hold suspects for up to seven days was necessary in the fight against terrorism and that it was not possible to introduce 'a satisfactory procedure for the review of detention of terrorist suspects involving the judiciary'.[110] Consequently the government lodged a derogation under art 15 of the Convention to enable it to continue to detain for up to seven days without any judicial involvement in the procedure.[111] Indeed, the detention order need not even be signed by the Secretary of State personally (s 19), in contrast to statutory warrants for the interception of communications.[112]

In *Re Gillen's Application*[113] the applicant was arrested on 27 January 1988 under the Prevention of Terrorism (Temporary Provisions) Act 1984 on suspicion that he had been concerned in the commission, preparation or instigation of acts of terrorism. On the following day the detention was extended for three days by order of the Secretary of State until 1 February. On 29 January an application for a writ of habeas corpus was made for the applicant, alleging that he had been assaulted in the course of interviews to induce him to confess and that as a result the detention was unlawful. Hutton J held, 'The discretion to arrest and to hold the suspect in custody in order to question him in relation to crime is a discretion to be exercised for the purpose of lawful questioning; to hold a person in custody whilst detectives try to extract a confession from him by assaulting him is an exercise of the discretion for a wrongful purpose. And under a well established principle where a power is exercised for a wrongful purpose the exercise of the power becomes unlawful' (p 53). The court ruled that the applicant would be entitled to a writ of habeas corpus if the claims were substantiated.

Additional parts IVA (Offences Against Public Security) and IVB (Cordons and Protective Powers) were inserted by the Criminal Justice and Public Order Act 1994 and the Prevention of Terrorism (Additional Powers) Act 1996 respectively. By virtue of s 16A of the former a person is guilty of an offence if he or she has in possession any article for a purpose connected with the commission, preparation or instigation of acts of terrorism (as defined above). It is a defence to prove that the article was not in the possession of the individual for a terrorist purpose (and it appears that the onus is on the defendant), though sufficient evidence of possession may be established where the accused and the article in question were both present in any premises. Under s 16B it is also an offence for a person 'without lawful authority or reasonable excuse (the proof of which lies on him)', to collect or record any information which is of such a nature as is likely to be useful to terrorists in planning or carrying out any act of terrorism, or to have in

---

[109]   *Brogan* above, at 136.
[110]   HC Deb, 14 November 1989, col 209 (WA).
[111]   In *Brannigan v UK*, the Strasbourg Court upheld this derogation: (1994) 17 EHRR 539.
[112]   *HM Advocate v Copeland* 1988 SLT 249 (order signed by higher executive officer in the Scottish Home and Health Department).
[113]   [1988] NILR 40.

possession any record (including a photograph) or document containing such information. In each case an offender may be sentenced on conviction for up to ten years. The 1996 amendments (inserting 16C and 16D), empower the police to impose cordons for up to 28 days in the course of terrorist investigations and to impose parking prohibitions and restrictions in order to prevent acts of terrorism. Of these the former is perhaps the most significant constitutionally, not only because it again permits the authorisation to be made by a senior police officer (of the rank of superintendent or above).[114] There is no reporting to the Home Secretary or to anyone else on the exercise of this power, and not even an annual reporting obligation of the number of times the power has been used. People within the cordoned area must leave immediately if ordered to do so by a police constable in uniform, and a police officer of the rank of superintendent or above may authorise in writing the search of premises for material likely to be of substantial value to a terrorist investigation.

Part V of the 1989 Act confers powers on the police to obtain information for the purposes of terrorist investigations. A justice of the peace may issue a search warrant if satisfied that a terrorist investigation is being carried out and that there are reasonable grounds for believing that there is material on the premises which is likely to be of substantial value to the investigation and does not consist of items subject to legal privilege, or excluded or special procedure material.[115] In the case of excluded or special procedure material, a constable may apply to a circuit judge for an order requiring the person in possession to produce it for the constable to take away or have access to it.[116] Unlike PACE, there is no provision in the 1989 Act requiring that the application for an order should be made inter partes.[117] Where any order is not complied with, or where access to the material is needed more immediately, the constable may apply to the circuit judge for a warrant to search the premises for the excluded or special procedure material.[118] In addition to these measures, which bear a close resemblance to those in PACE, three points call for attention. First, a written order to conduct a search (including a search for excluded or special procedure material) may be issued by a police officer of at least the rank of superintendent where there are 'reasonable grounds for believing that the case is one of great emergency and that in the interests of the state immediate action is necessary'.[119] Secondly, a circuit judge may on an application made by a constable order any named person to provide an explanation of materials seized in pursuance of a warrant or an order to produce material. It is a criminal offence to make a false or misleading statement under this provision.[120] Thirdly, apart from judicial

---

[114] In cases of 'great urgency', the power may be exercised by a constable of lesser rank.
[115] Prevention of Terrorism (Temporary Provisions) Act 1989, Sched 7(2). See now Sched 7(2A) inserted by the Prevention of Terrorism (Additional Powers) Act 1996, s 2, making it easier to obtain a warrant for non-residential searches.
[116] 1989 Act, Sched 7(3)–(4).
[117] See *R v Middlesex Guildhall Crown Court, ex p Salinger* [1993] QB 564 for detailed guidance on procedure to be followed in this type of application.
[118] Prevention of Terrorism (Temporary Provisions) Act 1989, Sched 7(3).
[119] Ibid, Sched 7(7). Cf Official Secrets Act 1911, s 9 (see ch 24 above).
[120] Prevention of Terrorism (Temporary Provisions) Act 1989, Sched 7(6).

officers in normal cases and senior police officers in urgent cases, the Secretary of State may in some circumstances (relating to offences under part III of the Act) issue orders having the same effect as search warrants.[121] This is additional to the power of justices and circuit judges and is an example of legislation conferring power on ministers that would be better conferred on judges.

Northern Ireland (Emergency Provisions) Act 1996[122]

Part I of the Northern Ireland (Emergency Provisions) Act 1996 deals with what are referred to as scheduled offences, defined to include both common law offences (for example, murder, manslaughter, riot and kidnapping) and statutory offences (for example, under the Offences against the Person Act 1861, Explosive Substances Act 1883 and the Firearms (NI) Order 1981).[123] Three points of particular note arise. The first is the limitation of the power to grant bail in the case of scheduled offences. In these cases bail may not be granted by magistrates but only by a judge of the High Court or Court of Appeal, and in determining whether to grant bail, the judge must take into account factors which include the character, antecedents and community ties of the person (s 3(4)(b)). Secondly, a trial on indictment for a scheduled offence shall be held only at the Crown Court in Belfast, unless the Lord Chancellor after consulting with the Lord Chief Justice of Northern Ireland directs otherwise (s 10). All such trials 'shall be conducted by the court without a jury'. These are the so-called Diplock Courts, introduced following a recommendation by Lord Diplock in 1972 to deal with the problem of intimidation of jurors.[124] Thirdly, part I also deals with questions of evidence and onus of proof in scheduled offence prosecutions. Courts must exclude or disregard statements where there is prima facie evidence that 'the accused was subjected to torture, to inhuman or degrading treatment, or to any violence or threat of violence (whether or not amounting to torture), in order to induce him to make the statement' (s 12(2)(b)).[125] In other cases, statements may be excluded if it is appropriate to do so to avoid unfairness to the accused or otherwise in the interests of justice (s 12(3)).[126] Otherwise the onus of proof is effectively transferred to the accused on a charge of possession of explosive substances, petrol bombs, or firearms: where it is proved that the accused and the offending item were both present on any premises, 'the court may accept the fact proved as sufficient evidence of his possessing ... that article at that time unless it is further proved that he did not know of its

---

[121]   Ibid, Sched 7(8).
[122]   See HC Deb, 9 January 1996, cols 31–8.
[123]   Northern Ireland (Emergency Provisions) Act 1996, s 1 and Sched 1. For a full commentary, see B Dickson [1992] PL 592.
[124]   Cmnd 5185, 1972. For a consideration of this measure, see Cm 2706, 1995 and Cm 3420, 1996. See also Gearty and Kimbell, above, pp 56–7.
[125]   Cf *Ireland v UK* (1978) 2 EHRR 25.
[126]   See *R v Cowan* (1987) 1 BNIL 15; *R v Mullen* (1988) 10 BNIL 36; *R v Howell* (1987) 5 BNIL 10; *R v Latimer* (1993) 3 BNIL 45. See Cm 2706, 1995, pp 18–19.

presence in the premises in question, or, if he did know, that he had no control over it' (s 13(1)).[127]

Part II of the 1996 Act confers wide powers on the police and the armed forces. Thus any member of the armed forces on duty or any constable may stop any person 'so long as it is necessary in order to question him' for the purpose of ascertaining the person's identity and movements, as well as what he or she knows about a recent terrorist incident (s 25). None of the safeguards of the kind laid down in part I of PACE appear to apply here.[128] Moreover, a constable may arrest without a warrant any person whom he or she has reasonable grounds to suspect is committing, has committed or is about to commit a scheduled offence, or any other offence under the Act (s 18).[129] A member of the armed forces on duty may also arrest without warrant, and detain for up to four hours, a person who he or she has reasonable grounds to suspect is committing, has committed or is about to commit any offence (s 19). The power of arrest by the armed forces under the Act thus appears wider than that of the police, while the requirements for executing a lawful arrest are also different. A member of the armed forces making an arrest 'complies with any rule of law requiring him to state the grounds of arrest if he states that he is effecting the arrest as a member of Her Majesty's forces' (s 19(2)).

In *Murray v Ministry of Defence*[130] the plaintiff had been suspected of the offence of collecting money for the purchase of arms for the IRA in the United States. At 7 am armed soldiers arrived at her house to arrest her and take her to a screening centre in Belfast. One of the soldiers told Mrs Murray to get dressed while the others searched every room in the house and asked all the occupants to assemble in one room downstairs. After the plaintiff had dressed and come downstairs, she was told by a soldier 'As a member of the armed forces I arrest you', and was taken to the screening centre where she was released several hours later. One issue in subsequent proceedings for wrongful imprisonment was whether the failure to tell the plaintiff that she was being arrested until the soldiers were about to leave the house rendered the arrest unlawful. The House of Lords held, however, that the arrest was lawful and that it was

---

127 The Criminal Evidence (Northern Ireland) Order 1988, SI 1988 No 1987, removes the right to silence of arrested and accused persons in criminal proceedings generally. Art 4 provides, for example, that if an accused person refuses to give evidence, the court or jury may draw such inferences from the refusal as appear proper, and may 'treat the refusal as, or as capable of amounting to, corroboration of any evidence given against the accused in relation to which the refusal is material' (art 4(4)(b)). The regulations are in Zander, *The Police and Criminal Evidence Act 1984*, pp 454–8.

128 See ch 21 C above.

129 There is no longer a right, as there was in s 11 of the Northern Ireland (Emergency Provisions) Act 1978, for a constable to arrest without warrant any person whom he suspects of being a terrorist. As interpreted by the House of Lords in *McKee v Chief Constable for Northern Ireland* [1985] 1 All ER 1 (the suspicion need not be reasonable but must be honestly held), the power was found to violate art 5(1) of the European Convention on Human Rights (no one to be deprived of liberty except on *reasonable suspicion* of having committed an offence) in *Fox v United Kingdom* (1991) 13 EHRR 157. However, the wide power of arrest in similar circumstances in the Prevention of Terrorism (Temporary Provisions) Act 1989, s 14, applies to Northern Ireland and appears to take the place of s 11.

130 [1988] 2 All ER 521. See C A Gearty [1988] CLJ 332, C Walker (1989) 40 NILQ 1.

proper to delay speaking the words of arrest until all reasonable precautions had been taken to minimise the risk of danger and distress. According to Lord Griffiths, 'If words of arrest are spoken as soon as the house is entered before any precautions have been taken to search the house and find the other occupants, ... there is a real risk that the alarm may be raised and an attempt made to resist arrest, not only by those within the house but also by summoning assistance from those in the immediate neighbourhood'.[131]

Part II of the 1996 Act also contains wide powers of entry, search and seizure. Thus, any member of the armed forces or any constable may enter any premises 'if he considers it necessary to do so in the course of operations for the preservation of the peace or the maintenance of order' (s 26). Such a person may enter and search any premises or place other than a dwelling-house for the purpose of ascertaining whether there are any munitions (s 20). A police officer at least of the rank of chief inspector may authorise the entry and search of a private dwelling where there are reasonable grounds to suspect that munitions or a transmitter are being kept there.[132]

Part III of the 1996 Act deals with offences against public security and public order. This effectively makes similar provision for Northern Ireland to that contained in part I of the Prevention of Terrorism (Temporary Provisions) Act 1989. Thus, membership, support for and the organisation of meetings on behalf of a proscribed organisation are criminal offences (s 30). However, the list of proscribed organisations under this Act is longer than that under the Prevention of Terrorism (Temporary Provisions) Act. For in addition to the IRA and INLA, the 1996 Act proscribes the Ulster Volunteer Force, the Irish People's Liberation Organisation and five other organisations.[133] As with the Prevention of Terrorism (Temporary Provisions) Act, the Secretary of State may add or remove an organisation from the Schedule (s 30(3) and (4)). Even more far-reaching is s 29, containing a measure first introduced in 1991,[134] whereby it is an offence for any person to direct at any level the activities of an organisation concerned in the commission of acts of terrorism,[135] far-reaching because it carries the possibility of life imprisonment. In practice, however, evidence is very difficult to obtain, and there has been only one conviction. Other offences include the possession of items intended for terrorist purposes (s 32) and the collection of information likely to be useful to terrorists (s 33). In the case of both these offences, the onus of proof lies with the accused to show that the item was not in his or her possession for terrorist purposes; or that he or she was not collecting information without lawful authority or reasonable excuse. The public display of support for a proscribed organisation is an offence under the 1996 Act (s 31) as it is under the Prevention of Terrorism (Temporary Provisions) Act

---

[131]   [1988] 2 All ER 521 at 527. It was also held in *Murray* that the army could question a suspect about activities other than those in connection with which he or she had been arrested.

[132]   In 1993, 4,166 premises were searched under what is now s 20: Cm 2706, 1995, p 77. See generally Cm 2706, 1995, pp 21–9.

[133]   1996 Act, Sched 2.

[134]   Northern Ireland (Emergency Provisions) Act 1991, s 27.

[135]   Terrorism is defined by s 58 as having the same meaning as in the Prevention of Terrorism (Temporary Provisions) Act 1989; see note 89 above.

(s 3). It is an offence for any person without lawful authority or reasonable excuse to wear in a public place any hood, mask or other article adapted for use for concealing his or her identity or features.[136] Again the onus is on the accused to prove lawful authority or reasonable excuse.

Part IV of the 1996 Act deals with internment, referred to as 'the detention of terrorists and persons suspected of being terrorists' (s 36). Internment, ie detention without trial, which has a long history in Ireland, was discontinued in 1975, having proved to be not only highly controversial but also of questionable effect.[137] Although the practice was discontinued, there continues to be power to re-introduce it on the advice of the Chief Constable of the RUC on security grounds.[138] In *Ireland v United Kingdom*,[139] the European Court of Human Rights held that previous internment procedures violated art 5 of the European Convention on Human Rights, but that derogation from this commitment could be justified under art 15.[140] However, the techniques employed for the interrogation of interned suspects violated art 3 of the Convention as inhuman and degrading treatment.[141] Part V of the Act contains 'anti-racketeering' measures. The intention behind the introduction of these measures in 1987 'was to cure a mischief whereby bogus firms supplying "security services" extorted money from builders, contractors and businesses of all kinds. The money went to paramilitary organisations'.[142] To combat this, a licensing system was set up, with firms offering security services being required to apply for a licence annually.[143] Applicants must supply information about the business, including details of any persons employed as security guards (s 38). Personnel records are subject to inspection by the police, who may enter the premises of a company providing security services and require the records to be produced (s 41). The Secretary of State may refuse a certificate only if satisfied that a proscribed organisation or a 'closely associated' organisation 'would be likely to benefit from the issue of the certificate' (s 39). The Secretary of State may revoke a certificate on the same grounds, but the holder must be notified of such an intention and be given a reasonable opportunity to make representations (s 39(6)). There is no statutory right to a hearing before a certificate is refused, though the common law duty to act fairly may apply to require some right to make representations.[144] This, however, is likely to be rather perfunctory, particularly as the minister's decision will be based to some extent on intelligence information which the courts will not normally require to be disclosed.[145]

---

[136] Cf Public Order Act 1936, s 1. See ch 23.
[137] For background, see Cm 1115, 1990, ch 11. A full account of the procedures is given in *Ireland v UK* (1978) 2 EHRR 25; and see ch 6 above.
[138] HC Deb, 9 January 1996, col 37. According to J J Rowe QC, however, these powers 'ought not to stay' (Cm 2706, 1995, p 33).
[139] (1978) 2 EHRR 25.
[140] Art 15 provides that in time of war or other public emergency threatening the life of the nation, the government may take measures derogating from some Convention obligations to the extent strictly required by the exigencies of the situation.
[141] Ch 6 above.
[142] Cm 1115, 1990, p 58.
[143] See now 1996 Act, s 38.
[144] See ch 29 B.
[145] See ch 24.

Part VI of the 1996 Act deals with the rights of persons in police custody detained under s 14 of the Prevention of Terrorism Act 1989. Such persons have a right to have someone informed of their detention (s 46) and a right of access to legal advice (s 47), though in each case this may be delayed where there are reasonable grounds to believe that this may damage the investigation or make it more difficult to prevent acts of terrorism or to apprehend terrorists.[146] In *Murray v United Kingdom*,[147] however, this power to delay access was questioned in the context of the Criminal Evidence (Northern Ireland) Order 1988 which allows adverse inferences to be drawn from an accused's failure to mention particular facts when questioned by a police officer. In such circumstances, said the court, 'it is of paramount importance for the rights of the defence that an accused has access to a lawyer at the initial stages of police interrogation'. Under the Order the accused is confronted with 'a fundamental dilemma relating to his defence. If he chooses to remain silent, adverse inferences may be drawn against him in accordance with the provisions of the Order. On the other hand, if the accused opts to break his silence during the course of interrogation, he runs the risk of prejudging his defence without necessarily removing the possibility of inferences being drawn against him'. It was concluded that 'the concept of fairness enshrined in Art 6 [of the ECHR] requires that the accused has the benefit of the assistance of a lawyer already at the initial stages of police interrogation'.[148] The question which flows from this is whether there is also a right to have a lawyer present while the accused is being interrogated by the police. The matter has exercised the courts in Northern Ireland on a number of occasions and it has been held that in the absence of any statutory right to this effect not only is there no common law right to have a solicitor present during an interview, but the decision in *Murray* 'does not guarantee a right to access to a lawyer during pre-trial examinations'.[149] Although the police 'have undoubted power and therefore a discretion, to be exercised properly, to allow a terrorism suspect to have his solicitor present during interviews', it is 'not incumbent on the police to justify refusal of access, rather it is for the police to give access only if special circumstances exist', the court emphasising that in doing so the police would be granting a concession rather than complying with an obligation.[150] In his review of the 1991 Act, J J Rowe QC was not prepared to recommend that suspects should have the right to have solicitors present during interrogation, even though such a restriction 'may be a breach' of art 6 of the ECHR.[151]

Finally, Part VII of the 1996 Act contains compensation measures for persons whose 'real or personal property is taken, occupied, destroyed or damaged' or who suffer any other interference with their private property rights

---

[146] These correspond to the Police and Criminal Evidence Act 1984, ss 56 and 58, which applies in England and Wales only.

[147] (1996) 22 EHRR 29.

[148] Where a terrorist suspect wishes to exercise the right to consult with a solicitor, an interview may take place before the solicitor arrives in order to avoid unreasonable delay in the investigation. A confession should not be excluded 'merely because interviewing continued whilst the arrival of the solicitor was awaited'. See *R v Harper* (1997) 1 BNIL 20.

[149] *In re Begley* (1996) 5 BNIL 39, and *in Re Russell* (1996) 9 BNIL 33.

[150] See esp *Russell*, above. See also *Harper*, above.

[151] Cm 2706, 1995, pp 49–50.

(s 55). This is additional to any common law action for negligence or nuisance which might be available, and arises from damage caused, for example, by the cutting of fences or the spoiling of property due to the search of the inside of a house. Applications are made to the Secretary of State for Northern Ireland, from whom an appeal lies to the county court. In practice, 'it is most unusual for a settlement not to be reached', and it is the policy of officials to do this quickly, 'especially in respect of damage done in house searches, or in temporary occupation by the security forces'.[152] The amount paid out in compensation has risen at an 'alarming rate' from a total of £34,156 in 1973–74 to £2,600,591 in 1993–94. This was explained partly on the ground of an increase in fraud and partly to a willingness by some people to pursue minor infringements, though no reference was made to the possibility of an increase in the amount of damage which is actually being inflicted. But whatever the reason, Rowe nevertheless had 'reservations' about some of the government's proposals for reducing the scope of compensation and the time within which complaints should be made. He recommended an extension of the statutory compensation scheme to victims of property damage arising from the exercise of powers under the Prevention of Terrorism Act 1989;[153] it does seem peculiarly anomalous that entitlement should depend on the source of the power by which the damage was authorised. This would be consistent with Rowe's more general recommendation for the two statutes to be merged into a single code. Part VII also empowers the Secretary of State to make regulations 'to make provision additional to the foregoing provisions of the Act for promoting the preservation of the peace and the maintenance of order' (s 49). The potential scope of such regulations is very broad indeed.

Reform and future prospects

Various provisions of the legislation relating to terrorism have been strongly criticised, though it seems likely that it will become a permanent feature of our law, in one form or another. Although much will depend on a permanent ceasefire being established in Northern Ireland, it is the case that certain provisions of the legislation are not readily compatible with civil libertarian concerns, and as such have been widely criticised. These include the powers in respect of exclusion orders, the power in s 14(1)(b) of the 1989 Act to arrest a person without suspicion that he or she has committed an offence, the powers of the police and the Home Secretary to authorise the search of domestic premises, the power to deny access to legal advice during police interrogation, and the absence of trial by jury. On the other hand, it is widely accepted that 'there is no obligation on a democratic nation to prove its liberal bona fides by allowing itself to be destroyed by its enemies',[154] though there is scope for debate as to how best the criminal law could be most effectively deployed in a manner which respects both the liberty of the individual and the security of the state. The *Inquiry into Legislation against Terrorism* conducted by Lord Lloyd in 1996 concluded that in common with the practice of a number of other countries there should be in this country permanent legislation to deal with

---

152   Cm 1115, 1990, p 61.
153   Cm 2706, 1995.
154   Gearty and Kimbell, note 30 above, p 69.

terrorism in its various manifestations, even when lasting peace is established in Northern Ireland.[155] It would be an offence to be a member of a terrorist organisation and to be concerned in the preparation of an act of terrorism. In respect both of domestic as well as international terrorism, it is proposed that while a number of the controversial provisions of the Prevention of Terrorism (Temporary Provisions) Act 1989 and the Northern Ireland (Emergency Provisions) Act 1996 should be repealed, others should be retained (with modifications).[156]

---

[155]   Cm 3420, 1996.
[156]   For a comprehensive account of how these problems are addressed elsewhere in Europe, see Vercher, *Terrorism in Europe.*

PART IV

Administrative law

CHAPTER 26

The nature and development of administrative law

During the last 25 years, there has been, and continues to be, a remarkable growth in litigation seeking judicial review of the decisions of public authorities.[1] This may be why the law of judicial review is sometimes thought to be the only part of administrative law which lawyers need to know. But this is no more correct than to say that employment lawyers need study only the law of unfair dismissal, or tort lawyers only the law of negligence. Certainly, the law of judicial review, outlined in chapters 29 and 30, is a vital part of administrative law, but the part must not be mistaken for the whole.

A formal definition of administrative law is that it is a branch of public law concerned with the composition, procedures, powers, duties, rights and liabilities of the various organs of government which are engaged in administering public policies.[2] These policies have been either laid down by Parliament in legislation or developed by the government and other authorities in the exercise of their executive powers. On this broad definition, administrative law includes at one extreme the general principles and institutions of constitutional law outlined in earlier chapters; and at the other the minutely detailed rules contained in statutes and ministerial regulations that govern the provision of complex social services (such as social security), the regulation of economic activities (such as financial services) and environmental law.

As we will see below, there is no 'bright line' demarcating constitutional and administrative law. Building on the account of the institutions and principles of constitutional government already given, this part of the book deals with aspects of administrative law which are relevant to all areas of government. These are the powers of the executive to make secondary, or delegated, legislation; the procedures whereby specialised tribunals and

---

[1] In 1981, 533 applications for judicial review were made, of which 376 were allowed; in 1987, 1,529 were made and 767 allowed; and in 1994, 3,208 were made and 1,260 allowed: Bridges, Meszaros and Sunkin, *Judicial Review in Perspective*, app 1. And see M Sunkin (1987) 50 MLR 432 and [1991] PL 490.

[2] For fuller accounts, see the textbooks on administrative law by (respectively) Cane, Craig, Foulkes, Wade and Forsyth. See also Richardson and Genn (eds), *Administrative Law and Government Action*; Harlow and Rawlings, *Law and Administration*; and the collections of case materials by Beatson and Matthews, and Bailey, Jones and Mowbray.

inquiries, and the Parliamentary Ombudsman, make decisions or provide redress for individual grievances; judicial review of public authorities; and the liability of public authorities, notably central government, to be sued for damages. The aim will be to identify principles upon which public administration ought to be based.[3]

Functions of administrative law

One important function of the law is to enable the tasks of government to be performed. Administrative agencies are created by law and equipped with powers to carry out public policies on behalf of the state and in the general interest. A second function of the law is to govern the relations between various public agencies, for example, between a minister and a local authority,[4] or between two local authorities.[5] A third function of the law is to govern the relations between a public agency and those individuals or private bodies over whose affairs the agency is entrusted with power. By providing a public agency or other body with legal powers to perform its tasks, the legislator also imposes a measure of control since an agency is not authorised to go outside its powers. The granting of powers may be subject both to express conditions or limitations, and also to implied requirements, such as the duty to exercise powers in good faith and not corruptly. The extent of the powers granted will reflect the system of social, economic, and political values recognised in a given society.

Individuals are affected by administrative powers in many ways, sometimes to their benefit and sometimes to their detriment. An individual's rights are seldom absolute: thus a landowner whose farm is required for a new motorway does not have an absolute right to prevent the acquisition of that land for a purpose considered to be in the general interest of the community. Nor, to take a very difficult example, do parents with a seriously ill child have an absolute right to medical treatment for him or her in the NHS when this is not recommended on clinical grounds.[6] Conversely, the powers of public authorities should not themselves be regarded as absolute. Few would dispute that individuals, local communities and minority groups have a right to legal protection when confronted with the coercive powers of the state. The difficulty comes in determining the form and extent of that protection, and the basis on which such disputes may be resolved. The more fundamental the rights of the individual affected, the greater ought to be the degree of protection.[7]

The constitutional background to administrative law

Earlier chapters described the structure of central government and the civil service; the responsibility of ministers to Parliament; the use of public bodies to regulate public utilities and other services; and the effect of public powers

---

[3]   Cf de Smith, Woolf and Jowell, *Judicial Review of Administrative Action*, ch 1.
[4]   Eg *Education Secretary v Tameside MB* [1977] AC 1014, ch 29 A below.
[5]   Eg *Bromley BC v Greater London Council* [1983] AC 768.
[6]   *R v Cambridge Health Authority, ex p B* [1995] 2 All ER 129.
[7]   See Lord Browne-Wilkinson [1992] 397 and Sir J Laws [1993] PL 59.

on the individual's rights and liberties. The legislative supremacy of Parliament is relevant to administrative law, since no court may hold that the statutory powers of an agency are unconstitutional. Despite that supremacy, the courts play an important role in interpreting the legislation that applies to public authorities. They have developed that role to a point where they may enforce standards of lawful conduct and good administration, even if these are not directly derived from the legislation itself.[8]

In a modern legal system, the way that disputes arising out of administration are handled is of constitutional significance. Where, as in Germany, there are separate superior courts, one entrusted with interpreting the constitution and one dealing with disputes between the citizen and the administration, a distinction between constitutional and administrative law can be based on the actual work done by the two courts. In the United Kingdom, however, it is impossible to draw a hard and fast line between constitutional and administrative law.[9] Public law disputes are handled by the same courts that have jurisdiction in matters of private law. The leading judicial review cases are likely to have a broad significance in public law.[10] In *Wheeler v Leicester City Council*,[11] the House of Lords held that a local authority had acted unlawfully in depriving a rugby club of the use of the council's playing fields because members of the club had played rugby in South Africa. The case involved aspects of local government and race relations law as well as the freedom of expression. Decisions based on the royal prerogative (such as the issue of passports) or those that affect the individual's fundamental rights (such as the control of immigration) are likewise important in public law generally. Both European Community law and the European Convention on Human Rights have many implications for administrative law. The criminal law as such falls outside administrative law, but management of the police and the penal system often gives rise to disputes about the exercise of official powers (for example, over the rights of convicted prisoners to legal protection against the prison authorities).[12] The procedures of Parliament fall outside administrative law, but the rules of public audit directly affect the working of government departments[13] and so do parliamentary procedures for the scrutiny of delegated legislation.[14]

Administrative law and 'droit administratif'

The study of administrative law in Britain was formerly dominated by the comparison which Dicey drew between the system of administrative jurisdiction (*le contentieux administratif*) in France, under which a special hierarchy of administrative courts (headed by the Conseil d'Etat) deals with most disputes concerning the exercise of administrative power, and the common law in

---

[8]   See D Oliver [1987] PL 543; Lord Woolf [1995] PL 57. Cf C Forsyth [1996] CLJ 122.
[9]   And see Craig, *Public Law and Democracy*, ch 1.
[10] Eg *R v Home Secretary, ex p Fire Brigades Union* [1995] 2 AC 513 and *R v Foreign Secretary, ex p World Development Movement* [1995] 1 All ER 611.
[11] [1985] AC 1054.
[12] Eg *R v Deputy Governor of Parkhurst Prison, ex p Hague* [1992] 1 AC 58.
[13] See Turpin, *Government Procurement and Contracts*.
[14] Ch 27.

England.[15] Dicey contrasted the disadvantages involved in a system of administrative courts handling disputes between officials and citizens with the advantages enjoyed in Britain through the absence of such a system. The common law, as Dicey saw it, subjected executive actions to control by the same courts and according to the same principles as governed the relationships between private citizens. Dicey concluded that the common law gave the citizen better protection against arbitrary action by the executive than the French system. Unfortunately, Dicey's denial that 'droit administratif' existed in England led many to suppose that there was no such thing as administrative law in the United Kingdom.

Old beliefs died hard[16] but today administrative law in Britain needs no proof of its existence. In 1987, the government circulated a leaflet bringing to the notice of civil servants the existence of what it called 'The Judge Over Your Shoulder', accompanying it with a secret Cabinet memorandum entitled, 'Reducing the Risk of Legal Challenges'.[17] The judiciary in Britain are now well aware that their power to control the actions of public authorities is of constitutional significance. Lord Diplock described the rapid development of 'a rational and comprehensive system of administrative law' as having been 'the greatest achievement of the English courts' in his judicial lifetime.[18] One judge has written that in this area of common law, 'the judges have in the last thirty years changed the face of the United Kingdom's constitution'.[19]

Despite these developments, there are many differences between the English and French approaches to administrative law. The French system lays emphasis on the use of separate administrative courts whereas the British system relies heavily upon the superior civil courts. In both systems, the essential principles of judicial control are judge-made and do not derive from either codes or statutes. But in France, the price paid for a separate administrative jurisdiction is a complex body of law dividing jurisdiction between the civil and the administrative courts (that is, between private and public law); questions of conflict must be settled by the Tribunal des Conflits or by legislation. Where the French system gains is that administrative courts develop rules of procedure (for example, regarding the obtaining of evidence from government departments) and rules of substantive liability (for example, regarding administrative contracts, or the state's liability for harm caused by official acts) which take account of the public setting of the disputes. These rules may confer special duties upon the administration (for example, liability without fault in certain circumstances),[20] not merely immunities.

---

[15]   *The Law of the Constitution*, ch 12 and app 2. See F H Lawson (1959) 7 Political Studies 109, 207; Brown and Bell, *French Administrative Law*; and, for a critique of Dicey's approach to administrative law, H W Arthurs (1979) 17 Osgoode Hall LJ 1.

[16]   Mr Maudling, when Home Secretary, said in debating a clause of the Immigration Bill 1971: 'I have never seen the sense of administrative law in our country, because it merely means someone else taking the Government's decisions for them' (Official Report, Standing Committee B, 25 May 1971, col 1508).

[17]   See A W Bradley [1987] PL 485 and [1988] PL 1; and D Oliver [1994] PL 514.

[18]   *Re Racal Communications Ltd* [1981] AC 374, 382, and *R v Inland Revenue Commissioners, ex p National Federation of Self-Employed* [1982] AC 617, 641. And see Lord Diplock [1974] CLJ 233; Lord Scarman [1990] PL 490.

[19]   Sir S Sedley, in Richardson and Genn, op cit, p 36.

[20]   R Errera [1986] CLP 157.

By contrast, the British approach, manifest in case-law and in the Crown Proceedings Act 1947, has been to apply general principles of liability in contract and tort to public bodies as well as to private citizens. It was by application of the general law of negligence that the liability of the Home Office was decided in respect of harm done by escaping Borstal boys.[21] In respect of the judicial control of official decisions, however, public law principles have developed since the jurisdiction to review the validity of official acts has no counterpart in private law. Particularly in the 1950s, the British courts were very reluctant to exercise jurisdiction over public authorities; such remedies as were available (the former prerogative orders)[22] were subject to technical restrictions and were little used. Since the mid-1960s, the judges have been more willing to play an active role in umpiring administrative law disputes; today they could not be accused of reluctance to find for the citizen against the government. While gaps in legal protection for the citizen undoubtedly exist,[23] the British courts are capable of providing an effective, authoritative and timely remedy to individuals who challenge the legality of official acts.

Historical development

One effect of the constitutional settlement in 1689 was to restrict the power of the King's government in London to supervise the conduct of local administration by such persons as justices of the peace for the counties, who met quarterly to dispense criminal justice and to govern their locality. The powers of the justices in such matters as the poor law, licensing and highways, were derived from Acts of Parliament. Although there was little, if any, central control over the activities of the justices, their exercise of power could be challenged in the Court of King's Bench on grounds of legality and jurisdiction by recourse to the prerogative writs.[24] Particularly after 1832, new bodies were established by Parliament such as the poor law guardians, public health boards and school boards. When modern local authorities were created and new departments of central government emerged, the Court of King's Bench extended its controlling jurisdiction to include all these bodies. In his lectures at Cambridge in 1887–88, Maitland argued for a broad approach to constitutional law that would include these new organs of government:

Year by year the subordinate government of England is becoming more and more important. The new movement set in with the Reform Bill of 1832: it has gone far already and assuredly it will go further. We are becoming a much governed nation, governed by all manner of councils and boards and officers, central and local, high and low, exercising the powers which have been committed to them by modern statutes.[25]

Since these bodies were exercising statutory powers, disputes about the limits

---

21 *Dorset Yacht Co v Home Office* [1970] AC 1004; ch 31 A. And see Bell and Bradley (eds), *Governmental Liability: a Comparative Study*.
22 Ch 30.
23 See eg *Hoffmann-La Roche & Co v Trade & Industry Secretary* [1975] AC 295, 359 (Lord Wilberforce).
24 See Henderson, *Foundations of English Administrative Law*; de Smith, Woolf and Jowell, *Judicial Review of Administrative Action*, ch 14.
25 Maitland, *Constitutional History*, p 501.

of their power were settled by the courts, often by recourse to the prerogative writs. Thus the procedures of judicial control, which originally checked the powers of inferior courts, were used to review the exercise of statutory powers first by local authorities and then by ministers of the Crown.[26] It is a long step from reviewing the rate levied by county justices to pay for repairs to a bridge[27] to reviewing a decision by the Home Secretary to introduce a new and less costly scheme of compensation for criminal injuries.[28] Yet in both instances the court's role is to ensure that those who exercise executive power observe due standards of legality in doing so.

Inevitably, the supervisory role of the courts has changed and developed as patterns of government have changed. Judicial control of central government is complementary to, not a substitute for, the responsibility of ministers to Parliament. The grounds of judicial control have never been defined in legislation. However, by the common law doctrine of precedent, unsystematic and haphazard as it is, principles have developed both for policing the outer limits of powers and for reviewing the use of discretionary powers. In 1992, an eminent New Zealand judge summarised administrative law in this way: 'The administrator must act fairly, reasonably and according to law. That is the essence and the rest is mainly machinery'.[29] Such principles apply whenever public power is exercised, regardless of its legal source.[30]

In Scotland, the detailed history of the law is different but the general form of the development has been similar. After the abolition of the Privy Council for Scotland, following the Union with England in 1707, the Court of Session adopted a supervisory role comparable to that of the Court of King's Bench in England. Since the prerogative writs were never part of Scots law, and since a separate court of equity was never created, the remedies for controlling inferior tribunals and administrative agencies were obtained from the Court of Session by the procedures used for civil litigation between private parties. But the principles upon which judicial control was founded were remarkably similar to those developed in English law.[31] The sheriff court exercised an important but more specific role in enabling many local administrative disputes to be settled judicially.[32] In the 20th century, much of the development in government has been by statute law which applies both in England and Scotland, and the response of the Scottish courts has been very similar to that of the English courts.

Reform of administrative law

The explosion of government in the 20th century did not wait for lawyers and academic writers in Britain to acquire an understanding of administrative law.

---

26 Eg *Board of Education v Rice* [1911] AC 179 and *Local Government Board v Arlidge* [1915] AC 120, on which see Dicey, *The Law of the Constitution*, app 2.
27 *R v Glamorganshire Inhabitants* (1700) 1 Ld Raym 580.
28 *R v Home Secretary, ex p Fire Brigades Union* [1995] 2 AC 513.
29 Sir Robin Cooke, quoted in *R v Devon CC, ex p Baker* [1995] 1 All ER 73, 88.
30 Eg *CCSU v Minister for Civil Service* [1985] AC 374.
31 See eg *Moss Empires Ltd v Glasgow Assessor* 1917 SC (HL) 1. Also *Stair Memorial Encyclopaedia, The Laws of Scotland*, vol 1, title Administrative Law.
32 *Brown v Hamilton DC* 1983 SC (HL) 1.

The first textbooks on the subject appeared in the late 1920s.[33] At first a narrow approach was taken to the subject, confining it to delegated legislation and the exercise of judicial powers by administrative bodies. Only later was a broader definition of administrative law adopted as covering all administrative powers and duties as well as judicial control of the administration.

The hesitant development of administrative law in Britain since the 1920s may be illustrated by reference to three committees appointed by the Lord Chancellor to inquire into aspects of the subject. The first, a committee that examined the archaic law protecting the Crown and government departments from being sued, made no effective progress.[34] The second, the Committee on Ministers' Powers, was appointed in 1929 at a time when a storm of criticism was directed against departments by some judges and barristers, by academic lawyers at Oxford and a small group of MPs. Indeed, the Lord Chief Justice (Lord Hewart) had just published a strident book, *The New Despotism*, in which he argued that Britain was experiencing administrative lawlessness rather than the rule of law. The terms of reference of the committee were:

to consider the powers exercised by, or under the direction of (or by persons or bodies appointed specially by), Ministers of the Crown by way of (*a*) delegated legislation, and (*b*) judicial or quasi-judicial decision, and to report what safeguards were desirable or necessary to secure the constitutional principles of the sovereignty of Parliament and the supremacy of the law.

The committee vindicated the civil service from the charge of bureaucratic tyranny, analysed in terms of constitutional principle the legislative and judicial powers vested in ministers and made recommendations to improve delegated legislation and administrative justice.[35] No government adopted its recommendations, but it had some influence on the drafting of Bills which conferred powers on departments, and eventually the House of Commons in 1944 established a select committee to scrutinise delegated legislation.[36]

In 1955, when the government machine was again under attack from sections of political opinion,[37] the Committee on Administrative Tribunals and Inquiries was appointed to review:

(*a*) The constitution and working of tribunals other than the ordinary courts of law, constituted under any Act of Parliament by a Minister of the Crown or for the purposes of a Minister's functions.

(*b*) The working of such administrative procedures as include the holding of an inquiry or hearing by or on behalf of a Minister on an appeal or as the result of objections or representations, and in particular the procedure for the compulsory purchase of land.

This committee (the Franks committee) reported in 1957.[38] In examining tribunals and inquiries, it covered again ground which the Committee on Ministers' Powers had already reviewed (judicial and quasi-judicial decisions taken by or for ministers) but, unlike that committee, it found great difficulty

---

[33] Robson, *Justice and Administrative Law*, and Port, *Administrative Law*.
[34] See Cmd 2842, 1927, discussed by J Jacob [1992] PL 452; and ch 31 A.
[35] Cmd 4060, 1932.
[36] Ch 27.
[37] The attack was intensified by the Crichel Down affair; ch 7.
[38] Cmnd 218, 1957.

in distinguishing formally between judicial and administrative decisions. Adopting a more pragmatic approach, it examined one by one the procedures within its terms of reference and inquired how far the characteristics of openness, fairness and impartiality applied to each. The committee concluded that judicial control, whether by direct appeal to the courts or by review through the prerogative orders, should be maintained and where necessary extended. These recommendations led directly to the Tribunals and Inquiries Act 1958, which set up the Council on Tribunals, and to other action implementing the committee's report.[39]

The Franks committee's attention was confined to areas where recourse to a tribunal or a public inquiry was already available. The committee could not consider those areas of governmental power where neither safeguard existed. Nor could the committee consider the provision of redress for individuals suffering from maladministration. These two problems were examined in 1961 by a non-governmental committee appointed by Justice.[40] The report, *The Citizen and the Administration*, recommended (*a*) that, except where there are overriding considerations of government policy, a citizen should be entitled to appeal from a departmental decision on a matter of discretion to an impartial tribunal; rather than the creation of many new tribunals, a general tribunal should be created to hear miscellaneous appeals against discretionary decisions, and (*b*) that a Parliamentary Commissioner (Ombudsman) be appointed to investigate complaints of maladministration. Nothing came of the former recommendation, but the first appointment of a Parliamentary Commissioner for Administration was made in 1967. The creation of an Ombudsman did not affect the rules and procedures of administrative law. In 1969, the government decided not to appoint a royal commission to examine the whole of administrative law, and asked the English and Scottish Law Commissions to study separately the effectiveness of administrative law remedies in the English and Scottish courts. In 1976, the English Commission recommended important procedural reforms[41] and these were implemented between 1977 and 1981, creating the current procedure of application for judicial review.[42] Since 1977, increased use of this procedure has enabled the High Court to deal with many complaints of injustice which would previously have gone by default. A similarly named procedure was introduced into Scots law in 1985.[43]

The continuing refusal of governments to make a general inquiry into administrative law led in 1979 to a further initiative by Justice, with All Souls College Oxford, to create a committee to review administrative law in the United Kingdom, under the chairmanship of Sir Patrick Neill QC. In 1988, the committee recommended inter alia that a permanent Administrative Review Commission be appointed for consultation and review of admin-

---

[39]   Ch 28 A and B, and see J A G Griffith (1959) 22 MLR 125.
[40]   For comment, see I M Pedersen [1962] PL 15, J D B Mitchell [1962] PL 82 and A W Bradley [1962] CLJ 82. Justice is the British section of the International Commission of Jurists.
[41]   Cmnd 6407, 1976; and see the Scottish Law Commission, *Remedies in Administrative Law*, Memorandum No 14, 1971.
[42]   Ch 30.
[43]   See note 31 above and A W Bradley [1987] PL 313.

istrative procedures, that the grounds on which judicial review may be sought should be enacted in legislation and that reasons be given for all administrative decisions.[44] None of the committee's recommendations were adopted by government.

In 1994, the English Law Commission completed a review of the mechanism of judicial review and of the statutory procedures for appeals to the High Court from inferior courts, tribunals and other bodies.[45] It proposed some limited changes in procedure and nomenclature, which (inter alia) would enable public interest challenges to official decisions to be made by interest groups, and advisory declarations to be made by the court. By 1997, the proposals had not been implemented and the issues had become subsumed within Lord Woolf's much broader review of the conduct of civil litigation.

It must be emphasised that, except for the creation of the procedure of applications for judicial review in 1977, the development in the public law role of the courts in recent years owes more to changing attitudes on the part of the judges than it does to formal procedures of law reform.

Law and the administrative process

The principle that government must be conducted according to law means that for every act performed in the course of government there must be legal authority. That authority is usually derived expressly or by implication from statute or sometimes from the royal prerogative. Moreover, the Crown has at common law the same capacity as any other person to make contracts, own property etc.[46] It is particularly necessary for a public body to be able to show that it is acting in accordance with legal authority when its action (for example, the levying of a tax) adversely affects the rights or interests of a private individual. Exceptionally, the public interest may require the government to satisfy a court that its decisions are lawful even if no private individuals are affected except as members of the public at large.[47]

It is not possible to describe the administrative process in terms of law alone. There are many tasks (for example, budgeting, coordination and planning) to which law is not of primary relevance. Many politicians and administrators are likely to view law instrumentally as a means of achieving social or economic policies. In areas of government such as taxation, the detailed rules may be found in statutes or in judicial decisions interpreting the statutes. Even here, circumstances may arise in which the revenue authorities exercise an extra-statutory discretion not to enforce payment of tax in a situation which neither Parliament nor the government can have foreseen.[48] But the practice of granting extra-statutory concessions would

---

44   *Administrative Justice: Some Necessary Reforms*, discussed by P McAuslan [1988] PL 402 and
      C T Emery [1988] PL 495.
45   Law Com No 226; HC 669 (1993–94). See also Lord Woolf [1992] PL 221, R Gordon
      [1995] PL 11 and C T Emery [1995] PL 450.
46   B V Harris (1992) 108 LQR 626.
47   See eg *R v Foreign Secretary, ex p Rees-Mogg* [1994] QB 552; *R v Foreign Secretary, ex p Worldwide
      Development Movement* [1995] 1 All ER 611; and ch 30.
48   See eg Annual Report of Parliamentary Commissioner for 1970, HC 261 (1970–71), p 36
      (refusal to refund gaming licence duty to casino in Scotland).

defeat the whole purpose of imposing taxes by law if it became widespread; by the nature of a tax concession, it may escape challenge in a court of law.[49]

By contrast with taxation, in many areas of government the nature of the legal framework is deliberately skeletonic, so as to allow for wide discretion on the part of the department concerned in promoting policies which are nowhere laid down in statutory rules. Thus an agency responsible for grants to industry may wish to make selective grants to certain forms of industry or to discriminate between areas of high and low unemployment.[50] Wide discretion is found in many other areas of government, such as the control of immigration and the control by central government of local authority expenditure. In principle, discretionary powers are subject to control by the courts. In practice, the exercise of discretion is often closely controlled through policy decisions taken by ministers, or departmental rules which lay down how officials should exercise their powers.[51] The creation of the Social Fund in 1988 for discretionary payments to those in need of the basic necessities of life was a deliberate return to a scheme of administrative discretion in place of a scheme of entitlement based upon statutory regulations.[52]

The work of many officials is therefore concerned with the administration of government policies rather than with the administration of the law as such. It is often difficult to separate the administration of an existing policy from the making of a new policy. When a department is exercising discretionary powers and a case arises that raises new features, a decision on the facts will serve as a precedent for future decisions of a similar kind. Thus the process gives rise to the formulation of a more detailed policy than had previously existed.

Decision-making within a department is very different from the process by which a court settles a dispute between two parties. A civil case, for example, is decided by the judge after hearing evidence and legal arguments brought before the court by the parties in an adversary procedure. Oral proceedings usually take place in public before the judge, in the presence of the parties and their lawyers. A reasoned decision is announced in open court; when made it can be challenged only by appeal to a higher court. By contrast, a departmental decision is typically taken in secret, without an adversary procedure. Often it is not known at what level in the department the decision has been taken. Political pressure may be brought to bear on the department both before and after the decision. Except where a statute so requires, reasons for the decision need not be given, although political pressure may often bring about some explanation.

Although the two processes of administrative and judicial decision-making are different, it would be wrong to assume that one method is superior to the other or to suppose that a department should always seek to adopt the methods of a court. Everything depends on the type of decision to be made

---

[49]   But not judicial criticism: *Vestey v IRC* [1980] AC 1148. And cf *R v IRC, ex p National Federation of Self-Employed* [1982] AC 617.
[50]   See eg *British Oxygen Co v Board of Trade* [1971] AC 610.
[51]   On departmental rules and 'quasi-legislation', see ch 27 below.
[52]   See Social Security Act 1986, s 32 (1); R Drabble and T Lynes [1989] PL 297; T Mullen (1989) 52 MLR 64.

and on the results which it is desired to achieve from a particular scheme.[53] However, decisions that are made on the basis of general rules and after a procedure that enables the specific facts to be ascertained and the competing considerations to be weighed up by a reasoned process are likely to be fairer and more soundly based than if made without such aids to decision-making.[54] Thus many classes of decisions are taken not by civil servants in the department but by independent tribunals, which apply a modified form of judicial procedure in making decisions. In other cases, Parliament has provided that a stage of the administrative process should be exposed to view in the form of a public inquiry, while leaving the final decision in the hands of the minister or department.[55] The use of executive agencies under the 'Next Steps' initiative to handle many tasks of government has not changed the legal nature of the decisions to be made, but it could lead to greater openness in the structure of decision-making and to more use of formal schemes of delegation.[56]

Powers, duties and discretion

As Lord Diplock said,

> The very concept of administrative discretion involves a right to choose between more than one possible course of action on which there is room for reasonable people to hold differing opinions as to which is to be preferred.[57]

Only rarely is there placed on an official the duty of taking a specific course of action; for example, the duty of a local government official to produce council minutes for inspection by an elector.[58] In general, administrative action involves the exercise of discretion. While the law does not regulate all forms of official discretion,[59] there are many important principles of administrative law which govern the exercise of discretion. Administrative discretion, although it may be wide, is very rarely unlimited. Even where a statute confers a wide discretion on a minister, it is possible to seek a remedy in the courts on the ground that a particular decision is beyond his or her legal authority, for example because it seeks to achieve policies which are not authorised by the statute.[60]

If an Act which confers authority to administer a branch of government is analysed, it will often be found to confer a broad duty on the minister or on local authorities to fulfil certain policy objectives; it may also confer narrower duties to act in specified situations; and it will also confer various powers intended to promote the purposes of the Act. In administrative law, 'power' has two meanings, which are not always distinguished: (*a*) capacity to act in a certain way (for example, power to provide services, or to purchase land by

---

53   G Ganz [1972] PL 215, 299. Cf *Local Government Board v Arlidge* [1915] AC 120.
54   See J Jowell [1973] PL 178 and (the same author) in Jowell and Oliver (eds), *The Changing Constitution*, ch 3.
55   Ch 28 A and B.
56   Ch 13 D.
57   *Secretary of State for Education v Tameside MB* [1977] AC 1014, at p 1064.
58   Local Government Act 1972, s 228.
59   See Davis, *Discretionary Justice*, and Galligan, *Discretionary Powers*.
60   *Padfield v Minister of Agriculture* [1968] AC 997; *Congreve v Home Office* [1976] QB 629.

agreement with the owner); and (*b*) authority to restrict or take away the rights of others (for example, power to acquire land compulsorily, whether or not the owner wishes to sell; power to license a trade or occupation). Powers, duties and discretion are often very closely related to each other. There is often a duty to exercise a discretion. If a public authority is to fulfil the broad duties laid on it by Parliament, it must be equipped with powers which may adversely affect the rights of individuals. If use of these powers is challenged in the courts, the authority may rely on its broad duty as a justification for its action, while the individual may seek to show that the powers in question have not been lawfully exercised.

A no less difficult question arises when, under severe constraints on expenditure, a public authority takes its budgetary position into account in deciding whether it can provide a certain benefit to an individual or must, for example, close down valuable community services. Here the legal answer may depend on the exact terms of the legislation under which the service or benefit is provided.[61] The statute may impose a duty which must be performed in any event, or confer a qualified duty or a discretion, whose exercise may depend on the individual's situation and other matters. In such cases, the court is not concerned with the political merits of the authority's policy, but it must protect individual rights where these are granted by statute. Questions inevitably arise before a court as to where the dividing-line comes between matters that a public authority should decide and those that should be decided by the judges.[62]

These matters will be considered more fully in later chapters. In the rest of this chapter, we first consider two general matters, namely the classification of powers and the distinction between public and private law, which are relevant to the process of judicial control. Thereafter the significance of local government in administrative law will be outlined.

Classification of powers

Under a written constitution which is founded upon the separation of powers, it may be necessary for a court to decide whether legislative or executive action has improperly infringed the judicial power.[63] Although this is not the case in the United Kingdom, there are several purposes in administrative law for which attempts have been made to classify the powers of government as being legislative, administrative or judicial in character. Thus under the Statutory Instruments Act 1946 in its application to earlier statutes, a distinction was drawn between instruments which were legislative and those which were executive in character.[64] The jurisdiction of the Parliamentary Ombudsman applies to 'action taken in the exercise of administrative functions' by a government department, which may mean that he is not concerned with the functions of departments which are legislative in charac-

---

61   *R v Gloucestershire CC, ex p Barry* [1997] 2 All ER 1; cf *R v Cambridge Health Authority, ex p B* [1995] 2 All ER 129.

62   Eg *Bromley BC v Greater London Council* [1983] AC 768 and *R v Environment Secretary, ex p Hammersmith Council* [1991] 1 AC 521; and ch 29. Also Lord Devlin (1978) 41 MLR 501.

63   *Liyanage v R* [1967] 1 AC 259; *Shell Co of Australia Ltd v Federal Commissioner of Taxation* [1931] AC 275. And ch 5.

64   SI 1948 No 1, reg 2(1); ch 27.

ter.[65] Under the Crown Proceedings Act 1947, s 2(5), the Crown is not liable for the acts of any person who is discharging responsibilities of a judicial nature.[66] There are also other purposes for which it may be necessary to decide whether a particular procedure may be described as judicial. Thus, absolute privilege at common law protects a witness who gives evidence at a statutory inquiry into a teacher's dismissal.[67] In contrast, the law of contempt of court extends to industrial tribunals and mental health review tribunals,[68] but not to a local valuation court which decides disputes about the valuation of property under the rating system.[69] Under art 177 of the EC Treaty, only a court or a tribunal has power to refer questions for a preliminary ruling to the European Court of Justice and this would exclude an administrative body without judicial functions.[70]

There were formerly two main purposes for which emphasis was placed on the classification of functions. First, arising out of the history of the prerogative writs, certiorari and prohibition were seen as means by which to control inferior tribunals and other bodies which exercised jurisdiction or were required to act judicially. These writs were used against many administrative bodies yet, to legitimise the intervention of the Court of King's Bench, administrative functions were often described as judicial. Secondly, the rules of natural justice were held to apply when administrative bodies were performing judicial functions and were therefore required to act judicially.[71]

While many powers may be described without difficulty as legislative (for example, the power to make statutory regulations), administrative (for example, the power to decide where a department's offices should be located and when they should be open to the public) or judicial (for example, the valuation in a disputed case of land which has been compulsorily acquired), many powers are so classifiable only with difficulty and others defy such classification. The body upon whom the power is conferred affords no reliable test of the nature of the power. Laws are not always general in application; legislative form may be used to apply government policy in an individual case.[72] Government departments exercise both formal and informal powers of rule-making: is the issue of a circular which delegates executive powers to be regarded as a legislative act?[73] How should we classify the decision to build a motorway,[74] the issuing or revocation of a licence,[75] or the dismissal of a chief constable?[76] Does a decision change its character from being judicial to administrative if it is vested in a government department instead of a court?[77]

---

[65]   Parliamentary Commissioner Act 1967, s 5(1); ch 28 D.
[66]   Ch 31 A.
[67]   *Trapp v Mackie* [1979] 1 All ER 489.
[68]   *Peach Grey & Co v Sommers* [1995] 2 All ER 513; *P v Liverpool Daily Post plc* [1991] 2 AC 370.
[69]   *AG v BBC* [1981] AC 303; ch 18 B.
[70]   See Ellis and Tridimas, *Public Law of the European Community*, pp 471–8; and ch 8 A.
[71]   Ch 29 B.
[72]   *Hoffmann-La Roche & Co v Trade Secretary* [1975] AC 295.
[73]   *Blackpool Corpn v Locker* [1948] 1 KB 349.
[74]   *Bushell v Environment Secretary* [1981] AC 75.
[75]   *Boulter v Kent Justices* [1897] AC 556.
[76]   *Ridge v Baldwin* [1964] AC 40.
[77]   *Local Government Board v Arlidge* [1915] AC 120.

Questions such as these were formerly asked because it was thought that the answers would determine the extent to which the courts could review the diverse decisions being made by government departments and other public authorities. Particularly in the 1930s, there was much dispute in the literature of public law over the nature of administrative and judicial functions.[78] The debate was reflected in the case-law of the period, and the term 'quasi-judicial' came into vogue to describe a function which could not easily be classified as either judicial or administrative. It was used variously to describe judicial functions vested in a body which was not a court and also powers vested in a department which gave rise to a public inquiry. In the latter case, the term quasi-judicial was sometimes applied to the whole process of public inquiry and the resulting decision, and sometimes merely to the inquiry itself.[79] Today it is best to avoid use of the term quasi-judicial.[80]

Fortunately, the expansion in the scope of judicial review now makes it unnecessary to enter into the earlier debate, which often led to circular argument and involved the court in the process of 'labelling' particular functions. An extreme example of this is the case of *Nakkuda Ali v Jayaratne*, where the Privy Council held that a textile licensing controller had no duty to act judicially in revoking a dealer's licence because he was not required by statute to give a hearing to the dealer before deciding to revoke.[81] In 1997, a court would simply ask whether it was fair to the dealer to act in this way.

The heresy that a public authority's powers had to be described as 'judicial' before its decisions could be subject to judicial review was dispelled by the House of Lords in *Ridge v Baldwin*. Lord Reid stated that in situations where officials had power to make decisions affecting the rights of individuals, the duty to act judicially was readily inferred from the nature of the decision; it was not necessary to look for any express judicial elements, such as the duty to give a formal hearing.[82] In the light of *Ridge v Baldwin*, the courts today rarely need to classify a power as judicial or quasi-judicial in considering the scope of judicial review. Administrative functions are subject to the controlling juris-diction of the courts without it being necessary for a court first to apply the appropriate label:[83] 'it is the characteristics of the proceeding that matter, not the precise compartment or compartments into which it falls'.[84] The language of judicial, quasi-judicial and administrative functions may still be heard in some judgments[85] but the classification of functions has lost its earlier signifi-cance. Even where the rules of natural justice do not fully apply, administrat-

---

[78]   See D M Gordon (1933) 49 LQR 94, 419; Robson, *Justice and Administrative Law*, ch 1; and Jennings, *Law and Constitution*, app 1.

[79]   Eg *Errington v Minister of Health* [1935] 1 KB 249, 273 (Maugham LJ).

[80]   And see *R v Commission for Racial Equality, ex p Hillingdon BC* [1982] AC 779, 787.

[81]   [1951] AC 66. See also *Franklin v Minister of Town Planning* [1948] AC 87, criticised by H W R Wade (1949) 10 CLJ 216; ch 29 B.

[82]   [1964] AC 40; ch 29 B.

[83]   See eg *R v Hillingdon BC, ex p Royco Homes Ltd* [1974] QB 720; *R v Commission for Racial Equality, ex p Cottrell and Rothon* [1980] 3 All ER 265, 271.

[84]   *Re Pergamon Press Ltd* [1971] Ch 388, 402 (Sachs LJ).

[85]   Eg *R v Environment Secretary, ex p Ostler* [1977] QB 122; *R v Home Secretary, ex p Tarrant* [1985] QB 251, 268. In *R v Army Board of Defence Council, ex p Anderson* [1992] QB 169, the Army Board's power to decide on a soldier's complaint of racial discrimination was held to be judicial; cf *R v Department of Health, ex p Gandhi* [1991] 4 All ER 547.

ive bodies are under a duty to act fairly.[86] The application of general principles to the exercise of public power must be welcomed, but questions may arise as to how those principles apply in particular situations. Thus judicial review may vary in intensity according to the nature and context of what is under review,[87] and may not apply at all to certain decisions.[88]

Public and private law

While the need to label functions as legislative, administrative or judicial no longer exists, a different problem of classification arises from the prevailing tendency of the courts to resolve questions about jurisdiction, liability and procedure by asking whether the matter is one of private or public law. This formal distinction is reflected in the structure of many European legal systems. Thus in France it determines whether a dispute is decided by the administrative courts or by the civil courts. By contrast, in Britain the superior civil courts exercise an undivided jurisdiction over all justiciable disputes, whether they concern private citizens or public authorities.[89]

Lord Woolf has described public law as 'the system which enforces the proper performance by public bodies of the duties which they owe to the public'; and private law as 'the system which protects the private rights of private individuals or the private rights of public bodies'.[90] This is a deceptively simple distinction. Even apart from the burgeoning effects of privatisation, there is no clear-cut line between public bodies and private persons; and many acts of public bodies are subject to private law.[91] Moreover, in the common law tradition the system which protects the private rights of private individuals *is* to an important extent the system which enforces the performance by public bodies of the duties which they owe to the public, at least if the public is regarded as comprising all private individuals.[92] To take personal liberty as an example, one's liberty is protected both by the law of habeas corpus[93] and by the law of tort (the action for false imprisonment): does the former remedy come within public law (as it may lead to an order against an official if the applicant's detention is unlawful) and the latter private law (as it may lead to damages being paid to the plaintiff)? In the area of property, many disputes (over compulsory purchase, for example) arise exactly at the interface between a person's private rights and the powers and duties of the public authority.

In this difficult matter, it is worthwhile considering (1) the different levels of separation between public and private law that may arise, and applying this analysis to (2) the broad tasks of the courts in administrative law.[94] (*a*) The

---

86   *Re HK (an infant)* [1967] 2 QB 617; ch 30 B.

87   See eg *R v Environment Secretary, ex p Notts CC* [1986] AC 240; ch 29 A.

88   Eg *R v Lord Chancellor, ex p Hibbit & Saunders* [1993] COD 326.

89   Cf J D B Mitchell [1965] PL 95, advocating the creation of a new public law jurisdiction.

90   [1986] PL 220, 221. Also Woolf [1995] PL 57, 60–5.

91   See note 88 above. Wade's argument in (1985) 101 LQR 180, 195–7, that *CCSU v Minister for the Civil Service* [1985] AC 374 concerned private law issues has not received support.

92   Eg *Entick v Carrington* (1765) 19 St Tr 1030, ch 6; and *Cooper v Wandsworth Board of Works* (1863) 14 CB (NS) 180.

93   See chs 21 F and 30.

94   This analysis draws upon Craig, *Administrative Law* (1983), pp 11–21, a passage which does not appear in later editions.

most extreme separation occurs where the two bodies of law are administered by separate courts and judges, according to separate rules of substance and procedure. (*b*) Separation is less marked when private law and public law are applied in different branches of a coordinated court system, by judges sharing the same training, but applying distinct rules of substance and procedure. (*c*) An even weaker form of separation exists when public law and private law are administered in the same courts, but *some* of the substantive and procedural rules depend on whether a dispute is between private persons or whether it raises questions of public power. (*d*) Finally, there may be no separation at all, regardless of who the parties to a dispute are and what it concerns.

There are two broad tasks that the courts perform within administrative law. The first (which we may call 'judicial review') arises when an individual seeks to review the legality of a decision taken by public authorities or specialised tribunals, and the court must in exercise of this supervisory jurisdiction decide whether to uphold or set aside the decision. This task has no close equivalent in private law, although in areas of law such as trusts, company and trade union law, disputes may arise as to the validity of decisions taken by trustees, company directors and trade union committees. The second broad task ('governmental liability') arises when individuals seek compensation in the form of damages for loss caused by a public authority's unlawful acts (for example, a tort or a breach of contract). This task plainly has much in common with the general law of tort, contract and restitution.

To apply to these two tasks the analysis of levels of separation made above, France provides a strong example of (*a*), entrusting both 'judicial review' and most 'governmental liability' questions to separate administrative courts. Germany and Italy are examples of category (*b*): 'judicial review' is entrusted to the administrative courts, but all 'liability' questions are decided by the civil courts. The United Kingdom is an example of (*c*), both 'judicial review' and 'liability' questions being decided by the ordinary civil courts. Nonetheless, 'judicial review' questions are decided by a separate procedure; and some 'governmental liability' questions are decided by rules that do not apply to ordinary actions in tort or contract.[95] However, in 1995 the House of Lords held that an individual's claim for damages from a local authority must be based on a private law cause of action; and that public authorities are liable in damages for defective performance of their functions only in situations where there could be liability in the ordinary law of negligence.[96] On this basis, public law concepts are relevant to 'judicial review', but irrelevant to questions of 'liability'.

Accordingly, the use of the public law/private law distinction emphasised by Lord Diplock in *O'Reilly v Mackman*[97] may be limited to indicating when it is that the procedure of making an application for judicial review *must* be used and when it would be an abuse of process to sue by ordinary writ. Adopting the distinction, the House of Lords in 1983 made a complex analysis of a local authority's duties under the Housing (Homeless Persons) Act 1977. Some of these duties (for example, to inquire whether a family was homeless) were held

---

[95]   Eg *Town Investments Ltd v Department of Environment* [1978] AC 359 (interpretation of lease of government offices governed by public law); C Harlow (1977) 40 MLR 728.
[96]   *X (Minors) v Bedfordshire CC* [1995] 2 AC 633; and ch 31 A.
[97]   [1983] 2 AC 237; ch 30.

to be essentially public law functions, but others (such as the duty to rehouse a family once it had been found to be homeless) were held to be private law duties. Although the public law and the private law duties concerned the same parties, they were said to be enforceable by different procedures in the courts.[98]

This approach to duties arising under a single Act of Parliament is over-elaborate and likely to lead to undue complexity of reasoning. It has proved difficult to explain the procedural choices that an intending litigant must make solely with reference to the public/private law distinction.[99] In *O'Reilly v Mackman*, for example, a convicted prisoner's interest in ensuring that the prison authorities observed the law in deciding his period of remission was described by Lord Diplock as no more than a 'legitimate expectation' so far as private law was concerned, but a matter of 'sufficient interest' to him in public law to justify the prisoner in seeking a remedy in the courts.[100]

The most difficult questions that have arisen concern the choice of procedure when the same dispute raises both questions of private law rights and public law duties. In *Davy v Spelthorne Borough Council*, the House of Lords held that an action in damages for negligence against a local council was 'an ordinary action for tort' which did not raise 'any issue of public law as a live issue'.[101] In a separate judgment, Lord Wilberforce urged caution in use of the public/private law distinction:

> Before the expression 'public law' can be used to deny a subject a right of action in the court of his choice it must be related to a positive prescription of law, by statute or by statutory rules. We have not yet reached the point at which mere characterisation of a claim as a claim in public law is sufficient to exclude it from consideration by the ordinary courts.[102]

Subsequently, in *Roy v Kensington Family Practitioner Committee*[103] the House of Lords allowed an NHS doctor to sue by ordinary action for statutory payments to which he claimed to be entitled, even though as a defence the NHS committee relied on a decision that it had taken under statutory powers reducing the amount of the payments.

This matter will be considered further in chapter 30, but three brief comments may be made here. First, the popularity of the procedure of application for judicial review has led to it being used to extend the scope of the supervisory jurisdiction of the English courts, with success in relation to bodies that exercise regulatory powers in which there is a strong public interest[104] but with less success in respect of bodies concerned with sporting or religious affairs.[105] Secondly, the public/private law distinction has proved

---

98   *Cocks v Thanet DC* [1983] 2 AC 286. The legislation is now the Housing Act 1985, part III.

99   See C Harlow (1980) 43 MLR 241; P Cane [1981] PL 322, [1982] PL 202; G Samuels (1983) 46 MLR 558; and J Beatson (1987) 103 LQR 34. And see Law Commission, *Administrative Law: Judicial Review and Statutory Appeals* (1994), part III.

100   [1983] 2 AC at 275.

101   [1984] AC 262; and see P Cane [1984] PL 16.

102   [1984] AC at 276. And see *Mercury Communications Ltd v Director General of Telecommunications* [1996] 1 All ER 575, 581 (Lord Slynn).

103   [1992] 1 AC 624; and see P Cane [1992] PL 193.

104   *R v Panel on Take-Overs, ex p Datafin plc* [1987] QB 815.

105   *R v Jockey Club, ex p Aga Khan* [1993] 2 All ER 853; *R v Chief Rabbi, ex p Wachmann* [1993] 2 All ER 249.

awkward in relation to public sector employment.[106] Thirdly, the problems under discussion do not arise in Scots law, where the supervisory jurisdiction of the Court of Session does not depend on the distinction between private and public law.[107]

Local government – a note[108]

The emphasis in this book is on the constitutional structures that underly the democratic government of the United Kingdom. In the context of administrative law, we are concerned with what public bodies are actually doing in providing services, exercising regulatory powers and so on. At a national level, the government undertakes such tasks as oversight of the economy, control of the physical environment, the provision or supervision of services such as the National Health Service and education, management of the state's revenues, the promotion of 'law and order' and the maintenance of the judicial system. As the example of the police shows,[109] it is neither necessary nor desirable that all public services should be provided directly from Whitehall.

During the 1980s, local government in Britain (which had been thoroughly re-organised early in the 1970s)[110] went through one of the most troubled decades in its long history. The policies of central government were hostile to the maintenance of a vigorous local democracy and much legislation was passed at Westminster imposing new restrictions or obligations on local government. The Greater London Council and the metropolitan county councils were abolished by the Local Government Act 1985. The Local Government Finance Act 1988 replaced the established system of local taxation (rates on domestic property) with the disastrous community charge, or poll tax. This in turn has given way to a new local tax, the council tax.[111]

Within local authorities, their management methods have been affected by such matters as the imposition of new standards of openness and the provision of information,[112] compulsory competitive tendering,[113] and new restrictions on officers and councillors.[114] Under the Local Government Act 1992, part I, a Local Government Commission for England reviewed the structure of local authorities in different areas of England, with a view to moving towards the creation of unitary authorities in non-metropolitan counties. A compromise solution emerged, with county and district councils being preserved in areas where unitary authorities were not created. In Scotland and Wales, a new pattern of unitary authorities was imposed.[115]

---

[106]   See eg de Smith, Woolf and Jowell, *Judicial Review*, pp 186–91.
[107]   *West v Secretary of State for Scotland* 1992 SLT 636; and see W J Wolffe [1992] PL 625.
[108]   For the law, see Bailey (ed), *Cross on Local Government Law*. See also Loughlin, *Local Government in the Modern State*; Byrne, *Local Government in Britain*; and Stewart and Stoker (eds), *Local Government in the 1990s*. In these footnotes 'LG' stands for 'Local Government'.
[109]   Ch 21 A and B.
[110]   By the LG Act 1972 (for England and Wales) and the LG (Scotland) Act 1973.
[111]   LG Finance Act 1992, chs III–V.
[112]   LG (Access to Information) Act 1985.
[113]   LG Act 1988, part I (as amended subsequently).
[114]   LG and Housing Act 1989, part I. See also the report of the Widdicombe Committee of Inquiry into the Conduct of Local Authority Business, Cmnd 9797, 1986; the Government Response, Cm 433, 1988; P McAuslan [1987] PL 154 and G Ganz [1990] PL 224.
[115]   Local Government etc (Scotland) Act 1994; Local Government (Wales) Act 1994.

It must be hoped that the essential qualities of local government will survive despite the pressures on them from central government and from local opinion in a changing society. The constitutional importance of elected councils is that they promote local democracy and thus also a wider democracy. Local authorities must be enabled to provide local services effectively, including powers of regulation and licensing. A working relationship has to be re-built between central and local government, based in part on the unfashionable notion of partnership.[116]

Local authorities are still the providers (or enablers) of many local services. In view of the conflicting demands being made on them and on their limited resources, they are often involved in the contentious side of administrative law, whether seeking judicial review against central government[117] or other local authorities,[118] defending applications for judicial review brought by individuals,[119] regulatory agencies[120] or government departments, or resisting actions for damages in tort resulting from alleged failures of duty.[121] Their powers of providing services are essentially all derived from statute and they are subject to the ultra vires doctrine.[122] Local councils have never had the privileges and immunities that government departments enjoy because of their identification with the Crown.[123] Local government officers are not civil servants, and local methods of management are usually very different from those in government departments. Even where schemes of delegation exist,[124] the most important local issues should be decided by a committee of councillors, or by the whole council. Councillors operate in a political context, and the legality of party groups has been recognised.[125] They must observe certain standards of public conduct[126] and must be accountable where they depart from these standards, either in the quality of their administrative decisions or in their management of public finances.[127]

---

[116] Works on central–local relations include Griffith, *Central Departments and Local Authorities*; M Loughlin, in Jowell and Oliver (eds), *The Changing Constitution*, ch 10; and (the same) *Legality and Locality: the Role of Law in Central–Local Government Relations*.

[117] Eg *R v Environment Secretary, ex p Hammersmith BC* [1991] 1 AC 521; *R v Environment Secretary, ex p Greenwich BC, The Times*, 17 May 1989.

[118] Eg *Bromley Council v GLC* [1983] 1 AC 768.

[119] Eg *Wheeler v Leicester Council* [1985] AC 1054; *R v Gloucestershire CC, ex p Barry* [1997] 2 All ER 1.

[120] Eg *R v Birmingham Council, ex p EOC* [1989] AC 1155.

[121] *X (Minors) v Bedfordshire CC* [1995] 2 AC 633.

[122] See ch 29 A.

[123] Eg *Mersey Docks Trustees v Gibbs* (1866) LR 1 HL 93; ch 31 A.

[124] As authorised by the LG Act 1972, s 101, and the LG (Scotland) Act 1973, s 56. See *Western Fish Products v Penwith DC* [1981] 2 All ER 204, and ch 29 C. The principle in *Carltona Ltd v Commissioners of Works* [1943] 2 All ER 560 (p 127 above) does not apply in local government.

[125] *R v Waltham Forest BC, ex p Baxter* [1988] QB 419; and see I Leigh [1988] PL 304.

[126] See LG and Housing Act 1989, s 31, authorising the National Code of Local Government Conduct for councillors (1990); and also LG Act 1972, s 94, and LG (Scotland) Act 1973, s 38 (disclosure of interests).

[127] See, on maladministration, the Commissioners for Local Administration (ch 28 D below); on finance, the Audit Commission (LG Finance Act 1982, part III, as amended) and, in Scotland, the Commission for Local Authority Accounts (LG (Scotland) Act 1973, ss 96–106).

CHAPTER 27

Delegated legislation

Although the legal source of administrative powers may be found either in common law or in statutes, the great bulk of domestic administration is today carried on under statutory powers. Government departments may indeed exercise powers derived from the royal prerogative, that is, from the common law powers of the Crown that are not shared with subjects: for example, in relation to foreign affairs. But as was held long ago in the *Case of Proclamations*,[1] there is no residual prerogative power in the Crown to impose obligations or restrictions upon the people.[2] For the vast area of public action which is a feature of the modern state, it is almost exclusively in statute that the source of power lies.

The term statute law covers both Acts of Parliament and delegated legislation. Most delegated legislation, or what may be called subordinate or secondary legislation, is made in the form of statutory instruments. One function of legislation is to create the organs needed if new tasks of government are to be performed, and to provide the powers that are needed for the operation of a public service.[3] It is in fact very rare for an Act to contain all the provisions which are essential if a complex service is to be provided. An Act frequently does no more than outline the main features of the scheme, leaving the details to be filled in by subordinate legislation. In complex areas of government such as education, planning and social services, a lawyer must have access to publications which bring together primary and subordinate legislation, along with codes of practice, ministerial circulars and often a digest of the case-law. The bulk of statutory instruments is now formidable. In 1994, there were enacted 41 Public General Acts which were contained in 3,012 pages. In the same year the total of statutory instruments issued was over 3,300; although many of these were local in effect, the eleven published volumes of general instruments amounted to some 10,120 pages.

---

[1] (1611) 12 Co Rep 74, p 55 above; and ch 12 D.
[2] In *R v Criminal Injuries Compensation Board, ex p Lain* [1967] 2 QB 864, it was held that the Crown had power under the prerogative to enact a scheme which conferred financial benefits upon victims of criminal violence: ch 12 D.
[3] See eg Social Security Contributions and Benefits Act 1992, part VIII (power of Secretary of State to make regulations and give directions prescribing rules of Social Fund).

Historical development

The formal process by which a Bill becomes an Act has never been the sole method of legislation. In the earliest years of Parliament, it was difficult to distinguish between enactment by King in Parliament and legislation by the King in Council. Even when legislation by Parliament had become a distinct process, broad power to legislate by proclamation remained with the Crown. In 1539, by the Statute of Proclamations, royal power to issue proclamations 'for the good order and governance' of the country was recognised to exist and such proclamations were to be observed and enforced as if made by Act of Parliament. One reason given for the Act was that sudden occasions might arise when speedy remedies were needed which could not wait for the meeting of Parliament; the Act contained saving words for the protection of the common law, life and property. The repeal of the statute in 1547 made little difference to the Tudor use of proclamations and only in the 17th century were the limits of the prerogative power to legislate defined.[4]

The supremacy of Parliament today means both that such prerogative powers of legislation as exist have survived by grace of Parliament, and that other subordinate legislative powers must be derived from the authority of Parliament. As long ago as 1531, Parliament granted legislative powers to the Commissioners of Sewers, forerunners of the modern rivers and land drainage authorities. After 1689, the annual Mutiny Acts delegated power to the Crown to make regulations for the better government of the army, but in general it was not until the 19th century that delegation of wide legislative power became common. The first modern Factories Act in 1833 conferred power on the four factory inspectors appointed under the Act to make orders and regulations, breaches of which were punishable under the criminal law.[5] A very wide power that remained law for over a century was the power, first vested in the Poor Law Commissioners, 'to make and issue all such rules, orders and regulations for the management of the poor ... and for carrying this Act into execution ... as they shall think proper'.[6]

The late 19th century saw a great increase in the delegation of legislative power to government departments and other subordinate bodies, granted piecemeal as need arose. The resulting confusion of terms, the variety of procedures by which powers were exercised, and the great difficulty of discovering what the law was, led to a system of official printing and publication in 1890 and to the Rules Publication Act 1893. This introduced the general expression, 'statutory rules and orders', helped to unify procedures and introduced a safeguard of prior publicity. During the First World War, the Defence of the Realm Acts granted power in very wide terms to the government to make regulations for the conduct of the war.[7]

After 1918, many lawyers became aware for the first time of the wide legislative powers of government departments. The Committee on Ministers'

---

[4] Ch 4 A.

[5] Labour of Children etc in Factories Act 1833. See now Health and Safety at Work etc Act 1974, ss 15 and 80.

[6] Poor Law Amendment Act 1834, s 15.

[7] Ch 25 D. And see Carr, *Concerning English Administrative Law*.

Powers[8] concluded that unless Parliament was willing to delegate law-making powers, it would be unable to pass the kind or quantity of legislation which modern public opinion required. The committee drew attention to certain dangers in delegated legislation and suggested the introduction of greater safeguards against abuse. Subsequently the Statutory Instruments Act 1946 replaced the Rules Publication Act 1893 and promoted a greater uniformity of procedure. Since 1944, a scrutinising committee has been regularly appointed by Parliament, first by the Commons and today by the Commons and Lords jointly. The practice of delegated legislation has been reviewed by several parliamentary committees,[9] but the flood of subordinate legislation shows no sign of abating. In 1986, the Joint Committee on Statutory Instruments reported that the volume and complexity of instruments had increased in the period 1981–86: 'Instead of simply implementing the "nuts and bolts" of Government policy, statutory instruments have increasingly been used to change policy, sometimes in ways that were not envisaged when the enabling primary legislation was passed'.[10]

Justification of delegated legislation

Delegated legislation is an inevitable feature of modern government for several reasons:

1 Pressure upon parliamentary time.   If Parliament attempted to enact all legislation itself, the legislative machine would break down, unless there was a radical alteration in the procedure for considering Bills. The granting of legislative power to a department which is administering a public service may obviate the need for amending Bills. Although many statutory instruments are laid before Parliament, only a minority of them gives rise to matters which need the consideration of either House, and Parliament spends a very small proportion of its time on business connected with them.[11]

2 Technicality of subject-matter.   Legislation on technical topics necessitates prior consultation with experts and interests concerned. The giving of legislative power to ministers facilitates such consultation. Draft Bills are often regarded as confidential documents and their text is not disclosed until they have been presented to Parliament and read a first time. No such secretive custom need impede the preparation of delegated legislation. There is also a good reason for keeping out of the statute book highly technical provisions which do not involve questions of principle, and which only experts in the field concerned can readily understand.[12]

3 The need for flexibility.   When a new public service is being established, it is

---

[8]   Ch 26.
[9]   Reports of Select Committee on Delegated Legislation, HC 310 (1952–53); Joint Committee on Delegated Legislation, HL 184, HC 475 (1971–72) and HL 204, HC 468 (1972–73); Select Committee on Procedure, HC 588–1 (1977–78), ch 3.
[10]   HC 31–xxxvii (1985–86), p 2.
[11]   In 1984–85 and 1994–95, the whole House of Commons spent respectively 10% and 7% of its time considering statutory instruments (*Sessional Returns*, 1984–85 and 1994–95). These figures do not include time spent by committees considering statutory instruments.
[12]   J A G Griffith (1951) 14 MLR 279, 425.

not possible to foresee every administrative difficulty that may arise, nor to have frequent recourse to Parliament for amending Acts to make adjustments that may be called for after the scheme has begun to operate. Delegated legislation fills those needs. When the community charge, or poll tax, came into operation under the Local Government Finance Act 1988, as amended by the Local Government and Housing Act 1989, no less than 47 sets of regulations were made in the years 1989–91. But even such extensive exercise of delegated powers could not prevent the tax from being a failure. A power commonly delegated to ministers is the power to make a commencement order, bringing into operation all or part of a statute. Often there are practical reasons why a new Act should not come into effect as soon as the royal assent is given. There is no duty on the minister to exercise a commencement power, but the minister must not act so as to defeat Parliament's expectation that the Act will come into operation.[13]

4 State of emergency. In times of emergency a government may need to take action quickly and in excess of its normal powers. Many written constitutions include provision in emergency for the suspension of formal guarantees of individual liberty. Although the Crown possesses an ill-defined residue of prerogative power capable of use in time of national danger, the Emergency Powers Act 1920 makes permanent provision enabling the executive to legislate subject to parliamentary safeguards in the event of certain emergencies.[14] Following the unilateral declaration of independence by the Rhodesian government in 1965, Parliament granted exceptionally wide legislative powers enabling the Queen in Council to take all necessary steps to bring about the resumption of lawful government in Rhodesia.[15] Upon the return to direct rule of Northern Ireland by the British government in 1972, wide power to legislate for Northern Ireland was conferred on the Queen in Council.[16] So long as direct rule continues, laws may be made for Northern Ireland by Order in Council, a procedure which does not allow full scope for democratic discussion.[17]

Exceptional types of delegated legislation

While much delegated legislation is essential, governments are often tempted to obtain from Parliament greater powers than they should be given. Criticism centres upon particular types of delegated legislation.

1 Matters of principle. There is a clear threat to parliamentary government if power is delegated to legislate on matters of general policy, or if so wide a discretion is conferred that it is impossible to be sure what limit the legislature intended to impose. There is no formal limit to the delegation of legislative powers, and Acts of Parliament frequently confer legislative powers in wide terms. One reason for this is that if powers are phrased more narrowly, this

---

[13] *R v Home Secretary, ex p Fire Brigades Union* [1995] 2 AC 513.
[14] Ch 25 D.
[15] Southern Rhodesia Act 1965.
[16] Northern Ireland (Temporary Provisions) Act 1972, s 1(3) and Sched, para 4; Northern Ireland Act 1975, Sched 1, para 1.
[17] See Hadfield, *The Constitution of Northern Ireland*, ch 5; and HLE, vol 8(2), p 82.

will make it more likely that the department will need to seek increased powers from Parliament in future. A proposal that Parliament should adopt a policy of passing framework legislation, with all details left to delegated legislation, was rejected by the House of Commons Committee on Procedure in 1978, on the ground that this would further weaken parliamentary control.[18] Another reason against framework legislation is that if the power of the courts to declare delegated legislation ultra vires is to be of value, the delegated powers must be defined with reasonable precision. But there are few absolutes in this debate and legislative practice is often a compromise between different attitudes to delegation.

2 Delegation of taxing power.   We have seen how vital to the development of parliamentary government was the insistence that Parliament alone could authorise taxation.[19] This insistence survives in an attenuated form, but modern pressures, particularly associated with the economy, have made it necessary for Parliament to delegate certain powers in relation to taxation to the government. In particular, the working of a system of customs duties combined with the development of the European Community has made necessary delegation of the power to give exemptions and reliefs from such duties.[20] Since 1961, the government has also had power to vary certain classes of indirect taxation by order of the Treasury.[21] Each of these powers is subject to parliamentary control in that orders imposing import duties or varying indirect taxation cease to have effect unless they are confirmed by a resolution of the House of Commons within a limited time.

3 Sub-delegation.   When a statute delegates legislative power to a minister, exercisable by statutory instrument, it may be assumed that Parliament intends the statutory instrument itself to contain the rules. Is it a proper use of such powers for the instrument to sub-delegate legislative power, by authorising rules to be made by another body or by another procedure? The legal maxim, *delegatus non potest delegare*, means that a delegate may not subdelegate his or her power, but the parent Act may always override this by expressly authorising sub-delegation, as did the Emergency Powers (Defence) Act 1939. Without express authority in the parent Act, it is doubtful whether sub-delegation of legislative powers is valid. Where sub-delegation occurs, control by Parliament becomes more difficult. In 1978, the Joint Committee on Statutory Instruments criticised the recurring tendency of departments to seek to by-pass Parliament by omitting necessary detail from statutory instruments and vesting a wide discretion in ministers to vary the rules without making further statutory instruments.[22] Under the European Communities Act 1972, sub-delegation is prohibited except for rules of procedure for courts or tribunals.[23]

---

[18]   HC 588–I (1977–78), ch 2.
[19]   Ch 4 A.
[20]   Customs and Excise Duties (General Reliefs) Act 1979.
[21]   Excise Duties (Surcharges or Rebates) Act 1979.
[22]   HL 51, HC 579 (1977–78), p 10; and see *Customs and Excise Commissioners v J H Corbitt (Numismatists) Ltd* [1981] AC 22.
[23]   European Communities Act 1972, s 2(2) and Sched 2.

4 Retrospective operation. It follows from the supremacy of Parliament that Acts may have retrospective operation.[24] But in principle retrospective legislation is repugnant to the rule of law. If on occasions retrospective legislation is considered necessary, as in the case of the War Damage Act 1965, this should be done by Parliament itself and not through delegated legislation.[25]

5 Exclusion of the jurisdiction of the courts. The power of the courts in reviewing delegated legislation is confined to declaring it ultra vires, whether on grounds of substance or procedure.[26] While control over the merits of delegated legislation is a matter for ministers and for Parliament, the possibility of control by the courts should not be excluded. It should never be for a minister to determine the limits of his or her own powers.[27]

6 Authority to modify an Act of Parliament. Sometimes power is delegated to modify a statute. Thus on a reform of local government boundaries after a review by the Local Government Commission, the Secretary of State may make regulations that extend, exclude, amend, or repeal 'any enactment'.[28] Particularly criticised has been the so-called 'Henry VIII clause' enabling a minister to modify the Act itself so far as necessary for bringing it into operation.[29] Yet some Acts dealing with schemes of social and industrial control empower a minister to broaden or narrow the scope of the schemes in the light of experience.[30]

Two instances of delegated power to modify Acts of Parliament may be given. The European Communities Act 1972, which introduced Community law into the United Kingdom,[31] by s 2(2) authorises the making of Orders in Council and ministerial regulations to implement Community obligations of the United Kingdom, to enable rights under the European treaties to be exercised and 'for the purpose of dealing with matters arising out of or related to any such obligations or rights'. Schedule 2 to the Act excludes certain matters from the general power, including the imposition of taxes, retroactive legislation and the sub-delegation of legislative power (other than power to make rules of procedure for any court or tribunal). Subject to these limitations, Orders in Council or regulations under s 2(2) may make 'any such provision (of any such extent) as might be made by Act of Parliament' (s 2(4)). The intention must have been to use such wide language so as to exclude the possibility of judicial review on grounds of vires in the case of instruments made under s 2(2). But it is doubtful whether this intention has

---

[24] Ch 4 B.
[25] And see eg HC 70–ix (1970–71). The unsatisfactory decision in *R v Social Security Secretary, ex p Britnell* [1991] 2 All ER 726 upheld regulations that had been made as 'transitional provisions' and retrospectively modified an earlier Act.
[26] See p 729 below.
[27] Yet under the Counter-Inflation Act 1973, Sched 3, para 1, an order made under part II of the Act could 'define any expressions used in the provisions under which it is made'. And see *Jackson v Hall* [1980] AC 854.
[28] Local Government Act 1992, s 26(4).
[29] MPR, pp 36–8; Carr, *Concerning English Administrative Law*, pp 41–7.
[30] Health and Safety at Work etc Act 1974, ss 15 and 80; Sex Discrimination Act 1975, s 80, esp sub-s (3).
[31] Ch 8 C.

been achieved; instruments under s 2(2) are not valid if made to give effect to *future* Community obligations.[32]

The Deregulation and Contracting Out Act 1994, part I, authorised ministers to amend or repeal Acts which imposed on any person 'carrying on a trade, business, profession or otherwise' a burden which, without removing necessary protection, could be removed or reduced. Part II of the Act made possible the contracting out of public powers to private contractors: ministers may authorise the functions of ministers, other office-holders and local authorities to be performed by other persons (but not the exercise of jurisdiction by a court or tribunal; powers of entry, search and seizure; nor powers to make subordinate legislation). These remarkable powers made necessary the creation of new procedures within Parliament for preventing their misuse.[33]

Nomenclature

Despite the Statutory Instruments Act 1946, terminology is often confusing. The term 'statutory instrument' is a comprehensive expression to describe all forms of subordinate legislation subject to the 1946 Act.[34] Within the scope of the Act are many legislative powers conferred on ministers by Acts passed before the 1946 Act came into operation. As regards Acts passed thereafter, there are two categories of statutory instrument: (*a*) legislative powers conferred on the Queen in Council and stated in the parent Act to be exercisable by Order in Council; (*b*) legislative powers conferred on a minister of the Crown and stated to be exercisable by statutory instrument. The first of these, the statutory Order in Council, must be distinguished from prerogative Orders in Council, which are not statutory instruments at all, though for convenience some are published as an appendix to the annual volumes of statutory instruments. One reason why some legislative powers are vested in the Queen in Council and others are vested in a named minister is that some powers may need to be exercised by any department of the government whereas others concern only one department; also the greater formality of an Order in Council is thought appropriate to some classes of legislation. The expression 'statutory instrument' does not include local byelaws, nor does it include such acts as the confirmation of compulsory purchase orders by a minister. Moreover there are other kinds of rule made under statutory authority which are not statutory instruments, for example immigration rules under the Immigration Act 1971.[35]

Although statutory instrument is the generic term, a variety of names apply to different kinds of statutory instrument: rules, orders, regulations, warrants, schemes and even licences and directions. Several of these terms may be used in a single Act to distinguish different procedures applied to different powers. In practice, the term 'regulation' is used mainly for matters of wide general

---

[32]   HL Deb, 17 February 1976, cols 399–417, and HL 51, HC 169 (1977–78), pp 17–18. Cf *R v HM Treasury, ex p Smedley* [1985] QB 657. And see ch 8 E, esp page 151.

[33]   See [1995] PL 21 (M Freedland) and 34 (C M G Himsworth); and p 728 below.

[34]   The official abbreviation for statutory instruments is SI followed by the year and number eg SI 1993 No 252 (or SI 1993/252).

[35]   See also *R v Clarke* [1969] 2 QB 91 and HC 588–III (1977–78), apps 22, 23.

importance, such as social security regulations. Where the legislation deals with procedure, rules are generally enacted, for example, the Rules of the Supreme Court. With the term 'order' there is less uniformity; thus an Order in Council may bring into effect all or part of an Act of Parliament, and in town planning law a general development order contains detailed rules for the control of development. These different terms for delegated legislation should not be confused with the many forms of administrative rules that are current, such as codes of practice and guidelines: these do not have the full force of law, but adverse consequences may follow if they are not observed.[36]

Control of delegated legislation

'There is now general agreement over the necessity for delegated legislation; the real problem is how this legislation can be reconciled with the processes of democratic consultation, scrutiny and control'.[37] The process of subordinate legislation differs significantly from that of legislation by Bill; it is equally important that there should be effective forms of control. The existing means of control will be described under four headings: (1) consultation of interests; (2) control by Parliament; (3) publication; (4) challenge in the courts.

1 Consultation of interests. Unlike the procedure of legislation by Bill, whereby the proposals are considered publicly in principle and in detail as the Bill passes through both Houses, most delegated legislation comes into force as soon as it is made public, either at once or after a short interval stated in the document itself.

There is no general requirement of prior publicity, and an ordinary member of the public has little chance of getting to know about proposed statutory instruments.[38] But the department proposing to make a new statutory instrument frequently takes steps to ensure that interests affected by the proposal are consulted. Some Acts make this obligatory. Many kinds of social security regulations must be submitted in draft to the Social Security Advisory Committee, whose disagreements, if any, with the Secretary of State must be reported to Parliament along with the regulations.[39] So too the Council on Tribunals must be consulted before rules of procedure for administrative tribunals and inquiries are made.[40] Several Acts do not specify the bodies to be consulted, leaving it to the minister to consult with such associations and bodies as appear to him or her to be affected.[41] Even where there are no express requirements, advantage may be gained from consulting organisations or interests likely to be affected by the proposed legislation. Consultation may ensure that the contents of subordinate legislation are as

---

[36] See text accompanying notes 86–99 below.

[37] Memorandum by the late Aneurin Bevan MP quoted in HC 310 (1952–53).

[38] J F Garner [1964] PL 105.

[39] Social Security Administration Act 1992, ss 170, 172–4.

[40] Tribunals and Inquiries Act 1992, ss 8, 9. See also Deregulation and Contracting Out Act 1994, s 3.

[41] Eg Industrial Training Act 1964, s 1(4), considered in *Agricultural Training Board v Aylesbury Mushrooms Ltd* [1972] 1 All ER 280; also *R v Social Services Secretary, ex p Association of Municipal Authorities* [1986] 1 All ER 164.

acceptable as possible to the interests concerned, and may secure the benefits of specialised knowledge from outside government. In some instances, a ministry's legislative proposals must be published and the interests affected have the right to present their objections before an inspector appointed by the minister. Where there is a duty to consult, fairness may require disclosure to an interested person of the scientific advice on which the minister is proposing to rely.[42]

2 Control by Parliament.[43]   Parliamentary control of delegated legislation originates in the fact that legislative powers derive from statute. There is therefore always some opportunity of giving consideration, at the committee stage of a Bill, to clauses delegating legislative power. But how effective is this control? The Ministers' Powers Committee recommended that all Bills conferring power to legislate should in each House be referred to a small standing committee to report whether there were any objections of principle to the proposals.[44] It was 60 years before the House of Lords in 1992 appointed a Committee on the Scrutiny of Delegated Powers, to consider clauses in Bills proposing the delegation of legislative powers and to receive for each Bill a government memorandum justifying the proposals. In reporting on such proposals, the committee aims to save debating time, to discourage the inclusion of excessive powers in Bills and to ensure that appropriate safeguards are included in the legislation.[45]

The general responsibility of a minister to Parliament for his or her department enables questions about the minister's delegated powers to be raised in questions and during debates. Parliament has also provided additional means of control specially for ministerial legislation. However, two basic reasons for delegating legislative power are pressure on Parliament's time and the technical nature of the subjects; the very object of delegation would be frustrated if Parliament had to approve each instrument in detail. The procedure through which a statutory instrument must pass depends on the terms of the parent Act. The principal procedures are the following:

(*a*) laying of draft instrument before Parliament, and requiring affirmative resolution before instrument can be 'made';
(*b*) laying of instrument after it has been made, to come into effect only when approved by affirmative resolution;
(*c*) laying of instrument that takes immediate effect, but requires approval by affirmative resolution within a stated period as a condition of continuance;
(*d*) laying of instrument that takes immediate effect, subject to annulment by resolution of either House;
(*e*) laying in draft, subject to resolution that no further proceedings be taken – in effect a direction to the minister not to 'make' the instrument;
(*f*) laying before Parliament, with no further provision for control.

---

[42] *R v Health Secretary, ex p US Tobacco International Inc* [1992] QB 353.
[43] Erskine May, ch 22; Kersell, *Parliamentary Supervision of Delegated Legislation*; reports cited in note 9 above; J D Hayhurst and P Wallington [1988] PL 547; St J Bates, in Ryle and Richards (eds), *The Commons Under Scrutiny*, pp 200–5.
[44] MPR, pp 67–8. Cf HC 310 (1952–53).
[45] See C M G Himsworth [1995] PL 34.

Finally, some statutory instruments are not required to be laid before Parliament at all.

In cases (*a*)–(*c*) (positive procedure), an affirmative resolution of each House (or in the case of financial instruments, of the Commons alone) is needed if the instrument is to come into force or to remain in operation. In cases (*d*) and (*e*) (negative procedure), no action need be taken in either House unless there is some opposition to the instrument.

Of these procedures, by far the most common is case (*d*) (subject to annulment); the most common of the positive procedures is case (*a*). Under the positive procedure, it is the minister concerned who must secure the affirmative resolution and, if necessary, the government must allot time for the resolution to be discussed in Parliament within ordinary business. Under the negative procedure, it is for any member who so wishes to 'pray' that the instrument should be annulled. It has often been impossible in recent years to ensure that time is found to debate prayers for annulment which have been tabled.[46] The situation has been eased by the greater use of standing committees to debate statutory instruments and by other changes in the timetabling of House of Commons business.[47] In practice, the positive procedure is reserved for more important measures, for example, orders made by the Treasury varying indirect taxation, or regulations made under the Emergency Powers Act 1920.

A novel provision made by the European Communities Act 1972 was that a statutory instrument made under s 2(2) should be subject to annulment by a resolution of either House unless a draft of the instrument had been approved by each House before the instrument was made.[48] Thus the government may choose whether the negative or positive procedure should be used. Both Labour and Conservative governments have been criticised for choosing the negative procedure for important measures modifying Acts of Parliament.[49]

One feature common to all these procedures is that neither House may amend a statutory instrument, except for very rare instances where amendment is expressly authorised by the parent Act.[50] If this were possible, it might involve the House in detailed consideration of matters which Parliament had delegated to a minister. Where a House is not satisfied with an instrument as it stands, the minister should withdraw it and start again.

The Statutory Instruments Act 1946 introduced some general provisions to promote uniformity of procedure. By s 4, where an instrument must be laid in Parliament after being made, it must in general be laid before it comes into operation; every copy of such an instrument must show on its face three dates, showing when it was made, laid, and came into operation respectively. What constitutes laying before Parliament is governed by the practice or direction

---

46   A Beith (1981) 34 Parliamentary Affairs 165; Griffith and Ryle, *Parliament*, pp 345–50.
47   HC 20–I (1991–92), p xxii and HC 491 (1994–95), p xvi. Also HC Deb, 12 December 1994, col 1456 and 2 November 1995, col 405.
48   European Communities Act 1972, Sched 2, para 2.
49   HL 51, HC 169 (1977–78), para 36; HC 15–viii (1981–82); and see Cmnd 8600, 1982. The Deregulation and Contracting Act 1994 requires the affirmative procedure for certain orders under the Act (compare s 1(4) and ss 5, 6).
50   Emergency Powers Act 1920, s 2(4), and Census Act 1920, s 1(2).

of each House[51] and an instrument may be laid when Parliament is not sitting. The rule that an instrument be laid before it comes into operation is so clearly expressed that, although there is no binding judicial authority on the matter, it is submitted that failure to lay an instrument prevents it from coming into operation.[52] But the position is doubtful in the case of delegated legislation that is outside the 1946 Act. While under the 1946 Act an interval of one day between laying and operation is sufficient, in practice departments try to ensure that the interval is not less than 21 days.[53]

By s 5 of the 1946 Act, where an instrument is subject to annulment, as in procedure (*d*) above, there is a uniform period of 40 days during which a prayer for annulment may be moved, exclusive of any time during which Parliament is adjourned for more than four days or is prorogued or dissolved. Where, as in procedure (*e*), an instrument is laid in draft but subject to the negative procedure, there is a similar period of 40 days during which the resolution may be moved. In the case of instruments which need an affirmative resolution before they can come into operation (procedure (*b*)), no set period is provided as it is for the government in each case to decide how urgently the instrument is needed. Under procedure (*c*) the length of time during which the affirmative resolution must be secured is stated in the parent Act and varies from case to case. The standing orders of each House and an official publication, *Statutory Instrument Practice*, seek to ensure that proper laying procedures are observed.

Although a parent Act may expressly confine control of statutory instruments to the Commons, as in the case of fiscal measures, the House of Lords is usually granted the same powers of control as the Commons. Moreover, the procedure under the Parliament Acts 1911 and 1949 for bypassing the Lords applies only to Bills and not to statutory instruments. But it is extremely rare for the House of Lords to exercise its legal veto over subordinate legislation. When on 18 June 1968 the House rejected an order containing sanctions against the Rhodesian government made under the Southern Rhodesia Act 1965,[54] this caused the Labour government to propose that the power of the Lords to veto statutory instruments should be abolished.[55] Although the present power of veto could be abused as a means of harassing a government in political difficulties, a reformed second chamber could provide a valuable safeguard against misuse by the executive of legislative powers.

When a vote is taken on a statutory instrument in the Commons, it is extremely rare for the government not to obtain a majority. Both in 1972 sand in 1982, the Conservative government was defeated on proposed new

---

[51]   Laying of Documents before Parliament (Interpretation) Act 1948, and see *R v Immigration Appeal Tribunal, ex p Joyles* [1972] 3 All ER 213.

[52]   Cf de Smith, Woolf and Jowell, *Judicial Review*, pp 274–5, and A I L Campbell [1983] PL 43. The point was assumed but not decided in *R v Social Services Secretary, ex p Camden BC* [1987] 2 All ER 560 (A I L Campbell [1987] PL 328).

[53]   HL 51, HC 169 (1977–78), pp 11–12.

[54]   A month later, on 18 July 1968, an identical order was approved by the Lords. On the right of the House to reject a statutory instrument when it considers it necessary to do so, see HL Deb, 20 October 1994, col 356.

[55]   Cmnd 3799, 1969, pp 22–3; Parliament (No 2) Bill 1969, clauses 13–15. And see ch 10 B.

immigration rules, but modified rules were subsequently approved by the Commons.[56]

Joint Committee on Statutory Instruments All general statutory instruments laid before Parliament, as well as other statutory orders, come under scrutiny by the Joint Committee on Statutory Instruments, consisting of seven members appointed from each House. The members from the Commons also meet separately to scrutinise those instruments which are laid only in the Commons. The joint committee is advised by the Speaker's Counsel and by Counsel to the Lord Chairman of Committees.

The committee's duty is to consider whether the attention of the Houses should be drawn to an instrument on any of the following grounds, namely:

(*a*) that it imposes a charge on the public revenues or contains provisions requiring payments to be made to the Exchequer or any government department or to any local or public authority in consideration of any licence or consent, or of any services to be rendered, or prescribes the amount of any such charge or payments;

(*b*) that it is made in pursuance of an enactment containing specific provisions excluding it from challenge in the courts, either at all times or after the expiration of a specified period;

(*c*) that it purports to have retrospective effect where the parent statute confers no express authority so to provide;

(*d*) that there appears to have been unjustifiable delay in the publication or in the laying of it before Parliament;

(*e*) that there appears to have been unjustifiable delay in sending a notification under the proviso to s 4(1) of the Statutory Instruments Act 1946, where an instrument has come into operation before it has been laid before Parliament;

(*f*) that there appears to be a doubt whether it is intra vires or that it appears to make some unusual or unexpected use of the powers under which it was made;

(*g*) that for any special reason its form or purport calls for elucidation;

(*h*) that its drafting appears to be defective.

The committee may also report an instrument on any other ground which does not impinge on its merits or on the policy behind it. The committee is therefore concerned with the scrutiny of instruments on technical grounds, that is, legal and procedural matters. In practice, the grounds that arise most frequently are grounds (*h*), (*g*) and (*f*), in that order, and it is rare for other grounds to arise. Under ground (*f*), the committee may express doubts about the vires, or validity, of an instrument, but the committee is not able to give a binding decision on such an issue. That is a matter exclusively for the courts to determine. Before an adverse report on an instrument is made by the committee, the department concerned is given an opportunity to furnish its explanation of the position. Relatively few instruments are reported to the two Houses.[57] The report by the committee on a particular instrument has no

---

56 HC Deb, 22 November 1972, col 1343, and 15 December 1982, col 436.

57 In 1994–95, 1,524 instruments were examined by the joint committee and 174 were reported, including 87 on ground (*h*) above, 38 on ground (*g*), and 26 on ground (*f*): HC 132 (1995–96). The yearly average of instruments reported on grounds of vires rose from four in 1978–85 to 34 in 1987–90 (HC Deb, 28 February 1991, col 544 (WA)).

effect on the instrument, although it may encourage a member to table a prayer against the instrument.

This committee does not examine the merits or policy of an instrument. These matters may be discussed by the whole House if a debate is held on an affirmative resolution or on a prayer for annulment. The impossibility of finding enough time in the Commons to debate the merits of instruments which MPs wished to discuss led in 1972 to a proposal that committees should be used to debate instruments on their merits.[58] For this purpose, several standing committees are regularly appointed, on the lines of the standing committees used for the committee stage of Bills.[59] An instrument may be referred for debate to a standing committee on the proposal of a minister, unless 20 or more MPs object. In the committee, one and a half hours are allowed for considering each instrument.[60] After this consideration, a vote on the affirmative resolution or the prayer for annulment may be taken in the whole House without further debate. A debate in standing committee may be better than no debate at all, but the procedure does not exercise any effective political power over the government.[61]

In 1994, the Deregulation Committee of the Commons, was appointed, jointly with the Lords' committee on delegated powers, to oversee the use of powers under the Deregulation and Contracting Out Act 1994; its remit was adapted from that of the Joint Committee on Statutory Instruments, but its procedures enable it to delay or influence departmental action.

In order that each House may inform itself about EC secondary legislation, committees of the two Houses have been appointed which have functions comparable with those of the committees which deal with statutory instruments.[62]

3 Publication. Although it is desirable that all legislation should be publicised before it takes effect, there are some matters, for example changes in indirect taxation, where the object of the legislation would be defeated if it had to be made known to the public in advance of enactment. This is recognised by the Statutory Instruments Act, which allows that for essential reasons a statutory instrument may come into operation even before it is laid before Parliament, with the safeguard that the Lord Chancellor and the Speaker must be provided with an immediate explanation. Apart from this, publicity is now secured by the following rules:

(*a*) A uniform procedure exists for numbering, printing, publishing and citing statutory instruments.[63] An instrument classified as local by reason of its subject-matter and certain classes of general instrument may be exempted from the requirements of printing and sale. Each year is published a collected

---

[58]   HC 475 (1971–72), para 123.

[59]   Ch 10 A.

[60]   In the case of instruments concerning Northern Ireland, 2½ hours: HC SO 101(4).

[61]   In 1994–95, 126 instruments were considered by standing committees (HC 132 (1995–96)). Since 10 January 1995, all affirmative instruments are in principle referred automatically to a standing committee.

[62]   Ch 8 C.

[63]   Statutory Instruments Act 1946, s 2, amended by the Statutory Instruments (Production and Sale) Act 1996.

edition of all general instruments made during the year which are still operative.

(*b*) The rule that where an instrument has to be laid before Parliament it must be laid before it comes into operation has already been mentioned.

(*c*) It is a defence in proceedings for contravention of a statutory instrument to prove that it had not been issued by HM Stationery Office at the date of the alleged contravention, unless it is shown by the prosecutor that reasonable steps have been taken to bring the purport of the instrument to the notice of the public or of persons likely to be affected by it or of the person charged.[64] Thus ignorance of a statutory instrument is no defence but failure to issue it may in certain circumstances be a defence. This defence is necessary because these instruments may otherwise operate without any warning of their enactment.

4 Challenge in the courts. If made in accordance with the prescribed procedure, and within the powers conferred by the parent Act, a statutory instrument is as much part of the law as the statute itself. The essential difference between statute and statutory instrument is that, unlike Parliament, a minister's powers are limited. Consequently, if a department attempts to enforce a statutory instrument against an individual, the individual may as a defence question the validity of the instrument. The courts have power to decide this question even though the instrument has been approved by resolution of each House of Parliament.[65]

The validity of a statutory instrument may be challenged on two main grounds: (*a*) that the content or substance of the instrument is ultra vires the parent Act, (*b*) that the correct procedure has not been followed in making the instrument. The chances of such a challenge succeeding depend on the terms of the Act by which legislative power has been conferred. If a minister is given power to make such regulations as appear to him or her to be necessary or expedient for achieving a particular purpose, the minister is unlikely to be successfully challenged unless the power is used for a totally different purpose. But even in such a case there is a judicial presumption that Parliament does not intend certain forms of legislation to be made unless by express words or by necessary implication it has clearly authorised them. The principles that no one should be deprived of access to the courts except by clear words of Parliament and that there is no power to levy a tax without clear authority are illustrated in cases arising out of defence regulations made during the First World War.[66] The former principle was applied in 1997, when an order by the Lord Chancellor increasing the court fees payable for litigation and requiring them to be paid by someone on income support was held to deprive that person of the constitutional right of access to the courts.[67]

---

[64]   Statutory Instruments Act 1946, s 3(2); *R v Sheer Metalcraft Ltd* [1954] 1 QB 586. For the argument that at common law delegated legislation must be published before it can come into force, see D J Lanham (1974) 37 MLR 510 and [1983] PL 395; for the contrary view, A I L Campbell [1982] PL 569.

[65]   *Hoffmann-La Roche v Trade Secretary* [1975] AC 295.

[66]   *A-G v Wilts United Dairies Ltd* and *Chester v Bateson*, discussed in ch 25 D. And see *Kerr v Hood* 1907 SC 895.

[67]   *R v Lord Chancellor, ex p Witham* [1997] 2 All ER 779.

That basic principles can cut down the width of even such expressions as 'power to make such regulations as seem to the minister to be necessary' was illustrated in *Commissioners of Customs and Excise v Cure and Deeley Ltd.*

The Finance (No 2) Act 1940 empowered the Commissioners to make regulations providing for any matter for which provision appeared to them to be necessary for giving effect to the statutory provisions relating to purchase tax. Regulations were made under which, if proper tax returns were not submitted by manufacturers, the Commissioners might determine the amount of tax due, 'which amount shall be deemed to be the proper tax due', unless within seven days the taxpayer satisfied the Commissioners that some other sum was due. *Held* that the regulation was invalid in that it purported to prevent the taxpayer proving in a court the amount of tax actually due, and substituted for the tax authorised by Parliament some other sum arbitrarily determined by the Commissioners.[68]

By similar reasoning a court might declare invalid a statutory instrument which purported to have retrospective effect in the absence of clear authority from Parliament. In 1973, the Court of Session declared ultra vires a regulation made by the Secretary of State for Scotland which sought to remove from qualified teachers the right to continue teaching without first registering with a statutory Teaching Council.[69] In 1976, the House of Lords by 3–2 held ultra vires a regulation which authorised the levying of sewerage charges on houses not connected with public sewers,[70] and in 1982, the Home Secretary's power to make rules for the management of prisons was held not to permit him to make rules fettering a prisoner's right of access to the courts.[71] But in *McEldowney v Forde*, which concerned the freedom of association in Northern Ireland, the House of Lords by 3–2 upheld a remarkably phrased ban on republican clubs imposed by the Northern Ireland Minister for Home Affairs.[72] In 1990, byelaws made by the Defence Secretary barring access to Greenham Common, then a nuclear missile base, were held ultra vires because they ignored the provision in the Military Lands Act 1892 that such byelaws must not take away or prejudicially affect the rights of the commoners.[73] Social security regulations which deprived an asylum-seeker of all benefits while his or her appeal for asylum was pending were unlawful because their effect was to prevent the right to appeal from being exercised.[74]

In reviewing the contents of delegated legislation, the courts do not lightly strike down a statutory instrument, but if necessary they may apply a test of unreasonableness where a regulation is so unreasonable that Parliament cannot be taken as having authorised it to be made under the Act in question.[75] Where an order by the Environment Secretary 'capping' selected local councils' expenditure was subject to approval by resolution of the House of Com-

---

68   [1962] 1 QB 340. See also *R v IRC, ex p Woolwich Building Society* [1991] 4 All ER 92.
69   *Malloch v Aberdeen Corpn* 1974 SLT 253; and see Education (Scotland) Act 1973.
70   *Daymond v South West Water Authority* [1976] AC 609.
71   *Raymond v Honey* [1983] AC 1.
72   [1971] AC 632. And see D N MacCormick (1970) 86 LQR 171.
73   *DPP v Hutchinson* [1990] 2 AC 783. And see n 84 below.
74   *R v Social Security Secretary, ex p B* (1996) 9 Admin LR 1.
75   *Maynard v Osmond* [1977] QB 240; *Cinnamond v British Airports Authority* [1980] 2 All ER 368.

mons, the House of Lords held that if the order came within the 'four corners' of the parent statute it was subject to review for unreasonableness only on the extreme grounds of bad faith, improper motive or manifest absurdity.[76]

A serious procedural error by the department concerned could lead to an instrument being declared invalid. Thus where there was a duty to consult interested organisations before regulations were made, it was held that the mere sending of a letter to an organisation did not amount to consultation;[77] and no effective consultation occurred when a department failed to allow sufficient time for this.[78] But not every procedural error vitiates the statutory instrument; some procedural requirements are held to be directory (that is, of such a kind that failure to comply with them does not invalidate the instrument) and not mandatory or imperative.[79]

Where either on grounds of substance or procedure an instrument is to some extent defective, this does not necessarily mean that the whole instrument is a nullity; it may still be operative to its lawful extent or be binding upon persons not affected by the defect of procedure.[80] The decision of when such 'severance' is permissible may involve a textual, or 'blue pencil' test (does deletion of the offending phrase or sentence leave a grammatical and coherent text?) and also a test of whether after deletion of the unlawful part the substance of the provision remains essentially unchanged in purpose and effect from what had been intended.[81]

It was at one time believed that if the parent Act provided that regulations when made should have effect 'as if enacted in this Act', the courts were precluded from inquiring into the validity of the regulations; but in 1931 the House of Lords were of the opposite opinion[82] and this expression in the parent Act adds nothing to the binding effect of a properly made instrument. The power of a court to rule on the validity of a statutory instrument should not be excluded, however rarely the power may need to be used. Where a tribunal must adjudicate upon the rights of an individual, and the extent of those rights is directly affected by a regulation, the tribunal must if necessary decide whether the regulation is valid;[83] the tribunal's decision on this issue will be subject to appeal or review. So too, if someone is prosecuted for breach of a regulation or byelaw, it is in principle a defence to show that the instrument in question is invalid.[84]

Byelaws are a form of delegated legislation that generally applies only in a

---

[76] *R v Environment Secretary, ex p Hammersmith BC* [1991] 1 AC 521, applying *Notts CC v Environment Secretary* [1986] AC 240 (C M G Himsworth [1986] PL 374, [1991] PL 76).

[77] The *Aylesbury Mushrooms* case, note 41 above.

[78] *R v Social Services Secretary, ex p Association of Metropolitan Authorities* [1986] 1 All ER 164.

[79] de Smith, Woolf and Jowell, *Judicial Review*, pp 265–74, and ch 29 B.

[80] *Dunkley v Evans* [1981] 3 All ER 285; the *Aylesbury Mushrooms* case, note 41 above.

[81] *DPP v Hutchinson* [1990] 2 AC 783 (A W Bradley [1990] PL 293); and *R v IRC, ex p Woolwich Building Society* [1991] 4 All ER 92.

[82] *Minister of Health v R* [1931] AC 494.

[83] *Chief Adjudication Officer v Foster* [1993] AC 754 (and see D Feldman (1992) 108 LQR 45; A W Bradley [1992] PL 185).

[84] Eg *Kruse v Johnson* [1898] 2 QB 91; *R v Reading Crown Court, ex p Hutchinson* [1988] QB 384 (A W Bradley [1988] PL 169); *Bugg v DPP* [1993] QB 473 (D Feldman [1993] PL 37) and C Emery [1992] CLJ 308. Cf *R v Wicks* [1997] 2 All ER 801 (HL) and A W Bradley [1997] PL 365.

particular locality or certain public places (for example, airports). They are usually made by a local council or a statutory undertaking, but are subject to ministerial confirmation before they take effect. The courts formerly exercised greater control over byelaws than over departmental regulations.[85]

Administrative rule-making

Legislation by statutory instrument is more flexible than primary legislation, since the law can be changed without need for a Bill to pass through Parliament. Nonetheless, statutory instrument procedures are today complex and the instruments are expressed in formal language. In government business today, many less formal methods of rule-making are used. Such methods are sometimes directly authorised by Act of Parliament, but rules so made have an uncertain legal status (for example, the immigration rules made under the Immigration Act 1971).[86] Two forms of rule-making that are often authorised by statute are codes of practice and administrative guidelines or notes of guidance.[87] They do not have the full force of delegated legislation and generally do not have a mandatory effect,[88] but a department may be expected either to observe them or take steps to change them[89] and adverse consequences may follow for an individual who does not observe them.

Depending on the parent Act, these rules may totally evade the procedures for parliamentary control described above. Indeed, many administrative rules are issued without direct statutory authority. This phenomenon was once described as 'administrative quasi-legislation'[90] when it was related to the practice of issuing the official interpretation of doubtful points in statutes and of stating concessions that would be made in individual cases. The practice has continued ever since, for the revenue authorities have often chosen to waive the application of over-harsh laws rather than seek changes in the legislation. In 1979, the Inland Revenue's use of executive discretion rather than a statutory basis for assessing tax was described by the House of Lords as unconstitutional.[91] As Walton J had said, 'One should be taxed by law, and not be untaxed by concession'.[92]

In 1976–78, when the minority Labour government was pursuing a non-statutory incomes policy, a wide range of powers was used to bring pressure to bear on industry, including the awarding of government contracts.[93] The use of such powers had a quasi-legislative effect, but the policy collapsed when the

---

85   Cf *Powell v May* [1946] KB 330; *Burnley BC v England* (1978) 77 LGR 227; *Cinnamond v British Airports Authority* [1980] 2 All ER 368.

86   See ch 20 B.

87   See eg Police and Criminal Evidence Act 1984, part VI. Also HL Deb, 15 January 1986, cols 1075–104, and (1989) 10 Stat LR 214; and A R Mowbray [1987] PL 570. On the Social Fund, see R Drabble and T Lynes [1989] PL 297, *R v Social Services Secretary, ex p Stitt, The Times*, 5 July 1990, and D Feldman (1991) 107 LQR 39.

88   See eg *Laker Airways v Department of Trade* [1977] QB 643.

89   *R v Home Secretary, ex p Khan* [1985] 1 All ER 40 (and A R Mowbray [1985] PL 558).

90   R E Megarry (1944) 60 LQR 125; Ganz, *Quasi-Legislation*; R Baldwin and J Houghton [1986] PL 239. See also Baldwin, *Rules and Government*.

91   *Vestey v IRC (No 2)* [1980] AC 1148.

92   *Vestey v IRC* [1979] Ch 177, 197. And see D W Williams [1979] British Tax Review 137.

93   G Ganz [1978] PL 333, R B Ferguson and A C Page [1978] PL 347, and T C Daintith [1979] CLP 41; and ch 17 E.

House of Commons voted against it in December 1978. Central government continues through the exercise of its contractual power to be able to impose non-statutory policies, subject to the constraints of Community law, but the same power has been taken away from local councils.[94]

In many areas of government, such as town planning, education and health, ministerial statements of policy and circulars to local authorities have a practical effect which falls little short of modifying the law. On important matters of general policy where controversial issues are involved, government by circular is not a satisfactory substitute for legislation. Nor can such circulars require the performance of unlawful acts.[95]

Informal rule-making is frequently adopted by departments in order that wide discretion vested in ministers by statute may be exercised by officials in a reasonably uniform manner.[96] Some departments which rely on such rules make a practice of publishing them; others have attempted to keep them secret, which causes problems when a person affected by the rules has a right of appeal to a tribunal, or wishes to know the reasons for a decision. Secrecy has been maintained when changes have been made in published rules or policies, and the government wishes to avoid being criticised for the changes. This occurred notably with the changed policies on the export of defence-related equipment to Iraq, which the Scott report found caused ministers repeatedly to give misleading answers to MPs.[97] Like any large organisation, a department may wish to give instructions to its staff on purely internal matters without publishing them. But rules which directly affect the interests of the citizen should be published. Problems arising out of the use of departmental rules have frequently come before the Parliamentary Ombudsman, most notably in the Sachsenhausen case.[98]

We therefore may conclude that, while delegated legislation in the form of statutory instruments and byelaws has, not without difficulty, been accommodated within the legal system, many executive powers of rule-making present a continuing challenge to the notion of government according to law.

Recent steps to encourage greater openness in government may alleviate some of the problems relating to departmental rules. The non-statutory code of practice on access to government information, which is policed by the Parliamentary Ombudsman, obliges departments (inter alia)

to publish or otherwise make available explanatory material on departments' dealing with the public (including such rules, procedures, internal guidance to officials, and similar administrative manuals as will assist better understanding of departmental

---

[94] See T C Daintith, in Jowell and Oliver (eds), *The Changing Constitution*, ch 8; Local Government Act 1988, part II.

[95] *Royal College of Nursing v DHSS* [1981] AC 800; *Gillick v West Norfolk Health Authority* [1986] AC 112.

[96] Eg Local Authority Social Services Act 1970, s 7 (guidance of Secretary of State) and s 7A (directions by Secretary of State) (added by NHS and Community Care Act 1990, s 50); and see *R v Islington Council, ex p Rixon, The Times*, 17 April 1996: council must follow statutory guidance except if there is good reason to depart from it).

[97] See HC 115 (1995–96) (Scott Report) esp vol IV, para K. For an absurd attempt by the Treasury, to keep secret changes in published rules, see the Compton Bassett affair, recounted in Gregory and Hutchesson, *The Parliamentary Ombudsman*, pp 593–9.

[98] Ch 28 D, and see A R Mowbray [1987] PL 570.

action in dealing with the public) except where publication could prejudice any matter which should properly be kept confidential under Part II of the Code.[99]

Publication of administrative rules may lead to criticism in Parliament and the media or to judicial scrutiny, but a regular practice of publication should generally make it easier for departments to explain their decisions and, as the code also requires, to give reasons for those decisions.

---

[99]   *Code of Practice on Access to Government Information* (2nd edn, 1997), para 3(ii). The grounds for confidentiality in part II include defence, security and international relations; internal discussion and advice; management of the economy; personnel matters affecting civil servants; individual privacy; and commercial confidences. And see ch 13 E.

CHAPTER 28

Administrative justice

The title of this chapter might seem a contradiction in terms: there are such marked differences between the way in which decisions are made by civil servants and ministers on the one hand, and by the courts on the other, that the two systems, administration and justice, should be kept quite separate. However, as we will see in relation to the judicial control of administrative action, there is a strong tendency in public law in Britain for principles derived from the courts, such as the doctrine of natural justice,[1] to be applied to administrative decisions. The same tendency applies to the development of institutions within government. In his seminal book, *Justice and Administrative Law*, first published in 1928, Robson described the extent to which 'trial by Whitehall' had developed in the British constitution. He argued that the judicial powers given to administrative bodies served to promote the welfare of society and that administrative justice could become 'as well-founded and broad-based as any other kind of justice now known to us and embodied in human institutions'.[2]

In this chapter we examine institutions and procedures concerned with an extensive area of public decision-making that lies somewhere between the world of government departments on one hand and that of the law courts on the other. This territory is liable to become a battleground as competing interests from the administrative and legal worlds struggle to occupy it. In one sector of the disputed territory that was formerly under strong departmental influence, namely administrative tribunals, the judicial model of decision-making now holds sway. The British system of tribunals, today best referred to without the adjective 'administrative', will be outlined in section A of this chapter. In another sector, that of public inquiries (considered in section B), government departments exercise the dominant influence over the procedures and the decisions that are made. Again, when things go wrong in government, impartial means are needed for discovering what happened so that those responsible may be called to account. In section C will be described one constitutional device, the 'tribunal of inquiry' appointed under the Tribunals of Inquiry (Evidence) Act 1921, that allows techniques of judicial investigation to be applied to scandals and disasters of special importance. By contrast, section D is concerned with the Ombudsman. The mission of this

---

[1] Ch 29 B.
[2] Robson, *Justice and Administrative Law*, p 515. And see W A Robson [1979] CLP 107.

office is to investigate individual complaints about governmental action and to remedy injustice that official errors have caused, but the Ombudsman carries out this mission by investigatory means which owe little to traditional court procedures. Before we examine these sectors of administrative justice separately, a brief discussion of the role of tribunals and inquiries may be helpful.

When Parliament authorises new forms of social service or state regulation, it is inevitable that questions and disputes will arise out of the application of the legislation. There are three main ways in which such questions and disputes may be settled: (*a*) by conferring new jurisdiction on one or other of the ordinary courts; (*b*) by creating new machinery in the form of special tribunals; (*c*) by leaving all decisions to the authority with primary responsibility for the scheme, whether it be local authority or central department. In case (*c*), the Act may create rights of appeal (for example, from a local council to a central department), or it may require a hearing or public inquiry to be held before any decision is made. If decisions are entrusted entirely to local authorities, as is the case with the homeless persons provisions of the Housing Act 1985, part III, the procedure of judicial review exists to supervise the legality of decisions. But reliance on judicial review, which should be an exceptional remedy, is not adequate to ensure the quality of numerous decisions at first instance (for instance, those concerning rights of the homeless, or the award of housing benefit).[3]

There are important distinctions to be drawn between tribunal decisions and departmental decisions involving a public inquiry. The Franks report of 1957 made it clear that tribunals and inquiries differ in their constitutional status and functions. No tribunal should appear merely to be part of the departmental structure, for the typical tribunal exercises functions which are essentially judicial in character, although of a specialised nature. Indeed, most tribunals could be regarded as specialised courts. As the Franks committee stated,

We consider that tribunals should properly be regarded as machinery provided by Parliament for adjudication rather than as part of the machinery of administration. The essential point is that in all these cases Parliament has deliberately provided for a decision outside and independent of the Department concerned.[4]

On the other hand, the public inquiry, while it grants citizens affected by official proposals some safeguard against ill-informed and unreasoned decisions, is essentially a step in a complex process which leads to a departmental decision for which a minister is responsible to Parliament.

Several trends during the 1990s were causing some concern. One was that in some local government services, a limited right of 'appeal' or 'review' had been created.[5] Another was that in some central services, an appeal to a

---

[3] See report of Council on Tribunals for 1990–91, pp 29–30; for 1991–92, pp 21–2; Lord Woolf [1992] PL 221, 228–9; and Law Commission, *Administrative Law: Judicial Review and Statutory Appeals*, p 15.
[4] Cmnd 218, 1957, p 9; ch 26 above.
[5] See eg the rights of appeal in school admission decisions (now Education Act 1996, s 423) and the procedures for review of housing benefit decisions (report of Council on Tribunals for 1994–95, pp 2–5); R Sainsbury and T Eardley [1992] PL 551.

tribunal had been downgraded to a process of review by officials.[6] In neither case was there the right to a decision by an independent tribunal. A third was that financial pressures were endangering the tribunal system, causing excessive delays in busy tribunals or inferior documentation, and leading some departments to require tribunal users to pay for the full costs of a tribunal.[7] As the Franks committee concluded in 1957, both with tribunals and inquiries the ordinary administrative procedures are not enough to protect the individual's interests. All powers of government should be exercised fairly – but principles of openness, fairness and impartiality are more likely to be maintained when there are statutory procedures designed to promote these qualities. In fact, developments in real life often overtake textbook distinctions. We will discover in section B that some public inquiries today lead directly to a decision being made by the official who conducts the inquiry, not by the department concerned; thus a new form of 'tribunal' has developed under the guise of an inquiry.

A. Tribunals[8]

Reasons for creation of tribunals

For many centuries Britain has had specialised courts in addition to the courts of general jurisdiction. Medieval merchants had their courts of pie poudre; the tin-miners of Devon and Cornwall had their courts of Stannaries.[9] The growth of the welfare state led to the creation of many procedures for the settlement of disputes. The National Insurance Act of 1911, which created the first British social insurance scheme, provided for the adjudication of disputes by new administrative agencies. The present social security scheme includes a complex structure for the settlement of disputes concerning the benefits or pension payable to claimants.

The creation of tribunals has sometimes been considered to endanger the position of the judiciary and the authority of the law administered in the ordinary courts.[10] The right of access to the courts is indeed an important safeguard for the citizen, but the machinery of the courts is not suited for settling every dispute which may arise out of the work of government. One reason for this is the need for specialised knowledge if certain disputes are to be resolved fairly and economically. Areas such as taxation, social security or immigration embody complex systems of regulation which require innumer-

---

6   See R Sainsbury, in Richardson and Genn (eds), *Administrative Law and Government Action*, ch 11; and note 37 below.

7   Report of Council on Tribunals 1995–96, pp 2–6.

8   See report of the Franks committee, Cmnd 218, 1957, parts II and III; Spencer (ed), *Jackson's Machinery of Justice*, part III; Wraith and Hutchesson, *Administrative Tribunals*; Farmer, *Tribunals and Government*; Richardson and Genn (eds), *Administrative Law and Government Action*, part II.

9   See *R v East Powder Justices, ex p Lampshire* [1979] QB 616.

10   See eg Lord Scarman, *English Law – the New Dimension*, part III. For an historical critique, see Arthurs, *Without the Law: Administrative Justice and Legal Pluralism in the 19th century*.

able decisions to be made by officials trained in what is required. The ordinary courts could not deal with the mass of appeals from such decisions unless they, the legal profession and legal aid were organised quite differently. While policy decisions and oversight of a department's work are entrusted to ministers, most schemes require a structure of rules which officials may apply without constant recourse to the minister, a fact which underlies the present use in Whitehall of executive agencies.[11] In such schemes, individuals may more readily have a right of appeal from official decisions to a tribunal designed with a particular area of government in mind. This is a better remedy against poor decisions than the principle of ministerial responsibility.

In other areas of government, there may be more need to retain power to decide in the hands of the department and the minister. In some fields, notably the regulation of civil aviation, a special agency such as the Civil Aviation Authority exists with power to develop policies through the mechanism of licensing, but with ultimate control being retained by the minister, to whom appeals against the Authority's decisions may be brought.[12] In other fields, such as social security, the principles applicable have been laid down in statutes or statutory instruments, and the duty of applying them has been vested in a hierarchy of tribunals, for whose decisions no minister is responsible, and which the government can control only by amending the relevant statutory rules. Here the relationship between minister and tribunal approaches that which exists between the government and the judiciary. Such tribunals exist not because they must exercise a political discretion which it would be inappropriate to confer on the judges, but because they can do the work of adjudication required more efficiently than the courts.[13]

This claim can be justified on several grounds. As was said in relation to claims for social security benefit, 'For these cases we do not want a Rolls-Royce system of justice'.[14] Practical factors that have favoured the setting up of tribunals include: the desire for a procedure which avoids the formality of the courts; the need, in implementing a new social policy, for the speedy, cheap and decentralised determination of many individual cases; the need for expert and specialised knowledge on the part of the tribunal, which may include not merely lawyers but also other professionals with relevant experience. Another important characteristic of tribunals is that the legal profession has no monopoly of the right to represent those appearing before tribunals. This fact alone makes tribunals more accessible to the public than the courts, since an individual's case may often be presented effectively by a trade union official, an accountant, a surveyor, a social worker or a friend.

It used to be said that a reason for preferring tribunals to courts was that many lawyers, including judges, were out of sympathy with changing social policies. Today the profession appears better able to respond to the needs of

---

[11]   See ch 13 D.
[12]   See *Laker Airways Ltd v Department of Trade* [1977] QB 643; G R Baldwin [1978] PL 57 and (the same) *Regulating the Airlines.*
[13]   Cf the distinction between 'policy-oriented' and 'court-substitute' tribunals: Farmer, op cit, ch 8, and H Genn, in Richardson and Genn (eds), op cit, ch 11.
[14]   Street, *Justice in the Welfare State*, p 3.

the time than it used to be; and the contribution of lawyers at all levels to the operation of tribunals is not seriously questioned.

The necessity for administrative justice should not lead to the creation of tribunals for their own sake when the ordinary courts could well take the decisions in question. In the view of the Franks committee, 'a decision should be entrusted to a court rather than to a tribunal in the absence of special considerations which make a tribunal more suitable'.[15] Moreover, granted the need for specialised tribunals, the essential merits of the court system should so far as is practicable be incorporated in the tribunal system. Thus, if independent decisions are to be made in accordance with the law, the appointment and dismissal of members of tribunals must not be solely in the hands of the department concerned. Again, there is danger as well as merit in informal procedures. In general, tribunals are not bound by the rules of evidence observed in courts and could not reach decisions simply and speedily if they were. Some tribunals follow procedures that are inquisitorial rather than adversary, but minimum standards of evidence and proof must be observed if justice is to be done.[16] One safeguard lies in the appointment to tribunals of legally qualified chairmen, another in maintaining in all cases the right to legal representation – although if this right is to benefit those who most need it, legal aid or assistance must be extended to more tribunals.[17] A further safeguard is the right of appeal, either to a higher tribunal or to the ordinary courts: in particular, it should always be possible to challenge in the superior courts a tribunal's ruling on points of law, and tribunals should give reasons for their decisions.

Since the Franks report of 1957, acceptance of these principles has removed much earlier distrust of tribunals. But there will continue to be tension between those lawyers who believe that tribunals should come to resemble courts in all but name, and those who insist that tribunals must be flexible, informal and accessible to the ordinary person in a way in which the courts are not. The latter would argue that it is the courts which must learn from tribunals, rather than vice versa.

Classification of tribunals

It is not easy to classify the 70 or so systems of tribunal which exercise judicial functions in relation to specific branches of government, nor to draw a sharp line between those bodies which may be classed as tribunals and those which may not. A list of tribunals under the supervision of the Council on Tribunals is published annually in the council's report. In the report for 1995–96, this list included agricultural land tribunals, child support appeal tribunals, the Civil Aviation Authority and the Director-General of Fair Trading in their licensing functions, criminal injuries adjudicators, the Data Protection Registrar, education appeal committees (dealing with admission of pupils to schools) and the Special Educational Needs Tribunal, immigration adjudicators and the Immigration Appeal Tribunal, industrial tribunals, the two Lands

---

[15]   Cmnd 218, p 9.
[16]   See eg *R v Deputy Industrial Injuries Commissioner, ex p Moore* [1965] 1 QB 456.
[17]   Report of Council on Tribunals for 1994–95, pp 5–9; for 1995–96, pp 32–3. And note 24 below.

Tribunals, mental health review tribunals, the Comptroller-General of Patents, war pensions appeal tribunals, rent assessment committees, social security appeal tribunals and the Social Security Commissioners, disability and medical appeal tribunals, the general and special commissioners of income tax, traffic commissioners and parking adjudicators, valuation tribunals, VAT and duties tribunals and, in Scotland, children's hearings and the Crofters Commission.

It is possible to group these tribunals by subject-matter, for example, (*a*) social security, health and social services; (*b*) land, property and housing; (*c*) economic activities, licensing and taxation; (*d*) others, including industrial and immigration tribunals.[18] But it is also possible to analyse tribunals in terms of the general considerations which are discussed below: thus in some tribunals the parties are private individuals (landlord/tenant, employer/employee) but in many tribunals a citizen is in dispute with a government department or local authority. Moreover, some bodies which are not subject to the Council on Tribunals may claim to be regarded as tribunals. These include the Gaming Board, legal aid committees, the Parole Board,[19] local appeal committees for council tax and housing benefit and the many professional discipline committees. There is no invariable legislative practice of calling a tribunal a tribunal (thus the Pensions Ombudsman is a tribunal in all but name).[20] Nor does the fact that a tribunal is styled a court by Parliament mean that it has all the attributes of a court, such as the power to commit for contempt of court.[21]

Problems of classification arise because the system of tribunals is not subject to an overall plan and each year new tribunals are created by legislation. One solution to the organisation of administrative justice might be to create a series of higher administrative courts or tribunals, each covering a range of related jurisdictions. On matters of social security and other aspects of income maintenance, the Social Security and Child Support Commissioners serve as a national appeal tribunal within a variety of different adjudication structures. There has also been a definite policy of concentrating disputes relating to the valuation of land on the Lands Tribunal, and those relating to employment on the Employment Appeal Tribunal. Attempts to resist the proliferation of tribunals are often made by the Council on Tribunals,[22] not always with success, for the department concerned with new legislation can often discover reasons for establishing a more suitable tribunal than any which exist. The Franks committee rejected the general principle that tribunal service should be based on whole-time salaried employment. There are in fact many exceptions to that principle (for example, the Social Security Commissioners, the Lands Tribunal and the full-time chairmen of industrial tribunals), especially at the national or appellate level, but most tribunals depend on part-time service from lawyers and others.

---

18   Cf Wraith and Hutchesson, op cit, ch 2; and Farmer, op cit, chs 7 and 8.
19   Report of Council on Tribunals for 1994–95, p 40.
20   Report of Council on Tribunals for 1989–90, pp 26–8.
21   *A-G v BBC* [1981] AC 303; ch 18 B. See also N Y Lowe and H F Rawlings [1982] PL 418; Contempt of Court Act 1981, s 19; and *Peach Grey & Co v Sommers* [1995] 2 All ER 513.
22   See eg reports of Council on Tribunals for 1990–91, pp 26–8, and 1995–96, pp 46–7.

General considerations

Tribunals are concerned with a wide range of activities but certain questions are of general application. (*a*) What is the composition of the tribunal? Tribunals are not composed of government officials. Often they are constituted of lay members of the public, sometimes coming from groups such as employers' organisations and trade unions. But in certain tribunals specialist qualifications are required (for example, in medicine or psychiatry, land valuation, local government, or the needs of disabled persons); usually provision is made for a legally qualified chairman. (*b*) Who appoints the members of the tribunal and who has power to dismiss? Usually appointments are made for a fixed period of years, either by the minister concerned, by the Lord Chancellor, or by both minister and Lord Chancellor jointly; in general dismissal now requires the concurrence of the Lord Chancellor.[23] (*c*) What are the powers and jurisdiction of the tribunal? In particular, how extensive is the tribunal's discretion? Many tribunals, like the Lands Tribunal and the commissioners of income tax, exercise strictly judicial functions. Some, like the Civil Aviation Authority, base their decisions on wider aspects of policy, exercising regulatory functions in a judicial form. (*d*) What procedure is followed by the tribunal and how formal is it? Are hearings in public or in private, and do individuals appearing before it have the right of legal representation? In 1997, legal aid was available before the Lands Tribunal, the Commons Commissioners and the Employment Appeal Tribunal; legal assistance by way of representation was available before mental health review tribunals and other proceedings including the discretionary lifer panels of the Parole Board and (in cases when representation is permitted) prison disciplinary hearings. Legal advice and assistance without representation could be obtained in connection with all tribunal proceedings.[24] (*e*) Are the tribunal's decisions final, or is there the right to appeal, whether on law, on fact, or on the merits? The Franks committee considered that the ideal appeal structure took the form of a general appeal from the tribunal of first instance to an appellate tribunal; that as a matter of principle appeal should not lie from a tribunal to a minister; and that all decisions of tribunals should be subject to review by the courts on points of law.[25] The structure of social security appeals complies broadly with this pattern but other tribunals depart from it. (*f*) Are the tribunal's decisions published and, if so, do they have authority as binding or persuasive precedents for future tribunals? (*g*) What is the relation between the tribunal and the department with whose work it is associated? What opportunities are there for the department to influence the work of the tribunal other than by formal legislation?

The structure of some leading tribunals will now be outlined. The tribunals chosen for this purpose do not include tribunals that have already been mentioned in earlier chapters, such as the commissioners of income tax and the immigration appeals structure.[26]

---

[23] Page 745 below.
[24] Legal Aid Act 1988, part III. And see Genn, *The Effectiveness of Representation at Tribunals.*
[25] Cmnd 218, 1957, p 25.
[26] See chs 17 C and 20 B.

Social security appeals[27]

In common with the income tax system, the social security system requires each year millions of decisions directly affecting the financial position of individuals to be taken by civil servants. Whenever a decision is taken that adversely affects an individual (for example, when a claim to benefit is refused or when less benefit is paid than an individual has claimed), he or she should be able to appeal against it, if only because such decisions must be founded upon a sound legal base, not upon the arbitrary decision of an official. As we have already seen, the right of appeal to an independent authority was recognised in the National Insurance Act 1911. When after 1945 the social security scheme became more complex as new benefits were provided, the adjudication procedures also became more diverse and elaborate. An important distinction formerly existed between the structure of appeals for contributory benefits under national insurance (such as retirement pension) and that for non-contributory means-tested benefits, such as income support and payments to relieve need (now made from the Social Fund). One reason for the distinction was that a scheme based on compulsory insurance necessarily created substantive rights to benefit. Such rights are absent from a scheme of means-tested discretionary payments, as with supplementary benefits before 1980, and the Social Fund since 1988. Even so, all claimants for benefit are entitled to have their claims decided by a proper procedure and in accordance with the relevant legal rules. Moreover, even where benefits are discretionary, no public body can operate a scheme responsibly without developing administrative rules to govern the exercise of official discretion.

Claims for most forms of benefit (such as disablement benefit, retirement pension and income support) are decided in the first instance by adjudication officers appointed by the Secretary of State for Social Security. These officers are full-time civil servants, who act subject to advice from a chief adjudication officer.[28] From an adjudication officer's decision, there is a right of appeal to a social security appeal tribunal. This tribunal, which sits locally, comprises a chairman, who must be a lawyer of five years' standing,[29] and two persons drawn from a panel of those with knowledge of conditions in the area and representative of persons living or working there. The chairman is selected to sit by the President of the Independent Tribunal Service[30] from a panel of lawyers appointed by the Lord Chancellor or, in Scotland, by the Lord President of the Court of Session. From the tribunal's decision, there is an appeal on a point of law, subject to leave being granted, to the Social Security Commissioners, who are qualified lawyers of ten years' standing. Normally an

---

[27] See now Social Security Administration Act 1992, part II (cited as the 1992 Act), and the Social Security (Adjudication) Regulations, SI 1995 No 1801. Also Ogus, Barendt and Wikeley, *Social Security Law*, ch 17; H Genn, in Richardson and Genn, op cit, ch 11; T Buck, *The Social Fund – Law and Practice*; Baldwin, Wikeley and Young, *Judging Social Security*; R Sainsbury, in Finnie, Himsworth and Walker (eds), *Edinburgh Essays in Public Law*, 335–49. On the earlier tribunals, see eg Harlow and Rawlings, *Law and Administration*, chs 18, 19; Adler and Bradley (eds), *Justice, Discretion and Poverty.*

[28] 1992 Act, s 39. And R Sainsbury [1989] PL 389.

[29] Ie a five-year general qualification under the Courts and Legal Services Act 1990, s 71.

[30] The Service administers social security, disability and medical appeal tribunals and also child support appeal tribunals.

appeal is heard by a single Commissioner, but the Chief Commissioner may direct that an appeal involving a question of law of special difficulty should be heard by a tribunal of three Commissioners.[31] There is an appeal with leave on a point of law from a Social Security Commissioner to the Court of Appeal in England, and to the Inner House of the Court of Session in Scotland.[32] Selected decisions of Social Security Commissioners are published and bind adjudication officers and local tribunals, although the law may be changed by Act of Parliament or by fresh regulations made by the Secretary of State under delegated powers.

Some questions on which a social security claim may depend (for example, a claimant's contribution record) are reserved for decision by the Secretary of State, and are not decided by a tribunal. From such a decision, there is a right of appeal on law to the High Court or Court of Session.[33] Various medical questions (for example, the extent of disablement caused by an industrial injury or disease) are decided by an adjudicating medical practitioner employed by the DSS, with an appeal to a medical appeal tribunal, consisting of two independent medical members sitting with a legal chairman. From the medical appeal tribunal, appeal lies on a point of law and with leave to the Social Security Commissioners.[34] In addition to these rights of appeal, decisions taken by the adjudicating authorities are subject to administrative review, for example if there has been a relevant change of circumstances since the decision was made.[35]

Appeals about disability living and disability working allowances are decided by disability appeal tribunals, who sit with a lawyer as chairman, one member from a panel of medical practitioners and the other from a panel of persons experienced in dealing with the needs of disabled persons. Before such an appeal can be considered by the tribunal, it must first have been subject to a review by an adjudication officer.[36]

In the case of payments from the Social Fund, intended to be a residual way of meeting hardship, the first decision is made by a social fund officer and is subject to review by another such officer and then by a social fund inspector, acting under the guidance of the Social Fund Commissioner. This system of review was created following the government's decision that there should be no right of appeal to a tribunal.[37] There is also no right of appeal to a tribunal in the case of housing benefit decisions taken by a local authority's benefit

---

[31]   1992 Act, s 57.

[32]   Ibid, s 24. And see *Chief Adjudication Officer v Foster* [1993] AC 754. The structure of appeals described here is broadly replicated by the Child Support Act 1991 for appeals against assessments of child support maintenance (ss 16–28, 1991 Act).

[33]   1992 Act, s 18. And M Partington, *Secretary of State's Powers of Adjudication in Social Security Law*.

[34]   1992 Act, s 48.

[35]   Ibid, ss 30–5, 42, 43. And N Wikeley (1992) 11 CJQ 227.

[36]   1992 Act, ss 19, 25–9, 35, 47. And see R Sainsbury, in Richardson and Genn (eds), op cit, ch 12.

[37]   1992 Act, ss 64–6. For the Council on Tribunals' opposition, see Cmnd 9722, 1986. Also R Drabble and T Lynes [1989] PL 297. A right of appeal to a tribunal applies to Social Fund payments for maternity and funeral expenses and cold weather heating: 1992 Act, s 20(6)(e).

review board.[38] Both with the Social Fund and with housing benefit, decisions that are taken improperly or in breach of the law are subject to judicial review, although this may not in practice always provide due relief.

The present structure of social security appeals is complex, and the quality of first instance decisions is uneven. But the Independent Tribunal Service enables the tribunals to be administered from outside the Department of Social Security. This has enhanced the independence of the tribunals. The requirement of lawyers as chairmen is vital to the effectiveness of the tribunals; and it remains important that the tribunals should be accessible to claimants, avoid undue legalism, and promote better decision-making within DSS offices. Yet in 1996 the government was considering making radical changes in the scheme.[39]

Lands Tribunal

The Lands Tribunal Act 1949 authorised two Lands Tribunals, one for Scotland and one for the rest of the United Kingdom.[40] The latter tribunal has jurisdiction over a variety of matters relating to the valuation of property, including the assessment of compensation for compulsory acquisition of land and rating appeals from the local valuation courts and the variation of restrictive covenants.[41] The jurisdiction can be enlarged by Order in Council. The President of the Lands Tribunal, who must have held judicial office or have a seven-year general qualification under the Courts and Legal Services Act 1990 (s 71), is like the other members appointed by the Lord Chancellor. These members must be lawyers or persons qualified by professional experience in the valuation of land. There is no fixed composition for the tribunal; this is varied according to the particular case as the president may determine. Thus a single surveyor may sit, or the president together with members who are lawyers and surveyors. On the application of any party a case may be stated on a point of law for determination by the Court of Appeal; otherwise the decision of the Lands Tribunal is final.

The composition of the Lands Tribunal ensures that it has access to expertise both in legal and valuation matters. While procedure before the tribunal can be as formal and elaborate as litigation in the courts, particularly when large sums of money are at stake, the tribunal may adopt a simpler procedure in smaller cases. Legal aid is available before the tribunal.

Industrial tribunals[42]

Industrial tribunals were first established in 1964 to determine disputes arising from the imposition on certain industries of a levy to meet the expenses of industrial training boards. They rapidly acquired a wide jurisdic-

---

[38]   1992 Act, s 63; Housing Benefit (General) Regulations 1987 (SI 1987 No 1971), part XI. Also N Wikeley (1986) 5 CJQ 18; R Sainsbury and T Eardley [1992] PL 551.

[39]   See *Improving Decision Making and Appeals in Social Security* (Cm 3328, 1996). Cf report of Council on Tribunals for 1995–96, pp 50–4.

[40]   The Lands Tribunal in Scotland was established in 1971, to deal with matters arising under the Conveyancing and Feudal Reform (Scotland) Act 1970 and with valuation of land for planning, compulsory purchase and tax purposes.

[41]   See eg *Westminster Council v Duke of Westminster* [1991] 4 All ER 136.

[42]   See now the Industrial Tribunals Act 1996, part I.

tion, which now includes disputes under the Equal Pay Act 1970 and many important issues of employment law, in respect of such matters as guarantee payments, facilities for trade union activities, maternity pay, redundancy payments and (in practice the most numerous) unfair dismissal. In a field that continues to grow in importance, the tribunals deal with alleged discrimination in relation to employment, under the Sex Discrimination Act 1975, the Race Relations Act 1976 and the Disability Discrimination Act 1995. An industrial tribunal consists of a lawyer chairman and two lay members drawn from panels representing each side of industry. The tribunals are organised on the presidential system. The two presidents of industrial tribunals, in England and Scotland respectively, oversee the administration of the tribunals, convene conferences of chairmen and members, and represent the tribunals in their relations with the government, the Council on Tribunals and other bodies. Many of the chairmen hold full-time, permanent posts. Associated with the tribunals, but separate from them, is an advisory and conciliation service.

Appeals on law lie from industrial tribunals to the Employment Appeal Tribunal.[43] It consists of nominated judges of the High Court and the Court of Session, one of whom is appointed by the Lord Chancellor to be president of the tribunal, sitting with lay persons with special knowledge or experience of industrial relations. The tribunal is a superior court of record but conducts its business with less formality than the High Court and lawyers have no monopoly of representation.

Tribunals and Inquiries Act 1992

The main conclusions of the Franks committee on the status of tribunals have already been mentioned. As well as making detailed recommendations for improving existing tribunals, the committee proposed certain general reforms that were mainly implemented by the Tribunals and Inquiries Act 1958, re-enacted in 1971 and again in 1992. Thus the chairmen of certain tribunals are now selected by the minister concerned from a panel of persons approved by the Lord Chancellor (s 6), a provision that should help to ensure that chairmen are either legally qualified or have suitable alternative experience; in the case of most tribunals, the minister's power to terminate membership of a tribunal can be exercised only with the concurrence in England and Wales of the Lord Chancellor, and in Scotland of the Lord President of the Court of Session (s 7); appeals on points of law lie from certain tribunals to the High Court or the Court of Session (s 11); and all tribunals are under a duty, if requested on or before the giving or notification of the decision, to give reasons for their decision, such reasons whether written or oral being deemed to form part of the record for the purpose of review by certiorari (s 10).[44] In practice, many rules of procedure for particular tribunals require reasons to be given in every case.

---

[43]   See now the Industrial Tribunals Act 1996, part II; and ch 18 A.
[44]   Ch 29 A.

Council on Tribunals[45]

The Tribunals and Inquiries Act 1992 continued in being the Council on Tribunals, first established under the 1958 Act. The members of the council (in number between 10 and 15) are appointed by the Lord Chancellor and the Lord Advocate (in respect of Scotland), and the council has a Scottish committee. The council is under a duty to keep under review the constitution and working of a large number of tribunals, both those named in the First Schedule to the 1992 Act and also those subsequently included by statutory instrument made by the Lord Chancellor and the Lord Advocate (s 13). The Lord Chancellor and the Lord Advocate may ask the council to consider and report on matters concerning any tribunal other than ordinary courts of law. In one instance, concerning those administrative procedures which involve a statutory inquiry, the council may itself take the initiative on a matter determined to be of special importance.[46] The council's functions are essentially advisory and consultative; it has no power to interfere with the decision of a tribunal, although it may comment on the way in which tribunals operate. The council has no executive powers: the Franks committee's recommendation that members of tribunals should be appointed by the council was not accepted by the government, and the council merely has power to make to the appropriate minister general recommendations on the appointment of tribunal members (s 5).

The council makes an annual report to the Lord Chancellor and the Lord Advocate, and other reports by the council are made to these ministers (s 4). The council may take the initiative in reporting on any tribunal placed under its general supervision, but the government departments concerned will not necessarily take any action on its reports. The council has no rule-making powers but it must be consulted before procedural rules are made for any tribunals subject to its supervision (s 8) or for any procedures involving a statutory inquiry (s 9). Often the council is consulted by the government on proposed legislation to create new tribunals and similar procedures,[47] but some departments are reluctant to accept the expert advice given or leave consultation until the last minute. In 1991, the Department of Health was criticised by the council, over the strange devolution of certain NHS appeals by the Health Secretary to the Yorkshire Health Authority, for 'a major failure to observe the basic principles advocated over 30 years ago by the Franks committee as to the ... establishment of new tribunals and their procedures'.[48]

The council seeks to remind departments of the qualities of fairness, openness and impartiality which the Franks committee stressed that tribunals should possess. Its extensive work on procedural rules gives detailed expression to those qualities. It has neither the resources nor the power to

---

[45]   Accounts of the Council include D G T Williams [1984] PL 73 and (1990) 9 CJQ 27; Harlow and Rawlings, *Law and Administration*, ch 6; D L Foulkes (1993) Eur Rev of Public Law (special issue) 262.

[46]   Section B below.

[47]   Report of Council on Tribunals for 1991–92, app H (Code for Consultation).

[48]   Report of Council on Tribunals for 1990–91, pp 11–14. In 1995, the functions were transferred to a new Family Health Service Appeal Authority.

investigate complaints about particular tribunals[49] but its members regularly visit tribunals and hearings.[50] In 1994, the jurisdiction of the Parliamentary Ombudsman was extended to include complaints against the administrative staff of certain tribunals, but not against tribunal decisions.[51] The council has often drawn attention to a backlog of cases building up in particular tribunals, for example in immigration and mental health appeals. Where a department does not accept the council's advice, the council can publish the fact in its annual report. In 1991, the council published a comprehensive collection of model rules of tribunal procedure.[52]

In 1980, the Council on Tribunals published a special report examining its own functions, recommending inter alia that it should be granted power to act as an advisory body over the whole area of administrative adjudication, that its right to be consulted about relevant legislation should be clearly defined and that its resources should be strengthened.[53] Although the government agreed that a 'code' for consultation between the council and departments should be prepared, the other proposals made by the council were peremptorily rejected.[54]

In 1988, the Justice/All Souls report recommended that an administrative review commission be created on the lines of the Administrative Review Council in Australia to provide independent scrutiny of all administrative procedures and to work alongside the Council on Tribunals.[55] No such commission was appointed. However, it must be recorded that in the 1990s the Council was prepared broadly to advocate proper structures of administrative justice and to exceed its formal remit for good reason.[56]

B. Public inquiries

We have seen that the Franks committee concluded that tribunals should be regarded as machinery for adjudication rather than as part of the machinery of administration. The same conclusion is not applicable to public inquiries, whose role is deeply embedded in the whole process of government and administration. We examine below the attitude of the courts to inquiries in the context of natural justice.[57] Generalisation is difficult in view of the many purposes which inquiries serve, but two views on the nature of inquiries have often been expressed. As seen by the Franks committee in 1957, the 'administrative' view was to regard the inquiry as a step leading to a ministerial decision in the exercise of discretion, for which the minister was responsible only to Parliament. By contrast, on the 'judicial' view, the inquiry appeared 'to

---

49 See Cmnd 7805, 1980, ch 7.
50 D L Foulkes [1994] PL 564.
51 Parliamentary Commissioner Act 1994; and section D.
52 See report of Council on Tribunals for 1990–91, pp 23–4; and Cm 1434, 1991.
53 Cmnd 7805, 1980.
54 Report of Council on Tribunals for 1980–81, p 7; and for 1981–82, app C. See now report for 1990–91, pp 37–8.
55 *Administrative Justice – Some Necessary Reforms*, ch 4; and cf A W Bradley [1991] PL 6.
56 Eg report of Council for 1995–96, pp 6–8 and app A (non-statutory inquiries); section C below.
57 Ch 29 B. And see generally Wraith and Lamb, *Public Inquiries as an Instrument of Government*.

take on something of the nature of a trial and the inspector to assume the guise of a judge', so that the ensuing decision must be based directly upon the evidence presented at the inquiry.[58]

The Franks committee rejected these two extreme interpretations. In the committee's view, the objects of the inquiry procedure were (*a*) to protect the interests of the citizens most directly affected by a governmental proposal by granting them a statutory right to be heard in support of their objections; and (*b*) to ensure that thereby the minister would be better informed of the whole facts of the case before the final decision was made. To ensure a reasonable balance between the conflicting interests concerned, the committee recommended (1) that individuals should know in good time before the inquiry the case they would have to meet; (2) that any relevant lines of policy laid down by the government should be disclosed at the inquiry; (3) that the inspectors who conduct inquiries should be under the control of the Lord Chancellor, and not under that of the minister directly concerned with the subject-matter of their work; (4) that the inspector's report should be published together with the letter from the minister announcing the final decision; (5) that the decision letter should contain full reasons for the decision, including reasons to explain why the minister had not accepted recommendations of the inspector; (6) that it should be possible to challenge a decision made after a public inquiry in the High Court, on the grounds of jurisdiction and procedure.[59]

Except for the recommendation that the inspectors should be transferred to the Lord Chancellor's department, these recommendations were accepted.[60] Moreover, the Council on Tribunals was given power to consider and report on matters arising out of the conduct of statutory inquiries. In this context, 'statutory inquiry' includes both an inquiry or hearing held by or on behalf of a minister in pursuance of a duty imposed by any statutory provision, and also what is known as a discretionary inquiry, that is, an inquiry initiated by a minister other than in pursuance of a statutory duty where such an inquiry is designated for this purpose by statutory instrument.[61]

The inquiries examined by the Franks committee mostly concerned such matters as procedure for the compulsory purchase of land that was needed for public purposes (for example, the construction of a new town, a power station or a motorway, or for slum clearance), and disputes under town planning law about the use and development of land. Inquiries and related procedures also serve other purposes, for example to inquire into electoral boundaries,[62] or to investigate the causes of a public disaster (such as an aviation accident) or the failure by a local authority to maintain proper standards of care in relation to children.[63] Another form of procedure occurs when there is a right of appeal

---

[58]   Cmnd 218, 1957, p 58.
[59]   Ibid, part IV.
[60]   Ministry of Housing circular 9/58; report of Council on Tribunals for 1963, app A.
[61]   Tribunals and Inquiries Act 1992, s 16(1); and see SI 1975 No 1379, as amended by SI 1976 No 293, SI 1983 No 1287 and SI 1992 No 2171.
[62]   Ch 9 B.
[63]   See Justice/All Souls report, *Administrative Justice*, pp 312–27; S Sedley (1989) 52 MLR 469; and eg the (Butler-Sloss) report of inquiry into child abuse, Cm 412, 1987; the (Fennell) report of the inquiry into the Kings Cross fire, HC 499 (1987–88); and section C below.

to a minister against certain decisions and the individuals concerned must be heard before the minister determines the appeal. Thus, the Director-General of Fair Trading may refuse to grant a consumer credit licence (or may revoke an existing licence) if the individual is not a fit person to hold the licence: an appeal lies from the Director-General to the Secretary of State, who may arrange for the appeal to be heard by a panel of independent persons, but the minister retains the right to make the final decision.[64]

Rules of procedure for public inquiries

Under the Tribunals and Inquiries Act 1992, s 9, the Lord Chancellor (or the Lord Advocate, in the case of Scotland) may, after consulting the Council on Tribunals, make rules regulating the procedure at statutory inquiries. Rules have been made in respect of inquiries held for many purposes, including inquiries into compulsory purchase orders, both by ministers and by other public authorities; inquiries into the purchase of land for highway purposes; and appeals against the refusal of planning permission.[65] On a compulsory purchase of land by non-ministerial public authorities, if an inquiry is to be held the Secretary of State must give notice to the acquiring authority and those entitled to object, and may cause a pre-inquiry meeting to be held to discuss procedural matters. At least 42 days' notice of the inquiry must be given to the public authority and to every owner of an interest in the land affected who has objected to the making of the compulsory purchase order. At least 28 days before the inquiry, the public authority must send to every objector and to central departments a full statement of the reasons for the order. Both objectors and the public authority have a right to appear at the inquiry and to be represented, either by a lawyer or some other person. In advance of the inquiry, a written statement of evidence (and a summary) may be required from any person entitled to appear at the inquiry. Objectors must be informed of the views of any government departments which support the order, and departmental representatives are required to attend the inquiry in order that they may give evidence about departmental policy. However, the inspector may disallow a question put to such a representative if in the inspector's opinion it is 'directed to the merits of government policy'. Subject to the rules, procedure at the inquiry is determined by the inspector. The degree of formality depends on the circumstances of the inquiry, particularly the extent of legal representation. The inspector may visit the land alone before or during the inquiry, but if he or she makes a formal visit during or after the inquiry, notice must be given to the public authority and to the objectors, who have the right to be present. The inspector's report must include his or her conclusions and recommendations, if any; it will be sent to the parties when the minister's decision is notified to them.[66]

One important rule deals with the situation where the minister, after considering the inspector's report, either differs from the inspector on a

---

[64] Consumer Credit Act 1974, part III, esp ss 25, 32, 41. And see G Borrie [1982] Jl of Business Law 91.

[65] See respectively SI 1994 No 3264 and SI 1990 No 512; SI 1994 No 3263; SI 1992 No 2038 and SI 1992 No 2039.

[66] When this requirement applies, *Local Government Board v Arlidge*, ch 29 B below, is to this extent reversed.

finding of fact or, after the close of the inquiry, 'takes into consideration any new evidence or new matter of fact (not being a matter of government policy)'. In such a case, if the minister proposes not to follow the inspector's recommendation because of this new material, the public authority and objectors must be informed and they have the right to require the inquiry to be reopened. The background to this lies in what was known as the chalk-pit affair.[67]

At an inquiry into a planning authority's refusal of permission for the digging of chalk in North Essex, neighbouring owners brought evidence to show that their land would be seriously harmed if this were permitted. On the strength of this evidence, the inspector recommended that permission should not be given. Subsequently the Ministry of Housing consulted privately with the Ministry of Agriculture, and later granted planning permission, inter alia on the ground that the chalk workings would not harm neighbouring land. The neighbouring owners tried unsuccessfully to seek a remedy in the High Court, and then complained to the Council on Tribunals about this apparent abuse of inquiry procedure. Following pressure from the Council on Tribunals, the Lord Chancellor finally accepted the point of principle and agreed to make the rules of procedure from which the present rules are derived.

One effect of the statutory rules for inquiries is to give the individuals most closely affected by compulsory purchase and planning proposals better legal protection, since the rules are enforceable in the courts and an objector is not restricted to relying on a breach of natural justice at common law.[68] But rules of natural justice, or fairness, apply to any inquiry not governed by statutory rules of procedure.[69] Although the rules define those who are entitled to statutory notice of an inquiry and to take part in it, they give the inspector a discretion to allow members of the public to appear at the inquiry. In practice, community associations and other interest groups are permitted to take part. By taking part in the inquiry such groups acquire a right to come to the court to enforce the rules of procedure.[70]

Similar rules apply to many public inquiries in Scotland. Two differences may be noted. The person appointed to conduct an inquiry is known as the reporter, which may describe his or her duties more accurately than the term 'inspector'. After the inquiry, the reporter must circulate to all the parties a draft of that part of the proposed report which contains the summary of the evidence and the findings of fact, in order that inaccuracies may be corrected.[71]

Through consultation, the Council on Tribunals has taken an active part in the preparation of these rules and in seeking to secure the award of costs to those taking part in inquiries, at least for owners who successfully object to the compulsory purchase of their land. But in circumstances of serious abuse, the courts have the power to give an effective remedy to an owner which

---

[67]   See J A G Griffith (1961) 39 Public Administration 369; and *Buxton v Minister of Housing* [1961] 1 QB 278.
[68]   Ch 29 B.
[69]   *Fairmount Investments Ltd v Secretary of State for Environment* [1976] 2 All ER 865; and see *Bushell's* case below.
[70]   *Turner v Environment Secretary* (1973) 72 LGR 380.
[71]   See SI 1976 No 1559.

the council lacks.[72] Moreover, the council has neither the powers nor the resources properly to investigate complaints about inquiries. If someone is aggrieved by the improper conduct of an inquiry, or by the acts of the department related to the inquiry, he or she may take the complaint to the Parliamentary Ombudsman, who can conduct a full investigation into the matter.[73]

Developments in the use of public inquiries

The public inquiry continues to be an aspect of the process by which certain decisions are made, especially those concerning the use of land for developments of environmental significance. Although the Franks committee sought to steer a middle course between the 'judicial' and 'administrative' views of the inquiry, its report led inevitably to greater legalisation. Increased involvement of the legal profession in inquiries was one aspect of the pressure on the planning process that led to delays and over-centralisation of decisions on many local issues. It is not possible to summarise here the changing role of the local inquiry in the planning process under the Town and Country Planning Act 1990. One variant of the full-scale inquiry, used for examining proposed revisions or replacements for 'structure plans', is the *examination in public*, generally held by the planning authority before a panel appointed by the Secretary of State and which deals with such matters as the authority considers ought to be examined or as the Secretary of State directs.[74] By contrast, a district council's 'local plan' to which objections are received is subject to a full public inquiry held before an inspector appointed by the Secretary of State. The inspector reports on the inquiry to the council, but decisions on the report are subject to directions by the Secretary of State and the council must give reasons for rejecting the inspector's recommendations.[75]

As regards the control of development, government policy has been to reduce delay by transferring the power to decide planning appeals from the Secretary of State to the inspectorate. Since 1981, all appeals in respect of applications for planning permission and all appeals against enforcement notices may be decided by an inspector.[76] An inspector's decision is subject to review in the courts as if it were the decision of a minister, but the Secretary of State is not responsible to Parliament for it. The inspector's decision should take account of relevant ministerial policies, but is essentially based on the evidence given at the inquiry. Moreover, most planning appeals are now decided not after a formal inquiry nor even after a hearing in private, but by a simpler procedure based on the exchange of written representations between the parties.[77] Where this procedure is used, the public at large have no scope

---

72 For the rebuff suffered by the Council on Tribunals in the Packington Estate case, see [1966] PL 1 and Crossman, *Diaries of a Cabinet Minister*, I, pp 450–1, 456–7, 467–8, 528.

73 Section D below.

74 Town and Country Planning Act 1990 (as amended by the Planning and Compensation Act 1991), ss 35, 35A and 35B; and SI 1991 No 2794.

75 1990 Act (as amended by the 1991 Act), ss 36, 42–5; and SI 1991 No 2794, regn 16.

76 1990 Act, Sched 6 and SI 1981 No 804. The Secretary of State retains power to decide particular appeals; and see 1990 Act, s 77 (power to call in applications).

77 See SI 1987 No 701.

for effective participation.[78] There was formerly uncertainty over the role of planning inspectors and the extent to which they were independent of central government. The Planning Inspectorate is now an executive agency, which in 1996 comprised over 200 full-time and 130 part-time inspectors, whose position is quite distinct from that of civil servants in the Department of Environment.

While the transfer of power to decide planning appeals was possible because in most cases only local issues arose, the role of the inquiry in matters of national importance has often been controversial. During the 1970s, government policy in promoting motorways led to stormy scenes at inquiries, as objectors came to realise that proceedings at an inquiry might have little effect where the Department of Transport had already decided that a new motorway was needed. In 1978, a review of highway procedures made detailed proposals for improving the assessment of need for new trunk roads and for restoring public confidence in the inquiry system.[79] So far as the courts were concerned, the history of motorway inquiries culminated in *Bushell v Secretary of State for the Environment.*[80]

During a lengthy inquiry held concerning two sections of the M40 extension near Birmingham, the inspector allowed the objectors to bring evidence challenging estimates of future traffic growth, but refused to allow civil servants to be cross-examined on the matter. After the inquiry but before the minister took his decision, the department revised its traffic estimates, but the minister did not allow the inquiry to be re-opened for examination of the new estimates. The objectors claimed that natural justice entitled them (*a*) to cross-examine officials on the traffic predictions and (*b*) to a re-opening of the inquiry. The House of Lords upheld the motorway orders, holding that natural justice had not been infringed. The judges stressed that an inquiry was quite unlike civil litigation. An inspector had wide discretion to disallow cross-examination if it would serve no relevant purpose. The methods of predicting future traffic growth were an essential element in national policy for motorways, and were not suitable for investigation at local inquiries. Lord Edmund-Davies, dissenting, held that the objectors had been denied 'a fair crack of the whip'.[81]

This decision was a reminder of the fact that a public inquiry into a controversial proposal put forward by a government department is only part of a broader political process. In this process, it is not possible to expect the minister concerned to assume a cloak of judicial impartiality and detachment.

The strain placed upon the inquiry in relation to proposals of national importance has been evident in inquiries such as that conducted (exceptionally) by a High Court judge into the proposal by British Nuclear Fuels Ltd to

---

[78]   For the rule that inquiries must in general be held in public, see Town and Country Planning Act 1990, s 321. In 1994–95, out of about 13,080 planning appeals that were dealt with in England, inspectors decided 1,252 appeals after a public inquiry; 1,364 after a private hearing; and 10,246 after written representations. The Secretary of State decided only 218 appeals: report of Council on Tribunals for 1995–96, app H, part III. In 1996, the Department of the Environment began a review of both development plan and planning appeal procedures: see DOE circular 15/96 and related consultation papers.

[79]   Cmnd 7133, 1978; report of Council on Tribunals for 1977–78, p 25 and app C; also P H Levin (1979) 57 Public Administration 21.

[80]   [1981] AC 75. And see *R v Transport Secretary, ex p Gwent CC* [1988] QB 429.

[81]   [1981] AC at 118.

establish a nuclear fuel reprocessing plant at Windscale,[82] the marathon Sizewell B inquiry conducted into the proposal by the Central Electricity Generating Board to build a PWR nuclear power station in Suffolk,[83] and the long-running inquiry into the projected fifth air terminal at Heathrow. Lengthy and expensive as such inquiries are, and difficult as it is for interest groups to take part, they afford a means of scrutinising in public the technical and environmental aspects of a proposal and of ventilating issues of public concern. This scrutiny may not lead to a reversal of government policies, but it would be rash to suppose that better decisions would be made if there were no public inquiries. Could the system be improved? In 1978, a non-governmental committee proposed a new procedure for the investigation of projects with major national implications; this involved a two-stage 'project inquiry' conducted by an impartial committee, followed if necessary by a local inquiry into issues relating to a specific site.[84] These proposals were not adopted, but in 1988 the government gave further guidance on the procedures that should be followed for major public inquiries.[85]

Important new powers of authorising transport projects (including railway and guided transport systems) and schemes affecting harbours and canals were given to ministers by the Transport and Works Act 1992, which aimed to reduce the need for special powers to be obtained by private Acts.[86] For schemes of national significance, before the Secretary of State may make an order for a scheme, each House of Parliament must first have adopted a resolution approving the proposal. The Secretary of State may (and in some cases must) hold a public local inquiry or grant a hearing into objections to such schemes that are received, but these proceedings are held within the limits of any parliamentary approval that has been given.

C. Tribunals of inquiry

Both tribunals and inquiries form part of the regular structure of administrative justice and many thousands of decisions are made each year by recourse to these procedures. The 'tribunal of inquiry' is a much rarer happening, only 22 having been appointed since the Tribunals of Inquiry (Evidence) Act 1921 was passed. In the 19th century, parliamentary committees were occasionally appointed to inquire into matters of concern, for example allegations of corruption amongst officials or politicians. The use of such committees was discredited in 1913 when a Commons committee investigated the conduct of members of the Liberal government in the Marconi Company affair and in reaching its conclusions produced three

---

82 See the Parker Report 1978 and P McAuslan (1979) 2 Urban Law and Policy 25.
83 See M Purdue et al [1985] PL 475, [1987] PL 162; O'Riordan et al, *Sizewell B: An Anatomy of the Inquiry.*
84 Outer Circle Policy Unit, *The Big Public Inquiry.*
85 See Cm 43, 1988, *Planning: Appeals, Call-In and Major Public Inquiries;* also Joint Circular 10/88, Code of Practice on Big Public Inquiries.
86 For the background, see HL 97 (1987–88) and Cm 1110, 1990. Also report of Council on Tribunals for 1989–90, pp 42–5, and for 1991–92, pp 44–7.

conflicting reports.[87] Under the 1921 Act, when both Houses of Parliament resolve that it is expedient that a tribunal be appointed to inquire into a matter of urgent public importance, a tribunal may be appointed by Her Majesty or by a Secretary of State. The instrument of appointment may confer on the tribunal all the powers of the High Court, or in Scotland the Court of Session, with regard to the examination of witnesses and production of documents. Where a person summoned as a witness before the tribunal fails to attend or refuses to answer any question which the tribunal may legally require to be answered, or commits any other contempt, the chairman of the tribunal may report the matter to the High Court or the Court of Session for inquiry and punishment.[88]

Tribunals of inquiry have been appointed to investigate serious allegations of corruption or improper conduct in the public service, or to investigate a matter of concern which requires thorough and impartial investigation to allay public anxiety. In the former category fall the tribunals appointed in 1936 to inquire into a leakage of Budget secrets, in 1948 to investigate bribery of ministers and civil servants, in 1957 to investigate the premature disclosure of information relating to the raising of the bank rate, in 1971 to investigate circumstances relating to the collapse of the Vehicle and General Insurance Company, and in 1978 to investigate the disastrous financial operations of the Crown Agents in 1968–74.[89] In the latter category fall the tribunal of inquiry into the Aberfan coal-tip disaster in 1966, the inquiry into the 'Bloody Sunday' shootings in Londonderry in 1972 and Lord Cullen's inquiry in 1996 into the Dunblane shootings.[90]

The task of a tribunal of inquiry is to investigate certain allegations or events with a view to producing an authoritative account of the facts, attributing responsibility or blame where it is necessary to do so. Tribunals of inquiry do not make decisions as to what action should be taken in the light of their findings of fact but they may make recommendations for each action. The chairman is normally a senior judge, assisted by one or two additional members or expert assessors. Exceptionally, the 'Bloody Sunday' inquiry was conducted by Lord Chief Justice Widgery sitting alone. The subject-matter is presented publicly to the tribunal by a Law Officer or senior counsel, instructed by the Treasury Solicitor, whose duty it is to call all relevant witnesses, whether or not they are suspected of impropriety. The tribunal allows witnesses to be legally represented and their costs may be met ex gratia out of public funds. There may be cross-examination of witnesses by counsel appearing at the tribunal and witnesses may be questioned by members of the tribunal. Because of the inquisitorial nature of the proceedings, it is difficult to provide the same facilities to a witness for answering an accusation as he or she would have in answering a criminal charge. Thus the proceedings may result in severe criticism of a witness who has not been called on to meet definite charges and may not have an

---

[87]   See Donaldson, *The Marconi Scandal.*

[88]   See *A-G v Mulholland and Foster* [1963] 2 QB 477; ch 18 B (imprisonment of two journalists for refusing to disclose their sources).

[89]   See Cmd 5184, 1936; Cmd 7616, 1948; Cmnd 350, 1957; HC 133 (1971–72); HC 364 (1981–82). And see Keeton, *Trial by Tribunal*, and Z Segal [1984] PL 206.

[90]   HC 553 (1966–67); HC 220 (1971–72) and Cm 3386, 1996. In June 1996, a tribunal of inquiry into child abuse in North Wales was appointed.

adequate opportunity of answering any accusations.[91] The Attorney-General may, however, inform a witness that no criminal proceedings will be brought against him or her in respect of matters arising out of the evidence.

In 1966, a royal commission on tribunals of inquiry under the chairmanship of Salmon LJ reported that tribunals of inquiry should be appointed only in cases of vital public importance, but that it was necessary to retain the possibility of inquisitorial procedure.[92] The commission did not favour changes such as a preliminary inquiry or a subsequent right of appeal. Sittings in private were discouraged. In what have come to be known as the six Salmon 'cardinal principles', the commission laid emphasis on protecting persons whose reputations might be involved; for example, a witness should be told beforehand of any allegations affecting him or her and should be entitled to legal representation, to cross-examine those giving evidence adverse to him or her and to call relevant witnesses. The dual role of the Attorney-General as a member of the government and as independent counsel to the tribunal should be avoided through the appointment of another Queen's Counsel to act for the tribunal.

In 1966, at the time of the Aberfan disaster, concern arose about the permissible extent of press comment on the disaster, having regard to the uncertain operation of the sub judice rule once the tribunal had been appointed. In 1969, a departmental committee, also chaired by Salmon LJ, examined the rules of contempt of court in relation to tribunals of inquiry.[93] When the law of contempt of court was reformed in 1981, the changes then made were in general extended to tribunals of inquiry; in particular, the proceedings of such a tribunal are deemed to be 'active' from the time at which the tribunal is appointed until its report is presented to Parliament.[94]

The public procedures of a tribunal of inquiry were not considered suitable for a review of events leading to the outbreak of the Falklands Islands hostilities that involved access to many secret Cabinet, diplomatic and intelligence documents; instead, a committee of privy councillors was appointed.[95]

Apart from the 1921 Act, many Acts confer powers of investigation for specific purposes, for example by inspectors inquiring into the proper conduct of companies.[96] In 1963, Lord Denning's inquiry into the Profumo affair was conducted informally and with no statutory powers: the Salmon commission recommended that such inquiries should not be repeated to investigate any matter causing nation-wide concern.[97] However, in 1992 Bingham LJ completed a non-statutory inquiry into the role of the Bank of England in the collapse of BCCI; and from 1992 to 1996 Sir Richard Scott

---

[91]   This criticism was made of the tribunal which investigated the collapse of the Vehicle and General Insurance Company and found a senior civil servant to have been negligent in his work: HC 133 (1971–72); and ch 7.

[92]   Cmnd 3121, 1966.

[93]   Cmnd 4078, 1969. And see Cmnd 5313, 1973.

[94]   Contempt of Court Act 1981, s 20; and see ch 18 B above.

[95]   Ch 12 C above and cf the abortive proposals for a joint parliamentary committee into the Rhodesian oil sanctions affair, headed by a Lord of Appeal in Ordinary: HC Deb, 1 February 1979, col 1709 ff, and HL Deb, 8 February 1979, col 849 ff.

[96]   Companies Act 1985, part XIV.

[97]   Cmnd 2152, 1963; and Cmnd 3121, 1966, pp 19–21.

carried out his inquiry into the Matrix Churchill affair and the export of arms from Britain to Iraq.[98] Such inquiries are 'judicial' in that they are conducted by a judge. But their procedure is investigative and they have no power to compel witnesses to attend and may not take evidence on oath. Since they are not protected by the law of contempt of court, the subject-matter can be discussed freely in the media. In the Matrix Churchill inquiry, Sir Richard Scott was assured that if he needed them, powers under the 1921 Act would be granted to him; in fact, he was eventually satisfied that he had full access to all official witnesses and papers.[99] Despite abundant efforts made by the inquiry to avoid unfairness, the procedure for taking evidence orally in public received some criticism for its effect on witnesses, who could have legal assistance but not representation.[100] In Sir Richard's view, the Salmon 'principles' mentioned above did not apply fully to an investigatory inquiry, and a balance was needed between aspects of fairness, efficiency and cost.[101] As a sequel to the Scott inquiry, the Council on Tribunals advised the Lord Chancellor on procedural issues affecting such inquiries, stressing that the Salmon 'principles' were recommendations, not rules of law, and that it was 'wholly impracticable' to devise a single set of rules to govern every inquiry.[102]

D.   The Parliamentary Ombudsman

Before the creation of the Parliamentary Ombudsman, the main safeguards for the citizen against oppressive or faulty government were the following: judicial review of administrative action, through remedies to be described in chapter 30; the right of appeal to a tribunal against an administrative decision; the opportunity of taking part in a public inquiry held before a ministry's decision was made; redress by parliamentary means with the aid of an MP; and a request for administrative review of a decision already taken. Although each of these procedures may be effective in particular situations, each has its limitations.[103] For example, many discretionary decisions affecting the individual are made without the possibility of recourse to a tribunal or inquiry. Judicial review is expensive and often uncertain, and is not an ideal procedure for investigating the process of official decision-making. Parliamentary procedures are not well suited to the impartial finding of facts nor to the resolution of disputes according to sound principles of administration.

---

[98]   See respectively HC 198 (1992–93) and HC 115 (1995-96) (the Scott report), on which see articles at [1996] PL 357–527; also I Leigh and L Lustgarten (1996) 59 MLR 695.

[99]   Scott report, section A, ch 1.

[100]   See Lord Howe [1996] PL 445; and Scott report, app A, part D. Also B K Winetrobe [1997] PL 18; L Blom-Cooper [1993] CLP 204 and [1994] PL 1; C Clothier [1996] PL 384; M C Harris [1996] PL 508; and Leigh and Lustgarten (above), pp 694–701.

[101]   Scott report, sections B and K, ch 1; and R Scott (1995) 111 LQR 596.

[102]   Report of Council on Tribunals for 1995–96, app A.

[103]   Cf *The Citizen and the Administration* (the Whyatt report), ch 26 above; Cmnd 2767, 1965; and Birkinshaw, *Grievances, Remedies and the State*.

The office of Parliamentary Commissioner for Administration was created in 1967. The legal title of the office is very cumbrous, and in 1994 the government agreed that 'at the first opportunity' of legislation it would be changed to 'Parliamentary Ombudsman'.[104] Although it derived from the Ombudsman in Scandinavian countries and New Zealand,[105] the British model was designed to fit within existing British institutions, without detracting from existing remedies. While the Parliamentary Ombudsman has close links with the executive, the office is designed as an extension of Parliament; and it has virtually no links with the judicial system. As Sir Cecil Clothier, then the Ombudsman, said in 1984:

> The office of Parliamentary Commissioner stands curiously poised between the legislative and the executive, while discharging an almost judicial function in the citizen's dispute with his government; and yet it forms no part of the judiciary.[106]

On one view, the essence of the Ombudsman idea for the ordinary person is accessibility, flexibility and informality. On another view, the Ombudsman provides an authoritative means of 'judging' the behaviour of officials, thus helping to maintain standards of administration that are publicly acceptable. In the British version of the Ombudsman, the latter view often seems to prevail over the former.

Status and jurisdiction[107]

The Parliamentary Ombudsman is appointed by the Crown and holds office during good behaviour, although he or she may be removed by the Crown following addresses by both Houses (s 1). By a practice dating from 1977, the government consults the chairman of the House of Commons committee on the Ombudsman before making an appointment.[108] The Ombudsman's salary is charged on the Consolidated Fund (s 2). He or she appoints the staff of the office, subject to Treasury consent as to numbers and conditions of service (s 3). The staff are mostly recruited from the ranks of the civil service. Of the six Ombudsmen who served between 1967 and 1996, four came to the post from civil service careers, and two were practising Queen's Counsel.

The main task of the Ombudsman is to investigate the complaints of citizens who claim to have suffered injustice in consequence of maladministration by government departments and many non-departmental public bodies in the exercise of their administrative functions (s 5). The area of

---

[104] See HC 619 (1993–94).
[105] On comparative aspects, see Rowat (ed), *The Ombudsman*; Gellhorn, *Ombudsmen and Others*; Hill, *The Model Ombudsman*; Stacey, *Ombudsmen Compared*.
[106] Report for 1983 (HC 322 (1983–84)), p 1.
[107] References in the text are to the Parliamentary Commissioner Act 1967, as amended subsequently. The literature includes Gregory and Hutchesson, *The Parliamentary Ombudsman*; Seneviratne, *Ombudsmen in the Public Sector*; Harlow and Rawlings, *Law and Administration*, ch 7: I Pugh (1978) 56 Public Administration 127; A W Bradley [1980] CLJ 304; C Clothier [1986] PL 204; G Drewry and C Harlow (1990) 53 MLR 745.
[108] Cmnd 6764, 1977. See HC 619 (1993–94) for the government's agreement to amend the law so that appointment by the Crown would give effect to an address by the Commons moved after consultation with the Opposition.

jurisdiction is defined by the 1967 Act, Sched 2 of which (as amended by Parliament in 1987) lists the departments and other bodies subject to investigation. This list may be amended by Order in Council (s 4), a power which is exercised when departments are abolished or created. Section 4 in its 1987 version restricts the bodies which may be entered in Sched 2 to (*a*) government departments; (*b*) bodies exercising functions on behalf of the Crown; (*c*) bodies established under an Act of Parliament or Order in Council or by a minister that fulfil certain criteria as to the source of their income and the power of appointment to them.[109]

The Ombudsman has no jurisdiction over authorities which are outside central government, for example, local authorities, the police, and universities, although he or she may investigate complaints about the way in which central departments have discharged their functions in these fields. However, many matters are excluded from investigation for which ministers are or may be responsible to Parliament (s 5(3) and Sched 3). Thus the Ombudsman may not investigate:

(*a*) action taken in matters certified by a Secretary of State to affect relations between the UK government and other governments, or international organisations;

(*b*) action taken outside the UK by any officer representing or acting under the authority of the Crown;[110]

(*c*) the administration of dependent territories outside the UK;

(*d*) action taken by a Secretary of State under the Extradition Acts;

(*e*) action taken by or with the authority of a Secretary of State for investigating crime or protecting the security of the state, including action so taken with respect to passports;

(*f*) (1) the commencement or conduct of civil or criminal proceedings before any court in the United Kingdom, court martial or international court; (2) action taken by persons appointed by the Lord Chancellor as administrative staff of courts or tribunals, and being action taken on the direction or by authority of persons acting in a judicial capacity;[111]

(*g*) any exercise of the prerogative of mercy;

(*h*) action taken on behalf of central government by authorities in the National Health Service;

(*i*) matters relating to contractual or other commercial transactions on the part of central government;[112]

(*j*) appointments, discipline and other personnel matters in relation to the civil service and the armed forces, and decisions of ministers and departments in respect of other branches of the public service;

(*k*) the grant of honours, awards or privileges within the gift of the Crown.

---

109 Bodies within jurisdiction include the Arts Council, the Charity Commission, the Commission for Racial Equality, OFSTED, and the utility regulators such as OFTEL and OFWAT.

110 The acts of British consuls abroad, other than honorary consuls, are within jurisdiction, if the complainant is resident or has a right of abode in the United Kingdom: 1967 Act, s 6(5).

111 By the Parliamentary Commissioner Act 1994, acts of the Independent Tribunal Service (note 30 above) may be investigated, although the Service is not appointed by the Lord Chancellor.

112 This is subject to an exception for transactions relating to compulsorily purchased land and other land bought under threat of compulsory powers. But for this exception, a latter-day Crichel Down affair (ch 7 above) would be outside the Commissioner's jurisdiction.

In respect of each exclusion, different policy considerations arise. It was these restrictions which led to criticism that the legislation sought to carve up areas of possible grievances in an arbitrary way.[113] Those restrictions which have been most criticised are in (*i*) and (*j*) above. The government has power by Order in Council to revoke any of these restrictions (s 5(4)), but despite frequent recommendations from the House of Commons committee that the restriction on personnel matters in (*j*) should be revoked, successive governments have refused to do so.[114]

Another limitation is that the Ombudsman may not normally investigate any action in respect of which the complainant has or had a right of recourse to a tribunal or a remedy by proceedings in any court of law, although he or she may do so if in a particular case the citizen could not reasonably be expected to exercise the right (s 5(2)). If a citizen is dissatisfied with a decision about a social security benefit, or an award of compensation on a compulsory purchase of land, he or she should appeal to the relevant tribunal. But the Ombudsman often accepts that a complainant cannot be reasonably expected to embark on the hazardous course of litigation.[115]

There is no rule that the complainant must be a British citizen, but in general either he or she must be resident in the United Kingdom or have been present in the United Kingdom or on a British ship or aircraft when the offending action occurred, or the action concerned must relate to rights or obligations arising in the United Kingdom (s 6(4)).

There is also a time bar: the Ombudsman may investigate a complaint only if it is made to an MP within 12 months from the date when the citizen first had notice of the matter complained of, except where special circumstances justify the Commissioner in accepting a complaint made after a longer interval (s 6(3)).

It is for the Ombudsman to determine whether a complaint is duly made under the Act; in practice, many complaints identify the injustice that has been suffered more closely than the maladministration which caused it.[116] The Ombudsman has an express discretion to decide whether to investigate a complaint.[117] But the Act does not protect the Ombudsman if he or she takes up a complaint on a matter outside jurisdiction and the Ombudsman's acts are subject to judicial review, though the court is unlikely to intervene concerning his or her discretionary decisions.[118] If the Ombudsman were to act outside jurisdiction, for instance by investigating the actions of a local authority, no one could be held liable for obstruction or contempt for refusing to supply information (s 9). Questions as to the extent of the Ombudsman's powers may involve difficult legal issues, for

---

[113]   HC Deb, 18 October 1966, col 67 (Quintin Hogg MP). Cf report by Justice, *Our Fettered Ombudsman*, 1977.

[114]   See eg HC 615, 1977–78; and Cmnd 7449, 1979. Some aspects of employment relating to overseas development are within jurisdiction: 1967 Act, Sched 3, para 10(2).

[115]   Cf *R v Commissioner for Local Administration, ex p Croydon BC* [1989] 1 All ER 1033, 1044–5.

[116]   Cf *R v Local Commissioner for Administration, ex p Bradford Council* [1979] QB 287, 313.

[117]   Section 5(5), 1967 Act. And see *Re Fletcher's Application* [1970] 2 All ER 527.

[118]   *R v Parliamentary Commissioner for Administration, ex p Dyer* [1994] 1 All ER 375; N S Marsh [1994] PL 347. In October 1996, in *R v PCA, ex p Ballchin* (unreported), Sedley J quashed the Ombudsman's decision rejecting a complaint against the Department of Transport.

example regarding the extent to which the acts of court officials may be investigated.[119]

Procedure

One important feature of the Ombudsman idea is that the Ombudsman should be accessible to the individual. But in Britain the citizen has no right to present a complaint to the Parliamentary Ombudsman. In the first instance, a complaint of maladministration must be addressed by the person who claims to have suffered injustice to an MP (s 5(1)). It is for the MP to decide whether to refer the complaint to the Ombudsman. Usually complainants will send the complaint to their constituency MP but the Act does not require this. When the Ombudsman receives a complaint from a private person that is clearly investigable, it may be sent with the complainant's agreement to his or her MP, with a statement that the Ombudsman will investigate it if the MP wishes this is to be done.[120] Although many critics would wish to see it removed in favour of direct access, the 'MP filter' was upheld by the select committee of the Commons on the Parliamentary Ombudsman in 1993.[121]

When the Ombudsman receives a complaint from an MP, it must first be decided whether it falls within jurisdiction. If so, and if the Ombudsman decides to conduct an investigation, the department concerned and any person named in the complaint must be given an opportunity of commenting on any allegations made (s 7(1)). The investigation must be carried out in private (s 7(2)); normally one of the Ombudsman's staff examines the relevant department files. The Commissioner has wide powers of compelling ministers and officials to produce documents and has the same powers as the High Court in England or the Court of Session in Scotland to compel any witness to give evidence (s 8). The Ombudsman's investigation is not restricted by the doctrine of public interest immunity (s 8(3)). The only documents which are statutorily privileged are those certified by the Secretary of the Cabinet, with the approval of the Prime Minister, to relate to proceedings of the Cabinet or a committee of the Cabinet (s 8(4)).

When the investigation is complete, the Ombudsman must send to the MP concerned a report on the investigation (s 10(1)). If the Ombudsman considers that injustice was caused through maladministration and has not been remedied, he or she may lay a special report before Parliament (s 10(3)). Such a report and other communications relating to an investigation are absolutely privileged in the law of defamation (s 10(5)). A minister has no power to veto an investigation, but may give notice to the Ombudsman that publication of certain documents or information would be prejudicial to the safety of the state or against the public interest; this notice binds the Ombudsman in making his or her report (s 11(3)).

The Ombudsman has no executive powers. Thus he or she cannot alter a departmental decision or award compensation to a citizen, although an

---

[119]   See now Courts and Legal Services Act 1990, s 110 (extending jurisdiction to certain administrative staff of courts and tribunals, but not if acting on judicial authority), and the Parliamentary Commissioner Act 1994.
[120]   Report of PCA for 1978 (HC 205 (1978–79)), p 4.
[121]   See HC 33–I (1993–94), pp xv–xx.

appropriate remedy may be suggested. A minister will usually be under a strong obligation to accept the Ombudsman's findings and take corrective action, but a report might have such political implications that a minister could come under pressure not to accept the recommendations.[122] To support the Ombudsman in such a situation, and to watch over the office, a select committee is appointed by the House of Commons to examine the reports laid in Parliament. This committee takes evidence from the departments concerned and reports to the House on the Ombudsman's work. The committee has been more successful in helping to ensure the provision by departments of adequate remedies and the improvement of defective procedures than in efforts to remove limits upon the Ombudsman's jurisdiction.[123] In 1993, the committee made a valuable study of the powers and work of the Parliamentary Ombudsman and the Health Service Ombudsman,[124] following this in 1995 with an excellent report on the theme of maladministration and redress.[125]

The Ombudsman's casework

What is meant by the phrase, 'injustice to the person aggrieved in consequence of maladministration' (s 10(3))? No definition and no illustrations of maladministration and injustice are given in the Act. Maladministration includes such defects as 'neglect, inattention, delay, incompetence, ineptitude, perversity, and arbitrariness'.[126] Many examples of maladministration may be found in the Ombudsman's reports. They include failure to give effect to assurances given to a citizen;[127] incorrect advice about social security or tax matters; failure to give proper effect to a department's policy guidance;[128] dilatory enforcement of regulations against asbestosis;[129] failure to make departmental policy known in the press[130] and even the making of misleading statements by a minister in Parliament.[131] In 1984, Home Office officials were criticised severely for having failed to deal promptly with complaints from a prisoner that his conviction for murder had been based on evidence from a forensic scientist whose evidence in other trials was known to be incompetent and unreliable.[132]

Even if maladministration has occurred, this does not in itself mean that injustice has thereby been caused to the individual. Conversely, injustice or

---

122 In 1975, the government was supported by the Commons in rejecting the Ombudsman's finding that the government had some responsibility for holidaymakers' losses arising from the collapse of the Court Line group: HC Deb, 6 August 1975, col 532.

123 R Gregory [1982] PL 49.

124 HC 33–I (1993–94). See also HC 619 (1993–94); R Gregory et al [1994] PL 207; P Giddings and R Gregory [1995] PL 45.

125 HC 112 and 316 (1994–95).

126 HC Deb, 18 October 1966, col 51 (R H S Crossman MP).

127 See A W Bradley [1981] CLP 1, 8–11.

128 A R Mowbray [1987] PL 570. See also A R Mowbray [1990] PL 68 and P Brown, in Richardson and Genn, op cit, ch 13 (remedies for misinformation).

129 HC 259 (1975–76), p 189.

130 HC 680 (1974–75).

131 HC 498 (1974–75).

132 HC 191 (1983–84). On the PCA's response to official delay generally, see S N McMurtrie [1997] PL 159.

hardship may exist which has been caused not by maladministration but, for example, by an Act of Parliament or a judicial decision.

One difficult matter has been the relation between maladministration and discretionary decisions. Unlike the New Zealand Ombudsman, who is empowered to find that a discretionary decision was wrong, the British Ombudsman may not question the merits of a discretionary decision taken without maladministration (s 12(3)). Where errors have been made in the procedures leading to a discretionary decision, the Ombudsman can report accordingly. But what is the position where a discretionary decision has caused manifest hardship to the individual, but no identifiable defect has occurred in the procedures leading up to it? In such a case, the Ombudsman may infer an element of maladministration from the very decision itself. Similarly he has been prepared to inquire into harsh decisions which may have been based on the over-rigorous application of departmental policies.[133] A catalogue of maladministration for the 1990s prepared by Sir William Reid, Ombudsman from 1990 to 1996, includes 'unwillingness to treat the complainant as a person with rights', and 'failure to mitigate the effects of rigid adherence to the letter of the law where that produces manifestly inequitable treatment'.[134]

Two leading examples of the Ombudsman's investigations may be given. The Sachsenhausen case was the first occasion on which he found a department to be seriously at fault.[135]

Under the Anglo-German Agreement of 1964, the German government provided £1 million for compensating UK citizens who suffered from Nazi persecution during the Second World War. Distribution of this money was left to the discretion of the UK government and in 1964 the Foreign Secretary (Mr Butler) approved rules for the distribution. Later the Foreign Office withheld compensation from 12 persons who claimed under these rules because of their detention within the Sachsenhausen concentration camp. Pressure from many MPs failed to get this decision reversed and a complaint was referred to the Ombudsman. By this time the whole of the £1 million had been distributed to other claimants. After extensive investigations, the Ombudsman reported that there were defects in the administrative procedure by which the Foreign Office reached its decisions and subsequently defended them, and that this maladministration had damaged the reputation of the claimants. When this report was debated in the Commons, the Foreign Secretary (Mr George Brown) assumed personal responsibility for the decisions of the Foreign Office, which he maintained were correct. He nonetheless made available an additional £25,000 in order that the claimants might receive the same rate of compensation as successful claimants on the fund.[136]

At the time, the prevailing view was that the 'Butler rules' were not enforceable in law since they conferred no rights on the claimants, but on similar facts today the claimants could seek judicial review of the Foreign Office decisions.[137] In 1968, parliamentary pressure alone would not have been successful. Indeed, the Ombudsman's report was based on information

---

[133] HC 9 (1968–69); HC 350 (1967–68), and see G Marshall [1973] PL 32.
[134] Report of PCA for 1993, HC 290 (1993–94), p 4.
[135] HC 54 (1967–68); HC 258 (1967–68); G K Fry [1970] PL 336; and Gregory and Hutchesson, op cit, ch 11.
[136] HC Deb, 5 February 1968, cols 105–17.
[137] Compare *Rustomjee v R* (1876) 2 QBD 69 with *R v Criminal Injuries Compensation Board, ex p Lain* (ch 12 D) and the *CCSU* case (ch 12 E).

about the Foreign Office decisions which parliamentary procedures could not have discovered. In retrospect, it appears that the Foreign Office erred in deciding to distribute the money itself, rather than entrusting this to the Foreign Compensation Commission, a judicial body for whose decisions the Foreign Secretary is not responsible.[138]

The most elaborate investigation ever undertaken by the Ombudsman was into the Barlow Clowes affair, which no fewer than 159 MPs had referred to him.[139]

In 1988, the Barlow Clowes investment business collapsed, leaving millions of pounds owing to investors, many of whom were elderly persons of modest means. The Department of Trade and Industry had licensed the business under the Prevention of Fraud (Investments) Act 1958 (which later gave way to the more rigorous Financial Services Act 1986), though there were indications that the business was not properly conducted. The Ombudsman found that there had been maladministration in five respects on the part of civil servants. As a result, the eventual losses to investors exceeded what they would have been had the department exercised its regulatory powers with a 'sufficiently rigorous and enquiring approach'.[140]

The government took the unusual course of rejecting the findings of maladministration, but nonetheless undertook ex gratia to provide £150 million to compensate investors for up to 90% of their loss. Had the investors attempted to sue the DTI in negligence, they would almost certainly have been unable to establish in law that the department owed them any duty of care.[141]

At one time, the services of the Ombudsman were not well publicised and seemed under-used. During the 1990s, the work-load has increased each year. In 1996, 1,933 complaints were referred by 566 MPs to the Ombudsman (in 1991, 801 complaints were referred by 432 MPs). Of the 1,679 cases dealt with during 1996, 1,419 (84%) were rejected as being outside jurisdiction (for example, because they did not concern administrative action). Out of 260 cases that were investigated, in 189 (73%) the complaints were fully upheld and in 57 (22%) they were upheld in part, leaving only 14 cases (5%) in which no maladministration was found.[142] The two departments giving rise to most complaints were Social Security (47%, of which over half were against the Child Support Agency) and the Inland Revenue. The remedies provided included payments of ex gratia compensation, the repayment of claimants' costs, the payment of arrears of benefit, in one tax case the waiving of an interest charge of over £15,000, and for a veterinary student the funding of his clinical years at a cost of £37,000. The Ombudsman has no power to compel a department to provide a remedy; but where injustice caused by maladministration has not been remedied, he or she may lay a report before Parliament

---

[138] HC 385 (1968–69). And see *Anisminic Ltd v Foreign Compensation Commission* (ch 29 A) and [1968] CLJ 42.
[139] See PCA, HC 76 (1989–90); also HC 671 (1987–88) (the Le Quesne report); HC 99 (1989–90); and R Gregory and G Drewry [1991] PL 192, 408.
[140] HC 76 (1989–90), para 8.12.
[141] *Yuen-Kun Yeu v A-G of Hong Kong* [1988] AC 175 and *Davis v Radcliffe* [1990] 2 All ER 536; ch 31 A.
[142] Report of PCA for 1996 (HC 386 (1996–97)).

(s 10(3)). The first such report in 1978 led to a government decision to introduce legislation enabling the injustice to be remedied.[143]

In 1995, the second such report resulted from the government's refusal to accept that the Department of Transport had acted wrongly over the planned Channel Tunnel rail link and the blight on properties in Kent affected by the plans.[144] In 1997, the department adopted a scheme for compensating certain owners which the Ombudsman considered acceptable.

The 1967 Act does not allow the Ombudsman to give publicity to the report on an individual's complaint, but a quarterly selection of reports is published in an anonymised form. In the mid-1990s, Sir William Reid laid in Parliament several reports on investigations which he considered to be of general interest to MPs: these included reports on the Department of Agriculture's deliberate decision to deprive poultry farmers of their full right to compensation, excessive delays by Social Security in handling the new disability living allowance, and the innumerable errors made in relation to the Child Support Agency.[145]

In 1994, an additional role was assumed by the Ombudsman under the non-statutory code of practice on access to official information, issued under the government's policy of open government.[146] Where a department fails to make available information which should under the code be produced, the individual's complaint can be referred to the Ombudsman, who may deal with it as a complaint under the 1967 Act. Few complaints of this kind have been received (in 1996, only 44, of which 12 were investigated).[147]

Other Ombudsmen in the public sector

The Ombudsman model has been applied in other areas of government.[148] As we have seen, complaints about the National Health Service were excluded from the jurisdiction of the Parliamentary Ombudsman. A scheme of Health Service Commissioners (Ombudsmen) for England, Wales and Scotland was later introduced.[149] Complaints about the acts of health authorities, NHS trusts and other bodies may be referred directly to the appropriate Ombudsman by a member of the public. The Ombudsman operates against a changing background of procedures for NHS complaints; in 1996, the jurisdiction was enlarged to include complaints against those providing primary health functions such as general medical, dental and ophthalmic services, and

---

[143] HC 598 (1977–78); Local Government, Planning and Land Act 1980, s 113; [1982] PL at pp 61–3.

[144] HC 193 (1994–95); report of PCA for 1995, HC 296 (1995–96), pp 42–5. Also HC 270 and 819 (1994–95) and HC 453 (1996–97); R James and D Longley [1996] PL 38.

[145] See respectively HC 519 (1992–93); HC 652 (1992–93); HC 135 (1994–95). Also A W Bradley [1992] PL 353, [1995] PL 345; and W Reid [1993] PL 221.

[146] See *Open Government* (Cm 2290, 1993). A revised version of the code was issued in 1997. See ch 13 E.

[147] Report of PCA for 1996 (HC 386 (1996–97)), pp 28–33.

[148] For Northern Ireland, see the Parliamentary Commissioner (NI) Act 1969, the Commissioner for Complaints (NI) Act 1969, and the Ombudsman (NI) Order 1996 SI 1996 No 1298.

[149] See the consolidating Health Service Commissioners Act 1993; also Seneviratne, *Ombudsmen in the Public Sector*, ch 3.

by the removal of the statutory bar which had prevented the Ombudsman from investigating complaints about clinical judgment.[150] Many aspects of the Health Service Ombudsmen are modelled directly on the Parliamentary Commissioner Act 1967; in practice the Parliamentary Ombudsman also holds the three posts of Health Service Ombudsman, whose reports in that capacity are considered by the House of Commons committee on the Parliamentary Ombudsman.

So far as local government is concerned, there are Commissions for Local Administration in England and in Wales (of which the Parliamentary Ombudsman is an ex officio member) and a Commissioner for Local Administration in Scotland.[151] Again the scheme resembles the Parliamentary Ombudsman model, with certain differences. Individuals may complain to the Local Government Ombudsman for their area regarding alleged maladministration by local authorities, joint boards, police authorities (other than the Home Secretary) and certain other local bodies. Since 1988, the individual has been able to complain either directly to the Ombudsman or by referring the matter to a member of the body in question. The complainant must specify the conduct which he or she considers to be maladministration, or at least identify the action giving rise to complaint.[152] An Ombudsman may not investigate complaints about action which affects all or most of the inhabitants in the area of a local authority, nor complaints about such matters as public passenger transport, the provision of entertainments and markets, nor complaints which relate to the giving of instruction or the internal organisation, management and discipline of local authority schools. Reports on cases investigated are sent to the local authority and to the complainant. The greatest number of complaints have related to housing and town planning.[153] Just as with the Parliamentary Ombudsman, the local Ombudsman has no means of compelling the provision of a remedy for maladministration, although a council has power to pay compensation where the Ombudsman reports in favour of a complaint.[154] In some 6% of cases where the Ombudsman has found there to be maladministration, councils have refused to provide any remedy. If no satisfactory response is made by the council to the Ombudsman's first report, he or she may issue a second report with a recommendation on the action that should be taken, and may require local publicity to be given to the matter; a decision not to comply with a further report must be taken by the full council.[155] A strong case may be made for imposing a legal obligation on a council to provide a remedy in such

---

150   Health Service Commissioners (Amendment) Act 1996. Even before this enlargement, the number of complaints increased from 990 in 1990–91 to 1,784 in 1995–96: report of Health Service Commissioners for 1995–96, HC 465 (1995–96).
151   Local Government Act 1973, part III; Local Government (Scotland) Act 1975, part II. And see Local Government Act 1978 (local authorities may pay compensation for injustice caused by maladministration).
152   *R v Local Commissioner, ex p Bradford Council* [1979] QB 287.
153   Seneviratne, op cit, ch 3 and p 107. See generally Lewis and Gateshill, *The Commission for Local Administration*; Justice, *The Local Ombudsman*; D C M Yardley [1983] PL 522; C Crawford [1988] PL 246; G Marshall [1990] PL 449.
154   Local Government Act 1974, s 31(3), as amended.
155   Ibid, s 31(1)–(2H), as amended by the Local Government and Housing Act 1989.

circumstances.[156] As with the NHS, the work of the Local Government Ombudsmen has emphasised the need for councils to have in place effective complaints procedures.[157] In 1996, the government concluded after a review of the Local Government Ombudsman service that there should continue to be a voluntary approach to the provision of complaints systems by councils and that the main role of the Local Government Ombudsmen should be to provide an independent means of investigation into complaints of maladministration.[158]

Although there are statutory provisions which enable the various Commissioners to cooperate with each other,[159] it would take an exceptional citizen to know how and to whom he or she could refer complaints about officialdom. From the individual's viewpoint, a uniform and simple right of access to all Ombudsmen is highly desirable. Attention also needs to be given to the relationships that should exist between the system of Ombudsmen and other forms of remedy for individual grievances, notably the remedies that may be obtained through recourse to the courts.[160] The Maastricht Treaty required the European Parliament to appoint an Ombudsman with power to receive complaints from EU citizens regarding maladministration on the part of Community institutions, except for the Court of Justice and the Court of First Instance acting in their judicial role.[161]

The Citizen's Charter initiative that was launched by the Conservative government in July 1991 sought inter alia to improve the quality of service provided by public bodies, to create more effective complaints procedures and to provide better redress for the individual when services go badly wrong.[162] One result of this initiative has been to encourage the appointment by departments of so-called 'lay adjudicators' to deal initially with claims for redress which have not been dealt with satisfactorily by the officials concerned. The Inland Revenue were first in the field with the appointment of a Revenue Adjudicator;[163] in 1995, the Home Office appointed a Prisons 'Ombudsman' for England and Wales,[164] and in 1997, the Child Support Agency appointed an Independent Case Examiner.

The Ombudsman concept has spread from the public sector into the private sector, with the building societies, banks, insurance companies and others agreeing to appoint their own Ombudsmen to deal with complaints

---

[156]   Cf Commissioner for Complaints (Northern Ireland) Act 1969, s 7 (power of county court to award damages). See also HC 448 (1985–86), C M G Himsworth [1986] PL 546 and Justice/All Souls Committee report, *Administrative Justice – Some Necessary Reforms*, ch 5.

[157]   See Lewis, Seneviratne and Cracknell, *Complaints Procedures in Local Government*; Commission for Local Administration, *Devising a Complaints System* (1992).

[158]   See HC Deb, 12 February 1996, col 402 (WA), and 28 November 1996, col 333 (WA).

[159]   Eg Local Government Act 1974, s 33; Health Service Commissioners Act 1993, s 18.

[160]   Cf A W Bradley [1980] CLJ 304, 320–32.

[161]   EC Treaty, art 138e.

[162]   See Cm 1599, 1991; HC 158 (1991–92). Also A W Bradley [1992] PL 353; A Barron and C Scott (1992) 55 MLR 526.

[163]   See P Morris [1996] PL 309.

[164]   The title is inappropriate, because of potential confusion with the Parliamentary Ombudsman: see HC 33–I (1993–94), p x.

from dissatisfied consumers.[165] In 1990, the legal profession in England and Wales acquired a Legal Services Ombudsman, appointed by the Lord Chancellor, to investigate complaints made about the way in which a particular grievance against a lawyer has been handled by the professional body with control over that lawyer.[166]

---

[165]   See A R Mowbray in Finnie, Himsworth and Walker (eds), *Edinburgh Essays in Public Law*, pp 315–34.
[166]   Courts and Legal Services Act 1990, ss 21–6; and for Scotland, see Law Reform (Miscellaneous Provisions) Act 1990, s 34.

CHAPTER 29

Judicial control of administrative action – I

Judicial control of administrative action raises some of the most difficult problems of public law. As we have already seen, many tasks of public authorities in administering public services (for example, decisions by a central department as to what level of expenditure by local councils is permissible)[1] are not of a character suitable for decision by a court. Control of these functions is essentially a matter for administrative and political means. Yet public authorities regulate private activities, by licensing and other controls, and may confer benefits and impose burdens upon individuals. While administrative and political control is of no less importance in these matters, the law is also relevant, for it determines both the extent of public powers and the rights and duties of the individual. Where Parliament has provided an appeal to a tribunal or to a court against an administrative decision, a further right of appeal or recourse to the superior courts generally follows: it is now accepted that tribunals and inferior courts should be bound by decisions of the higher courts on matters of law and jurisdiction.[2] In many fields Parliament has provided no right of appeal against administrative decisions. Nonetheless the superior courts still exercise a supervisory jurisdiction on matters such as the limits of an authority's powers, which affect the *legality* of official decisions. Judicial control is no substitute for administrative or political control of the *merits, expediency* or *efficiency* of decisions. But the courts may ensure that decisions made on such grounds conform to the law and that standards of fair procedure are observed.

In exercising this jurisdiction, the courts take account of the principles of administrative law that have developed from judicial decisions, and also the specific legislation that applies to the subject-matter. The role of the judiciary has been said to be essentially that of a football referee, the judge's task being to intervene when a breach of the rules has occurred. While the background of common law rules does not change overnight, 'Parliament, understandably and indeed inevitably, tends to lay down different rules for different situations'; the judges 'are continually being faced with the need to study, interpret and apply new versions of the rules'.[3]

---

[1] R v Environment Secretary, ex p Hammersmith Council [1991] 1 AC 521, pp 708, 731 above.
[2] Tribunals and Inquiries Act 1992, ss 11, 12; ch 28 A.
[3] R v Environment Secretary, ex p Hammersmith Council (above) at 561 (Lord Donaldson MR).

The legislation that applies to public authorities is made up of many separate Acts, varying widely in the powers conferred, the agencies in whom they are vested, and the extent of protection for private interests. In its operation judicial control always has a tendency to fragment into disparate branches of law, such as education, housing, and immigration law. Yet general principles have emerged from numerous judicial decisions affecting public authorities, and awareness of those principles is essential when specific statutes are before the court.

Judicial review of administrative action involves the judges in the task of developing legal principles against a complex and often changing legislative background. In this dynamic branch of the law, precedents must be used with care. As Lord Diplock warned in 1981, 'Any judicial statements on matters of public law if made before 1950 are likely to be a misleading guide to what the law is today'.[4] Some areas of government (such as immigration) give rise to many more cases of judicial review than others, and it has been said that judicial review of administrative action 'is inevitably sporadic and peripheral' when set against the entire administrative process.[5] But the general principles which emerge from the judicial process should be neither haphazard, incoherent nor contradictory.[6]

The legal solution to many administrative disputes inevitably involves some form of judicial discretion. Even if the relevant principles are clear, their application to a particular dispute is seldom clear-cut. This fact, taken with the political impact that a judicial decision may have when it concerns the policy of a minister or large local authority, leads sometimes to criticism of the judges for political bias.[7] A prominent instance of this occurred in 1981, when the cheap-fares policy for London of the (Labour) Greater London Council (GLC) was challenged in the courts by the (Conservative) Bromley Council. Some extravagant language was used by two judges in the Court of Appeal (Lord Denning MR and Watkins LJ) in condemning the actions of the GLC, but that court's decision was upheld in more restrained terms by a unanimous House of Lords.[8] It is impossible for anyone to consider the cheap-fares issue without some social or political prejudice, but it does not appear from the record of events that the GLC had given any attention to the relevant legal issues before issuing the disputed direction that fares be cut; and there were certainly substantial arguments for and against the GLC's position that merited a judicial decision. In another leading decision, the House of Lords held that a city council acted unlawfully in withdrawing the use of its rugby pitch from a club that refused to make a statement on apartheid in South Africa in terms stipulated by the council.[9] Various explanations are given for the decision in the Lords, but the dispute certainly raised fundamental issues relating to race relations as well as freedom of

---

4 *R v IRC, ex p National Federation of Self Employed* [1982] AC 617, 640.
5 de Smith, Woolf and Jowell, *Judicial Review of Administrative Action*, p 3.
6 For a perceptive critique of the underlying theories, see D J Galligan (1982) 2 OJLS 257.
7 Eg Griffith, *The Politics of the Judiciary*, chs 3–7.
8 *Bromley Council v Greater London Council* [1983] AC 768; and see the sequel *R v London Transport Executive, ex p GLC* [1983] QB 484. Also J Dignan (1983) 99 LQR 605; H Sales [1991] PL 499.
9 *Wheeler v Leicester City Council* [1985] AC 1054.

speech and opinion, as was stressed by Browne-Wilkinson LJ in the Court of Appeal.[10]

The increase in the number of judicial review cases since 1980 has made both public authorities and the judges increasingly aware of the principles of administrative law. This increase would not have occurred unless the courts had taken an independent stance to the disputes coming before them. But the judicial process is better suited to remedying acts of individual injustice, like the case of the probationer police officer dismissed without a hearing by his chief constable, than to determining the legality of economic and financial policies.[11]

In the GCHQ case in 1984, Lord Diplock classified the grounds on which administrative action is subject to judicial control under three heads, namely 'illegality', 'irrationality', and 'procedural impropriety'; he accepted that further grounds (for example, 'proportionality') might be added as the law developed.[12] In 1986, the President of the New Zealand Court of Appeal commented that 'the substantive principles of judicial review are simply that the decision-maker must act in accordance with law, fairly and reasonably'.[13] This is an admirable summary of the policy behind the law, but a great deal needs to be known about the meaning attached to each of its three strands if it is to serve as a guide to decision-making. This chapter deals first with what Lord Diplock termed illegality and irrationality before turning (in section B) to issues of a procedural kind, such as fairness. Although the emphasis is on English law, the principles of judicial review in the law of Scotland are very similar. Chapter 30 deals with the judicial remedies by which review may be obtained. These remedies are very different as between England and Scotland, although some statutory remedies are common to both systems.

A. Illegal and irrational use of powers

The ultra vires rule

When a power vested in a public authority is exceeded, acts done in excess of the power are invalid as being ultra vires. The ultra vires doctrine cannot be used to question the validity of an Act of Parliament; but it serves to control those who exceed the powers which an Act has given. The simplest instance of the rule is where a local council, whose capacity to act and to regulate private activities is derived from statute, acts outside the scope of that authority. Three examples may be given.

1 In *R v Richmond upon Thames Council, ex p McCarthy and Stone Ltd*, a local planning authority began charging a fee of £25 for informal consultations between its planning officers and developers intending to seek planning permission for new development. The council was required by law to determine all applications for planning permission

---

[10] Ibid, p 1061.
[11] Contrast *Chief Constable of North Wales v Evans* [1982] 3 All ER 141 with the poll-tax capping case: *R v Environment Secretary, ex p Hammersmith Council* (note 1 above) (and see C M G Himsworth [1991] PL 76).
[12] *CCSU v Minister for Civil Service* [1985] AC 374, 410; cf p 414 (Lord Roskill).
[13] Sir Robin Cooke, in Taggart (ed), *Judicial Review of Administrative Action in the 1980s*, p 5.

that were made, whether or not such informal consultations had been held. *Held*, by the House of Lords, while it was conducive or incidental to the council's planning functions that its officers should have informal consultations with intending developers, the fee of £25 was not lawful, since making such a charge was not incidental to those functions. The House applied the principle that no charge on the public can be levied by a public body without clear statutory authority.[14]

2 In *Hazell v Hammersmith and Fulham Council*, the local authority (as other councils had done) in 1983 established a fund for conducting transactions in the capital money market, by which the council could benefit from future movements in interest rates. These transactions included interest rate swaps, options to make such swaps, forward rate agreements and so on. If interest rates fell, the council would benefit; in fact, rates went up and large capital losses were made by the council. In a second stage of the policy, the council made further swaps, but solely to limit the extent of its losses while extricating itself from the market. The district auditor applied for a declaration that all the transactions were unlawful. *Held*, by the House of Lords, a local council had no power to enter into interest swap transactions, which by their nature involved speculation in future interest rates, since they were inconsistent with the statutory borrowing powers of the council and were not 'conducive or incidental to' those powers.[15]

3 In *R v Barnet Council, ex p Johnson*, the council owned a public park, Cherry Tree Wood. Under the Public Health Act 1875, byelaws regulated use of the park and these prohibited certain activities (eg construction of stalls and erection of tents) without the council's permission. Each year the council allowed a local community festival to be held in the park, promoting local artists and community groups. In 1988, the council sought undertakings from the organisers that no political party and no group 'likely to indicate support for or opposition to any political party or any political cause' would take part in the festival or engage in such activities. The organisers agreed to let no political parties take part in the festival, but this did not satisfy the council. *Held*, by the Court of Appeal, the power to regulate use of the park did not include power to prevent individuals resorting there peacefully for their own political purposes; the council was placing an impossible task on the organisers; and the conditions were meaningless and incapable of reasonable enforcement.[16]

As these cases illustrate, the limits of an authority's power are often not obvious. The powers of an authority include not only those expressly conferred by statute but also those which are reasonably incidental to those expressly conferred.[17] While it was held to be within the management powers of a housing authority to enable its tenants to insure their household goods with a particular insurance company,[18] a council's implied powers do not protect what on other grounds is objectionable.

In *Crédit Suisse v Allerdale Council*, the council set up a company to provide a leisure pool complex (which was plainly within the council's powers) together with time-share accommodation (which eventually was held not to be); since the council was restricted from itself borrowing the necessary capital, it guaranteed repayment of a loan of £6

---

14   [1992] 2 AC 48.
15   [1992] 2 AC 1; and see M Loughlin [1990] PL 372, [1991] PL 568.
16   (1991) 89 LGR 581. The council relied without success on the Local Government Act 1986, s 2 (councils not to support political organisations).
17   In the case of local authorities, see Local Government Act 1972, s 111; Local Government (Scotland) Act 1973, s 69.
18   *A-G v Crayford UDC* [1962] Ch 575.

million made by the plaintiff bank to the company. The company did not earn enough from selling time-shares to repay the loan. *Held* (Court of Appeal) the guarantee was void and unenforceable, as the Local Government Act 1972 had established a comprehensive code of borrowing powers. The project was 'an ingenious scheme designed to circumvent the no-doubt irksome controls imposed by central government'.[19]

The ultra vires principle applies to all public authorities created by statute, but its application to government departments is modified. They benefit from the rule that the Crown as a legal person is not created by statute and has capacity at common law to own property, enter into contracts, employ staff etc.[20] However, a department that is exercising statutory powers of regulation may not go against the statute.

Laker Airways Ltd v Department of Trade concerned the Civil Aviation Act 1971, under which the Civil Aviation Authority (CAA) regulates scheduled services to and from the United Kingdom. The CAA was bound by s 3(1) of the Act to ensure that the publicly-owned British Airways had no monopoly of long-distance routes and that at least one other British airline could compete on each route. By s 3(2), the Secretary of State could give written guidance to the CAA regarding its functions. In 1972, the CAA granted Laker Airways a licence to run a cut-price service, Skytrain, between London and New York, but the US authorities delayed their consent. In 1975, the Secretary of State adopted a new policy, deciding that the British licence for Skytrain should be revoked and issuing 'guidance' whereby, except with the consent of British Airways, no more than one British airline should operate on long-distance routes. This 'guidance' was approved by resolution of each House of Parliament as required by the 1971 Act. *Held* (Court of Appeal) the Secretary of State's 'guidance' was ultra vires, since it conflicted with the 1971 Act by giving a monopoly position to British Airways. The power to issue guidance did not include power to alter the objectives set out in the Act.[21]

Nor may a department incur expenditure which does not meet the relevant conditions imposed by Parliament.[22] When a public body's conduct is challenged as ultra vires or contrary to statute, the court's attention focuses on the Act which is claimed to be the source of its authority. Often an answer is found by interpreting that Act. But the process of judicial review goes well beyond a narrow exercise in statutory interpretation. One reason for this is that acts taken under the prerogative or from another non-statutory source may themselves be subject to judicial review.[23] A second reason is that many statutes confer broad discretion on public authorities; judicial control of such discretion, to which we now turn, goes beyond the process of statutory interpretation.[24]

---

[19] [1996] 3 WLR 894, 916 (Neill LJ); and see *Crédit Suisse v Waltham Forest Council* [1996] 3 WLR 943.
[20] See B V Harris (1992) 108 LQR 626.
[21] [1977] QB 643, discussed by G R Baldwin [1978] PL 57; and see *R v Transport Secretary, ex p Richmond Council* [1994] 1 All ER 577.
[22] *R v Foreign Secretary, ex p World Development Movement* [1995] 1 All ER 611.
[23] See *CCSU v Minister for the Civil Service* [1985] AC 374; *R v Panel on Take-overs, ex p Datafin plc* [1987] QB 815.
[24] J Jowell and A Lester [1987] PL 368.

Abuse of discretionary powers[25]

Under the ultra vires rule in its simplest form, the courts may prevent powers from being exceeded. However, this is no more than a starting-point[26] and the courts may also prevent powers from being abused; it is unlawful to exercise a discretion for an improper purpose or without taking into account all relevant considerations. This does not mean that the courts may substitute their own decision for that of the body or person to whom a discretion has been entrusted; unless any material errors are shown to exist, the decision taken must stand.[27]

In *Associated Provincial Picture Houses Ltd v Wednesbury Corporation*, the council gave the company permission for Sunday cinema performances subject to the condition that no children under 15 should be admitted to Sunday performances, with or without an adult. The Sunday Entertainments Act 1932 gave a local authority power to sanction Sunday performances, 'subject to such conditions as the authority think fit to impose'. The Court of Appeal held that the council had not acted unreasonably or ultra vires in imposing the condition.[28]

Lord Greene's judgment in this case is often cited today in decisions involving judicial review of powers for unreasonableness. What is referred to as the *Wednesbury* test is the proposition that a court may interfere with the exercise of discretion for unreasonableness only when the authority has come to a conclusion 'so unreasonable that no reasonable authority could ever have come to it'. It is clear from Lord Greene's judgment that unreasonableness as a ground of review is closely related to other grounds such as irrelevant considerations, improper purposes and error of law. The meaning of 'unreasonable' was central to the decision of the House of Lords in the *Tameside* case.[29] Lord Diplock there said that 'unreasonable' denotes 'conduct which no sensible authority acting with due appreciation of its responsibilities would have decided to adopt', a formula which seems very likely to give rise to conflicting interpretations.

Where an authority has discretionary powers, control of the merits of its decisions is primarily a political or administrative matter. Sometimes by statute a local decision requires ministerial confirmation or is subject to an appeal to the minister. Exceptionally, when statute has provided a full right of appeal to a court against an official decision, the court may apply its own view of the merits, provided it has due regard to the opinions of the authority which made the first decision.[30]

In some cases the language of the statute seeks to confer an absolute

---

25 See de Smith, Woolf and Jowell, *Judicial Review of Administrative Action*, ch 6; Wade and Forsyth, *Administrative Law*, chs 11, 12; Craig, *Administrative Law*, ch 11. And see Galligan, *Discretionary Powers*.

26 As to whether the ultra vires rule is the fundamental basis for judicial review, contrast D Oliver [1987] PL 543 with C Forsyth [1996] CLJ 122.

27 *R v Lancashire CC, ex p Huddleston* [1986] 2 All ER 941; *R v Trade Secretary, ex p Lonrho plc* [1989] 2 All ER 609.

28 [1948] 1 KB 223. See also *R v Somerset CC, ex p Fewings* [1995] 3 All ER 20 (decision to ban deer hunting on council's land not taken for 'benefit, improvement or development' of the county); cf G Nardell [1995] PL 27.

29 Note 53 below. On principles of *Wednesbury* review, see P Walker [1995] PL 556, Lord Irvine of Lairg [1996] PL 59 and R Carnwath [1996] PL 245.

30 *Sagnata Investments Ltd v Norwich Corpn* [1971] 2 QB 614.

discretion on the administrator; where this is so, the powers of the court may be much reduced, but they are not completely excluded. Even the power to refuse naturalisation to an alien without giving reasons may be subject to a procedural requirement of fairness;[31] and a power to grant what would otherwise be a 'conclusive' certificate may be reviewed if the power is inconsistent with Community law.[32] In the past, the courts were readier to accept that executive discretion was immune from judicial review than they are today. During the Second World War, power was given to the Home Secretary to detain anyone whom he had reasonable cause to believe was a person of hostile origin or association. In *Liversidge v Anderson*, it was held by the House of Lords, Lord Atkin dissenting, that the court could not inquire into the grounds for the belief which led to the making of a detention order; the matter was one for executive discretion. In regard to such an issue, an objective test of reasonableness could not be applied, but only a subjective test. The statement of his belief by the Home Secretary was accepted as conclusive.[33] But *Liversidge v Anderson* is an extreme example of judicial unwillingness to review executive discretion, best explained by wartime circumstances.[34] The present attitude of the courts to claims that a minister has unfettered discretion is shown in *Padfield v Minister of Agriculture*.

Under the Agricultural Marketing Act 1958, the milk marketing scheme included a complaints procedure by which a committee of investigation examined any complaint made about the operation of the scheme 'if the Minister in any case so directs'. Padfield, a farmer in south-east England, complained about the prices paid to farmers in that region by the Milk Marketing Board. The minister refused to direct that the complaint be referred to the committee of investigation, and claimed that he had an unfettered discretion in deciding whether or not to refer such complaints. *Held*, the minister would be directed to deal with the complaint according to law. The reasons given by the minister for his refusal were not good reasons in law and showed that he had not exercised his discretion in a manner which promoted the intention and objects of the Act of 1958. 'The policy and objects of the Act must be determined by construing the Act as a whole, and construction is always a matter of law for court'.[35]

This decision was also significant in that the judges, after examining the reasons given by the Minister of Agriculture to see whether they conformed to the Act, were prepared to assume that he had no better reasons for his decision. The willingness of the judges to impose limits upon the minister's discretion in *Padfield* matches the way in which they have frequently cut down the width of local authority discretions. Thus a local planning authority may grant planning permission 'subject to such conditions as they think fit', but the courts have severely limited the apparent width of this power.[36]

Some grounds on which the courts may hold that a power has been abused

---

[31] *R v Home Secretary, ex p Fayed* [1997] 1 All ER 228.
[32] Eg *Johnston v Chief Constable RUC* [1987] QB 129.
[33] [1942] AC 206; ch 25 D.
[34] See R F V Heuston (1970) 86 LQR 33, (1971) 87 LQR 161; Simpson, *In the Highest Degree Odious*.
[35] [1968] AC 997, 1030 (Lord Reid). *Padfield* was criticised by R C Austin in [1975] CLP 150 but Lord Denning MR considered it 'a landmark in our administrative law' ([1977] AC 1014, 1025).
[36] Eg *Hall and Co Ltd v Shoreham-by-Sea UDC* [1964] 1 All ER 1; *R v Hillingdon Council, ex p Royco Homes Ltd* [1974] QB 720.

will now be described. In practice, these grounds overlap and are often not easily distinguished from each other.[37]

1 Irrelevant considerations. Powers must be exercised in accordance with the intention of Parliament as may be inferred from the Act in question. Thus local authorities acted unlawfully in cancelling purchase of *The Times* for public libraries (provided under the Public Libraries and Museums Act 1964) because they disapproved of the publishers' actions in an industrial dispute between the publishers and their employees.[38] A decision to award a council house to a councillor, enabling her to get ahead of others on the housing list, was unlawful, having been influenced by the view of the chairman of the housing committee that it would help her to be re-elected.[39] Where rates of over £50,000 had been overpaid to a council on an unoccupied warehouse, the council did not lawfully exercise its statutory discretion to refund overpaid rates when it refused to do so for reasons which the House of Lords held to be irrelevant and in disregard of the statutory purpose of the discretion.[40]

The court's power to rule that certain considerations are irrelevant may severely limit the scope of general words in a statute,[41] but the courts do not always interpret statutory discretion narrowly.[42] The converse of the proposition that an authority must not take into account irrelevant considerations is that it must take into account relevant considerations. However, to invalidate a decision it is not enough that considerations have been ignored which *could* have been taken into account: it is only when the statute 'expressly or impliedly identifies considerations *required to be taken into account* by the authority as a matter of legal obligation' that a decision will be invalid because relevant considerations were ignored.[43] Thus there are factors which the decision-maker *may* take into account, but need not do so.[44] While it is for the court to rule whether particular factors are relevant or irrelevant and whether they were taken into consideration, it is for the decision-maker to decide what weight to give to a relevant consideration that is taken into account.[45]

2 Improper purposes. The exercise of a power for an improper purpose is invalid. Improper purposes include malice or personal dishonesty on the part of the officials making the decision, but examples of this kind are rare. Most instances of improper purpose have arisen out of a mistaken interpretation by

---

[37] See G D S Taylor [1976] CLJ 272.

[38] *R v Ealing Council, ex p Times Newspapers Ltd* (1986) 85 LGR 316. See now Local Government Act 1988, part II. See also *R v Somerset CC, ex p Fewings* (above).

[39] *R v Port Talbot Council, ex p Jones* [1988] 2 All ER 207.

[40] *R v Tower Hamlets Council, ex p Chetnik Developments Ltd* [1988] AC 858.

[41] See eg *Mixnam's Properties Ltd v Chertsey UDC* [1965] AC 735 (G Ganz (1964) 27 MLR 611) and *R v Somerset CC, ex p Fewings* (above).

[42] Eg *Roberton v Environment Secretary* [1976] 1 All ER 689 (risk of assassination of Prime Minister relevant to diversion of footpath on Chequers Estate); *R v Westminster Council, ex p Monahan* [1990] 1 QB 87 (relevant to permission for office development near Covent Garden that profits would fund improvements in opera house).

[43] *CREEDNZ Inc v Governor-General* [1981] 1 NZLR 172, 183 (Cooke J) (emphasis supplied), approved in *Re Findlay* [1985] AC 318, 333.

[44] See *R v Somerset CC, ex p Fewings* [1995] 3 All ER at 32 (Simon Brown LJ).

[45] *Tesco Stores v Environment Secretary* [1995] 2 All ER 636; *R v Cambridge Health Authority, ex p B* [1995] 2 All ER 129.

a public authority of its powers, sometimes contributed to by an excess of zeal in the public interest. Thus a city council which was empowered to buy land compulsorily for the purpose of extending streets or improving the city could not validly buy land for the purpose of taking advantage of an anticipated increase in value of the land.[46] In *Congreve v Home Office*, where the Home Office had threatened certain holders of television licences that their licences would be revoked by the Home Secretary if they did not each pay an extra £6, the Court of Appeal held that it was an improper exercise of the Home Secretary's power of revocation 'to use a threat to exercise that power as a means of extracting money which Parliament had given the Executive no mandate to demand'.[47] Despite the duty of local councils under the Race Relations Act 1976, s 71, to have due regard to the need to eliminate racial discrimination, it was improper for a council to use its powers over its playing fields to exercise pressure on officers of a rugby club to denounce a rugby tour of South Africa; and to boycott a company's products to induce the company to end its trading links with South Africa. It was unlawful for a council to switch its advertisements for teachers from the *Times Educational Supplement* to another paper simply because the leader of the council was suing the newspaper's publishers for libel.[48]

Difficulty arises when the authority is motivated both by lawful and unlawful purposes.

The Westminster Corporation was empowered to provide public conveniences but not pedestrian subways. Underground conveniences were designed so that the subway leading to them provided a means of crossing a busy street. It was sought to restrain the corporation from proceeding on the ground that the real object was the provision of a crossing and not of public conveniences. The court refused to intervene. 'It is not enough to show that the corporation contemplated that the public might use the subway as a means of crossing the street. In order to make out a case of bad faith, it must be shown that the corporation constructed the subway as a means of crossing the street under colour and pretence of providing public conveniences not really wanted'.[49]

In such cases a distinction has sometimes been drawn between purpose and motive, so that where an exercise of power fulfils the purposes for which the power was given, it matters not that those exercising it were influenced by an extraneous motive. But the motive–purpose distinction is difficult to maintain, and it has sometimes given way to the test of what was the dominant purpose, or to the rather stricter rule, already outlined, that the presence of any extraneous or irrelevant considerations invalidates the decision.[50]

---

[46] *Municipal Council of Sydney v Campbell* [1925] AC 338. In *Crédit Suisse v Allerdale Council* (above), the scheme was designed to evade a statutory borrowing restriction.

[47] [1976] QB 629, 662 (Geoffrey Lane LJ).

[48] See respectively *Wheeler v Leicester City Council* [1985] AC 1054; *R v Lewisham Council, ex p Shell UK Ltd* [1988] 1 All ER 938; *R v Derbyshire Council, ex p Times Supplements Ltd, The Times,* 19 July 1990. By the Local Government Act 1988, part II, councils must not now take into account non-commercial considerations in placing contracts.

[49] *Westminster Corpn v London and North Western Railway Co* [1905] AC 426, 432 (Lord Macnaghten); cf *Webb v Minister of Housing* [1965] 2 All ER 193 (and see [1965] CLJ 1).

[50] De Smith, Woolf and Jowell, op cit, pp 340–6.

3 Error of law.   An authority which is entrusted with a discretion must direct itself properly on the law or its decision may be declared invalid.

In *Perilly v Tower Hamlets Borough Council*, the council wrongly believed that it was under a statutory duty to deal with applications for trading licences in the Petticoat Lane market in the strict order in which they were received; it therefore refused a licence to Perilly on the death of his mother, although she had had a pitch in the market for 30 years. The court quashed a licence which the council had granted to a newcomer to the market, and ordered that the licence be issued to Perilly.[51]

The notion of error of law goes wider than a mere mistake of statutory interpretation. A minister commits an error of law if (inter alia) he or she acts when there is no evidence to support the action or comes to a conclusion to which, on the evidence, he or she could not reasonably have come.[52] These principles, developed by the courts in relation to planning and compulsory purchase decisions, were highlighted in 1976 when a Labour Secretary of State and a Conservative council clashed over the re-organisation of secondary education.

Under the Education Act 1944, s 68 (now s 496 of the Education Act 1996), if the Secretary of State was satisfied that an education authority was proposing to act unreasonably, he or she could issue such directions to the authority as appeared expedient. When in May 1976 the newly elected Tameside council proposed, contrary to an earlier plan, to continue selection for entry to five grammar schools in the coming September, the Secretary of State directed the council to adhere to the earlier plan. The House of Lords refused to enforce this direction, holding that it was valid only if the Secretary of State had been satisfied that no reasonable authority could act as the council was proposing to. 'Unreasonable' in s 68 did not mean conduct which the Secretary of State thought was wrong. On the facts, there was no material on which the Secretary of State could have been satisfied that the council was acting unreasonably. He must therefore have misdirected himself as to the grounds on which he could act.[53]

Reliance on error of law as a ground for controlling discretion places the courts in a position of strength vis-à-vis the administration since it is peculiarly for the courts to identify errors of law. As the *Tameside* case indicated, error of law is a sufficiently pliable concept to enable the judges, if they feel it is necessary, to make a very close scrutiny of the reasons for an official decision and the facts on which it was based. We consider later in this chapter whether it is now a general rule that a tribunal which makes an error of law in reaching a decision must be held to be exceeding its jurisdiction.

4 Unauthorised delegation.[54]   A body to which the exercise of discretion has

---

51 [1973] QB 9.
52 *Edwards v Bairstow* [1956] AC 14; applied to ministers' decisions in *Ashbridge Investments Ltd v Minister of Housing* [1965] 3 All ER 371; *Coleen Properties Ltd v Minister of Housing* [1971] 1 All ER 1049; *R v Transport Secretary, ex p de Rothschild* [1989] 1 All ER 933. On error of law generally, see J Beatson (1984) 4 OJLS 22; Emery and Smythe, *Judicial Review*, ch 3. See also note 116 below.
53 *Education Secretary v Tameside Council* [1977] AC 1014 and D Bull (1987) 50 MLR 307.
54 Cf the approach taken in two decisions of great importance: *R v Home Secretary, ex p Fire Brigades Union* [1995] 2 AC 513 and *R v Foreign Secretary, ex p World Development Movement* [1995] 1 All ER 611.

been entrusted by statute cannot delegate that exercise to another unless from the statute it is clear that the delegation is authorised.

Barnard v National Dock Labour Board concerned a statutory scheme for the registration of dockers, under which the disciplinary powers of the National Dock Labour Board had to be delegated to local dock boards. The London board purported to delegate its disciplinary function to the port manager, who during a trade dispute suspended Barnard from work. *Held,* that disciplinary powers could not be lawfully delegated to the port manager; the purported suspension was declared a nullity.[55]

The rule against unauthorised delegation of powers might seem to require all powers vested in a minister to be exercised by him or her personally. That the courts have accepted the exigencies of departmental administration was shown in *Local Government Board v Arlidge*:[56] powers and duties conferred on a minister may properly be exercised by officials, for whom the minister is responsible to Parliament, or by a junior minister.[57] But where a statutory duty is vested in one minister, he or she may not adopt a policy by which the decision is effectively made by another minister.[58] And, where a discretion is vested in a subordinate officer, it may not be taken away by orders from a superior.[59] Somewhat similar principles apply to statutory agencies. Thus the Police Complaints Board could not adopt a rule of taking no action on complaints which the Director of Public Prosecutions had decided should not lead to criminal proceedings;[60] but the Commission for Racial Equality may delegate to its staff the task of conducting formal investigations into alleged discrimination.[61] In local government, there is now wide authority for councils to delegate their functions to committees, sub-committees and officers.[62] But a committee or sub-committee may not consist of a single councillor.[63]

5 Discretion may not be fettered.   A discretion may not be surrendered, whether the surrender takes the form of contracting in advance to exercise it in a particular way or of pre-judging the way in which it shall be exercised. Licensing committees have full discretion in licensing matters, but they must hear all applications and apply their minds in each case presented to them, whatever general policy they may have decided upon. Each applicant must have the opportunity of urging that the particular circumstances of his or her case should be taken into account before a decision is made.[64] A public authority may adopt a general policy and indicate to an applicant that the policy will be applied unless there is something exceptional in the case; but

---

[55]   [1953] 2 QB 18. And eg *Young v Fife Regional Council* 1986 SLT 331.
[56]   [1915] AC 120; and Section B below.
[57]   *Carltona Ltd v Commissioners of Works* [1943] 2 All ER 560; *Re Golden Chemical Products* [1976] Ch 300. See also *R v Home Secretary, ex p Oladehinde* [1991] 1 AC 254; D Lanham (1984) 100 LQR 587; *R v Home Secretary, ex p Doody* [1994] 1 AC 531, 566 (power of Home Secretary to determine penal element of life sentence for murder); and ch 13 D.
[58]   *Lavender & Son Ltd v Minister of Housing* [1970] 3 All ER 871.
[59]   *Simms Motor Units Ltd v Minister of Labour* [1946] 2 All ER 201.
[60]   *R v Police Complaints Board, ex p Madden* [1983] 2 All ER 353.
[61]   *R v Commission for Racial Equality, ex p Cottrell & Rothon* [1980] 3 All ER 265.
[62]   Local Government Act 1972, s 101; Local Government (Scotland) 1973, s 56.
[63]   *R v Environment Secretary, ex p Hillingdon Council* [1986] 2 All ER 273.
[64]   *R v Torquay Licensing Justices, ex p Brockman* [1951] 2 KB 784.

the authority may not adopt a rule that applications of a certain kind should always be refused.[65]

These principles apply to the exercise of discretionary powers vested in government departments. In practice it is often essential that departments should formulate policies and apply them.

Under a scheme for discretionary investment grants to industry, the Board of Trade applied a rule that grants could not be paid in respect of items costing less than £25 and refused to pay a grant to a firm which had spent over £4 million on gas cylinders costing £20 each: the House of Lords accepted that the department was entitled to make such a rule or policy, provided that it was prepared to listen to arguments for the exercise of individual discretion.[66]

In such a case, individuals may find it very difficult to persuade officials that they should receive preferential treatment. Their right might be more realistically described as a right to ask that the general policy should be changed.[67] Even so, the courts could be readier than they are to hold that public authorities are entitled to adopt definite policies without this interfering with the proper exercise of discretion.[68] Thus, as regards discretionary awards for further and higher education, local authorities have found it very difficult to reconcile budgetary constraints with the need for fair and consistent treatment of individuals.[69]

6 Breach of a local authority's financial duties. One controversial ground of review that applies to local government is that councils are expected to observe due standards of financial responsibility to the council taxpayers, but the limits of this duty are difficult to determine. In *Roberts v Hopwood*, the House of Lords held invalid a decision by the Poplar council in 1923 to pay a minimum wage of £4 per week to all adult employees, regardless of the work which they did, their sex and the falling cost of living; the judges considered that the council had exceeded its power to pay such wages as it saw fit, by making gifts or gratuities to its staff which it had no power to do.[70] Fifty years later, the principle that local authorities owe a fiduciary duty to their ratepayers in the management of local finance was again prominent in *Bromley Council v Greater London Council*.[71] The House of Lords held that the Greater London Council must exercise its powers in relation to London transport with due regard to ordinary business principles; the decision that fares be cut by 25% had caused both a big increase in the subsidy payable by ratepayers and also a sharp loss in rate support grant paid from central government. The council was thus in breach of the fiduciary duty which it owned to London ratepayers. However, a modified scheme of subsidy for London fares later

65 *R v Port of London Authority, ex p Kynoch* [1919] 1 KB 176, 184 (dictum of Bankes LJ). See D J Galligan [1976] PL 332 and *R v Police Complaints Board, ex p Madden*, note 60 above.
66 *British Oxygen Co v Board of Trade* [1971] AC 610. And see *Schmidt v Home Secretary* [1969] 2 Ch 149 and *Cumings v Birkenhead Corpn* [1972] Ch 12.
67 *British Oxygen Co v Board of Trade* (above) at 631 (Lord Dilhorne).
68 Cf *A-G ex rel Tilley v Wandsworth BC* [1981] 1 WLR 854, *R v Environment Secretary, ex p Brent BC* [1982] QB 593 and *R v Rochdale BC, ex p Cromer Ring Mill Ltd* [1982] 3 All ER 761.
69 Eg *R v Warwick CC, ex p Collymore* [1995] ELR 217; *R v London Borough of Bexley, ex p Jones* [1995] ELR 42.
70 [1925] AC 578. And see *Prescott v Birmingham Corpn* [1955] Ch 210.
71 [1983] AC 768.

survived legal challenge[72] and in *Pickwell v Camden Council* the court accepted as lawful a local pay settlement made by the council during national strikes which was more favourable to workers in Camden than was the national settlement.[73] Excessive expenditure on a lawful object may in extreme circumstances be restrained by the court; but much will depend on the decision-making process and on how relevant considerations were taken into account.

7 Failure to give reasons.　Although the giving of reasons 'is one of the fundamentals of good administration',[74] at common law there is no general duty to give reasons for decisions.[75] However, in a growing number of situations the duty to give reasons may arise. Thus, under the Tribunals and Inquiries Act 1992, s 10, there is a duty to supply reasons on request where decisions are made by tribunals or following a public inquiry, and specific statutes or regulations often require reasons to be given for certain decisions (for example, the refusal of planning permission). Moreover, the nature of a particular discretion may entail giving reasons, for example if a right of appeal depends upon it.[76] Fairness may require the giving of reasons,[77] and reasons may be necessary to explain a decision which otherwise might appear arbitrary:[78]

if all other known facts and circumstances appear to point overwhelmingly in favour of a different decision, the decision-maker who has given no reasons cannot complain if the court draws the inference that he had no rational reason for his decision.[79]

European law requires the giving of reasons when this is necessary to secure effective protection of a Community right.[80] If some reasons are given for a decision, and these are all bad, the court may infer that there were no good reasons for the decision.[81] Where there is a duty to give reasons, 'proper, adequate reasons must be given' which are intelligible and deal with the substantial points in issue.[82] Failure to give such reasons may cause the court to quash the decision for error of law, or to remit the matter to the decision-maker in order that proper reasons be given.

[72]　*R v London Transport Executive, ex p GLC* [1983] QB 484.
[73]　[1983] QB 962 (and C Crawford [1983] PL 248). See to opposite effect, *Allsop v North Tyneside Council* (1992) 90 LGR 462.
[74]　*Breen v AEU* [1971] 2 QB 175, 191 (Lord Denning MR). G Richardson [1986] PL 437; Justice/All Souls Committee report, *Administrative Justice*, ch 3; P P Craig [1994] CLJ 282.
[75]　*R v Trade Secretary, ex p Lonrho plc* [1989] 2 All ER 609; *R v Higher Education Funding Council, ex p Institute of Dental Surgery* [1994] 1 All ER 651; *Public Service Board of New South Wales v Osmond* (1986) 63 ALR 559.
[76]　*Minister of National Revenue v Wright's Canadian Ropes Ltd* [1947] AC 109.
[77]　*R v Home Secretary, ex p Doody* [1994] 1 AC 531 (and Craig, note 74 above); *R v Lambeth Council, ex p Walters* (1993) 26 HLR 170.
[78]　*R v Civil Service Appeal Board, ex p Cunningham* [1991] 1 All ER 310 (and J Herberg [1991] PL 340).
[79]　*R v Trade Secretary, ex p Lonrho plc* [1989] 2 All ER 609, 620 (Lord Keith). Cf *R v Lancashire CC, ex p Huddleston* [1986] 2 All ER 941 (and A W Bradley [1986] PL 508).
[80]　See eg Case 222/86 *UNECTEF v Heylens* [1989] 1 CMLR 901.
[81]　*Padfield v Minister of Agriculture* [1968] AC 997.
[82]　*Re Poyser and Mills' Arbitration* [1964] 2 QB 467, 478. Contrast *R v Home Secretary, ex p Swati* [1986] 1 All ER 717.

Proportionality

In varying forms, the concept of proportionality is found in the constitutional law of countries such as Germany, the USA and Canada as well as in French administrative law and Community law.[83] In outline, if action to achieve a lawful objective is taken in a situation where it will necessarily restrict a particular right of the individual, the concept requires that the effect on the individual right should not be disproportionate to the public purpose sought to be achieved. As the European Court of Human Rights has said, a restriction on a fundamental right cannot be regarded as 'necessary in a democratic society' unless it is proportionate to the legitimate aim pursued.[84] If, for example, in a given situation there is a need for public action that restricts the freedom of expression, the interference with the right 'must be necessary and proportionate to the damage which the restriction is designed to prevent'.[85] Any further restriction is unjustifiable. May this test be adopted in United Kingdom courts? So far as the test overlaps with that of *Wednesbury* unreasonableness, it is already part of the law. But the House of Lords held in 1991 that proportionality is not open to the courts as a distinct means of assessing the merits of an executive decision.[86] In so far as the test of proportionality can arise in Community law, it is already applicable in the United Kingdom. But the majority of the House in *Brind* was not prepared to extend the power of the courts to review the merits of executive decisions, nor to adopt the European Convention in the course of applying the law of judicial review.

Failure to perform a statutory duty

We have so far been considering how a public authority may exceed its powers or misuse its discretion. Such a body may also act unlawfully if it fails to perform a duty imposed upon it by statute, for example to perform a public service or to grant a benefit to a specified class of individuals. The remedies appropriate for enforcing such a duty will be considered in the next chapter. A few comments on the problems of identifying an enforceable duty are made here. In some cases, the statutory duty is clear and precise and is plainly enforceable by the persons concerned. Thus any elector for a local authority area is entitled to inspect the authority's minutes and to make copies or extracts of those minutes.[87] But there are many statutory duties which are more general in character and may not be clearly enforceable in the courts. Thus the Education Act 1996, s 9, obliges both the Secretary of State and local education authorities to pay regard 'to the general principle that pupils are to be educated in accordance with the wishes of their parents, so far as that is compatible with the provision of efficient instruction ... and the avoidance of unreasonable public expenditure'. How far does this statutory duty create enforceable rights in the parents of children of school age? It has often been

---

[83] See J Jowell and A Lester, in Jowell and Oliver (eds), *New Directions in Judicial Review*, pp 51–72. See also de Smith, Woolf and Jowell, op cit, pp 593–606; Craig, op cit, pp 411–21; and Schwarze, *European Administrative Law*, ch 5.

[84] As in *Dudgeon v UK* (1981) 4 EHRR 149; ch 19 B.

[85] *R v Home Secretary, ex p Brind* [1991] 1 AC 696 at 751 (Lord Templeman).

[86] Ibid. And see Lord Hoffmann, *A Sense of Proportion*.

[87] Local Government Act 1972, s 228.

held that this duty requires local authorities to take parental wishes into account but does not oblige the authorities to give effect to them.[88] Thus in regard to school admission policies, it was only by the Education Act 1980 (now s 411 of the 1996 Act) that local authorities were placed under an enforceable duty to respect parental wishes.[89]

By contrast, under s 8 of the Education Act 1944, education authorities had a duty 'to secure that there shall be available for their areas sufficient schools ... for providing full time education' suitable to their pupils. In *Meade v Haringey BC*, a local authority was faced with strike action by school caretakers and ancillary staff and decided that all schools should close until further notice. The Court of Appeal held that parents who suffered as a result of this decision to close the schools had a remedy in court, and that the council would be in breach of its duty if it decided to close the schools in sympathy with a trade union's claims at a time when the closure could reasonably have been avoided.[90] However, later decisions have referred to the duty in issue in *Meade* as a 'target duty': 'the metaphor recognises that the statute requires the relevant public authority to aim to make the prescribed provision but does not regard failure to achieve it without more as a breach'.[91] Thus the duty may be enforceable by the Secretary of State under default powers but not by a private individual.

Even where a statutory duty is binding on public bodies, the question of enforcement may be difficult. Sometimes enforcement is expressly left to the relevant government minister using default powers;[92] sometimes a private law right of action in damages for breach of duty may be available; but more frequently the individuals affected have no more than an interest in seeking a public law remedy, such as an order of mandamus.[93] Thus prison authorities must observe the statutory rules made for the conduct and discipline of the prisons, but no right to sue for damages accrues to prisoners who are affected if the rules are broken.[94]

Finally, the statutory language is not always decisive of whether a public authority has a duty or a discretion on a certain matter. In some circumstances, the word 'may' used in legislation is equivalent to 'must'.[95]

The concept of jurisdiction[96]

Our discussion so far of the ultra vires doctrine has been phrased in terms of powers, discretion and duties. In many cases, however, use is made of the language of jurisdiction. For historical reasons, as we saw in chapter 26, the

---

[88] *Watt v Kesteven CC* [1955] 1 QB 408, applied in *Cumings v Birkenhead Corpn* [1972] Ch 12.
[89] See eg *R v Greenwich Council, ex p Governors of John Ball School* (1989) 88 LGR 589.
[90] [1979] 2 All ER 1016. The duty is now found in the Education Act 1996, s 14.
[91] *R v London Borough of Islington, ex p Rixon, The Times*, 17 April 1996 (Sedley J) citing *R v ILEA, ex p Ali* (1990) 2 Admin LR 822.
[92] See eg *R v Environment Secretary, ex p Norwich Council* [1982] QB 808.
[93] Ch 30.
[94] *R v Deputy Governor of Parkhurst Prison, ex p Hague* [1992] 1 AC 58. See also *X v Bedfordshire CC* [1995] 2 AC 633; and ch 31 A.
[95] *Padfield v Minister of Agriculture* [1968] AC 997.
[96] See de Smith, Woolf and Jowell, op cit, ch 5; Wade and Forsyth, op cit, ch 9; and (for a rewarding re-statement) Craig, op cit, ch 10. Also Rubinstein, *Jurisdiction and Illegality, Stair Memorial Encyclopedia of Laws of Scotland*, vol I, pp 94–9.

concepts of vires (powers) and jurisdiction are closely linked. Often it makes no difference whether a certain matter is regarded as being ultra vires or in excess of jurisdiction. But an inferior tribunal or a body such as a licensing authority may be said to have jurisdiction to hear and determine certain questions, whether it be a claim for a social security benefit or a taxi-driver's licence. In the past these decisions were often taken in judicial form and they are subject to control by the superior courts on jurisdictional grounds. This supervision does not provide a fresh decision on the merits but ensures that the body in question has observed the limits which are a condition of its power to make binding decisions. According to a famous dictum in *R v Nat Bell Liquors*:

> That supervision goes to two points: one is the area of the inferior judgment and the qualifications and conditions of its exercise; the other is the observance of the law in the course of its exercise.[97]

Thus all tribunals and like bodies are subject to control by the superior courts on jurisdictional grounds, whether or not there is a statutory right of appeal from their decisions. While important differences exist between judicial review and remedies available by way of appeal, there is a wide overlap between the two, since many decisions made by a tribunal could give rise both to an appeal (if such a right exists) and to judicial review. In the discussion which now follows, the inferior body whose decisions are under review will be described simply as a tribunal, but the principles involved also apply to many bodies (such as licensing authorities) which are not classified as tribunals for such purposes as supervision by the Council on Tribunals.[98]

The limits of a tribunal's jurisdiction

Tribunals have both a positive duty to decide the questions that the legislature intended them to decide and a negative duty to refrain from exceeding their jurisdiction. Many jurisdictional questions may arise at the outset of proceedings: for example, is the complaint one with which the tribunal may deal?; has any essential prior procedure been observed?;[99] are the members of the tribunal properly appointed? The first duty of a tribunal is to decide such preliminary matters, if questions about these are raised. But it is well established that no tribunal has power to decide conclusively the limits of its own jurisdiction.[100] Thus, if a tribunal refuses to 'hear and determine' a particular matter, saying that it falls outside its jurisdiction, that decision may be challenged in the High Court. So too can the decision of a tribunal to go ahead and decide a matter against the objection of one party. The aggrieved party may immediately request the High Court to intervene and prohibit further proceedings in excess of jurisdiction; or, if a decision on the merits has been made, the court may hold that the whole dispute was outside the

---

97   [1922] 2 AC 128, 156.
98   Ch 28 A.
99   Eg *R v Paddington Rent Tribunal, ex p Bell Properties Ltd* [1949] 1 KB 666.
100   See the famous passage in *R v Shoreditch Assessment Committee, ex p Morgan* [1910] 2 KB 859, 880 (Farwell LJ).

tribunal's jurisdiction,[101] even if at the time the aggrieved party did not challenge the jurisdiction of the tribunal.[102]

Although it was formerly argued to the contrary,[103] jurisdictional control applies not just at the outset of a case but throughout the time that the matter is before the tribunal. Thus if a tribunal, after properly conducted proceedings, reaches a decision (such as to impose a penalty on one party) which is outside its power, the aggrieved person can have the decision quashed by the High Court as unlawful.

These rules maintain the principle that tribunals do not have unlimited jurisdiction. To give an illustration used in the *Anisminic* case, a tribunal established by Parliament to give protection to wives against their husbands may not exceed its jurisdiction by seeking to protect unmarried women against their male partners.[104] In practice very difficult questions have arisen in distinguishing between (*a*) elements in a tribunal decision which amount to an excess of jurisdiction if they are, in the opinion of a superior court, decided incorrectly; and (*b*) elements in a tribunal decision which arguably may be incorrect but are nonetheless 'within jurisdiction' and can be put right only by an appeal on the merits, if one exists. One reason for these difficulties is that the courts have often gone far into the merits of a decision to correct what they consider to be a mistake by a tribunal, while justifying their action on jurisdictional grounds.

Jurisdictional fact and law

What has been called the doctrine of jurisdictional fact and law provides one approach to the problem of distinguishing between jurisdictional and non-jurisdictional elements in a tribunal decision. Assume that by statute the Home Secretary is empowered to deport an alien when he deems this to be conducive to the public good.[105] If the Home Secretary proposes to use this power against X, believing X to be an alien, X's status may be said to be a preliminary or collateral question, or a matter of jurisdictional fact, which X can ask the High Court to resolve. If X is found by the court not to be an alien but a British citizen, then the Home Secretary has no power to deport him or her. This means that the court must review the evidence relevant to X's nationality and decide the matter for itself, whereas (if X is indeed an alien) the court will not interfere with the Home Secretary's discretionary decision that X should be deported unless it can be shown that the Home Secretary has abused the discretion.

Although this is a fundamental principle of law, it was virtually ignored by the House of Lords in 1980 in *R v Home Secretary, ex p Zamir*.[106] Fortunately, that decision was overruled by the House three years later in *Khawaja's* case.[107]

---

[101] See eg *R v Monopolies and Mergers Commission, ex p South Yorkshire Transport Ltd* [1993] 1 All ER 289 (Commission's jurisdiction dependent on whether South Yorkshire area a 'substantial part of the United Kingdom').

[102] *Essex Congregational Union v Essex CC* [1963] AC 808.

[103] By D M Gordon, whose articles include (1931) 47 LQR 386, 557, and (1971) 34 MLR 1.

[104] Lord Pearce in *Anisminic Ltd v Foreign Compensation Commission* [1969] 2 AC 147, 194.

[105] An illustration used in *Khawaja's* case (below) by Lord Bridge.

[106] [1980] AC 930.

[107] *R v Home Secretary, ex p Khawaja* [1984] AC 74.

These cases both concerned the power of the Home Secretary under the Immigration Act 1971 to remove from the United Kingdom persons who were 'illegal entrants' under the Act. In *Zamir*'s case, the House held that it was not a condition precedent of the power to remove that the immigration officer should satisfy the court that the individual was indeed an illegal entrant. This approach was tantamount to treating the individual's status as an illegal entrant as if it were a matter of Home Secretary's discretion. But in *Khawaja*'s case, the House of Lords applied the principle that (in Lord Scarman's words) 'where the exercise of executive power depends upon the precedent establishment of an objective fact, the courts will decide whether the requirement has been satisfied'.[108] On this test it was not sufficient that the immigration officers believed Khawaja to be an illegal entrant; Khawaja's status as an illegal entrant was an objective fact which had to be established by evidence before the power to remove him could be exercised. This stricter test is particularly suitable when the individual's liberty is at stake.

Jurisdictional issues may involve the court not only in looking again at the evidence but also in reviewing the decisions on matters of law which were made by the tribunal. The difficulty of drawing the line between jurisdictional and non-jurisdictional matters is illustrated by the complex litigation in *Anisminic Ltd v Foreign Compensation Commission.*[109]

The Foreign Compensation Commission was a tribunal created by the Foreign Compensation Act 1950. It had rejected a claim made by a British company (Anisminic) under a scheme for compensating British subjects who had lost property in Egypt during the Suez affair in 1956. The reason for rejection was that, on the commission's interpretation of the relevant Order in Council, it was fatal to the claim that Anisminic's assets in Egypt had after 1956 been acquired by an Egyptian company, since the order required that any 'successor in title' to the British claimant had to be of British nationality. In the absence of any right to appeal, Anisminic had to establish not only that the commission's interpretation of the order was erroneous, but also that the commission's decision rejecting the claim was a nullity, since the 1950 Act excluded the power of the High Court to review errors of law made within the jurisdiction of the commission. *Held*, by a majority in the House of Lords, the commission's interpretation of the Order in Council was wrong (since the Egyptian company was not Anisminic's 'successor in title'); and that this error had caused the commission to take into account a factor (the nationality of the Egyptian company) which was irrelevant to Anisminic's claim. Thus the commission had exceeded the limits of its jurisdiction and the decision rejecting the claim was a nullity.

This decision has been much discussed.[110] The main issue for present purposes is whether the *Anisminic* case established the rule that *all* errors of law made by a tribunal cause the tribunal to exceed its jurisdiction. On a reading of the speeches in *Anisminic*, this does not seem to have been intended, but in *Pearlman v Keepers and Governors of Harrow School*, Lord Denning MR said that the distinction between an error which entails absence of jurisdiction and an error made within the jurisdiction should be aban-

---

[108]   [1984] AC at 110.
[109]   [1969] 2 AC 147; and see ch 30 below. See also *R v Home Secretary, ex p Bugdaycay* [1987] AC 514 (distinguishing *Khawaja*) and *Tan Te Lam v Superintendent of Tai Detention Centre* [1997] AC 97 (applying *Khawaja*).
[110]   See H W R Wade (1969) 85 LQR 198, B C Gould [1970] PL 358, L H Leigh [1980] PL 34.

doned and that the new rule should be that 'no court or tribunal has any jurisdiction to make an error of law on which the decision of the case depends'.[111] In supporting this view, Lord Diplock said:

> The breakthrough made by *Anisminic* was that, as respects administrative tribunals and authorities, the old distinction between errors of law that went to jurisdiction and errors of law that did not was for practical purposes abolished.[112]

Other judges for a time sought to maintain the traditional rule that tribunals may commit errors of law while remaining within their jurisdiction.[113] One reason for this could be found in the ancient remedy of certiorari, which for a long time was available to review both matters affecting jurisdiction and errors of law 'on the face of the record' ie errors of law which were apparent from the text of the tribunal's decision.[114] The implication from this was that errors of law which neither went to jurisdiction nor were apparent from the decision itself could not be reviewed. This branch of doctrine is now merely of historical interest. In *R v Hull University Visitor, ex p Page*, the House of Lords held unanimously that *Anisminic* had rendered obsolete the distinction between error of law on the face of the record and other errors of law 'by extending the doctrine of ultra vires'. Parliament must be taken to have conferred power on a tribunal subject to it being exercised 'on the correct legal basis'; a misdirection in law in making the decision therefore rendered the decision ultra vires.[115]

While all material errors of law go to jurisdiction, this does not apply to all errors of fact although, as in *Khawaja*, some key findings of fact may go to jurisdiction.[116] Moreover, even where the facts are not disputed, a reviewing court will not impose its own view on what the decision should have been if the relevant statutory criterion is 'so imprecise that different decision-makers, each acting rationally, might reach differing conclusions when applying it to the facts'.[117]

B. Procedural propriety

Even if an official decision is within the powers of the body taking it, the decision may be challenged on procedural grounds; the issue then is whether the procedural requirements on which the decision's validity depends have

---

[111] [1979] QB 56, 70 (and H F Rawlings [1979] PL 404). And see *R v Chief Immigration Officer, ex p Kharrazi* [1980] 3 All ER 373.

[112] *Re Racal Communications Ltd* [1981] AC 374, 383, and see *O'Reilly v Mackman* [1983] 2 AC 237, 278 (Lord Diplock).

[113] *Re Racal Communications Ltd* (above) at 390, and *South East Asia Fire Bricks v Non-Metallic etc Union* [1981] AC 363.

[114] *R v Northumberland Compensation Appeal Tribunal, ex p Shaw* [1952] 1 KB 388; and eg *Baldwin and Francis Ltd v Patents Appeal Tribunal* [1959] AC 663.

[115] [1993] AC 682, 701. Also held, by 3–2, that a visitor's decision could not be reviewed for alleged errors as to the internal law of the university (applied in *R v Visitors to Lincoln's Inn* [1994] QB 1).

[116] On the law/fact distinction, see W A Wilson (1963) 26 MLR 609, (1969) 32 MLR 361; E Mureinik (1982) 98 LQR 587. See also note 52 above and T H Jones [1990] PL 507.

[117] *R v Monopolies and Mergers Commission, ex p South Yorkshire Transport Ltd* [1993] 1 All ER 289 at 298 (Lord Mustill).

been observed. Many such requirements are found in the statutes which confer the power of decision. Others are derived from the common law doctrine of natural justice or, as it is now widely known, the doctrine of fairness.

Statutory requirements

Where statute authorises a certain power to be exercised after a stated procedure has been followed, failure to observe the procedure may result in the purported exercise of the power being declared a nullity.

In *Ridge v Baldwin*, the Brighton police committee summarily dismissed their chief constable following his trial at the Central Criminal Court on charges of conspiracy; his acquittal had been accompanied by serious criticism of his conduct by the trial judge. Disciplinary regulations made under the Police Act 1919 laid down a procedure by which a formal inquiry had to be held into charges brought against a chief constable before he could be dismissed. The committee contended that this procedure did not apply to the power of dismissal under the Municipal Corporations Act 1882. The House of Lords held inter alia that the disciplinary regulations did apply; 'inasmuch as the decision was arrived at in complete disregard of the regulations it must be regarded as void and of no effect'.[118]

But not every procedural error invalidates administrative action. The courts have often distinguished between procedural requirements which are mandatory (breach invalidates) and those which are directory (breach does not invalidate). But this distinction does not take account of whether there has been a total failure to observe the procedure, or substantial compliance with it; nor of whether the procedural defect caused any real prejudice to the individual.[119] In 1979, Lord Hailsham, commenting upon the distinction, suggested that the courts are faced with 'not so much a stark choice of alternatives but a spectrum of possibilities'. He continued, 'The jurisdiction is inherently discretionary, and the court is frequently in the presence of differences of degree which merge almost imperceptibly into differences of kind'.[120] In that case, a planning authority's failure to notify landowners about their right of appeal to the Secretary of State invalidated a decision by the authority which adversely affected the land.

Natural justice

The requirements of natural justice are essentially rules of the common law; on many matters they have been embodied in enacted law, for example where statutory procedures enable someone who objects to a proposed decision to be heard at a public inquiry. As an unwritten principle, natural justice evolved largely through the control exercised by the central courts over bodies of inferior jurisdiction, such as local justices and the governing bodies of

---

[118]   [1964] AC 40, 117 (Lord Morris of Borth-y-Gest).

[119]   Compare *Coney v Choyce* [1975] 1 All ER 979 (no prejudice caused by failure to notify school closure at school entrance) with *Bradbury v London Borough of Enfield* [1967] 3 All ER 434 (complete failure to notify proposed changes in composition of schools).

[120]   *London and Clydesdale Estates Ltd v Aberdeen DC* [1979] 3 All ER 876, 883; and see *R v Tower Hamlets BC, ex p Tower Hamlets Traders Assn* [1994] COD 325 and *Wang v Commissioner of Inland Revenue* [1995] 1 All ER 367.

corporations.[121] The rules of natural justice were also applied to arbitrators, and to the disciplinary functions of professional bodies and voluntary associations. With the development of new governmental powers affecting an individual's property or livelihood, natural justice served to supplement the shortcomings of legislation. Public authorities were bound to observe natural justice in many of their functions, and it was for the courts to determine the limits of this obligation. Before considering how the courts have performed this task, it is convenient first to illustrate the two main rules of natural justice with examples drawn from the ordinary courts themselves.

The rule against bias

The essence of a fair judicial decision is that it shall have been made by an impartial judge. The main rule against bias[122] is that disqualification of a judge from acting in a particular case can arise in two ways: (*a*) where he or she has any direct pecuniary interest, however small, in the subject matter of inquiry – thus a judge who is a shareholder in a company appearing before him or her as a litigant must decline to hear the case, save by consent of all the parties;[123] (*b*) where, apart from direct pecuniary interest, there is a real danger, in the sense of a real likelihood or possibility, that the judge or tribunal member would have a bias for or against one of the parties.[124] Where bias is alleged, the reviewing court does not have to decide whether the decision was in fact biased, since 'bias operates in such an insidious manner that the person alleged to be biased may be quite unconscious of its effect'.[125] Lord Hewart's much-quoted dictum, that it is 'of fundamental importance that justice should not only be done but should manifestly and undoubtedly be seen to be done', comes from *R v Sussex Justices, ex p McCarthy*.

The acting clerk to the justices was a member of a firm of solicitors who were to represent the plaintiff in civil proceedings as a result of a collision in connection with which the applicant was summoned for a motoring offence. The acting clerk retired with the bench, but was not asked to advise the justices on their decision to convict the applicant. *Held*, that, as the clerk's firm was connected with the case in the civil action, he ought not to advise the justices in the criminal matter and therefore could not, had he been required to do so, properly have discharged his duties as clerk. The conviction was accordingly quashed, despite the fact that the clerk had taken no part in the decision to convict.[126]

To disqualify a person from acting in a judicial capacity, an unreasonable suspicion of bias is not enough, particularly when further facts could readily

---

[121]   Ch 26 above; and see de Smith, Woolf and Jowell, op cit, chs 7–12; Wade and Forsyth, op cit, chs 13–15; Craig, op cit, chs 8, 9; Flick, *Natural Justice*.

[122]   *R v Rand* (1866) LR 1 QB 230; *R v Sunderland Justices* [1901] 2 KB 357; and *Wildridge v Anderson* (1897) 25 R (J) 27.

[123]   *Dimes v Grand Junction Canal (Proprietors of)* (1852) 3 HLC 759. And see R Cranston [1979] PL 237. Cf *R v Mulvihill* [1990] 1 WLR 438 (judge's shareholding in bank no bar to conducting trial of bank robber).

[124]   *R v Gough* [1993] AC 646 (juror realised after G had been convicted that she lived next door to his brother).

[125]   Ibid at 672 (Lord Woolf).

[126]   [1924] 1 KB 256; cf *R v Rand* (above).

have been verified.[127] It was formerly uncertain whether in establishing bias it was enough that an observer had a reasonable suspicion that members of the tribunal might be biased, or whether it must be shown that there was a real likelihood of bias.

In *Metropolitan Properties Ltd v Lannon*, a rent assessment committee had fixed the rent for three flats in one block of flats. The chairman of the committee was a solicitor who lived with his father in a second block of flats owned by the same property group. The chairman's firm was negotiating about rents with the landlords on behalf of his father and other tenants in the second block. *Held*, that the decision of the committee must be quashed. 'No man can be an advocate for or against a party in one proceedings, and at the same time sit as a judge of that party in another proceeding.'[128]

This outcome was correct, but the court's judgments left doubt as to the proper test[129] and differing tests were applied to justices, tribunal members and jurors. Since *R v Gough*, the single test applying to all persons acting in a judicial capacity (in the absence of a pecuniary interest) is the 'real danger' test, namely whether, in all the circumstances ascertained by the reviewing court, there was a real likelihood, in the sense of a real possibility, of bias.[130]

The right to a fair hearing

It is equally fundamental to a just decision that each party should have the opportunity of knowing the case against him or her and of stating his or her case. Both parties must have the chance to present their version of the facts and to make submissions on the relevant rules of law. Each side must be able to comment on all material considered by the judge, and neither side must communicate with the judge behind the other's back. Although the rules of court procedure embody these general principles, there is scope for the unwritten right to a hearing to operate even in the courts. Thus the High Court cannot order a solicitor personally to bear costs caused by his or her misconduct without giving the solicitor an opportunity to meet the complaint,[131] nor can a witness to proceedings for assault be bound over to keep the peace unless the magistrates give him or her an opportunity of being heard.[132] The requirements of natural justice are not invariable: although a party to civil proceedings is normally entitled to know all the material considered by the judge, the nature of the High Court's jurisdiction over children is such that in exceptional cases the judge may take into account confidential medical reports on the children which are not disclosed to the parents.[133] But the Court of Appeal acted in breach of natural justice when in

---

127   Cf *R v Camborne Justices, ex p Pearce* [1955] 1 QB 41.
128   [1969] 1 QB 577, 600.
129   Eg *R v Altrincham Justices, ex p Pennington* [1975] QB 549; and see F Alexis [1979] PL 143.
130   See *R v Inner West London Coroner, ex p Dallaglio* [1994] 4 All ER 139 (coroner's refusal to resume inquest into *Marchioness* disaster quashed for bias); and *R v Environment Secretary, ex p Kirkstall Valley Campaign Ltd* (below).
131   *Abraham v Jutsun* [1963] 2 All ER 402. And Rules of the Supreme Court, Order 62, r 11(4).
132   *Sheldon v Bromfield Justices* [1964] 2 QB 573; cf *R v Woking Justices, ex p Gossage* [1973] QB 448.
133   *Re K (Infants)* [1965] AC 201. Contrast *McMichael v UK* (1995) 20 EHRR 205.

a case concerning the wardship of children the court read and acted upon a letter by a social worker which the parties had not seen.[134]

Natural justice and administrative authorities

The rules of natural justice have had a notable effect on many decisions made outside the ordinary courts. From them is derived the important emphasis now made in administrative law on the duty of public authorities to act fairly in making decisions. The question that was often asked was whether in reaching a particular decision there was a duty to observe the rules of natural justice. Thus, if the exercise of power affected a person's rights, property or character, it was more likely to be subject to natural justice; so was a decision which followed a procedure involving the confrontation of two opposing views, in a manner resembling litigation.[135] Thus a university may not impose penalties upon students or senior members without informing them of the charges and giving an opportunity of answering them.[136] Nor can a trade union expel members without giving him or her adequate notice of the charges giving rise to expulsion.[137] The same principle was applied in a classic 19th-century decision to action by a local authority under statutory powers directed against an individual's property.

In *Cooper v Wandsworth Board of Works*, the plaintiff recovered from the board damages in trespass for demolishing his partly-built house. He had failed to notify his intention to build the house to the board, which by statute thereupon had power to demolish the building. *Held*, that the board should have given a hearing to the plaintiff before exercising their statutory power of demolition. 'Although there are no positive words in a statute requiring that the party shall be heard, yet the justice of the common law shall supply the omission of the legislature'.[138]

In a similar manner the rule against bias has been applied to local authorities. Thus a local authority's decision to grant planning permission for the development of an amusement park by a private company was declared to be void because the council had previously made a contract with the company by which it was liable to the company in damages if planning permission was not granted.[139] When an education sub-committee had confirmed a decision by the governors of a school to terminate a teacher's employment, the decision was quashed because the fact that three members of the sub-committee were also governors of the school gave rise to the possibility of bias.[140] And when the Barnsley markets committee revoked a stallholder's licence for a trivial and isolated misdemeanour, that decision was also

---

134 *B v W, Wardship: Appeal* [1979] 3 All ER 83.
135 See R B Cooke [1954] CLJ 14. Cf *Durayappah v Fernando* [1967] 2 AC 337, 349, and see G D S Taylor (1975) 1 Monash Univ LR 258.
136 *Dr Bentley*'s case (1723) 1 Stra 557; see also *Ceylon University v Fernando* [1960] 1 All ER 631.
137 *Annamunthodo v Oilfield Workers' TU* [1961] AC 945; cf *Breen v AEU* [1971] 2 QB 175.
138 (1863) 14 CB (NS) 180, 194 (Byles J).
139 *Steeples v Derbyshire CC* [1984] 3 All ER 486, distinguished in *R v Amber Valley DC, ex p Jackson* [1984] 3 All ER 501. See also *R v Environment Secretary, ex p Kirkstall Valley Campaign Ltd* [1996] 3 All ER 304 (rule in *R v Gough* applied to members of urban development corporation).
140 *Hannam v Bradford Corpn* [1970] 2 All ER 690.

quashed: not only did the committee hear the evidence of the market manager (who was in the position of a prosecutor) in the absence of the stallholder, but the manager was present throughout the committee's deliberations.[141]

Natural justice and ministers' powers

The older instances of natural justice date from the period before the development of modern government. Today the granting of new powers is often accompanied by complex procedures designed to reconcile executive needs with safeguards for the individual. To what extent may additional unwritten rules of fair procedure be applied by the courts?[142] Is the rule that no person should be judge in their own cause relevant if the settlement of disputes arising from the execution of policy is entrusted to the minister whose department is responsible for that policy? There are some powers where the courts have allowed little scope for natural justice, notably the powers of the Home Secretary in relation to the deportation of aliens where aspects of national security are affected.[143] Where ministers' powers have involved public inquiries, the courts have had to decide how far common law principles of natural justice may supplement the procedure adopted by the department in question. In 1915, the House of Lords in *Local Government Board v Arlidge* held that natural justice required little more from a department than the carrying out in good faith of its usual procedures.

The Hampstead council had made a closing order in respect of a house which appeared unfit for human habitation. The owner, Arlidge, exercised a statutory right of appealing to the Local Government Board. A public inquiry was held before an inspector and, after receiving his report, the board confirmed the closing order. Arlidge applied to the court to declare the decision invalid, on the grounds that the board did not disclose which official of the board actually decided the appeal; that he, Arlidge, had not been heard orally by that official; and that he had not seen the report of the inspector who conducted the public inquiry. The House of Lords rejected these claims, holding that Parliament, having entrusted judicial duties to an executive body, must be taken to have intended it to follow the procedure which was its own and was necessary if it was to be capable of doing its work efficiently. So long as the officials dealt with the question referred to them without bias, and gave the parties an adequate opportunity of presenting the case, the board could follow its own established procedures, even though they were not those of a court of law.[144]

Similarly, in *Board of Education v Rice* it was held that in disposing of an appeal the Board of Education was bound to act in good faith and to listen fairly to both sides, since that was a duty which lay on everyone who decided anything. The board was not, however, bound to follow the procedure of a trial. It could obtain information in any way it thought best, always giving a fair opportunity to those who were parties in the controversy to correct or contradict any relevant statement prejudicial to their view.[145]

These decisions of the House of Lords did not mean that departments were

---

141   *R v Barnsley Council, ex p Hook* [1976] 3 All ER 452.
142   See *Wiseman v Borneman* [1971] AC 297, 308 (Lord Reid); *Lloyd v McMahon* (note 173, below).
143   See eg *R v Home Secretary, ex p Cheblak* [1991] 2 All ER 319. And ch 20 B.
144   [1915] AC 120.
145   [1911] AC 179.

totally freed from the duty to observe the essentials of fair procedure. In the 1930s, in litigation concerned with procedures for slum clearance and the compulsory purchase of land, the courts found great difficulty in applying common law rules of natural justice to the duties of the minister. In *Errington v Minister of Health*, the court quashed a slum clearance order made by the Jarrow council: the facts were that, after the public inquiry into the order had been held, private discussions took place between council officials and civil servants, and a Whitehall official visited the houses affected in the presence of council officials but without informing the owner. The court held that an order made in such circumstances was in breach of natural justice.[146] In such cases, the courts attempted to distinguish between the judicial and administrative functions of the minister. Thus the judges accepted that the final decision of the minister could be based on matters of policy, and was thus administrative, but asserted that the department exercised judicial or quasi-judicial functions at the public inquiry stage.[147] This approach was called into question in *Franklin v Minister of Town and Country Planning*, where under the New Towns Act 1946 a public inquiry had been held into objections to a controversial draft order that the minister had made designating Stevenage as a new town. Rejecting the objectors' argument that the minister was biased in confirming his own order, the House of Lords held that there was no evidence that the minister had not genuinely considered the report of the inspector on the inquiry. The House also stated that at no stage was a judicial or quasi-judicial duty imposed on the minister: his duty to consider the inspector's report was purely administrative.[148] It is hard to reconcile this analysis with cases such as *Errington v Minister of Health*, save for the obvious distinction between a minister required to consider a scheme initiated by a local authority, and the new towns procedure by which a minister must decide whether to uphold his own scheme or give way to the objectors.[149] However, at common law the right of owners to be heard in defence of their rights did not depend on the two-tier situation of a central department confirming the proposals of a local authority.[150]

Today, as a direct consequence of the Franks report in 1957, most public inquiries are governed by detailed procedural rules which set high standards of fairness.[151] But such rules have not been applied to all public inquiries; and common law rules of natural justice may still be relevant. In 1976, a decision of the Secretary of State confirming a compulsory purchase order was held to be in breach of natural justice, since it was based on an opinion formed by the inspector on a matter which had never been considered at the public inquiry.[152] But in *Bushell v Secretary of State for the Environment*, which concerned a controversial motorway inquiry, the House of Lords adopted an approach which, as in *Franklin*'s case, stressed the administrative character of the

---

[146]   [1935] 1 KB 249.
[147]   This followed the analysis made in the Ministers' Powers Report, ch 26 above.
[148]   [1948] AC 87.
[149]   See H W R Wade (1949) 10 CLJ 216 and cf *Wednesbury Corpn v Ministry of Housing* [1966] 2 QB 275.
[150]   *Ridge v Baldwin* [1964] AC 40, 72–3 (Lord Reid).
[151]   See ch 28 B.
[152]   *Fairmount Investments Ltd v Environment Secretary* [1976] 2 All ER 865.

minister's decision and protected crucial aspects of the official process from full investigation at the inquiry.[153]

The present scope of natural justice

The importance of natural justice in the judicial review of administrative action has not been in doubt since the landmark decision of the House of Lords in *Ridge v Baldwin,* which as we saw above also involved a failure to observe statutory procedures.

In this case the Court of Appeal had held that natural justice did not require the Brighton police committee to grant the chief constable a hearing before the committee exercised its power to dismiss 'any constable whom they think negligent in the exercise of his duty or otherwise unfit for the same';[154] in dismissing the chief constable, 'the defendants were acting in an administrative or executive capacity just as they did when they appointed him'.[155] The House of Lords overruled this view: quite apart from the procedure laid down by the discipline regulations, natural justice required that a hearing should have been given before the committee exercised its power. The failure to give a hearing invalidated the dismissal, and the subsequent hearing given to Ridge's solicitor did not cure the earlier defect.[156]

This decision could have been regarded narrowly as an interpretation of a particular statute. In fact, *Ridge v Baldwin* was the first of a group of House of Lords decisions during the 1960s which laid the foundations for the operation of judicial review today. Of first importance was the holding in *Ridge* that the duty to observe natural justice was not confined to powers classified as 'judicial' or 'quasi-judicial'. Since 1964, courts have applied the principles of natural justice in a very wide variety of situations. By 1970, this development led Megarry J to remark that the courts were tending to apply principles of natural justice to all powers of decision unless the circumstances indicated to the contrary.[157] The benefits of *Ridge v Baldwin* have spread to many other persons, including students,[158] police officers,[159] school teachers,[160] market stallholders,[161] residents of local authority homes at risk of closure,[162] those affected by decisions of self-regulatory bodies,[163] and, most notably, convicted

---

153 [1981] AC 75; ch 28 B above.
154 Municipal Corporations Act 1882, s 191(4).
155 [1963] 1 QB 539, 576 (Harman LJ).
156 [1964] AC 40; and see A W Bradley [1964] CLJ 83.
157 *Gaiman v National Association for Mental Health* [1971] Ch 317, 333 (power to expel members of company limited by guarantee); cf *Bates v Lord Hailsham* [1972] 3 All ER 1019 (delegated legislation).
158 Eg *R v Aston University Senate, ex p Roffey* [1969] 2 QB 538; and *Glynn v Keele University* [1971] 2 All ER 89. And see, on the visitor's jurisdiction, P M Smith (1981) 97 LQR 610; *Thomas v University of Bradford* [1987] AC 795; and (as to judicial review) *R v Hull University Visitor, ex p Page* [1993] AC 682.
159 *R v Kent Police Authority, ex p Godden* [1971] 2 QB 662; *Chief Constable of North Wales v Evans* [1982] 3 All ER 141.
160 *Hannam v Bradford Corpn* [1970] 2 All ER 690; *Malloch v Aberdeen Corpn* [1971] 2 All ER 1278.
161 *R v Barnsley Council, ex p Hook* [1976] 3 All ER 452; *R v Wear Valley Council, ex p Binks* [1985] 2 All ER 699.
162 *R v Devon CC, ex p Baker* [1995] 1 All ER 73.
163 *R v LAUTRO, ex p Ross* [1993] QB 17; and A Lidbetter [1992] PL 533.

prisoners in respect of prison discipline and the parole system.[164] In 1980, on an appeal from the Bahamas concerning refusal of an individual's constitutional right to citizenship, the Judicial Committee held that natural justice must be observed by any person with authority to determine questions affecting the rights of individuals.[165] But natural justice is not limited to situations in which individuals can show that their private rights are in issue, and the courts protect a wide variety of individual interests against unfair action by public bodies.[166]

Fairness and natural justice

The scope of natural justice is best understood against the broad perception that it is the duty of the courts to ensure that *all* administrative powers are exercised fairly, that is, in accordance with principles of fair procedure. It has always been difficult to describe the contents of natural justice except in general terms. As Tucker LJ said in 1949:

> There are ... no words which are of universal application to every kind of inquiry and every kind of domestic tribunal. The requirements of natural justice must depend on the circumstances of the case, the nature of the inquiry, the rules under which the tribunal is acting, the subject-matter that is being dealt with and so forth.[167]

In *Ridge v Baldwin*, in rebutting the view that natural justice was so vague as to be meaningless, Lord Reid referred to the test of what a reasonable person would regard as fair procedure in given circumstances.[168] In 1967, in *Re HK*, which concerned the kind of inquiry that an immigration officer should make when seeking to discover the age of a potential immigrant, Lord Parker CJ said that good administration required that the immigration officer should act fairly: 'only to that limited extent do the so-called rules of natural justice apply, which in a case such as this is merely a duty to act fairly'.[169] Even where an executive body does not need to conduct an adversarial hearing before reaching a decision, it must act fairly.[170]

Many judges have explained natural justice purely in terms of fairness.[171] Lord Diplock stated that whenever statutes give power to make decisions which 'affect to their detriment the rights of other persons or curtail their liberty to do as they please', Parliament is presumed to have intended that the administrative body should act fairly towards them.[172] In 1988, the position was summarised by Lord Bridge in *Lloyd v McMahon*:

---

[164] Eg *R v Hull Prison Visitors, ex p St Germain* [1978] QB 678 and *(No 2)* [1979] 3 All ER 545; *Leech v Deputy Governor of Parkhurst Prison* [1988] AC 533; *R v Home Secretary, ex p Tarrant* [1985] 1 QB 251; and *R v Home Secretary, ex p Doody* [1994] 1 AC 531.

[165] *A-G v Ryan* [1980] AC 718.

[166] Cf *O'Reilly v Mackman* [1983] 2 AC 237, 275, 283 (Lord Diplock). For the protection of new social interests, see eg *R v Wandsworth Council, ex p P* (1989) 87 LGR 370; *R v Norfolk CC Social Services Dept, ex p M* [1989] 2 QB 619.

[167] *Russell v Duke of Norfolk* [1949] 1 All ER 109, 118.

[168] [1964] AC 40 at 65.

[169] [1967] 2 QB 617, 630, applied in *R v Home Secretary, ex p Mughal* [1974] QB 313.

[170] *Pearlberg v Varty* [1972] 2 All ER 6.

[171] Eg *Wiseman v Borneman* [1971] AC 297 (especially Lord Morris); *Maxwell v Dept of Trade* [1974] QB 523; and *Selvarajan v Race Relations Board* [1976] 1 All ER 12. See also D H Clark [1975] PL 27; C P Seepersad [1975] PL 242.

[172] *R v Commission for Racial Equality, ex p Hillingdon Council* [1982] AC 779, 787.

[The] so-called rules of natural justice are not engraved on tablets of stone. To use the phrase which better expresses the underlying concept, what the requirements of fairness demand when any body, domestic, administrative or judicial, has to make a decision which will affect the rights of individuals depends on the character of the decision-making body, the kind of decision it has to make and the statutory or other framework in which it operates. In particular, it is well established that when a statute has conferred on any body the power to make decisions affecting individuals, the courts will not only require the procedure prescribed by the statute to be followed, but will readily imply so much and no more to be introduced by way of additional procedural safeguards as will ensure the attainment of fairness.[173]

In *Lloyd v McMahon* itself, local councillors who were in breach of duty by preventing their council from setting the level of local rates, claimed the opportunity of making oral representations to the district auditor before statutory sanctions were imposed. It was held that the auditor had acted fairly, as he had given them notice of the case against them and had received and considered their written representations. In 1993, concerning parole for convicted murderers serving mandatory life sentences, Lord Mustill said that it was for the courts 'to decide what the elements of fairness demand' in the regime by which Home Secretaries had chosen to exercise their powers; he stressed that standards of fairness are not immutable and depend on the context of those powers.[174]

The procedural effects of natural justice and fairness

Assuming that natural justice or fairness must be observed before a decision is taken, what in practical terms must the public authority do? A great deal depends on the nature of the decision. In a situation where a public office or other benefit is being withdrawn for reasons of misconduct or incompetence, the 'irreducible minimum' at the core of natural justice is (*a*) the right to a decision by an unbiased tribunal; (*b*) the right to have notice of the charges against the individual; and (*c*) the right to be heard in answer to those charges.[175]

In cases where no misconduct is alleged (for example, in the case of school or residential home closures, where parents or residents must in fairness be consulted by the local authority), then (*a*) the process must take place at a time when the proposals are at a formative stage; (*b*) sufficient reasons must be given for the proposal to permit intelligent consideration and response; (*c*) adequate time must be allowed; and (*d*) the product of consultation must be conscientiously taken into account.[176]

Many detailed procedural questions arise to which there are no general answers. We have seen that in some contexts individuals do not have the right of an oral hearing,[177] but if the body in question has to decide questions as to someone's conduct or competence, the individual is entitled to know what evidence is given against him or her and must have a fair opportunity to rebut

---

[173]   [1987] AC 625, 702–3.
[174]   *R v Home Secretary, ex p Doody* [1994] 1 AC 531, 557.
[175]   Lord Hodson in *Ridge v Baldwin* [1964] AC 40, at 132.
[176]   *R v Brent Council, ex p Gunning* (1985) 84 LGR 168 (P Meredith [1988] PL 4); and *R v Devon CC, ex p Baker* [1995] 1 All ER 73.
[177]   *Lloyd v McMahon* [1987] AC 625.

it.[178] Regulatory bodies that expect officials to do preliminary work for them must nonetheless be in a position to come to their own decisions.[179] Where a soldier claimed that he had been subject to racial harassment, members of the Army Board could not decide on the complaint judicially without meeting to consider the matter; and the soldier was entitled to see all the material on which the Board reached its decision, other than documents for which public interest immunity was properly claimed.[180] An individual has no universal right to be legally represented regardless of the nature of the proceedings in question,[181] but there may be circumstances in which a body with power to permit legal representation may not reasonably refuse it.[182] No breach of natural justice occurs when the opportunity of being heard is lost through the fault of a party's lawyer.[183]

There is no absolute rule that natural justice does not apply in the case of preliminary investigations, inspections or suspensions pending a final decision,[184] but the right to a hearing is often excluded because of the need for urgent action or because the individual's rights will be observed at a later stage.[185]

Many aspects of procedure raise issues of fairness: thus it may be unfair for a tribunal to refuse adjournment of a hearing.[186] The manner in which evidence is obtained by tribunals is subject to constraints of natural justice[187] but hearsay evidence is usually permitted.[188] Natural justice may entitle a party to cross-examine those giving evidence against him or her[189] or obtain the names of potential witnesses from the other side.[190] But it is sometimes sufficient that only the gist of allegations against an individual is made known.[191] Considerations of national security may seriously reduce the scope for natural justice.[192] It has been held contrary to natural justice for a commission of inquiry with investigative powers to make findings of fact that individuals have been guilty of serious misconduct, when the findings are supported by no evidence of

---

[178]　*Kanda v Government of Malaya* [1962] AC 322; *Chief Constable of North Wales v Evans* [1982] 3 All ER 141.

[179]　*Selvarajan v Race Relations Board* [1976] 1 All ER 12; and *R v Commission for Racial Equality, ex p Cottrell and Rothon* [1980] 3 All ER 265.

[180]　*R v Army Board of Defence Council, ex p Anderson* [1992] QB 169.

[181]　*R v Maze Prison Visitors, ex p Hone* [1988] AC 379.

[182]　*R v Home Secretary, ex p Tarrant* [1985] QB 251.

[183]　*R v Home Secretary, ex p Al-Mehdawi* [1990] 1 AC 876 (and J Herberg [1990] PL 467).

[184]　*Rees v Crane* [1994] 2 AC 173 (Trinidad judge entitled to notice of complaints against him at initial stage of dismissal procedure).

[185]　*Wiseman v Borneman* [1971] AC 297, *Furnell v Whangarei High Schools Board* [1973] AC 660, *Norwest Holst Ltd v Trade Secretary* [1978] Ch 201.

[186]　Eg *Priddle v Fisher* [1968] 3 All ER 506.

[187]　*R v Deputy Industrial Injuries Commissioner, ex p Moore* [1965] 1 QB 456, *Crompton v General Medical Council* [1982] 1 All ER 35.

[188]　*T A Miller Ltd v Minister of Housing* [1968] 2 All ER 633.

[189]　*R v Board of Visitors, ex p St Germain (No 2)* [1979] 3 All ER 545. Cf *R v Commission for Racial Equality, ex p Cottrell and Rothon* (above).

[190]　*R v Blundeston Board of Visitors, ex p Fox-Taylor* [1982] 1 All ER 646.

[191]　*R v Gaming Board, ex p Benaim and Khaida* [1970] 2 QB 417; *Maxwell v Dept of Trade* [1974] QB 523.

[192]　*R v Home Secretary, ex p Hosenball* [1977] 3 All ER 452; *R v Home Secretary, ex p Cheblak* [1991] 2 All ER 319.

probative value and individuals have had no opportunity to rebut them.[193] Fairness does not in general require reasons to be given for decisions, but may sometimes do so.[194]

Three matters may be mentioned briefly. First, if fairness or natural justice would otherwise entitle someone to be heard, a court should be slow to brush aside that right on the ground that a hearing would make no difference to the outcome.[195] The second matter is whether the failure by an authority to give a hearing to which the individual is entitled is cured by a full and fair hearing given later by an appellate body. No absolute rule can be laid down on this matter; sometimes the appeal proceedings may take the form of a full re-hearing and this may cure the earlier defect, but in other situations the individual may be entitled to a fair hearing at both stages. In intermediate cases, the court must decide 'whether, at the end of the day, there has been a fair result, reached by fair methods'.[196]

The third difficulty concerns the legal effect, if any, of a decision reached in breach of natural justice. When a breach of natural justice is established, then it was held in *Ridge v Baldwin* that the decision in question is void and a nullity. In *Durayappah v Fernando*, however, the Judicial Committee held that failure to give a hearing when one was due made the decision voidable and not void.[197] This decision was plainly contrary to legal principle. In 1979, the Judicial Committee accepted that a decision reached in breach of natural justice was void rather than voidable, but added that until it was declared to be void by a court it was capable of having some effect in law and could be the basis of an appeal to a higher body.[198]

Fairness and legitimate expectations

Accompanying judicial reliance on fairness has been the evolving concept of legitimate expectations.[199] A concept by this name exists in many other systems of public law (including those of Australia, Germany and the EU).[200] The link in English law between fairness and legitimate expectations has not always been clear, but the courts have invoked the latter concept to justify imposing a duty to act fairly in public law. In 1969, Lord Denning MR distinguished (obiter) between aliens required to leave Britain when their leave to remain expired, and aliens whose leave to remain was terminated by the Home Office prematurely: the latter, but not the former, had a 'legitimate

---

193   *Mahon v Air New Zealand Ltd* [1984] AC 808.
194   Note 77 above.
195   *John v Rees* [1970] Ch 345, 402; and *R v Chief Constable, Thames Valley, ex p Cotton* [1990] IRLR 344, 352.
196   *Calvin v Carr* [1980] AC 574, discussed by M Elliott (1980) 43 MLR 66.
197   [1967] 2 AC 337, criticised by H W R Wade (1967) 83 LQR 499 and (1968) 84 LQR 95; see M B Akehurst (1968) 31 MLR 2, 128, and D Oliver [1981] CLP 43.
198   *Calvin v Carr* (above). And see S Sedley [1989] PL 32.
199   See R Baldwin and D Horne (1986) 49 MLR 685; P Elias, in Jowell and Oliver (eds), *New Directions in Judicial Review*, pp 37–50; C F Forsyth [1988] CLJ 238; P P Craig (1992) 108 LQR 79.
200   See Schwarze, *European Administrative Law*, ch 6. In *Minister of State for Immigration v Teoh* (1995) 128 ALR 353, the High Court of Australia held that ratification of an unincorporated treaty created a legitimate expectation that executive decisions would conform to the treaty. See R Piotrowicz [1996] PL 190; and ch 15 B.

expectation, of which it would not be fair to deprive [them] without hearing what [they have] to say'.[201] In contrast, where unlicensed cab-drivers had frequently been convicted for breaching regulations at Heathrow, Lord Denning held that in view of their conduct they could not have had a legitimate expectation of being heard before byelaws were made excluding them from the airport.[202]

Two propositions are well established. First, an express undertaking by a public body to receive and consider representations may entitle the individual to a hearing on the matters in question: 'when a public authority has promised to follow a certain procedure, it is in the interest of good administration that it should act fairly and implement its promise, so long as implementation does not interfere with its statutory duty'.[203] If the individuals would otherwise have no right to be heard, it will be vital for them to show that such an undertaking was given.

Secondly, the consistent practice of a public authority in consulting with those affected before changing its policies may give rise to a legitimate expectation of consultation, as it did in the *GCHQ* case over civil service conditions of employment.[204]

What if there has been no express undertaking and no consistent practice? In 1984, Lord Diplock stated that the law may protect legitimate expectations which arise where individuals have been permitted to enjoy a benefit or advantage which they can reasonably expect to continue until some rational ground for withdrawing it has been communicated to them on which they have been able to comment.[205] It has indeed been held to be unfair for a public authority to withdraw certain benefits without affording an opportunity of consultation.[206] However, since the entitlement to a hearing or consultation here may be inferred from the nature of the benefit itself, reliance on a 'legitimate expectation' adds nothing to the proposition that before such a benefit is withdrawn the authority must act fairly. Indeed, there is no need for the law on fairness to be re-stated in terms of legitimate expectations.[207]

Other matters relating to legitimate expectations are still evolving. First, when the term 'fair' is used in this context, it relates essentially to the procedure to be followed and does not generally go to the substance of the decision itself.[208] Certainly, decisions may be manifestly 'unfair' if, for example, they are biased, discriminatory, partial or malicious,[209] but these will in

---

[201]   *Schmidt v Home Secretary* [1969] 2 Ch 149; also *McInnes v Onslow-Fane* [1978] 3 All ER 211.

[202]   *Cinnamond v British Airports Authority* [1980] 2 All ER 368.

[203]   *A-G of Hong Kong v Ng Yuen Shiu* [1983] AC 629, 638 (Lord Fraser); and *R v Liverpool Corpn, ex p Liverpool Taxi Operators Association* [1972] 2 QB 299.

[204]   *CCSU v Minister for Civil Service* [1985] AC 374, 401 (Lord Fraser); and see *R v Brent Council, ex p Gunning* (1985) 84 LGR 168.

[205]   *CCSU v Minister for Civil Service* [1985] AC 374, 408 (Lord Diplock).

[206]   Eg *R v Devon CC, ex p Baker* [1995] 1 All ER 73.

[207]   See *R v Devon CC, ex p Baker* (above) at 89, citing *A-G for New South Wales v Quin* (1990) 93 ALR 1.

[208]   See *R v Barnsley Council, ex p Hook* [1976] 3 All ER 452; *Chief Constable of North Wales v Evans* [1982] 3 All ER 141.

[209]   *R v IRC, ex p National Federation of Self-Employed* [1982] AC 617, 650 (Lord Scarman). And see *HTV Ltd v Price Commission* [1976] ICR 170.

any event be ultra vires. Secondly, while a legitimate expectation may arise from enjoying an existing benefit or advantage, that expectation is in general protected by the court requiring the administration to observe a certain procedure, not by requiring it to provide a particular, substantive outcome. However, there are authorities to the effect that the court may attribute a substantive content to what is legitimately expected.[210]

Finally, it is sometimes argued that a legitimate expectation arises from current policy which may prevent the public body from changing that policy for the future. In principle, such an argument will fail: where the Home Secretary changed his policy on parole for convicted prisoners, with the effect that certain serving prisoners ceased to be eligible for parole, it was held that all that a prisoner could expect was that his case would be examined in the light of whatever lawful policy the Home Secretary saw fit to adopt.[211] However, the effect of a proposed change in policy may require those affected to be consulted[212] and a failure by the policy-maker to consider effects of the change could be a ground for judicial review by those affected. In Community law, because of the need for legal certainty, a public authority may be restricted from making changes in its substantive policies which adversely affect accrued interests.[213]

C.   Binding nature of official acts[214]

In their dealings with government agencies, private persons often need to know if they can rely on statements made to them by officials, or on decisions which have been notified to them. In business and commercial affairs, an individual is entitled to hold others to their word when a *contract* has been concluded between them. But official decisions like the issue of a licence, the granting of planning permission or the payment of a subsidy usually do not take a contractual form. When is a citizen entitled to hold a public authority to its word, or to the word of one of its officials? Is an authority free to change its mind, or to disavow an official whose conduct has led the citizen to believe that the authority has made a certain decision?

These questions raise a wide variety of issues, and answers to them take diverse legal forms. It is not possible to treat informal advice, assurances about future conduct, misleading statements, properly taken decisions and errors in communicating decisions as if they all had the same legal effect.[215] Here it is possible only to outline a few of the situations which may arise; one issue in

---

210   *R v Home Secretary, ex p Ruddock* [1987] 2 All ER 518; *R v Ministry of Agriculture, ex p Hamble Fisheries Ltd* [1995] 2 All ER 714, 723–4 (Sedley J). Also Forsyth (note 199 above) and section C below.

211   *Re Findlay* [1985] AC 318; *R v Home Secretary, ex p Hargreaves* [1997] 1 All ER 397.

212   *R v Health Secretary, ex p US Tobacco International Inc* [1992] QB 353 (B Schwehr and P Brown [1991] PL 163).

213   See Schwarze, op cit, ch 6, and *R v Ministry of Agriculture* (above); but note *R v Home Secretary, ex p Hargreaves* (above).

214   See P P Craig (1977) 93 LQR 398, A W Bradley [1981] CLP 1 and M Akehurst [1982] PL 613. And, for contrasting accounts, Craig, *Administrative Law*, ch 18, and Cane, *Administrative Law*, ch 10.

215   Cf M A Fazal [1972] PL 43.

these situations is sometimes stated to be whether or not a public body is subject to the doctrine of estoppel in administrative matters, but this formulation of the difficulty is no more satisfactory than other attempts to produce a clear-cut line between private and public law.

First, if an official agency takes a decision affecting the rights of the citizen and communicates it to that person, without qualifying it by words such as 'provisional' or 'subject to review', the agency has exercised its discretion in the matter and may not thereafter alter the decision to the citizen's disadvantage.[216] This general principle applies subject to express statutory provision. Thus in tax and social security matters the statutes give express authority for reviewing decisions, for example when fresh information is available.[217] Some statutes provide that when a decision has been made, for example to grant planning permission for development, it may be revoked only on payment of compensation.[218] Apart from such provision, a public authority which has conferred a continuing discretionary benefit upon an individual under a mistake of fact may revoke the benefit for the future once it has discovered the true position.[219] Where the error is one of law (for example, if an agency refused to award a benefit because of an interpretation of a statute which is later held in another case to be wrong), the agency may take a fresh decision based on the correct view of the law; under some circumstances, it must do so.[220]

Secondly, where there has been a full inquiry by proper procedure resulting in a considered decision (say, as to the status of certain land in planning law, on which there has been an appeal to the Secretary of State), the decision may under a principle analogous to 'res judicata' be binding on the parties by what has been called a 'cause of action' estoppel.[221]

Thirdly, as we have already seen, an assurance about its future conduct given to citizens by a public authority may, on principles of fairness, be held to bind the authority where the assurance is compatible with the authority's statutory duties.[222] In clear cases, the courts may protect the legitimate expectations created by such assurances. Where a Nigerian woman in the United Kingdom wished to return home for Christmas and was given a firm assurance by the Home Office (confirmed in her passport) that she could come back to Britain by 31 January, the immigration officer could not refuse to admit her when she returned from Nigeria before that date.[223] When the Home Office stated the criteria that it would apply in deciding whether to permit children to come into the United Kingdom for adoption and this statement was relied on, it could not in that case apply more restrictive criteria, although it could change its policy for the future.[224] As Bingham LJ said in 1989,

---

[216]   *Re 56 Denton Road Twickenham* [1953] Ch 51; and see G Ganz [1965] PL 237.
[217]   Eg Social Security Administration Act 1992, ss 25, 30.
[218]   Town and Country Planning Act 1992, ss 97, 107.
[219]   *Rootkin v Kent CC* [1981] 2 All ER 227.
[220]   *Cheung v Herts CC, The Times,* 4 April 1986; C Lewis [1987] PL 21.
[221]   *Thrasyvoulou v Environment Secretary* [1990] 2 AC 273.
[222]   See note 203 above.
[223]   *R v Home Secretary, ex p Oloniluyi* [1989] Imm AR 135.
[224]   *R v Home Secretary, ex p Khan* [1985] 1 All ER 40 (A R Mowbray [1985] PL 558).

If a public authority so conducts itself as to create a legitimate expectation that a certain course will be followed it would often be unfair if the authority were permitted to follow a different course to the detriment of one who entertained the expectation.[225]

Where the Inland Revenue give a prior assurance to a taxpayer as to how a transaction will be treated, the Revenue are bound by it if in dealings between private persons it would create a contractual duty or an estoppel.[226] However, the taxpayer must have 'put all his cards face upwards on the table', and the statement relied on must be 'clear, unambiguous and devoid of relevant qualification'.[227] Even in the absence of a representation, the Revenue's previous practice may disable it from enforcing a statutory time-limit.[228] By contrast, certain assurances, for example those relating to future executive action in the conduct of a war, may by their nature be incapable of having a binding effect.[229]

Fourthly, an official who appears to the citizen to have authority to bind the agency may act as if he or she has such authority when this is not the case. If in this situation the citizen relies on the official's statement to his or her detriment, the agency may be estopped (that is, barred) from denying the truth of the statement. In *Robertson v Minister of Pensions*,[230] Denning J applied the following principle:

Whenever government officers, in their dealings with a subject, take on themselves to assume authority in a matter with which the subject is concerned, he is entitled to rely on their having the authority which they assume. He does not know and cannot be expected to know the limits of their authority, and he ought not to suffer if they exceed it.[231]

This principle was soon buffeted by a conservative House of Lords,[232] and its scope needs to be qualified in the interest of maintaining the rules of criminal law and the ultra vires doctrine. Should an official be able to authorise persons to commit criminal offences with impunity?[233] An estoppel (which is a rule of evidence) does not enable an agency to avoid performance of its statutory duties[234] nor confer jurisdiction where none exists.[235] Subject to these considerations, there are good reasons why public authorities, including the Crown, should be subject to the operation of estoppel in administrative matters. It was said in *Southend Corporation v Hodgson (Wickford) Ltd* that estoppel could not hinder the exercise of a statutory discretion[236] but in *Lever Finance*

---

225 *R v IRC, ex p MFK Ltd* [1990] 1 All ER 91, 110. Also *R v Jockey Club, ex p RAM Racecourses Ltd* [1993] 2 All ER 225, 236 (Stuart-Smith LJ).

226 *R v IRC, ex p Preston* [1985] AC 835 (assurance not binding on the facts) (C Lewis (1986) 49 MLR 251).

227 See note 225. Also *R v IRC, ex p Matrix-Securities Ltd* [1994] 1 All ER 769.

228 *R v IRC, ex p Unilever plc* [1996] STC 681.

229 The *Amphitrite* case, ch 31 B.

230 [1949] 1 KB 227. For the facts, see ch 13 D.

231 *Falmouth Boat Construction Co v Howell* [1950] 2 KB 16, 26.

232 *Howell v Falmouth Boat Construction Co* [1951] AC 837.

233 Cf *R v Arrowsmith* [1975] QB 678 and authorities there cited.

234 *Maritime Electric Co v General Dairies Ltd* [1937] AC 610, *Rhyl UDC v Rhyl Amusements Ltd* [1959] 1 All ER 257 and J A Andrews (1966) 29 MLR 1.

235 *Essex Congregational Union v Essex CC* [1963] AC 808.

236 [1962] 1 QB 416, discussed in [1961] CLJ 139.

Ltd v Westminster Council, a local planning authority was held to be bound by a mistaken statement made on the telephone by a planning officer, in the exercise of his ostensible authority.[237] A growing tendency to rely on estoppel in planning matters was curbed by the Court of Appeal in *Western Fish Products Ltd v Penwith DC*, which criticised *Lever Finance* and asserted that no estoppel could prevent a statutory body from exercising its discretion or performing its duty.[238] While this forceful decision is likely to hold sway in the area of planning, situations may arise in other contexts in which a public authority in exercising a discretion must take account of previous statements or assurances which have been given to the individual.[239]

Fifthly, where the citizen reasonably relies on inaccurate advice given by an official (for example, a social security clerk who wrongly advises a citizen that he or she is not eligible for a certain benefit), the appropriate remedy seems to be to require the department to compensate the citizen for any loss, either as a matter of legal liability or by recourse to the Parliamentary Ombudsman.[240] But it would not be reasonable for a large company with abundant information and resources to take advantage of a junior civil servant's statement on a legal or technical matter.[241]

Finally, and most difficult, a department makes known its current policy or practice but later decides to alter this, to the possible prejudice of those who have already acted upon the earlier information. We have already seen that a department must be able to change its policy for the future,[242] unless the court considers that a particular change would create inconsistency or unfairness for the individual.[243] Issues of legal certainty and the desirability of avoiding retrospective executive action may arise. A reasoned decision as to what transitional exceptions, if any, should be made to the new policy might well resist judicial review.[244] Possibly the individual's challenge to the effect of the new policy could be based on a combination of *Wednesbury* grounds and the concept of legitimate expectations, especially if rights under Community law are involved.

---

[237]   [1971] 1 QB 222, discussed in [1971] CLJ 3.
[238]   [1981] 2 All ER 204. And see *Newbury Council v Environment Secretary* [1981] AC 578.
[239]   See cases cited in notes 203 and 223–226 above.
[240]   Chs 31 A and 28 D.
[241]   Cf the facts of *R v IRC, ex p Matrix-Securities Ltd* (above).
[242]   See notes 211 and 212 above.
[243]   *HTV Ltd v Price Commission* [1976] ICR 170; and *R v IRC, ex p Unilever plc* (above).
[244]   *R v Ministry of Agriculture, ex p Hamble Fisheries Ltd* [1995] 2 All ER 714, 722–3.

CHAPTER 30

Judicial control of administrative action – II

In chapter 29 we considered the principles which the courts apply to the exercise of administrative powers by public authorities. We now examine the procedures by which the courts exercise their supervisory jurisdiction.[1] Review may take place indirectly, when an issue as to the validity of administrative action is decided in the course of ordinary civil or criminal proceedings.[2] So too the validity of action by a public authority may be relevant to a private law action in contract or tort (chapter 31). But here we are concerned with the procedures enabling there to be a direct review by the court of acts and decisions of public authorities.

The primary procedure in English law is now that of *application for judicial review*, often referred to in short (sometimes misleadingly) as 'judicial review'.[3] It was brought into being by a group of reforms between 1977 and 1982 which, like many procedural reforms of the common law, did not go back to first principles and make a fresh start. In particular, the sphere of application of the new procedure was not defined, and certain aspects of the common law appeared to have been left intact. We therefore must look briefly at the earlier position in English law before we deal with the procedure of application for judicial review itself. Thereafter this chapter will deal with statutory remedies created for the review of certain decisions, the legislative exclusion of judicial review, and the different system of remedies in Scots law. The chapter concludes with an account of habeas corpus. This ancient writ is an important remedy against executive action which takes away individual liberty.

Forms of relief

When administrative action is challenged in the courts, the individual will ask the court to provide one or more of the following forms of relief:

(*a*) to quash, or set aside as a nullity, a decision that is ultra vires or in excess of jurisdiction;

---

[1] In addition to the books on administrative law already cited, informative works on procedural aspects are Gordon, *Crown Office Proceedings*; Supperstone and Goudie (eds), *Judicial Review*; and Lewis, *Judicial Remedies in Public Law*.
[2] See text accompanying notes 101–108 below.
[3] A similar but not identical procedure was created in Scotland in 1985; see below. For Northern Ireland, see P Maguire, in Hadfield (ed), *Judicial Review, A Thematic Approach*, app.

(*b*) to restrain the authority from acting ultra vires or in excess of jurisdiction;

(*c*) to order the authority to perform its lawful duties;

(*d*) to declare the rights and duties of the parties;

(*e*) to order the authority to provide financial redress for loss or damage suffered; and

(*f*) to secure temporary relief, pending the outcome of the proceedings.

The main defect in English law used to be that while procedures existed for all these forms of relief to be obtained, there was no single procedure for doing so. Often the procedures for obtaining one or more of these reliefs were mutually incompatible, and the law was fragmented into the law of different remedies. Today, the reforms have established what should be viewed as a comprehensive procedure for securing whatever relief is appropriate. The main effect of the reforms was that certain remedies which had long been available – notably the prerogative orders (mandamus, prohibition and certiorari), injunctions and declarations – were for purposes of administrative law transformed into *forms of relief*[4] obtainable by a single procedure known as an application for judicial review. These changes in procedure were accompanied by judicial reorganisation so that, according to one expert view, without Parliament having directly authorised it, an administrative court has been established.[5] The court, which exists within the Queen's Bench Division of the High Court, deals with what we see below is known as the 'Crown Office list' of cases.

The prerogative orders

The prerogative writs of mandamus, prohibition and certiorari (later restyled orders)[6] were the principal means by which the former Court of King's Bench exercised jurisdiction over local justices and other bodies.[7] Although the writs issued on the application of private persons, the word 'prerogative' was apt because they were associated with the right of the Crown to ensure that justice was done by inferior courts and tribunals. They share with the writ of habeas corpus distinctive nomenclature (for example, *R v Bristol Council, ex parte Smith*) which indicates that the High Court has been moved to intervene against the named authority on the application of a private person. The Crown as such plays no part in the proceedings, except when a government department is itself the applicant. Since the prerogative orders upheld the public interest in the administration of justice, aspects of the procedure (for example, the need for leave from the court, the summary procedure and the discretionary remedies) were vitally different from litigation designed to protect the plaintiff's private rights.

Mandamus is an order from the High Court commanding a public authority or official to perform a public duty, in the performance of which the applicant has a sufficient legal interest. The order does not lie against the

---

[4] Supreme Court Act 1981, s 31(1).

[5] L Blom-Cooper [1982] PL 250, 260.

[6] Administration of Justice (Miscellaneous Provisions) Acts 1933, s 5, and 1938, s 7.

[7] de Smith, Woolf and Jowell, *Judicial Review of Administrative Action*, ch 14; Henderson, *Foundations of English Administrative Law*.

Crown as such. However, mandamus may enforce performance of a duty imposed by statute upon a minister or on a department or on named civil servants, provided that the duty is one which is owed to the applicant and not merely to the Crown.[8] In practice, mandamus is used to enforce the performance of many departmental duties which directly affect the individual.[9]

Mandamus will not lie if the authority has complete discretion whether to act or not. But there may be a duty to exercise a discretion, such as the duty of a tribunal to hear and determine a case within its jurisdiction. Thus the Home Secretary was required by mandamus to hear and determine the application made by the wife of a UK citizen for a certificate of patriality.[10] So too the duty of a tribunal to give reasons for its decisions under the Tribunals and Inquiries Act 1992, s 10, may be enforced by mandamus. Where a minister has power to give directions to a local authority, for example in the exercise of default powers, such a direction may be enforced by mandamus, provided that the direction is lawful.[11] Failure to comply with an order of mandamus constitutes contempt of court and is punishable accordingly.

Prohibition is an order issued primarily to prevent an inferior court or tribunal from exceeding its jurisdiction, or acting contrary to the rules of natural justice, where something remained to be done which could be prohibited. *Certiorari* served originally to bring a case or decision from an inferior court into the Court of King's Bench for review. Today it is a means of quashing decisions by inferior courts, tribunals and public authorities where there has been (*a*) an excess of jurisdiction or an ultra vires decision; (*b*) a breach of natural justice; or (*c*) an error of law.[12] By setting aside a defective decision, certiorari prepares the way for a fresh decision to be taken.

As means of jurisdictional control, prohibition and certiorari cover broadly the same ground. The main difference is that certiorari quashes an order or decision already given, and prohibition prevents an order or decision being made which if made would be subject to certiorari.[13] It is convenient to seek both remedies in the same proceedings when a decision in excess of jurisdiction has already been made and other similar decisions have yet to be made.[14] Likewise certiorari and mandamus may be sought in the same proceedings, certiorari to quash a decision in excess of jurisdiction and mandamus to compel the tribunal to hear and determine the case according to law.[15]

Despite the judicial origins of certiorari and prohibition, for many years they have been available against ministers, departments, local authorities and

---

[8]   *R v Special Commissioners for Income Tax* (1888) 21 QBD 313, 317. Cf *R v Lords of the Treasury* (1872) LR 7 QB 387. And see Harding, *Public Duties and Public Law*, pp 87–96.
[9]   Eg *Padfield v Ministry of Agriculture* [1968] AC 997.
[10] *R v Home Secretary, ex p Phansopkar* [1976] QB 606.
[11] *Education Secretary v Tameside MB* [1977] AC 1014.
[12] The error of law, if it was an error within the tribunal's jurisdiction, had formerly to be on the face of the record for it to be reviewed by certiorari, but this requirement is now obsolete: ch 29 A above.
[13] Eg *R v Minister of Health, ex p Davis* [1929] 1 KB 619.
[14] *R v Paddington Rent Tribunal, ex p Bell Properties Ltd* [1949] 1 KB 666.
[15] Eg *R v Hammersmith Coroner, ex p Peach* [1980] QB 211 (inquest into death of Blair Peach).

other administrative bodies. The courts at times found difficulty in accepting such broad use of the remedies. Formerly, a dictum of Atkin LJ, in *R v Electricity Commissioners, ex p London Electricity Joint Committee*, had special authority:

Wherever any body of persons, having legal authority to determine the rights of subjects and having the duty to act judicially, act in excess of their legal authority, they are subject to the controlling jurisdiction of the King's Bench Division exercised in these writs.[16]

Interpreted narrowly, this dictum prevented certiorari being available where (for instance) a court held that a public body was not under a 'duty to act judicially'.[17] In 1967, in a decision involving the Criminal Injuries Compensation Board, Lord Parker CJ said:

the exact limits of the ancient remedy by way of certiorari have never been, and ought not to be, specifically defined. They have varied from time to time, being extended to meet changing conditions ... We have ... reached the position when the ambit of certiorari can be said to cover every case in which a body of persons, of a public as opposed to a purely private or domestic character, has to determine matters affecting subjects provided always that it has a duty to act judicially.[18]

However, the 'duty to act judicially' was already ceasing to be a condition of the availability of certiorari. In 1982, Lord Diplock stated that certiorari lay in respect of statutory tribunals or other bodies 'having legal authority to determine questions affecting the common law or statutory rights or obligations' of other persons.[19] We examine below the difficult line between the decisions of public bodies that are subject to judicial review and those of other bodies that are not.[20] But it is now established that the prerogative orders lie against public authorities of all kinds making decisions that affect individuals, whether the power is derived from statute or from another source. It is not necessary to show that an authority is under a duty to 'act judicially' for it to be subject to review.

When a public body's decision is challenged by a private individual, the question may arise of the individual's standing to sue, i.e. whether he or she has sufficient interest in the decision to justify the court's intervention. Some would wish the courts to entertain a challenge to an authority's conduct from any member of the public. But English law has never openly recognised an *actio popularis*, and the applicant for a prerogative order usually had to show a personal right or interest in the matter. According to the case-law, the nature of the right or interest required could vary with the particular remedy being sought.[21] Although judicial attitudes fluctuated,[22] by the 1970s the trend of judicial decisions appeared to be developing a single test of locus standi for all

---

[16]   [1924] 1 KB 171, 205.
[17]   See Lord Reid's analysis in *Ridge v Baldwin* [1964] AC 40 (the duty to act judicially is to be inferred from the nature of the power); and eg *R v Board of Visitors of Hull Prison, ex p St Germain* [1979] QB 425.
[18]   *R v Criminal Injuries Compensation Board, ex p Lain* [1967] 2 QB 864, 882.
[19]   *O'Reilly v Mackman* [1983] 2 AC 237, 279.
[20]   See text accompanying notes 66–84 below.
[21]   de Smith, Woolf and Jowell, op cit, pp 626–31, 634–5; Thio, *Locus Standi and Judicial Review*.
[22]   Contrast *R v Lewisham Union Guardians* [1897] 1 QB 498 and *R v Metropolitan Police Commissioner, ex p Blackburn* [1968] 2 QB 118.

the prerogative orders,[23] and the creation of today's judicial review procedure reinforced that trend. Before examining that procedure, we will consider two remedies, the injunction and the declaration, which, unlike the prerogative orders, are available in all branches of the law.

Injunctions[24]

While the prerogative orders enabled the courts to exercise a supervisory jurisdiction over inferior tribunals and public authorities, the injunction is an equitable remedy available in all branches of law, public and private, to protect a person's rights against unlawful infringement. In the public law field an injunction may be claimed against a public authority or official, to restrain unlawful acts which are threatened or are being committed, for example unlawful interference with private rights[25] or ultra vires action such as improper expenditure of local funds.[26] An important exception relates to the position of the Crown. Injunctions are not available against the Crown as a legal entity, and they are not available in private law proceedings brought directly against the Crown.[27] In place of an injunction in private law proceedings against the Crown, the court may make an order declaring the rights of the parties, but no interim relief may be obtained.[28] However, Community law may require injunctive relief to be available against the Crown[29] and such relief may also be given in judicial review proceedings against government departments and civil servants.[30]

Where the injunction concerns private rights (for example, liability in private nuisance), the ordinary rules of the law of property or tort apply as to who may seek an injunction. But when the injunction concerns a matter of public right (for example, the public nuisance caused by the obstruction of a highway), an injunction can be obtained by the Attorney-General, either at his own instance or at the instance of a relator (ie one who informs). A relator need have no personal interest in the subject-matter of the claim save his or her interest as a member of the public. The consent of the Attorney-General to the proceedings prevents any objection being taken to the relator's standing in the matter.

There are two cases where a person can sue without joining the Attorney-General:

(*a*) if interference with the public right also constitutes an interference with the plaintiff's private right; for example, where an obstruction upon a highway is also an interference with a private right of access to the highway;[31]

---

23   *R v Liverpool Corpn, ex p Liverpool Taxi Operators Association* [1972] 2 QB 299; *R v Greater London Council, ex p Blackburn* [1976] 3 All ER 184.
24   de Smith, Woolf and Jowell, op cit, pp 637–42; Wade and Forsyth, op cit, pp 581–91.
25   Eg *Pride of Derby Angling Association v British Celanese Ltd* [1953] Ch 149.
26   *A-G v Aspinall* (1837) 2 My & Cr 406.
27   Crown Proceedings Act 1947, s 21; ch 31 C.
28   *R v IRC, ex p Rossminster Ltd* [1980] AC 952.
29   *R v Transport Secretary, ex p Factortame Ltd* [1990] 2 AC 85; *(The same) (No 2)* [1991] 1 AC 603. See also the Public Supply Contracts Regulations 1991, SI 1991 No 2679, reg 26, authorising injunctive relief against the Crown for breach of the regulations.
30   *M v Home Office* [1994] 1 AC 377; and note 61 below.
31   *Boyce v Paddington BC* [1903] 1 Ch 109; *Barrs v Bethell* [1982] Ch 294.

(*b*) where no private right of the plaintiff is interfered with, but he or she suffers special damage from the interference with a public right, for example, where as a result of a public nuisance a plaintiff's premises have been rendered unhealthy.[32]

A third exception, under the Local Government Act 1972, is that a local authority may institute proceedings in its own name when it considers it expedient for promoting or protecting the interests of inhabitants of its area, even though the object of the proceedings is to enforce public rights which before the 1972 Act would have required the Attorney-General's consent to relator proceedings.[33]

Relator actions can be used to restrain unlawful action by a public authority, even though its validity could have been tested by certiorari.[34] One use of relator proceedings, that goes far outside administrative law, is to provide additional means of enforcing the criminal law when existing penalties and procedures are inadequate to deter repeated breach.

In *Attorney-General v Sharp*, the owner of a fleet of buses had been prosecuted 48 times for breach of local regulations in operating his buses without a licence. He continued to run his buses without a licence, since despite the fines he found it profitable to do so. *Held* that, since the rights of the public were involved and as the remedies provided by the local Act had proved ineffective, there was jurisdiction to grant an injunction at the instance of the Attorney-General by way of ancillary relief.[35]

In comparable circumstances, relator proceedings have been used to enforce planning control and fire precautions against those who find it profitable to break the law.[36]

In practice, the Attorney-General never consents to relator proceedings against departments of central government. He appears to have absolute discretion in deciding whether to consent to relator proceedings. Although he is accountable to Parliament for his decisions, he cannot be required to justify them to the courts nor have the courts power to overrule the decisions. These questions were settled conclusively in 1977 in *Gouriet*'s case.

The Union of Post Office Workers had asked its members to boycott South African mail for one week as a protest against apartheid. Gouriet, claiming that the boycott would be criminal conduct under the Post Office Act 1953, asked the Attorney-General to consent to proceedings for an injunction against the union. This consent was refused. Gouriet then obtained an interim injunction against the union from the Court of Appeal. Lord Denning MR went further than the majority of the court in holding that the Attorney-General's refusal could be reviewed by the court and if necessary over-ridden. On appeal to the House of Lords, *held* that when the Attorney-General has refused consent to relator proceedings, a private citizen who asserts that the public interest is affected by a threatened breach of the criminal law, may not go to the civil courts for a remedy, whether injunction or declaration. Public rights may be

---

[32] *Benjamin v Storr* (1874) LR 9 CP 400.
[33] *Stoke-on-Trent Council v B & Q (Retail) Ltd* [1984] AC 754; *Kirklees Council v Wickes Building Supplies Ltd* [1993] AC 227. And see B Hough [1992] PL 130.
[34] *A-G v Tynemouth Corpn* [1899] AC 293.
[35] [1931] 1 Ch 121; and see *A-G v Harris* [1961] 1 QB 74 and note 33 above.
[36] *A-G v Bastow* [1957] 1 QB 514; *A-G v Chaudry* [1971] 3 All ER 938.

asserted in a civil action only by the Attorney-General as representing the public. The Attorney-General's discretion may not be reviewed in the courts.[37]

In the sensitive political circumstances of the *Gouriet* case, a difficult discretion had to be exercised in the public interest and it would have broken new constitutional ground for the Attorney-General's decision to be subject to judicial review. Yet in not dissimilar circumstances involving the imminent breach of a local authority's duty to maintain its schools, the court was willing to assume jurisdiction.[38] The proposition of the Lords in *Gouriet* that public rights can be asserted only by the Attorney-General applies both to injunctions and to declarations sought by ordinary action. However, the proposition was not intended to apply to applications for judicial review[39] where, as we shall see, individuals may with leave of the court bring proceedings against public authorities in which the Attorney-General plays no part.

The High Court may grant an injunction to restrain a person from acting in an office to which he or she is not entitled, and may also declare the office to be vacant. This procedure takes the place of the ancient procedure of an information in the nature of a writ of quo warranto.[40]

Declaratory judgments[41]

A declaratory judgment is one which merely declares the legal relationship of the parties and is not accompanied by any sanction or means of enforcement. The authority of a court's ruling on law is such that a declaratory judgment will normally restrain both the Crown and public authorities from illegal conduct. Order 15, r 16, of the Rules of the Supreme Court provides:

No action or other proceedings shall be open to objection on the ground that a merely declaratory judgment or order is sought thereby, and the Court may make binding declarations of right whether or not any consequential relief is or could be claimed.

It is an obvious convenience in many public law disputes to be able to have the law determined in relation to particular facts without seeking a coercive remedy. An early example arose in *Dyson v Attorney-General*, where a taxpayer obtained a declaration against the Crown that the tax authorities had no power to request certain information from him on pain of a £50 penalty for disobedience.[42] The jurisdiction to grant declarations is as wide as the law itself, except that the judges may as a matter of discretion impose limits upon its use. Thus an action for a declaratory judgment must be based on a concrete case which has arisen. The courts will not give answers to questions propounded in the form of hypothetical cases and are reluctant to grant a

---

37 *Gouriet v Union of Post Office Workers* [1978] AC 435; and see P P Mercer [1979] PL 214, B Hough (1988) 8 LS 189, and Edwards, *The Attorney-General, Politics and the Public Interest*, pp 120–58.
38 *Meade v Haringey BC* [1979] 2 All ER 1016; ch 29 A.
39 See *R v IRC, ex p National Federation of Self-Employed* [1982] AC 617.
40 Supreme Court Act 1981, s 30; cf Local Government Act 1972, s 92.
41 de Smith, Woolf and Jowell, op cit, ch 18; Zamir and Woolf, *The Declaratory Judgment.*
42 [1912] 1 Ch 158.

bare declaration that can have no legal consequences;[43] however, courts have reviewed the legality of advisory guidance which in itself has no legal effect.[44]

Nor will the court give an opinion on a point of law which is in issue in concurrent criminal proceedings.[45] But in administrative law the declaration may be available when other remedies are not and, before the creation of the judicial review procedure, there were procedural advantages in declaratory proceedings (for example, in discovery of documents).[46] In *Pyx Granite Co Ltd v Ministry of Housing*, the House of Lords held that a statutory procedure for obtaining a decision on whether planning permission was needed for development did not exclude the owner's right to come to court for a declaration.[47]

The declaration was formerly considered to be both alternative and preferable to the prerogative orders. Thus the judgment of a tribunal could be declared invalid as being in excess of jurisdiction.[48] But the declaration could not be used as a means of correcting errors of law on the face of the record of a tribunal's decision.[49] Nor could the court by a declaration decide de novo a question entrusted by statute to a minister or a special tribunal.[50] The advantages of suing by ordinary action for a declaration were sometimes considerable despite these limitations, but the choice between the prerogative orders and the declaration as a means of seeking judicial review was transformed by the reforms of 1977–82, to which we now turn.

Reasons for creating the present judicial review procedure

Amongst the main reasons for what was described by the Law Commission in 1976 as 'the dilemma of the litigant seeking judicial review'[51] were the following:

(*a*) While two or more of the prerogative orders could be sought in the same proceedings, and an injunction and declaration could be sought together, the two classes of remedy could not be combined, nor could a litigant who made the wrong choice convert one procedure into the other. Damages could be sought with an injunction or declaration, but not with the prerogative orders.

(*b*) The rules of standing to sue differed as between the prerogative orders and injunctions/declarations; they also had formerly differed as between the various prerogative orders.

---

43   *Maxwell v Dept of Trade* [1974] QB 523.
44   Eg *Gillick v West Norfolk Health Authority* [1986] AC 112. In 1994, the Law Commission recommended that the High Court be authorised in its judicial review jurisdiction to make advisory declarations on points of general importance: Law Com No 226, pp 74–6. And see J Laws (1994) 57 MLR 213.
45   *Imperial Tobacco Ltd v A-G* [1981] AC 718.
46   *Vine v National Dock Labour Board* [1957] AC 488.
47   [1960] AC 260.
48   *Anisminic Ltd v Foreign Compensation Commission* [1969] 2 AC 147; *Ridge v Baldwin* [1964] AC 40.
49   *Punton v Ministry of Pensions (No 2)* [1964] 1 All ER 448; P Cane (1980) 43 MLR 266.
50   *Healey v Minister of Health* [1955] 1 QB 221; *Argosam Finance Ltd v Oxby* [1965] Ch 390.
51   Report on Remedies in Administrative Law, Cmnd 6407, 1976, p 15.

(*c*)   The summary procedure used for the prerogative orders did not allow for discovery of documents, or the cross-examination of witnesses.

(*d*)   Certiorari had to be sought within six months, but no fixed limit of time applied to the declaration.

(*e*)   Leave from the court was required for prerogative order proceedings but not for injunctions/declarations; relator actions needed consent from the Attorney-General.

(*f*)   The declaration lay in respect of all forms of official act, including delegated legislation, and against all public authorities, including the Crown. But a declaration could not quash a decision made by a tribunal within jurisdiction, nor could interim relief be obtained against the Crown.

Accordingly, the Law Commission proposed a draft Bill to create the procedure of application for judicial review. The Commission emphasised that the new procedure was not to be an exclusive remedy, and litigants would remain free to seek an injunction or declaration if they so chose. In the event the procedure was created by amending the Rules of the Supreme Court to provide a new Order 53.[52] This came into effect in 1978 and was amended in 1980 to allow a single judge to hear matters previously heard by the Divisional Court of two or three judges.[53] The Supreme Court Act 1981, s 31, enacted the main features of the application for judicial review and the High Court's business was reorganized by forming a Crown Office list, to include applications under Order 53, statutory appeals to the High Court and related proceedings.[54] In 1982, the House of Lords in *O'Reilly v Mackman* and *Cocks v Thanet DC* gave added impetus to the reforms by holding that, for most purposes of judicial review, application under Order 53 had become an exclusive remedy, contrary to the aim of the Law Commission in 1976.[55]

Applications for judicial review: the Order 53 procedure

By s 31 of the Supreme Court Act 1981, applications to the High Court for an order of mandamus, prohibition or certiorari (and for an injunction restraining a person from acting in a public office to which he or she is not entitled) *must* be made, in accordance with rules of court, by an application for judicial review. Neither the Act (s 29(1)) nor Order 53 sought to alter the existing scope of the prerogative orders at common law. The High Court has a discretionary power (by s 31(2) of the 1981 Act) to make a declaration or grant an injunction whenever an application for judicial review has been made seeking that relief, if it would be 'just and convenient' to do so. In exercising this discretion the court must have regard inter alia to the nature of the matters in respect of which the prerogative orders apply, the nature of the persons and bodies against whom the orders lie and all the circumstances. Thus within what may be called the 'public law' field of the prerogative orders, declarations and injunctions may now be granted on an application for judicial review. But the Act leaves it entirely open whether within this field

---

[52]   SI 1977 No 1955, discussed by J Beatson and M H Matthews (1978) 41 MLR 437.
[53]   SI 1980 No 2000.
[54]   *Practice Direction* [1981] 3 All ER 61.
[55]   See p 816 below.

an application for judicial review is to be the sole means of obtaining an injunction or declaration.

Leave of the court is needed for every application for judicial review (s 31(3)). Since 1980, leave is generally a matter decided by a single judge without a hearing, but if necessary (for example, if the applicant seeks interim relief) the decision may be made after a brief hearing;[56] the hearing at the leave stage may be of the applicant alone, but the intended respondent may be present to argue against the granting of leave. The requirement of leave operates unevenly, but it protects the court, and public authorities, from a flood of 'hopeless' cases and vexatious challenges, and may facilitate access to the High Court for deserving cases.[57] Where leave is refused without a hearing, the application for leave may be renewed in open court before a single judge or a Divisional Court; it may be further renewed in the Court of Appeal but not the House of Lords.[58] When leave is obtained, the substantive hearing of the application takes place before a single judge or a Divisional Court. In 1995, 23 judges were designated to hear cases on the 'Crown Office list'.

The court may refuse to give leave or relief if it considers that there has been undue delay in making an application and if the granting of relief would be likely to cause substantial hardship to or prejudice any person's rights, or be detrimental to good administration.[59] By Order 53, an application for judicial review shall be made promptly, and in any event within three months from when grounds for the application first arose, unless there is good reason for extending the period; statutory time limits for review are not affected.

If the relief sought is prohibition or certiorari, the granting of leave for the application operates as a stay of the proceedings challenged if the court so directs; when other forms of relief are sought, the court may grant such interim relief as could be granted in an action begun by writ.[60] The 1981 Act did not expressly provide for interim relief against the Crown, as recommended by the Law Commission, but in *M v Home Office*[61] it was held that the language of s 31 enabled coercive orders (including interim injunctions) to be made against ministers of the Crown in judicial review proceedings.

On an application for judicial review, the court may award damages if these have been sought by the applicant and the court is satisfied that damages could have been obtained by an action brought for the purpose (s 31(4)). But the 1981 Act did not alter the substantive rules of liability in damages and the

---

[56]   Order 53, r 3 (as amended in 1980).

[57]   See A Le Sueur and M Sunkin [1992] PL 102; Bridges, Meszaros and Sunkin, *Judicial Review in Perspective*, chs 7, 8. In 1994, the Law Commission recommended that 'preliminary consideration' should replace the leave stage: Law Com No 226, part 5.

[58]   *Re Poh* [1983] 1 All ER 287.

[59]   1981 Act, s 31(6). *R v Dairy Produce Tribunal, ex p Caswell* [1990] 2 AC 738 seeks to resolve inconsistencies between s 31(6) and Order 53, r 4; and see A Lindsay [1995] PL 417.

[60]   Order 53, r 10. See *R v Education Secretary, ex p Avon Council* [1991] 1 QB 558 (CA) interpreting 'stay of proceedings' more widely than did *Minister of Foreign Affairs v Vehicles and Supplies Ltd* [1991] 4 All ER 65 (PC). On the criteria for interim relief, see *R v Kensington and Chelsea BC, ex p Hammell* [1989] QB 518 and *R v Inspectorate of Pollution, ex p Greenpeace Ltd* [1994] 4 All ER 322.

[61]   [1994] 1 AC 377 (H W R Wade (1991) 107 LQR 4; M Gould [1993] PL 368). For the Crown Proceedings Act 1947, s 21, see ch 31 C.

fact that an individual suffered financial loss because of a decision that is quashed as invalid gives rise to no liability.[62] Thus even successful applicants for judicial review seldom obtain damages.

An application for judicial review must be supported by one or more affidavits as to the facts relied on, and the respondent authority may file affidavits in reply. Although the powers are rarely used, the court may allow the discovery of documents, interrogatories, and cross-examination of witnesses, but without prejudice to any privileges of the Crown.[63] When certiorari is sought, the court may both quash the decision under review and also remit it with a direction to the body in question to reach a fresh decision in accordance with the findings of the court (s 31(5)). When the relief sought is a declaration, injunction or damages, and the court does not consider this appropriate on an application for judicial review, the court may allow proceedings to be continued as if they had been begun by writ.[64] The court does not have the converse power to permit proceedings by writ to be continued as if they had been begun as applications for judicial review.[65]

Significant issues which have arisen in relation to the public law character of applications for judicial review include (*a*) the scope and extent of review, (*b*) standing to apply for review, (*c*) whether Order 53 procedure is exclusive and (*d*) the discretion of the court in granting review.

The scope and extent of judicial review

Much greater use is made of the Order 53 procedure for judicial review than was formerly made of the prerogative orders. If an application for review concerns decisions of central government, or any public authority or official, the courts readily accept jurisdiction in judicial review, except if a reason to the contrary is shown.[66] Thus decisions taken under prerogative powers are subject to review, unless in their subject-matter the court considers them to be non-justiciable.[67] Also reviewable are decisions by local authorities in controlling access to public property, initiating legal proceedings, and in matters preliminary to the award of contracts.[68] Such decisions arise from an exercise of public power susceptible to control on principles of public law. Two broad exceptions to the availability of judicial review exist. First, some decisions are subject to statutory appeals and similar procedures which, to a greater or lesser extent, exclude review under RSC Order 53.[69] Secondly, public authorities are in general subject to the ordinary law of contract, tort and property. Since *O'Reilly v Mackman*,[70] such branches of law may be said to be within 'private law' to distinguish them from the rules of 'public law' applied on

---

[62] Ch 31 A; eg *Dunlop v Woollahra Council* [1982] AC 158.
[63] Order 53, r 8.
[64] Order 53, r 9(5).
[65] For the proposal that the power should exist, see Law Com No 226, pp 27–8.
[66] See de Smith, Woolf and Jowell, op cit, ch 3; Lewis, *Judicial Remedies in Public Law*, ch 4; and D Pannick [1992] PL 1.
[67] See the *CCSU* case, note 72 below; and eg *R v Ministry of Defence, ex p Smith* [1996] QB 517. Cf *Reckley v Minister of Public Safety (No 2)* [1996] AC 527.
[68] Respectively *Wheeler v Leicester City Council* [1985] AC 1054; *Avon CC v Buscott* [1988] QB 656; and *R v Enfield Council, ex p TF Unwin (Roydon) Ltd* [1989] 1 Admin LR 51.
[69] See text accompanying notes 121–148 below.
[70] [1983] 2 AC 237, p 817 below.

judicial review. An application for judicial review may not be used in place of an ordinary action in contract or tort, just because the defendant is a public authority.

Thus, when such an authority dismisses an employee, the employee's primary remedy is a claim for unfair dismissal, or a claim under the contract of employment.[71] However, depending on the circumstances, decisions by public authorities as employers may stem from or involve issues of public law.[72] Public sector employees such as NHS hospital staff[73] and civil servants[74] must generally use procedures open to them in employment law rather than seek judicial review. This does not apply to holders of public office such as police and prison officers[75] whose position is 'under-pinned' by statute. Judicial review may be available if a public employment dispute raises issues as to the powers of the public authority, or other matters suitable for redress by judicial review.[76]

A difficult question is what constitutes a 'public law dispute' for judicial review purposes. The prerogative orders were not, and judicial review is not, available against bodies such as trade unions or commercial companies. Membership of a trade union is based on contract. If a trade unionist complains that expulsion from the union was in breach of union rules or infringed natural justice, he or she may sue the union for damages and an injunction. Bodies such as the National Greyhound Racing Club and the Jockey Club are not subject to judicial review under Order 53, even if they regulate major areas of sport, but contractual remedies will often be available.[77] Nor are decisions by religious bodies subject to judicial review.[78] Judicial review extends to visitors to the universities but, unusually, the scope of review is for historical reasons confined to jurisdictional grounds.[79]

The most difficult case is that of regulatory bodies which derive their powers neither directly from statute[80] nor from contract. Despite having no formal legal status, the City Panel on Take-Overs and Mergers is subject to judicial review, since its functions 'de facto' are in the nature of public law powers and are indirectly supported by statutory sanctions.[81] The effect of

---

[71]   *R v BBC, ex p Lavelle* [1983] 1 All ER 241.

[72]   Eg *CCSU v Minister for Civil Service* [1985] AC 374; cf H W R Wade (1985) 101 LQR 180, 190–6.

[73]   *R v East Berks Health Authority, ex p Walsh* [1985] QB 152.

[74]   *R v Lord Chancellor's Department, ex p Nangle* [1992] 1 All ER 897.

[75]   *R v Home Secretary, ex p Benwell* [1985] QB 554. By the Criminal Justice and Public Order Act 1994, s 126, prison officers acquired the same employment rights as other civil servants; this may deprive them of access to judicial review: G S Morris [1994] PL 535.

[76]   See *McLaren v Home Office* [1990] ICR 824. Also B Walsh [1989] PL 131; S Fredman and G Morris [1988] PL 58, [1991] PL 484, (1991) 107 LQR 298.

[77]   *Law v National Greyhound Racing Club Ltd* [1983] 3 All ER 300; *R v Disciplinary Committee of the Jockey Club, ex p Aga Khan* [1993] 2 All ER 853. And see M Beloff [1989] PL 95; N Bamforth [1993] PL 239. Cf *Finnigan v New Zealand Rugby Football Union Inc* [1985] 2 NZLR 159 (private association exercising function of major national importance).

[78]   *R v Chief Rabbi, ex p Wachmann* [1993] 2 All ER 249.

[79]   *R v Hull University Visitor, ex p Page* [1993] AC 682.

[80]   Unlike the Law Society; see eg *Swain v Law Society* [1983] 1 AC 598.

[81]   *R v Panel on Take-overs and Mergers, ex p Datafin plc* [1987] QB 817 (C F Forsyth [1987] PL 356; D Oliver [1987] PL 543); *R v Advertising Standards Agency, ex p Insurance Service plc* (1990) 2 Admin LR 77.

privatisation and 'market testing' of public services has produced some conflicting decisions.[82] Publicly owned undertakings such as British Coal are subject to judicial review in respect of some of their functions.[83] Inferior courts, such as magistrates' courts and county courts, are subject to judicial review. So is the Crown Court, 'other than its jurisdiction in matters relating to trial on indictment',[84] an imprecise limitation which makes it necessary to distinguish between those decisions of the Crown Court that are subject to judicial review and others which can be challenged only by appeal after a trial.

Standing to apply for judicial review

At the stage when leave is sought for an application for judicial review, the court must not grant leave 'unless it considers that the applicant has a sufficient interest in the matter to which the application relates' (s 31(3)). The test of 'sufficient interest' was proposed by the Law Commission as a formula which would allow for further development in the rules of standing. The test plainly allows the court discretion to decide what is to constitute 'sufficient interest'. To what extent did it alter existing rules of locus standi?

In *R v Inland Revenue Commissioners, ex p National Federation of Self-employed and Small Businesses*, a body of taxpayers challenged arrangements made by the Commissioners for levying tax on wages paid to casual employees on Fleet Street newspapers. For many years the employees had given fictitious names to evade tax, but the Commissioners agreed with the employers and unions on a scheme for collecting tax in future and for two previous years, in return for an undertaking by the Commissioners not to investigate any earlier years. The Federation, complaining that their members were never treated so favourably, applied under Order 53 for a declaration that the arrangement was unlawful, and a mandamus ordering the Commissioners to collect tax as required by law. The Court of Appeal held, assuming the agreement to be unlawful, that the Federation had sufficient interest in the matter for their application to be heard. The House of Lords *held* that the question of sufficient interest was not merely a preliminary issue to be decided when leave was being sought on an application for judicial review, but had to be resolved in relation to what was known by the court of the matter under review. On the evidence, the tax agreement was a lawful exercise of the Commissioners' discretion. In general, unlike local ratepayers,[85] a taxpayer did not have an interest in challenging decisions concerning other taxpayers' affairs. In the circumstances, the National Federation did not have sufficient interest to challenge the Commissioners' decisions.[86]

The speeches in this case contain many comments on the significance of Order 53, but they also include a perplexing diversity of opinions about the test of 'sufficient interest'. The account above seeks to summarise the views of three judges (Lords Wilberforce, Fraser and Roskill), although Lord Fraser also stressed that the test of 'sufficient interest' was a logically prior question which had to be answered before any question of the merits arose. Lord

---

[82] Compare *R v Lord Chancellor's Dept, ex p Hibbit & Saunders* [1993] COD 326 (D Oliver [1993] PL 214) and *R v Legal Aid Board, ex p Donn & Co* [1996] 3 All ER 1.

[83] *R v British Coal Corpn, ex p Vardy* [1993] ICR 720. See ch 14.

[84] Supreme Court Act 1981, s 29(3); R Ward [1990] PL 50; *in re Ashton* [1994] 1 AC 9 and *R v Manchester Crown Court, ex p DPP* [1993] 4 All ER 928.

[85] *Arsenal FC v Ende* [1979] AC 1.

[86] [1982] AC 617 (P Cane [1981] PL 322). And see de Smith, Woolf and Jowell, ch 2.

Scarman paid lip-service to the existence of a test of standing separate from the merits, but his conclusion (that the Federation had no sufficient interest *because* they had not shown that the tax authorities had failed in their duties) virtually eliminated any prior test of standing separate from the merits. Lord Diplock, who advocated a very broad test of standing, was alone in holding that the Federation had sufficient interest in the matter; in his view the case simply failed on its merits. What emerges from the various speeches is that the judges were reluctant to turn away the applicants without hearing something of their case, and unwilling to hold that the tax authorities were immune from judicial review.

In most applications for judicial review, the question of sufficient interest presents no problems, although for the parties not to raise the issue does not confer on the court jurisdiction that is otherwise absent.[87] An ordinary taxpayer had interest to challenge the government's proposal to designate as a 'Community treaty' a treaty providing extra funds to the Community.[88] The Equal Opportunities Commission had standing to challenge statutory provisions which discriminated against women employees in breach of their Community rights.[89] Organisations such as trade unions acting in their members' interests and environmental groups have standing to challenge decisions on relevant issues[90] but difficulties can arise with some public interest litigation. Thus a non-profit-making company formed to protect the site of a Shakespearian theatre had no standing to review a minister's decision refusing to schedule the site as a historic monument.[91] In 1994, the Law Commission recommended that if the applicant for judicial review was not directly affected by the decision under review, the court should have discretion to decide whether it was in the public interest for the application to be heard.[92]

Does Order 53 provide an exclusive procedure?[93]

Although the House of Lords failed to sound a clear note in the *National Federation* case, the House in two later cases was unanimous in holding that litigants seeking judicial review of administrative action must proceed by application under Order 53. The question arose because the Supreme Court Act 1981 did not expressly exclude the individual in public law cases from suing for an injunction or declaration, or for damages for breach of statutory duty. The issue had arisen in numerous cases concerning immigrants, prisoners, homeless persons and others.

---

[87] *R v Social Services Secretary, ex p CPAG* [1989] 1 All ER 1047.

[88] *R v HM Treasury, ex p Smedley* [1985] QB 657; *R v Foreign Secretary, ex p Rees-Mogg* [1994] QB 552. See also *R v Felixstowe Justices, ex p Leigh* [1987] QB 582.

[89] *R v Employment Secretary, ex p EOC* [1995] 1 AC 1.

[90] *R v Inspectorate of Pollution, ex p Greenpeace (No 2)* [1992] 4 All ER 329; *R v Home Secretary, ex p Fire Brigades Union* [1995] 2 AC 513; *R v Foreign Secretary, ex p World Development Movement* [1995] 1 All ER 611. And P Cane [1995] PL 276.

[91] *R v Environment Secretary, ex p Rose Theatre Trust Co* [1990] 1 QB 504. See also Sir K Schiemann [1990] PL 342 and P Cane [1990] PL 307.

[92] Law Com No 226, pp 41–4. And see report by Justice, *A Matter of Public Interest* (1996).

[93] See de Smith, Woolf and Jowell, op cit, pp 191–201; Wade and Forsyth, op cit, pp 680–95; Craig, op cit, ch 15; A Tanney [1994] PL 51.

In *O'Reilly v Mackman*, convicted prisoners who had lost remission of sentence in disciplinary proceedings after riots at Hull prison sued for a declaration that the disciplinary awards were null and void because of breaches of natural justice.[94] The defendants applied to have the action struck out on the ground that the decisions of boards of visitors could be challenged only by an application for review under Order 53. *Held* (House of Lords) while the High Court had jurisdiction to grant the declarations sought, the prisoners' case was based solely on rights and obligations arising under public law. Order 53, by its requirement of leave from the court and by its time limit, protected public authorities against groundless or delayed attacks, and had removed previous defects in the system of remedies. It would 'as a general rule be contrary to public policy, and as such an abuse of the process of the court, to permit a person seeking to establish that a decision of a public authority infringed rights to which he was entitled to protection under public law to proceed by way of ordinary action and by this means to evade the provision of Order 53 for the protection of such authorities' (Lord Diplock).[95] And in *Cocks v Thanet DC*, the House held that a homeless person who sought to challenge a decision by a local authority that he was not entitled to permanent accommodation must do so by application under Order 53, and not by suing in the county court for a declaration and damages for breach of statutory duty.[96]

Although neither the Supreme Court Act 1981 nor Order 53 had established the application for judicial review as an exclusive remedy in public law matters, these two decisions left no doubt that the Lords wished to carry further than either Parliament or the Law Commission had done the reforms associated with Order 53. The step taken in *O'Reilly* was indeed justified on practical grounds, namely that litigants could now be required to use the Order 53 procedure as the former defects hampering use of the prerogative orders had been cured. But in expressly seeking to protect public authorities from a flood of litigation,[97] both *Reilly* and *Cocks* relied heavily on the public law/private law distinction, despite the difficulties that this presents in English law.[98]

One consequence of *O'Reilly* has been that much effort in litigation has been spent in testing the procedural choices made by litigants, rather than in deciding the merits of their grievances. Sir William Wade's view in 1994 was dramatic: 'The need for law reform is clearly greater now than it was before 1977'.[99] However, this understates the general benefits resulting from the 1977 reforms, and the Law Commission in 1994 did not share this view of the difficulties created by *O'Reilly*.[100] Decisions by the Lords since *O'Reilly* have shown that the rule of procedural exclusivity is not absolute. An action for negligence against a planning authority relating to an agreement over a disputed enforcement notice was held to raise no question of public law, since the action did not seek to quash the notice and assumed that it was valid.[101] In

---

94   See *R v Board of Visitors of Hull Prison, ex p St Germain* [1978] QB 678.
95   [1983] 2 AC 237, 285. And see C F Forsyth [1985] CLJ 415; and Justice/All Souls Report, *Administrative Justice*, ch 6.
96   [1983] 2 AC 286; and see *Mohram Ali v Tower Hamlets BC* [1993] QB 407.
97   See Woolf, *Protection of the Public – A New Challenge*, ch 1; and (the same) [1986] PL 220; [1992] PL 221, 231.
98   Ch 26.
99   Wade and Forsyth, op cit, p 685.
100 See Law Com No 226, part 3.
101 *Davy v Spelthorne Council* [1984] AC 262.

O'Reilly, Lord Diplock stated that an exception to the rule requiring use of Order 53 might exist where the invalidity of an official decision arose 'as a collateral issue in a claim for infringement of a right of the plaintiff arising under private law'.[102] The converse of this situation arose when a local council sued one of its tenants for non-payment of rent, and the tenants raised the defence that rent increases made by the council were ultra vires. Although the tenant could have sought review of the increases under Order 53 (and had not done so), the defence was held to be no abuse of process but a proper defence of the tenant's private rights.[103] In 1992, Lord Diplock's suggested exception was applied directly in *Roy v Kensington Family Practitioner Committee.* An NHS committee, acting under statutory powers, had deducted 20% from money which was due to Dr Roy for providing medical services to the NHS; in suing by ordinary action for the full amount, Dr Roy was entitled to seek a declaration that the deduction had not been properly made.[104] This decision by the House of Lords was a significant step towards re-assessing the proper limits of the principle in *O'Reilly v Mackman.* Lords Bridge and Lowry would evidently favour restricting the *O'Reilly* rule to situations in which the individual's *sole* aim was to challenge a public law act or decision, and would not apply it when an action to vindicate private rights involved some questions as to the validity of a public law decision.[105] In 1995, the Lords further limited the effect of *O'Reilly*, holding that a decision by the regulator of tele-communications interpreting a statutory licence might be questioned by originating summons in the Commercial Court. Emphasising the need for some procedural flexibility, Lord Slynn said that the main question was whether the proceedings were an abuse of process, and they were not.[106]

An exaggerated view of the procedural exclusivity required by *O'Reilly v Mackman* threatened for a time to erode the rights of individuals who have to defend themselves against enforcement action by public authorities. It is important that an individual who is prosecuted for breach of subordinate legislation such as byelaws can as a defence plead that the legislation is invalid, and is not barred from doing so by failure to seek judicial review.[107] And tribunals whose task it is to decide whether a statutory disability benefit should be paid to an individual must be able to decide on the validity of the relevant regulations.[108]

Judicial discretion in granting relief[109]

One important aspect of the question of remedies is the principle that the prerogative orders are residual, and should not be granted when other

---

[102]   [1983] 2 AC 237, 285.
[103]   *Wandsworth Council v Winder* [1985] AC 461.
[104]   [1992] 1 AC 624 (and P Cane [1992] PL 193).
[105]   [1992] 1 AC 624, at 653 and 629.
[106]   *Mercury Communications Ltd v Director General of Telecommunications* [1996] 1 All ER 575. Cf *British Steel plc v Customs and Excise Commissioners* [1996] 1 All ER 1002.
[107]   See *R v Reading Crown Court, ex p Hutchinson* [1988] QB 384, distinguishing *Quietlynn Ltd v Plymouth Council* [1988] QB 114 (see A W Bradley [1988] PL 169). Cf *Bugg v DPP* [1993] QB 473 (D Feldman [1993] PL 37) and *R v Wicks* [1997] 2 All ER 801; also p 731 above.
[108]   *Chief Adjudication Officer v Foster* [1993] 1 All ER 705 (D Feldman (1992) 108 LQR 45 and A W Bradley [1992] PL 185).
[109]   de Smith, Woolf and Jowell, op cit, ch 20.

redress is available. In a leading case from the 19th century, mandamus was refused where a statute created both a duty and a specific remedy for enforcing it (a complaint to central government).[110] Where there is an express right of appeal, the court does not grant a remedy if the appeal would fully meet the individual's case,[111] but may do so if the statutory remedy is not a satisfactory or effective alternative to a judicial remedy.[112] So too, no declaration is granted in respect of a statutory duty if the Act which created the duty also provides the remedy (for example, application to the magistrates' court).[113] In this situation, the High Court has no original jurisdiction to exercise. On similar grounds, the court may hold that before seeking judicial review applicants must exhaust all statutory remedies available to them. However, the default powers of ministers in respect of local social services may be able to deal with the merits of a particular complaint, but do not enable points of law to be resolved.[114] Judicial review is not an optional substitute for an appeal to the statutory tribunal that has jurisdiction over, say, the tax liability of the individual seeking review.[115] But circumstances may arise in which a judicial remedy may be justified, if the decision at first instance is manifestly ultra vires[116] or there has been abuse of the statutory procedure by the public authority.[117]

The court's approach to alternative remedies is only one aspect of the discretion that a court may exercise in deciding whether to grant relief. Amongst the matters that may move a court to withhold relief when grounds for review have been established are factors going to delay in bringing the application, the applicant's conduct and motives,[118] and the public inconvenience that a remedy might entail.[119] This flexibility was invoked when, in reviewing decisions of the City's Take-over Panel, the Court of Appeal stated that in that context the court would see its role as 'historic rather than contemporaneous', ie that the court would seek to guide the panel in its future conduct of affairs, not to intervene in ongoing take-over battles.[120]

Statutory machinery for challenge

The technicalities of the prerogative and other remedies in their unreformed state often led in the past to legislation providing a simpler procedure for securing judicial review. Such legislation was always related to specific powers of government and usually included provisions excluding other forms of judicial review. An important example is provided by the standard procedure

---

110   *Pasmore v Oswaldtwistle Council* [1898] AC 387.
111   *R v Paddington Valuation Officer, ex p Peachey Property Co* [1966] 1 QB 380.
112   *Leech v Deputy Governor of Parkhurst Prison* [1988] AC 533.
113   *Barraclough v Brown* [1897] AC 615.
114   *R v Devon CC, ex p Baker* [1995] 1 All ER 73.
115   *R v IRC, ex p Preston* [1985] AC 835.
116   *R v Hillingdon Council, ex p Royco Homes Ltd* [1974] QB 720.
117   *R v Chief Constable, Merseyside, ex p Calveley* [1986] QB 424. Cf *R v Home Secretary, ex p Swati* [1976] 1 All ER 717 and *R v Birmingham Council, ex p Ferrero Ltd* [1993] 1 All ER 530.
118   Eg *R v Commissioners of Customs and Excise, ex p Cooke* [1970] 1 All ER 1068. See generally Sir T Bingham [1991] PL 64.
119   *R v Social Services Secretary, ex p Association of Metropolitan Authorities* [1986] 1 All ER 164.
120   *R v Panel on Take-overs and Mergers, ex p Datafin plc* [1987] QB 815. And see C Lewis [1988] PL 78.

for the compulsory purchase of land. After a compulsory purchase order has been made by the local authority and, where objections have been raised by the owner concerned, an inquiry has been held into the order, the minister must decide whether to confirm the order. If he or she decides to confirm, there is a period of six weeks from the confirmation during which any person aggrieved by the purchase order may challenge the validity of the order in the High Court[121] on two grounds: (1) that the order is not within the powers of the enabling Act; or (2) that the requirements of the Act have not been complied with and that the objector's interests have been substantially prejudiced thereby.[122] These grounds have been interpreted as covering all grounds upon which judicial review may be sought, including in (1) matters affecting vires, abuse of discretion, and natural justice and in (2) observance of all relevant statutory procedures.[123] When an aggrieved person makes an application to the High Court, the court may make an interim order suspending the purchase order, either generally or so far as it affects the applicant's property. If the order is not challenged in the High Court during the six-week period, the order is statutorily protected from challenge; any other form of judicial review of the order is excluded, before or after the confirmation of the order.[124]

This effective method of challenge was first provided by the Housing Act 1930 at a time when there was strong feeling against legislative attempts to exclude judicial review of ministers' actions altogether. Today it is found in the Housing Act 1985 in regard to clearance orders and in many other statutes relating to land.[125] Resort to this remedy has often enabled the High Court to give its entire attention to the principles of judicial review in issue, uncomplicated by the procedural and jurisdictional questions which may arise in regard to the prerogative orders.[126] The imposition of a time-limit on the right of challenge is necessary in order that, if no objection is taken promptly, the authorities concerned can put the decision into effect. Other statutory rights of appeal include the right to appeal to the High Court on matters of law from many tribunals[127] and on points of law affecting planning decisions.[128] Although these remedies are outside the scope of the application for judicial review under Order 53, they are heard in the High Court by the same judges.[129]

It is however necessary for an applicant to the court to come within the scope of the procedure, and the question of locus standi depends on the statutory provisions. The six-week right to challenge compulsory purchase orders and planning decisions is given to 'any person aggrieved'. This clearly

---

[121]   Or in Scotland in the Court of Session. On when the six weeks begin to run, see *Griffiths v Environment Secretary* [1983] 2 AC 51.

[122]   Acquisition of Land Act 1981, s 23 (consolidating earlier Acts).

[123]   *Ashbridge Investments Ltd v Minister of Housing* [1965] 3 All ER 371; *Coleen Properties Ltd v Minister of Housing* [1971] 1 All ER 1049; *Seddon Properties Ltd v Environment Secretary* (1981) 42 PCR 26.

[124]   Acquisition of Land Act 1981, s 23; and see below.

[125]   Eg Town and Country Planning Act 1990, ss 286–8.

[126]   Examples include *Fairmount Investments Ltd*, p 792 above, and *Bushell*, p 752 above.

[127]   Tribunals and Inquiries Act 1992, s 11; and see RSC Order 57.

[128]   Town and Country Planning Act 1990, ss 289, 290.

[129]   Note 54 above.

includes the owner who objects to his or her land being compulsorily purchased but in 1961 it was held not to include neighbouring owners who had objected at a public inquiry to proposed new development; they were considered to have no legal interest that would render them aggrieved persons in law.[130] In 1973, Ackner J gave a more generous interpretation to the phrase 'person aggrieved', including within it the officers of an amenity association who had opposed new development at a public inquiry.[131] This decision was welcome, for those who take part in a public inquiry have a definite interest in ensuring that the decision which follows conforms to the law.

Statutory exclusion of judicial control[132]

There is a strong presumption that the legislature does not intend access to the courts to be denied. But where Parliament has appointed a specific tribunal for the enforcement of new rights and duties, it is necessary to have recourse to that tribunal in the first instance. Unless an appeal to the courts is provided by the statute, their jurisdiction is limited to the general methods of judicial review. But many statutes have contained words designed to oust the jurisdiction of the courts. Such provisions have been interpreted by the judges so as to leave, if at all possible, their supervisory powers intact. At one time the prerogative orders were often excluded by name, but even the express exclusion of certiorari was not effective against a manifest defect of jurisdiction or fraud committed by a party procuring an order of the court.[133] One frequent clause was that a particular decision 'shall be final', but it is settled law that this does not restrict the power of the court to issue certiorari, either for jurisdictional defects or for error of law.[134] Such a clause means simply that there is no right of appeal from the decision. Another clause which does not deprive the courts of their supervisory jurisdiction is where it is stated that a statutory order when made shall have effect 'as if enacted in the Act' which authorised it; the court may nonetheless hold the order to be invalid if it conflicts with the provisions of the Act.[135]

It is then only by an exceptionally strong formula that Parliament can effectively deprive the High Court or the Court of Session of supervisory jurisdiction over inferior tribunals and public authorities. Exclusion clauses today frequently accompany the granting of an express right to challenge the validity of an order or decision during a limited time. Thus the statute which permits challenge of a compulsory purchase order within six weeks of its confirmation provides that subject to the possibility of challenge in that time, 'a compulsory purchase order ... shall not, either before or after it has been confirmed, made or given, be questioned in any legal proceedings whatsoever ...'.[136]

In *Smith v East Elloe Rural District Council* the plaintiff, whose land had been taken

---

[130]   *Buxton v Minister of Housing* [1961] 1 QB 278; cf *Maurice v London CC* [1964] 2 QB 362.
[131]   *Turner v Environment Secretary* (1973) 72 LGR 380.
[132]   de Smith, Woolf and Jowell, op cit, pp 231–49; Wade and Forsyth, op cit, pp 729–42; Craig, op cit, ch 16.
[133]   *Colonial Bank of Australasia v Willan* (1874) 5 PC 417.
[134]   *R v Medical Appeal Tribunal, ex p Gilmore* [1957] 1 QB 574.
[135]   *Minister of Health v R* [1931] AC 494.
[136]   Acquisition of Land Act 1981, s 25.

compulsorily for the building of council houses nearly six years previously, alleged that the making of the order had been caused by wrongful action and bad faith on the part of the council and its clerk. She submitted that the exclusion clause did not exclude the court's power in cases of fraud and bad faith. The House of Lords held by a bare majority that the effect of the Act was to protect compulsory purchase orders from judicial review except by statutory challenge during the six-week period. Although the validity of the order could no longer be challenged, the action against the clerk of the council for damages could proceed.[137]

A very different attitude towards an exclusion clause was taken by the House of Lords in 1968 in a decision which we have already considered in relation to jurisdictional control.

In *Anisminic Ltd v Foreign Compensation Commission*, the Foreign Compensation Act 1950, s 4(4), provided that the determination by the commission of any application made under the Act 'shall not be called in question in any court of law'. The commission was a judicial body responsible for distributing funds supplied by foreign governments as compensation to British subjects. It rejected a claim made by Anisminic for a reason which the company submitted was erroneous in law and exceeded the commission's jurisdiction. *Held*, by a majority in the House of Lords, s 4(4) did not debar a court from inquiring whether the commission had made in law a correct decision on the question of eligibility to claim. 'Determination' meant a real determination, not a purported determination. By taking into account a factor which in the view of the majority was irrelevant to the scheme, the commission's decision was a nullity. Lord Wilberforce said, 'What would be the purpose of defining by statute the limits of a tribunal's powers, if by means of a clause inserted in the instrument of definition, those limits could safely be passed?'[138]

The decision is a striking example of the ability of the courts to interpret privative clauses in such a way as to maintain the possibility of judicial review. Although the authority of *Smith v East Elloe RDC* was questioned in the *Anisminic* case, the former decision was not overruled: indeed, the issues involved in considering the finality which should be given to a compulsory purchase order are different from those involved in considering how far an award of compensation should be subject to review. In 1976, the Court of Appeal held that the statutory bar on attempts to challenge the validity of a purchase order after the six-week period was absolute: an aggrieved owner could not bring such a challenge some months later, even though he alleged that the order had been vitiated by a breach of natural justice and good faith which he had only discovered after the six-week period.[139] Even if the purchase order must stand, this should not prevent the owner from seeking compensation from those responsible for the alleged acts of bad faith.

Tribunals and Inquiries Act 1992, s 12

The Franks committee in 1957 recommended that no statute should contain words purporting to oust the prerogative orders. Section 12 of the Tribunals

---

137 [1956] AC 736.
138 [1969] 2 AC 147, 208 (and ch 29 A above). For the legislative sequel, see Foreign Compensation Act 1969, s 3.
139 *R v Environment Secretary, ex p Ostler* [1977] QB 122 (N P Gravells (1978) 41 MLR 383 and J E Alder (1980) 43 MLR 670). Also *Hamilton v Scottish Secretary* 1972 SLT 233 and *R v Cornwall CC, ex p Huntington* [1994] 1 All ER 694.

and Inquiries Act 1992 (re-enacting the Tribunals and Inquiries Act 1958) provides that:

(*a*)   any provision in an Act passed before 1st August 1958 that any order or determination shall not be called into question in any court, or
(*b*)   any provision in such an Act which by similar words excludes any of the powers of the High Court,
shall not have effect so as to prevent the removal of the proceedings into the High Court by order of certiorari or to prejudice the powers of the High Court to make orders of mandamus.

There is a corresponding provision to restrict exclusion of the supervisory jurisdiction of the Court of Session. These provisions do not apply in two cases, namely (*a*) to an order or determination of a court of law, or (*b*) where an Act makes special provision for application to the High Court within a specified time, for example, the power to challenge a compulsory purchase order within six weeks of its confirmation. This means that s 12 of the 1992 Act has no effect on the decision in *Smith v East Elloe RDC*.[140]

The effect of s 12 largely depends on the interpretation placed on the words 'order or determination'. To take one example from the Parliament Act 1911, by s 3, 'any certificate of the Speaker of the House of Commons ... shall be conclusive for all purposes and shall not be questioned in any court of law'. Such a certificate would seem to be a determination within the meaning of s 12 of the Tribunals and Inquiries Act. But it is doubtful whether that Act is to be construed as setting aside the common law rule which prevents the courts from inquiring into any matter relating to the internal proceedings of the House of Commons.[141]

Two common forms of statutory provision are not affected by s 12 of the 1992 Act. First, a provision that a registrar's certificate is 'conclusive evidence' that certain procedures have been complied with has been held not to exclude the jurisdiction of the courts in judicial review, since it is limited to matters of evidence.[142] Secondly, the jurisdiction of the courts may to an extent be restricted if a power is conferred upon an authority in terms which allow it to act 'if it is satisfied', 'if it thinks fit', 'if it appears to it', 'if in its opinion'.[143] The literal interpretation of such formulae would leave little room for effective judicial review[144] and the courts often exercise their supervisory jurisdiction in the face of subjectively worded powers.[145]

It is increasingly anomalous that the effect of s 12 of the 1992 Act is limited to legislation enacted before August 1958. Statutory provisions which intend to exclude judicial review are still sometimes enacted.[146] However, clauses enacted at any date that seek to exclude judicial review on matters affecting

140   *Hamilton v Secretary of State for Scotland* (above).
141   Ch 11 A. And cf Scotland Act 1978, s 17(4).
142   *R v Registrar of Companies, ex p Central Bank of India* [1986] QB 1114. And see *R v Foreign Secretary, ex p Trawnik, The Times*, 21 February 1986.
143   For examples, see Housing Act 1985, part III (Housing the Homeless), ss 62, 65–7.
144   Eg *Robinson v Minister of Town and Country Planning* [1947] KB 702.
145   *Commissioners of Customs and Excise v Cure and Deeley Ltd* [1962] 1 QB 340; *Padfield v Minister of Agriculture* [1968] AC 997; *Durayappah v Fernando* [1967] 2 AC 337. And see Wade and Forsyth, op cit, pp 442–53.
146   Eg Security Service Act 1989, s 5(4), and Intelligence Services Act 1994, s 9(4); ch 24.

directly effective rights in Community law are not enforceable by the courts.[147] More generally, a legislative policy of excluding judicial review of official decisions would be controversial for constitutional reasons and would create a risk of breaching the right to a fair hearing under the European Convention on Human Rights, art 6.[148]

Remedies in Scots administrative law[149]

The prerogative orders have never been part of Scots law, except to the extent that they were introduced into Scotland by legislation for the purposes of revenue law, nor did a separate court of equity develop in Scotland. Apart from statutory remedies like the six-week right to challenge a compulsory purchase order, which apply both in Scotland and England, administrative law remedies in Scotland are essentially the same remedies as are available in private law to enforce matters of civil obligation. The most important of these remedies (which are now available subject to the procedural changes made in 1985 described below) are (*a*) the ancient remedy of *reduction*, by which any document (including decisions of tribunals, local byelaws, the dismissal of public servants and disciplinary decisions) may be quashed as being in excess of jurisdiction, in breach of natural justice or in other ways contrary to law;[150] (*b*) the no less ancient remedy of *declarator*, from which the English declaration of right was derived; (*c*) the remedy of *interdict*, corresponding to both injunction and prohibition in English law; (*d*) the action for damages for breach of civil obligation; and (*e*) a summary remedy to enforce performance of statutory duties, comparable with but not identical to mandamus.[151] By contrast with the former English law, all relevant forms of relief may be sought in the same proceedings.[152]

Several points of comparison with English law may be noted. First, it was established in *Watt v Lord Advocate* that while the remedy of reduction may be used to quash decisions of tribunals which are in excess of their jurisdiction, it is not available (as certiorari is in English law) to review errors of law made by a tribunal within jurisdiction.[153] However, at a time before the right of appeal on points of law from decisions of the Social Security Commissioners had been created,[154] the court also held that the error of law in question had led the tribunal to exceed its jurisdiction, since it had caused a statutory entitlement to unemployment benefit to be withheld on an extraneous consideration. This decision applied to Scots law the principle in *Anisminic Ltd v Foreign Compensation Commission*.[155]

---

147   Case 222/84 *Johnston v Chief Constable RUC* [1987] QB 129.
148   See eg *Zander v Sweden* (1993) 18 EHRR 175; A W Bradley (1995) 1 European Public Law 347.
149   *Stair Encyclopedia of the Laws of Scotland*, vol I, pp 147–96; C M G Himsworth, in Supperstone and Goudie (eds), *Judicial Review*, ch 19; and in Hadfield (ed), *Judicial Review, A Thematic Approach*, ch 10; T Mullen et al [1995] PL 52.
150   See eg *Malloch v Aberdeen Corpn* [1971] 2 All ER 1278; *Barrs v British Wool Marketing Board* 1957 SC 72.
151   Court of Session Act 1988, s 45; *T Docherty Ltd v Burgh of Monifieth* 1971 SLT 12.
152   Eg *Macbeth v Ashley* (1874) LR 2 HL (Sc) 352.
153   1979 SC 120.
154   See now Social Security Administration Act 1992, s 24; ch 28 A.
155   Note 138 above, and ch 29 A.

Secondly, in Scots law there is no direct equivalent to relator proceedings. The Lord Advocate in this respect never assumed the role played by the Attorney-General. For this reason, and because Scots law does not favour the granting of an interdict by a civil court to restrain further criminal conduct, *Gouriet*'s case[156] has no direct application in Scotland. The lack of relator proceedings is partly made good by broader rules on title and interest to sue, which permit individuals to sue directly to enforce many public rights.[157] In *Wilson v Independent Broadcasting Authority*, members of a group campaigning in the referendum on devolution had title and interest to sue for an interdict to restrain the showing of a series of political broadcasts which did not maintain a proper balance between the two sides. The judge, Lord Ross, could see 'no reason in principle why an individual should not sue in order to prevent a breach by a public body of a duty owed by that public body to the public.'[158] This welcome statement of principle was, however, not supported by some earlier decisions.[159] In 1987, the organisation Age Concern Scotland was held to have title but no interest to challenge as ultra vires official guidance that limited the making of supplementary payments to old people for severe weather conditions;[160] but a teachers' association had title and interest to challenge a university's unlawful action where its members could not be expected to do so individually.[161]

Thirdly, difficult situations brought about by official failures may sometimes be resolved by the power of the Court of Session to exercise an extraordinary equitable jurisdiction in the form of the *nobile officium* of the court.[162]

Finally, since 1985 Scotland has had its own procedure of application for judicial review, which is similar to but by no means identical with the English model.[163] It was introduced later in Scotland than in English law because the procedural difficulties relating to the prerogative orders did not exist in Scots law. However, the ordinary procedures of civil litigation were not ideal for the prompt resolution of disputes arising in areas such as housing and immigration; and the decision of the House of Lords in *Brown v Hamilton DC* that the sheriff court had no power at common law to review decisions of local authorities caused Lord Fraser to recommend the introduction of a new summary procedure in the Court of Session.[164]

In 1985, rules of court[165] established a new procedure of petition, known as an application for judicial review, which *must* be used whenever an application is made to the supervisory jurisdiction of the Court of Session for one or more of the remedies mentioned above. The rules seek to provide for the rapid handling of every application, with the main procedural steps being

---

[156]   Note 37 above.
[157]   *Duke of Atholl v Torrie* (1852) I Macq 65; *Ogston v Aberdeen Tramways Co* (1896) 24 R 8.
[158]   1979 SC 351.
[159]   *D & J Nicol v Dundee Harbour Trustees* 1915 SC (HL) 7; *Simpson v Edinburgh Corp* 1960 SC 313.
[160]   *Scottish Old People's Welfare Council, Petitioners* 1987 SLT 179.
[161]   *Educational Institute of Scotland v Robert Gordon University*, The Times, 1 July 1996.
[162]   *Ferguson, Petitioners* 1965 SC 16.
[163]   See A W Bradley [1987] PL 313.
[164]   1983 SLT 397 at 418, and see *Stair Encyclopaedia*, above, p 191.
[165]   See now Rules of the Court of Session (made by SI 1994 No 1443), ch 58.

under the control of individual judges designated for the purpose. The leave of the court is not required for an application, but an application without merits can be briskly rejected by the judge for that reason. The major problem that has arisen is that the 'supervisory jurisdiction' of the Court of Session is not defined in legislation, though it has often been described in judgments.[166] It cannot be identified with the scope of the remedies that may be granted on a successful application for judicial review since those remedies are available in the whole of the civil law. Some judgments after 1985 drew for this purpose upon the private law/public law distinction made in English law,[167] but in 1992 the Court of Session in *West v Secretary of State for Scotland*[168] robustly rejected that distinction. It held that the court has power under its supervisory jurisdiction 'to regulate the process by which decisions are taken by any person or body to whom a jurisdiction, power of authority has been delegated or entrusted by statute, agreement or any other instrument', in particular where there was a 'tripartite relationship' between the decision-maker, the individual affected and the person or body from whom the power to decide was derived. On the facts in *West*, it was held that a prison officer could not obtain judicial review of a decision made by the Scottish Office that he should not receive a home removal grant after he had been transferred from one penal institution to another. This dispute was seen as one arising from a contract of employment, with no features bringing the dispute within the 'supervisory jurisdiction'.[169] The court's approach to jurisdiction was based on an analysis of the process of decision-making and its review, not on any discussion of the political or social context of the powers of public authorities. There is no divergence between the substantive principles of public law in English and Scots law, but *West* may enable the Scottish courts to apply their supervisory jurisdiction to regulatory and similar powers of private organisations, where in England this would be impeded by the private/public distinction.

Habeas corpus[170]

As has already been seen,[171] the prerogative writ of habeas corpus is in English law an important remedy in respect of public or private action which takes away individual liberty. Today its use as a means of securing judicial control of executive acts arises mainly in extradition and immigration law,[172] but it is potentially available in other areas of power, such as detention or internment under emergency powers[173] and when the liberty of mental patients is

---

[166]   Eg *Moss Empires Ltd v Glasgow Assessor* 1917 SC (HL) 1.

[167]   Including *Tehrani v Argyll Health Board (No 2)* 1990 SLT 118 and *Watt v Strathclyde Council* 1992 SLT 324. See Himsworth in Supperstone and Goudie (note 149 above) and Lord Clyde, in Finnie, Himsworth and Walker (eds), *Edinburgh Essays in Public Law*, pp 281–93.

[168]   1992 SLT 636 (and see W J Wolffe [1992] PL 625).

[169]   See also *Naik v Stirling University* 1994 SLT 449 and *Blair v Lochaber Council* 1995 SLT 407.

[170]   For a full account, see Sharpe, *The Law of Habeas Corpus*. On the history, see HEL IX 108–25 and Forsyth, *Cases and Opinions in Constitutional Law*, ch 16.

[171]   Ch 21 F.

[172]   Ch 20 B, C.

[173]   Ch 25 D, E.

restricted. Unlike the prerogative orders, the writ has not recently been the subject of legislative reform. The writ originally enabled a court of common law to bring before itself persons whose presence was necessary for pending proceedings. In the 15th and 16th centuries, the courts of King's Bench and Common Pleas used habeas corpus to assert their authority over rival courts, and to release persons imprisoned by such courts in excess of their jurisdiction. In the 17th century, parliamentarians used the writ to check arbitrary arrest by order of the King or King's Council.[174] In 1640, it was enacted that in the case of any such detention, the common law courts must issue the writ and inquire into and rule upon the true cause of the detention.

It was of the essence of habeas corpus that it was a procedure by which the court could determine the legality of an individual's detention, and that the procedure should be efficient. Habeas Corpus Acts were enacted in 1679, 1816 and 1862.[175] These Acts did not need to widen the jurisdiction of the courts but sought to enhance the effectiveness of the writ and to ensure that applications were dealt with promptly by the judges. Thus the 1679 Act prohibited evasion of habeas corpus by transfer of prisoners detained for 'any criminal or supposed criminal matter' to places outside the jurisdiction of the English courts (for example, to Scotland, Ireland or to any 'island or places beyond the seas') on pain of heavy penalties. The 1816 Act inter alia gave the judge power in civil cases to inquire summarily into the truth of the facts stated in the gaoler's return to the writ, even though the return was 'good and sufficient in law'.[176] The 1862 Act provided that the writ was not to issue from a court in England into any colony or foreign dominion of the Crown where there were courts having authority to grant habeas corpus and with power to ensure its execution. Detention within Northern Ireland and Scotland is a matter for the courts in those jurisdictions.[177]

Habeas corpus is described as a writ of right which is granted *ex debito justitiae*. This means that a prima facie case must be shown before it is issued but, unlike the prerogative orders, it is not a discretionary remedy and it may not be refused merely because an alternative remedy exists.[178] However, habeas corpus is a remedy against *unlawful* detention: clearly an order for detention issued by an inferior tribunal is unlawful if the tribunal had no jurisdiction to issue it. But is habeas corpus a remedy for correcting every error made by an inferior tribunal? The question of how far the High Court will go in reviewing the validity of an order for detention which appears to be lawful cannot be answered simply, 'for the case-law is riddled with contradictions'.[179] In *Rutty*'s case, habeas corpus issued to release a woman who had been detained for eight years on a magistrate's order under the Mental Deficiency Acts 1913–27: the High Court exercised its power under the 1816 Act to examine the truth of the facts stated in the return and established that there was no evidence before the magistrate on which a valid order could

---

174   For *Darnel*'s case and the Petition of Right, see ch 12 D.
175   For the detail, see Taswell-Langmead, *English Constitutional History*, pp 432–6.
176   See eg *R v Board of Control, ex p Rutty* [1956] 2 QB 109.
177   *Re Keenan* [1972] 1 QB 533; *Re McElduff* [1972] NILR 1; *R v Cowle* (1759) 2 Burr 834, 856.
178   *R v Governor of Pentonville Prison, ex p Azam* [1974] AC 18, 31 (CA).
179   de Smith, Woolf and Jowell, op cit, p 678; and see Rubinstein, *Jurisdiction and Illegality*, pp 105–16, 176–86.

have been made.[180] But in a wartime internment case, the Home Secretary was not required to give the grounds for his belief that the applicant was of hostile origin and association, and the internment was upheld without further inquiry into the facts.[181]

Similar difficulties have arisen concerning immigration law. In one line of cases during the 1970s, the courts were most reluctant to make effective use of habeas corpus as a means of reviewing executive decisions, for example in the case of someone about to be removed from the country as an illegal entrant.[182] We have seen that in *Khawaja's* case the House of Lords reversed this trend.[183] Lord Scarman there considered that the Habeas Corpus Act 1816 imposed a duty on the court to examine the truth of the facts set out by the executive, where an individual's liberty was in issue; he added that the nature of the remedy sought could not affect the principle of the law. However, the Court of Appeal has distinguished between the scope of habeas corpus and the grounds of judicial review. Thus the court has held that habeas corpus is not a substitute for an application for judicial review when a detained immigrant facing removal from the country seeks to challenge the original administrative decision refusing leave to enter, not on grounds that there was no power to make it but on grounds such as procedural error or failure to take relevant matters into account.[184] The distinction drawn by the Court of Appeal between habeas corpus and judicial review has been authoritatively criticised for eroding the power of habeas corpus.[185] In 1995, the Court of Appeal distinguished *Muboyayi* when a mental patient had been compulsorily detained on the basis of a defective application by an approved social worker;[186] but in the case of young persons wrongly imprisoned for non-payment of fines, the Divisional Court held that their detention could be challenged by judicial review, but not by habeas corpus.[187] This uncertainty affecting habeas corpus is reflected in case-law at Strasbourg: the European Court of Human Rights held in the case of a mental patient that habeas corpus did not enable the English court to determine both the substantive and formal legality of the detention,[188] but reached the opposite conclusion in the case of persons suspected of terrorist offences.[189]

Normally the applicant for habeas corpus will be the person detained, but any relative or other person may apply on his or her behalf if the detainee cannot do so. Application is made *ex parte* (that is, without the other side

---

[180] Note 176 above.
[181] *Greene v Home Secretary* [1942] AC 284, following *Liversidge v Anderson* [1942] AC 206.
[182] The decisions include *R v Home Secretary, ex p Mughal* [1974] 1 QB 313 and *R v Home Secretary, ex p Zamir* [1980] AC 930. And see C Newdick [1982] PL 89.
[183] *R v Home Secretary, ex p Khawaja* [1984] AC 74 and ch 29 A.
[184] *R v Home Secretary, ex p Cheblak* [1991] 2 All ER 319; *R v Home Secretary, ex p Muboyayi* [1992] 1 QB 244. In *Muboyayi*, habeas corpus was issued urgently to restrain the removal of an individual pending decision of his application for judicial review; the court could now issue an interim injunction against the removal: *M v Home Office* (note 61 above).
[185] Law Commission, Law Com No 226, part XI, and H W R Wade (1997) 113 LQR 55. Also A Le Sueur [1992] PL 13; M Shrimpton [1993] PL 24.
[186] *Re S-C* [1996] QB 599.
[187] *R v Oldham Justices, ex p Cawley* [1996] 2 WLR 681.
[188] *X v United Kingdom* (1981) 4 EHRR 188.
[189] *Brogan v United Kingdom* (1988) 11 EHRR 117.

being heard) supported by an affidavit to the Divisional Court or in vacation to a single judge.[190] If prima facie grounds are shown, the court ordinarily directs that notice of motion be given to the person having physical control of the person detained (for example, a prison governor) but notice may also be served on a minister (for example, the Home Secretary) who is responsible for the detention. On the day named, argument on the merits of the application takes place. If the court decides that the writ should issue, it orders the prisoner's release forthwith. Under this practice there is no need for the respondent to produce the prisoner in court at the hearing (exceptionally, an applicant may be allowed to present his or her case in person)[191] and no return to the writ is made as the writ itself has not yet been issued. In exceptional cases the court may order the issue of the writ on the *ex parte* application if, for example, there is danger of the detainee being taken outside the jurisdiction. Disobedience to the writ is punishable by fine or imprisonment for contempt of court and there may also be penalties under the Act of 1679. Officers of the Crown are subject to the writ.[192] Rights of appeal from the High Court's decision are subject to detailed provision in the Administration of Justice Act 1960 (ss 5, 14, 15): in a civil matter, the appeal goes via the Court of Appeal to the House of Lords and in a criminal matter (for example, in extradition proceedings) from the Divisional Court to the Lords, with leave.[193]

The writ of habeas corpus has no exact counterpart in Scots law, but ever since the Scottish Parliament's Act for preventing Wrongous Imprisonment in 1701 there has been strict provision restricting the length of time within which a person committed for trial may be held in custody.[194] As regards civil detention, the Court of Session has jurisdiction to order the release of any person who is unlawfully detained. If no other more convenient remedy is available (for example, by a suspension and interdict), the detained person may petition the Inner House of the Court of Session for his or her release in the exercise of the nobile officium of the court.

---

190   RSC, Ord 54.
191   *Re Wring* [1960] 1 All ER 536.
192   *Re Thompson* (1889) 5 TLR 565; *Secretary of State v O'Brien* [1923] AC 603.
193   On the civil/criminal distinction, see eg *Amand v Home Secretary* [1943] AC 147, 156. On the right to make successive applications, see Administration of Justice Act 1960, s 14(2).
194   For the '80 day' and '110 day' rules, see now the Criminal Procedure (Scotland) Act 1995, s 65.

CHAPTER 31

Liability of public authorities and the Crown

In chapters 29 and 30, we examined the law that enables the courts to review the decisions of public authorities on grounds such as ultra vires, error of law and breach of natural justice. We now consider the position of public authorities in relation to civil liability, in particular the law of tort and contract.[1] In principle, public authorities in English law are subject to the same rules of liability in tort and contract as apply to private individuals and companies. There is no separate law of administrative liability for wrongful acts.[2] In practice, however, public authorities require powers to enable them to maintain public services and perform regulatory functions; these powers are generally not available to private individuals. Many new public works, such as motorways and power-stations, could not be created unless there was power in the public interest to override private rights that might be adversely affected. Parliament has often legislated to give public authorities special powers or protection from liability. The courts have also recognised that the public interest may require a public authority to be treated differently from private individuals.

At several points in this chapter, the special position of the Crown will be emphasised. In the past, important distinctions were drawn between (*a*) the Crown, including departments of central government, and (*b*) other public bodies, such as local authorities and statutory corporations. While many of these distinctions have been removed, notably by the Crown Proceedings Act 1947, others still survive. This chapter deals in section A with the liability of public authorities and the Crown in tort, and in section B with contractual liability. Section C deals with other aspects of the law relating to the Crown, including such procedural immunities and privileges as survive and the rules of evidence relating to the non-disclosure of evidence in the public interest.

Relevant aspects of the law in Scotland will be mentioned briefly in each section. Although the common law in Scotland regarding the position of the Crown differed from the law in England, the same broad approach to the

---

[1] Wade and Forsyth, *Administrative Law*, chs 20–21; Craig, *Administrative Law*, chs 17, 19, 20; de Smith, Woolf and Jowell, *Judicial Review of Administrative Action*, ch 19; Arrowsmith, *Civil Liability and Public Authorities*; Hogg, *Liability of the Crown*; Harlow, *Compensation and Government Torts*.

[2] As was stressed in Dicey's account of the 'rule of law': ch 6 above.

liability of public authorities in general has been followed in both legal systems, especially since the Crown Proceedings Act 1947.

A.　Liability of public authorities and the Crown in tort

Individual liability

In the absence of statutory immunity, every individual is liable for wrongful acts that he or she commits and for such omissions as give rise to actions in tort at common law or for breach of statutory duty. This applies even if an officer representing the Crown claims to be acting out of executive necessity.

In *Entick v Carrington*[3] the King's Messengers were held liable in an action of trespass for breaking and entering the plaintiff's house and seizing his papers, even though they were acting in obedience to a warrant issued by the Secretary of State. This was in law no defence as the Secretary had no legal authority to issue such a warrant.

Obedience to orders does not normally constitute a defence whether the orders are those of the Crown, a local authority,[4] a limited company or an individual employer.[5] The principle that superior orders are no defence to an action in tort would, if unqualified, have placed too heavy a burden on many subordinate officials. At common law an officer of the court, such as a sheriff, who executes an order of the court, is protected from personal liability unless the order is on its face clearly outside the jurisdiction of the court.[6] Moreover, it has been found necessary to provide protection for certain classes of official. Thus certain statutes exempt officials from being sued in respect of acts done bona fide in the course of duty.[7] The Constables Protection Act 1750 protects constables who act in obedience to the warrant of a magistrate, though the magistrate acted without jurisdiction in issuing the warrant. Again, the Mental Health Act 1983, s 139, affords constables and hospital staff some protection against civil and criminal liability in respect of acts such as the compulsory detention of a mental patient, unless the act was done in bad faith or without reasonable care.[8] The liability of individual officials will therefore turn both on the powers which they may exercise and also on the privileges and immunities which they may enjoy. But no general immunity is enjoyed by officers or servants of the Crown.[9]

Vicarious liability of public authorities

While the individual liability of public officials was historically important in establishing that public authorities were themselves subject to the law,

---

[3]　(1765) 19 St Tr 1030; ch 6 above.
[4]　*Mill v Hawker* (1875) LR 10 Ex 92.
[5]　For the position of the armed forces, see ch 16.
[6]　*The Case of the Marshalsea* (1613) 10 Co Rep 76a.
[7]　Eg National Health Service Act 1977, s 125; Financial Services Act 1986, s 187.
[8]　On the earlier law, see *R v Bracknell Justices, ex p Griffiths* [1976] AC 314; *Carter v Metropolitan Police Commissioner* [1975] 2 All ER 33; and *Ashingdane v UK* (1985) 7 EHRR 528.
[9]　The suggestion to the contrary in *R v Transport Secretary, ex p Factortame Ltd* [1990] 2 AC 85, 145 was rightly disapproved in *M v Home Office* [1994] 1 AC 377.

individual liability is not today a sufficient basis for the liability of large organisations. It is now essential to be able to sue an individual's employing authority, if only because the authority is a more substantial defendant: a successful plaintiff wants the certainty of knowing that any damages and costs awarded will in fact be paid.

We examine below the process by which vicarious liability came to be imposed on the departments of central government. In cases not involving the Crown, it has long been the law that a public authority is, like any other employer, liable for the wrongful acts of its servants or agents committed in the course of their employment. It was established in 1866 that the liability of a public body whose servants negligently execute their duties is identical with that of a private trading company.

In *Mersey Docks and Harbour Board Trustees v Gibbs,*[10] a ship and its cargo were damaged on entering a dock by reason of a mud bank left negligently at the entrance. The trustees were held liable and appealed to the House of Lords on the ground that they were not a company deriving benefit from the traffic, but a public body of trustees constituted by Parliament for the purpose of maintaining the docks. That purpose involved authority to collect tolls for maintenance and repair of the docks, for paying off capital charges and ultimately for reducing the tolls for the benefit of the public. It was held that these public purposes did not absolve the trustees from the duty to take reasonable care that the docks were in such a state that those who navigated them might do so without danger.

In spite of the argument that a corporation should not be liable for a wrongful act, since a wrongful act must be beyond its lawful powers and therefore not attributable to it, a corporation is, like any other employer, liable for the torts of its employees acting in the course of their employment. Thus a hospital authority is liable for negligence in the performance of their professional duties by those physicians and surgeons who are employed by the authority.[11] Under general principles of vicarious liability, a public authority is not liable for acts committed by an employee who is acting outside the course of employment 'on a frolic of his own'. But where a prisoner is ill-treated by prison officers, the Home Office may be vicariously liable even if those acts amount to misfeasance in public office, when the ill-treatment is a misguided or unauthorised method of performing their duties.[12] Even where an official is appointed and employed by a local authority, the authority is not liable for acts which he or she commits under the control of a central authority or in the exercise of a distinct public duty imposed by the law.[13] There was formerly no vicarious liability in respect of police officers, but the chief constable is now vicariously liable for their acts committed in the performance of their functions.[14] Such vicarious liability has been held not to arise when police officers commit the statutory tort of racial discrimination.[15]

---

[10] (1866) LR 1 HL 93.
[11] *Cassidy v Minister of Health* [1951] 2 KB 343. For the vicarious liability of education and social service authorities, see *X v Bedfordshire CC* [1995] 2 AC 633 (below).
[12] *Racz v Home Office* [1994] 2 AC 45; and text at notes 82–85 below.
[13] *Stanbury v Exeter Corpn* [1905] 2 KB 838.
[14] Police Act 1964, s 48 (now 1996, s 88); Police (Scotland) Act 1967, s 39; ch 21 F.
[15] *Farah v Metropolitan Police Commissioner* [1997] 1 All ER 289.

Tortious liability of the Crown

There were two main rules which until 1948 governed the complicated law relating to the liability of the Crown: (*a*) the rule of substantive law that the King could do no wrong; (*b*) the procedural rule derived from feudal principles that the King could not be sued in his own courts. The survival of these rules into the 20th century meant that before 1948 the Crown could be sued neither in respect of wrongs that had been expressly authorised nor in respect of wrongs such as negligence committed by Crown servants in the course of their employment.[16] Nor were government ministers vicariously liable for the tortious acts of staff in their departments, since in law ministers and civil servants are alike servants of the Crown.[17] It was anomalous that this immunity of the Crown applied to the activities of central government. The rigour of the immunity was eased before 1948 by concession. Acting through the Treasury Solicitor, departments were often prepared to defend an action against a subordinate official and pay damages if he or she was found personally liable for a wrongful act. From this there developed the practice by which the Crown might nominate a defendant on whom a writ could be served. This practice was however disapproved by the House of Lords in 1946, in a case in which the nominated defendant could not have been personally liable for the alleged tort.[18] It became urgently necessary for the law to be changed to permit the Crown to be sued in tort. As early as 1927, a draft Bill had been recommended by a government committee, but opposition from within government prevented reform of the law.[19] The law was at last placed on a new basis by the Crown Proceedings Act 1947.

With important exceptions, this Act (which applies only to proceedings by and against the Crown in right of Her Majesty's Government in the United Kingdom)[20] established the principle that the Crown is subject to the same liabilities in tort as if it were a private person of full age and capacity (*a*) in respect of torts committed by its servants or agents, (*b*) in respect of the duties which an employer at common law owes to his servants or agents, and (*c*) in respect of any breach of the common law duties of an owner or occupier of property (s 2(1)). The Crown is therefore vicariously liable for the torts of its servants or agents, for example, negligent driving by a Crown servant while in the course of his or her employment.

The Crown is also liable for breach of a statutory duty, provided that the statute is one which binds the Crown as well as private persons (s 2(2)) such as the Occupiers' Liability Act 1957. The Act of 1947 imposes no liability enforceable by action in the case of statutory duties which bind only the Crown or its officers, such as the duty placed upon the Secretary of State for

---

16 See eg *Viscount Canterbury v A-G* (1842) 1 Ph 306 (negligence of Crown servants causing Houses of Parliament to burn down).
17 *Raleigh v Goschen* [1898] 1 Ch 73; *Bainbridge v Postmaster-General* [1906] 1 KB 178. And see *M v Home Office* [1994] 1 AC 377, 408–9.
18 *Adams v Naylor* [1946] AC 543.
19 Cmd 2842, 1927. And see J Jacob [1992] PL 452 and Jacob, *The Republican Crown*, ch 2.
20 S 40(2)(b), (c). And see *Franklin v A-G* [1974] QB 185, *Tito v Waddell (No 2)* [1977] Ch 106, *Mutasa v A-G* [1980] QB 114, *R v Foreign Secretary, ex p Indian Assn of Alberta* [1982] QB 892.

Education by s 1 of the Education Act 1944 (now s 10 of the Education Act 1996), to promote the education of the people.

Although the principle of Crown liability is established, the Act of 1947 elaborates this in some detail. Thus the vicarious liability of the Crown is restricted to the torts of its officers as defined in the Act (s 2(6)). This definition requires that the officer shall (*a*) be appointed directly or indirectly by the Crown and (*b*) be paid in respect of his duties as an officer of the Crown at the material time wholly out of the Consolidated Fund,[21] moneys provided by Parliament or a fund certified by the Treasury. This excludes, for example, the police. There is no vicarious liability for officers acting in a judicial capacity or in execution of judicial process (s 2(5)),[22] nor for acts or omissions of a Crown servant unless apart from the Act the servant would have been personally liable in tort (s 2(1)). The general law relating to indemnity and contribution applies to the Crown as if it were a private person (s 4). The Act does not authorise proceedings to be brought against the Sovereign in her personal capacity (s 40(1)) and does not abolish any prerogative or statutory powers of the Crown, in particular those relating to the defence of the realm and the armed forces (s 11(1)).

Under the 1947 Act, there were formerly two principal exceptions from liability in tort. The first related to the armed forces. By s 10, neither the Crown nor a member of the armed forces was liable in tort in respect of acts causing death or personal injury which were committed by a member of the armed forces while on duty, where (*a*) the victim was a member of the armed forces on duty at the time or, if not on duty as such, was on any land, premises, ship, aircraft or vehicle which was being used for the purposes of the armed forces, and (*b*) the injury was certified by the Secretary of State as attributable to service for purposes of pension entitlement. This certificate did not guarantee an award of a pension unless the conditions for entitlement were fulfilled.[23] There certainly must be a public scheme for compensating members of the armed forces who suffer injury or death during their service. But should this exclude the right to sue for common law damages? In 1987, Parliament legislated to put into suspense s 10 of the 1947 Act.[24] Section 10 can be revived if it appears to the Secretary of State necessary or expedient to do so, for example by reason of imminent national danger or for warlike operations outside the United Kingdom. Until it is so revived, members of the armed forces (and in the event of death, their dependants) may sue fellow members (and the Crown vicariously) for damages in respect of injuries or death arising out of their service. However, when a soldier sued for personal injury caused during the Gulf operations in 1991 (for which s 10 was not revived), the Court of Appeal held that no duty of care was owed to him by his fellow soldiers during battle conditions.[25]

---

21   Ch 17.
22   On s 2(5), see *Jones v Department of Employment* [1989] QB 1 (functions of adjudication officer not judicial) and *Welsh v Chief Constable of Merseyside Police* [1993] 1 All ER 692 (prosecutor's administrative functions not judicial).
23   *Adams v War Office* [1955] 3 All ER 245. On s 10, see also *Pearce v Defence Secretary* [1988] AC 755, overruling in part *Bell v Defence Secretary* [1986] 1 QB 322.
24   Crown Proceedings (Armed Forces) Act 1987; and see F C Boyd [1989] PL 237.
25   *Mulcahy v Ministry of Defence* [1996] QB 732 and ch 16.

The second exception from liability for tort formerly applied to the Post Office, at that time a government department, for acts or omissions in relation to postal packets or telephonic communications (s 9). Nor was there any liability in contract.[26] When the Post Office ceased to be a government department and became a public corporation, the existing limitations on liability for postal and telephone services were continued.[27]

Subject to these two exceptions, the Crown Proceedings Act in principle assimilated the tortious liabilities of the Crown to those of a private person. However, in many situations involving the potential liability of the government the analogy of private liability is not directly helpful. Some claims against the Crown are held to be non-justiciable,[28] but in general the courts seek to apply to governmental action rules derived from, for example, the ordinary law of negligence.[29]

In the law of Scotland, the position of the monarch in respect of Crown proceedings was not identical with the position in English law, the Court of Session being less willing than the English courts to grant the King immunity from being sued.[30] However, it was held in 1921 that the Crown was not vicariously liable for the wrongful acts of Crown servants.[31] Section 2 of the 1947 Act established such liability in Scotland, although the terminology is modified. Thus 'tort' in the Act's application to Scotland means 'any wrongful or negligent act or omission giving rise to liability in reparation'.[32]

The Act of 1947 thus enabled the Crown to be sued in England in the law of torts, and in Scotland in the law of delict, or reparation. We will now consider some aspects of the substantive law governing the liability in tort of public authorities generally.

Statutory authority as a defence

Where acts of a public body interfere with an individual's rights (whether these concern property, contract or liberty), those acts will be unlawful unless legal authority for them exists. Such authority may be found in legislation or in common law. Where Parliament expressly authorises something to be done, to do it in accordance with that authority cannot be wrongful. It will depend on the legislation whether compensation is payable for the rights which Parliament has authorised to be taken away. The undertaking of many public works affecting private rights of property (for example, the construction of nuclear installations or motorways) is subject to detailed rules of compensation in the relevant legislation.[33] But often express provision for compensation is not made. It is then for the court in interpreting the legislation to decide what powers are authorised and whether any compensation is payable. In that process of interpretation, it is assumed that, when

---

26   *Triefus & Co Ltd v Post Office* [1957] 2 QB 352.
27   Post Office Act 1969, ss 6(5), 29, 30; British Telecommunications Act 1981, s 70.
28   Eg *Tito v Waddell (No 2)* and *Mutasa v A-G* (note 20 above).
29   Eg *Dorset Yacht Co v Home Office* [1970] AC 1004; note 67 below.
30   See J D B Mitchell [1957] PL 304.
31   *MacGregor v Lord Advocate* 1921 SC 847.
32   Crown Proceedings Act 1947, s 43(b).
33   See eg Nuclear Installations Acts 1965 and 1969 (as amended by Energy Act 1983, Part II); Land Compensation Act 1973.

discretionary power is given to a public body, there is no intention to interfere with private rights, unless the power is expressed in such a way as to make interference inevitable.

In *Metropolitan Asylum District v Hill*, hospital trustees were empowered by statute to build hospitals in London. A smallpox hospital was built at Hampstead in such a way as to constitute a nuisance at common law. *Held*, in the absence of express words or necessary implication in the statute authorising the commission of a nuisance, the building of the hospital was unlawful. 'Where the terms of the statute are not imperative, but permissive, when it is left to the discretion of the persons empowered to determine whether the general powers committed to them shall be put into execution or not, ... the fair inference is that the Legislature intended that discretion to be exercised in strict conformity with private rights and did not intend to confer licence to commit nuisance in any place which might be selected for the purpose'.[34]

If, however, the exercise of a statutory power or duty inevitably involves injury to private rights, there is no remedy unless the statute makes provision for compensation.[35]

In *Allen v Gulf Oil Refining Ltd*, the House of Lords held that a local Act which envisaged the building of an oil refinery at Milford Haven, though it gave the company no express power to construct the refinery and did not define the site, did give authority for the construction and use of the refinery. Such authority protected the company against liability for nuisance caused to neighbouring owners which was the inevitable result of the construction of the refinery, even though the Act gave the owners no compensation for the loss of their rights.[36]

While the courts may, as in *Allen v Gulf Oil Refining Ltd*, hold that the right to sue for nuisance has been taken away, the courts will rarely hold that a body exercising statutory powers is at liberty to do so carelessly. As a leading dictum of Lord Blackburn put it,

... no action will lie for doing that which the legislature has authorised, if it be done without negligence, although it does occasion damage to anyone; but an action does lie for doing that which the legislature has authorised, if it be done negligently.[37]

This statement must be read in context: it applies only where a statute authorises an act to be done which will necessarily cause some injury to private rights, and where the act is performed carelessly so causing unnecessary injury to those rights.[38] Such additional injury is outside the protection afforded by the statute. However, if a public authority which merely has a power to act, and not a duty, decides to take action but acts inefficiently, it is not liable unless the inefficiency causes extra damage to an individual: this was so held in 1941, in the difficult case of *East Suffolk Catchment Board v Kent*, when the use by a river board of an ineffective method of removing flood water from a farmer's land was held to create no liability towards the farmer.[39]

---

[34]   (1881) 6 App Cas 193, 212–13 (Lord Watson).
[35]   *Hammersmith Rly Co v Brand* (1869) LR 4 HL 171.
[36]   [1981] AC 1001.
[37]   *Geddis v Proprietors of Bann Reservoir* (1878) 3 App Cas 430, 455–6.
[38]   *X v Bedfordshire CC* [1995] 2 AC 633, 733.
[39]   [1941] AC 74. And see M J Bowman and S H Bailey [1984] PL 277. Cf *Fellows v Rother DC* [1983] 1 All ER 513, 522.

Statutory duties[40]

It was at one time the view that anyone who had been harmed by a failure to perform a statutory duty could bring an action for damages against the person or body liable to perform it.[41] If this were the law today, it would have a very broad impact on public bodies required to provide services or to exercise regulatory or protective functions. However, the enormous variety of duties imposed by statute means that there can be no single form of proceedings for enforcing public duties. Some duties, for example the duty of the Secretary of State for Education to promote the education of the people of England and Wales,[42] are effectively unenforceable by legal proceedings of any kind.[43] Some public duties may be enforced by proceedings for an injunction brought by the Attorney-General in the public interest, or by a local authority in exercise of statutory powers.[44] Some are enforceable only by recourse to statutory compensation.[45] Very many public law duties may, as we have seen, be enforced by an order of mandamus obtained on an application for judicial review.[46] Some statutes provide for a criminal penalty in the event of a breach of duty. Where the statute that creates a duty expressly provides a sanction for breach (for example, prosecution of the person responsible) or a remedy for those affected to use, the courts may well hold that no other means of enforcing the duty exists.[47]

In some situations, particularly where the statutory duty closely parallels a common law duty (for example, to use care not to cause personal injury) the breach of statutory duty gives rise to a private right of action for damages; such an action is akin to an action for negligence, except that liability depends on the breach of the duty itself, not on there being a lack of care.[48] Such an action for breach exists if it can be shown by interpretation of the statute that the duty was imposed for the protection of a certain class and that the legislature intended to confer on members of that class the benefit of a right of action.[49] It is notoriously difficult to evaluate all the factors that may be relevant when a court is deciding whether a statutory duty is enforceable by an action for damages, where the statute is silent on the point.[50] In 1969, the English and Scottish Law Commissions recommended that the courts should be able to assume in interpreting statutes that the remedy of damages was

---

[40] R A Buckley (1984) 100 LQR 204; Harding, *Public Duties and Public Law*, ch 7.
[41] Dicta to this effect in *Couch v Steel* (1854) 3 E & B 402 were disapproved in *Atkinson v Newcastle Waterworks Co* (1877) 2 Ex D 441.
[42] Education Act 1996, s 10.
[43] Ch 29 A (text at note 91).
[44] Ch 30.
[45] Note 33 above.
[46] Ch 30.
[47] See *Cutler v Wandsworth Stadium Ltd* [1949] AC 398; *Lonrho Ltd v Shell Petroleum Co Ltd* [1982] AC 173, 185; *Scally v Southern Health Board* [1992] 1 AC 294; *Wentworth v Wiltshire CC* [1993] QB 654.
[48] Eg *Reffell v Surrey CC* [1964] 1 All ER 743.
[49] See *X v Bedfordshire CC* [1995] 2 AC 633, 731.
[50] See Bennion, *Statutory Interpretation*, Code, s 14 (revised at [1995] All ER Rev, p 496). Such difficulties do not arise where an Act specifies the means of enforcement; see eg Local Government Act 1988, s 19(7) (excluding criminal penalties but authorising judicial review and claims for damages).

available for breach of statutory duty, unless the statute expressly provided to the contrary.[51] This proposal, which was not adopted, did not take account of the relations between government and the individual which are the concern of administrative law, where often damages would not be an appropriate remedy. Indeed, recent judicial policy has severely limited the availability of damages as a remedy for breach of public duties.

In *X (minors) v Bedfordshire CC*,[52] the House of Lords considered a group of claims for damages arising from the defective performance by local councils of duties relating to the education and welfare of children. The alleged breaches included the failure of a social service authority to take children into care who were badly in need of protection and at risk of abuse; a converse error by social workers in taking a child into care believed to be at risk of sexual abuse, when the identity of her abuser was mistaken; and failures by education authorities to identify the special educational needs of children and to provide special schooling which was appropriate. The councils had applied to have these claims struck out as disclosing no cause of action. *Held*, so far as the actions were based on breach of statutory duty, they were disallowed. The duties in question gave rise to no private rights of action; nor were the councils under a duty of care in performing the statutory duties. The education cases were allowed to proceed so far as they were based on the councils' vicarious liability for the professional negligence of teachers and educational psychologists; there was held to be no such vicarious liability for social workers and psychiatrists reporting to the councils on alleged child abuse.

This decision is notable for Lord Browne-Wilkinson's analysis of the common law rules of liability that apply to statutory functions of local authorities. He emphasised that very different policy considerations applied to (a) public law remedies obtainable by judicial review, and (b) the private right to sue for damages. His speech dealt also with difficult issues affecting the liability of public authorities in negligence, including the relation between the duty of care and official discretion and the distinction between direct and vicarious liability. In a different context, an earlier decision of the House reflects a similar approach to that in *X v Bedfordshire CC*: a prisoner adversely affected by a breach of prison rules was held to have no action in damages arising from the breach. Lord Jauncey said:

The fact that a particular provision was intended to protect certain individuals is not of itself sufficient to confer private law rights upon them, something more is required to show that the legislature intended such conferment.[53]

Tort liability and judicial review

In respect of both statutory duty and the law of negligence, *X v Bedfordshire CC* is the culmination of much case-law which, in an era when the use of judicial review has expanded dramatically, has resisted an equivalent expansion in the liability of public bodies to be sued for damages.[54] We have seen that in France

---

[51]   HC 256 (1968–69), para 38.
[52]   [1995] 2 AC 633; see P Cane (1996) 112 LQR 13 and L Edwards (1996) 1 Edin Law Rev 115.
[53]   *R v Deputy Governor of Parkhurst Prison, ex p Hague* [1992] 1 AC 58, 171 (Lord Jauncey); see also *Becker v Home Office* [1972] 2 QB 407.
[54]   *Meade v London Borough of Haringey* [1979] 2 All ER 1016 (P Cane [1981] PL 11) and *Thornton v Kirklees Council* [1979] QB 626 are inconsistent with the thrust of recent case-law.

both the judicial review of official decisions and the power to award compensation for wrongful acts committed by public authorities are entrusted to the administrative courts.[55] Under the French system, rules of public liability have developed which differ from the ordinary rules of liability in civil law. In English law, by contrast, public authorities and officials are in principle subject to the same law of civil liability as private persons. Thus a claim in damages against a public authority must be based on one of the ordinary torts (including negligence, nuisance, trespass to the person and breach of statutory duty), or on a specific right of action created by statute. Yet the existing categories of tort do not include all instances in which a public body may cause loss to an individual through acts or omissions that as a matter of public law are in some way wrongful.

In particular, English law does not accept that an individual has a right to be indemnified for loss caused by invalid or ultra vires administrative action.[56] The current procedure for judicial review, whereby an applicant for review may seek damages together with the prerogative orders, has not changed the substantive rules of liability.[57] Thus a prisoner may successfully seek judicial review of a prison governor's decision to put him in solitary confinement for 28 days, but has no right to sue the governor or the Home Office for damages, whether for breach of prison rules or for false imprisonment.[58]

When a trader's licence for a market stall is cancelled in breach of natural justice, he or she may by certiorari recover the licence[59] but has no right to recover compensation for the intervening loss of income unless, exceptionally, he can prove that the market authority acted with malice.[60] The Judicial Committee has twice affirmed that a public authority's decision may be invalid, in the sense of being ultra vires, without this giving rise to a right to damages.

In *Dunlop v Woollahra Council*, an owner of building land suffered financial loss when the local council imposed restrictions on prospective development which were later quashed as ultra vires. *Held*, the owner had no claim in damages for the loss resulting from the invalid restrictions. Moreover, the council had not acted negligently in imposing the restrictions, having taken legal advice before so doing. The council had acted in good faith and, in the absence of malice, could not be liable for the tort of abuse of public office.[61] In *Rowling v Takaro Properties Ltd*, a New Zealand Cabinet minister had acted ultra vires in refusing consent to the proposed development of a luxury hotel; this had caused the Japanese investors to lose interest in the project. When the minister was sued for damages by the developer, the Judicial Committee *held* (reversing the New Zealand Court of Appeal) that even assuming that a duty of care was owed by the minister to the developer, he was not in breach of that duty: his

---

55   Ch 26 above. Brown and Bell, *French Administrative Law*, ch 8. And see C R Harlow (1976) 39 MLR 516; Bell and Bradley (eds), *Governmental Liability*.
56   *Hoffmann-La Roche v Secretary of State for Trade* [1975] AC 295, 358 (Lord Wilberforce).
57   See ch 30; and see eg *Page Motors Ltd v Epsom and Ewell BC* (1982) 80 LGR 337, and P Cane [1983] PL 202; *Davy v Spelthorne BC* [1984] AC 262.
58   *R v Deputy Governor of Parkhurst Prison, ex p Hague* [1992] 1 AC 58.
59   *R v Barnsley Council, ex p Hook* [1976] 3 All ER 452.
60   *David v Abdul Cader* [1963] 3 All ER 579 (and A W Bradley [1964] CLJ 4); and *Roncarelli v Duplessis* (1959) 16 DLR (2d) 689.
61   [1982] AC 158.

decision had been based on a tenable view of his powers and was neither unreasonable nor negligent.[62]

The distinction between judicial review and the right to sue in damages for breach of a statutory duty has been applied in the context of Community law.

In *Bourgoin SA v Ministry of Agriculture*,[63] the Minister of Agriculture had banned the import of turkeys from France, claiming to do so on health grounds. The European Court of Justice held that the real reason for the ban was to protect British turkey farmers, and that the action breached art 30 of the EEC Treaty;[64] the French turkey companies then sued the Ministry for damages, claiming inter alia breach of statutory duty. *Held*, in the Court of Appeal (by 2–1), it was a sufficient remedy for the companies in English law that they could have had the ban quashed by judicial review. Oliver LJ dissented, holding that the protection of individual rights under Community law involved the payment of compensation to cover the period between the commission of the wrong and its rectification.

In some circumstances, maladministration by a government department or local authority may cause an individual to suffer injustice. In this event, by complaining to the appropriate Ombudsman the individual may succeed in obtaining compensation, but the authority is not liable to be sued in damages for maladministration by such a person.[65] It was against this background that in 1988 the Justice/All Souls committee on administrative law recommended that the law should permit compensation to be recoverable by any person who sustains loss as a result of acts or decisions that are for any reason wrongful or contrary to law or as a result of any excessive delay.[66] There is however no prospect of any such change in the law being acceptable to the government. Thus in practice the liability of public authorities will continue to depend on tort law, in particular the tort of negligence.

Public authorities and liability for negligence

Although the Crown Proceedings Act 1947 assimilated the tort liability of central government to that of a private person, the duties of government may give rise to issues of liability which are not easily resolved by applying legal principles that relate primarily to the acts of private persons.

In *Dorset Yacht Co v Home Office*,[67] the Home Office was sued for the value of a yacht which had been damaged when seven borstal boys absconded at night from a borstal summer camp on an island in Poole harbour. The plaintiffs alleged that the boys were able to abscond because of the negligence of their officers. The Home Office argued that the system of open borstals would be jeopardised if any liability was imposed on

---

[62]   [1988] AC 473.
[63]   [1986] QB 716.
[64]   Case 40/82 *EC Commission v UK* [1982] ECR 2793.
[65]   Ch 28 D; and *R v Knowsley BC, ex p Maguire* (1992) 90 LGR 653.
[66]   *Administrative Justice, Some Necessary Reforms*, ch 11.
[67]   [1970] AC 1004; and see C J Hamson [1969] CLJ 273, G Semar [1969] PL 269 and M A Millner [1973] CLP 260.

the government for the wrongful acts of those who absconded. The House of Lords *held*, Lord Dilhorne dissenting, that the Home Office was liable for the negligence of the officers; in the circumstances the officers owed a duty of care to the yacht owners, the damage to the yacht being reasonably foreseeable as the direct consequence of a failure to take reasonable care.

This decision had broad consequences for the developing law of negligence, but it did not establish that the Home Office was liable regardless of negligence; nor did it govern the situation in which it was alleged that an executive discretion (for example, to transfer someone to an open prison) had been improperly exercised. Lord Diplock in *Dorset Yacht* suggested that questions of liability for the exercise of discretion were to be settled by applying the public law concept of ultra vires rather than the civil law concept of negligence.[68] The relationship between the two concepts arose again in *Anns v Merton Council*,[69] in which the Lords held that both a failure by local inspectors to inspect, and a failure to inspect properly, the foundations of a new building (which later suffered structural damage because the foundations were inadequate) could make the council liable for the cost of repairing the building. In the leading speech, Lord Wilberforce distinguished between the discretion of the council in adopting its policy as to inspection, and the operational tasks involved in carrying out that policy: the more 'operational' a power or duty might be, the easier it might be to impose a common law duty of care.[70]

An immense amount of litigation arose directly from *Anns v Merton Council*, caused in part by Lord Wilberforce's analysis of the approach which the courts should adopt in applying the law of negligence to new fact situations, and in part by the problems that arose for public authorities from the broad way in which *Anns* caused them to be liable for not having prevented the commission of wrongs by others.[71] In *Murphy v Brentwood Council*, on similar facts to those in *Anns*, a seven-judge House of Lords declared that *Anns* had been wrongly decided, and held (inter alia) that the defendant council owed no duty of care to the plaintiff when it approved the plans for defective foundations for the plaintiff's house.[72]

Apart from the *Brentwood Council* decision, the courts have sought in many contexts to restrict liability on the part of public authorities, particularly in respect of claims for economic loss arising out of regulatory functions[73] and of claims seeking to impose a private law duty of care upon the public functions

---

68   [1970] AC 1004, at 1067; cf *Fellowes v Rother DC* [1983] 1 All ER 513 and Harlow, *Compensation and Government Torts*, pp 54–7.

69   [1978] AC 728.

70   On this distinction, see D Oliver [1980] CLP 269, S H Bailey and M J Bowman [1986] CLJ 430 and P P Craig (1978) 94 LQR 428; and Craig, op cit, pp 618–32. See also *X v Bedfordshire CC* [1995] 2 AC 633, 736–8.

71   The decisions include *Peabody Donation Fund v Sir Lindsay Parkinson & Co* [1985] AC 210 and *Curran v Northern Ireland Co-ownership Association* [1987] AC 718. And see M J Bowman and S H Bailey [1984] PL 277; T Weir [1989] PL 40; A W Bradley (1989) 23 The Law Teacher 109.

72   [1991] 1 AC 398. And see I N D Wallace (1991) 107 LQR 177.

73   *Yuen Kun-yeu v A-G of Hong Kong* [1988] AC 175; *Davis v Ratcliffe* [1990] 2 All ER 536. And see H McLean (1988) 8 OJLS 442.

of the police,[74] on the Civil Aviation Authority[75] and on the civil servants who decide claims for social security benefits.[76] In a case of physical injury, as opposed to economic loss, the House of Lords by 3–2 refused to impose a duty of care on a highway authority which failed to remove an earth bank that it knew obstructed visibility at a dangerous road-junction; in the majority view, it was 'important, before extending the duty of care owed by public authorities, to consider the cost to the community of the defensive measures which they are likely to take to avoid liability'.[77]

By contrast, on the authority of *Hedley Byrne v Heller*,[78] a person who relies to his or her detriment on inaccurate statements made by an official in the course of the latter's duties may have a remedy against the official and the department concerned. In *Culford Metal Industries v Export Credits Guarantee Department*, the department was liable in negligence for having given advice to an English company which caused the company to be uninsured when German contractors failed to pay for work carried out abroad.[79] So too was a local authority liable where an environmental health officer negligently required expensive and unnecessary alterations to be made to a farm guest house.[80] In general, however, it is now plain that 'novel categories of negligence' will develop 'incrementally and by analogy with established categories, rather than by a massive extension of a prima facie duty of care' restrained only by indefinable policy considerations seeking to limit the scope of the duty of care.[81]

Other aspects of governmental liability

Other aspects of the liability of public authorities may be briefly mentioned. First, liability in tort for misfeasance in public office arises when officials knowingly abuse or exceed their powers, either intending to inflict injury on the plaintiff or knowing that loss will be caused to the plaintiff.[82] In *Bourgoin v Ministry of Agriculture*, on the basis that the minister knew he did not have the powers that he purported to exercise, the Court of Appeal held unanimously that such liability would arise.[83] It appears that a local council would be liable for misfeasance where it was not exercising public law functions but acting as

---

[74] *Rigby v Chief Constable of Northampton* [1985] 2 All ER 985; *Hill v Chief Constable of West Yorkshire* [1989] AC 53; *Calveley v Chief Constable, Merseyside* [1989] AC 1228. Also *Elguzoli-Daf v Metropolitan Police Commissioner* [1995] QB 335 (no duty of care in respect of prosecution decisions).

[75] *Philcox v Civil Aviation Authority, The Times*, 8 June 1995.

[76] *Jones v Department of Employment* [1989] QB 1; W J Swadling [1988] PL 328.

[77] *Stovin v Wise* [1996] AC 923, 958 (Lord Hoffmann).

[78] [1964] AC 465; cf J Stapleton (1991) 95 LQR 249.

[79] *The Times*, 25 March 1981. And see *Meates v A-G* [1983] NZLR 308; Aronson and Whitmore, *Public Torts and Contracts*, pp 108–14.

[80] *Welton v North Cornwall DC* (1997) 9 Admin LR 45.

[81] *Sutherland Shire Council v Hayman* (1985) 60 ALR 1, 43–4 (Brennan J) quoted in *Murphy v Brentwood Council* [1991] 1 AC 398, 461.

[82] See note 60 above. Also *Micosta SA v Shetland Islands Council* 1986 SLT 193 (C T Reid [1986] PL 380) and J McBride [1979] CLJ 323.

[83] [1986] QB 716. For a valuable review of the law, see *Three Rivers DC v Bank of England* (No 3) [1996] 3 All ER 558 (and C Hadjiemmanuil [1997] PL 32).

the owner of property if, intending to damage the interests of a lessee, a majority of the council voted for a resolution cutting down the lessee's use of a building leased by the council.[84] Vicarious liability may arise in respect of misfeasance in office if the misconduct is an improper way of performing an official's duties.[85]

Secondly, ever since the general warrant cases in the 1760s in which exemplary damages were awarded for unlawful search and seizure, the courts have had power to award exemplary damages for oppressive, arbitrary or unconstitutional acts in the exercise of public power.[86] The power is limited to torts for which exemplary damages had been awarded before 1964, and does not apply to negligence or public nuisance.[87] For the same reason, exemplary damages may not be awarded in respect of the statutory torts of racial and sexual discrimination (which were created after 1964), significant as these are to public authorities both as employers and also as the providers of services to the public.[88] Juries considering the award of exemplary damages against the police must be directed by the trial judge as to the permissible range of such awards.[89]

Thirdly, the developing law of restitution was applied by the House of Lords in resolving a fundamental question as to the obligations of public authorities in *Woolwich Building Society v Inland Revenue Commissioners (No 2)*.[90] Nearly £57 million in tax had been paid under protest by the society under regulations which were later held to be ultra vires.[91] The House held by a majority of 3–2 that at common law there was a general restitutionary principle by which money paid pursuant to an ultra vires demand by a public authority was recoverable as of right, not at the discretion of the authority. This, said the majority, was required both by common justice and by the principle in the Bill of Rights that taxes should not be levied without the authority of Parliament.[92] Amongst the questions left open by Lord Goff's speech was whether the same principle applies if taxes are levied wrongly because the tax inspector misconstrued a statute or regulation. On this point Lord Goff commented that 'it would be strange if the right of the citizen to recover overpaid charges were to be more restricted under domestic law than it is under Community law'.[93]

Finally, as Lord Goff's comment suggests, the requirements of European law, including such issues as the liability of governments for failure to imple-

---

84   *Jones v Swansea Council* [1990] 3 All ER 737, 741. See also *Bennett v Metropolitan Police Commissioner* [1995] 2 All ER 1.

85   *Racz v Home Office* [1994] 2 AC 45.

86   *Wilkes v Wood* (1763) Lofft 1; *Rookes v Barnard* [1964] AC 1129, 1226. And see *Lancashire CC v Municipal Mutual Insurance Ltd* [1996] 3 WLR 493.

87   *AB v South West Water Services Ltd* [1993] QB 507, applying *Cassell and Co Ltd v Broome* [1972] AC 1027.

88   *Bradford Council v Arora* [1991] 2 QB 507 was over-ruled by *AB v South West Water Services Ltd*.

89   *Thompson v Metropolitan Police Commissioner* [1997] 2 All ER 764.

90   [1993] AC 70; and see P B H Birks [1980] CLP 191, [1992] PL 580; and J Beatson (1993) 109 LQR 401.

91   *R v IRC, ex p Woolwich Building Society* [1991] 4 All ER 92.

92   See chs 2 A and 17.

93   [1993] AC 70, at 177. For the duties of public bodies to make restitution, see also *Westdeutsche Landesbank Girozentrale v Islington Council* [1994] 4 All ER 890 (CA).

ment EC directives,[94] will increasingly effect the liability of public authorities, not only in the law of tort and restitution, but also in the law of contract.

B.   Contractual liability

In English law, the contracts of public authorities are in general subject to the same law that governs contracts between private persons.[95] There is no separate body of law governing administrative contracts, as there is in France.[96] There are however certain qualifications which must be made to this general statement. Contracts made on behalf of the Crown are subject to certain exceptional rules, which will be examined below together with relevant provisions of the Crown Proceedings Act 1947. Contracts made by statutory bodies such as local authorities are subject to the rules of ultra vires, both as regards matters of substance and matters of procedure. Thus a contract which it is beyond the power of a local authority to make (for example, because it conflicts with a statute which binds the authority) is void and unenforceable.[97] A contract made by a public authority is also void if it seeks to fetter the future exercise of the authority's discretionary powers.[98] Thus where a local planning authority in Cheshire agreed with Manchester University to discourage new development within the vicinity of the Jodrell Bank radio telescope, the purported agreement was without legal effect.[99] Moreover, a local authority remains free to exercise its power to make byelaws even though the effect of doing so may be to render the future performance of contracts it has made impossible or unprofitable for the contractor.[100] Other restraints may also apply to contracts of public authorities: thus the nationalised industries are subject to statutory duties regarding the terms on which they provide their services.[101] In the case of a local authority, its standing orders normally regulate the procedure by which contracts are placed and these may not be ignored by a council.[102] Where the officers of a local council purport to execute a contract in terms which have never been approved by the council, the contract is wholly void and not binding on the

---

[94]   See Case C – 6/90 *Francovich v Italy* [1993] 2 CMLR 66; P P Craig (1993) 109 LQR 595; C Lewis and S Moore [1993] PL 151; and ch 8 B.

[95]   Street, *Governmental Liability*, ch 3; Mitchell, *The Contracts of Public Authorities*; Turpin, *Government Procurement and Contracts*; Hogg, *Liability of the Crown*, ch 8 and see eg *Blackpool Aero Club v Blackpool Council* [1990] 3 All ER 25.

[96]   Mitchell, op cit, ch 4; Brown and Bell, *French Administrative Law*, pp 192–201.

[97]   *Rhyl UDC v Rhyl Amusements Ltd* [1959] 1 All ER 257; *Hazell v Hammersmith Council* [1992] 2 AC 1; *Crédit Suisse v Allerdale Council* [1996] 3 WLR 894; and ch 29 A.

[98]   *Ayr Harbour Trustees v Oswald* (1883) 8 App Cas 623; *Triggs v Staines UDC* [1969] 1 Ch 10; *Dowty Bolton Paul Ltd v Wolverhampton Corpn (No 2)* [1973] Ch 94.

[99]   *Stringer v Minister of Housing* [1971] 1 All ER 65.

[100]   *William Cory & Son Ltd v City of London* [1951] 2 KB 476.

[101]   Eg *South of Scotland Electricity Board v British Oxygen Co* [1959] 2 All ER 225 (duty to avoid 'undue discrimination' in fixing tariffs) and see ch 14.

[102]   *R v Hereford Corpn, ex p Harrower* [1970] 3 All ER 460. Also *R v Enfield Council, ex p Unwin (Roydon) Ltd* (1989) 1 Admin LR 51.

council.[103] An important control in the public interest is that contracts entered into by local authorities are subject to retrospective scrutiny by the system of local government audit. The contractual freedom of local authorities was further restricted by the Local Government Act 1988, which both required local councils to put specified services and activities up for compulsory competitive tendering, under the supervision of the Department of the Environment, and also barred councils from taking into account 'non-commercial' considerations in the placing of contracts for works and supplies. The economic importance of public procurement contracts has long been recognised in Community law and the Community directives on this matter are the subject of delegated legislation within the United Kingdom, creating rights and duties enforceable in the ordinary courts.[104] Changing attitudes to the management of government during the 1990s sought to expose those providing public services to market disciplines, within central as well as local government and also the NHS. The procedures devised for this purpose make use of the language of contract but often, as with the internal market of the NHS, stop short of creating legally enforceable contracts.[105]

Contractual liability of the Crown

In English law before 1948, the Crown's immunity from being sued directly in the courts was not confined to liability in tort and extended to all other aspects of civil liability. But it had long been regarded as essential that the subject should be able to obtain judicial redress under a contract made with the Crown or government department. The petition of right was originally a remedy for the recovery of property from the Crown, but it became available to enforce contractual obligations. The practice was simplified by the Petitions of Right Act 1860. A petition of right lay in respect of any claim arising out of contracts by which the Crown could be bound, but not in respect of claims in tort. It lay also for the recovery of real property, for damages for breach of contract[106] and to recover compensation under a statute.[107] Before a petition could be heard by the court, it had to be endorsed with the words *fiat justitia* (let right be done) by the Crown on the advice of the Home Secretary, who acted on the opinion of the Attorney-General. There was no appeal against the refusal of the fiat. A judgment in favour of a suppliant on a petition of right took the form of a declaration of the suppliant's rights and, being observed by the Crown, was as effective as a judgment in an ordinary action.

By s 1 of the Crown Proceedings Act 1947, in all cases where a petition of right was formerly required, it is possible to sue the appropriate government department or, where no department is named for the purpose, the Attorney-

---

103   *North West Leicestershire DC v East Midlands Housing Assn* [1981] 3 All ER 364.

104   See the Public Supply Contracts Regulations, SI 1991 No 2679, the Public Works Contracts Regulations, SI 1991 No 2680, and the Utilities and Works Contracts Regulations, SI 1992 No 3279; Craig, op cit, pp 685–9.

105   See Harden, *The Contracting State.* Also M Freedland [1994] PL 86 and, on the NHS, D Longley [1990] PL 527 and J Jacob [1991] PL 255.

106   *Thomas v R* (1874) LR 10 QB 31.

107   *A-G v De Keyser's Royal Hotel* [1920] AC 508.

General, by ordinary process either in the High Court or in a county court. No prior fiat from the Crown is required.

While the Petitions of Right Act 1860 was repealed by the Crown Proceedings Act 1947, it appears to have been kept in being for the purpose of proceedings in matters of contract or property against the Sovereign personally.[108] Since the 1947 Act applies only to proceedings against the Crown in right of the government of the United Kingdom, a procedural problem faced holders of Rhodesian government stock in 1974 when they attempted to force the British government to pay arrears of interest that had accrued since 1965. As the 1860 Act had been repealed and Rhodesian matters lay outside the remedies provided by the 1947 Act, it was necessary for the stockholders to bring their petition in the pre-1860 form.[109]

In Scotland the petition of right procedure had never existed, since it was always possible to sue the Crown as of right in the Court of Session on contractual claims or for the recovery of property.[110] Accordingly, s 1 of the Crown Proceedings Act 1947 does not apply to Scotland.

In general the ordinary rules of contract apply to the Crown: thus an agent need have only ostensible authority to bind the Crown and there is no rule requiring the actual authority of the Crown.[111] Those who make contracts on behalf of the Crown, as its agents, are in accordance with the general rule not liable personally.[112] Statutory authority is not needed before the Crown can make a contract, but payments due under the Crown's contracts come from money provided by Parliament; if Parliament exceptionally provides that no money is payable to a certain contractor, payments that would otherwise be due may not be enforced.[113] If a contract expressly provides that payments thereunder are to be conditional upon Parliament appropriating the money, the Crown is not liable if Parliament does not do so. But, in general, 'the prior provision of funds by Parliament is not a condition preliminary to the obligation of the contract'.[114] Payments due under contract are made out of the general appropriation for the class of service to which the contract relates, and not from funds specifically appropriated to a particular contract. It is usually accepted that the Crown has full contractual capacity as a matter of common law,[115] but this cannot entitle the Crown to make contracts which are contrary to statute. There is moreover a rule of law, the exact extent of which it is not easy to determine, that the Crown cannot bind itself so as to fetter its future executive action.

In *Rederiaktiebolaget Amphitrite v R*, a Swedish shipping company, Sweden being a neutral in the First World War, was aware that neutral ships were liable to be detained

---

[108]   Crown Proceedings Act 1947, s 40(1); *Franklin v A-G* [1974] QB 185, 194.

[109]   *Franklin v A-G* [1974] QB 185; *Franklin v R* [1974] QB 202.

[110]   Mitchell, *Constitutional Law*, p 304.

[111]   See *A-G for Ceylon v Silva* [1953] AC 461 on the difficulties of establishing ostensible authority in relation to the Crown. Cf *Re Selectmove Ltd* [1995] 2 All ER 531.

[112]   *Macbeath v Haldimand* (1786) 1 TR 172; and see *Town Investments Ltd v Department of the Environment*, note 145.

[113]   *Churchward v R* (1865) LR 1 QB 173.

[114]   *New South Wales v Bardolph* (1934) 52 CLR 455, 510 (Dixon J.); Street, *Governmental Liability*, pp 84–92.

[115]   See eg BV Harris (1992) 108 LQR 626; cf M Freedland [1994] PL 86, 91–5.

in British ports. They obtained an undertaking from the British government that a particular ship, if sent to this country with certain cargo, would not be detained. Accordingly the ship was sent with such a cargo, but the government withdrew the undertaking and refused clearance for the ship. On trial of a petition of right, *held*, the undertaking of the government was not enforceable as the Crown was not competent to make a contract which would have the effect of limiting its power of executive action in the future.[116]

It has been suggested that the defence of executive necessity only 'avails the Crown where there is an implied term to that effect or that is the true meaning of the contract';[117] or again that the defence has no application to ordinary commercial contracts made by the Crown. A preferable view is that the *Amphitrite* case illustrates a general principle that the Crown, or any other public authority, cannot be prevented by an existing contract from exercising powers which are vested in it either by statute or common law for the protection of the public interest.[118]

In *Commissioners of Crown Lands v Page*, the Crown sued for arrears of rent due under a lease of Crown land that had been assigned to the defendant. The defence was that the land had been requisitioned by a government department and that this constituted eviction by the Crown as landlord. The Court of Appeal held that the arrears were payable. Devlin LJ said: 'When the Crown, in dealing with one of its subjects, is dealing as if it too were a private person, and is granting leases or buying and selling as ordinary persons do, it is absurd to suppose that it is making any promise about the way in which it will conduct the affairs of the nation.'[119]

There are other problems arising from government contracts to which the accepted principles of English law provide no answer, for example, the power of a department to place contracts and to remove a firm from its list of approved contractors.[120] This power was used by the Labour government in 1975–78 to require companies who were granted contracts to observe a non-statutory pay policy.[121] This is an outstanding example of a government's ability to achieve public goals without recourse to formal legislation.[122]

The pre-contractual procedures observed in central government appear not to be subject to judicial review.[123] However, government contracts are subject to the scrutiny of the Comptroller and Auditor-General. Much government practice in placing and administering contracts derives from rulings of the Public Accounts Committee.[124] In view of the number and value

---

[116] [1921] 3 KB 500.
[117] *Robertson v Minister of Pensions* [1949] 1 KB 227, 237 (Denning J).
[118] Street, op cit, pp 98–9; Mitchell, *Contracts of Public Authorities*, pp 27–32, 52–65.
[119] [1960] 2 QB 274, 292; see also *William Cory & Son Ltd v City of London* [1951] 2 KB 476.
[120] Turpin, *Government Procurement and Contracts*, ch 4.
[121] G Ganz [1978] PL 333.
[122] T C Daintith [1979] CLP 41. Until it was rescinded by the House of Commons on 16 December 1982, the Fair Wages Resolution had for many years required uniform conditions on fair wages to be included in all government contracts.
[123] *R v Lord Chancellor, ex p Hibbit & Saunders* [1993] COD 326. Reliance on the public/private law distinction here is unconvincing (D Oliver [1993] PL 214). Cf *R v Legal Aid Board, ex p Donn & Co* [1996] 3 All ER 1, and see S Arrowsmith, *Government Procurement and Judicial Review* and (1990) 106 LQR 277.
[124] Ch 17.

of government contracts awarded each year, remarkably few disputes arising from such contracts reach the courts. Such disputes in practice are resolved by various forms of consultation, negotiation or arbitration. The Review Board for Government Contracts, established in 1969 under an agreement between the government and the Confederation of British Industry, reviews such matters as the profit formula for non-competitive government contracts and it may also examine in relation to a particular contract a complaint by either party that the price paid is not 'fair and reasonable.'[125] Government contracts are excluded from the jurisdiction of the Parliamentary Ombudsman.[126]

Service under the Crown

Service under the Crown is another instance of the special contractual position of the Crown; for it is generally held to be part of the prerogative that the Crown employs its servants at its pleasure, whether in the civil service or the armed forces.[127] The Crown has always claimed that its freedom to dismiss its servants at will is necessary in the public interest. Certainly the case-law suggests that the relationship between the Crown and its servants gives rise to few rights on the part of the servant against the Crown. Thus, in the absence of statutory provision,[128] no Crown servant has a remedy for wrongful dismissal. Where a colonial servant failed in a claim that he had been engaged for three years certain, Lord Herschell said: 'Such employment being for the good of the public, it is essential for the public good that it should be capable of being determined at the pleasure of the Crown, except in exceptional cases where it has been deemed to be more for the public good that some restriction should be imposed on the power to dismiss its servants.'[129]

The Crown's power at common law to dismiss its servants at pleasure has sometimes been explained on the basis that a term to this effect is implied into every contract of employment made by the Crown. If this were so, the Crown's power to dismiss at pleasure could be excluded by an express term in the contract of employment, but the court might disregard any such attempt to depart from the normal rule as a clog or fetter on the overriding power of the Crown.[130]

Although civil servants have no tenure of office in law, in practice they have a high degree of security. This security by tradition depended upon convention rather than law, and the collective agreements on conditions of service which were applied to civil servants did not give rise to contractual

---

[125] See eg Report of the Board on the 6th General Review of the profit formula for non-competitive government contracts, 1990.

[126] Ch 28 D.

[127] See *CCSU v Minister for the Civil Service* [1985] AC 374 and cf Sir William Wade (1985) 101 LQR 180.

[128] Eg the rule that judges hold office during good behaviour (ch 18 A), *Gould v Stuart* [1896] AC 575 and *Reilly v R* [1934] AC 176.

[129] *Dunn v R* [1896] 1 QB 116; G Nettheim [1975] CLJ 253. See also *Dunn v MacDonald* [1897] 1 QB 401.

[130] *Terrell v Secretary of State for the Colonies* [1953] 2 QB 482.

rights.[131] Indeed, it was for long uncertain whether Crown service is a contractual relationship at all. Many provisions of the Employment Rights Act 1996 apply to the armed forces;[132] although those relating to protection of wages are expressly excluded, it may be questioned whether the old rule that members of the forces cannot sue for their pay[133] still applies. In respect of the civil service, the Crown may now be liable for arrears of salary.[134] In 1991, it was held that civil servants are employed by the Crown under contracts of employment, since all the incidents of a contract of employment were present in that case and the civil service pay and conditions code dealt in detail with many aspects of the relationship; despite the statement in the code that the relationship was governed by the prerogative and civil servants could be dismissed at pleasure, neither the Crown nor civil servants intended the contents of the code to be merely voluntary.[135] However, the same court held that an aggrieved civil servant could not seek judicial review of a dismissal or other action.[136]

Many of the older arguments in favour of the Crown's privileged position as a civil employer were superseded in 1971 when the statutory right to bring proceedings in an industrial tribunal for unfair dismissal was conferred on civil servants.[137] However, the Crown may in the interests of state security exempt classes of civil servants from enjoying employment rights. This power was used in 1984 to exempt the civilian staff of the Government Communications Headquarters at Cheltenham from the Act. At the same time, the government used the prerogative powers of the Crown to impose a new condition of service barring GCHQ staff from union membership.[138] Subject to the statutory remedy for unfair dismissal, the Crown retains power to dismiss its servants at pleasure. In its employment practices, the Crown must not in general discriminate on racial or sexual grounds.[139]

C. The Crown in litigation: privileges and immunities

As we have already seen,[140] 'the Crown' is a convenient term in law for the collectivity that now comprises the Sovereign in her governmental capacity, ministers, civil servants and the armed forces. Lord Templeman said in 1993,

---

131   *Rodwell v Thomas* [1944] KB 596; cf *Riordan v War Office* [1959] 3 All ER 552. And see *CCSU v Minister for the Civil Service* [1985] AC 374.
132   Employment Rights Act, s 192, as amended by Armed Forces Act 1996, s 26.
133   *Leaman v R* [1920] 3 KB 663; *Kynaston v A-G* (1933) 49 TLR 300.
134   *Kodeeswaran v A-G of Ceylon* [1970] AC 1111; cf *Cameron v Lord Advocate* 1952 SC 165.
135   *R v Lord Chancellor's Department, ex p Nangle* [1992] 1 All ER 897 (and see S Fredman and G Morris [1991] PL 485 and (1991) 107 LQR 298), not following *R v Civil Service Appeal Board, ex p Bruce* [1988] 3 All ER 686. For proposals to provide senior civil servants with full written contracts, see Cm 2627, 1994 and M Freedland [1994] PL 224.
136   For the reasons for this, see ch 30, text at notes 71–76.
137   See now Employment Rights Act 1996, s 191.
138   *CCSU v Minister for the Civil Service* (above); and ch 12 E.
139   Sex Discrimination Act 1975, s 85; Race Relations Act 1976, s 75. Ch 19 A.
140   Ch 12, text at notes 1–4.

'The expression "the Crown" has two meanings, namely the monarch and the executive'.[141] However, difficulties may arise from confusing the two meanings. When the Sovereign governed in person, royal officials properly benefited from many of the Sovereign's immunities and privileges. But despite the ending of personal government by the Sovereign, the personnel of central government continued to benefit from Crown status. The shield of the Crown extended to what was described not very satisfactorily as the general government of the country or 'the province of government',[142] but not to local authorities nor to other public corporations. Notwithstanding the Crown Proceedings Act 1947, for several reasons it may be necessary to know whether a public authority has Crown status.[143] It is good legislative practice for an Act which creates a new public body to state whether and to what extent it should enjoy Crown status,[144] but this does not always happen. Whether because of express legislation or judicial interpretation, a public agency may be regarded as having Crown status for some purposes, but not for others.

In regard to central government, the concept of 'the Crown' has various consequences. Contracts are generally concluded in the name of individual departments and ministers, acting expressly or impliedly for the Crown.

In *Town Investments Ltd v Department of the Environment*, it had to be decided whether a rent-freeze imposed by counter-inflation legislation applied to two office-blocks in London, of which the Secretary of State for the Environment was the lessee 'for and on behalf of Her Majesty'; the offices were occupied by a variety of departments, and in part by the US navy. The House of Lords *held* (Lord Morris dissenting) that the Crown was the tenant and that the premises were occupied for the purpose of a business carried on by the Crown; the leases were therefore subject to the rent-freeze. Lord Diplock stated that it was public law that governed the relationships between the Queen in her political capacity, government departments, ministers and civil servants: executive acts of government done by any of them 'are acts done by "the Crown" in the fictional sense in which that expression is now used in English public law'.[145]

This decision revealed a striking anomaly in the legislation, namely that the Crown as tenant could take the benefit of the rent-freeze, whereas the Crown as landlord was not barred from increasing the rents which its tenants had to pay. The legal reasons for this inequity will be examined below. Although in 1991 the Court of Appeal considered 'the Crown' not to be a legal person, the House of Lords later held that 'at least for some purposes' the Crown has legal personality.[146] Whether the Crown is to be described as a corporation sole or a corporation aggregate[147] seems immaterial, given that the long-standing practice of Parliament has been to legislate on the basis that the Crown is a continuing legal entity.

---

[141]   *M v Home Office* [1994] 1 AC 377, 395.

[142]   *Mersey Docks Trustees v Cameron* (1861) 11 HLC 443, 508; *BBC v Johns* [1965] Ch 32.

[143]   Eg liability to taxation and the criminal law; whether staff are Crown servants (*R v Barrett* [1976] 3 All ER 895). And see ch 14.

[144]   See eg National Health Service and Community Care Act 1990, Sched 6, para 21 (NHS trusts not to be servants or agents of Crown).

[145]   [1978] AC 359, 381 (and see C Harlow (1977) 40 MLR 728).

[146]   *M v Home Office* [1992] QB 270; [1994] 1 AC 377, 424.

[147]   Eg *Re Mason* [1928] Ch 385.

Application of statutes to Crown[148]

As we have already seen, under the 1947 Act the Crown may be sued for breach of statutory duty. But nothing in the Act affects 'any presumption relating to the extent to which the Crown is bound by an Act of Parliament' (s 40(2)(*f*)). The rule that Acts do not bind the Crown, that is, that the Crown's rights and interests are not prejudiced by legislation unless a statute so enacts by express words or by necessary implication, significantly limits governmental liability for breach of statutory duty. It is by the operation of this rule, for example, that Crown property is in law exempt from taxation and much environmental legislation. This immunity of central government from regulation that applies to private persons goes much further than is justifiable, and Parliament has begun to remove the immunity piecemeal.[149] In 1947 the Judicial Committee took a strict view of the test of 'necessary implication', holding that in the absence of express words the Crown is bound by a statute only if the purpose of the statute would be 'wholly frustrated' if the Crown were not bound.[150] In 1989, as we saw in chapter 12, in *Lord Advocate v Dumbarton Council*, the House of Lords for the first time considered the legal basis of Crown immunity. The Court of Session had held that in some instances (for example, where its property was not affected) the Crown could be bound by town planning and highways legislation. Reversing this decision, the House held that the Crown is not bound by any statutory provision 'unless there can somehow be gathered from the terms of the relevant Act an intention to that effect'.[151] For an Act to bind the Crown it is sufficient for it to be shown that if the Act did not do so its purpose would be frustrated in a material respect, not that its purpose would be wholly frustrated. It is good legislative practice for new Acts to state expressly whether and to what extent they apply to the Crown.[152] Where an Act does not apply to the Crown or its servants acting in the course of duty, a Crown servant is not liable criminally if he or she disregards the statute.[153] But these rules do not prevent the Crown deriving benefits from legislation. Even though the Crown is not named in an Act, the Crown may take advantage of rights conferred by the Act, as in the *Town Investments* case.[154]

Procedure

Where the Act of 1947 enables proceedings to be brought against the Crown in English courts, whether in tort or contract or for the recovery of property, in principle the normal procedure of litigation applies. The action is brought against the appropriate department, the Minister for the Civil Service being

---

[148] Street, *Governmental Liability*, ch 6; Hogg, *Liability of the Crown*, ch 10.

[149] Eg National Health Service and Community Care Act 1990, s 60.

[150] *Province of Bombay v Municipal Corpn of Bombay* [1947] AC 58 and *Madras Electric Supply Co Ltd v Boarland* [1955] AC 667.

[151] [1990] 2 AC 580, 604 (ch 12 D above and J Wolffe [1990] PL 14). Contrast *Bropho v State of Western Australia* (1990) 171 CLR 1 (and S Kneebone [1991] PL 361).

[152] Eg Race Relations Act 1976, s 75, considered in *Home Office v Commission for Racial Equality* [1982] QB 385.

[153] *Cooper v Hawkins* [1904] 2 KB 164. See now Road Traffic Regulation Act 1984, s 130.

[154] Crown Proceedings Act 1947, s 31; and note 145 above.

responsible for publishing a list of departments and naming the solicitor for each department to accept process on its behalf; in cases not covered by the list, the Attorney-General may be made defendant. The trial follows that of an ordinary High Court or county court action, but several differences arise in respect of remedies and enforcement. The most important is that in place of an injunction or a decree of specific performance, the court makes an order declaring the rights of the parties (s 21(1)); nor can any injunction be granted against an officer of the Crown if the effect 'would be to give any relief against the Crown which could not have been obtained in proceedings against the Crown' (s 21(2)). Although at common law an injunction lay against an officer of the Crown who was threatening to commit a wrong such as a tort,[155] for many years after 1947 section 21 was interpreted broadly so as to deprive the court of power to grant such relief.[156] The inability of the court to grant injunctions excluded the power to grant interim injunctions, and English law does not allow an interim declaration to be made in place of an interim injunction.[157]

It is now clear that the powers of the court in respect of the executive are not limited as severely as previously seemed to be the case. First, the court may grant injunctive relief where necessary to protect rights under Community law.[158] Secondly, the House of Lords held in *M v Home Office*, applying ss 23(2) and 38(2) of the 1947 Act, that the restrictions on injunctive relief do not apply to applications for judicial review, which are not 'proceedings against the Crown' for the purposes of the 1947 Act.[159] Thirdly, it was also held in *M v Home Office* that s 21(2) of the 1947 Act does not prevent injunctive relief being granted against officers of the Crown (including ministers) who have personally committed or authorised a tort and applies only in respect of duties laid on the Crown itself. As Lord Woolf said, 'it is only in those situations where prior to the Act no injunctive relief could be obtained that s 21 prevents an injunction being granted.'[160] But he added that declaratory relief against officers of the Crown should normally be appropriate.

Other provisions maintaining the special position of the Crown may be briefly mentioned:

(*a*) judgment against the department cannot be enforced by the ordinary methods of levying execution or attachment; the department is required by the Act to pay the amount certified to be due as damages and costs (s 25);
(*b*) there can be no order for restitution of property, but the court may declare the plaintiff entitled as against the Crown (s 21(1));
(*c*) in lieu of an order for the attachment of money owed by the Crown to a debtor, a judgment creditor may obtain an order from the High Court directing payment to himself or herself and not to the debtor (s 27); for this

---

155   *Tamaki v Baker* [1901] AC 561.
156   *Merricks v Heathcoat-Amory* [1955] Ch 567.
157   See *International General Electric Co v Commissioners of Customs and Excise* [1962] Ch 784; *R v IRC, ex p Rossminster Ltd* [1980] AC 952. On the case for interim declatory relief, see Zamir and Woolf, *The Declaratory Judgment*, pp 81–7, 301–10; Law Com No 226 (1994) pp 61–4.
158   *Case C-213/89, R v Transport Secretary, ex p Factortame Ltd (No 2)* [1991] 1 AC 603; ch 8 D.
159   [1994] 1 AC 377 (and M Gould [1993] PL 568).
160   [1994] 1 AC 377, 413, disapproving *Merricks v Heathcoat-Amory* (above); and see HWR Wade (1991) 107 LQR 4.

purpose the Crown is within the jurisdiction of the English courts, even in respect of savings accounts held with the National Savings Bank, whose head office is in Glasgow.[161]

An action for a declaration may be brought against the Crown without claiming any other relief, for example where a wrong is threatened,[162] but not to determine hypothetical questions which may never arise; for example, as to whether there is a contingent liability to a tax.[163]

In private litigation, when the plaintiff seeks an interim injunction against the defendant to maintain the status quo pending the final decision, the court grants such a request only if the plaintiff gives an undertaking as to damages, so that the defendant's loss may be made good if the plaintiff's action ultimately fails. When the Crown is seeking to assert rights of property or contract, the Crown may be expected to give such an undertaking. But when the Crown takes proceedings to enforce the law, an undertaking as to damages is generally not appropriate.[164]

In Scotland, where civil procedure is different from that in England, actions in respect of British or United Kingdom departments (like the Ministry of Defence or the Inland Revenue) may be brought against the Lord Advocate;[165] in respect of Scottish departments, actions are brought against the Secretary of State for Scotland.[166] So far as remedies against the Crown are concerned, the Court of Session in *McDonald v Secretary of State for Scotland*[167] held that the reasoning in *M v Home Office* did not apply in Scotland, where the statutory and procedural background differs from that in England; sections 21(1) and 42 of the 1947 Act permit a declarator but not interdict to issue against the Crown and ministers. Actions may be raised by and against the Crown in either the Court of Session or the sheriff court.

Non-disclosure of evidence: public interest immunity

Discovery of documents is a procedure in civil litigation by which a party may inspect all documents in the possession or control of an opponent which relate to the matters in dispute. Formerly it could not be used against the Crown. By s 28 of the 1947 Act, the court may order discovery against the Crown and may also require the Crown to answer interrogatories, that is, written questions to obtain information from the other party on material facts. But the Act expressly preserves the existing rule of law (formerly known as Crown privilege) that the Crown may refuse to disclose any document or to answer any question on the ground that this would be injurious to the public interest; the Act even protects the Crown from disclosing the mere existence

---

[161]   *Brooks Associates Inc v Basu* [1983] 1 All ER 508.
[162]   *Dyson v A-G* [1912] 1 Ch 158.
[163]   *Argosam Finance Co v Oxby* [1965] Ch 390.
[164]   *Hoffmann-La Roche & Co v Trade Secretary* [1975] AC 295 (department seeking to compel company to observe price control for drugs.) And see *Kirklees Council v Wickes Building Supplies Ltd* [1993] AC 227.
[165]   Crown Suits (Scotland) Act 1857; Law Officers Act 1944, s 2; and see *Lord Advocate v Argyll CC* 1950 SC 304.
[166]   Reorganisation of Offices (Scotland) Act 1939, s 1 (8).
[167]   1994 SLT 692. Contrary to the view taken in the text above, the Lord Justice Clerk (Ross) (at p 695) regarded Lord Woolf's views on s 21 of the 1947 Act as 'clearly obiter'.

of a document on the same ground. Public interest immunity (which became known as PII in the wake of the Matrix Churchill trial in 1992 discussed below) is not restricted to proceedings in which the Crown is a party and applies also to civil proceedings between private individuals. The need for some power to protect documents from publication in the interests of state security was illustrated by *Duncan v Cammell Laird & Co.*[168] What is more difficult is to determine the extent of the power, when it may be exercised and how use of the power may be controlled by the courts. These matters were not finally settled in *Duncan v Cammell Laird & Co*, as was once thought to have been the case.

Early in 1939 a new naval submarine sank while on trial with the loss of 99 lives, including civilian workmen. Many actions in negligence were brought by the personal representatives against the company, who had built the submarine under contract with the Admiralty. In a test action, the company objected to the production of documents relating to the design of the submarine. The First Lord of the Admiralty directed the company not to produce the documents on the ground of Crown privilege, since disclosure would be injurious to national defence. *Held* (House of Lords) the documents should not be disclosed. Although a validly taken objection to disclosure was conclusive, and should be taken by the minister himself, the decision ruling out such documents was that of the judge. In deciding whether it was his duty to object, a minister should withhold production only where the public interest would otherwise be harmed, for example, where disclosure would be injurious to national defence or to good diplomatic relations, 'or where the practice of keeping a class of documents secret is necessary for the proper functioning of the public service'.[169]

On this basis, documents might be withheld either because the *contents* of those documents must be kept secret (as in *Duncan's* case itself) or on the much wider ground that they belonged to a *class* of documents which must as a class be treated as confidential, for example civil service memoranda and minutes, to guarantee freedom and candour of communication on public matters. Thereafter the practice developed of withholding documents simply on the minister's assertion that they belonged to a class of documents which it was necessary in the public interest for the proper functioning of the public service to withhold.[170] Where documents were withheld, oral evidence of their contents could not be given; and it seemed that the courts could not overrule the minister's objection if taken in correct form.

Concern at these wide claims of privilege was eased by government concessions. In 1956 the Lord Chancellor stated that privilege would not be claimed in certain types of litigation for various kinds of documents in a department's possession; these included factual reports about accidents involving government employees or government premises and, where the Crown or a Crown employee was being sued for negligence, medical reports by service or prison doctors. In 1962 the government stated that statements made to the police during criminal investigations would not be withheld where the police were sued for malicious prosecution or wrongful arrest, and that in other civil proceedings the question of whether statements to the

---

[168]   [1942] AC 624. For the subsequent history, see J Jacob [1993] PL 121.
[169]   [1942] AC at 642.
[170]   See *Ellis v Home Office* [1953] 2 QB 135 and *Broome v Broome* [1955] P 190 for the harsh operation of the rule; and J E S Simon [1955] CLJ 62.

police should be withheld would be left to the trial judge, subject in each case to the names of police informers not being revealed.[171] Despite these concessions, it was still considered that in English law the courts were bound by the minister's objection. By contrast, it was already established in Scotland that a court must take account of the minister's decision but is not bound by it and in exceptional circumstances may overrule it if the interests of justice so require.[172] After decisions of the Court of Appeal had cast doubt on the conclusiveness of the minister's objection,[173] in 1968 the House of Lords overruled an objection taken by the Home Secretary to the production of certain police reports. This established that it is for the court to hold the balance between the public interest in the administration of justice and the public interest in efficient government.

In *Conway v Rimmer*[174] a former probationary constable sued a police superintendent for malicious prosecution after an incident of a missing electric torch had led to the acquittal of the plaintiff on a charge of theft and to his dismissal from the police. The Home Secretary claimed privilege for (*a*) probationary reports on the plaintiff and (*b*) the defendant's report on the investigation into the incident. He certified that these were confidential reports within a class of documents production of which would be injurious to the public interest. *Held*, the court has jurisdiction to order the production of documents for which immunity is claimed. The court will give full weight to a minister's view, but this need not prevail if the relevant considerations are such that judicial experience is competent to weigh them.

The House of Lords thus departed from the wide rule laid down in *Duncan v Cammell Laird*, which it accepted had been properly decided on the facts. English law was thereby brought broadly into line with Scots law, Lord Reid considering there to be no justification for the law on this matter of public policy being different in the two countries.

Since *Conway v Rimmer* enabled the courts to have the last word on ministerial objections to disclosure, they must decide when, on a balancing of the competing public interests, the withholding of evidence is justified. In subsequent cases, the issues arising have included (*a*) the use as evidence of material which is subject to constraints of confidentiality; (*b*) the disclosure of documents relating to the formulation of government policy; (*c*) the grounds which must be shown before the court will inspect documents; and (*d*) the use of public interest immunity in criminal proceedings.

In *Rogers v Home Secretary*,[175] the House of Lords refused to order production of a secret police report to the Gaming Board about an applicant for a gaming licence, holding that the report fell into a class of documents which should not be disclosed. It was emphasised that power to withhold evidence on grounds of public interest was not a privilege of the Crown as such and that 'Crown privilege' was a misnomer. The fact that documents may be regarded as confidential by their authors and those who possess them is no reason why they should as a class be immune from disclosure on grounds of public

---

[171]   See HL Deb, 6 June 1956, col 741–8 and 8 March 1962, col 1191.

[172]   *Glasgow Corpn v Central Land Board* 1956 SC (HL) 1; *Whitehall v Whitehall* 1957 SC 30.

[173]   Including *Merricks v Nott-Bower* [1965] 1 QB 57 and *Re Grosvenor Hotel London (No 2)* [1965] Ch 1210; D H Clark (1967) 30 MLR 489.

[174]   [1968] AC 910; D H Clark (1969) 32 MLR 142.

[175]   [1973] AC 388.

interest. Where a government department holds material supplied to it in confidence by companies regarding commercial activities, the court's decision on public interest immunity will depend on an assessment of factors such as the reasons for disclosure and the harm that disclosure might cause to the public interest.[176]

In *D v National Society for the Prevention of Cruelty to Children*, the House of Lords held that public interest as a ground for non-disclosure of confidential material was not confined to the efficient functioning of government departments.[177] In that case, the Court of Appeal had ordered the NSPCC to reveal the identity of someone who had informed the society of a suspected case of child battering. The society, established by royal charter, had a statutory responsibility to take proceedings for the care of children. The House of Lords held, by analogy with the rule protecting the identity of police informers from disclosure, that the names of informants to the society should be immune from disclosure.

In *R v Chief Constable of the West Midlands Police, ex p Wiley*,[178] the House of Lords held (overruling decisions by the Court of Appeal)[179] that confidential statements made during investigation of complaints against the police were not as a class immune from disclosure in civil litigation. In Lord Woolf's view, 'The recognition of a new class-based public interest immunity requires clear and compelling evidence that it is necessary'; no sufficient case had ever been made to justify a general immunity for such statements held by the police. The House accepted that a specific statement might be withheld from disclosure if, for instance, it revealed the identity of a police informer.

In *Science Research Council v Nassé*,[180] the House of Lords held that on an employee's complaint of unlawful discrimination in employment, no question of public interest immunity could arise in respect of confidential reports on other employees held by the employer. Lord Scarman stated that public interest immunity was restricted 'to what must be kept secret for the protection of government at the highest levels and in the truly sensitive areas of executive responsibility'.[181] However, the language of public interest immunity was used in *Campbell v Tameside Council*, where a teacher had been assaulted by an 11 year old pupil and wished to see psychologists' reports held by the council; the Court of Appeal ordered discovery after inspecting the reports, since the public interest in the administration of justice outweighed any harm to the public service resulting from production of the reports.[182] When in unfair dismissal proceedings a former diplomat wished to rely on material relating to the activities of the security and intelligence services, the Court of Appeal, without inspecting the documents, upheld the Secretary of

---

176   Compare *Crompton Amusement Machines Ltd v Commissioners of Customs and Excise* [1974] AC 405 and *Norwich Pharmacal Co v Commissioners of Customs and Excise* [1974] AC 133.

177   [1978] AC 171.

178   [1995] 1 AC 274.

179   *Neilson v Laugharne* [1981] QB 736; *Makanjuola v Metropolitan Police Commissioner* [1992] 3 All ER 617; and *Halford v Sharples* [1992] 3 All ER 624. *Neilson v Laugharne* had been distinguished in *Peach v Metropolitan Police Commissioner* [1986] 1 QB 1064 and *Ex p Coventry Newspapers Ltd* [1993] QB 278.

180   [1980] AC 1028.

181   [1980] AC at 1088.

182   [1982] QB 1065.

State's certificate claiming immunity for them in view of the actual or potential risk to national security.[183]

In *Conway v Rimmer*, Lord Reid had expressed the opinion that Cabinet minutes and documents concerned with policy-making within departments were protected against disclosure, so that the inner working of government should not be exposed to ill-informed and biased criticism.[184] In *Burmah Oil Co Ltd v Bank of England*,[185] the House of Lords had to consider the extent to which such high-level documents should be protected from disclosure.

In 1975 the Burmah Oil company had with government approval agreed to sell its holdings in BP stock to the Bank of England as part of an arrangement protecting the company from liquidation. Later the company sought to have the sale set aside as unconscionable and inequitable. It wished to see documents held by the bank, including (*a*) ministerial communications and minutes of meetings attended by ministers and (*b*) communications between senior civil servants relating to policy matters. The Crown contended that it was 'necessary for the proper functioning of the public service' that the documents be withheld. The House of Lords held that the Crown's claim of immunity was not conclusive. If it was likely (or reasonably probable) that the documents contained matter that was material to the issues in the case, the court might inspect them to determine where the balance lay between the competing public interests. Having inspected the documents, the House ordered that they be not produced since they did not contain material necessary for disposing fairly of the case. Lord Wilberforce dissented from the decision to inspect; in his view, it was a plain case of 'public interest immunity properly claimed on grounds of high policy'.[186]

In the *Burmah Oil* case, judicial opinion had moved far beyond the position in *Conway v Rimmer*. Even Lord Wilberforce envisaged that there might be circumstances in which a high-level governmental interest must give way before the interests of justice.[187] Even Cabinet papers may not be immune from disclosure in an exceptional case where the interests of justice so require.[188] In the Watergate tapes case, it was the public interest in criminal justice that led the US Supreme Court to order President Nixon to deliver his tapes to the special investigator.[189]

Apart from such exceptional circumstances, did the *Burmah Oil* decision mean that the judges should regularly inspect and if necessary order the production of documents relating to policy-making within government departments? In *Air Canada v Trade Secretary*[190] the House of Lords upheld the Secretary of State's claim for immunity and refused to inspect the documents. In ordinary litigation, one party may inspect relevant documents held by the other side when discovery is *necessary* either for disposing fairly of the action or for saving costs.[191] In *Air Canada*, the House applied to a case alleging ultra vires acts by a department stricter rules than would apply to litigation between

---

[183] *Balfour v Foreign and Commonwealth Office* [1994] 2 All ER 588.
[184] [1968] AC 910, 952; see also Lord Upjohn at 993.
[185] [1980] AC 1090; D G T Williams [1980] CLJ 1.
[186] [1980] AC at 1117.
[187] [1980] AC at 1113.
[188] As in the Australian case of *Sankey v Whitlam* (1978) 21 ALR 505. See also *Air Canada v Trade Secretary* [1983] 2 AC 394, 432 (Lord Fraser); I G Eagles [1980] PL 263.
[189] *US v Nixon* 418 US 683 (1974).
[190] [1983] 2 AC 394; Lord Mackay (1983) 2 CJQ 337 and T R S Allan (1985) 101 LQR 200.
[191] RSC Ord 24, rr 2(5), 8, 13(1); see also r 15 (public interest immunity).

private parties where public interest immunity was not claimed. The majority (Lords Fraser, Wilberforce and Edmund-Davies) held that for a court to exercise the power of inspection, it was not sufficient that the documents *might* contain information relevant to the issues in dispute; the party seeking access to the documents must show that it was reasonably probable that the documents were likely to help his or her case. A speculative belief to this effect was not enough. The minority (Lords Scarman and Templeman) considered that the applicant must show only that disclosure of the documents was likely to be necessary for fairly disposing of the issues in dispute; on the facts, Air Canada had failed to do this.

The majority view in *Air Canada* emphasises that even where the applicant is seeking judicial review of a policy decision, the litigation has an adversary character, and the court does not have an inquisitorial power to inspect documents held within government. While the *Air Canada* case does not question the power of the courts to override executive claims to privilege, it makes more severe the obstacle which an applicant for discovery must surmount to persuade the court to exercise its powers.

Although public interest immunity has mainly arisen from the civil procedure of discovery, the immunity extends to criminal proceedings, albeit in a different form.[192] Plainly the public interest in keeping material secret can be damaged by disclosure wherever it occurs, but the public interest in the administration of justice is at its strongest when, if evidence were to be withheld from production in a criminal trial, this would prevent the defendant from establishing a defence. While all or part of a trial on charges under the Official Secrets Acts may be held in camera,[193] if material is too secret for the judge to decide the issue of immunity under such restrictions, any prosecution must be abandoned.[194] In November 1992, the collapse of the Matrix Churchill trial for unlawful export of arms to Iraq brought these issues into public controversy. Before the trial, four ministers had signed PII certificates dealing with documents that related to the question whether the defendants' involvement in the export of machinery to Iraq was known to the security services and thus to the government. The claims for PII were made on a variety of 'class' grounds, including the protection of the proper functioning of government as well as the interest in keeping secret security and intelligence operations. Having inspected the documents, the trial judge ordered disclosure.[195] Sir Richard Scott's subsequent inquiry into the export of defence equipment and other goods to Iraq extended to decisions by the prosecution and to the PII certificates in the Matrix Churchill case.[196] His report makes a penetrating study of the use which departments and their

---

[192] *R v Governor of Brixton Prison, ex p Osman (No 1)* [1992] 1 All ER 108; *R v Davis* [1993] 2 All ER 643. See A Wharam [1971] Crim LR 675. For the place of PII in the changing law of criminal procedure, see eg Corker *Disclosure in Criminal Proceedings,* ch 6.

[193] Official Secrets Act 1920, s 8; and ch 24.

[194] *R v Ward* ([1993] 2 All ER 577) at p 633; and cf *R v Davis* (above).

[195] See A W Bradley [1992] PL 514, A T H Smith [1993] CLJ 1, I Leigh [1993] PL 630. On the Scott report generally, see [1996] PL 357–507; also I Leigh and L Lustgarten (1996) 59 MLR 695.

[196] In the Scott report (HC 115, 1995–96), see on PII vol III, chs G.10–15 and G.18; vol IV, ch K.6. Also A Tomkins [1993] PL 650; R Scott [1996] PL 427.

legal advisers had made of PII certificates. Of their use in Matrix Churchill, his main criticisms were:

(i) class claims were made which ought to have had no place in a criminal trial; (ii) the claims extended to some documents 'of which no more could be said than that they were confidential'; (iii) ministers were advised that they could not take into account when considering the class claims whether the documents were so material to the trial that they ought to have been disclosed to the defence; (iv) one minister, Mr Heseltine, had been advised that it was his duty to make the PII claim, despite his view that the overall public interest required disclosure.[197]

On this last point, the Attorney-General's advice to Mr Heseltine had been based on a view of the law[198] which had been widely held but was declared to be wrong during the course of the Scott inquiry. In *R v Chief Constable of West Midlands Police, ex p Wiley*,[199] the House of Lords held that, in principle, documents which are relevant and material to litigation should be produced unless disclosure would cause substantial harm. 'A rubber stamp approach to public interest immunity by the holder of a document is neither necessary nor appropriate'.[200] This was a welcome clarification of the duty of ministers, but other questions relating to the use of PII certificates required to be answered.

In December 1996, the Attorney-General announced the results of a review made after public consultation into the operation of PII in relation to government documents in England and Wales. He stated that the government would no longer rely on the former division into 'class' and 'contents' claims for PII. Ministers would in future claim PII 'only when it is believed that disclosure of a document would cause real harm to the public interest'. Future PII certificates would seek to identify in more detail the contents of a document and the damage which disclosure would do, and this 'will allow even closer scrutiny of claims by the court, which is always the final arbiter'. It was hoped that the effect of *ex p Wiley* and the government's new approach woud be to reduce the number of PII claims.[201]

This branch of the law has thus come a very long way in the half century since *Duncan v Cammell Laird* first distinguished between 'contents' and 'class' as a basis for witholding documents in the public interest. It remains to be seen whether this important change in official policy, which applies both to civil and criminal cases, will in fact achieve its objectives.

---

[197] Scott report, para G18.104.
[198] Derived mainly from the *Makanjuola* case (note 179 above).
[199] Note 178 above.
[200] [1995] 1 AC 274, 281 (Lord Templeman).
[201] HC Deb, 18 December 1996, cols 949–50. And see M Supperstone [1997] PL 211.

Bibliography

ADLER, M, & BRADLEY, A W (eds), *Justice, Discretion and Poverty*, 1976

AITKEN, J, *Officially Secret*, 1971

ALDERMAN, G, *Pressure Groups and Government in Great Britain*, 1984

ALDERMAN, R K, & CROSS, J A, *The Tactics of Resignation*, 1967

ALLAN, T R S, *Law, Liberty and Justice: The Legal Foundations of British Constitutionalism*, 1993

ALLASON, R, *The Branch: A History of the Metropolitan Police Special Branch 1883–1983*, 1988

AMERY, L S, *Thoughts on the Constitution*, 2nd edn, 1953

ANDREW, C, *Secret Service: The Making of the British Intelligence Community*, 1985

ANDREWS, J A (ed), *Welsh Studies in Public Law*, 1970

ANSON, W R, *The Law and Custom of the Constitution*, vol I, *Parliament* (ed M L Gwyer), 5th edn, 1922; vol II, *The Crown* (ed A B Keith), 4th edn, 1935

ARLIDGE, A, & EADY, D, *The Law of Contempt*, 1982

ARMSTRONG, W (ed), *Budgetary Reform in the United Kingdom*, 1980

ARNSTEIN, W L, *The Bradlaugh Case*, 1965

ARONSON, M, & WHITMORE, H, *Public Torts and Contracts*, 1982

ARROWSMITH, S, *Civil Liability and Public Authorities*, 1992

ARROWSMITH, S, *Government Procurement and Judicial Review*, 1988

ARTHURS, H W, *Without the Law: Administrative Justice and Legal Pluralism in the 19th Century*, 1985

AUBREY, C, *Who's Watching You?*, 1981

AUSTIN, J, *The Province of Jurisprudence Determined* (ed H L A Hart), 1954

BAGEHOT, W, *The English Constitution* (introduction R H S Crossman), 1963

BAILEY, S H (ed), *Cross on Local Government Law*, 8th edn, 1991

BAILEY, S H, HARRIS, D J, & JONES, B L, *Civil Liberties: Cases and Materials*, 4th edn, 1995

BAILEY, S H, JONES, B L, & MOWBRAY, A R, *Cases and Materials on Administrative Law*, 2nd edn, 1992

BALDWIN, J R, WIKELEY, N, & YOUNG, R, *Judging Social Security: The Adjudication of Claims for Benefit in Britain*, 1992

BALDWIN, R, *Rules and Government*, 1995

BALDWIN, R, *Regulating the Airlines*, 1985

BALDWIN, R, & KINSEY, R, *Police Powers and Politics*, 1982

BALDWIN, R, & MCCRUDDEN, C, *Regulation and Public Law*, 1987

BARKER, A (ed), *Quangos in Britain*, 1982

BARNARD, C, *EC Employment Law*, 1996

BARNETT, J, *Inside the Treasury*, 1982

BASSETT, R G, *1931: Political Crisis*, 1958

BATES, T ST J N, et al, *In Memoriam J D B Mitchell*, 1983

BEATSON, J, & MATTHEWS, M H, *Administrative Law, Cases and Materials*, 2nd edn, 1989

BEDDARD, R, *Human Rights and Europe*, 2nd edn, 1980

BEER, S H, *Modern British Politics*, 1965

BEER, S H, *Treasury Control*, 2nd edn, 1957

BELL, J S, *French Constitutional Law*, 1992

BELL, J S, & BRADLEY, A W (eds), *Governmental Liability: A Comparative Study*, 1991

BENNION, F, *Statutory Interpretation*, 2nd edn, 1992

BENTHAM, J, *Handbook of Political Fallacies* (ed H A Larrabee), 1962
BERCUSSON, B, *European Labour Law*, 1996
BERGER, R, *Impeachment*, 1973
BERKELEY, H, *The Power of the Prime Minister*, 1968
BIRCH, A H, *Representative and Responsible Government*, 1964
BIRKINSHAW, P, *Grievances, Remedies and the State*, 1985
BIRKINSHAW, P, *Reforming the Secret State*, 1991
BIRRELL, D, & MURIE, A, *Policy and Government in Northern Ireland: Lessons of Devolution*, 1980
BISHOP, M, KAY, J, & MAYER, C, *Privatisation and Economic Performance*, 1994
BISHOP, M, KAY, J, & MAYER, C, *The Regulatory Challenge*, 1995
BLACKBURN, R, *The Electoral System in Britain*, 1995
BLACKBURN, R (ed), *Constitutional Studies: Contemporary Issues and Controversies*, 1992
BLACKBURN, R, *The Meeting of Parliament*, 1990
BLACKSTONE, *Commentaries on the Laws of England*, 10th edn, 1787; 14th edn, 1803
BLOM-COOPER, L J, & DREWRY, G, *Final Appeal*, 1972
BOGDANOR, V, *Devolution*, 1979
BOGDANOR, V, *The Monarchy and the Constitution*, 1995
BOGDANOR, V, *Multi-party Politics and the Constitution*, 1983
BOGDANOR, V, *The People and the Party System*, 1981
BONNER, D, *Emergency Powers in Peacetime*, 1985
BOTTOMLEY, A (ed), *Feminist Perspectives on the Foundational Subjects of Law*, 1996
BOYLE, K, & HADDEN, T, *Ireland: A Positive Proposal*, 1985
BRAZIER, R, *Constitutional Practice*, 2nd edn, 1994
BRAZIER, R, *Constitutional Reform: Re-shaping the British Political System*, 1991
BRAZIER, R, *Constitutional Texts*, 1990
BREWER-CARIAS, A R, *Judicial Review in Comparative Law*, 1989
BRIDGES, Lord, *The Treasury*, 2nd edn, 1966
BRIDGES, L, MESZAROS, G, & SUNKIN, M, *Judicial Review in Perspective*, 2nd edn, 1995
BROMHEAD, P A, *The House of Lords and Contemporary Politics, 1911–1957*, 1958
BROMHEAD, P A, *Private Members' Bills in the British Parliament*, 1956
BROWN, A N, *Criminal Evidence and Procedure*, 1996
BROWN, R G S, & STEEL, D R, *The Administrative Process in Britain*, 2nd edn, 1979
BROWN, L N, & BELL, J S, *French Administrative Law*, 4th edn, 1993
BROWN, L N, & KENNEDY, T, *The Court of Justice of the European Communities*, 4th edn, 1994
BROWNLIE, I, *Basic Documents on Human Rights*, 3rd edn, 1993
BROWNLIE, I, *Principles of Public International Law*, 4th edn, 1990
BRYCE, J, *Studies in History and Jurisprudence*, 1901
BUCK, T, *The Social Fund – Law and Practice*, 1996
BUCKLAND, P, *The Factory of Grievances*, 1979
BUNYAN, T, *The Political Police in Britain*, 1976
BURROWS, F, *Free Movement in Community Law*, 1987
BUTLER, D (ed), *Coalitions in British Politics*, 1978
BUTLER, D, *Governing without a Majority: Dilemmas for Hung Parliaments in Britain*, 1983
BUTLER, D, & HALSEY, A H (ed), *Policy and Politics*, 1978
BUTLER, D E, *The Electoral System in Britain since 1918*, 2nd edn, 1963
BYRNE, T, *Local Government in Britain*, 6th edn, 1994

CALVERT, H, *Constitutional Law in Northern Ireland*, 1968
CALVERT, H (ed), *Devolution*, 1975
CAMPBELL, C, *Emergency Law in Ireland 1918–1925*, 1994
CAMPBELL, C M (ed), *Do We Need a Bill of Rights?*, 1980
CANE, P, *An Introduction to Administrative Law*, 3rd edn, 1996
CARD, R, *Public Order: The New Law*, 1989
CARNALL, G, & NICHOLSON, C (eds), *The Impeachment of Warren Hastings*, 1989
CARR, C, *Concerning English Administrative Law*, 1941
CARTWRIGHT, T J, *Royal Commissions and Departmental Committees in Britain*, 1975
CHAPMAN, L, *Your Disobedient Servant*, rev edn, 1979
CHESTER, D N, *The Nationalization of British Industry, 1945–51*, 1975
CHESTER, D N, & BOWRING, N, *Questions in Parliament*, 1962
CHITTY, J, *Prerogatives of the Crown*, 1820

CHRISTIE, M, *Breach of the Peace*, 1990

CHUBB, B, *The Control of Public Expenditure*, 1952

CLARKE, R, *New Trends in Government*, 1971

CLAYTON, R, & TOMLINSON, H, *Civil Actions Against the Police*, 2nd edn, 1992

CLAYTON, R J (ed), *Parker's Law and Conduct of Elections*, 1996

COOMBES, D, *The Member of Parliament and the Administration*, 1966

CORKER, D, *Disclosure in Criminal Proceedings*, 1996

COSGROVE, R A, *The Rule of Law: Albert Venn Dicey, Victorian Jurist*, 1980

CRAIES, W F, *Statute Law* (ed S G C Edgar), 7th edn, 1971

CRAIG, P P, *Administrative Law*, 3rd edn, 1994

CRAIG, P P, *Public Law and Democracy in the UK and the USA*, 1991

CRAIG, P P, & DE BURCA, G, *EC law: Text, Cases and Materials*, 1995

CRICK, B, *The Reform of Parliament*, 2nd edn, 1968

CRIPPS, Y, *The Legal Implications of Disclosure in the Public Interest*, 2nd edn, 1994

CRITCHLEY, T A, *The Conquest of Violence*, 1970

CRITCHLEY, T A, *A History of the Police in England and Wales*, 2nd edn, 1978

CROMBIE, J, *Her Majesty's Customs and Excise*, 1962

CROSS, R, & TAPPER, C, *Evidence*, 8th edn, 1995

CROSS, R, *Precedent in English Law* (eds R Cross & J W Harris), 4th edn, 1991

CROSS, R, *Statutory Interpretation*, (eds J Bell & G Engle), 2nd edn, 1987

CROSSMAN, R H S, *The Diaries of a Cabinet Minister* (vol I), 1975

CURRAN, J, & SEATON, J, *Power without Responsibility*, 4th edn, 1991

DAALDER, H, *Cabinet Reform in Britain, 1914–1963*, 1964

DALE, W, *The Modern Commonwealth*, 1983

DALYELL, T, *Devolution, The End of Britain?*, 1977

DASH, S, *Justice Denied*, 1972

DAVIES P L, & FREEDLAND, M R, *Labour Legislation and Public Policy: A Contemporary History*, 1993

DAVIS, K C, *Discretionary Justice*, 1969

DENNING, LORD, *What Next in the Law?*, 1982

d'ENTREVES, A P, *The Notion of the State*, 1967

de SMITH, S A, *Constitutional and Administrative Law* (ed R Brazier), 7th edn, 1994

de SMITH, S A, *The New Commonwealth and its Constitutions*, 1964

de SMITH, S A, WOOLF, Lord, & JOWELL, J, *Judicial Review of Administrative Action*, 5th edn, 1995

DEAKIN, S, & MORRIS, G S, *Labour Law*, 1995

DEVLIN, LORD, *The Criminal Prosecution in England*, 1960

DICEY, A V, *The Law of the Constitution* (ed E C S Wade), 10th edn, 1959

DICEY, A V, & RAIT, R S, *Thoughts on the Union between England and Scotland*, 1920

DONALDSON, A G, *Some Comparative Aspects of Irish Law*, 1957

DONALDSON, F, *The Marconi Scandal*, 1962

DONALDSON, G, *Edinburgh History of Scotland, vol 3, James V–James VII*, 1965

DOYLE, B, *Disability, Discrimination and Equal Opportunities*, 1995

DREWRY, G (ed), *The New Select Committees*, 2nd edn, 1989

DRUCKER, H (ed), *Scottish Government Yearbook 1980*, 1980

DRZEMCZEWSKI, A, *European Human Rights Convention in Domestic Law*, 1983

DUMMETT, A, & NICOL, A, *Subjects, Citizens, Aliens and Others: Nationality and Immigration Law*, 1990

DWORKIN, R, *Taking Rights Seriously*, 1977

EDWARDS, J LI J, *The Attorney-General, Politics and the Public Interest*, 1984

EDWARDS, J LI J, *The Law Officers of the Crown*, 1964

ELLIS, E, & TRIDIMAS, T, *Public Law of the European Community: Text, Materials and Commentary*, 1995

ELTON, G R, *Studies in Tudor and Stuart Politics and Government* (2 vols), 1974

EMERY, C T, & SMYTHE, B, *Judicial Review: Legal Limits of Official Power*, 1986

ENGLEFIELD, D (ed), *Commons Select Committees*, 1984

ERNST, J, *Whose Utility?: The Social Impact of Public Utility Privatisation and Regulation in Britain*, 1994

ERSKINE MAY, *Parliamentary Practice* (*The Law, Privileges, Proceedings and Usage of Parliament*) (ed Sir C Gordon), 21st edn, 1989

EVANS, G (ed), *Labor and the Constitution, 1972–1975*, 1977
EVANS, J M, *Immigration Law*, 2nd edn, 1983
EVATT, H V, *The King and His Dominion Governors*, 1936
EVELEGH, R, *Peace Keeping in a Democratic Society*, 1978
EWING, K D, *Britain and the ILO*, 2nd edn, 1994
EWING, K D, *The Funding of Political Parties in Britain*, 1987
EWING, K D, *Trade Unions, the Labour Party and the Law*, 1983
EWING, K D, & FINNIE, W, *Civil Liberties in Scotland: Cases and Materials*, 2nd edn, 1988
EWING, K D, & GEARTY, C A, *Democracy or a Bill of Rights*, 1991
EWING, K D, & GEARTY, C A, *Freedom under Thatcher: Civil Liberties in Modern Britain*, 1990
EWING, K D, GEARTY, C A, & HEPPLE, B A (eds), *Human Rights and Labour Law*, 1994

FARMER, J A, *Tribunals and Government*, 1974
FARRAR, J H, *Law Reform and the Law Commission*, 1974
FAWCETT, J E S, *The Application of the European Convention on Human Rights*, 2nd edn, 1987
FAWCETT, J E S, *The British Commonwealth in International Law*, 1963
FELDMAN, D J, *Civil Liberties and Human Rights in England and Wales*, 1993
FERGUSON, W, *Edinburgh History of Scotland*, vol 4, *1689 to the Present*, 1968
FFORDE, J S, *The Bank of England and Public Policy 1941–1958*, 1992
FINDLATER, R, *Banned!*, 1967
FINE, B, & MILLER, R (eds) *Policing the Miners' Strike*, 1985
FINER, S E (ed), *Adversary Politics and Electoral Reform*, 1975
FINNIE, W, HIMSWORTH, C, & WALKER, N (eds), *Edinburgh Essays in Public Law*, 1991
FLICK, G A, *Natural Justice*, 1979
FOLEY, M, *The Silence of Constitutions: Gaps, 'Abeyances' and Political Temperament in the Maintenance of Government*, 1989
FORD, P & G (ed), *Luke Graves Hansard's Diary, 1814–1841*, 1962
FORSEY, E A, *The Royal Power of Dissolution of Parliament in the British Commonwealth*, 1943
FORSYTH, W, *Cases and Opinions on Constitutional Law*, 1869
FOULKES, D L, *Administrative Law*, 8th edn, 1995
FRANKLIN, M N, & NORTON, P (eds), *Parliamentary Questions*, 1993
FRANSMAN, L, *British Nationality Law*, 1989
FREDMAN, S, & MORRIS, G S, *The State as Employer: Labour Law in the Public Services*, 1989
FREEMAN, E A, *The Growth of the English Constitution*, 1872
FRIEDMAN, W G, *Law in a Changing Society*, revised 1964
FRIEDMANN, W G (ed), *Public and Private Enterprise in Mixed Economies*, 1974
FRIEDMANN, W G, & GARNER, J F (ed), *Government Enterprise*, 1970
FRYDE, E B, & MILLER, E (ed), *Historical Studies of the English Parliament 1399–1603*, 1970
FULLER, L L, *The Morality of Law*, 1964

GALLIGAN, D J, *Discretionary Powers: A Legal Study of Official Discretion*, 1987
GANZ, G, *Quasi-Legislation: Recent Developments in Secondary Legislation*, 1987
GEARTY, C A (ed), *European Civil Liberties and the European Convention on Human Rights*, 1997
GEARTY, C A, *Terror*, 1991
GEARTY, C A, & KIMBELL, J A, *Terrorism and the Rule of Law*, 1995
GEARTY, C A, & TOMKINS, A, *Understanding Human Rights*, 1996
GELLHORN, W, *Ombudsmen and Others*, 1966
GENN, H, *The Effectiveness of Representation at Tribunals*, 1989
GIDDINGS, P J (ed), *Parliamentary Accountability: A Study of Parliament and Executive Agencies*, 1995
GILBERT, G, *Aspects of Extradition Law*, 1991
GORDON, G H, *Criminal Law of Scotland*, 2nd edn, 1978
GORDON, R, *Crown Office Proceedings*, 1990
GOUGH, J W, *Fundamental Law in English Constitutional History*, 1955
GRAHAM, C, & PROSSER, T (eds), *Waiving the Rules: The Constitution under Thatcherism*, 1988
GRANT, J P (ed), *Independence and Devolution, the Legal Implications for Scotland*, 1976
GRANT, W, & MARSH, D, *The Confederation of British Industry*, 1977
GREGORY, R, & HUTCHESSON, P G, *The Parliamentary Ombudsman*, 1975
GREY, Earl, *Parliamentary Government*, 1864
GRIFFITH, J A G, *Central Departments and Local Authorities*, 1966
GRIFFITH, J A G (ed), *From Policy to Administration*, 1976

GRIFFITH, J A G, *Parliamentary Scrutiny of Government Bills*, 1974
GRIFFITH, J A G, *The Politics of the Judiciary*, 4th edn, 1991
GRIFFITH, J A G, & RYLE, M, *Parliament*, 1989
GUEST, A G (ed), *Oxford Essays in Jurisprudence*, 1961
GURRY, F, *Breach of Confidence*, 1984

HADDEN, T, & BOYLE, K, *The Anglo-Irish Agreement*, 1989
HADFIELD, B (ed), *Judicial Review, A Thematic Approach*, 1995
HADFIELD, B (ed), *Northern Ireland: Politics and the Constitution*, 1992
HADFIELD, B, *The Constitution of Northern Ireland*, 1989
HAGUE, D C, MACKENZIE, W J M, & BARKER, A (ed), *Public Policy and Private Interests*, 1975
HAILSHAM, Lord, *On the Constitution*, 1992
HAILSHAM, Lord, *The Dilemma of Democracy*, 1978
HALL, P, *Royal Fortune: Tax, Money and the Monarchy*, 1992
HANHAM, H J, *The Nineteenth Century Constitution, 1815–1914*, 1969
HANSON, A H, *Parliament and Public Ownership*, 1961
HARDEN, I, *The Contracting State*, 1992
HARDING, A J, *Public Duties and Public Law*, 1989
HARLOW, C, *Compensation and Government Torts*, 1982
HARLOW, C, & RAWLINGS, R, *Law and Administration*, 1984
HARMAN, H, & GRIFFITH, J A G, *Justice Deserted*, 1979
HARRIS, D J, *The European Social Charter*, 1984
HARRIS, D J, O'BOYLE, M, & WARBRICK, C, *Law of the European Convention on Human Rights*, 1995
HARRISON, A J, *The Control of Public Expenditure, 1979–1989*, 1989
HART, H L A, *The Concept of Law*, 1961
HART, H L A, & HONORE, A M, *Causation in the Law*, 1959
HARTLEY, T C, *The Foundations of European Community Law*, 2nd edn, 1988
HAWKINS, W, *Pleas of the Crown*, 6th edn (by T Leach), 2 vols, 1787
HAYEK, F A, *The Constitution of Liberty*, 1963
HAYEK, F A, *The Road to Serfdom*, 1944
HEARN, W E, *The Government of England*, 1867
HECLO, H, & WILDAVSKY, A, *The Private Government of Public Money*, 1974
HEDLEY, P, & AYNSLEY, C, *The D-Notice Affair*, 1967
HENDERSON, E G, *Foundations of English Administrative Law*, 1963
HENLEY, D, et al, *Public Sector Accounting and Financial Control*, 1984
HENNESSY, P, *Cabinet*, 1986
HENNESSY, P, *Whitehall*, rev edn, 1990
HEPPLE, B A, *Race, Jobs and the Law in Britain*, 2nd edn, 1970
HERBERT, A P, *Uncommon Law*, 1935
HEUSTON, R F V, *Essays in Constitutional Law*, 2nd edn, 1964
HEUSTON, R F V, *Lives of the Lord Chancellors 1885–1940*, 1964
HILL, L B, *The Model Ombudsman*, 1976
HOFFMANN, Lord, *A Sense of Proportion* (J M Kelly Memorial Lecture, 1996), 1997
HOGG, P W, *Liability of the Crown*, 2nd edn, 1989
HOGG, P W, *Constitutional Law of Canada*, 2nd edn, 1985
HOGGETT, B, *Mental Health Law*, 4th edn, 1996
HOLDSWORTH, W, *A History of English Law* (14 vols), 1923–64
HOLLAND, P, *The Governance of Quangos*, 1981
HOLT, J C, *Magna Carta*, 2nd edn, 1992
HOOD PHILLIPS, O, & JACKSON, P, *Constitutional and Administrative Law*, 7th edn, 1988
HOOD PHILLIPS, O, *Reform of the Constitution*, 1970
HOPKINS, P, *Parliamentary Procedures and the Law Commission*, 1994
HOWARD, C, *Australian Federal Constitutional Law*, 3rd edn, 1985
HUNNINGS, N M, *Film Censors and the Law*, 1967

JACOB, J M, *The Republican Crown: Lawyers and the Making of the State in 20th Century Britain*, 1996
JACOBS, F G, & WHITE, R C A, *The European Convention on Human Rights*, 2nd edn, 1996
JACONELLI, J, *Enacting a Bill of Rights, the Legal Problems*, 1980
JAMES, S, *British Cabinet Government*, 1992
JANIS, M, KAY, R, & BRADLEY, A W, *European Human Rights Law: Text and Materials*, 1995

JEFFERSON, T, & GRIMSHAW, R, *Controlling the Constable: Police Accountability in England and Wales,* 1984

JEFFERY, K, & HENNESSY, P, *States of Emergency: British Governments and Strikebreaking since 1919,* 1983

JENKINS, R, *Mr Balfour's Poodle,* 1954

JENNINGS, I, *Cabinet Government,* 3rd edn, 1959

JENNINGS, I, *The Law and the Constitution,* 5th edn, 1959

JENNINGS, I, *Parliament,* 2nd edn, 1957

JENNINGS, I, *The Sedition Bill Explained,* 1934

JENNINGS, R, & WATTS, A, *Oppenheim's International Law: the Law of Peace,* 9th edn, 1992

JOHNSON, N, *In Search of the Constitution,* 1977

JOHNSON, N, *Parliament and Administration; the Estimates Committee 1945–65,* 1966

JOHNSTON, A, *The Inland Revenue,* 1965

JONES, A, *Extradition,* 1995

JONES, J M, *British Nationality Law,* 2nd edn, 1956

JONES, R (ed), *Mental Health Act Manual,* 2nd edn, 1988

JONES, T, *Whitehall Diary,* vol 3 (ed R K Middlemas), 1971

JOSEPH K, *Freedom under the Law,* 1975

JOWELL, J L, & OLIVER, D H (eds), *New Directions in Judicial Review,* 1988

JOWELL, J L, & OLIVER, D H (eds), *The Changing Constitution,* 3rd edn, 1994

JUSTICE, All Souls Committee, *Administrative Justice: Some Necessary Reforms,* 1988

JUSTICE, *The Local Ombudsman,* 1980

KEATING, M J, & MIDWINTER, A, *The Government of Scotland,* 1983

KEETON, G W, *Trial by Tribunal,* 1960

KEIR, D L, & LAWSON, F H, *Cases in Constitutional Law,* 6th edn, 1979

KELLAS, J G, *The Scottish Political System,* 4th edn, 1989

KELLY, J M, *The Irish Constitution,* 3rd edn, 1994

KERMODE, D G, *Devolution at Work: A Case Study of the Isle of Man,* 1979

KERR, J, *Matters for Judgment,* 1979

KERSELL, J E, *Parliamentary Supervision of Delegated Legislation,* 1960

KINLEY, O, *The European Convention on Human Rights: Compliance Without Incorporation,* 1993

KITSON, F, *Low Intensity Operations,* 1971

LASKI, H J, *A Grammar of Politics,* 5th edn, 1967

LATHAM, R T E, *The Law and the Commonwealth,* 1949

LAUNDY, P, *The Office of Speaker,* 1964

LAWRENCE, R J, *The Government of Northern Ireland,* 1965

LAWSON, N, *The View from No. 11,* 1993

LEE, H P, HANKS, P, & MORABITO, V, *In the Name of National Security: the Legal Dimensions,* 1995

LEGOMSKY, S H, *Immigration and the Justiciary: Law and Politics in Britain and America,* 1987

LEIGH, D, *The Frontiers of Secrecy,* 1980

LESTER, A, & BINDMAN, G, *Race and Law,* 1972

LEVY, H P, *The Press Council,* 1967

LEWIS, A, *Make No Law,* 1991

LEWIS, C B, *Judicial Remedies in Public Law,* 1992

LEWIS, N, SENEVIRATNE, M, & CRACKNELL, S, *Complaints Procedures in Local Government,* 1987

LEWIS, N, & GATESHILL, B, *The Commission for Local Administration,* 1978

LIKIERMAN, J A, *Cash Limits and External Financing Limits,* 1981

LINKLATER, M, & LEIGH, D, *Not Without Honour,* 1986

LODGE, J (ed), *Institutions and Policies of the European Community,* 1983

LOUGHLIN, M, *Legality and Locality: the Role of Law in Central–Local Government Relations,* 1996

LOUGHLIN, M, *Local Government in the Modern State,* 1986

LOUGHLIN, M, *Public Law and Political Theory,* 1992

LOVELAND, I D, *Constitutional Law, A Critical Introduction,* 1996

LOVELAND, I D (ed), *Frontiers of Criminality,* 1995

LOWE, N V, & SUFRIN, B E, *Borrie and Lowe's Law of Contempt,* 3rd edn, 1996

LUSTGARTEN, L, *Legal Control of Racial Discrimination,* 1980

LUSTGARTEN, L, *The Governance of the Police,* 1986

LUSTGARTEN, L, & LEIGH, I, *In From the Cold: National Security and Parliamentary Democracy,* 1994

MacDONALD, I A, & BLAKE, N, *Immigration Law and Practice in the United Kingdom*, 4th edn, 1995
McCABE, S, & WALLINGTON, P, *The Police, Public Order and Civil Liberties: Legacies of the Miners' Strike*, 1988
McCRUDDEN, C, & CHAMBERS, G (eds), *Individual Rights and the Law in Britain*, 1993
McELDOWNEY, J F, *Public Law*, 1994
McILWAIN, C H, *Constitutionalism, Ancient and Modern*, 1947
McILWAIN, C H, *The High Court of Parliament*, 1910
MACKINTOSH, J P, *The British Cabinet*, 3rd edn, 1977
MACKINTOSH, J P, *The Devolution of Power*, 1968
MACKINTOSH, J P, *The Government and Politics of Britain* (ed P G Richards), 7th edn, 1988
MACKINTOSH, J P, *Specialist Committees in the House of Commons – have they failed?* (rev), 1980
McNAIR, Lord, *Law of Treaties*, 2nd edn, 1961
McNAIR, Lord, & WATTS, A D, *The Legal Effects of War*, 4th edn, 1966
MAITLAND, F W, *The Constitutional History of England*, 1908
MALLORY, J R, *The Structure of Canadian Government*, 1971
Manual of Military Law, 13th edn, 1992
MANN, F A, *Foreign Affairs in English Courts*, 1986
MARGACH, J, *The Abuse of Power*, 1978
MARKESINIS, B S, *The Theory and Practice of Dissolution of Parliament*, 1972
MARSHALL, G, *Constitutional Conventions*, 1984
MARSHALL, G, *Constitutional Theory*, 1971
MARSHALL, G, *Parliamentary Sovereignty and the Commonwealth*, 1957
MARSHALL, G, *Police and Government*, 1965
MARSHALL, G, & MOODIE, G C, *Some Problems of the Constitution*, 5th edn, 1971
MATHIJSEN, P S R F, *A Guide to European Community Law*, 6th edn, 1995
MEGARRY, R E, & WADE, H W R, *The Law of Real Property*, 5th edn, 1984
MICHAEL., J, *The Politics of Secrecy*, 1982
MIDDLEMAS, K, & BARNES, J, *Baldwin*, 1969
MIERS, D R, & PAGE, A C, *Legislation*, 2nd edn, 1990
MILL, J S, *Representative Government*, 1861
MILLER, C J, *Contempt of Court*, 2nd edn, 1989
MILLER, J D B, *Survey of Commonwealth Affairs: Problems of Expansion and Attrition, 1953–1969*, 1974
MILLETT, J D, *The Unemployment Assistance Board*, 1940
MILNE, D, *The Scottish Office*, 1957
MITCHELL, J D B, *Constitutional Law*, 2nd edn, 1968
MITCHELL, J D B, *The Contracts of Public Authorities*, 1954
MOORE, W H, *Act of State in English Law*, 1906
MORGAN, J, *Conflict and Order: The Police and Labour Disputes in England and Wales 1900–39*, 1987
MORGAN, J P, *The House of Lords and the Labour Government, 1964–1970*, 1975
MORISON, J, & LIVINGSTONE, S, *Reshaping Public Power: Northern Ireland and the British Constitutional Crisis*, 1995
MORRIS, A (ed), *The Growth of Parliamentary Scrutiny by Committee*, 1970
MORRIS, G S, *Strikes in Essential Services*, 1986
MORRIS, H F, & READ, J S, *Indirect Rule and the Search for Justice*, 1972
MORRISON, H, *Government and Parliament*, 3rd edn, 1964
MORTON, J. *Criminal Justice and Public Order Act 1994*, 1994
MOSLEY, R K, *The Story of the Cabinet Office*, 1969
MOUNT, F, *The British Constitution Now: Recovery or Decline?*, 1992
MUNRO, C R, *Television, Censorship and the Law*, 1979
MUNRO, C R, *Studies in Constitutional Law*, 1987

NICOLSON, I F, *The Mystery of Crichel Down*, 1986
NICOLSON, H, *King George V*, 1952
NOEL, E, *Working Together – The Institutions of the European Community*, 1994
NORMANTON, E L, *The Accountability and Audit of Governments*, 1966
NORTON, P, *The Commons in Perspective*, 1981
NORTON, P, *The Constitution in Flux*, 1982
NORTON, P, *Dissension in the House of Commons 1945–1974*, 1975; *1974–1979*, 1980

O'CONNELL, D P, & RIORDAN, A, *Opinions on Imperial Constitutional Law*, 1971

OGUS, A I, BARENDT, E M, & WIKELEY, N, *The Law of Social Security*, 4th edn, 1995
O'HIGGINS, P, *Censorship in Britain*, 1972
O'RIORDAN, T, KEMP, R, & PURDUE, M, *Sizewell B: An Anatomy of an Inquiry*, 1988

PAINE, T, *Rights of Man* (ed H Collins), 1969
PANNICK, D, *Judicial Review of the Death Penalty*, 1982
PARRIS, H, *Constitutional Bureaucracy*, 1969
PARRY, C, *Nationality and Citizenship Laws of the Commonwealth*, 2 vols, 1957–60
PARTINGTON, M, *Secretary of State's Powers of Adjudication in Social Security Law*, 1991
PATERSON, A, *The Law Lords*, 1982
PATERSON, A, & BATES, T ST J, *The Legal System of Scotland: Cases and Materials*, 3rd edn, 1993
PATTEN, J, *Political Culture, Conservatism and Rolling Constitutional Change*, 1991
PELLING, H, *The British Communist Party: A Historical Profile*, 1975
PIMLOTT, B, *The Queen: A Biography of Elizabeth II*, 1996
PLIATZKY, L, *The Treasury under Mrs Thatcher*, 1989
POLYVIOU, P G, *The Equal Protection of the Laws*, 1980
POLYVIOU, P G, *Entry, Search and Seizure: Constitutional and Common Law*, 1982
PONTING, C, *The Right to Know: The Inside Story of the Belgrano Affair*, 1985
PORT, F J, *Administrative Law*, 1929
PROSSER, T, *Nationalised Industries and Public Control: Legal, Constitutional and Political Issues*, 1986

RAWLINGS, H F, *The Law and the Electoral Process*, 1988
REID, G, *The Politics of Financial Control*, 1966
REINER, R, *The Politics of the Police*, 1992
RICHARDS, P G, *Parliament and Conscience*, 1970
RICHARDS, P G, *Patronage in British Government*, 1963
RICHARDSON, G, & GENN, H (eds), *Administrative Law and Government Action: The Courts and Alternative Mechanisms of Review*, 1994
RIDER, B, ABRAMS, C, & FERRAN, E, *Guide to the Financial Services Act 1986*, 1989
RILEY, P W J, *The Union of England and Scotland*, 1978
ROBERTS, C, *The Growth of Responsible Government in Stuart England*, 1966
ROBERTS-WRAY, K, *Commonwealth and Colonial Law*, 1966
ROBERTSON, A H, & MERRILLS, J G, *Human Rights in Europe: A Study of the European Convention on Human Rights*, 3rd edn, 1993
ROBERTSON, G, *Freedom, the Individual and the Law*, 6th edn, 1989
ROBERTSON, G, *Obscenity*, 1979
ROBERTSON, G, *The People against the Press*, 1983
ROBINSON, A, *Parliament and Public Spending – The Expenditure Committee 1970–76*, 1978
ROBSON, W A, *Justice and Administrative Law*, 3rd edn, 1951
ROBSON, W A, *Nationalised Industries and Public Ownership*, 2nd edn, 1962
ROLPH, C H, *The Trial of Lady Chatterley*, 1961
ROSEVEARE, H, *The Treasury*, 1969
ROWAT, D C, *The Ombudsman*, 2nd edn, 1968
ROWE, P, *Defence: The Legal Implications*, 1987
ROWE, P (ed), *The Gulf War 1990–91 in International and English Law*, 1993
RUBIN, G R, *Private Property, Government Requisition and the Constitution 1914–1927*, 1994
RUBINSTEIN, A, *Jurisdiction and Illegality*, 1965
RYLE, M, & RICHARDS, P G (eds), *The Commons under Scrutiny*, 3rd edn, 1988

SAWER, G, *Federation under Strain*, 1977
SCARMAN, Lord, *English Law – The New Dimension*, 1974
SCHWARZE, J, *European Administrative Law*, 1992
SENEVIRATNE, M, *Ombudsmen in the Public Sector*, 1994
SHARPE, R J, *The Law of Habeas Corpus*, 2nd edn, 1989
SHELL, D, *The House of Lords*, 2nd edn, 1992
SIMPSON, A W B, *In the Highest Degree Odious*, 1992
SIMPSON, A W B, *Pornography and Politics – the Williams Report in Retrospect*, 1983
SINGER, P, *Democracy and Disobedience*, 1973
SMITH, A T H, *Offences Against Public Order*, 1987
SMITH, I T, & THOMAS, G H, *Industrial Law*, 6th edn, 1996

SMITH, J C, & HOGAN, B, *Criminal Law*, 8th edn, 1996
SMITH, T B (ed), *The Laws of Scotland: Stair Memorial Encyclopedia*, vols 1 & 5, 1987
SORENSEN, M (ed), *Manual of Public International Law*, 1968
SPENCER, J R, *Jackson's Machinery of Justice*, 8th edn, 1989
SPENCER, S, *Called to Account*, 1985
STACEY, F, *Ombudsmen Compared*, 1978
STALKER, J, *Stalker*, 1988
STEEL, D, *A House Divided; the Lib-Lab Pact and the Future of British Politics*, 1980
STEEL, D, *No Entry*, 1969
STEPHEN, J F, *Digest of Criminal Law*, 1877
STEPHEN, J F, *History of the Criminal Law of England* (3 vols), 1883
STEVENS, R, *Law and Politics: the House of Lords as a Judicial Body, 1800–1976*, 1979
STEVENS, R B, *The Independence of the Judiciary, The View from the Lord Chancellor's Office*, 1993
STEWART, J D, *British Pressure Groups*, 1956
STEWART, J, & STOKER, G (eds), *Local Government in the 1990s*, 1995
STONE, R T H, *Entry, Search and Seizure: A Guide to Civil and Criminal Powers of Entry*, 3rd edn, 1997
STREET, H, *Freedom, the Individual and the Law*, 5th edn, 1982
STREET, H, *Governmental Liability*, 1953
STREET, H, *Justice in the Welfare State*, 2nd edn, 1975
SUPPERSTONE, M, *Brownlie's Law of Public Order and National Security*, 2nd edn, 1981
SUPPERSTONE, M, & GOUDIE, J (eds), *Judicial Review*, 1991
SWINFEN, D B, *Imperial Appeal: The debate on the appeal to the Privy Council, 1833–1986*, 1987

TAGGART, M (ed), *Judicial Review of Administrative Action in the 1980s*, 1987
TARNOPOLSKY, W S, *The Canadian Bill of Rights*, 2nd edn, 1975
TASWELL-LANGMEAD, T P, *English Constitutional History* (ed T F T Plucknett), 11th edn, 1960
TERRY, C S, *The Scottish Parliament 1603–1707*, 1905
THIO, S M, *Locus Standi and Judicial Review*, 1971
THOMPSON, E P, *Whigs and Hunters: the Origin of the Black Act*, 1975
THOMPSON, E P, *Writing by Candlelight*, 1980
TOWNSHEND, C, *Making the Peace: Public Order and Public Security in Modern Britain*, 1993
TRIBE, L, *Constitutional Choices*, 1985
TURNBULL, M, *The Spycatcher Trial*, 1989
TURPIN, C C, *British Government and the Constitution: Text, Cases and Materials*, 3rd edn, 1995
TURPIN, C C, *Government Procurement and Contracts*, 1989

UGLOW, S, *Policing a Liberal Society*, 1988
UNSWORTH, C, *The Politics of Mental Health Legislation*, 1987

VAN DIJK, P, & VAN HOOF, G, *Theory and Practice of the European Convention on Human Rights*, 2nd edn, 1990
VERCHER, A, *Terrorism in Europe: An International Comparative Legal Analysis*, 1992
VILE, M J C, *Constitutionalism and the Separation of Powers*, 1967

WACKS, R, *The Protection of Privacy*, 1980
WADE, H W R, *Constitutional Fundamentals*, 1980
WADE, H W R, & FORSYTH, C F, *Administrative Law*, 7th edn, 1994
WALKER, C, *The Prevention of Terrorism in British Law*, 2nd edn, 1992
WALKER, D M, *The Scottish Legal System*, 6th edn, 1992
WALKER, J, *The Queen has been Pleased*, 1986
WALKER, P GORDON, *The Cabinet*, rev 1972
WALKER, S, *In Defense of American Liberties*, 1990
WALKER, C P, & STARMER, K, *Justice in Error*, 1993
WALKLAND, S A (ed), *The House of Commons in the Twentieth Century*, 1979
WALLINGTON, P T, & McBRIDE, G, *Civil Liberties and a Bill of Rights*, 1976
WARD, I, *A Critical Introduction to European Law*, 1996
WEATHERILL, S, & BEAUMONT, P R, *EC Law*, 2nd edn, 1995
WEATHERILL, S, *Law and Integration in the European Union*, 1995
WEILER, P, *In the Last Resort*, 1974
WEST, N, *A Matter of Trust: MI5, 1945–72*, 1982

WEST, N, *MI5: British Security Service Operations 1909–45*, 1983

WHEARE K C, *Modern Constitutions*, 2nd edn, 1966

WHEARE, K C, *The Constitutional Structure of the Commonwealth*, 1960

WHEARE, K C, *The Statute of Westminster and Dominion Status*, 5th edn, 1953

WHEELER-BENNETT, J, *King George VI*, 1958

WHITLAM, G, *The Truth of the Matter*, 1979

WILLIAMS, G, *Media Ownership and Democracy*, 2nd edn, 1996

WILLIAMS, D G T, *Not in the Public Interest*, 1965

WILLIAMS, D G T, *Keeping the Peace*, 1967

WILLIAMS, E N, *The 18th Century Constitution, 1688–1815*, 1960

WILLIAMS, O C, *History of Private Bill Procedure*, 2 vols, 1949

WILLSON, F M G, *The Organization of British Central Government, 1914–1964*, 2nd edn, 1968

WILSON, H, *The Governance of Britain*, 1976

WILSON, H, *The Labour Government, 1964–70*, 1974

WILSON, S S, *The Cabinet Office to 1945*, 1975

WINDLESHAM, Lord & RAMPTON, R, *Report on 'Death on the Rock'*, 1989

WOLFE, J N (ed), *Government and Nationalism in Scotland*, 1969

WOODHOUSE, D, *Ministers and Parliament: Accountability in Theory and Practice*, 1994

WOOLF, Sir H, *Protection of the Public – A New Challenge*, 1990

WRAITH, R E, & HUTCHESSON, P G, *Administrative Tribunals*, 1973

WRAITH, R E, & LAMB, G B, *Public Inquiries as an Instrument of Government*, 1971

WYATT, D, & DASHWOOD, A, *European Community Law*, 3rd edn, 1993

YOUNG, H, *The Crossman Affair*, 1976

YOUNG, T, *Incitement to Disaffection*, 1976

ZAMIR, I, WOOLF, Lord, & WOOLF, J, *The Declaratory Judgement*, 2nd edn, 1993

ZANDER, M, *Cases and Materials on the English Legal System*, 7th edn, 1996

ZANDER, M, *A Bill of Rights?*, 4th edn, 1997

ZANDER, M, *The Police and Criminal Evidence Act 1984*, 3rd edn, 1995

Index

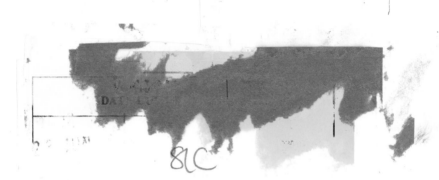

Constitutional and administrative law